Josephine Young Case

Everett Needham Case

Owen D. Young
and
American Enterprise

OWEN D. YOUNG
AND AMERICAN
ENTERPRISE

❧

A BIOGRAPHY

❧

Josephine Young Case
Everett Needham Case

DAVID R. GODINE · BOSTON

First published in 1982 by
David R. Godine, Publisher, Inc.
306 Dartmouth Street
Boston, Massachusetts 02116

Library of Congress Cataloging in Publication Data
Case, Josephine Young, 1907–
Owen D. Young and American enterprise.

Bibliography: p. 911
Includes index.
1. Young, Owen D., 1874–1962. 2. Household appliances, Electric—
United States—History. 3. Businessmen—United States—Biography. I. Case,
Everett Needham, joint author. II. Title.
HD 9971.5.E542Y683   338.7′6213′0924 [B]   80–83945
ISBN 0–87923–360–5

Manufactured in the United States of America

OWEN D. YOUNG AND AMERICAN ENTERPRISE

was set in linotype Caledonia, a typeface designed by the great American
calligrapher and graphic artist W. A. Dwiggins, a long-time resident of
Hingham, Massachusetts. This clear and classic face was inspired by the
work of Scotch typefounders, and particularly by the transitional faces cut
by William Martin for Bulmer around 1790. The display face for the
essay openings and title page is, in fact, Monotype
Bulmer, also cut by Martin and used in the
famous 'Boydell Shakespeare' of 1791.

The book was designed by Edward Foss and set by Service Typesetting of
Austin, Texas. Halliday Lithograph of West Hanover,
Massachusetts printed it on S.D. Warren's 1854
Medium, a totally acid-free sheet.

Jacket and title page calligraphy
by Richard Lipton.

For the ten grandchildren

Contents

Illustrations follow pages 20, 116, 276, 404, 500 and 692

Owen D. Young
and
American Enterprise

Part I

Roots and a Branching Out

1874–1912

A Country Boyhood and
a Country College

G RANDPA waited at the little bridge at the foot of the farm road, as he did every school day, for Owen to come home. The old man's temper was short at the best of times and now, heated by the fear that something might have gone wrong on the mile walk home, it was boiling. Owen could see the anger as he came over the hill; he knew he was at least an hour late, for teacher had kept him almost that long after school to rewrite the multiplication tables. He walked slowly down to Grandpa and explained. The storm broke, indeed, but not on him. It fell on the young teacher who had dared to keep him late. She was lucky not to hear the blistering barnyard description of her defects.

Owen was the only child on the farm which his grandfather owned and his parents, Smith and Ida Young, worked. They had lost a son before Owen was born; approaching middle age—by the standards of the time—they saw before them the bleak prospect of a childless family on a farm. So there was much rejoicing when, on October 27, 1874, a second son was born to them in the little farmhouse on the hill above Van Hornesville. Names for males in the Young family had always been biblical (Smith's first name was Jacob) but an imaginative aunt suggested Owen, with a middle initial D. to make it sound better, and so he was named.

There had been Youngs on these central New York State hills south of the Mohawk River since 1750. Driven from the Palatinate on the Rhine by the constant warring of their rulers and by religious persecution, the Jung family and thousands of their countrymen fled first to England. They were fed and housed by "good Queen Anne," a Protestant like themselves, but soon became too much of a burden to support. In 1710 the queen was persuaded by Pastor Joshua Kochertal of Newburgh in New York to send the refugees over to provide naval stores for the British fleet from the forests along the Hudson River.

It was not long, however, before the German immigrants tired of what they called "slavery"; they began to move north and west, taking up land from the Indians along the Schoharie River and farther north along the Mohawk.

They knew good land when they saw it, they knew how to work it, and they had the labor for it in their families of a dozen or more children. They built stone churches for worship and for forts against the Indians. They were free and they thrived.

One part of the Jung family went up the trail from the Mohawk at Fort Plain, south and west along the Otsquago creek. At its headwaters they found rich land on easy slopes, well watered. It was nearly half a century since the family had left the Rhine, but this was the end of the journey—and some of their descendants still live upon those hills.

Of these Jungs, a name soon Anglicized, the firstborn on the land above the Otsquago was Jacob A. His father was probably named Adam and his mother was probably an Indian; persistent family tradition calls her the "Frenchwoman"—then the current name for a squaw. And it is true that in the raids and kidnappings and destruction of the years of war, she and her children were never harmed. Owen Young always liked to feel that his blood was aboriginal as well as European.

Jacob A. Young served in the wars, as did his son Jacob I. Young in the later years. And by the time Jacob I.'s eldest son was born, in 1807, the area was well populated and most of the land taken up. A village of some size had developed at the edge of the Young farm— a church, houses and a store—but it was not destined to survive, for it lacked waterpower.

Below the Young farm lay a deep valley half a mile long, where the Otsquago was strong and swift in a series of falls. When General James Clinton's army made its difficult way in 1779 from the Mohawk to Otsego Lake and the Susquehanna, the right wing followed the trail along the Otsquago, passing through this narrow valley and putting down planks in the creek bed itself for the cannon and the wagons. A member of the Third Regiment of the Tryon County Militia noticed with interest the untouched waterpower of the stream; this was Quartermaster Abram Van Horne, an immigrant from New Jersey who had come to the Mohawk country eight years before. A descendant of early settlers of New Netherland, he was an enterprising pioneer, a member of the local Committee of Safety and later high sheriff of Tryon County, which at that time included all the Mohawk country.

When the war was over Abram Van Horne came back to the little valley with two of his sons, Richard and Daniel, and harnessed the Otsquago. They built dams and mills, houses, and set up a store. They were smart and energetic millers and merchants, and the new settlement soon outdistanced the old ones on the hills. They were a different breed from the German farmers, although their homelands were not far apart; they were "Low Dutch" from Hoorn on the Zuyder Zee, the Youngs were "High Dutch" from the upper Rhineland provinces. There was not much in common between the families, though the Youngs did use the Van Hornes' gristmill, and if in the records of Richard Van Horne's store the name of Young appeared, it usually did so only for a "gill of rum."

Nevertheless, two young people from the families found interests in common, for Jacob I. Young married Eve Van Horne and they had fourteen children, of whom Peter was the eldest. Peter Young married Magdalen, daughter of a blacksmith, Gersham Smith, who had come to the Otsquago hills from Princeton, New Jersey, in a cold winter after the Revolution in a covered sleigh.[1] They had four children, of whom the eldest was Jacob Smith Young, born in 1831, and always known as "Smith." Peter Young was a person of consequence and held several offices in what was by then the town of Stark. He owned a number of farms at different times, and in the spring of 1856 bought the one that came to be known in the Young family as the Home Farm. It was across the valley to the east from the original Young land, cleared a hundred years before, and it too had fertile acreage and good water.

Smith Young was married that same year, at Thanksgiving, to Ida Brandow, and Peter invited them to live on the Home Farm and do all the work. Magdalen died the following year, and Peter with his daughter Eliza and his son Aaron settled in with the Smith Youngs. But Peter was an opinionated and strong-willed paterfamilias, and at one time or another his children could stand him no longer and moved away. Aaron went permanently to Illinois, Eliza was disowned when she secretly married—with Smith's and Ida's connivance—Seneca Herkimer,[2] and Smith and Ida left for a few years on neighboring farms. When they returned it was to stay, and the Home Farm was where Owen Young was born.

ii

The boy grew up alone on the farm with the three older people. There were no very close neighbors, and the farm was separated from the road by a great fold of hill, beyond which could be seen only the blue Adirondacks far to the north. Sometimes he would run to the top of that hill when he heard a team passing by, just to see some other people. The village of Van Hornesville, always referred to as "the Holler," was a mile down the steep road to the west.

The village itself was wholly contained along its single street winding through the narrow valley beside the stream which had attracted Abram Van Horne a hundred years before. There were the red schoolhouse, two stores, a church, a blacksmith shop, the post office, and the big four-story stone gristmill built by Daniel Van Horne to replace the early wooden one.[3] Along the stream, both above and below, were a number of other mills powered by the constant flow of water: a distillery, a cheese factory and cheesebox factory, several sawmills, and a big stone cotton-spinning mill, where the local girls worked before they got married. The church was a "Union" church, which, when the shaky union broke down, became the Universalist church, and the Methodists converted the old Van Horne store into a church of their own. There were also two hotels, as they were called, although they were more like pubs or small country inns. The goings-on within their walls were reputed to be high, wide and handsome, and Van Hornesville had rather a bad name in the country around. Owen Young wrote many years later, when he heard that a nearby one had burned down: "That old building carries with it many memories—the anticipation of a boy looking forward to the time when he would be big enough to go in the hotel and the realizations of a man once in and anxious to get out."[4]

The family on the Home Farm made their visits to the post office and the store, to the Universalist church on Sunday, to the hotel if there was a social or an entertainment in the "ballroom." A stagecoach ran through the town—known locally as the "Van Hornesville Express"—from Fort Plain to Cooperstown and back, carrying mail and passengers. A telephone was put into the store about 1883; a year later Owen, aged ten, stood on a box listening to the report of the election returns and giving the news to the group around the stove that Grover Cleveland had been elected.

Smith Young was a reserved and gentle man who worked to the limit of his strength every day of his life. Blue-eyed like all his mother's family, he talked little, but his upright character was so evident that he was a widely felt influence in the community. A captain in the militia in his younger days, later a justice of the peace, he was respected and beloved by his neighbors, his many relatives, and by his son. He spent his life making ends meet, or trying to; from the first his boy knew how much labor resulted in how little money. The farm gave them food—meat, milk, butter, fruits and vegetables—in return for the endless work on the land, in the barn, in the house. For cash, they sold butter, milk to the cheese factory, and, especially, hops. Hops were raised in central New York State, at that time, in large quantities; it was a chancy crop to grow, and prices were as uncertain as the weather, especially in the 1890s when cash was hard to come by. Smith had to borrow money to keep things going, to raise the barn he had to have, to buy the few necessaries they could not grow or make. Like Ida's dresses, all that they had was patched and turned and used over and over again. But year after year, in spite of his wife's objections, Smith continued to grow the beautiful, fragrant, back-breaking crop, tied to its high poles and strings, never knowing whether he would get five or fifty cents a pound for the dried and pressed product during the coming year. There was certainly something of the gambler under Smith's quiet exterior.

Ida Brandow Young was the daughter of a Holland Dutch family, which after the Revolution had settled on the hills southwest of Van Hornesville. One of seven children of John Worden Brandow and Catherine Connine, Ida was born in their log cabin in 1839, and was married at seventeen. A thin, wiry, gray-eyed and dark-haired woman, she had a beautiful wide forehead and well-cut features. Her quiet manner seldom betrayed her firm character and strong will, though her husband and son—and even her father-in-law—came to know them well. She too worked hard through the endless hours of the farm wife. She helped with the chores, for they could seldom afford a hired man, as well as taking care of the milk, making butter to sell, minding the chickens and the garden, cooking, preserving, feeding thirty or forty hop pickers in season, doing the washing and ironing and darning, and making new clothes. The boy never forgot the sight of his mother working almost every day of the year from dawn to dark.

Grandpa Peter, however, would do no work whatever. His retirement was total and he refused to lift a hand. If a thunderstorm threatened as the last of the hay was being got in, he would not ride the hayrack. If the baby cried in the cradle and his busy daughter-in-law called to him to rock it with his foot, he shouted, "I will not! Goddammit, woman, you'll have me taking care of the brat!" But the boy, as he grew older, was the apple of his eye; he would even act as congregation when Owen, at six or seven, would stand on a chair in the parlor to preach a sermon. The minister was the only public speaker Owen had ever heard, and when Peter would not listen, he would go to the barn, climb on the milking stool, and preach to the cows. But this worried Grandpa considerably, for he did not want a preacher for a grandson, even though the boy's mother thoroughly approved. The old man died just before Owen was eleven, so he did not have to suffer when Owen did, occasionally, preach real sermons in church when he was eighteen and nineteen.

In the summers Owen had playmates from distant Brooklyn, Warren and Rob Herkimer, sons of his aunt Eliza. They were considerably more sophisticated than he, and the three were often in trouble, although the worst crime that Owen remembered was smoking corn silk out back of the barn. But for the most part the boy's life revolved, with that of his parents, within the lonely cycle of the farm year. Here were the important things in life: first the weather, then the crops, the animals, and the prices for farm products. In his first years away from the land he thought and wrote constantly about the farm, knowing as he woke each morning what was to be done that day at home.

The Home Farm year, as the deep snows faded along the hills and the higher sun made the sap start, began in March with sugaring. Owen had a "bush" he called his own, where he had given numbers to the trees and kept records of their individual production from year to year. Then the cows began to freshen and there was more work in the barn in looking after the calves and the milk; as soon as the cheese factory opened for the season, Pa drew the milk to sell. Then plowing and sowing began, the hop poles were set in the hopyard, and the burden of "spring's work" was well under way.

The handsome, greedy, fast-growing hop vines demanded constant care; Owen stood on the back of a farm horse to tie them to overhead strings as soon as they had climbed their poles. Then there were the other crops to look after: hay and corn, buckwheat and potatoes. Owen helped in the fields and with the cows and calves, pigs, and three horses—the farm team and Dan, the driving horse, who was his pet. When his father could afford it he would get a hired man for the whole summer, but much of the time he did the work himself, with what help the boy could give. Ida worried constantly about the overload upon her husband's frail frame.

September brought the hardest work of all—the harvesting of the hops. When the vines were bright with the yellow-green cones, a crowd of pickers arrived to be housed and fed. They were neighbors and family, but included also some outlanders looking for a little money and some fun. And fun there always was; for all the hard work, it was the gayest time of the year. Everyone enjoyed it, even the harassed women in the kitchen, and Smith Young perhaps most of all—the crowd of pickers, young and old, the laughter and clowning, the beauty of the fruited vines, through it all the fragrance of the hops. He spent the nights in the hop house, tending the fire and turning the drying crop. Who knows, he thought, perhaps this year they will bring some real money.

When picking was over it was time to go to the Fair, perhaps to both Otsego County's at Richfield Springs and Herkimer County's at Herkimer. Here again it was a party, a group driving over the hills together, seeing the sights, running knowledgeable hands over the cattle, visiting with friends in town, driving home by moonlight. And before the winter set in—it comes early on the hills above Van Hornesville—there were apples to be picked and cider made, potatoes to be dug and stored, pigs to be slaughtered and the meat dressed and smoked, the last grain to be harvested—all the winter's provender for man and beast to be carefully put away in the barns and the cellar.

Ida was busy canning and preserving while the men—Smith kept the hired man, when he had one, till November—did the fall plowing, pressed the hops, and cleaned up the hopyard; the cattle were brought into the barn but there was not much milk, for the cows soon dried up. The steam threshing machine and its crew arrived in November and Ida had more mouths to feed for a few days, but there was plenty of buckwheat flour and syrup for the pancakes.

The neighbors got together for cornhuskings as election time came on, when there was always a great deal of political discussion and argument, in which Smith was almost alone in upholding the Democratic cause and candidates. Then as soon as the roads were frozen and the snow was deep enough to get out the sleighs, the winter season of socials and dances and entertainments began. In some of these Smith and Ida took part, but they were often snowed in at the farm. The evening dark came early, and Pa read his newspapers by the lamp. He took several—one from New York City, weeklies from the surrounding towns; later Owen sent him the Canton *Plaindealer* and the Boston papers. Newspapers had good solid reading matter in those days, in big pages of fine print. Or Smith would weave new seats for the straight wooden chairs with hop twine, while Ida sewed or wrote letters to their relatives in Brooklyn and Illinois.

There was company when the roads were good; the surrounding hills were populated by relatives and there was visiting back and forth when farm work slackened. From her kitchen window Ida could look out to the west, toward the house where she was born and her mother still lived, where the sun shone earliest in the morning. In the other direction lived their best friends, Abram and Hannah Tilyou, whom they could always count on for companionship or help. One of Ida's brothers, John Worden Brandow, kept the hotel in Jordanville seven miles away, but came often to see them. He was a keen horse fancier and liked to drive his beautiful team or a lively single around the country. He had a great sense of fun and kept them laughing while he helped with the work; he wrote Owen when the boy was first from home: "You know I have to Milch all the cows that give Big Pails full. The Red Bull and the White Bull had too fites. But I kept rite on milking and Paid no Tention gol want it fun."[5]

Smith's uncle Wick, a much younger brother of Peter Young, lived with two sisters over the hills to the north; he never married and Smith's family was his, Owen becoming almost like a boy of his own. For all the loneliness of the farm, Owen was brought up with a strong sense of family support; none of them was rich, or even well-off, but there were many willing hands and warm hearts in days of rejoicing and times of need.

Thus the first dozen years of Owen Young's life, spent entirely on the farm, established with his parents the deep and close relationship which lasted all their lives. Working and playing, going to church or to the Fair, they were always together. In the slow rhythms of the farm year, there was time to talk and to think. Neither Smith nor Ida had had more than an elementary education, but they were thoughtful, observant people, interested in and learning from all that came to their notice—the world in the newspapers, the smaller world under their eyes. They were educated in the important things—life and death, the slow turn of the seasons—and possessed the strengths and principles to cope with them.

And for all the back-breaking work they enjoyed the beauties their lives provided: the fruit trees in bloom, the new grass "like a carpet of Green Plush," cattle turned out into green fields, fat sleek horses, the pleasures of gliding, swift and soundless, over the snow in a sleigh, the primroses flowering in the house in the winter, the delights of food—such as a Sunday dinner of "Sausage, Potatoes, Ripe tomatoes, Plum Sauce, apple Pie, Molasses Cake"—the "hammock under the apple shade," the antics of kittens and their dog Shep, and best of all, the healthy growth, good looks and lively intelligence of their boy.[6]

iii

Owen went to school for the first time in the spring term of 1881, when he was six years old. The little red schoolhouse had three terms: spring and fall were for the younger children, with a few older girls, and were taught by women teachers. The winter term was for the older children who worked on the farms the rest of the year, and was taught by a man, who could keep the big boys in order. From October through March the one room was crowded with fifty or sometimes even sixty pupils.

The teacher who did the most for Owen as he grew older was Menzo McEwan, who taught him for a number of years. McEwan was a big, powerful Scotsman, a cheesemaker by trade, who taught school in the winters when the cheese factory was closed. "He was very independent in his judgments," wrote Young years later, "and he made cheese and taught school his way or not at all."[7] His way as a teacher was to maintain perfect discipline—he was such an intimidating person that there was no difficulty in this—and to concentrate on those students whom he considered educable and to pay little attention to the rest. For this he received five dollars a day, a salary unheard of in Van Hornesville or the country around. It outraged the villagers, not to speak of the women teachers, who got from seven to ten dollars a week. But McEwan gave them their money's worth, to such an extent that big boys from surrounding districts were sent to him at the Van Hornesville school.

It was McEwan who was responsible for Owen's going on to the academy at East Springfield. He took the boy there in the spring of 1887—McEwan lived in the cheese factory nearby—for the regents exams. This competition was a kind of local horse race: each schoolmaster entered his prize pupil, the reward being the enhancing of his own as well as his student's reputation. There were sometimes other rewards as well; Young learned many years later that McEwan, in a heated discussion around the stove in the East Springfield store, had bet five dollars against the pot that the student he would bring to the examinations would win. And he did, for "if there was ever a student prepared for an examination, thoroughly and completely, I am sure that I was," remembered Owen Young.

There were few opportunities for secondary education near Van Hornesville. The Clinton Liberal Institute at Fort Plain and the academy at Cazenovia were excellent schools, but "one had to be courageous as well as rich to go that far away from home." East Springfield was only seven miles away over the hills, and tuition varied from seven to nine dollars a term. Owen entered the academy in the fall of 1887, staying there Monday through Friday. His father drove him over with a cheesebox full of food and called for him at the end of the week. A room in a house was a dollar for the week; eight boys lived together, swapped the food in their boxes, and fared well.

The boy was needed on the farm, but his mother said, years later,

"From the first he had a great leaning toward books and study. He cared more for books than he did for the farm, though he always did his work and helped his father. . . . When the time came and he decided that he wanted to go away to school, we felt that he ought to go."[8]

The academy was housed in a simple frame building in the village of East Springfield on the Cherry Valley Turnpike. The students were housed with local families; Owen roomed about half a mile away that first year, walking back and forth. One of those walks almost ended his story before it was well begun. It was March 12, 1888, and as Owen went across the fields the snow, which had been coming down all day, grew thicker and the wind stronger. It was extremely cold, and as the tall, skinny thirteen-year-old floundered on, blinded and breathless, he felt he could not make it. The temptation to lie down and rest was powerful; but he was experienced enough to know that this would be fatal. He fought on, and succeeded in finding and reaching his house; but he never forgot how close a call he had had in the famous blizzard of '88.

Not many miles away his mother fretted all that day and lay awake all night. When at last the snow let up a little she sent the hired man, George, down to the store to telephone the store at East Springfield to find out if Owen was all right. George reported in later years that "I damn near got buried in the snow myself," but made it, and got back with the word that quieted the mother's well-justified fears.

East Springfield Academy was small, coeducational, and fun. The graduates of this period reported without exception that they had had not only a good education but a good time. This was due in great part to a remarkable man who served as principal from 1888 to 1893, which included two years of Owen Young's attendance. Mark Hollister was a native of Otsego County, a poor farm boy who by enormous effort had made his way through Hamilton College. Although he had to teach school to support himself even during the college years, he graduated with his class in 1887, at the age of twenty-five. A year later he came to the academy, which was just about his age. His salary as principal was to be whatever was left over from tuition payments, after he had paid his assistant—the only other teacher and part-time at that—and bought heat and light for the building, for which he was also janitor.

In the fall of 1888 hop picking was late because of bad weather; when the school opened in September, one pupil appeared. The new principal postponed the opening for a week and spent the time visiting the parents of former and possible pupils, including the Youngs (Owen had had one year there already). His efforts were effective, and thirteen students presented themselves the following Monday. More came later as farm work slackened and Hollister's reputation grew, and by winter the school was the largest it had been in years.

Mark Hollister taught nearly everything: basic subjects such as grammar, arithmetic and geography, as well as advanced mathematics, physiology, chemistry, geology, physics, zoology, mental and moral philosophy, rhetoric, government, and Greek, Latin, French and German—all with a competence and enthusiasm that his boys and girls never forgot. He also taught them to stand and walk properly, to develop good study habits, always to use correct English, and to learn by heart and to recite passages of prose and poetry.

Perhaps his favorite subjects were the history and literature courses, and he taught his pupils to use and love books. The little library upstairs in the academy building had only about two hundred volumes, but they were good ones. The authors whom Owen Young read and admired all his life, and of whose works he collected first editions, he saw first in East Springfield.[9] On the Home Farm there were not many books: the Bible, the doctor book and the horse-doctor book, a few others. But upstairs in the academy, with the sun coming through the big, small-paned windows, Owen found on the shelves— and read—Scott, Dickens, Thackeray, Hawthorne; Cooper, of course, since the academy lay in Deerslayer country; also Carlyle, Gibbon, Macaulay, Bancroft, Prescott; Defoe, Swift, Sam Johnson, Goldsmith, Washington Irving; Bryant, Burns, Longfellow, Milton, Poe, Pope, Tennyson, Whittier, Wordsworth and Shakespeare—of the last, the poems but not the plays. After he had left school Mr. Hollister wrote him a postcard: "Dear Owen—I find Greene's History of England charged to your ac'ct. If convenient come to see us before you go to Canton and bring along the book. Send us word when you can come and we will be prepared with chocolate pie. Yours truly, Mark Hollister."[10]

Young took a general course, which included in his first year American history, physical geography, civil government, rhetoric and English composition, English literature, bookkeeping, astronomy, and political economy. Later he did a great deal of math, at which he was good. Hollister described him as not a brilliant student but a clear-thinking one, and thought because of his proficiency in math he could get him a state scholarship at Cornell; but state scholarships were not awarded to students under sixteen years of age and Young graduated from the academy at the age of fourteen. Disappointed in this, he took a year of postgraduate study with Hollister, devoted mainly to Greek and Latin, of which he had had little before.

Owen made lifelong friends at the academy, and tried to attend all the reunions that were held over the years. A pile of tiny folded notes (obviously passed around in school hours) from his feminine school-mates fills a good part of his boyhood trunk: "I do not believe I quite understand your plans"; "I did not mean to cry"; "Do you *care* about what has happened?"—indicating how much he enjoyed their company and how he teased them. Indeed, there were plenty of parties and picnics and expeditions, in which Mark Hollister joined, for he was always in favor of fun. And one night, when Owen and his best friend Frank VanDeveer of Fort Plain got into more serious trouble than usual, Mark helped them out. Young reminded him of it years later:

The incident occurred in the fall of 1889. . . . Frank and I had embarked on an escapade which kept us out until nearly four o'clock in the morning. At that time we were both worried and contrite. Worried, because our landlady was very faithful in reporting our conduct to our parents. We were satisfied that no apology, however sincere, would appease her conscience and keep her quiet. What were we to do in this tragic and critical situation? We decided to go to the Principal's house, wake him up, and see if he would not take us in for the rest of the night. He did, without a word of reproach, and the next morning sent word to our landlady that we had spent the night with him. He even assured her that if on other nights we were not in, she was not to worry. A few times, subsequently, that assurance was useful, too. What was the result of that kind of treatment by a teacher of his pupils? What kind of relationship did it establish? I can testify that it was the most effective method of discipline which could have been adopted.[11]

It was a fortunate circumstance that brought Hollister and Young together in the simple little academy at the crucial point in the boy's life. But for a time it seemed as though the road the schoolmaster had opened for him—to history, to literature and science—would lead nowhere. College seemed impossible, although he was fully prepared; there was no money at home, and he was too young to win a scholarship. The only practical course appeared to be a combination of farming and teaching school, with the hope of saving up some money, like Hollister, for college. This was a program he did not want.

iv

In the summer of 1890 Owen Young, not yet sixteen, was superintendent of the Sunday school in the Universalist church in Van Hornesville. It was the custom of the church, then and for many decades after, to invite theological students from St. Lawrence University to preach during the summer. It was a cheap way to hear something new—perhaps—from the pulpit.

St. Lawrence, in Canton, New York, had been founded by Universalists, and included a liberal arts college as well as a theological school. It was a small institution, struggling to keep alive, and in serious need of both money and students; the president, Dr. Alpheus Baker Hervey, was, at this time, actively seeking both. So when a young "theologue" named Potter, who had preached at Van Hornesville, reported that he had found a likely-looking candidate, Dr. Hervey decided to go and see for himself. An indication that he would like to come brought him a letter from Owen Young on June 11, and Hervey wrote back promptly; he would arrive on Saturday, June 21, on the 3:36 P.M. train at Fort Plain and would preach in Van Hornesville on Sunday. He went on to say: "Mr. Potter tells me you are thinking of going to college this fall. I believe I sent you a catalogue and paper at his request. I shall wish to have some talk with you about the subject and shall hope to make you convinced that St. Lawrence is the College which you will wish to attend."[12]

From later reports it is clear that he liked what he saw at the small, white, frame church beside the milldam in the valley: the fifteen-year-old boy, his wrists and ankles projecting from his Sunday suit, his hazel eyes smiling, shy but eager. It did not take Hervey long to find out that the boy was well prepared for college; and he liked him, immensely, at once. He talked to his parents, and to Uncle Wick, urging them to send him to St. Lawrence. But after the visit he heard nothing from them all summer.

On the Home Farm they were discussing it, and the answer was not easy. In the first place the boy was needed on the farm, now more than ever. His father was fifty-eight, far older than Peter Young when he retired from farming, and not strong. Ida was fifty-one, and they were both worn and harried and stooped from too much work. If Owen—who now did a man's work—should leave, they must have a man to take his place, and the cost of hiring one would be an added burden. Second, the cost of college looked prohibitive: tuition was forty-five dollars a year, there would be the train fare back and forth, board and lodging, books, and certainly a need for more clothes than he had ever had in his life. (His outfit for East Springfield had come to $12.25, including an overcoat for $6.50.)

Their relatives and neighbors thought the Smith Youngs were crazy even to consider sending the boy to college. In Van Hornesville, boys—much less girls—did not go to college; why spoil a farmer with education? Only Abe Tilyou and Uncle Wick stood by; they could not offer much, but might be able to help with the work and lend Smith a little to get along.

No one knew all the objections better than Owen, who had shared the farm work, and gone without, since he could stand. But he knew also that he must go.

On the twelfth of August Dr. Hervey wrote again. As he read the letter Owen knew that he *could* go:

My dear Young,

I have not heard from you since I left you that day in Ft. Plain. I hoped I might, before this, and hear that you were surely coming to St. Lawrence this fall. That is the thing really for you to do. You are abundantly able to come here now and take our full Classical Course in the next four years. You can easily make up what you are behind in during the first year, and this will save you a year's time.

You have talents my dear boy that should not be neglected. I do not mean to flatter you, and I think you are too manly a fellow to be harmed by such words, but I tell you that I have seen a good many young men in my day, and I have seen none who had a better promise of a distinguished career than you have, if you will only train and cultivate the gifts, mental and moral, which God has given you.

It would be the mistake of your life not to go on and get a college education. It is within your reach, and no matter what may be your natural powers you would be hampered and crippled all your life if you do not take it, and the time to take it is now. You are young in years and it may seem as though you need not be in haste, that you may safely wait. You cannot safely wait, if you possibly can come now, because you do not know what influences may arise or what circumstances may surround you, in one year, or two, to divert you, or hold you back from a college course—influences and circumstances which *could not take you from it*, if you were *once started* in it.

I do not think you need to consider your age, in your case, because you are unusually mature for your years. I would advise you to come, and I never advise against what I think is safe and wise. I often advise young men to wait a year or two years, or even three when they are of your age.

Now as to the money, I do not think you need to hesitate on account of that. I judged from what your guardian said that you had money which you could avail yourself of. I will say this, that if there is any difficulty about that, you may look to me for a part or all that you may need. If I cannot lend it to you from my own funds I will find some one who will.

You see my boy that I am determined to have you go to college. Well, the reason is, I believe in you. I have great expectations in regard to you, expectations which I know you will modestly disclaim but which I am sure will not be disappointed if you will follow the right course.

Let me hear from you soon. Convey my kindest regards to your parents

Cordially yours—
A. B. Hervey[13]

Smith and Ida were persuaded; if the president of the college thought this much of their boy, they should not stand in his way. Owen answered the letter, saying that he would come. Dr. Hervey wrote: "I am very glad and I am sure that neither you nor your parents will ever regret this step." He told Owen to come on September 8, and that he would find him a good boarding place before then—"I can I think get you one in the best place in town for $3.50 a week. This includes a furnished, lighted and heated room with care of the same." He told him which train to take from Utica, "which should bring you here at 6 in the evening. I shall expect you then."[14]

Owen made his plans to leave according to instructions, with a heart far lighter than those of his parents. They were worried and anxious at the parting, and about the money. But as it turned out that burden was lightened by Smith's excellent crop of hops, which that fall was far better than his neighbors'. He sold them for a thousand dollars and Ida put the money, more than she had ever seen, under the mattress of their cherry four-poster and—as she told her grandson Philip—didn't sleep a wink all night. Now they could pay some of the debts and send Owen a draft for fifty dollars for first-term tuition and lodging and for books. When it was most needed, Smith's gamble paid off.

v

Owen Young's association with St. Lawrence University began on September 8, 1890, but it did not end at graduation on June 27, 1894, for the college was a part of the rest of his life. The history and character of the institution are vital to the history and character of Owen Young. Indeed, it is incredible to those who knew him and St. Lawrence that he could have gone anywhere else. Even Hollister must have admitted that it was the place where the influences, at that time, were right for him, as it proved to be the place where, then and later, Owen could bring the greatest influence to bear.

In the background of both the man and the university was a moving force not to be underestimated—the Universalist faith. In Van

Hornesville there were two churches, the Methodist and the Universalist; the difference was hellfire, which belonged in the former but not in the latter. Removed from the extremes of belief in universal sin and damnation, and equally from emotional evangelism, the Universalists lived in the conviction of God's fatherly concern for all the brotherhood of man, among whom Jesus, a man, was first and best. It made, both at home and on the campus, for a peaceful faith which allowed space for happiness and hope. A strict moral code was enforced, of course; standards were high and demanding in both places. But the Puritan gloom, lit by flashes from hell, was absent. Soul-searching, carried to neurotic lengths, was not in order, and reason and loving-kindness were taught as the necessary basis for religion as for life.

Thus, Universalism allowed a degree of intellectual freedom unknown to many other sects in their seminaries and colleges. The curriculum at the St. Lawrence Theological School, for instance, had been quick to include study of the biological theory of evolution, and within the liberal arts college there were no rules as to what could or could not be taught. This atmosphere, *and* faith, combined with a pervasive friendliness, inspired in faculty and students alike an extraordinary devotion to the institution.

The founders of the College of Letters and Science, as distinguished from the New York State Convention of Universalists, who were mainly interested in the Theological School, were the town fathers of the village of Canton. Having their origins in New England, their inherited passion for education had loosened their purse strings to the extent of fifteen thousand dollars, which provided twenty acres of land and a building. The college was to be nonsectarian and coeducational, and was chartered by the state of New York in 1856.

The institution was so small at first that all classes, meetings and chapel were held in the one college building. Indeed, in the earliest days, the students lived and boarded there; it was surely one of the first coed dorms in the country.[15] Over the years the minuscule university surmounted the crises of the Civil War and of constant lack of funds only by the devotion, persistence and self-sacrifice of the men at its helm. Absalom Graves Gaines, president from 1873 to 1888, was a many-faceted teacher, and established for the institution high standards and won for it wide support. These the succeeding president, Hervey, continued and developed; like all the early presidents of St. Lawrence, he taught so many subjects that he was fond of saying he occupied "not a chair but a settee."

Hervey was born on a farm in an even more remote section of New

York State than Van Hornesville—Triangle, in Broome County—in 1839. From the first he was determined to get an education—"Nature seemed to have stamped my mentality all over with interrogation marks," he said years later. He worked hard to get money, came to Canton when he was nineteen, and graduated with the first class that entered the ministry. He became a successful minister, pursuing at the same time his scientific interests, writing books on flowers and algae and ferns, and translating German works on microscopy.

It was a day of continuous controversy over the relation of science to religion, but to Dr. Hervey there was no dichotomy; both were equally manifestations of God. From the fusion of his scientific knowledge and his belief in a Divine Order he worked out an understanding of the world that owed as much to Emerson and Wordsworth and the Greeks as to Darwin and German science. In spite of personal vicissitudes which a lesser man might have taken as evidence of serious flaws in the Divine Order, he taught, wrote and lived a grand and optimistic conception of man, God and the natural world to the end of his long life. His students never forgot this or him—especially Owen Young.

Hervey was president of St. Lawrence for six years, wearing himself—not to the bone, for he was a heavy man—but almost to breakdown. He increased the endowment by $50,000 and the number of students from 60 to 150, for he searched the high schools not only of New York but of a dozen states. As later years proved, many of those he brought to the college did it, and him, honor; they could say with Owen Young, "Of all the people outside my own family, there is no one in the world to whom I owe as much as to you."[16]

When Owen got off the train from Utica to Canton on September 8, 1890, the first person he saw was Dr. Hervey. In his frock coat and black, broad-brimmed hat he was smiling happily and greeting his boys and girls. There were twenty in the freshman class and he had arranged places for them all to stay; the college building was no longer large enough for everyone, and the students were put to board in private houses in the town.

The president introduced Young to Clifford Spurr from Rochester, who was to room with him at Mrs. Simmons's at 12 Pine Street, and took them there himself, a few blocks from the depot. There were two others in the comfortable house, which the boys called the "Pink Villa"—James F. McKinney and George I. Woolley. The four became known as the "Simmons Gang." Their picture shows them nattily dressed, wearing hats and vests, wing collars and watch chains (except Owen), holding a curious assortment of weapons—a cane, a spear, a racket, a golf club—and looking ready for anything in the way of a fight or a frolic.

They were serious about study, at least at first. Young said that "a college man should establish a reputation as a student during the first two years of his course so that afterwards as an upperclassman he would have more time to devote to outside interests without any loss of reputation or standing."[17] This reflected a fair assessment of the situation, and in general he followed it, though the record indicates that he must have done some studying in the last two years as well.

At first he was perhaps a little overconfident. "An isolated country boy," he wrote many years later, "with a reputation for precocity is liable to get some ideas that will not hold water and the first thing college did for me was to help me adjust myself." It was a story he loved to tell. He had been tutored so intensively by Hollister that he did not see why he should waste his time taking freshman math; he applied to the professor for permission to take an advanced-standing exam:

He invited me to his room one morning at ten o'clock. I went and sat alone with the formidable professor. He wrote on the blackboard one question: 2 plus 2 = what and why? After a half-hour spent in trying to get at least one sentence which was not inane in explanation of the "why," I reluctantly and humbly confessed that perhaps my earlier teachers had overlooked something in my mathematical instruction. Whereupon he laughed heartily and said, "I think you had better come along in the regular classes. I need someone to help me there."[18]

That first term he took, besides mathematics, ancient history, rhetoric, German, Virgil and Caesar, and got top marks in all, except the Algebra exam.

The class of 1894, twenty freshmen of whom four were girls, was the largest yet enrolled; more than half were from New York State, but there was one apiece from Ohio, Maine, Vermont, New Hampshire and Texas, and two from Massachusetts.

The two struggling fraternities were delighted to have so many new boys, and they set to work immediately on the serious business of rushing them. The "Simmons Gang was overwhelmed with attention from both." But at Young's suggestion they stuck together as a unit—not a negligible one considering the size of the class—and enjoyed the hospitality and importuning of both the Alphas and the Betas until they made up their minds and accepted in a body the invitation of Beta Theta Pi. Owen had worried very much about joining because of the cost—seven dollars for the first year, a very large

The Home Farm as it looked when Owen Young was a boy

The house where Owen D. Young was born

Ida Brandow Young at the kitchen door, about 1902

Owen at age thirteen, when he first went east to Springfield Academy

Smith and Ida Young, with Owen's horse Dan

Graduation 1889: Professor Hollister, center; Owen standing at left

Owen Young, not quite sixteen, when he entered St. Lawrence University, 1890

The university in 1890

The Simmons Gang: Young, on the ground, with George Wooley, Cliff Spurr and James McKinney

Josephine Sheldon Edmonds at St. Lawrence

sum in his budget. He consulted his parents, and his mother replied:
"Pa says go in if you want to it is all right—we are willing to do
anything that is going to be of any benefit to you."

The twenty-acre campus was for the most part bare; the college
catalogue of 1890–91 described it as "spacious." It looked very much
like the farmland it was, and was mowed, like a hayfield, occasionally.
Behind the college building were barns, a pump where the students
drank, and a sizable gable-roofed edifice, in one end of which coal
and wood were stored; the other end was partitioned into HE and SHE
compartments.[19] Besides the college building there were Fisher Hall,
the home of the Theological School, and the little stone Herring Library. There were a few trees and more were planted every year on
"Tree Holiday."

Owen was impressed with the town. He wrote home: "Canton is
a beautiful town, has fine lawns and houses and county buildings . . .
they have electric lights and force water." As he came to know it
better, he found there were other differences from home. Unlike Fort
Plain or Herkimer in the longer-settled Mohawk Valley, Canton retained in the 1890s many characteristics of the frontier. Its proximity
to the "Big South Woods"—as the great Adirondack wilderness was
called in Canton—and to the great boundary river of the north gave
its industries and many of its people a different character from those
of the valley towns with which Owen was familiar. He was interested
in the sawmills and the logs—"the most logs that ever I lay [sic] eyes
on." And he soon found that the local paper had numerous accounts
of fights, bloody accidents, murders, swindles, and chases by the sheriff—many of these confirmed by trials in the county courthouse, which
he attended regularly.

The town's Main Street, east and west from the hill down to the
two bridges over the Grass River, which supplied the power for the
sawmills, was wide, unpaved, treeless, and bordered by brick buildings with metal awnings over the sidewalk, hitching posts and horse
troughs. The largest building was the town hall, with a belfry, and
there were three hotels. Owen was right, however, in his description
of an area of elegance; big, handsome houses indicated Canton's importance as a county seat and population center, and numerous
churches on the square or nearby streets pointed not only to piety
but worldly wealth.

The university, small as it was, exercised considerable influence.
There were concerts and plays, both professional and amateur; readings and lectures, numberless meetings, commencements and other
college celebrations, track meets and baseball and football games. In

all of these the local citizens took as much interest as members of the college, and attended them in force. The faculty was made up, for the most part, of intellectually sophisticated men and women with solid educations behind them. They provided a contrast for the town to the world of lumber mills and the saloons bursting with loggers and woodsmen, so typical of the '90s; east though it certainly was, Canton, when Owen was an undergraduate, was a frontier town.

The college catalogue of the year Owen Young entered describes the town as "pleasant and thriving. . . . The student is peculiarly free from undue distraction . . . while no place is free from evil to such as persistently seek it, the unavoidable temptations to vice and dissipation are here at a minimum, and are utterly discountenanced, not merely by the discipline of the School, but also by the general sentiment of the students and of the neighborhood." It goes on more explicitly: "frequenting bar-rooms, billiard rooms, or saloons, is absolutely forbidden." For maintenance of proper behavior, the students' "sense of duty and honor, and the generous feelings natural to young men and women engaged in honorable pursuits are appealed to as the best regulators of conduct."

This seemed to work, by and large, though of course sometimes the fun went too far. If there was trouble, Dr. Hervey would call in the students concerned and speak seriously to them. "He talked so reasonably and friendly," Charles Gaines recalled, "that when he got through somehow the trouble had disappeared. . . . Dr. Hervey never seemed to have any trouble with the discipline. That was not because the students of the time—the students that he brought here—were a particularly tame and docile crowd. I can testify, and I think that they will confirm it, that they were anything but that."[20]

There was one instance, however, when Hervey was not completely successful. In the fall of 1891 the constant rivalry between freshmen and sophomores was particularly intense, and there was some hazing of freshmen. One of the sophomores who took part said: "We proceeded on the theory that ignorance of ancient customs was no excuse; and so endeavored to impress upon them the fact that they were not yet entitled to the full privileges of the campus. Young, I believe, was one of the lecturers, and assigned to the duty of laying down the law to the captured freshmen." The sophomores were called in by the president for a sharp rebuke:

"Gentlemen [he ended], you must tell the [freshman] class you are sorry for what you have done." There was silence for a moment, and then Young arose and said, "Doctor, it was not our wish to do anything of which the Faculty disapproved; and we are willing to do anything which you ask us to do; but the fact is, we are not sorry for what we have done to these freshmen. If we say we are sorry we shall have to lie about it. Still, if you ask us to lie, and you say it is the proper thing to do under the circumstances, we are ready to lie." The good doctor winced a little, then allowed just the trace of a smile to appear, finally withdrawing the demand for an expression of sorrow to the underclassmen.[21]

There were plenty of opportunities for fun on the campus. Few students had pocket money to spare, but poverty was no barrier. In a coeducational college so small that everyone knew everyone else, there were endless chances for parties and dates. In the winter, besides the more formal "hops" and banquets, there were skating and coasting and an imposing toboggan slide—all of these especially popular by moonlight. In spring and fall there was boating on the river—upriver on a Saturday for a picnic, and drifting home late in the afternoon with banjos and singing; all boats had to return by sunset. Hiring a horse and rig was too expensive to do very often, in spite of the advertisement of the local stable in the *Laurentian:* "College boys will find it to their advantage to call at this livery." Owen wrote home longingly: "How is Dan? I tell you sometimes I ache for him." But occasionally a group would get together and hire a surrey to go to a concert or a game at Potsdam Normal—an exciting expedition of eleven miles. Mostly, however, they walked, even sometimes all the way to Potsdam.

Young could not attend any parties that required a dress suit, for he did not have one. It was possible to hire one from Utica, but that cost two dollars and did not fit anyway. He was so tall his clothes could not keep up with him. A classmate wrote him many years later: "I can see you now—your trousers too short—sleeves ditto—and the derby tilted over your nose—you used to have a sort of challenging look on the world."[22] His mother worried about his clothes and inquired anxiously, "How does your school clothes compare with the others?" His freshman account book shows purchases of collars, cuffs and neckties, and two pairs of rubbers. When cold weather came and he had to have an overcoat, he wrote pages and pages home about the expense, and finally settled for one at twenty-two dollars. In his last years at college, when he was earning some money by tutoring, he sported a felt hat and a long overcoat with a fur collar.

His total expenses for his freshman year were $258.80. This included tuition at $45.00, board and lodging at $105.00, and three trips home, $30.54; books were $14.30 and postage for those weekly letters home not quite $4.00. The rest was spent on clothes, fees, gifts, photos, haircuts ($2.80 a college year, payable in advance) and medical ex penses—he had a terrible cold in March and went to the doctor, which cost a dollar.

He put a nickel in the collection plate every Sunday. The students were required to go to church as well as to daily chapel, but they could choose which one.[23] Owen tried every church in town, including the Catholic, and wrote home sage comments on the preaching. But usually he attended the Universalist, a brick building on the "Park" in the center of town. If he did not report that he went to both church and Sunday school, he heard about it from his mother in the next letter.

He denied that he was lonesome and homesick when she asked him. But he was, he admitted later. And he was worried about the additional burden on his parents caused by his absence from the farm:

> Remember I don't want you to work yourself sick (that is both of you) for me. Be careful of yourselves for you (you know) are all I have in this world. Of course I will have to come home if I take too much money, but I think I can get through for $225 per year and later I can earn some for myself you see. I fully appreciate what you are doing for me and while I am here I will try to do honor to you.

He usually signed his letters home "Goodbye" or "As ever, Owen," but here, after he repeated "I am not homesick," he signed "Yours in love and hope, Owen D. Young."

He was learning fast that first fall. He had written home in September, "There are so many things about a college you don't know until you get here," but by November he felt he had learned "an immense lot." It was wonderful to go home for Christmas; but he was homesick again when he returned. Things went well, however, and he was soon in the swing again; he was elected chairman of the Executive Committee of the class—"that runs the whole business." The Simmons Gang had discovered early that if they stuck together they could run things as they pleased in the Class of '94, and they did, throughout their college years. And in tests in March the Simmons Gang came out the four highest in the class.

Owen got home for Easter, in spite of the $9.60 for the round trip of more than seven hours each way. His parents were delighted, for they had feared they would not see him from January until June. Life on the Home Farm was very different without the boy. His mother, who was the letter writer for both parents, said bravely but transparently: "We get along nicely only it seems a little lonely that we can manage as long as goes all right with you." They lived for his letters, read them over and over, and demanded every detail of his life in Canton. In their replies, admonishments were few but serious: "Be careful what you say or do we feel very anxious that you make no mistakes you are so young yet but you know how it has been always, looking and expecting more from you than most boys of your years."

His mother's letter of November 2 of that freshman year sets a scene repeated many times throughout his years away:

Dear Boy I walked down after your welcome letter Tuesday the stage gets up so late on acount of pore roads it was nearly dark when I got Home . . . Pa wanted me to take Dan but I took your school path across Mr Kelley Lot had a nice walk Pa brought the cows and was milking and I hurried and got Supper we have your letter for a Desert every Tuesday night glad to hear you are well and pro[s]pering in your Studies may it be a year of Prosperity we talk it over and over if only you do not make any mistakes always stop to consider and get the right . . . Your Pa is very much interest in your school work has never regreted that he Started you on this year's Job.

And again in February 1891:

You know what we told you when you were here about all you ought to make that one of your studies to Studie yourself that is worth everything. Do not think we are borrowing trouble but we talk about you and this is the only way that we can talk it to you. You get so anxious to accomplish a good deal in a short time you forget yourself unless we remind you ocassionly and this we feel is our dutie.

She was looking forward already to the summer, and teased him about coming back to the farm: "it wont be so funny to be fetching cows and scaring birds off the roost but Shep will help you if you are afraid when it is kindy dark yet. Your Blue shirts and Overalls hang upstairs waiting." In June he came home, put them on, and whistled for Shep to get the cows.

Chapter 2

A Bachelor's Degree—and Jo

Owen took a brief vacation from farm work, before the busy days of hop picking, in August of 1891. His friend Caleb Fisher, who had just graduated in June from the Theological School at St. Lawrence, invited him to go on a trip to New England; it was to be Caleb's treat. Fisher's sister lived in Campello, near Brockton in Massachusetts, and they spent some time with her and her family. They splurged for a night or two in Boston at Young's Hotel, and Owen wrote home: "As you see I am at a hotel with a good name. It is the most fashionable one in the city and the best."[1] He was impressed by the chandeliers, and by the bathroom, but most of all by a theater Caleb took him to, and by a visit to Harvard College. Then they took a steamer to Rockland, Maine, for Caleb had an appointment to preach at Orland; they were both very seasick on the boat. But on the way home they braved the Fall River Line to return via New York City to see the sights.

It was Owen's first expedition into the world beyond New York State and his first visit to big cities. Caleb, who was not rich but shared all he had with his younger friend, delighted in showing him around, and this was the first of many such trips—always with a stint of preaching for Caleb, which helped pay expenses.

After hop picking was over Owen was back in Canton, tanned and healthy; Caleb was in Herkimer, where he had been appointed to the pulpit of the Universalist church. He gave the new sophomore a good send-off with a present of "a first class dinner, 6 pair black socks, a necktie and a solid gold stud."

Young's later boast to his children and grandchildren that he spent some of his college days in jail was literally true of a good part of his sophomore year. The sheriff of St. Lawrence County had invited him and Cliff Spurr to lodge with him in the comfortable living quarters which were part of the brick and wood building directly behind the courthouse. This was not as extraordinary an idea as it might seem, but one that was typical of Sheriff Erastus Backus. A native of the county, "Rast" had fought in the Civil War; a minié ball at the Battle of Cold Harbor shattered his right elbow, and delayed and inadequate care had left him with a useless and often painful arm. This did not keep him from owning some very spirited horses, which he used on his trips out to his farm at Russell, or in going about the county to serve official papers or even to collect prisoners, with one of "his" boys to drive.

Backus's interest throughout his career was aid to delinquent boys; Young of course pointed out that this accounted for his interest in Spurr. Both in St. Lawrence County and in Kings County, where he later worked as a parole officer for his well-known brother, District Attorney Foster Backus, he spent the major part of his time and money working with boys who had come up against the law, trying to put them back on their feet. He was an early advocate of farm schools, and his work became so well known that he was called the "Father of Probation." He was "a temperance man with strong convictions as to right and wrong," Owen wrote home, and also a hospitable man, a bachelor, and a firm friend to the students.

The sheriff asked Young and Spurr to help him with his clerical work, with the prisoners, and to tutor another boy who lived there, Ernest Chilton. Ernie was the star of the football team, of which Backus was a great supporter, but he needed help with his studies. In return the sheriff offered room and board to Young and Spurr.

They had an unforgettable experience.[2] Young said later that the schooling he received from Mr. Backus was far more valuable to him than any experience he ever had elsewhere. And at the time, feeling something of this at the age of seventeen, he wrote home: "I tell you there is a world of human nature to study as well as books."

There were many advantages for the boys; the trusties (and most of the prisoners were trusties under Backus's regime) blacked their boots and brushed their clothes, harnessed the horses, which the sheriff let the boys take out alone sometimes, and cleaned the rooms. The boys had a bathroom of their own and did not have to wait for baths on Sundays only as they had at the Simmons house. They did not have to go out to church, for a service was held in the jail every Sunday afternoon, with a different minister each week; there was good singing and good preaching, Owen reported to his parents. And they used the library of the courthouse for study; it was a pleasant place, with a fire in the stove and plenty of good heavy legal paper for notes—or letters.

Backus was not elected to another term as sheriff (possibly because one of his trusties got away), and at the beginning of the year 1892 he moved out of the jail and into a house at 20 State Street, not many blocks from the courthouse. It was a large, comfortable house and the three boys went with him. It was while they were living there that Spurr and Young drew up their elaborate Conduct Schedule, which was pinned to their wall thereafter.[3]

It was a good walk across town to the college, but Owen enjoyed it. In this second year he began to find himself and to emerge as a leader. "He was in the middle of every worthwhile College activity except sports," wrote James McKinney. "When he wasn't in the middle he was one jump ahead leading the pack. Young never protruded his personality violently into any situation, so that it is difficult to recall in any case whether he actively participated in the matter or whether he contented himself with 'egging' the rest of us youngsters on."[4]

All sophomores took a course with Professor Charles Kelsey Gaines in parliamentary law. Gaines had established its format in 1886. It was known as the Sophomore Assembly, and was actually a miniature parliament on British lines. Legislative positions were set up—a prime minister with a ministry, and an opposition; bills were introduced, debated and voted upon. If the ministry was supporting a bill which was defeated, it fell, and a new one was elected. The class of '94, known as "a talking class," threw themselves into this with an enthusiasm remembered for years to come. "Vote-getting turned out to be the chief business of the opposing parties, and voters were influenced not so much by the speeches as by tactics employed outside the classroom," reported Spurr. "Nothing in the line of politics or wire-pulling was neglected. Young's ability as a leader began at once to manifest itself. He did his share of debating but the greater part of his attention was devoted to planning and running the campaign which his side happened to be interested in, rallying and posting his forces and bringing his personality to bear upon doubtful voters."[5]

On one occasion a bill was introduced in favor of a protective tariff; a hot issue of the day, this divided the Assembly on party lines. The Republicans were greatly in the majority, and the Democrats, of whom Young was one, called a worried conference. Then, to the Republicans' surprise, Young announced that he would speak in favor of the bill.

He arose and in a very carefully worded speech began to outline some of the then well-known arguments in favor of protection. The Premier and the other members of the ministry listened with the greatest of interest and nodded their heads in approval as Young made his apparently telling points. But at the appointed place in the speech the leader of the opposition arose and asked Young if he would submit to a few questions. Young seemed rather annoyed at the interruption but graciously consented and then the questioning began. Young was apparently driven into one corner after another by the questions, finally being forced to admit his arguments in favor of the bill were all unsound. This went on for some forty minutes to the great chagrin of the ministry and the intense amusement of the opposition.

And the bill was defeated.[6]

When he was living in jail, and thereafter, Owen faithfully attended the trials in the courthouse. Court Week brought together the lawyers of the county—and often distinguished outside ones—and a great variety of cases. Fascinated by the law, the lanky boy spent as many hours as he could spare in the back of the courtroom observing fine points and good speeches, transgressors and famous lawyers. He was fascinated also by the procedures in the court—the formality of dress and behavior, the measured tread of the age-old routine of justice; for these traditions he never lost his appreciation. One of his children, going with him into the successor of that very courtroom decades later, could hear that enthusiasm in his voice as he described his early impressions of the law.[7]

All these interests and activities would seem enough to fill the life of a seventeen-year-old sophomore; but the class that entered in the fall of 1891 brought to him a new, demanding and time-consuming pursuit. That year the freshmen numbered more than ever before—as indeed each successive class did in those days; there were fourteen boys and twenty-one girls. Among the latter was a special find of Dr. Hervey's from Southbridge, Massachusetts. Hervey had been pastor of the Universalist church there in 1864–66, and was a good friend of two members of the congregation: Charles Sidney Edmonds—perhaps the church's most prominent member—and his wife, Altha Josephine Hobbs Edmonds, the church organist. Their only daughter had graduated from Southbridge High School in 1888, and had wanted very much to go to college; it was "her favorite dearest ambition."[8] This was hardly the fashion in a town like Southbridge in those days, and she received little encouragement. An illness of her father and the need to help her mother—she was the eldest, with two brothers—had thwarted her hopes. But Dr. Hervey, on a visit there in the summer of 1891, encouraged her to come to St. Lawrence. Her father, who was secretary and a director of the American Optical Company, which his father had helped to found, could afford it, and she was eager to go. Dr. Hervey promised that she should live in his home, where he had three other girls under the care of his housekeeper, Mrs. Foster (his wife had died in 1884). He was, as always, very persuasive, and with this encouragement her parents allowed her to go so far from home.

Josephine Sheldon Edmonds was a slender, dark-haired girl of middle height, beautiful, lively and intelligent. She was interested in the intellectual life, and perhaps even more—at that age—in social life. She had already had a good time in the latter, in the simple amusements of Southbridge: church socials and local dances, amateur theatricals and benefits, buggy rides, or just going downtown for milk shakes. But she had also made visits, long ones in the fashion of the day, to cousins in Washington and friends in Baltimore, where she had enjoyed a more sophisticated round of concerts, theaters and balls. Although she considered Canton a hick town, there is no indication that she found college life dull.

The letters she wrote during her freshman year at St. Lawrence to her high-school mate Blanche Winter gave an inimitable picture of life at the college—and of Josephine Edmonds. She wrote a proper "Journal" to her parents, about her daily life and studies, but to Blanche she wrote about the main topic of the girls' concern: men. Her first letter is marked in the corner "please Cremate"; after mentioning briefly Greek roots and quadratic equations, she goes on to the matters of real importance. First, the Latin professor, who is "so nice," then the Freshman Reception:

Of course everybody was there—and have you heard of Mr. Spurr and Mr. Young . . . they are two sophs, and I spotted Y almost as soon as I saw him . . . the cleanest cut face imaginable. Beautiful eyes and complexion. . . . As Y—— doesn't dance, didn't see very much of him during the reception—only long enough to filch a piece of Soph red ribbon. Well, when we came out—no, before, about the time of the last dance he asked if I had other company home,—I said no, unless it was the Dr.— 'Oh, he didn't count.' . . . Well, we had a glorious time,—shortest way round, oh no,—I mean the reverse. . . . He will start to say something,— get me all interested and excited and then drawl off into something else,— I flare up and tell him to go on, and he gets intensely amused and I get provoked, and that is just the way it is every time I see him . . .

The girls at Dr. Hervey's accepted Young's and Spurr's invitation to go upriver next day; they had a wonderful time. Jo wrote: "Came to the conclusion that Y—— is worth cultivating—await further development. He and S—— were around the other evening to look up something in the Dr.'s study. Dr. was away so we helped them."

Though she was older than most of the freshmen—and some four

years older than Owen—Jo plunged into college life with the greatest
enthusiasm, and became immensely popular. She was elected vice-
president of the class, initiated into Kappa Kappa Gamma, the "ladies'
fraternity," and went to the Beta Ball with "Owen D. Y——." Young
and Spurr had rented dress suits for the ball—they arrived from Utica
in the nick of time: "We both felt good to think we were properly
dressed."9 But as usual Owen did not dance. He had never learned,
and was afraid to try. So Jo spent most of the evening dancing with
Professor Clement P. Baker.

Most of the time Jo and Owen were together they spent in "con-
fabs" and "sessions," arguing, teasing, laughing: "I scold and blow him
sky-high—he sits back and smiles, and says 'Now don't get excited.
You look very pretty that way, but I wouldn't trouble myself.' He
certainly is as handsome as he can be and goes stalking off in the most
fascinating way." They managed to meet during the winter even in
class hours: "We both got out of recitation at 11 A.M. and meandered
into the reading room. Great luck, it was deserted. We managed to
get up quite a respectable little quarrel over almost nothing, but
finally got down to serious business. O.D.Y. remarks 'What is the matter? We seem to have been drifting apart a little lately?' I was profoundly ignorant." They decided that they did not really trust each
other: " 'If,' he continued, 'we could see each other oftener, we might
in this way **** get rid of the distrust in time.' . . . you see the
reading room was deserted . . ." (Jo's earlier letters to Blanche indicate the special meaning of what she called "punctuation marks.")

She did not, however, spend all her time with "Owen D. Y——."
There was hard studying to do, and dates with other boys—and with
Professor Baker as well, who was extremely attentive. A graduate of
the college in the class of '85, Baker had taught Latin and rhetoric
there ever since. A charming, rather plump bachelor—Jo called him
"Pickwick"—he was not very strong as the result of an accident some
years before. But he invited Jo to whist parties, church, concerts,
dances, or called upon her at Dr. Hervey's to help her with her Latin.
He sent her flowers, and candy in beribboned baskets, while her girl
classmates teased her and the boys glowered. She tried to discourage
him, but his persistence and charm undermined her resolve and, half
angry, half enchanted, she continued to go out with him.

Of his new preoccupation Owen said nothing in his letters home.
He knew well that any indication of serious interest in a girl would
worry his parents, and mentioned Jo's name only once or twice that
year, as in his report of the leap-year party in February of 1892:
"The young ladies did very nicely with it. Spurr and I both went—

got home at one o'clock. Miss Edmonds from Dr. Hervey's invited me." His mother teased him in her reply: "Did they have to coax you bet you did not want to go but dare not say No (Poor Boy)." She knew he did not like dances or dancing, but she did not know how well he liked Miss Edmonds.

ii

Charles Kelsey Gaines was the member of the faculty, after the president, who had the most influence on both Owen and Jo. The son of President Absalom Graves Gaines, he was a member of the class of '76, and taught at St. Lawrence from then until 1932, with only a few years' absence. Like all the professors in the little college, he taught a number of different subjects, and different ones at different times; but his favorites were Greek, English and his parliamentary law course, the Sophomore Assembly. He wrote poetry, a romantic novel, *Gorgo*, laid in the time of Pericles, and a revised version of Cushing's *Manual of Parliamentary Practice*, which was widely used.[10] A small, wiry man, with short-cropped hair and beard that in later years were snow-white, he was a serious and imaginative scholar, and a teacher whose gentle voice and manner concealed a firm taskmaster. He liked to be with his students and was always willing to talk or listen, sitting in his special mission-oak rocker in his study (he had designed it himself, with a writing arm). His wife, Cammie, who had been his classmate, was a woman of accomplishment, influence and wit. She also taught in the college, and guided the dramatic productions, as well as being the most-wanted chaperon; Jo described her to Blanche as "always ready for a lark, always on hand whenever we want her, and the best company I ever saw."

It was from Charley Gaines that Owen Young learned the rules of parliamentary law, the techniques of debating and how to handle a speech and an audience. Oratory, Gaines thought, should be direct and telling; fanciful ideas and fanciful sentences had no place in it. And it was with Gaines that Jo entered not only the world of English literature and literary history, an interest which lasted all her life, but ancient Athens as well. Gaines said, at the end of his teaching career, that he had never had a better Greek student than Josephine Edmonds.

Professor Baker, for different reasons, also had a deep effect upon them. He proposed to Jo in November of 1891; she refused him, and resolved not to see him anymore. This of course was impossible, as she saw him every day in class, and in spite of the rebuff he did not

cease his attentions. Owen was very worried; his feelings were ambivalent, for he too admired and enjoyed the company of "P.B.," as
did everyone in the college. Owen's fragmentary diary for parts of
1892 indicates that he could see nothing but trouble and pain for
Jo—and himself—in her relationship to Baker. When he talked to Jo
about it, she "denied that he had the *slightest right* to know how
matters stood between me and P.B." She wrote Blanche Winter in
January of 1892: "We fought like cats and dogs for the better part
of an hour. I wouldn't give in, but told him he needn't worry himself
about that third party . . . he said that of course he took my word for
it and we wound up with a delightful little time . . ."

Dr. Hervey was no help in solving their problem. He was fond of
the young professor, who was his distant cousin, and invited him often
to the house to play whist—the doctor's favorite pastime—with Jo and
Carolyn Foster making up the four. Afterward he would ask for music
from Baker's violin, accompanied by Jo at the piano. Either oblivious,
or slyly planning, the president made things difficult.

This tense and emotional situation continued for some weeks. P.B.
was alternately charming and cold to Owen. And Jo, the boy confided
to his diary, "appears a little cranky and I scare her a little . . . we
have a talk of about two hours . . . on the ending which is best so far
we *kiss*." Their own affair seemed suddenly "a desperate flirtation,"
and he said to himself, "I fairly detest her in one way."[11]

The problem was tragically resolved. Baker developed Bright's
disease, a result of his earlier accident, and died in April. Jo was overwhelmed. Brief as was the time she had known him, she had come to
love, if not him, his charming and thoughtful companionship, their
music together, their many expeditions, the roses he sent her which
meant so much in the bleak Canton winter. She had not hesitated a
moment in refusing his proposal, and never considered—as he hoped
so much she would—retracting her no. But for both Owen and Jo,
in this early experience of the loss of an admired companion, there
was a tragic sadness tinged with a touch of guilt.

Jo wrote Blanche: ". . . so much has happened since I came off out
here last Fall that I hardly feel like the same person," and she told
her friend how wonderful Owen had been through it all. But as spring
came she recovered enough to go on picnics with her classmate Mark
Manley, or boating on the river with George Woolley and Lorenzo
Case, and to Potsdam with Owen for a ball game and a play, behind
the "brown ponies—best team in town."

In June Mr. and Mrs. Edmonds came to Canton to take Jo home,
via Saranac and Saratoga. They met Owen and liked him, but the

college year ended without any definite understanding between the young people. Jo wrote Blanche about the situation:

O.D.Y. wouldn't be caught dead going regularly and constantly with any girl. He *says* he thinks it is all nonsense for a fellow to get so dead gone he can't brace up, but must always be tagging a girl around. So to the casual observer we are friendly enough without any special interest in each other,—while in reality there is the deepest interest on both sides. He confesses to it, and I don't mind telling you that I am as much bewitched by his indifference, his dignity, his "don't-careness" as I ever was by that of the Hon. John A. [a Southbridge suitor not otherwise identified]. And I don't mind adding considerably more fascinated.

It makes not the slightest difference to him how much I go sky-larking off, when I come back to him he is always just as sweet and calm. He advises me to do the sky-larking for he says "Of course, Jo, you want to be popular, and so don't think of confining yourself to one fellow. It wouldn't be a good thing for you." When I receive invitations, I talk them over with him, tell him all about the larks, etc. He got to wondering the other night how ever such a strong feeling sprang up between us. We had to give it up,—there was no accounting for it.

Owen's marks had been consistently in the top bracket, and he went home to work on the farm with satisfaction in his record. He looked forward to the farm work, to building up his strength, and to enjoying the company of his parents. "I am *Happy*," his mother had written in April, "when we are all Home and well and am counting weeks for that time."

He went to work in the hayfield, which he liked. He also liked, after a long day in the fields, the hammock under the apple tree and a book; and he liked his mother's cooking and the wild strawberries in the orchard. And he liked thinking about Jo. He had written her that he would "come east" in August, for he and Caleb Fisher were planning a trip to Cape Cod, where Cale would preach. She, on her part, wrote him every week, "dreaming and remembering," reviewing the past year: "Owen, my boy, I know we must put on brakes when we return to Canton."[12]

In the spring Owen had shown his mother a picture of Miss Edmonds, and asked her to tell him what sort of a girl she was. Ida Young stared at it for a long time, then sized her up as proud, quick-tempered and brilliant—a fair enough assessment. One day in the fields that summer Smith Young asked his son, "Who is this Miss Edmonds Cale tells about?" Caleb, who came often to the farm from Herkimer and who was devoted to Owen's parents, had been telling tales out of school. Jo reported to Blanche that Owen answered this question "meekly as though he had been telling about Miss V—— (a chump at college). His father went on to say that his mother had spoken to him about the aforesaid before. And then he delivered O.D.Y. a long lecture on its not being good policy for any two parties to have their name constantly associated etc. all of which had a great [?] effect on Owen."

But of course he visited her on his way to the Cape, got to know her family better, met her friends, including Blanche, and went with Jo to Walker Pond, her favorite spot, where the Edmondses had a summer place—"six miles with Daisy and the surrey." (Daisy was Jo's own little mare.) There they went boating on the quiet lake; it was a very satisfactory visit.

iii

The great excitement of the fall of 1892, at the college as throughout the country, was the presidential election. Owen Young was head of the Democratic Club, as well as president of his class. The college political clubs were both branches of national college leagues. The president of the Republican Club, which at St. Lawrence was by far the larger of the two, was Professor Lewis Beals Fisher; described as a "genial giant," he taught economics, political science, evolution and pastoral theology at the Theological School. The stated aim of this school's curriculum was to give the student "the knowledge which should underlie a rational faith." This included, obviously, encouragement to take part in politics.

Owen Young had listened to political discussions from his earliest days, at home and around the stove in the Van Hornesville store. His father was that rare bird for upstate New York, a native rural Democrat, and was deeply interested in politics, local, state and national. In this, as in so much else, the boy followed his example. An early picture from St. Lawrence shows him, tall and handsome in a rented dress suit, in the small group of young men and women who made up the college Democratic Club.

The campaign of 1892 was not one of the most exciting of the century. The conservative, rather dull Grover Cleveland inspired no popular devotion; but he had proved to be a capable and forthright leader, who shone by comparison with the devious Benjamin Harrison. The young Democrats approved Cleveland's position on the tariff and were eager to support him. For many of them it was their first presidential election, and although not all—including Young—could vote, their enthusiasm ran high.

Spurr, McKinney and Young set up a meeting in the town hall for the Friday before election. This astonished the predominantly Republican community so much that it attended in a body, if only to complain that such upstarts should be arrested. Young and Professor Fisher presided jointly—"the most important position to fulfil that I have ever yet been called upon to do," Owen wrote home to his admiring parents. Two students spoke for the Republican side, two for the Democrats—Spurr and McKinney—and all four spoke forty-five minutes each; political audiences were hardier in those days. A quartet sang party songs (the singers were all Democrats), and the homegrown orators provided, the local paper reported, "a feast of reason." There was also, it noted with surprise, no "vilification or abuse," and the audience remained attentive to the end although "no formal decision was rendered."[13]

The formal decision was rendered on the Tuesday following, and Owen and his crew were wild with delight at Cleveland's victory, though "Mr. Backus felt almost sick." There was a victory parade with fireworks, a banquet at a dollar a plate, dancing and singing. And when the boys found that the manager of the cheese factory, an old Republican enemy, was still flying his party's banner over the building, Owen and McKinney climbed up by night and tore it down, weighted it with stones, and sank it in the Grass River.[14]

During this, his junior year, Young took on a tough job for the college magazine, the *Laurentian*. Like most academic publications it struggled along on an inadequate budget, and was deeply in debt. The new "temporary business manager" cleaned up the mess he found in the accounts, borrowed money from the bank to pay the bills, and worked successfully to get more advertisements; he also planned to extinguish the debt through alumni contributions, in which he also was successful.

His next project was raising money for a gymnasium, but as Owen soon discovered, 1893 was not a good year for raising money for any purpose.[15] In June the board of trustees voted to make "a vigorous effort . . . during the coming year to add $100,000 to the endowment of the College," which at that time was about $155,800. But they too picked the wrong year; the depression made funds scarce everywhere and even Dr. Hervey could not find them, though he wore himself out trying. Tuition was still $45 a year, and faculty salaries were minimal, averaging about $1,100. The university was run on a shoestring, but even string was hard to find.

The college may have been almost starving, but the education it provided continued to be excellent. Young had an interesting year; he did well in chemistry, and Professor Priest gave him a key to the laboratory, making him the only student who had one. He was continuing French and German, and took English history, psychology and a physics class in "Electricity and Light with Applications." He was also keeping up his public speaking. It made a very full course, but he wrote home that he could carry it easily enough.

He had time, too, to take his first trip out of the country. Canada is next door to Canton, but it was not until January 1893 that he went to Montreal with friends from Herkimer—Caleb, and Mr. and Mrs. Helmer. He took the Central Vermont to Malone, and thence the "new railroad" to "the imperial and matchless Montreal." They drove up Mount Royal in sleighs to see the view—"the finest sight that I ever witnessed . . . I would not have missed it for worlds," he wrote home about the trip from the St. James Hotel opposite the Grand Trunk Railway depot.

He was beginning to realize how green he had been when he came to college; he wrote his parents: "I presume that these [his current letters] will never appear quite so peculiar as those [his first letters] do to me now. I was surely a boy when I started out, and I guess and hope that I shall never get over it—however I have seen quite a considerable of the world now in comparison with then."

In April he was elected by his fraternity to be their delegate to the Beta District Reunion at Union College in Schenectady. He worked hard on his "Toast" (really a speech), rented a dress suit in Utica, and set out. He wrote home, "I was not frightened at all—perfectly at ease. . . . I spoke nearly twenty minutes and had them perfectly under my control . . . they frequently interrupted me with applause and once the Union boys gave their college yell . . . of course I felt very fine over it."[16]

In spite of this busy program he was well, and wrote home that he weighed 180 pounds. The relationship with Josephine Edmonds had both calmed and deepened as the year went by; they quarreled less and had fewer doubts about each other. The flare-up of a previous affair in Southbridge, before she returned to college for her sophomore year in the fall of 1892, had unsettled Jo briefly. Her father was growing very impatient with her; she reported to Owen that he was beginning to think her fickle, because she had sent away the seventh man last month. But all this confirmed her preference for Owen. And at New Year's, 1893, she was writing to him in Van Hornesville: "After our parents, the first greeting of the New Year goes to the one dearest of all in the world."

They made a strenuous effort to conceal how much they cared for each other. But her roommates, she told Blanche, were not deceived:

" 'Oh Jo,' says Amy and Charlotte to me the other day, 'You know you think a tremendous lot of Owen. When he comes into the room, even if you don't look at him, your whole face changes, and your eyes look different.' " In another note she told Owen that she had heard that she had been called "the most sensible girl in the college" by a number of people. "What do you suppose those good people would think of Miss E—— if they could—for instance—read this note? In fact Miss E—— astonishes herself when she begins to put a hundredth part of what she feels on paper."

They managed to meet frequently, sometimes in Dr. Gaines's classroom after class hours, for this was private, though not wholly unsuspected by Charley Gaines; or in the library, when it was deserted and the stove was going. And when Dr. Hervey was away, which was often, they sat in his study, both of them together in his big old chair. There were always parties at the Hervey house—candy pulls ("You know what a gale you can have that way," wrote Jo to Blanche), potato races, or music and singing. Owen was by no means the only young man to come to see Jo, and he too dated someone else. There was a very pretty, very bright girl in the freshman class that year named Elinor White. He had many interesting conversations with her, for she had, he thought, "an enigmatic character."[17] Elinor was very good friends with Lorenzo Case (who was also a beau of Jo's), and campus gossip reported that they were engaged. She had, however, a very serious and very jealous beau at home in Lawrence, Massachusetts, who was frantically suspicious and unhappy about Elinor's life at St. Lawrence, and jealous of both Young and Case. He won out in the end, for after finishing college in three years Elinor went home to marry this high-school sweetheart and became Mrs. Robert Frost.

When the end of that college year came, and Owen and Jo parted for the summer, Jo considered herself an engaged girl. But she wrote to Owen: "It isn't quite right for you to bind yourself when you are so young."

iv

The Edmonds family was close-knit, entrenched and conservative, moving in a small circle of relatives and friends, all of whom shared the same ideas, stability, and English descent. William Edmonds, the immigrant ancestor, came over with Governor Winthrop in the sizable group that landed in Massachusetts Bay in the summer of 1630. The Edmondses settled in Lynn, but early in the eighteenth century moved southwest to the vicinity of Southbridge, where they remained. Charles Sidney Edmonds, Jo's father, was born in 1835, and worked with his father and grandfather in the optical glass business which became the American Optical Company. After his first wife died, he married Altha Josephine Hobbs, the daughter of Hartwell Hobbs and Josephine Augusta Clark.[18] She bore him three children: Josephine Sheldon, Charles Howard and Stuart Clark.

The large frame house at 154 Main Street on the hill at the north end of town was a pleasant and comfortable home. Charles and his wife liked good furniture and pictures and rugs and could afford to buy them. He was fond of wine and good cigars, and they both loved music. There were always evenings when friends came in, "piazza parties," with delicious food and lots of music. Papa played the flute, Mama the parlor organ as well as the big one in church, Josie the piano and the boys wind instruments; Stuart also did some composing. There were handsome horses and carriages in the stable, pet dogs and kittens, a maid or two, and constant visitors. There was, however, a good deal of illness; Charles, in spite of his tough and long-lived ancestry (Jo knew her great-grandparents as well as her grandparents Edmonds), was often ill, and died in 1903 at the age of sixty-seven. Josie—as the daughter was called at home—herself was not strong, and was seriously ill in the late summer of 1893, so that her family insisted she should not return to college for her junior year. Her father, indeed, never wanted her out of his sight. But the girl had a will of her own, as well as a special reason for returning, and insisted on going back to Canton, which was, she wrote Blanche, "the dearest, dirtiest, pleasantest and worst place on the face of the earth."

Owen spent a few days with the family at Walker Pond that summer; he and Jo rowed on the lake, drove Daisy in the bright new phaeton around the pretty countryside of small hills and pinewoods, and spent a good deal of time in the hammock talking, kissing, and planning their future. When they got back to college they were more settled and assured, and the year turned out to be for both a happier one. They knew it would be a long time before they could be married; the Edmondses had accepted Owen, at least as a serious suitor, but he had to be able to earn enough money to support a wife, and to give sufficient earnest of future success to persuade Charles Sidney Edmonds to part with his darling daughter.

They both became increasingly conscious, as Owen's senior year progressed, of how short a time remained for them to be together in college; and Owen became more and more concerned about his future. IIis position as the leader of the college was now assured and taken for granted by everyone in the community, including himself. And his academic work was no problem, although he was taking twenty-two hours: chemistry, jurisprudence, logic, political economy, ethics, rhetoric, and English literature.

Owen moved for his senior year from Mr. Backus's to the Beta "Club House"; Spurr went too, and they were together again in a room that was better than any they had had for study. There was always fun and music in the house, with—as Owen wrote home—"many nice boys of excellent family." The band of brothers was small and close; they studied and played and got into trouble together, entertained the Kappa girls and fought with the Alphas. This spirit of community, and his Beta friendships, meant much to Owen Young.[19]

During the summer Young had preached in the Universalist church in Utica; Caleb Fisher had been called there from Herkimer and Owen substituted for him during a few weeks in the summer, as he had done in previous years in Herkimer and Mohawk. At Utica the congregation was much larger and more sophisticated, but Owen's sermons were well received and his parents were very proud.

The great excitement of the fall of 1893 for the Young family was the World's Columbian Exposition in Chicago. They did not, however, go together. Ida and Smith went at the end of September, after hop picking was over, with their good friends and neighbors the Tilyous. They spent more than a week in Chicago—a tremendous experience, to go so far and to stay away so long from the farm. They lodged near the fairgrounds, in rooms at a dollar a night and "only a few steps to Restrants where we get nice meals very reasonable," wrote Ida in her letter to Owen.

Just as his parents returned, Owen and Caleb took off. Fisher's church had given him ninety dollars to go to the exposition, and he insisted that Owen accompany him. So Owen cut classes and they had a wonderful time. The exhibits foreshadowed the age in which Owen was to live and work, and he felt something of this as he stood in the brilliance of the electric light and watched the great dynamos.

Senior year was not far advanced before he was writing home of his worries about the future: "All day so far I have been thinking of where I am going and what I am to do next year. . . . Sometimes I wonder whether I had not better try and teach one year." But Dr. Hervey had told him that "first of all he wanted me to go to some large city and live up against some of the best intellects in the country and see what I was made of."

By May he had finished all his college work except for the graduation essay which had to be presented as a speech at commencement;

its title was "Morals in the Evolution of Political Science." Actually he never did get it in proper shape, for he was far too busy, and after it was over Dr. Gaines, with his usual twinkle, congratulated him on his excellent extemporaneous speech.

His parents did not come to commencement. Early in the year Mr. Backus, thoughtful as always, had invited them to come for the whole week and stay with him. Owen wrote them in April, urging them to come: "You better think about it and not treat it all as an impossibility." But that was what it seemed to them. It was an extremely busy time on the farm; the cows were giving a lot of milk, the hops were growing rapidly and had to be tied, the strawberries and cherries were ready to can. Money was very scarce, for the depression was bearing down hard on the farmers; they could not afford the railroad fare to Canton plus hiring someone to tend the farm while they were away. And, a truer reason, perhaps, there was about them a shyness which lay at the root of their decision not to come; even, perhaps, a wholly unjustifiable idea that they could not live up to Owen, the leader of the college, the most distinguished, most-likely-to-succeed student in the eyes of the faculty and his fellows. It is visible between the lines of his mother's letter: "Circumstances will hardly allow me to [come] as it would cost quite a little for me to get ready you know."

Commencement indeed was no simple matter in the 1890s. The week was a full one, from the two sermons on Baccalaureate Sunday, Alumni Association meetings and a Senior Class Concert on Monday, through trustees' meetings and the President's Reception on Tuesday, to Commencement on Wednesday morning. This was followed by an Alumni Dinner in the afternoon, where Young in "a very loyal speech represented the Class of Ninety-four," and in the evening a reception and ball at Miner Hall, downtown, which went on until daylight.

The ceremonies included the sad and surprising announcement of Dr. Hervey's resignation. In spite of his largely successful efforts to obtain money and students, his effective teaching, his close rapport with the young people, there was apparently dissatisfaction in the board of trustees—which at that time was a thoroughly stuffy group. The students were shocked and thought that the resignation should not have been accepted. But two weeks before commencement, the doctor had told Owen privately of his plan to return to preaching.

It was a time of parting. Owen was happy and satisfied that the college years were finished with a good record behind him. But to part with Jo was a wrench that hurt them both deeply. She was uncertain of her own future plans—to return in the fall to a college without him, to go elsewhere, to give up college entirely as her family wanted her to do. Owen's resolve to do well in the years ahead was more than ever confirmed now for her as for his parents. He had decided what his career would be; after the summer on the farm he would go into law.

v

It was by no means a new idea. In the spring of 1888, after a winter at the East Springfield Academy, Owen had come home to help hoe the hopyard. It was hot weather, and hoeing hops was not his favorite work on the farm. His uncle John Brandow came by to ask him to go to Cooperstown with him, and the boy accepted with pleasure. Uncle John, a horse trader as well as an innkeeper, was involved in a lawsuit with a man to whom he had sold a horse; Owen had been present at the deal and was needed as a witness.

They drove fifteen miles in the hot sun to the courthouse on the hill above Otsego Lake. On the lawn under the trees were lawyers and clients waiting their turn, talking and laughing, some reading books or briefs. When they went into the courtroom it was cool, the breeze blowing in the windows. The judge sat calmly, listening to the well-dressed, well-spoken lawyers. "It was a new idea to me, I had never seen anything like it," Young said years later to his daughter. "I had never known before any way of earning a living outside of farming except by preaching or teaching. Neither of those had particularly appealed to me. There wasn't enough reading of books, as I saw it, in either, or enough companionship. Here was something that just suited me. And so I went home to say that I was going to be a lawyer and from that day I never expected to be anything else." (But he never told his daughter how the horse-trading case came out.)

Grandpa Peter and his mother had been sure he would grow up to be a preacher. But at Christmas 1893, in the middle of his last year at college, he gave his last sermon, at Caleb's church in Utica. Cale reported that it had been very well received, but Owen wrote his parents from Canton: "Now I think I had better stop preaching and get at law."

In his last semester he had time left over from his studies, and he felt the future at his heels. In mid-February he wrote home:

Now that I have all my afternoons to myself as soon as everything can be arranged I shall begin to study law. . . . I shall get and file my application for the bar with the Court of Appeals in a week or so and then that will allow me to be admitted at the June term 1896. If it be possible I think that I shall try to get in the office of the District Attorney of St. Lawrence Co. here in Canton which will be a fine one & will recommend me in other offices probably. This will give me quite a start you see.

And he did. In April he went to see Ledyard P. Hale, St. Lawrence '76 and a Beta, who was the district attorney, and asked if he could come into his office. "Why I should be glad to have you come," said Hale, and promised to map out a course of study for him. A week later Owen wrote his parents:

I feel that at last I am started on what is to be my life's work provided it will yield any bread or money for us. . . . My table in the office is in the District Attorney's room & I sit at his right hand where I hear him talk over all his cases and give counsel to others. . . . A good way to learn law as [it is] a good way to learn medicine is to see the case & hear a Doctor prescribe, for law is a remedy for violation of men's rights as physic is a remedy for violation of laws of health. I am at present reading cases on Real Estate Law from the textbooks which are used in the Harvard Law School.

Hale took great pains with the nineteen-year-old boy, and a warm relationship ensued which lasted all the life of the older man. Owen had not been there a month before he was offered a permanent job— "to take charge of the junior end of the business."

But by then he had his heart set on going to Boston. Long before, he had decided that Boston was preferable to New York for the making of his career. Caleb Fisher had been influential in this decision, and in his easygoing, sanguine way had assured Owen that when the time came he could help to find him a place there. Indeed, St. Lawrence had always faced more toward Boston than New York. Both the college and the Theological School maintained close ties with the eastern seaboard and its Universalist churches, and there were many alumni throughout the New England states.

There was also, for many young men of the 1890s, an attraction in Boston that outshone New York. A rich and cultured city, one of the great investment centers of the country, pouring money into railroads and mills, sparking western expansion, Boston offered opportunities in business and the professions that were hard to match elsewhere. The most famous preachers spoke from Boston pulpits, the most famous lawyers in Boston courtrooms, the most widely read books and periodicals were produced by Boston authors. There was the oldest and most famous university, and others besides; there the theater and music thrived. To the young man at college in a region where the first settler took up land in 1800, Boston looked as ancient, as rich in history and culture, as London itself.

This particular young man, of course, had also his particular reason for looking to the east. Josephine Edmonds's plan, developed over the summer, to transfer to Radcliffe assured him of the companionship he most desired. Whether Owen's intention to go to Boston persuaded Jo, or her decision for Radcliffe clinched his move, history does not say. They probably worked it out together.

So he refused Hale's offer of a job, although much pleased by the confidence it indicated. His first idea, he told his parents, was to get into a law office in Boston, "where I can meet the best men of the country & if they would have confidence in me and happen to offer such a thing—*why* then none of us would have to worry any more because I could earn a farm a year."

But in May he wrote again: "There is another excellent thing to do which will carry me into Harvard Law School next year & then I can get a good place besides knowing lots of law . . . I shall be all right."

At this point Smith and Ida Young raised serious objections; they were not at all sure he would be all right. A place in a law office would at least supply a pittance to live on; but Harvard Law School! They wrote the boy, saying in characteristic understatement that this idea was "not the best thing." The barrier of course was money, and it seemed insuperable. Times were still bad in agriculture as everywhere else after the panic of '93, and in agriculture on the hills above Van Hornesville the margins were very narrow. Smith was in debt, and afraid of going deeper still. The costs of keeping Owen at St. Lawrence, small as they were even by the standards of the time, had been all that he could bear. This new prospect seemed utterly impossible.

His son was writing long, passionate letters full of heavy pen marks and underscorings: "I guess that I don't understand you or you don't understand me one of the two. First of all I don't see why I should not go to Boston next year if *possible*. Now what do you mean when you say it is not the best thing and you have always tried to grant my *wishes* ect. ect. [sic]." They had, he repeated again and again, done all for him that he desired or that they should do:

You have given me the opportunity of a college education which in my case has opened up ways and means that without it I could never have hoped or dreamed of; it has brought me from a country boy *somewhere* in the ways of at least a little influence and being known quite widely for a boy of my age—All of it is due to you—All the care and trouble and worry which you have been under in sending me I have not nor shall I forget it. *You* have done a great deal for *me*. Now from the time I graduate in June *on* you ought not and shall not give me another cent of money. I shall start on my own feet and I *shall not* take any more money . . .

He went on to say that if it were absolutely necessary to clear up the debts at home he would put off studying law for three years "and go to teaching or something like that and guarantee you $1000 at the end of three years. . . . in any case whether I teach or study law or do something else I must be left to do what seems best under the circumstances *to do*."

His mother wrote back:

Your letter last night found us in hopyard tieing them for the second time . . . Pa sent [the hired man] for the mail so I sat down on ground and read your letter. I think you have it right when you say you do not understand but I tried to make it plain as it is hard to write what we could talk better, did I not say your Pa had no objections to Boston but could see no way to furnish you necessary means to start as he would like to have you and would gladly grant your wish in regard to Boston if he only had the money for you . . . You talk about doing something to pay the debt that is not what we meant at all as we can do that if we stay well in a year or two.

She did not want Owen to feel that he should not have any more money from them: "We are not a divided house . . . will do all we can for you as who else have we to do for . . . Think you were a little nervous when you wrote keep yourself Steady my Child dont get to anxious all is meant well if you do not understand." This calmed him down, and he replied that he would go to Boston at the end of May— Caleb had offered to pay his way—and try to find something there:

If it is impossible I shall do the next best thing . . . I shall stop off when I come back and stay a few days and then we can talk over everything and have a good long visit and this summer I can get up a good muscle in the hayfield and hopyard. . . . Now don't either of you work too hard *because* you are getting where it isn't best to try to do too much. We will all work out in some kind of shape before many years. Don't work too much or worry any.

He stayed with Caleb's family in Campello, and saw several of Cale's friends in Boston about a place in a law office, with no results. Then he applied to Harvard Law School, his goal from the beginning. But there he met the first serious disappointment of his life. Dean Christopher Columbus Langdell agreed that his qualifications were without flaw; but when he discovered that, even with tuition remitted, Young would have to work to support himself during the course, he refused him admission. It was not possible, he said, to fulfill the requirements of Harvard Law School and at the same time earn money to live. The no was definite.

At the Law School of Boston University the dean and assistant dean were two brothers, Edmund C. Bennett and Samuel H. Bennett. Young went there, saw the assistant dean, and found at his hands help and understanding which he never forgot. Again, he was readily acceptable, but also, though nothing definite could be promised at the time, there were good possibilities not only of a tuition scholarship but also of a job in the school that would pay a small wage. Samuel Bennett told the boy to come to the Law School in September.

So Owen went back to Van Hornesville to tell his parents the news and have that good long visit. In June he returned to St. Lawrence for his graduation with the confidence that his future course was assured, and that the goal determined upon in the Otsego County Courthouse could be attained.

During that summer, when the first rush of work on the farm was over, Owen took a job in Herkimer with his and his parents' friend Mr. Helmer, with whom he had visited Montreal. Helmer had a large wholesale and retail flour business, and wanted to go on a month's vacation. Owen managed the mill and the books, and came home to the farm on Sundays. He was grateful for the opportunity to earn a little money; both he and his parents looked to the fall with some apprehension. But at the end of July a letter came from a friend of Caleb's in Boston, who had a brother on the faculty of the Boston University Law School; the brother reported that Young was practically sure of securing "that position" in the school. (Caleb had undoubtedly instigated an inquiry.) This was the job as assistant in the library which Owen held throughout the next year and which paid five dollars a week. He also received a tuition scholarship for the whole year, of a hundred dollars. This financial help may not have wholly convinced his parents that his projected course was "the best thing," but at least it now appeared possible.

Chapter 3

A Law Degree—and Tyler

Y OUNG went to Boston at the end of September 1894. Hop picking was over, and he was brown and healthy and ready for the new adventure. He was not yet twenty, but he was definitely engaged to be married. Jo had written Blanche Winter that Owen would be coming "to interview the folks" sometime in the summer: "We think now that we will have it regularly settled this year—although not make any public announcement. . . . But we are not foolish enough not to expect a good many trials and tribulations in the future. We are prosaically matter of fact." (The last statement is not confirmed by her letters to Owen.) In July the Edmondses agreed to the engagement, and Owen informed his parents; to neither couple could this have been a surprise.

Jo's father and mother, she wrote Owen, were much pleased at her plan to transfer to a college nearer to them: "Pa and Ma are both, in fact, carried away with the idea of having me within gunshot of home." Dr. Hervey was visiting her family at the time—he had acted as special pleader for the young people's engagement with the Edmondses—and she had a long talk with him about Owen and marriage, which she duly reported. The doctor told her: "You will be very exacting of a husband, demand from him in many ways—more than the ordinary man would be capable of giving,—but Owen will never fail you." He also went with her to inspect Tufts, Wellesley and Radcliffe. She had no doubt about her first choice: "We took the new electrics out to Harvard Square and found Radcliffe. Somehow or other I felt at home at once."

Professor Gaines sent a "charming letter of recommendation" for Radcliffe, and she was accepted. "Do you think," she wrote Owen at Herkimer, "it is really probable that we are to be comparatively *together* in Boston—our Mecca—next winter?"

Boston in the 1890s was a city of half a million people. Of these, by the turn of the century, the foreign-born from more than two dozen countries, plus their children, outnumbered the Yankees by three to one. The changes which produced the urban problems of the twentieth century were spawning, and the tight little political entity of the earlier years was slowly becoming a sprawling metropolitan region. The resulting tensions gave a new cast to politics, and there was agitation for reform.[1] In the winter of 1894–95 the city was in more of a ferment than ever. The panic of '93 had brought widespread bank failure, disruption of production and business, and high unemployment. Boston had its share of strikes. It sent a determined contingent to join Coxey's Army in Washington in the spring.

To the young man from the farm and the little freshwater college, both the people and the problems were new. In college he had read *Looking Backward* and *Progress and Poverty*, but in later years he told Ida Tarbell that in youth he had been essentially conservative and ready "to accept things on authority and to learn about them rather than to question them. . . . I do not think that I ever related thought in those years to any practical program." But as he walked the streets, among strange faces and strange tongues, noting the stunning contrast between the mansions in Back Bay and the slums of the North and South Ends, he received impressions he never forgot. Yet "for the first few years after I went to Boston I gave very little time or thought to economic and social problems. Every minute of time and ounce of energy I had I put into the law, first, to get through the law school, next, to earn a little something by teaching it, and last and most important, to establish a place for myself in its practice."[2]

Nevertheless, in spite of his heavy work schedule and his light purse he took advantage of every opportunity to learn from the city and its citizens. And to report what he found to his parents. Boston offered much that was free for the taking: public lectures, libraries, the streets themselves. He explored the wharves, watching the small boats unloading codfish, the big steamers setting out "and the people on board who probably the next time they set their foot on land will be on the old world." Sundays he saw the fine people in fine clothes, walking or driving in elegant "turn-outs" on Beacon Street and Commonwealth Avenue, and wished that his father and mother were there to see it all with him.

Perhaps of all the free entertainment and instruction offered by the city, he enjoyed most the churches. He went every Sunday, often twice; once he went four times and heard twelve men speak. This was not from an excess of piety, although his family were faithful churchgoers; nor was it only because it offered a regular—and unchaper-oned—opportunity to see Jo. It was also because there were great preachers in Boston in those days, and oratory—the use of words, the manner of delivery, the art of persuasion—had been of consuming interest to him since childhood. They heard Minot Savage, "the great Unitarian"; Edward Everett Hale, who was eighty years old but still a powerful voice; Lyman Abbott in the chapel at Harvard, of whom Owen wrote home, "It will be safe to die now for I have heard the greatest preacher in the world of this day. A simple plain wonderful sermon." They went to hear younger men too, such as Jo's ex-beau Frank Oliver Hall, when he preached one Sunday in the Universalist church in Roxbury. And they went often to the vesper service in the Arlington Street Unitarian Church to hear the music.

He was fascinated by the theater, then and always, but he could not afford to go. Fortunately he was occasionally invited to go with friends; the Edmondses were fond of the theater and whenever Josie's parents came to town they would invite Owen out for dinner and the play; it was hard to tell which he enjoyed more.[3] A friend at the Law School, Vere Goldthwaite, had a wealthy father who lived in Boston and did the same for his son and Owen.

ii

The Law School at Boston University was only twenty-three years old. Although Harvard's was a half-century older, the idea of a school for law was still not general, and most young men learned their profession as apprentices in offices, as Owen had started to do in Canton. The Boston University school offered an ambitious program, demanding a liberal-arts degree for admission. Its faculty was excellent, for it attracted many first-class practicing Boston lawyers as instructors; and it attracted good students. The dean did not care where they came from if they were able and industrious and ambitious.

The boy from St. Lawrence was all three. He had not been there a week before he was writing home that he could finish the three-year course in two years. He went to school at eight in the morning and stayed until six at night. His job in the library required him to be there most of the day, but it allowed him time to do a good deal of studying when he was not in class.

From the first it was a struggle to live, and he had to go back on his proud statement of the spring that he would never take any more money from his parents. He had hoped to live on three dollars a week for all expenses, but this he was never able to do. He took a room on Joy Street at $2.50 a week; it was just around the corner from the school at 10 Ashburton Place, near the statehouse and the law courts, which the students were encouraged to attend. It was on the fourth floor of an old brick house

way up on the hill and so free from any malaria or disease of any kind; it is really quite an aristocratic part of Boston . . . convenient and *pleasant*. . . . Now do you suppose you could let me have $1 or $2 a week for a few weeks—I deliberated a long time before I asked you but I lack just about that much now—I questioned whether I had better get out of school for a while and earn more but I am started and I want to finish the course in two years and with $20 or $30 now I can do it. I hate to ask for a cent *more* but I think I can get it and pay it back to you this vacation coming. You have done so much for me already that I ought to do for myself now.

They replied promptly: "About the money it is close business with us Pa sends you what he has now. That is not much but will try to send some more next week . . . that is one thing you surely must have to live in Boston and if we only had it how gladly we would send it on." And they did—two or three dollars at a time, sometimes only one, never more than five, except that when Owen first arrived in Boston somehow they found fifteen. They also worried constantly— and with reason—about his working too hard. His mother wrote: "I think I see you studying when I lie down at night that is my last thought."

He always felt guilty when he was not studying; but occasionally he admitted, especially when his stomach or his eyes were bothering him because of overwork, that he needed a change and a rest. One day he took a trip to Concord with a Beta brother from Amherst; it cost thirty-six cents on the train, and he was deeply impressed by the battlefield beside the stream, as he was by all the reminders around Boston of the Revolution. He remembered hearing Dr. Hervey say that his aunt had heard the guns at Bunker Hill and told him about it when he was a little boy. And in Concord too were the homes of the writers whose work he had come to know and admire—Emerson, Hawthorne, Alcott.

Happiest of all were the times he spent with Jo in Cambridge or Boston, or at her home in Southbridge. The last was the best, for Mrs. Edmonds delighted in feeding the hungry boy. Jo took him to parties with her friends, and best of all, in the winter they could go sleigh riding, in the cutter with her little horse. If there was one thing more than another that Owen missed in city life, it was sleighing; when the snow began to fall, his letters were full of how much he longed for Dan and the cutter.

Parties in Cambridge were not so much fun. He sent home for the dress suit he had had made, at his parents' insistence, in his senior year, because Jo had invited him to an Idler Club reception; he didn't think much of it, but was impressed by "as finely an educated set of people as there are in the United States."

Jo played an important role, besides that of the beloved companion, during her two years at Radcliffe and the following two in Southbridge. With the greatest ease and enthusiasm she shared with him her own more sophisticated background; she suggested books to read, current magazine articles that had interested her, and invited him to lectures at Harvard, such as Charles Eliot Norton's on Dante.[4] She took him to art exhibitions, talked about pictures to him, and bought some small paintings and etchings herself, with their future home in mind.

Owen was shy with her family at first, and reluctant to visit too often lest he seem to be pushing; but they were becoming very fond of him. Jo reported to him that her mother had said, "There isn't much frosting about Owen—but he is a true gentleman—with the best kind of breeding that comes from the heart—and that is the noblest, best kind after all." But Jo was equally shy in regard to his parents: "You make me very anxious, and curious, when you say that you are talking about me with your father and mother. *Have* they accepted me, dear?" She was not to meet them for another year, and she worried about what they would think of her, well knowing how they doted upon their boy.

At the end of Owen's first months so far from Van Hornesville his father sent him the money to come home for Christmas. The train from Boston got into Fort Plain very early in the morning, and he waited at the hotel until, as soon as it was light, Smith came with the sleigh and they traveled the twelve cold uphill miles home. It was a wonderful vacation; he got rested, and filled with home food, and when he returned he was very homesick. His mother wrote: "We all turn to our work feeling if Christmas presents were not plenty we were all *happy* and well, which will wear longer than presents."

In January he moved from Joy Street to a room in a house at 656 Massachusetts Avenue, where a friend named Bunnell lived; he had been very lonely in the room on Beacon Hill. Here he had a spacious third-floor room with lace curtains at the windows—and bedbugs in the bed. But when the landlady had got rid of the latter, he was satisfied. It was a forty-minute walk from the school, but he believed the exercise was important for his health, and it saved carfare. It was expensive in shoe leather, however, even though he wore rubbers to protect his shoes, for new soles cost a dollar. When he was home for one vacation, he left his shoes to dry by the stove at night, and came down in the morning to find his mother looking at the holes in them with the tears running down her face.

Food cost money too, and he was always hungry. He tried to keep expense for meals to ten cents for breakfast, ten cents for lunch, and fifteen cents for dinner. Even at depression prices it was not enough food for a hardworking twenty-year-old who was over six feet tall. The longing for food was part of his homesickness:

Nights when I am walking home I think how I used to come up through the snow and then I think about you and wonder how you are and all about you. The thinking is not all on your side and now while I have an excellent place to eat *yet* I would gladly turn that plate over and eat with you— for the eating and more than that to be with you. But never mind the day is coming when we can rejoice together and we won't need to shovel snow or milk cows for some bread—mind what I tell you—believe in me.

At the beginning of the next term he was one of the first 3 chosen from 150 for the legal fraternity, Phi Delta Phi: "If I can keep up that sort of ratio I will someday be one of the greatest lawyers in the country and such men charge and get what they please for their services. It encouraged me greatly." But in the meantime he was hard put to it to pay the five-dollar initiation fee. In March he was the winner of an important debate; the subject was "Is personal effort or environment more important to a man's success?" Young had the side for environment, and expected to lose; "it is useless to say that I felt pretty good. My stock went up 100% in the Law School. . . . Of course I was proud of it, but I put good work on the question and with it achieved a good result so I am more than satisfied." At home they "talked it over and over again . . . My *Boy* you are the Life and Light of this home."

As the school year ended he reported that his marks were high, and "I am proud of my year's work." In one year he was well beyond halfway in a three-year course.

iii

Owen Young did not spend the summer of 1895 at home on the farm; he became involved in a new enterprise, with his friend Vere Gold-thwaite. When they had first become acquainted at the Law School,

Owen thought Goldthwaite "a peculiar fellow"; certainly the boy from Van Hornesville had never known anyone like him. "Goldie" was a tall, attractive boy with long black curly hair, who had grown up in the West and was better with horses than lawbooks. His mother was an Indian, his father a wealthy medical man with a house on Beacon Street and another in fashionable Roxbury, to both of which Owen was often invited. When Vere had first come east, on the death of his mother, he had worked on the construction of street railways in Haverhill, near Boston, and then had gotten into the bill-collecting business there. As early as January 1895 he had suggested to Owen that they go into partnership, take rooms, and open an office in Haverhill. Dr. Goldthwaite, who had acknowledged his son and given him his name, was willing to fund the operation, especially if the bright boy from New York State would help Vere with his law studies, in which he was not doing well. Owen could not take time from his course during term, but as a summer job it appealed to him; there would be some experience gained in minor aspects of the law, and some money to be earned.

The plan was that the boys would set up a bill-collecting office as a sort of subsidiary of a Haverhill law firm. Dr. Goldthwaite enlisted the help of Dean Bennett in recruiting Young, and the dean encouraged Young to try it out for two weeks; if all went well he should have a month's vacation at home and then return to the firm. Owen wrote home about the plan, knowing how disappointed they would be not to have him there for the whole summer. Coming in from the hopyard, where she had been helping to tie the hops, his mother replied to his letter with an unwilling agreement; she wanted him home "to get recruited up," but she knew the experience would be valuable and the earnings essential. And at least he would be home for a month.

The trial period went well, he went off happily to the farm "to turn somersaults all around the orchard." He wrote Vere that "such days are lived over many times in the memory."[5]

The "firm" lasted a little over a year. His stationery bore the proud heading:

Office of Vere Goldthwaite and Owen D. Young
204 Merrimack Street, Room 5, Haverhill, Mass.
Office Hours 7 a.m.–8:30 p.m.

If it did not make the partners rich, it helped Owen's finances appreciably and, as well, Vere's knowledge of the law. They both gained practical experience, and they had a lot of fun. The firm had a team

of horses, which was used for business, but which also took them to
the shore for clam and fish dinners, and to lie on the sand and watch
"the surf come in and listen to the roar of the great Atlantic." But
even there Owen's thoughts were on the farm: "I suppose you are all
done haying now and about ready for the grain which is early this
year and that is good so you can get it easily out of the way before
hop-time. By the way, how are the hops looking now?"

The boys had plenty of business. Owen worked hard, collecting
bills, drawing wills, conveyances, writing contracts; the more he did,
the more fees he got. And he enjoyed it. In August he wrote proudly
to his parents:

We have a man now to take care of the team, drive us around and do general work such as to go out and notify people that we have bills against
them. He is a young fellow, older than I am, I imagine, who thinks that
it is quite an honor to be doing work for lawyers. He is doing exactly the
sort of business I should have to do were I in a large office with no one
behind me. As it is he takes my orders and does my errands. . . . It makes
me smile to think what a lucky dog I am and somehow or other how things
turn up right for me. Of course everyone in this city really thinks we are
full fledged lawyers.

Indeed, the local paper printed a paragraph which did them no
harm: "The tallest law firm in Haverhill is that of Goldthwaite and
Young, 204 Merrimack Street. The senior member stands 6 feet high
and the junior member 6 feet 2 inches. Both are very young men, but
both are very gentlemanly, courteous and able. I am not surprised to
learn that they are already doing a first class business.[6]

They got their first big fee in an action against the Lowell, Lawrence and Haverhill Street Railroad for negligence in the death of a
man. The next week they were retained by the owner of a bicycle
shop to find a man who had rented a bike and gone off with it. The
boys set out with their team, found the man in Concord, New Hampshire, and triumphantly brought back the bicycle in the wagon.

Although after the dissolution of the little firm the following summer Young did not see much more of Goldthwaite, who died young,
he never forgot him. The handsome half-breed, with his Indian features set off incongruously by a delicate gold pince-nez, his long black
hair, his tall frame always elegantly dressed in a frock coat, was a
memorable figure. He insisted too that Owen should always be well
dressed, and gave him money for a new suit. Easy with money, easy
with women, he was a great talker and a humorous companion. Although he was not a good student, he was very fond of poetry and
knew pages of Byron and Pope by heart; he would recite the *Essay*

on Man, entire, to his partner, who learned from this a permanent pleasure in Pope. And when Buffalo Bill, an old friend from western days, brought his Wild West Show to Boston, Vere rode a bucking bronco in his Prince Albert coat, to the amazement and delight of the spectators and the members of the show. His letters to Young testify, in lengthy and ornate sentences, to his warm affection and deep respect for and dependence on his partner.

There was not much time that summer to get to Southbridge to see Jo. But letters flew back and forth twice or thrice a week, and he managed four days with her on his way back from Van Hornesville. They wrote of the small things in their daily lives, but also of life and death and love, and their plans for the future. She was delighted by the success of the Haverhill venture, but he said that what he really admired as a profession was that of the scholar. "You puzzle me," she answered, "with your desire to lead the life of a scholar. . . . I'd rather a hundred times over that [you] were a man of affairs . . . you *will* be a scholar . . . but you will be something else too—a man with a knowledge of the outside world, of men, of events, and a man with a thorough understanding of life in its broadest sense."

iv

Young awaited the opening of his second year at the Law School with anticipation, and, after his taste of real practice, with an eagerness to be done with it. He took some advanced-standing exams, in Agency and Bills and Notes, and did well after the summer's experience. Best of all, he won a larger scholarship—$150 instead of $100.

It was a different story from the uncertainty, lack of confidence, and homesickness of the year before. But the pressure was even greater, for he was still living and working at Haverhill, since the money earned there was necessary for living expenses. He left by train in the morning at 10:05 or 10:44, and returned from Boston by 5:15, working in the Haverhill office before and after.

He had neither time nor money to go home for his twenty-first birthday, so he settled for the next best thing—to go to Southbridge. Jo was going too, for October 27 fell on a Sunday, and it was her parents' twenty-seventh wedding anniversary. They had a great cele-bration, church in the morning, a drive, a "swell dinner," and in the evening "plenty of music." When he got back to Haverhill he wrote his parents all about it; he seldom mentioned Jo in his letters home, but this time his enthusiasm carried him away: "Josie, of course, went up from Cambridge with me and came back yesterday too; she is surely an educated and cultured girl, sensibly and well brought up. I am more and more impressed with the fact that the family and their surroundings are most excellent and I flatter myself that I am not very easily imposed on either." But he went on quickly to say: "Through it all my thoughts kept going to you and I spent much of the day with you in thought, wondering what you were doing and *why* I could not have arranged it to go there with you. . . . I have my box—it came Friday and that night I took it up here in my room and opened it—and ate some of the candy and then sat a long time thinking of you until I got quite lonesome and homesick."

The shoe business was dull that fall; it was the lifeblood of the Haverhill, Lawrence and Lowell area, and when it was bad nothing was good. So Goldthwaite and Young did not do so well; but there was still plenty to keep Owen busy. He tried a case in the municipal court and made his first extended plea in a criminal case; the defendant was charged with larceny, and Young got him off with a ten-dollar fine "where he ought to have had a year's imprisonment.[7] I got $15 for my work. We also have a case for the alienation of a wife's affections which is quite a famous one in this city and if we get on the right track will give us no little notoriety."

In contrast to the previous year, he felt that he could take a day off "without feeling that I must make up for the money out of my dinners." He did so on election day, when he had not registered and did not vote, '95 being an off year. Besides, as he wrote home, "The Republicans have it all their own way, and I am not at all interested in it." Instead, he and Jo went to Concord, to see again the house and grave of Emerson, and "the old battleground where stands the monument, the speech for the dedication of which I used to read last summer out in the hammock."

There were other pleasant occasions. Caleb Fisher had been called from Utica to the Universalist church in Lowell, Massachusetts, at an increase in salary from fifteen hundred dollars to two thousand dollars a year, and Owen was happy to be "connected by the electric cars" with Cale. It was a disappointment to the Youngs on the farm, however; Fisher had become almost like a son to them in his years at Herkimer and Utica, when he came often to the farm to talk with Smith and eat Ida's delicious meals: "We awfully hate to have both our Boys so far from us."

For Christmas Owen was home with his parents; Jo asked him, "Do you think the postmaster at Van Hornesville will mind if I write you very often?" And she did, almost every day. It was a short holiday,

for he had exams immediately before, and after there was all the work
at Haverhill to make up—"I am pushed to death." But 1896 began
auspiciously; Young was chosen one of the twenty "honor men," from
whom the candidates for the competition for commencement speaker
were selected; even the *Herkimer Democrat* reported this honor. Also,
he had three offers of positions in law offices in Boston, two of them
partnerships. And when the Boston papers announced his election as
one of the two competing commencement speakers, he wrote home
happily, "I have proved to them that a graduate of a little unknown
college in the wilds of northern New York could hold his own against
the graduates of Harvard and Yale."

In March of 1896 the firm of Goldthwaite and Young moved into
new offices, in the Academy of Music Building in Haverhill; business
was much better, and Owen sent his father enough money to get a
hired man, and bought himself a spring overcoat for thirty-five dollars.

In May, when he had five exams coming up, plus all the work in
the office, he had to give his oration in the competition for commencement speaker, the top honor at Boston University Law School. On
May 13 he wrote his father and mother: "The best fortune yet has
smiled on us. Yesterday I was chosen winner at the Law School Contest. . . . I am happy in having honored you." This brought him honor
also in the city, for the competition was well known as a stiff one.
"When I got up I knew I was going to win. I could feel it tingling
all over me that I was going to make every soul within reach of my
voice listen to me and I did," although "I had to make some of it up
as I went." He told them he was to repeat the winning oration at
commencement on June 3 and wished they would come, and Uncle
Wick too.

By June 1 he had passed all his exams with flying colors, and but
for commencement his days at school were over—although in his
letter home he put in his customary caveat: perhaps something might
happen so he would not get his diploma. His parents did not come
to graduation, for the hops were growing too fast, and Uncle Wick
would not come because he did not have a dress suit. But his mother
wrote that they would feel proud even at home "and we have a right,
too; as Honor upon Honors have you sent back to us." She asked
"at what hour are the exercises as we shall think of you, imagine we
see you . . . hope you will feel in a speaking mood." Jo, also, had invited them to Class Day at Radcliffe, which pleased them.

Graduation exercises for Boston University were held in Tremont
Temple, near the Common, with three thousand people present—including the entire Edmonds family, Josie pink-cheeked with pride.

Owen Young's oration was entitled "Professional Honor"; it was a plea for adherence to the principle and reason of the law rather than its word and form.

We must first be men, then lawyers. Our duty is to use, not abuse the law. . . . The question is never what a lawyer can do but what a man ought to do. . . . The regime of anarchy on the one hand and that of centralized power and corporate wealth on the other, are dangerous to a stable equilibrium and a constant rule. . . . Never before has there been more need of the great conservative power in the state exercised by the law. . . . The great lawyer of the future will be the man who has the faculty for seeing right; the man who has the courage to tell what he saw; the man who has the stability to maintain what he said.[8]

v

After the triumph, bar exams lay ahead. They were to take place in the old courthouse in Salem on June 18, 19, 22 and 23. It was the first time the exams had ever taken up more than one day, and they turned out to be the most difficult ever given in the state. The first one came on Jo's Class Day, and Owen took his dress suit along to Salem, and went directly to Cambridge in the evening. (Fortunately her commencement was on the twentieth, between exams.) Owen was seriously worried about passing; the strain was great. But he did, although many of his fellows did not. Then he went home to the farm over the Fourth of July to rest; he was worn out.

On the thirteenth of July, Owen Young was duly sworn in at Salem and received his certificate to practice in the courts of the Commonwealth of Massachusetts. He had an offer of a job immediately. The chairman of the examining board for the bar exams had been Judge Elbridge Burley, a distinguished lawyer with offices in Boston and Lawrence, where he conducted a prosperous business as counsel for many textile manufacturers in the region. He asked Young to take a place in one or the other office, on a salary, in the fall. The old man and the young took to each other on sight; Owen accepted promptly.

The firm of Goldthwaite and Young was dissolved at the end of July, much to Vere's distress; at first angry and hurt, he refused to say good-bye when Owen left. Later he wrote that "the blow which our untimely separation has given me completely crushes me." But he testified to "the tender and most commendable regard with which I have ever and do still contemplate you," and tried again and again to get Owen back as partner.[9]

Owen wrote his parents that he would be home by August 1 to stay a month or six weeks: "Happy prospect and I am as happy a boy as there is in Massachusetts tonight. I shall be able to have weeks of happy time with you without the least bother about business nor any trouble of any kind. Just a good vacation pure and simple."

It was indeed a good vacation, for Jo came for ten days in the latter part of August. It was a meeting both she and his parents approached with fear. She knew well how close the little family of three had always been, and understood, she said, "the pain your mother must feel." But she was eager to know them, to have them like her and not resent her—"how anxious I am to love them—if they will only let me." The next year, when Owen was planning to invite her again, his mother wrote him: "I shall not dread her as last summer since I know her." "Can your mother stand our happiness?" wrote Jo before she came the first time.[10] Owen too was very nervous at this first encounter of the two women, both of whom he loved deeply. But he was lucky; they established almost at once, and maintained for the rest of their lives, an understanding and affection that set at naught the differences in their backgrounds and temperaments, and united them in love and care, not only for Owen, but for each other.

When Owen had written with such joy about his bright prospects for the fall, he had forgotten to put in his usual caveat. In September he received a message from Judge Burley that he was ready for Young to come into his office in Boston. Shortly thereafter came another telegram; his mother watched his face as he read it, and never forgot the look. The wire reported that Burley had dropped dead.

It was a staggering blow; Owen felt that his whole future had been destroyed. His brief acquaintance with Burley had given him a deep respect and admiration for the man, as well as exactly the kind of position in Boston that he wanted. He went to Boston, attended the funeral, and a little later called on Mrs. Burley. But he did not know where to turn for help. His friends the Bennetts were still away on vacation, and the law offices he knew were also closed for the summer; the partners were on the Cape or the Vineyard, in the mountains of New Hampshire or on the coast of Maine. He visited Jo in Southbridge, then came back to the farm.

In September, however, Samuel Bennett wrote that he had learned of a place in the city which would pay enough to support him: "If you are inclined to accept, it would be wise to come to Boston as soon as practicable." The boy left at once. On September 25, Friday, at 4:30 in the afternoon, he addressed his parents from the office of *Charles H. Tyler, Counsellor at Law, Sears Building, Boston*: "I am settled in the position as above and have been working at it all day. You may send my bag to Room 505 Sears Building. . . . I am settled at $50 a month as a starter, with some extras outside and pretty fairly brilliant prospects. Mr. Bennett thinks the prospects very bright indeed." Mr. Tyler, he reported, "is a young man but has an extensive practice and one which handles large sums of money. I am very glad to be so well started. I have an office of my own and shall have a student in it as soon as the school opens."

Thus began an association which was to last sixteen years and to become a lifelong friendship, full of affection and respect on both sides. In 1896 Charles Tyler was thirty-five years old; active, hard-working and demanding of himself and of those in his office, he had a large and lucrative practice, mainly in real-estate and corporation law. He expected a great deal of the young men working for him, but he paid them well. The usual salary in law firms for a recent law-school graduate was twenty-five dollars a month. It was typical of Tyler, when he asked Dean Bennett for a new clerk, to expect the young man to appear the next day and begin work immediately.

In spite of his bright prospects, Young did not intend to take any chances on overspending; he had had too many thin times in Boston already. After a brief stay with Caleb in Lowell, he took a room at 4 Columbus Square for six dollars a week, shared equally with a roommate. It was a long way from the Sears Building, but this gave him the walk he always counted on to keep him in good health. A friend from the Law School was the roommate, Arthur DeGoosh: "the only man in the Law School I would room with . . . he is a fine boy . . . our careers and tastes and ambitions are much the same. He is quiet, a hard student with a character very estimable in every way." DeGoosh, called "the Squire," was a Tufts man, a Vermonter and a Universalist; the boys ate together at a restaurant nearby, and read aloud or talked law in the evenings.

The room was big and square with a bow window, hot and cold water, two folding beds and four or five rocking chairs. Owen asked his parents to send "your pictures and Josie Edmonds' pictures—it is less lonesome if I have them." The following year Jo was able to come there herself, for her brother Stuart, who was studying in an architect's office in Boston, was rooming there also and could act as chaperon.

Charles Tyler soon found out the capabilities of his new clerk. Young had not been in the office a month before he was writing home: "I have my own work under the direction of no one not even Mr. Tyler. He turns it over to me and lets me handle it." His letter gave careful instructions as to what he wanted sent from home, and what he did not want—neither the worn overcoat nor the extra-heavy underwear. "As to books, I wish you would send my Curtis in three volumes and my Constitutional History of England in four volumes and Wilson's 'The State' if you can find it." And finally he reported that Mr. Tyler had invited him to his house on Beacon Street the previous evening—"a very swell place you know."

By the latter part of November he was sending money home, sometimes as much as fifteen dollars at a time, and having a new winter overcoat made. When Jo came to town he took her to dinner at Young's Hotel, the object of his longing appetite during the previous hungry years.

Jo was now living at home in Southbridge, helping her mother, teaching a class of girls, and writing letters to Owen two or three times a week. Her record at Radcliffe had been excellent; she had continued her Greek, with the great Professor William Watson Goodwin, done a good deal of French and German, and taken several writing courses. The final year she had lived on Buckingham Place in Cambridge with the Goodhues, who became good friends, especially Bertram Goodhue, who was to make his mark as an architect.

During her two years at Radcliffe Jo and Owen had seen each other at least once a week; church, the theater, a concert or an art show served to bring them together, and they also met often at Jo's aunt's in Waltham. They enjoyed most Owen's visits to Southbridge, especially when they could go to the cottage at the lake. The Edmondses were fond of entertaining company, but there were times when they could be alone. During these long years of engagement—they met in the fall of 1891 and were not married until June of 1898—they became lovers; Jo in her numerous and passionate letters addressed Owen as her "dear Husband," and told him she lived for his visit, and for the day when they could be together for good.[10]

It was fortunate that she had the teaching to take up much of her time. This was a course on English literature she gave to a young women's club, the Entre-Nous. She worked at her lectures very faithfully; Owen sent the books she wanted from Boston, and in her letters she kept him in close touch with her work. The lecture on Walter Scott "ought to be very simple—yet it ought to be rich, somehow, like one of the old-fashioned silks that stood alone." She hoped he would like the lecture on Macaulay and Carlyle, which she thought the best she had done yet; but "it would spoil my disposition if I should spend over much time on Carlyle—cross old genius!" She told him to get cheap editions of the Rossettis and Mrs. Browning—"By

and by we will have them in morocco. . . . I've buried Keats, am
about to drown Shelley," and she romped through the Victorians—
"I gave a lecture on Clough and Arnold yesterday, next Tuesday
Dickens, Thackeray and George Eliot." But she said wanting him all
the time "consumes too much vital energy" and she was tired out.

She loved to be outdoors, and driving the horses was her favorite
pastime; whenever the weather and the roads were good, and her
father would permit, she was out with them, looking for flowers in
the spring, chestnuts in the fall, the beauty of the gentle countryside
always. At home she tended her garden, walked the dogs, helped
with the housework, made barberry jelly and grape wine, and looked
after her father and her brothers, who were often ill.

There was the very active social life of Southbridge as well, church
affairs, bazaars, amateur theatricals—the last a great favorite of her
father's—dances and visits. She went to Meriden, Connecticut, to stay
with her dearest friend from St. Lawrence, Julia Hull, and to New
York with other friends; there she went to a "cinematograph," which
made her seasick, and bought some new gowns, and spent hours
among the paintings in the Metropolitan Museum.

Best of all she liked reading, and each book that she liked she recommended to Owen. She insisted on his reading Pater, *Marius* especially, and Grahame's *Golden Age*, and a short story she found in the
Century for December 1895—"The Brushwood Boy" by Rudyard
Kipling, then and since the favorite of so many lovers: "It's about
the best short story I have seen in a great while."

Owen spent both Thanksgiving and Christmas in Southbridge;
there was too much work at the office for him to take the time to go
home. His parents' loss was Jo's gain; she wrote Ida Young after
Thanksgiving, "best of all Owen was here—the first Thanksgiving he
ever spent with me and it made me very happy. Mama and Papa
laugh at me and say I think the sun rises and sets on Owen; but I
notice nothing is too good for Owen with them, and if he wants
anything he *must* have it." And she spoke of Van Hornesville, and
asked Mrs. Young to write her about "the people that I feel very near
to me, because they are Owen's people."

Young received the offer of a job in Chicago in November of '96:
this was the result of an effort on the part of his devoted uncle Wick,
who had moved there, except for summers in Van Hornesville, to
live with his sister Ellen Young Moyer, and thought it would be
wonderful to have Owen near him. But Chicago had no attractions
for Owen, or Jo either. An offer that he did accept, however, was to
teach in the Boston University Law School the following year, in

addition to his job at Tyler's. It meant extra work, but also extra pay, and he was sure he could do it. He was to be an associate of Homer D. Albers, at that time dean of the school, in teaching common-law pleading. He told his parents, "It will give me a good standing at the Boston Bar because the subject is very large and influential and one which most lawyers of our day know only too little."

In March 1897, when his name appeared in the Law School catalogue as instructor, Mr. Tyler called him into his office and asked him if his current salary of seventy-five dollars a month was enough. Young answered, "Do you think it is enough?" The next day Tyler offered him one hundred dollars, and the time needed for the Law School job, which paid between three and four hundred a year.

With such prospects, he told his father to hire what help he needed on the farm. When Smith hesitated Owen insisted:

I am getting into a position for next year where I can assure you that [a hired man] will be paid and I can do so much better work if I feel that you have a good man. . . . I shall feel hurt, discouraged and disheartened if you do not. . . . You speak of a few hundred dollars just as if I were not capable of making any; as if I were a hod carrier out of work . . . you worry over these things just as if you had no one in the world to help push the wheel when the time comes.

Already he could see that in the expanding Tyler office his prospects were, as Dean Bennett had prophesied, very bright. They would be also at the Law School if he should find that he preferred teaching law. He could not only support himself, but he could help on the farm. And it was time to persuade Mr. Edmonds that he could also support a wife.

In this he was successful. When Jo came again to the farm in the summer of 1897 it was as one of the family. Owen fell ill while she was there, and she helped Ida nurse him. He was not able to go back to the office until the end of August; Tyler was so glad to see him he paid him for the weeks of absence. Ida Young wrote: "Mr. T paid well for sick help out of the state, kind of him." Owen gave his parents the check; "I demurred to taking it but he was so persistent that I could not refuse very well without making him mad and afterward I thought it would help pick the hops too."

The office was extremely busy all fall with a big railroad case on which Young did the major part of the work. His Law School lectures were beginning, four days a week; these went well, and he enjoyed doing them. Before Christmas he went to Southbridge and gave Josie a ring, a rose-cut diamond of respectable size, very bright. They began to discuss wedding plans; Charles Edmonds, now it was settled that his girl was leaving, wanted to get it over with. But it was not until February 1898 that Owen wrote home—in the midst of a record-breaking Boston snowstorm that gave him time to write a five-page letter because the office was closed—that he was "thinking of getting married during the year. . . . I am thinking now it would seem best to be married the very last of June and spend all of July with you at home—Do you think you could board two as well as one?" He quoted figures to prove the ancient fallacy that two can live as cheaply as one. Mother wrote back, "It is all right with us as you think you can get through certainly it would be pleasanter to live in your own home."

In March Josie wrote Ida a rather nervous letter—"I'm ever so glad that it seems all right to you," and hoped it would not be too much trouble for them to come during the busy summer work on the farm. Then she plunged into an account of preparations—handmade sheets and pillowcases, towels, quilted puffs, underwear—with considerably more assurance; "Mr. Young will not be interested in all this business."

Perhaps not to Owen and Jo but to the rest of the country the news of war overshadowed all else that spring of 1898. The U.S. battleship *Maine* was blown up in Havana harbor on February 15; Congress declared war against Spain in April. On the farm Pa was worrying about it, as he worried about the sugar bush where so many limbs had been broken by a devastating ice storm that the sap all ran away. If he were younger, Ma wrote, "I would expect to see him shoulder a gun and start—he laughs—says you and he know too much for that." When the papers reported that the Massachusetts coast was in danger she wrote Owen to come home: "We can farm it for a time have plenty to eat and safe place to sleep I am no Hero myself unless I have to be."

From Chicago Uncle Wick wrote Josie, whom he had got to know well from the summers on the farm, in his characteristic vein:

It needs no prophet to foretell that after the fall of Boston the invading army will march on Southbridge hence I prayerfully entreat you to let no old-fashioned Yankee patriotism deter you from turning your back on New England and flee for safety to this City always take time by forelock better come at once . . . will only add to see your way clear the city fathers led by Hinky Dink and Bath House John will vote ample appropriations for defense of City. Funds will be faithfully applied for purposes contemplated if they have no chance to steal them. It is the consensus of opinion the victorious Enemy will attack this City. After the fray there will be no Spanish Army to advance or retreat. Will meet you at Station — W.H.Y.[11]

Owen wrote his parents in April that he expected the war "would be soon upon us," and that it would hurt the law business but help the farmers—"you will be the money-makers of the country now. I guess I will come home to help you farm it—what do you say?" In May he reassured them: "Boston Harbor is entirely out of danger . . . mines and forts and torpedoes . . . the beginning of the end is here." He was right; the country celebrated, the law business looked up, farm prices did not rise spectacularly, and the young couple could be married in a time of peace.

Chapter 4

Marriage and the Boston Bar

OWEN and Jo were married on Thursday, June 30, 1898, in the square, white Universalist church on the main street of Southbridge, only a few blocks from the Edmonds home. There were two ministers; the young couple insisted on being married by Dr. Hervey, "our patron saint," but since he was not at that time licensed in Massachusetts the pastor of the church, Dr. Penniman, tied the knot. They went off on the train to Hartford after a party at home with plenty of champagne for the several hundred guests, and after speeches and fun on the part of Owen's friends and Josie's brothers. They stayed that night at the Heublein Hotel, and on Friday their first stop was a bookshop: Owen bought his wife a copy of *Don Quixote* in Charles Jarvis's translation. She wrote her new name in it, and the date.

From Hartford they went to New York, and spent Friday night at the Waldorf on Fifth Avenue at Thirty-fourth Street. On Saturday they took the Hudson River boat to Albany, where they stayed the night; and on Sunday they went home to Van Hornesville on the train. Owen's parents had not made the trip to Southbridge for the wedding because the couple were coming so soon. Pa was at the Fort Plain station with the horses, and a warm smile.

Once again Charles Tyler was generous, and gave Owen a month's vacation. It was a happy time; Owen had his three best-loved people together on his native soil, there was plenty of hay to toss in the bright days, and cool evenings to swing in the hammock after Jo had washed the dishes from one of Mother's good farm meals.

They set up housekeeping in Cambridge at 97 Avon Hill Street, in half a big double house rented from Samuel Usher for fifty dollars a month. The situation was good, on the high land above Linnaean Street and not far from the train and trolley stations on Massachusetts Avenue. The house was too big and too expensive for them to manage alone, so Jo's brother Stuart, who was in an architect's office in Boston, and "Squire" DeGoosh, Owen's former roommate, lived there too, sharing meals and general expenses.

Cambridge was then a town of about eighty thousand people; it possessed not only an interesting history and great educational institutions, but numberless churches and social and benevolent societies in the proper New England tradition. They were already familiar with it from Jo's two years at Radcliffe, had many friends there, and enjoyed it.

Jo went to Smith Hawes in Boston, a wholesale firm well known for housewares. Her list of some ninety items (eggbeater, puff pans, ash barrel, clothes horse, and so on) came to $21.80 and the bill was sent to Owen's office in the Sears Building. A little later they invested in a piano; Josie played, and Stuart, like their father, was an enthusiastic amateur musician.

Jo had a maid, whom they paid four dollars a week, with Thursday afternoons off, and Sunday morning to go to church. Jo had a butcher's book which she took when she went to buy meat; it was added up at the end of the month and if it looked as if she was spending too much Owen scolded and Jo cried. But four pounds of pot roast was only forty-eight cents, and besides, the folks on the farm sent ham and pork as well as butter and eggs, apples, potatoes and preserves regularly, so she had plenty of victuals for her three hungry young men.

The only flaw was that Owen was so busy and away so much. Mr. Tyler knew a good thing when he saw one and loaded him with work, both in Boston and in distant cities. Jo was very much annoyed and considered "C.H." a slave driver. But he did one very pleasant thing for them; he made them a present of two bicycles. (Owen had to wait two weeks for his, for it had to be made especially for his long legs.) Up to then, their outings had been trips to the country on the "car," there to take long walks—she at least was an interested bird and flower watcher. But now she made herself a short skirt and, she wrote Mother Young, "bloomers to wear under it," and learned to ride; Owen "rode right off." He wrote home: "I am riding a wheel and I have never had more fun since I have been here." The roads were good, the sport gave him air, exercise and a terrific appetite— "Josie says Mr. Tyler ought to give me $100 more for increase in meat bills in addition to the wheels." And Owen often bicycled to work in Boston.

Owen was still teaching at the Law School in addition to the work in the office, and spent many evenings and Sundays preparing lectures and reading papers. But once in a while as a special celebration they got to a theater or concert in Boston: for her birthday Owen took Jo to see Bernhardt. And they saw their friends. Frank Oliver Hall lived across the street and they went to his church, the Third Universalist in North Cambridge; he would come in evenings sometimes and the talk usually ended in violent arguments, for Owen and Frank seldom agreed. Their friends Edmund and Florence Whitman—the latter from St. Lawrence—were not far away at 23 Everett Street. But Caleb Fisher, a bachelor, felt hurt that Owen did not have time to visit him in Lowell as often as he did before his marriage.

An especially great pleasure for the young couple was to welcome Owen's parents to their home. Many pressing invitations had been sent before the folks finally made up their minds to come, in February of 1899, a slack time on the farm. Smith Young had traveled occasionally to Albany, once to New York, and they had both been to Chicago to the Columbian Exposition, but most of their lives had been bounded by the hills above Van Hornesville. So the visit to Boston required many letters to be exchanged in advance; the young people were anxious for them to make the trip in daylight so as to see the country; a train was chosen, and Owen sent them twenty-five dollars for the fare.

They spent most of February in Cambridge; Mother helped around the house and mended their clothes and Father tended the furnace and took out the ashes. He was sixty-seven and she was fifty-nine; a winter month in a centrally heated house with indoor plumbing was a pleasure, quite apart from the company of the children whom they loved so much.

The following summer, 1899, was a hot one, as most summers were and are in Boston. Jo was pregnant, and her father took her off to Nantucket. He loved the sea and fishing and sailing, and she too always felt her best by salt water, breathing salt air. As a child she had loved the family's vacations at Oak Bluffs on Martha's Vineyard, and the excursions by boat to Gay Head, where they went ashore from the fishing boat in oxcarts to examine the bright clays in the cliffs above the rocky beach. But now she was worrying about Owen keeping house in Cambridge in the heat; he and "Squire" DeGoosh came to the island weekends when they could; it was one hundred degrees in Boston and seventy in Nantucket. Owen wrote his parents about catching a twelve-pound bluefish—"he makes one hustle before you get him into the boat too." But as usual he was thinking about the farm: "When are you beginning haying? I am sorry not to be there at the start, when the barns are empty and I can show my strength.

I do hate to bother about putting little forkfuls way up in the roof."

The baby was born December 17, 1899, in the house on Avon Hill Street and was named, for his two grandfathers, Charles Jacob (C.J.) Young. It was a difficult birth and a slow recovery for Jo; the nurse stayed on more than five weeks (her total bill was $111).

Owen was not allowed to stay home very much with his little family; in January 1900 he was in Appleton, Wisconsin; Springfield, Illinois; Cleveland; and Chicago—the last he enjoyed because he had a visit with Uncle Wick. And always when he got home he had to make up for lost time in the office and with his Law School classes.

When the hot weather came around again Jo took the baby to her family's cottage on Walker Pond, which she and Owen had enjoyed so much before they were married. Her father was not well; it was the beginning of a year and a half of illness which ended in his death. Owen could not get away that summer except for brief weekends with his family. At the end of August he sent his mother twenty-five dollars to hire help in the house at hop-picking time, and told his father if he needed money to pay the pickers to let him know, "as I have enough for us." He never forgot the exhausting labor demanded of both his parents in harvesting their main cash crop. In October they all went to Van Hornesville—"C.J. yelled bloody murder on the train."

On his return to Cambridge he wrote his parents, on his twenty-sixth birthday:

Dear Father and Mother;

It is cool enough today so that we stay down in the parlor by the fireplace. The lights are just started—C.J. is on the floor and a roaring fire in the grate makes me feel like using Josie's desk and write you how I wish you were here, too. I was glad enough to know that the hops were gone—there is a good margin of profit in them for you this year and that is sufficient. I'm glad the horse wasn't lame going home—write about him and also the other one when you get her for it is interesting to know what is going on and how you like them. Josie has already written you all the news and how well we came down. I got back in the harness on Tuesday and while the first two or three days seemed rather slow and confining as against golf and Cooperstown yet now I am in the harness again and I tell you it is mighty interesting when one is in it. My Law School work begins tomorrow and from now until March 1st will be my busy time—"plow and mow and reap and sow" ect. [sic]. I went to Harvard and Carlisle football game yesterday at which 15,000 people sat out in a drizzling rain to see the game—it was good sport however. There is no politics but there is considerable fear lest Bryan win—I have never seen C.H. so bitter in politics as now—he is getting to be one of the bloated bondholders in earnest now and free silver would mean a large loss to him undoubtedly. I had the best

vacation I ever had this time, so it seems to me—do take good care of yourselves—watch all chances to find a girl and do not stop at the price—if you
need any money now tell me—with love—Owen.

Jo's letter, which he refers to, completes the picture of the household
at 97 Avon Hill Street on that Sunday in October of the last year of
the century: "Stuart drawing, Arthur reading some English newspapers, and Owen is working on his lectures—they begin tomorrow
morning." The baby was teasing the pug-dog—Jo's old dog Jingo,
which she had brought from home when she was married—who had
just had a bath; she said Owen missed the "Pumpkin Hook golf
course," and asked them to send some fresh eggs to her papa.[1]

ii

Charles Hitchcock Tyler was a native of Cambridge, where his father
was registrar of probate. He graduated from Harvard in the class of
1886, and took his law degree at Boston University Law School. Perhaps the new law school in the city appealed to him more than Harvard. After his graduation he taught the law of landlord and tenant
there for a few years, and was no sooner admitted to the bar, in 1889,
than he set up his own office, in the Sears Building at 199 Washington
Street.

He was successful from the first, for success was natural to him.
By the time he hired Young, in the fall of 1896, he was doing a
thriving business. Hard-driving, active, tenacious, he was described
by contemporaries as a "dynamo" and a "go-getter," and it was said of
him that he was almost as much of a son-of-a-bitch to have on your
side as on the opposing one. Many years later he wrote Young, "As
you know, I have always played with the Results Family and they
are a pretty good family to play with." "I know," his former clerk had
answered to a similar remark, "how important 'now' always is to you."[2]
It was typical of him that when Boston's first skyscraper was built—
the Ames Building of twelve stories—he moved in, in 1901, and eventually took the two top floors, where the firm still does business today.

Tyler was a big man, 215 pounds, with the height to carry it, but his
energy was inexhaustible. He worked long hours—and in those days
the workweek included all day Saturday—and expected his staff to
do the same. Brilliant and impatient, he could be sharp, but his lifelong confidential secretary, Karl Singer, told the authors that he was
always fair. He was also meticulous about detail; no letter went out

of the office without being read and approved by him and he never talked on the telephone without Singer on an extension.

But Charles Tyler's life was not only that of a hardworking and successful corporation lawyer. He was a connoisseur and collector in many fields, and became one of the first great collectors of eighteenth-century American furniture. He had the taste and acumen to buy beautiful pieces at a time when they were readily available, and his houses—in Boston at 83 Bay State Road, his estate in Beverly, even his little farmhouse at Sanbornton, New Hampshire—were full of elegant old furniture and objets d'art. He was an amateur of prints and engravings, rare china and silver, books and ship models.[3] Intuitively selective, he always demanded excellence, and in later years applied his talents to several living collections, breeding handsome brahma poultry, English setters and Guernsey cattle, all champions of their kind.

Charles Tyler never married. He admired and adored his mother, with whom he lived until the end of her long life. He told Young in later years that he had never been able to find anyone to equal her and had given up the search. When he was away from Boston he called her every night—an attention more unusual in her day than in ours. A lady of the old school, intelligent, amusing and charming, herself a connoisseur, Mrs. Tyler lived into her nineties and her son was desolate at her death.

His gentleness and devotion to her, the kindness he showed from the beginning to Owen and Jo, with his remarkable appreciation of things of beauty and his constant and durable sense of humor, made up the other side of the "go-getter." Young was to stay with him until the end of 1912, to continue to be his friend until his death in 1931, and never to forget—or forget to say to him—what he owed him. They corresponded and met fairly often in later years, exchanging jokes and stories as well as information and professional advice. Tyler wrote Young in 1926: "I have just taken a young man into the office who, they say, is the ablest man graduated from the Law School with one exception and you were named as the exception. He is better looking than you are." A postscript says, "Than you *were*."

For Tyler, Owen Young was an apt pupil from the first, to be taught the nitty-gritty of the daily practice of the law, to be worked to the limit of endurance—long hours, few or no vacations—to be given responsibility as fast as he could handle it, which indeed was almost from the very first day. But he was also to be taught the collecting of old furniture and fine prints and rare books, the appreciation of good food and wine, good clothes, above all the necessity for excellence in all things. In these too he was an eager pupil, retaining and perfecting this knowledge throughout his life. In only one area did he fail his teacher; Mr. Tyler had him down to Beverly and taught him to play golf. But the pupil, although he practiced on the fields at home and on the little course at the north end of Lake Otsego, reached neither then nor ever any standard of excellence and soon gave up the game.

The walls of the offices in the Ames Building were—and are—hung with fine steel engravings. Mr. Tyler's corner office, with its fireplace, handsome old furniture and chandelier, was full of old prints and ship models. The big windows opened on a miles-wide view of the city and its surroundings. Through the great landlocked harbor the ships came and went to the docks below. The Old Statehouse and the New, Faneuil Hall with its grasshopper weather vane, King's Chapel were all nearby; only the spires of the churches rose higher than the trees of the Common. Young eventually became the inhabitant of the other corner office on the south side, which looked out to sea beyond the islands, and had engravings of his own on the walls.

Although Tyler dealt mainly in corporation law, there was every sort of case passing through the office. Young was allowed to handle lesser ones alone, and was sent hither and yon—to Delaware, New York City, New Haven and, nearer home, Plymouth, Fall River, Cambridge. He tried cases himself, which he described to his parents: "We have just finished a three days' trial of a case in which $40,000 is involved for the Old Colony Trust Company of Boston on some forged checks; it was quite interesting."

But it was natural that a young lawyer in Boston at the end of the nineteenth century should cut his teeth on a railroad case. New England has been rightly called the mother of railroads; wherever tracks were laid down throughout the nation, wherever the fast-growing industry, which offered both romance and profits, needed men and money, there were Boston dollars and Boston men: engineers, promoters, executives, financiers—and lawyers. In the 1880s the general offices of the Chicago, Burlington and Quincy, the Union Pacific, the Santa Fe were not in Chicago or New York; they were in Boston, where Charles Francis Adams headed the Union Pacific, and Thomas Nickerson and after him Thomas Jefferson Coolidge the Santa Fe.

The Union Pacific had moved its head office to Boston in 1869, after some Tweed-inspired roughhousing, and subsequent complications, at a stockholders' meeting in New York. With Thomas C. Durant and Oakes Ames as moving forces, Boston financiers bought up a considerable interest in the expanding road; by 1884 over one-third of UP stock was held by New Englanders "including distinguished members of the Boston aristocracy."[4] But the enormous expense of bridging the continent was too great, even with substantial subsidies from the federal government; wasteful and often corrupt contracts, during the period of Crédit Mobilier control, left the road in a weakened condition, and traffic was never adequate to turn a profit. The panic and depression of 1893 was the final blow; the UP collapsed, and the road began to deteriorate.

In 1895, in New York, Jacob H. Schiff of Kuhn Loeb and Company formed a reorganization committee, which included Boston financiers Oliver Ames and T. Jefferson Coolidge. Schiff invited E. H. Harriman to join the committee; Harriman, the financial manager of the Illinois Central, had had some notion of reorganizing the UP himself, and at first refused. But a compromise was worked out, Harriman agreed to participate, and early in 1897 the committee filed articles of incorporation. In Boston, Tyler was hired to represent stockholders and creditors of the railroad, including the holders of first mortgage bonds, which represented a large proportion of the total.

In November 1897 a syndicate headed by Kuhn Loeb and Company bought up the UP at a sale in Omaha, agreeing to pay the debt to the government and purchase the first mortgage bonds; the UP, described by General Tecumseh Sherman as "a work of giants," was in business.[5] Harriman leaped into prominence, Tyler was the richer by an enormous fee, and Owen Young had learned at first hand what a big railroad case was like.

Not unconnected, perhaps, with his work on this case was the invitation, in June of 1897, to become assistant attorney general for the Commonwealth of Massachusetts. He felt honored by the offer, he wrote his parents, but "a public office is no sinecure for a poor boy," and he refused it. He was also greatly pleased that summer when "Richard Olney was retained as senior counsel in the [UP] case. I am mighty glad to come in contact with him." Olney had been Cleveland's attorney general in 1893–95, and secretary of state from 1895 to March 1897, and it meant much to the young man that Olney approved of his work.

The fall was frantically busy for him, for the November sale by no means terminated the lawyers' work. He told his parents he could not possibly come home for Thanksgiving; Van Hornesville was too far out of the lines of communication:

U.P. matters are in such a state that I dare not get out of reach so far for the present. You see I cannot be got at either by telephone or telegraph very quickly and then so far from trains when two or three hours might mean as many millions of dollars. . . . I am so much more clearly in touch with the situation at present than either Mr. Tyler or Judge Harrow that I would not be doing right by them to go away when the crisis is liable to come.

It was, he said, "quite fun to dabble in a scheme when your opinion counts for something in the distribution of such an immense fund." Smith and Ida may have been saddened because he could not come home for the holiday, but they must have been impressed—as he meant them to be.

The lectures at the Law School suffered, however; there was not much time to prepare them. He had a class of over a hundred; among them were several whom he described as "middle-aged—35 or 40," including two judges from Connecticut. DeGoosh reported that one of the students told him that Young was the most interesting lecturer in the school next to Professor Melville M. Bigelow, who was the best.

Owen did get home for Christmas, but only for the day; one of the UP cases came up in court in the week before New Year's, and he wrote home that he won it. He was back and forth to New York and working from eight in the morning till eleven at night, for Tyler was trying to settle the final details. The firm was successful in getting not only the creditors but the stockholders paid off; Young told his daughter fifty years later that this was a landmark for this kind of case, and that he considered it his first big success. Tyler's fee was very large: "things are on easy street so far as money goes," he wrote home. But "Mr. Tyler has got another big railroad case—about twice as big as the one just finished which came in the office on Monday and it will be hurrah boys again." This case was the settlement of legal and financial details of the proposed purchase by Harriman of the Oregon Short Line, which had been part of the UP, but was not included in the 1897 sale.

These big cases were tough and useful training. Young learned much in a short time about complicated financial structures, about dealing with government and politicians, about negotiation with a variety of men motivated by diverse influences. When a third railroad case came into the office in the spring of 1898 Tyler let him handle it by himself. It did not interfere with the June wedding, but beginning with the fall it kept Owen away too much to please his bride.

The search for prestige and profits was not confined to the great transcontinental roads. In Vermont the prospect of connecting the Great Lakes with the seaport of Boston promised both, and there was no lack of hardheaded—and often avaricious—Yankees to try to do it.

The Vermont Central Railroad started out bravely in 1849 with a line from Windsor to Burlington. Much more trackage was built in the next forty-five years and mergers were made establishing links to Montreal and the west, such as the lease of the Ogdensburg and Lake Champlain, which provided an eastern terminal for a water route to Chicago.

But over the years the enterprise failed to deliver payment on its promises; the Central Vermont (it switched its name in 1873) suffered from simple problems: traffic inadequate to meet expenses, cutthroat competition, and—as George Pierce Baker puts it with Yankee under-statement—"a financial management far from outstanding."[6] It was bankrupt in 1896, defaulting on the bonds of the Ogdensburg and Lake Champlain, among others, and was reorganized as the Central Vermont Railway Company, with a controlling interest owned by the Canadian Grand Trunk Railway.

In the fall of 1898 the Tyler firm was representing, among others, the bondholders of the Ogdensburg and Lake Champlain and the tiny Lamoille Extension, but Tyler himself, after introducing Young to the problems, went off to Minneapolis, involved in a newer and more exciting industry.

The reorganization, with the Grand Trunk in control, could not be brought into effect without the approval of the Vermont legislature, and there was considerable objection to the acquisition of this great Vermont railroad by "foreign intervention." In Brattleboro, Burlington, St. Albans and Montpelier, Young sat up late nights in hotel rooms consulting with railroad men and their lawyers, with politicians and representatives of the creditors, drafting compromises and new pro-posals for settling the claims of the bondholders, while Jo fretted at home, worrying that he was smoking his pipe too much.[7]

Finally, however, a bill was passed that was satisfactory to the newly inaugurated governor of Vermont, Edward C. Smith, who, coin-cidentally, was president of the railroad and the son of the man who had built it. But before this could become operative, the Central Ver-mont had to be put up, *pro forma*, for public sale.[8] This occasion, held at the main office of the railroad in St. Albans on March 22, 1899, brought Owen Young to the notice of the Vermont newspapers. Lawyers in such a controversy rarely appear in the public prints; it would be many years before it happened to Young again.

A reporter from the *Burlington Free Press* described the scene. The front steps of the massive office building, a Romanesque edifice near the tracks in St. Albans, was the place appointed for the sale. As a small group of men appeared there—officers of the Central Vermont and lawyers representing various interests—a considerable crowd gathered to watch. The master designated to conduct the sale read the notice and announced that "he would offer the property to the highest bidder. 'How much is offered for the entire property?' exclaimed the master, whereupon Owen D. Young stepped forward and read the following protest." The protest was printed in full, in all the glory of its legal language; it was of course merely a *pro forma* proceeding on the part of the bondholders of the Ogdensburg and Lake Champlain Railroad. The reporter concluded, "This protest was no surprise and the sale accordingly proceeded."[9] The Grand Trunk became the owner of the Central Vermont.

This glimpse of the tall, skinny young lawyer, reading his legal paper from the steps to the assembled crowd on a bleak day in northern Vermont, is one of the few surviving from his early days in the law. The case, complicated, exhausting and largely unsuccessful, was nevertheless his first venture alone upon that battlefield where politics, public service and private enterprise were locked in a struggle which no one of them could wholly win. It was a field which was to command his energies and talents for much of his life; the long negotiations through late nights, the aroused emotions of the participants, the compromises between irreconcilable positions, the effort to maintain the rights and interests of all under the law—for him all these had only just begun.

iii

Next, Tyler handed him a textile-mill case in Maine—the consolidation of the Pepperell Manufacturing Company and the Laconia Company—while he himself went off to Cleveland and Chicago. These cotton mills were heirs to a number of predecessors dating back to the early years of the nineteenth century; situated on the Saco River at Biddeford, they were owned and directed largely by Boston men. Their "countinghouses" were in Boston—in fact, that of the Pepperell Company was for some years in the Sears Building, though before Tyler's day. In the countinghouses the directors met—men with Boston names like Bowditch, Wigglesworth, Welch, Codman, Grew—the majority Harvard men. The treasurer of Pepperell at the time of the consolidation was George Dexter, Harvard '55. (In the cotton manufacturing industry the title of "treasurer" indicated the chief executive officer.) Dexter was also treasurer of the Laconia Company, and many of the directors as well as the stockholders were the same.

Pepperell was by far the stronger company, and it was to the advantage of both to consolidate. But the plan had been twice defeated, in 1878 and in 1886, by unwilling stockholders, so that when the question came up again, in 1899, careful preparations had to be made.

For legal advice the companies turned to Tyler, and in April of that year he went to Portland to meet with them, taking Young with him. Then he left for Cleveland. Owen wrote his parents from the Congress Square Hotel in Portland: "I am organizing a corporation here to take over the business and property of several large cotton mills—the property is worth several millions of dollars and so it has to be done with some care."

It did take "some care," but not much time. He worked out the details of the merger and devised a letter that went out to the stockholders when the plan was set: a new company was to be formed to take over the properties; stockholders were to receive the shares of the new company in exchange for the old ones, plus a cash dividend, on a prorated basis. The offer must have been sufficiently attractive, for this time, on May 10, the stockholders voted unanimously for it, and the consolidated company came into being as one of the largest textile concerns in the nation, to the satisfaction of its young lawyer.

Unlike the Central Vermont, this job was relatively brief and posed no serious problems for Young; but it provided him with valuable experience with manufacturing companies, mergers and financial affairs on a large scale. And like the UP and the Central Vermont, it put him in a position where he could show the men in charge in Boston what he could do.

In other fields too Young was working for them. In spite of the hard times of the '90s Boston had retained much of its wealth and leadership. As the new century came in, the city itself was changing; new buildings were rising, new offices, stores, theaters, many of them on land in downtown Boston long and closely held by old-fashioned trusts on whose rosters the same names appeared again and again. For living quarters the population had sprawled out beyond the city, where suburbs were encouraged by the development of electric street railways. There were more than a million people within a radius of ten miles of the statehouse. To serve them, the commercial center, crowded on the narrow streets and hills of the original port, had to develop extensively. Land values rose as this demand increased.

Where property pressures develop, lawyers thrive, and Charles Tyler was not one to miss opportunities. The result was that Young was involved in many real-estate cases, most relatively small, some large. The largest was one in which Young, as the principal attorney for Edward A. Filene, handled the acquisition of numerous small parcels of land to make up the block on which the Filene department store was built. This was a successful achievement, the result of endless negotiations with small-property owners, who were often recalcitrant, greedy, or stubborn; it was excellent training, but Young never cared much for real-estate work or handling estates. Of the latter he had a good deal, although he had been told he would never get anywhere as a lawyer in the midst of the "entrenched privilege" of Boston. But when he was asked to do a special job for John Ames, of the wealthy and prominent Boston family, and received a large retainer, he asked Mr. Ames why he had chosen him, rather than one of the equally able young Boston lawyers, such as Thomas Nelson Perkins. Ames's answer implied that although both were equally good lawyers, men of perfect integrity with whom secrets were absolutely safe, Young was chosen *because* he was an outsider.

In the spring of 1899 Tyler took on a new man in the office, C. F. (Fred) Weed, who had been a student of Young's at the Law School. (Weed's notebook for the course in common-law pleading ended, in a flourishing hand, "All Owen.") The two young men became firm friends and remained so all their lives, although Weed gave up the law to go into banking.

There was plenty of work in the office for everybody, for as the new century moved in, Tyler was taking on more and more jobs, most of them of a new kind, in a new field where the law was far behind the problems. It was a field exactly suited to the abilities and tastes of both Charles Tyler and Owen Young—electric power.

Chapter 5

Ubiquitous Utilities:
Tyler Takes a Partner

W HEN Owen Young was a boy on the farm, Thomas Edison was working on the dynamo and the electric light, and before he went to college, central power stations for the production of alternating current were being set up throughout the country. In many cities the horse or the mule had been unhitched from the streetcar, and a trolley harnessed overhead to an electric wire instead. There were electric lights on Boston Common when Owen first saw it, and even Van Hornesville was brought nearer to the outside world by the construction of interurban electric railways to Cooperstown from Oneonta, and later from Herkimer to Jordanville, only seven miles away. When Owen went to the Columbian Exposition at Chicago in October of 1893 he saw, like the rest of the world, the various and spectacular possible uses for electricity. There was not only lighting of unparalleled brilliancy, but electric stoves and irons and even dishwashers, which made him think of Mother in the farm kitchen back home; and the whole fair was supplied with power from the dynamos which so much excited Henry Adams when he first laid eyes on them that he saw in them, prophetically, the introduction of a whole new phase of history. As the boys of the following generation grew up with the idea that man could fly, so the generation which came to manhood at the turn of the century was equally excited by the limitless possibilities of electric power.

Perhaps the new development that captured the American imagination most widely at this time was the electric railway. It had taken some time to perfect a dependable trolley car. Early models used batteries, which were impractical, or a third rail—Edison worked on this type—which tended to give horses and pedestrians shocks, and proved impractical at street level. But the development of the trolley and the overhead wire made possible not only the city streetcar but the speedy interurban, with its luxurious cars, low fares, and an amuse-

ment park at the end of the line. It was an American dream come
true. Every city in the country had to have streetcars, and an interurban to somewhere else, just as decades later it had to have an air-
port. The newspapers called the first decade of the century the interurban era, and foresaw closer and happier relations between city and
country—heretofore deeply separated—and wider horizons for everyone. "Life is motion," wrote an anonymous author in the Stone and
Webster *Public Service Journal* of June 1909, "and the interurban is
by far the greatest exponent of human motion today. . . . Its promoters are providers of a larger material, intellectual and moral life
for the American people." And there was also just the pure joy of
going fast, in a vehicle where you could really feel it, like the open
summer trolley car which whizzed through the woods to the amusement park, to see the trained white horse dive off a platform into the
pond.

In 1908 there were more than 38,000 miles of electrified street and
interurban railways in the country, on which ran more than 86,000
cars; 120,000 hard-worked horses and mules were definitely out of a
job.[1] All this was not accomplished without massive requirements for
technical, managerial and legal skills, as well as capital. The law
indeed was limping far behind the new technology. State and municipal governments had to make up the rules when—or after—the
electric utilities moved in. It was exactly the kind of situation for
Charles Tyler to operate in; he was not only astute and hardheaded,
he was also forward-looking, romantic, and creative—and Young was
much the same. They were as much excited by the implications of
what seemed limitless power as the engineers and the capitalists were;
and in the control of this power for service to all the people there
were opportunities to build and to create in the law.

Not far from the offices in the Ames Building were those of a young
firm whose business was the uses of electricity. Charles H. Stone and
Edwin S. Webster graduated from the Massachusetts Institute of
Technology in 1888, and the following year set up a partnership in a
few rooms in Post Office Square. They planned to act as middlemen
between electrical manufacturing companies and consumers, and
almost at once they found themselves overwhelmed with jobs. Capable engineers themselves, they soon found that public utilities on
every level, in every state, were crying out for technical and managerial help. There were not enough experts to go around, and the
little firm expanded rapidly. Even the depression years, when many
new public-utility companies were in trouble, helped Stone and Web-

ster, who examined their procedures, advised changes—hard times forced better engineering—and in some cases helped in financing.

As times grew better, they were instrumental in organizing new companies and building new properties. By 1900 they were managing seven or eight public-service companies and were involved in many more.[2] Almost every move they made required legal advice. They had local lawyers in each area where they operated; these areas were primarily the still small but rapidly growing cities, like Dallas, Seattle, Minneapolis, Terre Haute. But they retained also, at their headquarters in Boston, Charles Tyler and his bright young men. For Tyler himself, and increasingly for Young, the early years of the century were filled with travels throughout the nation, from Seattle to Galveston, from Minneapolis to El Paso. It was fortunate that both of them enjoyed it, for it took up a great deal of time—three days from Boston to Dallas, two to Minneapolis, five to Seattle. But, for the most part, the trips were comfortable: private rooms, excellent food, top-notch service. And they provided the time to study the papers and prepare for the meeting, look at the country, and think. Young was interested in everything new he saw, especially in agriculture, and wrote his father details about the crops in Texas or Minnesota.[3] It was not long before he had been in every state of the union, and knew the leaders in business and government, as well as the law, in most of them. He grasped quickly the essential qualities of men and places, and never forgot them—nor they him. This far-reaching acquaintance and thorough understanding were always among his greatest assets.

The first case on record which Young handled for Stone and Webster was the reorganization of the Houston Electric Street Railway Company. A notice went out on July 2, 1900, to the bondholders that Eliot Wadsworth and Owen D. Young had been "requested to act as a committee and to prepare a plan for the reorganization of the Houston Electric Street Railway Company and its constituent companies. They have prepared such a plan and a reorganization agreement, and submit them herewith for your consideration."[4] Eliot Wadsworth, Harvard '98, worked for Stone and Webster and later became a partner in the firm. At the time of the Houston affair he was twenty-four years old; Young was not yet twenty-six. But Young at least had had some experience in this kind of thing, and their plan, over a period of time, was successful.

The following year Young did a great deal of traveling for Stone and Webster, to the annoyance of his wife. In June he was in Terre Haute, where the street railway was an s&w property. The night he arrived, Monday, June 3, the employees went out on strike. "Not a car was running on Tuesday morning," he wrote his parents on June 8;

we were up all Monday and Tuesday nights treating with the strikers and the Mayor and Common Council and everybody else who for political reasons or otherwise could get an excuse for putting their finger in—In the street were mobs of angry men and so it went on until early [Wednesday] morning the strikers weakened and went back to work at six o'clock. It was a most interesting experience for me because coming direct from Boston I was supposed to be the personal representative of Stone and Webster. We were mighty lucky not to get something blown up with dynamite.

It was in Terre Haute, on this or a subsequent visit, that Young and his companion, Guy Tripp of s & w (later chairman of Westinghouse Electric), became annoyed at the inadequacy of the hotel's service. They had difficulty in getting a bellboy; when he finally came, they locked him in the closet, and phoned to ask, "Where is that boy?" Another was sent, and was locked in the closet. They had three before they relented.

From Terre Haute he went to Minneapolis, where s & w owned the Minneapolis Power and Light; he was amused by an incident at the hotel, which he described to his parents: "When I came in the hotel this morning from the train, the hotel clerk told me that he was very sorry but all his rooms with baths which were large enough to show samples in were taken. I finally assured him that the samples of the goods which I had for sale would not require a great amount of space for display. Well, I am what you may call a commercial traveler but I do try and carry exclusive samples so as to discourage competition."

Then he was back in Terre Haute—no wonder Jo wrote his mother, "I don't like it *at all.*" Her father was very ill, the baby was sick with teething and summer heat, and Owen was no sooner home from the Middle West than he went off to Texas. The court in Houston "was about to enter a foreclosure decree in our railway case so I had to start south," he wrote to Van Hornesville. When this was finished he went to Galveston, which was just beginning to come back to life after the hurricane of September 1900 in which the city was devastated and five thousand people killed. Then he was in Dallas, putting up at the Oriental Hotel, the "Finest Hotel Structure in the South," it boasted on its stationery, where the all-inclusive rates ran from $2.50 to $5.00 a day. It was his first acquaintance with the place and people with whom he would have much to do in the years to come. The time of year was not ideal; he arrived in the midst of a heat wave which frizzled most of the country. The *Dallas Morning News* was reporting in big headlines the numbers of dead from the heat in New

York and Boston, although it contained little comment on local conditions: the forecast for Dallas was "warm"—the temperature was 107 degrees. But Owen wrote back to the farm that the heat was more bearable than in the north; the air was dry, for Texas was suffering from drought, water was a good deal scarcer than oil, and the crops were parched.

Nevertheless, Dallas was an exciting place to be, and Young, for all the dust and heat, found the city and many of its citizens agreeable and interesting. Dallas was in the process of completing its metamorphosis from a frontier cattle town to a modern city. The population increased by more than eighty thousand from 1880 to 1910; when Young arrived in 1901 it was already up to forty-three thousand. The open range had been turned into farms and ranches, and Dallas became the second largest distributor of farm machinery in the nation. Oil was omnipresent; the sixth big new oil company was chartered in Houston while Young was there.

Growing, pushing, with an eye on the fast buck, Dallas was not by any means a hick town. Broadway shows were presented at the opera house (twenty-five cents in the upper balcony), and the local bookstore reported that the American novelist Winston Churchill's *Crisis* was its best seller. Dallas had had since 1885 one of the best newspapers in the nation; established by Colonel Alfred Horatio Belo, a Civil War veteran, as an addition to his thriving publishing business in Galveston, the *Dallas Morning News* produced for its readers a fair and thorough coverage of international and national news, if not of the local weather. Admired by both Adolph Ochs and Alfred Harmsworth, it maintained its standards over many years. Young became a friend of the Belo family, and when the colonel's son, who succeeded him as publisher, died at an early age, Young was legal consultant to the executors and to the widow—a job which went on for many years.

But even as a cow town Dallas had been known as an "electrical city." A company as far back as 1882 asked the city government for permission to build a lighting plant; by 1883 the dirty streets and many of the innumerable saloons were lit by arc lights. A number of small companies sprang up, and competition was perhaps more widespread than technical improvements; at one point the city electrician complained in his report that electricity was escaping into the water pipes on Commerce Street.[5]

Stone and Webster were not interested in the bigger cities, where public utilities were well established, nor in rural electrification, which was hardly thought of, but in the middling cities, like Dallas. Young's visit in the summer of 1901 was to scout the acquisition of the Dallas

Electric Company; this came about in 1902, with the formation of the
Dallas Electric Light and Power Company. The addition of the word
power to the title was no accident, for at the same time, s&w acquired the Dallas Consolidated Street Railway Company, an originally
mule-powered road electrified in 1892. Nor was it an accident that an
ordinance was passed allowing lighting companies to provide power
for street railways.

Behind all these acquisitions, ordinances and new franchises, and
essential to their successful conclusion, were the lawyers. No newspaper notice was given them, and records of the long, wearing and
often acrimonious hours of negotiation do not—and never did—exist.
In a business so closely involved with politics, the discussions into the
small hours were forgotten as soon as the end was attained. Young
was beginning to find out that the ability to negotiate was his strong
point. Intuitive and understanding, sensing, underneath the talk, what
his opponents *really* wanted from their bargaining, he was calm and
relaxed, never showing any anger or impatience. He seems also to
have had a faculty, not too common at the time, for remembering the
interests not only of his clients, but of the citizens who depended
upon the utilities he was setting up. Many years later he described to
his first biographer "my original idea of what a municipality or private interest taking over a public utility should agree to," in this case
a street railway:

Here is what I would say to a town council. You have certain properties
which we want to take over—make your own valuation, suit yourselves
about that, let it be a historical or a replacement valuation. We will accept
your decision.

There are certain things you must look out for in the contract. Your roads
must earn replacement expenses, that is, take care of depreciation; they
must earn interest on the value which you have placed upon them, not over
seven per cent, preferably six per cent.

You must provide for a reserve which will enable you to take care of the
growth of your town, for your town will expand and your roads must expand with it.

If at any time your earnings overflow, that is, do more than provide
necessary expenses, this overflow should be divided between the stockholders and the consumers; that is, if the dividend goes up the rates must
come down. The dividend must never go in any case beyond ten per cent.

Let the franchise be indeterminate, and if at any time the town should
want to take over the franchise they can do so for a sum to be fixed by
negotiation.

On the board of the utility the town must have a representative to watch
the operations. The town should have monthly reports and if this representative does not object to a report within thirty days it stands.

These reports will be published so that the consumers will know what is going on. If there is any objection on the part of this representative voicing a dissatisfaction in the community, this shall be settled by arbitration.[6]

When this Dallas job was finished—there would be many more—Young was ready and eager to come home. But a wire arrived from Tyler, asking him to "step over" to El Paso to look into the street railway business there; it was a step of more than six hundred miles. On the way he stopped in San Antonio for a day—"the quaintest and most historic town in Texas," as he wrote his parents, and added that at last he had seen some rain, that the corn was ripe and cut and the cotton beginning to show—"there are plenty of peaches and melons of all kinds." His father had an atlas, and Owen explained how to find El Paso. It must have looked a long way from Van Hornesville, the farthest he had ever been away from them.

It looked far to Jo, too: so far, so hot. Distressed by the long illness of her father, worried by the effects of the extreme heat of the summer on the baby, she wrote her mother-in-law that she was "tried clean through," which from her was an extremely strong expression. Fred Weed came out from the office to see her, but he hardly had a reassuring effect when he quoted Mr. Tyler as saying, "Why Young's all right—having a good time!"

El Paso's public utilities had had the usual history of too many competing companies, inadequate capital and rudimentary technology, with the addition of international complications. In the '80s one street railway company—mule powered—was given the exclusive right to build a bridge over the Rio Grande—but only halfway, to the international boundary; the necessary franchise from the city of Juarez, Mexico, was not forthcoming. Early in 1901 Stone and Webster moved in; their man Goodrich was granted a franchise to construct and operate an electric car line in El Paso, with six miles of track.[7] There was competition, however, and politics was of course involved—both American and Mexican, for this too included a bridge. It was a lucrative line, especially when, at a later date, the state of Texas closed all saloons on Sunday while the other side stayed wet. Permission was granted by the Mexicans for the building of the bridge and Goodrich speeded up the construction schedule, promising an operating railway by the new year—a promise which was kept. On New Year's Day the last mule retired. That summer of 1901 s&w sent several of their men down, including Eliot Wadsworth; Young was charged with getting a franchise for expanding the line, since a developing El Paso would need more than the six miles of track, and s&w looked forward to buying out the competition.

Young drew what he considered a perfect franchise and the city council accepted it; it embodied most of his ideas about dividends and rates, and gave s & w a right-of-way on all streets in El Paso, present and future. In later years he liked to tell the story, half ruefully, of how he was fooled on this contract; he had been as sure that it was perfect as he had been that he knew too much mathematics for the freshman class. But an oil man named Barnsdall, a promoter, succeeded in getting a contract from the council that gave him the right-of-way down the *middle* of all the streets in El Paso, present and future—which left s & w climbing the sidewalks. The competitor sold his franchise, of course, to Stone and Webster for a good-sized block of stock, but Young liked to say, "That was the bitterest humiliation of my professional life."[8]

For the time being the job was done in Texas, it was time for his vacation in Van Hornesville, and he wanted to see his wife and son. But he was not "all right and having a good time," for he had caught malaria. Somehow he made it home, but he was a very sick young man. Jo wrote his mother that he was dreadfully thin and yellow; "he had a pretty close call—I think it was nothing but his grit and determination that brought him home in as good shape as he is." Friends rallied around, Fred came frequently, Vere Goldthwaite appeared one day. It was a hard pull back, but as soon as he could get about—and much sooner than Jo liked—he was back in the office, and it was not long before he was off on his travels again.

Texas malaria did not keep him from returning to Texas many times, maintaining ties in Dallas and Houston and Galveston, straightening out legal problems in Stone and Webster properties. He was indeed their Texas man, and they regarded him as practically a member of their firm.[9] Those days were a special part of Young's life, important for the experience they gave him in handling new and intractable situations—"There I began my work on the firing line of the development of public utilities"[10]—but also for the friends he made there, with whom he kept up in succeeding years. The atmosphere of life in Dallas was novel and heady, and although the working days were strenuous and exhausting, the evenings were often pleasant: dinner with friends, sometimes a poker game into late hours. He delighted his children—all of whom he taught to play poker—with his descriptions of games in Texas, when guns must be placed in plain sight before the cards were dealt, and he had to prove that he wasn't carrying one.

There were many other jobs in other states, all far away, which continued to displease his wife. In August of 1902, their second son, John, was born, and she was completely tied down with the two little ones. It was eleven years and two more children later that she went with Owen for the first time on a business trip—to Texas.

Minneapolis was his destination many times in and after 1901. On June 3, 1901, he wrote his father and mother from Cambridge—"I am off tonight on the midnight train for New York and then over the Pennsylvania to Terre Haute and Indianapolis"—the details were included so Smith could get out his atlas and follow the little thin lines of railroad tracks across the country. Minneapolis was the next stop, where the Minneapolis General Electric Company, taken over by Stone and Webster in 1899, was at this time the largest property managed by them. Many of their properties were powered by steam generated by coal or oil; but they were always much attracted by the power of white water, and some years after this visit of Young's they built a huge plant—dam, powerhouse, substations and lines—at Taylor's Falls on the St. Croix River. This enabled "Minneapolis to boast of having one of the notable recent engineering feats of the country at its service."[11] Development in this northern city was rapid, and as the main industry shifted from lumbering to milling, the demands for power increased. Young went there many times, for there was plenty of legal work involved, and he enjoyed the place and the people.

Far west of Minnesota, more powerful white water roared down from the mountains to the state of Washington. The young cities of Seattle and Tacoma were thirsty for power. When the Northern Pacific Railroad tunneled the Cascades to Puget Sound in 1885, the little settlements there—Seattle had but four thousand people—saw a great future before them. S. Z. Mitchell—later head of Electric Bond and Share and a close associate of Young's—as the youthful agent for the Edison Electric Company had put in a central station and the first street-lighting system west of the Rockies in that year, when Washington was still a territory. It was a chancy business. Needed equipment was slow in coming so far from the manufacturers, and capital costs were great compared with initial income; but as "S.Z." once said, "If the light shines you know your money is safe."[12]

Electrical companies proliferated in the Northwest, with—as usual—a good deal of Boston capital behind them; the Tacoma Railway and Power Company, for instance, listed among its organizers Robert Treat Paine, Thomas Jefferson Coolidge, Gordon Abbott and other Boston entrepreneurs. The Seattle-Tacoma Interurban, one of the earliest on the West Coast, had been financed by Kidder Peabody, and was acquired by Stone and Webster in 1902; s & w also owned the Tacoma and Seattle city systems, and renamed them the Puget Sound Electric Railway Company.

All these companies needed constant infusions of capital, which s & w usually stood ready to provide; over the years they acquired most of the electric railway, light, and power companies in the Puget Sound area. Twenty years after Washington became a state, in 1909, when Seattle had over 300,000 people, the white water was mostly harnessed: the Pulyallup, the White, the Nooksack and others were providing power for the cities of the northwest coast. Obviously there was plenty of work for s & w's lawyers, and Owen Young was introduced to a new and beautiful part of the United States—mountains, seacoast and rivers such as he had never seen before. It happened to be there, as Ida M. Tarbell quotes him, that he met his first and only request for a bribe. He had come on the public-utility scene too late in its development for the open passing of money; but in the Northwest an old-time councilman had asked Young, "Who is getting the money? There has none come my way."[13]

From his very first day in the field Young had recognized that there was no feasible alternative to open and honest dealing between public-service corporations and local and state governments. The railroad cases had taught him something of the devious influences that could be brought to bear on contracts and franchises; and he had learned a great deal more in a dozen medium-sized cities as counsel for Stone and Webster. His apprenticeship in the development of fair public-utility law made him recognized, long before he left Boston, as an authority in this field; his opinion was frequently asked as states and eventually the federal government set up regulatory commissions, and he was ready with suggestions to safeguard the rights of the consumers and the ability of the company to give good service.[14]

He was recognized also as a skillful and imaginative negotiator, whose integrity was unquestioned. Burton Eames, who came into the Tyler office in 1905, told Ida Tarbell that "Owen Young would get at the root of a complicated case more quickly and more accurately than any other man I have ever known. He was resourceful in argument, leaning always toward compromise; did not get angry," and, he added, was "absolutely unyielding when he had come to a decision."[15]

Public utilities, other corporations, estates and real estate—his success in dealing with all these and more made Young feel, halfway through his years with Tyler, that he was ready for a new status.

ii

Charles Tyler had never expected to take a partner; autocratic and individualistic, he preferred to command the troops alone. But his young men, as they attained—and were conscious of—their competence, grew restive. This was true of Owen Young and Fred Weed; as early as 1901 there was a crisis in the office. Weed felt he was underpaid and Young supported him; neither was satisfied with the other man in the office, Parsons. They plucked up their courage and talked to C.H., and by the middle of May, Jo would write her mother-in-law, "Affairs in the office have about settled down. C.H. did very well by Weed, and they are expecting Parsons to take another position; and if he does his salary will be divided between the boys— Everything is lovely at present." Parson did not leave, but by 1903 all three of them had their names on the letterhead as associates.

In 1905 Tyler was not well, and in July he had an operation; his doctor forced him to take a long rest. He went off to Europe for almost six months, leaving the office under Young's command. Things went well; morale was high, the s & w business was handled expertly, and, in spite of shorthandedness, other business as well. When Tyler came home in 1906 he was extremely pleased. He offered Young a salary raise, up from the five thousand dollars he was getting. But the younger man knew it was the right moment to suggest what he wanted—a partnership.

It took Tyler some time to make up his mind to this iconoclastic step; but Stone and Webster were strongly for it, in fact (as Stone told Young in later years) they would have liked to have him all to themselves. Finally, in January 1907, notices were sent out, and the letterhead thereafter read *Tyler & Young*. He was not required to put up any capital—in fact, no partner of Tyler's ever did; he was the sole proprietor of the firm. But Young shared in the earnings, which were considerable. Tyler knew that what he offered his clients was first-class, and he charged first-class prices.

The new partner was thirty-two years old. He had two sons, and another child about to make her appearance. He had rented a big house, which he was soon to buy, and with Jo's careful New England management they could be very comfortable, even as more children came along. Fifty years later he said to his daughter, "I was always lucky, I never had to worry about money. I always had enough to get along." Perhaps he had forgotten the hungry days in the Law School. But now, in Lexington, he could give his family what he wanted for them, and best of all, he could do what he wanted in Van Hornesville.

As early as 1901 Owen and Jo had felt that the living arrangements in Cambridge were not satisfactory; "the boys"—Stuart Edmonds and Arthur DeGoosh—were (as she wrote Ida) "an expense rather than helping any." They began to think of moving, but it was not until June of 1905 that Owen wrote his parents: "We have a new house out in Lexington on top of a hill where Dr. Stevens says there is no malaria where it is otherwise considered as healthy as any place in Massachusetts. We shall probably move in two or three weeks."

With the help of the devil which always attends to such occasions, Mr. Tyler fell ill just at the time of the move; Owen wrote, "I am necessarily here every minute when he is away." But they managed, or Jo managed, and they were in the new house by July 7. He told his parents jokingly that just Lexington, Mass., was sufficient address, as they were "prominent citizens."

The house was at the corner of Warren and Washington streets; the road leading up to it turned off at the Revolutionary Munroe Tavern on Massachusetts Avenue. The Youngs rented it from Mary B. Brooks for $60 a month for the first years; in 1909 they bought it for $12,500, with several acres of land. Later another piece of land out front was purchased for $3,300, and a garage was built in back for $1,700. Inside the house, they had all the plumbing replaced, and renovated the third floor at a cost of $3,000. When at length Young came to sell it, which was not until 1919, he asked $17,500 for it.

They thought the situation might be a little blustery in winter; but the view was splendid. The house itself was not very old, big, dark-brown-shingled, unpretentious and comfortable looking; there was a long porch around the front and a grove of pine trees behind. The pleasant rooms set off the antique furniture they were beginning to collect, and upstairs there was plenty of room for all the children and the two Irish maids. The garage was designed by C.J., at the age of eleven—the first of many attractive family buildings designed over the years by him as a strictly amateur architect—and housed a bright red Peerless, vintage 1910. This, and the big touring car which succeeded it, was driven by a chauffeur—neither Owen nor Jo ever learned to drive a car.

The place was lived in by the Young family until the summer of 1913, and they always remembered it affectionately. The daughter, Josephine, and the third son, Philip, were born there, and the older boys spent most of their childhood there and attended the Lexington public schools. The father walked down the hill to the station at the foot, called Munroe Station, and took the train to Boston. C.J. made model airplanes that really flew, and rigged up electrical contrivances, sometimes to the annoyance of the neighbors. There were plenty of playmates about and plenty of fields and woods to roam in. Lexington was still a small country town, where April 19 was more important than the Fourth of July, and each year saw a Paul Revere gallop into town, followed later in the day by a spectacular—or so it seemed to the children—parade.

Young had had to give up his teaching at the Boston University Law School in 1903, after seven years as lecturer in common-law pleading. In spite of the difficulties of fitting it in with the increasingly demanding work and travel of the Tyler office, he had enjoyed it immensely. Jo complained that evenings and Sundays were taken over by the preparation of lectures and the reading of papers, but Owen was a natural-born teacher and the work meant much to him. Both the dean and the students were satisfied as well.

In 1897 a "volume of test cases" was prepared by Professor Homer Albers and Owen Young, and published for the use of students. And in 1902 another book, *Problems in Practice and Pleading at the Common Law*, was published by Young and James T. Keen. This, according to the preface, was "designed to assist students in the application of the abstract theories of this subject to concrete cases."[16]

In 1902 the Law School tried to get him full time, as professor of corporations and trusts, at four thousand dollars a year; it was tempting, and Young took his time in deciding: "C.H. is having ten thousand fits in the meantime," he wrote to the farm, "telling me how soon I can get rich on the division of earnings scheme which he proposes to put in full force in the fall. The total net earnings for the [last] nine months . . . shows $87,000 which rather influences me not to leave." Nor did he.

He was also offered, at one point during his teaching, the post of assistant dean, with the implication that the deanship would follow; although he could not afford to take it, it was "a tremendous temptation," and was only declined after he had talked it over long and carefully with Jo.[17] In later years he looked back to see that this was indeed a dividing of the ways for his career; he liked teaching, he liked the Law School, he would have liked to be dean. He never forgot the struggle of that decision.

But if Young gave up teaching in a formal sense, he was ready to expound and advise about the law whenever need arose. A young man from Maine, Clement Robinson, fresh out of Harvard Law, joined the Tyler firm in 1906, but became restless and dissatisfied within a year. Young invited him to lunch at Young's Hotel and they talked for two hours—or the partner talked and the clerk listened. This

disquisition on the choices a lawyer faces was reported by Robinson
in a letter to his parents (a copy of which he sent to Young almost
forty years later). It illuminates how Young assessed the practice of
law after eleven years' experience: "ODY said that in the legal profession, nobody can forecast one's future, not even a man himself . . . in
his opinion the thing to do is to think oneself over, his capabilities,
opportunities, etc. coldbloodedly looking the problem in the face,
and then forecast for oneself the course which he will take today,
tomorrow and the next day, and let the forecasts of others go hang."
In the legal profession, he went on, there are three types of worthy
ideal. The first was the one whose field of action is the courtroom,
where if he is successful he will gain fame; this, Young had decided,
was not for him. The second was the "allround lawyer" of "conventional ambition"; him Young admired, but money was necessary to
get started. But the third kind, "equally noble and as honorable and
profitable as either," was one who was part of "a big machine"—
that is, a large and powerful law firm. "For himself he tentatively
chose that ambition years ago and has not deserted it." In spite of the
advice of friends he stuck it out, and "he is pretty well satisfied with
the results already." And here Robinson put in a parenthesis: "(ODY is
an exceptionally modest man. He never talks about himself. So to have
all this revelation of his own hopes etc. was most impressive.)" And
in conclusion Young praised the boy's work, told him to give any other
opportunity a very close look, advised him to stay where he was for
a year or two, ask Mr. Tyler for a raise, and stick it out.[18]

Young's interest in politics was always lively, and his habit of careful newspaper reading lifelong. He read not only the Boston and New
York papers, but on his travels the *Springfield Republican*, the *Cleveland Plain-dealer*, the *Baltimore Sun*, the *St. Louis Globe-Democrat*,
the *Dallas Morning News*, and many others of less importance. Conscious of the conflicting currents of the day, he followed closely not
only the general course of events but the varying temperatures of the
political and economic climates which were so important in the public-
utilities field. He had been, as he told Ida Tarbell, a conservative in
college, ready to accept authority and the world as it was—or as it
was supposed to be in the American dream. In law school he was too
busy studying and working to stay alive to occupy himself with large
issues such as reform or economic affairs—except for his own, and
the price of hops. But later, as Tyler sent him on errands around the
country, he met not only new places but new men—strikers and
strikebreakers, entrepreneurs of all types, grafters, reformers and bu-
reaucrats—and had to deal with them. The problems he read about
in the papers took on flesh and confronted him on the job.

If the last decade of the 1800s had been disturbed by depression, agricultural unrest and industrial warfare, the first of the 1900s had problems of its own. The growth of nationwide businesses, of the holding companies, of the labor unions, the concentration of wealth, the expansion of the cities and the corruption of government—all developed far wider support for progressivism, which embraced modern industrial society, than populism, which did not, ever had in its effort to preserve an earlier, largely agricultural, way of life. The cry for reform was no longer limited to a few leaders on the margins of society. Theodore Roosevelt as President set a new stage. He was pictured by himself and others as the champion of the people against "the malefactors of great wealth." He did not and could not go as far as the reformers—notably Robert M. La Follette—and the socialists—notably Eugene V. Debs—desired, but the climate in the White House, as in the country, had changed markedly from the wide-open laissez-faire atmosphere of the last century.

McClure's Magazine and the others which followed its lead in exposing evils of the "Trusts" and seeking civil service and other needed reform became for the time truly "mass media." The articles describing the malfunctions and greeds of the day were widely read, for they were often sensational; but in *McClure's* they were responsible journalism, soundly researched and documented. S. S. McClure himself, though eager for increased circulation and advertising, had a strong moral strain, and the magazine put before a large section of literate America new questions about the morality of many contemporary social ideas, corporate practices and accommodating politicians. Ida Tarbell and Lincoln Steffens, both of whom Owen Young came to know well in later years, were driven, like most of the others writing for *McClure's*, by high ideals and anger, and in its relatively brief career as a muckraking publication *McClure's* symbolized the voice of reform. With this, and with other outraged cries in print— the novels of Frank Norris and Upton Sinclair, the sharp humor of Finley Peter Dunne's Mr. Dooley—Young was, of course, acquainted.

Family letters seldom discuss politics and national affairs at length, and what the young lawyer, working all over the nation in the public-utility field was thinking about these currents of change cannot be documented. But his model franchise, providing for the consumer a share of rising profits, and for the community knowledge of and ultimate control of the utilities which served it, indicates the philosophical framework within which he thought and worked. He said once to his younger cousin, John Worden Elwood, who was his assistant from 1917 to 1922, "Think radically and act conservatively—but keep on thinking."[19]

Chapter 6

And Loses Him to Industry

M ARRIAGE sometimes causes the loosening of ties with home and parents; it was not so with Owen Young. His relationship with his father and mother, and with the farm and the community, remained intimate, concerned and rewarding through all the vicissitudes of his busy life. Jo's appreciation of the place, and her warm relationship with Ida Young, supported and encouraged his attitude. It was not possible for him to get home often, but letters flew back and forth each week. Mail service was excellent; a letter mailed in Cambridge or Boston, even in the afternoon of one day, was in Fort Plain at seven the next morning, and at the Van Hornesville post office by noon, where, if he was expecting a letter from Owen, Smith Young was probably waiting when the mail-carrier's buggy or cutter drove up to the store.

As money became more plentiful, Owen was able to carry out some of his plans for the farm. But he worried more and more about both of his parents working too hard, and finally decided that there was only one solution—to get them off the farm. He bought a house in "the Holler," at the center of the village, and moved his parents into it in 1903. It was a big, square, flat-roofed house, built some twenty years before by Walter Shumway, the local storekeeper. The store was across the street, and Mr. Shumway had wanted the handsomest house in town—big, with two porches, a double-arched front door, and elegant brackets under the eaves. There was also a barn and stable, a chicken house and run, and plenty of space for a garden. Drinking water—bright-shining, pure, and hard as a rock—had to be brought in pails from the spring, but there was also a cistern for rainwater for washing, with hand pumps on both floors. At the back of the house was a big summer kitchen and wood house, and back of that a comfortable three-holer, so it was not necessary to go outdoors. There was a little room off the kitchen with a bathtub in it, to be filled with hot water from the reservoir in the wood stove—though the grand-children remembered being washed in a round tin tub on the kitchen floor.

On the main floor were a parlor, a small, seldom-used dining room, and a comfortable sunny living room; upstairs, two large front bed-rooms, heated by stovepipes from the stoves below, and three smaller ones. The ceilings were high, the rooms airy; soon there were flowered carpets on the floors and lace curtains at the tall windows. Compared to the little house on the farm, it was a mansion.

In 1903 Owen began as well the acquisition of land and farms to which he devoted much time and money for most of the rest of his life. He bought the farms on either side of the Home Farm, and later the original Young farm from his cousins. And he bought cattle, plan-ning the development of a first-class Holstein-Friesian herd. The plan was for Smith Young to organize and supervise these farms; careful, wise, foresighted and patient, Smith was well qualified by a lifetime of farming. And although his son could not come often, he kept his finger on everything: "Nobody can find much fault with the price of cheese—How much milk are you getting now? What about the hay crop—if I can't see it before you begin cutting write me a letter about it . . . I am saving all the statements—How are your new cows doing?"

Smith Young had been in the dairy business all his life; but it was not until the 1880s that purebred Holsteins were imported from Hol-land in any numbers into New York State. And it was many years before the idea of a wholly purebred herd, developed for uniformity, beauty and large milk production, was accepted by the ordinary farmer. Of the early breeders in this country, Owen Young was not only one of the first, but one of the most persistent, intelligent and devoted. Today, in the pastures which once were his, and in thou-sands of others throughout the nation, graze the handsome black-and-white descendants of his program.

It was a pastime and a business which came naturally to him. His innate passion for excellence, nurtured by Charles Tyler, demanded the finest animals that could be produced. Breeding animals of any sort requires a combination of the gambling instinct and a good deal of intuition—a "feel" for it; these were strong in him, and with the years of experience he became very successful. His sense of business demanded low costs and high production; and, not least, he loved the animals, which, in turn, responded to him. To visit the barn with him was to see these characteristics in every move he made, as he ran a hand over the satiny hides, over the big bones, feeling the great bags of milk, scratching the calves' heads where the horns were sprouting, or petting the enormous bull that would let no one else touch him. He wrote his parents in the spring of 1905, "I was very glad to get your letter with so much cow news; it is one of my greatest pleasures and next to seeing them which I should so much like to do, the best thing is hearing about them especially at this time when so many new results are coming about which we have been working for and arranging more than a year."

Young was not, and never was, a "gentleman farmer." Born and bred to the work, in the earlier days he took an active part in his barns—so much so, that his mother made him change his clothes when he came back to the house. He had as well a strong desire to show his neighbors what could be done to improve herds, buildings and land without major expenditures. His barns were never polished-up showplaces, like those of some of the breeders from whom he purchased stock; they were ordinary red wooden Herkimer County barns, but tight, clean and workable. He bought machinery as it was developed, but only after careful study of cost and efficiency.

On purebred "individuals" he spent considerable sums. But again, he did his homework before he bought. He collected all the available literature on the breed—herdbooks, Canadian and Dutch as well as American. He corresponded with other breeders, comparing notes: "I am satisfied now that you are absolutely right in your belief that inbreeding to the extent which you are practising will only accentuate desirable traits without loss of physical power." By 1910 he was writing his uncle in Van Hornesville that "we are now commencing to deal with the best there is. In fact there are only about three or four breeders in America which have such stock as I am shipping you."[1]

Much of his happiness with his program in the beginning was the pleasure and occupation it gave his father. Over seventy, Smith Young was worn by a lifetime of hard work; but he did not know how to do nothing. Owen was delighted with his solution for his father, and looked forward, sanguine as always, to many years of working with him on his program. But it was not to last; on the sixteenth of January, 1906, Smith Young died of a heart attack, aged seventy-four.

Owen had always worried about his parents, and there must have been some such fear in his heart; he had hoped he had put it off by the move from the farm. He took it very hard, for his mother's sake and his own. The three of them had been so close a family, had shared all the good times and bad times throughout his life, and the older ones had so recently come into sunshine and ease that the death was far more of a blow than it usually is for a grown-up son with an elderly father. Three years before, he had written to his mother on his birthday:

Twenty-nine years old—that does not sound very old; somehow I believe I am older—that you have made a miscount. At any rate no one appreciates so well as I all you and Pa have done for me in these years—one never can understand these things fully until they have children of their own and then it does all come over them what that day—their birthday—meant to others as well as themselves.—There is really no occasion for my writing because I am coming so soon, but I just feel that on this birthday I ought to bow down and make acknowledgement to you—with best love—

He felt somehow when Pa died that he had not paid his debt in full, though his parents would not have agreed. His mother was to live twenty-five years more, and for her, she felt, he did far more than she had ever done for him. Their relationship became even closer, and, as she now spent more time visiting them, it became closer also with the rest of the family. The younger children knew only one of their four grandparents, but she made up for all the rest.

The Holstein program had to go on, and it did so for many years. Owen's uncle John Worden Brandow, and his wife, Maria (Van Horne), came to live with Ida in the big house in Van Hornesville, and Uncle John took over the management of the farms. It was not an ideal arrangement for John Brandow was not by nature a farmer; he had been at various times a carpenter, an innkeeper, a horse breeder—he greatly preferred horses to cows, and always had a handsome team, or a spirited one for his buggy, in the stable, and had been run away with so often it became an old story. But he worked hard at the job and did as well as he could, and Owen of course gave the program his constant attention.[2]

His trips to Van Hornesville, and the family's summers and Christmases with Grammy, kept them in close touch with the village and its people. Ida Young had been one of eight children, and four of them were still living in or near the village. Dr. Will Young, a cousin of Owen's, lived up the street, and looked after the family when needed—he once sent Owen a bill for fifty dollars "for the last six years." Owen kept up with everything and was active in initiating or supporting improvements in the village: an association for care of the cemetery, agitation for sidewalks to replace the mud of the roadside, better telephone service; and, as automobiles became more common, he took up the cause of good roads. A letter to Abram Tilyou, who, since Smith's death, had taken the place of a father to Owen as much as anyone could, described in 1912 the dreadful condition of the roads through and near Van Hornesville:

I doubt if there is another point in the entire State where such fertile lands lie so remote from transportation facilities as [this] area. . . . It is accessible only by a poor dirt road from the middle of June to the middle of September and by sleighing for a month or two in the winter. During the remainder of the year the roads are practically impassable for heavy or satisfactory teaming. . . . The want of transportation facilities, either by railroad, electric road or even good highways has done more than anything else to depreciate the value of these rich agricultural lands. Within a generation these lands have depreciated from about $100 per acre to from $20 to $35 . . . due almost wholly to lack of accessibility.[3]

It was some years, however, in spite of his efforts, before a new road was built; but eventually he had the satisfaction of seeing a paved road through Van Hornesville, connecting—like the old stage— Fort Plain and Cooperstown, the Mohawk and the Susquehanna.

ii

Every man, every family, has years which are turning points, when— often suddenly—new courses are charted and new directions taken. Nineteen twelve was such a year for Owen and Josephine Young. The first three-quarters were usual enough; Owen was away a great deal, mostly in Texas, and when he was in Boston he was working long hours. He had been a partner of Tyler's for more than five years, there was always more work than he could do, and he was making all the money he wanted. The house in Lexington had been fixed up the way they wanted it and was extremely comfortable. Their family—they thought—was complete; C.J. would be thirteen at the end of the year, John was ten in the summer; they were both doing well in the Lexington schools. Little Jo was five, and, under the tutelage of the local librarian, could read and write. The baby, Philip, was two, and kept his mother busy. Grandmother came several times a year, with a lively correspondence in between; they all went to "the Holler" in the summer and for Christmas, looked at the new calves in the barn, and walked or skied over the hills. Life was good, and settled.

Owen Young had that type of physical constitution which suffers headaches and intestinal upsets (called in that day "bilious attacks") and colds, but is never seriously ill. In the fall of 1912, however, he was troubled by pain which did not go away in spite of his efforts to disregard it. On October 19 he had to have an operation for appendicitis. This was wholly successful, but it took him some time to recover his strength. The convalescence gave him time to think about and to discuss with Jo the possible new turning in the course of their lives.

More than once, in his legal work for Stone and Webster, Young had come up against the General Electric Company—in Texas, in Seattle, beside the Hudson River. As a boy he had seen from the train the great plant at Schenectady, built by the Edison Company and much enlarged when it became part of General Electric; it looked enormous to him, mysterious and fascinating. He had listened to the stories, around the stove in the Van Hornesville store, of the magic that went on in that plant, told by men who had worked there. And as a public-utilities lawyer he knew all about the size and importance of the company. In that very summer of 1912 the *Electrical World*, an influential paper in the industry, published a financial review of the company, on the occasion of the issue of a 30 percent stock dividend:[4] its "strong position financially is due in large part, aside from its phenomenal growth, to the conservative policy of charging off assets of an intangible character and providing amply for depreciation." Its capital was $125 million, its sales and earnings respectively $89 million and $13 million—including $5 million of "other income." And Herbert Knox Smith, the former commissioner of corporations, was quoted as saying, "The General Electric influence in this field is larger than that of any other single group of interests and comprises nearly one-half of the developed power."[5]

For a company which had commenced its corporate existence only twenty years before, this was—even for those days—a massive record. The story of the combination of good timing and good management which brought this about was familiar to Young, and through it moved the figure of a man whom he knew and respected, and whom he was to know far better and to respect even more.

A year before Owen Young was born, Charles Albert Coffin at the age of twenty-nine set up his own shoe-manufacturing firm in Lynn, Massachusetts. He had already spent ten years in the business in his uncle's firm, which he entered immediately after school. For his own firm, he built a new and larger plant, right next to the railroad station, so he caught his customers as they got off the train. Born in Fairfield, Maine, in 1844, Charles Albert Coffin was a descendant of Tristram Coffin, the seventeenth-century governor of Nantucket; Charles's grandfather had taken up free land when it was offered in Maine, and had become a farmer, and a Quaker. This heritage gave his grandson the Down East qualities of working hard, squeezing the pennies and never giving up, combined with the gentleness and spiritual qualities of the Friend. He was also a young man of acute intelligence and remarkable prescience; he was always looking for something new, and not averse to taking a risk.

Shoes were a good steady business and his company was doing well. But more exciting things were happening, and when Coffin had a chance through a fellow leather manufacturer in Lynn to buy into a little electrical company in Connecticut, he took it. He soon found himself moving it to Lynn, renaming it in 1883 the Thomson-Houston Company after the two inventive high-school teachers who had started it originally, and finally managing and developing it. For Coffin it was the end of the shoe business and the beginning of a long and remarkable career in the electrical industry.

Throughout the last decades of the nineteenth and the first of the twentieth century both the United States and Europe were full of inventors working on the practical uses of electricity: lamps, batteries, motors, dynamos, railways, central stations, and transmission of current. As workable solutions appeared, such as alternating current, they were adopted, and caused immediately a need for manufacturers, organizers, plant builders, financiers and salesmen. Coffin was all of these; he said to a former shoe customer, to whom he was offering a job in the Thomson-Houston Company, and who protested that he didn't even know what electricity was: "We've too many men who know what electricity is, or think they do. What we want now is somebody to care for the commercial side. Perhaps the less you know about what electricity is, the better!"[6] It was an observation of which Owen Young, later on, would develop his own version.

Numberless small electrical companies sprouted throughout the country, mainly to supply light; they needed lamps, alternators, transformers. Where cash was short, as it often was, Coffin took securities of the companies as part payment. In the financing of the Thomson-Houston Company itself, he persuaded a formidable array of Boston capitalists to take part, among them T. Jefferson Coolidge, Henry Lee Higginson, Endicott Peabody. The manufacturing end, under E. W. Rice, Jr., a former student of Elihu Thomson, as general superintendent, was surmounting the endless problems of a wholly new industry. Coffin decided that the company should go into the street-railway business; he added men and companies for this and other developments. Between 1889 and 1891 one of the first really successful street-car lines was built in Cambridge and the West End of Boston by the Thomson-Houston Company—a confirmation of Coffin's confident predictions to his Boston investors.

In New York City and New York State another big electrical manufacturing company was making the same kind of progress. The numerous companies which bore the name of Edison were gradually merged into one: the Edison General Electric Company began its existence in 1889, a powerful competitor to the Thomson-Houston Company.

To the development of both, however, and to the extension of the use of electricity to the people, there was one mammoth obstacle: conflicting patents. A jungle of private territories had grown up over the years of invention; infringement suits were legion, such as the famous one in 1889 between Edison's company and the U.S. Electric Lighting Company over the incandescent lamp. That one the Edison General Electric won, but at enormous cost. It was obvious to the Thomson-Houston Company that there was only one solution to its competition with Edison: a merger. Edison was slightly larger, in capitalization, gross business, number of employees, plants and customers; but Thomson-Houston had Charles A. Coffin.

The General Electric Company was born, after protracted labor pains, on April 15, 1892, and started business on June 1. Coffin was elected president, and on the new board was an impressive list of names from both Boston and New York, supplying to the newborn corporation not only know-how and respectability but assurance of financial support.[7]

A magnificent exhibit at the World's Columbian Exposition in Chicago celebrated the birth of the company; among the marvels were an electric railway encircling the grounds, generators of—for the day—enormous power, a motor-driven sidewalk, boats with electric motors, and a galaxy of incandescent lamps. But 1893 held less fortunate days for the young General Electric. Even while the bright lamps flashed on in Chicago, times were worsening. The financial panic of the summer brought desperate times. As the company's business declined, its indebtedness grew; and the notes and securities it had taken from small companies in payment for equipment became so many frozen assets. It was a true liquidity crisis and it really looked as though the new company might go under. But Coffin, under sharp criticism from both within and without, would not give up, though he is quoted as saying, many years later, "There were months that seemed like scalding centuries." And he succeeded; his plan to liquidate the securities of the local companies held by GE, by offering them eventually to the stockholders of the main company at a substantial discount, was accepted by his directors. But four million dollars in cash was needed for the initial transaction—the purchase of the securities by a syndicate. At the last moment J. P. Morgan, from his Maine summer home, agreed to put up the final million. The company was saved, and from 1894 its business grew and grew.[8]

Surviving both the panic of 1907 and an antitrust suit in 1911, General Electric and Charles Coffin maintained their position at the head of the electrical industry, and looked forward to new developments. Coffin, one of whose major assets was an unerring eye in choosing good men, had assembled a first-class top echelon for the company. Heading the list was E. W. Rice, Jr., the highly respected senior vice-president in charge of engineering and manufacturing, and Coffin's likeliest successor. In financial and corporate affairs, Coffin counted heavily on his onetime assistant Anson W. Burchard, widely experienced and now a vice-president too. Rice's tested assistant was Francis C. Pratt, destined for future recognition. Actually vice-presidents were few at the time, the only other one being Jesse R. Lovejoy;[9] but there were other old-timers, like George Emmons and George F. Morrison, William Roy Emmet and William R. Burrows, who knew the company's products, procedures and people like a book they had written themselves.

Coffin had realized early how important it was that the manager of GE's Patent Department be a man of parts as well as probity—and by common consent Albert G. Davis was both. Not only that, Davis had taken extraordinary measures to encourage invention to proliferate. In this effort his collaborator was a keen-eyed and indefatigable hunchback who had so impressed Rice that in his first year, 1893, when all salaries beginning with Coffin's were cut, Rice ventured the unorthodox recommendation: "Charles P. Steinmetz, electrical engineer, no conditions, service indispensable, increased compensation warranted."[10] Together Davis and Steinmetz waited on Rice in 1901 to propose that a basic research laboratory—separate from the plant—be forthwith established in Schenectady. Although basic research was then almost as rare in the universities as in industry, Rice supported the proposal and soon thereafter Schenectady was recruiting to the new center such creative scientists as Willis R. Whitney and W. D. Coolidge, both from the Massachusetts Institute of Technology, and Irving Langmuir from Stevens Tech. It was such work as theirs which helped in turn to bring in others—like the young Swedish engineer with the overriding interest in wireless, Ernest F. W. Alexanderson.[11]

But in April 1912 Coffin lost one of his stalwarts, Hinsdill Parsons, vice-president and counsel for GE, who was killed in an automobile accident. Coffin, as usual, took time and care in finding the right man to replace him. It was not until September, when Owen and Jo were in New York for a few days, that Coffin asked to see him. Young knew that the president of the General Electric Company was well acquainted with his work, for he had met GE lawyers more than once, in negotiation or in court. Which particular case brought him especially to Coffin's notice is not known, but it was probably a series of successes against Electric Bond and Share, a GE subsidiary. Hence, as Owen left the hotel, he said to his wife, "I am going to get spanked." But Coffin offered him the position of counsel and vice-president.[12]

Young was very much involved in Dallas affairs at that time, and he had to go to Texas for a week or so; on his return he went to Van Hornesville to see his mother and talk to her about the offer. He also talked to Abe Tilyou, for he always valued highly Abe's advice. On October 9 he was again in New York, and not feeling well. On that day he wrote his mother from the Holland House, at Thirtieth Street and Fifth Avenue, where he usually stayed: "Mr. Coffin came in to see me this afternoon—he evidently wants me to come pretty badly— his offer of $24,000 per year for first year and $30,000 the second is almost more than I can refuse." He also told her that he felt "pretty sore" and would go to the doctor as soon as he got back to Boston— which he did, and was told an operation was recommended.

On October 17, Owen dictated a letter which, in draft in Jo's handwriting, survives.

My dear Mr. Coffin—
Dr. Mixter finally advised this afternoon that I be operated on for appendicitis not as a matter of necessity but as a matter of insurance. He stated that I must give up not less than four, probably not more than six weeks for the purpose, and that I must slow down in my work for several weeks after that. I stated to you in New York and I still feel that I should like to accept your proposition to become a Vice-President of the G.E. CO.; with a salary of twenty-four thousand dollars for the first year if I were in fit physical condition to do your work; if not, you certainly would not want me. I have said this same thing to Mr. Tyler.
It may be that owing to the delay caused by the operation, you will feel that you must withdraw your proposition. If so I beg you to believe that I shall always cherish the honor which you have done me in making the suggestion. I shall be operated on at the Eliot Hospital in Boston on Saturday morning.[13]

But Mr. Coffin was not one to be put off so easily; his answer came promptly: "I have your letter of the 17th. I hope that by this time the operation which you were to undergo has proven a success and that you are already on the way toward recovery. I do not want to withdraw my suggestion and shall look forward when you recover to the association which we have contemplated."[14] And again, we have a draft in Jo's writing, of the answer to the answer: "I thank you for your letter of the twenty-first. The operation was a complete success and I expect in due time to be in fit physical trim for any work which may present itself."

Owen and Jo were excited by the new prospect. For her it meant leaving her native Massachusetts, where she had spent all her life except for the years at St. Lawrence; but she was ready and willing to try it. As for Owen, it meant freedom from the routine of the law office, where for sixteen years he had taken all jobs that came to his desk, whether interesting or dull, large or small. By now the firm of Tyler and Young was, in its field, the most important in Boston; in its entrepreneurial, hard-driving, profit-making atmosphere Young had served a hard apprenticeship, a demanding partnership. Now he saw great and different opportunities ahead. It was an escape, he told Ida Tarbell, "from the mediaeval, a chance to operate in what was still the no man's land of the law."[15]

But there was one person for whom the prospect was dark: Charles Tyler. It is fortunate that his letter of October 17, 1912, survives, for it illuminates not only the situation at the time but the whole relationship between the older and the younger man. He had talked to Jo on the phone that day and learned of the coming operation; his letter in reply was sent out to Lexington by hand.

My very dear Young:

I am *glad* to learn that you are to have an operation on Saturday, for I think it is the very wisest thing you can do whether regarded from the standpoint of insurance or necessity. I asked your wife to say to you that I wanted to talk with you before you wrote to New York, feeling very sure that you would understand what I meant. I do not propose to advise you, or attempt to advise you, in reference to the New York situation, for I think my advice would be tinged with self-interest, but I do think that before reaching any conclusion one way or the other you should talk with some of your very good friends such, for example, as Mr. Webster, Mr. Robb, Mr. Bradlee, Mr. Cotting, Mr. Welch or Mr. Hooper. So far as I know, only Mr. Webster and Mr. Robb know anything of what you have in mind. I do not think you ought to attempt to reach any conclusions upon your own judgment unaided, for I know that you are very greatly distressed and that you are troubled about the present and the future, but really I do not believe there is the slightest reason for you to be troubled or to have any fear but that everything will come out absolutely all right. I have, as you know, been through four operations in my life and I know that no matter how normal or well balanced a man may be, his judgment on the eve of a surgical operation, no matter how slight, is not either well balanced or judicial or what he should rely on.

What you need, I think, is a good talk with some of the people I have suggested above,—a perfectly good, straightforward talk. They all love you very dearly and whatever they tell you they will believe.

You do not need to have me tell you how fond I am of you and how anxious I am to be of any service to you whatever.

Believe me to be with ever so much love,

Very truly yours,
C.H.T.

Again we have the draft of a letter in reply in Jo's hand:

My dear Mr. Tyler—

Your note was delivered by messenger tonight. . . . I shall be operated on at the Eliot Hospital on Saturday morning, but after reading your note and thinking the matter over, I have concluded that there is very little if anything to add to what has been said already—I have stated to Mr. Coffin as I told you that I should like to accept his proposition, and come to New York, if I were physically fit to do the work. The time of leaving my work in Boston would have to be adjusted to your satisfaction, which I have no doubt would meet his necessities. The delay occasioned by the operation may put an entirely different phase on the matter. I realize fully that I may make a grave mistake on a matter of business judgment in going to New York. Of that, however, I am willing to take the risk. The only thing which influenced me at all and made me hesitate the most was breaking up my personal relations with you, which have grown from those of mere business to those of the highest affection and admiration. I am sure that discussion of the matter even with our warmest friends would be unprofitable for us both.[16]

There was no doubt about Coffin's eagerness to get Young to New York, for on November 27 he was writing again: "I have not heard from you for some time, and I am anxious to know if you are still making rapid progress toward complete recovery." Early in December his new man was well enough to go to New York and spend a week-end at the Coffins' place in Locust Valley. And on December 30, the day of the General Electric board meeting in Boston, Coffin made an appointment to see Young and Tyler together. The day after, Tyler handed his partner the final document:

Tyler and Young
Attorneys and Counsellors at Law
Ames Building
Boston

December 31, 1912

Charles H. Tyler
Owen D. Young

———

M. J. Dwyer
B. E. Eames
J. H. Ellis
R. A. Pritchard
J. P. Wright

Our partnership is this day terminated.

Young has received his full share of the partnership profits and assets, as per partnership agreement, and everything that is coming to him.

Tyler takes whatever is left.

Each releases the other, except that Tyler is to hold Young harmless from firm liabilities, which he hereby agrees to do.

Charles H. Tyler

Public notices were sent out by both the law firm and the General Electric Company, and on Thursday, January 2, 1913, the new vice-president and counsel sat in his office at 30 Church Street, New York.

Part II

*The New Freedom and
Big Business*

1913–1921

Chapter 7

Lag of the Law:
The Wilsonian Version—and Young's

T HE pace and productivity of Owen Young's first nine weeks at General Electric suggest that he had not forgotten his college maxim: work hard and establish a reputation for yourself at the outset. They also suggest what he later confirmed: that his recent appendectomy had left him "feeling better than I ever did in my life."[1]

It had been, of course, a great nuisance to be hospitalized in that eventful fall: to have to celebrate his thirty-eighth birthday in an antiseptic room instead of at home with cake and candles and the children; to be anesthetized, of all things, just as the fabulous triangular presidential campaign of 1912 was reaching its climax; worst of all, to be kept from the polls on that fateful Tuesday, November 5, and so from casting his vote (for once!) for the winner, Woodrow Wilson. Nevertheless, it had its compensations. Still regarded as a major operation, an appendectomy meant long and leisurely weeks of convalescence, and if in the hospital this left the patient restive, home was another matter. To be able to sit all day and every day in his wing-back rocker, getting up to poke the fire or reach down a favorite book, and then to spend the evenings with Jo and the children was to feel a kind of renewal of body, mind and spirit. Never had he experienced such freedom from the pressures and responsibilities of a six- to seven-day workweek. Never had there been such an opportunity to read, reflect, and take stock, to think and—in his own phrase—"keep on thinking."

In mid-October he had confessed to his mother that he was preoccupied almost to the exclusion of all else with his health and his new assignment.[2] But Young was an inveterate newspaper reader and the papers were full of the dramatic race, now entering the home stretch, between Teddy Roosevelt's New Nationalism and Woodrow Wilson's New Freedom—with President Taft, Jo's Republican favorite, a badly winded third. And as concern about his health—the only possible barrier to his new assignment—diminished daily, Young's sense of insulation rapidly wore off; stirring in themselves, the political race and its outcome had obvious bearing upon the future of his new employer and so upon the very nature of his job.

There were certain more basic questions. He knew that Coffin wanted him, but why? He knew that he was going to join GE, but why? What, with big business under fire, did he plan and hope to accomplish there? What was Coffin expecting of him?

One thing was clear: he was not being asked to reorganize GE's engineering, production or marketing operations—except perhaps for the marketing of its incandescent lamps. So far so good; these after all were fields in which the company was preeminent and he was not. And its preeminence offered good assurance that so far as GE's growth and prosperity were concerned, the next two decades could well match—or even outrun—the last two. Certainly he knew enough about the industry, and the company, to be sure of the potential.

What, then, *did* Coffin have in mind? Was Young to safeguard these potentials against all hazards, and if so, what were the major hazards? Panic and depression, of course, but Coffin himself would have to cope with these. *Fear* of depression then, or of depressing circumstances? That was getting warm, perhaps, but it was pretty nebulous. It was also worth pursuing, for, with all its fabulous growth, with all its resources and wide horizons, business—and especially big business—was operating under a cloud of public suspicion and private apprehension. Coffin himself still felt this cloud and couldn't get away from it. Priding themselves on their integrity, he and his colleagues were still smarting from the ignominy of the antitrust suit filed in 1911 by a Republican attorney general—and a Wall Street lawyer at that! True, they had finally settled for the consent decree as drawn by the government, but apparently they weren't too happy about that either. And with indictments and threats of indictment against corporate directors being bandied about, they were clearly apprehensive of worse to come, whether at Wilson's hand or Roosevelt's. What was Mr. Dooley's phrase about such options? "You pays your money and you takes your choice."

By the time that Young was home again, the American people had made their choice, and had done so greatly to his satisfaction. Whether or not Young had then read Herbert Croly's *Promise of American Life*, Theodore Roosevelt, as the Progressive, or Bull Moose, candidate, had made its thesis thoroughly familiar: competition being self-destructive, corporations should be permitted their natural growth, with abuses curbed and the national interest protected by the sweeping and continuous play of federal regulation.[3] Wilson, on the other hand, had been insisting (with Louis Brandeis) that as corporations grew too big for their britches they became inefficient as well as antisocial; a progressive government must therefore be concerned with the means of restoring and constantly renewing the conditions of fair competition.[4]

Familiar with both theses, and not completely happy with either, Young had put his money on Wilson and not only for party reasons. As attorney for Stone and Webster, he had come to feel at home with regulated monopoly, but it was only in situations which ruled out competition that monopoly and government regulation made sense. Certainly he wanted none of it for a great manufacturer like General Electric, which would far better go on testing its mettle against competitors like Westinghouse and Western Electric, as well as the scores of smaller specialty companies.[5]

What else did he want for General Electric? Well, for one thing he'd like to show Wilson that a business *need* not be inefficient or antisocial just because it was big. This would involve finding out more about Wilson's legislative program on the one hand and GE's contracts, policies and ways of doing business on the other. Wilson had suggested, and Young believed, that only a progressive administration could afford to be fair to business—especially big business.[6] But that meant that business, for its part—especially big business—could not afford to be anything but fair: to its customers and competitors, to the government and general public. Here the rules were pretty fuzzy, and certainly Young was not the man to fault Wilson for insisting that the lag of the law was chiefly to blame.

As a matter of fact he could tell the President-elect a thing or two about this lag. It wasn't only science and invention and engineering—General Electric's stock-in-trade—which had so changed the face of industry that the law could scarcely recognize it. It wasn't only the energy from steam or electric power that kept accelerating the pace. No, in order for these new forms of energy to produce the large-scale enterprise to which they pointed, invention had been busy in other fields too—even in the law. Or here, perhaps, the important thing was not so much invention as adaptation and ingenious application.

Take the concept of limited liability. It had been around for a long time with no noticeable impact. Then, suddenly, it had come alive as a new and dynamic force because it matched a need: the need of the railroads and their suppliers for large-scale capital investment. And once the limited-liability company proved itself the magnet required to attract large capital, there had been no stopping it. It gave the signal for the corporate explosion which, since about the time Young was born, had transformed the industrial scene and ways of doing business—with its mergers, pooling of patents and the rise of the great capital markets of Philadelphia, Boston, even Chicago, but especially New York. There were new problems for management too: the need to concern itself not with one market only but with two— for securities as well as goods and services. Hence the demand for prominent bankers as corporate directors, GE's Lee Higginson and J. P. Morgan, for example. Hence, too, the spawning of corporate subsidiaries, like GE's securities companies.[7]

Finance capitalism, in short, was fairly bristling with new questions of policy, public and private—including labor problems of a sort to baffle the old guard that would nevertheless have to be resolved. As for the status of the laws—local, state and federal—Wilson was essentially right. By and large, they were, as he had said, "still meant for business done by individuals." And Wilson had a way of putting it— even to quoting Lewis Carroll—that this sometime pedagogue relished. This relish was confirmed following publication a year or so later of Wilson's campaign speeches, under the title *The New Freedom*. Then, and especially after adding to his personal library an autographed first edition of this volume, Young liked to turn the pages until he came to Wilson's "parable of progress": Alice's breathtaking race with the Red Queen which left them both just where they had started. And then the Wilsonian sequel: "The laws of this country have not kept up with the change of economic circumstances in this country; they have not kept up with the change of political circumstances, and so we are not even where we were when we started. . . . They have not been satisfactorily adjusted to business done by great corporations and we have got to adjust them. I do not say we may or we may not; I say we must."[8]

Stirring words but, coming down to earth, just what did they mean for Young's new client's future—and so for his? Congress, to be sure, had made a few attempts at catching up, setting up the Interstate Commerce Commission and—as GE had good reason to know—enacting the Sherman law. Now Wilson promised other and more searching reforms; and those would bear watching—part of Young's job. In the meantime, he had better know all there was to know about the Sherman act, and specifically about the 1911 suit and the consent decree that terminated it.

Actually the consent decree, like the bill of indictment, was limited and specific; both were directed solely against the patent agreements and pricing procedures involved in the manufacture and marketing of the incandescent lamp. As general counsel, then, his first and obvious duty was to be sure that GE scrupulously observed the cease and desist orders to which it had consented. But as vice-president for policy he could hardly be content with mere conformity. What was needed to dispel that blanketing cloud was a business initiative that did not wait on government; an affirmative demonstration by GE— and why not?—that its continued and prosperous growth was wholly compatible with, and actually served, the public interest.

So—that was where he came in. *That* was what he wanted for General Electric—tough to achieve but worth the effort. The fact was, come right down to it, that the company's only discernible weaknesses were in two related fields: law and policy. *His* fields. It was here that Coffin had felt the need of a fresh eye. Coffin was right. And Young was ready.

ii

On the morning of January 3, 1913, before leaving his rooms in the Murray Hill Hotel, Young penned a brief note to his mother which undoubtedly told her what she most wanted to know. The move was made. Owen's new appointment was confirmed. His first day at the office had been "interesting and satisfactory" and she knew where to reach him. He had good company and expected better—Jo, no less— if only his small daughter's "bilious attack" would go away. (It did, but not in time.) And there was promise of a story to come with Owen's next visit.

For other reasons, too, the low-key recital was appropriate. At thirty-eight, this "Yorker" who had spent almost half his life in Boston was coming back to his native state; if, for the balance of the school year, his wife and children stayed behind, it was better that the absent husband and father be in New York than in Dallas or Seattle. Nor, at first reading, was any great leap involved professionally. A promising young lawyer was taking on a new and quasi-permanent client, whose problems and concerns he was prepared to make henceforth his own. In the meantime, he would look about for a new home, and visit his family whenever he could.

That wasn't often. If Young found his new environment strange it was undeniably exhilarating, and even at the workaday level the new job as he defined it proved endlessly demanding. The weekend of January 11 found him in Washington, where new tariff legislation was in the making, asking to be "instructed" about waterpower.[9] Before the end of the month he and Coffin had spent two crowded days in Schenectady which left Young wanting more.[10] The second week-end in February he devoted to his mother in Van Hornesville, taking the Friday-night sleeper to Herkimer and the interurban trolley over the hills to Jordanville, where his uncle John met him with the sleigh. He had intended to stop over in Schenectady on his return, but, as he wrote Allan Jackson, head of the Law Department, this was pre-cluded by developments which called him back to Washington early in the following week.[11]

Old responsibilities, moreover, were not so easily sloughed off. Dallas, last visited just before his operation, was once again clamoring for Young's attention, as Charlie Stone and Tyler did not scruple to remind him. Having talked with Coffin and satisfied himself that on the problems currently at issue there was no serious conflict of in-terest between Stone and Webster and GE's wholly owned subsidiary, Electric Bond and Share, Young agreed to go.[12]

Accustomed as he was to travel, Young was quick to appreciate the convenience of his new headquarters. Thirty **Church** Street was in the Hudson Terminal Building, whence—thanks to electric power and the notable persistence of one William Gibbs McAdoo—one could take the tubes to Jersey and there board the Pennsylvania for Wash-ington, Chicago or St. Louis—where, incidentally, one changed for Dallas. Often there were options. When his destination was Washing-ton, Young usually chose the three-block walk to the Jersey Central's Liberty Street Ferry, and the five-minute crossing of the lower bay which brought him to the B&O's Jersey City Terminal. Heading for Cleveland or Chicago, he preferred the New York Central, which also took him to Schenectady or Herkimer or Canton. And the New York Central, like the New Haven, was only a stone's throw from his rooms at the Murray Hill.

So, of course, was the Forty-second Street station of the Lexington Avenue subway, Young's customary point of departure for an office which was confronting the new general counsel with a series of major assignments. The downtown express—also electrically propelled—cost him a nickel and even at the rush hour took only about twelve min-utes. On his way home, after crossing Broadway and looking down toward Trinity Church, Young had a fine view of the Singer Building, only a block south, and still among the tallest. Looking north toward St. Paul's and the city hall, he could see the latest claimant, the un-finished Woolworth Building, rising to make good its challenge.

He never saw these sights on his way to the office, for the down-town subway exit debouched the passengers on Dey Street, well down the block from Broadway; but as he walked the half block to Church, breasting the streams of Jersey commuters flowing toward their offices from tube or ferry, he could sometimes catch a whiff of salt spray in the air. New York, like Boston, was still very much a seaport town.

But across Manhattan Island the currents of change were far more heady than in Boston, and however one newly arrived might deplore the destruction of old landmarks, there was something breathtaking about the thrust of its new skyscrapers. Pulses quickened with the tempo of life in this cosmopolitan metropolis, which sooner or later summoned everybody who was anybody—or, like Young, intended to be.

iii

The first of Young's assignments plunged him at once into the thick of GE's legal and policy problems. House hunting—even Dallas— would have to wait. At the January meeting of the directors, questions had been raised regarding the propriety of the General Company's continuing to be represented on the boards of its so-called securities- holding companies. The new general counsel had been asked to pre- pare and submit an opinion.

Fortunately, Young was no stranger to these subsidiaries or to the considerations which had prompted their formation. He knew only too well the difficulties that beset newly enfranchised utilities in financing the purchase of needed equipment, and sympathized with Coffin's desire to keep his customers alive by accepting their junior securities in partial payment of their bills. He had learned how Coffin had moved even before GE's liquidity crisis of 1893 to avert just such a contingency by creating and capitalizing the United Electric Securi- ties of Boston, which could then be expected to raise cash against these junior securities by issuing its own debentures or borrowing from the banks. He understood that so far as that panic was con- cerned, this had been a case of too little and too late and that the other heroic measures then invoked had barely saved the day.

But Coffin's faith had survived, and so had United Electric Securi- ties. After all, GE needed the orders, its customers needed something more than short-term credit, and Coffin had confidence in their future. This time the event had more than justified his confidence. Adequate- ly capitalized by General Electric, United Electric had indeed taken over, and nurtured, such of these customer obligations as had escaped the liquidating pool—plus, of course, new and diversified issues—and against them sold debentures and borrowed from the banks at need.

With time, many of these securities were finding a ready market. Indeed, by 1904, when a second subsidiary, Electrical Securities Corporation, was established with an eye on the New York market, a good number not only paid high interest or good dividends but commanded a premium. Thus the General Company was profiting both from expanded orders and from substantial returns on its customer investments.[13]

With the creation in 1905 of Electric Bond and Share (Ebasco)— a satellite originally intended to relieve the securities companies of their "cats and dogs," but whose concern to finance and interconnect the smaller utilities increasingly involved it in their engineering and management problems—GE's customer relations had taken on a new dimension. In a financial sense, certainly, Coffin's ingenuity had earned him full honors in the panic of 1907, which sent the Westinghouse Company into temporary receivership. It had other implications, however, which were not so generally acclaimed; mutterings about a power trust were beginning to accompany the louder outcries against the money trust. If these mutterings encouraged the antitrust suit of 1911, they also survived it. So did GE's relationship with Bond and Share.

From the outset, Coffin had accepted the stipulation of S. Z. Mitchell, whom he had summoned from Oregon to head Bond and Share, that GE name only one-third of the new company's directors and Mitchell the rest, with the further understanding that the parent company's representatives agree to support Mitchell's policies so long as he stayed in office. Also accepted was the stipulation that while the parent company was free to solicit business from Ebasco's "clients," it could expect to make a sale only if it offered "a proposition as good [as] or better than that of any other manufacturers." Under Mitchell's leadership, moreover, Bond and Share's financing of its domestic clients always stopped short of retaining a majority of their voting stock; legally, control remained vested in the client.[14]

Whether for these or for other reasons, continuance of the GE–Bond and Share relationship was never enjoined. In bringing suit against GE and its thirty-four codefendants on March 3, 1911, the attorney general might have denounced "what is alleged to be one of the most powerful and complete monopolies in the country," but the formal charge was a "violation of the Sherman . . . law in the marketing of incandescent lamps," plus a long list of related practices held to be in restraint of trade. Neither here nor in the consent decree of October 12, with its stipulation of major changes in GE's corporate and con-

Young's graduation picture, 1894

Young after graduating from Boston University
Law School

Josephine Edmonds in her Radcliffe graduation
picture

Smith Young at Owen's house on Avon Hill Street in Cambridge

Smith Young at the village house in Van Hornesville with his grandsons
Charles and John

Owen, young Jo and his mother, Lexington, September 1908

The Young house in Lexington, 1910

Little Point in the twenties: a fisherman and his daughter

Josephine Edmonds Young, about 1920

tractual arrangements, had Bond and Share been cited, even though the "cats and dogs" had mostly become valuable assets.[15]

Unofficial critics were not disarmed, however, and interlocking directorates and holding companies remained among their favorite targets, both in the congressional investigation of the "Money Trust" and in the presidential campaign of 1912. In the five-page opinion Young submitted to Coffin on February 5, 1913, he duly recognized this fact. Confessing to a "very sensitive feeling regarding interlocking boards and holding companies generally," he addressed himself first to what he held to be the fundamental question: namely, the "propriety of stock ownership of the Securities Companies by the General Company."

As bearing on this question, he found the Supreme Court's decision in the United Shoe Machinery case both illuminating and reassuring. From its language he inferred that

so long as a Company keeps within the limits of its charter it may manufacture goods and it may sell them; in selling them it may extend its agencies to reach the ultimate consumer; it may aid in creating markets, and if it is advisable, in order to create a market, to assist in financing or to maintain Securities Companies to assist in financing [its customers], there seems to be no objection to this course simply because of the size of the institution resulting. . . . The important thing is to keep the development within the powers of the parent concern and in a straight line. If there be involved any attempt to connect up parallel and competing lines then it may be that under the Union Pacific case, it is objectionable, even though it may not result in monopoly.

Clear as he was that "the General Company has the power, under its charter, to do directly what the Securities Companies are doing," he held that "the powers . . . exercised through the subsidiary companies have sufficiently direct and close relationship to the principal purpose of the General Company to make the holding of the stock of the Securities Companies not only within the letter but also within the spirit of the law." It followed, then, that GE's substantial investment in these subsidiaries made representation on their boards both natural and proper. It would be quite otherwise were the situation such that interlocking boards might serve as "substitutes, through implied understanding between men having common interests and power to control, for the formal agreements, which, if made, would be objectionable to the law or public policy."[16]

So that was that. On February 27, Young wrote the secretary of Bond and Share one of his more businesslike notes:

Dear Sir:

Owing to my absence from the city, your notification of my election as director of the Electric Bond and Share Company has not been acknowledged.

I accept the office.

Yours truly . . .

iv

It was the call to Dallas which accounted for Young's absence. An unwelcome interruption this trip might well have been, but for his saving stipulation that, this time, his wife must go with him.

And so it was arranged. Grandmother and Uncle John Brandow stayed in Lexington with the children; little Jo was annoyed because both parents were away over her sixth birthday, but so many wonderful things had been planned by Mother before she went that they were forgiven.

It was new country for Jo senior and a rare opportunity to see her "man of affairs" in action on one of his old stamping grounds. Dallas had become over the years one of the great electric-railway cities of the nation; it now boasted 136 trains daily, over 138 miles of track, with 123 more miles building. In 1909 it was said there was "less complaint against the street car service than perhaps in any other city in the country."[17] By 1911 the city was growing so fast that there were complaints: more tracks and trains were needed, as well as new terminals. But more extensive lines and new equipment would require longer-term franchises from the city; only a franchise of at least thirty years was attractive to the investors who must provide the money for the new developments. And the provision of new franchises was no simple matter in Dallas at that time; under a new Texas law, cities were empowered to amend their own charters, if the popular vote concurred—and an amendment was required for a new franchise.

It was Young's job, representing as he was both the companies owned by General Electric and those owned by Stone and Webster, to see that any amendment provided them with what they needed for expansion. But he must also work with the city government and representatives of the public, with the politicians and lawyers and the press. Fortunately his wide acquaintance in Dallas, and the reputation he had built there, enabled him to do this, and an amendment that apparently satisfied all parties was finally hammered out. But there was one serious barrier to its adoption; the process of setting up a popular "election" to amend the city charter was so new that no machinery had been developed for the voting. Hence the proposed amendment to approve the new franchises, needed by the public and the companies alike, was tossed into the general city election for mayor and other officials. This complicated the picture with political and personal rivalries, and under this pressure the amendment was defeated when it came up in the spring.

But at least Owen could feel that he had created a sound basis for future consideration, and he and Jo had a good time with his Texas friends, and Texas hospitality. They made a trip to Galveston, on the interurban built by Stone and Webster, fifty miles long from Houston to Galveston, two dollars for the round trip. This too Young had worked on and he now enjoyed showing off to his wife. An impressive new station had been built; an early picture shows a handsome new "coach" on the track in front of the flag-bedecked building, but sticking out its brass nose from behind the huge electric car, a little Model T awaits its day.[18]

It was Thursday afternoon, February 27, when Owen and Jo got back to New York, to spend the night in his rooms at the Murray Hill. As an interlude the fortnight had been strenuous, and Young still had a long report to write for Tyler.[19] He was preoccupied too with major policy questions on which he felt impelled to write his new chief at some length—after reciting to his wife, as usual, what he intended to say. Nevertheless, such shared experiences were rare enough to be precious and, thanks to the Pullman Company, the trip by rail from Dallas to St. Louis to New York had afforded the restorative of long if cinder-flecked hours of privacy. Something of this warmth remained to ease the Sunday evening parting when, having seen Jo safely home and enjoyed a rare weekend with the children, Owen left Lexington in time to catch the midnight for New York.

v

Young's appearance at 30 Church Street on the morning of Monday, March 3, marked the beginning of his third month with General Electric. His healthy respect for his new client is evident in his response to Caleb Fisher's plea on behalf of a job-seeking protégé; before he could help he would have to learn "the machinery of this organization somewhat."[20] But he had made his presence felt: in Schenectady as well as Lynn, on the Washington scene as well as in Boston, and of course in New York. The directors knew that he was on the job, thanks to his "opinion" of February 5, and so did Bond and Share. The Texas chore was behind him, and he had completed and dispatched his comprehensive report to Tyler on Friday the twenty-eighth before leaving with Jo for Lexington. (He had also sent Tyler his expense account, for *half* of its $583 total, taking care of his wife's half himself.)

Now his second and third policy reports for Coffin were beginning to take shape. Tuesday, March 4, found him far too busy to consider going to Washington for the inauguration of Woodrow Wilson—the first Democrat to be elected President since Young's undergraduate days and his youthful efforts on behalf of Grover Cleveland. On Wednesday, the fifth, one of these reports was ready—a four-page *magnum opus* in which he came to grips with GE's central problem as he saw it. The other—twice as long if only half as arresting— followed two days later. "Dear Mr. Coffin," the first of them began:

By way of educating myself I have been giving some attention to the more recent federal monopoly cases, and as a result of such preliminary investigation I desire to make a tentative suggestion. Before stating the suggestion I should like to state briefly the basis for it.

There are at least two ways of creating a monopoly in any business; one is through the combination of competitors, and the other is through the ruination of competitors. The first has been a favorite ground of complaint under the Sherman Law; the second is being developed as a ground of complaint. The first involves a conspiracy, that is, the action of more than one to restrain trade; the second may involve the action of only a single individual or company.

The cases indicate that in the past both methods have been carried on very openly and frankly. The combinations were often the result of expressed agreements under which the profits of monopoly were frankly capitalized. The ruinous competition was established as an open and avowed policy, and, to judge from some cases, permeated the entire organization of the victorious concern. The method of combination and ruinous competition had been in existence from time immemorial between small competitors, and naturally men of business did not realize that a combination of large competitors, creating or tending to create monopoly, was, as a matter of law, different in kind. They naturally thought that it was only different in degree; in fact, the lawyers themselves had but little appreciation of the evolution of the modern law regarding restraint of trade. The very frankness of the older methods, as shown by the cases, is the best evidence of the good and honorable intentions, in fact, of the so-called conspirators.

So much for historical analysis—a kind of nonpunitive version of Wilson's lag of the law. But what about the present—and the future?

As knowledge of the limitations of the law increased, the managers of business fell into two classes; one, those honestly desiring to obey the law, and two, those anxiously trying to evade it. The latter class, instead of creating monopoly through combination by expressed agreement, or promoting ruinous competition openly and frankly, endeavored to obtain the same results by doing the same things indirectly. The consequence has been that the government, in order to meet such conditions, has adopted the procedure of stating a large number of facts more or less related, and asking a jury or a court to infer from the facts stated that there must have been, precedent to such accomplishment, a formulated plan intentionally devised by the governing officers of the concern to create such results, either by combination or ruinous competition, as the case may be.

The danger is, especially in a large company, that a number of isolated transactions, each perhaps legal in itself, may be grouped together as the basis of an inference that the company complained of, and its managers and officers, had intended to restrain competition in violation of the law. It is these inferences from isolated cases, often comparatively few in number, which are dangerous to the large concern whose officers and directors desire to obey the law, but who, being concerned with questions of general policy, cannot personally oversee even many important transactions of the concern, to say nothing of the acts of a remote but over-enthusiastic salesman who, although conscientiously striving to promote the interest of his company, may be creating the very situations out of which grow future complaints.

All well and good, but what, specifically, was Young's suggestion?

In order to avoid any unjust or unfounded inferences of conspiracy or secret understandings, I recommend that it be adopted as the policy of the company that no agreement or understanding, either express or implied, with any competitor, large or small, be made until the same shall have the written approval of the Law Department. I recommend that this written approval be filed and retained as a part of the records of the company.

In order to avoid any unjust or unfounded inferences of unfair competition, I suggest that the Legal Department send to the Board of Directors a statement indicating the line, so far as it is now possible to do so, between fair competition on the one side, and unfair competition on the other. I recommend that then the Board of Directors transmit to the selling departments of the company such instructions as may be consistent only with fair competition, in order that the selling departments may not be uninformed as to the proper limitations of their activities. I think it should be the duty of the Legal Department to transmit, from time to time to the Board, such additional information as may be derived from new statutes or new cases on the subject.

Finally:

I believe it to be of the utmost importance to the company and to its officers and agents, not only that the greatest effort be made to confine all activities of the company strictly within the law, but also that contemporaneous records be made showing that, so far as possible, every precaution has been taken to prevent the activities of the company, by accident, extending beyond the law.[21]

Two days later, in his letter of March 7, Young was analyzing for Coffin the propriety as well as the legality of the General Company's holdings in various supply and jobbing concerns. Satisfied of their legality from his recent study of the applicable state and federal laws, as well as the relevant stipulations of the consent decree, he urged a policy of full public disclosure as the best answer to any intimation that the company had something to conceal. Options which would assure control of such concerns should either be exercised or canceled. Drawing by way of example upon his firsthand knowledge of the Hobson Electric Company (of Texas)—recently renamed the South-West General Electric—he further declared that open acknowledgment of GE's interest most certainly entailed the removal of its "nominees" from the shareholders' lists. Henceforth its holdings were to be recorded—as it was to do business—only in its own name.[22]

There was also an echo and an affirmative application of a point made in his letter of March 5. "I realize well," he wrote, "that it is unsafe to test the legality of a course of action by deciding merely on the legality of its associated unit parts. It is entirely possible . . . to come to an illegal place through entirely lawful individual steps. It is impossible, however, to do this if lawful steps are taken not individually but collectively with a lawful purpose and intent." In the light of this dictum he was prepared to approve GE's contractual arrangements with its jobbers as legal steps all taken with the "lawful purpose and intent" of promoting distribution of its products. Indeed, he went on to recommend the acquisition of any odd shares found to be outstanding in jobbing houses where GE had a controlling interest.

The presumption is that Coffin's acknowledgment of these three reports was mostly face-to-face; on that of March 5, however, he did request that Young "present a draft of record to be inserted in the minutes of the Executive Committee," which Young transmitted on the following day.[23]

Two of the reports at least were shown to E. W. Rice, the senior vice-president, who wrote Young from Schenectady on March 22 in most commendatory terms. "I wish to confirm," his letter began, "the statements already made to you verbally expressing my delight and satisfaction with the straight-forward, clean-cut and altogether honest position which you advise in these matters." Going on to say that in manufacturing and engineering, which he knew, this kind of dealing had always been the rule but that "general conditions throughout the business world have not been in entire accord" and could have become a source of infection, Rice reiterated his satisfaction with Young's guidance as reaching every department. "I am particularly delighted," he concluded, "because I firmly believe that a large corporation should not only take the lead in obeying the law but in setting a good example of honest dealings with all men."

Impending changes in top management were to lend this letter added force. Coffin undoubtedly knew, if Young did not, that at the board's June meeting Rice was slated to succeed him as president— though Coffin as chairman would remain GE's chief executice officer.

In the meantime, sending Rice's letter along to his wife with a handwritten note, Young dubbed it characteristic. So was his acknowledgment. "Your cordial letter of the 22nd," he wrote on March 25, "is welcome beyond all measure. I feel sure that I can rely on you for as full, direct and frank criticism when you disapprove. While it will not be quite so pleasant to receive . . . it will be even more helpful . . ."[24]

Chapter 8

General Electric
and "Fair Competition"

N EW as he was to the human and procedural problems of a large
corporation, Young had a shrewd notion of all that he was
letting himself in for. To recommend a comprehensive code of
fair competition was one thing; to devise and apply such a code was
quite another. As a newcomer, moreover, he must tread warily, lest
he be accused of being merely meddlesome, or, worse still, one of
the "holier than thou" breed.

Well, he would tread warily, but he would get on with the job. He
would seek help and thus involve his colleagues. He would keep his
voice low—someone once remarked that he never raised it, even in a
letter—but he would also keep a sharp eye out for what concerned
him. And that might take him anywhere; after all, the demonstration
he was seeking from GE involved its entire nexus of relationships—
with customers and competitors, agents, jobbers and suppliers, employees and, more broadly, government and public—and many of
these relationships were contractual.

Thanks to Coffin, there was little need to worry about customer
relations. Thanks to Rice and his tested associates, this was also true
of engineering and manufacturing. Much the same, indeed, could be
said of employee relations—in part because skilled workers were still
in the ascendancy, in part because GE, by contemporary standards,
was generally considered a fair employer. Young found this all the
more reassuring because, as his new colleagues were aware, he had
had little or no experience in labor relations. It was a field he would
have to learn, no doubt, if GE's labor policies were to keep pace with
changing standards and the problems incident to growth. But for the
moment that could wait.

So long as GE was scrupulous in observing the terms of the consent
decree, relations with President Wilson's government looked promising enough. After all, the President had declared that "there is ab-

solutely nothing for the honest and enlightened business men of the country to fear" at his hands, and Young was disposed to take him at his word.[1] Young liked to know the people he was dealing with, however, and having some acquaintance with William McAdoo—the lawyer and entrepreneur who had built the Hudson Tubes and was now named secretary of the treasury—he took occasion to improve it. Writing ostensibly to inquire about McAdoo's now deserted house in Ardsley-on-Hudson as a possible haven—if it wasn't too large—for his own "temporarily abandoned family," he offered the new secretary heartiest congratulations, not only on his high office but also on the way his appointment had been received. He also chided him for leaving 30 Church Street "so promptly after my arrival," promising not to forget "that possession has been turned over to me."[2]

As for the public, Young deeply shared Coffin's concern about the damage which the antitrust suit might have done to GE's reputation— or what Madison Avenue would one day call its "corporate image." Rumblings about a power trust, disturbing in themselves, invited exaggerations and distortions which, unless tracked down and dealt with, could and would compound the damage. He was also coming to feel that the public was entitled to know far more than it did about the industrial leaders who, like Coffin, held positions of great power and responsibility. Big corporations were far too impersonal and certainly GE, with a man like Coffin at the helm, could only profit from wider public awareness of his character and stature. Coffin, however, remained totally unreceptive to any such suggestion, as an intolerable invasion of privacy. This, too, it seemed, would have to wait; and indeed it was not until some years later, when Young succeeded in turning the spotlight on the "little wizard," Charles P. Steinmetz, that this notion of "public relations" was put to the test.[3]

In the meantime, Coffin was pressing him to follow through on his recommended code of fair competition. At the same time he was expected to uncover and correct any failure fully to meet the stipulations of the consent decree, plus any existing practices which smacked of unfair competition. This would involve the prodigious task of reviewing and, where necessary, renegotiating and revising the hundreds of contracts and licensing agreements which GE had, or had under consideration, with its competitors, suppliers, jobbers and agents.[4]

All three of these tasks were so closely interrelated as frequently to overlap. Under the terms of the consent decree, GE might presume—as it had done—to fix the retail price of its lamps *only* as title passed directly from the company to the consumer. Pending judicial review of this assumption, both practices and contracts must make it plain beyond peradventure that all dealers and jobbers involved in marketing GE lamps were indeed doing business as agents of the company and not on their own account.

Thus even before submitting his first, or February, report to Coffin, Young had inquired of Allan Jackson, head of the Law Department in Schenectady, whether all such contracts could be said to meet that test.[5] Somewhat later he was urging F. S. Terry, who with B. G. Tremaine had developed what was now GE's National Lamp Division, to make certain that all lamps sold under the new agency contracts clearly bore GE's name as maker and seller. This too had been stipulated in the decree and GE's Edison Lamp Department had already been similarly cautioned, lest practice here should lag behind the law.[6] And any such lag must speedily be corrected because, despite the attorney general's objections to its previous marketing arrangements, GE could justifiably boast that the price of its lamps—one of its few consumer products and certainly the most profitable—had consistently been reduced as their quality improved.[7] It was jealous, therefore, to retain control of both lamp producers, as well as to regularize its "agency" contracts, not least with Western Electric.[8]

Young was testing out the Law Department in more ways than one. Through Jackson's good offices, he sought and later acknowledged the aid of young Darius Peck, one of Jackson's more promising associates, in preparing for his letter of March 7, a reexamination of the laws regarding supply houses. He explained to Jackson that this exercise implied no doubts regarding earlier examinations but simply fulfilled a personal commitment; "I shall not make any recommendations," he said, "until I have come to a mature conclusion . . . and I shall . . . seriously doubt my own view if you disagree with it."[9]

On March 8 he sent Jackson a copy of his opus of March 5, together with a copy of "resolutions of the Executive Committee in regard thereto." Recognizing the legal problems these entailed, Young inquired whether Jackson had "a digest of the recent cases, whether federal or state, relating to unfair methods of competition. If not, have you someone in your office who could abstract these cases carefully?" Should his limited force be tied up in other work, Jackson was to say so and Young would look elsewhere. Two weeks later, on learning that Jackson himself was laid up, Young wrote him about his health like a Dutch uncle, offering to come to Schenectady and "spend as much time as is necessary" to help work things out.[10]

Young had already relieved Jackson of one chronic headache. The

Ferguson Electric Company was making extravagant claims against GE's lamp division for alleged breach of contract; and its irascible counsel, Frank Y. Gladney, had made himself so objectionable to Jackson and others that Young had been warned never to let himself become involved. When Gladney next wrote Jackson, Young ignored the warning. Sending Jackson the draft of his proposed reply inviting Gladney to call, he asked that Jackson "please exhibit your confidence in me by criticizing it freely and frankly." Next day the letter was sent unchanged.[11]

When Gladney came storming in to see the general counsel, he was ushered into Young's office with disarming courtesy. Momentarily disconcerted by Young's long and thoughtful survey of his person, he seems to have been delighted as well as astonished at what followed. "They told me," said his now smiling host, "that you had horns and a tail but I can't seem to find them. So let's sit down and see what kind of problem you have that the two of us can't solve." Gladney sat down, and if the problem in all its ramifications was not to be resolved for several months, during which Young sought help from others and showed himself to be no pushover, the encounter did ultimately prove to have been the turning point. Gladney even became of counsel to GE.[12]

ii

Others too were finding Young considerate but no pushover. In February, Anson Burchard had proposed the organization of a holding company to take over electric-bulb machine patents and license the various manufacturers thereunder. In his comment of March 3, Young assumed "that the license from your holding company would not attempt to fix either manufacturers' prices or allotments," thus leaving the competitive situation as between the several bulb manufacturers unchanged. But GE, as he pointed out, was also a consumer of bulbs, and any differential in its net purchasing price accruing from the plan would seem on its face to violate clause three (which was quoted verbatim) of the federal decree.

A differential in the cost of bulbs in favor of the General Company resulting from the organization of a patent holding company participated in by all the bulb manufacturers in the United States certainly sounds like an ominous charge. . . . In making this statement I am really attempting to put the opposing view as strongly as possible . . . without intending at this time to express an opinion. It is submitted only for your criticism, and as a basis for further discussion. . . .[13]

Was it from the Law School, from Tyler or his clients that Young had learned the virtues of this approach? Here, for example, he was not presuming to tell the experienced Burchard what to do; he simply confronted him with certain of the hazards implicit in his proposal and put the next move up to him. From that next move, moreover, one could learn much about the man one was dealing with.

Throughout the spring Young continued to sow but was also beginning to reap. On May 14 he wrote Barton Corneau, Tyler's new partner, asking his help in completing a file "of all the bills of complaint and indictments brought by the federal government under the Sherman Law." A week earlier, in asking counsel in Dallas about the implications for GE of the Texas attorney general's recent move against a Standard Oil subsidiary, Young reminded him that at least a clear majority of South-West General Electric shares were to be transferred promptly into the General Company's name—a move which was "extremely desirable . . . for reasons other than the local situation in Texas." In addition, his earlier inquiries were bearing fruit. On April 9 he had written to thank Gerald Dahl, counsel for Bond and Share, for giving him all that he had asked for and more about the securities companies, their directors and ramifying influences, adding that "it is a great . . . comfort to me that with your superior knowledge of these companies, you have your eyes open to see that nothing takes place that can by any possibility subject the General Company to criticism. . . ."[14]

With regard to the Sherman law he was at special pains to keep his information at once comprehensive and up-to-date. At the end of May he asked a member of the solicitor general's staff in Washington whether "copies of complaints and petitions" under that act could not be sent along to him, "after they were filed, printed and ready for distribution to the public."[15] He had already asked his old St. Lawrence friend Clifford Spurr for help in defining what was actually prohibited by the Sherman act, and he found Spurr's responsive "statement and the theory on which it is based . . . interesting" enough to send along to Charles Neave, junior partner in the firm—Fish, Richardson and Neave—that had long been GE's chief legal advisers.[16] This was the most satisfying way Young knew of repaying a friend and he practiced it whenever he could.

As summer approached, efforts to complete the code were intensified. Young was concerned about state laws, with their widely differing definitions of monopoly and unfair competition, and here again sought Jackson's help. He also set up a special office in room 1923, at 30 Church Street, in which a young lawyer, W. J. Jenks, was installed expressly to collect and analyze reports from Wisconsin and other "western" states.[17] Having enjoyed a three-day breather with Jo at the St. Lawrence commencement and got his family settled in for a long summer visit with his mother at Van Hornesville, Young went back to the office and really took his coat off. With Jackson and especially with D. R. Bullen, manager of the Commercial Department, he began the extraordinary series of dialogues that enabled him not only to complete his thirteen-page report on "fair competition" for submission to Coffin on August 1, but also to test it thoroughly in advance and item by item.[18]

Happily for the student of *lex mercatoria*, as developed in the United States just before World War I, the twenty-two pages which Young devoted to listing and answering Bullen's two dozen questions are preserved in his old-fashioned letter-press copybooks. To such a student, his letter to Bullen may be even more rewarding than the letter to Coffin which it helped to refine and inform. Bullen's interest in such issues as the right to purchase a competitor's business was downright and specific: "Does [such and such a clause] prohibit purchasing, for example, the Hot Point Flat-Iron Company, whose business" together with GE's "amounts to approximately 50% of the total business on heating devices?" Inasmuch as GE was one day to purchase control of Hot Point, Young's cautious answer is interesting too, but the lay reader may be willing to settle for his concluding commentary, or a reasonable facsimile thereof. For all his efforts to spell out the rules, Young was saying that their application is necessarily limited and so the rules themselves are less important than the discussion and attention they provoke, for it is these that give form and substance at any given time to the "underlying policy and spirit of fair play [that] enable us to deal . . . with situations which cannot . . . be covered by any specific rule."[19]

As for the letter to Coffin, it essayed to put down in black and white *first*, the activities involving or tending toward monopoly which the law expressly forbade, and *second*, the kinds of actions involving unfair competition, which were constructively proscribed. Because, in the second category, the defendant's *intent* was held to be determining, any listing of actions to be avoided save the obviously unfair could hardly be definitive. For example, an individual, natural or corporate, could act in his own interest with purely incidental hurt to his competitor; he could not take action primarily to harm his competitor which had only incidental benefit to himself.

Inasmuch as a nice distinction such as this was a better guide to conscience than to conduct, Young's letter did specify classes of action *tending* toward monopoly which the courts had generally construed to be unfair. Young was suspicious too of apparent loopholes: any act or procedure of GE's involving a competitor must be beyond reproach and above suspicion too. Large companies, especially, could not afford to give themselves the benefit of the doubt, nor could they indulge in certain practices common to their smaller competitors whose actions posed no threat whatever of monopoly. In marketing its wares—heavy equipment as well as lamps—GE must always take pains to distinguish between its agents, who do not take title, and others—including jobbers—who usually do. As a measure of safety, *all* contracts thereafter drawn should have the express approval of the Law Department before being executed. As for "unspoken understandings," they could be "just as dangerous as a written contract if not more so," because they are so easily misrepresented.[20]

Certainly GE's new legal broom was sweeping clean, even though the dust it turned up was partly cobwebs. Young took a stern view particularly of the company's obligations under the consent decree, many of whose provisions he spelled out as matters calling for further and continuing checks. Nevertheless, he had accepted the validity of GE's action—on which the attorney general had quite correctly declined to pass judgment—in converting its lamp dealers and jobbers into agents, the device by virtue of which the company continued to set the retail prices of its lamps. And either because he himself was essentially sanguine or because he sought to give Coffin all possible reassurance, his letter of August 1 ended with these words: "I am happy to say that investigation of these cases and of the complaints made by the Department of Justice leads me to believe that no business, however large, when fairly and honestly conducted with due regard to the spirit of the law herein set forth, is in serious danger of prosecution, much less conviction."

Before the year was out, this comfortable view was facing a formidable challenge in the court of public opinion. The charges were only too familiar, dealing as they did with GE's alleged control—principally through Bond and Share—of the "lion's share" of the nation's water-power and street railways; it was their authorship and sponsorship which made them of special concern. To be sure, the series of articles which the redoubtable Louis Brandeis had written during the late fall for *Harper's Weekly* had been directed against the so-called Money Trust, of which the Power Trust that he envisaged was no more than a "ramifying influence."[21] In his brief piece on power, Brandeis had drawn heavily on the recent report by the commissioner of corporations, Joseph E. Davies; thus Young's first move was to procure a copy of this in order to test its credibility against the already familiar report of Davies's predecessor, Herbert Knox Smith.[22] Certainly Brandeis could hardly be faulted unless his source was proved vulnerable.

On this Young seems to have suspended judgment, but he had no hesitation in advising Rice and Coffin that the concurrent piece in *World's Week*, by one Herbert Bruce Fuller, was grossly inaccurate. Having lately come to know Arthur Page, who had replaced his father as editor on the latter's appointment to the Court of St. James's, Young arranged to meet him soon after New Year's Day, sending him a copy, "not for publication," of his August letter to Coffin. He also armed himself by procuring from Dahl and S. Z. Mitchell a currently accurate statement on the dimensions of Bond and Share control.[23] Of what transpired when they met we find no record, but as the first of many, their meeting undoubtedly helped to establish the mutual respect and confidence that was to mark a long and cordial relationship. And largely because of Young's conviction that, "given the facts," the press could normally be counted on, even at its most critical, to treat business fairly, this relationship proved to be the first of many such which Young would one day enjoy with editors, publishers and reporters.

iii

Owen Young had been too busy with the intricacies of the Sherman law and the consent decree to give primary attention to the legislative program through which President Wilson was spelling out and hoping to assure the New Freedom. Besides, the measures he was most concerned about, involving a federal trade commission and new anti-monopoly laws, were scheduled to come later.

For political and tactical reasons, a lower tariff was commanding first priority in the Congress, but it was hard pressed by Carter Glass's determined moves in the House toward banking and currency reform. By the close of the year both the Underwood tariff and the Federal Reserve Act had been placed on the statute books; so far as the latter was concerned, Young—a future chairman of the New York Federal Reserve—had been little more than a passive observer.[24] But his education may have been advanced somewhat by a letter of November 10 from his senatorial friend Henry F. Hollis of New Hampshire. Expressing, as one of the four Senate committee Democrats, his hopes of reporting shortly a "perfected bill," Hollis said in conclusion: "I find that President Wilson is thoroughly informed on banking and currency matters. Every time I see him I am impressed with his size."[25]

As for the tariff, Wilson was no expert, but he knew what his party stood for, and saw in the Payne-Aldrich type of tariff a protective shield for the trusts.[26] Having controlled the previous Congress, the Democrats had been at work in committee on tariff and banking bills alike well before Wilson took office, and Young's first trip to Washington was to have a look at the way the new tariff schedule was shaping. He had been brought up as a low-tariff Democrat, and a year or more after the enactment of the Underwood tariff, with the economy still depressed by "the war disturbances abroad and uncertainties at home," he found a novel way of defending it to a friend as, after all, a good thing for business. This was so, he said, because— like depression itself—the loss of tariff protection subjected a large corporation to the discipline of having to take the tough measures, too often neglected in fat times, which restored its competitive stance.[27]

It is improbable that this view would have been widely popular in GE, and Young did what was expected of him in reporting on prospective rates, especially for bulbs, incandescent lamps and such of their ingredients as carbon and tungsten. For GE, these were the principal items of concern, and Young had been quick to establish rapport with J. M. Woodward of Ohio, counsel to the National Lamp Division, who was very much at home in Washington. He also arranged for his Boston friend Arthur Weed (Fred's brother) to join Woodward for the time being. In an early letter to Woodward on bulbs, he wrote, "I am extremely anxious that we be conservative in the method of handling the whole matter."[28] In April he was advising Coffin that Ways and Means had adopted a 30 percent rate on bulbs and incandescent lamps; in September he reported that the Senate had rejected a La Follette amendment proposing a 20 percent rate. Once the Underwood tariff bill had been enacted, he recommended to Coffin a fee of eighty-five hundred dollars for Weed and one thousand dollars for John T. Beasley of Terre Haute, whose counsel he had also sought. "The above items, plus travelling expenses," he said in conclusion, "represent the total expenditure of the General Company incurred through me on account of tariff legislation."[29]

What was Young doing, then, with his spare time? For one thing he was in Albany to clear with the Public Service Commission a flotation of bonds by the Schenectady Illuminating Company, then a direct charge of the General Company. He was in Buffalo shortly thereafter for an emergency board meeting of the Buffalo General Electric, to protest a new valuation and rate schedule handed down by the commission, which he held to be based on an evaluation theory that no utility could live with. Then he was back in Albany for long discussions of the Buffalo problem with officials of the commission, including its chairman: the same Ledyard P. Hale who had once invited Young to join his law office in Canton and was now chairman of the St. Lawrence University Board of Trustees.[30]

That neither his reports to Coffin on these matters nor Young's other correspondence of the period contain any reference to the current passage by the New York legislature of the so-called Murtagh-Petrie bill, which, but for Governor Sulzer's veto, would have put the generation of electricity from waterpower in the hands of the state, suggests that the power companies must have been pretty confident of the veto and of its being upheld. It was some years before Young publicly declared that the important thing was to get these natural resources somehow developed, adding that so long as the energy they released was made available for distribution by the power companies, ownership might very well rest in the state—or preferably in a public nonprofit corporation.[31]

Of more immediate concern was some means of simplifying, or keeping abreast of, the diverse laws and regulations affecting the burgeoning public utilities. As power systems crossed state lines, which was rapidly becoming the rule rather than the exception, the multiplicity of jurisdictions to which these natural monopolies were subject was not merely an annoyance; it was a source of confusion to investors and management, and so, too often, of public suspicion. Finding this situation profitable to no one save the politician in search of an issue, Young first worked with the group that was drafting for the National Civic Federation a model utility bill for submission to the Congress. He joined the committee in January 1913; early in February he got his friend Clifford Spurr to work on it; by May the bill was ready, but nothing came of it.[32]

Failing such a law, the next best thing was to provide a guide for utilities and investors in the form of case reports on state laws and relevant decisions of the courts and public service commissions. Young had had a "hazy plan in mind" for such a central information source since he came to GE; working with several others of like mind, he called in Spurr to help. With the assistance of Coffin and Bernard Flexner of Chicago—whose clients then included Samuel Insull—and such other rising young lawyers as H. Alexander Smith, Young found sufficient financial support. By the end of 1914, guaranteed subscriptions were adequate, and material was being actively collected from the commissions. Four months later, the first volume of *Public Utilities*

Reports, Annotated, was duly issued, with Clifford Spurr as editor; its reception and subsequent history indicated that something approaching a vacuum had been filled.[33]

Far more demanding, both of energy and time, was Young's self-imposed obligation to review the entire spectrum of GE's contracts and licensing agreements. What one learned from the process was cumulative and it was not until 1914 that renegotiation really became the order of the day. Nevertheless, the more important contracts renegotiated in his first two years included those with Western Electric, Phoenix Glass, Otis Elevator, Pacific States Electric, South-West General Electric, Ferguson Electric, and *all* of GE's agents for the distribution and sale of lamps. Western Electric was still at that time a potent competitor in many lines and Burchard was encouraged to renegotiate with them most of the existing contracts, foreign and domestic. The main trouble spot here continued to be the lamp contract which, until the new agency system was set up, had given mutual satisfaction. In June of 1914 it was decided that any revision should await the return from Europe of the contract's principal author, Western Electric's Gerard Swope.[34] Fortunately for both companies, Swope succeeded in returning during the summer despite the outbreak of war.

A few months later, a new standard form of contract was ready; Young wrote Jackson that if the Law Department approved it, any who questioned it should put their objections in writing, with unresolved questions going to GE's so-called Advisory Committee and, with its recommendations, to the board. In the meantime, new developments meant new and still evolving contractual relationships—notably to cover electric lighting and self-starters for an auto industry that began to look as if it were here to stay.[35] From all this constructive ferment, not the least significant outcome was the strengthening of Young's comprehension of the range and reach of the company's business, with all that this suggested of new opportunities to be assessed and, where appropriate, pursued.

Certainly he showed no signs of relaxing the sharp lookout he was keeping for anything smacking of the illegal or unfair. A proposed new motor agency contract he dismissed as establishing no agency at all. Vice-President Jesse Lovejoy was advised that participation in an Electric Power Club was permissible only if discussions confined themselves in fact to standardization as a means of advancing the art and not of limiting competition. On the same day Jackson was warned against joining any conference of licenser and licensee, simply because freedom from suspicion was important. Young was particularly sensitive to any disparagement of competitors' apparatus; maintaining

samples of the same even for the "sole purpose" of training salesmen
was, he wrote Francis Pratt, a temptation to abuse. More disarmingly,
he wrote A. G. Davis of the Patent Department in June of 1914: "Can
you state to an ignoramus like me just why the new form of maximum
demand indicator . . . is not a device on which royalty should be paid
to the Chicago Electric Meter Company under our contract with it?"
Two months later, he made a handsome bow to a competitor, the
chairman of Allis-Chalmers, to whom he had passed along a colleague's allegation of a patent infringement. He found the chairman's
vigorous disclaimer so convincing as to warrant an expression of the
hope that he would always be able to answer complaints against G E
as effectively and well.[36]

By this time, it was becoming something of a habit in G E to clear
everything with Young. In the single week of June 22, 1914, he was
called upon to attend not only the regular fortnightly meeting of the
Advisory Committee, of which he was a member, but also (by invitation) meetings of the Manufacturing Committee, the Executive Committee and the board.[37] The Advisory Committee met that month at
"Association Island," in the St. Lawrence River, where G E maintained
a "camp" spacious enough for industry-wide as well as company-wide
meetings. A year earlier, when an industry-wide meeting was scheduled there for the week after Labor Day, Young had found himself
charged with procuring the speakers. His first choices at the time
were Louis Brandeis and the British chancellor, Lord Haldane; the
suggested topic, "Big Business and the Law." Here Young's reach
exceeded his grasp; some would say fortunately. Though his inquiries
had preceded by some months publication of Brandeis's strictures on
the power trust, Young must have been aware that even such Wilson
supporters as Henry Lee Higginson (a G E director) had looked askance
at his proposed appointment as attorney general. The fact remains—
and only the fact is known—that Young went ahead, writing Brandeis's partner to ask about his availability.[38] And to him the reply
was disappointing; only good could come, he believed, from this kind
of confrontation.

Toward the end of his first year with G E, Young moved to strength-
en his ties with the Law Department by arranging to spend one day
every other week with Jackson and his colleagues in Schenectady.
Perhaps this arrangement encouraged him to respond as he did on
December 24 to the complaints of M. F. Westover, the company's
courtly secretary, that he never stopped by when visiting the plant.
"Being now convinced," he wrote, "that I am unable to get in or out
of Schenectady without subjecting my trail to your mighty hunter's

eye, I will give up trying. . . . My New Year's resolution will be that hereafter I shall always come and see you. Subject to that affliction, I wish you a happy New Year."[39]

iv

The transition from law to industry, and from Boston to New York, was pretty well effected—and dramatically confirmed—within twelve months. Nineteen thirteen had been quite a year, both for the new administration in Washington and for Young's new undertaking. Hints of the depression—but not of the war—which was to ensue had begun by December to make themselves heard, but General Electric's Annual Report for 1913 made it hard to take them seriously. Orders received of $111,819,000, and sales billed of $106,477,000, set new company records; so did profits from sales, which, at $10,270,000, were up 25 percent from 1912.[40] If GE's sense of corporate responsibility was in fact to keep pace with its growth, 1913 was providing an uncommonly searching test.

Young too had faced such a test and seemed to thrive on it. Certain aspects of the law, especially those relating to real estate and trust management, he had usually found less than satisfying; later he was to suggest that while industry was constantly opening new and untraveled roads, the law, and too many lawyers, followed after as a kind of street-cleaning department—another sort of lag.[41] If he had complaints about his new job, he would need more time to identify them; for the moment, he was far too busy.

But absorbed as he was in his work, Young still relished good company. His suggestion of April 28 to Robert Gorham, the much admired senior partner of the Ropes & Gray firm of Boston, that he (Gorham) plan to miss the five o'clock one day soon in order to dine and spend the evening was echoed in similar letters to Gorham's junior partner, Thomas Nelson Perkins, and to old friends like Senator Hollis of New Hampshire, or Ralph Whelan of Minneapolis, and, of course, Charles Tyler. If, missing his wife and children, Young sought the company of the fair sex, the record is discreetly silent. Certainly his old St. Lawrence friends like Spurr and Edward Adler appeared from time to time, and what with his work and their company, there is no evidence that Young's evenings were lonely. Old friends and extracurricular chores were also serving to widen his acquaintance. Introduced by Eliot Wadsworth of Stone and Webster, Sam Fordyce of St. Louis and Wadsworth's class at Harvard was soon handling some matters for GE, and became Young's loyal and often entertaining admirer. Before the year ended he had even helped to settle the Gladney affair.[42]

Even when he was borrowing himself, Young helped old friends like Caleb Fisher. To Wallace Donham, vice-president of the Old Colony Trust, Young wrote brief notes about his personal account and his still-modest investments. When, in February 1913, he needed a four-month loan of two thousand dollars, he concluded his letter by saying: "I am troubling you with this because I do not desire to 'fuss' your smaller officials with such an extremely large and important matter."[43] Donham, better known later as the innovative dean of the Harvard Business School and, like Coffin, pure New England, was the first president of the Employers Mutual Company, set up under Massachusetts's newly enacted Workmen's Compensation law, a circumstance which Young found useful when he recommended that the Lynn plant adopt and test out this program despite the added initial expense.[44]

But the real proof of Young's earlier achievement, as well as a searching test of his new commitment, came in October 1913 when Nelson Perkins came over from Boston, following Robert Gorham's sudden death, to offer his friend Young a partnership in the distinguished Ropes Gray firm. According to Perkins, a thorough discussion ensued, with Young expressing his gratification but also his inner conviction that he had better stay put. Young did, Perkins added, tell Coffin that this was GE's opportunity to get rid of its new vice-president, but Coffin was more disturbed than amused. The incident was closed with an exchange of grateful and regretful letters. Perkins expressed the pious hope that Young would let him know if he were ever to change his mind. But Perkins knew when he was licked and chose prescient words when he wrote: "I take it that this decision practically anchors you in New York for the rest of your working life."[45]

Young moved promptly to strengthen the anchorage. On October 29, he wrote Chief Justice Arthur P. Rugg, of the Massachusetts Supreme Court, about "transferring" from the Massachusetts to the New York bar. On November 5, after acknowledging Judge Rugg's regretful but cordial response, he wrote Judge Irving R. Devendorf at Herkimer that he had strong sentimental reasons for wishing to be admitted to the New York bar "up in Herkimer County," adding that Judge Rugg had written to indicate that "he is ready to get me out of his own jurisdiction by vouching for my admission to another."[46]

In the meantime another anchor was being dropped—tentatively at first. In August 1913, after he and his wife had inspected various possibilities, Young had rented the Clyde Fitch house in Greenwich, Connecticut, from the playwright's mother. Its Italianate garden, pool, and somewhat pretentious gewgaws were fun for the children until the baby fell into the pool, but it was far from the kind of home the family wanted. It was spring of 1915 before this was found: the old Lincoln Steffens house in Riverside, Connecticut. The Steffens place was known as Little Point and, facing the Long Island Sound, with a generous stretch of beach and spacious lawn, the house had developed gradually from its eighteenth-century beginnings into a rambling and unpretentious structure which Mrs. Young pronounced just right. The rest of the family agreed: for the next twenty years it was a home that they lived in whenever they could and loved always.

Originally it was rented, partly furnished. When a little later Young proposed to buy it, he had the property appraised by three real-estate experts and offered Steffens the highest figure; as Young said later, he was taking no chances with "these muckrakers." Steffens had no such scruples. He was ready to sell, he said, and no doubt Young's offer was fair. But he wouldn't know what to do with all that money. What he needed was a good annuity; if Young would agree to pay him annually for life 7 percent of the purchase price, the place was his.[47] Young agreed and when, some fifteen years later, Steffens was still collecting and the house had, in effect, been more than paid for without any amortization of the mortgage, Young ruefully complained about the sharp deal this high-minded reformer had put over on him. Steffens was delighted and loved to tell his friends that these big-business barons weren't so tough if only one knew how to handle them.

When Steffens had agreed to "sell," much of his furniture and many of his books went with the house and are still in use by various members of the family. Two notable volumes were to be added to the shelves when, in March 1931, Steffens presented an autographed copy of his newly published autobiography, inscribed in the author's hand:

> To Owen D. Young
> with the compliments of his
> banker and fellow-prophet
>
> Lincoln Steffens[48]

Chapter 9

War in Europe,
Reform and Neutrality at Home

W HETHER, in the summer of 1914, their chief preoccupation was the gospel of progress, the progress of reform, or, more simply, a good vacation and the progress of the baseball season, the American people were wholly unprepared for the brutal war that so swiftly seized and ravaged the Old World. So was their government. Skeptics might deride Secretary of State Bryan's "cooling-off treaties," but there had been bipartisan support for the President's peace proposal of April 1913, recommending that "all questions in dispute, which diplomacy should fail to adjust, should be submitted to an international commission, pending whose investigation and report war should not be declared nor hostilities begun." As Wilson reported to the Congress on December 2, the secretary's efforts to implement this proposal had already won "the assent, in principle, of no less than 31 nations representing four-fifths of the population of the world." Germany, to be sure, had made difficulties, but by the following summer thirty treaties, including those with Britain and France, had been negotiated and twenty-eight ratified by the Senate.[1]

Setting an example, moreover, for his diplomacy of peace, Wilson had reversed his position on special privileges for American coastwise vessels using the Panama Canal, and persuaded the Congress to the unpopular course of restoring equality of treatment for all ships of whatever flag. This had been stipulated in the Hay-Pauncefote Treaty which, as Britain pointed out, and Elihu Root confirmed, had originally cleared the way for the digging.[2] Finally, the offer of the Argentine, Brazil and Chile, the so-called ABC powers, in April 1914 to mediate the vexatious involvement of the United States with Mexico had been accepted by Washington with an alacrity which did much to allay Latin-American suspicions of the Giant of the North.[3]

In such an atmosphere, the spectacle of the "civilized" nations of Europe at each other's throats was hard to credit. Wall Street's immediate response was panic, and the stock exchange was closed. Other emotions flared as German armies moved against the French by violating Belgian neutrality, and so brought Britain into action. The neutrality of the United States, however, was proof for some two years and eight months against all pressures from within and without. What it could not do was to shield the American people from the war's economic and emotional involvement, nor ultimately from the war itself.

At the outset, there was a disposition to proceed with the business at hand, however dismaying the news from abroad. Again the White House set the example: until his antitrust legislation was enacted President Wilson's program of reform was anything but complete, and he quickly made it clear that he was not to be diverted from his purpose. This could hardly have come as a surprise to those who knew him best or to others who recalled his response to the astonishing New Year's announcement of J. P. Morgan (junior) and George F. Baker (senior) that "an apparent change in public sentiment in regard to directorships" had persuaded them to withdraw from some thirty of the sixty-nine they held.[4] Advised by Colonel Edward House and Joseph Tumulty, his two most trusted men, to regard this "surrender" as an act of good faith—others mistrusted it as a device to blunt the edge of reform—the President did indeed tell Congress on January 20 that "the antagonism between business and government is over. . . . The government and businessmen are ready to meet each other half way in a common effort to square business methods with both public opinion and the law."

Nevertheless, in Ray Stannard Baker's words, Wilson

went on to recommend exactly the program of legislation which he had all along in mind:

1. Laws to prohibit interlocking directorates.
2. Laws giving more power to the I.C.C. to "superintend and regulate the financial affairs of the railroads."
3. Laws clarifying the anti-trust act. "Nothing hampers business like uncertainty."
4. A law creating a federal trade commission to advise, guide, and inform business.[5]

However ambiguous business may have found his response, Wilson seemed deaf to all complaints—even to the *New York Times*'s pointed warning in May of a "severe business depression" which might well have repercussions at the polls in November. Nor did the guns of August divert him from his purpose. True, the chaotic state of the market following the outbreak of war did produce agreement to post-

pone for the duration such statutory changes in the methods of railway financing as the Rayburn bill provided. Under presidential
prodding, however, Congress had authorized by September 10 establishment of the Federal Trade Commission, and on October 15 the
President signed the Clayton Anti-Trust Act. The fact that both measures differed significantly from the original Clayton bill as adopted
by the House on June 5 is ascribable chiefly to decisions antedating
the outbreak of war.[6]

On June 10, Owen Young had advised A. G. Davis of GE's Patent
Department not to be concerned about the House bill since the Senate
was sure to alter it beyond recognition.[7] Either this was a shrewd
guess, or its author was remarkably well informed. On that very day
Wilson had summoned Louis Brandeis and his friend George Rublee
to the White House and told them that their antitrust program, as
developed after intensive study and embodied in a bill introduced by
Congressman Stevens (Democrat, New Hampshire), was henceforth
his. In contrast to the original House bill, Stevens's proposal envisaged
a strong trade commission with plenary authority—subject only to
judicial review—to oversee business, to hear or file complaints of unfair competition and, after due hearings, to issue cease and desist
orders as warranted by the evidence. This was substantially what the
Congress authorized and the President approved in the Federal Trade
Commission Act of September 10, although many Democrats complained that it was nothing less than a surrender to the New Nationalism. But Brandeis now saw it as necessary to ensure fair competition.

However Brandeis and Rublee may have felt about other aspects of
the original Clayton bill, it soon became apparent that Wilson, overcome by the death of his wife on August 6, had lost all interest in it.
Left to its fate at the hands of a weary and beleaguered Senate, the
act finally emerged in mid-October with many of its teeth drawn or
blunted: exclusive selling contracts, or interlocking directorates, for
example, were prohibited only "where the effect may be to substantially lessen competition or tend to create a monopoly in any line of
commerce."[8] On its face, to be sure, this afforded small business a
measure of freedom which big business might claim only at its peril;
everything depended, however, on the way in which the powers
vested in the Federal Trade Commission might be exercised.

For his part, Young was more concerned to understand the implications of the Clayton act than to join in defending or opposing it.
His initial reactions were practical: declining in November a good
customer's invitation to speak because of the pressures of the times,

he wrote: "Those abroad result mostly from the disturbed conditions due to the war. Those here result largely from the uncertainties due to new legislation."[9]

Meanwhile, Young's efforts to see that GE's trade practices were unexceptional by Sherman-act standards had not ceased nor was he ready to desist. To Frederick P. Fish of Boston, GE's senior counsel, Young had written on August 17, 1914, enclosing "copy of my letter to Mr. Coffin of August 3rd which sets forth the prohibited trade practices covered by a decree in the case of United States against American Thread Company and others." He had also enclosed "copy of letter from Mr. Jackson of August 14th to me, in which he calls attention to certain trade practices of the General Company which would require careful consideration if the practices prohibited in the thread business were applicable to our own." In conclusion he suggested that "the directors should have an expression of your views on Mr. Jackson's letter. I will be very glad to discuss the matter with you if you so desire."[10]

Now he lost no time in seeking advice on the specifics of the new law as they might apply to GE's contracts and business procedures. On October 30, he requested Gilbert Montague, a young attorney who admitted to some expertise on the antitrust laws, to analyze for him both the trade commission and the Clayton acts. What, Young asked, does "substantially lessen competition" really mean? And "is it now lawful to make a contract with a distributor conditioned on his not handling the goods of a competitor?"—a device, he added, which GE had seldom but its competitors had frequently employed.[11]

Some three weeks later, Young was again writing Fish, this time to propound two questions for discussion with him as well as Charles Neave: (1) Is a contract to supply a customer for all his requirements (single or multiple lines) for one year with a quantity discount and rebate a violation of the third section of the Clayton act? (2) Can we, under Section 2, or 2 and 3 together, "discriminate between jobbers and other distributors except on the basis of quantity?"[12]

Equally suggestive of Young's approach to such new problems and to his new GE relationships is his letter dated Boston, November 25, 1914, to A. K. Baylor of the New York office:

I have just had an opportunity of reading your letter of November 11th to me on the application of the Clayton Act to our various forms of future delivery contracts, and also your letter to Mr. Rice of November 4th on holding company contracts.

These letters are very illuminating and make me feel for the first time that if I bask in their sunlight long enough I may absorb some understanding of the actual and intended operation of this method of doing business.

Without expressing any official view, I think we may find it desirable to eliminate exclusive obligations from our contracts, and also to set the minimum under non-exclusive contracts at such point, as compared with the purchaser's total requirements, that it could not in fact be found to be exclusive, even though in terms non-exclusive.

Is it not the custom of the government of the United States or municipalities to contract for a year's supply? I do not believe that anyone has ever thought the effect of such contracts might be to substantially lessen competition. . . .

Whatever problems Young was having with the new antitrust act, about the trade commission he was sanguine. In May of 1914 he had essayed two speeches, the first at a General Electric dinner for its leading customers in New York, and the second at the Hot Springs meeting of the Manufacturers Club. In both, his theme betrayed his earlier experience as lecturer in common-law pleadings: legal restrictions on the use of private property which had developed since the middle of the nineteenth century were not so much a new phenomenon as a reversion to restraints traditional to the common law and their adaptation to the modern corporation. Business—and certainly the public utilities—should recognize that relief from unfair laws or excessive statutory restraints had best be sought from the legislatures rather than the courts.[13]

For these speeches his friends Clifford Spurr and more particularly Edward Adler had dug up any number of early cases in which private property was held to be affected by a public interest limiting the owner's right of use. Able in the allotted time to cite only a few of these cases (his allusion to Noah as the holder of a God-given monopoly of which the Almighty had speedily repented was without judicial sanction), Young urged Adler to develop his thesis on the public aspects of business and submit it to the *Harvard Law Review*.[14]

When Adler did so and his essay on "Business Jurisprudence" was accepted for publication, Young set about, as friend and mentor, to give it wide if selective circulation. As head of the Bureau of Corporations, Joseph E. Davies of Wisconsin was a likely candidate to head the trade commission; he had recently made the report to the President on the ramifications of GE's power interests which Brandeis quoted at length in his *Harper's Weekly* pieces and again in *Other People's Money*. Nevertheless, it was to Davies, a recent acquaintance, that Young sent a proof copy of the Adler piece with this suggestive comment: "I think his point that all business is public is a new one. . . . It shows, it seems to me, how deep and stable the foundations are for such legislation as that creating the Federal Trade Commission."[15]

In December Young was sending copies of the *Law Review* to Dwight Morrow at Morgan's, to Walter Hines Page at the Court of St. James's, and to Walter Lippmann, who was helping Herbert Croly to launch the *New Republic*. He was particularly delighted when *World's Week* gave Adler editorial praise in its February 1915 issue. In writing its editor, Arthur Page, to that effect, he also expressed full agreement with the latter's dictum that as a kind of "common sense court without too much red tape or delay" the Federal Trade Commission could be useful, "if ably manned and directed."[16] He refrained from offering suggestions regarding appointments, but in succeeding months he kept note of its proposed and actual personnel. Early in 1915 he wrote one H. C. Clark (who had asked for a copy of his speech at the General Electric dinner) that he hoped "that when the Trade Commission is organized and the people who are interested in the subject get into an investigative, as distinguished from a combative, frame of mind, I may be able to render some service."[17]

By June he was writing his old friend and colleague in Dallas, the lawyer Edwin B. Parker of Houston, a full assessment of the commission and its members, in answer to a query from Parker:

I think I know the characteristics of the different persons comprising the Federal Trade Commission pretty well, and as a whole I am quite ready to say that I believe they intend to be broad-minded, fair and liberal. At the present time you can be assured of a patient and fair hearing without reference to political expediency; in fact, I think you will get a sympathetic hearing. . . .

The Chairman, Mr. Davies . . . was successful in carrying his delegation for Mr. Wilson and assisted Mr. Wilson in many of the adjoining states. . . .

He is of Welsh extraction; a man of great personal charm, somewhat emotional, highly ambitious, conscientious and courageous. His views in college and immediately after were quite radical, but he has been making progress with increased knowledge and experience in the conservative direction.

Mr. Davies has great ambition for the Federal Trade Commission. He accepts fully and literally the President's statement that the creation of the Commission signified a constitution of peace between the Government and business. It is his personal desire, I think, to be helpful in every way to legitimate business interests and at the same time to protect the public from some of the more unscrupulous managers of business.

The present weakness of Mr. Davies lies, I should say, in his inexperience in business matters; his somewhat emotional approach; his firm belief that [a] governmental agency can and ought to exert itself to correct in a short time many evils which have grown up with our commercial and social organization during a long course of years. . . .

Mr. [Edward N.] Hurley, who was formerly president of the Hurley Machine Works of Chicago, is a very different type of man. He is a hard-headed business man, is fairly familiar with the ways of business, and has very decided opinions as to what is right and what is wrong in business. When his mind is once made up it is impossible to move him. You may expect from him, I think, absolutely fair treatment.

Young went on to discuss Barry, "a man of sound sense and of general business experience" and "progressive ideas"; Harris, a political appointee; and George Rublee,

an excellent lawyer of somewhat radical views—a disciple of Mr. Brandeis —a man who has capacity either to be very helpful or very dangerous. Intellectually he is undoubtedly the strongest man on the Commission. . . .

Speaking of the Trade Commission as a body, I have at present a good deal of confidence in it, and I hope that it will not become prejudiced and sour as the Interstate Commerce Commission has. It will have to face, however, great difficulties and disappointments, and if the individual members are able to maintain their spirit of co-operative helpfulness in the face of such disappointments, I believe there is considerable hope for the future.[18]

Young's education in federal regulation was progressing rapidly; he was already, thanks to the years with Stone and Webster, something of an authority on state and local regulation of public utilities. He was prepared, moreover, sharply to challenge views of others in the industry which he found unfair to the regulatory authorities. A case in point is his six-page letter of September 12, 1916, addressed to O. B. Willcox of Bonbright and Company, who had written Coffin attacking a recent decision of the Public Utility Commission of Colorado. To him Young wrote in part:

In this case the Commission holds that a public utility cannot make charges for service exceeding the value of the service rendered even though the return is less than a fair return on the fair value of the property devoted to public use.

My views differ substantially from all the views expressed in [your] letter . . . because I think that the Colorado Commission, in making the decision aforesaid, is absolutely on safe ground. The rule that the public should pay the fair value of the service rendered is, in my judgment, the right rule, and if followed to its logical conclusion will give the public utilities exactly what they ought to receive; that is to say, the successful and efficient ones will obtain a handsome return on a successful business; and the poor and misjudged enterprises will starve. I think there is nothing more detrimental to the development of the public utility business than the adoption of the labor union dead levels; that is that all concerns are entitled alike to a fair return and only a fair return on their investment irrespective of their ability to serve their public economically and well. . . .

In the old days if a . . . grocer served his customer . . . without a pre-arranged price and a dispute arose, the courts . . . determined the fair value of the groceries furnished, and that was what the customer was obliged to pay. In the case of the grocer, that is the law today. . . . That, I believe, was the law with reference to the public service, and, in my opinion, it should be the law today. . . .

The chief difficulty in the situation has been to find a way of fixing the fair value of the service rendered. The governmental regulating authorities, always in fear of the courts upsetting their orders on the ground of con-fiscation, have considered it to be their duty not to find the fair value of the service but rather to ascertain whether a given charge for service would yield such a return on the value that the courts could not upset their order when made.

This led to the very erroneous notion, which has existed in the minds of those who ought to know better, that a rate just above the point of con-fiscation was a fair rate and, therefore, represented the fair value of the service. The fair rate must necessarily be substantially above the con-fiscatory point in order to induce the necessary capital to go into public service enterprises. Any rate below the point which will enable the public service company to live as a business institution and command the necessary capital to meet its needs is an unfair rate, even though it may not be con-fiscatory. On the other hand, the fair value of the service may yield an amount substantially above a "fair return," and, if it does, it has always seemed to me that the company should be compensated for its ability to earn a large return at a fair rate.

Unless this rule is adopted I feel sure that the next generation of public service managers will largely deteriorate in comparison with our existing managers. Young men in these days are not going into a business which, in the nature of things, can yield no recognition for special ability or unusual effort. If the stupid and inefficient manager succeeds in getting exactly as much, in the shape of return on capital, as the efficient manager, then the efficient manager must disappear.[19]

Young was also on the side of the commission in the matter of judicial review; he wrote Anson Burchard in the spring of 1917 in regard to the Martin bill which was then pending in Albany:

The question of court review of Public Service Commission decisions has been up many times, and in each instance the Commissions have strenuous-ly opposed what is known as a broad review; that is to say, an entire re-hearing. The Commissions desire that their finding of the facts should be final, and that there should be an appeal only on the strictly legal questions involved.

I am personally on the side of the Commissions so long as the personnel of the Commissions is such as to inspire confidence. The men now on the Second District Commission are certainly as competent as the average judges. If that be the fact, then what the public service companies are looking for by the Martin bill is not a review by some more competent authority but two shots at the target instead of one. I think that the Commissions are more competent to handle public service questions than the judges.[20]

ii

Nineteen fourteen was not a good year for the General Electric Company, or for most American corporations. The Annual Report noted, with Coffinesque understatement, a "marked contraction" in the company's business. The same number of orders were received as in 1913, but with a decrease of 25 percent in value; and there were fifteen thousand fewer employees—that is, a total of about fifty thousand.

As a stimulant, then, the impact of the European war was gradual, but 1915 showed a substantial increase in GE business. This was true even without counting orders for munitions of almost thirty-four million dollars, which were kept separate in the Annual Report for tax purposes. Orders for munitions, stated the report, "have been so restricted as to interfere as little as possible with the regular product of your company." The number of employees was up to sixty thousand, and for 1916 raises were in order—5 percent for all employees who had served at least five years, except for directors and general officers.

At first the war matériel manufactured by GE consisted mainly of ammunition for field artillery, destined for Russia; the contract was made with the British government through the agency of J. P. Morgan, but Russian technical officers as well as British were present to oversee and inspect. As it became clear that the war would *not* be over in a few months, and that the United States might at some point be involved as a combatant, orders poured in: more for munitions, many for guns and cannons and all kinds of supplies, such as searchlights and large electric motors. The 1916 Annual Report described "an extraordinary demand for General Electric products"; all facilities were being operated "to the limit of their capacity," and orders received were 70 percent greater than in 1915. There were extensive additions to manufacturing plants, and many contracts were let to smaller companies.

The war, even prior to the United States' entry, forced new developments and accelerated many already in train; GE took new products from the drawing boards and put them into the service of the nation in as short a time as possible—sometimes only after overcoming violent objections on the part of conservative officers of the government and the armed forces. In 1913 William Roy Emmet of GE had, with enormous difficulty, persuaded the U.S. Navy to allow his company to equip a naval collier with a turbine generator instead of the conventional steam propulsion. It worked so well that, after a long fight, Emmet convinced Secretary of the Navy Josephus Daniels that turbine drive, and complete electrical equipment, would work for a battleship. GE got the contract, and in 1915 the "all-electric" ship *New Mexico* was launched, as was the General Electric Company in the business of ship propulsion, a business of massive size during the war and after.[21]

Another field due to develop great strength was first important in these years also: radio, which leaped from a fascinating toy and a means of communication limited by distance and the Morse code to an ocean-spanning instrument vital in both war and peace.

Meanwhile, in all aspects of GE business, new and old, Young had his part. He wrote J. M. Woodward early in October of 1915 that "the pressure of the war contracts and the subsidiary contracts has kept me tied up so excessively as to prevent my consideration of the many other important matters such as yours which have been brought to my attention."[22] Other immediate problems claimed his attention also; the next week he spent with Rice in Schenectady because of a strike at the plant. He was well into his apprenticeship in labor problems. Concerned at this time with the study of various types of profit-sharing schemes for employees, he wrote to many others who had such plans, including Gerard Swope at Western Electric. He was puzzled as to how to allocate shares of profits according to merit; in a letter to M. F. Westover he said he objected to the theory of dividing profits because it might impair "the credit of an independent concern," and insisted that "due protection to the stockholders and the employees sharing in the profits requires in my judgment that the right to share shall be measured by the contribution which the individual makes to the business."[23]

Western Electric, he noted, had a plan for increased compensation for salesmen, and Young suggested that perhaps

all employees not directly concerned in making sales might have profits arbitrarily distributed, the amount of which should be based upon the aggregate amount of supplementary compensation which the salesmen get. This would center the entire energy of the organization on the outlet and, I should think, would tend to encourage everybody, from the office boy up, to assist in the sale of goods. In suggesting a plan, I am, of course, getting into a field in which I have no experience and in which my judgment at best can be of little value. . . .

Two days later he wrote again to Westover on the same subject: "people whom the Socialists call non-producers such as you and I, would have to take pot-luck . . . would it not be better to call us lubricants instead of non-producers? That sounds a little slippery, I know, but it does recognize to a slight extent our reason for existence."[24]

For all the papers in the "Immediate Attention" pile on Young's desk in 1915 and 1916, he was not allowed to sit there all the time. GE's stepped-up production increased the problems too, and the presence of counsel—and of a man beginning to be known as someone to depend on in a tight situation—was required in Washington, Boston, St. Louis, Chicago and—of course—Dallas, as well as on the GE circuit of Schenectady, Lynn, Fort Wayne, Erie and elsewhere.

One at least of these trips was a long and pleasant one, for Jo accompanied him, and so did Mr. and Mrs. Rice, who were very congenial companions. In 1915, San Francisco, to celebrate its post-earthquake reconstruction and burgeoning development, and the further rich prospects offered by the opening of the Panama Canal, invited the world to the Panama-Pacific International Exposition.

Within the bright and graceful buildings on their incomparable site at the Presidio, art and culture were the theme, rather than science and invention as at Chicago twenty-two years before—although airplane rides and movies were available. The exposition was strikingly beautiful at night; extensive electrical illumination, more imaginatively used than at Chicago, brought a magic brilliancy to the buildings and grounds. This lighting had been designed and installed by Walter D'Arcy Ryan, director of GE's Illuminating Engineering Laboratory. The architects and officials of the fair had been initially extremely dubious about it. Ryan used new concepts of floodlighting, installing a locomotive to provide steam for a "scintilator" played upon by colored searchlights. He also had made in Austria 130,000 cut-glass "jewels," which he hung upon the 400-foot central tower to glow and flash in myriad colors under still more searchlights—a daring scheme which was stunningly successful.[25] No wonder E. W. Rice, Jr., and Owen Young felt they had to see this; they took their wives and set out in November of 1915.

It was a sight-seeing trip with some business thrown in. They went to the Grand Canyon, and when they arrived in California stayed first at the famous Hotel del Coronado in San Diego. There they visited another exposition in honor of the Panama Canal; after all, the General Electric Company had supplied the central control system for the canal's enormous locks. And Jo wanted to see the handsome Spanish buildings of the San Diego Panama-California Exposition, which had been designed by her old friend from Cambridge, Bertram Goodhue. Then, on the way home, after San Francisco, there was business to be done in Dallas, interspersed with Texas hospitality, which gave Jo a chance to renew her acquaintance of 1913. They did not return home until December 24, when they gathered up the children and set off at once for a very cold and snowy Christmas at Van Hornesville with Owen's mother. The children thought it was rather a close thing.

In 1916, if Young was not at his desk in New York, or visiting a GE plant, he was in Dallas. Jo was certainly used to his absences by this time, but she had not grown to like them, nor, indeed, did he, as the "Dallas situation" heated up again. No one—Charles Tyler, Stone and Webster, Gordon Abbott, GE or the people in Dallas, both opponents and proponents—thought that anybody could negotiate and settle and soothe and hand-hold in Texas except Owen Young. So off he went, again and again. At this point the interests of the General Company and Stone and Webster were much the same, which simplified things somewhat. But in 1916 he was in Dallas for many days in every month of the first six, and even in 1917 he was there five or six times. This was not all, for a good portion of the lengthy and complicated negotiations of 1916–18 were carried on in New York and Boston.

As suggested in previous chapters, a volume could be written on the "Dallas situation" over the years, and its importance in Young's experience. The trips of the war years were his culminating effort to supply the fast-developing city on the banks of the Trinity River with adequate and fair-priced electric light, power and transportation. Dallas is an interesting case study, first of the problems of providing public services for a population accelerating at a dizzying rate, and second of Young's method—and it was a method by now—of handling conflicts between competing men and interests, conflicts exacerbated by personality clashes, legal tangles and a not always responsible press.

General Electric and its subsidiaries, Electric Bond and Share and the United Electric Securities Company of Boston, had begun to take an interest in Stone and Webster's Dallas properties after Young's visit there with Jo in 1913. s&w continued to manage them, without, however, great success. Many of the reasons for this were beyond their control, as Young explained in a long letter to Charles Coffin: the city charter's restrictions on the granting of franchises, and the Texas law forbidding mergers of the small competitive street railways which had sprung up in horse-drawn days, had by this time resulted in great inadequacy of both power and streetcar services. Public opinion, irritated especially by the lack of good transportation, was further inflamed by the attacks of the *Dallas Dispatch* and of city politicians who attempted to further their own power and popularity by coming out against "foreign landlords and corporate interests." Nevertheless, efforts by local businessmen to improve the situation by amending the charter were defeated by popular vote—and once apparently by the "telephone interests."[26] The blame was put on Stone and Webster's shoulders for all the inadequacies the citizens suffered; the people wanted local management and local investment, and it was these, in the long run, which Young provided.

It was clear that the situation would improve if Stone and Webster moved out of both ownership and management. If acceptable franchises could be obtained, with appropriate amendments to the city charter, the General Electric interests were willing to take over the properties. It was a big *if*, and a big job for Young.

The crucial election of April 4, 1916, was preceded by enormous excitement. The incumbent candidate for mayor, Henry Lindsley, was running on a platform of settlement of the utilities problem, although the franchise he had drafted was unacceptable to the utility companies, as they had informed him in advance. So was the proposed bond issue for a municipal lighting plant, although the charter amendments to be voted upon were agreed to by both sides. When Young arrived in Dallas—for the fourth time that year—on March 29, feelings were running high. Although he had written Jo on his previous visit in February that he "was not taking it as seriously as I used to," he was soon caught up in the excitement of the electioneering. "I have never seen a community so stirred up," he wrote her on March 31; "speeches at noon, afternoon and night—Bands and flags—all sorts of things to attract attention and create enthusiasm—the papers are full of it. . . . It is exciting—no man can tell tonight whether we win or lose but I feel that I have been able to contribute better cooperative effort in the last twelve hours"—the last a reference to the fact that the different utility managers had been bickering among themselves. That same day the *Dallas Daily Times Herald* quoted Lindsley as saying, in a rabble-rousing speech: "Stone and Webster had supplanted Brig. Gen. Wallace [the president of the Dallas Light and Power Company] with Major General Young, who is now in command. Major General Young gets a salary of $75,000 a year, so I am told. He sits in his room at the Adolphus Hotel directing and moving men in this campaign."[27]

From Young's own account of the fray, written for Coffin, we cite only the outcome: the mayor had carried the day by the narrowest of margins, "something like eighty votes out of a total of more than twelve thousand."[28]

The result of this defeat was to leave conditions in Dallas "so chaotic as to make consideration of any specific matter almost impossible."[29] But in the next few days Young spent his time talking to people in Dallas—his wide acquaintance there was invaluable at this point—canvassing the situation and the sentiment. The upshot of his efforts was, first, the withdrawal of the discredited Stone and Webster firm from the scene, with an offer of an option on all their holdings to the United Electric Securities Company; and second, a plan for the organization of local companies, with local men at the head and local investors cooperating in the reorganizing and refinancing of the properties.

This plan, which "met with the instant approval of the people of the town," Young laid the groundwork for during the next year. It was not easy. The mayor again made difficulties with the franchises, and numberless compromises were made in return for the promise of his support; and there were endless details to be worked out among the General Company, Bond and Share and United Securities. "Here," Young wrote Gordon Abbott, "is an opportunity for the President's term 'mutual accommodation.' "[30]

The entire project hinged upon the acceptance by the city and its citizens of the new franchises, for without them the option with Stone and Webster would not be taken up, and public-service affairs would return to chaos once more. In March 1917—when other and more important affairs were heating up for the nation—Mayor Lindsley threw a monkey wrench into the machinery. He had stated publicly that he thought the new franchises "would be of immediate benefit to Dallas," but when Young came to see him, shortly thereafter, he said that as a citizen he would vote for them, but "as Mayor taking into account the future he felt obliged to say he would vote 'no.' "[31] This was in spite of the many concessions made to him, and the fact that he had given Young "his express assurance that . . . he would not only vote for the franchises as Mayor but would support them on a referendum." Young's own comment was, "I have had some experience in dealing with men, but my experience has not yet been wide enough to enable me to explain the present attitude of Mr. Lindsley."[32]

In another letter, to Tom Camp, a lawyer who was reported to be dissatisfied with the franchises, Young made a statement about franchises in general:

The day has gone by, in my own opinion, when utilities could afford to take, even if they could obtain, unfair franchises. It would be unfortunate enough if the unfairness were on the face of the franchises, but if any hidden traps were concealed in them, it would and should be disastrous to the utilities. On the other hand, from my point of view, the municipality cannot afford to force, even if it has the power, unfair franchises on its utilities. If the unfairness is in favor of the utilities, it will involve reprisal, competition and ultimate disaster to the investment. If the unfairness exists in favor of the city, and the utilities are unprofitable for that reason, it will necessarily restrict the amount of capital which will be invested and the service which can be rendered.

The ideal situation for a city like Dallas, is to have franchises such that the capital invested will have maximum safety, so that money can be raised at the cheapest rate and also yield such a return on the capital as to make it of interest to the utilities to substantially increase their capital investment and thereby add to their facilities. This will mean that the facilities will always be a little in advance of the needs of the community, rather than lagging behind, as has been the case under the old franchises. New capital could not be obtained under the old franchises for the reason that the existing capital was in jeopardy.

I have some reason to think that you will accept my personal statement to you at its face value, and so I am presuming on this to say that in my opinion the franchises as worked out are, on the whole, fair alike to the City and to the utilities, and that there is nothing in the franchises or out of them regarding which I should not welcome the freest and frankest discussion.

A person examining the franchises could properly find here and there detailed criticism. I would myself. . . . The question is not whether the franchises are beyond criticism—that would be too much to expect—but whether they substantially reflect the arrangement which is fair and desirable both to the community and to the utilities. As to this I have no doubt.[33]

This time, Young's efforts paid off. In April 1917, "the franchises carried practically on a two-to-one basis . . . Mr. Lindsley has been defeated," Young wrote to Jeanette Belo Peabody in Cambridge, thanking her for the support of the Belo family newspapers—which did not include the *Dallas Dispatch*. "I am very happy," he added, "to have drawn the franchises which have merited the support of the *News* and the *Journal*."[34]

The United States was now at war with Germany, but in October, Young was in Dallas again, this time with Gordon Abbott and S. Z. Mitchell, of United Securities and Bond and Share, respectively. It was a trying journey and for once Young showed signs of impatience. "We were eighteen hours late getting into Dallas and on arriving found things pretty unsatisfactory," he wrote to his wife, "so I used strong arm methods." What he found was disagreement between the local utility managers as to who was to manage what; what he did was to reallocate responsibility. "This was taking it away from people who did want it and putting [it] on people who did not want it. It seems to me I never had a more difficult or disagreeable job. However it is now done and so far as it is humanly possible to foresee I am completely discharged from the Dallas utilities."[35]

He was not, of course. Nevertheless, in reporting to Coffin at the end of the year (1917) Young could say with some satisfaction that "the attitude of the public and of the Municipality towards these properties is the best I know in any public utility situation . . . and it does seem that . . . these public utilities should be successful in reasonable earning power and safe as to capital invested."[36] So, in a sense, he had his reward.

iii

Far from Dallas, there was one area of business, of steadily growing importance to the General Electric Company, in which Young considered himself the merest apprentice—but one eager to learn. He had never been out of the United States, except for trips to Montreal and a stroll across the bridge from El Paso to Juarez, but GE had interests all over the world, and here too it was the responsibility of counsel to pass on the contracts.

Like many American companies, GE had sought business abroad almost from the beginning. In 1896 the Annual Report stated that "we have sold a large amount of our apparatus in foreign countries during the past year," and in 1897 the Foreign Department was set up because of the volume of business: "design, cost and efficiency compare most favorably with that of European manufacturers."[37] By the turn of the century GE had sold power plants utilizing waterpower to Mexico, the Argentine, Japan (at Hiroshima) and Canada. An especially large one was set up by GE in southern India, bringing electricity a hundred miles from the hills for use in the Kolar goldfields in the state of Mysore.

In 1900 an office was established in London, for the company was eyeing not only England but the "British Dominions." Power plants and electric railways were the major items. GE provided the equipment for the London Underground, the Paris Métro, and all the tramways in Tokyo; the last was "the largest electric plant in Asia."[38] Turbines were sold all over the world, in South America and Australia as well as Europe and Asia. Close financial and manufacturing relationships were maintained with the British Thomson-Houston Company and the French Thomson-Houston Company, and a patent exchange— but no financial interest—was arranged with the Allgemeine Elektrizitäts Gesellschaft (AEG) in Germany; GE had also holdings in the Shibaura Engineering Works in Japan.

In 1914 foreign orders were over seven million dollars, and Young, as he worked on the contracts, became more and more interested in these areas, which he knew little about and had never seen. His tutor was Maurice Oudin, manager of GE's Foreign Department, with whom he developed a close relationship. Immediately after the outbreak of war in Europe, Young and Oudin were dining together, and the latter, deeply depressed, said he might as well leave now for his vacation. Young, in a rare emotional explosion—resulting no doubt from his own dismay at the course of events—attacked Oudin for this attitude. On the following day Young wrote a letter of apology: "I felt guilty all last evening, and I still feel so. I do not think that you ought to let my childish prattle affect your plans. . . . Just now the whole world, outside of nations at war, are endeavoring to regain consciousness. Until we and until they do I do not think much progress will be made," especially in the foreign field. And, he added, no better time than the next two weeks was apparent for Oudin's proposed holiday.[39]

Oudin taught him about Japan as well as Europe, and there also he received help from J. R. Geary, GE's representative in Tokyo. "Your letters are very interesting and instructive to me," Young wrote Geary in July of 1914,

and I cannot let this opportunity go by to tell you how much I appreciate the cordial and sympathetic way in which you have handled every matter about which I have written you. You must make allowances for my ignorance both generally and specifically of your Japanese situation, and I feel that I can rely upon you to write me very frankly in the future in case you think my point of view is wrong or that I am asking something unreasonable.[40]

Young's initial concern for the foreign field was occasioned less by the war than by his own antecedent responsibility for contracts and for the effect of the Clayton act on foreign trade. He sent Arthur Weed, the brother of his former colleague in Tyler's office, now with the United States Chamber of Commerce, a study prepared at Young's suggestion by Carman F. Randolph, a lawyer in New York, on the desirability and possibility of securing legislation to facilitate exports by removing all doubt as to the applicability of the antitrust laws to foreign trade. In this regard Young was anxious that export associations should be declared legitimate, by legislation if necessary. The attorney general, he wrote Thomas Thacher of Simpson, Thacher and Bartlett, who had written a letter to the *New York Times* on the subject, "appeared unwilling to rule that export associations are permissible. Both Secretary Bryan and Secretary [of Commerce] Redfield favor legislation expressly permitting such associations."[41]

Young was interested also in the settlement of international commercial disputes by arbitration. In a letter to H. A. Toulmin of Dayton, he drew a distinction between domestic and foreign commercial arbitration, pointing out that there was no judicial machinery in the international field to deal promptly and effectively with disputes: "The very difference in the fundamentals of the substantive law and procedures in the Latin American countries and in our own presents unusual difficulties." He continued:

After active practice of nearly twenty years I am more and more impressed with the view that the lawyers must correct not only the form of procedure in the courts but their own dilatory habits in order effectively to keep the judicial machinery in step with the needs of business. I venture the opinion, relatively speaking, that the delays in the courts today, compared with the speed with which business transactions are handled, are greater than they have ever been in the history of the world before. This means that the law is lagging further and further behind business.

If this is true in the domestic field, as I believe it is, and on these difficulties is superimposed the difference in law and procedure in the international field, I think it is quite apparent that there is unquestionably room for commercial arbitration in the international field without bad results.[42]

In spite of the war in Europe, American businessmen continued to travel about the world in 1915–16 and even 1917 with what seems a remarkable disregard of submarine warfare. Young himself did not go abroad until well after the war was over, but he was in constant touch with many who did. In 1916 he was worried about the British Thomson-Houston Company's position in the field of turbine manufacture. A relatively small branch of the General Company at first, British Thomson-Houston had become an important, in fact *the* important, maker for British territory of the Curtis turbine, which GE had been manufacturing and improving since 1903. Now a rival company was threatening their supremacy, and Young knew a man must go over. He and his associates were completely tied down at home, and he thought of Thomas Nelson Perkins, his old friend from Boston, and himself a skilled negotiator.

Four years older than Young, Nelson Perkins was a partner in the firm he had asked Young to return to Boston to join in 1913, now Ropes, Gray, Boyden and Perkins. A Bostonian of old family, married to an Adams, he was well traveled, sophisticated, imperturbable—in fact a perfect legal ambassador to England. Young wrote him a long, informative, half-persuasive, half-commanding letter about the mission. He was eager for Perkins to take on this job, as a prelude to his helping G E "deal with the many new problems which are sure to arise in the future."[43]

Perkins rather grudgingly agreed to go. But at the last moment plans were drastically changed; he was sent on a far-flung mission, but in the opposite direction. G E was affiliated with a Russian company, Wseobschtschaja Kompania Elektritschestwa (w K E), and just before Perkins was to sail for England an even more critical situation arose in Petrograd; it was clear a man must go there at once. The Russian company had obtained its patent rights from General Electric by way of A E G, the German company, and as a result of the war the Russian government had canceled these rights; w K E was crying for help.

In haste, Young, in consultation with Rice, drew up a new contract; G E would be willing, they decided,

to authorize Mr. Perkins to make an interval contract with the Russian Company and an obligation to purchase such material as it did not make from us. I assume that we should also be willing to go so far as to authorize Mr. Perkins to commit us to the organization of a lamp company of which we should have control. . . . Mr. Perkins would not be authorized to commit the General Company to any financial obligations outside of its participation in the lamp company.[44]

So Perkins, with Oudin, set off in the middle of January 1917, crossed the Pacific, did a little business for G E in Japan, crossed Siberia, and arrived in Petrograd on February 25. It seemed hardly the moment for peaceful negotiation on electric lamps between businessmen. Many workers were on strike, and massive discontent was seething underneath. Eleven days after the Americans arrived this exploded in gunfire in the streets, and the Revolution was on. Nevertheless, a month later, Perkins was cabling details of a completed contract to Young, who was worrying about what kind of a caldron he had tossed his friend into.

Perkins finally got home on June 3, by the same route, reported to the board of General Electric at its meeting in Boston on June 7, and from then on was GE's Russian expert. When he sent in his bill to Young in October of that year, he wrote: "If things in Russia keep on going as they now are, I am not sure that your directors won't try to assess me instead of paying me."[45]

On his return, Perkins went into government service and was in Washington during the war, working with the surveyor general of army purchases, Edward Stettinius, under Secretary of War Newton D. Baker. He became very impatient with Stettinius and, as he confided to Young, felt himself useless. In answer Young sent a handwritten note typical of their close relationship:

I deny all the allegations in your letter about yourself. You are all right— you are helping Stettinius a lot and just the sort of help he needs. . . . The best way to get cooperation in an organization is to assume (and really believe) that you are going to get it. There is no use complaining to anyone unless he has power to remedy the complaint. So I wanted you both to adopt as a principle of action, saying the good things about the Dept. and everybody in it—making them feel happy and also that you are satisfied and contented with your present place. That will create confidence and good feeling. To the Secretary and his Assistant I should be frank, firm, disagreeable if necessary as he only can apply the remedy. . . . Throw off your indigestion and be cheerful as you naturally are—no better antidote could be had for that most difficult situation than Mr. Stettinius' great experience and ability and wisdom plus the charm of your personality and your all around good sense.

I am very serious—very confident of the outcome both for you and for the country.[46]

Young and Perkins were to work closely together in international affairs in later years; it was perhaps the closest friendship either of them had, and was a friendship shared by Josephine Young and Louisa Perkins. In the midst of important and difficult jobs there were many happy interludes—at the Auteuil or Longchamps races, at dinners in little restaurants, where Nelson and Owen and Jo and Lulu forgot their burdens and enjoyed themselves with their own particular brand of humor. At the moment, however, such peacetime pleasures could hardly be anticipated or even dreamed of.

Chapter 10

The Yanks Are Coming:
Crusade and Its Aftermath

Y OUNG voted for Woodrow Wilson in the close election of 1916, although in September he was writing to the director of the Hughes National College League:

As a Democrat I hope to be able to support Mr. Wilson for President. If, however, the issue is, as Mr. Hughes is now making it, that any combination of men, whether they be laborers or employers or farmers, can go to the Government of the United States and demand special legislation under threat of starving the people of the United States, then I am in favor of the independence and dominance of the Government. I am not, however, at the moment, ready to make contributions in any form to Mr. Hughes' campaign.[1]

But two weeks before the election he had made up his mind in spite of his objections: "I have been strongly in sympathy with all of Mr. Wilson's policies except his handling of the labor situation," he wrote Tom Chadbourne, of Chadbourne, Stanchfield and Levy. "That I do not object to as a labor situation, but I do object to any body of men in the United States threatening the Government of the United States and getting results from the threat. Other than this I am an enthusiastic supporter of Mr. Wilson's administration. And in this respect I do not think that the Republican party, outside of Mr. Hughes, has made a demonstration which is satisfactory."[2]

Temperamentally no less opposed to war than Woodrow Wilson himself, Young, like the majority of his countrymen, had been shocked by the invasion of Belgium and the nightmare of submarine warfare. Neither Anglophile nor Francophile, he had no wish to see the ordered world he knew destroyed or new arches of triumph erected in honor of the kaiser. His wife, of unmixed English descent, deeply shared his feelings, and even the younger children sensed them. His daughter at the age of nine was stunned by the look on her father's face as he read the news of Verdun.

When unrestricted submarine warfare was resumed by the Germans at the beginning of February 1917, it was clear that President Wilson could no longer maintain neutrality. Immediately after the White House severed diplomatic relations with Germany, Young composed a telegram to the secretary of war and the secretary of the navy for the signatures of C. A. Coffin and E. W. Rice, Jr.:

The General Electric Company tenders the cooperative assistance of its organization and of its technical and manufacturing facilities to the United States Government in any measures which may be adopted in the present situation. Our Research Laboratory will be at the disposal of the Naval Consulting Board or any other agency of the Government. Our executives and engineers will be available to attend any conferences which the Government may suggest with view to devising means of utilizing our facilities most effectively. We wish through you to express to the President our desire to render sympathetic and helpful service in every practicable way.[3]

This was not quite the kind of demonstration that Young had envisaged for GE as its response to the challenge of the New Freedom, but the challenge to which it was addressed was moving closer daily. March news only confirmed the need for such support throughout the country: the Zimmermann telegram, the arming of U.S. merchant ships, increased financial aid to Britain and France, the threat of a railroad strike, the news of the Russian Revolution, the continued sinking of American ships—all these resulted in a reaction expressed by Theodore Roosevelt's outraged yell for immediate entry into the war and national unity to support it. There were demonstrations and meetings, mostly on the eastern seaboard but Chicago and Denver were included, in favor of war. On April 6 Congress approved Wilson's message and the President signed the bill declaring that a state of war existed.

Young was at Little Point with his wife and younger children for a weekend visit. The newspapers, even six-year-old Philip noticed, had colored American flags above the enormous headlines. Like all American families on that fateful morning, they wondered what it meant for them. The father was forty-two, young enough to don a uniform if needed; the older boys, at school, were seventeen and fifteen. Owen Young knew well that to stick to his job would be more useful to his country than to be a soldier, but he needed the reassurance Nelson Perkins provided with his characteristic "Don't be a damned fool."

A war two thousand miles away was new business for the American people. At first they did not know what to do about it; indeed, they hardly believed they were in it. Young found this especially true on his trips to the South and the West. At the end of May he wired the president of the United States Chamber of Commerce:

I favor strongly resolutions of Executive Committee May 24th. Have just returned from trip to Texas and found sentiment everywhere ready to back the President *quote* if we get into this war seriously *unquote* Until people are made to understand that we are now in war seriously and informed of things to be done and general order of their importance it will be difficult to get prompt and decisive action stop Until intelligent public opinion demands that certain things be done and be done promptly we shall not get cooperative and effective action between governmental and producing agencies Resolutions of Executive Committee go to root of our present difficulties Please record General Electric Company in favor of resolutions.[4]

In July Young wrote J. W. Kirkland of the South African General Electric Company, who had been in the United States earlier in the year, a long letter, congratulating him on his safe return, and describing at some length the last three months in the United States:

The declaration of war in this country produced enthusiasm which was thrilling, especially among all the people on the Atlantic seaboard. The great concerns offered their facilities to the Government and many thousands of people went to Washington to offer their personal services to the Government. Many of them were men and women whose individual services would be valuable, but, of course, there was no organized machinery to make them of value to the Government. Accordingly, hundreds of them came home disappointed, ready to criticize an Administration which was not in a position immediately to accept volunteer services.

Repeating his concern about the "if the war becomes serious" attitude he had found in Texas, he added: "I must say, however, that I think Congress, under the lead of the President, whose influence is very great and indeed almost controlling, has done very well. It voted the large loan, and the $2,000,000,000 was more than fifty per cent oversubscribed."

He went on to report oversubscription of the Red Cross campaign for $100 million—not least because of the "special Red Cross dividends" authorized by GE and the larger corporations generally. Business, he said, was operating under heavy pressures, with GE orders steady at an unprecedented $4 million a week. Then he described Washington's committees for national defense, as well as the conscription act and its impact on manpower and supplies. Pointing out that sale of government bonds had made heavy drains on investment funds, he found the utilities feeling the pinch when it came to paying for their orders; nevertheless, "while there is considerable confusion,

I think that on the whole we are doing pretty well, and I believe that we shall be able to demonstrate here that we can handle a war question efficiently."[5]

The General Electric Company, as an important part of American machinery for making war, demanded almost every minute of Young's time. In the spring of 1918 he wired General Hugh S. Johnson, the director of purchase and supply, who wanted him to come to Washington:

The executives of the General Electric Company have so distributed their work that some of them are free to do and are now doing war work while others stay on their jobs. A very large percentage of the business of the Company is Government work. In this distribution I have agreed to stay on the job and so I am not available for the service you propose. Under the above conditions I am sure my greatest service can be rendered here. Thanks for your consideration of me.[6]

After all, someone had to mind the store. Refusing to be pressured by Washington, Young also replied sharply to correspondents who wanted him to do things he considered unessential: "There is one thing," he wrote early in the war, "and only one thing for every man woman and child to do at the moment and that is to make their contribution toward *winning the war.* Everything else should be held in suspense and energy and money diverted to that end." And to this creed he stuck throughout: when Rice wanted him to go to Japan and China with him—for business and for their daughter Mabel's wedding to Philo Parker of Standard Oil—Young refused, for there were "too many problems now arising."[7]

The General Company, which was already operating to the limit of capacity in 1916, was expanding its facilities rapidly. In 1917 $22,000,000 went into new buildings and tools, with $13,000,000 more planned for the following year. Profits were large, but new taxes were catching up; in 1917 GE paid $1,789,508 in federal income tax and $7,289,508 of excess-profits tax. At the time such payments were novel; Young found the figures so astounding that he instigated a study of the tax situation and proposed setting up a separate department to deal with it.

All of GE's products, old and new, were greatly in demand, and were selling at high wartime prices. As noted, a major part of their war effort was in ship propulsion, and this demanded much of Young's time. In May of '17 Edward Filene of Boston wrote Young, asking him to be a member of a committee working to arouse and educate public sentiment in favor of more and faster shipbuilding—one of Filene's innumerable good causes. This of course Young could not do:

To any shipbuilding program the General Electric Company is one of the largest, if not indeed the largest, contributor in the United States because of its large facilities for the manufacture of steam turbines—the most efficient and economical prime mover for ship propulsion. Because of my connection with the General Company I feel sure that my membership on such a committee would be a handicap to the committee. . . . When it comes to the more definite work of organizing the machinery to build the ships as distinguished from the organization of public sentiment to build the ships, I think I can be of service. In that work I am now engaged entirely unofficially in our own organization and in connection with others.[8]

He spent many hardworking days in Washington at the Navy Department, and retained Thomas F. Logan, then Washington correspondent for the *Philadelphia Inquirer*, to watch general developments throughout the government. When the President appointed E. N. Hurley—who knew that ships were "immediately and imperatively necessary"—as head of the U.S. Shipping Board, replacing William Denman, Young applauded. "Nothing in the administration of the war has caused us such great concern as the failure to go forward with the shipping program," he wrote Hurley, "because we know full well the difficulties of obtaining adequate propulsion apparatus quickly, and we also have fairly complete figures as to the rate of sinkings and the relation of speed to the safety of the ship." He was therefore much pleased that the President had "cut the Gordian knot" and lodged the power in Hurley's hands.[9]

Delays, however, were not wholly due to problems within the Shipping Board. America entered the war with a totally inadequate number of ships for the transport of armies and supplies, munitions and food for its allies, so shipyards had to be built and shipbuilders trained—men taken from bridge and skyscraper construction, and others less experienced, women among them—and all this at enormous expense. "The men in the yards worked in three shifts, hammering away on unfinished ships all night under the glare of electric lights. Riveters earned almost as much as bank presidents," wrote William G. McAdoo in his memoirs.[10]

In Schenectady, where the works resounded with the rapid construction of ship-propulsion machinery, they heard about this and the machinists struck. But compromises were hastily made and they went back to work. Strikes and lockouts were general in 1917, for the cost of living was shooting up and pressures on everyone increased as the war went on. It was not until the National War Labor Board went into action in the spring of 1918, under rules which provided a fair deal for labor, that strikes were banned for the duration.

There was a massive strike at the Erie plant just after the armistice, however, when the prospect of the cancellation of war contracts darkened the whole industrial scene, and Young spent many days there. Indeed, his education in labor relations, as in foreign business, was greatly accelerated by war, and he was able to form certain guiding principles. Nelson Perkins remembered him saying, "The more unreasonable seem the grievances for which men strike, the more it is pretty certain to be the fault of the management that they do strike."[11]

Problems in wartime were more than enough, but Young, as counsel, had also to keep his eye on the future. In the General Electric Research Laboratories were numerous scientists working for the U.S. government; Young wrote to A. G. Davis on December 7, 1917: "It seems to me that we should expressly recognize the right of the Government to use for military purposes any inventions without royalty during the period of the war, but that subject to such use the inventions should belong to us. I regard it as important with the increasing scope of governmental activity that we do not recognize an unqualified right in the Government to use inventions."

Taxes too—even before America entered the war, counsel was worrying about the 12½ percent tax on profits from munitions manufacture: "a super-tax on profits above 10% introduces a principle into our revenue legislation which may well be considered permanent. . . . Whenever a new way to raise money is pointed out or adopted as an emergency measure which is capable of continuance after the emergency has passed, my observation is that the tax is not likely to cease with the emergency."[12]

Young kept close watch during 1917 on the war revenue bill, which in the summer of '17 was in conference committee. J. F. Zoller, GE's tax attorney, was spending much time in Washington and reporting progress—or lack of it—to Young. To Paul Cravath, the prominent corporation lawyer, later to be briefly chairman of Westinghouse, Young wrote in July:

Unless the base of the Senate bill can be made high enough to cover the annual earnings of the corporation I should prefer to gamble on the early ending of the war to the extent of accepting the House rate. A progressive rate of taxation, I fear, is going to be disappointing as a revenue producer when it gets into the higher percentages. I am not at all certain that some concerns may not feel that they should build good will with their customers for the future rather than to make profits, 50% or more of which will be paid out in taxes. If I am right in this the surest revenue producer on the excess profits would be a flat rate and not a progressive rate.[13]

He changed his mind, however, when the *New York Times* published a series of articles by Professor E. R. A. Seligman on the war revenue bill which Young thought excellent; he sent copies to influential friends, such as Bernard Flexner in Chicago, saying that the public should be properly informed and asked to support the Senate committee's version of the bill.

Young's own lobbying efforts, however, were chiefly on behalf of an amendment attached to this bill by Senator Henry F. Hollis of New Hampshire, exempting from taxation gifts from income to the Red Cross and charitable and educational institutions. Originally a war measure to support the Red Cross, at Young's urging it was broadened to include other gifts, and so had far-reaching effects. He was, of course, especially interested in the provision of gifts to educational institutions because of St. Lawrence, which, like other small colleges, was having a hard time during the war. Young lobbied for this amendment as a member of a committee headed by Professor Samuel Mc-Cune Lindsay of Columbia; he wrote his friends asking them to write their senators and also to send money to support the committee's work. He got an excellent response; Dwight Morrow was especially helpful and the amendment was finally passed. The act, as signed in October 1917, posed a 6 percent tax on corporations, and an excess-profits tax graduated from 20 to 60 percent on the earnings of individuals and corporations—the latter being raised a year later to 35 to 70 percent.

Young had little time for other interests: he served on Mayor John Purroy Mitchel's Committee on National Defense in New York City, and worked, as he could, for the Red Cross, as did his wife. Perhaps his greatest contribution, outside of GE, was his knowledge of acceptable candidates for war jobs. His unmatched acquaintance across the continent among experienced and capable men provided him with a reservoir of suggestions, from which he could draw at a moment's notice and of which Washington made good use. Nelson Perkins was at the top of the list, and would have had to be ten men in order to take all the jobs his friend recommended him for.

The war came even closer to the Young family when, in the spring of 1918, the eldest son volunteered as an ambulance driver in a Red Cross unit. C.J. had entered Harvard in the fall of 1917, at the age of seventeen, and his father and mother, like all parents when the first child goes away to college, worried about him. In October '17, when Owen was on an extended trip—Dallas to Salt Lake to Spokane—he wrote Jo from Salt Lake City: "I was very glad to get your wire here saying you were all well and especially glad that Charles was at home to relieve the Sunday for you as well as for him. I have thought about him a lot—and wondered whether he was getting started well and was happy. Unless he is he won't do well and we are so anxious to have him do well."[14]

The boy was now eighteen, but not eligible for the draft—which in the early part of the war began at twenty-one—and nearly finished with his freshman year. The ambulance unit was being recruited at Harvard, and many of his friends were going; it was to serve on the Austrian-Italian front, and the boys would not be allowed to sign up for more than six months. C.J. sent a telegram to his father asking his consent and saying he would have his academic credits for the year past: "Telegraph me tonight so I can settle in morning there is rush for places am very very anxious to go."[15]

There were, naturally, telephone talks before he could "settle," but on May 3, his father wrote the letter confirming his consent, ending it: "I congratulate you, first on your volunteering, second on your acceptance."[16]

The unit sailed for Italy later in May, and saw very active service under shellfire on the dizzy mountain roads of northern Italy. Communications to the United States were not good, letters were long delayed, and Owen and Jo had five months of anxiety until he returned, safe and sound and very much grown-up, in October. By this time the draft age had been lowered to eighteen, and he enlisted at once in the Harvard unit of the Marine Corps. John, who was sixteen, was drilling in the Hackley School uniform and wishing he was older.

ii

But even in wartime, families must somehow attend to their own concerns. The Youngs had moved into the Lincoln Steffens house in Riverside, Connecticut, on April 19, 1915—an auspicious day for a Lexington family. The occasion was somewhat less than happy, however, for the move almost two weeks ahead of plan was forced by the imminence of a case of the measles in little Jo, and her mother wanted to get settled. It was not too bad; from her sloping-ceilinged bedroom the little girl could see out across Cos Cob Harbor to the islands at the mouth, and beyond the islands to the Sound, where, at night, the lighthouse on Great Captain's Island winked white and red and white. Measles or not, she, like the rest of the family, was satisfied from the first day, and always loved it.

Lincoln Steffens had loved it too, and he was glad to have it lived in by appreciative tenants. He had found it years ago, when he was spending some time in the "art colony" of Cos Cob with the writers and artists there. He often rowed or sailed about, looking for a place of his own: "I knew all the time that the place I liked best was right in the harbor, a tiny cape in Riverside, that I called Little Point . . . with a sandy beach, a bay, and an old house under trees on a hill."[17] He bought it, and lived there—as much as he lived anywhere—for some years with his first wife, Josephine Bontecou, and her mother. They all loved it, but after both women died, Steffens did not live there again.

Young, as Steffens expected, took excellent care of the property, saw that all needed repairs were properly made, and when the barn burned in January 1916, Young—with C.J.'s help—supervised the designing and building of a new one. Their landlord, for the most part absent in California or Mexico or Europe, considered it an ideal arrangement.

The Youngs kept cows and chickens; the cows were not Holsteins but Guernseys, probably at Jo's request. She loved the small brown-and-white creatures, and also they gave more cream. There was a motorboat anchored off the Point, and a dory in the old-fashioned boathouse, and later the children had a small sailboat and a canoe; no wonder they loved the place.

In his own way, Owen Young was an enthusiastic saltwater fisherman. His enthusiasm was evidenced first by a trip to the beach at low tide with a clam-digging fork, usually in the company of the younger children, who had been taught that digging in the mud for clams for bait was fun. This exercise was followed by long silent hours of sitting—in a disgraceful old coat and hat—on the seawall at incoming tide, or out on the Sound in the anchored motorboat, with an occasional eel or flounder or, in season, mackerel as reward. He was no sailor, and never learned to swim, so the expeditions out to sea took place only in the calmest weather, and usually only as far as the rocks at the entrance of the harbor, where Jo could keep an eye on him with the field glasses. His companions were sometimes his sons, but usually the chauffeur, faithful, stolid Theodore Sharpe, who knew how to run the boat and could be counted on to keep quiet. Fish may have been few, but there was plenty of sea air and sunshine, and many problems were considered, and often solved, over the years—for General Electric, for the family, even for the nation.

It was, from the first, when she found it, Jo's place. It was what she wanted: in New England, on the salt water, an old house that needed fixing up, with plenty of space for the trees and flowers she loved. She planned and supervised the gardens—flowers and vegetables, fruit trees and flowering shrubs, climbing roses and grapevines. Her children remember her in an old tweed coat, out in all weathers with Barney the Irish gardener, who was always surprising her with some new and unwelcome idea: "What kind of a tree is that you've put in there, Barney?" "Oh, ma'am, that's just a forest tree." In Van Hornesville, the place was Owen's and his mother's; in Riverside, it was all hers.

Although Young continued to rent and eventually "bought" Little Point from Steffens, the family lived there over the whole winter only that first year of 1915–16. Not far away upriver the New Haven trains rattled over the bridge to the Riverside station, which was just the right distance for a good walk morning and evening. But the schedule at General Electric, accelerated by the war, with all its demands for evenings and trips away, was too full for constant commuting. Owen rebelled at these enforced absences from his family, and after that year Little Point became a weekend and holiday haven, near enough by train or automobile to visit often.

And so in the summer of 1916 Young took a five-year lease on an apartment at 830 Park Avenue, on the southwest corner of Seventy-sixth Street, and the two younger children were entered in a small private school in a brownstone on Fifth Avenue opposite the Plaza. Their move in the fall was delayed, however, by the infantile paralysis epidemic and resultant quarantine of that year. The family, growing a bit too large and obstreperous to spend a long vacation in Grammy's house in Van Hornesville, had rented a cottage on Otsego Lake, ten miles south, for August. And there they stayed, even after school began, to the children's delight. September and October colored the tree-clad hills across the still lake; the two older boys were finally allowed to leave and go directly to their boarding school at Tarry-town, but Jo remained until November, at the cottage and then in Van Hornesville, with little Jo and Philip—a season of beauty and peace which they never forgot.

Meanwhile, Owen, taking rooms at the Ritz in New York, struggled alone with the new apartment. It was to be "done" by a decorator, a procedure that turned out to be very expensive and resulted in an effect quite different from the Youngs' original—and permanent—taste for considerable simplicity, with American antiques and Oriental rugs. But the apartment came equipped with Gothic stone fireplaces, and the decorator, inspired by these and by a then-current fashion in New York for Mediterranean decor, produced Italian and Spanish tables and chests as well as Jacobean chairs, gold brocade curtains and wall-to-wall carpets. The effect was handsome, and different, which perhaps was what Owen Young wanted. The younger children, brought from up-country into this splendor, were amazed; they had each a bedroom complete with carved Italian beds and inlaid chests, and each was done in their favorite colors—Josephine's in green and Philip's in purple.

But no luxurious quarters could make up to country-bred children for the loss of freedom, grass and water. Confined in city schools— Jo went in a year or two to the Brearley and Philip to Buckley—and not allowed to go out alone except to walk to school or walk the dog around the block, they could not wait for Friday and the weekend at Little Point. Their mother too felt the loss of country things, and did not like the feeling of isolation of eleven floors up on Park Avenue, but for her this was certainly compensated for by the increased hours with Owen.

Thus the pattern of family life was established for the next dozen years: 830 from October through May, with weekends at Riverside— if it was not every weekend the children screamed; Christmas at Van Hornesville with Grammy; and the long summer (private schools in those days ended in May and did not begin until October) divided between the delights of swimming and sailing at Little Point, and running over the hills above "the Holler."

Through this pattern moved Owen Young at his own pace, now at home in one of the three places, now shuttling between New York and Boston and Washington and Schenectady, or away on longer trips. It was Jo who cared for the family day by day, watching and planning for the children, making the decisions, running two homes. There was plenty of help—maids, a cook, a laundress and a chauffeur, as well as Young's friend and devoted valet from the early days in the Murray Hill Hotel, Tom Gairy, a handsome, slight West Indian, with an excellent British education and accent. Tom was butler and valet and self-appointed supervisor of everything. He lived in Harlem and on his days off played cricket on the top team in the city.

But Jo found time to enjoy, and teach her daughter to enjoy, the music, art, theater and opera which living in the city provided. Not since her days at Radcliffe had she had such opportunities, and few weeks went by without their visiting a new exhibition, seeing a new play, or just driving about New York to tour museums and old houses, historic sites and beautiful churches. The children's education was by no means confined to school.

From the start in New York, Owen and Jo avoided, insofar as possible, the demands of society. They had a number of good friends in the city (mostly with St. Lawrence backgrounds), but beyond social occasions with them, they did not go out. There were obligatory dinners with GE or other officials, and they always went as a matter of course to St. Lawrence functions. But their evenings together were rare enough anyway, and they prized them too much to accept invitations unless they had to. Life at Little Point was even more isolated. Quite consciously they made no close friends there; it was to be a haven, a refuge for Owen from the demands which grew more harassing with each year. Time there, valuable and too brief, must be saved for the lawn and the garden, the hammock under the crab-apple tree, the beach and the boats and the fish.

There developed, over the next few years, two exceptions to this established family pattern. The first was a move to a larger apartment in the same building, on the south side with sunshine and a magnificent view downtown—until a new apartment house was put up in front of it. There were two floors with a curving stair, and in later years two more were added; this was their New York residence for the rest of their life together.

The second exception was a stunningly unexpected surprise. One day in the late fall of 1918 Jo said to her husband, "I don't know why I don't feel very well." And he answered, "Have you thought you might be going to have a baby?"

It was true. Jo was forty-eight, her youngest child, Philip, was eight, and a family of four children was just right. But she got used to the idea, and when, on June 23, 1919, a little boy was born, everyone was delighted. Little Jo and Philip named him Richard and assumed proprietary airs. The father came in for some teasing from his friends, one of whom asked, "Series B?"

Jo's convalescence was slow, and she looked about for someone to help take care of the baby. Soon the proprietary airs were assumed— in the most modest way possible—by someone else. Recommended by a friend of a friend, a young Irish girl came for an interview; as soon as Jo saw how she looked when she saw the baby, and how she touched him, Jo knew this was the one she wanted. Margaret Carey, recently from Ireland, had been taking care of an old lady; but her real love was children and her ambition was to be a baby nurse. She knew nothing of professional training, and very little of anything else, which was exactly what the mother wanted—"Now I can teach her everything myself." Apt teacher, and apt pupil, for Margaret remained throughout her life a special member of the family, with her store of love and loving care undiminished by devotion to five generations of Youngs.

iii

The two areas in Young's life which he never allowed to be slighted were, first, the family, then Van Hornesville; and after them St. Lawrence. He said once, "One of the things I like to know about a man is whether he is loyal to his college, or whether he forgets."[18] When he first came to Boston as a law student he was very conscious of the little freshwater college in his background, to whose name the response was usually, "What? Where?" His pride in his record at the Law School and his success in the Tyler firm was first for his family, but it was also a tribute to his college.

He became a trustee of St. Lawrence in 1912, and was active in the search for a successor when President Almon Gunnison retired in 1914—although he was perfectly happy about the college with his old friend and mentor Charley Gaines as acting president.

In the New York years, Owen and Jo attended St. Lawrence dinners and meetings regularly, as well as making trips to Canton for commencements and other occasions. And in 1915 Owen had the great pleasure of taking his mother to Canton for the first time. Ida Young saw at last the streets, houses and college buildings where she had lived vicariously for four years, and met many of the people whom she had come to know through Owen's letters more than twenty years before.

With Dr. Hervey the Youngs were always in touch. In his later years the good man lived in Bath, Maine, in the summer and in Bermuda in the winter, where he collected algae in the pursuit of his research, and a new wife as well. He often stopped off with the Young family in between, in Lexington and later at Little Point. To the children, Dr. Hervey was a wonderful and mysterious figure, incredibly old, like a prophet from the Bible. He told them stories from the Old Testament—their favorite was Elisha and the bears. Or at table he might take a stone from the date he had just eaten, turning it over in his fingers before their eyes, saying, "See the rainbow colors, the network of silken lines, the perfection of this seed which God has made and hidden away until now." They knew the story of how Dr. Hervey had brought their parents together, and, staring at him, wondered where, without him, they would be.

The voluminous correspondence in Owen Young's personal letter books about St. Lawrence is matched by that relating to the farms in Van Hornesville and his cows. His letters disclose throughout a Jeffersonian concern for the land, the animals and the crops. The tenant on the Home Farm was prodded to plant more corn, to get on with the additional plowing for more feed crops, including not only corn but rye and some millet. Uncle John Brandow, now the manager of the farm operation, was admonished to keep a sharp eye on expenses and above all to report the outcome of the testing of the herd. When his Stone and Webster friend Henry Bradlee wrote to inquire about the Holsteins, Young replied, "It is a matter of great pride to me that you connect my name with the most important and least profitable business in which I am engaged."[19]

During the years of the war he came as often as possible to visit his mother; when he could not come he wrote her. Telephoning was more difficult; Ida had a telephone with a crank hung on the wall near her rocking chair, but there was no service nights and Sundays. It was not until after the war that—under pressure from Young—the Otsego and Delaware Telephone Company improved the situation.

Even during the war the family managed to come for the summer and the Christmas visits that were the best of all. After one of the latter, which Owen spent "riding down hill" with his boys, he said it was the best vacation he ever had. And in both seasons the days ended with a visit to the barn at milking time, then a gathering around the kitchen table, where the family made short work of Grammy's abundant food. Owen sat at the end next to the sink and hand pump, where his long arms could reach for a cloth to wipe a child's sticky face and fingers.

The war took manpower from both the farms and St. Lawrence; but Young did his best to keep them both going. With the help of many others both survived, to move into greatly expanded development in the postwar years.

The end of 1918 brought Young to the completion of six years at General Electric, six years of a new life in New York. He had built well upon his experience in Boston with Tyler, and had developed new areas of knowledge and expertise forced by the war. Now the war was over, the country was in a turmoil, a whole set of new problems awaited government, business and education. The first half-dozen years had been busy for Young, but the next were to be busier still.

Chapter 11

Wireless versus Cables:
Creation of RCA

T HE story of the creation of the Radio Corporation of America
has often been told—more than once, indeed, by its creator. His
first or synoptic version is recorded in the hearings held in January 1921 by the subcommittee on Cable Landing Licenses of the
Senate's Interstate Commerce Committee. Young had suggested that
the invitation to testify might well be premature, but the chairman,
Senator Frank B. Kellogg of Minnesota, hastened to explain that his
subcommittee was also concerning itself with the role and future of
the wireless and wanted Young's views now.[1]

The temptation to let this early testimony of Young's speak for
itself has been resisted for two reasons: fresh and crisp as it is, it
occupies some seventy-five pages of the stenographic transcript; and
even so, it was selective and necessarily incomplete. Much, like the
following summer's cross-licensing agreement with Westinghouse, remained to be accomplished. Much that was germane remained to be
told when Young felt free to tell it, as he finally did when testifying
before the Interstate Commerce Committee of the Senate in December 1929. But that, it could almost be said, was in another country,
so sharp was the contrast in circumstance and context. Certainly the
reception given in 1929 to Young's recital of Woodrow Wilson's urgent message from the Paris peace conference about wireless and the
future, its virtual branding as apocryphal by at least one senator, and
the hitherto unpublished story of the way in which that challenge was
met and answered when the hearings resumed belong to another
chapter.[2]

Of immediate concern are the how and the why of Young's involvement in a field largely foreign to his prior interests and experience.
For the decade prior to the war, thousands of amateurs and youthful
experimenters—including Young's eldest son, C.J.—had responded to

the excitement generated by the wireless.[3] Within the family, more-over, C.J. was to enjoy an unchallenged monopoly of anything approaching scientific curiosity or engineering skill with respect to this new phenomenon.

Nor did Young display, either before or during the war, any note-worthy grasp of radio's commercial or cultural potentialities. Like most of his generation, he had felt the magic of this fantastic new device which needed no wires to transmit its electrical impulses over-seas; its larger message was simply not for him.

In 1915, to be sure, Young had met Guglielmo Marconi when the latter visited Schenectady on behalf of the company that bore his name for the express purpose of inspecting, and then contracting for the exclusive use of, the so-called Alexanderson alternator.[4] Young was aware that the same war which had twice interrupted these nego-tiations had witnessed an impressive demonstration of the virtues of this generator of high-powered alternating current, whose high-frequency waves provided the most efficient means so far developed for long-distance wireless transmission. He knew that the navy had com-mandeered for the duration all existing wireless stations, including American Marconi's station at New Brunswick, New Jersey, where first a fifty-kilowatt and later a two-hundred-kilowatt Alexanderson machine, complete with multiple-tuned antennas and other late im-provements, had been installed at GE's own expense. Like his asso-ciates, he had taken pride in the role of these machines in transmitting to Europe the President's famous "Fourteen Points," and in the in-fluence which this and subsequent messages had in accelerating the enemy's decision to sue for peace.[5]

In addition, because of his position and responsibilities, Young could not have escaped knowing that the navy, less than a year after commandeering the stations, had directed the manufacturing com-panies—with the promise that they would be held harmless—to dis-regard all patent restrictions on radio devices in meeting government orders.[6] Here, for the first time, and by government mandate, the science, the art and the industry found themselves free—and indeed constrained—to pool their patents and mobilize their technical re-sources with an eye singly focused to producing the best possible equipment in the shortest possible time. Nor was it any secret that Navy Secretary Josephus Daniels hoped to perpetuate a government monopoly in wireless communication, despite the fact that a bill to effectuate that purpose had, in January of 1919, died in committee.[7]

With the war over and the navy instructing GE to hold up work on the second of the two-hundred-kilowatt alternators it had ordered in December, the company was becoming deeply concerned to find a market for these devices, in the development of which it had by now a substantial investment. Renewed interest, as displayed in March by the Marconi companies—British and American—looking toward the purchase of some two dozen units, was therefore more than welcome, especially as the navy—already committed to the rival Poulsen Arc transmitter—was most unlikely to enter the lists.[8] Of this Young was certainly aware, and although the Marconi negotiations were principally in the hands of Anson Burchard—ably assisted by C. W. Stone and E. P. Edwards, commercial manager of the Radio Department— Young would have to pass on any new contract and so was kept informed. By early April the Marconi companies had agreed to buy twenty-five alternators at $125,000 each, and had offered $1,000,000 additional cash in lieu of royalties. GE still resisted an exclusive contract, however, and insisted on continuing royalty payments.[9]

So matters stood—or more accurately, were rapidly moving toward a climax—as that April day of 1919 approached which Young's testimony always underscored as decisive. His description fitted nicely the conference which he, Rice, Davis, Edwards, and later Charles Coffin had with Admiral William Bullard and Commander Sanford C. Hooper in New York on Tuesday, April 8. That Young later named the date as April 5 may have reflected faulty briefing, or a natural confusion resulting from the fact that April 5 was itself decisive in a crucial if negative sense. For it was on that day, with Burchard sailing for England and conferences with the managing director of British Marconi, Godfrey Isaacs, that Edwards's fresh draft of a "final" proposal on royalty payments was interrupted by a phone call from Commander Hooper of the U.S. Navy, urging GE not to close with Marconi until representatives of the navy could confer with GE's top officials.[10]

This call had an interesting background and was to have a still more interesting sequel, both involving Young. Under the date of February 25, Admiral R. S. Griffin of the navy's Engineering Bureau had written GE requesting the "professional services of your research engineer, Mr. E. F. Alexanderson, to visit the naval radio station, Sayville, Long Island, to make a report on the speed control system for the high frequency alternator installed at that station." Coinciding as it did with resumption of the Marconi negotiations and other matters on which Alexanderson was working, this postwar request was decidedly irksome to Schenectady; and when Young urged patience and cooperation, Davis and Edwards, together with Francis Pratt— Rice's onetime assistant and now a vice-president—descended on him in protest. Evidently Young found this trio persuasive, for the reply he suggested that Pratt draft for him was promptly signed and sent unchanged.[11]

Thus Pratt's draft became Young's letter of March 29, addressed in Admiral Griffin's absence to another Yorker, Franklin D. Roosevelt, then assistant secretary of the navy. After quoting Griffin's request and rehearsing GE's cordial wartime relations with the navy, Young went on to explain the status of the current and highly promising negotiations with the Marconi companies. In conclusion, he suggested the wisdom of an early opportunity "to talk this situation over fully for the purpose of arriving at a mutually satisfactory understanding, whereby we would be in a position to furnish such equipment and engineering advice to the Navy as may be required from us, and at the same time to retain a reasonable protection for the commercial interests of the General Electric Company." Young added that he and his associates would be "pleased to go to Washington to discuss this matter with you and others of the Navy personnel who are immediately interested."[12]

Clearly it was Young's letter, on which Roosevelt had evidently consulted Hooper, and possibly Admiral Bullard—newly returned from Paris to assume direction of Naval Communications—that precipitated Hooper's telephone call to Edwards on Saturday, April 5. On Friday, April 4, Secretary Roosevelt had already replied to Young expressing his appreciation for the "spirit of your letter of March 29," and explicitly requesting that "before reaching any final agreement with the Marconi companies, you confer with representatives of the department," naming as the time and place 10:00 A.M., Friday, April 11, at the Navy Department in Washington.[13] Evidently this failed to satisfy the sense of urgency which Young's letter had instilled in Bullard and Hooper, who felt that it was already the eleventh hour.

Whether or not Young had heard from Edwards of Hooper's Saturday call, it was not until Monday morning, April 7, when Roosevelt's letter reached his office, that he went into action. At once Young wrote Stone at the New York office a hand-delivered note asking him to see that the Marconi negotiations were "suspended until after Friday." He was also in touch with Edwards, asking him to withhold—and subsequently to destroy—his unmailed "final" proposals, dated April 7, to the Marconi people.[14] By or through whom the conference with Admiral Bullard and Commander Hooper was arranged for the following day is no part of any record the authors have discovered, nor is it of any discernible importance. What matters is the conference itself and the effect it was to have on the future—Owen Young's not least.

ii

It is clear from all of Young's subsequent testimony that the conception of RCA dates from this Tuesday session in New York, which took the place of the Washington meeting Roosevelt had scheduled for the following Friday.[15] If years were to pass before Young felt free to mention President Wilson's plea from Paris, he never did allude to the Roosevelt correspondence and its arresting impact on negotiations in progress. It is as if the drama of this meeting and its consequences for him made all that had gone before of no further importance.

What made it, then, so memorable? The most nearly contemporaneous account by a participant is set forth in a long letter to Young dated June 30, 1919, and written—quite possibly at Young's prompting—by his respected colleague A. G. Davis. Since in his 1921 testimony Young drew heavily on this record (except that he confused the date, which Davis stated correctly), the relevant paragraphs have a double interest. Wrote Davis:

On Tuesday, April 8, 1919, Admiral Bullard and Commander Hooper met Mr. Rice, you, Mr. Stone of the General Company, Mr. Edwards and myself, in our New York office.

At this meeting Admiral Bullard explained to us the importance to American interests and to the League of Nations of free and cheap communication between Nations and told us that if at this critical period in the history of radio we sold to the American or British Marconi Companies the Alexanderson machines they wanted and our radio system, which he frankly said was the best in the world and the only system capable of full competition with the cables, we would fix indefinitely in a concern dominated by the British Government a monopoly of international radio communication. He represented to us that the British interests now dominated cable communication and the manufacture of ocean cable, and dwelt on the dangers to the interests of the United States which would result from British monopoly of all communications.

He strongly urged the officers of the General Company as patriotic Americans, to decline to sell these machines to either Marconi Company, and suggested that the Navy Department would be sympathetic with the formation by the General Company and other clearly American interests of an American-owned, world-wide, radio-operating company, which would be strong enough to deal with the Marconi Companies as an equal.

He also suggested that the Navy Department owned valuable wireless patent rights and desired licenses and releases under the radio patent rights of the General Company.

The War Department as well as the Navy Department has used during the war quantities of apparatus involving inventions of the General Company. The Patent Board has asked the General Company to submit a statement of any claim which it has against the Government in this respect. Admiral Bullard suggested that if full licenses for Government work and releases to the Government could be obtained the Government would be willing to turn over to the American Corporation above referred to extensive rights under Government patents and generally that the Government would cooperate in assisting the New Company to obtain concessions and otherwise.

The interest of the General Company up to that time in the radio business was purely the interest of a manufacturer which had invented and developed certain apparatus which it desired to sell at a profit.

The Marconi Companies were the largest and in fact substantially the only potential customer for this apparatus.

But the Officers and Directors of the General Company were unwilling to deal with this situation in any manner which the Navy Department might regard as unpatriotic; I was instructed to go to Washington to work out with the Navy Department a contract along the lines of Admiral Bullard's suggestions. You wrote Mr. Nally stopping the Marconi negotiations.[16]

So, the conference had indeed ended on a note of decisive action. In later years, relaxing in his library and fussing with his pipe, after a ten-hour day of office appointments, phone calls and meetings—with dictation filling any gaps—Young liked to remark that, being essentially lazy, he never did a lick of work he could avoid, or, better still, get somebody else to do. What, then, was so compelling about Admiral Bullard's plea as to persuade him to take on this adventure into the unknown in addition to an already sufficiently taxing job? Or why didn't he get somebody else to do it?

The answer to the latter question is clear: from the moment that, Coffin concurring, it was decided to go ahead, it was the evident consensus that the ball was Young's to run with. Others would make such "interference" as they could. As for the prior question, Young's experience as a lawyer had accustomed him to the task of mastering in short order the complex concerns of a new client. He was only forty-four, his wartime role had been one of unremitting work and no glamour, and the prospect of emerging as the architect of a new American company, strong enough to compete on equal terms with the British-dominated cables, undoubtedly exerted a powerful appeal. Even before the conference was over, his mind was busily identifying and measuring some of the building blocks which he would have to fit together: the putative contract with the navy; the radically different deal with the two Marconi companies; a mobilization of technical resources, beginning with patents, as nearly parallel to the navy's wartime achievement as the law might allow in time of peace; an effective means to approach and deal with South America, China and

Japan as well as Europe. And all this starting, as it were, from scratch, except for the Alexanderson alternator, which would still for GE be a major bargaining counter.[17]

Whether these influences alone would have been sufficiently potent to stir Young to action is one of those teasing questions to which there can be no final answer. As far as the world knew then, and for some years to come, they had been sufficient, and that impression could have done Young no harm.

The fact remains that other influences were present—influences of which none of the original participants save Young, Coffin and Bullard could be aware—and for Young these could only have been decisive. Admiral Bullard, as Young recalled years later, had "explained President Wilson's part in the affair not in the open conference but privately. . . . At the moment there was uncertainty as to what action the directors might take." It was then that Bullard had called him aside and imparted to him "as a state secret" the President's concern to checkmate British domination of world communications and his personal appeal for Young's cooperation toward that end. It was then that Young went next door to brief Coffin—the only person except his wife to whom he confided the message—following which Coffin joined the meeting and the decision to proceed was made. As Young saw it, the fact that "for diplomatic reasons the head of the nation could not openly show his hand in the matter" was only less obvious than the obligation he shared with Bullard to respect it.[18]

The indelible impression this message made on Young is evident in the relish with which he recounted it as soon as he felt free to do so, well after the day when presidential messages held any novelty for him. Although the authors doubt that he knew President Wilson personally, as he was to know all of his successors from Coolidge to Eisenhower, his ingrained respect for the office was matched in this instance by increasing admiration for the man. If with the years, embellishments appeared in his accounts—Young was not one to let a story suffer in the retelling—the substance never varied. Here was the embattled President, in Paris, struggling to save his League of Nations and at least some vestiges of his Fourteen Points from emasculation at the hands of Lloyd George and Clemenceau, but nevertheless giving realistic attention to such basic factors affecting America's postwar parity with Britain as petroleum, international transportation and world communications. With our (then) dominant position in oil matched by Britain's dominance in shipping, a roughly equal posture clearly required an American initiative in wireless development strong enough to challenge Britain's control of cables. Never mind who had told Wilson that Owen Young was the man to take such an initiative; the President's appeal had been delivered and it was sufficient.[19]

iii

Young's design for RCA was partly intuitive and partly pragmatic: the building blocks he was continuing to identify as essential to the kind of structure he had in view were often hard to come by. The contract with the navy, Davis's first assignment, looked promising enough as long as he had to clear it only with Admiral Bullard and Assistant Secretary Roosevelt, but in answer to a Roosevelt message, Secretary Daniels cabled from Paris that it would have to await his return. A conference in his office on May 23, attended by Roosevelt and Young as well as Davis, found the secretary still wedded to his hopes for a naval radio monopoly; should Congress reject that plan and authorize him to proceed with the proposed contract, he would do so. The rejection but not the authorization ensuing, hopes for the contract finally petered out.[20]

In the meantime Young was finding himself engaged in a major exercise in intercorporate and international diplomacy, in which the effectiveness of a move in one segment was typically dependent on the outcome of others. There was little use, for example, in approaching the telephone company for an exchange of patent rights until RCA was something more than a gleam in the eye. The new company could not begin to operate, however liberal its charter (which was yet to be secured), unless and until American Marconi could be induced to turn over its wireless stations, patents and other working assets in exchange for a stock interest in RCA, in an amount to be negotiated. Since American Marconi was being invited virtually to lose its corporate identity, it was hardly surprising that its initial response was not enthusiastic; as the pressure was applied (and it was), American Marconi reluctantly came around, subject always to the proviso that GE succeed in purchasing the entire stock interest of the parent, or British, company in its American subsidiary. And that, as Davis and Young soon discovered, was to take some doing, especially since the transaction could be of little use without comprehensive cross-licensing and traffic agreements.[21]

As for the U.S. government, the President was not to return from Paris until July, and then only to find himself locked in the struggle which was to end in rejection of his League of Nations by an effective minority in the Senate and the paralyzing illness which interrupted his last-ditch effort to carry his appeal to the people. Young duly reported every important move that he was making to the secretary of the navy and, where it was appropriate, to the attorney general, but a confused and leaderless government did little or nothing to help.[22] Indeed, the American Marconi stations, like all the rest, were still in the navy's hands and were to remain there until the last day of February 1920. And so new was the phenomenon of wireless, the Congress had done little or nothing to protect the limited number of wavelengths available from the chaos of free use and constant interference.[23]

In such circumstances, it is doubtful that Young's "diplomatic trump card," as the historian of broadcasting in the United States, Eric Barnouw, describes the President's message, would have done him much good, even if he had been free to play it. Without it, moreover, Young had forces working for him that reflected the timeliness and broad appeal of his objective which, totally ignoring broadcasting, was simply "an American-dominated system of world communication."

"This objective," in Barnouw's percipient words, "could be viewed in a variety of ways; in idealistic terms—*let nation speak to nation;* in business terms—*we can undersell the cables;* in patriotic terms— *we need it.* With such a background of forces working for him," Barnouw declares, "Young negotiated deftly and with mounting success."[24]

Barnouw's statement is hard to fault, except as it masks the endless complications these negotiations entailed. To spell these out in detail here would obviously profit no one; as for the nexus of ensuing contracts and contingent agreements, the curious are referred to the Federal Trade Commission's *Report on the Radio Industry* of December 1, 1923, where they occupy upwards of two hundred pages of the appendix. For the most part these contracts were actually worked out by others—Young was able to muster an extremely able supporting cast—but all drafts had to meet his penetrating eye and more than once his intervention was determining.[25]

iv

Since effective agreement with the Marconi companies was the prime requisite of the whole design, key points in the negotiations with them may serve to illustrate the lot—as well as Young's own *modus operandi.* For a man so new to the field that his handwritten notes on the Bullard-Hooper conference simply identify, with their respective owners, the principal stations, Atlantic and Pacific, with which he might find himself concerned, Young learned fast.

First, of course, there was the business of briefing Burchard on developments since his sailing, and before he met with Isaacs of British Marconi; Rice took care of this in a coded message sent to the British Thomson-Houston Company. Young also arranged with Dwight Morrow, now a GE director, for Burchard to call at Morgan Grenfell, with whose officers J. P. Morgan and Company had their own lines of communication. Burchard quickly got the picture; by May 17 he was writing Young from Paris to remind him of all that Britain's wartime censorship of cables had yielded of useful and carefully filed commercial information and of the "strong feeling here" that Britain's control of cables would now be used to continue that practice. "This emphasizes," Burchard concluded, "the importance to any nation having large foreign commercial interests of having under its control a system of telegraphic communication. . . ."[26]

Young's appetite needed no such whetting. If, for the month following April 8, he was largely waiting on Washington, he had nonetheless launched various inquiries on American Marconi's financial standing, profits and net worth, the character and value of their principal patents and the quality of their officers and staff. Reports, some brief, some (from the lawyers) voluminous, began to reach his desk.

On May 12 he had a long luncheon conversation at the Bankers Club with E. J. Nally, American Marconi's rotund but able vice-president. Young was at pains to explain GE's decision not to let control of the alternators pass to foreign hands and their sense of the necessity of deferring to Washington on such a matter "even though the people who urged us not to sell . . . have no alternative policy which they can definitely carry out." Nally answered that the navy seemed to be playing a double game; on the one hand, urging GE not to let the British control the alternators, however indirectly, and on the other hand, promoting a sale to Marconi of the Poulsen Arc system. Nally's inquiries in Washington concerning this and other questions had evoked, he said, less than satisfactory answers. His experience in cabling New York of his recent success in broadening the rights his company already enjoyed in the Argentine had convinced him that the cables were by no means inviolate, even in the United States; it was quickly obvious, he said, that his message had been leaked to the Poulsen people.[27]

Young let Nally do most of the talking. After a long and knowledgeable—if *ex parte*—disquisition on the Marconi company's patents,

Nally partially disclosed his hand. What, he asked, would Washington's attitude be if GE were to form a new company and the British interest in American Marconi were to be "purchased by a syndicate" and sold to the new company? "I can not say," Young answered, "but I will say this, Mr. Nally: the American Marconi interests are greatly menaced because of the English holdings in the Company and the attitude of the Government toward such holdings. . . ." As for GE, "I recognize the right of the Government to stop us from negotiating with you, but I am almost inclined not to recognize their right to force us into competition with you."[28]

This reciprocal partial disclosure had its effect: Nally promised to talk with Isaacs about the advisability of the parent company's disposing of its American Marconi holdings. On meeting Young a week later, Nally said that he had cabled Isaacs confirming earlier intelligence of Washington's action to keep U.S. control of the alternator, and requesting Isaacs's presence here, which was now promised for June 20. To Young's rejoinder that it would not be possible to mark time for another month, Nally replied that "he could not expect that." Young's own memorandum of this meeting indicates his understanding that Nally's board was favorably disposed toward cooperation with GE in working out a program acceptable to Washington and recognized that this "would probably mean the necessity of [GE's] taking over the interests of the British Marconi Company" in American Marconi.[29]

During this conference Hooper called to ask Young to attend the May 23 conference with Secretary Daniels. Young agreed and so informed Nally. When negotiations resumed on June 2 Nally pressed Young to let him see a copy of the proposed contract with the navy; Young replied that he had sought permission to do so and found Hooper and Bullard sympathetic but Daniels not immediately available and Roosevelt apparently unwilling to act for his chief. Young expressed sympathy for the reluctance of Nally's directors to make commitments, as it were, in the dark; he offered to try to persuade Roosevelt to give his consent or, alternatively, to work out with Nally the "basis upon which a trade could be made if it were feasible for the Marconi Company [American] to become a participant in the new company."[30]

After Young had answered to Nally's satisfaction specific questions about the contract, Nally at last broached the question which, as Young knew, had been troubling him most. "Mr. Young," he said, "of course I have devoted . . . my life . . . to the wireless art and before entering into any kind of [new] arrangement, it is quite necessary to know what position our organization would assume . . . how we are going to be taken care of."

Young was ready with his answer. "I assume," he said, "that if an arrangement is made for the [American] Marconi Company to participate, . . . their present organization would do the operating and the General Electric Company would do the manufacturing." Certainly, he continued, GE was "best fitted to do the manufacturing. As far as operating is concerned, we know nothing about it and we ought to take advantage of your experience."[31] One Marconi official whose experience, ambition, and imaginative grasp of radio's future were thus to become a part of RCA was its commercial manager, young David Sarnoff. At this point, however, Young was not concerning himself with the names and numbers of the players, much less with anything so nebulous as broadcasting.

So that was that. The two men parted after quickly agreeing that the patent situation should be so cleared up as to assure, as Young put it, "control of as many patents as there is a possibility of our owning or using." Obstacles of great complexity remained to be surmounted but they were inherent and of neither party's making. Dating from this meeting, Young found Nally to be an eminently loyal and indefatigable ally in persuading first his board and then—in company with Davis—his British chieftain, Godfrey Isaacs, of GE's good faith and of the vast potentialities he discerned in the proposed new Radio Corporation.

June 12 found Nally actually completing his own draft of a proposed contract, which Davis forwarded to Young a few days later. On the thirteenth, Davis lunched with Nally and with American Marconi's able counsel, the junior partner, L.F.H. Betts, of Sheffield and Betts; Young joined them after luncheon. James R. Sheffield, the senior partner, was himself a director of American Marconi, whose president, John W. Griggs, sometime governor of New Jersey and a former U.S. attorney general, had left executive direction of the company pretty much in Nally's hands. Davis now reported that Sheffield, Betts and Griggs seemed ready to proceed so long as the new company was not to be dominated by any one interest. Young had no intention that it should be, though it would take time to interest others. Since Nally believed that the Radio Corporation (as it was coming to be called) would need at least a dozen alternators, to be paid for in its own preferred stock, Young asked Edwards—at Davis's prompting—for estimates of current manufacturing costs on the improved machine as well as total development expense. He also arranged for

GE's controller, C. E. Patterson, to review American Marconi's earnings and balance sheet with a view to determining the value of its assets "on a going concern basis"; Patterson's estimate of July 1 confirmed Nally's own figure of twelve million dollars.[32]

Young was getting ready to make a trade. His growing awareness of what international wireless communication involved as a business proposition is reflected in the two pages of notes he made on his June 30 meeting with Nally and Betts. Certainly he was asking the right questions: what key stations complemented each other; what territorial rights American Marconi enjoyed vis-à-vis the British in respect of international traffic and especially of patent arrangements; which companies owned what shares of the so-called Pan-American (or Latin America) Company; how to protect the United States against British transmission via Canada.[33]

The contract, on which so many people had worked and were to work, was beginning to take shape. By Saturday, July 12, a draft agreement involving GE and its international subsidiary, IGE, as well as American Marconi and the proposed new Radio Corporation, was ready. Significantly, it stipulated that representatives of GE and American Marconi would endeavor to purchase for GE all American Marconi shares held by the British company. Incidentally, this draft still took into account the possibility of a contract with the navy, but this contingency had now become so remote that with due notice to Secretary Daniels it was eliminated in the revisions made during the ensuing week.[34]

Other contingencies, however, were inherent and so refused to go away. The contracting parties were ready to cancel wartime claims each held against the other, but only if and when the Radio Corporation became an operative reality. This in turn depended on the prior consenting vote of American Marconi's shareholders, of which British Marconi was easily the largest. Would the latter sell its 18 percent interest to GE, and then urge other foreign shareholders to vote with GE in favor of the "merger"? The answer to these questions promised to be determining, especially in the light of opinion rendered by special counsel on July 22, when the contract was virtually complete, that "the transaction could be successfully assailed by a shareholder of the [American] Marconi Company."[35]

The outcome was a tripartite series of contracts, two of which were duly signed and executed by Young and Nally on July 25. The first, mutually canceling all outstanding claims against the other party, was to become effective only if the Radio Corporation were chartered prior to January 1, 1920; in the meantime counsel was to hold it in escrow. The second recorded the agreement of both parties with respect to the substance of the third or "main agreement," execution of which was mutually assured as soon as the consent in writing and the vote of a majority of the stockholders of American Marconi had been secured. Toward that end, American Marconi pledged its continuing best efforts.

As for the "main agreement," it recited first GE's undertaking to "cause to be formed . . . a corporation organized under the laws of Delaware . . . (herein called the Radio Corporation) which shall have authorized . . . 2,500,000 shares" of 7 percent preferred stock, par value $10, and "3,000,000 shares of common stock without par value"—soon changed to 5,000,000 of each, with the preferred having a $5 par value.[36] It went on to recite the patent rights to radio devices, and especially the exclusive rights to market the same, which GE and IGE, as owners and manufacturers, contracted to assign to the new company if and when formed; the plan for the latter to purchase a dozen alternators from GE and, far more important, to "acquire all assets of the [American] Marconi Company [except for certain claims designated as "reserved assets"], including its subsidiary companies" and "three-eighths of the stock of the Pan American Wireless Telegraph & Telephone Company, a Delaware Corporation"; GE's prospective purchase of the British company's 364,826 shares and all related rights in American Marconi, with the sums to be earmarked for that purpose and certain others; the right to terminate the agreement at either party's option on or before January 1, 1920, "if a satisfactory arrangement [with British Marconi] be not promptly reached"; and, finally, the respective number of preferred shares (for cash or other tangible assets) and common shares (for patents and goodwill) in the new company to be issued to each contracting party.[37]

This last item, representing at once an evaluation of each party's contribution to and prospective stake in the new company, was for Young supremely important. Profoundly distrusting a trade which left either contracting party feeling genuinely injured, he had been conservative in limiting GE's preferred allocation to 235,174 shares—plus of course its 2,000,000 of common. He had also been scrupulous in applying the whip of the government's antagonism toward the Marconi interests as an inducement to negotiate rather than as a means for driving a sharp bargain. Obviously the goodwill of the Marconi people was not to be valued at the traditional GE figure of one dollar; it was indispensable, as an active agent to the consummation of the deal.

Thus if transfer of the Marconi assets involved no cash, the Radio

Corporation stock to be issued in exchange therefor must reflect fair value beyond all question. Its fairness is suggested, *prima facie*, by analysis of the Marconi Company's balance sheet for June 30, 1919. As against total assets before depreciation of $13,840,000, current liabilities and stated reserves for depreciation were $1,710,000, leaving net assets of $12,130,000. Some $2,130,000 of this total represented patents and goodwill, leaving $10,000,000 of tangible assets, and these included the plant at Aldene, New Jersey, which G E was given the right to buy for $500,000. Thus, Marconi's tangible assets were fully, even generously, covered by the stipulated issue of $10,000,000 par value of Radio preferred, with intangibles cared for by two million shares of no-par common.[38] More significant was the test of acceptability: when Marconi stockholders came to vote on the recommended trade, minor threats of opposition were quickly overwhelmed in a ground swell of approval.[39] Evidently they had no fears about the ultimate test; namely, R C A's future earning capacity.

v

But this is getting ahead of the story. Before such a vote could be taken much remained to be done and, with the departure of Nally and Davis on the *Aquitania* three days after the signing of the July 25 agreements with American Marconi, the scene shifts to the British company's headquarters in London. Isaacs's promised visit of June 20 had never materialized and it was now up to this intrepid pair to smoke him out. With Burchard and Gerard Swope already abroad on I G E business, Young wisely chose to stay at home with his wife and infant son, holding himself in reserve against the unforeseen.

Davis, in the meantime, was seeking Young's advice at every stage of his arduous negotiations. For his part, Young forwarded information as requested and sometimes offered tactical suggestions. Indeed, the volume of coded cables exchanged during the month of August 1919 on behalf of this effort to establish transoceanic wireless must have sweetened rather substantially the short-run profits of the cable companies. Only one—Young to Davis of August 22—is cited here, and because it illuminates at once Young's approach and the scope and complexity of the issues at stake, it is quoted in full:

Your long cables not entirely clear result of transmission errors stop Our understanding is One New Radio Corporation has exclusive rights in United States territory and mandatories stop Two British Marconi has exclusive rights British Empire and mandatories except special agreement

will be made restricting Canadian stations to Canadian business and giving new radio corporation opportunity to acquire substantial interest
in Canadian company if it so desires stop Three satisfactory contracts
for exchange of business will be made between all present or future
stations of both companies in their exclusive territory stop Four all
South American transoceanic rights to be conveyed to New South American
company and new radio corporation will own majority of its stock and
operate stations stop Limitation Brazilian rights not clear to us stop Regard
full Brazilian rights very important stop Five New radio corporation will
have full licenses for Central America Mexico and West Indies stop This
is essential to trade with [United] Fruit Company and licenses should be
exclusive if possible stop Six New radio corporation will have such Chinese
rights as will enable it to control absolutely Chinese-American communications stop Seven Rest of the world will be neutral territory in which each
company licenses the other on the understanding that neither has already
acquired exclusive rights in any neutral country stop This license will be
subject to our foreign contracts stop Eight New radio corporation will
acquire interest British Marconi in Tuckerton [Long Island] station and
will have British Marconi cooperate in obtaining satisfactory contract French
Company for exchange of American business stop Ten Net cost to new
radio corporation of all of the above except interest in Tuckerton is approximately three million dollars ($3,000,000) stop On these understandings
would approve trade if satisfactory to Burchard and you but we think
British Thomson Houston should have substantial interest in Wireless manufacturing business.[40]

Fortunately Davis, as well as Swope and Burchard, was aware of
the British Thomson-Houston Company's stake in the proceedings as
the holder of GE's manufacturing and patent rights in Great Britain;
his consultations with Howard Levis and Gray, respectively president
and counsel of that company, were frequent and mutually helpful, as
Young was confident they would be.

Young was sanguine in part because he trusted Davis, in part because he could not believe that Godfrey Isaacs, whose dynamic direction of British Marconi had earned him at long last the grudging
recognition of his peers, could fail to see the proposed contract as one
in which he had much to gain and little to lose. Of what good to him
or to Britain was a controlling interest in an American subsidiary
which had no future precisely because of that control? On the other
hand GE was offering not only to buy out the British investment but
also to place its engineering and financial resources behind a new
American company with which British Marconi would be sharing
increasingly valuable reciprocal rights to patents as well as traffic. The
alternators were a case in point: given an American company with

rights to their use, it became a matter of interest to the U.S. government, as well as to GE, to see that British stations with which this company wished to exchange messages were similarly equipped. As for South America and the Far East, an awakened America was likely to prove more helpful as partner than as antagonist. And with traffic still largely undeveloped, competition here could only be disastrous.[41]

Young's reckoning was largely justified by the contracts, dated September 5, which Davis brought home, or rather sent, in the first instance, by Nally. They substantially reflected the understandings set forth in Young's cable of August 22. Isaacs had jibbed, to be sure, at the sale of their 365,000 American Marconi shares at par, and even when "additional considerations" lifted the price, in effect, by slightly more than a dollar a share, it was stipulated that the sale should be consummated only as the American Marconi contracts became effective; in short, as RCA was actually chartered. In the meantime, the U.S. government consenting, the British company's proxies would go to American Marconi to be voted for the "merger." All of this added up, of course, to another series of contingent agreements, the "principal agreement" taking effect only as it could be executed by a still nonexistent Radio Corporation.[42]

But Young was satisfied. Giving him much of the credit for the outcome, Davis—for whom it had been a grueling month—never ceased to be grateful for his unfailing support. If Young had urged him on occasion to consult with Burchard or Swope on this or that sticky point, he did not press matters when Davis complained that time was short and they were not available; indeed, Young later explained to Davis that his primary concern had been to assure these colleagues' full understanding and support. On one occasion when Burchard had made a proposal which Davis found wholly unacceptable, Young took Burchard gently but firmly off his back.[43] If his own replies to Davis's long cables could be explicit and comprehensive in defining what he hoped to see achieved, his views were more often put forward as "suggestions for your consideration," and on September 2 he was at pains to assure Davis that "our cables are not intended to limit your authority." Once the contracts were *faits accomplis,* moreover, he urged Burchard to send Davis his congratulations and assurances. Young's own cable to Davis, sent after a conference with Nally, said that he was "very much pleased with your London trade. It was an excellent piece of work and we will try to put our end through here."[44]

And so they went to work on "our end." Nally, with some help from Griggs, and with Davis, Betts and Young reviewing his drafts, developed the circular which was to assure a maximum stockholder vote for the merger, and did. Because of his Marconi connections, Nally was under some suspicion in Washington, but Isaacs had said he could not urge the other foreign shareholders to support the merger unless Nally were to head the new company—as indeed he already had Young's assurance that he would. In the event, as already noted, the affirmative vote of American Marconi stockholders, meeting on November 20, 1919, was virtually unanimous.

On the same day, the newly chartered Radio Corporation of America held its first stockholders' meeting, elected eight directors, and executed the "main agreements." Nally was duly named president and, with an eye to Washington, Young agreed to serve—at least temporarily—as chairman. The Marconi interest was represented on the new board by Griggs, Sheffield, Edward W. Harden (of Colgate and Company) and, of course, Nally. In addition to Young, the GE directors were Rice, Gordon Abbott and the redoubtable A. G. Davis—who on his return had also been elected a vice-president of General Electric.[45]

As the RCA charter had duly restricted alien voting rights to 20 percent of the total stock issue, so the bylaws now provided for the U.S. government to designate an official observer to sit with the board, having a voice but not a vote. In January of 1920, Admiral Bullard was so designated, on nomination of the acting secretary of the navy and with President Wilson's signed approval.[46]

Subject only to return of its high-powered stations by the navy, Young's new company was ready for business. On March 1, 1920, the effective date of such return, the Radio Corporation of America transmitted its first commercial wireless message to Great Britain. According to the Federal Trade Commission report a few years later, "cable rates between New York and Great Britain had for more than 30 years remained unchanged at 25 cents per word. . . . The rate charged [initially] by the Radio Corporation was 17 cents . . . on January 1, 1921, increased to 18 cents [and] on April 15, 1923, . . . to 20. . . ." Five days later "competitive cable companies reduced their rates . . . to 20 cents per word."[47]

With the opening of this service under American auspices, less than a year after Admiral Bullard's delivery of the President's message from Paris, Young could feel that a fair part of his mission had been accomplished. True, much remained to be done, especially in the mobilization of patents. Toward that end, and with such help as Young was free to give, GE and AT&T had been negotiating since the first of the year; but well before that time Young had found himself involved—in part at the President's request—in negotiations of a very different order. Wireless was important to the national interest, but so was industrial peace.

Chapter 12

Public Business:
A Bill of Rights for Labor

ROBLEMS which surfaced after the armistice may have been
less lethal than those of open warfare, but, as Wilson had discovered at Paris, they could be harder to get at. Preoccupied as
he was with the peace treaty and the League of Nations, the President
was to find on returning to Washington in July of 1919 that other
problems too were demanding and elusive: inflation, for example, and
labor unrest. And these two problems were closely related—to each
other and to the war.

By the fall of 1917, workers were bitterly complaining—and sometimes with reason—that wages had not kept pace with the rise in
living costs. Since strikes and lockouts posed intolerable threats to
war production, the secretary of labor, William B. Wilson, had
promptly set up the War Labor Conference Board, with instructions
to draw up a national code governing labor-management disputes for
the duration. Five employer representatives were chosen by the National Industrial Conference Board, five representatives by the American Federation of Labor; Frank P. Walsh of Montana and former
President William Howard Taft were appointed joint chairmen.[1]

By spring the code was ready, and on the first anniversary of the
U.S. declaration of war, April 8, 1918, a presidential proclamation declared its provisions now in force and set up the National War Labor
Board (identical in membership to the drafting group) to see to its en-
forcement. This the board proceeded to do in no uncertain fashion,
bearing down severely but impartially on all recalcitrants, employer
or employed.[2] But important as this was to the war effort, it was the
code itself—underwriting at a stroke "rights" which labor leaders had
asserted long and in vain—that was to have the more far-reaching influence.

True, the code was to apply for the duration only and, for that
period, the workers affected must waive the right to strike. In the

meantime, however, these same workers were assured protection against the hated "yellow dog contract" (join the union and you're fired) and promised a great deal besides—including, in principle at least, a "living wage." Also, the code "recognized and affirmed . . . the right to unionize and bargain collectively" as something "not to be denied, abridged or interfered with in any manner whatsoever." While employers could also associate to bargain collectively, they "must not discharge workers for union membership nor legitimate trade union activities." Existing union shops were to be continued, and where shops included both union and nonunion workers, the organization of a closed shop—albeit by noncoercive methods—was not precluded. Maximum production in all war industries was of course the goal—to be pursued, however, with due regard for the workers' health and safety. While wages and hours—including a minimum wage—were to take account of local conditions, it was stipulated unconditionally that "women doing men's work shall receive the same wages as do men."[3]

It was against this background that, following the armistice of November 11, 1918, labor and capital prepared for a showdown. In labor's view, the no-strike pledge had ceased to be operative, even though no peace treaty had been signed; and most employers, fearful of the unions, were impatient to recover their "war-damaged" prerogatives. The pendulum was swinging away from all these emergency concessions to labor, and liberal employers—Young among them—feared that its swing would be excessive, and dangerously so. Labor, they argued, could hardly be expected to give up its hard-won gains without a struggle: they had come to be regarded as rights, and why not? Surely some of these gains should now be so recognized, or labor would quickly be exercising its temporarily suspended right to strike.[4]

And so it did. In General Electric, trouble started in Erie, where some 20 to 25 percent of the men walked out, and soon spread to Schenectady, Fort Wayne and Lynn. Meeting in New York on Tuesday, January 7, 1919,[5] the plant managers told Young that it was just the usual, wages and hours; but he was skeptical enough to give his assistant, John Elwood, a special assignment: visit the plants, talk with the men, study their grievances and give him the lowdown. Elwood's report, as abridged by Ida Tarbell, reads as follows:

1. The workmen feel that the foremen are inhuman beings who lack any sense of what the personal touch in business means.
2. The men desire to have some system of profit sharing or stock pur-

chase plan inaugurated so as to take advantage of the thrift instinct instilled during the Liberty Loan campaign.

3. They desire some sort of a representative plan.

4. They desire to have the welfare work increased so that it will be evident that the Company is taking a personal interest in them inside as well as outside of the plant.

5. They desire to have what might be called a "Manager of Man Power."

6. They desire to have thorough education and instruction—an opportunity for promotion and scientific selection of men and jobs.[6]

Helpful as far as it went, Elwood's report served to whet Young's appetite for more. The problem was how to secure it. If the men were to talk freely, any investigator would need credentials that placed him above suspicion; no management "stooge" could hope to win their confidence. Yet management's confidence in the investigator's integrity and objectivity was equally essential.

By early March, Young and Elwood had found their man and launched him on what was to be a two-month investigation of workers' gripes and attitudes—toward the company and each other—at Schenectady, Lynn, Pittsfield, Erie and Fort Wayne. The investigator, an author, editor and Chatauqua lecturer with a deep concern for labor and its problems, was also to analyze the deficiencies of management as he saw them—in the several plants and overall—in coping with the workers' grievances, actual and alleged. As an experienced reporter, now planning a series of labor studies for *McClure's Magazine*, Atherton Brownell could expect a cordial reception in all quarters—especially if he began (as he did) by consulting the local papers.

The immediate outcome was a seventy-five-page report—later slightly compressed but in no sense emasculated—which pulled no punches. It reached Young and Elwood in the thick of their Marconi negotiations, but it made a profound impression on them both. In the light of Young's own attitudes and predilections, its second paragraph leaves one wondering whether he himself had originally inspired it, or was rather to find it a source book for his later pronouncements. "General Electric," wrote Brownell,

. . . is spending eight or ten millions of dollars annually to maintain a great scientific research laboratory . . . to search out the secrets of Nature. It employs no psychologists to study the mental attitudes of its men. It employs the greatest engineers available to install and keep in a state of the highest efficiency all of the machinery in its several plants. It employs no specialized human nature engineers [sic] to keep its human machinery frictionless.

Proceeding to document his assertion that although "in all other branches of its activities the work of the company, wherever performed, is coordinated, there is no coordination between the several plants in the . . . vital matter of industrial relations," the investigator reported a strong sense of solidarity among the workers generally, however local conditions might vary. His proposed solution was to establish "an executive department of the corporation under a Director of Industrial Relations." But because any such step would necessarily be experimental if it was to command the confidence of men and management alike, he suggested as a preliminary move the creation of a "Joint Board of Men and Management," representative of all the plants; five appointees of management would be matched by five members elected by the men, and all ten would choose an eleventh, "of national prestige and reputation," who would mediate and presumably resolve any deadlock.[7]

While these conclusions were not submitted lightly, Young was far more interested in the author's spirit of approach and in the facts he had come up with than in any specific recommendations. But if no director of industrial relations was to be appointed during Young's long tenure at GE, the far-reaching influence of Brownell's findings on his own approach to labor's problems—at GE or nationwide—would be apparent before the year was over, and for many years thereafter.[8]

At the moment, Young's primary concern was to understand why the old-time skilled workers seemed no less restless and unhappy than the others. *Their* views, if properly interpreted, might impress his superiors sufficiently to encourage remedial action, and here the study was most helpful. Thus, finding that at Erie, union members were being dismissed on flimsy pretexts, Young protested to the board of directors that this was a "denial of a man's constitutional right of association." In the final settlement of the strike, he saw to it that the strikers suffered no penalty—not even the usual forfeiture of seniority and pension rights. Not having denied their right to strike, he said, the company was in no position to penalize them for having exercised that right.[9]

From the outset, Young found himself at odds with the majority of the employers, who were determined to break the power of the unions, once and for all, by insistence upon a completely nonunion shop. (They even called this an "open shop" and dubbed their program the "American plan.") But Young was not alone. A minority, led by John D. Rockefeller, Jr., was equally determined that more enlightened views prevail. At the least, they felt, management had responsibilities toward its employees which dictated policies consciously directed toward their greater security and welfare. After all, workers were people and entitled to something more than their hire. Surely welfare capitalism (as it came to be called) was better for all concerned than mere belligerency.[10]

Thus at about the time of Admiral Bullard's call in the spring of 1919, Young was joining A. C. Bedford, of Standard Oil, in creating the so-called Special Conference Committee as a forum for discussing and developing enlightened labor policies. Their mentor was the same Mackenzie King—a future prime minister of Canada—who had convinced Rockefeller that in labor disputes like the Colorado Fuel and Iron case, management is not automatically or universally right, nor does it have any monopoly of rights at issue.[11] The conference group embraced top officers and industrial-relations executives of ten to twelve of the largest companies. With notable exceptions, it was persuaded that this was the moment to meet labor at least halfway, conceding, for example, workers' rights to representation and collective bargaining, so long at least as they stayed within bounds (that is, within the plant). Outside unions and their "extraneous" influences were still eyed askance by most of the group, but up to that point, the employers were prepared to go far.[12]

This Special Conference Committee, representing large interests, was initially regarded with suspicion by the unions and employer groups alike. The typical stance of the latter at this juncture was simple insistence on the *status quo ante;* the prerogatives of management were sacred and not a proper subject for negotiation with any union. So, in effect, spoke Judge Elbert H. Gary for Big Steel. And so the issue was about to be fought out, at Gary, Indiana, and elsewhere.[13]

ii

That the country was in the grip of something like an acute industrial crisis was only too clear by midsummer of 1919. In the words of one recent and perceptive student of the period, Haggai Hurvitz, "Labor disputes spread like wild-fire from coast to coast, flaring up in most industrial centers. . . . Reaching their dramatic climax in the Big Steel strike [which began in September], these industrial struggles seemed to be dragging the nation into an economic chaos."[14] Six months earlier, a general strike in sympathy for the dockworkers had paralyzed Seattle. The Boston police strike began September 9, only a few days after President Wilson had embarked upon his ill-fated tour on behalf of the League of Nations, which was terminated in late September by his paralyzing stroke. If the obscure governor of Massachusetts who asserted, in putting the police strike down, that "there is no right to strike against the public safety by anybody, anywhere, anytime" achieved overnight fame with these fourteen words, too many industrial managers were ready to equate their company's interest with the public safety. Such equations, certainly, labor was in no mood to tolerate.[15]

In mid-September, Wilson acted by convoking a kind of domestic peace conference—this one charged with discovering means of establishing industrial harmony. It was a large order, especially since the fifteen representatives which labor and employer groups were each invited to name were largely committed to opposite views on basic issues. Partly to mediate this conflict, the President himself named twenty-five, headed by Bernard Baruch, to represent the public. Apparently an ill-assorted lot—John D. Rockefeller, Jr., and Ida Tarbell, Dr. Charles W. Eliot and the socialist John Spargo, John J. Raskob and Lillian Wald, not to mention the perennial absentee, Judge Gary—this so-called public group proceeded to display a cohesion and breadth of view that delighted its friends and astonished the rest. Failing in its efforts to mediate such crucial issues as the rights and status of the unions—and employers—the group found itself usually siding (by vote of a majority) with labor. Only the employers' group, as such, proved adamant.[16]

Having accepted appointment by the U.S. Chamber of Commerce as an adviser to the employers' group, Young was not happy. Fearing the worst but hoping for the best, he had taken his assignment seriously enough to brave the heat of Washington's late September in order to study in advance some of the issues that this so-called Industrial Conference would face when it convened on October 6. On September 15, he had met and dined with Franklin K. Lane, Wilson's secretary of the interior, who was to be conference chairman. When the Chamber of Commerce advisers were asked to meet just prior to the opening of the conference, Young was present if tardy, and except for one or two brief trips to New York, he remained at the Shoreham until the bitter end. How hard he was working in the frustrating effort to moderate the employers' stand is suggested by the October 14 letter of his indefatigable assistant to E. J. Nally. After reminding Nally that his chief would welcome news of progress on American Marconi's letter to its stockholders, and of legislative prospects for radio as they were developing in the hearings of Senator Poindexter's Committee on

Naval Affairs, Elwood added: "We were very sorry [not to see you] on Thursday night, but it so happened that we worked until 12:15 without any dinner. . . ."[17]

As Young wrote E. W. Rice, Jr., on Sunday, October 19, the situation was critical. On the Wednesday following, Secretary Lane was to make his final effort to hold the conference together by reading a moving plea from the stricken President asking the delegates whether "we were to confess" to a world desperately seeking to avoid war "that there is no method to be found for carrying on industry except in the spirit and with the very method of war." A hush fell as these words were read, but in the event, the employers would not budge. To defenders of a sacred principle, as Young was discovering, room for compromise can be the smallest in the world.[18]

Two days earlier, a message from the President's secretary, Joseph Tumulty, had advised Young that because of the illness of a public member, Fuller Calloway of Georgia, "the President has designated you to attend the Industrial Conference." Young having left for the long-scheduled meeting in New York of the American Street Railway Association, of which he was the current chairman, Elwood duly acknowledged the letter and promised an early reply in his chief's behalf. In the meantime, the appointment was given wide publicity, not because Young was named but because, for the first time since the President had been stricken, he was reported to have sat up and signed the document himself.[19]

Young was embarrassed. Not wishing to refuse such an invitation, he had no stomach for coming in only to join a wake. He also saw his position as equivocal. On Wednesday morning, immediately after his return, he wrote Harry Wheeler, president of the U.S. Chamber of Commerce, a hand-delivered note, saying that of course he could not serve except with the full consent of the group he had been advising. At that stage, evidently, this posed no problem; Young's letter of acceptance was dispatched to Tumulty on the same day.[20]

And so Young joined the conference in time to hear Lane's brief obituary of it on October 23. He did remain for the wake next day as a member of the public group and approved their final report, with its recommendation that the President call a second conference, comprising new faces and organized on very different lines. Thus when he was invited on November 22 to serve, this time by a letter from the President himself, Young could hardly plead immunity, even though Secretary of Labor William B. Wilson, the new chairman, was the only full-fledged holdover. Nor had he any wish to refuse what he regarded as virtually a command performance—incidentally his second of the year.[21]

When this time GE's directors raised objections, Young's response was prompt and even drastic; it was a time, as he wrote Charles Coffin, not to argue but to act. Written on the Saturday following RCA's christening party of Friday, November 21, this letter is too revealing to condense or paraphrase.

Dear Mr. Coffin [he wrote]:

The members of the Executive Committee, at their meeting in Boston yesterday, seemed to be of the unanimous opinion that my acceptance of the President's appointment to the Industrial Commission and my participation in its work would be prejudicial to the General Electric Company, in at least two respects.

First, that it would deprive the Company of my services to the extent of the time taken by the work of the Commission.

Second, that inasmuch as I would be the only member of the Commission closely identified with a large employer of labor, I would be taken by the Commission, the employers of the country and by the public as a representative of the employers; that if the employers of the country felt that the work of the Commission, and especially any activities of mine thereon, were prejudicial to their interests, the General Electric Company would suffer.

I acquiesced in these views and stated that their decision disposed of the matter so far as the General Electric Company was concerned, but that the remaining question was as to my personal duty and obligation which, of course, I would have to decide for myself.

The simple question then is whether, under all the circumstances, I consider my obligation to serve on the Commission as paramount to my obligation to serve the General Electric Company. I have given this question careful and serious consideration and I have discussed it fully with Mrs. Young, and we are both of the opinion that under the circumstances, it is clearly my duty to accept the President's appointment and to serve on the Commission.

Therefore, in protection of the interests of the General Company, I resign as Vice President and General Counsel, effective as of December 1st next.

With your approval, I will make provision to have the work of my office carried along, and will render every assistance within my power to the end that no injurious results may come to the Company. My powers and my compensation will, however, cease on December 1st.

I take this important step after due deliberation and in full confidence that you and the other executive officers of the General Company and its directors, whose good opinion and friendship I value so much, will, even if you disagree with my decision, have some sympathy with my reasons for making it.

Very sincerely yours,[22]

Assuming that this letter reached Coffin on the following Monday, it is evident that he met action with action—not writing but telling Young that his resignation was wholly unacceptable and that he was entirely free to accept the President's call. Thus on Tuesday—still vice-president—Young addressed the following letter to the White House:

Dear Mr. President:

I will gladly accept appointment on the Industrial Commission and undertake to devote my time and thought to the important problems which may be presented to it, not only in the hope but with the conviction that some forward step may be taken toward their solution.

Very respectfully,
Owen D. Young[23]

iii

When the Second Industrial Conference convened on December 1, 1919, Young's hope and conviction were strengthened by the company he found himself keeping. The fifteen members, all appointed by the President, included Thomas W. Gregory of Texas, just retiring as attorney general of the United States; Stanley King, a New England manufacturer (and future Amherst president) who had worked with Herbert Hoover on Belgian Relief; Martin Glynn, a former Democratic governor of New York; Julius Rosenwald of Chicago; and Oscar Straus of New York. There was also the former Republican attorney general who, in 1911, had filed the antitrust suit against GE, George W. Wickersham; Professor Frank Taussig, the Harvard economist and tariff expert; and, fresh from Paris, two recent members of the Supreme Economic Council: Henry M. Robinson, the Los Angeles banker, already Hoover's great friend and soon to become Young's, and Herbert Hoover himself, now named vice-chairman. Except for the chairman, Secretary Wilson, a former miner and United Mine Workers official, no member of the conference could be called a representative of labor, but neither were they representing any organized employer group. Thus they were at pains to invite and weigh the testimony of leading representatives of each camp—especially the moderates.

The scope and *modus operandi* of the conference are well described in the introductory section of its final report, dated March 6, 1920.[24] Convening on December 1 of the preceding year, the conference issued on December 19, for publication ten days later, its tentative plan for the adjustment of industrial disputes "by conference, conciliation, inquiry and arbitration." In so doing, it was inviting constructive criticism of its plan for adjustment while devoting itself to the "further development of methods of prevention." Reconvening on January 12, it remained so engaged through much of February, taking criticism in stride and also turning it to account.

Aware that "prevention . . . is worth more than cure," the final report put great emphasis on employee representation and collective bargaining, freely and fairly applied. At the same time it so modified its tentative machinery for adjustment of disputes as greatly "to diminish the field of arbitration and enlarge the scope of voluntary settlement." Evidently these men were prepared to rely less on the argument of force than the force of argument—a refreshingly novel concept in the field of labor relations.

The report then proceeded to identify the two major sources of opposition to the idea of employee representation: the dictatorial and recalcitrant employer of the old but "disappearing" school, and the union leader trained to "regard shop representation as a subtle threat directed against the union." It paid the unions the compliment of addressing its arguments primarily to them and in no hostile vein. The occasional misuse of employee representation, it held, should not obscure the fact that the relationship between the shop committee and the union could and should be a "complementary and not a mutually exclusive one. In many plants the trade union and the shop committee are both functioning harmoniously. In some establishments the men are unionized, and the shop committees are composed of union men. In others, some men belong to the trade union while all belong to the shop organization."

After all, the "union has had its greatest success in dealing with basic working conditions and . . . wages . . ."; local grievances, on the other hand, "fall naturally within the province of the shop committees. . . . Except for trades in which the union itself has operated under a system of employee representation, as it does in shipbuilding and the manufacture of clothing . . . these internal affairs are likely either to be ignored" or to be mishandled.

Collective bargaining implied, moreover, "a clear recognition by both sides of the obligations it imposes and of the limitations of these obligations." A contract once agreed upon represented an act of mutual good faith, and good faith rather than legal sanctions must sustain it. Employee representation, in turn, should begin in the plant itself, whether union or nonunion, with elections free from coercion and conducted by secret ballot "to prevent suspicion on any side." The general acceptance of these principles, plus further testing of such incentives to workers as profit or gain sharing, and decent hours and working conditions, should do much to encourage productivity and discourage strikes or lockouts. Nor was the right to strike denied except to public employees, the nature of whose service makes them "part of the machinery of government, and servants of the people." But this very fact, it was argued, makes it all the more incumbent on their employers to safeguard and promote their interests, while granting them full rights of association in seeking redress of grievances.

To deal with cases in which collective bargaining failed to produce agreement, the conference proposed the establishment of Regional Adjustment Conferences, with a National Industrial Board as a kind of court of appeal. Arbitration by the national board was limited, however, to disputes involving wages, hours, and conditions of work which regional boards had been unable to settle by unanimous vote. On both, equal representation of management and labor was assured, with the chairmen or public members to be appointed by the President. Coercive power was left largely to the force of public opinion, as guided by published findings of the facts in any unresolved dispute.[25]

Dealing as this second conference did in so forthright a manner with such basic and controversial issues, the unanimity it achieved is its own best commentary on leaders and members alike. With an eye to Big Steel's twelve-hour day, their report roundly condemned—*ex cathedra,* if you please—the excessive hours of labor still required in certain "large basic industries." Assuredly these were men of conviction and deep concern; one who had served as a member of Wilson's cabinet called it the most distinguished group that he had ever sat with for so long a period.[26] But they knew the importance of consensus if they were to have any public impact, especially in issuing a report which counted so heavily on achieving a consensus in specific disputes. Indeed, the whole weight of their recommendations put a premium on reaching workable agreements through direct collective bargaining, thus obviating the need to activate the machinery of adjustment. On only one issue was unanimity flawed; Gregory and Henry Carter Stuart (of Virginia)—but significantly not Young—insisted that public-utility employees were so charged with the public interest as to warrant denying them too any right to strike.[27]

What was Young's contribution? Minutes of plenary sessions seldom tell much about individual roles, but in this case there are other if limited sources. Taussig reported that, in the December session, he and Young had developed the whole idea of the regional adjustment machinery, which Young no doubt would credit chiefly to him. If Young ever did so, it was not in answering the complaint which a good customer and friend directed at this particular proposal. To the contrary, he assumed full responsibility for shaping it, and proceeded briefly to expound his reasons. If management and men bargaining collectively can't agree, he stated, then the dispute should go in the first instance, not to Washington, but to a board near enough to the plant to know something of local conditions. While a central board was needed as a court of last resort, every effort should be made to minimize the number of appeals that reached it.[28]

That Young himself felt labor's fundamental case to be both reasonable and negotiable is evident in his personal memorandum of October 19—dictated prior to the collapse of the first conference, but carried to the second. It spells out in a single page many of the basic propositions, as well as several of the nice distinctions, which inform that body's report:

We believe in the right of men to organize into unions, shop industrial councils or other organizations.

We believe in the policy of collective bargaining, and we understand this term to mean that the men in a plant may bargain as a group with the management.

We believe that the men may deal with the management through representatives chosen by the men by a secret vote so that the management and the men may be assured that the representatives are the honest choice of the men.

We believe that management is entitled to know of any grievances in the plant from the men themselves through men chosen from within the plant.

We believe that if the men acting collectively and the management cannot agree that then a majority of the men, if they so desire, may by secret vote choose any man from outside the plant to present their case, and that the management should hear him on the questions affecting solely the interest of the men in the plant.

We believe that if then the management and the men cannot agree, the matters in dispute should go to some kind of public forum, the nature and jurisdiction of which shall later be defined by this Conference.[29]

Quite evidently Young's contribution to the conference was not limited to the machinery for conciliation and adjustment of disputes which he and Taussig devised in December. Nor did it reflect any notably original thinking: knowing that labor had taken the code of the War Labor Board as its basic bill of rights, Young had done the same, and then worked to refine it. But his memorandum was somewhat more explicit than the final conference report in recognizing the role and importance of the unions.

Certainly it went further than GE had so far gone in that respect. The company had recently established shop councils in certain of its plants, and in the view of old-timers like Coffin and E. W. Rice—and even of "liberal" plant managers like Richard Rice of Lynn—this was clearly as far as they should go. Young himself was not in charge; he was now only one of half a dozen vice-presidents and his own future was at stake. Nevertheless, his field was policy. He agreed that collective bargaining, like the airing of grievances and proposals for increasing productivity, should begin at home, and so did the conference as a whole. But Young, like others—Hoover and Robinson, for example—was sensitive to the unions' charge, already cited, that shop representation alone—a "company union"—could become "a subtle threat directed against the union."

Thus he was ready to subscribe to the doctrine that in the last analysis employees must enjoy full freedom in choosing their own representatives, whether union or nonunion, and that the relations between the union and the shop committees could and should be essentially complementary. This, of course, constituted the real basis for a *genuinely* open shop, with neither management nor the unions subjecting the workers to coercive or discriminatory pressures. Aware that perverted versions of the open shop like the so-called "American plan" reflected management's fears lest such untrammeled freedom lead to the closed, or union, shop, Young preferred acceptance of that risk to what he held to be a thinly disguised *anti*-union, or closed company, shop.

The report—Young was on the drafting committee—includes more than one phrase on which his signature, not visible, is all but unmistakable. Stressing the point, for example, that employee representation in shop councils affords no panacea and that everything depends on how well it is used to define and develop areas of common interest for "joint action of managers and employees," the report adds: "It should emphasize the responsibility of managers to know men at least as intimately as they know materials. . . ." This, like the report's later emphasis on the foremen's key responsibility for developing understanding and voluntary cooperation by and with employees, is characteristic. Though Young was but one of the original draftsmen, he felt so deeply the force of such homely truths as to make them increasingly his own.[30]

iv

The report, published on March 6, 1920, was stillborn. As Hurvitz puts it comprehensively but succinctly:

It appeared when the upheaval of the strikes of 1919 was subsiding, shortly after U.S. Steel had crushed the AFL in a dramatic contest, immediately after the passage of the Transportation Act had supposedly settled the railroad situation, and when the country had just passed the peak of the Red Scare. Thus the Report did not stir great controversies. Nor did it get favorable reception from either labor or management. The AFL opposed the plan for two reasons. The machinery seemed too intricate and liable to serve labor's foes; the espousal of shop-councils might encourage the "organizing of workers away from each other." Organized employers were "on the whole hostile, even harsh." Generally, they considered "the plan as an unwarranted interference in the affairs of the employers," and many thought that "if present laws regarding the conduct of strikes were properly enforced, there would be no need for other machinery to prevent industrial disturbances." The public seemed weary of the whole subject. Neither Congress nor the President were moved to act upon the recommendations. Like innumerable other reports, the conference's plan was simply dropped, destined to remain on dusty shelves.[31]

So that was that. So much goodwill, so much imaginative, intelligent, and conciliatory effort gone for nothing. Except for a few letters—including warm notes of thanks from Tumulty, written "at the President's direction"—nothing to show for all that expenditure of time and thought. But there is remarkably little evidence that the group felt sorry for itself. Its members had developed pride in their work, and had learned much from it. Durable friendships were formed or strengthened—in Young's case most notably with Henry Robinson and Herbert Hoover.

There were some attempts to follow through. In addition to the Special Conference Committee, Young had copies of the plan sent in March to all of General Electric's plant managers with requests for their criticisms—which, alas, are no part of any surviving record. In its report of March 10, 1920, approved by the President on March 19, and summarized for the press, the Bituminous Coal Commission, of which Robinson was chairman, said: "If the recommendations of the President's Industrial Conference are adopted in regard to industrial tribunals and boards of inquiry, this machinery is to be put to use in the coal industry. Otherwise a special board is to be set up."[32] A special board it had to be.

Hoover went further, even launching something of a personal campaign on behalf of the conference's recommendations. He quoted from them that spring, for example, in addressing the Boston Chamber of Commerce ("a very frosty audience"). He wrote several articles, including one for the *Saturday Evening Post* which appeared on December 27, 1919, while the conference was in recess. A review of these articles and speeches—the earlier ones in particular—suggests in some degree the indebtedness of the conference to this man of parts and promise who was currently committed to the view that autocratic industry must be *reformed* along the lines demanded by such AFL leaders as Samuel Gompers, John P. Frey and Matthew Woll. Fresh from his European experience, Hoover wanted for the United States a kind of purge which would restore something approaching our vaunted equality of opportunity, and assure labor of meaningful participation in decisions affecting the workers. The consonance of his views and labor's, Hurvitz suggests, is understandable once one grasps the fact that for both, "the key issue . . . was not a choice between capitalism and socialism, but rather how to accommodate a capitalist economy to a democratic society and an egalitarian value system."[33]

This could also be cited to account, in part, for the notable rapport between Hoover and Young, which was to survive, with little impairment, the vicissitudes of nearly a decade. It also goes far to explain why Hoover in 1920 was being courted by the progressives of both parties, including Franklin D. Roosevelt, who "wished we could make him President"; and why, on February 25, Young followed such Democrats as Ray Stannard Baker, Secretaries Daniels and Lane, and the distinguished jurist Charles Warren in publicly proposing Hoover for that office. (On the same day—the better to support Hoover?— Young wrote Homer Cummings, Democratic National Committee chairman, accepting his invitation to dine.) When Hoover, some five weeks later, declared himself a "progressive Republican," Young was regretful but remained a warm admirer.[34]

Relationships developed at the second conference also prompted a second essay into politics on Young's part, this one involving an immediate cabinet appointment for Henry Robinson, in place of Secretary Lane, who was resigning as secretary of the interior. Robinson demurred, pleading his imminent appointment as head of the First National Bank of Los Angeles, but Young was not convinced. To his friend John B. Miller, president of Southern California Edison and a leading director of that bank, Young promptly addressed two long coded telegrams, urging the importance to the country, to Robinson and to the future of the bank of deferring for a year Robinson's Los Angeles obligation, so that he could assume this public role. Miller, a conservative Republican, was unimpressed. The important banking situation to which Robinson had been called, he replied, needed his immediate and continuing attention; no leave of absence could even be considered. So that was that.[35]

Nevertheless, the two industrial conferences had extended, not only Young's grasp of the basic issues involving labor, but also the circles in which he had earned the respect and admiration of his peers. For obvious reasons, this applied less to the first than to the second conference, where he was no longer a mere extra in the wings. Certainly it was the second that, bringing Young center stage, introduced him to public service on a national scale; hence, the contemporaneous appraisal of his fellows there may be worth noting. Ida Tarbell has quoted at some length the complimentary remarks of Secretary of Labor Wilson—for instance, "this man Young not only thinks clearly and works hard but he has a wonderful sense of fairness"—and of Attorney General Gregory: "I had not expected from him the progressive views which he constantly advanced . . . one of the leaders in the conference . . . and in my judgment . . . its ablest member." She also quotes in full the tribute of a knowledgeable friend from the telephone company, E. K. Hall, who wrote to Young in part: "To those of us who know, as I do, something of the part you played in visualizing and then working out the general plan and bringing the members of the Conference so unanimously to its support, it will always stand out as your greatest single personal achievement. . . ."[36]

Nevertheless, Young's efforts to carry the gospel to his peers and associates had very limited success. No doubt he had counted on support from his colleagues of the Special Conference Committee at least in respect to the compromise position he had prepared for the employers in an effort to save the first conference.[37] In insisting, however, that collective bargaining meant a readiness to deal with whatever representative the employees might freely choose, the second conference had gone even further in leaving the door open to "outsiders." And this, as Young discovered on leaving the conference in mid-January to seek support from these same colleagues, was still too much for most of them. Hoover was to make the same discovery somewhat later in meeting with a similar group which included Charles Coffin.[38] Even then, however, Young seems to have entertained no apprehension on his own account. Possibly Tarbell was right in suggesting that by this time Coffin and Young were rather like father and son.[39] Some twenty-eight years Young's senior, Coffin had no sons; it would have been quite in character for him to admire Young's daring and respect his views even while clinging to his own.

But this is speculation. What does emerge too clearly to ignore is the growth in Young's comprehension of the need, and his own capacity, for negotiated settlements; of conciliation as the only practical alternative to conflict. The young law-school graduate's insistence that "the lawyer of the future must draw straight lines for principles and with the great Reformer say 'I hate that word compromise' " was turning out to be no more than brittle rhetoric. As the second conference noted in its discussion of collective bargaining: "The matter is not advanced materially by the assertion of the right, on one side, to bargain collectively or on the other side, the right to refuse to bargain collectively; *as abstract rights both undoubtedly exist.* The real question . . . is whether as a matter of policy, better relationships . . . will be promoted and a more effective industrial organization for the nation will be brought about if a system of collective bargaining is adopted."[40]

As a matter of policy, Young had come to believe it would, not least because it afforded the one best hope of securing labor's cooperation on such key issues as increasing productivity and respect for its own contracts.[41] One need not applaud this particular conclusion— few seemed to understand it at the time—to discern in Young in increasing measure those qualities of mind and temper which were to win him recognition as a trusted and skillful practitioner of the conciliator's arts. As he had demonstrated at St. Lawrence, the great advocate analyzes his opponent's case so well as to state it more persuasively than he can—the better to demolish it. A more judicial variant of this skill is the ability to pierce the screen of extravagant demands which parties to a dispute—or to negotiation of a franchise— typically set up, and see precisely what it is that each party *has* to have. One who learns this invaluable art, as Young was surely learning it, is able to expand as others cannot the room for effective compromise. And inasmuch as society has a vested interest in the constant enlargement of that small but elastic space, one who can effect this is apt to find himself very much in demand—from the public as well as the private sector.[42]

Chapter 13

RCA: A Peacetime
Patent Pool

A T THE moment, the demand for Young's services arose from familiar quarters and concerned further steps in RCA's development. In a New Year's appeal, set forth in identical letters to the telephone company and General Electric, the Department of the Navy had taken a second initiative of major significance to radio. Dated January 5, 1920, this letter came from the Bureau of Steam Engineering; the signature was Admiral A. J. Hepburn's but the drafting hand was Commander Hooper's.[1] Marked for A. G. Davis's attention, the letter to General Electric read as follows:

Gentlemen:

Referring to numerous recent conferences in connection with the radio patent situation and particularly that phase involving vacuum tubes, the Bureau has consistently held the point of view that all interests will be best served through some agreement between the several holders of pertinent patents whereby the market can be freely supplied with tubes, and has endeavored to point this out with concrete examples for practical consideration.

In this connection the Bureau wishes to invite your attention to the recent tendency of the Merchant Marine to adopt continuous wave apparatus in their ship installations, the Bureau itself having arranged for equipping many vessels of the Shipping Board with arc sets. Such installations will create a demand for vacuum tubes in receivers, and this Bureau believes it particularly desirable, especially from a point of view of safety at sea, that all ships be able to procure without difficulty vacuum tubes, these being the only satisfactory detectors for receiving continuous waves.

Today, ships are cruising on the high seas with only continuous wave transmitting equipment except for short ranges when interrupted continuous waves are used. Due to the peculiar patent conditions which have prevented the marketing of tubes to the public, such vessels are not able to communicate with greatest efficiency except with the shore and, therefore, in cases of distress it inevitably follows that the lives of crews and passengers are imperiled beyond reasonable necessity.

In the past the reasons for desiring some arrangement have been largely because of monetary considerations. Now, the situation has become such that it is a public necessity that such arrangement be made without further delay, and this letter may be considered as an appeal, for the good of the public, for a remedy to the situation.

It is hoped this additional information will have its weight in bringing about a speedy understanding in the patent situation which the Bureau considers so desirable.

A similar letter is being addressed to the American Telephone & Telegraph Co., New York City.

> Very respectfully,
> (signed) A. J. Hepburn
> Acting Chief of Bureau

The plea was unequivocal and so was the response. Whether or not A. G. Davis had been a party to any of these "numerous recent conferences [on] the radio patent situation . . . particularly tubes," it is probable that the merest hint might now have stung him to action. Small wonder. If, as Commander Loftin, another of the navy's wartime radio experts, was soon to report to the Federal Trade Commission, "the very soul of radio . . . is the three-electrode vacuum tube,"[2] neither GE nor Western Electric could afford to wait indefinitely for adjudication of their respective claims under the Fleming-Langmuir and deForest-Arnold patents. Davis was as sick of interferences and litigation as he was of post-armistice orders from the navy— the latest also signed by Admiral R. F. Griffin—to help them out at Sayville.[3]

The suggestion that Davis at least was not unprepared for the Hepburn letter finds support in the date—also January 5—of his note to Young, enclosing a summary of the points to be covered in any agreement with AT&T. Also enclosed was a copy of an AT&T memorandum of May 28, 1918, proposing collaboration with GE in setting up a new wireless-communication company. This interesting document, signed by George E. Folk as general counsel, proved to have been drafted by the same Gerard Swope who had resigned his vice-presidency at Western Electric at the end of that same year to become the first president of International General Electric. Also approved at the time by Swope's former boss, its relative simplicity must have been the envy of the negotiators as successive draft agreements became increasingly complex.[4]

It must also have delighted Young, whose admiration for the man who had negotiated with GE in 1910 both the redoubtable lamp contract and the sale of Western Electric's power-machinery business had been quickly confirmed by his masterly handling of his new job. Young knew too that the post-armistice offer Swope had accepted had been GE's—and Burchard's—third attempt to land him; and that this time Coffin himself had been a party to the effort—even acquiescing in Swope's stipulation that GE's foreign business be separately incorporated if he were to head it. Too bad that this man of parts should now prefer to stay away from the current radio negotiations with his old chief. But Young understood such diffidence and knew the job was his.

Agreement in principle on the cross-licensing of patents had been swift enough to encourage false hopes. Young's sessions in early January—during the recess of the industrial conference—with AT&T's president, Harry B. Thayer, had achieved that much, and the lawyers were left to work out the details when the industrial conference took him back to Washington on Monday, January 12.[5] Except for his brief return to New York on conference business, Young was busy in the capital through the rest of this month and indeed through most of February. Notes from his assistant regretted his inability to attend directors' meetings at Bond and Share, Bankers Trust and even RCA.[6]

Charles Neave, counsel to the telephone company as well as to GE, was working hard to reconcile conflicting claims and interests, with one eye on the antitrust laws. When Davis objected that his late-January draft watered down rights which should be exclusive to GE, Neave replied on the twenty-fourth that the Sherman act made it the part of wisdom to reduce exclusive features of the contract to a minimum.[7] Nevertheless, under pressure from both parties they soon were creeping back.

As problems arose, so did the clamor for Young. On Wednesday, February 11, his two assistants, John W. Elwood and A. W. Morton, sent him at the old Shoreham copies of the latest Neave-Davis draft. Davis, they reported, had hoped to meet Young Sunday in New York, but Elwood told him that his chief might stay in Washington, hoping to come home early next week "with the work of the commission . . . completed." Davis thought it very important that Young attend the RCA meeting on the following Wednesday, the eighteenth.[8] He did.

Aside from Davis's need for reassurance, Young seemed to be the one man who could talk to Thayer. A Vermont Yankee, several years Young's senior, Thayer had for the past twelve years been the head first of Western Electric and then—but only recently—of its parent company. His gentle manner could sometimes prove deceptive. If he was a hard man to pin down, GE's negotiators also complained that his assent, when finally won, was too often a signal for his colleagues to move in with fresh objections. By the middle of April, when AT&T again pleaded the necessity of taking into account the views not only of Western Electric but also of its associated operating companies, Davis threw up his hands. The following day AT&T's general counsel, Folk, sent Young their standard form of intercompany contract by way of explanation; a letter from Neave explained less cryptically that this intercompany relationship was indeed a fixed point, but not a fatal one, in any negotiations with the telephone company.[9] A "natural monopoly" of imposing size and strength, AT&T, it appeared, was yet no monolith.

At this point, Young was briefly in Washington again, this time in response to an urgent request from Admiral W. S. Benson, chairman of the U.S. Shipping Board. Benson's only problems—not to be Young's for long inasmuch as they were settled in a two-day conference—involved the disposition of the wartime Merchant Marine to private owners and its operation in the meantime.[10]

Returning to his more familiar problems, Young was ready to bear down. After all, as he wired Henry Robinson on April 23, he was due in Pasadena on May 17 for the National Electric Light Association (NELA) convention, and he had agreed to look in at the Atlantic City meetings of the International Chamber of Commerce on his way. (Somewhat later Dallas appeared on his calendar as a second stopover.) Now he let the others know that he must leave for the West Coast by the first week in May; if the license agreements could be ready by that time, he could board his train with a free mind.

It was asking a lot and Young knew it, but he also knew that without a target date, lawyers' drafts can proliferate forever. The analyses he sought from his colleagues involved for them no easy exercise; the very effort to project into the ether the distinctive areas in which each company felt itself at home was proving unexpectedly difficult. A must for GE and RCA was exclusive rights in wireless telegraphy, and this was conceded; but how deal with the complexities of rights in wireless telephony? Here the telephone company's interest was clear: Would they concede rights which GE and RCA badly wanted for overseas communication? And ship to shore? They were disposed to, but subject to complex reservations. Then there was the little matter of the domestic pickup and delivery of RCA's long-distance wireless messages—what would AT&T do about this and on what terms? Finally, how to deal with that little known but quite possibly important phenomenon called broadcasting? Assuming that this curiosity ever amounted to anything, who was to make and sell the "music box" of which young David Sarnoff—one of the hidden assets which RCA had acquired from Marconi—had been talking of to Nally and now wrote of to Young?[11]

In his analysis of April 12, sent to Davis, Ernst Alexanderson felt that the latest draft was satisfactory on most of these points, and notably the last. Davis was not so sure. The license granted GE "to establish and maintain . . . stations for transmitting or broadcasting news, music and entertainment" and "to make, use, sell and lease wireless telephone receiving apparatus for the reception of such news, music and entertainment so broadcasted [*sic*]" seemed clear enough on its face. It also seemed sufficiently comprehensive, except that it was nonexclusive and might well be in conflict with certain domestic wireless telephony rights reserved by the telephone company. There were other troublesome ambiguities, and arrangements for pickup and delivery of overseas wireless messages proved curiously hard to settle. That, however, was a problem for a traffic agreement; for the rest, when human ingenuity finds itself unable to achieve significant agreements without resorting to ambiguity, it may well be worthwhile to do so. Davis finally came to this view, and so, after consulting Sarnoff, did Nally.[12]

That was enough for Young. On May 5, however, when agreement had seemed assured, Thayer expressed dissatisfaction with three specific clauses of the section on wireless telephony and advised Young that he was asking Folk to revise them and show the new version to Young. In a handwritten postscript he added, "If you will give this your usual broad consideration, I think it can be easily arranged."[13] And so it was. There remained, however, one unsettled question of great moment: How much was AT&T to invest in RCA, which, in Young's view, still needed substantial new capital?

Not wishing to force this issue, Young won Thayer's agreement to the following procedure: they would initial the licensing contract as it stood and submit it to their respective boards for approval. If approved, the contract was then to be held in escrow by Neave, pending Young's return and further discussions with Thayer on the matter of AT&T's investment. This would also allow time to work out the vexatious matter of a traffic agreement.[14]

ii

And so Young went off on his transcontinental trip. In his absence, on May 13, Davis spelled out the agreed procedure in a letter to Rice, reciting Thayer's promise to seek approval of his executive committee, and Young's wish for similar action by GE. He also told of the arrangement Young had made for Sam Fordyce (now of counsel to GE) and the telephone company's E. K. Hall to show the contract to the attorney general. On his own account he expressed the hope for prompt action, so that he would feel free to take up and settle with Folk the Langmuir and Arnold patent interferences which were "seriously impeding RCA's business and the development of the art."[15]

Before the end of the month, GE's executive committee had followed AT&T's example in recording its approval, and the escrow arrangement had come into effect.[16] Davis seized the moment to pursue with Thayer the still unsettled aspects of the traffic agreement. Writing Young on May 29, he said he had told Thayer he "could come in as a partner or we would rent his lines"; he couldn't expect to have it both ways.[17]

But Young, once away, was in no hurry to get back. He had declined Henry Robinson's cordial invitation to be his guest, his reservations at the Huntington in Pasadena having been confirmed, but, he added—no doubt with an eye to the still novel Eighteenth Amendment—"I reserve the right to call on you daily at least once and sometimes twice." Young was putting business before pleasure but not neglecting either. He was there because the NELA convention meant that GE's best customers were conveniently gathered together. Nevertheless, he saw much of his new friend Robinson, now duly installed as president of the First National Bank, and highly regarded in Los Angeles circles.

Nor, the electrical convention over, did Young race home to resume negotiations with Thayer. In a warm note to Robinson of June 21 he confessed that he had not been able to "resist the temptation of stopping off in Chicago to visit the [Republican] convention"—incidentally his first and only appearance at a national convention of either party. It was held in sweltering weather from June 8 to 12, and of course his chief interest was in Hoover. To Robinson he quoted Charles D. Hilles of New York as saying that while practically all the delegates agreed to make Hoover their second choice, he was nobody's first. He also quoted Oscar Straus, a fellow member of the Industrial Conference, to the effect that "these fellows just didn't take the Hoover movement seriously"; adding that in his view that had been the whole trouble. Thus Hoover's announcement that he would support the Harding ticket and work as a progressive for the party and the League of Nations seemed to Young his only possible course under the circumstances.[18]

Young knew neither party's nominee, but his own Democratic and pro-League sympathies made Cox the easier to vote for. He did know, as it happened, both vice-presidential candidates, and so could congratulate, if not vote for, Calvin Coolidge. Doing both in the case of Franklin Roosevelt, he expressed full agreement with the suggestion of Coolidge's friends that "both tickets are wrong end to."[19]

Actually Young had not "stopped off" in Chicago for the convention; he had gone back there to attend it—apparently on the spur of the moment—after spending the first four days of June in his office and the weekend at St. Lawrence for a trustees' meeting. But he was not disposed to rush things with Thayer, and besides, certain proposals involving General Motors were commanding his personal attention.

Recently organized to meet the demands of an expanding market, that promising young company was actively seeking to strengthen both its capital position and its board. The Du Pont Company, acting on the advice of its treasurer, John J. Raskob, had recently invested heavily in General Motors and, with the cordial approval of GM's president, William C. Durant, Pierre du Pont had been named chairman. Anxious to market some $60 million of new stock without depressing the shares outstanding, GM had interested Morgan's in taking a substantial bloc both for their own account and for private placement in hands which could be depended on not to dump it on the market. Thus Edward Stettinius and Dwight Morrow, both Morgan partners and recently elected directors of General Electric, were now offering Young a $350,000 piece—no doubt at an "attractive" (if unrecorded) price.

Flattered by an offer which, coming from this source, could only mean that he had now "arrived," Young found its dimensions somewhat staggering. He was doing well: as vice-president of GE his salary was now $60,000 and as chairman of RCA, $15,000. These earnings, plus occasional "extras," and income from his still modest investments, enabled him to meet his rising obligations comfortably enough, but he was by no means a rich man in the sense that the offer implied. Having consulted Charles Coffin, he replied on Friday, June 4, 1920, that, appreciative as he was, he must limit his subscription to $50,000, since more than that would exceed—as nothing else should—his personal holdings of GE. Later in the month he did, to be sure, take on an additional $50,000, but this he would carry for the benefit of certain protégés in GE (presumably his two assistants, Elwood and Morton, who had helped so much in the creation of RCA). In order to do so, he wrote Stettinius, "I shall need some assistance . . . but I shall plan to keep it on a banking basis."[20]

In the meantime, it had become clear that something else was in the wind. GM, initially through Stettinius, was asking Young to become a director and this, he told Stettinius, was what he chiefly valued. By the middle of July, his election was official; on July 19, Young was thanking Pierre du Pont for his cordial note of welcome and enclosing a copy of the letter of acceptance he had just dispatched to William C. Durant. "No other industry," he had told Durant, "shows such growth and no other concern in that industry shows such sound and progressive growth as yours." So much for Henry Ford and his Model T, which still led the automotive parade by a wide margin. Nevertheless, the sheaf of financial reports Stettinius sent showed that GM's sales had doubled in the previous year, and for the long run its diversified line looked—and was to prove—a better bet than Ford's redoubtable single model.

For the short run, however, there were pitfalls of which Morgan's, like Young and indeed most of GM's leaders, seem to have been wholly unaware. The automotive industry was the first to feel the postwar depression which, by 1921, was to become general; in September 1920 the bottom suddenly dropped out of the car market and both the company and its president found themselves heavily overextended. By late November GM was quoted on the market at half its average price for June and Durant's speculative commitments had resulted in a crisis in both his finances and those of his company. It was simply the good fortune of the new director—and indeed of countless others—that GM's moment of truth, coming early in December, found both the Du Pont and Morgan interests prepared to mount a rescue operation of the magnitude required, with the office vacated by Durant taken over first by Pierre du Pont himself and, some two years and four months thereafter, by Alfred P. Sloan.

As for the new investor, this was his good fortune too, but any expectation of paying off his loan and rewarding his young protégés by selling at a profit was not to be realized for some years. It would be interesting to know the price at which Morgan's had "placed" his stock which, following a 10 for 1 split in the spring of 1920, had soared to 36 and, for the month in which Young bought it, was quoted on the market at around 25. By September it had fallen to 20 and not even December's rescue operation could arrest the decline in the company's business or its stock. According to Sloan, GM's share of the cars and trucks sold in the United States was 17 percent in 1920 and 12 percent in 1921; at the same time, Ford's share was rising from 45 to 60 percent. It was to be a long, hard pull before Sloan's reorganization plans could become productive; even in 1922, when recovery was general, GM shares dropped below 10 and never rose above 15.[21]

Thus it would appear that the "goodwill" which Morgan's plan of private placement was expected to generate was a chancy thing at best, and it was well that only those who could presumably afford the risk were tapped. If Young found the experience chastening, it was not to be the last occasion on which his awareness of powerful forces that promised a rosy future blinded him to the hazards that might and sometimes did intervene.

iii

In the meantime a host of other matters pressed for Young's attention, but none so insistently as radio. Davis's letter of June 9 discussed the possibility of Western Union's taking a stock interest in RCA, the first such suggestion the authors have discovered. Young was in fact to pursue with Newcomb Carlton a possible traffic agreement, since here the telephone company continued to show itself remarkably unaccommodating. In this negotiation, lasting well into 1921, Young failed; in the meantime, his search for additional capital for RCA had been directed not toward Western Union, with its interest in the cables, but toward United Fruit.[22]

Here Young had discovered a mutuality of interest worth cultivating on several counts. United Fruit had found radio important in the timing of its operations, first in harvesting bananas on its vast Colombian and Central American plantations and second in their shipment and delivery to North American ports. Its subsidiary, the Wireless Specialty Company, held the Pickard crystal and other patents having something more than a nuisance value to RCA; it also operated wireless stations in the West Indies. RCA, for its part, having acquired substantial control of Pan-American Wireless with a view to direct communication with South America, was not averse to patent exchanges that gave United Fruit limited licenses for the conduct of its business, against assurances of capital subscription and noncompetition. Young had reason to believe, moreover, as he later wrote his GE colleague Jesse Lovejoy, that the fruit company was sold on testing electric propulsion for its fleet. All this added up, he told Lovejoy, to something worth developing. Two years later, his hopes for GE were rewarded by a million-dollar order for electric turbines for the Great White Fleet.[23]

Also waiting on Young's desk was a long report from his friend Sam Fordyce. It recounted the call on the attorney general, and incidentally on Bullard and Hooper, which he and E. K. Hall of the telephone company had paid on May 12. Young's friend Gregory having resigned, the new attorney general was Mitchell Palmer, the Quaker whose anti-Red campaign was making his name a household word for good or evil, depending on the household.

While officially adhering to the customary formula that he could express no opinion on the legality of the proposed cross-licensing contract, Palmer seemed to Fordyce "entirely satisfied with our reasons for talking the matter over with him, and made what I considered the significant remark that in his opinion the transaction looked like an excellent business arrangement." As for Bullard and Hooper, "each said that he was very much pleased that the GE and AT&T had entered [sic] into this contract, as a result of the Navy's request for clarification of the [patent] situation." Hooper did express concern lest "the contract . . . result in a lessening of competition between the GE and Western Electric in the electrical appliances and machinery that the Navy needed." On receiving Fordyce's assurance that it would not, Hooper volunteered the further statement that "the GE and Western Electric were as much responsible for the success of the Navy as the Navy itself . . . and that they should very much regret any change in the attitude of these companies toward the Navy as a result of this contract, or otherwise."[24]

One paragraph in this letter pointed, however, to the problem still confronting Young. "Admiral Bullard told me," Fordyce wrote, "that a representative of the AT&T had called upon him after my first visit, and although he seemed pleased that the contract was to be executed, he seemed to think that the GE would benefit more than their company."

Here was a challenge to Young's thesis that the ideal trade left neither party feeling injured or unhappy. Much of what subsequently transpired between Young and Thayer took place in unrecorded conversations, but the letters they exchanged in July indicate Thayer's extreme sensitivity and occasional sharpness, as well as Young's refusal to be put off by either.[25] The issue had indeed come down to the character and size of AT&T's investment in RCA, with Thayer intimating that Young's suggested figure was exorbitant and cash payment out of the question. Patient but firm, Young explained that the purchase at par of 500,000 shares of RCA preferred, plus equal shares of no-par common, for $2,500,000, simply followed the pattern of GE's investment, and was designed to give AT&T a continuing stake in an enterprise to which it was making important contributions. As for terms of payment, RCA was quite ready to accept, and liquidate, any marketable securities, including the Southwestern Bell 7 percent debentures which Thayer finally offered.[26]

Time passed and now Davis was becoming worried. Late in June, after yeoman service in preparing and vetting the telephone agreements, he had sailed for England, confident that the contracts, dated July 1, 1920, would be speedily delivered. To his inquiry of July 6 from London, Young responded by wireless on the ninth: "Telephone and United Fruit negotiations still pending and uncompleted. Think we shall get at least two and one half millions but I may fall down." He was not to fall down on either, and the more important breakthrough came first. Young's relief was evident in his uncommonly euphoric message to Davis of August 4:

Telephone trade closed today. Will yield [RCA] treasury about two million four hundred thousand. Very hopeful additional million Fruit Company next week. Be sure and tie up French communication no matter who ultimately controls it. Urge Nally to push long term contract with Germany and secure if possible French and German cooperation Argentine. Now is the time to do business.[27]

In the event, consummation of the fruit company agreements required another six to seven months, but it was all but assured by October and it did bring RCA an additional million of new capital.[28] In the meantime, however, Young's enthusiasm over the delivery at long last of the telephone company contracts—plus extension agreements to Western Electric and RCA—had been tempered by sober second thoughts.

On August 25, attending the monthly meeting of RCA's Technical Committee, he recalled the extreme delicacy of his prolonged negotiations with Thayer, and cautioned the radio engineers not to offend disturbed sensibilities by rushing in to exploit the technical resources of the telephone group. Proceed warily, was his counsel, and consult your opposite numbers first on general matters or perhaps on possible practical application of things Western Electric has done. Only as you gain their confidence can you hope, he concluded, to enjoy the full potentialities of the new alliance. Developments still only dimly envisaged—notably in radio broadcasting—were to justify Young's cautionary words in unexpected ways.

Before the meeting ended, Young essayed a kind of global review of the outlook for RCA, which he found good. The minutes also record Young's two concluding observations: "He further stated that the one obstacle which may be found in the U.S. was the International [Radio] Company which had now received the backing of the West-

inghouse Company. On the other hand, he thought, . . . Westinghouse
. . . could hardly afford to begin a patent war on the General Electric
Company, and therefore this question left him without apprehension."[29]

Within ten days, however, Young was courting Westinghouse and
cabling J. R. Geary, GE's representative in Tokyo, for information
about International Radio Company's moves in Japan.

iv

Had Westinghouse been one of the original "building blocks" Young
envisaged in setting out to create the Radio Corporation? In the absence of any explicit contemporaneous evidence pro or con, it may be
doubted. After the event, to be sure, Westinghouse was always included in statements broadly justifying the entire RCA complex. But
that was after Westinghouse had demonstrated its determination not
to be left out.

Certainly its inclusion was to raise a whole new set of problems.
For GE to establish RCA as a simple subsidiary to handle all its interests in wireless communication was one thing. To extend their
original cross-licensing agreements affecting radio devices to AT&T
and Western Electric involved a step, however imperative, that was
taken only after the navy's explicit, and urgent, appeal. In electrical
manufacturing, moreover, Western Electric existed primarily and increasingly to supply the needs of AT&T; it no longer offered GE anything like the broad general competition that Westinghouse did. Why,
then, take the risk of entering into even a limited partnership with a
major competitor unless, indeed, there was no escaping it?

One answer is that Westinghouse had already set out to make it
inescapable. Confronted with a sudden end to their substantial wartime orders for radio devices, Westinghouse officials had naturally
viewed with increasing dismay the emergence of a Radio Corporation
allied not only with its traditional competitor but also with AT&T.
Especially they disliked the group's evident stranglehold on tubes.
Casting about for measures which might strengthen its own competitive position—and so its bargaining power—Westinghouse had moved
in the spring of 1920 to infuse new life (as Young had been quick to
note) into the ailing International Radio Company, by means of a
capital investment which in effect made International a Westinghouse
subsidiary. Cross-licensing agreements followed, on the GE-RCA pattern, and since International owned the Fessenden heterodyne pat-

ents, Westinghouse clearly stood to benefit. But when International's president went to Europe that summer for a slice of the promising overseas communication business, he came home empty-handed. The cables might be swamped and the outlook for wireless never better, but of this potential traffic RCA had already secured "the lion's share"—in the strict, and fabled, sense.[30]

Nevertheless, International now had sufficient capital as well as patents to pose something of a threat, and Young moved swiftly to meet it. On September 2, after dictating two letters to Guy Tripp, Westinghouse's chairman, which he decided not to send, Young telephoned Tripp and made him an offer. A handwritten note on the back of one of Young's unmailed letters recorded the offer as 700,000 shares of RCA preferred and 700,000 shares of common.[31] In exchange, RCA was to get the bulk of International's assets, including the $2,200,000 in cash still due from Westinghouse; and a general exchange of licenses in the radio field was to follow.

Under prodding, perhaps, from radio enthusiasts like his associates Harry P. Davis and Frank Conrad, Tripp not only held out for more but took additional measures to assure it. Westinghouse already held some of Major Edwin H. Armstrong's earlier patents, and in October moved to buy the so-called Armstrong-Pupin patents with their valuable super-heterodyne and improved feedback devices. In these, GE also showed some interest, but when Armstrong suggested to his attorney playing off one against the other, he was advised to take the Westinghouse offer now, lest the bidders combine and drive down the price. Prudently, Armstrong did so. In the same month, Young reported to the RCA board that he had offered Tripp one million shares each of RCA preferred and common.[32]

At about this time, crude local experiments with actual broadcasting in East Pittsburgh were capturing the speculative attention of Westinghouse officials. As these developed in the nick of time to produce the first, if local, broadcast of a presidential election—on November 2, 1920, over station KDKA—it became clear that Westinghouse was on to something. If this was of little immediate concern to Young, whose eye was still fixed on his overseas communications company, with its global ramifications, this was by no means true of Sarnoff— or of GE's radio engineers, who, in fact, were kicking themselves.[33]

For the moment, Young's immediate concerns were international. British Marconi had been complaining for some time that RCA had been given too dominant a voice in the South American company which their contracts called for, and yet had done little or nothing to promote its development. Ready as he was to defend the delay, Young was anxious on RCA's account to reassure Godfrey Isaacs. When the latter arrived in New York early in November, Young arranged for him an elaborate dinner party which probably did more for the cause than all of the settlements laboriously worked out in the course of a series of meetings. Certainly Isaacs's letter of thanks and farewell made it clear that he had been charmed as well as delighted by his reception. And he did win limited but definite concessions.[34]

The new year too was bringing its own quota of new problems. The American delegates to the so-called preliminary Conference on International Communications, which had been meeting in Washington during the late fall, had been singularly unreceptive to Young's urgent plea for separate cable and radio conventions. America, he had argued, was relatively weak in the first and potentially strong in the second; besides, the problems were distinct.[35] Indeed, it was partly for this reason that he had first asked to be excused from testifying before Senator Kellogg's subcommittee on Cable Landing Licenses, but it turned out to be a good thing for RCA that the senator insisted. Young's testimony of January 11, 1921—reference to which brings this account, so to speak, full circle—was remarkably sharp in explaining not only the why and how of RCA's creation (still excluding Westinghouse) but also the nature of the problems and potentialities it was currently confronting—notably in the Orient and South America.[36]

With an eye to the latter, Young thereupon arranged for Swope as well as Nally—accompanied by his own assistant, Elwood—to wait on Isaacs in London. Sailing on January 20, their first task was to clarify, and verify, the terms of Anglo-American cooperation in South America, and then—but only then—to bring the French and Germans in.[37] Such a four-party agreement was becoming a matter of some urgency if ruinous competition was to be averted. The Germans, quick to move in, were strengthening their position in the Argentine as well as Brazil; the French, like British Marconi and even RCA, had various rights and concessions.

Adding to the fun and games was a maze of intercorporate relationships in which a novice—as Gerard Swope was not—might easily get lost. Chartered to develop intercontinental communication between the Americas, the so-called Pan American Wireless Company, now controlled by RCA, had been owned three-eighths by British Marconi, three-eighths by American Marconi and two-eighths by the Federal Telegraph Company of California—which also had its eye on Trans-Pacific Wireless. How to transfer these interlocking rights and concessions—highly unequal in value—to the proposed cooperative venture on an equitable basis was puzzle enough. It was further complicated by echoes of the Monroe Doctrine—distant but distinct— which Young translated to mean that, in South America, any equal pooling of interests with its European counterparts must somehow leave R C A more equal than the others.[38]

v

If the delegation to Nally and Swope of this formidable assignment left Young free to pursue negotiations with Westinghouse, his pursuit at this stage was less than hot. Evidently he wanted the two presidents, Rice and Edwin M. Herr, to be fully involved, and until January of 1921, their meetings were mostly without him.[39] Having dealt with the financial question himself, he may have been curious to see how they would deal with the other problems identified in his two unmailed letters to Tripp of September 2, 1920. These accounted, indeed, for the entire text of the second letter, which read:

> My suggestion of the trade of the International Company, outlined in my earlier letter to you of today of course contemplates some arrangement satisfactory to the General Electric Company and the Westinghouse Company, regarding the manufacturing of radio apparatus. It goes without saying that such understanding must be in full compliance with the law because our effort here is not to restrict or control the manufacture and sale of radio apparatus, but to try to set up an American radio communications company, which, so far as patents and resources are concerned, will be best able to serve American interests in the radio communications field.[40]

The distinction was a nice one—too nice perhaps for transmission without further exposition—but valid nevertheless. In the domestic and ship-to-shore fields, continuing competition was to be expected, notably from the Poulsen Arc; in overseas communication, the problem was quite different. Here Young was utterly convinced that, in order to compete with the cables effectively—and incidentally to deal on equal terms with foreign wireless concerns—an American monopoly, public or private, was imperative. Navy Secretary Daniels agreed. They differed only in their priorities, Daniels putting a government monopoly first and Young putting it second; but, their first choice failing, both saw their second as the only feasible alternative.[41] As for broadcasting, when this letter was dictated, K D K A's November demonstration was still two months away.

In the meantime, under the watchful eye of A. G. Davis, Rice and Herr were far too busy with the manufacturing problem to worry much about the others. How divide the opportunities and obligations involved for the manufacturers in meeting RCA's needs? Certainly not by applying the formula which GE and Western Electric had adopted—namely, letting the type of apparatus ordered determine the maker. Davis, at one point, was so bothered by this problem, and more especially by fears of some such forced solution, as seriously to question the need of bringing Westinghouse in. Just as an anonymous memorandum of May 1919 had questioned whether the telephone company's patents were really essential, so Davis began to derogate the importance to radio reception of the heterodyne and Armstrong feedback devices; GE and AT&T could perfectly well make do with what they had, even if their receiving apparatus were admittedly not so good and not so cheap.[42]

As finally worked out over the succeeding months, with Young's occasional but determining assistance, the purchase by RCA of all manufactured radio devices not explicitly reserved to Western Electric was to be prorated: 60 percent to General Electric, 40 percent to Westinghouse. Davis wasn't too happy about this either, nor were the engineering and production people. As for RCA, the arrangement was cumbersome enough to nourish David Sarnoff's growing (if controlled) conviction that one day his company must acquire manufacturing rights and facilities of its own. Even Rice made some motions in the same direction.[43] On the other hand, as both readily acknowledged, any threat of competition from Westinghouse's International Company was about to be removed, once and for all.

In the final showdown, all parties agreed that the proposed contracts were a good deal better than none. Once again it was Young's imminent departure on a long trip—this time quite unpremeditated—which precipitated a solution of sorts. On March 25, 1921, the day before his deadline, Young and Tripp signed papers recording their agreement that the radio interests of Westinghouse and General Electric were to be joined, in accordance with a stated set of governing principles. Most of these—including extension and exchange of cross-licensing agreements—are explicit or implicit in the preceding account of the negotiations, but two deserve special mention.

First: To assure orderly progress toward definitive contracts, item nine expressly stipulated that "if the two companies fail to agree as to the methods of carrying out this arrangement, any matters in question will be decided by Mr. [Joseph P.] Cotton [of McAdoo, Cotton and Franklin, counsel to RCA] after hearing . . . both sides."

Second: The offer of a million shares each of RCA preferred and common, which Young had already made with the RCA board's approval, was now formally—and not surprisingly—accepted by Tripp. Thus, far from being deferred, as in the telephone negotiations, this matter was settled out of hand.[44]

So far, so good—or was it? Why had Young raised his original offer so sharply and so quickly? Had he lost his taste for a horse trade? Was he suddenly being magnanimous to GE's traditional competitor which in broadcasting, certainly, had stolen a march? Or was he ready, like any collector needing one last volume to complete a valuable set, to pay any premium necessary to acquire it?

The suggested and suggestive analogy to the book collector is, for Young, not out of character, except that his experience in that art was still only in its infancy. This was even more true of the art of broadcasting, where, in any event, the Westinghouse Company's assets were still largely intangible. While its newly acquired Armstrong-Pupin patents might call for additional RCA common, heretofore the issue of RCA preferred had been limited to the value of the cash and other *tangible* assets delivered in exchange. By this standard, Westinghouse would appear to have qualified for little more than half of its actual allotment of preferred; why then this gross discrepancy and why had the RCA board been so ready to approve it?

For one thing, this particular deal involved something more than a cross-licensing agreement coupled with a Westinghouse investment in the Radio Corporation; it involved the actual purchase of the International Radio Telegraph Company. Known to Young from the outset, moreover, as suggested by his original offer, was the fact that Tripp faced a problem of divided ownership with respect to the sale of "his" International company. Of the latter, Fessenden's original backers—whose interests were now vested in the Given Estate of Pittsburgh—had been sole owners until Westinghouse had come in with fresh capital; in the reorganized company, the preferred stock, with a par value of $1,250,000, went to the Estate. So did half of the no-par common, for the other half of which Westinghouse had agreed to pay $2,500,000. At that valuation the Given holdings alone would thus be worth some $3,750,000, and no sale could be made without the Given Estate's approval. If this could be assured simply by a generous issue of stock, why quibble?—especially since the assets accruing to RCA would include, as a welcome accretion to capital, the $2,500,000 cash subscription to International as pledged by Westinghouse. And was it sheer coincidence that in the final tabulation of stock ownership in RCA, GE's share was 30 percent to Westinghouse's 20—thus reflecting the 60-40 ratio which was to govern their division of manufacturing production for RCA?[45]

That this and other final contracts still to be worked out were nevertheless not executed until June 30, while Young was still away, and even then not finally delivered until the second week of August, indicates that the free-flowing "agreement in principle" of March 25 had left a great deal of unfinished business in its wake.[46] Nevertheless, it was substantially on these terms that the deal was finally closed.

v i

It was unfinished business of quite another sort that was to account for Young's long and unexpected absence. Nally and Swope had returned from Europe with reports of mission accomplished; subject only to final clearance and ratification, a four-power pact for the cooperative development of wireless communication with South America now seemed assured.[47] But for some months Young had been looking in a very different direction.

Transpacific communication by cable was slow, uncertain and expensive, and it was time that wireless mounted a real challenge. Moreover, if the United States was to become the center of a worldwide system of wireless communications, it was important to explore at once the possibilities of reciprocal arrangements with relatively small Japan and sprawling China.[48]

So far his exploration had been at second hand: putting increasingly searching questions to GE's representatives in the Orient and, through the good offices of the San Francisco banker Mortimer Fleischhacker, opening discussions with the president of the Federal Telegraph Company, R. P. Schwerin.[49] But with Swope's return from Europe, the prospect changed dramatically. Notified of the death of one of IGE's top officers in Japan, Swope said that Nally would have to return alone for the ratification ceremonies; he himself was bound for the Orient. And he urged Young to come along.

They would take plenty of time, he said, getting some rest on the long voyage, with leisurely visits to Japan, Peking, Shanghai, Hong Kong and Manila, plus a possible stopover in Honolulu. The word *leisurely* was no part of Swope's accustomed vocabulary, but by this time it sounded very good indeed to Young. Not for years had he had a real vacation, nor had he yet crossed either ocean. He had been toying with the idea of taking his two elder sons to Europe in late spring or early summer, but even that could wait. This trip with Swope offered singular opportunities: to visit a civilization much older than Europe's, to explore for himself the possibilities for wireless development in the

Orient, and not least to take the measure of this fellow Swope—in action and as a person.

By 1921 this last consideration had become all-important, because Charles Coffin, now seventy-five, was confessing privately to Young his determination to retire and his hopes that Young would then take over as president of GE. In response Young had said that when the time came Coffin would find him far better fitted for the post of chairman, adding that Swope would prove to be far better fitted than he for the president's role. Now he had an unparalleled chance to test out this suggestion, and more important, the consonance of their ideas and the possibilities of their working together as a really effective team.[50]

Young knew he had to go. So did Jo when he told her why, although the prospect left her heavyhearted. So too did his mother, who had welcomed him to Van Hornesville for a long weekend beginning March 19. His elder sons, he knew, had counted heavily on their planned trip to Europe; he would have to make it up to them later. And so, returning to his office on Tuesday morning, March 22, Young finally announced that he would be sailing with Swope.

He had left himself a slim margin. Swope had already booked passage on the Pacific Mail steamer *Ecuador*, leaving the Golden Gate for Yokohama on Saturday, April 2. If Young was to find time for some last-minute business in San Francisco, he must plan to leave New York by the Twentieth Century Limited not later than March 26. But first there was much to be done, and his office took on something of the atmosphere of bustle that was more characteristic of Swope's.

While his staff was busy with a hundred things, expediting passports and canceling engagements, Young summoned Walter Carpenter of Du Pont, A. V. Davis of the Aluminum Company of America and Paul Schoellkopf of Niagara-Hudson for urgent meetings on Niagara and St. Lawrence power developments. Expecting to be away until the middle of July, he was eager to do what he could to promote concerted action on that front. He also sent a disarming telegram to the new secretary of commerce, Herbert Hoover, whose tenure was scarcely more than two weeks old: "I am leaving for Japan on Saturday . . . and will probably be away for two and a half months. I do not want to sneak out of the country without advising my superiors." Responding in the same vein, Hoover gave his "reluctant consent."[51]

It was, of course, on the very eve of Young's departure that the agreement with Tripp was duly signed, following an exchange of letters by both principals with Joseph P. Cotton as counsel for RCA.

Cotton had given informal assurance that the terms of the agreement involved no violation of the antitrust laws—an assurance he was to confirm in writing when the contracts were executed and delivered the following summer. Nevertheless, Young's final act before departing was to call A. G. Davis with the request that he get in touch with GE's senior counsel, Frederick P. Fish, asking him to advise GE's directors whether in his opinion it was proper "from the point of view of the General Company that this arrangement should go through." Confident that Fish would indeed so find and the GE board acquiesce, Young could sail for parts unknown satisfied that, in terms of its corporate structure, he had now accomplished for RCA all that he had set out to do, and more.[52] What else was possible, in a global sense, he would now perhaps discover.

Chapter 14

International Dimensions: The Orient and Paris

THE San Francisco Limited pulled into its destination on March 30, and Young, joined shortly thereafter by Swope, spent three nights at the Palace Hotel. There were some business meetings, with Herbert Fleischhacker, Mortimer's brother, with Dr. Addison of GE's San Francisco office, and others, but what Young enjoyed most was an all-day trip north of the city to the radio stations. He described it in detail in a letter to his daughter: in a small Buick they set out, first across the bay by ferry, then on a narrow mountain road, to the radio sending station at Bolinas—"a small village remote from the railroad, set inland among high hills at the head of a long narrow bay"— with the towers of the sending station rising, as the local bus driver told him, like huge "fountain pens writing anywhere on earth." Thence they traveled thirty miles farther north to the receiving station at Marshall, "where I listened to Honolulu and Japan until I was tired." He described the housing arrangements for the operators and their families, and the beauty of the setting—"on the edge of a great inlet of the Pacific called Tomales Bay with mountains or high hills all around."[1] It was an appropriate beginning for a long journey made to further radio communication, to set up more "fountain pens."

But as the letter to his daughter indicated, his thoughts were turning eastward; he was well aware of his wife's feelings about so long a separation and of what he was asking of her. The baby was only twenty months old, Philip was eleven, Josephine was fourteen, and the mother would have her hands full with both Little Point and 830 Park to manage, and Mother Young to keep an eye on. The two elder boys, on whom she depended so much, were away at college, and now planning a trip to Europe by themselves. Certainly Jo was accustomed to being left alone with the younger children, but she was not resigned.

To be sure, the household was well staffed, with Tom, the butler/

valet, keeping his watchful eye on daily routines, and Margaret, whose principal job was the baby but who did much else besides, filling the rooms with Irish songs and irrepressible laughter. And also there was Elizabeth, who sewed and mended and helped the middle children— a German-speaking Swiss, taciturn, devoted. Best of all, at Jo's right hand was Gertrude Chandler, Owen's financial secretary, for not only in the office did she devote her time to the affairs of the Youngs. A Vermonter and a spinster, she was indefatigable in both places, receiving in return admiration and respect, and the warmest affection. A model of prim decorum at work, always chic with her gray curls and high-heeled shoes, Chan relaxed on weekends at Riverside, where, with as much pleasure as the children, she played games indoors and out. When she got her sneakers on she could run as fast as they.

Even though the paterfamilias was absent so often, the equable atmosphere of the home was not interrupted. The mother, New England to the core, was sometimes strict but never stern; the children had no doubt about how they were supposed to behave (even if there were exceptions in practice) and no doubt of what was expected of them—nor about what they expected of their parents. Nor did they feel that their father was neglectful; they knew that he was deeply concerned about each one. He had the ability to make each one feel that he was wholly interested in what he or she was thinking about at the moment, whether it was a summer job for C.J., choosing a violin for John, Philip's learning to ride a bicycle (Pops demonstrated), Josephine's learning to swim (Pops did *not* demonstrate) or Dick's new rocking horse. As they grew older they realized that he had this gift of total attention in dealing with everyone, but this did not diminish their pleasure.

But crossing the Pacific meant a long interim in other relationships too. There was the seventh member of his family, in Van Hornesville, for whom he retained to the end of her life a respect and filial regard that made him seem more the dependent than she. His mother lived wholly for him, but she did not hesitate to tell him off when occasion required—to the awe and delight of her grandchildren. And it did him good; supported by this continuity, talking over his affairs with her by the stove or on the vine-walled porch, teasing and being teased, he went away a new man.

It was still a source of satisfaction to him that the house in the village had proved such a good home for her and her brother, Uncle John Brandow, whose wife had died in 1912. Owen had put in a hot-air furnace for them, but when he suggested running water, Mother demurred. It wasn't necessary, she said; they had good soft wash water from the cistern filled by the rain, and they could go to the spring for drinking and cooking water. Apparently he lost this argument, for he wrote her a letter on his return to New York after a visit in the spring of 1919:

Dear Mother:

You and Uncle John may be young enough to trail out to an icy tub under the elm tree in order to get some water, but I am too old for that sort of thing and so if you don't mind, taking into full consideration my advanced age, I hope you will follow out the original plans of having water brought into the house. However, the matter is your job and not mine, and after I had asked the advice of my neighbors, I would finally put the water where I wanted it if I were in your place.

Affectionately—
Owen[2]

It had become difficult for him lately to pay as much attention to the farms as he wanted to, and as they needed, but here his assistant, young Elwood, could help. An upstate boy, grandson of John Brandow, he was not, like his cousin Owen, a farmer at heart, but he was familiar with both the land and the people. Also, he understood the newfangled ideas, such as keeping close records on each cow—what she ate and how much milk she gave—which were essential to a long-range breeding program. He insisted on these, and on detailed accounting, and kept the farms in order. And, of course, Owen could always take a hand when serious matters came up. Between sending off a message to Burchard in Paris about snagging some business for GE in Belgium, Greece and Rumania, and a wire to Tyler about the Dallas situation, he wrote Hale Mixer, the head farmer, about a misbehaving cow: "If she will not run with the others or you are afraid of her corrupting their good manners, put a halter on her and stake her out. I cannot think of selling her merely because she is a little bit hard to handle."[3]

As for St. Lawrence, Young had now a new reason for special attention to the college. The fall of 1920 saw his second son, John, a freshman on the campus—exactly thirty years after the first boy from Van Hornesville stepped off the train at the Canton depot. In 1919, moreover, after a brief and unsuccessful interlude, a new president had taken over. This time the trustees had been determined to find a Universalist minister, and Young had gone from church to church listening to possible candidates. He found what they wanted: Richard Eddy Sykes of the class of 1883, pastor of the Universalist church in Malden, Massachusetts, who was to relieve the board of trustees of this particular concern for sixteen years.

St. Lawrence, like other small colleges, eroded by the war, was in serious need of funds; endowment and buildings were totally inadequate. Young had written Frank Oliver Hall, an old friend and pastor of the Church of the Divine Paternity in New York City—himself a first, but unwilling, choice for the presidency of the college—that St. Lawrence was "capable of doing the bigger thing but she cannot quite afford to do it. My dreams for her future will have to be postponed." Nevertheless, he went to work to bring them about, and knew he had been an important factor in the successful million-dollar fund drive which Sykes instituted. His imaginative ideas, his constant rallying of alumni, and his pressure on his rich friends made all the difference.[4]

But now family, farms, college, as well as the infinite tasks and complications of the New York office were to be left behind for almost four months. On previous visits to San Francisco—including the one with Jo—he had seen the ships pass out through the Golden Gate; now he too was to leave, for the first time, American shores. He was tired, he was excited, he was ready to go.

ii

The *Ecuador* sailed on April 2, 1921, and reached Yokohama just before dawn three weeks later. It was a long voyage for a novice in ocean travel, and it took Young some days to get used to it. But, a week out, they stopped for a day and a night at Honolulu, where they were met by GE and radio people, and Young's St. Lawrence friend Floyd Griffiths, president of Oahu College.[5] They went to inspect the big radio sending station which Young had listened to in California, driving through the fields of cane and pineapple, and his first glimpse of Pearl Harbor impressed Young very much.

The stopover was a welcome break; but the long succeeding days spelled rest of a sort that he had never known:

I have never been quite so lazy in my life [he wrote Jo] and I have set some pretty good records. After leaving Honolulu I decided to adopt Mr. Swope's schedule—that is to have breakfast in bed between 8:30 and 9 o'clock—then read or doze until about 11:30, then have a bath and get out on deck about 12:30 for a half-hour's walk before lunch at 1. After luncheon we read and talk until about five o'clock then walk sharp for an hour—get up a good sweat—have another bath and dress for dinner for want of something better to do.

After dinner Swope and I play cards or shake dice and about ten have a bottle of *beer*—think of beer—and go to bed. This goes on day after day until you lose all track of time. . . . The monotony of it . . . does not get on my nerves but I feel like a vegetable.[6]

If, during those long days, the vegetable was engaged in any serious talk with Swope about their future, their words went unrecorded. But with such unparalleled leisure, and two such active minds, it can be assumed that in the walks around the deck, and from two adjoining deck chairs, there was wide-ranging assessment and analysis of every angle of American industry, with special attention to GE and RCA. And since both were of sanguine temperament, there was no doubt some long-range and optimistic planning, in case the power should come into their hands. Young was forty-six, Swope was forty-seven, and the world lay before them.

Not until they were nearing Yokohama had Owen put pen to paper, but then he wrote Jo five folios of letter paper, on all four sides. This was the first in a sequence of eight half-diary, half-travelogue communications in which the tyro traveler set down for his family his first impressions of the strange lands and people he was encountering.

There were four strenuous weeks in Japan, visiting with the heads of the firms—electrical manufacturing, public utilities and radio—calling on the appropriate government officials, being "entertained to death" and simply being tourists. They had a weekend at Miyanoshimas's hot springs, where they climbed a thirty-two-hundred-foot peak and had a glimpse of Fuji "with its head in the clouds and its sides dressed in white." They motored to Halcowe Lake, lunched at a lakeside inn, and taking a guide "walked twelve miles over the mountains to Atami," the barren mountain trail ending in a burst of orange trees and terraced vegetation—"every inch cultivated"—as they neared that seaside town. The following weekend found them in Nikko, visiting the shrines and the curio shops and admiring the famous cryptomeria. Owen told Jo that "it was in Nikko I wanted you so much, and we must arrange to come before long because it is so lovely . . . with all my love . . ."

Back in Tokyo, "while Swope was going over the accounts," [he wrote], "I went to a curio shop here and fell for . . . incense boxes and some small but exquisite pieces of gold lacquer. . . . Everybody tells me that when I go to Kyoto, I will surely go broke—to say nothing about Peking."

The days given over to business are duly mentioned but get short shrift. J. R. Geary, GE's head man in Japan, had met the ship and they visited his office before proceeding to Tokyo by the interurban, which, "tho' government owned and operated, gives excellent service." The first day they received calls, the second attended conferences, the third, went to the lamp works—"interesting but not worth writing about"—and the following week "we have been trying to do business."

On the very night of their arrival, a Japanese newspaper editor and owner, who was a classmate of Charles Stone of Stone and Webster, had given them an elaborate ceremonial dinner at a Tokyo teahouse, where Young could see for the first time the low tables and cushions, the endless succession of courses, the serving and geisha girls, the formal toasts in sake between the host and each one of his guests. Swope, "being both small and experienced, did pretty well," Young reported, but his own first efforts to cope with chopsticks might have been more successful if he had been able to dispose his long legs with greater grace. "If I got on my knees I was up too high and if I tried to fold my legs under me my knees stuck way up . . . I finally gave up trying to sit Japanese style and work my chopsticks . . . so I stretched out my legs which seemed to reach half way across the room and tackled my chopsticks with a will." All of this transpired, he wrote, "much to the amusement of everybody," the girls not least. On a later occasion, he told his children when he got home, he got three of the girls to sit in front of the long legs to hide them.

At a formal tea party given by the greatly respected Dr. Takuma Dan, Young, arriving in cutaway and top hat, found himself as tall as the house. It was there that he saw the traditional tea ceremony for the first time, and wrote a detailed account of it to Jo. To her also, knowing how she would have enjoyed them, he described the gardens and the flowers, especially beautiful at that season.

He was not sorry to leave Tokyo, even in a sleeper whose berths were so small he lay "doubled up like a jackknife." But he found Kyoto "the ancient capital and art center of Japan . . . a dangerous place to come to if you do not want to spend your money." He bought more lacquer, and beautiful kimonos and brocades for his wife and daughter. Charles Tyler would have been delighted to see his pupil adapt his taste to a whole new world of objets d'art.

For so relatively short a visit, by such an inexperienced traveler, Young learned a great deal, not only about art, not only about the electrical and communications industries in Japan, but about the Japanese people. He had good tutors in Swope and Geary, but he was able to assess for himself the man behind the mask. His antennae, like those of his radio stations, were extraordinarily receptive. And he was listening to leaders: Dr. Takuma Dan of the great Mitsui banking and industrial corporation, Iwahura of Shibaura Engineering Works and Dr. O. Asano of the Illuminating Engineering Society among them. He sensed at once their pride and their sensitivity, and soon came to understand their problems: overpopulation with its constant specter of famine, a great defense establishment resulting in heavy taxation, over which the people had no control. "We—or any other nation—cannot discriminate against Japan as an inferior people. They feel that they have attained the dignity and the advancement of Occidental nations and unless we—and all other nations—accord them the respect due to this equal position we may have trouble. On that point Japan is keenly sensitive."

He made these points in an interview for the *Brooklyn Eagle* upon his return. In answer to a question he said also: "I do not believe that there is any class of people in Japan, that wants war with America. On the contrary, they are very desirous of avoiding such a contingency."[7]

iii

They entered China by the port of Tsingtao, and went thence by rail to Peking, through Shantung Province, "as this is so much in the public eye just now." The Japanese had driven the Germans from their rich concessions in Shantung early in World War I, and although lip service was paid to neutral China for the eventual return of the province to Peking, the conquerors settled in.[8] Young saw the "elaborate fortifications the Germans constructed," which the Japanese were allowing to fall to pieces; in the interview for the *Eagle*, "Mr. Young refused to discuss the Shantung situation more than to say, in general, of the Orient that if Japan gains for itself an economic, scientific and commercial superiority in the East it will find itself with the sympathy of the whole world, but in case the little island kingdom attempts to exercise political domination it will find itself, on the other hand, with most of the world disapproving."[9]

On May 30 Young was writing from the Grand Hotel de Pékin that "this is the most fascinating place in the world." He had been there a week, too busy with the sights and the shops to write, falling into bed at night dead tired. "I have spent all my money. . . . I am writing this before breakfast as we leave for Shanghai this morning and there is no use my trying to write about Peking. How I want you to come here with me. . . ."[10]

On the way to Shanghai, he told his interviewer later on, they passed through the edge of "the famine district . . . and saw hundreds of women crowding against wire fences of the railroad stations, begging, holding aloft babies—nothing more than skin-covered skeletons, terrible, horrible sights . . . passengers threw them coppers and they fought among themselves for them. . . . With proper transit means," said Young, taking a long shot, "there probably never would have been any famine. There are not enough railways or waterways. In some parts of China there is rice rotting in the fields, in other parts starving people."[11]

From Shanghai he wrote Jo a brief letter, saying nothing of the "International City," except that he and Swope had been "busy night and day." They had seen Wilhelm Meyer of Anderson Meyer, and visited the British-owned and directed Hong Kong and Shanghai Bank, as well as other business people. They were sailing for Manila "this afternoon"; after four days there they would take the *Empress of Asia* for home, stopping over one week in Hong Kong, one day in Shanghai, and due in Vancouver about the twelfth of July. He said he expected to reach home before any further letters he might write, so he wouldn't write them, and concluded: "Your letters up to May 3rd are here, also C.J.'s. Have cabled you approving boys' plans [for Europe]. Think them very good. So glad to know you are well . . . I am getting homesick now and anxious to get back to you. No place seems so fine as Riverside. Love to you and the children."

The visit to Manila was an especially enjoyable and pleasant one; Young had letters of introduction to people there, including one from Mabel Rice Parker, E. W. Rice's daughter, who was now living in Hong Kong, where her husband represented Standard Oil. Young met Mabel's friend Louise Powis Brown at a dinner given by Samuel Stow of the Pacific Mail and his wife; Mrs. Brown, an attractive young widow, was also sailing on the *Empress*. She had come to the Philippines with her husband, who was with the Y M C A, and after his untimely death set up a business in Philippine embroideries to support herself and her two children. Young wrote Stow, after he got home, testifying not only to the pleasure their hospitality had given him, but to the "great help which [their friend] Mrs. Brown gave me in Manila and especially to her charming company on the *Empress*. We had a delightful trip across." To Philo Parker he wrote also, saying how much he had enjoyed seeing "you and Mabel again . . . I wish you every success, and what is better, I am confident that you will have it." And Philo was asked to "tell Mabel that I found her friend, Mrs. Brown, worthy of our best traditions."[12]

Copies of each of these went to Mrs. Brown, at her mother's home in Wayne, Illinois, with covering notes: "My dear Mrs. Brown," the first began, "I do not think it quite proper for me to have any communications with your friends in Manila, especially regarding you, unless you are advised about them. Dutifully, therefore, I enclose copy of my letters to Mr. Stow. If I said too much, you will correct it; if I said too little, you will generously ascribe it to my incapacity of expression." In the second, enclosing a copy of his letter to the Parkers, he wrote: "I am perfectly ready to disclose to you what I say about you to anyone in Hong Kong as well as in Manila. Please understand, however, that outside of these two places, I will say what I please."[13]

These letters were to acquire, with time, an unanticipated significance. But the sequel belongs to a much later chapter—in their lives and in this book.

During the stopover in Hong Kong, Young had taken a trip to Macao, where he had unusual (for him) bad luck in that city of gambling, and then to Canton, "where Dr. Sun's southern Republic of China is situated." He found it the cleanest city he had seen, and was impressed by Sun's attempts to rid his republic of gambling and opium—both rife in nearby Macao: "It is strange that a European nation should allow this while the Chinese are attempting to stamp opium and gambling out."[14]

The second stay in Japan was brief, and there is no further report on the voyage home. J. M. Cranston, GE's veteran manager at Portland, met the *Empress* at Victoria, and Elwood met the train in Chicago, bearing armloads of mail and reports of fresh difficulties with Godfrey Isaacs over the South American contract. Monday, July 18, found Young back in his familiar office at 120 Broadway, looking out at the Atlantic.

iv

Young's thoughts, like the huge batch of letters of acknowledgment he now dispatched, might still be directed toward the Pacific, but the transatlantic mails quickly confirmed E. J. Nally's reports of a crisis in the South American negotiation. For this Nally blamed Isaacs, for refusing even to consider certain amendments to the original agreement which the RCA board had directed him to propose and even press; returning the compliment with interest, Isaacs had threatened to proceed himself with the French and the Germans. RCA having countered this threat with one of its own, a stalemate ensued.

Now Nally reported receipt of Isaacs's five-page letter of July 12, denouncing delaying tactics in general and RCA's recent proposals in particular. Taking vigorous exception as well to a certain "clause seven" in the original Anglo-American agreement, Isaacs wrote in conclusion: "There appears to us to be but one practical business course open to us and that is to carry through the consortium to which all parties have agreed in principle and from which we should be sorry to see the Radio Corporation retire at the eleventh hour."[15]

That was the situation confronting Young on July 28 when, for the first time since March 25, he presided at an RCA board meeting. Nally having made a full report and the letter from Isaacs having been reviewed, the whole matter was referred to the chairman, who proceeded to Washington the following week as planned to make his report to Hoover. Within a fortnight, however, the chairman acted, sending Isaacs a cable which provoked an exchange that speaks for itself.

Young to Isaacs—August 11, 1921

Your formal letter twelfth Radio Corporation has been referred to me by Board of Directors stop This message is not to be considered as a reply to that letter because personally I desire to approach the matter constructively free from the restraints which some portions of your letter seem to impose stop The real question is whether your company and mine desire to carry out the spirit of the cooperative arrangement which you discussed with me in New York last November and later with Nally and Swope in London stop I understood that we were then in agreement as to fundamentals and your letter of the twelfth seems to confirm that view stop If you wish to deal with the matter in the spirit above outlined I should be glad to meet you first in London and immediately thereafter the Germans and French with you at some convenient place on the Continent stop I am notifying French and Germans direct of my willingness to attend such conference and I would appreciate having the time and place fixed before I sail . . . if this suggestion is not acceptable to you I will formally reply to your letter of the twelfth.

Isaacs to Young—August 12, 1921

I am very pleased to receive your telegram yesterday regretting only that any thought with you should have inspired the last sentence of your message stop I can assure you my company's desire to cooperate with yours as closely and as widely as possible has not changed stop I shall be very pleased to see you earliest possible date of your arrival I will at once fix meeting at a convenient place on Continent with French and Germans as you propose stop Hoping you contemplate sailing not later than August 18th otherwise Argentine representative will have sailed and Dr. Schapira will be on holiday

Young to Isaacs—August 13, 1921

Will do my best to leave Aquitania twenty-third will wire you definitely early next week

Young to Isaacs—August 15, 1921

Nally Elwood and I sail Aquitania twenty-third assume this date will be convenient for you stop Hope it will not inconvenience Doctor Schapira and that Argentine director will wait[16]

Clearly the significance of one "innocent" phrase in Young's first message had not been lost on Isaacs, nor had Young expected it to be. By "notifying French and Germans direct of my willingness to attend such conference" with them, Young had completely checkmated Isaacs's threatened move to proceed without the Radio Corporation. Isaacs, in short, was now on notice that RCA's absentee chairman was very much back on the job.

For the conference that ensued, source material is scanty. Young's papers record the texts of the two four-party agreements but not how they were arrived at. His letters to Jo tell of problems but seldom spell them out. Gleason Archer, whose *History of Radio to 1926* (1938) reprints the texts in full, writes of the negotiations with all the authority of one who has consulted the then-extant files, and perhaps even a participant or two. His account is flawed, however, first by want of documentation and second by a weakness for windy dramatization.[17]

Nevertheless, it is clear that, at the factual level, the drama afforded by the conference was superior. With Isaacs's acquiescence, Young had proceeded directly to Paris, where the British and the French— but not the Germans—were awaiting him. According to Archer, it was on Young's initiative and indeed at his insistence that the Germans were now invited to join them, and we see no reason to doubt it. For Young such an initiative was wholly in character; he had never been one to "wave the bloody shirt." And who else of the parties involved could or would have taken it?

More to the point, perhaps, is the fact that a conciliatory gesture to the Germans would have served Young's present purposes. Certainly he wanted the Germans on hand as foils to the British and the French, whom Isaacs could maneuver almost as he chose. In addition, the Germans, being strongly entrenched in South America, were indispensable to a practicable deal, and if the contemplated business consortium was ever to work, it was time to abate the emotional hangover of the war and get down to business.

Young's letters to his wife confirm—albeit in very general terms— the extreme difficulty of securing the kind of agreement he was after. As he wrote her on September 11: "Some nights I feel as if it were all over—like last night—then it clears up as it has today. . . . It takes so much time to negotiate for our talks have to be translated by our interpreter into two languages as we are using French, German and English. Tell [young] Jo that the interpreter takes full notes of the conversations in French and then translates them into German or English as the case may be. You can see how time goes and how misunderstandings arise and how difficult and tedious it is to clear them."

By the time, some two years later, that the Dawes Committee met in Paris in 1924 to untangle the vexed problem of German reparations, Young had learned how to turn these tedious delays to account: they gave him time, he said, to think out the next move. Here too this useful art would come in handy. In negotiating the proposed consortium, for example, equality was to be the key word, as it applied to the pooling of interests, investment and concessions, and of course to the division of profits. Thus it was natural to suggest that they now set up an International Trust Agreement, with each party naming two trustees to a central Board of Control. Where ultimate control was at issue, however, Young was aware from his talks with Admiral Bullard, Walter S. Rogers and others, that the U.S. government was deeply committed to the view that in the Western Hemisphere, America's voice must somehow be determining. How to assure this without upsetting the apple cart—and preferably by means less cumbersome and more certain than the controversial Article 7—was of course the really challenging question. He bided his time. More than once he was to find the conference in danger of imminent collapse, only to discover next day that all parties recoiled from the prospect. And he did find means which made Article 7 no longer worth bothering with— much to his own relief—though he was careful to make it appear to be a concession to Isaacs.

According to Archer, Young found his opportunity and proposed his solutions when Isaacs raised some question of special rights for Britain in the proposed consortium. To this the Germans naturally objected, and so did Young. There could be no thought, he said, of any departure from the principle of equality *except that,* to avert any possible deadlock among the eight trustees on the Board of Control, there should be added as neutral chairman an eminent American not connected with radio but selected by RCA. When the Germans, already smarting from a sense of isolation, protested that this would fatally stack the cards against them and threatened to walk out, Young responded with his masterstroke. To the contrary, he told them, the chairman should be empowered to veto any action by a majority which he found unfair to the minority.

Young said nothing to his wife about a German walkout or proposals to him for a separate pact with Telefunken. Archer reports not only this proposal but also that Young let Isaacs know that he was considering it very seriously, since there seemed so little chance of achieving anything else. It was then, according to this source, that Isaacs realized concessions were in order and that he and the French agreed to Young's proposal of a "neutral" American chairman, veto power and all. Young in turn hastened to assure them that he would indeed go to Berlin but only for the purpose of securing Telefunken's adherence to the four-party pact.

On Wednesday, September 21, some three weeks after the conference had opened, Young's presence in Berlin is recorded in a long letter to Jo which makes no mention of these issues but does refer to a daylong conference with the Telefunken people and a visit to "the big wireless station" at Nauen. It was his first visit to Berlin as it had been his first to Paris—where he had seen all too little of his son John; he had yet to see London and, especially with John now sailing for home, the outlook for that was not promising. Now, after visiting the great electrical concerns—the AEG and Siemens—with his friend Guy Tripp, he was leaving "tonight after dinner . . . by train for Paris, where our conferences are resumed on Friday."

His Telefunken conference had, he felt, been constructive, but even so, the fate of the negotiations hung in the balance. There followed, Young wrote Jo on October 22, "a week of struggle and strain and most of the time depression because matters looked so hopeless." But by this time there was good news too: "Yesterday, we came to an agreement much I think to everybody's surprise so we adjourned . . . until tomorrow" to let the lawyers draft the contracts. "Today we have many hurdles of details to cross but unless someone goes back on the main principles we shall complete the job . . . as the British, French and Germans are ready to cooperate in . . . South America under the leadership of the Americans—we always to have the final say. It has been a hard struggle but I am tremendously pleased today with the result. . . ."

He added—sweet words to the family at home—"I was never so homesick in my life." He had hardly seen Paris and there were "so many supplemental contracts with each of the parties that it looks now as though I would cancel my passage on the *Berengaria* and sail a week later on the *Aquitania*. My only consolation . . . is that I shall have a few days in London which I very much covet. I am tired of being in Paris without time to look about . . . [it makes] one feel like a dray horse . . . all my love to you and the children and Mother."

The hurdles were successfully negotiated, the main and supplemental agreements duly signed, and Young came home on the *Aquitania*, gratified, no doubt, at having succeeded where others had tried and failed. But this success had only served to whet his appetite. Now was the time to capitalize on his Paris experience and on his recent and unforgotten visit to the Orient.

Certainly Young had not long been home before he was exploring a similar consortium for the Pacific—with Japan and China as additional partners, and with a Chinese rather than an American serving as neutral chairman. He wrote Dr. Dan a long, explanatory letter about the European agreements for South America, and went on to suggest not only such a consortium for the Orient, but the formation of a kind of RCA in Japan—an RCJ, so to speak—to be supported by the Japanese electrical and engineering firms. He also wrote Secretary of the Navy Edwin Denby about the Chinese program, making a strong case for the use of only one private agency in the United States to deal with international communications; that is, a public utility under government regulation—RCA.[18]

And in January he wrote Elihu Root to advise him that inasmuch as Pacific communications were on the agenda of the Washington Conference on world disarmament, RCA had submitted a plan for international cooperation in the development of external communications in China.

"The real obstacle," Young told Root, "seems to be that some of your advisors are again raising that always effective cry of monopoly. I maintain that the external wireless communications of America should be done by a single public service company regulated by our own government as to rates, service, and return, and that there is no place for competition in the field of external communications . . . if the competitive theory be adopted, the foreigners will regulate our rates and service; if the monopoly theory be adopted our own Government will do so."[19]

The conference—like the State Department—saw it differently, however, and in spite of all Young's arguments and efforts, no resolution which would encourage such a cooperative venture in transpacific wireless communication was adopted. In writing Admiral Bullard, then commanding the Yangtze Patrol of the Asiatic Fleet, Young spoke frankly of his disappointment and some of its consequent problems:

I did my best to get the Disarmament Conference to recommend to the several governments for China such a cooperative plan as I had worked out in South America. Such a plan was acceptable to the British, French and Japanese, but I understand that Mr. Rogers and Commander Hooper both felt that it should be opposed by the Americans because it would tend to give the Radio Corporation a monopoly of external communications. Consequently . . . the advisers to the several governments entered into a memorandum as a result of which the British, French and Japanese agreed to adopt a cooperative program if it could be worked out, and I understand the Japanese tendered their Peking station to the cooperative group. Mr. Rogers dissented from the plan but said that the Federal [Telegraph Company] program should be supported, so far as radio was concerned. . . .

It was provided, however, that the British, French and Japanese might cooperate with other American companies than the Federal. This, of course, means that the door was opened for the Radio Corporation of America.

Walter S. Rogers had been adviser on communications to the American delegation at Versailles, and was performing the same service at the disarmament conference. The Federal Telegraph Company of California owned some concessions from the Chinese government, but had not progressed very far with them.

Accordingly [Young's letter to Bullard continued], today I am faced with the choice of cooperating with the Federal in the development of the Chinese communications or with the foreigners. I have stated unqualifiedly that I prefer to cooperate with the Americans, meaning the Federal, than the foreign interests in this development, but that I cannot go forward with the Federal unless Washington approves. Certainly the Radio Corporation does not want to run the risk of indictment because it cooperates with the American interests, when it will be entirely free under the law if it cooperates with the foreigner.[20]

Problems with Federal Telegraph were worked out in another year by the formation of a new company in which RCA had a major interest, but Young's dream that his South American Consortium might serve as a model for the transpacific area was to be forever frustrated. His one consolation was to find that his great friend Nelson Perkins was unanimously elected as the ninth, or "neutral," trustee of the consortium.

v

In radio Owen Young had found the new and exciting field which fulfilled his original hopes in leaving the law for General Electric. This was evident in his speech of November 5—his first in many years—celebrating the opening of Radio Central, with its twelve gigantic "fountain pens," at Rocky Point, Long Island. Confessing to the thrill it gave him that "today America is able to lay down in her name in twenty-eight countries . . . this message from the President of the United States," he mentioned both the new consortium for South America and the Washington Conference "just about to convene." He ventured the assertion that "underlying the success of any program of disarmament is the development of adequate communication" because "when you can no longer appeal to the armies . . . you must appeal to . . . public opinion. . . ." And this had better be informed.[21]

Reading the radio files and correspondence, it is hard to believe that Young was doing anything but dream of, and work for, making the United States the center of a worldwide wireless network. The record shows otherwise. He was in Paris when, in late September, President Harding's Unemployment Conference convened; citing the critical state of his current negotiations he successfully parried (without declining) Secretary Hoover's urgent plea for his attendance.[22] On his return, however, he found that Hoover had named him chairman of a small but broadly representative subcommittee set up by the conference to investigate the relationship of business cycles and unemployment.

That this was a novel undertaking for business, as for labor, had its own appeal for Young; so did the pledge of full cooperation from the newly chartered National Bureau of Economic Research. While a December bout with influenza hampered the chaiman's initial moves, his health was so far restored by a family Christmas at Van Hornesville that he was able with the new year to set things in motion— incidentally securing from the Carnegie Foundation the funding which the government had somehow neglected to provide. Such a study was, of course, no overnight assignment, but for that very reason Young was eager to get on with it.[23]

A second involvement which had its social as well as business implications stemmed quite naturally from Young's deep-rooted interest in the law and from his recent appearance on the international stage. Having been named by the U.S. Chamber of Commerce as chairman of its committee on commercial arbitration between nations, he was asked in October to present his views to the Council of the International Chamber. Here too, he felt, the need for constructive action was clear and urgent but was not to be met offhand. Characteristically pragmatic, he advised setting up machinery, not to deal with disputes in advance, but rather to indicate "certain conditions under which the Chamber is prepared to tender to business men its good offices in arranging for arbitration. . . . In this way the machinery of the Chamber can itself develop, step by step, to meet the demands upon it."

He discussed sanctions, pointing out that where legislation now existed in a country "it would be wise for the Chamber to take full advantage thereof, and a code for arbitration *within the law* is therefore . . . necessary. . . . The Chamber should look forward, certainly, to the time when every civilized country will have adequate legal provision for the carrying into effect of properly conducted business arbitration, but it must recognize the fact that at the present time, and probably for many years to come, it is equally important . . . for the Chamber to support and develop the moral sanction upon which arbitration outside the law must depend."[24]

This was to be the first of several expository essays Young made in a field that was close to his heart. But when, in March 1922, he was called again to Paris, the unfinished business he left behind included what for him was the most novel adventure of all. His deep-seated respect for the fourth estate—and not least for such a venerable institution as the *New York Evening Post*—had not been blunted by his devoted attachment to the new art of wireless; clearly the two were complementary. And when, finding the *Post* on the market and in need of an infusion of new blood—and funds—a notably public-spirited group had agreed in January to take it over, Young was among them. Assured of his freedom as editor, Edwin F. Gay agreed to stay on; only time could tell with what results.[25] Sanguine as usual, Young had such interest in this project that he almost hated to leave.

vi

But this Paris trip was different; the long sessions of negotiation were over, the contracts were signed, and this meeting was merely to organize and set up the International Board of Control for the South American Consortium. Nelson Perkins was indeed named chairman—no sinecure under the agreements—and he and his wife would be going; best of all, the meeting was to be held in Cannes—and Jo was going too.

It was her first trip abroad. In 1897 her parents had made the Tour; Josie had wanted to go, but, more, she had wanted to stay near Owen. But now she could have both, and although she was over fifty she approached it with the enthusiasm of a girl. When they arrived in Paris on March 22 she wrote a note to her daughter:

We landed at seven this A.M. at Havre—came up to Paris, arriving soon after one—Had such a nice dinner on the train, much better than our dining-cars. And I do wish you could see our apartment [they were staying at the Meurice] . . . gray paint all over curly decorations—old rose brocade in plenty—the bedroom in blue brocade etc! We are just waiting now for Mr. Boyden[26] of the Reparations Commission to come after us to go to dinner at some place noted for its snails! Pops has had numerous callers this afternoon,—a knock on the door—"Is Mr. Young—the great engineer of the Radio Company here?" All with French accent—and I have to precipitate myself into the bedroom to keep from laughing in their faces. Our bedrooms are on the court—so there isn't a sound and I cannot believe I am in Paris —It is a beastly day—snow flurries and cold, but coming through Normandy this morning there were violets and yellow primroses in blossom along the railway bank and the grass green—

Another letter, from Cannes on April 1—"perhaps the joke is that I'm over here at all!"—described beautiful drives to Grasse and along the coast, shopping with Lulu Perkins, the Mediterranean outside her windows: "I can see a little catboat beating across the bay—every reef in I judge—there are lots of aeroplanes around and a hydroplane that runs around here in front of the hotel—even saw a Ford this morning, but there are not many." Dinners at the Casino were fun—"fine music, good dancing, and after dinner went into the gambling rooms" (it certainly was easier for her to get her husband there than onto the dance floor).

Most interesting crowd—lords and ladies right from England, thick as spatter. An old Lady Kent last night had a wreath of green velvet leaves around her grey hair—all her diamonds on . . . she was just as busy as she could be at the high table . . . the King of Portugal was directing the play of one of his attachés at the same table. At the next table the Rajah of—— was taking a little chance—and Lady Beauchamp (they say Beecham's pills are responsible for her jewels) . . . M. Poiret the great French dressmaker wandering around . . . and M. Sern the French caricaturist . . . I saw him doing Mr. Balfour.

The Burchards were staying at Nice, and there were calls there, and an opera with Mrs. Isaacs where Jo "sat elbow to elbow with the Queen of Portugal—frowzy individual." Her only regret was that Owen could not be with her on all the expeditions.

The conference went off smoothly—how else under the combined power of Young and Perkins?—and Owen and Jo drove back to Paris through Avignon and Orange—"the Roman ruins fairly pursue you around here"—and north to Lyons.[27] By the eighth of May they were back in New York.

A week and a day after the Youngs' return, the directors of General Electric met to accept Charles Coffin's resignation and to elect his successor. Of these duties the first was the more difficult; the second was a foregone conclusion. And if the same could hardly have been said of the choice of Rice's successor, Coffin had neither lost his grip nor neglected his homework. Thus when he called the board to order on May 16, 1922, its action was swift and unanimous. The tributes and resolutions—more than ritual this time—once over, Rice was named honorary chairman and Burchard vice-chairman of the board. The new president was Gerard Swope, the new chairman Owen Young.[28]

This election came, of course, as no surprise to Owen and Jo and they greeted it calmly; the children took it as a matter of course. Yet Owen and Jo must have felt deep satisfaction and pride in this recognition of achievement and capacity. To Jo her husband was now indeed, and at the top, her "man of affairs."

Part III

*New Era and
Business Ascendancy*

1922–1930

Chapter 15

GE: Young and Swope
Find Room at the Top

THE new team worked, in both senses of the word. Swope might promise to do it all and Young to do as little as he must, but it would be hard to say which put in the longer or more productive hours. That neither could fault the other here had—just possibly—much to do with their extraordinary and continuing rapport.

As a team they looked an ill-matched pair. Swope, a five-foot-five engineering graduate of MIT, had become in his career at Western Electric, at home and abroad, a dynamic organizer and salesman who could talk the language of finance and accounting as well as production. A compact bundle of energy, he radiated decisiveness, knowledgeability and confidence. When his patience was tried, his manner could be chill and abrupt. What tried his patience most was waste—even of words, because words take time. Where the direction of so vast an organization as General Electric was concerned, time—everyone's time but especially his—was at a premium. Junior officers and even vice-presidents of long standing soon learned that their reports and recommendations had best be concise as well as precise if they wanted the president's favorable attention. If these criteria were met they got not only his attention but also a quick and clear directive, infrequently accompanied (as he bowed them out) by a brief but curiously disarming smile.

Young's presence and manner—legato to Swope's staccato—were in striking contrast, and so was his *modus operandi*. Tall and apparently relaxed where Swope was short and tense, he gave his callers the impression of being wholly at their disposal and so—if they had a real problem—he was. (If they hadn't, he was apt to be unavailable the next time they tried to see him.) On occasion his response could be as quick and direct as any man's, but if the question at issue were complex, he liked to turn it over and around and look at it from every angle. Thus he often discovered aspects which his visitor had not seen and these sometimes suggested a solution. But he was not to be hurried; if other engagements intervened and the question was left dangling, he might come up with a fresh clue to the answer days after his visitor had supposed the matter forgotten. Critics called him indecisive; admirers said that his subconscious mind worked overtime. An assistant once observed, with rueful admiration, that "his mind takes off where mine bogs down."

That the talents, training and disposition of the two were complementary was the easy, and the usual, explanation of their combined effectiveness. On the surface this explanation scans: both the lawyer and the engineer acknowledged limitations in the areas of the other's strength. Thus Young could admire without envy Swope's capacity to spot and speedily correct anything within the organization which threatened its current efficiency or the realization of its full potential; Swope could marvel in his turn at the patient ingenuity with which Young had designed and put together the Radio Corporation or reconciled disparate views in the Second Industrial Conference. Clearly, this sense of parallel but noncompeting aims was one source of the extraordinary mutual trust which was to make possible Young's extensive involvement in public affairs.

But that was not the only source. The two had also learned, if many of their colleagues had still to learn, how much they had in common in matters of great moment: their aspirations for the company, for example, or their convictions about the role of corporate management at this stage of industry's development. If their aspirations for GE were unbounded, some were also unorthodox, embracing as they did a *primary* concern for those who were "investing their lives" in the company.

Swope's social conscience had been sharpened early, by a year's residence at Chicago's Hull House, where his tutors had included Jane Addams and the remarkable woman who was to be his wife, Mary Dayton Hill. There he had seen at first hand the ruthless exploitation of the immigrant workers and their families who populated the district; what impressed him most was their need for "decent housing, adequate schooling and elemental security." Moreover, his early experience with Western Electric had convinced him that the evils and unfair practices which the critics saw as integral to business were nothing of the sort; certainly Enos N. Barton (his boss) had built a successful enterprise without them.[1] As for Young, his early labors on his father's farm had left indelible impressions, on which he drew in speaking to the Schenectady foremen early in 1923. "No man can tell me," he said on that occasion, "the difference between an income which provides only an uncomfortable house, inadequate food and insufficient clothes and *no* provision for the future and an income which provides margins above suitable living conditions for education and health and recreation *and* provision for the future. I know what that margin . . . is and no man can tell me—whether he be a politician or an economist or a financier."[2]

Here one finds the genesis of Young's subsequent insistence on a "cultural wage," rather than just a "living wage," for labor. Here too are clues to policies which, developed over the years, were to offer GE's workers a program of benefits and opportunities comprehensive enough to make Young's phrase something more than rhetoric. As for the recurrent threat of unemployment inherent in the so-called business cycle, that was at the moment Young's chief extracurricular concern.

The new team's emphasis on employee welfare, it should be said at once, was far from connoting an indifference to profits. To the contrary: only as profits rose could their hopes and plans for the workers be fully underwritten. Completing the circle was their conviction that only as the workers came to feel a genuine stake in the company's welfare could profits be sustained and maximized. True, they were not yet ready to face the full implications of the conviction. But as Young, in hailing Anson Burchard as IGE's new head, quickly made clear (Swope hardly needed to), there was nothing parochial in their view of GE's profit opportunities: "you" of the IGE, he said, "have all the world at your feet, undeveloped."[3]

It was in the divorce of corporate control from ownership that Young and Swope found the rationale for this new look at the nature and scope of management's responsibilities. Louis Brandeis, a decade earlier, had taken hopeful notice of this divorce as conducive to the professionalizing of business; R. H. Tawney was now expressing doubt that so desirable a change could be expected unless the Acquisitive Society of which he wrote were first transformed. In the meantime, Tawney added, the powers vested in management (or a mere handful of directors) were so nearly absolute as to invite their selfish exploitation.[4] Conceding the danger, Young and Swope insisted that all freedom was susceptible of abuse but that nothing else afforded so great an opportunity for creative and constructive achievement. They further shared the optimistic view that, in the long run, abuse could only be self-defeating; to them it was wholly incompatible with the natural ambition of the responsible executive to hand on to his successor an institution stronger in every respect than he had found it.

The practical problem then, both immediate and continuing, was to see where and how General Electric could be further strengthened—within itself and in the public esteem. If, under their leadership, GE could demonstrate that enlightened policies were also the most rewarding, surely others would be quick to adopt them. Then and only then could industry establish its claims to the confidence of the public—on which, after all, its whole future depended. On this last theme, especially, Young was to ring all the changes, and no theme could have been more appropriate to the time.

In the meantime, the younger men in industry could hardly fail to welcome Young's finding that instead of serving as "gentlemen attorneys for the investors," managers could now regard themselves as "trustees of an enterprise in which capital and labor cooperate."[5] But they might inquire whether the last word were factual or wishful. Not least of the many tasks awaiting the new team was that of translating the cooperation they hoped for into reality, step by careful step.

"Think radically and act conservatively but keep on thinking." Not all of Young's associates would have understood or, if they had, would have approved his aphorism. In Gerard Swope, Young had found a man who not only understood but practiced it.

However brilliantly Young and Swope were to vindicate their novel concept of team management, it did not spring full-blown from the board's meeting of May 16, 1922. Whether serving as president or chairman, Charles A. Coffin had always been the company's dominant figure and chief executive, and neither he nor his fellow directors intended any change in the pattern. Thus Young, as Coffin's successor, was to be responsible to the board for supervising all aspects of the General Company's affairs. Rice's area of concern was to be research and engineering; Burchard's, finance and the I G E; Swope's, the duties "customarily performed by the chief administrative officer." The primacy of the new chairman was confirmed by their respective salaries: although Young was to insist shortly thereafter that they be equal (as they soon became), his was initially fixed at $85,000, and Swope's at $75,000.[6] The press too hailed Young as the company's new head, while giving primary emphasis to Coffin's remarkable career.

Aware that as a newcomer, he had still to earn the confidence which Young had so demonstrably inspired, Swope was quick to seize the opportunities afforded by his new office. Young had suggested that he continue to concern himself with policy and Swope with operations, likening his own role to the pilot's or the navigator's, and Swope's to that of captain of the ship. Swope set out at once to make it clear to all concerned who the captain was, and why. His job as he defined it was endlessly to "analyze, organize, deputize, and supervise," and he was tireless in its performance. Before the year was out Young was congratulating him on having won the respect and admiration of all; and Coffin, seldom effusive, was also full of praise.[7]

High on their agenda was Swope's determination to diversify the mix of the company's products so that GE's monogram—now "the initials of a friend"—would mean as much to the ordinary household as to the generating plant. Young agreed: radio, in the shape of Sarnoff's little black box, was already entering the home. Consumer markets were apt to be less volatile than those for durable goods, and wider distribution of electrical products would also increase demands for heavy apparatus. Thus diversification might help iron out the sharper curves of the business cycle and help to stabilize employment, as the relatively constant upward curve of consumer demand for GE's Mazda lamps (as they were called) had always done. Insofar as this meant new and more imaginative advertising policies, the new team could, and did, devise them, substituting an institutional program for the hit-or-miss output of the various departments.[8] But advertising alone afforded no adequate response to public charges and suspicions that GE was the head—and possibly the shoulders—of a predatory power trust, controlled and directed from Wall Street.

This brought them smack against the problem that Young had vainly sought Coffin's help in solving earlier: the public's "right to know" what kind of people these high-powered and too often remote big-business leaders were. Public exposure had its dangers, including false image making and the kind of excessive adulation which the unwary subject comes at last to think of as his due, but which may turn to ridicule or worse at the drop of a hat—or a misplaced word. So far both men had avoided these dangers but, in 1923, Charles Steinmetz died, and as Young's extramural activities brought him increasingly to the notice of press and public, he had to recognize that what was happening to him was no different from what he had urged on Coffin as a matter of policy. Swope recognized it too, and insisted that it was a risk Young would have to put up with. In the meantime, he said, Young could count on him to mind the store and to help wherever he could.[9]

It was risk taking of a kind which Young and the company he was coming to personify seemed to thrive on. Most people relish attention and find a novel thrill in first seeing their name and views in print, and Young was no exception. His experience with the *New York Evening Post,* moreover, was continually reminding him that the journalists too had a job to do and appreciated help as much as the next man. So, making himself available whenever possible to those with bona fide credentials, he quickly learned the art of fair and effective dealing with the press—a skill he was to find much use for in the years ahead.[10]

Nor was it only the press that noticed Young and his willingness to take on responsibilities in the public as well as the private domain. Late in 1922, for example, the Federal Reserve Bank of New York—indisputably the dominant force in the Federal Reserve System so long as Benjamin Strong was governor—tapped him as a Class B (for industry) director, to take office on January 1; his acceptance meant resigning a less demanding but potentially lucrative directorship in the Bankers Trust. It also introduced him to those unfamiliar central and international banking problems which the United States, emerging from the war as the world's great creditor nation, was suddenly confronting. If Young was to gain a reputation in this field—especially in his subsequent role as a Class C, or public, director of the New York "Fed" and finally as its chairman, his entry was modest enough. "I shall need from time to time painstaking instruction and charitable treatment," he wrote the current chairman, Pierre Jay, in accepting the original nomination.[11]

ii

Meanwhile, Swope was bustling through the plants—typically beginning his rounds at eight o'clock—and creating in his progress a kind of constructive havoc. The Erie works manager who bragged of a "third horizontal 10% reduction in all day and piecework rates" was staggered when Swope branded such cuts as "disastrous." Swope believed that the piecework system was the fairest yet devised, *provided* that the rate was properly set and not reduced as soon as workers became more skilled. Nothing, he told the foremen, was better for the company than high piecework earnings, if only because they meant "greater production for the same amount of floor-space and equipment."[12]

However such hard-boiled reasoning may have impressed the foremen, the word that reached through to the men was that the new boss, who came to see for himself, was for higher wages. It was true; by the end of 1923, according to Swope's biographer, GE was employing some thirteen thousand additional workers and the *average* pay had nevertheless risen by 13 percent over that for 1922. Certainly Swope was satisfied that high wages and better working conditions supported rather than hindered his announced objective of "more goods for more people at lower prices." But it was not until the Schenectady workers had rejected a works council on the Lynn model and finally accepted a representation plan of their own that they were ready to test out Swope's piecework rates.[13]

Here and in Swope's continuing efforts to develop a comprehensive plan of workers' benefits—based as it came to be largely on the contributory principle to avoid the charge of mere paternalism—Young was himself an active and imaginative participant. During their first year in office, Swope met and talked with the foremen in every major plant about their dual role in interpreting company policy to the men and conveying their workers' gripes and suggestions to top management. As for Young, meeting first with some forty of the leading officers, he stressed the care with which GE's engineers were constantly testing their materials with an eye to their improvement, and wondered whether any comparable attention was being devoted to the "most valuable material we have. That material is not copper or steel or tungsten. You could strip the plant of these materials and within a week you could resume operations. The thing I am referring to is the *human material*. Strip the plant of this and you couldn't restore it for years. . . . We have four thousand engineers dealing with materials. I'll try to deal with the men."[14]

Here, too, his approach proved to be characteristically direct. Some excerpts from his remarks to the foremen at Schenectady in February 1923 have already been cited, but the following reveal his purpose more clearly. "What," he asked, "is this General Electric Company of ours?"

I say "of ours" advisedly because it belongs to every human being who contributes something of his own to its success. . . . Some would have you believe that it was a mere combination of soulless capital on one side and of a commodity known as labor on the other. It is not. Some would have you believe that it personified an imagined contest between Wall Street on one side and the laboring men of the country on the other. It does not. If you believe that I know, and knowing, that I tell the truth, then these old battle cries of hatred will not . . . be raised by you.

My purpose, however, is not to find what the General Electric Company is not;—my purpose is to find what it is. Let me tell you what it is. It is a group of a hundred thousand human beings and more, who are trying in organized form to accomplish something worth while for the world and for themselves. . . .

He went on to describe the importance, for effective progress toward this end, of organization and discipline—*without* creating "one man a master and another man a servant": "I abhor the notion of 'master and servant' in a free country, and I was glad when the so-called Compensation Laws put an end once and for all to that branch of our law which was known as the law of 'master and servant.'"

Going on to analyze the thirty thousand shareholders, approximately half of them women, most of them holding not more than a hundred shares, he pictured them as not fitting any notion of "impersonal grasping capital" but rather as "live human beings," choosing to invest their savings in GE and so helping to provide tools and equipment for the job. To these investors he promised the same fair return for their contribution that "you and I . . . are entitled to for our[s]."

Who then would determine the "fair share" for investors and workers—provided, of course, that cooperation yielded a sufficient total to divide? While economic conditions were basically determining, he said, in a more immediate sense, this "great responsibility rests on management":

It will not be just to every man. The question should not be whether it is wholly just to every man, but . . . whether the spirit of your management is to be wholly just to every man. . . .

That is the test which you have a right to make . . . of the men who have assumed the obligation of management—that is the reason why you are entitled to know them and make up your minds about them, and if the truth must be told that is the reason why you wanted me to come here and that is the reason why I am here.[15]

There developed from this informal talk a single-page statement of Young's industrial philosophy, which he sent to William McAdoo in the fall of 1923, at the request of the former secretary of the treasury. McAdoo's acknowledgment called it "just what I wanted," but it is quoted here for other reasons, not the least of which is Young's concluding suggestion of what should constitute for management an "indictable offense."

The problem of management in any industry is to accomplish three things.
1st.   To command an ample supply of capital in order that the tools required may be always available. To do this, capital must be safe. It must have a return large enough to command it in a competitive market, and the rate will be lower if there is assured uniformity and continuity of return.
2nd.   To command an ample supply of labor. As labor means human beings and not a commodity, it is desirable to interest these human beings in some form in the enterprise and to insure progressively increasing returns for their labor.

3rd. To improve the output, which means either a better product at the old price or the same product at a lower price.

It is entirely fair to test every industry and its management by these standards. To the extent which any industry or its management fails in the accomplishment of any one of these objects, it is subject at least to inquiry, and if it fails in more than one, it is subject to indictment.[16]

Although neither Young nor Swope seemed likely to be indicted on this count, this statement offers useful criteria for testing the moves they were making at GE. How far did their actions—vis-à-vis capital, labor and the public—square with their words? And how far were either, or both, sufficient unto the day?

On the face of it, GE dividends having been both generous and continuous over the years, provision of ample capital had ceased to be a pressing problem. Nevertheless, there had been in 1922 a legacy of bank loans and bonded debt, totaling some eighty million dollars, which these equity-minded executives did not like. According to Swope's biographer, "he promptly organized the retirement of them all and accomplished it within four years." Thanks to profitable operations, the bank loans were indeed quickly retired, and most of the funded debt was called for payment in 1925.[17] The implication, however, that in financial operations of such magnitude Young's role was one of passive acquiescence cannot fail to startle anyone who knew him or saw the team in action.

As for the public, Young's stipulation of "either a better product at the old price or the same product at a lower price" sounds today almost utopian. For the times, and especially for such companies as GE— and RCA—it was nothing of the sort. General Electric's incandescent lamps and radio tubes were cases in point. Both had been vastly improved in consequence of Irving Langmuir's research and experimental studies in high-vacuum bulbs, a second consequence of which turned out to be lower unit costs as volume rose.[18] Here as elsewhere productivity was increasing faster than wages, although the latter too were rising. The industrial revolution, in short, was feeling the accelerating effects of the spiraling revolution in science and technology, which seemed at first to solve far more problems than it posed. Even management was supposed to become scientific, though neither Swope nor Young became converts to "Taylorism," and it was clearly Swope's art which, finally and with marked finesse, converted GE's traditionally independent lamp divisions into a single entity. Placed under F. S. Terry's expert direction, this quickly proved itself far stronger than the sum of its parts.[19]

In the field of heavy apparatus, a lower price was far less likely than a better product, but when, by 1925, Swope's astonishingly patient efforts to organize the manufacture and distribution of a whole new spectrum of electrical products for the home had finally materialized, it was clear that he had not forgotten either target.

What, then, about Young's second criterion? On the one hand, development of constructive labor policies and programs also calls for patience; on the other, one has to make a start. Even a false step may be better than nothing, as Young had discovered a year or two earlier from his ill-fated experiment with the sale of GE stock to the workers at the plants. Offered shares at an attractive price, the men naturally grumbled, he reported, when the price went down; when it rose, too many of them sold out and handed the proceeds over to promoters of various get-rich-quick schemes. But at least the men had been made aware of management's concern and, as Young had been quick to concede, "management"—meaning himself—had learned that good intentions are not enough.[20]

They do, however, help, and even in the anti-union atmosphere of the times, successive steps were taken at GE which approached the goals—modest enough in retrospect but not so at the time—which Young had worked to define in the industrial conference report. First, as noted, came the works councils and plans of representation, open equally to union members and nonmembers, which the several plants were encouraged to set up. Next came the men's initially skeptical endorsement of Swope's piecework rates. Finding that his rates and the new joint channels for dealing with grievances could be trusted, the men were ready for other proposals, and over the next few years they came: a revised and comprehensive pension plan, for example, introduced after exhaustive study on Swope's part; medical assistance, life and disability insurance and loans to promote home ownership; plans for extra compensation as well as the productive investment of savings. In 1925, management even proposed a plan of unemployment insurance, to be financed by small but regular payroll deductions which the company undertook to match. At that time the dangers of unemployment seemed remote and payroll deductions were clear and present nuisances; the proposal was accordingly rejected.[21]

The savings investment plan, introduced in 1923, might be described as an indirect and far more sophisticated version of profit sharing, with a minimum of risk to the investors. It quickly proved to be not only acceptable but widely popular. In accordance with its provisions, workers with a year or more of service were eligible to invest up to $500 of their annual earnings—then a substantial percent-

age for most—in 6 percent bonds of the GE Employees Securities Corporation; GE, providing the risk capital, guaranteed an additional 2
percent so long as the bonds remained outstanding and the bond-
holder in its employ. The portfolio of this Employees Investment
Trust, management of which was vested in eight directors representing
the stockholder and seven elected by holders of the bonds, consisted
first of General Electric shares and second of the stock of its principal
customers, the leading utilities. The response was immediate and
cumulative: at the end of the first year 25,000 workers had subscribed
more than $6,000,000; by the end of 1925 the corresponding figures
were 30,000 and $21,100,000. A couple of years later, Young told his
new assistant that, with one exception, no stockholder, individual or
corporate, owned as much as 1 percent of General Electric stock. The
exception was the Employees Securities Corporation, which owned
some 2 percent.[22]

Granting, then, the new team's more than usually effective application of Young's formula, there remains the question of how adequately
the formula itself met the fundamental needs of the day. Clearly it
represented a notable advance over earlier concepts of management's
role, just as "welfare capitalism" was conceded even by its leftist critics to be more enlightened than the old "American plan" with its
yellow-dog contracts. These critics generally held, however, that welfare capitalism was at once overpaternalistic and overeager to set up
company unions as a means of keeping the real unions out. There is
much to support these charges and indeed their applicability to GE's
benefit program, at least in its earlier phases. It was never static for
long, however, chiefly because management, even more than the men,
could not bear to leave it alone.   •

Young's statement in response to McAdoo's request had been deliberately low-key. Clearly he had been more concerned to make the
point of management's threefold obligation than to elaborate it. If his
own involvement in the public sector went unmentioned, so—and for
excellent reasons—did the dramatic move which he and Swope had
under discussion: divesting GE, once and for all, of its holdings in
Electric Bond and Share. Obviously this great utilities holding company no longer needed to look to GE for capital. Obviously too it was
this historic relationship which, above all else, lent substance to the
insistent cries (and whispers) of a sinister power trust with GE at its
center.

Before December 29, 1923, when Young sailed for Paris with General Charles G. Dawes on their historic mission, the decision to divest
was taken. But timing was also important, in terms not only of mar-

kets but of winning board approval over Coffin's protests. Execution was therefore deferred until after Young's return, which, except for a brief interlude, was also long deferred. In the meantime, except for Coffin, the decision must remain their secret, but for them there was to be no turning back.[23]

iii

By 1922, the demonstration Young had set out to make in wireless point-to-point communication was impressive, but it was rapidly being overshadowed by sales of the little black box. According to the Federal Trade Commission, the total of paid words transmitted in the Atlantic and Pacific theaters rose from 7 million in 1920 to 18 million in 1921 and 23 million in 1922. While the cables, as noted earlier, lowered their rates to match RCA's in the case of French and British traffic, radio remained the cheaper elsewhere even where cable rates were cut. Thus gross income from transoceanic communications had shown a gratifying rise from $2,138,625 in 1921 to $2,914,283 in 1922, while revenue from marine service rose from $553,000 to $630,000.[24]

This was nothing, however, as compared to the rise in sales of radio apparatus for broadcasting. Here the demand had first set in during the closing months of 1921, a year for which RCA reported gross sales of $1,468,920. For 1922 the corresponding figure was $11,286,489. Total operating income jumped from a little over $4,000,000 to nearly $15,000,000; net income (including "other") from $426,800 to $2,974,-580. In the following year sales doubled; operating income rose to $26,400,000 and net income to $4,737,774. Suddenly RCA was "in the money"; it was also at the tumultuous center of the instant and tidal public demand for a product which, at the company's inception, had been at best a gleam in David Sarnoff's eye. Its financial policies, however, remained conservative; profits were used to amortize patents and write off organization expense, with a reserve for federal income tax making its first appearance. There were no dividends, even on the cumulative preferred stock.[25]

This sudden shift in fortune and in corporate priorities posed immense problems for RCA, both internal and external. Vast numbers had to be recruited overnight with little time for careful screening: salesmen, patent attorneys, accountants, troubleshooters and a host of others. Patents, mobilized for other purposes, were proving impotent to curb the host of infringers, who were chanting a kind of anvil chorus of monopoly. At the heart of this fracas were the vacuum tubes, where the Radio group's patent rights had been controlling but were almost totally ignored. Citing Department of Commerce estimates that close to two million receiving sets were now in the hands of the public, the Federal Trade Commission stated categorically that "of these sets, the Radio Corporation has sold only a small portion." Of 1922 sales, RCA's share was estimated at 20 percent.[26]

In the meantime, research and experimentation were subjecting both broadcasting and point-to-point communication to sudden and revolutionary change. In brief, Westinghouse was now demonstrating what Sarnoff had foreseen: the vast superiority of shortwave to long-wave even in long-distance transmission. Since shortwave required less costly equipment, multiplied many times over the number of usable channels, and promised to minimize dependence on long lines for linking up stations, the future looked to be theirs. For RCA this was soon to mean writing off as obsolete both the Alexanderson alternator and the huge and expensive towers so recently erected for its use. It was well that its chairman, accustomed as he was to rapid obsolescence, had insisted on ample capital resources and reserves for depreciation.[27]

In September 1922, Sarnoff, already general manager, was given the added title of vice-president and, with Nally concentrating largely on the company's original assignment, found himself in operating charge of all these new and burgeoning developments. He was not helped by the fact that GE and Westinghouse together could not manufacture sets, and especially tubes, fast enough to meet the insatiable demand or keep pace with obsolescence.

By the year's end, however, Young's efforts to find the kind of public personage whom he had long sought to head the company were rewarded. After consulting Newton Baker and, at some length, the man whom Baker recommended, Young persuaded Nally to resign the presidency in favor of General James G. Harbord, who knew little about radio but was well and widely known as General Pershing's chief of staff and a figure of towering integrity. If this appointment did not appease RCA's more vocal critics it was reassuring to its friends and to the general public. It also afforded the embattled Sarnoff, as well as Young, a welcome sense of timely reinforcement.[28]

Reinforcement was timely for another reason: under pressure of the new competition to broadcast, Young's original structure showed ominous signs of cracking. Under the agreements, as interpreted by all the other parties, AT&T's Western Electric was denied any part in manufacturing the receiving sets which GE and Westinghouse were now selling to RCA almost faster than they could make them, at cost plus

20 percent. Western Electric was free to make only transmitting devices, demand for which, as broadcasting stations proliferated, was
brisk, but only a fraction of the other. In addition, the telephone company was not accustomed to supplying toll-free service, and was now
insisting that, as broadcasting *could* be, so it *should* be revenue producing—and was therefore entirely their pigeon. This claim was made
when Young, and even Sarnoff, still saw broadcasting as a public service which, well and freely offered, would produce ample income
through the resultant demand for radios. Not strangely, this view left
the telephone people cold.

The crack in the facade first became apparent when AT&T, piqued
and frustrated, proceeded to sell its RCA holdings in the market. Beginning in February of 1922, while Young was in Europe, this operation naturally attracted notice well before its completion the following
January. Asked by the press to explain it, counsel for AT&T blandly
stated that "brokers were advertising this stock ownership to induce
the public to invest in the stock, which tended to create a moral
obligation on this company's part which it did not wish to assume."
In the meantime—in June 1922—Walter Gifford and Frederick Stevenson of AT&T resigned from the RCA board.[29]

At about the same time the Federal Trade Commission had begun
investigating a competitor's charge that GE, and others, had set up the
Radio Corporation as a "bogus independent," in the attempt to monop-
olize the manufacture and sale of radio apparatus. Whatever might
have been its outcome, the scope of the investigation was suddenly
broadened and sharpened when, on March 3, 1923, House Resolution
#548 directed the commission to study and report on all facts relating
to patents, contracts, agreements, or practices in the manufacture and
sale of radios as "may aid the House . . . in determining whether . . .
the antitrust statutes of the United States have been or now are being
violated by any person, company or corporation. . . ."[30]

What kind of doctrine was this? The commission, be it noted, was
directed to report "the facts" rather than its own conclusions, and report them not to the attorney general but to the House. Was this a
measure of the House's want of confidence, not only in Harding's
attorney general, Harry M. Daugherty, but also in the commission
itself? If so, what did it signify for RCA's—and industry's—future?

The commission's report, as published at the year's end, did not fully
answer these questions. It faithfully recorded the history of RCA's
creation and the operating results cited earlier in this chapter. It faithfully reproduced Young's letters to Edwin Denby, Charles Evans
Hughes and others, justifying a monopoly in overseas wireless trans-

mission as essential to American autonomy and effective competition with the cables. It then solemnly proclaimed that "the Radio Corporation has acquired all the high-power stations in the country with the exception of those owned by the Government and it has practically no competition in the radio communication field."[31]

This was tantamount to saying that Young's acknowledged purpose had been achieved, and he could hardly regard it as a serious indictment. What followed, however, reflected at best the extreme difficulty of distinguishing aims from actual outcome. "There is no question," said the commissioners, turning now to the little black box,

that the pooling of all the patents pertaining to vacuum tubes has resulted in giving the Radio Corporation and its affiliated companies a monopoly in the manufacture, sale, and use thereof. With such a monopoly, the Radio Corporation apparently has the power to stifle competition in the manufacture and sale of receiving sets, and prevent all radio apparatus from being used for commercial radio communication purposes.[32]

Whatever was intended by this final clause, the meaning of this paragraph as a whole was crystal clear. True, by "power to stifle competition," *legal* power must have been meant, for the *fact* of prodigious competition had already been attested in the report. The commission professed to be adhering to its instructions and so reporting only facts and not its own conclusions. Nevertheless, such findings made inevitable the formal complaint which—with Young abroad on *public* business—was filed toward the end of January 1924; and they hardly simplified the problem of a settlement with AT&T. To the commission RCA's board might reply bravely, as it did, but it was all too evident that as profits multiplied, so did complaints.[33] Nor could an end to either be foreseen.

iv

Such anticorporate forays, to be sure, were hardly typical of the times. Coolidge, succeeding Harding, took a narrow view of government's role, while organized labor was weak and apparently getting weaker.[34] Woodrow Wilson's two crusades—for the New Freedom and for the League of Nations—had spent themselves with little to show for the vast mobilizations they had entailed. Wilson's chief supporters, moreover, the progressives and the internationalists, were equally in eclipse; and such of the insurgents as had survived—chiefly nominal Republicans like William E. Borah, George Norris and Robert M. La Follette—would have no truck with the pro-League crowd. As one of the latter, Young was especially unhappy over the kind of isolationism which hailed this country's emergence as the world's greatest economic power while officially disavowing the political, economic and moral obligations that went with it.

On the other hand, this very primacy—and even its "new freedom," Coolidge style—offered American business unparalleled opportunities to show what it could do, and not merely for its own aggrandizement, at home and abroad. Teapot Dome and its related oil scandals had to be lived down, and John D. Rockefeller, Jr., lost no time in ridding Standard Oil of Indiana of its tainted leader. Meanwhile, to Young and Swope, the electrical industry—with its apparently infinite capacity to provide clean and mobile energy for machines and people alike—was the very epitome of responsible modern business and they took great pride in heading the company which was its acknowledged leader. But if their opportunities were boundless, so too were their obligations, especially if business were to demonstrate its full potentialities.

It was with a strong sense of such obligation that Young had accepted late in 1921 the chairmanship of the President's Committee on Business Cycles and Unemployment. Secretary of Commerce Hoover, at least, was urging business to face up to such unsolved problems, and if the government provided no funding for the Young committee, the extra effort involved in securing foundation grants—notably, through Senator Elihu Root's good offices, from the Carnegie Corporation—had its saving aspects.[35] That the committee was financially beholden to neither industry nor government was at least *prima facie* evidence of its objectivity.

Young saw promise in other factors too; the size and composition of his committee, for example, and its engagement with the new National Bureau of Economic Research. Unlike the typically unwieldy government commission, this one comprised only the chairman, the secretary (lent by Hoover) and four others. Two of the four were fellow industrialists: Clarence Woolley of American Radiator and Joseph H. De-Frees, a former president of the U.S. Chamber of Commerce. Labor, certainly a major party at interest, was represented by Matthew Woll, the vice-president of the AFL who was widely (and in the event mistakenly) regarded as Samuel Gompers's heir apparent. The fourth was Mary Van Kleeck, whose liberal voice and public-spirited concerns were in no sense limited to her official duties at the Russell Sage Foundation. A workable and hardworking group, it was prepared to credit the premise on which Wesley Mitchell's National Bureau had been founded: namely, that economic research—who knew?—might one day prove as rewarding as research in the physical sciences.[36]

Young, for one, was more than ready to put this proposition to the test. He felt, and was frequently to say, that "unemployment is the greatest blot on the capitalistic system"; insofar as the business cycle was to blame, it was high time to find out what business itself could do about it. As for the extraordinary commitment of the bureau's economists to a concurrent inquiry in depth, the sorely needed data it should produce were not, in Young's view, its sole importance. There was the opportunity it afforded for educating himself and his business—and labor—associates in the nature of the economic forces they were called upon to cope with. There was the opportunity of educating the economists whom he came to know on some of the concrete problems involved in business decisions.[37] Finally, the inquiry would lend credibility to his more ambitious hope of exciting the continuing interest of the press and the public in both the problem and anything which might make it more manageable.

In its form and context as well as in its content, the final report of Young's committee reflected these aims. Its recommendations, modest but unanimous, were followed and substantially buttressed by the hardcover edition of March 1923 of some twenty expert studies designed by the bureau to cover all important phases of the problem. For the lay public, however, the report itself—with Herbert Hoover's foreword—also appeared as a separate pamphlet, which was at once widely circulated and well received.

Emphasizing—as did the economists—the scarcity of relevant data and the consequent need for further study in depth, the committee proposed for initial consideration and action such commonsense measures as the following: restraint on the part of businessmen and bankers, including the Federal Reserve, as commerce and industrial production expanded to the point where credit became strained; deferring to less prosperous times major construction projects, public and private; the experimental creation, chiefly by industry and labor acting together, of unemployment reserve funds; the establishment (as recommended by the 1921 Unemployment Conference) of a nationwide system of employment bureaus—whose reports on the number of workers looking for jobs, and vice versa, would incidentally afford "another measure of business conditions."

But chiefly it was a cry for facts, including the constant flow of current statistical data required to inform businessmen of where they were, and where (and how fast) they were going. In this respect, the committee was, indeed, making a case for putting economic research on a par with scientific; and certainly the questions it addressed to wage earners, engineers, and citizens' organizations as well as to bankers and businessmen reflected its concern to enlist wide popular interest and participation. If, said the report, it should stimulate these things, "the committee will feel that its work has been successful." How could it feel otherwise in the light of its euphoric expression of confidence that, given these things, "the destructive extremes of business cycles can in large measure be controlled"?[38]

Whether or not this phrase was Young's, its optimism was. Irresponsible action, he liked to think, derived from ignorance; once given the relevant facts, most people could be trusted to reach responsible conclusions. This was an indestructible tenet of his political and educational credo, and if, in applying it to business leaders in this context, he ignored the compulsion of competitive short-run profits, it was because he believed that knowledge of the facts would persuade most businessmen to respond accordingly. Indeed, within three months of the report's publication, Young was telling an interviewer from *Collier's Weekly* that, in his judgment, the current boom in business and the market had gone far enough; it was a time, he said, for caution and restraint. Young's neck was out; the interview was widely circulated.[39]

Looking back on the committee's work and report, Young, in a letter to an officer of GE's Lynn plant, spoke of his initial doubts as to whether any study "of such a sprawling subject . . . would have . . . any appreciable effect." But, he wrote, the report was widely circulated and he believed that it had prevented a dangerous peak in the economic upswing of late '22 and early '23: "However that may be, I feel sure that for the first time we have had greater cooperation both by business managers and by labor leaders in trying to prevent a disastrous peak and that the result will be that we shall have in this country fairly good but not booming business for a considerable period."[40]

Listed among the many advisers to whom the committee acknowledged its debt was the eminent scholar who was also one of Wesley Mitchell's directors-at-large. Edwin Gay, however, had been far too deeply immersed in the unsolved problems of the *New York Evening Post* to take any part in the bureau's special studies; now, despite his best efforts—and Young's—it was becoming all too clear that such capital infusions as the *Post* had enjoyed or could reasonably expect from its new sponsors were simply not enough. Nor was Gay's ensuing and most reluctant resignation; by December 1923 the *Post* was sold to Cyrus H. K. Curtis of Philadelphia, whose publishing experience encouraged hopes of maintaining its solvency. Its identity was another matter.

Young had spent considerable time and money on the *Post*; but in spite of ultimate failure, he had enjoyed the venture enormously. Coming home in the evening to 830, he would wave the latest issue at his family: "Anyone want to read my paper?"[41]

v

Hard work for the *Post*, for GE, for RCA, and in the quasi-public jobs such as the committee on business cycles and the Federal Reserve, and the satisfactions which came to Young from his performance in a variety of roles, filled 1922 and 1923. But 1922 also brought sudden tragedy to him and his family.

While Young himself was moving into new fields, so were his two older boys, now nineteen and twenty-two. C.J. had spent a summer in the West, working for a power company in Idaho. He had enjoyed it immensely: a new kind of job, a new kind of country. So after his sophomore year at St. Lawrence, John, the second boy, wanted to do the same. John was the one of the children most like his father; to have him at St. Lawrence was for his parents a reliving of their youth. He did well at college, for he was a natural student, a reader and a questioner, and he thought he would probably go on to law school. He made many friends in Canton, for he was a favorite with both boys and girls. One of these was John Atwood, son of John Murray Atwood, dean of the Theological School and one of Owen's and Jo's oldest friends. Young Atwood, who was thinking about an engineering career, decided he would like to go west too.

The boys got jobs working for the Phoenix Utility Company at Hood River, Oregon, in the summer of 1922. It was spectacularly beautiful country, and the big construction gang was camped along the river, developing a power project for the Pacific Power and Light Company. The boys were made material checkers on the work train; a narrow-gauge railway had been put through to carry supplies, and the boys rode on it, checking gravel and other material. One day the camp dog, a little fox terrier named Skee, came along too and rode with the boys on the forefoot of the dinky engine. As the train slowed the dog jumped off, directly in front of the wheels. John Young reached to save him, but himself fell under the engine, which could not stop in time. The dog was unhurt.

John lived only a few hours. When the message came, the Young family was scattered: the father was dining with John Elwood in New York, the mother and sister and littlest brother were at Little Point,

Philip was at camp in New Hampshire, C.J. was in Schenectady. Father and mother and sister spent a long night together in Riverside, but by the next night the family was together in Van Hornesville. Only there, together, with Grandmother, could they have the strength to live through the days to come.

John Young was born August 13, 1902; he had just turned twenty the week before he died. A quiet, gentle, dark-haired boy, he had his mother's brown eyes and his father's warm smile. He was musical, like his grandfather Edmonds, worked hard at his violin and became a good player; his mother played accompaniments for him, as she used to do long ago at St. Lawrence for Professor Baker. John and C.J. were inseparable as boys, and his sister, almost five years younger, idolized him. He loved to read poetry, as she did, he loved her kittens, he wrote her letters when he was away.

The weeks at Van Hornesville were healing, though no member of the family, especially the mother, was ever quite the same again. Owen Young stayed close to his family, dropping all his concerns and not going back to work for nearly five weeks; his presence strengthened them all. There was comfort too in the extraordinary outpouring of messages; the Youngs knew they had many friends, but the love and sympathy which came in hundreds and hundreds of letters and telegrams was almost overwhelming. From men in high places, from neighbors and St. Lawrence people, from the boss and the construction gang itself came words of sorrow, of praise for the young man, of sympathy for the parents. And since the death was widely reported in newspapers all over the country, because of the father's position— and also because of the dog—strangers wrote as well. From all this the family could not help deriving some strength and solace.[42] But the greatest comfort of all was the youngest boy. Dick was three, too young to realize John would not be coming back, but he was an amusing and delightful child and a loving companion; Owen and Jo were thankful for the surprise of 1919.

The summer of 1923, however, brought happiness, for in August C.J. and Eleanor Lee Whitman were married. A beautiful and charming girl, she was the daughter of Florence Lee and Edmund Whitman, old friends of Owen and Jo from St. Lawrence and Cambridge; C.J. had been instructed to call upon the family when he went to Harvard—and that was that.[43]

They were married before Jo and Josephine, who were in Europe, got back, but they appeared in Paris, on their honeymoon, for a great reunion with mother and sister. (Owen had returned earlier for the wedding.)

This European trip—all July, August, and half of September for the mother and daughter—had been planned by her parents for Josephine, then sixteen, to show her England and France and to see more of both themselves. The Nelson Perkinses and the Harbords went over on the same boat, for the men had radio meetings in both London and Paris; when these were over there was much sight-seeing, fine dining, and—in Paris—attending horse races at the small, charming courses around the city. For all three Youngs, the summer was an alleviation of sorrow.

Chapter 16

The Dawes Plan:
Adventure in Business Diplomacy

W HEN Owen Young sailed for Europe with General Dawes on December 29, 1923, he was highly regarded rather than widely known; both men were to return a few months later to something very much like sudden fame. How explain, half a century later, the extraordinary acclaim with which isolationist America was to greet the Dawes Plan and especially the American businessmen who were everywhere regarded as its master builders? In June, Dawes was to find himself named by the Republicans to run with Coolidge; November saw him duly elected as vice-president of the United States. Young's treatment was less drastic but he too would become a public figure whose name was henceforth bandied about as a likely prospect for high office—including the highest.[1] Why?

Essentially, it was because the unofficial "experts" had succeeded where governments had signally failed in coping with what was proving to be postwar problem number one. That the United States, rejecting the Versailles treaty as well as the League of Nations, claimed no "reparations" from Germany was beside the point; the Allied countries which had suffered most from the war and its ravages were determined that Germany should foot the bill down to the last farthing. And the bill as they reckoned it was formidable: even though it included at the time only a fraction of the $10 billion or more of Allied borrowings on which the U.S. government was demanding full payment, it added up to the fantastic total of 132 milliard marks—or roughly $33 billion.[2]

The effect on Germany of this demand—fixed in 1921 at an Allied conference in London—had been disastrous. Recoiling from a burden which it denounced as utterly unbearable, Germany had moved through various stages of resistance to something approaching economic and financial collapse—hardly a good omen for its experiment in democracy. As reparation payments fell to a trickle, an apprehensive Britain was more than ready to moderate its claims; not so the French. Still smarting from two invasions, they chose rather to force the issue by marching their armies into the Ruhr and taking over its mines. War's aftermath was becoming more and more like war itself.[3]

American complacency was severely jolted. It was easy to tell ourselves that we were well out of that mess, but were we? With Germany's currency and credit—and its whole middle class—wiped out by runaway inflation,[4] with French troops in the Ruhr and British protests enfeebled by divided counsel and massive unemployment, the armistice itself seemed in danger. Wherever one looked, all roads to recovery ended in the barbed-wire entanglement of reparations. And unless such roads could be cleared, and soon, what about the markets for our industrial, and especially our agricultural, surplus? Or for the investment of our surplus capital? Or for the purchase of certain indispensable imports?

There were also appeals from press and pulpit for American intervention on humanitarian grounds; on this occasion humane and economic considerations clearly pointed the same way. But if there was any single determining factor, it was the growing realization that if Europe were allowed to fall apart, default on the war debts would be the least of our worries. Far more compelling was the virtual certainty that this would leave the United States isolated economically as well as politically—with revolutionary communism threatening Germany as well as eastern Europe.[5] And that, to put it mildly, was more than even Senator Henry Cabot Lodge had bargained for in his successful anti-League campaign.

In such an atmosphere, the confident departure and triumphant return of the American "experts" came as waves of fresh air. If certain pundits had a field day dissecting the plan they brought back—and indeed the wisdom and morality of the very concept of reparations and war debts—their audience was small and not notably receptive. Press and business comments were overwhelmingly favorable and even enthusiastic. As for the general public, it was the *fact* of the settlement that mattered, rather than its contents. At long last the reparations tangle had yielded to the kind of businesslike approach that Americans understood. At long last emotionally charged arguments about Germany's capacity to pay had been replaced by a workable program for testing that capacity in realistic terms. Final or not (of course it was not), it was a settlement that cleared away the lethal roadblock; now everyone could get back to work.[6]

In this eleventh-hour victory for common sense there was something that restored the American people's damaged sense of pride. Once again, never mind how tardily, Americans had embarked on an overseas mission to save Europe from itself; once again, American participation had made all the difference. Their consciences eased, die-hard supporters of the League and isolationists alike found it easier to get along with themselves and with each other.

As for the business community, the sense that two (or three) of its own had done the job inspired a new appreciation of its importance, actual and potential, on the national and international stage. What politicians could not do, businessmen could. And there was one thing more. Let Washington deny as it pleased any connection between the Allied war debts and reparations, their *de facto* relationship was now almost as visible on Main Street as on Wall. Only as Germany paid reparations could the United States look with any confidence to Allied repayment of our ten billion dollars in loans. It was as simple as that— and worth remembering.[7]

ii

Also worth remembering was the paradoxical fact that Washington's role in making the Dawes Plan possible had been controlling. It was the secretary of state, Charles Evans Hughes, who had suggested such an international conference of "experts," Americans included; it was he who went on to decide—the President having been consulted—who these Americans should be. How did this come about? And why was Owen Young one of those recommended, along with General Dawes and Henry Robinson?

As many of the younger, historians are discovering with some astonishment, not even the Harding and Coolidge administrations were wholly isolationist. Harding's cabinet, indeed, included two avowed friends of the League: Hughes at State and Hoover at Commerce; when Harding died on August 2, 1923, both stayed on at Coolidge's urging. And the Washington Disarmament Conference of 1921 had been called, of course, at Hughes's initiative.

Forced, however, to recognize the limits of the possible by successive rebuffs at the hands of a Senate which even balked at joining the World Court, Hughes had followed with mounting anxiety the downward spiral of subsequent developments in Europe. Fully aware of Europe's crying need for the mediation or "disinterested" leadership which only this country could provide, he was by no means unmoved by the successive appeals for American intervention—from Germany,

Britain and even from American diplomats abroad—which reached him in 1921, and especially in 1922. But he rightly felt that the United States could assume such a role, even unofficially, only if the invitation to do so was unanimous. Without the express concurrence of a still intransigent France he could not move; moreover, he would have to make it clear, for here he had no option, that in any conference on reparations in which Americans took part, Allied debts could not be on the agenda. That these debts were bona fide obligations, with only the *terms* of repayment open to negotiation, had been stipulated by Wilson himself as well as his successors, and now, most recently, by the Congress.[8]

Nevertheless, on December 29, 1922—a year to the day before Young and Dawes took ship—the secretary made his historic proposal at New Haven. If this was prompted by what Hughes privately described as "the voice of God," he had also lately seen letters from Berlin in which Ambassador Alanson B. Houghton wrote of the famished populace, undernourished children, and the growing menace not only of communism but also of a new movement in Bavaria led by a young fanatic named Hitler. So it was that Hughes put before the world a proposal he had already privately and vainly put before the French premier, Raymond Poincaré.

Calling Europe's problems world problems and its economic recovery a prerequisite to permanent peace, he suggested that the several European governments had so positioned themselves on the key question of German reparations as gravely to prejudice their capacity to negotiate, much less to reach a consensus. In this situation, he asked, "why not invite men of the highest authority in finance in their respective countries—men of such prestige, experience and honor that their agreement upon the amount to be paid [*by* Germany, as well as *how*,] would be accepted throughout the world as the most authoritative expression obtainable. . . . I have no doubt that distinguished Americans would be willing to serve in such a commission."[9]

This was innovative diplomacy at its realistic best, no doubt, but even with the promise of American participation its time had not yet come. London duly applauded and so of course did Berlin but, with the invasion of the Ruhr still up his sleeve, Poincaré prepared to play his own trump and within a fortnight did so. One consequence was that French troops were met by passive resistance on the part of the German miners, which ended only after the total collapse of the mark and the virtual paralysis both of the economy and of the government had brought a new and shaky coalition headed by Gustav Stresemann into what was left of power. A second consequence was the alarming weakness of the French franc; with this and the entente with Britain both in jeopardy, Poincaré himself was having second thoughts. The present state of the German economy, he observed, was no true index of its long-term capacity; doubtless some analysis by the experts should be encouraged but only if limited to a three- to five-year period. It was Hughes's turn to stand fast: thus shackled, he replied, no committee could command the kind of independent experts it required.[10]

It was almost the end of the year before the impasse was resolved. A visit to Montreal and Washington in October had prompted Lloyd George, no longer in office, to stir Stanley Baldwin's Conservative government—and notably Lord Curzon at the Foreign Office—to positive action in support of the Hughes proposal, which President Coolidge then publicly endorsed. Following the hassle with Poincaré, Louis Barthou, president of the Allied Reparations Commission and a former premier of France, urged on by the "unofficial" U.S. representative, Colonel James A. Logan, finally came up with a formula which both Hughes and Poincaré could buy.

As transmitted to Hughes in late November, Barthou's new formula was disarmingly simple and deceptively guileless. It proposed the appointment of two commissions by the Reparations Commission itself: the first to seek means of balancing Germany's budget and of stabilizing its currency, and the second to seek means of reversing the flight of German capital. Who indeed could take exception to such unexceptional aims? True, the second commission might be redundant, but that was unimportant so long as its members had the sense—as happily they did—to realize it.[11]

The secretary's real concerns were rightly focused on the first—or, as it was to be called, the Dawes—committee, and especially on its mandate. Was this, as stated, sufficiently broad to include, not to say require, a reparations settlement? If not, it would not serve; if so, why not be more explicit? When Logan transmitted these questions, Barthou was at pains to explain. There were occasions—obviously he felt that this was one—when the attempt to spell out a charge at too great length served only to defeat one's purpose. Could the secretary not be content with the assurance that the French yielded to none in their concern for a workable reparations schedule, and recognized this objective as indeed implicit in the charge? Hughes, satisfied at last, agreed to go along, and so did the British. So too—and this was Barthou's triumph—did Poincaré.[12]

By this time it was December, but Hughes had reason to be gratified. With American participation now assured, all of the governments concerned—Germany's included—had found his proposed experiment

The Dawes Committee—the working group aboard the S.S. *America*, late December, 1923: Young in the center; next on right, General Charles Dawes; on extreme right, Stuart Crocker

The Dawes Committee an informal meeting, breakfast at the Ritz; left to right: Stuart Crocker, Young, General Dawes, P. Pichon (their translator), Henry M. Robinson. Derso

In Berlin: from the right, General Dawes, Young, Rufus Dawes, Stuart Crocker. Copyright by Press-Photo-News-Service

Mrs. Young commissioned Jo Davidson to do a portrait bust of Owen while they were in Paris; it is now in the Owen D. Young Library at St. Lawrence University

Young and Philip Snowden, Chancellor of the exchequer, at 10 Downing Street, April 1924. London News Agency Photos Ltd

General Dawes, Young and Henry M. Robinson report to President Coolidge at the White House, April 30, 1924

Derso

Young visiting his uncle Cyrus on the latter's Alberta ranch, August 1925

THE SOCIALIST PARTY IN NEW YORK

Rollin Kirby, New York *World*, March 2, 1926

Left to right: David Sarnoff, vice-president and general manager, RCA; M. H. Aylesworth, president, NBC; and Owen D. Young, 1926

October 1929: Mme Curie and Young at St. Lawrence; behind them are St. Lawrence's President Sykes and "Missy" Meloney. Associated Press Photo

in indirect diplomacy eminently acceptable. And why not? Reserving full rights—as did the Reparations Commission—to ratify or reject the experts' findings, they had everything to gain and nothing to lose. Meanwhile, the very act of acceptance enabled Poincaré, for example, to shore up the shaky franc and even more shaky entente and so partially disarm his domestic critics.

Thereupon the pace quickened. Well before Christmas, Hughes had identified and settled with the President the Americans whom the Reparations Commission should be invited to invite. Since these "experts" were to serve unofficially—and indeed at their own expense— confirmation by the Senate was not in order, but the screening process had nevertheless proceeded almost as if it were. For Hughes, in particular, too much was at stake to admit of costly mistakes; he would move, therefore, but always with deliberate speed.

Thus, as early as October, Hughes had asked his economic adviser for suggestions, and these included Dawes. Hoover, in volume two of his memoirs, names November 5 as the date when three cabinet officers—Hughes, Andrew W. Mellon and Hoover himself—agreed on the "final" slate: Dawes and Young for the first committee, Henry M. Robinson for the second. It was a slate which Hoover, knowing all three, could endorse with confidence; Hughes, however, elected to pursue his inquiries.

Dawes presented no problem. As a former controller of the currency, wartime coordinator of the Allied Services of Supply, and thereafter the first director of the federal budget, he was well and favorably known at home and abroad. He was also the Chicago banker who had quietly refused Harding's offer of the treasury— which had then gone to Mellon. A man of rocklike integrity, Dawes had caught the public's fancy by his picturesque response to the pettifogging questions of the congressional inquisitors about the high cost of certain critically needed army supplies: "Hell'n Maria, we were fighting a war." His fellow countrymen, including Young, were soon to discover something equally quotable in Dawes's homely observation on being named chairman of the experts' committee: "Oh well, somebody has to take the garbage or the garlands."[13]

Robinson's credentials, if less well known, were also impeccable. There was his earlier involvement in Hoover's war-relief activities, in the course of which he had learned something of Europe and made General Dawes's acquaintance. There was his later membership in the Supreme Economic Council. Like the general, a banker and a Republican, but with headquarters in Los Angeles rather than Chicago, he too was presumably free of any Wall Street taint. On every count, moreover, it was important that the West Coast, as well as the Middle West, be strongly represented.[14]

Owen Young's credentials, financial and political, were clearly of a different order. No banker, he and Dawes had never met. Also he had been a lifelong Democrat—one of several disqualifications which he noted when asked by Hughes to serve. But Hughes, wanting a bipartisan committee, had also welcomed the circumstance that Young's only banking connection—as a recently elected director of the New York Federal Reserve—was strictly noncommercial. And given his position and experience in such key industries as electrical manufacturing and international communications, he seemed an admirable complement to Dawes.

The fact was that Hughes had spent too much time "vetting" his candidates—and especially this dark horse—to take no for an answer. He had learned, for example, that Roland Boyden, on resigning his post with the Reparations Commission as "unofficial observer," had told Logan, his successor, that if ever he wanted a real job done, he'd best call on Owen Young. In recommending Young to Hughes, as he later recommended Robinson, Logan also had the support of the ambassadors to France and Germany, Myron T. Herrick and Houghton. President Coolidge too had taken a hand, and the response to his inquiries about Young from General Harbord and Wilson's secretary of war, Newton D. Baker—not to mention his old Amherst friend, Dwight Morrow (now a Morgan partner)—was enthusiastic enough to clinch the matter. With the tentative slate of November 5 thus confirmed, invitations to serve were transmitted by the Reparations Commission and duly accepted.[15]

The chorus of praise—William Randolph Hearst always abstaining—with which the press greeted the pre-Christmas announcement that Dawes and Young would go was all that Hughes could ask. Its tone, to be sure, was often less than strictly nonpartisan, but that could be forgiven. According to the *New York Evening Post*, it was clear at long last that the United States was to return—unofficially, of course—to the council table which (of course) "we never should have left." (Muted applause from Young.) On the other hand, the *Detroit Free Press* roundly hailed Coolidge for "safeguarding the financial interests of this nation . . . [while avoiding] any entanglements in old world squabbles." But the secretary and his unofficial envoys could join in the fervent hope that the *New York Tribune* was right in pronouncing Hughes's move and their appointment to be "the first long step in the direction of solving the reparations tangle and bringing order out of the economic chaos in Europe."[16]

Of the more personal acclaim which the press reserved for Dawes and Young themselves, the former, as chairman, naturally reaped the larger share. But Young had no cause for complaint; for example, as quoted in the *World* for December 23, Newton Baker pronounced him a "statesman" whose selection was "inspiring." And the consensus was voiced next day by the *New York Herald*: Dawes and Young were, quite simply, the "right men for the place."[17] Robinson's appointment, announced a few days later, was also warmly applauded; in the event, he was to render notable service to both committees. But for Young the unforgettable words were Jo's: "Owen Young, this is a job for which you have no qualifications whatever—except that you can do it!"

iii

Once launched, Hughes's little experiment in arm's-length diplomacy deserved, and received, all appropriate support. Without advertising the fact, both State and Commerce arranged to furnish these American "experts" with expert advisers; indeed, Secretary Hoover's Alan Goldsmith, taking the same ship, undertook forthwith to initiate Dawes and Young into the more recondite mysteries of reparations. Shipboard entries in Dawes's journal, appropriately labeled "At Sea," record daily seminars of four to five hours "in the children's play room" (assigned them by the captain) and praise Goldsmith as "thoroughly informed." But, the general added drily, "I am able to see from our discussions the advantages that our aloofness . . . gives us . . . in . . . selecting the essentials for discussion. . . . Just now my mind is more upon those methods which I must adopt as chairman to determine the capacity of my Committee to act than it is upon Germany's capacity to pay."[18]

These advisers, however, were never obtrusive and if the Allied governments, now including Mussolini's, were to respect Hughes's stipulation against intrusive political instructions, it was imperative that he set an impeccable example. He did and it was followed. True, Dawes was to remark of his first meeting with the leading French delegate that "the circumference of the useful activity of our Committees, at least at the inception . . . is a circle whose radius is the length of the string which ties Parmentier . . . to Poincaré."[19] It was a shrewd observation, but he never had occasion to accuse Poincaré of pulling the string.

Such restraint was obviously essential to any fair testing of Hughes's happy invention; for it was above all else this assurance of their independence which had persuaded these Americans and their eminent European colleagues that, working together, they might accomplish something.

Of the European delegates, the key members were readily identifiable: Jean Parmentier, the intelligent and responsive French civil servant par excellence; Alberto Pirelli, leading Italian industrialist whom Young had encountered at meetings of the International Chamber of Commerce; Emile Francqui, Belgian banker, shrewd industrialist and salutary raconteur; Sir Robert Kindersley, chairman of Lazard Brothers and director of the Bank of England; and finally the redoubtable Sir Josiah Stamp, also a director of the bank and, as economic statistician extraordinary, the only one among these leading "experts" with a professional reputation at stake. Each was to make his distinctive contribution to the task in hand, but Stamp's, by common consent, proved easily the most substantial, and the friendship he and Young developed became, and was to remain, particularly close. Meanwhile, it was only from the sense of a shared responsibility that was theirs and no one else's that these "experts" could hope to develop that *esprit de corps* which made a consensus at once the goal and the crown of the Dawes Committee's efforts.

To be sure, there was no escaping such facts of life—and politics— as the U.S. government's stubborn denial of any relationship between reparations and the war debts, or its equally stubborn insistence on full payment of the latter. The first of the funding negotiations—with Britain—had commenced early in 1923, even as the French were entering the Ruhr; concluded the following June, the agreement called for sixty-two annual payments with interest at 3 percent for the first ten years and 3½ percent thereafter. The pattern thus established was to have far-reaching effects on other settlements, including reparations—especially when experience of the Dawes Plan at length suggested that a "final and definitive" settlement was in order. In the meantime, Hughes's statement that funding of the debts did not affect Germany's capacity to pay was just as true—and just as helpful—as Coolidge's reputed dictum about the loans to the Allies: "They hired the money, didn't they?"[20]

Nevertheless, as practical men, the so-called experts of the Dawes Committee were used to dealing with equations in which the givens were not of their own choosing, and so refused to be fazed. This was especially true of the Americans, whose sanguine temperament had yet to be seriously ruffled by any experience of problems which would not yield to shrewd persistence and patient ingenuity. No doubt this could be counted fortunate, for without the kind of leadership which inspires accumulative confidence and trust, a committee facing tough decisions "merely multiplies," as Young once put it, "the incapacities of the individuals who comprise it." Given the history and context of the problem at issue, such leadership could hardly have come from any source except the United States. It was indeed American disinterest, however flawed, which gave the Dawes Committee its capacity to act—and Dawes his garlands.

i v

Certainly General Dawes demonstrated his right to the chair at the first Paris meeting of his committee on January 14—with the Reparations Commission also present. Disarmingly modest, his address was also realistic and remarkably plainspoken. Of nagging rumors that the Americans had come over to dictate to Europe a ready-made solution, he said that, on the contrary: "We come, humble in opinion, knowing that there is no barrier against the acquiring of knowledge like the pride of preconceived opinion. We come, knowing that you know much more about your affairs than we do." To illustrate the necessity—and difficulty—of achieving unity, he drew upon his war experience in France: "What brought about complete Allied cooperation in time of war? Nothing but overwhelming emergency." Lest anyone miss the analogy, he drove it home in winged words: "Upon what does the success of this Committee depend? Upon powers of persuasion? Primarily no! Upon honesty and ability? Primarily no! It depends chiefly upon whether, in the public mind and conscience of the Allies and of the world, there is an adequate conception of the great disaster which faces each Ally and Europe unless common sense is crowned king."[21]

People everywhere could understand that kind of talk. Evidently Dawes realized that the force which a mere committee can bring to bear on an apparently immovable object can become irresistible only as public opinion makes it so. No wonder Young was to say of Dawes after the event, in publicly testifying to his all-important role:

Politicians of all countries knew well how to get away with an "experts'" report. They looked with anxiety on the approaching Dawes report. The point I desire to make is that the Committee followed the best commercial and financial practice by having its goods sold before they were manufactured. In the language of the advertiser a "consumer demand" was built up for the Dawes Report before anybody knew what it was to be and before a line of it had been put on paper. General Dawes was the Sales Department of our concern. In that department he had no associates or assistants and he needed none.[22]

What, then, about the making and the content of the report as unanimously adopted by the Committee? In reporting briefly on these matters on the same occasion, Young resorted to understatement in the grand manner: "The remaining members of the Committee, with General Dawes as leader, were all in the Manufacturing Department. . . . With a Manufacturing Department thus set up, it would have been a reflection indeed if we could not have made a relatively simple article which would meet the requirements of a well-advertised market all ready to receive it."[23]

This was all very becoming on the part of one who was reputed to have played the major role both in designing and shaping up the product. No less aware than Dawes of the determining force of public opinion, Young also knew that any product of which the public expects so much had better be good. Thus the "manufacturing department's" final product must be ingenious enough to reconcile, as none had so far done, the clashing claims of the several parties at interest. In addition, its price must be so nicely adjusted to the claims of distributive justice that each party—like Young's upstate neighbor who came to buy a cow—would finally pronounce it "most too dear to take and most too cheap to leave." This story, reported Young, they had kept constantly in mind.[24]

Happily, it was in ways that served only to complement the chairman's that, from the outset, Young's own talents had been coming into play. Both had accepted Dwight Morrow's conclusion that any attempt, however "expert," to fix Germany's total liability for reparations *now* would prove premature and thus abortive. They further agreed that measures to restore Germany's currency and credit—including a balanced budget and a new bank of issue, internationally supervised but free of government control—were the prerequisites of Germany's recovery and so of any reparation "dividend." Then why not, Young suggested, proceed to work out and recommend an admittedly *interim* schedule of payments which, geared to such annual progress toward recovery as the experts found it reasonable to expect, could be sustained by a German tax burden roughly equal to that of the Allies? This, he argued, would circumvent the endless arguments over Germany's will and capacity to pay, by subjecting both at last to a genuinely pragmatic test.

As for the other *bête noire*, the so-called transfer problem, this too could—and in Young's opinion should—be circumvented. To do so, one need only limit Germany's obligation to the annual *deposit* of marks in the stipulated sums, leaving to a creditors' committee (with an American chairman) the task of translating into creditor currencies, at any given time, as much as the state of the foreign exchanges would permit. No more than fair to the debtor, this would incidentally provide the first pragmatic test of the creditors' capacity to take. It would also substitute verifiable facts about Germany's exportable surplus for fruitless debate over problematical forecasts.

It was quite a packet and if, as Robinson and Goldsmith testified, Young had it already pretty well worked out on shipboard, he was too wise to inflict it on his colleagues—or even on the chairman—all at once. He preferred to introduce it piecemeal, as the need and occasion arose. Here, nevertheless, were the basic and distinctive features which set the Dawes plan apart from previous efforts. They were also chief among the features which were to commend it, so to speak, to the market. Could manufacturing and sales departments cooperate more often to such effect, the team of Dawes and Young might have been less celebrated than it was.[25]

v

Soon after its first meeting, the Dawes Committee summoned Hjalmar Schacht, the new president of the Reichsbank, to meet with them in Paris. In the ensuing negotiations with the Germans, Young became the key figure, as Dawes was with the French. His past experience, in the radio consortium, of reconciling Allied and German interests, of dealing in the electrical industry with his German counterparts, and his directorship in the New York Federal Reserve Bank, all contributed to this position. So did his long acquaintance and cordial relations with the American ambassador to Germany, Alanson Houghton.

On his arrival in Paris, Schacht at once precipitated an issue which caught his hosts off guard, required of them forced marches to regain the initiative, and so had the paradoxical effect of accelerating the pace of the "manufacturing department's" work. In Dawes's words, "Dr. Schacht . . . asked to be allowed to start a gold bank of issue, something on which our Committee had already come to a practical understanding. After Dr. Schacht's departure the quick mind of Young rose to the occasion. He told the Committee that we must act at once. If Schacht went back to Berlin without our action, he would establish with our implied assent his own conception of the relation of the Reichsbank and the new gold bank of issue."[26]

Two days later, on January 23, the Committee released a communiqué which announced its decision to set up a new and independent bank of issue as "part of the ultimate plan to secure budget equilibrium and stable currency." It expressed the view that in this connection "some features of the plan outlined . . . yesterday by Dr. Schacht may well prove useful," but also seized the moment to emphasize the need for "foreign cooperation" in the management of such a bank. Finally it announced that it had promised Schacht "in view of the necessity for prompt . . . action . . . to discuss a definite plan at Berlin on Wednesday, January 30."[27]

Having thus checkmated Schacht without causing him any damaging loss of face, the Committee had a deadline to meet. It was then—less than ten days after the Committee had first convened—that Young offered what Dawes characterized as "one of those sensible and illuminating statements which are so valuable in shaping important policy. Its competence resulted in practical unanimity of accord and its effect will be greatly to facilitate our program." Dawes's assessment of its importance finds ample support in his observation that, with the Berlin visit pending, "we are faced with the necessity of considering and formulating as quickly as possible our whole plan." What Dawes's "hastily and imperfectly" recorded summary suggests is that Young was offering a preview of the Plan that touched on all of its basic points—the finest possible briefing for the Committee's upcoming visit to Berlin. And certainly Young had been first to insist—with British support—that the whole Committee be involved in such a visit, lest it be accused of sitting in judgment without a firsthand look at Germany's economic and human problems.[28]

It was the first through train from Paris to Berlin since the war; as it pulled in, the news photographers were waiting. A photo taken on the station platform shows Young in a gray fedora and chesterfield, with a stick; Kindersley, even taller than Young, in a black bowler, a double-breasted overcoat and spats, with a big briefcase and an umbrella; Dawes, shorter than the other two, in a very long overcoat with a caracul collar, a gray fedora, and, of course, the underslung pipe.

They were received with every mark of respect and next evening Chancellor Wilhelm Marx and General Dawes exchanged felicitous speeches at a meeting held in Bismarck's old office. Young remarked in an aside to Dawes that this meeting was the first real entry of the Allies into Berlin, and wondered how the Iron Chancellor's ghost was behaving.[29] Certainly Bismarck's current successor was behaving well enough, but the real key to the German government at this point was

Marx's predecessor, Gustav Stresemann, who had accepted his urgent plea to stay on as minister of foreign affairs.

It was therefore to Stresemann that Dawes sent Young, and they met at Ambassador Houghton's the following day. Their discussion proved to be of determining importance, chiefly because Young at once confronted Stresemann with a rationale for maximum reparations payments that was wholly independent of the hated war-guilt charge. There was no getting around the fact, Young told him in substance, that the world had recently indulged in a prolonged and fearfully destructive binge, most of the physical damage of which had occurred not on German soil but on that of its neighbors. Cleaning up the mess was painful and expensive, and the question that naturally concerned its neighbors now was whether or not Germany was willing to stand its fair share of the cost. On Germany's answer would depend the respect accorded it by others, and so the extent to which these others—including the United States—were prepared to help.[30]

Finding Stresemann cordially responsive to this approach, Young went on to warn him that an affirmative answer and consequent help would necessarily mean—"make no mistake about it"—that Germany must tax itself at least as heavily as the Allies were already doing. As for a negative answer, its predictable consequences made it unthinkable. Young then outlined the kind of pragmatic test of Germany's capacity—and will—to pay its full share which the committee had in mind—not forgetting its flexible and graduated payments schedule, or the role and significance of its Transfer Committee. He made clear, however, that the Germans would normally be expected to make available for transfer the scheduled total in marks, and, by way of under-writing this obligation, would be called upon to mortgage in their creditors' favor both the railroads and the basic industries. These too, like the new bank of issue, would necessarily be subject to some Allied supervision. As Germany's good faith and credit were reestablished— and only then—could it expect the private loans from American and Allied sources which it needed to restore its working capital and currency reserves, and so shore up its recovery.

While Stresemann winced at any suggestion of the likely dimensions of a "normal" year's payment—to begin after four transition years—he agreed that the concept of testing Germany's capacity, on an annual basis, first to raise and then to deposit specified sums subject to transfer made sense. So did a fair degree of Allied economic supervision. But if he were to commit his government to such a program, he would need the Committee's assurance that Germany's territorial and economic integrity would be promptly restored and fully respected. He would also need firm assurances of German industry's full cooperation—and on this, he suggested, Young himself could help immensely.

Regarding his first condition, Young replied that while the military occupation of the Ruhr was a political and legal question and so outside the Committee's frame of reference, the Committee was fully agreed that the *economic* integrity of the Reich, including the Ruhr, was a prerequisite to the tests it was proposing and as such an inseparable part of an indivisible plan. As for the industrialists, Young had already begun the series of meetings he was to have with them— sad at the thought that the late Walter Rathenau, once of A E G, and subsequently Germany's most promising economic philosopher and statesman, was no longer among them.[31]

He first saw A E G's current head, Dr. Felix Deutsch, whose response was moderately reassuring. Other leaders of the electrical industry, like Karl von Siemens, posed no problem, but Hugo Stinnes, the steel magnate and since Rathenau's assassination Germany's most powerful industrial figure, was a bird of a different feather. When, after several meetings, including a dinner at Ambassador Houghton's and a discussion lasting until 2:00 A.M., Stinnes declared that he was "still unconvinced," Young bore down. "It is not for me to convince you," he retorted, "but rather for you to convince me, as a Report is going to be made quite regardless of the attitude of any person or even the whole group of industrialists." Apparently unable, so confronted, to convince even himself, let alone Young, Stinnes finally agreed to give the proposed new Plan his support, provided that Germany's untransferred deposits were used exclusively for internal loans, and so protected against the French using them to purchase stock control of German industry. Stresemann and Chancellor Marx were satisfied, and so was Young.[32]

The Committee also invited representatives of German labor and agriculture to speak for their respective interests. What Owen Young never forgot was Herr Grasseman's insistence, as labor's chief spokesman, that German labor's crucial need of the moment was not higher wages or shorter hours but a stable currency—so that the workers could know at long last what it was that their wages could buy. As for the farmers, was it sheer coincidence, in the light of Young's own background, that a proposal to mortgage agriculture was dropped while the mortgage on industry was retained?[33]

The rest of the story, following resumption of the Committee's sessions in Paris, involves almost two months of unremitting and generally undramatic labor. The amount to be designated as a "normal" reparations payment (beginning with 1928–29) had still to be fixed; the French were demanding a figure upwards of three milliard gold marks, the British (and most of the expert advisers) that it be not more than two. Each party cited evidence to support its views until Dawes, Young and the whole group were fed up with analyses and computations—including a notably complicated one of Stamp's—that only widened the rift. At this point, reported Stuart Crocker, Francqui of Belgium arose and said, in the Pidgin English which he had learned as a child in China, "Mr. President, I have only this to say about Sir Stamp's method. I have a ship. She goes to sea. She have two mast, one long one short, and she have a skipper and a mate. Question: What is the age of the captain? Answer: 6284 feet. That is all I have to say about Sir Stamp's figures."[34]

This so far broke the tension that even Stamp was forced to laugh. In the long hours and heavy concentration of the meetings, however, such moments were too few. Indeed, as early as January 11, Dawes made a plaintive entry in his journal which Young could well have echoed: "It is the irony of fate that Paris, the playground of the traveling American, is and always has been, for me, the place of strenuous anxiety night and day, and little else."

It was apparently Dawes who urged an early break in this routine, suggesting that Young invite him out to dinner and (as Young put it) that they devote the evening to a firsthand look at the civilization they were supposed to save. And so they did. Just what the look included is no part of the record, but it was well toward three in the morning when their taxi dropped them at the Ritz. Then it was that Dawes spoke up: "Damned if I think she's worth saving, Young. Why don't we join in the downfall?"[35]

vi

But there was not enough time off, for them or anybody else. Toward the end of February, Young showed symptoms of cumulative fatigue which alarmed his devoted assistant. To this fact and to Stuart Crocker's ensuing messages to Mrs. Young, who came posthaste to the rescue, we owe a series of hitherto unpublished observations on the last frantic month of the conference. In Jo's reassuring and cozy letters to her daughter, Owen was of course the central figure, but she also had a sharp eye for others—both on stage and off.

Dated from the Ritz in Paris, Monday, March 10, 1924, her first letter tells how the indefatigable Stuart Crocker had met her at Cherbourg early Saturday morning and escorted her to Paris, where

Popsie was at the station to meet us. It was time that I came—he looked badly and last weekend had a mean time—his old trouble of fainting—due without doubt to the terrible load he had to carry in Berlin and everything combined. Scared Stuie pretty well as he did not feel well for several days but he is now improving—back on the job although dreading this last week which is the crucial time. They are hoping to finish by Saturday. I am going to sit right here and catch every minute I can to get him out to ride and away from the crowd and strain. No one knows how difficult this thing is . . .

She had gotten him away from Sunday-morning callers for an afternoon at the races, and promised her winnings to her daughter: "Sir Robert Kindersley and his wife and children were there. He is magnificent, six feet four and so good-looking and so English. She is so English too, but small and awfully dressed. . . ." On the way back they stopped at the Gallia, where all three of them had stayed the year before, and encountered—of all people—Lincoln Steffens, "just the same dear little man and crazy to hear every last thing we have done at Riverside. This afternoon I am going with him to Yvonne Davidson's dress exhibition—wife of Jo Davidson the sculptor . . . friends of Mr. Steffens . . . Gen. and Mrs. Dawes have been in and out—I'm going to have great trouble to keep my time as free as I wish. . . ."

The following Saturday found the work of the Committee far from finished but, as indicated in her next letter (begun on Sunday, March 16, and concluded Thursday the twentieth), Jo's presence was making itself felt: ". . . Last night Pops and I dined here alone in our sitting room as he was so tired after a full day at the Conference." But by Wednesday he had felt well enough to take her alone to a "late dinner at Foyot's—certainly . . . the best place in Paris!" And the evening before they had dined with General Pershing, "the only dinner invitation we have accepted," where Jo was placed beside the guest of honor:

I sat beside Maréchal Foch, just the nicest little great man you ever saw. He and General Pershing are a wonderful pair—regard each other with so much affection and have such fun. They were teasing Foch about the speeches he made in the United States—said he made exactly the same speech three hundred and fifty times, but as it was in French, no one knew the difference! He protested with hands and shoulders and violent French that it was not so . . . I'm keeping the dinner invitation for you as it is in Pershing's own handwriting.

All this was definitely outside the theater of operations. Meanwhile, behind the scenes: "The work of the Committee is progressing very slowly—Pops says he begins to see the end but they have struck all sorts of snags this past week. . . . If he can only get through these next ten days all right!" The next ten days, during which Jo "went to the Louvre all by myself," and to Rheims with Stuart Crocker, failed to bring down the curtain, but gave rise to a concern about others. In her letter of Saturday, March 29, Jo wrote:

This last drafting of the report lays them out by the wayside. Sir Robert went home sick last night and Sir J[osiah] Stamp was on the ragged edge. Awful strain—Pops came home very chipper—when it gets down to an endurance race he is right there. He has to be awfully careful about eating, sleeping etc. But I think he'll come through all right. . . .

Mr. Houghton the U.S. Ambassador at Berlin is here today . . . so am anxiously waiting to hear the inside dope from Germany. The elections are approaching . . . and the Report is going to have much influence on them. Poincaré has just fallen, but has been asked to stay on and form a new cabinet which I understand he has done with a more favorable mind toward the report. But nearly all the Committee are optimistic and believe it will be accepted.[36]

It was Henry Robinson's testimony, not Jo's, which revealed the role Young played in resolving the long impasse over the maximum, or "normal," reparations figure. During the Berlin visit, Robinson told Crocker, Stamp had privately conceded the force of Young's contention that if the Germans were taxed as heavily as the British, they could fairly be expected to raise toward reparations in "normal" times at least 3 milliard marks annually—the very sum for which the French were holding out. In now reminding Stamp of this, Young was able to induce him to propose the compromise figure of 2.5 milliard marks, or roughly $625 million, which the committee finally adopted.[37]

Now at last complete, the schedule of payments envisaged by the Plan was carefully graduated from the initial year's milliard gold marks to 1.2 milliard for the next two years, 1.75 milliard for the fourth, and thereafter to the agreed standard figure of 2.5 milliard marks. Except for service on the contemplated Dawes loan (which would assure the first year's payment), Germany's responsibilities would cease and the Transfer Committee's begin as these sums were deposited in marks with the agent-general. They were to come from three sources: from Germany's ordinary (tax-supported) budget, from railway bonds and a specified transport tax, and from industrial debentures. The amounts and the proportionate share to come from the ordinary budget were to rise by slow degrees from zero in 1924–25, to half the total for the "standard" year—1928–29 and after—or 1.25 milliard marks (some $300 million). Thereafter debtor and creditors were to share in any increase in Germany's prosperity, as measured by a specified index.[38]

On this salutary compromise, and especially on the key question of the Ruhr, Dawes had been in constant touch with Jean Parmentier, who still had means of sounding out Poincaré. French acceptance of Stamp's proposal having been assured, fresh Allied differences nevertheless arose as the laborious task of drafting a definitive report proceeded. In resolving these, Dawes himself played an indispensable role, including the designation of Young to head the group responsible for drafting the all-important Part I. Comprising as it did "The Committee's Conclusions and Scheme," this section was addressed less to "expert" than to literate public opinion, and accounted for the first 35 pages of the 124 in the final printed report. Of Part II, Stamp was the principal draftsman; his "expertise," especially in dealing as he did with the German budget, should, Dawes thought, "successfully run the gauntlet of the economic critics as Part I will do in the case of ordinary business minds."[39]

Tuesday, April 1, however, found Jo in no mood for April foolery: "Pops is sitting this afternoon in what I hope is the final session—everybody is worn out and nervous. I shall be glad when it is over. I can't settle down to anything myself until I know whether the report is agreed on."

During the week that followed she finally knew. On Wednesday, April 9, 1924, the Dawes Plan, signed unanimously, was finally submitted to the Reparations Commission and released to the press. Its phenomenal coverage and warm reception—as attested by the hundreds of clippings deposited in the Owen D. Young Papers—fully vindicated Dawes's appeal to public opinion as the best means of bringing the politicians to heel. The economists, to be sure, might disagree with this or that—and with each other—but even John Maynard Keynes, archcritic of Versailles and all ensuing reparations schemes, was impressed in spite of himself as, with wry generosity, he publicly acknowledged in the *Nation and the Athenaeum* for April 12:

The report is the finest contribution hitherto made to this impossible problem. It breathes a new spirit and is conceived in a new vein. It achieves an atmosphere of impartiality, and exhibits scientific workmanship and sound learning. Though the language seems at times that of a sane man, who, finding himself in a madhouse, must accommodate himself to the inmates, it never loses its sanity. Though it compromises with the impossible and even contemplates the impossible, it never prescribes the impossible. The facade and these designs may never be realized in an edifice raised up in the light of day. But it is an honourable document and opens a new chapter.

Lest any further sampling of editorial comment expose the authors to a charge of biased selection, they turn instead to Jo's final report—totally unbiased, of course—written only a day before publication of Keynes's views:

> Claridge's, April 11th (Thursday)
>
> Would you believe it—here we are in London. The English experts were not contented without Pops coming over here to see the Governor of the Bank of England . . . and so this noon I suppose he had lunch in that room at the Bank—do you remember it? And this afternoon they were due at 10 Downing Street at four . . . there are many things here still to be done. But your father has been so encouraged by the reports in the daily press, that I think he feels rested already.
>
> The last week . . . in Paris was certainly exciting—the Experts all trying to make their final corrections—newspaper men all excited about getting it out—printer's proof flying back and forth—They all felt they had passed into a new existence, when they had each signed the other's copies—left the official copy with the Reparations Commission, and left the Astoria for the last time. All the newspapers comment on their skill, industry and fairness —I am sending a couple of French papers—with a picture and interview with Pops—I dread to think what pressure may be put on your father to continue in some form or other. But he's through.

In the event, Jo's apprehensions were to prove more realistic than her determined optimism, but in the meantime there were more immediate concerns: a call by the Kindersleys, messages from Swope to be decoded, Owen's report on his Downing Street visit, where he had called by invitation on Ramsay MacDonald, then plans to revisit Paris briefly to gather up a few last threads and even take in the races.

Owen's call on the prime minister was to have an important sequel: a letter to Francqui in Brussels, written from Paris on April 21 (his wife's birthday) "before sailing tomorrow on the Leviathan," and sent by special messenger—which made it clear that his attention had not been wholly centered on the races. After an introductory paragraph in which he paid full tribute to Francqui's "indispensable" role in the committee's work and its happy outcome, Young got down to business:

> Since my return to Paris from London [he wrote] I have been following the question of the acceptance of the Report by the Allied Governments very closely. Frankly, I am somewhat worried about France. She

is likely to demand from England a commitment now for military action in case Germany defaults. This, England will not give. I feel sure of my position on this because of my frank, but confidential, talk with the Prime Minister. England, I am sure, is quite ready to move in case default occurs, but she will not presume the bad faith of Germany by making a commitment now. It is, therefore, most important, in my point of view, that Italy and Belgium should promptly come through with an unqualified acceptance of the plan. I say promptly, because I think time is of the essence.

The M.I.C.U.M. agreements can not be financed much longer, and if they break down the Plan will be lost in the resulting confusion. There will be force in the Ruhr, and a breakdown in the Mark in Germany. Before leaving, therefore, I cannot resist making a most urgent appeal to you to do everything in your power to bring Belgium through with unqualified acceptance as soon as possible.

It will be time enough to discuss matters between the Allies after they shall all have settled a plan with Germany. To precipitate a discussion of those matters as a condition precedent to accepting any German plan will be not only to fail in getting the required agreements among the Allies, but it will be to make the plan itself fail. This letter, of course, is wholly personal and confidential. I feel my relationship with you is such that I may properly write it, and I know your devotion to the plan is, like mine, such as to command every effort possible in its favor.

Very sincere regards, and all best wishes.[40]

On the morrow they sailed indeed, with the Robinsons and General and Mrs. Dawes. The *Leviathan,* docking at New York on the twenty-eighth, was besieged by reporters who had to be content with a hand-out issued jointly by the three, praising their European colleagues, disavowing receipt of any instructions from Washington or Wall Street and refusing comments on the Plan: "as written it must speak."[41] C.J. came down from Schenectady to complete a warm but brief family reunion; the evening of the twenty-ninth found Young taking the midnight train to Washington. Back on May 1, he called at the Federal Reserve on the senior deputy governor, J. Herbert Case—presumably in Benjamin Strong's absence. After a brief visit to Canton, he began the week he had promised himself in Van Hornesville. His mother had followed with the greatest interest the progress of the work in Paris, in the press and in the reports that Gertrude Chandler had forwarded from the office. Young Jo and Philip had spent their spring vacations with her, sleigh riding in the first weeks of April; it was while they were there that the letter had come describing the dinner with Pershing and Foch. C.J. came as often as he could from Schenectady, where he was working in GE, but none of this was equal to seeing Owen and hearing the story from his own lips. They sat beside the stove and he told her and Uncle John the history of the Dawes Plan.

The desk at 120 Broadway was piled high, Swope and Harbord had waited four months to see him; with them as with diplomats, economists and bankers Young was in constant demand. It was May nineteenth before he managed a proper call on Charles Coffin, now in his eightieth year, at his Long Island home. The old gentleman welcomed him with quiet pride; he was deeply moved (and so was Young) by the extraordinary thoughtfulness of General Dawes in cabling him from Paris in April just to sing Young's praises. The cable, addressed to Coffin at GE, is reproduced here for the credit it reflects not so much on Young as on its author, to whom in this instance Jo would certainly concede the last word:

As the meeting of our Committee ends at which we have finally agreed upon the last details of our plan I cannot refrain from wiring to you, whose love and confidence mean so much to Young, something of his achievements in this long laborious and difficult work. No man has been more trusted and more followed by his colleagues and no one has left a greater imprint upon a plan which we pray may forward the cause of peace and goodwill on earth. To his ingenuity, courage and tact in presentation we owe unanimous agreement upon many critical points and his was our most constructive mind.

Charles G. Dawes[42]

Chapter 17

Germany in Receivership: "Owen the First"

L ATE in May, in a somewhat lighter vein, Young wrote his friend the general:

I have now finished playing with the cows and last week I made my last bow as a great man before the National Electric Light Association [where he congratulated Gifford Pinchot, the conservationist, on his speech, and his hosts for inviting him]. That is the end of my career and I am getting back on the job today dealing with margins of mils and cents, and occasionally dollars, in place of billions, trillions, and quadrillions, etc. which rolled off my tongue so easily when I was with you. I hope by this time you may have re-adjusted yourself to the absence of ciphers sufficiently to make you a safe and sound administrative head of a great banking institution. . . .

By the way, I see by the papers that various devices combining the portraits of the President and yourself are likely to be used to stampede the Republican convention in Cleveland. All I have to say is that unless there is an arrangement in advance to the contrary, Charles G. Dawes will be nominated by that convention in spite of what he or anybody else can do. . . . A ticket of Coolidge and Dawes would spoil my democracy. I will come and see you some day, not because I am of the visiting kind but in spite of it.

Affectionately yours,[1]

From the outset, it should be noted, a thoughtful government had been taking steps to minimize the risk of any undue inflation in Young's self-esteem. At the very moment, late in January, that the Dawes Committee was leaving Paris for Berlin, the Federal Trade Commission filed its complaint charging the Radio group with violation of the antitrust laws. Some two months later, the attorney general, Harry M. Daugherty, brought suit against General Electric on similar charges. This occurred at the critical moments of the final drafting of the report when, according to Jo's letter, the strain was taking its toll. But it was also a critical moment for Daugherty, whose connections with the oil scandals of the Harding administration were at length catching up with him. Indeed, within the week, he had resigned an office that was no longer tenable.[2]

If, in Young's absence, certain of his associates were heard to mutter darkly about stabs in the back—or at least about the hazards of responding to the government's call for public service overseas—Young's own reactions were more philosophical. True, the government had been privy to every step taken in setting up the Radio Corporation but, as Young was fully aware, the trade commission was a wholly autonomous body, certain of whose findings, published in December, had indeed foreshadowed its formal complaint. As for the attorney general, his position as a member of the cabinet might ordinarily have made him amenable to a hint that the timing of his suit was hardly opportune; under existing circumstances, any such hint would have been most *in*opportune. That "the law will wait for no man" was one of Young's favorite legal aphorisms; here was further proof that it was so.

Of these and other developments which awaited his attention, Swope and Harbord had kept Young fully advised—even to Swope's enlightening allusions to Daugherty's predicament. On one point Swope was openly gleeful and knew that Young would be delighted too: the indictment was directed solely against GE's lamp contracts— notably with its agents and with Westinghouse—and made no mention whatever of Electric Bond and Share.[3] Thus they had not lost the initiative in severing that connection, which they still planned to exercise at the first propitious moment.

Swope was right; Young was doubly reassured. Before the year was out they were indeed to bring about the total divestiture of GE's holdings in Bond and Share. As for the lamp-agency contracts, Young's minute examination as counsel had satisfied him that they would stand up in court and when, in 1926, this view was unanimously affirmed by the Supreme Court—neither Holmes nor Brandeis dissenting—his vindication was sufficient. To anticipate even further, his vindication seemed complete when, some two years after that, the Federal Trade Commission dropped its complaint against the Radio group.[4] For the moment, however, such double vindication remained a hope and an objective, the realization of which meant plenty of hard work.

Young's career "as a great man," it appeared, was not to end quite so abruptly as he had averred in his letter to Dawes. Earlier in June he had attended his thirtieth reunion at St. Lawrence, and on the seventeenth and eighteenth he had been made an honorary son of Tufts and also of Dartmouth, the very prospect of which had led him to ask the president of Harvard, who had confessed to similar designs, whether such a raid on New England's honorifics might not appear excessive.[5] Mostly he was fending off the importunities that followed public acclaim, but surely some of its sweets—especially of the academic sort—were there to be savored. And if, as President Lowell had indicated, he had to earn his Harvard degree on the nineteenth by speaking to the alumni, there were one or two things that he wanted to get off his chest. What better platform than Harvard's—especially since it necessarily involved visiting the ancient college town where he and Jo had first set up housekeeping? And that meant, of course, that Jo would have to come too.

She did, and so did others of the family. Thanks to his daughter's diary—young Jo was then seventeen—one need not rely upon old newspaper clippings for a contemporary account of the proceedings in the Harvard Yard. Here is her entry for June 20, 1924:

Yesterday morning Momie and Pip and Stuie and I were well seated in Sever Quad. at 9:45.[6] Some indefinite time later, well occupied by observing the large number of antique ladies who attend Harvard Commencement, the procession entered, professors with variegated hoods, Pres. Lowell, the Governor [Cox] with his aides, and the recipients of Honorary Degrees, among whom Popie loomed high, silk hat and all. Then the numerous and more youthful scholars [sic]. We had a prayer—after the Sheriff had rapped three peremptory raps with his sword to call the meeting to order after immemorial custom, and then a Dissertatio Latina, of which I managed to understand one sixth. Then two English speeches and the presentation of the degrees. Hon. ones to Justice Sanford, Robert Bridges, Roland Boyden, Major Goetz etc. as well as to Father. President Lowell's conferrings were very good. Then, the excitement over, Momie and I with Mrs. [Thomas Nelson] Perkins, went to luncheon at Mrs. Lowell's—a whole mob of hens, but good food and a nice house. Mrs. Lowell is very thin and wears big pink roses in her hat.

So much for commencement proper, and the luncheon for the ladies.

Then back to the Quadrangle for the Alumni meeting. All us dames sat on the side, with the men below in the middle. Stu and Pip and Houst Kenyon marched in as big as life and sat with the Class of '24. Well, Justice Sanford made a speech (flowery) and Pres. Lowell made a speech, and Bishop Lawrence rendered account of gifts to Harvard. [These included George F. Baker's $5 million to Dean Donham's Business School.]

Finally Popie made a speech—the one he had read to us the night before. Well I guess maybe I'm a prejudiced judge,—but I never heard a better. The meeting went mad; they clapped and laughed and yelled and ended up with the three "Harvards" for Young . . . Lowell said to Popie: "They have courage enough to cheer, but not enough to act." It was a direct hit at Henry Cabot Lodge—a pity dear Cabot was not there.

Radio was allowed no place at a Harvard commencement but even without it, Young's voice was beginning to carry. As a reasoned but by no means unemotional plea for America to come to Europe's aid without equivocation, the speech invited—and received—more attention from the editorial writers than from the news desks. Nevertheless, it was widely noticed, and the next morning's *Wall Street Journal* printed the full text.

What did Young have to say that—having first survived his family's, and especially his wife's, critical ear—commanded the applause of auditors, diarists and editors alike? He did not talk about the Dawes Plan; that was a "group accomplishment. The group was dissolved, the report must speak for itself." Hailing, however, his freedom as "a purely private citizen"[7] to speak his mind on other matters, he proposed to recite "the evolution of my own ideas in regard to the position which should be taken by the U.S. in foreign affairs."

Having been at the outset "unreservedly in favor of the League," Young could still accept "as a fact" its rejection by the United States. If the Foreign Relations Committee of the Senate had mishandled the question, so, on occasion, had the President himself. But there were other facts to reckon with as well. One was that America's "rejection of the League has created abroad a feeling of hopelessness and despair" that the "nation which had so unselfishly spent its treasure and its men to win the war in order that all war might end, should fail them at the moment when its aid would be most effective." Another was the unhappy domestic impact of our decision—moral as well as economic, agricultural as well as financial. In the face of such facts, alleviating influences such as "our bootlegging participation in a reparation settlement" were simply not enough. "My purpose now is to ask what, in the face of these facts, should America do?"

Let me say first, that what America should do in playing her part in the World's affairs is a great moral question. That question should be faced and decided as such, and I, for one, object to the method by which we are making that decision. I object to having the . . . question . . . confused by a discussion of the merits or faults of the machinery through which she should make that decision effective. Whether I should go to the relief of my friend and comrade in a hospital and render what aid I could is one question. Whether I should go in a Buick or a Cadillac or a Ford is another question. I object to delaying my decision or to being diverted from my main purpose by the sales talks of promoters of different vehicles.

The first thing that I want to do is to send word to my friend in the hospital that I am coming and then I will go by the best conveyance which expediency puts at my disposal, and if there be no other way, I will walk to his relief. That is what I should like to have America declare to Europe. . . . We need make no treaties at the moment. We need make no entangling alliances. We only need a definite and authoritative declaration of where America stands in order that isolationists may be rendered mute at home, monarchists and communists may be crippled abroad, and movements for democracy and peace in every country of the world may be given the encouragement which they ought to have from the United States of America.

Europe is confused. She does not know what the spirit of America is. In fact, I think we have confused ourselves. Will the men of Harvard demand a decision on the great issue? Will they lay aside for the time being their selling talk regarding particular methods of conveyance? If they will, America may yet fulfill her glorious duty to the world.[8]

ii

Young's office calendar for the rest of the month was full, but no more than normally so for a man who had recently returned from a long absence and expected to be around. Just before leaving for Canton he had called on Bernard Baruch, who had struggled valiantly at Versailles to cut reparations down to size; there were also meetings at the Federal Reserve. He agreed, moreover, to serve as one of the trustees for founding, and establishing at Johns Hopkins, the Walter Hines Page School of International Relations. From Wednesday, June 11, through the Saturday, his many appointments included calls from a visiting Japanese and the German ambassador, luncheons with Swope and Coffin, and meetings of the International Chamber of Commerce, the Merchants Association, and the Federal Reserve directors. Nor was RCA neglected. After a futile attempt to talk with Harry Thayer of AT&T, he responded to a two-pronged query from Charles Evans Hughes's son-in-law, Chauncey Waddell of Dillon Read, by asserting that RCA "has no intention of buying a building in uptown New York or anywhere else." As for a new stock issue, RCA's only relevant actions involved a recently authorized change from five to fifty dollars in the par value of its preferred stock, and an exchange of common at the rate of five shares of old to one of the new—all with a view to listing both issues on the stock exchange.[9]

Returning from Cambridge and Boston via Schenectady for a weekend in Van Hornesville—the Boston and Albany Railroad being then alive and reasonably well—he was in New York in time for a Monday meeting at the New York Fed, after which he paid a call on William

McAdoo, now a Democratic presidential aspirant. On Tuesday, June 24, he took the one o'clock for Washington, where he saw, among others, the N.Y. Fed's peripatetic governor, Benjamin Strong. Back in New York the following day, he agreed to discuss with a representative of the Democratic National Committee what its foreign-policy plank should be. Arguing that any popular referendum on the League of Nations should be wholly nonpartisan and not mixed up with the complicated issues of a presidential campaign, Young submitted a draft which he confirmed next day. Though not adopted at the convention, his draft nevertheless reflects one man's effort to salvage the maximum possible from the wreck of Wilson's hopes:

> More specifically, the Democratic party favors cooperation with or participation in such organizations, including the League of Nations, as may be helpfully functioning in the social and economic rehabilitation of the world—on such terms as will, on the one hand, protect the sovereignty and independence of our Government, and, on the other, enable it to render its full service and receive its full benefit from the common and enlightened action of all the nations.[10]

On the same day, responding to an inquiry from John D. Rockefeller, Jr., Young expressed great interest in the work of the "several Rockefeller Foundations" and in the suggestion that he "might possibly be of service to them"; this he would be happy to explore. The summer promised to be busy, but surely its pace would seem relaxed as compared with Paris in the spring. To be sure, the Dawes Plan had still to be ratified and put into operation, but that was no part of *his* responsibility. He was through.

Or was he? After all, it was not every day that a species of receivership was proposed, as the Dawes Committee had done, for a sovereign if defeated power; conceivably, Germany might object. He did not expect it to, if only because this was a benign receivership, designed not to liquidate but to rehabilitate an ailing economy. In addition, Americans would be playing a major role, and Germany obviously wanted American involvement not only as a moderating influence but also as an encouragement to overseas loans and continuing economic cooperation.[11] Nevertheless, with an eye to the French as well as the Germans, it was important to pick the right man as "receiver," or agent-general.

Though Morgan's Paris partner quoted Young as saying in April that the bankers should do the picking, when Morgan came to propose Dwight Morrow, Young was not so sure. As he wired Dawes on June 3, his own first choice was Hoover, whose European experience and reputation as a great humanitarian clearly put him in a class by himself. But Hoover, no favorite with the British, was not about to leave his government post for anything so chancy; and once Young's doubts about his friend Morrow's wholehearted dedication to the Plan and its success had been allayed, he readily gave him his support. So did Dawes; so too did the President and his secretary of state.[12]

So matters stood as plans for the London Conference, called for July 16 to iron out the political differences which stood in the way of final ratification of the Dawes Committee's report, were being consummated. On learning from Dawes late in June that Ambassador Frank Kellogg and James Logan (our unofficial observer with the Reparations Commission) would be attending the conference, Young expressed great satisfaction, ". . . as that gives more official recognition by the U.S. to our work which should be most helpful in Europe. I will come to Washington any day next week you fix and if there is no objection I should like to have Dwight come along too."[13]

In the event he brought not only Dwight but Jo, who was evidently determined to keep her man free of further involvement (June 30 was also their wedding anniversary). On July 1 Dawes, Young and Morrow had long and eminently satisfactory meetings with Hughes and President Coolidge; during that evening, with the general and Mrs. Dawes and Morrow as their guests, Jo could congratulate herself as well as Morrow on the latter's imminent appointment. Though for Morrow this would mean resigning as a Morgan partner, it would virtually assure the success of any loan to Germany, and Dawes found Morrow in some doubt but strongly "inclined to accept." So Morrow and the Youngs went back to New York that night, with Morrow going on in the morning to join his family in Maine.

On the evening of the second, however, the President summoned Dawes—his houseguest and running mate—to an after-dinner conference with Hughes and Ambassador Alanson Houghton. "This," Dawes wrote in his journal, "lasted until nearly midnight when, at the request of the President and Secretary Hughes, I left for New York to see Young and J. P. Morgan to apprise them of the result." As Dawes went on to report:

> Houghton, with great earnestness, pointed out that the appointment of a member of the firm of Morgan & Company would probably enable the Nationalists in Germany to defeat the Republican Government there by raising the demagogic cry that it was a scheme of the international bankers to crush the life out of Germany instead of helping her. He gave this as the private opinion of the German Government itself. As a result of Houghton's representations it was the consensus that . . . the Administration deemed it inadvisable that Dwight be selected. We agreed that I should try to get Young to agree to serve.[14]

But this Young would not do. At most, he said to Dawes and Morgan, who met with him, he would take the place only long enough to get the thing going "and subject to an agreement now on a permanent Agent-General whom Mr. Morgan and the Government both approved." According to Dawes, "Nelson Perkins of Boston was tentatively agreed upon. . . . It was also agreed that Young should leave for London on the next Saturday [this was Wednesday] to be present at the Conference of the . . . Allied . . . premiers." Young then undertook to explain matters by phone to Morrow, who authorized him to transmit to Montagu Norman at the Bank of England his request to have his name withdrawn. Young also informed Norman that having seen Dwight's message he was sailing Saturday on the *Leviathan*, bringing "new suggestion for discussion which has approval here."[15]

iii

And so, on remarkably short notice, Owen canceled his plans to settle down in Riverside and sailed again for Europe on July 5, 1924, this time with Jo. According to his calendar, callers at his office on Thursday the third included not only Dawes, Morgan and Thomas Cochran (a Morgan partner) but also Houghton and, of course, Swope. After these sessions and a Radio board meeting, Owen took off for Van Hornesville to bring his eighty-five-year-old mother up to date, leaving his wife to break the news to the children, and, of course, pack all the trunks. Their passports were still valid and somehow the *Leviathan* yielded accommodations. Stuart Crocker was not available to help; on June 28 he had been married in the presence of most of the Youngs, and was off on a month's honeymoon.[16]

The children swallowed hard. Plans for the summer, not to mention the Fourth, had suddenly been shattered, and with C.J. and Eleanor living in Schenectady, young Jo—always with Chan's help—was left in charge. Their mother tried to reassure them: this trip was going to be short; they would surely be back by late August or early September!

The London Conference impinges on this story only insofar as it impinged on Young himself—excessively, in Jo's view. The official reports list his attendance as an American "expert" at all eight sessions of a key committee; he also submitted a lengthy protocol on controls over Germany's economy which became part of a separate agreement between the Germans and the Reparations Commission. But chiefly his involvement was offstage: as adviser to Ambassador Kellogg, as a moderating influence in effecting a workable compromise between the bankers and the French on how best to deal with any future German default—the chief concern of his committee—and in persuading the Germans that French concessions vis-à-vis the Ruhr would follow fresh evidence of Germany's good faith rather than any display of truculence. In the event, these efforts paid off. When the Germans came to London early in August, it was not merely to initial, as *pro forma* participants, an Allied protocol, but also and primarily for direct negotiations with the Allies and especially the French.[17]

Unlike Dawes, Young kept no diary, and he wrote few letters from London. This was not for want of help. George P. Auld, the former accountant-general of the Reparations Commission, was a valued adviser and so was Leon Fraser, a young international lawyer who, like Auld, was to render important service in putting the Plan to work—and later with the Bank for International Settlements. As for his absent assistant, Young had found a highly satisfactory substitute in Fred Bate, a young American artist who had earned his bread in Paris on the secretariat of the Reparations Commission, which had lent him to the Dawes Committee and now lent him again to Owen Young. Married to a connection of the royal family, Bate had become both friend and confidant to the Prince of Wales—at that time widely admired, at home and abroad. Knowledgeable, sensitive, hardworking and devoted, Fred Bate was to develop with the Youngs an enduring relationship of mutual admiration and affection, which, even in its early stages, did much to brighten that summer.

More important was the fact that, this time, Jo was with Owen from the start, and again her running commentary enlivens the scene.[18] Writing her children from Claridge's on Sunday, July 13—a letter she completed on July 15—she offered this preamble to the conference, which was to open on the sixteenth:

Things have happened so fast I haven't been able to write a word— Col. Logan came to see Pops Sunday night—and I couldn't very well write while they were talking—Then Monday a.m. we set up a regular office here in the sitting room—stenographer—Mr. Bate as secretary—and the usual powwow began of calls, and photographers—"just look up a little please"—and newspaper men—Pops has spent some time with Mr. Kellogg —and this morning Sir Robert Kindersley came in, just back from Germany—and they are off somewhere, and I don't expect to see Pops again today. The situation here is peculiar—Mr. Kellogg is the American representative at the Conference which opens in the morning—but he poor man—doesn't know anything much about the Dawes Plan which *is* the Conference,—and he knows he doesn't, so he's just hanging on to Pops— and just what position your father is going to have is still in the air—

He's much amused over it—being absolutely on his own—The English
papers are giving *Dr.* Owen D. Young considerable publicity—mostly wrong
—and I've started a clipping bureau—and keep it all for Miss Chandler—
. . . Sunday we drove across country to Oxford, in the loveliest weather
and landscape you ever saw. Nothing can compare with the English countryside, at its best—and it does remind me of the Mohawk Valley—

Perhaps Jo was feeling homesick, but she was also busy and observant. "I think," she continued next day, "I have found one man who
could really paint your father's portrait acceptably, Sir Wm. Orpen."
But there was also more about the conference:

I've just finished the morning's batch of clippings. And Pops is having
M. Parmentier for a session in the other room—The Conference opens
formally this morning. The general tone is pretty pessimistic,—there is so
much politics to the fore. It remains to be seen after the politicians have
made their speeches—whether Sir Robert and Parmentier and your father
will be able to pull anything through. No one knows what is going to
happen— . . . I wish you were all here—and I do hope nothing will prevent our getting off on August 6th, as we have planned—

Her next letter, dated July 24, is almost too beguiling not to reproduce in full, but excerpts will have to serve. Prior to a garden party at
Buckingham Palace, put on for the American Bar Association but with
the embassy asking the Youngs to go, they had lunched—thanks to
Fred Bate—with the Prince of Wales, and Jo had to tell her daughter
all about it. "He" had come promptly, looking "very fit," and "it was all
as simple and friendly and easy as any luncheon." Jo was charmed.
"He [the prince] evidently admires Pops very much—and listens with
the greatest attention to every word he says. In the afternoon at the
Garden Party he got hold of your father and they walked for about
an hour. . . ." Since after the luncheon Owen had found a "summons
to come to Buckingham Palace half an hour earlier to meet the King,"
he was having quite a day. As for Jo, who had waited with friends in
the queue to make her curtsy, she found the king "not so good looking
as his pictures . . . but the Queen . . . much better looking."

Then back to business: "The Conference is at a deadlock—and
everyone pretty discouraged. But something will have to happen next
week. I wish I were with you all . . . but it won't be long now. . . .
Please pass this letter to C.J. and Eleanor and Gramie."

What Jo could not know was that on this very day an anxious President was wiring Ambassador Kellogg that, in the event of an imminent
breakdown, he had a proposal of his own to make. Neither then nor
later would he divulge its substance to Kellogg but the under secretary of state, Joseph Grew, declared that it proposed the chief justice

of the U.S. Supreme Court as arbiter of any issues which the conference left unresolved. Inasmuch as the United States had so far refused to join the World Court, sitting at The Hague—whose presiding justice the London conferees proposed to invoke as arbiter in at least two eventualities—it was just as well, perhaps, that the Coolidge proposal never saw the light of day.[19]

In the event, the presence in London—unofficial, of course—of Coolidge's secretary of state was sufficient to obviate the need. While Washington's decision to ask that Ambassador Kellogg, and James Logan, as unofficial observer on the Reparations Commission, be accorded an official if limited place at the London Conference was hardly the dramatic gesture that Young had called for at Harvard, it did mean a degree of American involvement which Ramsay Mac-Donald, for one, had so far welcomed as to assure the ambassador that the Allied debts would be no part of the agenda. And this was all the encouragement Hughes had needed to attend, as he did and as its president, that summer's London meetings of the American Bar Association.

Certainly his public appearances in that role found Hughes at the top of his form. Taking full advantage of his "cover" to pay his "personal" respects at 10 Downing Street as well as Buckingham Palace, he also managed a heart-to-heart talk with the new French premier, Edouard Herriot, at a small luncheon party of Kellogg's, which at least one foreign correspondent pronounced determining in its impact. Proceeding thence to "courtesy calls" in Paris and Berlin, Hughes took occasion to warn Raymond Poincaré as well as Herriot, and equally Wilhelm Marx and Gustav Stresemann, that the Dawes Plan was now the American policy, and if it was not accepted, America was through.[20]

This indeed was all that Young could ask—and more. Nevertheless, on August 19, Jo was writing the children about the mounting pressures on their father and how heartbroken she had been at having to cancel their scheduled sailing for a second time.

I said to Pops that perhaps I had better go, but he said "Oh no—don't go," so I knew I had to stay. And these last days since the signing of the "Pact of London" last Saturday night have really taken it out of him more than all the time before. Pressure has been brought to bear on all sides—the Germans will have no one else to set up the Plan—the English—the President, and our ambassador here—the bankers [sic] and all. God knows it is too much to put on any one man's shoulders and he has tried so hard to arrange for some one else to take it. . . . But he came to see it was no use—and I knew he wouldn't feel he was doing the square thing if he left now. Some one to take the permanent job of Agent General will be appointed in the next few weeks—as Pops has only agreed to act temporarily. Of course you are interested to know how long that means, and I can't tell you—at any rate I am planning now to sail soon after the first of September, so that I can be there before you and Philip plan to start. . . .[21]

Except in her reference to the bankers, Jo did not exaggerate, nor was it only in "these last days" that the pressures had been mounting. August, so far, had been all too reminiscent of Paris, leaving little time for book hunting or lesser recreations. For one thing, Young's sessions with the bankers, chiefly Governor Norman of the Bank of England and Thomas W. Lamont of Morgan's, had become increasingly taxing and even acrimonious. The "new suggestion for discussion" which he had brought with him had not been well received; in spite of its approval at home—partly tentative, as Dawes had written, on Morgan's part—Norman and Lamont and now, quite evidently, Morgan wanted neither Perkins nor any merely temporary appointee. Denied Morrow, they wanted the closest possible facsimile thereof, so as to assure the terms and conditions necessary, in their view, for a successful flotation of the German loan. Young would "do," if only he would agree to serve for at least three years; his limit remained three months. Early in August, as Morgan himself arrived in London, Young wrote him a long and revealing letter, urging in conclusion that Dwight Morrow's name be reconsidered; Morgan replied that the matter was closed. Thereupon, as Kellogg reported to Hughes—and Hughes (at Young's request) to Dawes—Norman and Lamont, Morgan concurring, proposed Norman Davis, a veteran of the Versailles conference who was currently managing the campaign of Coolidge's Democratic challenger, John W. Davis.[22]

Young, of course, fully shared the bankers' concern about the flotation of that all-important loan, and hence about the need for concessions by the French. He came at length to feel, however, that the pressure the bankers exerted on the French was so excessive as to be self-defeating. On reaching that conclusion he so advised Kellogg, to whose intervention the bankers' tardy acceptance of the compromise which was finally worked out owes much. On the one hand the French did promise to complete evacuation of the Ruhr within the year if, in the meantime, Germany met its full obligations under the Plan. On the other, they renounced recourse to further sanctions unless (1) *by unanimous vote* the Reparations Commission found Germany in willful default or (2) a majority vote to that effect were upheld by a three-man arbitral tribunal, the chairman of which should be an American citizen. And since Secretary Hughes had further agreed that the same circumstances which had led to Kellogg's role in the London Conference dictated something more than a nonvoting American presence on the Reparations Commission, the United States could exercise an effective veto in the commission itself against any otherwise unanimous adverse vote.[23]

Though Young's problems with Norman, and especially with Morgan, might rankle, as they did, he was actually in an enviable position. He was seeking nothing for himself, and if the bankers could find someone acceptable to Washington who would take on the full assignment at once, so much the better. Failing that, and for the interim, he had undertaken, at the President's request, to set up the new machinery of the Plan and find the men to make it work, and he was not one to default on such an undertaking. Moreover, he could now claim to know "everybody who was anybody" on both sides of the Atlantic, and was beginning to feel almost at home abroad. He was perhaps the only man who enjoyed the full confidence of the four prime ministers in attendance at London—French, German, Belgian and British—and if the bankers had found him not always easy to get along with, neither—it was beginning to appear—could they get very far without him.[24]

But if Jo fretted, so did Gerard Swope, who might enjoy "doing all the work" but was missing his teammate sorely. Conceding that "strictly it is none of my business," Swope's radiogram of August 19 urged that however great the political pressures to take on this new assignment, Owen should not forget that "there is great work in this country which needs you and you alone." And he sought reassurance to that effect.[25]

Relief was now in sight and reassurance very much in order. Some days before the conference recessed, a dark horse had been entered in the agent-general sweepstakes: a young and personable lawyer named S. Parker Gilbert, who had recently joined the Cravath firm after distinguished service as under secretary of the treasury. At Morgan's, Russell Leffingwell could and did vouch for his ability and character. But Treasury Secretary Mellon too was now in London, ostensibly on holiday, and in the conversion of this dark horse into the favorite, his voice and presence, through muted, were undoubtedly determining. After some show of reluctance, Gilbert accepted the designation, stipulating, however, the need for some delay so that he could adjust his plans and clear matters with his absent chief. Thus Young could hardly escape the *ad interim* assignment after all. But he was free of anything beyond that, and with the other problems affecting flotation of the Dawes loan well on the road to settlement, this slate was quickly adopted.[26]

Young did manage one letter from London, handwritten from the Foreign Office on August 16, 1924; the children to whom it was addressed preserved it with care:

Dear Josephine and Philip—

This is the final meeting of the International Conference—I am writing while it is in session and during the translations. The proceedings are carried on in English, French and German. Mr. MacDonald is presiding—he looks tired, very tired, but happy. His voice is rich and mellow—his manner firm and masterful—Next him sits Herriot—likewise tired—still apprehensive as to what will happen to his ministry when he returns to Paris and reports. Theunis of Belgium neither tired nor apprehensive—not happy but content. His is the only gov't of Europe which has a safe majority—One does not know what Italy or rather Mussolini has. Mussolini is not here—his finance minister de Stefani is—He was a professor of finance and is now advanced to head of Italian Gov finance. He is quite large with broad head—in fact I am struck with the breadth and in a sense the flatness of the heads of all these men in political power—This is true too of Marx the German Chancellor who sits at foot of table with an impassive and unperturbed air. Streseman his foreign minister looks cunningly pleased—How I would like to know what is going on in his mind! Now we adjourn until 9 tonight to come back and initial the protocol.

The business is done—the curtain rings down on the Conference and rises on a new day in Europe—

With love—Pops
Owen D. Young

P.S. I sign for the record and with a quill pen.[27]

i v

As the conference recessed on August 16, to reconvene on August 30, Young's confident allusion to a "new day in Europe" was still prediction rather than fact. The ensuing fortnight would determine the fate of the London Pact and so of the Plan itself; for the recess was expressly designed to enable the respective delegations to take home the agreements they had initialed, and there secure—or fail to secure—parliamentary authorization to sign them. Young might be confident of the outcome, but the French and especially the Germans had good reason to be apprehensive.

In the event, Herriot was sustained by a large majority, and Stanley

Baldwin promptly assured MacDonald of bipartisan support. In Berlin, however, the Marx government's encounter with the Reichstag was by no means lacking in drama, as Young was to testify at the dinner given in his honor on December 11, when he was safely home:

In Germany the Chancellor and his associates asked the Reichstag [in August] for approval of the London Agreement. Two parties were in opposition. The extreme left, namely the communists, opposed the Plan as a new machine of capitalistic bondage. The extreme right, the Monarchists and reactionaries, opposed the Plan on the ground that its burdens were too heavy, and incidentally as a matter of domestic politics, because [if it were adopted] the position of the central democratic parties would be strengthened. A large majority of the Reichstag, but less than two-thirds, appeared on the initial votes to be in favor of the Plan.

As Young proceeded to point out, a majority would suffice to approve reorganization of the Reichsbank and the industrial bond issue of $1.25 billion. Under the German constitution, however, the transfer of the railroads to a private company and the issue of $2.5 billion of first-mortgage bonds against them for reparations account required a two-thirds vote. Entering the Reichstag for this final vote, the chancellor

held the decree of the President of Germany for the dissolution of parliament in his pocket, and frankly stated that if the bill were not voted, the Reichstag would be dissolved and an appeal would be made to the country in new elections in behalf of the Plan. The vote in the Reichstag is taken by ballot, a white ballot meaning "yes" and a pink meaning "no." The nationalist party as opponents to the Plan walked to the ballot box with pink slips meaning "no" upheld in their right hands. With their left enough of them put in white ballots so that the railroad bill was carried. The strongest single political party in Germany did not dare reject the plan and go to the country on the propriety of their action. That their judgment was justified is shown by the elections on last Sunday. That election, which strengthened the position of the central parties at the expense of the right and the left, would seem to show that Germany has the will to pay. If the world is convinced of that, the greatest barrier to a final settlement of reparations will have been removed.

And so, to quote Young further: "On August 30th, the representatives of the powers finally signed the protocol and for the first time since the war, after due hearing and full discussion, after separate consideration of the terms in their home capitols, the great nations of the world, Germany included, meeting on equal terms, agreed. The plan was adopted."[28]

Young too had been putting this decisive fortnight to productive use. Aside from the final designation of Parker Gilbert as "permanent" agent-general, there were other key posts to be filled—notably, on the Transfer Committee, at the Reichsbank, and on the Reparations Commission itself. Respecting these and other matters related to the pending loan, Young was in almost constant consultation with the bankers, private and central, of London and New York.[29] And, assuming the pact's ratification, he must be prepared to take at once all necessary steps to declare the plan operative.

Ratification found him ready and two days later, the curtain rose on Act III of this curiously engrossing drama. The testing of the Dawes Plan was about to begin, and with it the further testing of the man designated—for the time being—to play the lead.

It was, by any reckoning, an awesome role, as the Berlin press was at pains to point out. As early as July 23, anticipating Young's appointment, the *Neue Berliner Tageblatt* had observed that the powers of "His Majesty Owen the First" would surpass even those of the former kaiser. This theme was to be echoed later, notably in the "biographical" sketch appearing in the *Berliner Abendblatt* for October 10, translation of which the general's brother, Rufus Dawes, thoughtfully sent to Mrs. Young. In the meantime, the *New York Times* had at once printed a digest of the earlier piece, which so tickled the fancy of Dr. John Finley that his lead editorial for September 1 hailed Young as "Owen the First." Fortunately Young had as general counsel Leon Fraser, an able young American who refused to take himself or his chief too seriously. It was Fraser who, on September 1, with Young still in London, officially opened the agent-general's Berlin office at the Hotel Adlon. And it was Fraser who addressed an envelope to Young containing a picture postcard purporting to be of that office but actually of the Adlon's spacious bar.[30]

But there was much to be done, and done quickly, and able help was needed at once. When Young went to Berlin on September 3, Jo went too but, alas, illness cut short her first (and only) visit to that city and she was soon dispatched to Paris. With the Youngs on September 3 went a small clerical staff, drawn from the Reparations and other commissions: ". . . with Mr. Rufus Dawes, Mr. Auld and myself as temporary volunteer associates, assistants, or advisors. A few days later, Mr. Henry M. Robinson and his brother . . . joined this volunteer staff."

The quotation is taken from a letter written by Pierre Jay, chairman of the New York Federal Reserve Bank, to the chairman of the Federal Reserve Board in Washington. Dated October 16, with a copy to Herbert Case for discreet circulation in the New York bank, it constitutes an eminently knowledgeable source of what was going on as well as why and how. Jay pointed out that the London agreement provided a transition period of five weeks, beginning September 1, in which to give effect to such requirements of the plan as:

a) the reconstitution of the Reichsbank.
b) the formation of a railway company to take over the German railways from the . . . Government and to create a mortgage thereon of 10 billion gold marks.
c) the provision of a mortgage of 5 billion gold marks on the German industries.[31]

Aside from the organizing process these involved, and the receipt and expenditure of funds for deliveries in kind, there remained final arrangements to assure the international loan of 800 million gold marks.

Wisely it had been decided that the commissioner of railways should be a Frenchman, of industrial debentures an Italian, of the bank a Dutchman, "who gets on famously with Dr. Schacht." Only on the bank board—and of course the all-important Transfer Committee— would the United States be represented: on the former by Gates Mc-Garrah, a well-known and highly responsible New York banker; on the latter, by the head of Price Waterhouse, Joseph E. Sterrett, who would preside in the agent-general's absence. While the Transfer Committee would not begin to function until late October, and would have little to worry about in the actual transfer of money payments for a couple of years, it had wide authority on other matters, including deliveries in kind and the protection of the German economy generally. At its first meeting, scheduled for October 31, Jay reported, "Young has several very important matters [not specified] to lay before it at once."

"Of course," Jay's letter continues, "the *sine qua non* of the whole Plan was the loan. About the 20th September," after Schacht had taken soundings on the continent,

Mr. Young and Dr. Schacht both came to London, where, after some preliminary discussion with Mr. Morgan and two of his partners, and Governor Norman and other English bankers, representatives from Sweden, Holland, Belgium, France, Switzerland and Italy were called in and Dr. Luther, the German Finance Minister, came to London as well. America was to take one-half, England about one-quarter and the rest of the countries combined, including Germany, the other quarter. . . . Although some of the smaller countries found great difficulty in providing for their quotas, it was felt to be of the greatest importance to have the loan a great international one with all important countries represented and finally, after nearly three weeks of discussion and negotiation, Mr. Young came back to

Paris on the 9th [of October] with a form of contract agreed upon, a form of bond agreed upon, and a set of decisions to be taken by the Reparation Commission, making it absolutely clear that the loan would be a first charge on Germany ahead of reparation and all other payments. These he presented to the Reparation Commission on Friday the 10th, while the bankers were gathered together in London awaiting the results over the telephone.

Mr. Robinson, who accompanied Mr. Young at the meeting, which lasted four or five hours, tells me that Mr. Young's handling of the situation was remarkable. The Reparation Commission which, as I wrote you before, had not heretofore been very prompt, to say the least, in making its decisions, has during the past month been called upon by Mr. Young to make promptly a large number of decisions on very important matters. The one they were called upon to make on the 10th without much previous opportunity for discussion, declaring for the absolute priority of the loan and dealing with a lot of other details, with the bankers at the other end of the telephone wire waiting to send cables that evening to the members of the underwriting syndicate in America, was an especially large order. Some references were made, all in the best of good nature and thoroughly appreciatively, to the speed with which the Commission was being asked to make these decisions and to Mr. Young's multifarious activities. But Mr. Robinson says that Mr. Young's handling of the situation was masterful, and the evening wound up with a complete decision on the part of the Commission, a telephone message to the London bankers, and their dispatches of the necessary cables to the underwriting syndicate.[32]

Known only to Robinson, whose story Stuart Crocker recorded in his interview of the following May, was a bit of interwoven drama to which not even Jay was privy. Robinson, Crocker reports,

told of a battle between the Reparation Commission and the bankers with regard to certain things the bankers insisted be put in in connection with the loan. Mr. Young didn't believe they had a right to insist on it, but had to put it before the Commission. He put it up before the Commission, declined to do what the bankers asked, but suggested a modified formula. Then he went into the other room in the Astoria, and called Lamont at the Bank of England on the phone, and told him what he had done, saying that he advised the change, and Robinson backed him. He advised them to accept it. Lamont said, after talking it over with some of the bank officials, "All right." That was the very last clause that had to be put in to make the whole machinery start. When Mr. Young put up the receiver, he turned to shake hands with Mr. Robinson. And just then in walked Dr. Meyer with the blanket issue of bonds of the German railroads under his arm!

Mr. Young told Mr. Robinson that he had expected to have all manner of trouble in getting the plan to working, but as a matter of fact they had none. Everybody, even the Germans, helped as soon as the loan was assured.[33]

Jo, too, was reassured. True, her scheduled September sailing had been a casualty too and young Jo had had to pack brother Philip off to Choate and herself to Bryn Mawr with no help from either parent except for the encouraging and reassuring radiograms that flew back and forth across the Atlantic. On October 4 her mother finally managed a proper letter; it was from London and was mostly about book hunting, especially at Spencer's, "which takes Owen's mind off his problems."

She did, however, have other news:

The business of the Plan is moving on well. He (Pops) has a horde of followers scattered through the Ruhr, and Berlin—all experts of some kind or another—and they are regulating Germany's finances—etc. etc. . . . We are staying here a week longer than we intended as the bankers are all here, and there is much to do on the Loan. I'm afraid I'm going to miss out on the Orpen portrait, as we were detained here—and Sir William detained in Paris. . . .

Yesterday Pops went to lunch with Mr. Norman, and this morning he has been called to 10 Downing Street by the Prime Minister [a rare Saturday summons]. We are planning to do a little final book-hunting late this afternoon when he is through, for we go back to Paris Wednesday. . . . There is a chance that Mr. Perkins may come over—he has refused once, but they are bringing all sorts of pressure to bear—I wish they would come before we go—

Owen fully shared that wish. Where Perkins was concerned he did not give up easily. His original proposal having failed, Young had been trying to persuade his friend how important it was for him to become the first American to serve as a voting member of the Reparations Commission, where he would be invaluable to Parker Gilbert. It was this plea that finally persuaded Perkins, and led him to Berlin in time to join Henry Robinson in celebrating Owen's fiftieth birthday on October 27.[34] This was a date that did not pass without notice elsewhere: in Paris Jo had to remember it alone and, as Ida Young wrote young Jo at college, "Chan said they were to send Birthday greetings so we sent messages from Van Hornesville. Sorry that he has to miss [sic] his 50th Birthday away from home. . . ."

On October 19 Jo had written her daughter: "We are going to sail on November 12, so your father says." She was becoming skeptical, but writing from the Ritz in Paris on Sunday, November 2, she was more confident, and her letter covers considerable ground:

This [is] positively my last letter from Paris. It is now eight o'clock and the last of the six trunks is packed and soon I'm going to order a modest repast. No champagne—as there is no fun drinking alone. Fred and Vera

Bate dined with me last night, and tomorrow night I hope to dine at the Savoy—London—But whether Pops will be in or not I don't know—as I received a message from Berlin last night, saying they were leaving for Amsterdam,—that means Hook of Holland and some landing place in England, an all night's run, and they may not get in until Tuesday a.m. . . . Mr. Robinson and Mr. Perkins are with him. . . . The International Radio meetings [at which Perkins would be presiding] are Tuesday and Wednesday—so he can't be later than that. . . . Had a letter from Lincoln Steffens. He and his wife—he was married last February, the wretch, and never told me—are staying at San Remo—awaiting a baby—then he thinks he may come to the U.S.

She was right about the baby, but Steffens had misstated the date of the marriage, which, according to his biographer, had only recently taken place.[35] Jo wrote nothing about her trip to Berlin with Owen, or her illness there. But she was prouder than ever of her "man of affairs," and if she had missed out on the Orpen portrait, she had been busy to good effect with that sculptor friend of Steffens: "I wonder if you will like your father's bust. I expected to have some good photographs of it, by this time, to send you. But Jo Davidson has failed to get them here yet. I like it very much, but you have to become accustomed to seeing a familiar face in clay—it stays in one expression, while you are used to so many. . . ."[36]

Young's face must have worn an expression mainly of relief as he prepared at last to welcome Parker Gilbert, introduce him to the proper authorities, wind up his own affairs and make his adieux. In reply to Swope's most recent inquiry Young sent him from Paris on October 17 a succinct outline of his schedule for these final weeks abroad: "subject to verification on Gilbert's arrival my present plan is spend next week Paris installing Gilbert here week following Berlin installing him there November fourth London for Radio meeting if Harbord approves and sailing November twelfth I think Homeric."

Young's files contain a manuscript draft or copy of his final report to the Reparations Commission: low-key and understated, it bears eloquent testimony to the solid beginnings and promise for the future which, with quiet authority, he ascribes equally to French forbearance, German good faith and the commission's patience. His concluding bow to the commission itself was repeated a little later vis-à-vis his English Dawes Committee colleagues. At a London dinner given in his honor by Sir Robert Kindersley, Young responded to Lord Balfour's more than gracious toast by paying tribute both to Kindersley and to Josiah Stamp as reflecting, by their skill, devotion and unfailing consideration for others, the finest traditions of British representation abroad. If he had been told, as possibly he was, that his own remarks were in the finest American tradition, he would have asked nothing better.[37]

The final word on Young's 1924 activities as an American abroad belongs to Pierre Jay. He had been spending some weeks taking the measure of this man, a few years his junior, whom he had previously known only as one of his directors at the Federal Reserve; a sophisticate himself, Jay was not given to easy enthusiasm or extravagant praise. Nevertheless, his report to Washington was unstinting in giving Young what he felt to be his due:

> Every day only serves more clearly to show Mr. Young as the mastermind of this whole situation. I gather that the central idea of the activities of the Transfer Committee was Mr. Young's. . . . He was in London all through the Conference and was instrumental in writing into the report of the London Conference two sentences . . . which protect the bondholders in case any further sanctions are imposed on Germany; and he was the final negotiator with the Reparation Commission in their decision to grant complete priority to the bond issue. Furthermore, he is steeped in the philosophy of the whole Plan; is thoroughly imbued with the limitations of the position of Agent General as well as with its powers and responsibilities and never steps over the line. . . . With all his grasp of the entire situation, his clear method of presentation and his ability as a negotiator, he is so fair and respectful of the rights and proper sensibilities of other authorities that he is completely master of the situation. After six weeks of his "activities" with the need for prompt decisions the Reparation Commission is today giving him a lunch party![38]

"Owen the First," it would appear, had no stomach for the role of absolute monarch. Indeed, of his own activities, the otherwise informative radiogram he dispatched on October 18 to his friend A. C. Bedford, as head of the U.S. Chamber of Commerce, says nothing at all. Rather, "the ease with which the machinery under the Dawes Plan has been installed and the smoothness of its operation" is again ascribed to "the full cooperation" of all parties, debtor and creditor alike, bespeaking "the existence of a new spirit determined to restore tranquility to Western Europe. . . . If this spirit can be maintained then the Dawes Plan will work."

Young's concluding sentence, however, is personal enough. Sending "my remembrances and warm regards to my business associates and friends," he asked Bedford also to tell them "that I regard the job of the American business man as the most satisfying in the world and that I am looking forward . . . to a speedy return to my own job at home."

Chapter 18

American Ascendancy and Business Horizons

C ONVENTIONAL, nostalgic, or both, Young's message to his friends and associates was thoroughly attuned to the times. Nowhere else, not even in Renaissance Florence, had the businessman achieved the status, not to say commanding role, which he now enjoyed in the United States. Even in the White House he had a surrogate of sorts: it was the very man who had solemnly declared that "the chief business of the American people is business" who, in 1924, was elected President in his own right—and with more votes than the combined total cast for John W. Davis and Senator Robert M. La Follette. Young, of course, had sent a message supporting Davis, but clearly it was not the moment for judgmental Democrats or die-hard Progressives; it was better to keep cool with Coolidge. "More business in government and less government in business" was a slogan the administration had made its own, and this the man in the street readily understood—or thought he did. Business got things done, while the politicians only talked—except, of course, for Coolidge.

Owen Young was in no position, or mood, to deny that business "got things done." Fresh from his latest diplomatic triumph, he had also witnessed at the London sessions of the Radio consortium the successful outcome of his earlier venture. Three days out on the *Homeric*—which this time he and Jo had actually caught—he had also received a jubilant radiogram from James G. Harbord, with tidings that referee Roland Boyden's "draft decision" had awarded *all* contested rights in the AT&T hassle to the so-called Radio group. Gratifying as it was, this news was nonetheless cause for concern. Clearly, concessions to AT&T were now in order, and no time was to be lost in determining what they should be.[1]

But Young was not about to focus wholly on specific issues, however pressing. Perspective too was important, and certainly the view from abroad had given him a fresh perspective on the American scene. Already Henry Ford's Model T and his unprecedented minimum wage of five dollars a day had become mere prototypes of the new conveniences, contrivances and rewards which were now pouring from industry's assembly lines. The key was mass production and, as its lower unit costs and higher wages opened the door to mass consumption, the scientist and the inventor felt the spur to develop not only new products adapted to this market but also, with the engineer and the technologist, new and ever more efficient tools of production. These in turn assured for the worker a steady rise in productivity, which supported wage levels already averaging roughly twice the prewar level. Thus with purchasing power further enhanced by stable prices and a wide range of cheaper products, the already nationwide market was experiencing a kind of vertical expansion too. The motorcar, like the radio and the movies, now belonged to all the people— or almost all; for workers who lacked cash, installment credit was readily available. As for profits, if margins were typically smaller, their swelling total was sufficient—after higher dividends were paid—to support a substantial capital investment in the search for still more efficient machines. And so this cycle—apparently self-regenerating— went on its repetitive way.

World without end? Was the business cycle itself about to be displaced? Here was another of the long-range problems which industry, and Young himself, would have to confront. For the foreseeable future, certainly, the world's ability to consume was limited only by its ability to trade or buy, on cash or credit. Repairing Europe's war-shattered credit—beginning with Germany's—was what the Dawes Plan was all about, and as the Europeans now went back to work in earnest and other currencies than the German were stabilized, perhaps the United States would find these countries truly credit-worthy. If so, all stood to benefit.

Back home, however, it was clear that not everyone was applauding. Not the farmers, whose economy, as Young well knew, was badly out of gear with industry's. Not the embattled insurgents who watched big business getting even bigger. Not the textile workers, especially in the southern mills. Not the union leaders, who were wringing their hands over declining membership; and not, initially at least, the skilled workers, who saw many of their hard-won skills devalued.[2]

At the same time more fastidious hands were being wrung over the vulgar standardization and ubiquitous sloganeering that accompanied production in volume for the mass market. The materialistic values which, according to André Siegfried, marked America's "coming of age" were already favorite targets of churchmen and editors, intellectuals and humane scholars, who even persuaded some college students that the good life and Wall Street were not synonymous. "Boosters," like Sinclair Lewis's Babbitt, were exposed to ridicule, occasionally tinged, as in *Main Street*, with compassion. Nor did the voices of despair, notably T. S. Eliot's, which pronounced America a cultural wasteland, lack responsive hearers.

Aware as he was of such voices, Young was also aware that many of them were curiously blunted. The Babbitts, it appeared, were prosperous and literate enough to help make Lewis's book a best-seller. Technology was creating not only new jobs but whole new industries. Millions of mass-produced radios enabled a Harry Emerson Fosdick to be heard, if not always heeded, by the multitudes who tuned in to his Sunday broadcasts. If some young writers chose to follow Eliot and Ernest Hemingway into exile, many others were deciding, with Carl Sandburg and Eugene O'Neill, to take a closer look at the American scene. And all, whether they wrote abroad or at home, were to make a decade unparalleled in productivity in fields other than business.[3]

It was, however, the productivity of American *business* that excited the envy even of Europeans who shuddered at the prospect of their countries' Americanization. The paradox excited Young's interest and so did the ways in which various countries tried to resolve it. The British, who did most of the shuddering, tended to cling to their old ways—forgetting (or remembering?) that Britain had served as midwife to the first Industrial Revolution. The United States, as the great creditor nation, had much to learn from England, and England had much to learn from us about the wider diffusion of rewards and opportunities. For all his admiration of the English at their best, Owen Young could never abide their complacency toward a caste system which supported the few at the expense of the many.

The Germans, eager to recover lost ground, did most of the emulating, and, once the Dawes Plan was operative, found little difficulty in importing American capital and know-how to "rationalize" their industry. Some of both came from General Electric; toward this effort Young was highly sympathetic, specifying only that GE should never take over the direction or control of its foreign counterparts. For American business, he felt, international dimensions were now essential, but the mutual benefits of economic penetration—through capital infusions, for example—were quickly lost once this took the shape of economic imperialism. To the kind of cooperative advance he sought, this spelled death.[4]

In point of fact, as Jo was well aware, it was Owen's own job that he found "the most satisfying in the world." His imagination was stimulated by its international reach as well as by the sense that GE— not to mention RCA—was close to the dynamic center of the accelerating revolution in science and technology, with all that this portended for the future. Certainly the research laboratory at Schenectady was for him, rather more than for Swope, a favorite haunt; if he missed Charles Steinmetz, there were others who were very much alive: Irving Langmuir and W. D. Coolidge, for example, and especially Willis Whitney, its highly articulate director. Scanning with them the future of the "art" and so of the industry, Young himself contributed— according to Whitney—a kind of intuitive sense of the scientist's current preoccupations and their likely—or unlikely—outcome. He liked to remind these men that their achievements to date were nothing to what the future held: "After all, what you fellows don't know is still our greatest asset."[5]

But if the prospect was one of boundless opportunity, one could ask nothing better than a secure and stable base from which to scan and test it. Like Swope, Young never underestimated the advantages of leading from strength; and the strength of GE's position meant that one could afford certain risks—adventures in ideas, unorthodox experiments—which were responsive to the times and added zest to life. Some of these creative ventures had now developed lives of their own: witness, for example, the fantastic development of broadcasting, which was to involve Young in a whole network of novel problems in corporate and public policy. Others, including his efforts to decipher and articulate some of the more radical implications of the corporate revolution, were still in embryo. In the meantime it was reassuring to reflect that in converting the primary sources of power—falling water, coal and oil—into the cheap, clean and instant energy which held the key to American productivity and wages, electricity had no peer. Nor, in the still-burgeoning industry which Young knew inside out, had General Electric—the future of which was now primarily in his hands.

And Swope's. Remembering this, Young speedily identified it as the extra dividend that made his job uniquely satisfying. More than ever he had come to feel that this singular partnership in top management was one of his happiest inventions, with the company as well as the partners sharing the benefits. For most of 1924, they had gone their separate ways, but it was to Swope that Young had turned when the Dawes Committee needed to know—without asking the bankers directly—what Morgan and the others felt the terms of the Dawes loan ought to be.[6] By the same token, when, in August, Young's absence threatened to be indefinitely extended, it was Swope whose messages to London carried urgent if delicate reminders that Young's responsibilities began at home, where he was sorely missed.[7]

In most institutions, room at the top means room for one, and its occupant is likely on occasion to find it lonely. Evidently, the team of Young and Swope had succeeded in minimizing this hazard and at the same time maximizing their respective contributions. Indeed, with Young's return, the synergistic character of their relationship was to become more apparent—and valuable—than ever.

ii

Certainly Young's first week back at his office was a fresh demonstration of his capacity to function under pressure. It was also proof positive that he had indeed been sorely missed. This he relished, as he did the reunion with tested friends like Swope and Harbord, who were anxious to report to him on the antitrust suits, the Bond and Share connection, and Boyden's preliminary and almost too satisfactory findings in the AT&T dispute. But if he were to feel truly back home, he had still to touch base at Van Hornesville, and Thanksgiving, 1924, found him there.

His mother, now eighty-five, was entitled to feel that he had come a long way, but she was not about to tell him so. There was no need: he knew and knew that she knew. She was frankly curious, however, about some of his new and highfalutin friends. Coolidge, like Hughes and Hoover, was no longer a novelty and Dawes was hardly a puzzle. But all those prime ministers and chancellors he'd been seeing all over Europe—what kind of folks were they? Not to mention the king and queen of England—and the prince? So he told her, marveling at the way her horizons were still expanding at an age when most people's were contracting.[8]

Of the problems and accumulative demands which awaited his return, he told her little or nothing. That things had piled up, she took for granted, as she did the need for work. Both knew what every member of Young's office staff could attest: that he worked best under the kinds of pressures that constantly tested his mettle and stretched his mind. But for the moment, at Van Hornesville, it was good to sit by the stove, talk about the family and the farm, and stretch nothing but his legs.

Owen stayed on for a long weekend, and Monday, December 1, brought them word from Schenectady that Ida Young was now a great-grandmother. C.J.'s wife, Eleanor Whitman Young, had just presented him with a son, John Peter, and in Van Hornesville there was great rejoicing. On Tuesday Young stopped off at Schenectady for a visit with all three, and while pressing engagements kept him in New York for the next two days, Friday was wholly devoted to his daughter in Bryn Mawr. She had come up to New York to meet his boat, but it had been a brief encounter, interrupted by the innumerable demands that crowded upon him as soon as he landed. Now he wanted a good look at her and at her college, and besides, she was having a spell at the infirmary with flu. He also wanted to celebrate with her the arrival of her nephew, and it was hard to say who found this news more cheering, the young aunt or the new grandfather.

Such visits with the older and younger members of his family were all the more precious because the public and private claims confronting the new grandfather were now commanding his immediate attention. On Thursday, December 11, he was faced with a "testimonial" dinner at the Waldorf, and that meant a major speech. He also had to decide how best to approach Harry Thayer, and with what concessions to AT&T. Swope, in the meantime, was rightly impatient to have the Bond and Share business settled, and with Coffin still opposed to divestiture, he was counting on Young to see it through. And indeed, once Young was back, no time was lost: at the board's December meeting, divestiture was duly recommended and authorized, and on December 30, it was announced that GE's entire holdings would be distributed to its shareholders. "GE Cuts a Melon," said the headlines, and both stocks soared.[9]

The significance and timeliness of this move toward diffusion of corporate control was widely recognized and generally applauded. Bond and Share was ready for independence, and GE's customer relations with utilities which complained from time to time that S. Z. Mitchell was trying to buy—as perhaps he was—a sizable interest in their stock were notably improved. More important was the fact that it defused, although it did not end, the familiar charge that General Electric was the dynamo at the center of an intricate and sinister power trust. Skeptics might and did insist with Senator George Norris that no real change had occurred, but they now faced a heavier burden of proof. That the move was made on GE's initiative was generally taken, like Swope's candid statement that "we can't carry water on both shoulders," as evidence of good faith.[10]

But this is getting ahead of the story: even before the Bond and Share business could be settled, Young had to cope with the little matter of the "testimonial dinner." His resolve, announced from shipboard, "to come home, take up my job and keep quiet" had fallen on deaf ears; certainly his fellow businessmen, headed by A. C. Bedford, president of Jersey Standard and of the U.S. Chamber of Commerce, would have none of it. It was quickly evident too that Bedford knew what he was about. At a pinch, the banquet hall of the Waldorf-Astoria could seat a thousand; well before the evening of December 11 the pinch was felt and seats were at a premium.[11]

Everybody who was anybody was there; indeed, a more representative turnout of the business and financial elites—all men, of course—could hardly have been imagined.[12] His hosts had arranged, however, for after-dinner seats in the gallery for the ladies; thanks to this and a radio broadcast, quite a number of Young's fellow citizens of both sexes heard what he had to say. They included his wife, sitting in the gallery, and his mother, listening in Van Hornesville. The words they heard told much about the Plan and its significance, actual and potential. They reveal very little of Young's role but quite a bit about the man.

First, of course, he had to listen to a spate of messages, with the heads of government, at home and abroad, chanting his praise. In addition to President Coolidge, the vice-president-elect, General Dawes, sent a characteristically warm and generous letter, and Henry Robinson wired that "whatever may be said in the way of praise will be less than one-half the truth." From the French ambassador came the ribbon of the Legion of Honor, which went well enough with Young's white tie and tails. Sir Robert Kindersley's handwritten message was sent by "photoradiogram," said the New York *World* in reproducing it next day. (C.J. Young, a dinner guest, would doubtless have preferred "facsimile transmission," on which he was now working at GE with Ernst Alexanderson.) Conspicuous by its absence was any message from Berlin, which Hjalmar Schacht sought to explain by letter; some months later, the German government was to honor Young with the Order of the German Red Cross.

Accolades typically make dull reading after the event, but a paragraph from Hughes's—which came after Hoover's—is worth quoting for the clue it affords to the respective and mutually reinforcing roles of the public and private sectors: "The greatest difficulty that we have in making our democratic institutions work is in securing play for expert ability. . . . In this instance, talent has had opportunity not to determine but to advise, not to bind governments but to inform them. Here is a lesson of which we may take advantage in many of our perplexities. . . ."[13]

At last, it was the guest of honor's turn. That he did not disappoint his audience was evident both in their standing ovation and in the phenomenal coverage his speech—and indeed the entire occasion—was given in the press.[14] Much of what he said has already been quoted; what is new is his recognition of the problems faced by the Allied and German *governments* in coming to grips with the related political issues which only they could settle—and doing so in full awareness that failure meant scuttling the Plan. Evidently London had taught him much, and he had much to say about the courage, good-will and good faith with which Ramsay MacDonald, Edouard Herriot and Wilhelm Marx—leaders all of minority governments—had sought and finally achieved mutual accommodation and approval of their parliaments.

In turning then to Washington's role, and especially to Hughes's initiative, what Young had to say was a far cry indeed from his almost scornful allusion at Harvard to "our bootlegging participation in a reparation settlement." Reminding his audience that the Plan "would not have been created or *adopted* without America," he gave the Coolidge administration full marks, citing the fact that not only the secretary of state and the secretary of commerce had been of inestimable assistance, but also our ambassadors in Berlin and London: "In a word let me say that in my opinion the present government has done everything which could properly be done to aid in the formulation and to insure the adoption of the Dawes Plan. Personally, being of a different political faith, I feel like killing the fatted calf. . . ."

Credit having been given where credit was due, Young went on to make what was, perhaps, his most important contribution of the evening—to focus the attention of his hearers upon the future. The Plan, he said, is simply a point of departure:

As stated in the Plan, the restoration of Germany is not an end in itself, it is only a part of the larger problem of reconstruction of Europe. It is not German credit and German currency alone which need to be restored in order that financial stability may return to the world. Our low bank rates and our greatly increased gold supply will, if used wisely, enable us not only to aid our neighbors but to help ourselves. By restoring foreign credits we will increase our export markets particularly for our excess food supplies; by stabilizing foreign currencies we will restore throughout the world the free flow of commodities, including gold. When that shall have been done we shall hear less in this country, and rightly so, of artificial price levels and arbitrary bank rates.

Evidently Young was beginning to view the Dawes Plan as a promising first step toward continuing economic cooperation. In the latter, moreover, he was finding a promising alternative to—or perhaps the necessary basis for—the political cooperation which the United States had rejected along with the League of Nations. Did this, then, point the road to peace, which for six disastrous years the world had somehow lost? If so, let the United States this time be counted in. That was the theme of his concluding appeal and it was a theme on which he was to ring all the changes:

The Plan cannot succeed without the cooperation of the people of America. Have we at last realized the responsibilities which are the counterpart of our own riches? This plan is an economic program. It is not a political one. It requires for its execution the continued economic support of the United States. It does not require any direct political support or involve any political entanglement. Our agencies of business must all cooperate in support of the Plan. Our men of commerce, industry, agriculture and finance, including the Federal Reserve system, must aid in the restoration of the credit and currencies of the principal nations. We may debate political participation in the affairs of the world as we will, but we must participate in its business, and business, like science, knows no political boundaries and in its dictionary there is no such word as isolation.[15]

iii

At about the time that Young was finally returning to private life, Hughes was advising his newly elected chief of his decision to do so too. His venture in arm's-length diplomacy—which had still left him room for a timely bit of infighting—was now beginning to pay off, and the New York bar looked vastly more inviting than a second four years at State. Thus on January 5, 1925, his resignation was duly announced, to take effect on March 4; on both dates, the homage of his colleagues was widely echoed in the press. As for Young, in a personal letter to the secretary dated January 26, he pulled out all the stops:

In my opinion, no minister of foreign affairs in any country in the world at any time had a more important or a more difficult problem before him than you. To find a way by which America could do what she ought to do for Europe was indeed a pressing obligation and a most difficult task. In my opinion, history will record your undertaking as the greatest piece of diplomacy, both at home and abroad, of all the many postwar efforts in the field.

Obviously moved, Hughes was not to be outdone. Finding it "impossible to express adequately my appreciation of your letter," he went on to say:

To have such commendation from one who has done more than anyone

else to find a way of escape from the chaotic economic conditions in Europe
is the most satisfactory reward I could have for my own efforts. While
you estimate these far too generously, you have understood fully the difficulties and the sincerity and earnestness of purpose with which we have
sought to overcome them.[16]

Implicit in this purely private exchange was a mutual recognition
of the stake which these correspondents shared in the outcome of the
Dawes Plan. It was this rather than any opinion of Young's which
would determine what history finally recorded—and how the western
world fared in the meantime. But with Hughes now abjuring public
office and Dawes fairly caught in its toils, the principal watching brief
over the Plan's operation fell to Young.

It was a watching brief and more. It meant keeping in close touch
with the press, foreign and domestic, as well as former colleagues
and officials abroad—especially in Germany. Parker Gilbert's reports—
unofficial as well as official—were duly read and pondered, with comments designed always to encourage and never to interfere. Schacht,
as correspondent, was a never-failing source of information, often
illuminating of the actual situation and always of the man. As for
Ambassador Alanson Houghton, Young had come to rely so heavily
on his reports from Berlin that his transfer to the Court of St. James's,
early in 1925, was an occasion for regret as well as congratulation.
Certainly Houghton's comments on developments in Germany had
been both enlightening and endlessly encouraging, as when, after a
candid disclosure of the political hazards which still beset the Plan,
he concluded his letter of January 12, 1925, with these heartening
words:

It may make your New Year happier to know that a year ago there
were well over a million unemployed in Berlin and to-day about fifty thousand. And further, that in the Reich as a whole there were from nine to ten
million unemployed and to-day somewhere between four and five hundred
thousand. And, further, that even these figures are being steadily reduced.
More than anyone else, the credit of this miraculous change is due to you.[17]

A new and welcome source of information was available, however,
in the long letters now coming from Young's old friend Nelson Perkins, whom he himself had persuaded to go to Paris as the first American to sit as a voting member of the Reparations Commission. Identified simply as "The American Citizen," Perkins himself exercised a
full-time watching brief, which included keeping a shrewd eye on all
parties involved in the Plan's operations, beginning with the agent-
general. Of him Perkins wrote on February 3:

Gilbert is very good, just minded, sound minded, clear headed, and when he gets a little more used to the manners and customs of Europe he will be about perfect, although I am afraid he will always be late for every appointment. Schacht told me that at first he had been a little doubtful about Gilbert, but that each time he had seen him he had liked him better, and that now he felt perfectly sure he was going to be a success.

As for his own job, Perkins was more modest: "So far as I can see I am accomplishing nothing, which of course is the job of an insurance policy which has not been called upon. So far as I can see anybody else in the world could do anything that I have done so far just as well as I. . . ." He was not complaining, however, for he was there at Young's behest, and "your directions and opinions of course are always conclusive with me. They are still pretty conclusive, I think, with everybody in Europe, including the farming population of the Baltic states, but I don't think quite as 100% all over Europe, Asia and Kamschatka [*sic*] as they are with me."[18]

In the meantime, at the New York Federal Reserve, Benjamin Strong had already set about the delicate task of stabilizing the other European currencies—beginning, as a matter of course, with the pound sterling. Despite the war, Britain's financial prestige was still a factor to be reckoned with; indeed, it was in no small part the determination to shore it up which had led the Baldwin government, in 1923, to accept a settlement of its debt to the United States on terms that extended payments over sixty-two years, at relatively high interest rates.[19] The pound, when the Dawes report was issued, was already quoted at $4.30 against the dollar, and as it rose by the following November to $4.44, restoration to its prewar parity of $4.86 seemed to Strong and to his counterpart at the Bank of England, Montagu Norman, both feasible and desirable.

For its part, the Coolidge administration was content once again to leave the problem to the experts. While under existing law, the secretary of the treasury was still *ex officio* chairman of the Federal Reserve Board, Mellon was content to follow the leader; indeed, his unfailing support of Strong's exercise in central-bank cooperation was in some respects reminiscent of Hughes's relations with the Dawes Committee. As for Young, he was more than content to leave the stellar roles to others, but his heightened prestige and quick grasp of the essentials of this—to him—still novel field made his supportive role by no means unimportant. This was especially true when it came to interpreting current policy in answer to its critics.

Of this, no better illustration can be cited than the very personal letter Young wrote to his friend Josiah Stamp on March 3, 1925. Many

British industrialists, including Stamp, greatly feared the deflationary effects of any current move to make the pound convertible into gold at the old parity. In a statement to *The Times* early in March, which the *New York Times* promptly quoted, Stamp declared his opposition in no uncertain terms, adding that the Bank of England's evident determination to follow the lead of the Federal Reserve in raising its discount rate—as a declaration of intent—could mean only that "Britain is a vassal to America," with New York now "cracking the whip."

This was too much for Young and he let Stamp know it on the day it appeared. Too long for quotation here—it ran to seven pages—Young's candid recital of the risks which the New York Federal Reserve had deliberately taken in order to facilitate Britain's return to gold is a case study par excellence of the central banker's typical dilemma. It was also, if incidentally, a running commentary on the recent course of American business—which Young found to have been less responsive than the speculative markets to the "cocktail" of Coolidge's election. Balancing the need to curb this speculative surge against the importance of stable currencies and freer international markets, the Fed, he reported, had waited to raise the rate as long as it dared, and even then had advised Norman of the prospect well in advance. Thus statements such as Stamp's could only play into the hands of those—and there were still many—who opposed any and all American aid to Europe.

Fortunately their relationship was of the sort that thrives on controversy and candor, with a seasoning of humor, as Young's postscript strongly suggests. "If your views cut less ice over here," he wrote, "I would not be wasting all this time and paper writing you about your *Times* article. Somehow, our folks are deluded into thinking that you know something about all this and that the rest of us are mostly pikers."

Stamp responded in kind—and took six pages to do it. Counting himself "very fortunate to have succeeded in extracting from you so long and interesting letter as yours of the 3rd instant," he suggested that if, like Young, their banking people had been less secretive and more candid, the British manufacturers' complaints—which he had attempted to voice—might have been less bitter. He then proceeded in the finest possible spirit to rehearse and explain these basic complaints which, in the light of Britain's growing unemployment, former Chancellor Reginald McKenna too had found warranted. It was a curious exchange: Young the industrialist instructing Stamp on international finance, and Stamp the budgetary expert instructing him on the manufacturer's concerns and gripes. But if neither correspondent was converted, both found the exercise illuminating and refreshing and each could now explain to his associates what the other had been up to—and why.[20]

Actually, Winston Churchill's official announcement, as chancellor of the exchequer, of Britain's return to gold was made on March 28, 1925—thus antedating Stamp's reply by three days. Stamp's fears had not been groundless: for example, the very success of the Dawes Plan, and especially the revival of German mining which followed French evacuation of the Ruhr, was having a disastrous impact on Britain's coal industry—an impact of which the miners themselves were expected to bear the brunt.[21] Nevertheless, the gods appeared, on balance, to be siding with the central bankers. Displaying unexpected strength, sterling was apparently quite capable of sustaining its return to parity, especially after Norman found it possible to institute a more sustained tight-money policy. In addition, by the end of 1926, when Britain had weathered both a coal and a general strike, "eighteen other countries had . . . stabilized their currencies in terms of gold and France, the only major country whose currency was not formally stabilized, was making rapid progress in that direction."[22]

In answering these questions as they did, Strong and Norman were certainly supported by the vast preponderance of currently influential opinion. Unlike Strong, Norman did encounter some opposition among his own directors, especially on his timing, but here too the march of events—and especially the action of Australia and South Africa in embracing the gold standard without waiting on London—was forcing Britain's hand. As Churchill reported to Parliament: "If we had not taken this action the whole of the rest of the British Empire would have taken it without us, and it would have come to a gold standard, not on the basis of the pound sterling, but a gold standard of the dollar."[23]

As for Young, who well understood the compelling force of Churchill's remarks, any concern he may have felt for British industry and especially the miners was overbalanced by other considerations as well. One was his vivid recollection of the German workers' plea for a stable currency. Another was his conviction that only a general stabilization could at once promote and sustain the international movement of goods and services on which the European economy—not to mention a market for our own agricultural surplus—was so dependent. As for the gold standard, if it was indeed something of a fetish to certain economists like Edwin W. Kemmerer, Young's view was essentially pragmatic. As he had written Stamp—with an implicit bow to John Maynard Keynes—in explaining the Federal Reserve's determination to restore it:

> Quite apart from the question of whether the gold standard is the best, I am satisfied personally that it is unwise to introduce into a situation where it is desirable to restore normal conditions, the speculative elements of any new experiment. I think we should use, so far as we can, well-known and well-understood machinery in order that we may the more quickly, and with greater certainty, get back to stable exchanges, and thereby take the first step toward freer international markets.[24]

iv

If this stabilization of Europe's currencies was giving evidence of meeting the pragmatic test, so too was the reparation settlement which had made it possible. Clearly the Dawes Plan was doing much more than rescuing Germany from chaos and Europe from the brink. The spectacle of an increasingly prosperous Germany scrupulously meeting its foreign obligations—as it continued to do for the full five years of the provisional settlement's life—was having a salutary influence on Europe's political as well as economic life. From 1925 dates not only the Franco-Belgian evacuation of the Ruhr but also the Pact—and the even more widely heralded spirit—of Locarno.[25] And when, in the following year, Germany was at last admitted to the League of Nations—as a full-fledged member of the Council—the promise of a peace based on conciliation seemed at long last something more than a pious hope.

It all gave point to Young's favorite dictum: "You cannot, whether it be in your own country, or in your own business, or in your own family—you cannot make progress toward high ideals until you get your money matters straightened out."[26] It also gave point to his continuing efforts to educate his fellow citizens on their stake in promoting peace and a shared prosperity.

In aid of these efforts he agreed, during the year following his return, to become chairman of the International Chamber of Commerce's American Section. He declined John D. Rockefeller, Jr.'s urgent invitation to address his Bible class but accepted a place on the General Education Board. Evidently he was not about to default on whatever obligation for further public service might accrue from his recent and conspicuously successful efforts.

When this obligation involved mounting the rostrum, it had its special appeal for the teacher—not to say preacher—which in Young was never very far below the surface. Once, in answering the anguished question of Crocker's successor as to how a concerned American citizen, in a democracy of a hundred million plus, could expect to make his voice heard on any public issue, he had gently suggested that perhaps as a practical matter, the individual must first earn the right to be heard. Having done so himself, he was apt to equate the right with the obligation to speak out—always assuming, as his wife would remind him, that one had something to say.[27]

He had. At the Johns Hopkins University's Washington's Birthday convocation, he used the recently enacted Japanese Exclusion Act and the bitter resentment it had provoked in the Island Empire to illustrate the need for establishing the Page School of International Relations, devoted as it would be to marshaling and assessing *all* of the facts and factors—economic, political and psychological—from which, in any given case, international friction and hostility did, or could, develop. "Facts, Mr. President," he said on this occasion, "are our scarcest raw materials. This is shown by the economy with which we use them." Thus, Congress had lately taken account only of such facts as were visible in California (or Washington), totally ignoring those which in Japanese eyes were vitally important.

This was simply a variation on one of Young's old themes: Can you see through the other fellow's eyes? Judging by the attention it commanded, however—including a cordial letter from the silent President—this particular variation was unusually timely and telling. Indeed, its very homeliness gave point to the decision of the proposed new school's trustees, as also announced by Young, to seek the one million dollars of required endowment not in great chunks from the wealthy but in thousands of small gifts from the American people. That the *New York Times* led the chorus of editorial applause was hardly surprising—and not only because "Dr. John" (Finley) was also a Page School trustee.[28]

The applause, however, was by no means unanimous, as Young noted a fortnight later in addressing a closed dinner of the St. Lawrence University Club. But his critics, it seems, in their patriotic zeal to defend the legislation in question, had played into his hands. They had provided him, he said, with "a complete statement of the facts before Congress on that important issue"—all of which he found to "relate to the interest of America alone. There was not a fact relating to the problems of Japan. . . . I am not saying," he continued, "that the question of Japanese immigration was decided wrong. I am only saying that it was decided with the consciousness on the part of Japan that we had only selfishly taken account of our own problems and given no consideration to hers."[29]

But he had more to say on this occasion. It was, he pointed out, precisely this kind of attitude, on the part of the European democracies and our own, which had led to the postwar morass from which the "purely private citizens" who comprised the Dawes Committee were called upon to extricate the world. How? First of all, by facing *all* the facts, as no political leader dared. And he proceeded to share with his auditors "the most important thing I learned in Europe"—not an answer but a question: *"Can* a democracy face all the facts?" And the further question: How long can a democracy survive unless it contrives the means of doing just that?[30]

These were sobering questions for men and women for whom bolshevism was still a new and frightening threat, and Mussolini's early fascist venture at best a doubtful quantity. True, by June, when Young reminded Yale's commencement audience of the dinosaur's fate, as a kind of parable for isolationists to ponder, he had recovered something of his normal buoyancy. But his most relaxed and therefore most revealing observations—especially on certain potentialities hidden in the Dawes Plan—were made off the record a week later, following a dinner given in his honor at the Harvard Club of Boston by his old Stone and Webster associates.[31]

Back among friends in Boston, with no reporters present, Young spoke without a manuscript and with a kind of confident exuberance. True, he noted that the presence of Roland Boyden, "who knows all about European affairs," and of his "dear friend and former partner, Charles Tyler, who knows all about me," had put something of a crimp in his style. But after citing, "as a great secret," Boyden's role in providing much of the material on which Hughes had based his historic speech at New Haven in December 1922, and reciting all the stories he knew about General Dawes and his determining role, he got down to the business of exploring how far—and how—international debts could in fact be discharged in ways that might benefit debtor and creditor alike. In the process, he broke new ground.

Stripped to its essentials, his argument ran as follows. In limiting Germany's obligation to the deposit—and not the transfer—of marks in stipulated sums, the Dawes Committee had in effect set up for the creditors bank accounts in Germany which gave them options on German production. How, then, were these options to be exercised? Not, in the long run certainly, for consumer goods whose import would raise hob with the creditor country's own producers. So far, the economists were right, and insofar as the creditor concluded that he could not afford to exercise his options, he could hardly sustain—as the Plan made clear—further claims against the debtor.

But surely the creditor's options were not so easily exhausted. They included the right—which few economists had so far recognized—to transfer his bank balances "in goods . . . to be used for plant account." To quote Young's illustration:

One of the things which France needs, perhaps as much as any other, is a great power plant in the Rhone Valley. She cannot finance that plant in the Rhone Valley for the time being. Suppose she were to give an order to the Germans for all the machinery and equipment which are necessary to go in that plant. Now that is paid for with marks which she could not otherwise transfer; therefore, they are valueless unless they are used. Suppose the French Government places an order for the generating machinery and all the equipment for that plant with Germany; suppose she takes income bonds, or any security, of the Rhone Valley power plant in her own country in payment and puts them in the French treasury: at least, she has got some stuff out of Germany, hasn't she? [And] she has an obligation of an organization in her country in place of it. . . .

The electrical manufacturer of France has not lost anything because he could not have gotten the order for that machinery anyhow—the plant would not have been built. On the other hand, his business is greatly increased because he is going to have large orders for transformers, switches, sockets, motors, and everything else, when that power goes into use through the ordinary consumers of France. . . . Meanwhile, the Germans have paid their reparations. The French Government has received payment in the shape of securities on a wealth-producing unit in her country. . . .

Such words "from the horse's mouth" were heard with rapt attention by an audience well acquainted with power plants and their financing. Sensing this, the speaker proceeded to point out that the United States had signally failed to accord its Allied debtors anything remotely equivalent to the transfer protection which they themselves had granted Germany. Not only that, but by raising tariff barriers against the goods they were ready to send us, the United States was denying its debtors the only means they knew of converting pounds and francs into dollars. Yet these debtors too could accumulate domestic balances which gave their creditor options on their production. Why, then, not exercise our option by ordering, say, new power plants which, not needed here, could be installed in such underdeveloped areas as South Africa, South America and China? This would translate political debts into equities in a productive enterprise, whose senior securities organizations like Stone and Webster should then find little difficulty in marketing. But all this, he warned, would not easily come about, and if the United States was ever to learn how to deal wisely "with its new privileges and responsibilities," the educative process would have to stem not from the politicians (who usually found the effort self-defeating) but "from groups exactly like this."

No such educative process ensued. However stimulating this particular group might find Young's imaginative exercise, it did not stimulate action—on their part or on his. The excitement of the moment over, all seem to have sensed that any such proposal vis-à-vis the Allied debts was too far out to command political or even popular support. Nor, for that matter, did the French ever exercise their option in favor of a power plant in the Rhone Valley. Nevertheless, Young's effort had been notable, first in elucidating some of the more constructive but little recognized potentialities of the Dawes Plan and, second, in exploring possible escapes from the damaging bind which the Allied debt settlements were rapidly creating. That he enjoyed the occasion was clear; for one whose every public utterance was now good copy, and so must be carefully measured, it was fun to let oneself go, for once, in an off-the-record talk with friends. Even so, the press managed to come up with a truncated and garbled version of his remarks.[32]

V

Was it these Allied debts and the terms in which they were being settled, rather than reparations, that now, in midsummer 1925, constituted the number-one postwar problem? Not, certainly, in the eyes of the U.S. commission which, in successive negotiations—not yet including the French—had invoked the principle of "capacity to pay" as warrant for ever more lenient interest charges. On an actuarial basis, as correctly computed by the accountants, this was of course equivalent to partial cancellation—the lower the rate, the more was being forgiven.[33]

So far, so good. But Young could also understand that it was by no means the whole story: debtor nations facing a sixty-two-year payment schedule could and did cite a very different set of facts. It was this which had prompted his adventurous suggestions at Boston, but with his friend Herbert Hoover a key member of a war-debts commission, which also included Andrew Mellon and Frank Kellogg, he was reluctant to interfere or even seem to volunteer advice. And for reasons which will presently appear, this reluctance was to be strongly reinforced before the end of the summer.

Nelson Perkins had no such inhibitions. His letter to Young of September 3—with the French negotiations now just around the corner—is quoted both for its candor and because Young seized upon it as something he could properly send along to Hoover. As Perkins, writing from Paris, put it in his best Yankee style:

Dear Owen:

If I am right in my belief that the re-establishment of Europe is one of the most, if not the most, important problems facing the world today, it follows that the problem of Inter-Allied debts is one of the most important problems of the world today.

I am not an economist—I am not a financier, but I am satisfied that any pressure which is put upon the Allies to pay results in an additional pressure by the Allies upon Germany to pay them, and tends to reduce the reasonableness of the attitude of the Allies toward the Germans.

Whether Germany is going to be able to meet the Dawes annuities the future alone will show. That there is a very general disposition in Germany to squeal is already apparent; that the attitude of the Allies towards Germany has grown more reasonable since I have been here is, I think, true; that a position by the United States that is regarded as reasonable will increase the Allies' reasonableness toward the Germans I think is true; and that an attitude on the part of the United States that they regard as unreasonable will decrease their reasonableness towards the Germans I think is also true. Every bit of pressure that the United States put upon the Allies is likely to result in at least a corresponding pressure upon the Germans, and the pressure is likely to be put on in a way which will be a threat to the establishment of good relations between the Allies and Germany.

If there is anything that you can do to bring about, or to help to bring about, a liberal attitude on the part of our Government toward the French, I think it is worth doing.

Personally I do not think there is the slightest chance that one nation will make substantial payments to another nation for 62 years, and I think we are just fooling ourselves, perhaps necessarily, but nevertheless completely, in adopting any 62 year basis.[34]

Hoover's reply of September 18—duly forwarded to Perkins—suggested that this exchange had not been notably fruitful. "My dear Young," he wrote from Washington:

It seems to me that . . . [Perkins's] idea drives us into one of two holes—either we have to cancel or reduce the debt in the pious hope that it will relieve pressure from the Germans, or alternatively we must require that any concessions we make to the Allies be passed on in reduction of the Dawes plan payment.

If we adhere strictly to the basis of the ability of all these different people to pay, it seems to me we avoid these issues as well as they can be avoided.

The hole that this leads into is to make a quantitative determination of ability which may be a process of trial and error.[35]

Young, it seems, was not surprised—not even by Hoover's blindness to the nature of the hole he was digging for himself. As for Young's own views—including his reluctance to volunteer advice—two of his subsequent letters are especially illuminating. In the first, dated October 30, 1925, and responding to another fervent plea—this time from his old colleague A. G. Davis—that he do everything in his power to bring about a generous settlement with the French, he disclosed the fact that J.M.A. Caillaux, as minister of finance, had urged him some weeks earlier to come over and work out a program for the rehabilitation of France's currency and fiscal mechanisms. He also quoted his reply, which stated that he could not accept "unless our Secretary of State, with the approval of the President, requests me to act as he did in the case of the Dawes Committee." That had been in August. No such request having been forthcoming, Young could only conclude that any suggestions he might now offer would be gratuitous. He added that the War Debts Commission's one trouble, composed as it was of high-minded and conscientious men, was that "it is not exercising its own judgment as to what should be done in the French settlement. It is exercising its judgment as to what the Senate will approve. . . ."[36]

If the second letter, addressed to Secretary Hoover on January 5, 1926, "en route to Cincinnati," was forthright enough, it was because Hoover himself had opened the door. In meeting Young a day or two before, at a dinner in New York, Hoover had sought to enlist his support in countering the highly disturbing efforts of certain foreign governments (in this case Britain and Brazil) to control the sale—*and fix the price!*—of commodities like rubber and coffee. Conceding that the secretary had reason to be disturbed, Young earnestly sought to enlarge his view of the revelant facts. "That this," he wrote,

. . . is a new and threatening development, I agree. If it continues it will lead the whole world to disaster. On the other hand, I am sincerely troubled by our national program, which is demanding amounts from our debtors up to the breaking point, and at the same time excluding their goods from our American markets, except those few raw materials which we must have. They can pay in nothing but goods or services, and I confess to a certain sympathy with their efforts to get as much out of us for those goods as possible.

The establishment and maintenance of sound currencies abroad, the export of our gold for that purpose, the creation of export markets for our agricultural and other produce is so much more important, in my mind, than the collection of these war debts that I wish there were some way we could clean them all up by a great international settlement, and the flotation wide-ly . . . of a great international loan. When we transfer *whatever is to be paid on these debts* [italics added] from government treasuries to private inves-tors, we shall begin to see economic safety and tranquility in the world. . . . We shall need very fundamental treatment, in my judgment, of the disease which is manifesting itself in the symptoms of which you rightly complain.

Here for the first time, perhaps, one detects a hint of impatience with Hoover the politician that suggests the beginning of a rift in their relations. It was also a singularly comprehensive statement of Young's views. True, he stopped short of urging outright cancellation, but if he embraced instead the current panacea of "commercializa-tion," that meant, by definition, a sum which the market could absorb, and the phrase "whatever is to be paid on these debts" clearly con-veyed his hope for their drastic write-down. In the event, the week-end visit suggested in Hoover's reply became a mere breakfast ses-sion with the Youngs on January 20. What was said went unrecorded but policy remained unchanged.[37]

As for Hoover's (and the government's) insistence—reasonable enough on its face—that "capacity to pay" should be the major criteri-on in settling all these debts, Young had good reason for impatience with the refusal of Hoover (of all people) to face up to its wider implications. As applied to Germany, it had indeed been a factor in moderating the Allies' unreasonable demands. As now applied to the Allied debtors who were also Germany's immediate creditors, its effect was very different; for, as Hughes had observed back in 1922, any quantitative determination of a debtor's capacity to pay must necessarily take account of his receivables—including, in Britain's case, the Allied debts still due the country, and for all the Allied powers, German reparations. Under the Balfour formula, the relief which Britain could now afford its own debtors was as slight as the relief the United States had granted Britain; and France, as a debtor to both, obviously needed the maximum possible from reparations. France would need this maximum, moreover—and so would the other Allies—for the full sixty-two years over which, like a long-term mort-gage which minimizes *annual* charges, debt payments had been spread. Here was an ominous fact hanging over the future, and spe-cifically over the moment when the powers might determine to sup-plant the provisional Dawes Plan with a definitive reparation settle-ment. In the meantime, and despite the legalistic protests emanating from Washington, it emphasized afresh the ineluctable link between the Allied debts and reparations.

Chapter 19

Private Enterprise or Public:
Waterpower and Broadcasting

T wo special problems, both associated with the public interest and both affected by political influences and governmental regulation, demanded a good portion of Young's time during the 1920s. The first was the development of waterpower in New York State, the second was radio broadcasting, the unexpected, speedily growing and unmanageable child of the radio-communications business.

The first, unlike the second, had been a familiar phenomenon to Owen Young since childhood. Walking down to school from the farm on the hill, he crossed the arched stone bridge over the swift-running Otsquago, and could see and hear its falls. The Otsquago is not large as rivers go, but as it goes it generates considerable energy. Dropping four hundred feet from its source to the village, its power was made use of by a variety of water mills from the days when the first Van Hornes settled on its banks.[1] The old schoolhouse itself looked out on the milldam above the gristmill, and in spring the sound of the water that turned the big wheel could be heard in the classroom. The boy had a sense of the power of swift water from the first.

Niagara had been harnessed for the production of electric power while he was in college, and, while he was working for Stone and Webster, Young had seen waterpower brought into use all over the country. He himself had been involved in the setting up of the big generating plant on the St. Croix to provide current for Minneapolis fifty miles away; in the utilization of the rivers of the Northwest for Seattle and Tacoma and of the Spokane River for eastern Washington. The development of the big hydraulic turbine and of long-distance transmission of alternating current made feasible the generation of power many miles from industrial centers. The General Electric Company manufactured the equipment for hydroelectric stations, and as the years passed Young continued to be concerned with putting white water to work.

In this field, his main interest was the development of the waters of his native state and above all of the St. Lawrence River. Its international rapids were capable of generating immense power, a matter of importance and potential profit to GE; but to Young it was more than that. In November of 1921—a depression year—he pointed out to the Federal Water Power Commission one unhappy contrast between the United States and the foreign countries he had recently visited. In Germany he had found the electrical factories busy to capacity with hydraulic machinery for Scandinavia and Italy; in the same year he had seen the enormous development of waterpower in Japan; "but the true fact is," he told them, "that American factories are empty and men are idle and power is going to waste." And four years later, speaking to the Empire State Gas and Electric Association, he said:

The wage curves of the world and the power production curves of the world . . . go pretty much hand in hand. Low wages are where there is very little power production and the highest wages are where there is a maximum power production . . . to the extent to which you make the individual man a director of power . . . so can you make him more of a producer, more of a contributor to the wealth of the world.[2]

In 1919, at Young's suggestion, the General Electric Company had organized a company to acquire a dam site on the St. Lawrence River. This company was succeeded in 1921 by the Frontier Corporation, owned jointly by GE, Du Pont, and the Aluminum Company of America, which owned riparian rights along the river. Colonel Hugh L. Cooper, probably the most experienced hydraulic engineer in the world, designer and builder of waterpower developments in many countries, was hired to make plans for what might be the largest project he had ever undertaken.

A boundary river, however, is subject to international as well as national, state and provincial politics. There were difficulties on all four sides; Canada and Ontario were slow to respond to American overtures for participation, and it was not until January 1924, when Young was starting on the demanding job of the Dawes Committee in Paris, that he received a message that Prime Minister Mackenzie King would discuss the project with the Americans and that he favored the immediate development of power.[3] In Washington, the Federal Water Power Commission, authorized by the waterpower bill signed by

President Wilson in July 1920, was slow to promulgate its rules; when it did, it was clear that much of its regulatory power was handed back to the states, although permits for projects had to be approved first in Washington. And all plans, wherever made, were subject to approval also by the International Joint Commission, which had been set up by the United States and Canada in 1909.

Meanwhile the major block was in Albany. Even more than electric railways, even more than radio communications and broadcasting, waterpower was considered to belong to the people, and the question of its utilization aroused anew, in the capitol and in the press, the perennial controversy over public versus private development of utilities. Inevitably both political and financial greed, as well as pure inertia, were involved; but the skirmishes were mainly between men of probity who held strong and honest convictions as to the best way to provide more and cheaper power to the people of the state of New York. In the forefront of these were Alfred E. Smith and Owen D. Young.

There was probably no one in the state more experienced in this particular field than Young. He had hammered out over the years of dealing with public utilities a definite and consistent position in a war which "has been continuous and at times severe."[4] Experience had convinced him that the consumers, given fair and effective regulation, got the best results in costs and especially service from private capital and private management. To this basic tenet he was ready to allow exceptions and to work out compromises, particularly in regard to public *ownership* of sources of energy such as waterpower. But he considered that private operation was essential to serve the public properly and to free it from political and bureaucratic hang-ups.

The lines were drawn early in the game. When Smith was elected governor for the second time, he stated in his message to the legislature of March 1923 that the state should develop its waterpower resources and transmit the power over its own lines, enacting legislation to that end so that "this priceless heritage bestowed upon us by the Creator himself" should remain in the hands of the people of the state.[5]

To Young it did not seem quite that simple. He had met with the governor on the February 20 preceding, having sent by letter a few days before a statement of his own position:

The only political question involved in the solution of the water power problem for the State of New York is the extent to which the State or the municipalities shall engage in that business. This is an important question, but it should not be permitted to cloud our thought regarding the power problem itself. The problem is how to develop power from our natural resources at the lowest cost and how to transmit it so that the largest number of our citizens can obtain the maximum service from that power with the least expense. The problem should be so solved as to be of benefit to the small householders in the cities, to the farmers in the country, to the railroads and other transportation companies throughout the State, and to all industrial users of power, whether large or small . . . the people of the State of New York cannot afford longer to let these great resources go to waste. They had better adopt one plan or the other. Personally I believe that a combination of the two can be worked out so as to provide cheaper power than either of the systems can alone. I shall take the liberty of suggesting such a plan at our conference on Tuesday.[6]

There were no notable results from this meeting; Smith was still burdened by the original—and wholly Republican—Water Power Commission, which he had inherited. He recommended in his message to the legislature in 1924 the establishment of a New York State waterpower authority, but in that year and again in 1926 the governor's proposal was defeated by the Republicans in the legislature. These proposals Young had supported in part, for they set up a public corporation funded by tax-exempt bonds, which he always considered necessary to provide "a referendum as to the economic usefulness and soundness of the enterprise."[7] He had reiterated in a meeting with Smith before the 1926 message, on February 8, the importance of a combination of "the elasticity and efficiency of private operation with the lowest possible cost of capital" in order to get "for this state the maximum development of her water powers and the most economic distribution of energy." This he favored, he said, both personally and as chairman of GE: "That Company has a greater interest in low cost power to the consumer than any other single concern in the State . . . only as power becomes cheaper will the consumer increase his devices for its use. Therefore, in such increase lies the future business of the General Electric Company."[8]

After the meeting Smith reported to the newsmen at the door, "We found we were not very far apart. Mr. Young left me with the distinct impression that he was anxious to be helpful in relation to the water power program as I have laid it down."[9]

Young said nothing, but wrote the governor another letter. Smith, however, was carrying the ball, and released on March 1 a statement quoting two paragraphs from this letter and naming the author:

2nd. The cost of energy developed from falling water is determined very largely by the cost of the capital employed in the development. A public corporation such as you propose whose securities would be exempt from taxation under the Federal Law and under the State Law should produce, if properly set up, the required money substantially cheaper than a private corporation could obtain it. . . .

4th. I see no objection, but on the contrary, I can see some advantages to the development of the great water powers on the St. Lawrence and in the gorge of Niagara by public corporation rather than by a private corporation, and to the ownership of all lands, water rights, flowage, power houses and structures by such a public corporation.[10]

And the governor added, referring to Congressman Ogden Mills's description of himself as Socialist, "If there exists in this State a Socialist Party on the question of Water Power, it contains . . . Charles E. Hughes . . . Nathan L. Miller . . . [and] knocking on the party door for admission . . . is Mr. Owen D. Young whose declaration in favor of State ownership and State control I have quoted."[11]

Since this quotation of paragraphs out of context was very misleading, Young immediately released the entire letter; both Smith's statement and the letter were published widely. But, as usual, the first impression remained, and there were numerous headlines such as that on the first page of the New York *World:* SMITH POWER PLAN INDORSED BY YOUNG, with the whole letter reproduced below which indicated their serious differences. There were others, however, like that in the *New York Commercial*, which headed its editorial on the subject DID NOT TELL ALL.[12]

Young wrote at once to Secretary Hoover, restating his position, for "I am exceedingly anxious that you should not misunderstand me." He explained that his firm belief in private ownership and management was the same as it had always been, but that in the case of boundary or multiple-purpose rivers like the St. Lawrence or the Colorado there was a place for public money and residual ownership. He also wrote Merlin H. Aylesworth of the National Electric Light Association, to make sure that people in the electrical industry knew that he had not sought the meeting with Smith, that he had given only his personal opinions, and was not *volunteering* advice either to the governor or to the industry.[13]

Letters, however, came into his office from all over the country; public-utilities officials protested, though others praised. As late as July Young was writing Henry Robinson in Los Angeles about a report he had heard that indicated West Coast utility people were offended and disaffected by his attitude. Henry replied that "in this state people in the hydro-electric industry are extremely sensitive on the subject of governmental and municipal control." He realized, he said, that "the so-called 'vested interests' . . . feel that no member of their group should ever make any statement that is not a special plea on behalf of their interests." And he thought it was time that the vested interests "should recognize that an attitude such as yours instead of being injurious is one method and maybe the best one of protecting their real interests."[14]

Just before sailing for Europe on March 11, 1926, Young had had a quick exchange of letters with Charles J. Bullock of Harvard, an expert on public finance whom Young had come to know through the Business Cycles Committee. Describing himself as "a poor damn professor," Bullock took issue with Young over his view (as reported by the *Boston Herald*) that a public corporation could produce electric power cheaper than a private one, and threatened to use this in his book on public finance as a "horrible example." Young was delighted with this, and the letters flew back and forth, with Young making constant reference to existing conditions and pragmatic solutions: "My job in the world, if I have any, and I sometimes doubt whether I have, is to try always to accommodate practical action to principle. That always has to be done. I do not want to ride principles so uncompromisingly that nothing can be accomplished, and I hope never to stand for a practical program which violates in substance any real principle, economic or moral."[15]

Then he was off to St. Lawrence commencement, to which he took his mother, back to Van Hornesville with her, then boarding the Italian liner *Duilio* with Jo and the Harbords, bound for the Mediterranean. Stuart Crocker was left to deal with the pile of letters that were still coming in, as well as stacks of press clippings on the subject of waterpower; he sent reports to Europe on these, complaining with typical Crocker devotion to his boss that some were unfair and should be answered. Young replied: "I am undisturbed by editorial comment and I would make no special effort to restrict it."[16]

The message Governor Smith sent to the legislature on March 14, 1926—a substantial part of which Crocker forwarded by radio to the *Duilio*—indicated that Young's ideas had had some real effect. Speaking "in words of one syllable in order that misunderstanding may cease," Smith made it clear that his proposed power authority would *not* distribute power; he quoted Young again about the cost of energy being determined largely by the cost of capital. This the New York *World* applauded in an editorial which noted the quote from Young. The *Herald Tribune*, however, after remarking that "the Governor's retreat from radicalism has set in," said: "Neither the Governor nor Mr. Owen Young has made the slightest effort to indicate where the economy for the public lies in exempting a corporation from taxes."[17]

ii

Soon the press had a new angle on these two favorites. The governor had stated earlier in the spring that he would not run for a fourth term. This announcement was taken seriously enough by the Democratic party in New York State to cause them to cast about for a substitute. On May 1 the front page of the *New York Herald Tribune* contained the headline SMITH'S FRIENDS BOOM YOUNG FOR GOVERNOR. The article appeared in several upstate papers also, in the *Glen Falls Post Star* under the line SAY AL SMITH WOULD SMILE ON O. D. YOUNG. Smith's part in this was attributed by political observers to his own projected move toward the Democratic convention of 1928: "If Mr. Young is elected and then throws his political strength and widespread connections through the South and Southwest to Smith for the nomination for President the Governor will have achieved a master political stroke." Smith, said the article in the *Herald Tribune* for May 1, would like best a ticket of Owen D. Young for governor and Franklin D. Roosevelt for senator.[18]

Crocker fired off a summary of the articles by radio to Young, now returning from abroad on the *Olympic*, and the reporters were on hand when she docked on May 5. Young made short work of the "boom." "Without taking the suggestion seriously," he told them, "I will say that to hold public office effectively requires political knowledge and political experience. I have neither. I have never undertaken a job for which my experience did not in some degree qualify me, and I hope I never may."[19]

This may have countered the allegations of those who saw political ambitions in the positions he had taken, but it disappointed some of his friends. Dr. John Finley of the *Times*, a great admirer of Young, wrote a lengthy editorial the following Sunday entitled "Political Ability." He took issue with the unwilling candidate on his statement that political experience was needed, and cited a distinguished example—Charles Evans Hughes, who had been an excellent governor although it was his first political job. Young replied in a brief note to "Dr. John," whose warm friendship he valued highly: "It seldom happens that in the same editorial one may be severely criticized for bad judgment and at the same time be paid a very high compliment. For the complimentary part of your Times editorial on Sunday, I thank you."[20]

There was one more attempt in 1926 to enlist Young in politics, this time by Eleanor Roosevelt. She was then vice-chairman of the Women's Division of the Democratic State Committee, and as the *Times* pointed out, "better qualified to discuss the position of the Democratic women than any other person," for her job took her into every county of the state.[21] The women, she said, were strongly for another term for Smith; they were behind him because of his attitude on welfare and waterpower. As for the senatorship, "I think Owen Young would be a wonderful candidate. He is in many ways ideal."[22]

Young wrote her, thanking her for the compliment, and repeating that he was not a candidate for political office.[23] In the event, Governor Smith decided to run again and was overwhelmingly elected, with Robert L. Wagner, for whom Young had outlined several campaign speeches, as senator.

Meanwhile, in addressing on May 18 the annual convention of the National Electric Light Association, Young had made a strong case for cooperation "in the public interest from the representatives of both the utilities and the public," especially in regard to "special water powers" which involved navigation or irrigation or flood control as well as the generation of power. And he returned again to his central theme of the human importance of the development of power:

> We must aim to make human beings directors instead of generators of power. We must aim to make the earning power of human beings so large as to supply them not only with a living wage but a cultural wage. . . .
>
> This industry in this country has stood for maximum development of all power resources which could be economically and wisely made. It is reflected in our wages and living conditions so superior to any other in the world. I beg of you not to hold back or by opposition, direct or indirect, prevent such development as still remains on the vast rivers to which I have referred. Make it your business not to oppose, but to find some constructive way, guided as you will be and as you must be, by the great human interests which you fundamentally serve.
>
> Public service is the goal . . . a public service which not only meets its own economic requirements, but supplies our social needs—that is the target of the industry.[24]

When Young spoke on a subject in which he was deeply interested, one close to his heart—and he rarely made speeches otherwise—he put into it all the knowledge and experience of speechmaking which he had begun to acquire as a boy in church pulpits and had continued under the tutelage of Charley Gaines in college. His powerful and well-managed voice compelled attention, as did his commanding figure; intonations, pauses, gestures—well learned but wholly natural in effect—made his points telling and memorable. It was rare that he did not win his audience.

On this occasion he did not. Indeed, many members of the "vested interests" were antagonized, as Young expected; but after all the chairman of G E shouldn't always cater to his customers—there were times when they needed to be "shook up." It was this speech, as well as the letter to Smith, that he had asked Henry Robinson about, and received the reply already quoted. In a second and more private letter, however, written the same day, Robinson, who was not ignorant of the New York State political situation, warned: "Were you in a position of great authority, and were you to act as I know you would . . . in the interests of the whole people, I am fearful that your present close friends, many of them, might become sharp and critical enemies."[25] The plain fact was, as Young knew well, that in the mossier corners of the public-utility industry he was regarded as a dangerous radical.

Meanwhile in New York State the stalemate in regard to water-power continued. In June of '26 the state engineer, Roy G. Finch, who, like Young, was anxious for action, published a long report recommending consideration of the license applications of two private corporations—Frontier and American Super Power—for the "practical development" of the St. Lawrence. Young, at the request of the press, issued a statement, pointing out the choice between the two methods proposed over the years for the development of power, and ending, "I have said frequently that getting the job done is of much greater importance to the people of the State than the choice of method. . . ."[26]

Toward the end of 1926—after Smith's landslide reelection—the Water Power Commission, which was about to go out of existence in January 1927 under the new organization of state government, planned to grant the recommended licenses for the St. Lawrence. Smith threatened legal action and hired the well-known lawyer Samuel Untermyer to support the threat. Frontier and Super Power then withdrew their applications, and Untermyer and Young made widely differing statements to the press. The projected leases were described by the famous lawyer as containing more "jokers" than almost any document he had ever seen.[27] Young described them as sound and acceptable, providing full protection for the state, even more than was provided for under the Federal Water Power Act. He pointed out that the General Electric Company's interest in additional power was "to stimulate and increase the use of electricity in the State of New York, and therefore the business of the General Electric Company. . . . The risks and engineering problems involved in building a dam in that great river and transmitting its energy hundreds of miles to a profitable market, are beyond anything yet undertaken." And that, for the time being, was that.[28]

The last—and public—confrontation on waterpower in 1926 took place in December. The Survey Associates, a research and publishing organization, put on a dinner meeting in New York on December 13, with the awkwardly stated subject "Water Power and the Social Stake in It." Governor Smith agreed to speak on his "Policy for Water Power Development under State Ownership and State Control." Young refused the invitation to speak, on the ground that waterpower was still "a football of politics." He did, however, reserve a table for the dinner at the Waldorf-Astoria, and invited GE officers as well as Colonel Cooper and George Bishop of Frontier. The last, in accepting, wrote, "I am sure it will be an interesting evening. I hope the copiousness of my tears will not indicate to the Governor that his threats have caused a leak in the alleged water power trust."[29]

Young did prepare a speech; he was apparently afraid that he might be called on for an impromptu statement, and he did not want it to be too impromptu. The governor's speech was lively, amusing, general, and contained nothing new about his position. After this long rambling discourse Young was either not called upon or refused to comment.[30]

The following day, however, in answer to requests from editors, Young released part of his cautionary remarks:

1. The state should *not* contribute any money to the enterprise, for this would destroy the economic check.

2. If bonds are to be sold, the returns from the sale of power must be sufficient and the term long enough to insure their safety, or they would not sell.

3. It is not likely that power developed from the St. Lawrence would be cheaper than power from coal; but this water power will put New York in control of her own basic power supply, and no longer dependent upon millions of tons of imported coal.[31]

Smith had begun his speech by saying "I take this [water power development] to be not a political matter at all. I take it to be a business matter." Young's final comment was: "The development of the River is the thing. As a matter of business let us get it done."[32]

During the last two years of Smith's governorship, however, no progress was made, although the new commission set up to replace the Water Power Commission consisted of three members, two to be appointed by the governor. But in 1927 and 1928 Al Smith had other things on his mind, with little time for waterpower. Senator George Norris, strong advocate of wholly public development and distribution, was supporting him for the presidency, and no further discussions on Young's public-private plan for the St. Lawrence were held. Young had said earlier, "The debate has been carried on with energy, but our water power has run to waste."[33] Still unchecked, the river flowed on.

iii

As Franklin D. Roosevelt came into power in New York State, Young tried again. A week before the election of 1928 Young had written him, in order, he said, to have "the record clear as between you and me":

November 1, 1928

My dear Frank:

I am under some embarrassment as a result of your campaign. It arises because of your charges as to the water power situation in New York. I happened to be in the country on Saturday night and heard your speech in Albany in which, if not in precise terms certainly by the strongest reference, you charged [Albert] Ottinger [FDR's opponent and former New York State attorney general] with complicity in an attempted steal of the water power resources of the State. Now I happened to be sitting figuratively on the other side of the table in that affair representing the General Electric Company, the Aluminum Company, and the duPont Company, and if Ottinger was trying to steal the water power rights of the State, then I was trying to steal them too.

He went on to say that of course he would make no public statement about this, "because I sincerely hope for your election." He recapitulated his discussions with Governor Smith which had resulted in Smith's proposal of the state waterpower authority, and with Ottinger on the form which the lease to Frontier should take, in which every concession was made to the state.

As a matter of fact, I do not believe that any private people could have financed the lease as it was prepared, except such great concerns as the General Electric Company, the Aluminum Company and the duPont Company. . . . When there has been yielded to the State under the private lease everything that can be given consistent with obtaining the private capital to do the job, then the State has the best possible terms on that theory of development. When, on the other hand, the State without pledging its own credit and its own funds has obtained the capital with tax exemption at the lowest terms and still owns the equity, then that is the best and soundest set-up under public ownership. The issues between the two can now be clearly set forth and defined. There is no room for such charges as stealing on the one side nor of socialism on the other. It is a plain business proposition for the people to choose between two sound alternatives.

He ended the six-page letter thus:

I do not expect you to read this letter now, nor am I writing you with any thought that it can influence your position in this campaign. I am writing first in explanation of the facts and second because I can not permit myself to be called a thief by one of my best friends, even taking into account all questions of political expediency, without trying at least to make my own position clear.

Roosevelt dictated an answer immediately after he read the letter, which was—understandably—not immediately. But the reply is dated November 4, at his house on East Sixty-fifth Street, and Roosevelt explained that he was asking Louis Howe to sign it as he had to go off to Hyde Park at once.

The five closely typed pages are marked "Personal and Confidential," and begin:

My dear Owen:

I am much troubled by your letter and wish that you had written me earlier so that I could have made clear in some way publicly my very firm conviction that you would not permit yourself to become a party to any contract which you believe would be unfavorable to the best interests of the public. . . .

I will try to be as frank as you are. . . .

He went on to explain that he had not had time to go into any details on the waterpower leases "after my unexpected nomination." In fact, he said, he had been so interested in national issues for a number of years, that—not expecting to be involved in New York State—he had neglected state issues.

I frankly did not know . . . that you had personally taken part in the negotiations and personally considered the proposed agreement as one which was entirely fair and equitable to the public as well as to the companies. Had I known all this, I would certainly have dropped all other matters and gone into the details myself, for so great is my belief in your personal integrity and high minded devotion to the public interests as to make me unwilling to accept even such apparently overwhelming evidence in the fact [*sic*] of the knowledge that the proposed transaction met your approval.

He continued with a general statement of his own views on water-power, which agreed in many points with Young's. But he betrayed his suspicion—or perhaps his politically acceptable belief—that public-utility companies could often get around the law to increase rates, and that the state should not permit long leases, or any leases, without watertight provisions of recapture. But he agreed that "priceless time is being wasted," and asked for Young's advice as to how to expedite development.[34]

After the election Young wrote the new governor thanking him for his letter and offering his aid and support in all ways. He also sent him twenty-eight pages of material on waterpower in New York State to make up the gaps in his education. This included copies of his letters to Smith and Hoover, a twelve-page statement describing the situation in the state, and plans for the future.[35]

It was not Young's habit thus to "dump the whole load," and whether or not the new governor struggled through these pages, there is no doubt that he was already turning to less pragmatic and more doctrinaire sources of information. There is also no doubt that Young himself was getting pretty well fed up with an issue which not only remained a football of politics but threatened to make him one. With the turn of the year he was again called to Paris for a "final" grapple with the reparations problem, which kept him abroad until June of 1929. Shortly after his return, however, he wrote his old friend Julius Henry Cohen, now counsel of the Port of New York Authority, that GE "had sold all its interests in utility operating companies," so that "if I am free on the one side from any suspicion of selfish interest, either personal or corporate, I am also on the other without influence."[36] And in September of that year General Electric sold its share of Frontier to Niagara-Hudson Power.

It is not easy to assess the effect on Young of this prolonged experience in frustration. Would it discourage, once and for all, any lurking temptation to enter the political arena—especially as he now watched Roosevelt, like Smith before him, vainly battling a recalcitrant legislature on this same issue? Would it put him on guard, once and for all, against the hazards awaiting the conciliator, whose efforts to reason with contending forces may, and often do, simply expose him to their withering cross fire?

Time alone would tell, and certainly Young would have to wait long for any returns on the time and patience he had invested in this protracted effort to accommodate action to principle.

iv

If the development of waterpower moved too slowly in the 1920s, that of radio broadcasting moved too fast. It was an overnight growth that amazed the country and flabbergasted the people in the radio business. In no time, after the amateur efforts of the early years of the decade had shown the possibilities, the air was full of music, politics, sports, vaudeville turns, church services and educational talks. In Van Hornesville, Young asked an old farmer if he had a radio set. "No, Owen," he replied, "on a clear night all I have to do is go down to the far corner of the fence beyond the barn and I can hear the music right out of the air. I don't need no set."

The story of the mushrooming industry has been told often and in great detail;[37] here we include only those phases which Young had to think about and deal with. He had had plenty of experience with the rapid development of new fields propelled by science and technology, but radio seemed to be raising far more new and wide-ranging questions. In 1922 he had scribbled a memo to himself: "Broadcasting—Who can establish?—Who can sell?—What is broadcasting station?"[38]

The following years were to bring him some of the answers, and they were not easy to deal with. Fortunately the leadership at RCA was strong; with both James Harbord and David Sarnoff, Young's relationship was frank and open. They worked together well, in spite of their different backgrounds and administrative styles—and this was fortunate, for their problems were legion.

By 1925 the difficulties with patents and manufacturing were almost overpowering. The cutthroat competition which developed in the field as soon as it was clear that radio business meant money brought widespread pirating of the Radio group's patents and constant litigation. Sarnoff and representatives of the independent radio manufacturers worked out a licensing policy which, in their view, opened the door for sublicensing to patent infringers and "promoted orderly growth," but it was not a problem which yielded easily or quickly to solution.[39]

The second difficulty and in some respects the more serious was the persistent shortage of radio apparatus. Catching up was a nightmare for the manufacturing companies, GE and Westinghouse, for new and better sets were being designed daily and six-month-old ones were obsolete. It was impossible to foretell the size of demand, and RCA seemed to be constantly in the situation of having the shelves of the store either too full or totally empty. Young wrote Hoover, who as secretary of commerce was supposed to supply whatever regulation was needed in the field, that "every effort is being made . . . to meet this demand which has come on us very much overnight and when you stop to remember that no apparatus was developed to meet these broadcasting needs and none had been tested or manufactured in any considerable quantity, I think that the progress being made is quite as much as fairly could be expected."[40]

Young, however, was far more impatient with the situation than he had indicated to Hoover. He wrote sharp letters, not only to Harbord and Sarnoff, but to GE and Westinghouse; he had suffered, he said to Francis Pratt of GE, "shock and disappointment at the diminished earnings of RCA in 1925"; if the situation could not be improved in 1926, "I shall be broken-hearted"—strong language for him. This he did not have to suffer, however, for in 1926 RCA's net profits were up a million and a half from 1925. In a letter of January 1926 to Isaac Marcosson of the *Saturday Evening Post,* Young described himself, in relation to RCA, as a "kind of fifth wheel to the coach"; he seemed at times to be the driving wheel.[41]

It was in 1926 also that the complicated and long-negotiated agreements with AT&T were finally signed and the protracted controversy came to an end. The Radio group conceded to AT&T the right to manufacture and market radio sets and parts, under a royalty agreement; this right, for which AT&T had fought for so long, was, in the event, never exercised. AT&T would go out of the broadcasting business and sell WEAF, its broadcasting station in Manhattan, to RCA, and would lease its wires for broadcasting by others, a potential source of large revenue. All in all, it was a rather lame conclusion to so fierce a war, but at least it was now possible for the Radio group to move ahead with its plans for national broadcasting in an orderly way.[42]

As early as 1922 Young and Sarnoff had been talking about a separate company for broadcasting. Sarnoff had been thinking about it for some time, for it was clear to him that a specialized organization was needed to handle the rapidly growing infant; and it was clear to Young that taking broadcasting out of the hands of its quarreling parents would make for peace in the family. After July of 1926, when the agreements with AT&T were signed, the new company took shape; the patent-licensing agreement with the independents provided further support. The situation in the industry was by no means settled— will it ever be in broadcasting?—but the field had been cleared of the greatest immediate dangers.

The National Broadcasting Company was born on September 9,

1926, preceded by a full-page announcement of the impending event in newspapers nationwide. In August Young had drafted this announcement and sent it to General Harbord with a note; he had dictated the draft of the announcement "very hurriedly," he said.

I have not had the benefit of anybody's suggestion regarding it, and so it may be quite unwise. On the other hand, it is not so composite as to lose its character, which is one of the great dangers of all communications which are the product of several hands. I have tried to make it clear why the Radio Corporation engages in the business . . . I have also tried to anticipate both the charge of monopoly of the air and unfair competition toward competitors.[43]

The people at RCA liked the draft so well that they used it verbatim, with only minor changes, such as changing "American" Broadcasting Company to "National" Broadcasting Company. There was also added the notice of the appointment of the president of the new company, M. H. Aylesworth, former chairman of the Colorado Public Utilities Commission, later executive vice-president of Utah Power, and most lately executive director of the National Electric Light Association.[44] "One of his major responsibilities will be to see that the operations of the National Broadcasting Company reflect enlightened public opinion, which expresses itself so promptly the morning after any error of taste or judgment or departure from fair play."[45]

The announcement stated that RCA was "the largest distributor of radio receiving sets in the world" and hence was more interested than anyone else in "the best possible broadcasting"; five million homes already had sets, "21,000,000 remain to be supplied. . . . Any use of radio transmission which causes the public to feel that the quality of the programs is not the highest, that the use of radio is not the broadest and best use in the public interest, that it is used for political advantage or selfish power, will be detrimental to the public interest in radio, and therefore to the Radio Corporation of America." It was to ensure such development that the National Broadcasting Company had been organized, WEAF bought for a million dollars, and programs made available to "other broadcasting stations throughout the country . . . so that every event of national importance may be broadcast throughout the United States."[46]

These statements were visionary in 1926; the man who made them was sticking his neck out, and he admitted that although the need for adequate broadcasting was apparent, "the problem of finding the best means of doing it is yet experimental." And he stated explicitly that RCA was not seeking a monopoly of the air, which would be "a liability rather than an asset."⁴⁷ Monopoly indeed would have been hard to achieve, with the number of independent stations broadcasting, and a new network, Columbia, soon to make its appearance.

This public statement also announced the formation of an advisory council "to be chosen as representative of various shades of public opinion, which will from time to time give [NBC] the benefit of their judgment and suggestion"; so that the public "may be assured that the broadcasting is being done in the fairest and best way, always allowing for human frailties and human performance." And at the end of the announcement was an invitation to the public "to make known its views to the officials of the company from time to time"; signed, Owen D. Young and James G. Harbord.⁴⁸

The announcement, which could be dismissed as golden promises in the style of the day, is important because in it Owen Young said what he believed about broadcasting when it was first launched: how it should be handled and what it could do. In broadcasting he saw a medium to reach all the people; like Jefferson, he believed that the success of a democracy depended upon an informed citizenry. In 1925 he had written John O'Hara Cosgrave, the Sunday editor of the New York *World*: "My first idea is to see if we can create a broadcasting company which will concern itself with national programs only . . . such as speeches of the President, music by nationally known artists, and brief speeches by people nationally known."⁴⁹ He had seen that the "box" could destroy the isolation of the woman on the farm, of the communicant far from a church, of the shut-in and the uneducated. Now he dreamed of a greater and stronger nation because of it.

The arts too would have a renaissance thanks to the new medium; young Shakespeares and Robert Burnses, not tied to the theater or to print, would appear, musicians would spring up to write great music for all the people. Restrained, in the office, by the multiple problems of this shapeless and uncertain business, at home Young dilated to his family upon radio's unparalleled opportunities—prophecies punctuated by his mother's "Who's going to be the boss of it?" and his wife's "Who's going to pay for all this?"

They were good questions. Many answers had been suggested in those early years for the financial support of broadcasting. In England every aspect, from technical operation to programming, was directly controlled by a government agency, with supporting funds largely supplied by a tax on receiving sets. In a discussion with Godfrey Isaacs, Young had told him that "we would not . . . surrender the control of the broadcasting stations and the development of the programs to any government agency." Isaacs had replied, "Well, you can squander some of your money trying to do it, but the ultimate outcome will be that in order to have broadcasting continue, the government in some form will have to take over."[50]

Young, however, believed that government programming would mean censorship, as well as programs supported by taxation. And some years later he was delighted by a perceptive article contrasting the two systems, by the journalist William Hard. Hard pointed out that the British and European systems promoted individual culture, while the American advanced political and general discussion, aimed at the listener as a citizen: "My thesis, then, is simple. I will concede that European governmental broadcasting generally exceeds American private broadcasting in the potential cultivation of good taste—by a graceful margin. I will contend that American private broadcasting exceeds European governmental broadcasting, in any European country, in the potential cultivation of free citizenship—by a vital margin."[51] Young quoted this elegant paragraph many times, for it said what he believed.

Where, then, was the money to come from? Sarnoff had suggested in 1922 that broadcasting should be supported by 2 percent of gross radio-set sales, that broadcasting itself should *not* be a money-making proposition, and that possibly it might eventually receive funds from the foundations and the public, thus avoiding the use of "direct advertising," which neither he nor Young was ready to accept. But for such a conception of "public broadcasting" it was both too early and too late. The phenomenal success of W E A F under A T & T's ownership in selling time to advertisers had set the shape of the future; the problem would be to keep the advertisers within bounds.

The National Broadcasting Company opened its career with a bang on November 15, 1926. On that evening it offered, reported the New York *Evening World*, "one of the most, if not the most, pretentious programs of entertainment that ever has been broadcast." It was, after all, the 1920s, and before a thousand guests in the Waldorf-Astoria, and from studio hookups in other cities, Mary Garden sang, Harold Bauer played, and Will Rogers spoke; not only did the New York Symphony perform but Goldman's Band and Vincent Lopez as well. The program was sent out over a network of twenty-three stations and the estimated number of listeners was ten million. Radio broadcasting, said the *Washington Post*, "has put aside its swaddling clothes and has become a potential giant."[52] Newspaper coverage was national, and listeners all over the country had the novel pleasure of reading about what they had already heard. Overnight the name of the National Broadcasting Company was known nationwide.

The Advisory Council of N B C was the final form of an idea which Young had had ever since he began seriously to think about the control of broadcast programs. By 1925 he was planning a body of distinguished persons, representatives of various shades of public opinion, which would have "the right to say whether the broadcasting facilities are being used in a way prejudicial to the public interest." Such a council should lay down rules for broadcasting, and the rules should be published "so that all may know the conditions under which the broadcasting may be available."[53] By the time of the announcement of the formation of the National Broadcasting Company he had made his specifications more precise and was ready to put together his list and write the letters of invitation.

It was a neatly balanced collection, representing most areas interested in broadcasting, and including, naturally, many persons whom Young himself knew and admired. It also included the minorities recognized in those days: one Catholic, one Jew, one woman; the rest were male W A S P s, with varying sharpness of sting. At the head of the list were Charles Evans Hughes and Elihu Root, who, like Hughes, had been one of Young's heroes from his earliest days. There were other public figures: John W. Davis, the bankers Dwight Morrow and Henry Robinson, William Green of the A F L, as well as representatives of religion, education, agriculture, and the parent companies. The historian of broadcasting, Erik Barnouw, comments that "this unique body outshone any presidential cabinet of modern times."[54]

The letter of invitation expressed Young's feelings of pride and excitement in this great new medium, and his apprehensions lest it be misused. He questioned the feasibility of government regulation or control of broadcast programs, and drew a parallel between a free radio and a free press. But the broadcasting of national programs

carries with it its corresponding responsibility. That responsibility can be more wisely exercised under the advice of a disinterested and impartial body of American citizens representing widely different interests. . . . We believe that in this interval while a Democracy is learning how to handle an instrument of such power, it is most important that the decisions of its executives relating to broadcasting programs and public service should be subject to review and correction by an Advisory Council.[55]

It was a persuasive letter. Elihu Root wrote in answer, "I am really very much surprised to find, as a result of reading your letter of November 6th that I cheerfully consent to be a member of the Advisory Council of the National Broadcasting Company."[56]

At the first meeting, in February 1927, Young reviewed the "Historical Development of Radio," a nonscientific account of the formation of

RCA, the story of NBC itself, and the reasons for the formation of the Advisory Council. Root, who had had his eighty-second birthday three days before, made a statement which must have delighted the chairman's heart. The council, he said, had to "consider how the greatest cultural effects might be had from radio broadcasting and, at the same time, to keep in mind that it must be developed in a business-like way and, if possible, in a profitable way for the company." He went on to say that "it might go far toward checking the movement [from the farm] to the city and, in [my] judgment, the programs for the great agricultural areas should be arranged as much with the idea of affording relief from farming as for giving farming talks and information."[57] He spoke also about the possibilities for adult education, and asked Aylesworth a number of shrewd questions on the selection of advertisers and programs. He was almost as old as Owen Young's mother, but, like her, he was taking the modern world in stride and, like her, was very much interested in radio.

Charles Evans Hughes summed up the area of action for the council in lawyerlike fashion; it must deal only with matters of first importance: "We must not put into the public mind the idea that the Council is responsible where it is not in fact responsible, nor as to matters with which it could not cope successfully," and added that actions taken by the members are "experimental efforts."[58]

All in all, Young must have been pleased with his creation in its first appearance. At succeeding annual meetings, reports were made by the committees on agriculture, church activities, education, labor, music, and women's activities, and Aylesworth reported on the progress of the company. Over the years the membership remained remarkably stable, and when vacancies did occur, they were filled by equally distinguished names: Newton Baker, Felix Warburg, James Rowland Angell, Henry Sloane Coffin, Ada Comstock, Robert Maynard Hutchins, Alfred E. Smith.

Young's optimism about the effective role of the council was not wholly justified by its performance. Serious people, seriously concerned, the members did not find, as the National Broadcasting Company grew into a powerful and varied medium along somewhat different lines than Young had prophesied, that they had much part to play. Nevertheless, their presence, as he had foreseen, forestalled much hostile criticism, whether from listeners, advertisers or government. And to have such an eminent and wide-ranging group conversant with NBC policies and programs was in itself of great value, for Young transferred to them his sense of radio's opportunities, and his deep-rooted desire that it should be used well. He knew that they were, in a sense, window dressing for NBC, but his hopes for them went much farther than the window. He wanted the council, he told Aylesworth at the beginning, to be "a living thing." He worked hard to educate its members, so that they could provide both imagination and common sense for broadcasting—which, in some measure, over the years they did.

v

Not all of Young's hopes for the new company came true; NBC, like others in the field, was subject to enormous pressure from advertisers who came posthaste, with fistfuls of money, to buy air time. What they wanted for their programs was entertainment: light music, dance music, comedians and comedy acts—of which the most famous was "Amos n' Andy." The people at NBC, from Aylesworth down, became "show business" people, and the new offices at 711 Fifth Avenue, with the newfangled air-cooled studios, appeared more often like a movie lot than a concert hall. Standards of presentations were high; they had to be met by all programs. And although there was advertising on the programs, it was, says Barnouw, "brief, circumspect, and extremely well-mannered"—at least at the outset.[59]

In NBC's own programs, called "sustaining," musical and dramatic series were developed which were truly educational; of these the best known was Walter Damrosch's "Music Appreciation Hour," which, with its accompanying notebooks, was used in some 150,000 schools. Other excellent programs were presented with only the name of the sponsor mentioned, no advertising. And every Sunday was crowded with religious services, featuring such new radio stars as Harry Emerson Fosdick, S. Parkes Cadman, Daniel Poling and Stephen Wise. In addition to these, there were public speeches by national figures, news, sports and information services. It is clear that broadcasting was beginning to fulfill at least some of Owen Young's hopes.

From the first, politics presented a difficult problem. In Boston in 1894 the young law student had heard William Jennings Bryan address a reputed ten thousand people on the Common; but few others could handle such a meeting. Since the 1920 election, when returns went on the air from station KDKA, the politicians had been pounding on the broadcasters' doors. RCA's station WRC in Washington had so many requests that its managers recommended that political speeches should not be broadcast unless they were delivered at important public meetings.

As the 1924 conventions drew near, Young suggested to Harbord that a certain amount of time should be assigned to political broadcasting, and that the national committee of each party should appoint a representative to decide how it should be used—which was done. The Republican convention went off well enough, but the Democratic convention in New York must have discouraged listeners: 15 days and 103 ballots exhausted not only the conventioneers and the broadcasters but the radio audience.

The presidential election of 1928 was the first the National Broadcasting Company was called upon to handle. By then, both the equipment and the speakers were more sophisticated, and both parties used radio extensively. The conventions were broadcast, the League of Women Voters went on the air, election returns were heard all over the country. Young had publicly declared for Alfred E. Smith, but it was clear that the "raddio" gave the governor, with his East Side accent, no help in the South and West.

In general, however, Young was very optimistic about the effect of broadcasting upon the nation's political life. He pointed out to the NBC Advisory Council the obvious differences between the political speaker's harangue to a "closely packed and often hysterical mass meeting," and "this vast invisible audience coolly sitting in judgment around the family fireside . . . let us consider the effect upon those sections of the country where, through habit or convention, one or the other of the great parties has had a practical monopoly of the political stage. In some cases the rival party has virtually never had a hearing." (He was certainly thinking not only of the Republicans in the South but of the Democrats in upstate rural New York.) "It is the radio which evens the scales, which assures a fair hearing to both sides. Who can say what radio may not accomplish in destroying sectionalism and creating a new national unity?"[60]

Agriculture too must benefit from the radio; when the General Electric station in Schenectady was opened in February of 1922, Young's main interest was that it should serve the farmers with both entertainment and information. His mother, fascinated like millions of other rural dwellers by this new voice in the kitchen, kept him informed about the programs she thought useful, or just the ones she liked. When, for a brief time in 1925, WGY's usually excellent transmission was blurred so that it was not received well in Van Hornesville, the chairman of General Electric was checking immediately at Schenectady. His neighbors, he said, agreed with him that something was wrong, but they did not complain to w g y as they felt "they were getting something for nothing and had no right to complain or criticize."[61]

There were, however, many who did both, and the need for regulation of the air was becoming increasingly apparent. Hoover, as secretary of commerce, had done what he could—although no one, including Hoover, knew whether he had the power or not. Young kept in close touch with him on this as on other matters, and did not hesitate to advise or try to educate him. One letter begins, "Because I am more interested in radio than almost anything else in the world," and goes on, "inasmuch as I have my heart set . . . on a national broadcasting program through several stations advantageously located . . . I should be very sorry to have regional [advisory] committees dealing with any questions affecting broadcasting. There is no such thing as a region in broadcasting. . . ."[62] To this Hoover replied rather despairingly that the latest radio conference he had called did not want any kind of advisory committees, regional or otherwise.

The Radio Act, passed by the Congress in January of 1927, was "obsolete when passed," but contained some strong and necessary statements about censorship—either by the licensing authority or by the radio station—and about monopoly. It set up an independent bipartisan commission, which with notable courage attempted to bring some semblance of order out of chaos by a series of "grand shuffles and shakedowns." Young, though grateful for the regulation of the technical aspects of broadcasting, which "will insure the largest beneficial use of facilities for all the people," was firm in his opposition to "Government control of programs as an incident of regulation." As always, he put his trust in the people: "Listeners have it in their power to compel such programs as they wish . . . no legislative body can do this—no commission ought to be expected to do it."[63] And he trusted that out of many good programs they would choose the best.

If Young found himself unexpectedly in the "entertainment world" through broadcasting, other developments brought him into it even more deeply. "Talking pictures" were beginning by 1926 to move out of the laboratory, or rather two laboratories, for General Electric and Western Electric were hotly competitive in this area. In that summer Young, at the suggestion of Will Hays, the "czar" of the movie industry, was talking with Hollywood producers, emphasizing that r c a would want not royalties from its patents but participation in the business. But a t & t and Western Electric had stolen a march on g e and r c a, signing contracts with Hollywood for *their* sound-on-film system.

In the spring of 1928, just before sailing for Europe, Young held a meeting in his office where GE, RCA and Westinghouse planned a new corporation, RCA Photophone. Within a few weeks the company was incorporated and ready to move; it already had the technical equipment in GE's Pallophotophone, and all it needed was a market. This was provided by an alliance with Joseph P. Kennedy's Film Booking Office and the Keith-Albee-Orpheum chain of movie theaters. RKO (Radio-Keith-Orpheum) was the result, and by the fall of 1928 that company too was ready for business and Young was taking a childish delight in escorting his children to RKO theaters, free on his pass.

While in these, and in the still more sweeping changes in corporate structure and relationships which lay ahead, the initiative was often Sarnoff's, Young's influence was generally decisive. At the same time he was always pushing the pace and scope of technical progress in radio. Emphasizing his own technological ignorance, he urged faster development of photo transmission; he wanted radio communications to handle more words per second more cheaply. Even in 1923 he had written E. W. Rice: "I want the Radio Corporation to keep closely in touch with everything that is going on in the world by which pictures may be transmitted, because I have the deep conviction, as you know, that some day all communications outside of telephony will be pictures; that is to say, pictures of the messages to be sent." Five years later he was pushing Sarnoff on the same subject: "I want to flash letters and checks by the thousand daily, and establish a real communications company. Let's go!"[64] Always fascinated by newspapers, he wanted, with his *New York Times* on the breakfast table, a copy of the London *Times* of the same date, transmitted by radio facsimile. This led Dr. Alfred N. Goldsmith, the versatile pioneer and "practical visionary" of radio to whom both GE and RCA owed much, to remark: "It's a fine thing to have an imagination wholly unrestrained by any knowledge of fundamental facts."[65] This tickled Young, who loved to quote it.

Young had a special reason for his interest in this development. His eldest son, the amateur who worked with wireless on the hill in Lexington in 1910–13, was now a professional, specializing in this very field in GE's Radio Department in Schenectady. "Both Pops and I," remembered C. J. Young,

were exercising imagination but in different areas, which had suddenly come together. Mine had to do with the parts and pieces which made it possible to send over wireless circuits, not just the dots and dashes of telegraphy and the sounds of speech and music, but also the black and white of charts and pictures. We had plenty to talk about on the long drives to Van Hornesville, and in Grandmother's sitting room: "Could you do this or that—and what were the likely complications?"[66]

C.J. moved over to the RCA Laboratories in Camden in 1930, and continued to work on facsimile transmission; the conversations on "Could you do this or that?" were also continued. The father was enormously proud of the son who had all the scientific expertise and scientific imagination which he had not.

Chapter 20

The Modern Corporation: Shall Labor Hire Capital?

E ARLY in 1925, Young and Dawes had two reunions to which neither reparations nor war debts was admitted. The occasion for the first, on March 4, was the new vice-president's inauguration. This time Jo could not go with Owen, and young Jo came from college as her stand-in—or more accurately, sit-in—being seated beside Mrs. Dawes in the vice-presidential box at the inaugural ball.

The second, as Dawes wrote to remind his friend some two months in advance, arose from a joint commitment to assist in celebrating the sesquicentennial of the Battle of Lexington and (almost) coincidentally, the midnight ride of *two* patriot couriers: Paul Revere and William Dawes. It was rumored that Paul had cornered all the fame chiefly because his name better fitted Henry Longfellow's rhyme scheme, and that the vice-president had come to rescue his ancestor from undeserved oblivion. Thus the Youngs were there on the anniversary of the ride as William Dawes's now-famous descendant shared the rostrum of Old North Church with Paul Revere's great-great-granddaughter, Mrs. Nathaniel Thayer of Boston. Neither speaker took horse that evening, they later reported, and in escorting their friend to Lexington next morning—Patriots' Day—Owen and Jo were back on dear and familiar ground. It was all sufficiently different from the usual impersonal celebration or the conventional ancestor hunt to warrant its own "listen my children" when the party was over.[1]

One by-product of this reunion, which was to prove of considerable importance to the Young family fortunes, is described in Stuart Crocker's letter of June to his friend and Harvard classmate C. J. Young. "A short time ago," he wrote,

when Mr. Young and General Dawes were "refighting the Battle of Lexington," one of the General's brothers said that he was planning to sell his interest in the New York and Richmond Gas Company. The General and Mr. Young expressed some regret that he was selling out . . . and it finally resulted in the General inviting your father "to play along with him" in buying control . . . and having Mr. Rufus Dawes . . . one of the leading Gas Company operators in the country, to take over and manage the property. The New York and Richmond Gas Company serves Staten Island. All of us here believe that Staten Island has great possibilities for growth. . . .

Crocker did not exaggerate, and, as he went on to explain, his chief had agreed to purchase a one-third interest in the property, at a cost of slightly over $500,000. Not wishing to become involved in its management, however, Young had suggested that his eldest son and his assistant represent this interest as directors—which Crocker hoped would appeal to C.J. as it did to him. It did and both accepted.[2]

In the meantime General Electric was thriving; for 1924 the company reported profits at the peacetime peak of $21.13 per share. Nor did the Bond and Share distribution do any harm to stockholder relations, though one correspondent did complain to Young about the unseemly gyrations it had occasioned in GE shares. Taking pains to explain that the alternative would have been for GE to market its Bond and Share holdings through a consortium of bankers at needless expense, Young agreed that the gyrations were excessive. But he added, prophetically enough, that it seemed impossible to "prevent a common stock in a growing and prosperous concern and in a rapidly developing industry from having market fluctuations much wider than we should like to see."[3]

In marked contrast was his letter of Monday, May 4, addressed to Samuel Untermyer, who, as counsel to the "People's Legislative Service," had just sent Young and concurrently released to the press what amounted to a broadside against GE and all its works. As reported by the *Times*, Untermyer complained that the General Electric Company had been "whitewashed" of the criminal and civil charges brought against it as head of "the Electric Light Trust" by the Lockwood Committee of New York State; this he attributed to the influence of J. P. Morgan and Company (especially Dwight Morrow as a GE director) on the Coolidge administration, and to the "sinuous and devious activities of the Department of Justice," starting when Harry M. Daugherty was attorney general. As for the Morgan influence at GE, Untermyer asserted that the firm "virtually dictates policies," and accused Young of having told his stockholders that the Lockwood Committee's findings against the company "were false."[4]

Young's rejoinder was uncharacteristically sharp and sweeping. This was also handed to the press, which, scenting a battle, tended to print much of its text; here excerpts must suffice:

Dear Sir [he began]:

Your letter of April 30th reached me today, first through the newspapers and then direct. It seems to make charges against the Federal Courts, the Department of Justice, J. P. Morgan and Company and the General Electric Company. In my reply I shall endeavor to mind my business by dealing only with those matters which affect the General Electric Company.

First. The General Electric Company is not controlled by J. P. Morgan and Company or any other banking group or interest. . . . Of its 37,000 stockholders, no one owns more than one percent of its capital stock, except the General Electric Employees Securities Corporation.

Going on to say that GE was not seeking special favors from the government, but on the contrary had supplied all the facts requested by the Department of Justice in its lamp suit, he reminded Untermyer that the federal court had recently found in GE's favor, and it was of this that he had naturally advised GE's stockholders. He then castigated Untermyer for charging GE with profiteering on its lamps, a matter "on which you have always misled yourself and others."

So far [then] from apologizing to you or to anyone for the way we have developed and handled our incandescent lamp business, I make bold to say that of all the contributions to this wonderful electric age, the incandescent lamp, both in excellence of service and in reasonableness of price, is the greatest. If you would study more thoroughly the technical history of the incandescent lamp, I feel sure that neither you nor any other American making similar study could or would honestly charge the General Electric Company with criminal monopoly, but that on the other hand, you would applaud the initiative, the courage, and the efficiency of the men who are responsible for that development and be proud of the American contribution to that art. I can say this with propriety because this work was done before I, personally, became connected with the General Electric Company.

Finally, may I ask in the name of more than 100,000 men and women who are interested in the General Electric Company as stockholders and workers that you carry on [any] controversies you may have with J. P. Morgan and Company, or the Department of Justice, without involving us either in your private quarrels or your political attacks.

Reflecting, perhaps, a new confidence in the strength of GE's position and his own, this letter evoked a reply which, as Young was quick to acknowledge, was notably different in tone. But if, as the exchange suggested, Young could be a formidable antagonist—whose spirited defense could also boost company morale—he soon concluded that, in the long run, taking public issue with such attacks profited no one save a press that thrived on controversy and too often fanned its flames.[5]

ii

During these early, or pre–New Era, years—1925, 1926 and the greater part of 1927—Young's letters, like his speeches, reflect not only his constant concern with the direction and interpretation of GE's corporate policy but also his own wide-ranging interests and unflagging optimism. Certainly the latter were abundantly evident in the time and energy he devoted to the series of speeches in which he sought to popularize the Page School and all that it could contribute to improved international relations. As chairman of its trustees, he took his brief on the road, speaking in a sequence of one-night stands to large and representative audiences in Pittsburgh and Philadelphia, Cincinnati and Detroit. New York City could wait; the trustees were agreed with Young that the first $600,000 of the $1,000,000 needed for the school's endowment should come from the rest of the country, preferably in small but numerous gifts. This Young undertook to secure, with others taking responsibility for the final metropolitan campaign. And by early 1927, thanks in no small measure to well-organized efforts in key centers, plus General Dawes's generous and widely publicized gift of his 1925 Nobel Prize award, some $500,000 had been pledged—of which two-thirds was paid in cash—by approximately 4,000 individuals. There were ancillary prospects too; notably those involving the Edward W. Bok Peace Prize and the possibility of special studies on "taking the profit out of war" to be funded by Bernard Baruch, who had popularized the theme. Nor, with an eye to completing a possibly more expansive effort, was Young neglecting the foundations.[6]

Gerard Swope never complained of these extracurricular activities of his colleague—which seemed, incidentally, to be doing General Electric no harm. Earnings remained good, despite a slight drop in 1925; for 1926 the increase was sharp enough to give a notable boost to the price of GE shares—and to management's extra compensation. Except for the latter, much the same sort of thing was happening at RCA—allowing always for the more volatile nature of its ramifying business and profits, and the limited supply of its shares.[7] And if, with the collapse of the Florida land boom, speculative interest had shifted to Wall Street, it was by no means of the feverish sort.

To some, Young's tour on behalf of the Page School inevitably suggested political ambitions. Be that as it may, it afforded rare opportunities to visit with GE directors, managers and important customers on their home grounds; in Cincinnati he even made a second speech in celebration of a Columbia Gas and Electric anniversary. And on occasion his radical turn of thought could delight even his conservative friends and critics, as when he suggested first to President Coolidge and then, early in 1926, to the American Bar Association that government would be better employed in investigating not the profitable but the unprofitable concerns, whose failure meant lost jobs, wasted capital, disappointed customers and a shock to public confidence.[8]

In addressing the Association, Young dealt also with a broad spectrum of other concerns, some serious. Certainly he began lightheartedly enough:

Mr. President and Gentlemen of the Bar:
There are two subjects which seem to command the continuing interest of the public, and therefore, I assume, of the Bar. One is the want of prohibition; the other is foreign relations. They are both sensitive subjects. Under the inspiration of Mr. Hughes, I experimented with one of them for a period of nine months in the year 1924, and during that time I was relieved of the necessity of considering the legal aspects of the other.

Noting, then, that in that same year the bar association had tested this experiment for itself by meeting in London—where at the Pilgrims' dinner, the Prince of Wales had welcomed "the distinguished American Secretary of State under the nom de plume of President of the American Bar Association"—Young announced that he had just found a job abroad for Hughes's successor as the association's president, Walter P. Cooke of Buffalo. Thus, he said, with a bow to both, we have "on this platform tonight the original volunteer and latest draft for the reparations settlement in Europe."[9]

The theme which he proceeded to develop was familiar but its variations were novel. Why, he asked, had so many lawyers—Roland Boyden, Hughes, Nelson Perkins, Parker Gilbert and now Cooke— been called upon to deal with such sensitive issues as reparations? Why, as business became increasingly complex, had so many lawyers been called upon to direct so many of the great corporations? Is it, he asked, because "they are accustomed to approach a problem as a new problem," because "they are accustomed to finding facts and facing them . . . ? No group in the community finds facts with greater determination or bows to them with greater acquiescence. . . . They have learned from this profession that it is never safe to look for what you want to find . . . that it is only sound to accept as final, whether one likes it or not, the inescapable conclusions which result from facts rightly found and principles correctly applied."[10]

It was on this same occasion that Young, after citing as *exemplum gregium* and quoting at some length from Secretary Hughes's New Haven address of December 1922, offered Hughes the finest tribute one speaker can pay another: "Mr. President, I wish I might some time have the experience of writing a statement which, three years after, could be so proudly read."

Young, it seemed, still relished the rostrum and shared the satisfaction most human beings feel in seeing his name and views in print. But, like lending to the Germans, this too called for moderation; as Young had warned at his testimonial dinner, the extension of credit "must not be overdone." Thus before the year's end, in responding to a request from his old friend "Missy" Meloney, now editor of the *Herald Tribune*'s Sunday magazine, that their mutual friend Irving Bacheller do a feature article about him, Young was moved to protest:

If anybody is to write anything about me I should prefer to have Irving Bacheller do it more than anyone else I know, and if there is any importance in publishing such an article I should be glad to have you publish it.

My point on the whole business is this: I have made no effort to hide myself from the public nor to aim at mystery by keeping myself unknown. When I became Chairman of the Board of the General Electric Company and of the Radio Corporation, I gave quite frankly my personal views on all questions related to those offices. I felt the public had a right to know. That has all been published. The facts about my life and my views are not concealed from any one who desires to know them. Nothing new has happened putting further obligation for public disclosure on me, and until it does I see no reason, from my standpoint, for further publicity. I certainly hope that my friends—among the best of whom I count Irving Bacheller and you—will not continue an exploitation to the point where every one will be sick and tired of seeing my name, and will get the impression that I am courting publicity either to gratify my personal vanity or to further some personal ambition.

Now that I have said this much, I leave the matter to you, and I will be content with whatever decision you may make regarding it. If the thing is to be done, I am only too glad to have Bacheller do it.[11]

Young had reason to feel that this publicity business was being overdone. On the one hand, a press which was finding him exceptionally good copy was constantly heaping honors upon him and pointing the way to new ones. For this, many reasons could be cited. One was that Young had *made* news often enough so that what he did (or even said) came itself to be treated as news. Another was his habit of treating journalists as human beings. A third was that, in the context of the times, reporters often found—sometimes to their surprise—that what he had to say made sense. If here no charges of monopoly could be laid against him, the competition (as the press saw it) was neither fierce nor widespread.

On the other hand, Young's refusal to conform to the usual stereotype left not a few reporters baffled, if not downright suspicious. Alfred Sloan of General Motors, for example, spoke and behaved as a tycoon should; if he proclaimed (as he did) that "the primary object of the corporation . . . [is] to make money, not just . . . motor cars" he was simply shaping up.[12] But to Young, one of Sloan's directors, this formula was evidently simplistic and outmoded: management, he would insist, had other if not prior obligations—to the workers and always to the public. Yet Sloan and Young seemed to get along all right, and GE's shareholders were hardly being shortchanged. This man Young was a deep one for sure; just what *was* his game?

And so, to the dismay of his staff, there appeared from time to time portraits purporting to be of Young which were drawn not from life but rather to conform to the artist's preconceptions. When suspicion or occupational skepticism directed the pen, the "portrait" could become sinister: a personification of the power trust, perhaps, hiding behind a smoke screen of pious platitudes, the better to rake in the profits. Even worse were the sycophantic caricatures in which their paragon appeared as a sickly composite of Sir Galahad, Horatio Alger and St. John.[13] Nevertheless, for Young, honors from various sources continued to mount: as early as July of 1925, his German decoration had been added to the Belgian, French and (much earlier) Japanese, and honorary degrees from Johns Hopkins and Columbia, Colgate and Yale now supplemented those from Dartmouth, Tufts and Harvard. This was too much for his old friend and colleague of the Tyler firm, Fred Weed, now a vice-president of the First National Bank of Boston, from whose office, under the date of July 18, 1926, Owen received the following unsigned communication.

The First National Bank of Boston presents its compliments to Mr. Owen D. Young and advises him that it has reserved a compartment in its vault for his decorations and degrees.

It has also set aside a room for exhibition purposes and will furnish an armed guard whenever the collection is on parade.

For Mr. Young's convenience it will notify its 18,115 foreign correspondents that it is prepared to accept in Mr. Young's behalf anything from the First Order of the Auk to the Charge of the Light Brigade and have them notify Presidents, potentates and bodies politic and otherwise.

The reply came to Boston promptly:

Mr. OWEN D. YOUNG

accepts with pleasure the compartment in the vault of the First National Bank for certain of his decorations and degrees. He has found it quite impossible to keep all of his decorations together in a single safe, not so much because of the vast space required, as because they do not seem to live entirely in harmony with each other. Their last debate as to which was the more important and more merited was accompanied by such threats of physical violence that Mr. Young now fears that they may destroy each other. Therefore, he welcomes the opportunity to put them in different safes and to separate them by several hundred miles.

Mr. Young feels it necessary in frankness to say that he has a very able organization in the field soliciting these decorations and orders and will therefore not require the services of the relatively small number of foreign correspondents of the First National Bank. . . .[14]

iii

From all of this fanfare, private correspondence often came as a blessed relief; an opportunity to speak his mind without fear of exploitation or distortion. Even before Lexington revisited, an inquiry from Felix Frankfurter—then professor of law at Harvard—gave Young the chance to develop and restate his views not only on the best ways of dealing with statewide (and even interstate) generation and distribution of power, but also on the virtues of actual investment versus reproduction value as the base for figuring a utility's rate of return. Not uncritical, Young's response to Frankfurter's stated views was nevertheless far more commendatory than his utility customers would have liked. This time, however, he need have no concern about publicity, misleading or not.[15]

In responding a few months later to Walter Lippmann's query about inheritance taxes, Young's only concession to the negative view of most of his peers was his declaration that such levies would more properly be made by the states than by the federal government. For the rest, he wrote:

. . . for more than twenty years, I have believed that inheritances, especially in the larger brackets, should be heavily taxed. I have believed this not only because it was an easy way and an effective way of raising substantial sums but more because I believe it beneficial to the community as a whole. The inheritance law should be careful to protect beneficiaries who really need protection and whom it was the duty of the testator to protect. In my judgment, [however,] it is harmful to the community to ruin able-bodied children or other heirs through large inheritances. They usually misuse the funds, and for the most part, they are a standing advertisement of the worst things in the capitalist system. Therefore, you will see I am not only in favor of the inheritance taxes, but under certain conditions, of most drastic ones.[16]

One letter, written that same summer to his friend John O'Hara Cosgrave of the *World*, suggests that Young felt less at ease with the divinities than with the humanities—or even the natural sciences. (Given their optimistic conviction that God was too good to damn them, perhaps the Universalists thought it wise not to dabble further in the mysteries of speculative theology.) Be that as it may, in acknowledging Cosgrave's kindness in sending him a copy of his "clear and helpful," if speculative, essay, as published in the June *Century*, Young chose his words with caution:

The basic notion expressed in [your essay] is one which has always appealed to me personally, and that is that the human body was the mere instrument through which a directing force made its personality known in this physical world. The immortality of the directing force I have never doubted. The question of whether we shall ever make any progress in its study is one about which I have not dared to think. On the whole, it has seemed to me perhaps safer to assume that we would never make any advances in that field of study and that it would be more profitable and perhaps less demoralizing to confine ourselves to the study of purely physical laws. I say less demoralizing because if we make a mistake in our theories regarding the physical laws, it is the occasion only of normal debate and a mistake in the end will be corrected without very serious consequences because of it. If we make a mistake in our theory regarding the other thing which affects the hopes and fears of human beings so profoundly, then almost irreparable damage might be done.

But he added, wistfully enough, "If we could learn something about it though, it would be the greatest possible contribution to the world."[17]

More mundane but in its way no less stimulating—and certainly more consequential—was a letter Nelson Perkins wrote Young in November 1926 urging that GE actively explore the very great potentialities of the Russian market for electrical equipment. Young saw to it that GE should heed his friend's advice—as he himself had done a year earlier in initiating a cordial exchange with Perkins's friend Winston Churchill. But it was a letter from a courageous younger friend, dated October 5, 1925, that Young found especially moving. Asking a small favor of "dear Owen," Franklin D. Roosevelt reported from Marion, Massachusetts, "I am up here taking a wonderful course of treatment which is getting rid of the braces on my legs, and I feel more encouraged than at any previous times." Such indomitable optimism not even Young's could match.[18]

iv

Young and Swope had been among the first to recognize, with the late Walter Rathenau, both the fact and the significance of the twentieth-century corporate revolution which had divorced ownership from control and thus profoundly altered the role of management. If this concern, translated into human terms, had been the theme of Young's 1923 talk with GE's foremen, a month or so later it was further articulated in an interview with the same Atherton Brownell who had reported to him on GE's labor problems. And it was precisely because in this new phase of corporate development managers were no longer the "gentlemen attorneys" of capital but the "trustees of an institution in which capital and labor cooperate" that he and Swope were still busily developing the various employee benefit plans already described.[19]

But Young was not satisfied that he had yet formulated, much less applied, the true equation. It was all very well to stress the importance of assuring the ready availability of capital if the workers were to be supplied with constantly better tools; but as profits justified extras or policy dictated distribution of tangible assets like Bond and Share, shouldn't the workers have some direct and material share? The question was sharpened when, in 1926, the directors authorized a four-for-one split in GE shares, to bring the price within reach of the ordinary investor—at the same time raising the customary eight-dollar dividend to the equivalent of twelve dollars (three dollars was the new rate). Evidently valuable rights still attached to legal ownership, but so far, these accrued to the workers only as investors and chiefly through the Employees Securities Corporation.

True, by 1926 employee earnings at GE were reported up 118 percent over the 1914 average, as against a 68 percent rise in living costs.

(Over the same span GE's average price scale was reported up 13 percent as against a 54 percent rise in wholesale commodity prices.)[20] Nevertheless, if the American worker, as Young never tired of pointing out, had indeed become a "director rather than a generator" of the power which produced the goods, didn't the consequent increase in his productivity justify all this and possibly more? Was management, as trustee, seeing to it that the worker got his full slice of the pie? And was there no better way than paternalism, however you dressed it up, of enlisting and assuring his cooperation?

That Young was groping for answers became particularly evident in that same year. In his May (1926) address to the National Electric Light Association, in which he called for a "cultural wage," he went on to say:

> You are not afraid of new inventions and new engineering in your physical plants. . . . May I suggest that invention, improved engineering and courage to take the road are needed now more in the social than in the physical sciences. *I recommend that we take the overhead of research and experiment in the social field now when the social balance sheet is stable and not postpone them to the day when it may be too late.*[21]

Some four months later, in responding to a personal letter from a young magazine editor in Chicago, he not only took another significant step, but also became somewhat more explicit. Insisting that business had many things yet to do before it met its full obligations, he told his young correspondent:

> The men who do the business of the General Electric Company, and I mean to include in that all men who think of that business as their business, (not simply floaters looking for a day's work) are seeking on the one side to obtain their capital—that is to say, their tools—at the lowest cost. . . . On the other side, these men have the job of using those tools so as to make the product which, because of its excellence and cheapness, will command the market. That position not only gives them business today, but insures them business tomorrow. *The margins which result from the exercise of their mental and physical effort in that undertaking, in my mind, should belong to them. . . .*[22]

This was unequivocal and, not being written for publication, was not open to the charge of political motivation. The rest of the letter is interesting, not least because of his concern to dispose of Professor W. Z. Ripley's call for some new scheme of effective control by the owners: "Stockholders know nothing about the business nor do they care anything about it. . . . They are only [buying or] selling a commodity . . . if it does not yield them adequate returns, they sell their shares." Nor was a meddlesome government in any better position: "The carrying on of the business of the corporations, especially those doing big business, should be in the hands of those who are making that business the business of their lives." So "this is my answer to all those, including Professor Ripley, who are demanding money control of corporations and likewise my answer to the socialists who are demanding community control."[23]

Having found an "answer" which satisfied his sense of the equities, Young was showing, if you please, curiously little concern about the niceties of corporation law. Moreover, he had still to determine whether to make his "answer" public, and if so, when and where. At this point his old friend Wallace Donham provided the opportunity. Thanks to the five-million-dollar gift of George F. Baker, first announced at that 1924 commencement which made Young an honorary Harvard alumnus, the Harvard Graduate School of Business Administration had now acquired a handsome local habitation as well as a name. Now, as Dean Donham wrote Young on the last day of January 1927, the new Baker buildings across the Charles were about to be dedicated and the authorities, including President A. Lawrence Lowell, were unanimous in wanting Young to deliver the principal address. The date was fixed for June 4, 1927; not until April 18 was the invitation definitely accepted.[24]

Young had wanted first to be sure that he could do the kind of job the occasion called for. Late in 1926 he had declined Lowell's cordial invitation to deliver the Godkin Lectures at Harvard on the ground that "the things one must . . . or ought to do" left little time for "the things one would like to do."[25] But this was, perhaps, a must.

Young's old friend Edward Adler, who had dug up most of the cases cited in his first speech as an officer of General Electric, back in 1914, was now summoned once again—this time from his office in the Law Department in Schenectady. The occasion demanded a "learned" as well as a forward-looking speech; could Adler help with some research? Adler could and did. Once again he came up with a plethora of cases. Young chose those which best illustrated the contrasts in business considered—"in Lowell's happy phrase"—as "the oldest of the arts and the youngest of the professions." As Adler's drafts were discussed and revised, Young's own versions multiplied until, with his fifth draft, he was finally ready to settle. By this time it was close on Memorial Day; Crocker was put to it to get the text ready in time for Harvard to release advance copies to the press.[26]

The great day came and the weather smiled. This was fortunate, because the exercises were held outside the new Baker Library, with the dignitaries under its wide portico and most of the thousand others in attendance—faculty, students and invited guests—seated below them. Mr. Baker, an octogenarian symbol of probity as well as conservatism and wealth, had the seat of honor; the speaker's wife and two of his children sat near him—and at the luncheon following, the daughter sat next to Mr. Baker, at his express invitation.

The speech itself was one to suggest that Donham knew his man. Offering "no apology for our devotion to business," Young drew alike upon the past (when business was individual and local and so subject to community sanctions) and the future (with "the research workers in pure science" as "explorers set[ting] sail for unknown lands") to put the current scene in perspective. That business had made law as well as history was evident, not least in his quoted passage from Malynes's *Lex Mercatoria*: separate from the law of nations the customs commonly observed by merchants "in the course of traffic and commerce and the remainder of the said law will consist of but few points." But after explaining how the rise of corporations required the kind of sanctions that only business could apply to itself—through trade associations and new codes of conduct, for example—the speaker made it clear that he was no mere apologist for business:

Let me say however that so far as the public is concerned, organized business has been quick to take the advantages of group action, but has been slow to assume group responsibilities. Too frequently business men have acquiesced, even if they did not participate, in objectionable practices until an outraged society compelled amateurs [viz., legislators] to interfere. . . . It is to be hoped that within these walls research . . . will not only inspire business men to adopt standards acceptable to the public conscience, but will also furnish the information on which wise laws may be drafted and wise decisions made.

This was now imperative because the modern corporation—in which "we have brought together larger amounts of capital and larger numbers of workers than existed in cities once thought great"—had become a public institution and its managers, trustees. "We have been put to it, however, to discover the true principles which should govern [the] relations" between those who have invested their savings and those who have invested their lives. "From one point of view, they were partners in a common enterprise. From another, they were enemies fighting for the spoils of their common achievement." Proceeding then to recount the ways in which the area of conflict was (as he felt) gradually being reduced, and insisting that labor more than shared the risks once thought of as a monopoly of capital, he delivered his charge:

Perhaps some day we may be able to organize the human beings engaged in a particular undertaking so that they truly will be the employer buying capital as a commodity in the market at the lowest price. It will be necessary for them to provide an adequate guaranty fund in order to buy their capital at all. If that is realized, the human beings will then be entitled to all the profits over the cost of capital.

I hope the day may come when these great business organizations will truly belong to the men who are giving their lives and their efforts to them, I care not in what capacity. Then they will use capital truly as a tool and they will all be interested in working it to the highest economic advantage. Then an idle machine will mean to every man in the plant who sees it an unproductive charge against himself. Then every piece of material not in motion will mean to the man who sees it an unproductive charge against himself. Then we shall have zest in labor, provided the leadership is competent and the division fair. Then we shall dispose, once and for all, of the charge that in industry organizations are autocratic and not democratic. Then we shall have all the opportunities for a cultural wage which the business can provide. Then, in a word, men will be as free in cooperative undertakings and subject only to the same limitations and chances as men in individual businesses. Then we shall have no hired men. That objective may be a long way off, but it is worthy to engage the research and efforts of the Harvard School of Business.[27]

This was the chairman of General Electric speaking in 1927. Was anybody listening?

Not over the radio, for NBC's offer to broadcast the exercises free of charge had been declined by Harvard as, presumably, *infra dig.* Not, among his immediate audience, with the stunned attention such doctrine would have provoked had the words been William Green's or any other labor leader's—as significantly they never were. If some of Young's auditors were puzzled or dismayed—if, as one enthusiast wrote him later, "old ladies of both sexes" were alarmed for the safety of their GE holdings—the speech as a whole was "well received," but this time without cheers. Nor is there anything in the record to indicate that the faculty of the Harvard Business School found Young's objective worthy of their sustained attention, much less of any systematic research.[28]

Young did, however, enjoy a "good press" as usual, and those who could not hear could read. The speech was reprinted verbatim not only in the *New York Times* and a few upstate papers but also in the *Boston Evening Transcript,* and generous portions of it were quoted in other papers of these and other cities. Generally speaking, however, its coverage was marked more by breadth than depth; seldom was attention focused, for example, on the climactic passage which has just been quoted here. The *Herald Tribune's* editorial of June 5 was fairly typical: the professional aspirations of business were altogether praiseworthy and so was Owen Young; as for his more radical proposals, they were best given the silent treatment. Even though, to its credit, the *Times* refused to follow suit, it was clear that Dr. John Finley was finding this same passage something of a hot potato.

As indeed it was—and not least to the labor unions. What indeed were they to do if the old and familiar adversary relationship were once overturned? William Green did write in for a copy of the speech, receipt of which was duly acknowledged by his secretary. *Law and Labor* featured the speech (without comment) in its July issue, but that was a publication for, rather than of or by, labor. Trade journals were among the least diffident; for example, the editors of the *Electric Railway Journal* (June 11, 1927) and the *Manufacturers and Industrial News* (June 1927) featured the key passage, examined it boldly, and pronounced it good. Like those "magazines of business," *System* and *Forbes,* however, they were disposed to hail Young's "professional" concerns as "significant signs of the times," showing the "lines in which the highest executive ability of our day is thinking and working."[29] In short, the whole occasion offered further proof that these were no ordinary times and that the leaders of business could be trusted to deal responsibly with whatever problems came their way. Best leave it all to them.

Was it then a mouse or something even more dubious that Young had labored so long to bring forth? By and large the economists and the pundits paid it little mind. Journals of opinion like the *Nation* simply ignored it. The *New Republic* for June 15 did give the occasion editorial notice and the speech a kind of grudging praise, chiefly for its insistence that business had developed to a point at which professional standards had clearly become imperative. But if, on its staff or elsewhere—for example, on *either* side of the Charles River—there were economists sufficiently concerned about the concept of workers' control to give this proposal their critical attention, they signally failed to show.[30]

Politics was another matter. Carter Glass, sometime secretary of the treasury and now senator from Virginia, had listened carefully, and publicly hailed the speaker as "fit to be President." This was seized on avidly by large segments of the press and was echoed nationwide in editorial columns. Such an exercise was much more fun than sober analysis. Nevertheless, one such editorial—in the *San Diego Independent*—did include this thoughtful comment on Young's key proposal: "It will take time, social sense and much of adjustment to fit the world for the realization of Mr. Young's vision. But that he should take occasion to proclaim the faith he has in his fellows, rich and poor, and the spirit to solve such a problem will do more to make straight the way than any other word spoken in this generation."[31]

Among Young's peers in industry, as well as the utility leaders, there was always (as noted) some disposition to write his more radical proposals off to political ambition. Others shrugged and said that if, for whatever reason, Young wanted to talk a radical game that was his privilege—General Electric seemed to be doing all right. Most industrialists, however, shared the concern of union labor over anything which might destroy the familiar adversary relationship; without it, where would they be and what would they do?

There were, however, notable exceptions. Young's old New England friend Henry Dennison—himself a pioneer in the field Young was now exploring—was openly enthusiastic. So was Herbert Straus of Macy's, and the chairman of Chicago's Union Trust Company asked for copies enough for all his officers and directors. Others who wrote in for copies included Wayland Smith of the Oneida Community, J. H. Rand of Remington-Rand, and, of course, Boston's Edward A. Filene. Acting through a surrogate, even Samuel Insull asked to see the text. Thanks to the reprints soon made available by the *Harvard Business Review*, these and hundreds of similar requests were promptly met, although the original supply was soon exhausted.[32]

But it was Young's old Texas friend Judge Edwin B. Parker who tried hardest to compel the attention of business to his words. Now chairman of the United States Chamber of Commerce, Parker ordered and distributed at his own expense one thousand copies to key leaders nationwide, with a request for the reader's criticism or other comment. The replies he sent on to Young were mostly disappointing—like the long letter from the head of the Union Pacific, Robert Lovett (Sr.), who assumed that Young's proposal could only mean stock ownership by individual employees. This, he said, would never work. He knew because he had tried it. When the price of their stock fell they were bitter; when it rose, they sold. Young resisted the temptation simply to reply "you're telling me."[33]

v

But if this was not what he had in mind, what was it? Who knows? Young had gone from Boston to Canton for commencement, and then to inspect the new stone schoolhouse he was building for Van Hornesville. Before the month was over he had taken ship, with his wife, C.J. and Josephine, for the Stockholm meetings of the International Chamber of Commerce. When he returned late in August, Crocker had left to become vice-president of United Electrical Securities, and his new assistant, Everett Case, was full of questions he had been pondering and sometimes parrying: for example, how *was* the GE work force to "hire" their capital and then divide up the residual profits? Young was amused but not forthcoming. "I've done my part," he said, "in posing the objective. If people really want to reach it, they'll find a way. Let's see if they do. In the meantime you might find a clue or two to work on yourself in some of my earlier statements—or even in some of the steps we've already taken in GE."[34]

Thus was one of the authors of this book introduced to GE's still incomplete program of employee benefits—including the savings-investment scheme which, through the Employees Securities Corporation, gave the men in effect more than twice the holdings of GE's next largest shareholder. Two percent of the outstanding stock was quite a block. On December 30, 1924, when the Bond and Share distribution was authorized, it was precisely 36,058 shares. Was this the indicated road, and if so, how much farther would the workers have to travel down it to reach the point of effective control? And did they want control?

In his Harvard speech, Young had described as the single greatest obstacle "the unwillingness of men to assume responsibility and take a risk," adding that "most men yet prefer a fixed income without risk to a share in the profits of the enterprise with the responsibility which that involves." But he also discerned progress as, "under the impact of our present prosperity," wage earners also became joint owners in an ever-widening scale.[35]

It was at about this time that his new assistant, searching the files for further clues, came upon the already mentioned interview of August 1923 with Atherton Brownell. As early as that, it seemed, Young's view of the corporation's new institutional status, with management working for the benefit of all components, had been substantially developed, beginning with his insistence that the first duty of management "is to ensure the constant flow of capital," if only to assure the tools and raw materials necessary "to do a job at all." As the interview quoted Young further:

That's what the people who work would have to do if they ran the company for themselves. They would have to insure the same things in order to get the capital. They would likewise have to establish a management to make the company function and that is all we are doing under the present scheme of things. . . . If all the stock were owned by the employees themselves, it would not change the position of management in the least, nor its duties, nor its responsibilities . . . [for] management's . . . sole purpose is to make these two other groups—investors and workers—function together . . . to produce something . . . of value. . . .[36]

So. Young had been thinking four years earlier of workers as owners, but, with ownership divorced from control, this in itself was hardly calculated to put them in charge. Was management—meaning management of a kind that could sustain the confidence of workers and investors alike—indeed the key, as Young had suggested to Brownell and (as his assistant now discovered) had repeated three years later at GE's Camp General? What else could account for the challenge which, in July 1926, Young put to the hundred or so of the company's top officials there assembled? Given—he asked on that occasion—the corporate revolution with its irrevocable divorce of ownership from control, on whom if not on every member of this group does responsibility for GE's future lie? And what then must be our aims? Having taken all possible steps to assure "command of capital which is our tools, and of the market, which is our output . . . we have only one great problem [and] it is the problem of every man here . . . to see how we . . . can make that of benefit to the 75,000 human beings that are devoting their lives to the . . . General Electric Company. That is the problem and that is the responsibility."[37]

Here at least his new assistant had proof positive that Young was not one to talk out of one side of his mouth in public and the other in private. Even among his colleagues his concern was not for the so-called prerogatives of management but rather for its new and broad responsibilities. Still unanswered, however, was the teasing question of *how* these responsibilities were to be so exercised as to realize the declared objective—especially as this was so strikingly developed at Harvard.

Hiring capital was of course no novelty: to issue bonds—or even preferred stock—was to do just that. Unlike the utilities', however, GE's capital was now almost wholly in common stock, the volume and current price of which made it impracticable to consider any large-scale transfer from investors to employees. But if profits, including extras, over and above a fair return on capital were really to be divided up among all bona fide employees (excluding "floaters"), existing schemes for profit sharing, extra compensation (in cash or stock), pensions, insurance and the like would, at the least, have to be developed and applied on a vastly broader scale. In the long run, moreover, and as a continuing check on management, boards of directors would no doubt have to become more broadly representative of the workers' interests.

Could any steps so far-reaching be taken at GE without alienating capital—that is, GE's investors, large and small? Perhaps the company had already taken with impunity steps sufficient to suggest that the answer depended on how and when—as well as what—further moves were made. Certainly Young and Swope were not about to be stampeded, but neither were they satisfied to stand pat. But perhaps the attitude of labor—or of GE's own wage earners—was the real question mark.

Offered a plan of unemployment insurance in 1925, the men had voted it down. And known only to their directors—and perhaps not all of them—was the invitation GE's top management had extended to William Green, a year later and also in vain, to come in and organize GE's wage workers into a bona fide AFL unit. If this had been prompted in part by fear of something worse, there is no doubt that it was designed to strengthen the hand of a cooperative-minded labor leader, while quietly supplanting with a "legitimate" brand the too-often-suspect company union. It was also pointed out to Green that success at GE would strengthen his hand in the industry generally— thus putting pressure on GE's competitors to match its program of benefits. That the offer was declined was not the fault of Young and Swope, nor was it, perhaps, so much the fault of Green as of rigidities inherent in the federation's craft structure.[38]

And now it was becoming evident that Young's more radical proposal at Harvard was producing little more in the way of effective response than this earlier initiative had. The event found Young at once philosophical and unrepentant. To raise a standard was, he felt, a good thing in itself,[39] nor could his critics now complain that he did not try, at least, to practice what he preached. Besides, the standard Young had raised at Harvard was designed to provoke research and thoughtful study, not precipitate action. And among those capable of the long view, not a few expressed in highly quotable words their sense of its historic importance.

To the president of the Foreign Policy Association, James G. Mc-Donald, who had sent him a copy of the Harvard speech, Gilbert Murray of Oxford wrote: "Owen Young's address is a very fine thing and if the Harvard Business School starts on these lines, it will do a real service to the world." In acknowledging his copy (from the same source), Lord Robert Cecil, a leading draftsman and supporter of the League of Nations who had served often as Britain's representative on the Council, was characteristically forthright: Owen Young's speech, he wrote, ". . . is one of the finest things I have ever come across. I need not say that with the general ideas about Capital and Labour I am in the heartiest agreement, and I particularly like the suggestion that in the future it may be that labour will hire capital rather than capital hire labour."[40]

Nearer home, the president of the National Broadcasting Company essayed the unaccustomed role of prophet. In the context of the times, M. H. Aylesworth's prediction seemed bold rather than extravagant; writing Young on June 21, 1927, he said in part:

I regret that the Harvard authorities were of the opinion that the exercises should not be broadcast. We offered our facilities without cost. This speech was entitled to a very great audience. Today your ideas will be considered quite original and will cause some people to shudder. Twenty-five years from today your prophesies would receive very little publicity, because there is little news value to business in practices that have been put into effect.

Finally, the response of two eminent European scholars to the copies they received suggests both the reach of Young's thought and the contradictory views it excited in thoughtful men who sought to classify the author and his doctrine. Writing to McDonald, his friend and Young's, from the Harvard Law School, where he was serving as a visiting professor, Joseph Redlich of Vienna said:

I beg you to receive my heartfelt thanks for your having sent me this truly marvellous speech of Mr. Owen Young's. It is a work both scholarly and thoughtful, expressed in a very impressive language and it shows not less the deep insight of the author in the last and greatest problems of modern economic and social life. I find particularly interesting the form in which Mr. Young utters his socialist hopes for the future: but, as he says, there will come a time when the producers of wealth, the workmen and their technical leaders will buy for the cheapest price the capital necessary to carry on their industrial activity. This is just the most opposite and the most efficient contrast to Bolshevism or usual Communism, which first destroys life and capital of the owners of capital in order to put the "State" in the place of the capitalist.

It is my old conviction that only by a kind of social liberalism or liberal socialism the problem of modern capitalistic economy and society can be solved in a satisfactory manner.[41]

The other, from Paul Devinot, the French head of the Institut International d'Organisation Scientifique du Travail, in Geneva, said in part:

My dear Friend:

I thank you for your thoughtfulness in sending me the speech of Owen D. Young. Doriot [of the Business School faculty] had already called my attention to it, and I have read it with very great interest. I have also had the opportunity to comment on it several times, particularly before the chief of the Italian Government, during a speech delivered at the Congress of the Organisation Scientifique du Travail.

It is of course unnecessary for me to tell you of my great admiration of Mr. Young for making this courageous utterance. I suppose it is also needless to say to you how little prepared the mentality of our European employers is to realize the profound truth of these affirmations. . . .

If Mr. Young should come to Europe, he would be classed, regardless of his qualities, among our socialists. Truly this would be a mistake. Mr. Young belongs to that class of neocapitalists . . . who feel that the age is past when capital had only rights, and that it will be able to justify its existence in our industrial society . . . by accepting fully the duties that its role . . . requires of it.

There is in this speech the elements of a whole philosophy, or at least of a whole social school. . . . You wanted a note; I have given a judgment. . . .

Reviewing these and other responses to the copies of his speech which an admiring McDonald had circulated, Young found it easy to settle for this "judgment," knowing that his capacity for systematic thought was most unlikely to produce another speech or paper in which an obviously knowledgeable and disinterested reader could detect "the elements of a whole philosophy, or at least of a whole social school."

For Young, 1926 and 1927 were years of manifold activities and accomplishments. But they were not happy ones for the Young family, for once again they lost a young member from their circle. C.J.'s wife, Eleanor Whitman Young, daughter of Owen's and Jo's old friends and mother of two baby boys, had been troubled for some time by a rheumatic heart condition. Although everything that was known at that time was done for her, it became clear by the fall of 1926 that she could not survive. She died on Christmas Day of 1926, at the age of twenty-five. The two families shared the care of the little boys, for C.J. himself was ill for many weeks. His mother stayed with him most of the spring, and his father came as often as he could. And in the summer of 1927 the trip to Scandinavia and England was good therapy for him and for the family.

Chapter 21

The Uses of Unexpected Wealth: ODY and Education

W HEN, in June 1922, in recognition of their new chairman's achievement in putting RCA together, GE's directors voted to offer him 100,000 shares of Radio common at sixty cents a share, Owen Young had to borrow to make the purchase. Though he had sold enough of these shares over the next two years to liquidate his loan, sale of the rest by early 1925 yielded profits sufficient to finance his new and promising venture, with General Dawes, in New York and Richmond Gas. By 1929 that promise too would be redeemed, many times over.

This was fairly typical of the way in which, during these seven fat years, the right stocks bought at the right time, with (say) $60,000 of borrowed money, could produce a not inconsiderable fortune. For the first fifty years of his life, Young had worked hard and long for whatever came his way; now these years of unremitting toil were paying off, and fabulously. Not even at the height of the "New Era" did GE's stated salaries for top management attain the six-figure level, but extra compensation, geared as it was to earnings and in large part payable in GE stock, was generous. Thus for the last five years of the twenties, Young's annual earnings averaged, not the often reputed million, but some $375,000—$50,000 of which (but no extras) came from RCA. As the market continued to soar, Young's capital gains soared with it, typically amounting to twice his total earnings.[1]

Sharing this unexpected wealth with Jo was great fun, but did not answer the basic questions of how they were to use it and finally dispose of it. The first was no problem; Young was already deeply interested in collecting rare books, and whatever he could do for Van Hornesville that would please his mother most. And both Owen and Jo had a concern to broaden and make more nearly equal educational opportunities for the young, beginning with St. Lawrence. Now they could afford to indulge these interests further without undue worry about the expense—and so they did. This too was fun, even though book collecting became increasingly expensive and Owen's increasingly valuable collection came to represent a considerable part of their disposable assets.

The imaginative and comprehensive plans they finally developed for the disposition of their residual assets, real and personal, will be recounted in a subsequent chapter. Suffice it to say here that, consistent with Young's letter to Walter Lippmann, they rejected at the outset any notion that their wealth must now be jealously guarded and built up in order to provide a fortune to each of their four children. Far better, they felt, to establish as they could—and did in 1928— modest trust funds for each, the income from which should provide for the children a sense of basic security while affording them a certain freedom to pursue careers of their own choosing, even of the less remunerative sort.

Had Owen himself been the beneficiary of such a trust, who knows what he might have done when offered the prospect of becoming a law-school dean? In any event, he and Jo agreed that after thus discharging their major family obligations they could give free rein to their own concerns—books, education, and individual help to young people.

ii

Owen Young's first heroes, after his father, were his teachers: Menzo McEwan, Mark Hollister, Alpheus Hervey, Charley Gaines. In answer to the question, "In the light of your career since graduating, what in your college education appears now to have been of greatest value to you?" he replied, "The character and point of view of the men who were my teachers. How you man your faculty is much more important than how you make your curriculum."[2]

Owen and Jo had never moved far from St. Lawrence; they returned often and maintained close ties with Laurentian affairs and people. As a trustee since 1912, Young had helped with money raising and financial management, and had established a loan fund with his own money. As a member of the search committee when Dr. Almon Gunnison resigned as president in 1914, he corresponded widely with other colleges' presidents and trustees, which, not by accident, brought St. Lawrence to their notice. Tufts, another Universalist institution, was looking for a new president at the same time, and Young suggested, tongue in cheek, that they exchange candidates. For St. Lawrence this might have improved the situation, for its trustees' final choice had but a brief and unsuccessful career.

In 1919, Richard Eddy Sykes became president of the university. A native of Canton, he was a graduate of the college in 1883, and of the Theological School. He had served Universalist churches in Little Falls—seventeen miles from Van Hornesville—and in Denver, Colorado, and Malden, Massachusetts. It did not take him long to discover what he wanted in a chairman of the board of trustees—called on that campus the president of the corporation—and Owen Young was it. In 1924, with Jo's concurrence, Young accepted the office. During John Young's brief years in the college, 1920–22, and at the time of his death, Sykes and Young had come to know each other well, with mutual respect and understanding. It was a good partnership.[3]

As president of the corporation, Young devoted over the next decade a considerable portion of his much-demanded time to the affairs of his alma mater. He went to Canton as often as possible;[4] when he could not go he tended to college business in New York. It was a rule in the office in the Equitable Building that, no matter who else was there or expected, callers or messages on St. Lawrence business were attended to first.

The college in 1924 was not so different from the one Owen Young and Josie Edmonds had attended. One new building had been added early in the century—a gift from Andrew Carnegie for the sciences. In 1912 the enormous sum of $210,000 was raised for endowment, one-quarter of it in the form of a challenge grant from John D. Rockefeller's General Education Board, on which Owen Young was later to sit. The organization of the college and the curriculum was much the same as it had always been, and Charley Gaines was still teaching Greek.[5]

When Sykes came in, in 1919, there were 295 students, three times as many as in the 1890s, but hardly a large number. The institution needed just what it had needed in Dr. Hervey's day—more money and more students. Young and Sykes knew this, and they knew also that to bring the college into the modern world, more space and more buildings were essential.

It did not take them long to get started. A million-dollar drive for new buildings was undertaken in 1925; the old St. Lawrence families were the first to answer, and others followed. A year after Young had taken office, the plans for the Gunnison Memorial Chapel—designed by Jo's old friend Bertram Goodhue—were under way, the site for the Hepburn Hall of Chemistry was being discussed, and the Brewer Field House was complete. At the end of June 1925, Young wrote Emily Eaton Hepburn '86, the donor of the laboratory and a trustee, a long letter about progress on the campus: when the new buildings were ready, he said, St. Lawrence would have equipment second to none in its class. He also persuaded her to help with a new women's dormitory; a devoted alumna, Emily Hepburn was the widow of A. Barton Hepburn, president of the Chase National Bank, who also had been a generous donor to St. Lawrence.

Indeed, Young asked for help from all his friends, even the non–St. Lawrence ones. Many responded handsomely; Clarence Woolley of the American Radiator Company, for example, provided heating equipment for the new buildings at cost, as well as expertise and installations from his company. Young wrote him often and gratefully, explaining, "That little college is very near my heart, and I feel a great responsibility toward it, and as a rule you know, one's affection for anything is quite likely to be proportional to its needs."[6] He induced Charles Coffin to give the organ in the new chapel, and the head of B. Altman and Company to present a rich Oriental rug for the president's office. Some years later he persuaded Andrew Mellon, secretary of the treasury, and his brother Richard Mellon to join with George F. Baker and himself in building the men's residence, one of the handsomest on the St. Lawrence—or any other—campus. With his wife, Young gave an outdoor theater in honor of Cammie Gaines, Charley's wife and the drama coach of their day, and made a drama workshop out of a shed. But the building they cared about most, for special reasons, was the smallest of all: the Beta Theta Phi temple. Joining with Mrs. Hugh Abbott, mother of two St. Lawrence sons, they built a perfect little Greek temple for the chapter, commemorating the Abbott boys and John Young. To the Beta house itself, home of his two younger sons as well as John, Young was friend, adviser and donor over many years.

Yet perhaps Young's greatest contribution to the physical character of the modern St. Lawrence was not buildings, but land. The margins of the university's finances were narrow enough, and its current needs far more visible than future expansion. But to Young, the future seemed already pressing. Starting in the spring of 1925, he picked up farmland along the Potsdam Road to the east of the college—the only feasible direction for expansion—paying for it with his own money, selling off the crops and the farm buildings like the good farmer he was, adding altogether about six hundred acres. Young had a practical program in mind: "What I intend to do is to have the ground surveyed and the plan of the campus laid out. Whatever is needed, or can be advantageously used by the college, I mean to transfer to it. The remainder I will use to salvage as much of the original cost as possible."[7] It was not only that: Canton needed new residential areas as much as the college needed more space; these farms could provide both.

It was Young's favorite project to plant, along the property south of the road and east of the college, a quadruple avenue of elms nearly a mile long, such as he and Jo had seen in England, to be focused on the new chapel spire. A golf course was also laid out, house lots were divided, and by the sale of these he did indeed recoup some of his original expenditure, which in 1926 and 1927 amounted to more than $75,000. He presented lots to Dr. Sykes and Dr. Atwood, dean of the Theological School, for retirement homes; for use as a new president's house, he had renovated, decorated and furnished—this was largely Jo's work—a beautiful old house which stood, symbolically enough, between the main street and the campus.

The whole operation, expensive and time-consuming as it was, brought much satisfaction to Young; he enjoyed almost every minute of it. He loved land, and when it was in a place he loved—Van Hornesville, Canton—he wanted to own it, and put it in shape, and give it away. He liked buying it—for as low a price as possible—making plans for it, planting trees on it. Whether for elms or cows, vistas or houses, he wanted it used properly for the purpose, with care, proportion and beauty. The project at Canton gave him the scope he liked. "I can hardly wait," he wrote Sykes in the summer of 1925, "to get to Canton to see what progress is being made up there."[8]

iii

What Young did for his alma mater, as described so far, could have been done by any devoted chairman of the board of trustees who had foresight and imagination, taste and time and the money to work with. But Young's concern for St. Lawrence extended much farther than the improvement of the physical campus. From the very beginning of his chairmanship he applied himself to the problems of its academic structure, which, like the campus, had remained largely unchanged since his own day. College organization, like that of governments, is slow to keep pace with the times. St. Lawrence was still run by a president, a dean, a secretary, a treasurer, and a few helpers; the small faculty—not more than twenty—bore many burdens besides their teaching.

In the summer of 1925, after he had had a year in office, and after many private conversations, outside assessments and his own observations, Young wrote Dr. Sykes:

While I would not admit this to anyone else in the world but you, I have some question as to whether or not our curriculum and our teaching force is as good as it should be. I think that is one of the things toward which you will have to direct a good deal of thought and attention. I am more concerned about the faculty than the curriculum. It may be open to question whether the student has as many advantages today as you had or I when we went to St. Lawrence. Then there were few students, a few great men as teachers, and all the students had access to them. Now we have many students, a few excellent men, and other members of our faculty more or less floating.

Young knew that both the president and the dean were too busy with details of administration, the dean especially. Edwin L. Hulett, a man of relentless energy and multifold capabilities, had his days so full of work with the students—every one of whom he knew—and with the business of the college that there was little time left for academic affairs. Young suggested, in the same letter, the appointment of a dean of the faculty, to plan, lead and inspire the academic program. "I have a great horror," he ended, "of increasing buildings on the campus and diminishing effectiveness in the classroom."[9]

Changes in academic institutions are not made overnight; a year later Young was repeating these suggestions to the president, in somewhat stronger language. He spelled out also what he thought to be the president's job—the big things, not the day-by-day administration. As for the faculty, it "should learn to work together like a team and should be taught to do what other people have to do who are working in concert, namely be tolerant of others' views and accommodating in spirit." (It is possible that such admonitions worked better in the General Electric Company than with a college faculty.) But Young was trying very hard to realign the machinery, get rid of the rust, and move it forward. At the end he concluded: "This letter expresses my personal views only. In it the President of the Board of Trustees does not speak."[10]

Pastorates had not provided Sykes with the training or experience for tough administration; he was tenderhearted, understanding and sympathetic. Young encouraged him to fire unsatisfactory people and to maintain his decisions firmly; but the chairman never failed to put in the "I do not wish this letter in any sense to seem to be an intrusion by me, nor do I wish to be in the position of rendering volunteer advice."[11]

He was, of course, but the relationship between the two was strong enough to take the strain. The letters flew back and forth; in 1926, for example, letters from Young to Canton—largely to Sykes—averaged twenty-seven a month. This was not concern alone; he enjoyed taking part in the college's affairs, even when he could not be in Canton. After one visit he wrote Dean Hulett: "It is a pleasure to go up there and see the things accomplished, and particularly the things to be done. All of us will have much more work than we can do during all our lives to make that college what we wish to see it. It is a great privilege, however, to belong to an institution in which there are so many things to do rather than to an institution in which everything has been done." And the following year he was writing Irving Bacheller, the author, who was a close friend and fellow trustee, urging him to come to the fall meeting:

We shall have the Dean and a special Committee of the Board, a complete review of the scholastic activities of the College, of the teaching force, and generally a complete review and inquiry into the educational work of the Institution. That is a subject to which we should now devote our best attention. We do not need to worry about students in the sense we used to in the old days, nor do we need to worry so much about physical accommodations. They are inadequate but they always will be, I hope. When an institution gets a plant and an endowment adequate, or which it thinks is adequate, that means that it is dead and has no growth.[12]

iv

Other aspects of St. Lawrence kept the president of the corporation busy as well. Under his leadership, the character of the board became more progressive, and more representative of the graduates. As the numbers of the student body increased, more scholarship money was provided, largely by Young himself. He was always interested in the college radio station, and in the *Laurentian*, which he had saved

from bankruptcy by sound management in his own college days. Most
of all, he cared about the library; whenever he received a fee for an
article or other writing, he sent it to Sykes for books. In November
1925 he wrote, sending eight hundred dollars received for an article
on household electrification in the *Delineator*, "I do not want the kind
of books which stay on the shelves. I want the kind of books which the
students will wear out—the quicker the better. Then I will write another article on something or other, and we will make the women of
the U.S. buy us some more books."[13]

Not least important of Young's off-campus activities for his college
were his efforts to make it better known. In one respect New York in
the 1920s was little different from Boston in the 1890s when Young
was in law school: most people had never heard of St. Lawrence. On
the upper levels of the academic world it was considered a sleepy little
freshwater college. The man who woke it up wanted it to be known
and well-known everywhere. Especially in the awarding of honorary
degrees Young raised the sights; the list during his term and after is
a roster of great distinction. Of these, the most widely publicized and
most satisfying to Young was that to Marie Curie in 1929, when she
dedicated the Hepburn laboratory and received the degree of Doctor
of Science *honoris causa*.

The Curie visit had been long planned and hoped for by Young.
For some years the General Electric Company had been presenting
the Curie laboratory with equipment, for which she wrote touching
letters of thanks to the chairman.[14] Mme Curie's best friend in the
United States was Mrs. William Brown Meloney, at that time editor
of the Sunday magazine of the *New York Herald*, and a formidable
figure in journalistic and other fields in New York City. She was the
instigator of a fund to buy a gram of radium for Marie Curie to present to her native Poland—which was the most passionate desire of
the scientist's heart, since Poland owned no radium at all. To this
fund Young had contributed generously, and persuaded others to do
the same; his *quid pro quo* was a visit to St. Lawrence when Mme
Curie came to the United States. "Missy" Meloney, who knew St.
Lawrence and had lectured there, agreed.

Marie Curie, in spite of her frailty, came to the United States in the
fall of 1929, attended the Golden Jubilee of Thomas Alva Edison (put
on by Henry Ford in Dearborn to celebrate the invention of the incandescent lamp), visited the General Electric laboratories in Schenectady, and even spent a night in Van Hornesville, to which Owen

Young had whisked her secretly to get her away from the crowds who gathered at the very mention of her name.

The following weekend, October 24–26, she spent at St. Lawrence, where, she discovered, she was already present in her image, like a stone saint, at the door of the Hepburn Hall of Chemistry. Ten thousand people attended the ceremony of dedication, though few heard the short and touching speech of the tiny gray-haired lady, the only one she made during her stay in the United States. Though her visit to this country coincided with the collapse of the stock market, the press gave her enormous coverage from start to finish, and St. Lawrence received more notice than in all its previous history. From there she went to the White House, where Young and Missy Meloney had arranged that the money for the gram of radium should be presented to her by President Hoover.

Owen Young and Marie Curie, because of their correspondence since 1925, were like old friends; face to face, they took to each other at once. To him, and to his family, whom she accepted immediately and warmly, from Ida Young to ten-year-old Richard, her visit was unforgettable. Her indomitable purpose shone through her body, almost destroyed by radium, like the incandescent lamp so recently celebrated. Her wrinkled face, her crippled hands were nothing compared to the light in her eyes, the warmth in her manner. To the world at that moment she was, as the press repeatedly called her, "the greatest woman scientist." Owen Young, in his introduction of her at St. Lawrence, called her "the greatest scientist."

In the hard years of the early thirties there were no more big projects on the campus. Owen Young was left with his pledge for the men's dormitory to pay, and the problems—common to all educational institutions—of guiding the college through the worst of the depression. In the fall of 1933 he was asked to stand for another ten-year term as president of the corporation, when the current term was up in June of 1934. It was certainly a *pro forma* request; St. Lawrence without Owen Young at the helm was unthinkable to the present regime. But he refused, saying younger men should take over; Sykes was planning to retire, after fifteen years as president, and there is no doubt that they felt they had done what they could for the college and would be glad to put it in other hands.[15] But it is also probable, though no record exists in the files, that Young had had intimations of something else coming up which would preclude his acceptance of another term at St. Lawrence. And it was so: in February 1934 he was elected by the legislature to the Board of Regents of the State of New York; a regent is not permitted to hold any office in any educational institution in the state.

v

Concurrently with the developments at St. Lawrence in the later years of the 1920s, another educational project was taking shape under Young's guiding hand. On this too he expended loving care and money, and, in a way, it meant even more to him than the college.

On the night of December 16, 1926, the little white wooden schoolhouse in Van Hornesville burned to the ground. It had stood on the same site as Owen's red schoolhouse, on a bank above the main road and below the cemetery, with very little space about it for playgrounds.[16] Silas C. Kimm, superintendent of schools for the southern district of Herkimer County, wrote Young at once, suggesting "a larger and better site" and a "modern up-to-date school building, one that will fit in with your village improvements and that will be the pride of Van Hornesville and the whole Town of Stark. Why not make the best little schoolhouse in Herkimer County?"[17]

Kimm knew his man, and Young knew Kimm. They had been friends for a long time; Young described him as concealing under a quiet exterior a burning volcano, and he knew that if he did not do as Kimm suggested he would have no peace. Besides, he wanted to do just that.

For some years Owen Young had been working on the "improvements" in Van Hornesville which Kimm referred to. His mother's place had always looked well, but lately he had put in beds of flowers and masses of flowering shrubs for her pleasure, and built a small greenhouse so she could have flowers in the long Van Hornesville winters. He remembered the little primroses she had enclosed in her letters to him at college, plucked from a plant on her kitchen windowsill at the farm.

The millpond, visible from the bay window where she sat in her rocker, was cleaned and deepened and its bank cleared and made into lawn. The Universalist church opposite her house was repaired and painted, the Methodist church on the north side of her house as well. The scrubby little pasture in the center of the village became a proper green with a flagpole, shrubs, trees and a pool with a rockery; no longer could Uncle John Brandow break down the barbed-wire fence around it when his Model T didn't "whoa" when he said "Whoa!" Streetlights surrounded it, and were set along the main street in both directions—old-fashioned lights, square lanterns on wooden poles. The switch to turn them on and off was in Mother Young's kitchen; she put them on at dusk, and off when she went to bed. On clear nights of full moon she did not turn them on at all.

Elms were planted up and down the main street (in Van Hornesville the main street is almost the only street), and the sidewalks were repaved. The old Van Horne House, built about 1803 by Daniel and Richard Van Horne, sons of Abram, the founder of the village (and hence remote cousins of Owen Young), had been falling to pieces for decades; this he bought, renovated and gave to his daughter. An even older house across the creek he repaired and gave to his eldest son. The next son, Philip, was given the Home Farm when he married. Repairs, fresh paint and newly planted trees began to appear at the homes of other citizens, and soon Van Hornesville was losing its run-down look; Sundays brought a slow-moving stream of admirers along the main street.

These changes gave Owen Young great satisfaction; they were to him, both in Van Hornesville and at St. Lawrence, a grateful return for the important influences in his own past, and an evidence of his concern not only for the present but for the future of his college and his hometown. He was critical of those successful men—some from nearby and similar background—who did nothing for their birthplaces, and indeed never returned.

Pleased as he was with the village, Young was not happy about conditions among his native hills. Life on the farm was little improved from what he had known forty years before; in some respects it was worse. Health services were much less good, education in the one-room schools had changed little for the better, the churches had declined in membership and influence, the Grange was dying. Electricity and hard roads were nonexistent outside the bigger towns; Van Hornesville, in spite of Young's best efforts, had neither until 1923. Sharing in the general agricultural depression of the 1920s, the local farmers saw their income and land values decline, their fixed charges increase, and their young people leaving the farms for the cities. Helpless against these larger trends, Young did what he could by demonstrating, on his own farms, how purebred cows gave more milk, modern methods of crop rotation and new varieties of seed and fertilizer produced larger crops, and modern machinery could be made to pay for itself. He fought for better roads to reduce isolation and to get the milk to

market, first in Albany with the commissioner of highways, and locally with the town board. Sometimes he donated money himself, when
public funds were inadequate, which they usually were as the tax
base shrank. When it came to getting a snowplow to keep the road to
Fort Plain and the railroad open in winter, Young bought it himself.

vi

Gradually, turning over the idea of a new school, Young came to see
that here was the opportunity, not only to make the most important
"improvement" of all, but, perhaps, to effect some lasting betterment
of conditions in the Town of Stark. In March of 1927 he began to
move; the schoolchildren, after all, could not do with makeshift quarters forever. He came home for his mother's eighty-eighth birthday,
stayed several days, and met with Kimm and the school trustee, Clyde
Smith. He bought from his neighbor the miller, Otis Harrad, farmland
at the north end of the village; some of it, between the main road and
the creek, was level enough for a building and playgrounds, with
space for ball fields. On March 14 Young presented Smith with a
proposal, to be acted on at a special school meeting. This offered
three acres of land, the construction of a schoolhouse, and the presentation of both to School District No. 1 at no cost to the taxpayers,
with the provision that the old site up the road be transferred to
Young.

The record of the meeting, held on March 22, indicates that of the
twenty-nine legal voters present all but one voted to accept the site
and convey the old one to Young; the vote to accept a new building
was unanimous.

It was a small beginning. On that same day Young replied to a
letter from a builder who had asked about the new school, "I shall
not be obliged to deal with any of the details of [the building's] construction."[18] He was never more wrong in his life. Over the next
months and years he became even more involved in construction than
he was at St. Lawrence.

Architects and contractors wrote in by the score as the news got
around, and Young was fortunate to find the perfect architect. Ernest
Sibley was a specialist in school buildings, and, as well, an architect
ready and willing to listen to his employer. He soon grasped the idea
that this building was to be more than a schoolhouse; his first general

specifications include the note that the school was to be brought "in direct touch with the living conditions and interests of the native inhabitants," and to "provide education that will put the rural child on a basis of equality with children of the urban communities"; important also would be "economy of plan and design as an object lesson to other rural districts."[19] The last was not to come true as fully as the first two, but in all three specifications we hear the voice of the number-one "native inhabitant."

Sibley and Young saw eye to eye on most of the details of the plans, and if they did not, they could work out their differences. This was well, for the method of construction of the building was unusual. Young described it at the ceremony of July 4, 1928, when the cornerstone was filled with the records, and the building was nearly complete:

> Now this building stands for the things which I like. We have developed it largely from our own resources, both of men and materials. The stones which make it have been gathered from our fields—not carelessly but selectively. The men who made it have been largely gathered from this immediate country and have understanding of this place. The stones have been picked for size and durability and color, and hundreds have been rejected where one was taken. The men have been picked for character and skill in their respective jobs. And so we shall have a building here, not only beautiful in its materials but a monument to the craftsmanship and devotion of the men who made it . . . while I personally get much public credit for this building, my contribution is the least of all. The only work I was qualified to do was to dig on the foundations, which I did long enough to have my picture taken with my friend and associate of many years, Mr. Abram Tilyou.[20]

When the building was wholly complete, a bronze tablet was placed in the entrance which named these men and their respective contributions—including C. J. Young, who planned the radio and movie equipment; and at the end it read:

THIS BUILDING WAS BUILT BY THE COOPERATION
OF THE MEN NAMED ABOVE AND MANY OTHERS
WHO AIDED AND ASSISTED THEM
AND WITHOUT THE SERVICES OF A CONTRACTOR
A SUPERINTENDENT OR A BOSS

Who needed them for a project whose list of participants ended "Abram Tilyou and Owen D. Young, Rocking Chair Consultants"?

vii

The building of the Van Hornesville School did not pass unnoticed; in the surrounding countryside it soon became a cause for pride and a monument to visit. In educational circles it was regarded as an innovation, a subject for study and—possibly—emulation. In the nation, the name of its donor assured it wide publicity. As more and more articles appeared about the school, especially the long ones with pictures in the *New York Times* and the *Knickerbocker Press*, letters flooded into Young's office. Many sought jobs or contracts, but many others expressed admiration of the gift and the plans. Friends and strangers wrote, some sent gifts—a book, a picture, money—for the school. All of these Young answered; his reply to Elmer Ellsworth Brown, chancellor of New York University, is typical: "I owe a debt of gratitude to my home village for the privilege which they have given me of providing a school building, and likewise a debt to you and my other friends who treat it as something worthy on my part to do. As a matter of fact, I am getting fun enough out of it so that nobody owes me anything."[21]

The letters which counted most were those which said, in effect, we want to do likewise. These he answered with many pages of detail. He asked Sibley to send out photos to all who requested them: "It will sharpen the taste of everyone who sees it for better school buildings architecturally." He wrote to another correspondent: "I am hopeful that the general character of this little school at Van Hornesville will have some influence on the type and character of rural schools. They have always been uninviting and, to some extent, inefficient plants."[22]

Inside as well as outside, Young had a hand in the planning. Everything that his little red schoolhouse did not have, and needed, must be included in the new school: a teachers' room, a lunchroom, flush toilets and hot showers, many windows and attractively furnished rooms. When he came to the library, he wanted special furniture; not finding in stores what he had in mind, he had a fine cabinetmaker in Fort Plain copy the "Pennsylvania Sofa" in Independence Hall in Philadelphia; the chairs and big table, all hand-carved and made of Mexican mahogany, were copied from beautiful Chippendale models. The result was the handsomest room in Van Hornesville. One thing was added to this room in later days, but not by him: his portrait, by Leonebel Jacobs, over the mantelpiece.

Young saw the library as a service for the community as well as the school. He was very conscious of the decline of the church as a communal center in rural villages; when he was a boy the worship and work and play in the Universalist church had been of paramount importance in the social as well as the religious life of the little family on the Home Farm. Over the years the local Universalist church, like the denomination in general, became smaller and weaker, until finally no services were held at all. The Methodist church, with Young's encouragement and support, made efforts to reach the larger community, and with the backing of its stronger denomination, it survived. But Young felt that the school must become the center, and it was for this that he provided, intitially, the library and the movies and the evening classes for adult education.

It soon became clear, even when the school was very new, that its two classrooms, library, teachers' room and other small spaces would soon be outgrown and an addition must be built. It was the beginning of the era of centralization; the State Education Department was anxious to merge as far as possible the small rural schools. In fact, when Young's school was first talked about, the department wanted to make centralization a condition of the gift. This Young refused to do; there had been "a great deal of antagonism to the closing of the district schools . . . a great deal of bitterness resulted. . . . Accordingly, I told the Department that we would try an experiment of persuasion as distinguished from coercion."[23] So he said in effect, "If they want to come, let them come."

They came. The school, which in its first form in Owen Young's mind was only a glorified version of his own little red schoolhouse, was tranformed into one of the first centralized schools in the state, with grades kindergarten to twelve, equipped to send its pupils on to college. A dozen or more small rural school districts merged, a board of education was organized, buses were bought, and as soon as the addition was finished, the Van Hornesville Central School was in business.

The new building, much larger than the first one, was built in 1931, also of stone and in the same style, but this time by a contractor. Owen Young, however, paid for it all. It contained not only additional classrooms, locker rooms, and so forth, but a cafeteria and a handsome auditorium, as well as the science laboratory which Young had promised Marie Curie that one day he would build and name for her. There was, too, outside, a swimming pool. Owen had never learned to swim as a boy; in fact, he never did learn, and he was determined that every child in his school should know how.

The new plant required still another building. Young was greatly worried about getting for his school teachers worthy of it. The village was still remote, or people thought it was, and salaries were no higher than in other, "more civilized" places. And, most important, there were almost no good places for teachers to live in Van Hornesville. So he built opposite the school another handsome stone building, which not he but the village people called the "Teacherage." The central part was the residence of the principal, the two wings provided small, completely equipped apartments for teachers; Jo Young furnished and decorated the whole building charmingly. "I want," Young used to say, "the building where the principal and the teachers live to be the handsomest place in town."

At the time of the cornerstone ceremony Young had paid tribute to his own old teachers, and had asked all of them who were still alive to attend and speak, beginning with Mark Hollister. In his own talk on the construction of the school he described his teachers as "architects and artisans dealing with intangibles—buildings of the imagination and understanding on a foundation of character." The "Teacherage" was another way to emphasize the importance of the teacher, in the school and in the community.

All in all, Young was very pleased with the institution he had created in Van Hornesville. He was especially pleased because the centralization had come about of its own accord, with no appreciable rise in school taxes—for, since the buildings were free and clear, there were no bonds to amortize or pay interest on. When the children saw the school they wanted to come to it; when the parents heard about the twice-weekly movies at the parent-teacher meetings, with newly released films straight from RKO, they wanted to come too. Young was delighted when a farmer from the hills, who had borrowed money from him, came to explain why he could not repay it within the stipulated time. His children, he said, of whom there were many, and upon whom he depended to do the work of the farm, had struck; no more work, they declared, unless he built them an inside bathroom "like the ones at school," white tiles, flush toilet, hot running water and all. "It's all your fault, Mr. Young," he said.[24]

viii

The cost to Young had been something over half a million dollars, but he thought it was worth it, especially as the youthful first principal, Maurice S. Hammond, proved equally eager to make the school known for the quality of its education. Young wrote Hammond many letters, as he did Sykes at St. Lawrence, about the high standards he must have in hiring teachers and in making effective use of all the school's resources, actual and potential. Rural medicine, for example, had always seemed to Young next in importance to, and closely allied with, rural education; he saw his school as a center for the improvement of both. He knew that many of the children on the farms in the hills were undernourished, that incipient diseases went undiscovered or were neglected. He wrote Dean Thomas Ordway of Albany Medical College: "When I was a boy, there were two doctors in Van Hornesville, and they rode out for a radius of three or four miles to the surrounding farms. There was not a family in that whole vicinity which they did not know intimately . . . it was practically impossible for any person in that vicinity to have anything much the matter with him without one of those doctors knowing it." There was, he pointed out, no such medical care now in the area; there were no doctors in the villages, and only rudimentary public-health services. He wanted to see what could be done, with the school as the center.[25]

Dr. Ordway came to Van Hornesville to see for himself. The visit fired him with enthusiasm. Consultations were held with the nearest doctors, all of whom were at least a dozen miles away. Dr. Ordway persuaded the Rockefeller Foundation to allow the Albany Medical College to use part of their grant to set up the program; he also produced from his own staff the perfect doctor to operate it—"a person," he wrote Young, "unusually well adapted . . . to the work we have in mind." In the fall of 1932 Dr. Dorothy Henderson began the work, and laid some foundations in both school and community. She won the confidence of the children and hence of their parents, and moved out from the school examining room into the farmhouses in the hills, where her skill and charming manner brought her immediate acceptance.[26]

The satisfaction which all this gave Owen Young was increased by the pleasure his mother took in it. Eighty-eight in that March of 1927 when the site was bought and the plans for the school begun, she watched with intense interest every move, from the first excavation to the last slate on the roof. Owen talked over the plans with her, asked for her ideas, thought out loud with her about future developments. She knew almost everyone that worked on the first building, some of them for decades past. She followed the expenditures, for her brother John Brandow was paymaster, and kept the payroll book in his oak rolltop desk in her sitting room. Rocking a little in her chair in the evenings, perhaps with a small nightcap in her hand, she would deliver pronouncements on wages, plans, personnel and how Owen was spending too much money. She too was a product of a tiny rural school, a mile and a half to the south of Van Hornesville, and had walked a mile from her home every school day, carrying in winter a hot baked potato in her mittens, to keep her hands warm and to eat for lunch. This new school was pretty fancy, she thought, but she approved of it; besides, Owen wanted it that way.

Chapter 22

The Young Collection:
"Next to My Family
Come My Books"

T HERE had been few books in the farmhouse on the hills above Van Hornesville: the big Bible in its coat of worn leather, the doctor book, the horse-doctor book, a fat edition of all the *Leatherstocking Tales* in double columns of fine print, perhaps *Our Home* in an elegant, embossed red cover. And there was little time to read. Owen met English and American literature for the first time on the shelves of the small library of the East Springfield Academy. At St. Lawrence there was no money to buy books except the essential textbooks; those saved from college days are mainly manuals for science courses and foreign grammars and dictionaries. There is also a notebook from a course in English literature—but a good part of the notes are in Josephine Edmonds's hand. A paperback of Whittier's poems, inscribed "Young and Spurr '94," volume two of the prose works of Emerson (with the bookplate of the college library), and *The Last Essays of Elia* in an edition so cheap in paper and binding that it almost disintegrates in the hand—these are the flotsam from the college years of a man who was to collect first editions of all these authors, especially of Lamb.

Owen Young's devoted friend Caleb Fisher encouraged from the first his love of books. Even on the salary of a Universalist minister, Fisher acquired over the years an impressive library of good editions, wide-ranging through English and American writers. When he died in 1923, many of these went to St. Lawrence, but Owen himself took the beautiful Scribner's 1902 edition of Stevenson to remind him of his first bookish friend.

After his marriage he had another book lover at his side; in the house on Avon Hill Street in Cambridge and the house on the hill in

Lexington the shelves were full. Josephine had brought with her from Southbridge a good collection of her own, which she had used at Radcliffe and in teaching her English literature class. Their children grew up surrounded by books. One of the daughter's first memories is of her father in his big winged rocking chair with a book on his knee; when she learned to read she ensconced herself there, trying to look as much like him as possible.

As their income increased they were able to buy more books, both old and new. Boston was full of bookstores, and, by modern standards at least, books were cheap. The Old Corner Book Store appears frequently in their checkbooks of the period, among the household bills and the music and dancing lessons for the children. In the year 1910, for instance, they spent $128 there and at Little, Brown—not a large sum but one that then bought a lot of books.

From its opening in 1898 Owen Young was often in Goodspeed's little basement shop on Park Street, where on winter days the wood fire crackled in the old fireplace. From Goodspeed he learned something of first editions and their values as he fingered the motley collection on the shelves and tables and floor. Goodspeed sold engravings to Charles Tyler, especially of American dignitaries, which were hung throughout his offices; Young often chatted with Goodspeed when he arrived with a roll of prints. Goodspeed described Young as "a genial dark-haired young man who was never too busy to make himself agreeable to the young print-peddler."[1]

By the time the family moved to New York, books were a substantial part of their household goods, and again the shelves were filled and more had to be built, both in the apartment at 830 Park and at Little Point. In the latter place, also, the Youngs acquired with the purchase of the house a considerable number of Lincoln Steffens's books, including many odd volumes collected on his travels.

It was not until he became chairman of the board of the General Electric Company that Young was able to move into the higher levels of collecting. He and Jo had bought engravings and early American furniture under Tyler's sophisticated tutelage, but when it came to serious collecting it was natural for both of them to turn to books.

Gabriel Wells, the well-known book dealer, pointed out, in an article published in the very month and year that Young began his serious collecting, that "collecting is grounded in sentiment," and that the collector must be "essentially actuated by his feelings" if he is to get "the true collector's thrill."[2] So it was with Owen Young; the emotional and sentimental nature beneath his quiet and relaxed exterior played a vital part in his collecting. His books and manuscripts were not *things*—objects of safaris or just the result of the expenditure of large sums of money. Each was a voice and part of a person. As his collecting progressed, he came to know each author better, and to be on an intimate footing with Thackeray, Dickens, Lewis Carroll and the Lambs. One only needed to see how he handled his books, turned over the leaves of manuscripts, drew a letter of John Keats's from its original envelope, to understand how close he felt to them.

ii

He began slowly. The first substantial purchases were, properly enough, from Goodspeed's, in April of 1923: a set of George Borrow's works—probably a present for Jo on her birthday, April 21, for Borrow was one of her favorite authors; Thackeray's *Virginians*, 1858, with an autograph letter; Lowell's *Bigelow Papers* in a first edition. The purchases totaled $210.

But it was England that set him on course. The trip to Europe in the summer of 1923, with both Josephines, turned out to be a literary pilgrimage—except when Owen spied a fine-looking herd of Holstein cattle and insisted on stopping to discuss them with the owner. They visited Lamb's grave at Edmonton, Dickens's house at Gadshill, and, it seemed, every old-book shop in the cathedral towns of England.[3] But it was in London that Young spent most of his free moments, then and in many visits thereafter. In 1924, during his long exile, first at the London Conference and then as acting agent-general for reparations, he explored the market whenever he had time, going from book dealer to book dealer, finding out about people and prices, making his own judgments on what and where he wanted to buy.

Days in Paris found him in bookshops too; he bought a whole set of firsts of Anatole France, an author whom he much admired, although he preferred to read him in English. His wife wrote home that she had had to buy a new trunk because Owen wanted to keep Anatole France always with him—even in French. Balzac too was a favorite, rated only below Thackeray; he bought an unpublished manuscript, *Les Fantaisies de la Gina*, and had it translated with an eye to publication, although this never came about.

The Owen D. Young Collection of rare books and manuscripts became, in the next five years, so extensive, and its putting together involved so much of his money, that it is important to ask what he was

trying to do—for it was no haphazard affair, something for a newly
wealthy man to spend money on. Yachts and mansions did not interest him or Jo, and they did not care to change their way of life. But
books were living things which had always been a part of that life,
and adding more—even rare and expensive ones—required no change.
In Riverside Owen still fished from the old motorboat, and in Van
Hornesville he still came in through the woodshed to leave his boots,
muddy from the barnyard, and ate supper with his mother next to the
woodstove in the kitchen.

Major responsibilities made great and constant demands upon
Young's time and strength in the short, crowded years between May
of 1922 and October of 1929. But they did not blot out the more private concerns for which he cared the most. His books, he said, next
to his family, were closest to his heart; but neither they nor the cows
were merely for pleasure and recreation. Whether he was studying the
Holstein-Friesian World with an eye to possible outcrosses, or the
latest lists from Charles Sawyer or Gabriel Wells—or a frantic scrawl
from Walter Spencer saying that he had just gotten in absolutely the
best thing that ever came into the shop—Young had always in mind
what he wanted to do and where he wanted to come out. There was
a purpose in both programs, and he studied hard to acquire the knowledge which would enable him to accomplish them. He soon learned
to read rare-book catalogues as easily as herd books, quickly extracting
the essentials he needed, and to examine the rare books themselves
with the same sharpness with which he once read public-utility franchises and General Electric contracts. He was painstaking and careful,
knowing well that the rare-book trade was at least as tricky as cattle
trading. And he exercised with his books, as with his cattle, his intuition, his "feel" for what was right in condition, in value, and what
was not. A contract, an animal, a book in his hands gave him some
message inexpressible in words. He tried to explain this in a letter
to a bookseller when he returned Trollope's *Macdermots*:

When I first saw the book, as you know, I did not somehow receive the
thrill from it which a volume of that character should give. Later, the top
of my head rather than the seat of my pants got busy, and I thought I liked
it fairly well. After having it around for a week or two, I felt a return of
the same old instinctive reaction, so that when I picked up the volume, it
not only failed to give me pleasure, but I kept wishing it to be different.
That, of course, is the test of whether one wants to keep a book in his
library.[4]

With this kind of knowledge and feel, he developed his plan. When,

The new Van Hornesville, about 1925: the road, sidewalk and streetlights are new but the horses are still there; the Universalist church, freshly painted, abides

The village house lived in by Ida Young and her family from 1903 until her death in 1931

Ida Young, her brother John Brandow and Abram Tilyou in the village house, with Owen's diplomas on the wall

Young and one of his cows, the Home Farm, fall 1941. Eric Schaal, *New York Times*

Young and others breaking ground for the new school

The Rocking Chair consultants upright

The new school

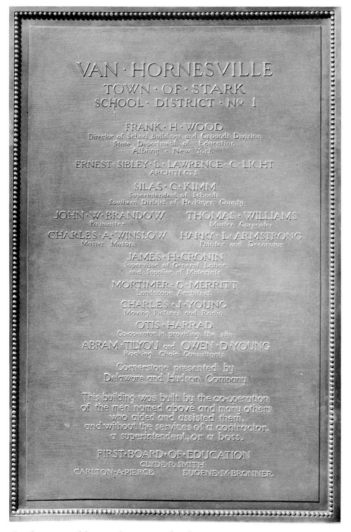

VAN · HORNESVILLE
TOWN · OF · STARK
SCHOOL · DISTRICT · Nº 1

FRANK · H · WOOD
Director of School Buildings and Grounds Division
State Department of Education
Albany · New York

ERNEST · SIBLEY · & · LAWRENCE · C · LICHT
ARCHITECTS

SILAS · C · KIMM
Superintendent of Schools
Southern District of Herkimer County

JOHN · W · BRANDOW   THOMAS · WILLIAMS
Paymaster   Master Carpenter

CHARLES · A · WINSLOW   HARRY · L · ARMSTRONG
Master Mason   Painter and Decorator

JAMES · H · CRONIN
Supervisor of General Labor
and Supplier of Materials

MORTIMER · C · MERRITT
Landscape Architect

CHARLES · J · YOUNG
Moving Pictures and Radio

OTIS · HARRAD
Co-operator in providing the site

ABRAM · TILYOU and OWEN · D · YOUNG
Rocking Chair Consultants

Cornerstone presented by
Delaware and Hudson Company

This building was built by the co-operation
of the men named above and many others
who aided and assisted them,
and without the services of a contractor,
a superintendent, or a boss.

FIRST · BOARD · OF · EDUCATION
CLYDE · R · SMITH
CARLTON · A · PIERCE   EUGENE · M · BRONNER

The bronze tablet in the new school

Henry Ford and Owen Young at a plowing contest, South Hartford, New York, August 21, 1938

in 1927, his friend Samuel Reyburn, the head of Lord and Taylor's department store, wrote asking for advice on collecting books, Young's reply gave, in the first sentence, his answer: "May I suggest that you first define in your own mind the field in which you think you would like to operate."[5] The area Young defined for himself certainly was wide enough: to put together a collection of the great books in English, each in its earliest appearance, each in as perfect a condition as could be obtained. To this central idea he adhered, although as he found unique treasures it was broadened to include manuscripts, letters, illustrations, and minor kinds of ancillary material, such as portraits of Thackeray, Dickens's tea caddy, Horace Walpole's traveling writing desk.

His main purpose he achieved. He had the money and the knowledge to do it, and somehow he found the time. New York booksellers—at least the really good ones—soon became accustomed, from 1925 to 1929, to seeing the tall figure bending over their best books around six in the evening, as he stopped in en route from 120 Broadway to 830 Park Avenue. Some, indeed, as they began to understand the breadth of his interests and the size of his purse, stayed open late on purpose. He went also to book sales, on the few occasions when a free evening coincided with one. Although book dealers did much of his buying for him at sales, he enjoyed the excitement of the auction and the thrill of bidding more than he should spend—as he did at the cattle sales in Earlville, New York.

He made some good friends in the field—Mitchell Kennerley, Barnet Beyer, Edgar Wells, Gabriel Wells, James Drake. It was to Drake that he wrote, when the dealer offered to negotiate for him the purchase of a large library: "I have a feeling that I can get more fun for my money in small thrills over a long period than one big thrill in a short period."[6] He wanted to do his own hunting and finding and "negotiate" his own purchases.

He did, however, accept negotiation in the case of his purchase of his Shakespeare First Folio, for a special reason. The folio was owned by James Fenimore Cooper, the grandson of the novelist, whose home was not far from Van Hornesville in Cooperstown, and whom Young knew as a friend. He asked Edgar Wells—who had been initially recommended to him by Nelson Perkins—to handle the purchase; the folio came into Young's possession for thirty thousand dollars, and Cooper wrote him: "We are glad to have the Folio in such good hands; it doesn't leave our neighborhood! I doubt if another as good ever will come on the market."[7]

A dealer and book friend of unique cast was A. W. S. Rosenbach of Philadelphia. There was only one "Rosy" in the book-collecting world, and Young came to know the idiosyncratic qualities of the "eye-twinkling, hard-selling, hard-drinking, scholarly bookman." They appreciated each other, from the early days of 1925 when Young bought Dickens and Thackeray items from Rosenbach; later his purchases were in almost every area of English and American literature, for no one had the stock that Rosy collected both at home and abroad. "Dr. Rosenbach was delighted with Young's excitement over his purchases," said Rosenbach's biographer, "his careful study of what he bought, and his willingness to pay the asked-for prices. Young loved the books he bought, and as far as money was concerned, the Doctor once summed it up very neatly, 'Owen Young is perplexed about the economics of this business; and so am I!' "[8]

When in 1929 the catalogues for the Jerome Kern sale appeared,

the huddles over whisky glasses and catalogues began at 15 East 51st St. [Rosenbach's New York house]. Owen Young of General Electric, whose stock, well over 200, had gone up fourteen points in the past week, was the richest and the hungriest of the private buyers—and the cagiest. He was spreading his bids among various dealers. He would not commit himself too deeply with the Doctor, but it was obvious that he was interested, greatly interested, and Dr. Rosenbach's keen eye noted those lots which set his pulse beating faster as they leafed through the catalogue together.[9]

As it turned out, Young bought most of his Kern items later on from Rosy; among these were two extremely high-priced items; one an autograph manuscript of part of Pope's *Essay on Man* at twenty-nine thousand dollars plus the 10 percent for the dealer. (Vere Goldthwaite was long in his grave, but how delighted he would have been to know that his friend and partner was able to spend so much money on a poem to which he had introduced him.) The other most expensive item was *Tom Jones*, at the same price; of Tom, more later.

The book dealer whose company Young enjoyed the most, and with whom he spent more time than any other, was the old rascal at 27 New Oxford Street in London, Walter T. Spencer. When the Youngs walked into his shop for the first time in the summer of 1924, and bought *Coloured Views of North America*, some old maps, an aquatint of a sea fight and the *Hunting of the Snark*, for a total of twenty-five pounds, none of them knew what a funny, sad, interesting relationship they would have over the years. But almost from that first day, and on every succeeding trip to London, Young spent many hours in the shop. It was no ordinary bookstore; Jo described it in a letter to her daughter of October 1924:

Today Pops wasn't busy—so went to Spencer's again. I shan't try to tell you about Spencer's—I'll just bring you over here sometime and set you down in this tiny old bookshop—provided his one chair isn't occupied, and you'll be surrounded by the loveliest books you ever saw—some fine bindings, of course, but more interesting from their contents. He reached behind me the other day—pulled down a piece of paste board tied up with white string and inside was Bobbie Burns' "O Scots wha hae with Wallace bled"— Bannockburn isn't it?—the original manuscript, stained and darned across the centre with zigzag stitches, but all there! Mr. Spencer has known all the literary men of forty years—I'm bringing home his book of Recollections— autographed—and rambles along about Stevenson and E. V. Lucas and Dickens' sister-in-law, of whom he got many things,—Tennyson and the Brownings—He showed me the little copy of Tennyson's "Maud," which Tennyson read aloud to the Brownings and the Rossettis one evening here in London. He knew Lewis Carroll well—and Tenniel who did the pictures —and we're bringing home a first edition with seventeen of the original Tenniel drawings—exquisite things.

Pops has developed a taste for Thackeray first editions, and he—and we—have visited bookshops—and studied catalogues, until the results will speak for themselves when we return. It is a blessed relief for him to have something to take up his mind when off duty.[10]

Young had his own room upstairs at Spencer's amid a great dump-pile of books and papers, where one might find anything or nothing. He spent a lot of time looking, sometimes with success.

In August of 1927 he was in London, after the meeting of the International Chamber of Commerce at Stockholm, and had some free time. He had hoped to see his friend Howard Levis, chairman of the British Thomson-Houston Company, but the Levises had left for a vacation in Scotland. Young wrote him:

I wanted at least an opportunity to tell you of what I am doing. Most of my hours are spent up in a little old room at the top of Spencer's building which he has fixed up for me, in which I am surrounded with pamphlets, plates and other literary junk, mostly of the 17th century. I say mostly, because there is no order to it and no dating—just a mass of stuff which is not very familiar. . . . No other such supply of material, I am sure, exists in the world, and Spencer has told me that if I wanted to go up and pick out what I liked I could do so, because he would never be able himself to sort out that material. . . .

Young's efforts paid off, for three days later he was writing Levis again:

Spencer and I were sitting up in the top room of the old building yesterday afternoon, pulling over a pile of dust-laden books and pamphlets, and we pulled out a volume in folio size, bound in old calf, with the title of "Miscellaneous" on the back, and when we opened it [it] contained first editions of Pope—one of them very rare—and best of all, a copy of Dr. Johnson's "London," which sold a few weeks ago at Sotheby's for 285 pounds. This one, because of its fine condition, I imagine would bring over 300 pounds. Spencer and I got up and danced around the room, and no winners at any form of gambling were ever more hilarious. This is just to let you know that all the sport is not on the links in Scotland. . . .[11]

When Young was not able to be in London to find things for himself, Spencer sent him numberless handwritten scrawls, for whenever amid the dust and scraps he found something good he never failed to let his favorite customer know: "I was going over some stock under the shop this morning and came across the two enclosed Thackeray letters, they are of such *great* importance"—and so on. When Young asked for Cruikshank material, Spencer went to work among the piles and produced a list of hundreds of Cruikshank items—drawings, manuscripts, prints, dozens of letters. But Young wrote back: "I must not permit myself to get in the habit of buying these large blocks in bulk for large sums and run the risk of feeling dissatisfied with them after I get them. That is not good business either for you or for me."[12]

Young knew well he was dealing with a rascal. Spencer knew he knew it; he noted in a letter that he was charging Young only half of what he did *before I had the pleasure of knowing you*—Spencer's own emphasis. Indeed, Spencer had a rather dubious reputation among dealers in London, and Young wrote him many letters of advice, and stern admonition as well. In one four-page letter he recommended that Spencer employ a competent bibliographer, have every book checked, mark perfect ones high, defective ones low—or not sell them at all— and develop buyers' confidence in his stock: "I write at such length because of my affection for you and because I think on this kind of subject my judgment is better than yours." The old man took all this well, and thanked Young for "your charming letter and wonderful advice to me," signing himself "with heartfelt thanks."[13] It was not very noticeable, however, that he took any of the advice.

With both Spencer and his wife, Owen and Jo had many amusing occasions, at the shop and socially. The two wives got along very well while the men were discussing bibliographical details, and as late as 1934 Spencer wrote Young: "My wife received a most charming letter from Mrs. Young, what a lovely homely letter your good lady can write."[14]

After 1930 Young did not go abroad again, nor did he buy books; the two men no longer met in the dusty little rooms full of junk and treasures, but they corresponded occasionally, and Young sent Spencer copies of his speeches. Spencer died in 1936.[15]

iii

Josephine Edmonds Young's knowledge and enthusiasm were an important ingredient in Owen Young's book collecting. Once his tutor in literature, she continued to read widely throughout her life, both modern and older authors. It was their joint appreciation of Thackeray and Dickens that led to his first important acquisitions; it was she who loved *Alice* so much that he made Carroll one of his serious interests. And her enjoyment of lesser authors prompted him to collect, not only Borrow and Ainsworth, but also Mary Wollstonecraft, Pepys and Southey; and because she was fond of *Evelina* he found himself with perhaps the greatest collection of Burney manuscripts in the world. Among the poets, he preferred the more classical—Dryden, Pope, Gray; but she was more interested in the Romantics, and they both loved Burns. It was she who pushed him into collecting later writers (Owen said he liked his books "seasoned"): Stevenson, Conrad, Hardy and Kipling, with all of whose books she was closely acquainted and whom she much admired.

She was certainly appalled by the amount of money he spent on the books. She never outgrew her New England character and training: the teachings of her careful mother, the precepts of thrift which even in a comfortable Massachusetts household were always practiced, the early years in Cambridge on a law-clerk's wages. It was some time after her husband began making a large salary that he succeeded in persuading her to spend more on her clothes, to go to New York's expensive shops, to buy beautiful materials and furs. This she did eventually—although when she succumbed to a Russian sable evening cape it took her a month to get over it—and she also, in a minor way, made her own collections of old English silver and furniture, and contemporary prints. Owen used to tease her and Lulu Adams Perkins about their New England upbringing, saying it did not keep them from spending money, but only from enjoying it. This was not really true of Jo: it gave her a fearful joy. And so it was with the books and manuscripts; Owen gave her over the years some beautiful, quiet jewelry, but she liked best his Christmas gift of 1928: Burns's "O, my luve's like a red, red rose," in the author's hand.[16]

Of their older children, the most bookish boy was gone; but the daughter, in college during the collecting years, taking wide-ranging literature courses, was awed and delighted by each addition to the collection. Every vacation or weekend at home provided some new pleasure, when her father opened the safe to show, perhaps, a Shakespeare quarto, Pope's own copy of Milton, or manuscripts of Dickens, of Stevenson, of Kipling—all her favorite authors; or it might be the 1488 Homer—like her mother she was a student of Greek—or, again, Keats's last letter to Fanny Brawne. Young did not need encouragement to make more purchases, but the enthusiasm of his two Josephines increased his own.

As the collection grew, there was not room enough for it and the safes which its value required in the apartment at 830 Park. So Young leased the apartment below, put in a stairway, and made a library— with a pool table—in what had been the dining room. It was a comfortable place, and when the curtains were drawn in the evening, the world outside was forgotten in the study of recent acquisitions or the deciphering of old manuscripts.[17] Young was always deeply interested in the changes in an author's manuscript: Why did he change that word, rearrange that sentence? Is it really better? What was in his mind? Young thought that crossed-out manuscripts should be used in teaching literature and writing. There were long discussions over these questions, with, for example, a copy of Tennyson's *Poems Chiefly Lyrical* in hand, studying the poet's own corrections and additions. Then—after an hour or more—there would be a hotly contested game of Kelly pool.

It was natural for Owen Young, in the first excitement and pride of "big" collecting, to want to share his acquisitions with St. Lawrence, and also characteristic that in arranging an exhibition he should invite others—all Laurentians, of course—to show their treasures. The exhibition was put on in the summer of 1925 in the Herring Library on the university campus. Only the catalogue, a minor triumph of fine printing, was designed by an outsider, William Edwin Rudge; of this Young distributed many copies, to friends and fellow collectors.

Another effort for his college arose directly from Young's plan to put together in his collection the great books in English. What, indeed, were the great books in English? Who could make up the list— and who would read them? With Dr. Sykes's enthusiastic support, the English department at St. Lawrence was set to work to compile the list, and with funds supplied by Young the designated volumes were bought in good but inexpensive editions which were within the reach of students. There were about 128 books, by 100 authors, not counting anthologies and the King James Bible.

At the dedication of the "Owen D. Young Fundamental Library of English Literature," Charley Gaines made the speech; the collection indicated, he said, how a student could collect a library of his own— "not difficult, not necessarily expensive. One may start with a little nucleus of good, well-chosen books, to be enlarged as inclination prompts and opportunity presents itself. Such a library soon becomes a priceless treasure; it becomes the mark and measure of its owner's quality; it gives the home a soul"—words which the donor must have read with satisfaction.[18] And some students, at least, took them to heart.

i v

Like all collectors, Young enjoyed talking shop with others in the same field. He and A. Edward Newton struck up a friendship immediately; they had not only books but electrical business in common, although the former were by far the more important, at least to Eddie Newton. His delightful writings on book collecting, the wit and charm which made him an amusing companion or correspondent, were enjoyed by Young. They exchanged lighthearted letters and met, when possible, in New York or Philadelphia. With Jerome Kern also Young exchanged warm letters; he had a good deal of sympathy for Kern's complaint that his books had enslaved him: "I never captured a prize, the prize always captured me."[19] When Kern sold his books, many of them ended up in Young's library; but when the composer wrote to ask Young if he had his *Queen Mab*, Young answered:

I am obliged to confess that I lacked two things, both of which were essential—"courage and money." Had there been no difficulty on the second, I think I might have screwed up the first. I find it is easier to raise the first than the second. Notwithstanding that I missed "Queen Mab" I think it must be true that I was still by all odds the largest single buyer at your sale. I used the opportunity largely to fill in the gaps or improve copies in my own collection . . . I am satisfied that I paid your collection the highest compliment in my power, more than any words can do. . . .[20]

There was little time for such exchanges with fellow collectors, but if it was at all possible Young always made time for the scholars who wished to consult his collection. He never lost the respect for learning and learned men he acquired at St. Lawrence, and in Cambridge, where Jo took him to hear at Harvard some of the most famous. Although he had not become the "scholar" that, as he wrote Jo in early days, he longed to be, he enjoyed the feeling that his collection was being made use of and contributing to scholarship; his sense of trusteeship was strong.

John Livingston Lowes was a friend of both the Youngs; Jo admired his books, especially *The Road to Xanadu*. Lowes wrote after a visit in 1928:

I'm afraid I was incoherent on Tuesday night, but the more I think of it, the less surprised I am that I was. I've never seen together so many unknown and unsuspected Coleridge manuscripts—let alone the Pope and the Keats and the Burney and the rest—and I'm not quite recovered yet. So I find it difficult to tell you with any approach to adequacy what rare pleasure you gave me. For I keep thinking of the bits of manuscript in that night's setting, and it has given them a curious added value.[21]

Bliss Perry wrote in the same vein after his visit, when he went off with the loan of some Emerson manuscripts to work on, for Young was always ready to lend material to trustworthy hands.

From England E. V. Lucas—one of Jo's favorite contemporary essayists—wrote that he was working on a new edition of Lamb's letters, and wanted very much to see those in the Young Collection. He was sent notes and copies of Lamb material, and very cordial letters were exchanged. Lucas asked permission for Edmund Blunden to write an article on one unpublished item in Lamb's hand—a review of Hazlitt's *Table Talk* with many corrections and deletions. Young replied:

If you think that it is worthwhile for Mr. Blunden or anyone else to make an article of it, please go ahead. I have no sympathy with this notion of hoarding things of that character. If a private person has a right to them at all, it is only as a kind of conservator and trustee for the public, to whom they really belong. Perhaps I too am being infected with radical ideas. If so, please come over again and cure me.[22]

Blunden replied directly to Young, thanking him for "the noble letter you wrote to Mr. Lucas. . . . Thank you very much for this Elian sanction. He (C.L.) would have rejoiced to read your letter, though whether (after what he said of Milton's mss) he would have felt comfortable at seeing his article with erasures and substitutions in the public eye is a question."[23]

v

Almost no American authors were included in Young's early collecting; from the collector's point of view, it was essential to begin with Edgar Allan Poe's first publication, *Tamerlane* (Boston, 1827, anonymous). Of this (in 1925) only four copies were known, all unavailable. Like the collector Walter T. Wallace, Young felt that "if I can't have a *Tamerlane* I will give up collecting"—of American books at least.[24]

It was not to be so. The story has often been told, but it is still an exciting one, even to this writer, who lived through it. Charles Goodspeed relates it in detail in *Yankee Bookseller*. In the summer of 1925 an article by Vincent Starrett appeared in the *Saturday Evening Post*; it was entitled "Have you a *Tamerlane* in Your Attic?" and it was read by a woman who had. In Worcester, Massachusetts, a city very familiar to the Edmondses of nearby Southbridge, lived Mrs. Ada S. Dodd, in two poor rooms with her elderly sister. She wrote to Starrett, but there was no reply; he was abroad. On the advice of the librarian of the Worcester Public Library, she wrote Goodspeed: "I understand this is a very rare book. I should like to sell it."[25]

Goodspeed did not for a moment believe it was a genuine *Tamerlane*; but he went to Worcester, and found it to be "a genuine and fine copy of the most valuable book in American Literature."

Goodspeed took it on commission, offering it first to Miss Greene at the Morgan Library, and then to another collector, without success. Then he remembered his old acquaintance Owen Young, and called his office in New York. Miss Chandler took the message and relayed it promptly to the boss. But Goodspeed was asking $17,500, and Young had spent his current allocation for books. He said no, but he left the door open: if it was not sold soon, let him know.

Goodspeed wanted Young to have it. He listed the *Tamerlane* in his next catalogue with full description, but before the catalogue appeared, he wrote Young again; this time he hit the right note: "There is a lot of satisfaction to find a book of this kind in the hands of someone to whom the money will mean a great deal."

Young was away, at a meeting in Atlantic City; he wired the book dealer to bring the book to New York. But Goodspeed was at Lake Placid on vacation. It was not until October 31, on a Saturday morning at nine, that Young, Goodspeed, and *Tamerlane* met at 830 Park, with Jo and young Jo in attendance. The little book and the large check were exchanged with great cordiality, and the following week Ada

Dodd received fourteen thousand dollars, an incredible sum to her. She wept, and according to Goodspeed said, "Is it really so? I can go to Boston to the sales and I can take a taxi when I want to? Why, I'm a rich woman!"

Young loved to tell the story of *Tamerlane*. It was not only his most exciting catch, but the stage was set in Worcester and Boston, and in the very shop and hands of the first rare-book dealer he knew. Although there were many other exciting moments in Young's book collecting, none pleased him more than the thought of Mrs. Dodd riding all over Boston in taxis. His Poe collection was begun, and grew to respectable size; it came to include, four years later, the other scarce Poe item, *Murders in the Rue Morgue*—a serendipitous find, this time in New York City—which Young bought from Dauber and Pine for twenty-five thousand dollars. From Poe he went on to his favorites: Emerson, Hawthorne, Cooper, Whitman and especially Mark Twain. In the end his American collection was a first-class one, though not as all-inclusive as the English one.

From the time when Young became chairman of General Electric to the crash and the depression, he was able to purchase almost anything he wanted to fulfill his plan for his book collection. His salary, augmented by the phenomenal rise of GE and RCA stock, was ample for the family and their homes, and for the large gifts to education which he made throughout the 1920s. He had, in his financial planning, an allocation for book purchases, and tried not to exceed it. But, as Rosenbach's biographer sagely remarks, "Money put aside to spend burns holes in a collector's pocket," and there is no doubt that he burst into flames more than once. And the stock market was not the only market that rose fantastically in the 1920s; rare books sold at record prices right up to the end of 1929. Young's largest expenditures for books were made in that year—until October. In spite of his long absence in Paris, where he paid all his own expenses as at the time of the Dawes Plan, he acquired some very costly items, beginning with the Kern sale. But the end of his collecting came with the end of the year; he was left with big bills to pay for what he had already bought, as well as no prospect of buying more—nor did he want to. In 1931, as the depression deepened, he wrote a dealer who had offered him some tempting items:

I have made it a rule now for two years not to spend any money in the rare book field until this period of terrific personal need for food and clothes is over. I would not feel justified in spending any money for anything, no matter how rare or how cheap just now, because such items instead of giving me pleasure in the future would always rise to curse me as a luxury purchase when luxuries should not be bought.[26]

But he could look back upon what he had done with satisfaction, writing to a friend:

I have been interested in the collection of books for a good many years, but my activities have followed the usual curves of human efforts. Sometimes I am aggressive and lucky, sometimes I am non-aggressive and lucky, sometimes I run into long barren spots. However, I can quite properly say that my collection owes me nothing. It has certainly paid more than its cost in education and pleasure.[27]

Chapter 23

Unfinished Business, Private and Public

WHEN the Assembly of the League of Nations held its regular public meeting at Geneva in September 1928, Allied and German representatives seized the occasion to meet in secret sessions that were no part of the scheduled agenda. Since the agent-general's latest reports had warned that there would be no final resolution of the reparations and related problems "until Germany is given a definite task to perform on her own responsibility, without foreign supervision and without transfer protection," these extracurricular activities did not escape the notice of the press. Thus when, on September 16, the Allies and Germany suddenly announced their accord on "the necessity for a complete and definite settlement" of reparations and "the constitution for this purpose of a committee of financial experts to be nominated by the six signatory governments," the correspondents were perhaps less surprised than the diplomats themselves.[1]

Owen Young was not surprised at all. In his speech at his daughter's commencement at Bryn Mawr in June of 1928 Young had spoken strongly of the dangers of overhanging intergovernment debts:

We have throughout the world [he said] a network of so-called political debts, a source of irritation and trouble today, and I venture the prediction that unless they are discharged, they will be a source of greater trouble tomorrow, and that means you. . . . To sell to private investors the obligations of debtor countries sufficient to discharge all political treasuries from intercountry debts . . . would remove the overhanging threat which now exists, not only to economic development but to peace.

Parker Gilbert, of course, had been keeping him fully advised, and on September 6, Nelson Perkins paid him a visit. So did George Auld, and on the twelfth Colonel James Logan was there. Two days later, still before the news had broken, General Dawes and Young were closeted all morning in his New York office.[2]

Young heard the radio announcement in Van Hornesville, where he spent the weekend; on Monday he was in Canton for the funeral of his and Jo's old friend Cammie Gaines, the wife of their favorite professor. But by Tuesday he was back at his desk and he and General Dawes were at it again. While, as usual, their conference went unrecorded, the fact remains that, except for Perkins, Dawes was the one person with whom Young would have felt wholly free to talk about reparations. Nor would it have been out of character for the general—still vice-president of the United States and so ineligible to serve himself—to make the trip from Washington especially to counsel with his most eligible friend.[3]

In any case, Young was shunning Washington and keeping his cards very close to his chest. It was all very flattering to hear and read— indeed to know—that the one thing all parties to the conference were agreed upon was that Owen Young should chair it. This might have been anticipated, and so it was—to a point which, for Young, would have made any other outcome profoundly disconcerting. Nevertheless, the prospect of this new call to conspicuous public service left him restive and unsure of his response.

For one thing, his wife was far from well. For another, the times and the auspices contrasted sharply with those that had led to the Dawes Plan. Instead of being tapped by a friendly secretary of state who had first proposed the conference, he would now be answering a call from abroad to which—with a presidential campaign in progress—Washington's response was ambivalent at best. So, in a sense, was London's; Britain had gone along with France and Germany but this time with misgivings.[4] Finally, the mix of opportunity and obligation that marked his own current business and personal agenda was not of the kind that is easily left or delegated.

The countryman's feeling for the seasons had been bred into Owen Young, and for GE and RCA alike, the coming harvest was full of promise. Technology was leading "his" Radio Corporation far afield: for example, into the pending merger with the Victor Talking Machine Company, and, through its Photophone subsidiary and lately acquired interest in Radio-Keith-Orpheum, into the production and distribution of the new "talking movies." Facsimile transmission by radio was developing apace and WGY in Schenectady had already begun an experimental series of television broadcasts. In the meantime, consolidation abroad of cable and radio communications was pushing Young to explore—notably with Newcomb Carlton of Western Union and Sosthenes Behn of ITT—what response to this challenge American companies could legally make.[5]

As for GE—or more strictly IGE—its recent acquisition of a control-ling interest in a second British electrical manufacturing concern, Metropolitan Vickers (Metrovick), meant that a merger of that com-pany with British Thomson-Houston could now be effected. Since this would force a break at long last in British resistance to Young's master plan for unifying and "rationalizing" the industry, Gerard Swope was going over and Young gave him a letter to Montagu Norman urging the latter's help. He also wrote Sir Josiah Stamp, Sir Robert Kindersley and above all the leading Scottish industrialist, Lord Weir, inviting them to suggest as directors of a new holding company, Associated Electrical Industries (AEI), four or five representative Britons who, if Young had his way, would serve the new company under the chair-manship of Weir himself.[6] Nor was this the only likely breakthrough on the international scene. Of far greater concern to press and public, certainly, was the door-opening twenty-six-million-dollar five-year con-tract with the Soviets which, after a year of the hardest kind of bar-gaining, was all but ready to be signed. Perkins's advice was bearing fruit.

Looking at the public sector, Young could congratulate himself that his involvement in the national and state campaigns of 1928 was strict-ly vicarious. True, with two friends competing for the presidency and another running for governor of New York, this involvement was by no means negligible, and from the Smith and Roosevelt forces he was under considerable pressure for supporting statements and funds. But the real pressure, from which Young could see no possible escape, was about to come from a nonpolitical source, the New York Federal Reserve. With its first and only governor, Benjamin Strong, now mor-tally ill, the directors of the bank—and in a special sense their deputy chairman—would shortly be confronted with the critically important and delicate task of naming his successor. Should attention center on the claims of Strong's fellow officers or should they look outside? With Washington waiting to move in, could anyone hope to maintain New York's ascendancy as Strong had done, or was that chapter about to end?

In the meantime, a number of Young's more private enterprises—chiefly up-country—were clamoring for time, money and attention. At Van Hornesville his new stone schoolhouse had opened early that year with a roster of thirty-four pupils, and he was concerned to see for him-self what still needed doing. His perennial interest in his Holsteins had become intensified with the progress of his breeding program, and there were charts to supplement his visits of inspection. At the same time he was setting up a new milk plant for the farmers, and renovating both the structure and the operation of the old stone gristmill, built by the Van Hornes some ninety years before. Could he assure a future for the mill, the milk plant and the new Central School, Van Hornesville too would have a future.

These developments pleased his mother, who would soon be ninety, not least because they brought Owen home so often. They were timely too because the long-awaited opening of the "Otsquago Trail"—which at last would join the Mohawk and the Susquehanna valleys—would expose Van Hornesville as never before to the world outside. And of course Owen would be coming up for the opening ceremonies and making a speech too—as he did.[7]

He was also committed to making a speech of a very different order at the October convocation of that metaphysical entity, the University of the State of New York. Of this unique institution, which boasts neither faculty nor students, the commissioner of education is the president, the regents are the trustees, and all New York State colleges and universities (then largely private) are the "members." For this assignment Owen and his old friend Edward Adler were already exchanging ideas. In that same month St. Lawrence, at Owen's and Jo's suggestion, was planning a major celebration of Dr. Hervey's double anniversary—of coming to Canton as a student, and as president of the university. The Youngs set up a fellowship in his honor, and joined him in the private car Owen had arranged to take their oldest friend to Canton in unaccustomed style.[8]

Jo was very much a party to these educational adventures, but her health was indeed giving Owen deepening concern. She had diabetes, but, thanks to insulin, it was under control. A tonsillectomy, however, performed to remove (it was hoped) the source of her concurrent eye infection had done nothing of the sort. Three months later, the pain and irritation were more pronounced than ever and their source, and so the remedy, remained elusive. So long as this was true, any notion of another European jaunt left Owen very cold indeed.

ii

Work as an anodyne for worry was still the accepted prerogative of the husband and Owen took full advantage of it. With Swope abroad,

he "ran" GE, and also looked in twice a week or more at the Federal
Reserve. While David Sarnoff handled the nitty-gritty at RCA, Young
had granted General Harbord a leave of absence to work for Hoover
and so was himself consulted on all questions of policy. In Cleveland
he made a widely reported speech at the Electric Railway Convention in which his call for private ownership of mass-transit facilities—
which still included streetcars—also made provision for reasonable
fares, buttressed where necessary by social subsidies to keep them
within reach of the ordinary citizen. Back in his office, he welcomed
Lord Weir and briefed Swope by radio on their ensuing talks. In a
second radio message to Swope he suggested they make *personal*
contributions of five thousand dollars each to the Democratic National Committee, and these were duly made.[9]

Young's action in releasing Harbord also prompted him to issue a
public statement on the great importance of an exercise in freedom of
choice at every level of industry. For his own part, he authorized
FDR to use his name as one of his business supporters for the governorship, and John J. Raskob to release his statement endorsing Al
Smith for President. This too was widely reported, winning editorial
notice in the *Times* and a warm response from the candidate; it was
also cited as having a "bullish" effect on the market, which needed no
new stimulus. If some such awareness prompted Young's cautionary
remarks to a Schenectady reporter against mortgaging one's future by
undue use of credit, this was the one observation he made which the
press contrived to play down.[10] Reporters and editors alike greatly preferred his address at the Regents' Convocation in which he discovered
the spirit of Shakespeare—a highly practical as well as curious and
imaginative spirit—newly incarnate in the research scientists of today.
Evidently the press relished the suggestion that thanks to the drama
and poetry of its laboratories, our business civilization might one day
develop its own version of an Elizabethan age. Indeed, a *Sun* editorial
went so far as to suggest that not all of industry's poets were at work
in the lab; one at least now sat at the desk of the chairman of the
board.[11]

When Owen's wife and daughter teased him about this, Young
retorted that he was not the first of the poets to be unappreciated at
home—look at Coleridge. Actually, he had enjoyed preparing a speech
which for once enabled him to draw on the riches of his experience
and his library, and indulge in an imaginative flight instead of problem solving. He also liked his "metaphysical" degree and what was

said in its conferring, and liked having his two Josephines on hand to see and listen. He was deliberately encouraging Jo senior on her own account to get out and around whenever she felt up to it; like the previous week's Hervey celebration at St. Lawrence, it served to minimize her troubles.

It was evident too that Owen was still enjoying the attentions of a press which reported his every word and move. The announcement in mid-October of GE's contract with the Russians was news indeed; but if press reactions were divided, it was Young who was handed the "garlands or the garbage." And if politicians found this interesting, any possible change in American policy was hardly made more likely by dispatches such as the *Telegram*'s Washington correspondent's, who wrote—without bothering about documentation: "The General Electric Company recognizes Russia regardless of the State Department. And when Owen D. Young has led, the State Department sometimes has been known to follow."[12]

One thing which State and Treasury were watching no less closely than Young himself was the constant speculation in the press about Europe's move to settle reparations and how far this would again involve American experts, notably Young. On the *desirability* of American involvement—widely recognized as inescapable—the weight of editorial opinion was positive, and there was something close to a consensus about Young's indispensability. Early in the year Young had written Paris headquarters of the International Chamber of Commerce a private letter urging that its Economic Restoration Committee explore the possibility of marketing German bonds in an amount sufficient to cover "present value" of the last forty annuities due on the Allied debts, which would thus be canceled out. Now Edwin L. James of the *New York Times* was reporting Paris hopes for a settlement much along these lines. But by this time one wondered whether the bond market would float enough to liquidate even the last twenty-five installments at present value. James was also presenting a shrewd summary of the irreconcilables present in the current equation: German insistence that reparations annuities be sharply reduced and limited in duration; Allied insistence that they be more than sufficient to cover net outpayments on the war debts for the full sixty-two years that these were to run; U.S. insistence that the debts as funded were sacred obligations and totally unrelated to reparations.[13] How were the experts to cope with these?

But thanks to the all but indomitable Benjamin Strong, who was indeed prepared to die but not to yield his concern for the future of "his" bank, Young had other and more pressing problems on his hands. When, in early October, Strong learned that he must return to the hospital for what would likely prove a terminal operation, he called Young at a late hour and asked him to come over. Recounting the story many years later, Young said that they had talked until 2:00 A.M., and that Strong had insisted on giving him his "last will and testament" with respect to the bank, stipulating that George Harrison should succeed him and proceed as a matter of top priority to "quiet" things with Washington. Finally Strong looked to Young as his "executor" to see to it that this was done. Less than two weeks later, Strong was dead.[14]

The charge could have been awkward, had Young's views made it so; fortunately, he was able to proceed for the most part in good conscience, while keeping Strong's testament very much to himself. But he would have to make haste slowly; Harrison was not the only contender for Strong's mantle, and in fairness to the others, time must be allotted for interviews with them as well as for consultation with senior officers and fellow directors. Nor was it wise to ignore the Federal Reserve Board in Washington, even though they were not officially a party to this election.

Young's interviews began with the senior deputy governor, J. Herbert Case, whom he greatly respected. When the United States entered the war, Case had left a promising career in commercial banking, at Strong's urging, to help the fledgling central bank in the unfamiliar task of financing the war effort. Working closely with such Treasury officials as Russell Leffingwell and Parker Gilbert, Case had won their confidence and friendship; Gilbert, indeed, had urged him strongly to come over in 1926 and head the Transfer Committee— which Pierre Jay had taken on only after Case had reluctantly but finally declined it. Largely self-educated, Case had a highly developed sense of the banker's role as trustee of other people's money, and if some of the highfliers in certain of the largest Wall Street banks dubbed him an old mossback, he had earned the respect and confidence of the banking community in general and of his Federal Reserve colleagues in particular. Whether or not his imaginative grasp of matters of high policy was judged to be sufficiently broad and sophisticated to qualify him for the highest post, it was important to his future and the bank's that he—and his colleagues—feel that he had been given full consideration.

Another who could hardly escape consideration was sixteen years Case's junior in age but only three in terms of service with the Fed. A Phi Beta Kappa graduate of Brown, with a Columbia doctorate in economics, Randolph Burgess was pointed to with pride as the intellectual of the family—a designation well suited to the demonstrated sharpness of his mind and pen but not always and everywhere equated with topflight executive ability. Even Young, as the nearest approach to an intellectual of which the New York board could boast, and for all his appreciation of Burgess's capacity to make the abstruse plain, was apparently beset by some such doubts.

In any event, George Harrison's credentials were formidable enough to impress others besides Ben Strong. A highly personable graduate of Yale whose slight lameness, as John Brooks so perceptively suggests, somehow inspired more confidence than sympathy, Harrison had gone straight from his honors degree at Harvard Law School to the coveted appointment of law clerk to Mr. Justice Holmes. Before coming to the New York bank as deputy governor in 1920, he had served the Federal Reserve Board in Washington, first as assistant and then as general counsel. Accompanying Strong on more than one of his European trips, he had come to know the leading central bankers of England and the continent far better than any of his colleagues did. A man—as indeed all three were—of unimpeachable integrity, he was also a man of parts who was not only at home in any company but was good company himself. His one drawback as Young saw it was his less than robust health, and remembering Strong's long and recurrent absences on that count, Young finally strayed so far from Strong's charge as to sound out Parker Gilbert—who was not available—before he and his fellow directors settled on Harrison. In his message to Gilbert, Young urged the advantages and rewards of his remaining in the public sector; the indications were that Gilbert was already committed, morally at least, to Morgan's.[15]

iii

For all the time Young had devoted to this issue, at the bank and elsewhere, he was absent from the board's meeting of November 22, 1928, which made official Harrison's election. His wife's eye infection was getting no better, and no one in New York seemed able to help. Thus, on November 14, he had finally taken her to a Philadelphia specialist, who held that an ailing sinus was the most probable source of the infection, and prescribed a good long exposure to Arizona air as the likeliest specific.

Young moved fast to test this out. Fortunately Swope was back from Europe, the Federal Reserve business was virtually settled, and the question of the reparations conference had not yet come to a head. A GE colleague, B. G. Tremaine, had a ranch not far from Phoenix, and with his help suitable accommodations were found in Chandler, at one of the San Marcos Hotel's attractive cottages. Determined to see Jo settled there and to stay if possible through Christmas, Young had canceled his planned trip to England, but in urging Weir to come over again in December, he had promised to meet him in New York if he did.[16] In the face of this contingency, and others, he urged young Jo to postpone her planned trip to Europe and come along to Arizona too, just in case. Nine-year-old Richard was also, of course, a member of the party.

And so on the twenty-second, having declined for unspecified but guessable reasons Newcomb Carlton's offer of his private car, they set out by train for Arizona. Their route was deliberately circuitous, and Young took advantage of it to prepare and to dispatch to FDR his voluminous postelection follow-up on waterpower.[17] Also there were stopovers, first in New Orleans (with dinner at Antoine's), and second in Texas, at the King Ranch, where C.J. met them and the Kleberg family were their hosts. The "invalid" enjoyed the trip, and found, when they arrived in Chandler, that their new winter home was much to her liking. Best of all, the warm sun and dry air soon improved the infection, and her general health as well. This was good news for her husband, who, two days after arrival, was called back to the office, thanking heaven that his daughter had come along to look after the family in the early weeks of their stay.

The occasion for Young's return was a call from Swope confirming Lord Weir's brief return and already imminent departure for Scotland. A message from Leon Fraser, however, as conveyed by Young's assistant, doubtless had a certain urgency as well. In his telephone call of November 28, made just after returning from Washington and just prior to sailing, Fraser had wanted Young to know that Secretaries Mellon and Kellogg and the German ambassador had each made it clear that "you were the essential factor to the success of the proposed final settlement . . . that a formal invitation would doubtless reach you within . . . the next ten days, and that the Administration would view it sympathetically."[18]

This was putting it squarely up to Young—especially since it echoed the prevailing sentiments from abroad as already conveyed by Gilbert and others. Young, however, was still keeping his own counsel, nor was this altered by his return to the city on Friday, December 7. He had come back unannounced, and except for a visit with Henry Robinson following that day's GE board meeting, and a luncheon at Morgan's on the following Monday with Thomas Lamont and Russell Leffingwell, he saw no one connected with reparations. On that same Monday the *New York Times* reported that he would be one of the experts; still no comment.

Even the zest with which he went to work that week was hardly enlightening. Was he simply demonstrating—to himself and others— that he had plenty to do at home without letting himself in for a return bout with reparations? Or was he cleaning up the docket in preparation for a long absence? The one thing certain was his eagerness to finish what he had come to do and get back to Arizona and his family.

But it wasn't quite that simple. On the day of his arrival, he was faced with successive meetings of his several boards: GE, IGE, RCA, NBC and RCA's new Photophone subsidiary. Also awaiting him that morning was a copy of the *Nation* for December 5 with a full-page "Open Letter to Owen D. Young," signed "The Editors." He had scarcely time to scan it before the first of his board meetings, and no doubt he took a quiet ribbing from some, at least, of his directors who had seen it. It began with a paragraph of high praise for the "very important, almost commanding position . . . you have achieved by your own efforts . . . in the field of electrical engineering and manufacturing. Your valuable public services," it continued, including "the creation and adoption of the Dawes Plan . . . have confirmed the high opinion held of you by the public and the press. . . ." Going on to cite his independence "as when you heartily approved Governor Smith's water power policy," and his "demonstrated understanding of public rights in . . . electrical power enterprises in sharp contrast to the views of many others," it listed a formidable series of abuses, including subversive and corrupting propaganda, of which the utilities stood accused by the Federal Trade Commission. Finally it called on Young to take a public stand which would do for this industry what Charles Evans Hughes had done for the scandal-ridden insurance business.

It was quite a letter with which to deal in an already crowded week. It was a touchy business too, asking Young publicly to sit in judgment on his own customers, not a few of whom were already irked by his incessant "preachments" and "unorthodox" public statements. Thus he was not about to attempt an immediate answer, but on the Monday, before lunching at 23 Wall Street, he did look in at the offices of the National Electric Light Association (NELA), of whose so-called Public Policy Committee he was a member. No doubt he also discussed the letter with M. H. Aylesworth, as NELA's sometime executive director. And that, for the moment, was that.[19]

Tuesday was completely given over to long discussions with Lord Weir, with Swope assisting. In 1926, Weir had been largely responsible for creating Britain's so-called electric grid, designed to unify and equalize distribution and delivery of electric power, and Young and Swope wanted him now to take the lead in doing as much for electric manufacturing. Still to be brought within the fold were two other companies of which by far the more important was General Electric Company Ltd., headed by Sir Hugo Hirst, and despite the name, no kin of GE's. Young urged the importance both for Britain and the dominions, as well as for the industry as a whole, of substituting a single strong manufacturing company, *of which Weir would be chairman,* for the half-dozen smaller concerns now cutting each other's throats. Toward this end the merging of British Thomson-Houston and Metrovick interests through a new holding company—AEI—was a significant first step, especially as it might make Hirst more receptive. Here strong British leadership was all-important and if Weir would undertake to provide it, GE would lend all necessary support, moral and financial.

Next day they let Weir alone, to think it over, but on Friday Young (and Swope) gave him a small dinner at the Metropolitan Club. That Weir's imagination was fired was quite evident before he left. So, unfortunately, was the ill health which, in the end, he pleaded in declining the stellar role—though he did agree to become a director of the new holding company. Thus his hosts, not content to drop the broader plan, were left to try a different tack.[20]

But if the mission that had taken him to New York had a disappointing ending, Young was at least free to leave the city and lost no time about it. As he wired Jo, he would return to Arizona via Schenectady—where he would stop off on Saturday to celebrate his grandson David's third birthday—and Van Hornesville, where he would have a good pre-Christmas visit with his mother. Then, as soon as son Philip came down from Canton, they would meet at Utica and board the Century, headed for Chandler. This they did on the nineteenth, wiring Jo to expect them late on the twenty-first.

i v

For the telephone and telegraph operators in Chandler and at the San Marcos, these messages served to introduce what was probably the busiest holiday season in their experience. Certainly the wires were kept humming almost from the moment of Young's arrival until January 3, when he and young Jo departed for New York. And January afforded little relief.

The shortest message, dated December 23, was Secretary Mellon's: "Shall telephone you important matter about ten o'clock there tomorrow morning." What transpired when he did is unrecorded. But the sequel makes it clear that Young fought shy of a final commitment.

On the twenty-fourth his assistant wired a long digest of a cable from Franklin Cutcheon, Perkins's successor as "the American Citizen" member of the Reparations Commission, summarizing official agreement on terms of reference and insisting that Young was "as essential to any practicable accord as any one can be." On the same day Gates McGarrah, Pierre Jay's successor as chairman of the New York Fed, had Parker Gilbert's long cable decoded and forwarded by airmail, having transmitted its substance by phone.

Next day they might expect a respite, and indeed the family's first Christmas in the desert was a happy one. But not even Christmas Day was to be immune. When Gerard Swope phoned his greetings, Young gave him a long message for Cutcheon and through the latter for Gilbert. On Boxing Day, Young's assistant sent a telegraphic summary of a lengthy letter from Sir Josiah Stamp, and on the twenty-seventh, his secretary wired Cutcheon's brief reply verbatim:

Thanks for cablegram repeated to Gilbert who sails today can say only that in your place if appraised conditions as I do would feel compelled accept provided health wife or self not prohibitive work will be reconciling apparently conflicting theses softening irritations preventing foolish declarations and convincing public opinion rather than laborious investigation prestige and contacts vital yours incomparably greater in situation than any others trust Mrs. Young much improved.

Not yet ready to accept the inevitable, Young tried compromising with it. He knew, however Washington might demur, that the chairman must be an American; if he could not escape that role, he could at least show Washington that he did not seek it. And press reports of the President's Christmas Eve conversation with Ambassador Sir Esmé Howard, dean of Washington's diplomatic corps, gave him an idea.

The United States, President Coolidge told Sir Esmé, would have no objection to the appointment of American experts should the Allied and German governments desire to appoint them; among those mentioned, said the press dispatches, were Owen D. Young, Henry M. Robinson, Nelson Perkins, Jeremiah Smith, Jr., and Dwight W. Morrow. Well, why not Dwight Morrow, the President's friend, as chairman, with Young playing the secondary role? With Perkins as his alternate, he himself could well come later with Stamp, when he would "help to get final agreement, sign the report and aid, so far as I could in getting acceptance by the governments. [In effect] that would give us the benefit and weight of three members of the Committees . . . the way we managed it with Henry Robinson on the Dawes Committee. In this way we could create the Morrow Committee and stand a very good chance of cleaning the matter up."

So in a wire of almost three hundred words, taken down in longhand by his daughter, Young spelled out his proposal. Dictated on December 27, for Secretary Mellon, it was first telephoned to Swope for transmission to Gilbert on the *Berengaria*; if Gilbert approved, it would then go to the secretary. Gilbert took it seriously enough to send back a hundred-word radio on December 31 which said that Secretary Kellogg "apparently told British Ambassador early this week that Washington will not permit American to be chairman"; that he had protested to Mellon that the committee should be allowed to choose its own chairman; that if Morrow were indeed available he believed that "every one on this side would be ready to accept the plan which ODY suggests though there will be general regret if he cannot see his way clear to come on the basis originally contemplated. Arriving New York January second."

But Young had not waited for Gilbert's comment before sending his message along to Mellon, who promptly wired him from Pittsburgh on the twenty-ninth as follows: "Thank you for your telegram of twenty-eighth stop Morrow has not been considered eligible by reason of his official position stop Am uncertain whether arrangement in line with your suggestion would be acceptable stop However your decision can be deferred until Gilberts arrival."

So that was that—or was it? Had Young any reason to think that

Morrow, weary of the embassy in Mexico City, would jump at the chance, or was his proposal disingenuous? As early as December 27 the *New York American* declared that Morrow would not serve, but ten days later the *New York Evening Post* reported that Gilbert "had conferred with Morrow immediately upon landing in New York (on Jan. 2nd) and again for several hours . . . in Washington." In the meantime Young could afford to inquire—as he did before leaving, in a second message to Mellon—whether Coolidge had, as reported, actually objected to an American chairman, thereby limiting the committee's freedom of choice. Mellon's reply is not among Young's papers and may have been given by word of mouth.

In any event, his train having been held up for seven hours by heavy snows in Kansas, Young finally reached New York on January 7, and on the eighth made what the *Schenectady Union Star* called a "secret" visit to Washington. Not since the middle of June had Young so much as set foot in the capital city, but two days later he was back again. This time there was no secret about it; as Owen wired Jo on January 10, he was off again "in response to invitation which is equivalent to command." But he still had no statement for the press next day—even after his long conference with Coolidge, Kellogg and Mellon, and his visit with Dawes.[21]

To Jo, however, he had plenty to report. First, he had told the President and the two secretaries that he would go "subject to encouraging word from you." Second, he had consulted Dr. Arthur F. Chace (her New York physician), who thought his decision right provided she would stay in Arizona till March—when General and Mrs. Dawes would probably be sailing and hoped that she would join them. Third, "Nelson [Perkins] will go as my alternate and take Lulu and Elsie with him," attending all meetings so that he could carry on "if there is any reason for me to leave at any time." Fourth, what would she think of his inviting Stuart Crocker and his wife to go along, and encouraging Josephine to spend some time in Paris? Fifth, he thought it likely that J. P. Morgan would be the second member and that they should finish by April 1. "It is a very hard decision to make and . . . heartbreaking to go without you; what do you say?" Her illness having been headlined in that morning's New York *World*, "we must answer quickly to stop that discussion. . . ." He would phone her next morning at "ten o'clock your time."

When he did and Jo told him to go, the *Times* had already hailed editorially on January 12 the "welcome good news . . . that Mr. Owen D. Young will agree, if not prevented by personal reasons, to serve on

the Commission of Experts which will revise the Dawes Plan. . . .
No American is better qualified. . . ." Who, then, would be his fellow—had Gilbert and Morrow settled that between them? On this
point, speculation had been wide-ranging, with no more than occasional mention of J. P. Morgan's name. But by January 15 the press
considered both appointments definite, and when, next day, a Paris
announcement made it official, Morgan was quoted by the *Herald
Tribune* as calling himself the second expert and Young the first, adding that if any American were to serve as chairman it would be Owen
Young. Two days earlier this same paper had reported Coolidge as
vetoing Gilbert's suggestion of Young as chairman; now the *Times*
declared that he had no objection.

Young had gone straight to Van Hornesville from his Washington
appointments but, back in the office on the fifteenth, he moved fast.
Asking the Paris Ritz to reserve the same suite he had had before,
for two months beginning February 7, he wired Jo next day that he
had it, that all in Van Hornesville were well, that the Crockers would
sail with him on February 1, that he was awfully busy but "feel fine
and weather is good." Young Jo, who had left Chandler with him, as
her cousin Altha Edmonds came on to stay with Jo senior, had already
embarked on her delayed trip to Europe; sooner or later they would
meet in Paris.

And Young was indeed awfully busy. He was conferring at length
with Bernard Baruch, David Sarnoff, and Thomas W. Lamont, who
had been named Morgan's alternate. He was sending radiograms to
old friends like Alberto Pirelli and Jean Parmentier, expecting to see
them about February 9; and to Stamp: "one of the few attractions
in the new job is the thought of spending some weeks with you again."
Acknowledging a message from Viscount Rothermere of the British
publishing empire, he said, "While I like my own business better than
other people's, there seems to be no escape for me."

On the eighteenth he presided at three board meetings—RCA,
Photophone, and NBC—and then wrote a junior at Princeton (John
Rockefeller III) a long reply to his letter of inquiry about a trip
around the world; it could be good if one took it seriously, kept an
inquiring eye and mind on the changing scene, met and talked with
people of all kinds, kept a diary, and so on. On the nineteenth the
American experts met with Sir Esmé Howard at the Morgan Library,
to accept the official invitation he was asked to extend; the *World*
reported that this ceremony took about three minutes, after which they
devoted themselves to Morgan's rare books and manuscripts. And on

Sunday, the twentieth, Young honored a commitment of long standing to speak at Harry Emerson Fosdick's behest from his Park Avenue Church pulpit, having somehow contrived to prepare a talk on the topic Fosdick suggested: "What's Right with Business."[22] Monday's papers gave his "sermon" so much attention that in his wire to Jo next day, knowing full well the grin it would get, he let himself crow: "I was a good enough preacher Sunday night to get Monday's front pages."

The ensuing week afforded no letup. Monday morning was spent at 23 Wall Street; his afternoon callers included General Harbord and his old friend Sam Fordyce. On that day and the next, he was sending radio messages to Leon Fraser and Governor Emile Moreau of the Bank of France about the forthcoming meetings and having alternates attend them all; he also answered a radio from Louise Brown (now Mrs. Clark) from the *Empress of Scotland* (she was returning from a business trip to Manila) promising to see her before leaving. Having dispatched wires of acceptance to the German ambassador and the Reparations Commission, he wrote Lamont that he would "come along . . . in the small investment corporation which you are organizing"— remembering, no doubt, that this kind of public service at one's own expense ran into money. Besides, if (as he wired Jo) his bids at the Jerome Kern sale had been overtopped (by Rosenbach), the *Times* reported on the twenty-fifth his purchase of Poe's *Murders in the Rue Morgue* for twenty-five thousand dollars.

On Wednesday, the first of several conferences with Leffingwell, a luncheon with Gilbert and Lamont, and a wire to Morrow ("see you Monday") were sandwiched between sessions on RCA business and the possible mergers with Harbord, Sarnoff, Paul Cravath and Sosthenes Behn. He also called on Alfred Sloan and John Pratt at General Motors, and Louis Howe came in to see him on behalf of New York State's new governor. On Thursday there was the regular luncheon and meeting of the Federal Reserve Bank directors followed by a second call on Leffingwell, Lamont this time assisting, and that evening a dinner of the St. Lawrence County Society at which Young was inevitably called on to "say a few words." Next day, between letters to Dr. Sykes about the St. Lawrence board's functioning in his absence and a warm letter to the President-elect of the United States, he saw (among others) S. Z. Mitchell, Clark Minor (who had succeeded Anson Burchard as president of IGE) and Ferdinand Eberstadt, a young investment banker who, on Joseph Cotton's recommendation, was going over to Paris as an adviser to the American experts. Again he called at 23 Wall, this time on Thomas Cochran as well as Leffingwell. And then, after tendering his resignation as a director of Mohawk-Hudson, he took the Friday afternoon train for Fort Plain and a weekend in Van Hornesville.[23]

There it snowed and snowed. What happened to Monday's projected meeting with Dwight Morrow is not clear; evidently one or both had been detained and they had to settle for an exchange of cordial telegrams. In the event Young spent most of Monday in Albany, conferring with F D R on waterpower, but on Tuesday the twenty-ninth he was back in the office, seeing Harbord, Sarnoff, and Behn as well as Leffingwell and Cochran. He wired Jo that C.J. was going to Cleveland (to see his future bride, Esther Christensen), leaving his two boys at Van Hornesville; that his mother was fine and said as he was leaving "that she thought this was my job and I ought to go." He also promised to telephone Jo on Friday. That same day he wrote Hoover, saying that his mother, who had cast her first vote for him, wanted more than anything else a "picture of my President"; would he autograph one for her? And then, since he and Morgan had been summoned to Washington to see President Coolidge next morning (Wednesday, January 30), he caught the midnight train—having first kept his promise to Louise, whom he saw that evening at the apartment.

At the White House, Coolidge agreed that Young should serve as chairman if he could not decently avoid it. He also surprised Young with an autographed photo. Then the two experts duly called first on the secretary of state and second on the secretary of the treasury. If they set special store on their session with the latter, it was partly because he, at least, was expected to stay on; but also because Young had accepted the appointment only after Mellon himself had strongly urged it. Thus there had been some truth in his wire of the twenty-third in response to a message from his G E colleague J. R. Lovejoy: "I did everything in my power to escape this job both for personal and business reasons but it seemed inevitable." At least he liked to think so, for, as he wrote on January 23 to his daughter's Bryn Mawr friend Jane Barth, who had heard him talk on reparations in June at young Jo's commencement, and now wrote to wish him well: "The bloom is off the rose on this reparations business for me so I am approaching it in the spirit of a disagreeable thing to be done rather than with the anticipation of a new experience."

And so, after a directors meeting on Thursday at the Federal Reserve and on Friday, February 1, with the boards of G E and R C A and its subsidiaries, Young had his telephone talk with Jo and got heartening word about her health: certainly by early March she would come over. Thus reassured he boarded the *Aquitania*, which sailed shortly after midnight, with Messrs. Morgan, Lamont and Eberstadt as his fellow passengers—as well as the Crockers and his traveling secretary, William E. Packer, who fortunately knew French. (Perkins, detained by illness in the family, would come a little later.) To the press, Young suggested that since the experts' task was simply to "complete the Dawes Plan," they should be known as the "Second Dawes Committee."[24] This suggestion did not take.

One letter which Young dictated and signed on the very eve of sailing helped to solace the assistant who—Crocker being a veteran of these wars—was being left behind. Oswald Garrison Villard, editor of the *Nation*, had written to wish Young well on his mission; Case urged the opportunity this afforded to reply to the open letter of December 5 quite personally, if not for publication. If his harried chief's reply was not all that his assistant could have wished, it was, all things considered, hard to fault. Acknowledging both the personal and the open letter, Young wrote:

Dear Mr. Villard:

I apologize for not having replied earlier to your very gracious letter of the twenty-third. I shall, of course, do everything within my power to bring to a conclusion this last unsettled item of the war's liabilities.

With reference to the Nation's open letter on the utility situation, I intended to answer it after the responsible people for the industry had presented their statement to the Federal Trade Commission. I do not wish to base a judgment of a great industry on the testimony and letters of widely scattered publicity agents writing to each other or writing to some subordinate in the industry. What I think we have a right to know is the attitude of the responsible managers toward what has taken place. I had expected that in the normal course that statement would already have been made. It has not, however, and therefore there is nothing for me to do now.

With many thanks for the compliment which you pay me in thinking that my views may have some real influence on the industry or on public opinion generally, I beg to remain,

Very sincerely yours,
Owen D. Young

Chapter 24

The Young Plan and
the International Bank

O F THE January 1929 conference in the Morgan Library and, incidentally, its long-drawn-out sequel in Paris, the British ambassador, Sir Esmé Howard, was to write some years later:

I was greatly impressed during this my first and only meeting with Mr. Owen Young. There are men who so impress us we hardly know why; but I carried away with me a strong belief that Mr. Young was a man who could easily attain to the highest place in any walk of life he might choose to follow. He had, it seemed to me, a sureness of touch and a rapidity of decision that singled him out as a great man.

Mr. Pierpont Morgan, after working closely with Mr. Young in Paris, confirmed this view by what he told me of that Conference. I remember he put it this way:

"All that the rest of us had to do at Paris was to hold up Owen Young's hands as the Children of Israel held up the hands of Moses during the battle of Rephidim against the Amalekites and the battle was won."

Morgan, justly priding himself on his invariably apposite but sometimes esoteric scriptural allusions, had perhaps forgotten that the Amalekites survived the battle to make further mischief for the Israelites. But he had good reason to recall—none better—his leader's dire need to have his hands upheld when, during the siege of Paris, the Amalekites seemed to have infiltrated the ranks of the experts themselves— even those of the supposed noncombatants stationed in Washington. Nor did Young ever cease to marvel at the way in which this associate, accustomed to command, sustained his self-imposed and invariably supportive role against the Amalekites whenever and wherever they appeared.[1]

Even to hint at ambush ahead, however, is to anticipate a story the full drama of which emerges only as it is allowed to tell itself. Taking at face value Owen's cable to Jo of February 8, it begins promisingly enough, with friend Fred Bate on hand to meet the ship:

Came from Cherbourg on special train the only time I ever did it comfortably stop Arrived Ritz three oclock and went immediately into rapid action stop Think committee organization will be announced Sunday's papers stop Telegram and letter from [young] Jo indicate she will be here about March tenth all settled at the Ritz with rooms overlooking south garden . . . so begins another adventure everyone asking about you and I am answering encouraging stop Am I right?

Owen's next message, dated February 14, suggests that Jo's reply had been positive but spare, New England style: "If my committee functioned with the . . . brevity and clarity of your last telegram we would get through before you had an opportunity to come over everything going fine and I am very well but it is very cold." In the meantime their nine-year-old son Richard, at the San Marcos with his mother, could boast of his own wireless message from Paris: "Dont you make fun any longer of my collection of chairmanships because I have just added another love to Momsie and Altha. Pops."[2]

So that vexed question had been settled. Not only had President Coolidge acquiesced, but a week before turning his office over to Hoover he had penned for Young in his own hand a handsome note of thanks "for the many ways in which you have been of help to me and especially for your going over to Europe to help in trying to settle the reparations. . . . The services you can render . . . will be of a wise and helpful character and will go far to secure a final adjustment. I trust you will find it all satisfying to your sense of public obligation." And if no such message about his present mission had come from Young's old friend, the President-elect, his New York office had received, on February 11, an autographed photo, inscribed in Hoover's hand "for Ida Brandow Young, mother of a great American." Three days later came a note in which he said to Young: "Just to indicate what I think of you, I would give five years of my life at the present time if you were on the right side of the political fence." Apprised by his staff of all these messages, Young was doubly reassured; evidently all was quiet on the home front.[3]

From Van Hornesville too came reassuring words. Ida Young was now finding wireless communication quicker and easier than writing letters, but her brother John, younger by two years, wanted to write himself to his beloved nephew: "I have been reading a few things about you that Rather Pleased me and thought you might want to get a few lines from your Home town. So here goes. . . ." There followed a report that 10 of his prize cows, milked 4 times a day, had been giving 830 pounds of milk daily. "I think it is Pretty Fine and Still going Strong." The snow was "fine for sleighing" and C.J. came up and took his boys home. So Owen had all the news.[4]

During the Christmas holiday Owen and Jo had talked of buying land near the San Marcos and building their own cottage, perhaps to a Frank Lloyd Wright design. On the seventeenth Jo had another Paris cable: "First week [is] over," it read, "and we still survive. Vercingetorix takes us to the races this afternoon. Hope you paid for the desert land because if not we shall be unable to do so tonight." How they actually fared that day is not recorded, but perhaps it was as well that Young's financial secretary—a Vermonter—was not notably lavish in parceling out his money.[5]

But Crocker records in his diary that his chief had been inwardly restive during that first week and the next. Finding the Allies and the Germans even farther apart than he had anticipated, he blamed his own "lethargic mind" for failing to come up with a creative proposal that would give all parties an additional stake in a settlement. According to Crocker, it was not until the following Sunday that "the flash came."[6]

ii

The genesis of the Bank for International Settlements, or BIS, is a classic instance of the way in which one man's mind catches fire from another's. Washington's Birthday had found Young still dispirited; so far he had come up with nothing. That afternoon Emile Francqui (of Belgium) looked in to suggest the need for a settlement agency which would handle reparation payments and transfers, *vice* the agent-general. Fair enough, but hardly exciting. Next morning, a Saturday, Hjalmar Schacht called to lay before Young a grandiose scheme for a new international agency or bank which would not only handle reparations but would also extend such credits to the underdeveloped countries as should greatly expand world trade—including, of course, the exports on which Germany's capacity to pay was finally dependent.[7]

Was this it? According to Schacht, Young's response was so immediate—and resonant—as still to be highly quotable a quarter century later: "Dr. Schacht, you gave me a wonderful idea and I am going to sell it to the world."[8] Schacht, who had first learned English in Brooklyn, could not be faulted on his American idiom, but for Young, the phrase was wholly out of character. Whatever his exact words, there was no denying that the next day's "flash" had been sparked by Schacht.

For the ten days that followed, Young was so deeply immersed in his own thoughts that, according to Crocker, he dined either alone or only with Nelson Perkins, who respected his long silences. But the chairman had lost no time in summoning the "real experts" to his aid: Randolph Burgess from the New York Fed, and two of Burgess's former colleagues: Walter Stewart, now economic adviser to the Bank of England, and Shepard Morgan of Parker Gilbert's finance office in Berlin.[9] On March 6, Burgess advised George Harrison in New York that they "had been working at the plan . . . both day and night," with Pierre Quesnay of the Bank of France and Schacht sitting in from time to time.[10]

Almost certainly the "sit-ins" were there at Young's suggestion. In a memo to the chairman, Quesnay had denounced Schacht's proposal as a scheme which, through credit, "would enable Germany to pay part of her debt and through inflation would cover the other part." What Young was demanding of himself and his aides, therefore, was a plan at once so intriguing and so soundly conceived that, when the American draft was ready, Burgess could report (as he did) that Schacht and Quesnay "largely concur."[11]

By March 19, in the second of his long cables to Frank B. Kellogg—marked "CONFIDENTIAL for the President [now Hoover], the Secretary of State and Secretary of the Treasury"—Young was able to report that the B I S had taken definite shape. As an international but nonpolitical bank for central banks, it would "terminate once and for all the war and post-war machinery" for handling reparations, replacing it with machinery "essentially commercial in character." By providing for regular meetings of the heads of the central banks, it would dissipate the aura of secrecy and suspicion of conspiracy which had hampered previous essays in cooperation. It would also provide a sorely needed financial channel for facilitating trade and foreign exchange, while economizing on the movement of gold. Finally, if and when market conditions made feasible the "commercialization" of some part of Germany's debt it would make the appropriate arrangements.[12]

In his earlier message of March 2, Young had given an extensive summary of the German position as presented by Schacht, of the contrasting Allied "requirements" and internal hassles over a fair division of the spoils, and of the genesis and early development of

the bank plan. He quoted Thomas Lamont's statement to the press
that the special subcommittee headed by Lord Revelstoke (Josiah
Stamp's colleague) had no plans for immediate commercialization of
the German debt, but was concerning itself only with future possibilities. He also reported that the Americans had vetoed Geneva as
the seat of the BIS. Now he quoted Lamont's latest reminder to the
press that payment of Allied debts to the United States had not been
questioned or even discussed—though of course (as everyone was
aware) the Allies were looking to Germany's annuities to cover their
own net outpayments and leave something over. Kellogg, in acknowledging receipt, promised to keep these candid messages strictly confidential.[13]

When, on March 10, plans for the new bank were first outlined to
the press, Young was especially concerned about American reactions.
This was not news to his New York staff, which had been briefing him
daily by radio on press accounts and commentaries. That the bank
plans were now hailed by the *Times* and the *World*, the *Herald Tribune* and the *Sun* was gratifying enough; more surprisingly, Hearst's
New York Evening Journal carried a long International News dispatch
from Paris which found that such a bank would meet a worldwide
need and help American business. True, the *Journal of Commerce*,
the *Washington Post*, and the Hearst papers generally took a dim
view, but it remained for the *Chicago Tribune* to denounce the plan
as a sinister plot of the international bankers for canceling the war
debts, or restoring London's financial supremacy, or both.[14] But since
any proposal for a new institution, especially one whose scope is
avowedly international, always excites similar charges—which, differing only in the identity of conspirators and victims, had also appeared
in the more chauvinistic sectors of the French, German and British
press—the experts were not unduly disturbed. More important was
the enthusiastic response of the "responsible" journals in all these
countries.[15]

iii

Perhaps the most pungent commentary on the significance of the proposed Bank for International Settlements appears in a handwritten
memo prompted by a statement of Schacht's, which is dated March 11
and signed "JPM." Apparently for the chairman, it reads as follows:
"Comes down to the fact that common interests are the only source of

friendship between nations; and this bank is one way of finding a common profit in common action."[16]

The chairman could not have agreed more. His efforts to break down the committee's overall problem into manageable specifics, and to focus attention first on those that looked most promising, had not worked out as he had hoped. As he had reported to Washington, subcommittees had been set up at the outset: one to deal with Germany's unconditional payments; a second, to work on "conditional" payments and the kind of moratorium that should attach thereto; and a third to propose new limits on deliveries in kind. He had reported Schacht's insistence that the Versailles treaty had provided—its "one redeeming feature"—that Germany's reparations debt should be liquidated in a single generation, versus the Allies' counterinsistence on annuities extending over the full period (now fifty-eight years) of their own debt settlements with the United States. He had also reported his efforts to get around this impasse for the moment by seeking agreement on workable annuities for, say, the first fifteen years. So far the fruits of these efforts had been meager; it was only as one looked beyond the committee's formal sessions—and notably to the proposed bank—that one could take heart.

But Young's reports, unfailingly objective and judicial in their tone, had failed even to suggest the increasingly formidable subjective barriers to a settlement. To review the contemporary record is to marvel first at the stubbornly cantankerous behavior of many members, and second at the equally stubborn persistence of their sorely tried chairman.[17] Soon premature obsequies were appearing in the press; in one of the more restrained, after duly noting that the committee had been in session for four weeks with little to show for it, the *Deutsche Allgemeine Zeitung* observed: "We do not believe that a favorable horoscope can be cast for the Paris Conference. Its chances decrease . . . the nearer it gets to the crucial problem of how much Germany can promise to pay honestly. . . ."[18]

And so indeed it seemed. How account for the reluctance of these experts—so many of them veterans of the Dawes Committee—to get down to hard negotiations? Why would no one even open the bidding? And why the interminable bickering among the Allies over the matter of "repartition"—the fancy name they gave to dividing up the still undetermined spoils?

Various answers suggest themselves: the frustrations of an inherently intractable assignment; the temper and rising tensions of the time; the difference between actual and nominal independence. Of these three, the third and least obvious may well have been first in importance. Unlike the Dawes Committee, the experts now meeting in Paris had come together in a peaceful and markedly prosperous year. Unlike the Dawes Committee, they could not expect any product they might come up with to have been sold in advance to an anxious and expectant world. Unlike the Dawes Committee, they were expected to effect a *final* settlement, the acceptable—and on their face irreconcilable—terms of which their respective governments had stipulated in advance and advertised widely. It was on finding their independence and their freedom to negotiate so narrowly constricted that the members of Young's committee alternately fumed and sulked.

What, then, were they doing in this galère? Such facts, however intractable, were not unknown to any participant and certainly not to Young. If his committee included members who still hoped against hope for a signal from Washington that in order to break the logjam and ensure a workable settlement, the great creditor nation was prepared to match in concessions to its debtors any reasonable concessions they might now offer Germany, Young was not among them. His two major efforts to persuade his friend Hoover to take a fresh look at the debts in their full context had got him nowhere and, as Young was aware, Hoover's own unsuccessful efforts to negotiate what he felt to be a generous settlement with the French had left him only the more exasperated.[19] And this was the man whose inauguration as President occurred less than a month after the committee first convened.

Young himself was there principally for the reason that his mother had stated when she said good-bye: it was his job. As for the others—especially the Germans and the French—they were playing for stakes that only a settlement could ensure; and these stakes were such as to rule out any ultimate refusal to face up to the problem just because one resented the givens in the equation. Finally, all shared in varying degree—the British probably least—Young's overriding conviction that a settlement at long last of this most conspicuously stubborn of the problems left by the war would release the funds, the human energy, and finally the widespread confidence required for a vast forward movement of the world's economy.

As his ace in the hole, then, the chairman had the comforting awareness that, in view of the stakes, no delegation, however disgruntled, was quite prepared to take public responsibility for walking out and breaking up the conference. Thus on the two or three occasions when a walkout was seriously threatened, he was able to call the bluff. Since it was recognized, moreover, that the Americans alone were in a position to walk out with something like impunity, any hint that an exasperated chairman was about to take that step and state the reason why was likely to prove an effective call to order. And so, when the chips were down, and in the face of one crisis provoked by sources outside the committee, it did.[20]

Owen Young was to need all the aces he could muster—including those somehow conjured up by Morgan's presence and support. Weeks passed before either side agreed to submit figures even to the chairman for possible discussion; even so, it was apparent that the gap was dishearteningly wide. How bridge it unless perhaps the chairman would propose figures of his own? To this suggestion, Young's first answer was that his role was that of mediator, not dictator, and if his colleagues had the will to narrow the gap, they would find the way. But by the end of March, just prior to Easter—having been importuned by all parties to intervene, and having by this time a pretty fair notion of what Schacht might be persuaded to accept—Young at last submitted a memorandum that suggested the extent to which any of the creditors might reasonably claim annual receipts over and above net outpayments to the United States. This memorandum—also sent to Washington early in April—had at least the virtue of exciting discussion, while ostensibly so angering the Germans as to warn the Allies against pressing them too hard. But the Allies, and most particularly Francqui and Emile Moreau, were slow to take the hint and the breakup so narrowly averted threatened again shortly after the Easter recess.[21]

In the meantime, the freedom of the experts was being further eroded by the Wall Street frenzy, which the authorities seemed unable or unwilling to control. Already the boom in common stocks, now apparently out of hand, had closed the door to further European borrowing and opened it to a flood of speculative funds, foreign and domestic. Treasury Secretary Mellon might mildly suggest, as he did in the middle of March, that this was the time to buy good bonds;[22] who but Mellon, answered the public, could afford bonds when you could buy stocks on margin and double your ante overnight? What, then, of the hopes that Young had once entertained, and the French had so fervently embraced, of discounting and paying off at "present value" the last forty scheduled installments of the Allied debt from the proceeds of marketing or "commercializing," say, the German railway bonds? Could the house of Morgan itself underwrite, under prevailing conditions, more than a fraction of the *unconditional* portions of Germany's still-to-be-determined annuities?

While the subcommittee headed by Lord Revelstoke struggled with such questions, Young and Harrison were exchanging anxious messages about remedial action by the Federal Reserve. Unhappily, Harrison had been unable to "quiet" things with Washington; with Benjamin Strong gone, the Federal Reserve Board had simply taken the bit in its teeth. On the very day Young and Morgan sailed, Governor Roy Young was dispatching letters from Washington advising the twelve regional banks of the policy they were to follow in lieu of a higher discount rate: to member banks that borrowed for the purpose of making or sustaining speculative loans to brokers, the discount (or rediscount) window was to be closed. Made public on February 6, this selective credit policy was both welcomed and, more frequently, denounced as ineffectual—"others" being more than ready to supply what the banks no longer could. Certainly Harrison and his directors were unhappy; so was his friend Russell Leffingwell at Morgan's. On February 11 the New York directors held a special meeting and on February 14—their first regular meeting since Young's departure—they voted unanimously to raise the discount rate to 6 percent. This, and some ten subsequent efforts, the Washington board promptly vetoed.[23]

As this stalemate persisted, Young became so exercised as to cable Harrison on March 11, urging him, if agreement with the board looked hopeless, to have Henry Robinson seek White House intervention, after first consulting Mellon. Doubtless prompted in some measure by his confidence in Hoover, this suggestion was nonetheless startling, coming as it did from one who, like Harrison, was jealous to preserve the central bank's independence. Harrison did confer with Mellon, who expected little of the board's directive and felt higher rates to be justified by the market; nevertheless, the secretary had failed to convince the board (including Hoover's friend Adolph Miller) and had so advised the White House. Harrison had thereupon concluded that the President would not intervene and did not attempt to approach him.[24]

But failure to curb the speculative mania in New York was distorting Europe's financial markets too, and thus writing a lame sequel to the chapter in which the stabilization of currencies and the restoration of world trade owed so much to the cooperation of the New York Federal Reserve and its counterparts abroad. And with two important central bankers—Moreau and Schacht—now members of his committee, Young felt this demonstration of impotence by the Fed as a kind of living reproach to his country and its institutions.

And so it was. For a central bank, the discount rate is at best a wasting asset; if a rise is to be effective it must above all else be timely. Thus, back home, with each veto of a higher rate, the Federal Reserve Board seriously weakened the only psychologically effective alternative to its policy of selective curbs which, in checking bank loans to brokers, had demonstrably left the field wide open to "loans for the account of others." Thus credit continued to feed the speculative fires—sensing which (as Harrison advised Young), the officers and directors of *all* the regional banks lined up solidly behind the New York Fed. This may have comforted Harrison, but it did not alter the case. The real tragedy of this disastrous impasse lay in its timing.[25]

iv

A more personal disappointment for Young was the inability of General Dawes to come over as suggested early in March. He was caught, it seemed, by an earlier commitment to the Dominican Republic, and could only send his friend warm messages of regret and reassurance. On March 15, however, young Jo turned up in Paris with her friend and classmate from Bryn Mawr, Polly McElwain, after a tour of half a dozen European countries; this gave her father a welcome excuse for taking both the evening and the weekend off. Then, only a week later, they went with Nelson Perkins and the Crockers to Cherbourg to meet Jo senior, arriving from New York with Mrs. Perkins, her son Jim and her sister Miss Elsie Adams—a riotously happy occasion.[26]

The Youngs settled in at the Ritz together, in the rooms overlooking the garden of the Ministère de la Justice; thus supported, Owen felt ready for anything—especially since Jo's eye and general health were greatly improved. And this was well, because it was not long after her arrival that Young found it necessary to work all night—much of it with his aides—on the memorandum proposing certain figures as a basis for discussion which he had finally promised to prepare for the committee. Next morning, March 28, it was ready, and since the committee was about to recess for Easter it would, as he told Jo, "give the members something to think about" over the holiday. It was not with that avowed purpose that he also sent a copy to Washington where, on that very day, Henry L. Stimson was succeeding Kellogg as secretary of state.[27]

Young himself, to Jo's dismay, had only a busman's holiday, having promised Swope to devote the Easter weekend to Sir Hugo Hirst and their joint effort to broaden the base of the British Thomson-Houston–Metrovick merger by bringing in Hirst and his General Electric Company Ltd. So, while the ladies planned a trip to Chartres for Easter, Young set off for London, taking with him only David Sarnoff, who had come over to lend a hand, and of course William Packer. It was at least a change of scene, and Hirst himself was so impressed with Young and his proposals that, but for the veto of adamant associates, Young's efforts—not forgetting Sarnoff's—would doubtless have paid off. But for Young time pressed; in the event he returned to Paris just in time to serve, along with Raymond Poincaré and Aristide Briand, Morgan and General Pershing, as a pallbearer at Ambassador Myron Herrick's funeral on April 4. Out of respect to the ambassador, the committee did not meet until afternoon; when it did, it seemed at first that all members were the better for the break.[28]

The relapse, however, came quickly. The "bill" as the several creditors, spurred by Young's memo, had reckoned it individually, was found to add up to more than the standard Dawes annuity! At this even the creditors were appalled, but several days of joint effort to reduce it left the total still so high that Schacht and Albert Voegler called it a "good ticket home." On the contrary, Young is quoted as responding, "it is now up to the German experts to tell us what they think they can manage." And so, on April 16, they did, but with conditions attached which were roundly denounced as political by Moreau and others. Thus the subjective gap, at least, was still being widened.[29]

It was in the midst of these tense sessions that, on April 9, a breathless Crocker delivered a long message for his chief which had just come through from the new secretary of state. Evidently prepared as a Treasury memorandum, it castigated Young and his American colleagues for so far ignoring their government's known concerns as to permit the unthinkable linking of war debts and reparations—not to mention proposing an international bank in which the Allies and the Germans would be arrayed as a solid debtor bloc against the United States. Certainly Washington would never permit the governor or other officer of any Federal Reserve bank to become a director of the BIS, nor could it countenance any reparations settlement based on the war debts rather than on Germany's capacity to pay.[30]

If Young was dumbfounded and incredulous. Morgan was apoplectic. Hurt and angry, Young talked of resigning and stating his reasons: how continue if your own government, speaking for your own people, gave you and all your works a rousing vote of no confidence? But Morgan would not hear of it; the United States government, he reminded Young, had refused any part in these proceedings. They themselves, as American citizens, had been appointed by the Germans and the Reparations Commission to help the European experts agree on the best possible settlement, and by God! he for one intended to stand by and see it through. Perkins agreed that the reply Young had been drafting should omit all talk of resignation. Lamont agreed too, but also wanted to excise the argumentative phrases and some of the strong language used by the chairman.[31]

Fortunately that eminent lawyer and elder stateman, Senator Elihu Root, was now in Paris, and Young, Lamont and Parker Gilbert lost no time in seeking his advice. After being briefed by Young on the background and reading Stimson's message three times over, Root advised that, rather than resign, Young and Morgan should make it clear to the secretary that

any such correspondence of debts as that to which you allude arises from . . . the necessity under which the [Allied] Governments . . . find themselves in order to meet their obligations to the U.S. Government. . . . To us it seems that they are clearly within their rights . . . in their efforts to arrange their affairs with their own great debtor in such a way as to facilitate payment of their own debts to the United States. . . . The correspondence between the two sets of debts may create an unfortunate impression but if there is a coincidence, . . . it is a coincidence of fact [and not of our creation].[32]

When, on April 11, Young's composite reply to Stimson was finally dispatched, it made that very point, adding that no settlement was possible which did not ease Germany's burdens in the event that its creditors' burdens were to be diminished. It also made clear the independent status of the Americans serving on the committee and so assumed that the Treasury memorandum did not constitute an official "instruction." Stressing that the committee's negotiations had now reached the critical stage, Young did insist on including his own statement—nothing else of his draft being left—on the services that the BIS could be expected to render, to the United States not least. On the same date, ex-Secretary Kellogg (who was also visiting Paris) sent Stimson a message of his own, both explaining and defending what Young and Morgan were in fact seeking to accomplish.[33]

It was now high time, Young told his colleagues, that they all get back to work, but he himself was not yet satisfied. He had a personal message to Secretary Mellon to get off his chest, and this he would prepare unassisted. Dictated on the evening of the twelfth after long and frustrating sessions with the so-called creditors committee, it was sent in code to his assistant in New York with instructions to decode and deliver it to the secretary by hand. "There," said Young sweetly to his still indignant wife and daughter, "now I've gotten that all out of my system," and going to bed he promptly fell asleep.[34]

When his New York assistant reached the office next morning—a Saturday—the instructions were on his desk; the three-hundred-word message, in code, came in later. Canceling whatever plans he had made for the weekend, the assistant decoded the long radiogram with rising astonishment. It was Case's first intimation of trouble with Washington; thus he wondered what could possibly have gone so wrong as to prompt his chief not only to dictate the bitter protest he was now deciphering, but actually to dispatch it. (In his brief experience, he had known his chief to do the one but not the other.)

Nevertheless, taking the sleeper to Washington, where the secretary had said he would await him in his home Sunday morning at 10:30, the assistant felt himself at last entrusted with a role of some consequence to the conference he had been so reluctant to miss. He remembers being admitted to the presence at 1785 Massachusetts Avenue—a vast and impersonal mansion—where a slight, silver-haired man rose to greet him with great courtesy and a somewhat tired smile. He remembers the expressionless face with which his host read and digested the message that the messenger now had almost by heart:

At the most critical and trying time of our negotiation here [it began] I received from the government of the United States quoting and adopting as the Government's position a memorandum prepared by you. That memorandum stated quote It is impossible for me to draw any other conclusion but that the American delegates have failed to maintain the position consistently taken by their government and that their failure . . . may have unfortunate consequences . . . insofar as the protection of the interests of America are concerned. Unquote. Such an indictment officially by one's country, based on a memorandum of one's friend in the first and only message thus far received from Washington, cannot fail to hurt, and it is difficult for us to believe it was not [so] intended. . . . You [also] criticized severely a program for amplifying International Settlements Bank and declared that quote Under no circumstances will George L. Harrison or any other official of the Federal Reserve System be permitted to serve as [or even to name] a director unquote. Such a declaration, with the meagre knowledge which we will all now have as to the ultimate functioning of such a bank, can scarcely be interpreted as a final decision by the United States but is [nonetheless] severely critical in form.

Reminding Mellon of his influential role in inducing him (Young) to take on this assignment, the message continued:

I should have expected to have received promptly your personal suggestions as to where we were going wrong and the extent to which our program as reported by me was inconsistent with the Administration's views [on] American policy. This seemed to me to be due to me personally from you personally, if not indeed from the President . . . personally. Instead . . . I get an official message based on your memorandum, condemnatory at every point and, with all due respect, in language which I regard as inexcusable. I am humiliated and hurt by one whom I have held in the highest admiration. . . . May I ask you to read my official reply and supplementary message of today to the Secretary of State, in order that you may be informed precisely of what has taken place here up to adjournment tonight. If the President saw your memorandum and authorized its transmission, I beg you to show the message to him. . . .

Owen D. Young[35]

Finishing his reading, the secretary looked for a moment into space and then said softly, half to himself, "Yes, I think I can understand just how Owen Young felt when he wrote this message." Then, addressing Young's messenger more directly, Mellon asked to be excused while he wrote out his reply—which perhaps Mr. Case would then have coded and sent off to Paris at once?

In due course the messenger received the beautifully penned manuscript—now deposited with Young's papers—and taking a room at the Mayflower to expedite matters, coded it there for immediate transmission to his chief. The tone was conciliatory enough. "I have your cable," Mellon's reply began, "and deeply regret that you should have interpreted memorandum prepared in Treasury Department as in any way intended as personal criticism you and your associates. It was not so intended. . . ."

But in substance—as Case indicated in a brief preliminary message to Paris—the secretary held his ground: "You ask why you were not more promptly advised of my views and those of the Administration. Until your cable received April 5, we had no official or direct information as to course negotiations were taking and no reason to feel apprehensive as to the joining of reparations with Allied debts to us. . . ." The memo, he went on, had been prepared as a department document, and was transmitted solely from a sense of the urgent need to warn you at once . . . of the very real dangers which we felt existed and might result in infinite damage to the entire situation in the future. . . . The purpose was not to criticize but to warn. . . . Stimson is cabling you fully today, and his cable will make clear . . . the basis of the very genuine apprehension felt here. I fully appreciate the enormous difficulty of your task and great public spirit you have shown. I am indeed sorry to have added to your burden but in all friendship I feel the exigencies . . . demand[ed] that you be warned at once. I am intending this as well for your American associates. With my warm personal regards and high esteem

A. W. Mellon[36]

Whatever else this meant to Young, he must have been puzzled by one overt statement and by one omission. If his cable received on April 5 had indeed been the administration's first direct advice from Paris, what had happened to his earlier and lengthy messages to Kellogg? And why had Mellon's reply included not one word about the BIS?

Stimson's following cable answered the second question; to its pejorative pronouncements on the bank and the need to keep the Federal Reserve's skirts entirely clear of it, Mellon, surely, could have added nothing. (Had it too been drafted in the Treasury— and by the same hand?) As for the first question, one remains perplexed. The Treasury memorandum of April 9, prepared—as Young was to learn—by Under Secretary Ogden Mills, had in fact referred to Young's earlier messages and specifically to the BIS; so did Mills's memo to Mellon on April 6. Had Mellon simply forgotten Young's earlier messages—or had only the last one really captured his attention? As for the new secretary of state, who had taken office only a few days earlier and avowedly with no knowledge of reparations or of the Young committee's background and purposes, the presumption is that he had simply not caught up with all the papers turned over to him by Kellogg when, on April 9, he was called upon to send that first cable.[37]

In any event, Stimson's second and even longer cable (of April 15) showed that he had fully caught up, if not with the committee's purposes and problems, at least with the way in which these were being viewed by the Hoover administration, including the President himself. And if Young's personal message was really intended less for Mellon than for Hoover, it brought no word whatever from the latter. It was this, try as he would to understand it, which really baffled Young. In the whole entourage of Republicans, from his wife to J. P. Morgan (and company), any mention of Hoover now aroused nothing but resentment and disgust. Young, the sole Democrat in the group except for his daughter, was the only one to come to his old friend's defense: as President, he said, Hoover could not let friendship stand in the way of what he and his advisers found to be politically expedient. But the insensate crudity of his methods still rankled. So did the evidence that not even the President could see in the new international bank what Morgan had seen so quickly.

It was necessary, of course, to put it all aside and, having at length secured Washington's assurance that its views were not to be regarded as "instructions," get on with the game as best one could. But a month or so later, relaxing in the privacy of his rooms after dinner with his wife and Stuart Crocker, Young showed that he had not forgotten. Had Al Smith made it to the White House, he told them, he would never have behaved that way. He would have been far less knowledgeable about international debts and reparations but, if politics had forced his hand, he would have sent a personal message to his friend in explanation. Someday, when all this was finished, Young continued, he himself would go to the White House and have it out on that basis—not as a citizen to the President but as Owen Young to Herbert Hoover. "Hm," said his wife. "If you do you will have to go alone; not only will I never again vote for Herbert, I shan't set foot in the White House as long as he is there." And she didn't.[38]

v

At committee headquarters in what young Jo's diary described as the "comfortable and splendidly new" Hotel George V, April continued to produce internal crises which the chairman met with outward composure. Under his prodding, the creditors did finally get together on a "bill" which reduced their separately computed Easter holiday figures to annuities averaging, for the first thirty-seven years, some 2.25 milliard deutsche marks. Since Schacht's responsive but "conditional" offer—for thirty-seven years only—proposed average annuities of some 1.65 milliard deutsche marks, the dimensions of the objective gap had at least become measurable. But with Moreau and Schacht storming at each other—and with Francqui chiming in at every worst possible moment—the Revelstoke Committee was finding it hard to make much headway, even on the chairman's sensible proposal to seek agreement on annuities payable for the first fifteen years. In determining what could fairly be expected of Germany for that period, Young pointed out, the committee should be able to function as experts or at least as practical men—anything beyond that involving at best only an educated guess. But on April 19, Lord Revelstoke's conscientious efforts ended abruptly in his death, and the chairman's quick action in adjourning out of grief and respect the plenary session scheduled for that day is generally credited with having averted a total break.[39]

What next? In replying on April 20—with the committee still in recess—to Stimson's second message, Young finally attempted a point-by-point rebuttal: initial efforts to concentrate on Germany's capacity to pay had failed because of Allied insistence that this was not absolute but relative. And if our debtors insisted on collecting the full debt they felt was due them, who were we, as Americans, to complain? Besides, insofar as they succeeded, their capacity to meet their debts to us was very greatly, and obviously, strengthened. Nor in this message did Young disguise the imminent possibility that he might feel forced to resign. Much as he shrank from the thought of defaulting on his obligations to the appointing authorities of Europe, even this was preferable to continuing on a course which his own government decried. He still hoped for an honorable escape from this dilemma; there was more than a suggestion that the failure of his own and his colleagues' best efforts might provide it.[40]

If this paraphrase puts the matter rather less subtly than Young did, it does give the substance of his lengthy dispatch. Except perhaps to his wife and Crocker, it was the one time he was to admit the possibility of failure, although his colleagues and even the press were now mostly prepared to accept it as inescapable fact. And as the chairman and his colleagues were aware, foreign offices were all buzzing with the news of the Hoover administration's failure to support the American experts.[41]

But whether Young's candid message, or talks with Root, or press reports of the committee's imminent demise, had now awakened Stimson to all that was at stake, the secretary's cable of May 2 was markedly different in tone, and suggested an intent, at least, to reassure. This Young was quick to acknowledge and when, a fortnight later, press reports of the secretary's reiterated denial of any possible participation by the Federal Reserve in the BIS created a furor in Paris and Berlin which suggested that the bank itself might be still-born, Stimson did have the grace to send a message of explanation and partial reassurance.[42]

This was fortunate because, during May, it was only through daily infusions from its chairman, so to speak, that the committee functioned at all. Plenary sessions were out; they had become counter-productive. Instead, the chairman met separately, and almost constantly, with one group or another—when he was not meeting with importunate individuals like Moreau or Francqui and, of course, Schacht. Somehow, with the aid of his American colleagues and advisers, he also found time to do what all—and especially Schacht—were now demanding: namely, to propose a compromise schedule of annuities that the Americans at least could back. But this he refused to submit to a plenary session unless and until he had satisfactory private assurance of support from creditors and debtor alike.

Under the circumstances, Will Rogers's column of May 6 in the *New York Times*—as transmitted in a radiogram from his sometime assistant, John Elwood—could hardly have been more opportune. A Will Rogers fan himself, Young found special relish in these shrewdly compassionate observations:

Sunshine and Perquisites are mighty scarce in us Democrats lives but just lest you forget this Owen D. Young that is doing such splendid work in Paris trying to divide one Bone with a half dozen dogs and not even having the bone to divide—its fallen to his lot to demonstrate to even the prize winners that war purses was greatly exaggerated and to be on the losers side is a downright discouragement—Well this Young man is a Democrat strange as it may seem and I have been his Mark Sullivan since 1920. I don't want to run him for President I just want to keep him to "point with pride" while we are "viewing our others with alarm."

Schacht visited Berlin following Revelstoke's death, and had returned chastened. Press reports of the imminent breakup at Paris had been followed by great pressure on the German mark, and while Schacht blamed this chiefly on the French, he also encouraged Young to make his compromise proposal. In undertaking to do so, Young had long since been apprised by Gilbert that in their early assessment of the conference and its probable outcome, Gustav Stresemann and others—with Schacht's knowledge—had reckoned on an annuity of at least two milliard (billion) marks as the price they could expect to pay for an end to the "receivership" and Dawes Plan schedules, *plus* evacuation of the Rhineland. And that was almost precisely the figure that Young now came up with—plus some fifty million for servicing the Dawes loan.[43]

While Young understood and admired Schacht's efforts to reduce the bill substantially, he also knew that Stresemann and Julius Curtius, then Stresemann's right-hand man, felt that on occasion Schacht had overreached himself. Thus Young reckoned on persuading Schacht that if he were the first to accept the chairman's compromise schedule, it would leave him in the strongest possible position and put Moreau and Francqui squarely on the spot. And as chairman he was the readier to help him because, as the lone debtor facing a solid creditor bloc, Schacht's position was even tougher than that in which the U.S. government feared so greatly to find itself within the BIS. It was also true that Schacht had helped him rescue the bank from the outrageous slings and arrows which first Stimson and then Moreau had launched in its direction.

His efforts seemed to bear fruit when, on May 4, Schacht accepted the chairman's figures—not, however, without conditions. As for the creditors, they backed and filled, with Moreau demanding a thorough airing of Schacht's new reservations. On May 17, Schacht's German colleague, Voegler, the Big Steel magnate, found a pretext to resign; Ludwig Kastl, his alternate and another industrialist, at once took his place. While Voegler's resignation closely followed the furor over Stimson's adverse comments on the BIS, there seems to have been no direct connection between the two. And somehow, these crises were surmounted.[44]

One reason was the chairman's steady pressure to move ahead with the report, stressing all they had accomplished and leaving the still unsettled items—like figures—to be filled in last. According to Crocker, he told Stamp in J. P. Morgan's presence that he (Stamp) would have to write the report because "you can always say what's in my mind so much better than I can." Morgan supported his plea. "Very well, Mr. Morgan," said Stamp, "I'll write it if you will underwrite it."[45]

The drafting process showed that a great deal had in fact been accomplished. First, of course, there was the bank. Second, there was the agreed division of the annuities into conditional and unconditional categories, with safeguards concerning the first which Germany alone could invoke. Third, deliveries in kind were to continue, but only for a limited time and on a wasting scale. Finally, the German receivership was to be lifted and all signs of foreign financial control removed. And though outside the committee's frame of reference, it was tacitly understood that evacuation of the Rhineland would follow hard upon agreement on the annuities.

Nor were the creditors far from finding Young's compromise figures acceptable; indeed, their latest figures were substantially closer to his than Schacht's had been. Had it been decided, as Young had vainly suggested, to leave "repartition" to the creditor governments—and why not?—agreement would not have been too difficult; unfortunately, every change in the annuity figures involved the creditors in a fresh debate on distributive justice. But at last, toward the end of May, they did agree; on Memorial Day, Schacht, who had escaped to Versailles for a sorely needed rest, returned and promised Young his full cooperation. Surely this was it. A day later Francqui's stormy insistence on a Belgian mark settlement *now* was again too much for Schacht, who stormed out himself. Instead of a final settlement, the final crisis had arrived.

Young could have wept. He had hoped to sail for home on June 2 with his wife and daughter; after all, his eldest son, C.J., and Esther Christensen were to be married in Cleveland on June 15 and there was little time to lose. His two Josephines must now go ahead on the *Olympic* and he would try to catch the *Aquitania* when she sailed on June 8. That would be his last chance to make the wedding, as the next few days would be his last chance to save the plan.[46]

Mirabile dictu, he did both. On June 4, after yeoman efforts by Sarnoff finally got Schacht off his high horse, a collateral solution of the Belgian marks problem was achieved and with that, ratification of all the basic agreements speedily followed.[47] On the evening of June 7, all members of the committee lined up to sign the report, while the press photographers pleaded for "just one more"—this time of Moreau and Schacht reaching across the chairman to shake hands. Amid great fanfare from the press Young actually caught the *Aquitania* when she sailed for New York next day.

But on the evening of June 7, when the ceremony of signing was over, Crocker reports that Young went to his rooms, took a bath, and set out from the hotel on foot, to dine alone. Even with all the invaluable and unfailing support of family, colleagues and friends, it had been a lonely struggle. And aside from his extraordinary patience, which the Japanese delegate, Kengo Mori, was so astonished to find in an American, the record leaves no doubt that the determining factor in this happy ending was the towering figure of Young, the American whom, with his powerful colleague Morgan, no government save their own found itself in any position to cross.

Indeed, in the final analysis, even Washington found it politic to congratulate Young and his colleagues on their "notable contribution to stability and to progress." In a "personal" message to Young, released to the press well before it reached him, President Hoover said that he had "heard with great satisfaction of the successful conclusion of the arduous work of the experts committee," which he called "a most important step toward the restoration of international confidence and national stability." Any temptation Young may have felt to reply, "Small thanks to you and the Treasury, Mr. President" was promptly—and no doubt properly—resisted.[48]

Chapter 25

Wall Street and Washington: The Crash of 1929

B Y THE skin of his teeth, Owen Young reached Cleveland on Saturday, June 15, in time for the wedding of his son Charles and Esther Christensen. He had to beg off from the hero's welcome which, with great fanfare, had been planned and announced by New York City mayor James J. Walker and his redoubtable chief of protocol, Grover Whalen. He had also to be rescued by special tug from the fogbound *Aquitania* on Friday evening in order to repack his bag and reach Grand Central Station before the 12:20 sleeper left for Cleveland. For the ubiquitous reporters he had only a prepared statement praising his colleagues; of the plan itself he would not talk. This was partly a matter of policy but there could be no doubt that he was thoroughly, and heartily, sick of reparations.[1]

Having gone down harbor on the tug to meet him, his assistant was deeply shocked at his chief's appearance; to Case he looked not so much five months as, suddenly, five years older. But the family reunion in Cleveland and a week or so in Van Hornesville—during which he made the commencement speech at nearby Hamilton College (which also awarded him a degree)—did wonders for him.[2] It was as well that he had not lost his powers of resilience. New York was still very much "where the action was"; also, before he could even make a start at his office he had a luncheon appointment to keep at the White House with his colleagues on June 25. Clearly his responsibilities vis-à-vis the plan had by no means ended with the ceremony of its signing.

The President was cordial enough, but this was hardly the occasion—would it ever arise?—for the man-to-man talk which Young had promised himself. Neither then nor later, moreover, did the administration alter its published stand against participation by the Federal

Reserve in the Bank for International Settlements. Rather, it was agreed, in conference with State and Treasury officials, that selection of alternative representatives (as provided in the plan) be left to Young and Morgan, with the understanding that they should be acceptable to Governor Harrison. The same procedure was to govern the choice of Americans to serve on the Organization Committee, which would see to it that the actual structure of the bank faithfully reflected its architects' blueprint. Here Young's first choice was Henry M. Robinson—still the President's close friend and adviser—but with Robinson definitely "unavailable," they finally settled on the respected heads of two First National Banks: of New York, Jackson Reynolds, and of Chicago, Melvin Traylor. Reynolds, indeed, was to serve as chairman of the committee, whose efforts were closely watched and abetted by J. P. Morgan from his vantage point in London.[3]

This was one item of the plan's unfinished business to which Young could devote himself *con amore*. Proceeding in Paris on the assumption that, in the context of the times, almost any settlement was better than none, he had contrived, improbably enough, to achieve one. Precarious as this doubtless was—by Perkins's standards, certainly—it was nevertheless true that Germany's annual obligations now averaged 20 percent less than the Dawes Plan's standard annuity and, for the next decade at least, the cut went half again as deep.[4] Free at last of foreign controls and troops, Germany was now on its own, and just conceivably might set out to prove that the gentlemen of the press wh had hailed the Young Plan and its authors as the true "makers of the peace" really knew what they were talking about. But such a hope made sense only as one could assume a sustained and rising level of prosperity, and it was precisely because this was not to be taken for granted that Young regarded the new international bank as a salutary as well as the one creative feature of the plan.

Thus, as he had told the American correspondents before leaving Paris, the BIS had implications for the future which far transcended the mere transfer of reparations. With industry and trade becoming increasingly international, new financial and credit facilities to match had now become imperative if the world's economic machinery was ever to function as it should. "You can't," he reminded them, "build a turbine in a blacksmith's shop"—adding, in a phrase which they were quick to broadcast, that "a capitalistic system in which millions in the other continents go hungry while wheat rots in the Dakotas" will not long survive. New tools would have to be fashioned if capitalism were to cope with new and emergent problems, and the Bank for International Settlements was one such tool.[5]

That Hoover, the great engineer, should fail to grasp all this was, for Young, still hard to credit. That as President of the country which had the most at stake he should see in the bank not a promise but a threat was worse than baffling; somehow it rankled. Was this the man who, six years earlier, in order to fire the imagination of the American people with something bigger than their petty concerns, had been so eager to promote "super-power" that Young had felt impelled to warn him of its political hazards?[6] Was he now being governed less by his generous hopes than by his fears? And if so, by *what* fears—of a European debtor bloc? Of the Congress? Or could they also be of Young?

Young's personal staff and closest friends found this last suggestion less farfetched than he himself professed to find it. "Saul hath slain his thousands and David his ten thousands" was a chant hardly calculated to endear David to the king, and while it was as peacemakers that Young and Hoover had both been honored, it almost seemed that for every favorable notice the press now gave the President it was giving ten to Young. Certainly his prestige, his reputation and his popular appeal had never been higher. Reparations might be remote from the daily life of the average American, but, as *Collier's* magazine proclaimed in a full-page editorial, the man who could settle that problem largely through his patience and powers of persuasion could doubtless settle almost any.[7]

Those who thought so were clamorous enough that summer to keep Young busy resisting their appeals. To William Green, president of the AFL, who was asking him to arbitrate a New Orleans streetcar workers' strike, he sent a sharply negative reply. To Schacht's colleagues, Ludwig Kastl and Carl Melchior, now at The Hague, he refused his interpretation of a clause in the Young Plan, reminding them that Sarnoff had already given it to Schacht. And if he did not altogether reject the plea of his old friend P. W. Litchfield, president of Goodyear Tire and Rubber, that he undertake once again to mediate the problems of that vexed'industry, his acceptance was limited and strictly conditional. If Nelson Perkins, he replied, could be induced to report on "the law and the facts" of the case, he would then offer his own recommendations based thereon; more than that he could not do.[8]

Unlike Hoover and even Coolidge, Young never gave the so-called New Era explicit public recognition, but to many of his fellows he personified it. If whatever he did or said was news, the editorial praise which typically followed was in part the honest tribute of men who knew and deeply admired him—John Finley, Walter Lippmann and Frank Kent, to name a few. But it was also in part a reflection of the need of a business-oriented society for some more-than-life-size figure in whom its virtues, actual and imagined, were writ large, and here Young seemed to fill the bill. Having what it takes to get things done, whether in business or public affairs, he also had, as Hoover did not, an ear for the telling phrase. And charisma. "Not a candidate," he might insist, but to the President's friends and advisers, a Democratic dark horse that would bear watching.

Indeed, on the very day that Hoover's message of congratulations had reached him in Paris came a cable from the publisher of the *New York Times* which read as follows:

Heartiest congratulations on agreement it is substantially what you prophesied two years ago stop You have established yourself as the wisest and greatest peacemaker of your time stop Having an abiding confidence in the wisdom of the American people I predict that you will be in the White House if not in four years in eight years.   Adolph S. Ochs

Young's reply—by radio, of course—was a model of circumspection. Ignoring the prediction, it credited Ochs himself with the idea of taking reparations out of "political treasuries." It then went on to testify to the "high regard" which Thomas Lamont and he had come to feel for the *Times* correspondent, P. J. Philip, who "has handled your reparations news superbly." Young was to do as much on his return for Leland Stowe of the *Herald Tribune* and Arnot Dosch-Fleurot of the *World*. Small wonder that the fourth estate tended to hold him too in "high regard"—not least, perhaps, as the lone capitalist who dared speak out about the weaknesses and the needs as well as the virtues and potential of the system.[9]

Not that Young did not have his detractors and his critics, from the well tempered to the harshly discordant. There were the tycoons who complained that he was too radical or too "preachy"—or both. There were the labor leaders who distrusted his proposed "cultural wage" and were baffled by his suggestion that labor hire capital. There were the liberals of the Norris-Brandeis stamp who found him bland, evasive, or "just too good to be true." And there were also such occasional paranoid figures as the "Swindled, Outraged and Embittered Inventor"—one Heard Respess—who, as Young was leaving for Paris, had written to "warn" him that the Victor Talking Machine Company had pirated an important Respess invention, and that the merger with

Victor would make the Radio Corporation accountable to him for the cumulative damage he had suffered. (This, according to his subsequent reckoning, amounted to a cool forty million dollars.) As Young's assistant had written to assure him, RCA's patent office was making its own investigation of his charges, but when General Harbord went farther and arranged a meeting of their respective counsel, Respess said he "smelled a trap" and refused to disclose—or permit his counsel to disclose—any part of the basis for his claims. Instead, he proceeded to exploit his undeniably inventive talent for vituperative abuse in a chain of letters which Young—now his favorite target—irked him further by totally ignoring.[10]

ii

Young, in any case, was finding himself far too busy to let scurrilous letters put him off his stride. July and August were months for catching up on a score of things: family, farms and St. Lawrence; GE, RCA, and of course the Federal Reserve, which had still come up with no effective means of curbing Wall Street's raging fever. And plans must be made with care for Marie Curie's visit in October, lest it prove too much for her.[11]

He was also keeping a sharp eye on the Allied-German conference on the Young Plan at The Hague, where Britain's Labour chancellor, Philip Snowden, was making trouble by demanding a bigger slice of the pie for Britain. Young, however, was apparently less worried about the outcome of Snowden's one-man show than about current British criticism of his friend Josiah Stamp for conceding too much at Paris. Certainly this was the burden of the singularly warm response which he dictated on August 26 to Stamp's long handwritten letter of late July:

If I were in your place I would say nothing and do nothing, and encourage my friends also to keep quiet. Snowden is riding the wave of popular acclaim at the moment. He will have that when he comes back from the Hague no matter what the settlement is, and when that cools down no one is likely to be more critical of what he has done than the very persons who have been beating the drums. Then will come the time for just appraisal of what you have done, and most all, a clear understanding of what Snowden has sacrificed. . . .

What follows is something rare for Young—a revelation of his innermost feelings about the whole structure of intergovernmental debts and so about the real nature of Snowden's lost opportunity:

The only thing that would justify Snowden in his position at the Hague would be a large policy of torpedoing the entire reparation and debt settlement program in the expectation that all the world would be brought sharply to its senses and that the slate would either be washed clean or nearly enough clean so that the figures remaining on it would be negligible. That is what statesmanship would be justified in doing at the Hague. . . .[12]

That so candid a letter is marked "Not Sent" is hardly surprising. Young's signature would have made it far too explosive to be entrusted to the mails or the hazards of accidental exposure. But it is too bad that Stamp could not have seen it—including Young's report on Washington's attitude and the more personal note with which it closed:

The Washington Government has not been friendly to the Plan. It has not dared to exhibit its unfriendliness except on the question of participation of the Federal Reserve in the International Bank. Nevertheless I have a feeling that the want of enthusiasm at Washington has served more or less as an encouragement to Snowden. In any event, there has been no influence from Washington to deter [him] notwithstanding the fact that we are the largest beneficiaries of the settlement. . . .

Josephine charged me this morning to send her love to Olive and to you. This I do with my own added.

In contrast to these incisive commentaries on the plan and its reception, Stamp might have detected in his friend's concurrent report on the business scene more than a hint of ambivalence.

I cannot say [Young wrote] that I have plunged into work in any such energetic way as you do, but I have been in the office daily getting reports of what happened during my five months of nightmare. Things move here so unbelievably fast that an absence of six months makes one superannuated as far as business is concerned. New alignments of interest, shifts in the center of gravity, new stars in the field of management, have come about in public utilities, banking and industry since I have been away. One has to take time to get his bearings. He must get familiar with the new lighthouses and the new sandbars, and he must learn that some of the old rocks in the channel have been torpedoed and disappeared. To try and sail the old course after six months absence would be nothing more than to demonstrate your want of skill as a navigator.[13]

New stars and old rocks notwithstanding, Young had no fear that his skill as a navigator was about to be challenged by his associates at GE, RCA, or the New York Federal Reserve. Whatever his part in resolving early in August the disastrous impasse over the discount rate, the Federal Reserve Board's tardy approval of the rise had come too late; not a few pundits condemned it and the market virtually ignored it. In industry, however—and notably with the Morgan-sponsored New York State utilities merger—the door was still wide open to the "new alignments of interests" of which Young wrote. Thanks to other negotiations begun in Paris, GE was making a substantial investment in the new share offerings of AEG, with Young and Gerard Swope becoming directors but in no sense challenging the Germans' full control. This was simply another step toward the realization of Young's master plan for the industry worldwide; perhaps it would give the British second thoughts about resisting—with Sir Hugo Hirst's key directors—his efforts to consolidate their still scattered and uneconomic units.[14]

As for RCA, its March takeover of the Victor Talking Machine Company assured it an even stronger position in recorded (and broadcast) music than its earlier Photophone and RKO ventures had provided in talking movies or the theater. More important, Victor's manufacturing facilities in Camden gave Sarnoff a potent asset to exploit in his ambitious plan for unifying radio research, manufacturing and sales in RCA itself. This ambition, thanks in great measure to Sarnoff's success in finally winning Young's support, was largely to be consummated before the year was out. In the meantime, the rapidly increasing numbers of motorcar owners were clamoring for radio sets and, as their installation became technically feasible, conferences between Young and Sarnoff and General Motors officials soon put the finishing touches on a joint and promising subsidiary, General Motors–Radio.[15]

In RCA's original field—instant point-to-point communication—the proposed merger with Western Union which Young had expected to conclude in Paris had never come off. That Newcomb Carlton, Western Union's president, had backed away at the eleventh hour was a disappointment to Young and others; as Lamont had written one of his partners from Paris, "Owen will make [this combination] blossom like the rose." Shortly thereafter, however, long talks with Sosthenes Behn had brought ITT into the picture—so much so that it had agreed to buy and take over bodily Radio's "wireless" subsidiary, RCA Communications. If to Young this was a less pleasing prospect than the other, it would at least help to unify our overseas communications which, with cables and radio already a joint enterprise in most of Europe, he now regarded as a curative move. Meanwhile, the price which he had fixed and Behn seemed ready to accept was calculated to be highly acceptable to the Radio Corporation's stockholders, of which GE was still by far the largest.[16]

There had been no trace of ambivalence in Young's own dealings with the stock market during that hectic spring in Paris. In September 1927, he had opened a brokerage account with George Pick of Chicago which to date had proved highly profitable to both. Buying only the equities he knew and always for the rise, in what seemed an ever-rising market, Young could draw on his credit to produce an abundant harvest from a small outlay of seed. If his consequent commitments to Pick were large, and they were—totaling some $2,200,000 on the eve of his departure for Paris—they were more than amply covered by the excellent securities held as collateral. And the same was true of his very substantial loans from the New York and Boston banks he knew best.[17]

As viewed in perspective from Paris, however, America's speculative orgy had its alarming and even sinister aspects. Decisive action was urgent, and if Young's best efforts failed to evoke it from the now-splintered central banking system, he could—and did—take it for himself. Thus by March 1, 1929, he had liquidated his brokerage account in full, and having also sharply reduced his outstanding bank loans, he was virtually out of the market.

And a good thing too—or was it? Back in New York that summer, with the stocks he had sold still soaring, Young was not so sure. Meeting in July with GE's senior and junior officials at their annual in-house gathering, Young confessed to a "sense of intoxication—notwithstanding the 19th Amendment" in being home at last, where the air was electric with enterprise in contrast to the static atmosphere of Europe. Of the market, he said nothing. His one word of warning was a reminder that Germany could pay reparations only as the goods and services it contrived to export exceeded its imports; this could happen without harming others, but only as such new instruments as the BIS operated to support the unprecedented forward advance in the world's economy for which he felt the stage was set. And in this drama, GE was clearly cast for the leadership role for which he and Swope had long sought to prepare it.[18]

During that summer, the sense of frustration and foreboding which prevailed at the New York Fed seemed pretty much confined to its four walls. Outside, from Cambridge to Berkeley, with notably few exceptions, economists, pundits and the press were playing their own variations on the theme of the "leading Chicago bank" (not Melvin Traylor's) which predicted that "1929 would be a banner year with every prospect for continuing prosperity."[19] Such caveats as appeared from time to time were somehow muted.

This was notably true of the reception given the report of the

Hoover Committee on Recent Economic Changes, which, signed in his absence, still bore Young's name as a member. Especially in Wesley Mitchell's concluding commentary, the presence of new sandbars and the need for new lighthouses were expressly and soberly noted, but the basic economy and its prospects appeared to have passed the National Bureau's comprehensive examination, with honors sufficient to produce a spate of reassuring and self-congratulatory headlines. Those crossing Young's desk included the *New York Sun's* EXPERTS VISION BRIGHT FUTURE FOR THIS NATION, and the *Chicago Journal of Commerce's* U.S. PROSPERITY BARELY BEGUN, SURVEY HOLDS. In its editorial comment on "A Disappointing Report," the *Times* of Hartford raised a discordant but lonely voice. More in tune was the *Watertown Times's* editorial on "Prosperity Ahead," which even discovered in Young's plea for a cultural wage the basis for the new and better balance between production and consumption of which the economy could already boast. Evidently discounting the future was no monopoly of the market.[20]

Such headlines and euphoric commentaries customarily left Young cold—but so, it would appear, did finding himself where the action was and having no part of it. To be at the races and place no bets— even when you knew the horses—was downright unsporting. True, when his broker first waited on him early in July, Young moved with caution, placing nothing more than a token bet. Yet here were his favorites—GE, RCA and the utilities—all setting new and breathtaking records; a storm was certainly brewing but, having made ample provision for his family, why shouldn't he have a final fling?

And so he did—somewhat, perhaps, to his own surprise—beginning with a second and very much more substantial bet on July 29. This time the horse was GE, which Young *knew* was having a banner year, but whose earnings could not come close to matching the exponential rise of its shares. Nevertheless, Young now instructed Pick to buy for his account 2,000 shares, currently quoted at 366, or just six times its (adjusted) price of some four years earlier. To these shares, over the next month, the same broker added, per instructions, 1,000 U.S. Steel at 237 and 3,500 RCA (new) at 93½. If he reminded Young that only 18 months earlier he had paid less than this for RCA's *old* shares, which had since split 5 for 1, it is not a matter of record.

These purchases, financed as usual by Pick and retained by him as collateral, now left Young his debtor by something more than $1,300,-000. Nor was this the whole story. Come September, still enamored as he was of certain old friends among the utilities, Young proceeded to buy at the market 1,000 shares each of American Power and Light, American Gas and Electric, National Power and Light, and Electric Power and Light. At current prices these purchases set him back by half a million, financed largely by his banks.

So far as his dealings with Pick were concerned, the record suggests that the urge was soon satisfied and that Young did not overstay his time. Before the end of September he had instructed his broker to sell all that he had bought for his account, except for 700 of the GE shares and his original token chip, 100 shares of Aluminium Ltd. This sale added a mere $33,000 to the vastly larger short-term capital gains he would be reporting to the Internal Revenue Service; far more important, it reduced his indebtedness to Pick by more than a million to some $250,000, duly secured by the remaining shares. At the same time he was advising Dawes by radio that the condition of the market made it now extremely urgent to dispose as planned of their joint and highly profitable holdings of New York and Richmond Gas.[21]

Nevertheless, he made no move to liquidate either his recently acquired utility shares or the bank loans on which they largely rested. What had happened to his vaunted prescience we can only guess. A storm of sorts he certainly expected, but apparently none so violent that he was not equipped to ride it out—"sound" common stocks, bank loans and all. Nor, it must be added, had anything in his experience prepared him for more than that. Certainly the present had nothing in common with the nineties; the coming storm would simply serve as a sharp reminder of all that we had to learn—chiefly, in Young's book, about the new responsibilities, national and international, which attached to our unprecedented prosperity and power. Thus chastened, we could resume our forward march with confidence and without illusions.

iii

Young's summertime affair with the market would have been news indeed; fortunately, he knew how to keep his own counsel and no leaks whatsoever occurred. Nor, being otherwise engaged, did he spend long hours with his broker or the heavily overburdened ticker tape. In early August, the executives attending the Harvard Business School's summer session voted him the "most outstanding" of American business leaders and the vote was duly featured and applauded by the press. That such eminence carries its own penalties was hardly news to Young; nonetheless, the summer abounded in reminders. One such had indeed anticipated the Harvard balloting: another "Open Letter" addressed to him in mid-July, this time by the editors of the *New Republic*.

The occasion was the merger of the Mohawk-Hudson and other New York State utilities into the Niagara-Hudson System, which, presumably because a Morgan-sponsored holding company was involved, the editors found tantamount to an unregulated private monopoly. Citing Young's support on the one hand of Governor Smith's waterpower program and of Roosevelt's subsequent candidacy as governor, and on the other his close association with Morgan in Paris, the editors urged that Young now owed it to himself as well as to the public—especially as a much-talked-of presidential nominee—to issue a statement which would clarify his current views.[22]

When this open letter appeared, Young was just completing a trip to the North Country. As he had radioed his daughter in London on July 11, her brother Philip was driving him up to Canton on the twelfth in her car, with a stopover at Association Island for Camp General and the speech already cited. Back in his office on July 18, Young saw no one, spending the day catching up on accumulated correspondence. His warm letter to Dawes of the nineteenth praised his friend's work as ambassador, especially his efforts to promote a U.S.-British naval accord, adding that here he was only echoing the President's praises. Evidently Morgan wanted to see him—whether about Niagara-Hudson, R C A – I T T, the B I S or possibly all three, one can only guess. And so, after meetings with Swope, Traylor and the R C A and N B C directors, he took the night train for Bar Harbor— whence he returned on Morgan's yacht, the *Corsair*. On the twenty-third the two met again, this time in Morgan's office at 23 Wall Street. And on the twenty-fifth, one Mr. Calvin Coolidge spent the morning in Young's office for a firsthand account of the Paris conference and the emergence of the Young Plan.[23]

That same afternoon, after writing Mme Curie, Young dispatched his reply to editor Herbert Croly at the *New Republic*. Citing the record as proof that he had "no hesitation in expressing my views . . . in regard to the appropriate solution" of such public questions, he found the present moment inopportune for any further statement. Pointing out that "the Legislature of the State of New York, at the initiation of and with the cooperation of the Governor, had set up a

Committee to investigate and report upon the very questions contained in your letter," he felt that "under such conditions it is inappropriate for me, as a private citizen, to volunteer my views."[24]

Presumably Governor Roosevelt would have agreed—though he might have called it pussyfooting. But Young's little talk to GE's customers at the September meeting of the Edison Illuminating Companies reveals concern of a kind which others shared but commonly found it expedient to suppress. Rejecting the notion that sensitive issues are best disposed of by sweeping them under the rug, he deliberately, if delicately, raised some: "After all, there are three great factors involved in the electrical industry, each of which we have to keep our eyes on. One is economics, the second is finance and the third is politics." Finding the first on the whole well handled, he confessed to "some reservation" about the second; certainly it would "bear investigation and consideration" by the industry—which was first to be affected:

We have recently seen situations, not satisfactory in themselves which had a tremendous repercussion upon every property in the industry. And so everybody is interested in everybody else's financing, especially . . . if in any sense it is bad financing. That is the kind of question which I think . . . might well be discussed, not alone privately in the rooms of half a dozen men but openly, in order that we may clear our minds frankly about what is going on, and whether it is well for the industry or ill. . . . Is there anything so sacred about finance that it shouldn't be exposed to . . . criticism?

As for politics, questions once purely local or parochial inevitably became statewide and even national as soon as the industry's financial pattern did. As such, they too deserved general attention and frank discussion: "And so, Mr. President, if I had any suggestion to make to you this morning, it would be in the future to add to your programs, which now deal practically exclusively with economic problems, problems of finance and, if you have the courage, problems of politics. Let men get on this platform . . . and propound their ideas. Let there be discussion and there will be, I promise you. . . ."[25]

iv

In the meantime, Young was concerning himself with the financing of certain nonprofit institutions, and for this the times promised good hunting. Unlike GE and RCA, St. Lawrence University and the Page School needed substantial new capital, and as chairman of both boards Young felt that it was up to him to find it. If so, he had better seize the moment.

Thus on August 21 he wrote Secretary Mellon—who owed him something after all—to invite a gift sufficient to build a Mellon library at St. Lawrence. He also wrote Floyd Carlisle (of Consolidated Gas) about a much-needed dormitory. Carlisle had other plans in mind, but before the year's end, Young had two pledges toward a new men's residence hall of $200,000 each, one from the brothers Mellon and the other from George F. Baker, Sr., whose father, a prominent Universalist layman in New York State, had been one of the charter trustees of the institution in 1856. As Young was to demonstrate afresh in raising funds for Mme Curie's gram of radium, it helped no end to do yourself what you were asking others to do. So now he did just that. The St. Lawrence venture, however, required a total of $600,000; this time Young's matching contribution would not be chicken feed.[26]

The Page School of International Relations was a very different story. Sparked by his earlier and well-publicized speeches on its behalf, contributions of nearly half a million dollars, largely in small gifts and pledges, had been raised, but efforts by his staff working with other key trustees to get the job finished during his absence in Paris had come to nothing. Having now become convinced that the original million-dollar target was grossly insufficient, Young attempted once again to use the force of example as leverage for large gifts from others. Late in August he wrote Dr. John Finley, a fellow trustee, that "I have . . . personally undertaken with Dr. Ames [who had succeeded Frank Goodnow as president of Johns Hopkins] to provide an income up to $50,000 a year for three years to start the work going." A few days later, on September 5, he wrote similar letters to Edward W. Bok and to his old friend Judge Edwin B. Parker—explaining to each the Page School's potentially unique significance as a central clearinghouse for all peace studies, here and abroad. That these efforts should have proved unproductive despite Judge Parker's undoubted concern, substantial resources and unlimited goodwill was a consequence of circumstances tragically unforeseen. Judge Parker, it developed, was now fatally ill; the two were not to meet again, and less than two months after Young had written him, he was dead. His two-million-dollar bequest to establish a school of international studies made no mention of the Page School; rather, it was to be set up at a university selected by the trustees named in his will. One of these, to be sure, was Young's friend Harlan F. Stone, but another, alas, had an overriding stake of his own in seeing that the funds went elsewhere. Thus the best efforts of Young and his staff to direct them toward Johns Hopkins were to prove unavailing.[27]

As August ended, Young was being roundly congratulated on the outcome of the Hague Conference, which had ended at last with relatively minor damage to the plan itself. Only then did he agree to accept the (Theodore) Roosevelt Medal, which was to be awarded on October 27—Roosevelt's birthday and his own. But Snowden's demands had left Schacht sorely disgruntled, and Aristide Briand's acquiescence in accepting them proved to be a prelude to his fall. And when, on October 2, Gustav Stresemann died, the prospect of ratification by Germany was seriously clouded.[28]

Young felt Stresemann's loss on other grounds as well, as his prompt, thoughtful and very personal telegram to the German ambassador made clear:

May I take the liberty of expressing to you and through you to Dr. Stresemann's family and personal friends my sorrow and my sympathy stop My acquaintance and I think I may properly say my friendship with Dr. Stresemann arose out of difficult situations and under circumstances where men in a short time come to know each other well stop He was a man of great understanding having the capacity to comprehend many facts and evaluate them correctly stop He was a man of great courage frankly facing the difficulties of his country and steadfastly meeting them stop He longed for a world at peace which meant to him something more than freedom from war and he was ambitious for his country to play its part in that accomplishment stop In his death Germany and all nations have suffered a serious loss.[29]

Science being international, Young had hoped that both Stresemann and Briand would attend the forthcoming Edison celebration in Dearborn, Michigan, and pay their respects to the octogenarian inventor. Now it seemed wise to eliminate all foreign politicos, letting Albert Einstein speak for Germany and Mme Curie herself for France. On October 4 he radioed Dawes to look after that indomitable little lady when they crossed on the *Ile de France*; General and Mrs. Dawes were then to come home with the Youngs.

After his usual board meetings, a dinner conversation with Winston Churchill, and sessions in his office with visitors as diverse as Samuel Insull and Mary Van Kleeck, Parker Gilbert and the mayor of Dallas,

Governor Harrison and the Salvation Army's General Booth, Henry Robinson and Missy Meloney, Young paid a flying visit to Henry Ford at Dearborn and returned just in time to meet the *Ile de France* when she docked on October 14. And when, on October 21, he and Mme Curie—along with Albert Einstein and the President—met in Dearborn for the great Edison celebration, it marked the beginning of the memorable week recounted elsewhere which he and his family devoted to this very special guest.[30]

For the purposes of this chapter, this series of engagements with Mme Curie is significant chiefly because it kept Young busy upstate while all hell was finally breaking loose on Wall Street. For the past six weeks a notable erosion in the market had been taking place; on "Black Thursday," October 24, a great fissure opened up and prices plummeted. That was the day when, to shield her from crowds and reporters, Young virtually spirited Marie Curie away from Schenectady to Van Hornesville. Coincidentally, this was also the day when the National Memorial Universalist Church in Washington announced that its newly completed "World Peace Tower" was to be named for that "great peacemaker," Owen D. Young. And so, on Sunday, October 27, it was, at a service attended by his daughter, Jo, and his son Philip; St. Owen, as his wife and children now dubbed him, could not be there himself. It was his fifty-fifth birthday and he had, as noted, a prior engagement.[31]

In the graceful speech with which, that evening, Young duly accepted the Roosevelt Medal for meritorious public service, he made no mention of the market whatever. Charles Evans Hughes, who had recently succeeded John Bassett Moore as a judge of the Permanent Court of International Justice, was also there and Young seized the occasion to compliment him once again on his ingenious use, as secretary of state, of arm's-length diplomacy. At the same time he disclaimed all title to the role of "expert"—a title which properly belonged, he said, to the professional economists who were the Dawes and Young committees' advisers. Likening them to GE's research scientists, he suggested that he and his colleagues were simply the application engineers who shaped the scientists' findings into marketable products. And with a shrewd eye to the goings-on at The Hague, he further suggested that the politicians were the "commercial engineers" whose function it was to package or repackage the product to meet the idiosyncrasies of local markets. Trouble arose, he said, only when one group or another forgot or overstepped its proper role.[32]

V

Returning to his office on Monday, October 28, Young still had nothing to say for the press about the market. Nor did he have anything to say in the black days immediately following, which were spent chiefly at the Federal Reserve. But the business of General Electric was not to be neglected; on the Monday he attended Swope's luncheon for Sir Felix Pole, with whom he met again—without notable result—on Thursday. On each of the days intervening he responded to urgent calls to join the so-called bankers group, now meeting daily in Lamont's office; he seems to have been the one industrialist present. And on Wednesday, October 30, following a climactic Tuesday of forced and panic selling—the "worst day in the history of the Exchange"—Young himself bought 1,700 shares of G E at the market, or 228—down from the September high of 396. It was an indicated but also a futile gesture; despite strategic support from a bankers' consortium reputed to involve more than $200 million, the market continued to sag and a fortnight later was staggering under the impact of another selling frenzy.[33]

It was only then, toward the middle of November, that Young finally consented to make a public statement. Interviewed by the New York financial reporters, he declared as quoted by B. C. Forbes in the *American* for November 14:

> Those who voluntarily sell stocks at current prices are extremely foolish. Our banking position is extraordinarily strong. Our general financial conditions never were sounder.
>
> Industry, not burdened by excessive inventories, is in excellent shape physically and financially. General business has been prosperous.
>
> Of course, if the frenzy in the stock market should be carried much further it will inevitably injure business. But there is no reason in the world why it should be carried further. It has already been carried nonsensically far.

In retrospect, it is tempting to suggest that Young's concluding paragraph might have been directed with even greater cogency to the frenzied market of the spring and summer months. Certainly Paul Warburg had done substantially that in his famous caveat of the preceding spring—famous not because it had more than momentary impact but because his voice was as lonely as it proved to be prescient. First castigating the Federal Reserve for "its failure promptly and effectively to reverse the engines at the critical moment," he went on:

The rudder then passed into the hands of the Stock Exchange operators. . . . If a Stock Exchange debauch is quickly arrested by prompt and determined action, it is not too much to hope that a shrinkage of inflated stock prices may be brought about without seriously affecting the wider circle of general business. If orgies of unrestrained speculation are permitted to spread too far, however, the ultimate collapse is certain not only to affect the speculators who sell, but also to bring about a general depression involving the entire country.

Whether any other voice, including Young's, could have been more effective at that time may well be doubted. Certainly it was never put to the test.[34]

Be that as it may, it almost seemed that in his efforts to arrest this later frenzy, Young had contrived to choose—or stumble upon—the psychological moment. And tone; for in castigating only those who sold stock *voluntarily*, he publicly recognized, as few had, the important distinction between forced and voluntary selling. To the harried and the harassed little people who were still struggling to hang on, such recognition offered at least some crumbs of comfort, and even perhaps of encouragement. In any event, and for whatever reason or concatenation of chance and circumstance, it was precisely from that date that the relatively orderly and convalescent market of 1929's final six weeks began to take shape.[35]

At the time, of course, such a prospect was no more than a pious hope, but at least Young's words bespoke deep-seated convictions. Certainly he could not be accused of any failure to "put his money where his mouth was"; indeed, he had done so well before opening his mouth. On October 30, only a day after the market's steepest decline so far, he had not only put up close to $400,000 for his 1,700 shares of General Electric but had written GE's old and valued customer, Samuel Insull, a letter which brought to some $150,000 his participation in the investment holding companies through which Insull was seeking to preserve family control of his far-flung empire against certain marauders who had dared to challenge it.

No, sir! [Young wrote.] You are not to construe my letter as meaning that I do not care for a participation in the undertaking. I wrote to explain that I was prevented from doing so by absence and to imply that I would always like to go along with your enterprises. Naturally the time having passed, I was in no position to make a request for a participation. However, notice came through allowing me a participation, so really that was in answer to your letter before I received it. Many thanks.[36]

For the first two weeks of November, the daily conferences on the crisis were held at Morgan's or the Federal Reserve or both. But on the thirteenth there was an all-day session at Young's office which brought together Julius Barnes—now head of the U.S. Chamber of Commerce and a close friend of the President's—Alfred P. Sloan of General Motors, Swope, Lamont and, for his first and only appearance there, Richard Whitney, then acting president of the New York Stock Exchange. Three days later, the President announced a series of White House conferences with industrial, farm and labor leaders; these took Young to Washington on the twenty-first and again on the twenty-seventh. They also produced agreement among the industrialists not to lower wages, plus pledges of substantial new construction, especially on the part of the utilities.[37]

The President had done well to summon business and labor leaders to his aid, for among the rank and file thousands upon thousands had already lost their jobs, their savings, or both. Jobs at least could be restored if only the quick recovery on which both Young and the President were clearly counting came quickly enough. Hindsight, of course, brands any such expectation as childishness or worse, but action after all must always be *prospective*, and the biographer's concern is therefore to recapture as best one can the scene and the prospect as his subject actually saw them. And in the final weeks of that memorable year—as we well remember—the scene was not unlike that following a hurricane: widespread damage, numerous and tragic casualties, ugly exposures and general disarray; but once the survivors set out to take stock, it was full of reminders that there was still much left to salvage and to work with. Thus in December Young could write to a disturbed North Country stockholder deploring (with her) a market psychology which had sent GE stock skyrocketing almost to 400 before the collapse, while assuring her that earnings for 1930 should approximate $9 per share with a dividend payout of $6. (He slightly overestimated the earnings but not the dividends.) For that year, the utilities too continued to prosper, and capital expenditures by the Insull group were reported at $197 million.[38]

The mood of the survivors, then, allowed no traffic with despair; rather, it was a composite of a sometimes fearful hope and an initially grim determination to carry on. As is usual in such circumstances, life for the more fortunate was soon taking on at least the semblance of its normal pattern. In November, Josephine Edmonds Young suddenly found herself sharing with her husband the spotlight she had always shunned. On the ninth, reported the *Times*, she was elected a vice-president of the national Girl Scouts—undoubtedly the result of a request to her from Lou Henry Hoover, to whom Jo did not extend her disaffection from the President. A few days later she presided at the Seven Colleges Dinner at the Astor, introducing as speakers Judge Hughes and Ada Comstock, the president of Radcliffe. This event was pictured in the Sunday rotogravure section of the *Times,* and Jo was teased about competing with Owen for public notice.[39]

Meanwhile, Owen was enjoying the comparative privacy of the Manhattan Club's dinner for its five honorary members—of whom he and former Governor Al Smith were two. And early in December he had the satisfaction of congratulating Jackson Reynolds and Melvin Traylor, just returned from Baden-Baden, on the outcome of their diplomatic but forceful work in organizing the Bank for International Settlements. Soon now, and none too soon, the bank should be in operation.[40]

vi

That American businessmen, if somewhat shaken, were still in the saddle was dramatically evident that fall and winter. The more serious the problem, the more their leaders talked only to each other—and sometimes to a press which waited on their words. And with the President, who had called them to his aid.

Congress, bypassed by the leaders but not by angry home constituents, was miffed. If it could not resolve the crisis, it could perhaps come up with a scapegoat, and monopoly, actual or prospective, was always a likely candidate. Thus in Resolution #80 the Senate authorized its Committee on Interstate Commerce to "make an investigation of radio, telephone, telegraph and power business"; and where were they to start if not with Owen Young? Accordingly its chairman, Senator James Couzens of Michigan, lost no time in requesting him to appear before the committee on Friday, December 6, and perhaps Saturday as well.

Young was not taken wholly by surprise. During the past few months the press had naturally been speculating about the prospects for the ITT and RCA Communications merger. In its November 15 issue, moreover, the *Saturday Evening Post* had published, under the title "Freedom of the Air," the old story of RCA's formation, as told to Mary Margaret McBride by Owen D. Young. And he had given her the whole story, making public disclosure for the first time of President

Wilson's message from Paris as transmitted by Admiral Bullard. Now, since the law would clearly need amendment if the proposed merger was ever to be consummated, he could offer no objection to the summons except that it conflicted with scheduled and highly important meetings of his boards, including RCA's. To his plea for a period of grace, the committee's response was to excuse him until the following Monday, December 9.[41]

To their prime witness, who this time took the offensive, the committee thereupon devoted three sessions: Monday and Tuesday mornings, and Tuesday afternoon. In his prepared statement, largely dictated on the Sunday afternoon train to Washington, Young emphasized once again the special reasons for RCA's creation, this time including as a matter of course President Wilson's determining message. He also stressed more forcefully than ever the need, as a matter of national policy, to counter foreign combinations of radio and cables by permitting—nay, requiring—an American combination to match them. Toward this, the contemplated merger of ITT and RCA Communications would be a constructive and timely move—always *provided* it were accompanied by effective government regulation. And again he said that we must learn how to regulate such privately directed combinations effectively, on pain of accepting the far less efficient alternative of a government monopoly.[42]

Young's appearance at this time to testify on this touchy subject caused something of a flurry in political and reportorial circles. The hearing room was full, and there was considerable infighting among committee members—the Democrats especially—some of whom were out to "get" Young while others were eager to "protect" him. Of the first group, the acknowledged leader was Senator Clarence Dill of Washington, who had found in radio the kind of issue that assured him public notice and had done his homework well. With liberals like Burton K. Wheeler of Montana, Young had little trouble; his views on the regulation of monopoly and the equation of a "fair return" for the utilities to *actual* investment were altogether too disarming. But there were times when the well-intentioned efforts of conservative senators like Alben Barkley and Harry B. Hawes must have reminded Young of the proverbial cry for protection from one's friends. Fortunately Senator Key Pittman of Nevada understood the virtue of silence, and the occasional intervention of New York's Senator Robert Wagner was most welcome.

Dill, however, had seized upon the use Young made of President Wilson's name, and was worrying it like a dog with an especially juicy bone. Why had Young failed to mention this alleged message from Paris in his 1921 testimony, when both Wilson and Bullard were still alive? Was there anything to substantiate it other than Bullard's alleged word to him? Was it in any event relevant to current issues involving RCA or to anything more than defending the Alexanderson alternator against a takeover by the British?

No stranger to the witness stand, Young seldom had difficulty in fielding tough questions but, perhaps because his briefing had necessarily been hasty and less than adequate, he fumbled Dill's initial— and key—question. He thought he had mentioned Wilson's message in his earlier testimony, and said so. Thus he missed the opportunity of simply reminding Dill that so long as a President is in office, and even for a decent interval thereafter, he is entitled to expect the privacy of such personal messages to be respected; that he (Young)—like Bullard—had thus been careful to respect it but that now, a decade later, disclosure was no longer anything but appropriate. And while he made a fair recovery, Dill continued to insinuate doubts about the accuracy of his memory and even his veracity, which the press could hardly fail to report and, in some cases, flaunt.

This disturbed his young assistant greatly, and was hardly calculated to sustain the buoyancy with which Young—sure now that the market had done its worst—had challenged the committee to disapprove of his pending merger. Over dinner that evening with Young in the hotel suite which they shared, Case could think of little else. Wasn't there someone, he asked, who could confirm the fact of Wilson's message and so put Dill in his place? If so, wouldn't Young talk with him now or as soon as his assistant could get him by phone?

"Yes to your first question and no to your second," answered Young. "Bernie Baruch knows something about it; he is also one of Dill's more important financial backers. But the man who really knows the full story is Admiral Grayson, who was in Paris with Wilson as his personal physician. He lives in Washington, your friend George Harrison is now his houseguest, and both know Key Pittman. So now you know as much as I do. For my part, I am going to bed and *I am not to be disturbed before morning by anyone on any account whatsoever.* And now, if I've made that perfectly clear, I'll say good night."

For all his lack of experience of such games behind the scenes, Case understood readily enough that it was now his ball. To figure out why, and what he was to do with it, took a little longer. A few minutes later, however, he found himself calling Cary Grayson's number and explaining the situation volubly to Governor Harrison. And when the latter, properly concerned, naturally insisted on talking with Owen himself, Case heard himself rehearsing politely but very, very firmly what his chief's explicit instructions had been—and why. Obviously Young was not about to lift a finger in his own defense or even to ask it of others; further, he wanted to be able, if charged with doing either, to deny it. Thus if anything was to be done—like introducing Grayson's testimony at the next day's hearings—it would have to be done by his friends, acting wholly on their own. Harrison gave ground grudgingly but finally saw the point and agreed to see what he could do—with his host and Pittman too.

Baruch was another matter.[43] Case's chief had mentioned casually that he would probably be out but that David Sarnoff, who had his box at the opera that evening, would know where and how to reach him. At last, during the final intermission, a person-to-person call got Sarnoff to the phone and Case was able both to brief him on Dill's behavior and to suggest that Baruch, as he understood it, might be the one to set Dill straight. Quick to understand that Case's information must have come from his chief, Sarnoff was even more insistent than Harrison had been about the need to talk to Young himself; in denying this as he had to, Case found himself calling on powers of resistance and diplomacy of which he had not been aware. Shortly before midnight this lengthy negotiation also ended happily with Sarnoff's undertaking to see what he could do, and Young's anxious but expectant assistant fell into bed.

Nothing happened in the morning session as the interrogation moved on to other subjects. Shortly after the afternoon session began, however, Senator Pittman asked permission to introduce a witness who, as he had reason to know, could illuminate a question which Monday's session had shown the need to clarify. Thereupon Admiral Grayson testified that President Wilson, during their early-morning drive in the Bois de Boulogne—he could not name the day—had asked to be reminded to "get in touch . . . today . . . with the Navy Department officially or with Admiral Bullard. I have an important message that I want to send to Mr. Owen D. Young relative to the protection of American rights and possibilities in radio communication." Asked by Pittman whether he had carried out those instructions, Grayson replied, "I did, sir."[44]

So that was that. Thanks chiefly to Harrison, the telephone calls had paid off handsomely. Sarnoff too had done his stint, but it was Grayson's testimony that enabled Dill to draw in his horns with such grace as he could muster. As for Case, if the truth be told, he cared less about the merger or even national communications policy than for his chief's good name. And it had been quite in character for Young, suspecting as much, to put his youthful assistant to the test by this implicit show of confidence.

Equally characteristic was his method of conveying his satisfaction with the outcome. Encountering Case senior at the Federal Reserve, he said without elaboration, "Everett did a good job for me in Washington the other day." Naturally this pleased the father and naturally he lost no time in repeating it to his son.

Part IV

Deflation and Depression:
Is Anyone in Charge?

1930–1932

Chapter 26

The Pivotal Year:
Convalescence and
the Radio Suit

HE fabulous decade that began with the sharp but brief recession of 1921 did not end with the market explosion of 1929; strictly speaking, it had another year to go. As that other year commenced, it seemed all too likely that the decade would end as it began with a sharp recession. Nevertheless, Owen Young was by no means alone in his hopes and determination that at least it should also be brief.

Named "Man of the Year" by *Time* in its first issue for 1930, Young was cited for many things but most particularly for the unfailing skill, self-discipline and fair-mindedness which had earned him the confidence of the warring members of the Young Committee, and so, ultimate success in coping with "the year's largest politico-economic job." And this success was further confirmed when, only a fortnight later, the Second Hague Conference reached agreement of sorts on all moot questions relating to the Young Plan—the last prerequisite to its ratification by the respective parliaments.[1]

Thereupon, to head the Bank for International Settlements—and without even waiting for ratification—Gates McGarrah resigned as chairman of the New York Federal Reserve, where J. Herbert Case was promptly chosen to succeed him.[2] Young's satisfaction with both appointments was expressed in many ways—not least in a letter to J. P. Morgan, the relevant portions of which he encouraged his assistant to show his father. And Young's attitude was the more important because he himself had recently been reappointed a Class C—or public—director and deputy chairman of the bank, notwithstanding his long letter of October 19 to the Washington board, urging that he had served long enough.[3]

In terms, too, of Young's other chief concerns, 1930 was developing auspiciously enough. True to his White House pledge, GE had been striving to contain the destructive impact of the crash, first of all through sales and orders sufficient to sustain both jobs and wages. So successful was this effort proving that, for the first few months of 1930, GE's earnings—net as well as gross—exceeded even their 1929 counterparts. Thus layoffs were minimal, affecting chiefly those most recently hired; and workers with five years or more of service had gotten their usual year-end bonus in December: 5 percent of their annual wage. Stockholders, too, were treated generously. With the new year, the extra dividend of $1.50 which in December the board had declared on the old stock became due and payable; also the 4-for-1 split in GE shares became effective. Partly in response to such moves, partly because of returning confidence, market quotations for the old stock had risen by December 31 to 243 from a November low of 168. Some two months later, GE was picked by Hornblower and Weeks "as the outstanding leader in the constructive market we expect for the balance of the year." And indeed, not long thereafter, its new shares touched 95—equivalent to 380 for the old.[4]

As for RCA, if important details relating to its Victor acquisition and its new quasi-independent status remained to be worked out, it was widely known that the change had been authorized in principle by GE and Westinghouse alike. Now, at its January meeting, the RCA board signalized the change by electing thirty-nine-year-old David Sarnoff president and General James G. Harbord chairman, with Young becoming chairman of its executive committee.[5] To this too, the market reacted favorably. Partly in anticipation of the change, and despite the sharp postcrash decline in the sale of sets and tubes, RCA's volatile common shares had risen from a November low of 26 to a year-end figure of 44; some three months later they were quoted at 69, equivalent to 345 on shares outstanding prior to the 5-for-1 split of the preceding spring. And at RKO, both business and profits were soaring.[6]

Other signs and portents were less heartening. Meeting in January to ratify the Young Plan, the Second Hague Conference seemed barely to have survived the emergence of fresh occasions for suspicion and dispute; only as Germany agreed to assume the (slight) additional burden which their resolution entailed did agreement finally ensue. Thereupon, the choleric Hjalmar Schacht cabled that he still stood by the Young Plan "but not the Hague bastard"; on March 7 he resigned the presidency of the Reichsbank, thus giving further aid and comfort to the Nationalists and the small but growing Nazi fringe who joined in opposing the plan. In Los Angeles, the mid-January bulletin of the leading bank—headed, of all people, by Henry Robinson—was expressing doubts about the B I S, and supporting Washington's decision not to let the Federal Reserve go in.[7] Robinson, of course, was first of all Hoover's friend, but Young could not forget that he had also been his own first choice to head the new institution. Small wonder that Robinson had turned him down.

Nor was this all. On January 8, the president of Western Union, Newcomb Carlton, ridiculed Young's contention that an international communications monopoly was essential to the national interest; Western Union, he told the Couzens committee, was doing very well under the existing competitive setup. This, of course, was meat and drink to Senator Dill and R C A's increasingly vocal band of disgruntled competitors, who were inveighing loudly against the Radio group as a conscienceless monopoly. It was also relished by sections of the press as diverse as the *Nation* and Hearst's *New York American*.

"The omniscience of Owen D. Young, alas," reported the *Nation* for January 23, "has been seriously questioned by two of his associated gods of the big business pantheon." (The other was Ellery Stone, president of Kolster Radio Corporation and Federal Telegraph Company). "Mr. Young," it continued, "wants to sell the communications system of the Radio Corporation . . . valued by Mr. Stone at $15,000,000 at the outside, to the International Telephone and Telegraph Company for $97,000,000. . . . The law of the United States (a foolish law, in our judgement) stands in the way [but] if Mr. Young wants to make a deal, let him not try to persuade himself and us that he is thereby saving his fellow-countrymen from imminent dangers." Agreeing that an intelligently unified system could effect substantial economies, the editors nevertheless "again point to Mr. Young as a striking example of the danger of accepting business men as safe guides in matters of public policy where their own interests are involved. . . . In public affairs, give us the leadership of impractical theorists."

The *New York American* (for March 3) was at once more simplistic and more devious. Its full-page editorial featured J. P. Morgan, an I T T director, as the villain-in-chief, "selling to himself [*sic*] for $100 million a heavily watered company which he knew to be worth $15 million." But Young too was castigated for waving the flag to disguise the true nature of the deal. And finally, the *American* took a gratuitous swipe at the B I S, labeling it "the financial department of the League of Nations and, incidentally, a device that is expected to eventually 'mobilize' America's gold for the benefit of the world, and bring about cancellation of Europe's war debt to us."

Of such sweeping indictments, perhaps the most significant aspect was that American business—and notably big business, as personified by Young—was increasingly being treated as a favorite, and vulnerable, target. Thanks chiefly to the crash, yesterday's heroes were suddenly discovered to have feet of clay—and there were those who did not stop at the feet. But in the art of casting stones, none could even approach in ingenuity and assiduity the aforementioned Heard Respess, the "swindled, outraged and embittered inventor," who now redoubled not only his output, but also his efforts to distribute it wherever it might do the most harm. Inasmuch as his mailing list now included the White House, the cabinet, and key senators like Dill, it was fortunate that his product was more than Young's most dedicated critics could stomach. What Young's friends found most disturbing was the increasingly paranoid nature of the malice and even venom which kept the ailing Respess typewriter working overtime.[8]

ii

Save for Newcomb Carlton's testimony—which Jo read simply as his revenge for having lost out on the Radio deal—Young's wife and three younger children were happily unaware of these slings and arrows. On January 11, they had taken ship for California via the Panama Canal— a new and leisurely route to their Arizona cottage. Four days later Young was writing GE's West Coast manager about the University of California's invitation to make the Charter Day address at Berkeley on March 24; "Would it suit you if I did this?" It did, and Young accepted; well before that time Swope would be back from Europe to take charge, and Young would be joining his family in Arizona.[9]

In the meantime, Swope's presence in Germany signified GE's determination not to slacken for a moment the promotion of its master plan for the industry worldwide. Next to AEG, Siemens-Halske was Germany's leading electrical manufacturer and with them, as Young reported to his wife, he and Swope were now "trying to run concurrent negotiations in Berlin and New York." Young had talked with several GE directors, he radioed Swope on January 24, about the general principle of "25% participation in all countries, and they believed in it thoroughly," so he was ready to buy enough of Siemens's new issue of debentures to achieve this level *if* Swope liked the general idea and would work out the best possible terms. Swope replied affirmatively, by phone to Young's apartment at 4:00 A.M., and Young sent an encouraging radiogram emphasizing the importance of such investment, which would benefit the GE stockholders at no cost to themselves, making them "the beneficiaries of the tremendous future growth of the industry throughout the world stop As I regard this our most important job sincerely hope you will not leave Europe until it is accomplished stop It will be the greatest thing you ever did stop Affectionate regards."[10]

Although Young himself met two days later with Siemens's Dr. Frank, the presumption is that Swope did his part well. On February 7, after the board had met, Young radioed him briefly that "directors approve our recent purchase." And when in July, at Camp General, Swope reported at length on his European venture, Young's response was enthusiastic:

I don't suppose [he said] that in the history of the industry, of the world, any story as thrilling as this could ever have been told before. Here is one concern, the General Electric Company of America, now holding a substantial interest in every principal electrical manufacturing company in the world . . . [and this] on the invitation of the management themselves. . . .

That advantage means nothing unless it is of real benefit to the world and if it be . . . it will inevitably, in my judgment, be of benefit to the General Electric Company, because for the first time you have something like an integration of a great industry on an international scale. . . . That may be a matter of great significance, because, as the world gets smaller, as competition becomes greater . . . it is quite likely to mean international disturbance, and one of the greatest insurances of peace in the world is the economic integration of the world. We shall never have, in my judgment, political integration until after we have first had economic integration . . . economics must lead . . . and politics must follow.[11]

There were, however, other missions to Europe of great import, as Young was well aware. On Secretary of State Stimson's departure for the London Naval Conference, he sent him a warm letter wishing him and his colleagues all success and offering to help in any way he could. Perhaps he was "heaping coals of fire," perhaps merely being politic; in any event the tone of the message was very much in character. So was his radio to Dwight Morrow, another American delegate, and his especially affectionate message to General Dawes, who, as the American ambassador, had performed yeoman service in preparing the way.[12]

Nevertheless, by the end of February, it was all too clear that the conference was foundering, and Young's assistant suggested that the general might welcome further words of encouragement. Young agreed, and went on to say:

It is a great pity that the General has been kept so much in the background at the London Naval Disarmament Conference. Stimson was certainly not the man to lead the American delegation because with all his conscientious qualities, he did not know how to appeal to the public imagination and arouse public opinion for results. This the General was admirably qualified to do. Beside the question of disarmament reparations was a dull business, and yet there public opinion had been enlisted to secure results far more effectively than was the case here. If Dawes had been given a free hand, we would have had the thing so dramatized that the public would be demanding action and really effective action. It looked a little as if some one did not want Dawes too much in the foreground. It looked a little like jealousy and suspicion. It looked a little as if the Engineering Mind were at work again.[13]

But Young was too busy to indulge himself in such criticism, which was rare enough in any of his pronouncements, even the most private. The tempo of the year was quickening and he had jobs to do.

Item: In the first week in January the American Federation of Labor, in the person of John P. Frey of the Metal Trades Union, asked Secretary of Commerce Robert P. Lamont to arrange a meeting with Young and other top industrialists to discuss the AFL's deep concern about the sharp decline in its membership. This Young welcomed, and insisted that the secretary be present at their first and private meeting, tentatively scheduled for Lincoln's Birthday. Even the most enlightened of Young's fellow industrialists gave him no support, however; and the meeting, which they feared could only be counterproductive, never took place. As Irving Bernstein, historian of American labor, noted later, only Young among the industrialists had "evinced any interest at all" in Frey's proposal "and it would be no exaggeration to describe it as slight."[14]

Item: On January 7 Young wrote the treasurer of the General Education Board, where he was a member of the Finance Committee, on a subject which had been bothering him for a year. The length of the letter is a measure of his concern, and we quote it only in part:

I signed last fall an authorization to loan on call such part of the Board's cash balance as might be from time to time convenient at current interest rates. At that time, I had grave reservations about the propriety of such authorization, but as the minute had already been signed by two members . . . and I was obliged to leave the city, I concluded to sign the authorization for the year 1929 and raise the question when similar authorization arose for the year 1930.

Personally, I think call loans on the stock market should be made by banks from their own resources and not made by private lenders even though such loans be placed by banks for the account of others. I have the very distinct feeling, and had it many months before the recent catastrophe in our market that if the banks were in control of the credit available for the market, there would have been a distinct brake put on market operations many months earlier, and we would have been saved from the crash with all its attendant ruin.

Noting the concern of banks to care for their own customers in difficult credit situations, he pointed out that when a private lender goes on the street with his money either directly or through a bank, it is simply a question of rate and collateral and there is no responsible banking control. "That was the history of our situation, especially during the six or nine months preceding the last break."

When the difficult situation arises, the lenders, feeling no responsibility to particular borrowers, withdraw their money abruptly and force the collateral on the market which thereby further destroys the stability of market conditions. In fact, there were many days during this recent break when so much collateral was being forced on the market through calling of these private loans that it seemed as if there were no buyers at all for the collateral. The bankers had to organize as buyers in order to keep the exchange open and preserve an appearance at least of safety and liquidity of loans.

Of this rescue effort, of course, Young had been a firsthand witness; the rest bespoke his long experience at the Federal Reserve. And indeed the Federal Reserve Board's "direct action" policy had been remarkably effective in curbing speculative lending *by the banks:* it was the ever-swelling volume of loans by and "for the account of others" that had fueled the speculative fires. What then should be done? Answering the question, Young said:

Some way, I think, must be found to keep market loans in the hands of responsible banking authorities and thereby to some extent under the influence and control of our Federal Reserve banks. . . . It is for this reason, among others, that *the corporations with which I am connected refused during all this period of high call rates to put money directly on the street.* They had the notion that irresponsible lending would lead to a crash in the stock market with its inevitable repercussions on business, and altho they were powerless to prevent that result merely by withholding their own funds, they did feel that their example with that of such other companies as the United States Steel, AT&T, and American Radiator, might act as some deterrent [emphasis added].

If, then, this corporation policy was right, it inevitably raised the question of whether "such institutions as our Board should set the example of direct loans on call." He was, he concluded, withholding his signature until the committee had expressed its views.[15]

Item: In thanking Samuel Crowther on January 10 for his booklet on Prohibition Young was more succinct. "I have a strong impression," he wrote, "that prohibition is an economic success. What will the American people ultimately do with an economic success and a moral and legal failure?"[16]

Item: On January 13, John D. Rockefeller, Jr., sent Raymond Fosdick to ask Young what he could do for education by radio. Young replied that the first thing that should be done was to mobilize for broadcasting purposes all of the city's great musical and dramatic enterprises—an opera house, a symphony hall, a Shakespeare theater— all to be brought together, along with RCA, NBC and RKO, in some such center as Rockefeller had planned for the opera. "It was not a question of subsidizing broadcasting . . . sooner or later radio could probably command the stars that opera now commands anyway . . . but rather of all interested parties cooperating to make possible a development which would bring to people everywhere the best in music, drama, arts and letters"—while still leaving a place for "Amos n' Andy." "Then the educators . . . could come in too and radio would really begin to do what it ought to do. . . ." And ample funds would still be needed if only because "some of the programs at least should be free of any suspicion of commercialism."[17]

Item: On January 15, Clarence Mackay of Postal Telegraph (now an ITT subsidiary) told the Couzens committee that Carlton was wrong and Young was right. For the press this was a less appetizing morsel than Carlton's testimony, but the New York papers did feature a story from Albany suggesting that Governor Roosevelt might appoint Al Smith to head his new State Advisory Power Commission, with Owen Young a likely member. Dismissing the latter as most unlikely, Young could attend without misgivings the luncheon which the Bond Club was giving to the governor next day. He was indeed curious to hear Roosevelt expound his plans and program for waterpower development, but that situation, as he wrote his wife, while "very much in his mind . . . is yet too indefinite to talk about very concretely." Especially (he might have added) to the Bond Club—and even perhaps to him.[18]

Item: On January 17—a labor of love—he went to Boston for the Tavern Club's dinner to Nelson Perkins, where he "said a few words"; and thence by sleeper for a weekend in Van Hornesville with his ninety-year-old mother.[19]

Item: On January 22, he wrote William Church Osborn about Princeton's new School of Public and International Affairs and its relationship to the Page School. He also sent Henry Luce congratulations on the first issue of *Fortune*—which had quite a story on RCA.[20]

Item: On January 23 he was in Washington for a meeting of President Hoover's Advisory Council, returning to New York in time to tell a dinner session at the Harvard Club how proud they should be of the behavior of Harvard alumni—Morgan, Lamont, Perkins, Jeremiah Smith and Parker Gilbert—during the interminable sessions of the Young Committee in Paris. And he confessed to a spinal thrill in Perkins's key role on the Reparations Commission, where, in terms reminiscent of the Roman Republic, he was known simply as "the American Citizen."[21]

Item: On January 29 he presided over the annual meeting of NBC's Advisory Council, which heard President Aylesworth report revenues of fifteen million dollars and no profits. (That was still the way it was supposed to be; but if this was to continue, the recession had *better* be brief.) As usual, he endorsed to St. Lawrence University his thousand-dollar honorarium—a fee which went to each member who actually attended. (Attendance was usually high.)[22]

Item: Next day, after George F. Baker's dinner to Jackson Reynolds, now back from organizing the BIS, he took the midnight for Van Hornesville, whence he had had word of his uncle John Brandow's death at eighty-five. "How could anyone's life be finer, full of sparkling brilliancy, zest, loyalty, and lovableness," read his telegram to Brandow's daughter Lena Loveland. A widow, she was soon persuaded to take the place her father had vacated in her aunt Ida Young's home. In the meantime, as Owen wrote Jo, his mother was "all right" and being looked after by three ladies, including the irrepressible and always loving Peggy Carey, now Mrs. Martin Egan of Van Hornesville.[23]

iii

When, in spite of Schacht, the Reichstag ratified the Young Plan on March 12, and Hindenburg signed it the following day, Young could feel that his own six years of inextricable involvement with the reparations question were happily over. And why not? In the spring issue of *Foreign Affairs*, no less sober an authority than Thomas W. Lamont had hailed the Young Plan—with an almost extravagant bow to its author-in-chief—as indeed the *final* reparations settlement.

Young himself was not so sure. Whether, as he put it more than once, Germany could in fact shoulder all the debts, chiefly to the United States, which the Allies had found unbearably heavy—plus 50 percent more for reparations proper—he declined to predict; but it now seemed that they were going to try. How hard they would try obviously depended in the first instance upon the pace and scope of recovery; for the rest, the matter was now out of his hands.

As for the bursting of the Wall Street bubble, it was a relief, of sorts, to have it now behind one; with that overhanging threat removed, one could get on with the business of rebuilding. Certainly that was what the new chapter now opening for RCA was all about. After a decade of uneasy subordination to its parents, an independent and greatly strengthened RCA would now manufacture its own products, in amounts and of a kind best calculated to suit its market. Since it would also assume responsibility for research and development in its field, RCA would become for GE and Westinghouse little more than a major investment—sufficient, to be sure, to give them each a potent voice on its board of directors and every expectation of profitable returns. If the parent companies would not be competing in the radio field, that had been true from the start; moreover, the Federal Trade Commission had recently reported that RCA's competitors—now chiefly its licensees—held some 75 to 80 percent of the market for sets and 60 percent of the tube market. As for the complaints of these licensees that the royalties they paid were excessive, even at 7½ percent, this was a reduced and recently negotiated figure which Young and Sarnoff saw as a fair charge on the capital their competitors had been spared the need of raising. After all, latecomers like Grigsby-Grunow had entered the market on a shoestring, and in two years had reaped fantastic profits. And if, with the market for sets still feeling the effects of the crash, some of the weaker units were now to go under, that could hardly be said to damage an industry which sorely needed stabilization.[24]

Young also liked the role for which these intercompany negotiations cast him. Happy to leave the nitty-gritty to the three respective presidents—Sarnoff, Swope, and Frank A. Merrick (of Westinghouse)—he was looked to by all three as impartial mediator of their disputes. Thus even before he left for the West to join his family, the new deal for RCA was rapidly taking shape and Young could feel that his precocious offspring was coming of age.

It was indeed, for him, a busy but also singularly relaxed and happy time—witness the entry for February 4 in his assistant's all too uneven and sporadic notes:

Mr. Young was in very good form today. His schedule was fearfully crowded and by three o'clock several people were clamoring to come in. Humphreys wanted to see him about the North American ("Wired Wireless") situation and insisted that rather than see Mr. Sarnoff, he ought to see Mr. Young. Sarnoff wanted to see Mr. Young before Mr. Neave (counsel) got back later in the week. A. G. Davis wanted to see him before Mr. Sarnoff saw him. Mr. Young sat back and scratched his head, looked up and smiled and said, "Of course, if I had a mind of my own, it would not matter so much which of these fellows saw me first. They all want to see me and make it up for me before I see anyone else." He paused a moment and then said, "You call Sarnoff and tell him if he wants to see me to come ahead." (Davis was not in town.) Then he asked Packer to get Humphreys on the 'phone. I waited to see what he told Humphreys before getting Sarnoff. I heard him say to Humphreys, "You want to see me and you don't want to see Sarnoff, is that it? . . . All right, I'll see you. But I have just learned that Sarnoff is on his way over, so I can't help it if you meet." That was my cue and I told Sarnoff to come right over. . . . They met and had it out, with O D Y in his favorite role.[25]

Two days later, still in a buoyant mood, Young set out to redeem a promise to Emile Francqui, the shrewd, sometimes amusing and frequently cantankerous senior Belgian member of the Dawes and Young committees. The letter he wrote to redeem it tells a good deal about the nature of his relationship to his prize Holsteins as well as to his old comrades-in-arms. "My dear Francqui," he wrote:

I have not forgotten that in Paris I told you about a wonderful record that one of my Holstein cows was making and that if she had a bull calf I would send him to you. Her calf last year was a bull but, unfortunately, it was born dead, so I awaited with patience the slow processes of nature to make my word good. I felt pretty sure that inasmuch as you had a vested interest in the calf, if it were a bull, nature would come to your rescue as she has always done so lavishly. I was correct about it. Two weeks ago, your bull came and the heifer is now increasing her record over last year when she was the champion point winner of the breed for her age. She is giving something over 100 pounds of milk per day, and she has made for the first seven days of her test something more than 30 pounds of butter. The calf is strong and large and gives every promise of becoming a beautiful animal. I have registered him under the name of "Van Horne Reparations." Van Horne is the name of my farms under which all cattle are registered and is taken from my Dutch ancestors.

He wanted, he said, to keep the calf for six months before putting him on one of Francqui's ships in New York; he was tuberculin tested and a certificate would be available for his entry into Belgium: "Sometime in June I will send him on his great adventure."

I recognize you as a dictator of finance, the master of radium, the arbiter of copper, but I am not so sure of your status in the live stock industry. Of course, I realize that you have aristocratic and expensive pigs, and I dare say that they have multiplied faster than you could eat them. After this bull calf is a couple of years old, if you have any trouble with Dr. Schacht, I suggest that you invite him over and let the bull settle it. One must always think of the peace of Europe.

Needless to say that this letter is personal and confidential, my dear Francqui, so goodbye before I say anything more indiscreet.[26]

Young liked this effort well enough to enclose a copy in the second transatlantic letter he dispatched on that same day. Long overdue, this went to Josiah Stamp, to whom he wrote in part:

Dear Jo:

This is not an application for a loan. I just want to relieve your mind because by this time I suppose you feel that I never would write you except under such compulsion. . . .

Now that the second Hague conference is over and the International Bank is fairly well on its way, I venture to congratulate you on the outcome of the whole business. I feel sure that the close perspective which you had to Snowden's activities when you last wrote me and the resulting disappointment, to put it mildly, has more or less cleared away. I hope it has all gone. I had occasion to tell Winston Churchill when he was here, not only what I thought about your work, but how unfortunate and unfair I felt the situation was in which you had been left. Winston said that he would undertake to see that that was corrected, because he had no thought that you had any feeling about it whatever. We have to remember that these political fellows get so hardened to that sort of thing that they forget how we unossified humans feel about it.

I also had an opportunity to speak to Ramsay MacDonald about the same thing and he expressed the greatest respect for you and concurred in my statement that you got everything there was to be had at Paris. The fact that Snowden could squeeze something more out of Stresemann, under the guise of taking it from someone else, did not mean that you could have gotten anything more out of Schacht, so I hope that you are happy again and have no recollection of Paris more serious or disturbing than the Derso drawings.

After quoting Schacht on the (second) "Hague bastard," and mentioning General Dawes's hope that when Stamp came over he and Young would each plant a tree in his brother's arboretum, Young went on to other subjects:

When Gerard Swope gets back—he is now in Europe—sometime the latter part of this month, I expect to go to Arizona and then up to San

Francisco to deliver the Charter Day address at the University of California on the twenty-fourth of March. I have a subject but no ideas. The subject is—"The Relationship of Economics to Politics in World Cooperation." If you have a stray idea or two, you might send them on. There is a great scarcity over here just at present. It would be a very good idea indeed for you to write a speech on this subject—excellent practice for you— then you send it over to me and I will restate it in my inferior language— you deliver yours in England, and I will deliver mine here, and everybody will say no wonder those two fellows could work well together—see how exactly their ideas match.

After the Charter Day address, we shall get home about the fifteenth of April and be ready for Lady Stamp and you when you come. If you think well of the tree business, you can tell General Dawes that we are trying to arrange it. I think any communication to him now from anybody which would show that they were in a helpful and cooperative spirit would cheer him up. . . .[27]

Having checked in with Stamp, Young now moved to get the Page School off dead center. Summoning the trustees to a luncheon meeting on February 14, he also wrote Judge Harlan Stone at length about the Parker bequest, and hoped that they might soon meet to explore its possibilities. On the day following the trustees' meeting, the *Times* announced that the school was ready to start, with the former minister to China, John V. A. MacMurray, as its head.[28]

February continued to be crowded and Young continued to take it all in stride. At least twice he met with Baron von Prittwitz, the German ambassador, and once with Sir Esmé Howard. He radioed Governor Moreau his support of Pierre Quesnay as general manager of the BIS—a move which left both Montagu Norman and Schacht unhappy. He wired the president of the University of California that he could not allow NBC—as, in part, his own creation—to broadcast his speech. He spent considerable time with Jackson Reynolds and especially with Gates McGarrah on BIS matters. He attended the morning-through-luncheon meeting of the Finance Committee of the General Education Board, and an all-day session of the Twentieth Century Fund trustees. He saw Sosthenes Behn about RCA—the ITT deal, they agreed, was now a dead letter—and wrote Melvin Traylor about the BIS. He bought some Riverside property adjoining Little Point, and paid several book dealers, including A. W. S. Rosenbach, all or part— mostly part—of what he owed them for his expensive 1929 purchases (among them Rosenbach's choice Kern items). And when, ostensibly to embarrass the Republican legislature, Governor Roosevelt prompted the minority leaders to propose Owen Young for election to the state board of regents, the latter was not visibly discomfited by his much publicized rejection. F DR professed to be, and this too was widely publicized—but if his interest was more than *pro forma*, a cynic would undoubtedly point out that regents were precluded from taking any active part in politics. More probably it was just another of the governor's little games.[29]

At the end of the month Young tidied up his affairs: saw to it that the St. Lawrence board authorized the building of the new dormitory, welcomed Swope back home, and—to quote the office boy's entry in the calendar—"went to his Taylor." Then he was ready to heed his wife's message from Arizona—"President of Yankee Republic [their ten-year-old son Richard] in urgent need of Chief Justice. All counting minutes until Tuesday"—and departed for Chandler and vacation.[30]

This was no ordinary trip; to Owen's delight his mother had asked to go west with him, so he hired a private railroad car to take her and her niece Lena Loveland across the continent. It was Ida Young's first long trip since she and Smith had gone to the Chicago world's fair in 1893—and this was far longer. She accepted the change from snow-buried central New York State to sunny Arizona with her usual aplomb. Sitting under the orange trees among the brilliant flowers, she looked as much at home as beside the stove in Van Hornesville. The family—Jo, Josephine and Philip—were well settled there after their long sea voyage, and together they celebrated her ninety-first birthday, in the little San Marcos cottage. The children lived in the private car, parked on a pine-sheltered siding; their father took refuge there when reporters became too attentive.

iv

Political pressures, indeed, were becoming too insistent to ignore, even in Arizona. To be widely hailed as "fit to be President" was the kind of public notice that even a purely private citizen must relish, and Young was no exception. On the other hand, he was certainly not envying the President his current responsibilities, and in protesting his own lack of political ambitions and his determination to stick to a job for which he had some qualifications, Young was being entirely honest.

Or was he? Not, certainly, in the eyes of a skeptical press and experienced politicians to whom such protestations meant only that Young fully understood the rules of the game. Nor did he, by word or deed—now more than ever the subjects of speculative scrutiny—succeed in persuading them to think otherwise. To them his professed indifference to politics, the wide range of his concerns, and his independent views and stance signified rather the emergence of a potentially astute campaigner. Nor, with it all, could he fairly be accused of failing to touch the more important bases.

This hint of ambivalence helped to keep Young's name linked with politics in the current scene; whatever he said or did or was involved in, the press saw to that.

The Charter Day speech was given as promised on March 24 in the Greek theater on the Berkeley campus, with Jo, Josephine and Philip in the audience. The man who delivered it had had more than two weeks of rest in the sunshine; economic recovery now seemed sufficiently assured to relieve him of major business or personal worries on that score. Reports from Europe were making it clear that the new plan would shortly become operative, with the agent-general for reparations being replaced by the Bank for International Settlements.

Thus on every count—even though Josiah Stamp had failed to come through with the suggested speech—Young could address his Berkeley audience with all the confidence, not to say aplomb, of a man who is at peace with himself and with the world. He could even indulge, as he did, in a sharp if good-humored denigration of politics, which, as in serving up to the Germans their first cocktail of inflation, found it so easy to "start something politics could not stop." The speech was amusing: politics was pictured as the lady of the manor, economics as the scullery maid. It was illuminating: since "roughly one half of the Dawes payments were needed by the creditors of Germany to pay their debts to the US" and since "that obligation was fixed," it followed that the 20 percent reduction in Germany's average annuity payments (as stipulated in the Young Plan) meant a 40 percent reduction in net budgetary benefits to Germany's creditors. That a reduction which looked so small to Germany looked so large to the Allies "was one serious problem in Paris." As for Young's analysis of the domestic scene, its grasp but not its reach might be open to challenge: "In our failure to achieve price stability," he said—and the year was 1930—"will be found the roots of those maladjustments which result in the unequal and unfair distribution of wealth, in unemployment, and in other serious problems." He was also consciously prophetic: "Let no man think that the living standards of America can be permanently maintained at a measurably higher level than those of the other civilized nations. Either we shall lift theirs to ours or they will drag ours down to theirs."

Small wonder that the speaker was given an ovation, first by his audience and then in the press, or that copies of the speech were in such demand. (Young sent one himself to Senator Dill.) Small wonder too, no doubt, that among the politically minded it should have delighted Young's friends and supporters and discomfited the rest.[31]

V

It was less than two months later, on May 13 to be precise, that Hoover's attorney general, William D. Mitchell, filed an antitrust suit against the Radio group: RCA, GE, Westinghouse, AT&T, and others. This of course was next morning's front-page spread; so, for much of the press, at least, was Young's concurrent release on RCA's behalf, rehearsing its origin and subsequent history and welcoming "this test of the validity of its organization . . . in every step of which the government has been advised."[32]

Reception was mixed. For RCA's competitors it was an occasion for dancing in the streets; from the senatorial insurgents of both parties who had been pressuring the attorney general to act, it brought varied sounds of relief and satisfaction; for "the swindled and embittered inventor," Heard Respess, it spelled vindication and even a chance to gloat, which led to fresh and frantic outpourings of vituperation. More soberly, there were many disinterested citizens who hailed the move as proof at long last that even a business-oriented government was not afraid to attack entrenched monopoly—even, as the more knowing added, usually *sotto voce*, where close personal friendships were involved. And there were not a few who felt that Young and especially that man Sarnoff had simply got what was coming to them.

On the other hand, the business and financial community—especially in its upper reaches—generally heard the news with dismay and consternation, and even, here and there, a wringing of the hands. For the past few weeks there had been an ominous pause in the uphill climb of business, and the stock market had been visibly sliding. What was Hoover thinking of to attack such a key group at such a moment? Could recovery, precarious at best, be expected to survive it? And, incidentally, why pick on Young, who for all his pains surely deserved something better at the hands of the President.

That nice legal questions were at issue exercised an undoubted attraction for many members of the bar; had Young himself been a disinterested observer, he might well have been among them. Not so his close circle of friends and admirers, who were, quite simply, out-raged. In some instances rage had rendered them wholly inarticulate; in others it might have been better so. For this group, certainly, the suit was nothing but an act of betrayal in high places, which could have been prompted only by the politics of jealousy and fear.

As for Young, the filing of the suit could hardly have come as a bolt from the blue. When the new RCA setup, as finally approved by the three boards, had been publicly announced on April 17, Senator Dill had stolen the next day's headlines—even in the *Times*—with a fiery speech denouncing Young's planned worldwide radio trust, per-petual control of which would now be vested in GE and Westinghouse. Mentioning Sarnoff's White House call just prior to the announcement, Dill "refused to believe that President Hoover approved any such monopoly as is being formed." He even dragged in the BIS as a likely party to Young's conspiracy and, like Senator Couzens, called for sum-mary action by the Department of Justice. So far as the press was con-cerned, Dill's speech fairly blanketed Swope's statement deprecating the need for any such action on the ground that there was "nothing particularly new to investigate." Incidentally, Swope's statement fol-lowed by a day his prophecy at the GE stockholders' meeting that the electric industry was facing one of its biggest years. What the Radio suit, now clearly threatened, would do to such a prophecy was not hard to guess, but when Young was urged to see "his friend the Presi-dent" about it, he flatly refused.[33]

On Saturday, May 3, with Young up-country and busy with his Holsteins, Sarnoff phoned Van Hornesville to tell him that the De-partment of Justice was apparently planning to seek an injunction against the meeting of RCA stockholders scheduled for Tuesday to ratify the new setup. Having heard him out, Young said he would "do nothing whatever about [it] . . . if the Department wishes to apply for the injunction they could go ahead as far as he was concerned." Evidently "they" had second thoughts; Monday's papers reported that no such step was contemplated.[34]

Young had stayed away from the White House even when he and Jo were spending the last weekend of April in Washington, attending the dedication of the National Memorial Universalist Church (the one with St. Owen's Tower) and staying on for meetings of the National Chamber of Commerce, where Melvin Traylor spoke on the Bank for International Settlements and the atmosphere was decidedly bullish. Clarence Woolley, ten years Young's senior and the President's close friend and supporter, had no such inhibitions; as a GE director he persuaded his chairman to prepare a statement on May 8, reviewing the whole history of R C A, which he undertook to deliver to the President.

Next day, Friday, May 9, Woolley did just that, reporting on his return that the attorney general had been misinformed of certain relevant data, and had even reported to the cabinet that Young's own statement of the facts was inaccurate. To this "charge" it appeared that Secretary Stimson, now back from London, had retorted that he would take the responsibility of guaranteeing that Mr. Young would never misstate or falsify his facts—an opinion in which, according to Woolley, "his Chief fully backed him up." Thereupon, Sarnoff reported, he and Woolley had prepared a telegram to be sent by Woolley to Secretary of Commerce Lamont on Monday, May 12, recommending that Young be given an opportunity to meet with the attorney general to clarify the facts, following which the Justice Department would of course take whatever action it thought fitting.[35]

Young being then at St. Lawrence for its Charter Day ceremony, these reports went to his assistant, whose notes also record the outcome. No meeting with Attorney General Mitchell was forthcoming, but the secretary of commerce was to be in New York on Monday and would be glad to see Young himself. Duly waiting on him that day, Young said he had only one request to make; namely, the courtesy of being informed as to whether the suit was to be brought on the declared assumption (1) that R C A was deliberately an illegal setup that had to be dissolved or (2) that charges brought against it were such as to warrant a thoroughgoing investigation of the facts which, in turn, would determine the government's proper course of action.

The secretary's reply was to assert that he, his chief, and most of their associates were decidedly in favor of the second procedure—but that certain parties in Washington felt very strongly that the political situation demanded the first. To this, Young told his assistant, his one retort had been that if the political situation was truly that precarious, he felt sorry for them.[36]

When, next day, the attorney general proceeded to file suit, Young was inevitably—if ruefully—reminded of Woodrow Wilson's dictum that only a liberal government can afford to be fair to big business. Moreover, like Secretary Lamont, General Dawes did not hesitate to give Young privately his view that politics had finally dictated the decision—and so, in a sense, it doubtless had. Hoover's dilemma was nonetheless a real one—even to the point of anticipating one of the issues which was to tease his successor: recovery versus "reform." But there was far more to it than that. Just before taking office, as noted, he had written Young to say that he would give five years of his life to have him in the Republican fold, and during the campaign General Harbord had employed his leave of absence—without pay—to work for Hoover's election. Henry Robinson, like Woolley, was a director of G E. Young knew and had the respect of most members of the cabinet, and Stimson's under secretary, Joseph P. Cotton, had headed the firm which from the beginning had been R C A's chief counsel. Should the President, no lawyer, now overrule his attorney general on a matter of law, the probable consequence was only too clear, with Mitchell's resignation giving point to the charge that the President was using his office to protect his friends. And after all, as the *Telegram* was quick to observe, this suit was designed merely to test the law and, having been welcomed as such by the defendants, should serve to clear the air.[37]

That Young himself came to understand the nature of Hoover's dilemma was evident in his subsequent behavior, but there is no doubt that, initially, he felt disheartened—a position far behind Jo, who did not hesitate to express, within the family, her anger and resentment. To Owen, what rankled most, perhaps, was the blow to his pride as a lawyer who had been at pains to keep abreast of all cases involving the Sherman and Clayton acts, and, checking his own views with those of eminent counsel, had never doubted that his cherished creation was well within the line. In any event, on May 20 he wrote Glenn Frank, president of the University of Wisconsin, that as a man now in effect under indictment on a very serious count, he could not and would not accept previously proffered academic honors, nor could he make the commencement address as planned. And when Frank suggested that this was silly, he wrote, most uncharacteristically, another letter, twice as long, to prove that it was not.[38]

If these letters constituted Young's own summary brief for the defense, more judicially minded comments did emerge from time to time. Even in the first of these two letters, after summarizing his reasons for supposing that the Department of Justice had "accepted the organization as lawful," Young observed: "As a matter of fact, I think they had until the gasoline cracking case was recently decided, which introduced a new element in the question of one's right to mobilize patents, even to release an art." And his earlier radiogram to counselor Charles Neave, currently vacationing in England, is too objective a summary of the issues and the outlook not to be allowed to speak for itself. Dated May 16, Young's message said:

Suit has been filed in Wilmington by the Attorney General against the Radio Corporation based on the theory that the original unification of patents violated the Sherman Act because they were competitive rather than supplementary and also on the ground that the agreements for subsequent patents taken with the stock interest which the General Electric and others will hold in the Radio Corporation will have the effect of extending the lawful monopoly of the patents beyond their expiration as well as to diminish competition when and as the patents expire stop All the original companies including the Telephone are deeply interested in establishing the legality of the original setup including the cross licenses resulting therefrom stop There will be a multitude of lawyers representing the special interests of the separate companies but there should be one representing the Radio Corporation who could assume leadership for all with the hearty cooperation and acquiescence of all stop I know of no such person except you otherwise I would not bother you stop Would it be possible for you to come home for a couple of weeks arrange for the answers to the bill outline the work of preparation and assign it and then return to complete your vacation stop Obviously no hearing can take place until fall stop I understand Telephone company will cooperate with us whole heartedly in defense and that John W. Davis will represent them stop Presume Cravath will represent Westinghouse and that Cotton's firm would be associated with you for Radio stop What suggestions have you for General Electric counsel stop [Ex-Senator George Wharton] Pepper who lives in the circuit and Silas Strawn have been considered but will do nothing until I hear from you stop Sorry to bother you but so am I sorry to be bothered affectionate regards.

Neave's response is implicit in Young's brief acknowledgment of May 19: "We are all delighted you are coming. Certainly you have never failed us."[39]

Thus reassured, Young evidently found his one private airing—to Glenn Frank—of his genuine sense of grievance sufficient to get it largely out of his system. For the rest of the year, at least, the suit was simply one of those things, a bothersome fact to be dealt with like any other business problem. And when, toward the end of June, first intervening as a "friend of the court," Grigsby-Grunow brought suit against the Radio Corporation, claiming thirty million dollars in damages on charges of "unfair competition," Young took it philosophically. Whatever grounds for an amicable settlement he and Grigsby might have found in their earlier exploration—of which Young's letter of June 3 had given Sarnoff a full account—had, not surprisingly, failed to bear fruit under what Young now referred to as "existing circumstances." The fact that the fiery ex-Senator James A. Reed, Democrat of Missouri, had been hired as their counsel and that their charges went far

J. P. Morgan, Owen D. Young, T. N.
Perkins   Derso

The Miracle-Man

Evans in Columbus Dispatch

New York Evening Post, June 7, 1929. Reprinted by permission of the
New York Post

H. M. Talburt, the *New York Telegram*, June 14, 1929

BETTER STAY TOGETHER   *By Sykes*

New York Evening Post, August 10, 1929. Reprinted by permission of the *New York Post*

At GE's Association Island, summer 1930; left to right: E. W. Rice, Jr., Gerard Swope, Richard E. Byrd, Owen D. Young

Brooklyn Daily Eagle, August 20, 1929

Man of the Year. Reprinted by permission from *Time*, The Weekly Newsmagazine; Copyright Time Inc. 1930

THE NEW SIGN

C. R. Macauley in the *Brooklyn Daily Eagle*, June 22, 1930

Clubb in the *Knickerbocker Press*, Albany, New York, May 20, 1932

"Would you recommend 'Owen D. Young' for a growing girl?"

Drawing by Kemp Starrett; © 1932, 1960 The New Yorker Magazine, Inc.

beyond any being pressed by the government itself was only to be expected. And if, as alleged, this was a source of some embarrassment to the Justice Department, that was just too bad. Any embarrassment RCA might feel derived chiefly from the fact that this plaintiff, entering the field in 1928, had sold more radio sets in 1929 than RCA had done. Evidently RCA's alleged "unfair competition" was proving marvelously ineffective.[40]

vi

On Friday, May 9, the only living ex-President of the United States wrote his friend Owen Young from Northampton suggesting, among other things, that business was making a mistake in not giving better support to the President. With his own wry brand of Yankee humor, he even turned Young's Berkeley gibe at politics around to intimate that business might be "starting something it could not stop."[41]

Replying some ten days later, Young made no reference to the suit which had been filed in the meantime, but expressed great surprise at Coolidge's complaint. Protesting that his own impressions were "all the other way"—that business, he had thought, "was making a great demonstration of helpful cooperation"—he pointed to the action of the railroads and the utilities in not even waiting for lower commodity prices before "going ahead in response to the President's call with [their] great construction programs." Citing also business support for the acceleration in public construction, he was satisfied that such cooperative efforts had "cut off a substantial part of the downward curve." And certainly the Federal Reserve System, "under the leadership of the Bank in New York," was doing all it could through open-market operations and successive reductions in the discount rate—now down to 3 percent—to make mortgage money cheap and plentiful as a boost to private construction.

As for GE, of the four roughly equal parts into which its business was divided—power and light, transportation, industry, and the general consumer—it was true that the industrial sector, and that alone, had fallen off. Attributing this primarily to the boom which had left the industrial plant overbuilt, Young added that industry was currently trying to anticipate its needs for new tools and equipment. Nevertheless, in his conclusion, he urged the former President to spell out his concerns, if only because "you have the very great advantage . . . of perspective . . . which I sadly lack."[42]

Did he indeed? In all fairness, the question calls for a look at Young's own operations in 1930's pivotal market, which at least make it clear that he was not talking out of one side of his mouth to Coolidge and another to his broker. Again in all fairness, the look must be prospective. However surprising Young's reentry into the '29 maelstrom, his sales of stock for that year had overbalanced his purchases at the rate of 7 to 1, thus enabling him (among other things) to reduce his year-end indebtedness to George Pick from $2,200,000 to a mere $250,-000 and his bank loans by half—from $1,575,000 to $800,000. Amply secured, as buttressed by his prompt response to calls for additional collateral, these residual debts evidently worried him so little that when, in early 1930, recovery looked about to make the grade, he put his money—or more accurately his credit—on the line to give it a timely boost, and not incidentally to acquire "sound stocks at bargain prices." By May 13, these acquisitions totaled just over $1,000,000— a third or more financed by his broker and much of the rest by additional bank loans. The largest block, however—5,000 GE—had been voted him as extra compensation for the banner year preceding, and so at the year-end figure of 60. Regarding this as a long-term investment, Young made no move to liquidate it, even as GE climbed to 95, or fell to 81, as it did just prior to the filing of the suit.[43]

In addition, on June 3 he instructed his broker to buy 1,000 of North American ("wired wireless" again) at 127½ and, toward the end of the month—after it had fallen to 91½—another 1,000 to average down his costs. By the middle of August he was so convinced that RCA itself was underpriced as to buy 12,000 shares at 38½, some 10½ points below its May 13 quotation, and some 53 points less than its cost to him a year earlier. Such staggering declines, he felt, meant simply that the nation was now moving from one extreme to the other; it was becoming as important to curb excessive deflation as it had been to check the runaway inflation. To buy now was a public obligation; it was also a private opportunity.

Young's own rise to prosperity and power, it will be remembered, had been of a sort that could only reinforce such determined optimism. So far—save only for the untimely deaths of his son John and of C.J.'s Eleanor—virtually everything in his life had turned out well: his marriage, his career in law and industry, his public service, his extracurricular concerns, even his latter-day adventures in the market. And if Jo's pride in her man of affairs did not preclude occasional sharp reminders about the fickleness of fame and fortune, both were well aware that Owen owed his fortune first of all to being in the right place at the right time. He had not "speculated" in General Electric or Radio or the utilities; he had merely held—or bought—them for the rise.

True, in the later stages of the New Era, he had increasingly backed his judgment by borrowing to buy more, and he had found it increasingly easy to let the rising price of his collateral pay off his very substantial loans. That it would not always and inevitably be that easy he recognized as a matter of course, but it was not, for him, the knowledge of experience. So now, banking on his conviction that the destructive forces released by the crash could not long prevail against the underlying and unspent strength of the American economy, he was simply doing more of the same. Aware that this involved rather more of a gamble than he was accustomed to, he was still betting, as usual, on the rise. To break this habit, regardless of the odds, would have gone against the grain; had he not found the auspices favorable, he would simply have stayed on the sidelines.

But perhaps the best documentation of his confidence in the future— the nation's and his own—is to be found in the new will he drew up for himself that summer and signed on August 26, 1930. Since its provisions document his own most intimate concerns about the future and, not least, his notion of the trusteeship and wise disposition of wealth, they have a special pertinence to the questions at issue. And since this testament of the moment may fairly be said to mark the end of a chapter—if for the moment only this one—its major provisions are here summarized, and in some part quoted.[44]

To his eldest son, Charles Jacob Young, he left all his property up-country, and for its maintenance a trust fund of $250,000, to be administered by C.J. and his sister, Josephine, as trustees "for any purpose which they may deem helpful to our home and property in Van Hornesville or its vicinity. It is to be used to any extent and for any purpose which my Mother may wish as long as she lives. . . . My hope is that my son Charles Jacob Young, will use and maintain such of the real and personal property as I have bequeathed to him and as he may decide to keep in such a way as to make it available to any members of the family who may wish to live there, either temporarily or permanently, just as I have done during my life-time." He went on to express the hope that C.J. would provide in *his* will for a successor among the children or grandchildren "to carry on the undertaking as I have done and he will do."

So much—not counting the school—for Van Hornesville and the perpetuation of the family interests and concerns that centered there.

The Riverside place and the New York apartment, with contents, he left to his wife, or if she did not survive him, to his daughter. When he came to his rare-book collection, which he had always intended to give away, and whose destination he had often discussed with his family, he provided a solution which reflected his overriding concern for education at all levels. Considering it to be worth more than a million dollars (it had cost at least twice that) he bequeathed it to St. Lawrence University, with the request that it be sold at auction and the proceeds used as follows:

(a) . . . the sum of Two Hundred and Fifty Thousand Dollars as a special fund to be known as the Van Hornesville School Fund, the income of which . . . shall be used for the maintenance and operation of the Van Hornesville School, it being my desire to maintain there a public school which will enable the children of that vicinity to secure not only a primary education, but a high school education up to the point of fitting them for college. . . .

(b) Five Hundred Thousand Dollars for the use of the University. The trustees of the University may have the broadest possible powers to deal with this fund. They may retain it as part of the endowment and use its income only or they may exhaust all or any part of the principal which they deem in the best interests of the institution. In fact, I would be glad to see the principal used sometime during the period of twenty-five years after my death rather than held as a permanent endowment. . . .

The testator also set up four funds to be used for "library purposes": the Josephine Sheldon Edmonds Fund of $100,000 to Radcliffe College; the Josephine Young Fund of $25,000 to Bryn Mawr College; the Charles Jacob Young Fund of $25,000 to Harvard University; and $25,000 to the Boston University Law School, for the library where he once worked. In addition, $5,000 each was left to fourteen colleges and universities which had given him honorary degrees. Should the books bring more or less than $1,000,000, all bequests tied to their sale were to be scaled up or down in the same proportions.

At the time this will was made, his two younger sons were minors; for all four children he had (as previously noted) set up in 1928 trust funds of moderate size. For his three secretaries he now left bequests of ten thousand dollars each, and his many debtors were forgiven their debts. The remainder of his estate was then left one-half to his wife and one-half in equal shares to the children; if she did not survive him, then equally to the children with the suggestion that they add the further sum to their trusts; "This is only a suggestion . . . I want them perfectly free to exercise their individual judgment as to the wisdom of this suggestion when the time arrives for action. . . ."

In his days as a lawyer, Young had drawn many wills and managed many estates—some of which hung on for years, even after his move to New York. The phrases "I express the hope," "this is only a suggestion," "I would be glad to see" indicate the lesson of this experience— the fear of the dead hand weighing upon his legatees. His estate, as of that date, would have been large; he merely sketched in the main outlines of what he wanted done—or would have liked to see done. He trusted his family and his college to carry them out as well as future circumstances would permit.

Chapter 27

The Pivot Unhinged:
End of an Era

ON TUESDAY, September 2, 1930, Young spent the night at the White House. It was his first visit with Hoover since the January meeting of the President's Advisory Council but the President had invited him down as early as June 10. This earlier message had caught Young on his travels; having assisted Swope in the induction of Karl Compton as MIT's new president, and then taken in the commencement at Canton, he was about to entrain for the West Coast and his scheduled speech at the utilities convention. So reporting to Hoover's secretary, George Akerson, he offered to come at once if, given the circumstances, the President still wished it; Hoover immediately wired that later would do as well. Back early the next month, Young had sent word, again through Akerson, that he was now free to come, but recognized that the President must now be wholly occupied with the all-important task of piloting the London Naval Treaty through the Senate. And so indeed he was, until its ratification of July 22, after which he had his own engagements in the West.[1]

What had prompted the President's invitation? Young's papers of the period yield little in the way of clues—least of all his three before-breakfast notes of September 3, written on White House stationery to his mother, wife and daughter. One may safely assume, however, that Hoover had not summoned him to Washington to discuss the Radio suit and also that Young would have left any such initiative to the President.[2] But the press would hardly have made this same assumption, and it was undoubtedly gratifying to both that Young somehow avoided the reporters and his visit went, for once, unpublicized.

There is little room for doubt that the President had taken the occasion to consult Young about Eugene Meyer's pending appointment as governor of the Federal Reserve Board, which he strongly endorsed and the President announced some three days later. But that was only by the way. Subsequent messages in Young's files are more illuminating, pointing as they do to Hoover's continuing concern to arrest the unchecked fall of international commodity prices. And the President's later appeal for Young's active help in stabilizing this market makes it clear that it was not his first; almost certainly that was made at the White House meeting.[3]

Now as later, Young would undertake to see what could be done, even as he asked himself whether the private sector alone could now find the means of reversing the trend. Thus he welcomed this current evidence of the President's deep concern, even while regretting earlier opportunities that had, in his view, been missed or fumbled.

To one of these Young had already paid his respects in his "little pinch-hitting" National Electric Light Association speech in June. "Pinch-hitting" as he did for Secretary of Commerce Robert P. Lamont, Young said that he "had drained off at short notice what was uppermost in my mind." What was uppermost was the problem of "our American surplus"; of goods, of gold, of capital, of labor—the last constituting "the most dangerous surplus any nation can have." That being so, it was the sheerest folly to raise fresh barriers against the very products Europe must send us in order to pay its debts *or* buy our surplus. Although no names were mentioned, this was a crack at the notorious Smoot-Hawley tariff, which Hoover's reluctant signature had just made into law. It was also fair game, especially for a lifelong Democrat, even though his party in Congress had not been notably faithful to its traditional low-tariff tenet. Told later—by Harry Robinson?—that Hoover's comment was, "Of course Owen Young is right but I wish he hadn't said just that just now," Young treated his assistant once again to a few mordant remarks on a favorite theme: the futility—and folly—of people in high places who had no natural nose for politics attempting to play politics with high policy.[4]

But it was not only by publicly inveighing against policies he found harmful and ill-timed that Young was now refusing to take recovery for granted. (Speeches never did any good, he said in reply to one letter praising his Berkeley address.) If unemployment was indeed, as he repeated at San Francisco, "the greatest blot on the capitalistic system," then there was no time like the present to attack it. Swope, who couldn't have agreed more, had already welcomed the initiative of the Works Committee at Schenectady in seeking to revive during the spring of 1930 the Unemployment Insurance Plan which, in 1925, the workers had turned down. Carefully updated, revised and edited, the plan was speedily resubmitted to the workers, and this time it was endorsed by some 75 percent of GE's 100,000 employees. And so, on June 20, the press was not only publicizing Young's NELA speech but was also heralding another timely GE innovation. In its next day's editorial, the *Times* even tied the two together.[5]

Certainly the plan's basic provisions made sense as far as they went. It was contributory, with the company matching the employees' 1 percent payroll deduction. Its management was joint, with the company guaranteeing 5 percent on the accumulative funds, or reserves. Relief payments, approximating one-half the normal wage, began when an employee was laid off or was working less than half time; they could continue for ten weeks in any given twelve months. While at first it was plant centered, a widespread emergency involved assessments on *all* salaried officers, including salesmen and top executives; all would thus have added incentives to promote recovery. Finally, policy would be geared to specific directives designed to limit expansion in good times and minimize contraction in bad.[6]

The editors of *Judge*—a magazine well known for its own dry brand of humor—could also be serious upon occasion, and so they were in hailing this GE venture. In the August 9 issue, "*Judge* on the Bench" warmly agreed with Frances Perkins, currently New York State's commissioner of labor, that it represented "Industrial Statesmanship of the First Order." The editorial rightly gave Swope full credit for being "directly responsible for the Plan," adding, however, that "it should not be overlooked that Mr. Young himself is the head of the General Electric Board. He stands today as he has stood for some years as our greatest industrial statesman."

Said Young himself, a few weeks later, in a widely syndicated and widely advertised interview by Earl Reeves, correspondent of the Hearst papers: "The greatest credit for the . . . plan . . . belongs to President Gerard Swope. It is due to his painstaking efforts that provisions were finally worked out which are satisfactory to the company and to the men." And in acknowledging their present limitations he proceeded to explain them:

. . . both Mr. Swope and I fully realize that it is only a beginning. We know that it is not, as it stands, adequate to meet the demands arising from periodic industrial and business emergencies. . . . The limitation upon the expansion of any such project, since it uses corporation funds, is the competitive situation in the industry. If . . . in the enthusiasm of our belief we were to enlarge such a plan to an extent which involved material increase in prices of our products, we might increase . . . the burden of unemployment [in our plants] because then our competitors might undersell us. . . .

Of the three things, Young went on, that "it is the duty of economic society to provide for the worker . . . a high wage . . . security of employment . . . [and] support for the years of retirement," all that had been done about the first and the third amounted to little unless ways could be found of coping with the second. Granted that it was the most difficult of the three, it was also the most important, because "*Insecurity* involves *Fear*, perhaps the most devastating . . . of all emotions."

In this interview, Young explicitly recognized that the business cycle had yet to be licked. Until it had been, efforts to maximize security of employment were, for business, both "a moral duty" and "an economic necessity." As others—especially its own competitors—recognized this truth, GE could and would go farther. And by way of encouraging the most hard-boiled to treat the proposition seriously, he said of GE's venture: "It is not an experiment in philanthropy. Although the heart may dictate that this or that thing should be done for employees, when it comes to working out a plan we have to call in the auditor."[7]

Evidently GE's top-management team was still functioning. Had private industry been prepared to follow their lead—as, quite evidently, it was not—it might just conceivably have been writing its own New Deal. But fear at this point was by no means confined to the wage earners; confronted with a choice between cooperative innovation and sitting tight, management was typically choosing the latter.

ii

Of Young's continuing efforts, early and late, to restore confidence and promote recovery, two call for special mention. Each concerned finance and credit—one international, the other domestic—and the second involved a major thrust on behalf of his own brand of reform, again directed at the utilities.

Of the international effort, dating from April 18, 1930, his assistant (who was present) left the following record:

This afternoon Mr. Young had an appointment with Bogdanov . . . Chairman of the Board of Amtorg Trading Corp., who wanted to discuss the whole credit situation. . . . The Russians, he said, are up against a situation in their search for credit in which every time there is a rumor about Russia the people from whom they are seeking credit are inclined to fight shy because they haven't time to investigate and they are getting skeptical, especially the smaller companies. Then, as they are refused credit at one place it is harder to get it at another because it creates a presumption against them. Smaller people cannot give them the same terms anyway as they can get from such companies as GE. They say they can pay cash in certain of the smaller cases but as soon as they do everyone wants the same terms and their credit is impaired to that extent. Moreover the banks will not discount their trade acceptances as they do in Europe.

[To remedy this situation] Mr. Young suggested that an American company be organized whose business it would be to mobilize the credit facilities available for Russia and extend credit to Russia at standard rates. Their rates would be based on a thorough knowledge of the situation because the head of the company would have to make it his job to be thoroughly informed. American companies would have far less hesitation in doing business with an American export company and if the Russians provided some sort of security against which the credits could be extended they would undoubtedly be able to finance their purchases with many companies, large and small. Then the Russians . . . would know where they were and have definite and uninterrupted credit facilities as long as they could satisfy officials of that one company that their policy was sound and their credit good.[8]

Young went on to emphasize the need of some such scheme to ensure the "uninterrupted flow of credit" which the "great constructive program" now under way would certainly require. He was referring to the huge dam and power project the Soviets were planning to build on the Dnieper River. It was not surprising, then, that a few months later America's foremost authority on the engineering problems involved— himself intrigued by the Soviets' plea for help—should have called to discuss it with Young; or that Young should have asked Secretary of State Stimson to give this same authority, Colonel Hugh Cooper, the briefing he wanted and should have before going over. Young's interest, of course, was twofold: in waterpower generally and in possible large orders for GE equipment. And here, as he explained to Stimson, his concern had been from the outset to meet Russia's demands promptly, in order that American rather than European (especially German) standards should become the norm and so prevail.[9]

The domestic effort took the form of an unusually long and cogent letter to his friend P. S. Arkwright, head of Georgia Power and currently president of the Association of Edison Illuminating Companies. Dictated and dispatched in July of 1930, this letter's theme was the same that had prompted Young's modest suggestion of the year before—namely, the need for the leaders of the industry to examine, openly and critically, all prevailing methods of utility financing—but this time he pulled no punches. Why, he asked, at a time when the light and power companies were rendering unexceptionable service, and badly needed public understanding and support, were they not getting it? Why wasn't the customer satisfied that even if he couldn't understand their new and complex financing, the Public Service Commissions would see to it that his rates were not thereby inflated?

Of these two questions Young disposed in short order:

In a word, [he wrote,] the ordinary man, feeling that the financing methods through complicated holding companies, etc., are a mystery which he cannot understand, believes also that the Public Service Commissions do not and cannot understand them. Therefore, while your service both physical and human is quite satisfactory to the public as a whole, I feel there is a great deal of doubt and restlessness in the minds of the public because of the mystery of these complicated setups. In some cases, this provokes active hostility, otherwise the politicians would not try to capitalize it. In other cases, it tends to keep people, otherwise friendly, from rising to the support of the utilities.

Not content with his general argument, Young proceeded to specifics. As examples of the questions which should figure prominently on the agenda of the association's next meeting, he suggested these:

1. —Basically what proportion of utility properties should be represented by bonds, preferred stock, and common stock? I do not mean by that what the capitalization of each operating company should be, but what the capitalization in the hands of the public should be.

2. —Is it, or is it not proper to issue bonds or notes of a holding company which owns nothing but stocks of operating companies? If so, what proportion of the holding company can properly be bonds or notes . . . and what proportion preferred and common stocks? Also, does it make any difference in these ratios whether the holding company has common stock only of the operating companies, or whether it also has preferred stock?

3. —How are these ratios affected when the holding companies are superimposed on other holding companies—sometimes two, three, four or five deep?

Young listed others, but these are sufficient to indicate that he was getting down to the essential issues. In conclusion he urged that if some simplification of utility financing was as important as he believed it to be, it was up to the Edison companies to do something about it; if the industry didn't, politics would. For his own part, if Arkwright agreed and would like him to write personal notes to Samuel Insull and S. Z.

Mitchell, urging their support, he would be glad to do just that. Arkwright's reply cannot be found in Young's files, but its nature can be deduced from the fact that the suggested letters to Insull and Mitchell were never written.[10]

A letter of comment and inquiry from his old friend Frank Kellogg, the sometime senator, ambassador and secretary of state who had now returned to Minneapolis and the practice of law, inspired Young a few weeks later to a further and at times impassioned exposition of his views on both the utilities and the tariff. On the impact of the latter, he cited a specific instance reminiscent of his early Page School speech on the failure of Congress, in passing the Japanese Exclusion Act, to take account of the facts as the *Japanese* saw them. Citing the current irritation abroad, which he felt could have been averted had Hoover publicly insisted that the new tariff bill be limited to agricultural schedules, Young wrote:

A Swiss lawyer was recently in this country, introduced to the Federal Reserve Bank by Governor Bachmann of the Central Bank of Switzerland. He said that one little schedule in the tariff bill, relatively insignificant to us, affecting certain types of embroidery, promised to throw out of work several thousand people in Switzerland, a number which, in percentage to the total population, would correspond to 875,000 being thrown out of work in this country. He said there were several cities and villages where mass meetings were held in protest, with the result that merchants, doctors, lawyers and political people no longer dared buy American motor cars, fearing a public boycott. He said that there was no question but that the American cars gave the best value for the money, but that the owners of new American cars were likely to be jeered on the streets and even the cars themselves, although not seriously damaged, were liable to be defaced. I have not investigated the particular schedule referred to, but it is an excellent illustration of how narrow-minded and inconsiderate tinkering with a small item may result in a boycott by a substantial market of one of our major exports.

As for the utilities, Young again rang all the changes on the suspicion aroused by the mystery and complexity of their financing arrangements, and here again multiple holding companies "out of public control" were his targets in chief. By way of illustrating the importance to the utilities themselves of steps to allay the gnawing irritant of public suspicion, he wrote of having noticed up-country "that every tree which shows diminished vitality and every animal which lacks its maximum fighting strength is the prey of all kinds of enemies." Nor could he resist the chance to restate his deeply held conviction about the proper rate base—which both the utilities and the Supreme Court had rejected: "I have always regretted," he wrote, "the rule which substituted reproduction cost for actual investment. That brings trouble from the public when the price level goes up, and it brings trouble to the utilities . . . when the price level goes down."[11]

Young may have taken some satisfaction, a month or two later, in finding himself quoted by Felix Frankfurter in the *Yale Review* as exponent of a rate base "fixed on the actual investment and not on reproductive value." Evidently Frankfurter had not forgotten their brief correspondence of 1925, nor had Young's conviction once wavered when rising construction costs in the New Era made his views anathema to most of his large customers. Now, as the *Times* suggested in its commentary on Frankfurter's article, falling costs might make these same customers more receptive to such views.[12]

iii

For broadcasting too 1930 promised to be a pivotal year. More than ever it was now clear that NBC and its competitors would derive their revenue chiefly from advertising; but this was still expected to support the noncommercial programs which the broadcasters regarded as a public obligation. And while the true professionals took special pride in these programs—which the more commercially minded put up with as sound public relations—they also resisted the advertiser's efforts to dictate the content of the commercial program itself, convinced that in the entertainment field they had already forgotten more than the advertising agency would ever know. Nor was there any hard-and-fast division between the commercial and the so-called sustaining program. NBC, for example, was rightly proud of presenting as a public service Walter Damrosch's "Music Appreciation Hour." When GE finally decided to sponsor a radio program of its own, it found nothing more likely to create the goodwill it sought than to take over this program unchanged, except for the hour and the announcement of its sponsorship.

But for a company which, like NBC, was the creature of others, there was something precarious about this nice distinction between operating for a profit and being merely self-supporting. The latter was all very well while radio sets were selling like hotcakes, but if the market continued cold, NBC would soon be under pressure to turn in maximum profits. As president, moreover, M. H. Aylesworth set great

store by his own independence, which he counted on Young to protect, and so eyed with some apprehension the new setup in RCA
which in fact made NBC its wholly owned subsidiary and David Sarnoff his boss. Realist enough to read the score, he had told Sarnoff
early in April that he was quite ready to go along *provided* that the
broadcasting company (meaning himself) were given responsibility
for the public relations of RCA and all its satellites. Reporting this to
Young via the latter's assistant, Aylesworth added that Sarnoff had
agreed.

"Well," said Young, "God bless him—but I have something bigger
in mind for him—which I want first of all to talk out with David":

I want [he said to Case] to group the Broadcasting Company with its
artists' bureau and its music company, together with RKO and the program and record department of RCA-Victor, under one concern and make
Aylesworth the head of it. This will centralize all activities of the radio
group which have to do with artists and amusement and which touch the
public most closely. It is quite natural in any such set-up that Aylesworth
should handle public relations for the whole group and so he should. Then
I want RCA-Victor to have complete charge of the manufacturing and selling operations so that that end of the business is centralized. That would
leave Sarnoff free to keep an eye on the finances of the group and on
the world situation and also to use his imagination in developing new
fields. He ought to be free to do that because just now nobody is doing
it and it's got to be done. He is an enormously able fellow and could be
doing a good job at that if his mind were not diverted by some of the
things that are now diverting it. I think that set-up would give him the
freedom he needs.[13]

Alas for the best-laid plans. Young had thought this one out, "sitting
around there in Arizona"; like so many others it had to be tabled when
the suit was filed in May.

But life went on, and so did broadcasting. By the middle of June,
the press was featuring Rockefeller's plans for "Radio City" and credit-
ing Young with the concept of making it a vast entertainment and
cultural center for all the people. True, his original conception would
suffer severely if the Metropolitan Opera, as it now appeared, were
fairly stuck with its old West Fortieth Street building and the Philharmonic remained wedded to Carnegie Hall. Even so there was to be
a great variety theater, directed by one Samuel Rothafel, known far
and wide in show business as "Roxy," together with "four other theaters for legitimate drama, musical comedy, concerts and talking pictures," whose patrons would "help to carry the cost of presentation

. . . to the 12 million owners of radio sets throughout the United States." Thus, said the front-page story in the *Times*, "Mr. Rockefeller . . . listened to the prospect of a cultural medium so young that it had no traditions, only a future; and so widely enjoyed that it could be presented to him as democratic rather than aristocratic." It would all add up not only to "the largest real estate project yet conceived by private interests in the history of the city but also [to the] formal installation of broadcasting as a new national industry." Said a *World* editorial next day, "Such a far-sighted and public-spirited program deserves to succeed."[14]

Finally, current readings of the clouded crystal ball indicated, according to the *Times*, that "as the distribution of television by wire seems to present engineering difficulties . . . television acts will have to travel from point to point, restoring the road to the legitimate theater and the variety stage just as it seemed to be slowly dying."[15] If such spreads suggested a new lease on life for R K O, they also served as a powerful rebuttal to fears that R C A, much less the economy, might be slowly dying. How could this Rockefeller project, with the thousands of jobs it would provide in the construction and allied industries, have been better timed?

It was time, too, for positive efforts to do something about education by radio, and before the year was out, two rival organizations had appeared on the scene to promote it. One saw no hope for education unless and until adequate special facilities were set aside specifically for the educators and free of commercial domination. The other, financed by the Carnegie Corporation, set out to test the broadcasters' contention that ample facilities would be readily available once the educators came up with challenging programs genuinely tailored to this new medium. And as the acting secretary of N B C's Advisory Council wrote the editors of the *New Republic*, this was the kind of challenge that American education, with its local control and decentralized traditions, was ill prepared to meet out of hand. It would take time as well as imaginative effort.[16]

Two developments of this same year afforded Young special and highly personal satisfaction. On April 4 the press had hailed the role of his son C.J., with Ernst Alexanderson, in their successful facsimile transmission of a San Francisco newspaper's front page to the laboratory in Schenectady.[17] And on July 1—with little notice from the press—his daughter Jo went to work at 711 Fifth Avenue for N B C's tiny education department. In that capacity she reported to Young's onetime assistant, John Worden Elwood, now an N B C vice-president.

Nor is it inappropriate, perhaps, to mention here that her job entailed more frequent meetings with Young's current assistant, who was also the acting secretary of NBC's Advisory Council.

As the summer progressed Young was still being teased by the purely legal aspects of the Radio suit. This is nowhere better illustrated than in his response to a young upstate correspondent who wondered if the study of law offered the best training ground for business. Wrote Young on August 11:

> The corporation lawyer of the future will be valuable to the extent [that] he is able to predict what the law will be as distinguished from advising merely what the law is. The law always lags behind business. It never develops until situations arise. Situations are being created constantly by adventures into new fields, and the question always is what will be the law to govern. In order to make such a prediction, one must have a background, not only of the law and its history, but of economics and the social sciences, and with it that flair for interpretation which enables him to determine the projection of the future curve. You see, the law in the last analysis is nothing more than the equilibrium which is arrived at in a tug of war by all these different forces. Precedents of the past, to which we all cling for safety, economic history and forecast, social and moral forces, all seem to have hold of a rope in a tug of war, and when it reaches equilibrium that is the rule of action. At what point it will reach equilibrium in the future is always the problem.

In conclusion Young advised law school—preferably Harvard's—if, and only if, his correspondent felt that he could meet these exacting requirements. Otherwise he suggested business school—notably Harvard's—where he would learn, along with certain techniques, that business "will have some of the aspects of a profession but . . . will retain much of the character of a trade."[18] Evidently the experience of the three years which had passed since his dedicatory address at Harvard had been somewhat chastening.

In the meantime—the suit and the slump notwithstanding—RCA-Victor had proceeded with its plans to celebrate Camden (Victor's home) as the new radio capital of the nation. September 19 was the day and the affair made a brave splash—but in waters that were becoming increasingly troubled. A week or so earlier, Merryle Stanley Rukeyser listed for *Forbes* magazine some sixty-odd companies that had "Never Heard of the Depression!"—having indeed reported increased earnings for the first six months of 1930. Not surprisingly, AT&T—and RKO—were among those present but GE and RCA were not.[19]

i v

With the approach of fall, and no hearing on the Radio suit impending, Owen and Jo felt a strong inclination to get away from it all and revisit England. As early as the previous spring Young had talked of going over on GE's account, and RCA's European contracts had since become a problem. During September, however, both the market and the economy continued their ominous decline, and in writing to Ambassador Dawes on the twenty-ninth Young confessed his doubts. After a "strenuous summer," he had "hoped that some signs of relief would come with the fall, but the outlook is not good . . . in fact all business here seems to be worse than ever. Perhaps it is the darkness before the dawn. That is what is keeping our spirits up at the moment." Whether, in the circumstances, he and Jo could come over as planned was still uncertain.[20]

Even to Dawes, Young made no mention of reparations and war debts, but the worsening business situation of which he complained was bringing them again to the fore. Rather against Young's advice, Hjalmar Schacht was now revisiting the United States; on Wednesday, October 8, Jackson Reynolds gave him a small luncheon which Young and former President Coolidge attended. Evidently Schacht behaved well but did not minimize the difficulties facing Chancellor Heinrich Brüning's efforts to effect far-reaching budgetary reform in the face of growing unrest and unemployment. At their after-lunch engagement Young presumably reported this to the Federal Reserve Board's Governor Meyer, whose biographer, M. J. Pusey, cites a meeting "soon after his appointment" at which George Harrison, Young and Under Secretary of State Joseph Cotton agreed with him that "reparations and war debts should be drastically cut."[21]

Following this conference, Pusey continues, "Meyer went to the White House with a plea that reparations and war debts be scaled down from 40% to 70% as a relatively painless contribution to world stability." Insisting that the two were inextricably interrelated in fact, and that drastic action alone could stave off certain disaster, Meyer is further quoted as warning the President that "Germany will default and repudiate and this will mean the economic collapse of everything in Germany and east of Germany. Then France and England will follow, and we will go in on top of the heap."[22]

Young could have predicted the outcome of the White House meeting—and probably did—but he could hardly have discouraged Meyer from making the attempt. He would certainly have questioned, however (if asked), the means Meyer is said to have proposed—that the President "call an international conference to slash both at the same time." In his view, it was a time not for bickering but for definite action by the principal creditor; besides, the Allies had already promised in their "concurrent memorandum" to pass along to Germany some two-thirds of any relief the United States might grant them. But Hoover, he knew, could have turned down this suggestion as readily as the other.

At about the same time Young's assistant was reporting Ida Tarbell's great desire to do a series of articles on his life and work that might even become a proper biography. To this Case urged his chief's consent—first, because Tarbell's ideas concerning the "unconscious" growth of our business organizations "about which we hadn't learned very much yet" spoke directly to his own. Case had a second reason too, only partially self-serving: giving her the assignment could afford a means of escape from the clamorous horde of journalists and would-be biographers he had been holding off. Young, who had met this sometime muckraker and admired her independent spirit, finally gave his consent, on the understanding that he would read not a word she wrote until it was in print. As Tarbell put it later, she became an "authorized" biographer but her book was not to be an "authorized biography."[23]

When, not long after, Owen and Jo decided to sail on October 18, there was much more to attend to than the usual passports and reservations. His new will, to be sure, had been drawn and executed in August; but the subsequent and curiously persistent decline in the index both of business and of the stock market now demanded and received his personal attention. In September, he sold some part of his recent acquisitions, including 5,000 shares of RCA, then down to 35; early in October he instructed his broker to sell 3,000 more, now quoted at 28½. But he was shifting rather than liquidating his portfolio: the following week his broker bought for his account 1,000 Radio B preferred at 57, 2,500 Bond and Share at 56 and 2,500 Electric Power and Light at 50½. Rather than sell out at present prices, Young was evidently determined to hold on for the rise—even though that entailed further borrowing and his wife's authorization to draw on her securities for additional collateral.[24]

As the *Leviathan* left the dock, reporters scurried off to file their stories, necessarily speculative because, for once, Young had given them no help. He was embarking, they wrote, on a secret mission to protect the gold standard or to arrange a moratorium on reparations and war debts. A wiser correspondent dryly observed that the most significant thing about his departure was that he was evidently not afraid to leave General Electric. And certainly it was with high hearts and few apparent worries that the couple had taken ship.[25]

That they had a relaxed and lovely time together is transparently clear in Jo's letters to her daughter. The crossing was good. Met at Southampton by a car from the Savoy, they enjoyed a leisurely drive to London, where their old friends of the Savoy staff and their favorite rooms fronting the Thames awaited them. They went often to the embassy to see Ambassador and Mrs. Dawes, and indulged their love of the theater frequently; among other productions, they saw *The Barretts of Wimpole Street*, *The Jealous Wife* at the Old Vic, and Bea Lillie in *Charlot's Revue*. And if Owen didn't do much buying, he still haunted his favorite bookshops and, on his fifty-sixth birthday, brought Walter Spencer and his wife back to the hotel. When he and Jo lunched at Lady Astor's, their fellow guests included Bernard Shaw. And on November 4, a radiogram to their daughter informed her that "[we] shall be dining at the House of Commons with your friend Lady Astor to receive the [U.S.] election returns."[26]

Aboard ship on the way over the Youngs had received a radio message signed only "Edward." "Who's Edward?" Jo had asked. It was an invitation from the Prince of Wales for a weekend in the country. They stayed with him November 1 and 2 at Sunningdale, in the old fort he had just made over for a weekend retreat; and there also were Fred Bate and his charming new American wife. Jo played the Japanese game Go with the prince, and beat him; Saturday night Owen sat up with him until after two. "I judge," wrote Jo to her daughter while she waited for him to come up, "that the affairs of the United Kingdom and the U.S. are all being settled!"[27]

There were days, however, that were spent differently. The diary of the secretary, William E. Packer, who traveled with them, lists calls and engagements enough to feed all sorts of speculation by the press of several countries. With Clark Minor of IGE, Young spent considerable time with Sir Felix Pole, now firmly installed as head of the new Associated Electrical Industries. (Although he reported to Pole on his one long visit with Sir Hugo Hirst of British General Electric, no new merger ensued.) With James Harbord he saw Guglielmo Marconi, and other radio figures, foreign but familiar; twice he visited Sir John Reith at the BBC, and once he met with his old friends of the South American Consortium. With J. P. Morgan he saw Sosthenes Behn of ITT. Also with Morgan and later with George Harrison of the New

York Federal Reserve he visited Montagu Norman at the Bank of England, lunching there on one occasion with his board. He was even reported, in error, to have visited the Bank of France, incognito.

Old friends who entertained them included the Stamps and the Kindersleys, and just before sailing for home Young attended a small luncheon with (among others) Winston Churchill. No moratoriums resulted, nor is it clear from Young's files whether anything came of the genuinely secret mission with which he was entrusted—word of which, in a coded radiogram from his office, had reached the Savoy on the very day of their arrival. Signed by Lillian Morrison and decoded by Packer, it read: "Following is from Baruch: Hoover discussed rubber cotton silk questions with Baruch who consulted with Robinson who in turn asked Baruch to advise Young to reopen discussion of rubber cotton silk in London and report."[28]

Though no trace of any consequent report appears in Young's files, the instruction to "reopen" discussion on these commodities suggests an earlier discussion to which Young had been a party. Hence the guess—already hazarded—that this was high on the President's agenda for their visit of early September. Had anything come of it, then or later, it would have been something of a miracle: currently, no nation was in a mood to make the concessions—private and public—which agreement would have required. Nor were the new high tariff schedules of any help. In any event, the price of raw materials played no part in the fanfare—described in a succeeding chapter—which attended Young's debarkation from the *Aquitania* on Friday evening, November 28. Suffice it to say that Monday, December 1, found him back in his office and in the presence of a series of unanticipated pressures, some of them explosive.

v

Precisely one week earlier—on Monday, November 24—the exhausted chairman of the New York Federal Reserve Bank, J. Herbert Case, wanted an urgent message flashed in code to his deputy chairman on the *Aquitania*. Coded, signed and sent by Young's assistant (now called upon to decode it), the message read:

Late Saturday night negotiations for dealing with Bank of U.S. situation completely and finally broke down. At request of clearing house banks and J. P. Morgan's, Father agreed to head combined banks as only way out. With banks and Morgan assuring support he talked with George Harrison yesterday morning [by phone to Berlin at 6:30 New York time] and Harrison very encouraging sees plan as only solution. Meyer C. E. Mitchell and Reyburn were also in close touch and gave endorsement. Case

Though neither the problem of the egregiously misnamed Bank of U.S.—it was not even a "national" bank—nor a saving merger with a stronger bank or banks was news to Young, a solution which called upon the Federal Reserve Bank's chairman to abdicate that office was startling indeed. How had things reached such a pass? When Young sailed for Europe, it was with every expectation that, thanks to Paul Warburg, the Bank of Manhattan Trust Company would take over the problem child. When Harrison sailed some two weeks later, Warburg's interest had visibly cooled, but he could leave with every assurance that the well-capitalized Manufacturers Trust and the smaller but even more liquid Public National Bank stood ready to effect a merger—which would include not only the Bank of U.S. but also—just for good measure—the much smaller International Trust Company.[29]

That much, at least, Young would have learned from Harrison in London, and so would have had no difficulty in interpreting the radiogram's reference to the "combined banks." Nor would he have needed any briefing on the importance at this stage of averting the failure of any metropolitan bank—especially one which, though state chartered, was a member of the Federal Reserve. Of the crash and its immediate aftermath, the most reassuring feature had been the absence of the money panic, or contagious runs on urban banks, which had been so conspicuous in the crisis of 1893 and again in 1907. Credit for this had been generally—and rightly—accorded to the Federal Reserve System, confidence in which had done much to buttress hopes for an early recovery.[30] Let small urban depositors, already having lost or fearful of losing their jobs, now fear the loss of their savings, and the ensuing panic would be doubly devastating. Already some of the weaker country banks had folded in numbers sufficient to point the moral.

But, as Young would learn when he heard the full story, it was first of all the bankers, not their depositors, who had become prey to fear. As the decline of business and the market became even steeper with the advent of November, one after another of those who had been most keen on the merger began to have qualms and so to set conditions. Warburg, as noted, was among the first to do so; the others bided their time. As late as the end of October the Manufacturers Trust had been sufficiently confident of the outcome to offer Case the post of chairman of the prospective new institution at twice his present salary. Neither the offer nor Case's firm refusal formed any part of the story on the expected merger which appeared in the *Sun* on the evening of October 28, and in all the morning papers next day. That the reported negotiations were not denied was naturally taken as a good omen. A week or so later, on November 6, negotiations were said to be progressing satisfactorily, but their quick conclusion was not to be anticipated owing to the many legal and financial problems remaining to be settled.[31]

And there, it appeared, was the rub. Having completed by November 12 their own examination of the misbegotten Bank of U.S., the two prospective partners, the Public and the Manufacturers, had advised the Federal Reserve and the state superintendent of banking, Joseph T. Broderick, that they wanted no part of it. Thus Case, in Harrison's absence the Fed's senior officer, had suddenly found himself holding a live bear by the tail. At the next day's meeting of the board, two fellow directors were named to assist him in its taming, but far more important was the unstinted support he could rely on from his fellow officers. And of these it was the same Randolph Burgess who had come to Young's aid in setting up the BIS whose deep dedication and negotiating skills now converted Case's otherwise lonely task into a genuine team effort.[32]

How invaluable this was, the next ten days would amply demonstrate. There were days—and nights—of endlessly taxing negotiations, involving not only the banks most directly concerned but also the so-called clearinghouse banks,[33] plus Superintendent Broderick and, especially and always, the chairman and/or Burgess, who, perforce, were virtually living at the Fed. Even so, the prospect was still gloomy when, on the evening of Saturday, November 22, they both left the bank for a meeting uptown with such Wall Street stalwarts as Russell Leffingwell of Morgan's, Walter Frew of the Corn Exchange Bank, Mortimer Buckner, chairman of the New York Trust and also of the clearinghouse, and Albert Wiggin of the Chase. But that meeting produced the bright idea which promised to revive the moribund merger. While all next day the Public National still held out for guarantees against loss, their midnight capitulation effected a consensus that the merger was now feasible provided—and this was the bright idea—that Case himself would give the new bank the all-important assurance of sound management by becoming its chairman and chief executive officer.[34]

For Case this proviso was a poser, giving to his efforts *pro bono publico* a curiously ironic twist. Asking nothing better than to stay on in the quasi-public post which promised more of the same, he was now under pressure to return to commercial banking as the greatest public service he could render. Very well, if nothing else would serve, he would do just that, *provided* that the bankers who were pressing this upon him were equally ready to do their part. First, he would require public announcement of the new bank's immediate admission to the clearinghouse. Second, as assurance of the clearinghouse banks' continuing commitment and support, he would require the consent of at least four representative new directors chosen from these banks, to serve on his new board—and he would do the choosing. These conditions having been accepted on the spot and his four new directors having by ten o'clock on Monday morning agreed to serve, Case consented to the draft. Released at once, the news was being hailed by the press at about the same time it reached Young.[35]

Although Young could only guess at the background of the cryptic message—to which he responded at once—he had no trouble in visualizing the impact of the news. And indeed his congratulatory message was only one of the spate with which Case was already being deluged, reflecting the intense relief and mood of self-congratulation which reached from Wall Street to the White House. Certainly Young found nothing surprising in the radio reports on the turn of the market, which *Forbes* pronounced "the most encouraging in weeks."[36]

Young's personal relief, after landing, that this crisis had been resolved could only have been strengthened as he reviewed his own calendar for the first week of December. Two days were completely given over to his board meetings: R C A-Victor and the Federal Reserve on Thursday; G E, R C A and half a dozen subsidiaries on Friday; after which he must get up to Van Hornesville for a visit with his mother. But first he had to devote himself, as he did on Monday and Tuesday, to catching up on things with Swope, as well as Harbord, Sarnoff and Aylesworth. Herbert Case, snowed under by his mail, was also busily planning for the kind of financial and legal staff his new post would require, but Harrison would be back—and taking charge at the Fed— before Thursday's directors' meeting. The nationwide drive to relieve the unemployed—by local and voluntary effort—had been entrusted to the Association of Community Chests and Councils, also headed by Case; but in New York a special committee led by Seward Prosser of the Bankers Trust was undertaking a drive to raise eight million dollars and Prosser wanted Young for its meeting that Wednesday. The same evening, December 3, he was scheduled—to quote another of his office boy's more memorable calendar entries—to "attend the Lotos Club dinner in honor of himself." And that, of course, meant another speech, on which he had already put in a few licks over the weekend. It was well that he had, especially in the light of his eleventh-hour decision to release it to the press, rather than risk a leaked and scrambled version.[37]

The Lotos Club dinner turned out to be quite an affair, at which Young was only one of several speakers, and briefer than most. Its inevitable political reverberations are discussed in a succeeding chapter, but his assistant, who was there, took note of other things. In an irresponsible moment this notetaker was reminded of Jeremiah Smith's reputed greeting to the expectant press correspondents in Paris after a particularly long and arduous session of the Young Committee: "Gentlemen, there is nothing to say, and it is important!" Sophisticated as it was, Young's immediate audience was almost as ready as the press to treat him as an oracle, and in some degree, Young obliged.

What he did not say, for example, was almost more significant than what he did. He spoke of radio as "one of the things I discussed in London," but not of the government suit. He mentioned the "abstract question" of whether the international debts which had given so much trouble "should exist at all" as one "on which certainly I would not express a view." He noted as important the question of our debtors' capacity to pay but did not answer it. As to what "action, if any" the U.S. government should now take, "it lies in the mouth of no private citizen to say." He urged only that it be "always definite"—uncertainty being stability's implacable enemy.

But the oracle did, perhaps, have something to say about the burden of these debts in time of deflation. If, for him, the analogy he drew between private and public debt had a poignancy unguessed by his auditors, the public message came through loud and clear. In measured words (which he had told Stuart Crocker and Everett Case he thought would not be unwelcome to the President at this point) he said:

It is quite natural in times of depreciated commodity and security prices that debtors should ask for a readjustment of their debts. I would be glad to do so myself. Unfortunately, it takes twice as many securities to pay my debts as it did when I incurred them. I could make a very good moral argument if anyone would listen to me, that my debts should be reduced, but I would not expect to get a hearing unless my creditor was satisfied of my incapacity to pay. If he was, then it would be for the creditor to say, not for me, what he wished to do about it. And as between nations, I should hope for a breadth of view and a sympathy of understanding in dealing with problems of this kind, greater than any individual has any right to expect from his own creditor. He, I have found, is very hard-hearted. Let not America be so.

Nor was there anything playful now in his treatment of politics versus economics. While the latter, with radio's help, was ignoring or overriding national and other artificial boundaries in its quest for wider and integrated markets, the former was increasingly engaged in magnifying the barriers—and the number of national governments busy at such tasks was vastly greater than before the war. How to reconcile these disparate aims was no longer an academic question; as a practical matter, no more urgent problem confronted this country and its leaders.

Was there, after all, in Young's peroration a veiled reference to the Radio suit which some of those present—and others not present— would know how to interpret? Emphasizing once again the importance to a disordered world of certainty as a prop to stability, he said:

Whether you apply [this criterion] to debts or reparations or rules of the game, it is all the same. . . . An orderly functioning world must play the game according to some rules, and they should only be changed after ample notice and with the greatest wisdom and care. The penalty of doing otherwise is destruction of confidence and consequent disaster.[38]

vi

After this crowded but satisfying week, and in preparation for the next, Van Hornesville was a predictably refreshing change. There too Young found plenty of problems, but at least the new stone schoolhouse and the handsome new principal's house—with teachers' apartments in its wings—were now fully operative, and paid for. But he had a very substantial personal payroll on his hands, temporarily including the teachers' salaries. Also Van Horne Farms was a major employer, and for many of the retired farmer-neighbors now living in the village, Young had found not too taxing chores for which he footed the bill. (Retrospectively one could almost say that his concern was their only social security.) It was not getting any easier to meet such problems and there would have to be some economies made, but for his mother's sake and his own, he would have to carry on. And here his farm manager, the brisk, able but sympathetic James Hagar from the Mohawk Valley, could and would be of help. So Young stayed on through Monday but that evening took the sleeper for New York and an all-day meeting of the Committee on Recent Economic Changes, deferred to this Tuesday in order to assure his presence.

What he had to say to the committee at luncheon on this Tuesday, the ninth of December, may help to explain their reluctance to meet without him. Avoiding pat solutions, he merely posed the current problem, but in words so simple and so lucid as to be in striking contrast to the President's verbiage about "mobilization of relief resources" and the "coordination of instrumentalities for recovery." Young put it this way:

We have an interesting situation in the world today. Raw materials are out of employment. They seek to work and are offering themselves at less than a living wage; that is, less than the cost of production. Fabricating plants are out of work. They seek employment, and are offering themselves, temporarily at least, without profit. Only a contribution to existing overhead is required. Money and credit are out of work. They are in ample supply, and are offering themselves at ridiculously low margins of return. Men are out of work. They seek employment, and nothing but a strong public opinion prevents them from slaughtering their wage scales for their necessities. In short, millions of people the world over need and want the things which could be made, yet the economic world seems to be set on dead center. We apparently have as perfect a balance in paralysis as we thought we had in activity two years ago.

Now the great question which everybody everywhere is asking is simply this: Why is it that men and money and materials, anxious to go to work to produce what millions everywhere are anxious to consume—why is it that they are denied the opportunity? That is the great, arresting question which any report must attempt to answer. Nothing but the most searching studies will meet the situation. No answers to subsidiary questions are of consequence unless they can be related directly to the answer to the big question. Therefore, I suggest that we make a survey of what we need to answer the big question and set against that need what we have and what we have not. What we have does not need to be duplicated but what we have not needs urgently to be supplied. I understand perfectly that the weighting of different factors will vary with individual judgment, but I do not think there should be much difficulty in getting an agreement on what are the important factors.[39]

Having delivered this charge, Young excused himself to attend the special meeting of the Federal Reserve directors which Governor Harrison, now back, had urgently summoned. Over the past weekend, Harrison now reported, the salutary merger which, in his absence, had been put together with such infinite pains had definitely come unstuck. The Public National, it appeared, had issued an ultimatum on Sunday demanding guarantees against possible losses on a scale which the clearinghouse banks found unacceptable; efforts had then been focused on how best to proceed without them. On Monday afternoon, however, the Manufacturers Trust had followed suit. That same night the officers of the Fed and Colonel Joseph Hartfield, the indefatigable counsel to the Bank of U.S., had worked out a plan which involved the resignation of all that institution's officers and directors, the pledge of all stock under their control, and the writing down of capital to five million dollars. This they hoped would induce the clearinghouse banks to put in the requisite fifteen or twenty million dollars of new capital, and this the latter were now actively exploring. Time was getting short but Harrison was apparently still hopeful.[40]

Next morning, Wednesday the tenth, Young attended the scheduled meeting of the General Education Board and conferred with Prosser about the relief drive (which exceeded its eight-million-dollar goal). In the afternoon, however, he was called back to the Federal Reserve, where he remained—taking time out only for a dinner of industry's Special Conference Committee—until two o'clock the morning after. During the day there had been large runs on several of the Bank of U.S. branches and the situation was desperate enough to command the serious attention which the Clearing House Committee was now giving it. Broderick subsequently reported that as late as 8:30 that evening Harrison had phoned to tell him that "everything looks fine" and that the reporters were being asked to come in around 9:30 to receive a statement which had already been prepared.

And then, shortly before midnight, the bottom dropped out. Spent and weary, Harrison emerged from a long session with the bankers, bearing catastrophic news. "One or two of the clearinghouse banks don't want to go along now," he said to Broderick, "and others say they won't unless these do. I am not in a position to press them."

Neither Young's files nor those of the New York Fed yield any record of that fateful meeting, but in the light of Broderick's subsequent testimony, it is clear that it followed a too-familiar pattern. Just as fear of possible contingencies had blinded the Public National and the Manufacturers to the vast potentialities for new and profitable service in what would have been the city's fourth-largest bank, so now fear that the required infusion of new capital might be risky, or even insufficient, gradually overcame the clearinghouse banks' more enlightened and public-spirited concerns. And once again the fears of the few had carried the day.[41]

Broderick's own last-ditch effort—at 1:00 A.M. on Thursday, December 11—offered final proof that no mere plea, however eloquent, could move the recalcitrant minority of the clearinghouse group or persuade the majority to act without them. In terms of numbers served, he pointed out, the Bank of U.S. was possibly the largest in the city; to its 400,000 small depositors—as well as to public confidence in banks and bankers generally—its closing could do irreparable harm. And because of its unfortunate name, news of its failure could have grave repercussions abroad. To these unanswerable arguments the only apparent response came from the First National's Jackson Reynolds, in whose opinion, as reported by Broderick, the impact would be "purely local."[42]

Later that same morning Superintendent Broderick took reluctant but final action: for the first time ever, a metropolitan "member bank" with sizable deposits was forced to close its doors. Harrison lost no time in dispatching explanatory and reassuring telegrams to the heads of the eleven other regional Federal Reserve Banks and especially to the governors of the European central banks; the worried replies from abroad amply vindicated his judgment in ignoring the view imputed to Reynolds.[43] As for the "purely local impact," the failed bank had some fifty-nine branches—which meant a lot of closed doors, each bearing the legend "Member of the Federal Reserve System." Its 400,000 depositors, including many recent immigrants, were permitted to borrow (by grace of the clearinghouse banks) up to half of their current deposits, but such relief as this afforded was hardly reassuring to small depositors elsewhere. The garment trades, whose needs the bank had best understood and served, were suddenly strapped for credit; the Manufacturers Trust, which might have helped, was suffering runs of its own—a contagion of fear from which not even the Public National was immune. As for business and the market, their recent rise ended abruptly as they went into a predictable tailspin. Confidence was in shreds, and so of course was all present hope of redeeming the promise of early recovery which had marked the spring of the year— a promise on which so many, including Owen Young, had banked so heavily.[44]

It had been widely expected of the New York Federal Reserve—and not least by its officers and directors—that in any such crisis it would exert a leadership no less masterful, and certainly more disinterested, than that of the elder Morgan during the panic of 1907. Now as then, it is fruitless to ask whether Harrison, had he been there from the start, could have put together and sustained this saving but slippery merger, or whether Case, left in charge throughout, would have proven the more masterful in the showdown. The fact was, and is, that each did his utmost—but lacked the magic touch of a Benjamin Strong. And the further, and ineluctable, fact was that the failure of the ill-starred Bank of U.S. was a shattering and most untimely blow to public confidence in the Federal Reserve itself.[45]

For the purposes of this book, its chief importance lies in Young's long and responsible association with the New York Federal Reserve— especially as he, if anyone, might be presumed to share something of Strong's "magic touch." Absent abroad during the first weeks of crisis and assured of its solution as he returned to face a crowded schedule, he had joined the final and unanticipated round-the-clock efforts to save the Bank of U.S. with full realization of what the bank's failure spelled for the depositors, the city, the Fed and the prospects for national recovery, as well as for his friends George Harrison and Herbert Case. Like Morgan in Paris, however, he was not in charge, and felt that his influence could best be brought to bear by upholding the hands of him who was. In a letter at the end of the year deploring the failure of the bank, he said only that "Governor Harrison made every effort to save it and I gave him my full support."[46]

In the event, this failure too became just one of those facts which Young, like others (Case included), had to live with. The pain it gave him was obviously not that felt by the small depositor, but his own purse was by no means immune from the "purely local" impact of the closing. On first returning home, Young had made a modest effort to buttress his brokerage account by buying 1,200 shares of Radio B preferred at the "ridiculously low" price of 37; after all, when the suit was launched it had been quoted at 81. Now on December 17 and 18, he took the painful step of selling 7,500 shares of Radio common at 12½. Had he said at the Lotos Club that it now took twice as many securities to pay his debts as when he had incurred them? Only last April this sale would have yielded better than $500,000; now it brought him less than $100,000. How at this rate was he to meet his extensive commitments and at the same time liquidate loans from his broker and three banks which now totaled some $3,000,000 and were constantly demanding additional collateral?

One thing he could do now and did. On December 16, the will he had drawn with such satisfaction only last August was marked CANCELLED and a new one drawn in his own hand. This time he simply left "all my property of every kind to my wife, Josephine Edmonds Young, who will be in a position to carry out our plans as circumstances may permit."[47]

And so, for Owen and Jo, ended this pivotal year.

Chapter 28

1931: Year of Adversity

S PEAKING at the Lotos Club on December 3, 1930, of the man who
came to dinner "in honor of himself," David Sarnoff used soberly
prescient words:

It is said that the true significance of a man is to be found in his works.
Perhaps—but not wholly. The years destroy the most enduring monuments.
Circumstances often vitiate the best laid plans. Only time can tell how
soundly we build.

For the occasion this evening I should like to amend the old law. I
should like to say that in his higher values a man cannot be measured
merely by his works; he must be measured by the things he works for; by
the courage with which he faces his tasks; by the purpose that moves him;
by the principles which sway his decisions. . . .[1]

If Young was moved, he gave no sign, least of all in his public
response. That he was severely shaken by the closing, only a week
later, of the Bank of U.S., was privately attested by his new will of
December 16. Nevertheless, he wanted no obituaries for what had been
lost, and his public stance remained strictly pragmatic. Let the fate of
all his "works"—including his most cherished creations and achievements—be determined as it would by the new decade, perhaps even
by the coming year. In the meantime there were pressing problems,
public as well as private, to confront and if possible resolve.

The fundamental question was the one Young put to the Committee on Recent Economic Changes in December: how to put idle plants
and credit, materials and men back to work. The immediate question
was how to arrest the ever more destructive spiral of deflation, while
doing everything possible to mitigate its ravages; here at first 1931
offered signs of encouragement. And it was a measure of the respect
and confidence still vested in the man himself that Young's advice and
counsel were now in greater demand than ever.

What should the Senate do to strengthen our fatally weak banking system? What should the House do about the veterans' bonus? Should the President propose a moratorium on all international debt payments, including reparations, and if so, when and for how long? How could state and local agencies for relief of the unemployed best be mobilized to maximize their yield? What measures to provide jobs and promote recovery could industry and government best take? These were conspicuous among the public questions on which Young was asked to testify, advise, or—as in the case of the relief and recovery programs—take active leadership.

Nor could one detect in his response to these successive calls any hesitation or self-doubt. When, on Tuesday, February 3, he boarded the 1:30 P.M. Baltimore and Ohio train for Washington, it was to meet a double test: at ten next morning to testify before Senator Carter Glass's subcommittee on ways of strengthening the banking system; on the same afternoon to give the Ways and Means Committee of the House his views on the bill calling for immediate payment of the bonus due the veterans in 1945. His January calendar, crowded as usual, had left him little time for preparation and it is not surprising that he devoted Monday afternoon to absorbing all that the New York Federal Reserve had to offer. Even more important for his testimony on the bonus, however, was his weekend at Van Hornesville. He "had to get away from this Wall St. atmosphere," he told his assistant, to find out what he "really thought."

What he really thought—especially about the bonus—made front-page headlines. YOUNG FAVORS CASH BONUS FOR NEEDY VETERANS ONLY; URGES FEDERAL BANK CURB reported Thursday's *New York Times* in a two-column spread. The *Times* also printed the full text of both his statements and an editorial strongly commending his bonus proposal—and him for making it. This proposal, as a startling departure from the orthodox opposition of other leading banking and industrial witnesses, was everywhere hailed as *news*; it also produced a renewed political buzz and hum. And a notable digest of what the witness said, in the context of the hearings, appeared in *Time*, where Young's testimony all but dominated its section on national affairs.[2]

In a column entitled "The Young Plan," *Time* briefly rehearsed the "chorus of adverse testimony [which] seemed to suffocate all bonus legislation. . . . Then," said its report,

as a final witness, Ways and Means Chairman Hawley put on the stand Owen D. Young, confident that that tycoon would merely reiterate the business world's objections to any form of certificate payments at this time.

But Mr. Young did not perform as expected. Like his banking friends, he did oppose a big bond issue to pay off the Bonus on the grounds that 1) such an issue probably could not be sold; 2) savings necessary for business recovery would be absorbed otherwise; 3) "we should end worse off than we began." Unlike his associates, however, Democrat Young favored a compromise, favored upping the loan value of service certificates (now 22½%) for the benefit of really needy cases. The Republican committeemen were thoroughly startled to hear a proposal so out of tune with the other songs of Big Business.

Mr. Young began with friendly words for veterans in distress: "They hold our promises to pay; they need money now. They, of all people, should not be left in want. We must approach the problem with a determination to do them not only justice but more."

Citing Young's estimate that some 30 percent of the veterans needed help, and needed it now, *Time* quoted him as suggesting "that the Government might advance"—to them and to them only—"a substantial percentage of the face value of their certificates." Involving by his reckoning "not less than $300,000,000 nor more than $500,000,000 . . . a diversion of funds in that amount would," in his words, "be wholly justified." Finally: "If veterans not in distress complained against this loan plan which would leave them out, Mr. Young said: 'I should pay no attention to it.' Remarked Congressman Garner, the committee's leading Democrat: 'You might if you came up for re-election next year.' Retorted Mr. Young: 'Well, I don't!' "

After a column or more devoted to the political repercussions of Young's statement, *Time* proceeded to the Senate hearing, which it entitled "Reserve Review." Again Young's testimony appeared in context. First it was explained that this investigation was not of the spectacular hit-and-run sort, but a serious effort to examine the strengths and weaknesses of a system which Chairman Glass had done so much to set up some seventeen years earlier. Having summarized the testimony of preceding witnesses, most of whom held the Federal Reserve Board largely to blame for the inadequacy of efforts to check the speculative boom, this report continued as follows:

Most impressive, most lucid, most constructive witness before the Committee was Owen D. Young, a director of the New York Federal Reserve Bank. Said he of the stock crash: "The low [rediscount] rates were continued too long. An active, firm and decisive policy of advancing rates should have been carried out in 1928. The Federal Reserve Bank of New York did not make its recommendations for rate increases early enough or advance the rates rapidly enough. I was quite as much to blame for that as anyone."

Mr. Young diagnosed present banking ailments as due to charter com-

petition between the U.S. and the States. He recommended that all commercial banks be *forced* into the Federal Reserve system, even if it required
a constitutional amendment, as a means of "fixing responsibility." He declared that "Member of the Federal Reserve System" painted on a bank's
window today meant, despite popular impression to the contrary, little or
nothing because the Federal Reserve exercised no real control over the institution, was in fact afraid to, lest it drive the bank out of the System.

"We have seen thousands of banks fail here," testified Mr. Young. "It is
certainly a great reflection on the American people that they cannot get a
banking system in hand that will prevent such awful tragedies." He favored
a limited form of branch banking, recommended prohibiting corporations
from putting their surplus cash into the call market, frowned on security
affiliates of banks which go unexamined.[3]

To Young's assistant, as a central banker's son, this testimony was a
natural source of pride. More memorable, however, was the way his
chief had refused in his bonus testimony to bow to "Wall Street" pressures—even those which emanated from the highly responsible and
conservative side of the street. The concern of this side to protect the
credit of the federal government was real and deep-rooted; so was the
fear that this would suffer from any concessions on the bonus. Thus
the two men "chosen" to accompany Young on the train—ostensibly
to add spit and polish to his banking statement but actually to dis-
suade him from any bonus compromise—were men who enjoyed his
special confidence: Randolph Burgess of the Fed and Morgan's newest partner, Parker Gilbert.

Respecting both his advisers for their overriding concern for the
nation's welfare, and only less for his, Young spared no effort to accommodate his views to theirs—save on the principle at issue. On that he
refused to budge. If they suspected (as his assistant did) that here he
was actually bowing to political ambitions, that was just too bad. Even
at its best, Young felt Wall Street's outlook tended to be parochial:
from Van Hornesville, one could see much farther.

It was well past midnight when his two final statements were ready
to be mimeographed for the press. Yet when Young took the stand
before the Glass committee next morning he seemed refreshed and
wholly in command. And when he appeared before the Ways and
Means Committee, it was to offer—for better, for worse—his own un-
altered views about the bonus.

A bill incorporating his proposal was quickly drafted but as quickly
discarded in favor of one which raised the loan value of *all* service
certificates to 50 percent—involving an outlay of $1.7 billion. Over-
whelmingly approved by the House on February 16, this measure was

promptly vetoed by a President who belatedly professed a willingness to sign any bill to help needy veterans only. He was never to have that opportunity—nor could he make his veto stick.[4]

Young sent off copies of both his statements to Ambassador Dawes in London, and wrote Treasury Secretary Mellon in regard to the bonus. He repeated his bonus statement for a newsreel, which was widely shown—the family went from theater to theater to see it half a dozen times. But politics, it seemed, was readier to ask than to follow Young's advice, and his next and almost pedagogical speech, at the annual St. Lawrence dinner in New York, was on the Federal Reserve System. If Congress would not act, his fellow alumni at least should understand just what it was up against—and why.[5]

ii

Early in March of 1931 came intimations of mortality that touched Young closely. Dr. Hervey, at his son's house on Long Island, was seriously ill; Young went at once to see the man to whom, he often said, he owed the most in the world outside his family. Almost ninety-two, Hervey recognized him when he came to the bedside, and they had a last talk. When Owen was in Van Hornesville for his mother's ninety-second birthday on March 10, they had news of the doctor's death.

Only the week before, Young had been home for the funeral of another old and dear friend, Abram Tilyou, to whom he had turned when his own father died, and who had become his fellow "rocking chair consultant" in developing the new school and many other local projects. Nor had Owen forgotten their innumerable games of pinochle, with Uncle John Brandow and the local storekeeper to make up the foursome. If these deaths lent a certain poignancy to his mother's birthday celebration, she seemed well and lively as they shared a drink beside the sitting-room stove. Soon now, he told her, he would be heading for Arizona, from which Jo and young Richard were sending loving messages. And indeed, after a frantically busy week in New York, Owen was back for one more visit on his way to join them in Chandler. A day in Chicago, meeting with Samuel Insull and Melvin Traylor, then he was in the bright sunshine under the orange trees, planning to stay at least a month.[6] (This year his mother had thought she had best stay at home.)

Less than two weeks later, on April 6, this idyll ended abruptly with word from Van Hornesville that Ida Young had suffered a disastrous fall. The Arizona contingent left at once. While they were en route, Jo suffered a serious heart attack, which laid her low for most of the year and left her future precarious at best. When they reached Van Hornesville, however, the immediate prognosis for both patients was encouraging enough for Owen to snatch a few days at the office, preparing for the Washington meeting with the attorney general on April 22, in which he saw some promise of an early settlement of the Radio suit. Early settlement would prove elusive but not for want of persistent effort on both sides.[7]

But as the days passed it became clear his mother could not survive, from April 25 to the day of her death, Owen left her bedside only to sit with his wife, who at least was now holding her own. The children were with them as much as possible, to give what help they could to their father. Ida Young drifted into a semicoma, and died on May 21; even as she moved away she knew him.

Mother and grandmother and great-grandmother, she had seemed to all immortal; she, and Van Hornesville, had been fixed indistinguishably in the lives of her family. The place was unthinkable without her. No house was ever more empty than hers when she left it.

Everyone who knew Owen Young knew how much she had meant to him and the letters and telegrams and radiograms poured in from home and abroad. The local newspapers ran streamer headlines, the city ones long accounts of her life. She was always distrustful of publicity, and one can imagine her tight little smile at the headline in the *Herkimer Evening Telegram*: MOST DISTINGUISHED GROUP EVER IN COUNTY ATTEND YOUNG FUNERAL.

Her son often said of her that until she was over fifty her normal world had a radius of about five miles; in the last decades of her life it was the globe. If Owen was in China or Europe, she wanted to know about the place and the people. She read several newspapers daily, and listened to the radio news. "She felt that she knew most of the important men in the world," he said to a sympathetic local reporter, "and she was interested in their activities. . . . I don't believe that she ever enjoyed life so much as she did from 75 to 85 years and on . . . it is possible to have the best part of your life ahead of you at 70. . . ."[8]

This fateful summer of 1931 was marked not only by death and illness in the Young family but by happier, more forward-looking occasions. Shortly after the first Van Hornesville School commencement, Josephine Young and Everett Case were married, the bride's father— in top hat and cutaway—escorting her along the village street to the little white church where he had been Sunday school superintendent at the age of fifteen. Philip too was married, in August, to Faith Adams, the daughter of H. H. Adams, the General Electric representative in Washington. Young Richard took a dim view of these proceedings, but his parents were happy to have one still at home.

From the long siege of illness and death, from the prospect of his young people setting up homes of their own, Owen Young, with his farmer's knowledge of the land and the seasons, drew renewed strength and intellectual power. Far from withdrawing from his usual round of widespread activities, he carried them forward with undiminished skill. Certainly he had never been more sensitive to the needs of others than he showed himself that summer, in the time and effort he devoted to the wants of diverse individuals—mostly the humble or the recently "humbled"—who sought his counsel and help in that time of troubles.

And the summer gave him deep satisfactions at both St. Lawrence and Van Hornesville. In Canton, at commencement in June, the new men's dormitory was dedicated in the presence of three of the donors, Andrew and Richard Mellon, and Young himself; the fourth, George Baker, Sr., had died in May. In August, at a second commencement, for the summer school, at which his son Philip was graduated just in time for his wedding, Young made one of his most telling and widely quoted speeches. It compressed in five questions a final examination for graduating seniors to give themselves; if the answer to all five was yes, you were educated:

First. Have you enlarged your knowledge of obligations and increased your capacity to perform them?

Second. Have you developed your intuitions and made more sensitive your emotions?

Third. Have you discovered your mental aptitude?

Fourth. Have you learned enough about the machinery of society and its history to enable you to apply your gifts effectively?

Fifth. Have you acquired adequate skills in communication with others?

Of the first he said, "Failure on the first question means failure altogether." The second question, to those who knew him, was equally characteristic. "I mean by it," he said, "that whole area of subconscious or superconscious activity which underlies our ordinary mental machinery. . . . I would endeavor to develop those thousand and one antennae which unconsciously absorb, especially in your contacts with other human beings, impressions of which the mind either cannot take account or comprehends all too slowly." The third and fourth were repeated again and again to young people, including his children, when they asked for help in making decisions. The fifth, he said, is that without which all the others cannot function. But it was the first which he emphasized most; he included both private and public obligations and urged—not least, perhaps, upon himself—a continuing study of "what your obligations are in this modern world and . . . how you intend to perform them."[9]

The first commencement of the Van Hornesville School was not only the culmination of the first phase of Young's effort for the improvement of education in his birthplace, but, in a sense, a crossroads where the paths of his educational, political and personal interests met. It was one of those landmarks in a life which, significant at the time, would grow more so as the years went by.

The governor of New York, Franklin Delano Roosevelt, whom Young had known since the days when he was assistant secretary of the navy, gave the address to the graduating class of seven girls and one boy. Young, in his brief talk, referred to the isolation of Van Hornesville in his own youth:

The Governor took less time today in coming to Van Hornesville than I used to take as a boy to get to Fort Plain. . . . Twelve miles was more than seventy now. The capital of the Empire State was far—oh so far away. Dr. Munn, one of the most distinguished residents of this village, took me to Albany in the '80s and presented me to Grover Cleveland, the Governor of the State of New York. . . . How little did I think that we should be able to welcome here Grover Cleveland's successor.

And he pointed out how greatly the educational program had to be revised for young people who now must become part, not of isolated communities, but of the nation and of the world. Turning to the governor beside him, he said that perhaps one day this school would provide a governor from among its alumni, "who will come here to carry on the high tradition this day begun. Then the Governor will be your friend as this Governor is mine."

Roosevelt spoke well and warmly, mentioning his own "rural" background, and referring to Young as "a very necessary factor in almost every forward-looking step of the nation." Politics was not mentioned; but in thanking the governor for coming, Young assured him that "our friendship and good wishes go with you in all the undertakings in which you now are *or may hereafter* be engaged" (italics added).[10]

If some of his neighbors muttered their dissent, it went unnoticed. And thanks to the flood of press reports which the occasion evoked, the Van Hornesville School became, almost overnight, the best-known rural school in the United States.

Indeed, by this time, the school was already on the threshold of the new and centralized phase described in an earlier chapter, for on May 1 the voters of the neighboring school districts had elected to join it. The substantial new building operation which this would entail meant a correspondingly large increase in Young's already large commitments; what would his creditors say? Nevertheless, he treated the action of the outlying districts as a vote of confidence and hence a mandate to proceed. "By the will of the people I build," was his half-humorous comment; after all, it would mean jobs, and building costs were low: somehow he would find the funds. And Jo agreed. She had had to miss the weddings and commencements, keeping to her bedroom in Van Horne House even when the governor came for luncheon, and leaving young Jo to do the honors. But she knew, none better, how much this program at the school meant to Owen, nor had her confidence in him once faltered. Thus, in a sense together, they embarked on this new and major contribution to education and to the kind of unemployment relief which began close to home.

This new undertaking, however, demanded that Owen come to grips with his own financial problems. During July and August he sold at the market upwards of 20,000 shares of GE, which, with some earlier sales and 5,000 of Radio B preferred, enabled him to meet his most pressing commitments and to retire a million or more in bank loans. While this decisive if tardy action left the Bankers Trust and his broker, George Pick, as his principal creditors on loan account, it also left him uncomfortably close to bankruptcy, at least in a technical sense. Against more than $2,000,000 in current obligations, all the collateral he could muster was now woefully inadequate, and such long-term assets as real estate, prize cattle and rare books would bring little in the current market. His uncommitted liquid assets now consisted chiefly of his earning power, itself facing every prospect of a sharp reduction. Nevertheless, the dimensions of his problem remained a well-kept secret, except from Gerard Swope, who—some months later—generously lent him $200,000 to meet his "liquidity crisis." Meanwhile, it was better to have applied these already shrunken assets to the reduction of his debts than to have sat by and watched them melt entirely away. Besides, the game was far from over; neither then nor later would he consent to let it go by default.[11]

iii

In that crowded June of 1931, consultation on world affairs also demanded Young's attention. With Parker Gilbert, he met in Washington on the thirteenth with Secretary of State Stimson, Acting Treasury Secretary Ogden Mills, George Harrison and Eugene Meyer on the precarious and worsening European situation. A week later—and none too soon—came the President's declaration of a one-year moratorium on all intergovernmental debts.

Beginning with the spring, developments abroad were now threatening to unravel the whole fabric of international credit. Germany, with unemployment rife, especially among the young, trade stagnant, and foreign loans cut off, was increasingly holding reparations responsible for all its troubles; but Chancellor Brüning rightly felt that unilateral moves to repudiate obligations would totally destroy his country's credit. Instead, with his somewhat reluctant consent, his government had been plotting a customs union with little Austria and, as word of this leaked to France, it caused a furor. Its denunciation on legal grounds was damaging enough, but when this was accompanied by sudden withdrawals of substantial funds—chiefly French—the predictable result was the collapse of Austria's major bank, the Creditanstalt. The ensuing international panic proved too much for Germany's key banks; except, perhaps, for France and presumably England, the specter of wholesale default had come to dominate the stage.[12]

Before taking action on the moratorium, President Hoover had consulted a few key members of the Congress and his cabinet; also the British government, Governor Meyer, Dwight Morrow, and (through Ogden Mills) Owen Young. To Germany and France, his declaration evidently came as a surprise, delighting the one but infuriating the other. Exasperated by Washington's alleged diplomatic slight, France was also fearful that any stoppage, however temporary, in the flow of the "unconditional" reparation payments would permanently jeopardize the Young Plan, in the future of which France, of all the Allied creditors, had easily the largest stake. It took critical days and weeks—and damaging concessions—before France grudgingly consented to go along, and by that time the psychological impact of Hoover's dramatic move had been all but vitiated.[13]

Young had urged with all the force at his command that the *duration* of the moratorium be at least two years, adding that it had best apply as well to the private short-term debts which were plaguing the German banks. Not only would this afford the world's ailing economy more time for recuperation; it would also largely remove from the campaign politics of the next, or presidential, year the sensitive issue of deferred payments or, alternatively, of scaling the debts down to size. Why, in the face of arguments so compelling, Hoover still elected the timid course is a question we must leave—half reluctantly, perhaps—to *his* biographers.[14]

To his family and close friends, Young made no pretense of concealing his disappointment: once again—and this time on a subject he might be presumed to know something about—he had given his friend Hoover the best advice he had to offer, only to have him fumble it. His public stance, however, was all that the President could ask, and certainly his statement supporting Hoover's proposal to suspend intergovernment payments "even for a year" was widely heralded at home and abroad. Choosing to put the best possible face on a move now irrevocably made, he even hailed it as proof that, in a crisis, a democracy can act "promptly, wisely and helpfully." Thus he went on to express the hope "that other governments [notably France?] can and will act also, and that private interests, with restored faith, will be helpful too. . . ." And when such all-knowing columnists as Drew Pearson and Robert S. Allen, in their "Washington Merry-Go-Round," credited Young himself, as the real author of the plan, with having prodded a timid President into action, he wrote Hoover at once, deploring any diversion to others of the credit which was rightly his and his alone.[15]

Meanwhile, invisible to the public, a related drama was being enacted at the Federal Reserve in which Young found himself taking an unexpectedly responsible role. With the failure of the Hoover moratorium to break or arrest Europe's accelerating spiral of deflation, government had in effect left it to the central banks to see what they could do through cooperative action to mobilize the credits of which Austria, but more particularly Germany, stood in dire need. And in the absence of the New York bank's chairman, Herbert Case, who was still recuperating slowly from the severe postoperative complications which had followed an emergency appendectomy in May, Young served throughout the long summer as acting chairman.

It was, as Young observed, high drama, but with its tragic outcome all but implicit, the price was high. True to its traditions, and with the experienced Montagu Norman still governor, the Bank of England led in the effort to marshal credits adequate to hold the deteriorating situation in Austria and Germany, with the Federal Reserve responding as it could but always insisting that the Bank of France play its part. And so, up to a point, it did, but always—and predictably—subject to its own stipulated conditions. Also, the Bank for International Settlements did what it could, but it was not yet geared to meet so punishing a test. Thus, by the end of July, it was only too clear that Germany's needs far transcended all that the central banks had been able to advance or believed they could.

At this point the exhausted Norman collapsed and had to leave the stage. Small wonder: not only had his best efforts failed to resolve the German crisis, but it soon began to appear that his nagging fears for England were more than justified. British merchant banks were heavily involved in German and middle-European ventures, now bankrupt or teetering on the edge, and London's hard-won "standstill agreement," designed to save the German banks, proved a boomerang to the British. As their plight was bruited about and invited runs on sterling, the Bank of England was to find that its rescue efforts had left it with all-too-limited reserves. Leaning heavily on Young's support and Governor Meyer's knowledgeable help from Washington, George Harrison was making heroic efforts to direct support to London, but here too he and Norman's stand-in were finding themselves powerless to check what was rapidly becoming a tidal drain on the Bank of England's remaining gold reserves.

The denouement came over the weekend of September 19–20, which Young spent with Harrison and the other responsible officers at the Fed, in constant touch by transatlantic phone with their British counterparts. At 6:30 A.M. (New York time) on Saturday, September 19, the acting governor of the Bank of England called to advise Harrison that Britain would be forced to suspend gold payments as of the following Monday, September 21. As word to that effect flashed around the world late Sunday night and Monday morning, markets were rocked and trade plummeted, while the speculators reaped their harvest. Young privately pronounced it the end of an epoch: London was finished and now it was New York's turn. Meanwhile, New York could do little more than watch as the numerous currencies with ties to sterling also went off gold and were left to seek their own levels.[16]

With another "fixed point" on the human compass once again fluctuating wildly, the epoch of central-bank cooperation had its own tragic ending. What it had labored so long and effectively to restore it could no longer sustain, nor in the demoralization of trade and exchanges that ensued was there any significant role left for it to play, with or without the help of the fledgling B I S. That "the collapse of a key currency thus signalled the end of the financial system established in the 1920s" was already clear; that it would also prove a "major factor in the final plunge of the depression to the depths of 1932" could have been no more than a fearful surmise.[17]

Even that, however, was enough to lend added poignancy to current plans for relief of the already swollen ranks of our own unemployed. When, in August of 1931, the President had invited Walter Gifford of A T & T to head the National Advisory Committee on Unemployment Relief, the press had been quick to note the absence of Young's name. That omission was speedily rectified and by the end of the month Young had agreed to head a subcommittee on the "Mobilization of Relief Resources" (though its Hooveresque title gave him fits). By the time this subcommittee had its first meeting in Washington, on Friday, September 18, Young and the President must have had more than an inkling of what the weekend promised to bring forth, and certainly the new and dynamic thrust which Young contrived to bring to this relief effort did credit at once to his concern and his resiliency.

Because of the political color which was attached to all that Young did and said in 1931, an earlier effort toward recovery never got further than the drawing board. His old friend William Donham, dean of the Harvard Business School, had pointed out in his book *Business Adrift* that business must now mount a concerted attack upon the depression and all its works. Young had read the book in May, and in June the two exchanged letters, Donham insisting that comprehensive planning had become a must, that with Hoover refusing the initiative, business must assume it, and that without Young's active leadership business would only fumble and flounder. Young's response had been to acquiesce readily enough on the first two points, but on the third to pass the ball straight back.

> You are quite wrong [he wrote] in thinking that I should lead. . . . If I were attempt to lead, and that means public leadership, the whole affair would immediately be embroiled in and bedeviled by politics. . . . Therefore, such a movement during the next six months would be entirely ineffective in my hands. I suggest . . . that while you have the public ear, as you have a right to have it, you move out and let me and others help you all we can.

Donham was dubious, but agreed to try if Young, Nelson Perkins and Melvin Traylor of Chicago would support him as a kind of steering committee. He would arrange their initial meeting if Young would give a time and place.

But the march of events was so swift as to be overwhelming. The calls to Washington, the unsettled Radio suit, the demands of the Federal Reserve, the conferences with doctors on Jo's illness, above all the political spotlight, prevented the man whom the *Outlook and Independent* had recently called the "great conciliator" from working on, much less heading, Donham's project. No record of an initial meeting can be found, nor of any other.[18] And indeed, Young was now privy to the making of another ambitious plan, which, as far as he was concerned, must have the right-of-way, a plan put together that summer by Gerard Swope.

i v

As far as recovery measures to promote and *restore* jobs were concerned, it was Swope who had taken the lead and—as of the fall of 1931—could be said to have stolen the show. His point of departure was GE's venture in unemployment insurance and his first step was so to buttress the original plan with company funds as to keep it functioning. From there his restless and logical mind went on to develop an industry-wide plan which, by bringing others in, would remove the competitive limitations on the GE experiment which he and Young had noted at the outset. But this was only a beginning. Workers generally, in his view, were entitled to all the benefits that GE had already set up for its own, and something more. If a whole industry were to recognize publicly the right of its employees to decent wages, limited hours, and insurance against death, disability, old age *and unemployment*, no one company could undercut its competitors by refusing to accept such charges as a permanent part of doing business. That in itself would help to lift and stabilize prices. It would also eliminate the worst kind of cutthroat competition while putting a competitive premium on quality of the product and its efficient marketing. And it should also, Swope insisted—this was something more—make it possible for an employee who chose, or was forced, to seek a job elsewhere, to take with him his equity in the several insurance plans to which he and his employer had alike contributed. Finally, with labor a full partner in setting up and administering such plans, labor-management relations could not fail to benefit.

In order to be effective, such industry-wide planning would necessarily involve overall production controls and the maintenance of minimum price schedules. Given a federal regulatory commission to prevent and punish all abuses, the obvious agencies for dealing with such matters were the trade associations which, as secretary of commerce, Hoover had done so much to foster—but they could act only as the antitrust laws were suitably amended. Not surprisingly, this was a common feature of the several similar proposals which were now engaging the attention of the U.S. Chamber of Commerce, the American Bankers Association and others. All of these—especially that of the Chamber's so-called Committee on Continuity—stressed stabilization of employment, but none went so far as Swope's in its comprehensive concern for labor.

Only Swope, it seemed, was both concerned and shrewd enough to know that the necessary amendment of the anti-trust laws would never be forthcoming "unless the public is assured of the constructive nature of the steps industry will take and that the interests of the public will be adequately safeguarded." Equally important was his recognition of the fact that consumption—that is, demand—could be restored to a high level and kept there only as people had money which they felt it safe to spend. Jobs were the prime requisite but a genuine sense of security would follow only if jobs carried with them protection against the hazards of old age and unemployment. And if industry failed to provide this protection, one day government would—less effectively, and at vastly greater expense.[19]

Working on his plan over the summer, Swope had discussed it often with Young, who encouraged him to think it through and get it down on paper. (According to Swope's biographer, Newton Baker also had a preview and pronounced it "too radical.") Following Young's advice, Swope had his plan ready to put before the National Electrical Manufacturers Association (NEMA) when they met in Washington on September 16. And that meant putting it before the public—which had been given something of a foretaste in Swope's radio address of two nights earlier. Young was not only on hand but was called upon himself to present the speaker. In so doing, reported the *Wall Street Journal*, he "revealed that the Swope stabilization plan had been submitted for study and comment to leading members of the electrical industry and that it had received support."[20]

Nevertheless, for Young it posed something of a dilemma. On the one hand, Swope had given unstinted and unfailing support to his own widely heralded efforts to effect a reparations settlement; could the author of the Young Plan do less than respond in kind now that the "Swope Plan" was about to command the headlines? Young recognized it too as the honest and thoroughgoing effort of his friend and partner to come up with an answer to the very question he himself had posed the previous December to the Committee on Recent Economic Changes: would anything less now suffice to put idle men and materials, idle plants and credit, back to work? On the other hand, he could not escape grave reservations about the nature of this answer in all its implications. To a Brandeis, Young's version of the New Freedom might be no better than a travesty of Wilson's concept, but neither had Young become a full-blown apostle of Theodore Roosevelt's New Nationalism. Yet the Swope plan now envisaged a cartelization of industry that carried the TR concept to its logical—and to Young, still dubious—extreme. Quite apart from the substantive issue, was it likely that his own continuing efforts—so far unsuccessful—to effect a settlement of the Radio suit would be abetted by his espousal of this bold new move to repeal or seriously weaken the antitrust laws themselves? And it is doubtless fair to add that if Young remained a balky horse where the presidential sweepstakes were concerned, he was far too canny to provide putative opponents with further means of crippling him should he still be drafted for the race.

That he and Swope discussed all this quite frankly can be taken for granted; unrecorded, the fact is implicit in their whole relationship. Thus Young could say from the platform with some confidence what he felt he had to say both to Swope's immediate audience and to the public. The disposition of the press at the time to quote his every comment is well illustrated by this passage (subheadings included) in the *Wall Street Journal's* report on the N E M A proceedings:

Proposal for Action Says Young

The plan is not free from criticism (Mr. Young said in discussing the proposal). Mr. Swope would be the first to admit that. There are grave questions both of public and of business policy lying at its very foundations. There are undoubtedly many improvements which could be made in detail. The significance of this event tonight does not lie in the possible criticisms of the plan but in the fact that a responsible industrial manager and the members of a great industry are ready to put to the public an offer to assume voluntarily responsibilities of vast consequence.

Its design recognizes obligations to employees and to general economic stability which have only been academically discussed before. At this stage, the plan is not only a definite proposition for debate but a proposal for action. It comes before the public with the willingness of an industry to adopt it, if public opinion supports it and the necessary authority can be had to institute it.

Price of Economic Planning

May I say, Mr. President, that economic planning will contribute to a standardized and so more stable prosperity, but in the same breath may

I remind you that like all other things in this world, it demands its price. A plan written on paper is of no service. A plan proposed for education is of some service but it is likely to become obsolete before it becomes effective. A plan to be productive of quick results must be executed promptly. No one concern can make it effective. Cooperation is required by the great majority of the participants and the coercion of the rest may ultimately be necessary.

　　If the government were ever to assume the great obligations which Mr. Swope's plan visualizes, then the price must be in the form of a surrender to political government. If industry itself is to perform these obligations, as is here contemplated, then the surrender of the individual units is to be made to the organized group, of which the unit is a part. If results are to be obtained, they call for surrender somewhere. The question for the public is to say whether they wish the results, and if so, by what agency they are to be accomplished.[21]

In the event, the Swope plan provoked widespread discussion and no action. Neither government nor business was yet ready for it, and if Hoover did not publicly denounce it, his silence was not friendly. Not until the advent of the New Deal was it to become clear that Gerard Swope's labors had not been wholly in vain.[22]

V

Of Young's activities from the end of September to Christmas, his present biographers were only distant observers. They had been married at the end of June, and their three weeks' honeymoon had already consumed Everett's precious company vacation. He had told his chief-turned-father-in-law that it was time to find himself a new assistant, though he was not about to quit until that had happened. But when Young discovered that the young couple had, as a matter of course, declined an invitation from the Institute of Pacific Relations to attend as American delegates its international conference at Shanghai in October, he strongly demurred. Go now while you can, he urged; if you wait you may be sorry—"contingencies" are likely to arise that will keep you home. (He was right.) Even with his urging it was hard to decide, for Josephine's mother and Everett's father were still far from well; but both young people were accustomed to listening to his advice and, with Everett assured a (payless) leave of absence from G E, they consented to be overruled. They left New York for Montreal and Vancouver (from which they sailed for Yokohama on the *Empress of Russia*) on the very eve of Britain's fateful announcement on gold.

That, at least, Jo's father told them as they left, won't worry the Chinese; if you want to help *them*, you'll have to do something for silver, or about the Japanese in Manchuria—a major item on the conference agenda.

It was a vicarious satisfaction for Owen Young to see them go; his own memorable trip to the Orient a decade before had left him with a strong desire to return—with his Jo. Now he would never return to Peking, for he would not go without her. But the younger generation's long letters from Japan and China, reflecting the same fascination he had felt, were a pleasure to them both.[23]

In that fall of 1931, Owen and Jo, for the first time since 1899, found themselves alone at home. C.J. and Esther, after the remove of radio research from Schenectady to RCA at Camden, were settled in Ardmore, Pennsylvania, with two small children of their own, plus C.J.'s two older boys. Philip, with the Harvard Business School in view, took his bride to Cambridge. And young Richard, on a venture of his own, had left home to enter Choate.

This new loneliness, the parents were quick to discover, had its compensations. Jo's continuing illness—and he was never again without anxiety for her—kept Owen very much at home, and there were no more long absences. Instead, he made it possible, even with his schedule, to spend hours with her each day. There, walking up and down the room or settled back in the big chair with his pipe, he talked out in characteristic fashion his problems and plans, his ideas both constructive and crazy, his disappointments and his successes. Often his long letters and speeches grew out of these hours, trimmed and deepened by her astute Yankee comments. They were rewarding sessions for him, as well as intellectually stimulating for her.

Van Hornesville saw little of Young that fall; he did not even go up to vote. Thanksgiving and Christmas were both spent at 830—with such children as were able to come. Young Jo and Everett made it back just in time for Christmas, which they spent half in Plainfield with his parents, half in New York with hers. Owen was able to get up-country for a few days early in December; his cows had been doing well even without his personal attention. Van Horne Aaggie Belle Colantha had made a record of milk and butterfat that put her fifth in the nation in her class.

In December his old friend and boss Charles Tyler died, and Young got away long enough to attend the funeral, and to have a visit with the Philip Youngs in Cambridge. He visited C.J. and Esther in Ardmore also, bringing back news of the grandchildren to Jo. But for

the most part he was tied down in New York, not only by his wish to
be constantly with his wife, but by the Committee on the Mobilization of Relief Resources, and by the succession of crises at the Federal
Reserve, from which, until the year's end, Herbert Case was still absent. Other invitations he refused; he told Senator La Follette that he
could not appear before his subcommittee on manufacturers—"I think
you will share with me the feeling that I should aid in the present
emergency rather than devote any time for long-range planning now."[24]

v i

No one went into mourning for the demise of 1931. Though the corks
that popped to welcome 1932 were still mostly illicit, their welcome
expressed the legitimate hope that with new numbers on the calendar
things could only get better.

They didn't, though. Evidently business now knew only one direction: down. Confidence, scarcely a memory, was just a word to jeer at.
Perhaps it was Young's rising impatience with the President's failure
to mount any effective counterattack that saved him from succumbing
to the prevalent despair. His own experience in hunting for "relief
resources" had convinced him—but not the White House—that local
and voluntary agencies could no longer meet the swelling needs of the
unemployed without federal help. As for recovery, if ever the pump
needed priming from federal sources, it was now; yet the President
had remained fearful that a bond issue, sufficient to finance a major
program of public works, would fatally impair the government's credit.
Nor, of course, whatever the merits of the case, could government
have chosen a worse moment for pressing its suit against the Radio
group.

True, the elections of 1930 had left the Democrats virtually controlling both houses of Congress, and like certain Republican insurgents, the so-called sons of the wild jackass were prescribing various
nostrums which it was incumbent upon the President to resist. But
when a responsible Democratic leader like Senator Joseph Robinson
of Arkansas sought Young's counsel in developing constructive measures which, incidentally, might head off the others, the President
remained on the defensive. And when he in turn sought Young's counsel as proof of his own nonpartisanship, he was apt to adopt only a
part of what Young felt to be an organic whole—as in his handling of
the moratorium—and so leave his adviser frustrated.

Actually Young's private apprehensions about the one-year moratorium were unhappily confirmed far earlier than he had feared. In October 1931, while Young was searching for a formula that might settle the Radio suit and at the same time mounting his relief program extraordinary, Hoover and the French premier, Pierre Laval, had met in Washington to discuss the future of the now-suspended intergovernmental obligations. Hoover had quite properly suggested that the Allied governments take the initiative in considering and proposing— prior to the expiration of the moratorium—such further "agreement regarding them [as] may be necessary covering the period of the business depression"; this had been embodied in their joint communiqué. On December 10, again quite properly, Hoover asked the Congress, now in special session, to reconstitute the War Debts Commission as the appropriate agency to receive and review such proposals. Apparently he did so, however, without adequate consultation with the congressional leaders, and only four days after insisting on the need for higher taxes to balance the budget. The predictable consequence was a disastrous double rebuff: not only did Congress refuse to reconstitute the commission; it promptly passed a resolution forbidding any reduction whatsoever in the debts. (It was a triple rebuff if one includes the rejection of the higher taxes.) Young was dismayed. It was, he confided to his assistant on the latter's return, another instance of retarded realism plus political ineptitude.[25]

Meanwhile, the shock waves released by Britain's suspension of gold payments had been playing havoc with what was left of international trade. They also led to the sudden repatriation of foreign gold from the vaults of the Federal Reserve and so to an involuntary tightening of Federal Reserve credit at the very moment that the hard-pressed banks needed it most sorely. For the smaller banks especially, the liquidity crisis had become acute; bond values, already disastrously low, were still falling, and their short-term liquid assets—which alone were eligible for rediscount—were virtually exhausted.

Like many others, Young therefore breathed more easily when the President, under constant prodding from Governor Meyer of the Federal Reserve Board, finally moved late in 1931 to set up the two-billion-dollar Reconstruction Finance Corporation, with its lending powers directed primarily to banking and other financial institutions, and incidentally to the railroads as well. Once Congress was assured of its bipartisan directorate, approval had come quickly, and the first week of February 1932 saw the RFC actually open for business. Dawes, recently returned from the London embassy, was named its first president but Meyer—as penalty for his prodding?—was made chairman, while continuing to head the Federal Reserve Board. Young cordially approved both appointments, and also endorsed, as Democratic member of the board, the Houston tycoon, banker and publisher Jesse Jones.[26]

Here at last was a major step forward—notably one that enabled the banks, under certain conditions, to borrow against assets not eligible (by law) for discount at the Federal Reserve banks. Then, before the end of February, eligible assets were themselves liberalized by the Glass-Steagall Act. Business, however, was still in the doldrums, and "Young's companies" were no exception. They too had had to lay off thousands while cutting both wages and salaries. At the GE stockholders' meeting of April 1932—the company's fortieth anniversary— earnings reported were way down, and quarterly dividends were abruptly reduced from forty cents to ten cents. RCA's position was even worse: 1931's net earnings were down almost to the vanishing point and, for the fourth quarter, dividends on its B preferred shares had been omitted. Moreover the suit was still going badly. The government's proposal of the previous summer for a settlement based on an open patent pool had won the support of the independents as well as the defendants, plus collateral concessions from the latter group, but when the government also insisted on drastic changes in the Radio group's intercorporate contracts and relationships, the defendants balked; given the times, they found this demand so destructive as to be unrealistic. Young's best efforts to explain the problem had got him nowhere: now, in March of '32, the Justice Department filed an amended petition which also complained of RCA's international contracts and licensing agreements. Meanwhile, feeling that its stake was not worth the effort, the telephone company had made a separate peace.[27]

Early in April, moreover, the public utilities—and especially their maze of holding companies which Young had vainly prodded them to simplify—were given a fresh black eye by the sensational failure of three Insull companies. Young had worked for weeks to avert it, but it was in character that Insull should have turned to him for help so sorely needed only after his affairs had reached the desperate stage. If at first Young's involvement appeared to damage nothing but his reputation as a problem solver, the whole affair promised plenty of ammunition for those who were branding the so-called Power Trust— and therefore Young—as the people's enemy number one. And this could hardly strengthen his hand, either as political *or* business leader.[28]

Having nevertheless concluded that a bold new federal program was now imperative if business was ever to be put back on course, Young was prepared to go all out to achieve it, come what might. His Easter visit to the capital, with his twelve-year-old son, Richard, was no more than a pleasant interlude—except as it may have served as a kind of prologue. Thus in late April and early May of 1932 Young was much in Washington—sometimes with Bernard Baruch—specifically to work with Democratic leaders like Senators Joe Robinson and Robert Wagner and Speaker John Garner in shaping up bills authorizing a two-billion-dollar issue of government bonds to do what the RFC was not yet empowered to do: first, to finance self-liquidating public works and so put men and materials back to work; second, to supplement local efforts to assure adequate relief for the unemployed. Since Young was also enlisting former Governor Smith's endorsement of this plan, and himself endorsing experimental adoption of the so-called equalization fee to aid the farmers, it was widely assumed by the press and members of the Senate that his hat was now definitely in the ring.[29]

Young could argue with perfect consistency that his Washington excursions were all directed toward a single end: business recovery. To eager friends and supporters who insisted that four years at the White House would better serve this end than a decade at GE, he could always answer that, like most seductive propositions, this one was highly chancy. Besides, to desert his first love, business, when she was under fire was to go against the grain; his first obligation was to stand by and do what he could on his own terrain.

And for the first time in many months he was glimpsing in this terrain what might become a genuine opportunity. For one thing, his Washington efforts began to look like paying off. Rather than see the Democrats pass the Robinson-Wagner-Garner bill, Hoover was reluctantly working on a face-saving compromise which would concede much in exchange for a strong revenue bill. The capital originally required to set up the RFC had cost the treasury only $500 million: the other $1.5 billion of the RFC's funds had come from the sale of its own debentures. If now the RFC were authorized to sell another $2 billion of the same to finance self-liquidating public works, while advancing $300 million more to state and local authorities for relief of the unemployed, the same ends would be achieved without vast new issues by the treasury. Although precious weeks and even a veto were to intervene before the final version, known as the Emergency Relief and Construction Act, was signed by the President on July 22, the bipartisan attack Young had worked for was beginning to take shape.[30]

Nor was this all. Free soon after the turn of the year from its restraining international obligations, and encouraged by the Glass-Steagall Act, the Federal Reserve could and did cooperate with the RFC by resuming its easy-money policy with the aim of making bank credit irresistibly plentiful and cheap. Work for idle funds could mean work for plants and idle people, but the times were such that even a bargain was greeted with skeptical eye. Thus if the syndrome were to be shattered, it could only be by carefully planned and concerted action on the part of business and financial leaders who could find or fashion the means of putting these funds to work. The high potential was there; skillfully tapped at strategic points, it might yet stimulate or shock the economy into forward motion.

Whoever was the first to sense this, George Harrison was the first to do something about it, summoning as he did a small group to discuss it at the New York Fed on April 28, 1932.[31] Young was there and once again found himself pressed to take the lead. Recalling his exchange of the year before with Donham, he could only make the same reply again, so long as he was presumed to be playing the political game. But what if he could finally contrive to be free of this political incubus—free to lead a business crusade without being suspected of ulterior motive—what then?

Time pressed, and by the middle of May 1932, Young not only came to grips with his problem but resolved it. It is idle now even to speculate on the more far-reaching consequences of his decision, though there was no dearth of speculation at the time. But where so much is at stake—even potentially—there is a certain fascination about the decision-making process itself, if only in the light it throws on a man's primary concerns and ultimate values.

Chapter 29

1932: Climax of
an Apolitical Career

Y OUNG had been accustomed, as a boy and a young man, to follow his father's example and take a constant interest in politics.
He made his earliest public statements in this field, at Jordanville and St. Lawrence in 1892, when he was just eighteen. It would be
forty years before he made another public speech in a presidential
campaign; but as a spectator he watched the game closely and judicially. The years with Tyler had been educational in this respect;
Boston was his first textbook in municipal politics, and after that there
were few surprises. Drawing franchises for public utilities had brought
him into close—and sometimes abrasive—touch with municipal, county
and state governments not only in Texas but all over the country. He
maintained consistently his voting residence in Van Hornesville and
his allegiance to the Democratic party. In the first dozen years with
General Electric, however, he had no time and indeed no taste for
political activity. When it came, it was forced upon him.

In the summer of 1923 *Collier's* magazine took a number of straw
votes of its readers for candidates for President in 1924; the leading
candidate turned out to be Henry Ford, well ahead of the incumbent
Warren G. Harding. The accompanying editorial surmised that perhaps the American people wanted the country to be "governed by a
great industrial mind. . . . America is rich in industrial generals, only
nobody has thought before of running one for President . . . suppose
just for instance some Democratic slate makers were inspired to think
of some name like—well, say Owen D. Young."[1]

This suggestion was the first, nationwide, of a long series of unofficial nominations, followed by mailbags of enthusiastic letters from
supporters, which cluttered up the desks at 120 Broadway and took
the time of Young and his staff to answer. But answered they were;

to an old school friend from Springfield Center, who wrote that he had bet a new hat that Owen would be President, Young replied: "I would do almost anything to help you win a new hat and prove that you were a prophet. I think on the whole that I would rather buy you the hat than be President of the United States. It would be cheaper, the job would be over sooner, the risk to the country would be less, and therefore, as a patriotic citizen, I think you should accept this solution of the hat question."[2]

After Calvin Coolidge had beaten John W. Davis two to one in 1924, the divided Democrats began immediately to look around. By that time Young's service on the Dawes Committee had made his a name to conjure with, and with Dawes already vice-president-elect, certain Democratic chieftains began to wonder if perchance they were missing a bet. In response to an inquiry from Governor Albert C. Ritchie of Maryland, Young wrote:

> I have tried to make it clear to my friends, and I especially desire to say to you that I do not wish any political office nor do I desire to engage in politics except as a private citizen modestly supporting the Democratic party as I always have done. . . . My field is business and my only desire is to carry on successfully my work in my own field. Please do not think I take these suggestions seriously. I make the above statement only to prevent my silence being taken seriously. . . . Congratulations to you on the things which you have done and the things which I feel sure you are to do.[3]

By 1926 the temperature was rising on the political front and the figures of candidates began to emerge from the jungle of the Democratic party. (The Republicans were in no quandary; they were happy with Coolidge, until he said he did not choose to run.) In a rasping article in the February 1926 *American Mercury* the journalist Arthur Krock, then with the New York *World*, described the pitiful condition of the Democrats: "In its pursuit of Prohibition votes in the South, and liberal votes in the North and East, and agrarian votes in the West, the Democratic Party has burst like the chameleon which, placed on a square of Scottish plaid, took its mission in life too literally." Al Smith was Krock's candidate, "the only strong personal leader in the United States," but he thought he could not be nominated because of his religion. Instead, "A moist Protestant messiah may arise. Even now glances of hope are being cast in the direction of Owen D. Young." But he, said Krock, would need a great deal of publicity to make himself known.

This Young was receiving by May, from the short-lived "Boom

Young for Governor" campaign, and Eleanor Roosevelt's suggestion that he run for senator. It was then that he made his statement that he had never taken a job for which his experience did not qualify him, which became his theme song for the next six years. Few people took it seriously, however, beginning with Dr. John Finley of the *New York Times*. Lincoln Steffens wrote Young from Italy at the end of May: "I see that you are going to be President of the United States. Nobody can decide it, either choose you or beat you except yourself, and by way of advising you how not to defeat yourself, I shall tell you a story. It's about Roosevelt." This, of course, was Theodore, at the time of the story police commissioner of New York City; Steffens as a police reporter saw a good deal of him. One day Steffens and a fellow reporter took their courage in their hands and asked Roosevelt if he was "out to be president." TR exploded: "What!" he shouted, "You ask me a question like that. Friends of mine! And you make me think of the Presidency. Go away." They didn't however, "and when TR had cooled off a bit he told us—what I want to tell you":

Don't you know that, secretly, every man who becomes prominent in any way wants, secretly, to be president. He does not tell his friends . . . they might encourage him and—ruin his chances. They might tell him he can be elected. And he must not think that. Nay, he must not let himself know that he even has a thought of being president . . . most possible candidates . . . defeat themselves. . . . Since you have spoken of it and I have been ranting here at you, I have been realizing all the time that I have been thinking of running for president . . . lying to myself about it. Pooh, I say to myself. You! Huh . . . Theodore Roosevelt as President. Impossible. Bull in a China shop! Cow boy on an engine! No. It is impossible.

"If you get me, I am Yours sincerely," ended Steffens.[4]

Young replied that when he read the letter to his wife she had said, "If Mr. Steffens is right, you had better announce your candidacy for the presidency right away. That will insure us against all trouble however remote." And Owen went on to say:

One of the things which I have endeavored to do all my life is not to fool myself about myself. I have been perfectly willing to fool myself about other people or fool other people about me. Having said this, I will now say not only that I have no desire to be President of the United States, but that I should consider that job as a most burdensome and thankless task. I much prefer to do what I am now doing. Perhaps you know me well enough to believe me—most people don't.[5]

But Steffens's letter made him think. On the same day he wrote his friend Jack Miller of the Southern California Edison Company, who had asked him about his political ambitions. He complained that even his best friends did not believe him, because of "that deep-seated feeling in all Americans not only that one could not refuse that great office, but that one could not avoid a desire to hold it. This attitude has been so apparent to me recently that I have wondered whether I was fooling myself."

He concluded that he would rather stay where he was, "to help to maintain the economic advance . . . and to prevent impairment of it by ill-advised political action." He had no feeling of obligation, he wrote, to undertake political office because there was now no particular crisis in American affairs, and there were others far better qualified, because "they have some taste for and understanding of politics. This element is important to successful administration, especially in normal times. It may be unimportant in a time of crisis."[6] It was a small loophole, but one he was to look through again in 1932.

Young supported both Al Smith for governor—who decided after all to run again in 1926—and Robert Wagner for senator. To both he contributed money and advice, and for Wagner he roughed out statements on issues of the day. The style in which these pages were written— easy in language, hard-hitting, sharply critical of the Republicans, indeed a style perfectly Wagnerian—indicated perhaps something of a desire on Young's part to make these speeches himself. They were "hastily jotted down at the very end of the day," he wrote Wagner, and were on "the general subject of inaction against affirmative leadership."[7] Wagner used them almost verbatim in some instances, both before and after election, with good effect.

In his own person, Young did not hesitate to make statements on issues of the day in letters to correspondents. He admitted to one that on the question of prohibition "my mind is not at all clear,"[8] but he considered that his experience qualified him to speak on affairs abroad and agriculture at home. He was totally out of sympathy with the current isolationism, he wrote one correspondent, for "contact is an insurance against undesirable entanglements precipitated by others." He believed the war debts should be canceled or substantially readjusted; payment of international obligations should not be exacted, he wrote, if it compels "greatly reduced standards of living for labor in any country." But these "political debts" must be settled in one way or another, otherwise they "will plague two generations yet to come and . . . will be repudiated or will cause sufficient irritation to threaten our peace."[9]

In March 1927, Cordell Hull, then a member of the House from Tennessee, asked Young for a memorandum which might be used in formulating the principles and program for the Democratic party in the months ahead. Young replied, "I am a Democrat but I am no politician. I do not use the last term in any sense offensively. I merely mean by it that I have no way of drafting a program or principles except to set down my own personal views. Whether they are politically expedient or suitable from a party standpoint is not for me to judge." He enclosed seven pages dealing with foreign and domestic affairs. Needless to say, the jerry-built platform adopted at Houston in 1928 reflected little of Young's unequivocal and clearly stated recommendations. The central ideas are those he consistently held to all through these years: he was for cooperation with the League of Nations, for the World Court and disarmament, for government help in dealing with the agricultural surplus, for retiring the government debt by taxes over a number of years ("Spreading the payments over a generation will serve as an ever continuing reminder that war is economically burdensome and wasteful"). He was against the tariff, and strongly against encroachment upon the rights of citizens:

Armies of investigators, spies, informers, exercising in fact arbitrary powers until the country is filled not with one absolute monarch, but with millions of little despots is inconsistent with the principles of the Democratic party and the dignity of citizenship in a great free republic. These were the principles of Jefferson, and the Democratic party will always be unsafe in fundamentals if it fails to formulate its platform and execute its policies in strict accordance with them.[10]

Throughout 1927 the press continued to worry his name, while he continued to make denials and to reaffirm his support of Governor Smith "for any office which he would accept."[11] But toward the end of the year his noncandidacy received a tremendous boost. On November 21 Young made a speech at the dedication of the Jordan Dam on the Coosa River, an important unit in the hydroelectric development of Alabama. It was not a great occasion and Young's speech was far from great, but it had consequences. In introducing Young at the ceremonies, the local congressman had suggested that he was an outstanding candidate for President, an act, commented the *New York Times*, of "customary politeness to a distinguished guest, who would be supposed to go away feeling that something had been lacking in hospitality if he had not been 'mentioned' as a possible president." Certainly Young took it as such. But in the party at the dam was Victor H. Hanson, president and publisher of the *Birmingham News* and the *Birmingham Age-Herald*. Hanson was idealistic, shrewd, powerful and courageous, and in spite—or because—of the fact that he was an inveterate enemy of the Ku Klux Klan he had enormous influence in the state and in the South. On November 23 his papers, with a tremendous spread, came out for this candidate. It was the beginning of a long, enthusiastic and almost daily campaign, totally undiscouraged by the complete lack of cooperation—indeed, the active noncooperation—of Young. His letters to Hanson were always appreciative; he thanked him "from my heart for your gracious proposal" as he reiterated his support of Smith.[12] The nomination was taken up at once by newspapers all over the South; Young said it just went "to show how dangerous it is for one to move in such a warm-hearted country as the South." Much of this support, naturally, was not so much pro-Young as anti-Smith. Young was worried about this; as soon as the Birmingham campaign began he wrote the governor: "The fact . . . that the proposal comes from a state which has not indicated its support of you induces me to send you this purely personal note stating my own position so as to avoid the risk of any possible misinterpretation of my silence." And he offered to repeat his support of Smith "with express application to the Presidency" to aid "your nomination which I so much desire" whenever he wanted him to. Smith replied, "I read [your letter] with a great deal of pleasure and satisfaction."[13]

Nineteen twenty-eight brought a new flood of newspaper and magazine articles on the reluctant candidate, and the mail grew heavier and heavier. Not only Democrats but lifelong Republicans and independents offered their help and their votes; applications for jobs on his campaign staff were numerous. All the letters were answered, appreciatively and negatively. To a fellow book collector, who wrote that every book collector in the country would vote for him, he replied, "Why force me out of the book market by such unnecessary cruelty as putting me into politics?" It was a conspiracy, he suggested, to kill him off and get his books.[14]

June came at last and the Democrats went off to Houston, where the temperature was nearly a hundred—and modern air conditioning not yet invented. Five days before the convention opened, Newton Baker, himself with considerable support as a candidate, wrote Edward A. Filene: "Nobody in the Democratic Party of whom I have any knowledge would make as good a president as Owen Young. He not only has a great mastery of the processes of modern business but is intelligent as well as a man of character and decision. Should anything happen to make the Smith nomination impossible, it would give me untold joy to be helpful in furthering Owen Young."[15]

Young refused to go to the convention, but when it was over he sent Franklin Roosevelt a telegram of congratulations on his speech nominating Al Smith, saying it came through beautifully on the radio.

Roosevelt's warm reply foreshadowed future successes when he said that the speech was "primarily for the radio audience and the press."[16]

Young was a faithful contributor to the Democratic party. In 1928 he made an early contribution of two thousand dollars and another of the same after Smith was nominated; he also shared with Gerard Swope a ten-thousand-dollar personal subscription to Smith's campaign in September. He supported Roosevelt's campaign for governor, and always contributed to Eleanor Roosevelt's "Women's Activities" of the Democratic State Committee. He did not play any official part in organized political activity, for the rules of the Federal Reserve Bank forbade its directors to do so, and Young was happy to obey. But John J. Raskob, chairman of the Democratic National Committee, consulted him often. At Raskob's request Young issued a long statement on October 1, giving in detail his reasons for supporting Smith:

First, I am a Democrat—one of those persons born in the party, as it were. All of my people for many generations have been supporters of the liberal party, just as they were communicants in the most liberal branch of the Protestant Church. So it would be strange indeed if being a liberal both in background and temperament, I failed to support the liberal party when it is under such true and courageous leadership as that of Governor Smith.[17]

Young made no speeches in the campaign, but exerted his influence where it would do the most good—in Boston, for example.[18] He also raised a good deal of money, and won on the one hand the gratitude and appreciation of Smith and other Democratic leaders, and on the other the amazement of his colleagues in business, who could not imagine a big industrialist as a Democrat.

On election day in Van Hornesville Owen and Jo, as usual, canceled each other's votes. Young Josephine, turned twenty-one that year, was a thoroughgoing Democrat. Ida Young had never availed herself of the new privilege of voting; after a lifetime of not being able to, she was, she said, not used to the idea. But when she discovered her granddaughter was going up to the Grange Hall to vote for Smith, she got up out of her rocking chair and went along—to vote for Hoover, whom she much admired.[19]

Owen Young had never got much sympathy from his family even for a nonexistent political career. His mother and his wife were firmly determined to keep him out of any political office. The idea of his being President was an amusing one for the children to contemplate, and considerable flights of fancy about living in the White House developed around the dinner table. But even they, sensing that the absences and the burdens would be even greater than now, were not eager for him to run. At home he was frank about the possibilities and impossibilities of the situation, and there were serious as well as joking discussions. He had never believed that he could be nominated, or elected, because of the big business and "Power Trust" tag, but he was still reexamining himself. His friend B. F. Sunny, of the General Electric Company in Chicago, wrote him begging him not to go into politics: "There are plenty of men to fill positions of [that] kind but there is no one to fill the position that you hold in the electrical industry."[20]

Young answered, repeating his position, and said: "The only thing which would lead me to change my mind and accept public office would be the conviction that I could not retain my own self-respect and the good opinion of the people whose judgment I value by declining on what might appear to them and would be to me purely selfish grounds."[21]

ii

It is untrue to say that Owen Young was not a political animal. He was, and the previous pages indicate it, no matter how hard he tried to keep himself out of politics. His whole career, from college days on, had been filled with action involving "political" skills: ability to go to the heart of a problem and state it simply; ability to listen, to understand not only what the other fellow wanted but why he wanted it; ability to give and take, to negotiate patiently, to be pliable and also to be firm; and above all the ability to *feel*, to come close to people and movements by intuition rather than analysis, to know the right time and to act upon it. He was also a handsome and commanding figure, and an excellent speaker; he had an easy, simple manner and a ready sense of humor. Exemplar of the American myth, the poor farm boy who made good, he knew his own abilities, he knew he would be good in politics, he knew he would make a good President.

In the years 1929–32 the pressures grew stronger. It was certain that Hoover would be the Republican candidate, and it was becoming increasingly certain that he would not win. As Franklin Roosevelt emerged as an important contender, those who did not care for him or his ideas cast about for an alternative. Smith had proved the country was not yet ready for a Catholic. So the stable of Democratic dark horses became well filled, and near, if not nearest, the door was Owen D. Young.

The undercurrent for Young was given new impetus at the end of 1929 by, curiously enough, his appearance to testify before the Senate Committee on Interstate Commerce, headed by Senator James Couzens of Michigan; they were meeting to discuss the setting up of a regulatory communications commission. Young's written statement, discussing the advantages for overseas communication of a government-regulated private monopoly, rather than government ownership and operation, put forth arguments which have been described elsewhere in this book. He also gave, with the greatest frankness, details on the proposed unification of communication services between ITT and RCA. This called for a transfer of 400,000 shares of ITT to RCA for the sale of its subsidiary; Senator Clarence Dill of Washington "wanted to know how the price was arrived at, and Mr. Young obligingly responded: 'It was arrived at because I fixed it.' "[22] Then he went on to give complete details.

What most impressed the senators, the spectators and the press were Young's "progressive" opinions: he said he had nothing in principle against government ownership and operation, but he had serious questions about efficiency and costs; and he stated again that the proper basis for regulating public utilities' charges was a fair return on actual investment. This, reported the special correspondent William Hard in his widely distributed column, was "the equivalent of a political bombshell," and put Young "straight out of the class of the ordinary public utility magnates of private life and threw him almost into the class of the members of the so-called left-wing of the Senate." And Hard pointed out that such a rate base—for railroads in this case—was one of the principles of Robert M. La Follette.[23] Senator Smith W. Brookhart of Iowa needled Young so sharply with irrelevant questions and insinuations that other senators—including Wagner—intervened. But the witness never lost his composure and, as the *Washington Post* commented, "did not come out second best."[24]

The politics of the situation were clearly apparent, said Hard, who obviously enjoyed the fireworks, and "Young returned to New York in the peculiar role of being highly regarded by conservative Democrats as a business man and highly regarded by most liberal Democrats as a progressive business reformer."

The speech which Young made on the Berkeley campus in March of 1930 was perhaps the most widely reported and discussed of any of his pronouncements at that time. The press, often reporting it entire, concluded that it would make him an outstanding candidate for President. It was not, of course, a political speech. Rather, it was, said Dr. John

Finley of the *New York Times*, "the essence of eleven years of history" presented with "wit, irony and imagination."[25] And that other great philosopher of the fourth estate, Will Rogers, put his money on Young for President in two of his brief daily paragraphs:

BEVERLY HILLS, CAL. March 25.
My original Democratic white hope come through great in a speech out here where a university conferred on him the degrees "doctor of dividends" and "purveyor extraordinary to financial conferences where hopes are high but funds are low." He said "economics had no business in politics." Now, some might think that was bad foresight to knock politicians, but it was on my advice that he did it. Everybody knew Mr. Hoover was not a politician, and that fact alone gave him a majority of nine million. Now, if my man can even go further and show that he knows politicians, but has no use for their methods, why he can win by 29 million. The old Democrats are perking up every day.

BEVERLY HILLS, CAL. March 26.
Yesterday I wrote about my Democratic candidate and didn't mention his name, I didn't think I needed to. I said he has been given a university degree for his advice in high finance. Well, what Democrat have we got that could get into a big financial conference (unless he was a watchman or messenger boy) outside of Owen D. Young? Well, Owen is my man.[26]

By May, Jouette Shouse, now the chairman of the Democratic National Committee, was saying, according to a headline in the *Schenectady Gazette*, OWEN D. YOUNG LOOMS AS CANDIDATE. And *Collier's* "Uncle Henry," on being asked if he thought Young could get the nomination, groaned:

Hopeless . . . the man's got a terrible record. At every point in his career he's damned by proof of brain an' achievements . . . if they try to offer him the nomination, you're goin' to see a new world's record for the marathon. Why should he want to give up his nice comfortable home for life in a cyclone cellar. . . . About the only chance I see for Owen Young to get more'n a handful of votes, if he's foolish enough to run for President, is his bein' turned down for the Board of Regents the other day in his own home state of New York. . . .[27]

But it was a few days later that the Department of Justice filed its suit against RCA; irritating as this was, the suit seemed at least to promise good protection against nomination.

In June, Young was back in San Francisco, to make his "little pinch-hitting" address before the National Electric Light Association convention. The occasion was publicized by a massive radio linkup with London and Berlin—a World Power Conference was taking place in the latter city and the secretary of commerce was to have addressed it. Guglielmo Marconi spoke from London, Thomas A. Edison from West Orange, New Jersey, the president of the power conference from Berlin, and Young from San Francisco. Wire, cable, telephone and radio facilities were combined to put on a broadcast heard all over the world—including Washington. It was a feat not to be accepted casually in 1930, and of a kind that never failed to thrill the creator of RCA.

In the fall, as noted elsewhere, Young got a little respite from political pressures by the trip to London with Jo. (There, incidentally, Lloyd George had told Admiral Cary Grayson in July that before he died he expected to see Owen D. Young the President of the United States.)[28] But returning home on November 28, Young found himself again assailed; the *Aquitania* had not left quarantine before his cabin was invaded by the press. There appeared "a small army of photographers and reporters chiefly concerned with his reaction to reports cropping up again that Democrats want to nominate him for President in 1932." The headline on this account read: "YOUNG RETURNS, BEAMING, CORDIAL, BUT QUITE DEAF. He Fails to Hear Ship Reporters' Queries as to His Stand Regarding Possible Candidacy." He was, said the *World* reporter, "impressively silent," until they asked about the adjustment clause which was omitted from the Young Plan.[29]

December was an active month for Young as a noncandidate. As noted earlier, his impressive silence was broken on December 3 when the Lotos Club gave him a dinner. His brief remarks were originally intended as an off-the-record speech; warned that the press would probably get, and print, a garbled account, he authorized its release at the last moment. The wisdom of this was vindicated by the widespread attention it commanded from friend and foe alike. The *Chicago Tribune*, predictably, would have none of it; predictably, the *New York Times* printed the full text, with commendatory comment.

Collier's of December 6, in an article headed by a cartoon of the Democratic donkey bringing crown and scepter to a locked door marked OWEN D. YOUNG; PRIVATE; KEEP OUT; DO NOT DISTURB, and titled "The Unwilling Moses," made a reasoned argument for Young. In the following week's issue another column stated, "Of all the names mentioned, Owen D. Young, who hasn't mentioned it himself, means the greatest change in the future of American politics." And in the South, Young continued to be a favorite; Victor Hanson continued to dash off editorials. Again Young thanked him for the compliment, but added, "Certainly in a horse race you would not bet on an unwilling and much less a balky horse."[30]

With a year and a half to go to the convention, candidacies both real and unreal could not be taken too seriously. Political writers could freewheel about possibilities, and candidates could say yes or no without meaning it. That Young did not mean his no was the hope of what Clinton W. Gilbert called his "unorganized but extremely ardent supporters."[31]

iii

The story of Young's noncandidacy in 1931 is similar to that of 1930, but more so. As plans were beginning to be made for the convention which would meet in Chicago in June of 1932, the press, the pundits in the back room, the Democratic party and its possible candidates grew more and more restless and itchy. Willy-nilly, Young was getting the kind of publicity which Krock had said he would need; in publicacations as diverse as the *New York Times* and the *Union Labor News*, *Harper's Bazaar* and the *New Republic*, his "candidacy" was being seriously discussed. *Fortune* published a three-part "Life of Owen D. Young," in its January, February and March issues, nonpolitical but informative, while the February *Review of Reviews* defended him against Senator George W. Norris and his allegations about the "Power Trust."[32]

After each session of his congressional testimony of February 4, 1931, Young said good-humoredly but firmly to the reporters crowding around him that he was "not a candidate." This inspired the *Daily News* to remark that Young could now be regarded as an active candidate; he has made "two statements of the 'what I would do if I were Congress and the President' variety and has twice told newspapermen that he did not want the nomination." Full reports of his testimony, with editorials—mostly sympathetic—sprouted on every side. The political columnist Frank Kent said, "If he wanted to be nominated he could hardly have taken a better line . . . he may not be a candidate, but when did a candidate do better?"[33] And other columnists noted that in these appearances he made a great impression as a *person*, where before, to most people, he was only a name.[34]

There were less admiring reports, however, notably by Paul Y. Anderson in the *Nation*. Anderson too was convinced that Young was definitely a candidate, and one to whom Republican businessmen would flock:

It is true that some of the older industrial cutthroats feel that his views on such subjects as labor and utility valuation are a trifle unorthodox, and by the same token the usual quota of dilettante liberals are ready to dis-cover messianic traits in him. Both groups do him injustice. If anyone can find in the history of Standard Oil or steel more ruthless examples of buc-caneering than attended the rise of the Radio Corporation under Mr. Young's enlightened guidance, I should like to hear of them. Let no one underestimate his capacity. A smoother piece of high-powered machinery has seldom been seen in action. He has brains, nerve and presence, and he is one of the best showmen since Barnum. If he can get the Democratic nomination there is every reason to expect that he will wipe up the earth with poor Herbert.[35]

A few months later, Justice Louis Brandeis, greatly exercised by "the multiplicity of problems confronting the nation," wrote his favorite correspondent, Norman Hapgood: "There never was, in our time, such an opportunity for effective blows. Of course, they cannot be dealt with without adequate detailed knowledge of past and present; and for this much study is indispensable. But with knowledge and skill—much might be done. For the enemy is demoralized. One of the first tasks is to protect this country from Owen Young."[36]

"Uncle Henry," however, thought Young would have trouble escap-ing the nomination: "They tell me he's keenly aware of his danger, an' is trying to grow a beard, besides wearing dark glasses. But Owen will find that even the most perfect disguise is of no use. The Royal Mounted has nothin' on the Democratic party when it comes to gettin' their man."[37]

But the newspapermen were quick to point out that there were two blocks—very large blocks—in the road to a nomination for Young: the so-called Power Trust, and Franklin D. Roosevelt. Clinton Gilbert re-ported that power interests were afraid of Young's nomination, for he was too radical for them. Progressives considered him "an octopus all in himself," and the Democratic politicians feared him because he was not one of them. In fact, said Gilbert, "he is the man whom nobody wants as President but who, nevertheless, remains one of the three or four most likely nominees."[38]

There was, however, a much more important hindrance in Owen Young's mind. In July of 1931, he had taken Jo to New York for ex-tensive examination and prognosis. Dr. Irving Wright, at that time a young physician with Dr. Arthur Chace, who was Josephine Young's physician, told the story of this episode, thirty-five years later, in *An-nals of Internal Medicine*. Dr. Chace was away in the Adirondacks, so that it was Wright with whom Young discussed the possible prob-lem of the Democratic nomination. He needed the best medical advice as to the effect of this—should it occur—upon his wife. Wright quotes him as saying:

I have been asked to accept nomination as the Democratic candidate for the presidency of the United States. I have reasonable assurance from the key leaders of the Democratic party that I could be nominated, and it is highly probable that whoever leads the Democratic ticket will be elected, in view of the poor economic state of the country. You must help me to make the decision. . . . One of the key factors in making my decision will be your determination as to whether Mrs. Young can be expected to carry on or survive four years at the White House.

The young physician was overcome by this, but he got busy and a panel of most distinguished medical men was convened, to whom all the evidence was presented. Their conclusion was that "the strains involved by living as the wife of the President of the United States could increase the risk of subsequent attacks and shorten both good health and life." In any case she was expected to live less than four years. Young told no one about this, even his children, and of course the doctors scrupulously respected the confidential nature of their task, until both principals had died.[39]

In that summer of 1931 Roosevelt and Young were considered, on all sides, as the most likely nominees, and it was widely believed that the choice lay in the hands of Al Smith. Neither FDR nor Young could be nominated "without Al's active cooperation," and Al had not yet spoken his mind. His rift with FDR had widened, and it was known that he was "fond" of Young. While the betting went on, so did the publicity.

Collier's "Gentlemen at the Keyhole" stated Young's problem neatly: "Among the Old Guard of the power industry Owen D. Young is almost as much of a radical as Senator Norris himself. It is one of the ironies of politics that the graybeards of power should be shocked at Mr. Young's opinions and at the same time the Progressives should regard Mr. Young as the wickedness of the power trust incarnate."[40]

To enlighten the public about the life, opinions, and achievements of this puzzling character, the *Daily News* ran a serial in sixteen sections on Owen D. Young, by Martin Sommers, the night city editor. The first was headed "Aladdin Quietly Awaits the Call to Presidency," and the series was billed as a life story that "reveals things never related before about this self-effacing and little known Man of Power." (What his family said to him about this can be imagined.) Actually it was a fairly accurate account, lively and interesting, with occasional moments of insight. For example: "Year by year, Young sharpened his ability to put the language of one field of endeavor into the language of an entirely different field so expertly that specialists in the two fields could understand one another" (from part three of the serial). Sommers asked him if he ever lost his temper: " 'I think I can say I reserve that great luxury for small matters. It wouldn't do to enjoy it where big things are involved' " (part four). In Van Hornesville, Sommers asked what the neighbors thought when they read about him in the papers "mediating with old European governments." "Well, I think some of them sometimes think there's some kind of fake about it" (part nine). And Martin Sommers thought that perhaps part of Young's success with Europeans was due to his commanding figure, dark hair and skin—the image of the noble red man they had read of in James Fenimore Cooper's novels![41]

A more serious article, "If Owen D. Young Were Nominated," appeared in the August *Harper's*; it was by Charles Merz, an experienced and judicious newspaperman, later a Pulitzer Prize winner and editor of the *New York Times*. He noted that Young's name had appeared in the *Times* over the last two years "on 326 occasions, an average of approximately three times a week. Even Henry Ford has had no press since the new model to compare with this." Merz gave him good marks on more substantial grounds, however, because he had "thought seriously and consecutively about questions of foreign policy," in which he differed from all other possible candidates, except for Newton Baker. His success in difficult negotiations at home and abroad, and in business, joined with his liberalism, made him acceptable to a variety of strange political bedfellows. If he were nominated, surmised Merz, the dominant issue of the campaign would be economic; business was restless and looking for a candidate. If Young were nominated, Merz ended, "we shall witness a great migration . . . with a little nostalgia but no real regret, big business will load its vans and cross the line."[42]

iv

For the fall of that year—aside from conferences designed to settle the Radio suit—Young was almost totally occupied by his fund-raising job for the Unemployment Relief Committee. Will Rogers said:

I think Mr. Hoover had overlooked Owen D. Young in his first relief committee and all the papers commented on it, and to make up for it he appointed him on a special one. Asking a Democrat to feed the country is almost a "believe it or not." Young is in a tough spot. If he feeds them through the winter, he will only be keepin' 'em alive to vote the Republican ticket next fall. Voters can't remember back over two months.

And the *Baltimore Sun* remarked that "it is of more than passing interest that a possible contender for the Democratic nomination next year should have been selected to take the lead in pulling out of the fire the relief chestnuts of the prospective Republican nominee. A more piquant political situation it would be difficult to imagine."[43]

The situation was growing more desperate daily throughout the country, with at least eight million unemployed in the summer, and William Green of the AFL estimating two million more by January. It was a mammoth job to find the funds to cope with such a problem. Young said, "I do not think we are going to let anyone suffer in the United States," and to this end he organized every resource available. Since the funds had to be raised locally, in every town and city of the nation, he attacked the job with all the tools of advertising: posters, newspapers, magazines, radio and the movies—all of which were donated for the purpose. It was like the Liberty Loan drives in the war.[44]

A national broadcast was set up for October 18, 1931, on which President Hoover opened the drive for funds. The star of the evening, however, was Will Rogers, who made perhaps the longest speech of his career; "new team on the radio," he said, "Hoover and Rogers." Will surveyed the scene with his usual humor and good sense, making a hard-to-resist plea for funds. Incidentally he took a crack at the Young Plan: "The Young Plan was that every nation that owed each other should pay what they could. But somebody came along with an older plan than the Young Plan; in fact it is the oldest plan there is. It was that nobody pay anybody anything. So that being an improvement over Young's plan, why it's the one Europe is working under now."[45]

The most popular and most publicized scheme that Young dreamed up to raise money took place on the gridiron. He suggested that each college and university football team play one game for unemployment relief. The idea ran through not only the colleges but the high schools like wildfire. The "Ivy" colleges—not including Harvard—worked out a postseason tournament of twenty-minute games; the Midwest conference said they might be able to raise a million dollars. St. Lawrence tried to arrange a game with Boston University, thus combining the alma maters of the scheme's inventor, but it did not work out.

Young called in the sportswriters to discuss plans to "fatten the gate" of the games; Joe Williams of the *New York World-Telegram* gave a good sportswriter's account of the meeting, with a picture of Young from a new angle:

The call came in the form of a very cordial telegram, which was signed Owen D. Young. It is a pleasure to report that most of the boys . . . responded on the instant. Only a few held back.

Mr. Francis Albertanti said he would not be duped by a phony telegram. "That's just a gag," insisted Mr. Albertanti, "I know Owen's handwriting when I see it."

Mr. Bill Farnsworth likewise declined politely but with iron determination. "I'd go if it was any place but the Bankers' Club. Times are too tough to run the risk of a touch by those fellows. . . ."

"This is not by any chance Mr. Cy Young, who used to pitch for the old Red Sox, is it?" your correspondent asked of Mr. W. O. McGeehan.

It developed not to be. He is a Van Hornesville (N.Y.) boy who made good in the city, and there is talk that his friends intend to put him up for the Presidency, or maybe it is his enemies. At any rate, Mr. Young is a tall, swarthy gentleman, with thin graying hair which he parts meticulously in the middle.

He effects [*sic*] sombre clothes, and there are state occasions when he drapes his nose with owlish spectacles moored to thin black ribbons. He has what the boys call a poker face and speaks with a soft even voice.

"I do not think a fellow would get very far trying to rush a hot check past him at that," commented Mr. Westbrook Pegler with evident chagrin.[46]

Then they got down to the business of promoting the games.

It paid off; Army and Navy played in Yankee Stadium December 12—fortunately a springlike day—before "a vast and distinguished assembly."[47] Army beat Navy to the tune of about $400,000 for relief; millions more "saw" the game through the familiar voice of Graham McNamee on the radio, and some were inspired to make contributions.

More than 132 institutions took part in other games, and there were also hundreds of high-school games throughout the country, which pleased Young even more, for he felt they gave the younger people a feeling of participation in a great cause. "The football games were done very well," he wrote Herbert Bayard Swope, Gerard's younger brother. "I suppose they have contributed two to two and a half million dollars in total to the fund."[48]

This effort of Young's for unemployment relief was successful as far as the fund was concerned; but it kept him in the political spotlight during the winter of 1931–32. To one reporter, who had asked him for an appointment, to get his "appraisal of political values," Young wrote: "I am always glad to see you and express my views quite fully and frankly on any subject on which I have views, but I do not wish at this time to be quoted publicly. I am not very keen about people who preach and refuse to act. As I do not intend to do the latter politically, I think at least I should eschew the former." The same columnist wrote later about Young, in describing the Democratic candidates and non-candidates: "He is probably the worst politician of the Presidential lot.

He has a way of saying just what he means regardless of consequences."[49]

As spring came on, the divided Democrats produced so many possible candidates that no one—not even Roosevelt—could count on winning the two-thirds vote in the convention still needed for the nomination. In March Mark Sullivan listed a possible sixteen candidates, including Young. Paul Y. Anderson, writing in the *Nation* at the end of March about the suit against RCA, was unusually kindly toward Young: "Owen hasn't been getting the breaks lately, which is unfortunate, because it is a delight to see him perform under fair conditions. He is the only industrial magnate I ever saw who could think rings around the average Congressman"—which could qualify as a bad break for both industrialists and members of Congress.[50]

Al Smith was still regarded as the kingmaker; would he support Roosevelt, who had nominated *him* in 1928? At Tammany Hall, Dudley Field Malone proposed a ticket of Young for President, John Nance Garner for vice-president; and Smith's admiration and affection for Young were well known.

Young himself was not hiding, as "Uncle Henry" had suggested he must. He spoke out on the new veterans'-bonus demands, strongly opposing printing money for an immediate cash settlement, but supported a two-billion-dollar bond issue for public works to make jobs for the unemployed. This latter was put forth in the Congress by Senator Joe Robinson of Arkansas, and had been worked out for him by Young.

In a speech in Canton he discussed the "crippling paralysis of business," suggesting that "our salvation may lie in the adoption of the equalization fee, which, if properly organized and administered, would give to the agriculturist something of the protection enjoyed by the industrialist." Political commentators studied his every word, and deduced, as stated in the *New York Times* headline of May 11, "Young Considered in the Race Now." Frank Kent said, "It is hardly possible to be more Progressive than Mr. Young is now, he really makes Governor Roosevelt . . . look like a reactionary."[51] "Whatever he has to say on national affairs," said the *Newark Evening News*, "becomes a campaign document."[52] And when the Democrats in New York City announced a special fund-raising dinner for May 17, every candidate watcher was sure this would be the hat-in-the-ring party for Owen D. Young.

The heat was increasing, and Young had not moved very far out of the kitchen. On April 28 John Crowley, editor of the *Little Falls Evening Times* (as near a hometown daily paper as residents of Van Hornesville could claim—seventeen miles away), had nominated

Young in a page-long double-column editorial. This was hardly news, for Crowley had been booming his Van Hornesville friend for years. In the Sunday *New York Times* of May 1, Arthur Krock reviewed the candidates, dwelling at length upon Roosevelt, and on the attempts to block him.

The only strange aspect of the case is that an eminent Democrat, who is not a candidate, who has not one instructed delegate, who has declined to allow an organization to be made for him or to have one penny spent in his interest, and who has even declined to attend the convention as a delegate, is the hope in the mind of all the leaders opposed to Governor Roosevelt. He is the real choice of most of them. Such professionals as Mayors Hague, Walker and Cermak and Mr. Curry have been quoted as saying to friends that, if this private citizen could be nominated, his election would be a certainty. . . . He is Owen D. Young.

Despite the dubious value of such professional support, Krock's statement was pounced upon by Victor Hanson and many others and reprinted all over the country. This noncandidacy, which the subject had paid little attention to—in the hope, perhaps, that it would go away— was beginning to look more and more like the real thing.

Young had had a frantically busy year. His efforts to alleviate the financial situation—both the nation's and his own, neither of which was good—had kept him occupied to the point of exhaustion. The Radio suit still defied settlement, extra efforts were demanded by his work upon the war-debts moratorium and the collapsing Insull empire. Frequent trips to Washington, to testify before the Congress, to meet with the secretary of state or the President, took up his nonexistent spare time. Jo's illness deprived him of his partner's active help, and he saved many hours to be with her.

But now, little more than a month before the national convention, he could not ignore the rising temperature of the political scene. To say he was not a candidate was no longer enough; he was not believed. He must make a stronger statement. But first he must make up his own mind. Was this the kind of call which, as he had written his friends, he could not reject without losing his self-respect? And what then about Jo?

He went out to Little Point for the weekend of May 13–15. Jo was living there now, with her flowers about her and the windows open to the salt air she loved. Owen went every weekend and as often during the week as he could. C.J. and Esther were spending this weekend there too. The three of them went out in the boat on Saturday, fishing, with Theodore, chauffeur and handyman, to cut bait. On Sunday, the three of them went out alone, anchoring off Little Point, with a line or two down for flounders; and Owen put the question to them.

"I want you two to help me decide. I'm not going to talk to anybody else about it—and when we finish it here, one way or other—it will be all that will be said on the subject."

They talked and talked for two hours (Esther wrote her mother) "from all angles of it and finally the statement . . . was evolved directly from our 'conference.' "[53]

"The statement" was a letter addressed to John Crowley at the *Little Falls Evening Times*, and was written on Monday, May 16; it appeared in Crowley's paper on the seventeenth, and soon thereafter throughout the nation.

My dear John Crowley:

Because you are my personal friend and because your paper circulates in my home community, your suggestion of my nomination for President by the Democratic party has raised again many inquiries regarding my attitude on that subject. I had hoped that my earlier statements had disposed of the matter.

While on the one hand I do not wish to put myself in the position of declining a nomination for the greatest office in the land which no one is in a position to tender, yet on the other hand, I must not, by silence, permit you and other good friends like you to put yourselves in the embarrassing position of making a wasteful and fruitless effort. Indeed, to do so, would put me under some obligation to the very people whose respect and good will I value most highly.

So may I say definitely and finally that I can not, for reasons which are so controlling as not to be open to argument, accept a nomination for the Presidency if made. With assurances of gratitude for the high compliment you have paid me, believe me to be,

Sincerely yours,
Owen D. Young

Even in the political arena, Young's withdrawal gave him a new sense of freedom. He always told his children that indecision was the worst state to be in: "Decide," he would say; "you may decide the wrong way, but decide."

On the very day his letter to Crowley appeared, he saw William C. Redfield of the Democratic Victory campaign and attended a fund-raising dinner for the party. Two days later, on May 19, he was writing Frank Altschul and half a dozen others to join him in making contributions to liquidate the party's overhanging debt ($250,000). He spoke out on the need for party unity and when FDR was nominated, wrote him a personal note repeating the warm best wishes he had extended a year earlier—not lightly, he said—at the Van Hornesville School commencement.[54] To inquiries from GE stockholders and employees, he refused advice on how to vote, insisting on the need for all citizens to consult their own intuition and considered judgment; just before the election he authorized the Democratic National Committee to release samples of these letters. And if his Metropolitan Opera House speech for Roosevelt just prior to the election had little influence on the outcome, his praise for FDR's "spirit of approach" did serve to reassure in some degree his apprehensive colleagues in business and finance.[55]

To be sure, Young's letter of renunciation had been hailed as a "national tragedy" by Victor Hanson and his Birmingham papers, and there were many who felt that way. And if the *Times* and the *Baltimore Sun* knew how to temper their expressions of regret, Young did not escape the criticism of those who felt, with the *New York Evening Post*, that "when the Republic calls, no man should have the right to say no." For the most part he remained unruffled, but to one correspondent who found his action unworthy and even cowardly, he responded briefly that "if you think my letter . . . was induced by lack of courage or other such low motive, you should feel greatly gratified that the country has escaped the risk, slight though it be, of such a President."[56]

Sometimes his critics resorted to humor—witness the "letter" printed in the *Providence* (Rhode Island) *Bulletin*, long one of Young's supporters:

Mr. Owen D. Young
Care of John Crowley
Little Falls, N.Y.

Dear Sir, etcetera,
The boys in the Van Hornesville Town Band, of which I play cornet, have asked me to make inquiry of you as to why you came out so flatfoot . . . against running for President. This sort of thing ain't being done by the big politicians, and it kind of makes all us folks up here look like hicks.

Jim Connors, who is a cousin of Cal Coolidge's twice removed, happened to run across Cal yestiddy and he asked Cal what he'd a done if he'd a been you, and Cal cal'ated that he'd of left a loophole in case worse comes to worst and he had a chance to run. . . . He says that a lot can happen to reasons in a month, and mebbe you could fix it to say at the convention that those reasons are now removed by circumstances and you will now accept the nomination for the prosperity of the country and the glory of all concerned, which includes us.

The boys in the band have asked me to suggest this loophole to you, because this means a lot to us. Mr. Coolidge, as you no doubt know, is very experienced in making statements. In fact, all the politicians but you are. And we can't make out why you went and done what you done.

Jim says it's because you're advisers are inexperienced, but I says you done it because you ain't got no advisers. Anyway, it's flabbergasted us to have you come out so straightforward, unless, of course, you meant what you said, in which case you've made a bad political mistake.

Please give this your immediate attention if convenient, and let John Crowley know your decision, if any.

Respectf'y y'rs,
Joshua Whiffle, 1st cornet.[57]

But of all the personal letters that poured into his office, few if any could have been more heartening than the one from Walter Lippmann, dated May 18:

My dear Owen:

Had I known the other day when we lunched together what the afternoon papers would carry, I should not have been able to proceed quite so impersonally. However, I probably wouldn't have been able to say as clearly then as I can now what I feel: that deeply as I regret the reasons which must have led to your decision, the real effect of it, in my opinion, will be greatly to enhance your own power in the present crisis. It's my honest belief that you can contribute more to the determination of fundamental policies in this country than any other man. And there is no one whom I would rather see exercise this great power. The circumstances which have made it impossible for you to have an active political career enable you to have a much more influential one. For in the present state of popular government the man in office is inevitably hopelessly compromised, and our ultimate salvation must lie in the influence of men who are listened to and are, at the same time, disinterested.

I send you warmest salutations,

Yours ever,
Walter Lippmann

Chapter 30

Banking and
Industrial Committees:
A Twice-flawed Effort

THREE days after publication of Owen Young's letter to John Crowley, his name was again dominating the headlines. On May 19, George Harrison announced that Young had agreed to head a newly appointed Committee of Twelve—six bankers and six industrialists—which, especially for the New York area, would consider "ways and means of making the large funds now being released by the Federal Reserve Banks useful affirmatively in developing business." That the public was hungry for some such initiative is strongly suggested by the four-column front-page spread with which the next morning's *Times* greeted this announcement. Faith in business leadership had no doubt suffered severely over the past two years, but in some quarters it died hard. Besides, this move seemed to promise a new kind of cooperative action, not only within the private sector but, on more than a token basis, with government as well. Mark Sullivan saw it as New York's first show of cooperation—and leadership.[1]

Governor Harrison, it seems, was somewhat taken aback by all the fanfare, which he rightly considered premature. If Young concurred, he could hardly have been unhappy to see his readiness to lead this businessmen's venture so widely advertised just after he had renounced all political ambition and its attendant obligations. Free at last to accept the challenge his friend Wallace Donham had tendered almost a year ago, he had lost no time about it. And perhaps the time was right; at least the particular series of disasters which had marked the intervening year was no longer waiting to pounce.

That Young had been giving much thought to the needs of the moment, and preferred taking risks to doing nothing, was already clear to those—including many members of the Congress—who had read, only two days earlier, his lengthy interview with John Owens of the *Balti-*

more Sun. Federal aid for the unemployed was now a must, he said, but measures that promised reemployment were worth ten times as much.

In outlining the kind of program that might redeem this promise, Young had spoken with deep compassion, but also with the authority that comes, perhaps, only with renunciation of personal ambition. First the federal budget must be balanced on current account—to quiet fears and also to establish a solid credit base. Then one must put that base to use: bond issues to finance self-liquidating public works could hardly impair the credit of a government whose revenues could come only from men and capital at work. And since corporations would be profiting from consequent new orders, let them pay a 2 percent tax to cover amortization of the bonds. As for the farmer, why not test the merits of the so-called equalization fee by applying it to a single commodity like wheat?

Here at last was a prospectus that invited a working consensus. Of the new committee Young was heading—Walter Gifford of A T & T, Walter Teagle of Jersey Standard, Alfred Sloan of General Motors, Clarence Woolley of American Radiator, Floyd Carlisle of Consolidated Gas, and half a dozen leading bankers[2]—not one would have questioned the need for balancing the budget, but very few would have gone farther on their own. On the other hand, impatient liberals in and out of Congress were proposing to go farther—sometimes much farther—without bothering about the budget at all. It had remained for Young to reconcile the two in a fashion that was hard to fault— especially when he added, and defended, a new corporation tax.

Certainly it made him good copy—not least because, in this instance, he refused to stop there. Typically, the so-called internationalists were insisting that domestic recovery must wait on world recovery, while their opponents reversed the order or simply dismissed the rest of the world. Yet here, as John Owens made clear, a foremost "internationalist" was bent on coping first with our urgent domestic problems: the plight of the jobless, of the small homeowner and of the farmer. According to Young, only when we had done everything possible to deal with these problems directly should we concern ourselves with such matters as tariffs, international debts and world markets. And only as we could contrive to do both—and this would require "liberal leadership"—could we hope to achieve a full measure of prosperity, especially for the farmer.[3]

Readers of this interview extraordinary could hardly have doubted that if Young had felt free to run for President, he would have had his program ready. What else did it signify? Was he challenging the President—or Governor Roosevelt—to demonstrate the kind of "liberal leadership" which such a program called for? Was it a kind of business manifesto, anticipating the aims and hopes of the new committee he was about to head? Or was it a nonpartisan plea for concerted action by government and business to rescue the stricken economy?

Hoover, in any case, was making it clear that he was very much a party to the act on which the curtain was now rising. Treasury Secretary Ogden L. Mills and Governor Eugene Meyer had indeed been actively involved in plans which led to creation of Young's so-called Banking and Industrial—or "B & I"—Committee; on their return from its first meeting (May 20) the President not only pointed this out but called for the appointment of similar groups in the other Federal Reserve districts. Then, he said, he would invite all the chairmen to meet in Washington, so that the program could be coordinated nationally. As for Young, his own involvement in planning this new initiative makes it clear that he was fully aware of this impending opportunity to serve "in his own field" when he finally scratched his name from the presidential lists.[4]

The decision against running was not new; essentially, it dated from the previous summer when the doctors had made their report on his wife's health. But if that remained the "controlling" factor, there were others to support it.

For one thing, the impact of that summer's catastrophic developments abroad, culminating in the "float" of the pound sterling, had been personal as well as global. Thus, if Young's autumn campaign to relieve the unemployed had brought him psychological relief, his own financial independence, like the collateral that "secured" his loans, was now a thing of rags and tatters. Also, the two companies for which he felt primary responsibility were finally feeling the full force of the depression, aggravated by the still unresolved Radio suit. If he felt limited enthusiasm for Roosevelt as his party's standard-bearer, he had even less for the "stop-Roosevelt" role for which he was evidently being groomed. And it had become increasingly apparent that avoidance of this role could be assured only by the drastic step he finally took.

ii

That Young felt an anticipatory sense of freedom even before dispatching his letter to Crowley is evident in the content and the timing of the letter he addressed to the President on May 11. Written when it was, and mailed to reach the White House on the second anniversary of the filing of the Radio suit, it was also the first time that Young had made an appeal directly to President Hoover for action affecting the suit.

My dear Mr. President [it read]:

Mr. Charles Neave, who is Counsel-in-Chief for the defendants in the Radio trust case brought by the Government, has just been in to tell me that the Department of Justice has indicated the intention of setting the case down for a hearing in open court in Wilmington on the third of October next. Mr. Neave has told Judge Olney that that is a date satisfactory to counsel, if the case is to be tried in open court.

In that trial, naturally, I will be one of the important witnesses, and if the case proceeds as suggested, it will be necessary for me to spend at least a month in preparation, because the testimony will involve complicated transactions covering at least twelve years, and after preparation, I must hold myself in readiness to appear at any or all times while the testimony is being taken.

You are somewhat familiar with my present problems and activities. The Secretary of the Treasury, Governor Meyer, and General Dawes are even more familiar with them. You and they will know better than I whether it is in the public interest to take me out of my present activities for two months or more in times like these.

One would think that if there were ever a time in which one could expect agreed statements of fact and clear and definitely framed issues, it was now. Lawyers, of course, are always talking about "color," but frankly, Mr. President, it seems to me that is child's play in serious times. I dare say that ninety or ninety-five per cent of all the really material facts in the Radio case are free from reasonable dispute. The Department has had full access to my personal files and to those of the various defendants, and has spent months going through them and taking copies; so the Department should be in full possession of the facts. Based on those facts, one or two simple issues of law might be framed for the convenience of the court.

In making these suggestions, I am not asking for favors of any kind in the trial of the Radio case, nor for personal advantage. I am merely trying to say that if perchance you feel as I do about such wasteful efforts, you may wish to ask the Attorney General to reach an agreement of facts, and if you come to that conclusion, I will ask the counsel for the defendants likewise to exhaust their efforts in making such agreements and so avoid the diversion of time and energy of myself and others, similarly situated, in the taking of testimony.

Very respectfully yours,[5]

The President's only response was officially impeccable; he directed his secretary to send Young's letter to Attorney General William D. Mitchell with a request for his "advice as to a reply." When, more than a month later, Mitchell's four-page response was ready, it was addressed to that same secretary, Lawrence Richey, in whose absence another secretary forwarded a copy to Young. No comment on either letter reached Young from Hoover.

The attorney general's reply, dated June 14, was nothing if not comprehensive. Noting that Young's "only direct request is that I be directed by the President to reach an agreement of facts with the defendants," he nevertheless found that "the first half of his letter, although not expressly asking for a postponement, carries the suggestion that the trial should be postponed because it is not in the public interest to require Mr. Young to give any attention to the case in these times." Based on that reading of Young's plea for an agreed stipulation of the facts which might reduce the court's adjudication and so the respondents' testimony to "one or two simple issues of law," Mitchell devoted several paragraphs to rehearsing the history of the case and reciting the manifold reasons why further postponement was not to be considered.

But if this was largely gratuitous—perhaps dictated for the record— his observations regarding stipulation of the facts were cogent enough to give Young pause. The government, he said in effect, would welcome the maximum possible agreement on the pertinent facts but, so far, its efforts to achieve this had found defendants' counsel almost wholly unresponsive. Nor was pursuit of such agreement now precluded merely by setting the date for the trial.[6]

What Charles Neave had to say about this retort when Young showed him Mitchell's letter is, alas, not a matter of record. The record is clear, however, that neither the long wait nor the attorney general's counteroffensive affected Young's determined efforts to promote recovery. The demanding job of getting his B & I Committee organized for action was interrupted at the outset by a special trip to consult the President, Secretary Mills and Governor Meyer on a new and emergent crisis marked by large French withdrawals of gold and rampant speculation against the dollar. This threat, which came to a head at the end of May, was sudden and dangerous; thanks to prompt action by the President and the Congress as well as by the Federal Reserve and the treasury, it was relatively brief. By general agreement, the first and urgent move in defense of the dollar involved prompt passage of the pending revenue bill, and it was precisely here that Young's influence with the Democratic senators was quite possibly decisive.[7]

This threat was not the first nor was it to be the last of the cruel shocks which hampered that spring's efforts toward recovery. The suicide and subsequent disclosure of fraudulent operations of the "Swedish match king," Ivar Krueger, had preceded by only a few weeks the Insull collapse. The kidnapping of the Lindbergh baby had its deeply tragic ending; this child was also the grandson of Young's old friend Dwight Morrow, whose funeral he had attended only a few months earlier. And by late June, with the Democratic convention, which would nominate Governor Roosevelt, assembled in Chicago, Young had barely finished handing out diplomas at the Van Hornesville School's second commencement when he was summoned to the phone—Chicago calling—by Jesse Jones, not on convention business but to ask his approval of a ninety-million-dollar emergency loan from the Reconstruction Finance Corporation to the so-called Dawes Bank.[8]

Sentiment aside, Young knew well enough that there was no feasible alternative to prompt approval; failure of this bank would presumptively have led to the closing of all Chicago banks. But the size of the loan, plus the fact that Dawes had so recently resigned from the presidency of the RFC, was to make it something of a *cause célèbre*. Too easily forgotten by the general's critics were his eight years of devoted public service: as vice-president, ambassador to Britain, and finally as the RFC's first president. Forgotten also—or brushed aside—was the drastic credit crunch of the past nine months, which had left the RFC so often the bankers' one recourse; at five billion dollars, the contraction in bank loans for that brief span had been double the total for the previous twenty-two months, beginning with the crash. From such a squeeze, with no market for their bonds, banks were suffering almost as acutely as their customers. If Dawes had erred, it was in waiting too long before leaving the RFC's responsibilities to others and assuming the one at home which only he could hope to discharge.[9]

Young had last seen the general at the White House conference of May 30, and the following day had wired the general's brother a copy of his schedule. Thus Gertrude Chandler's telegram of June 7 which awaited him in Riverside on his return from delivering the commencement address at Notre Dame contained few surprises: "Tax bill signed, Dawes resigns, Rockefeller letter favoring repeal creating tremendous stir, Tarbell book out today."

The Tarbell book was his biography—of which, true to his promise, he had not read a line. Also devoted to his wife, Ida Tarbell was quick to understand Young's withdrawal from the presidential race, but it must have been dismaying to Macmillan, her publishers. Reviewing it for the *New York Evening Post*, William Soskin found that it "has the distinctive flavor of a campaign document" and "would do very nicely as a Democratic Bible." He also found its protagonist something less than credible: "This man Owen D. Young—hasn't he any weaknesses?" Lewis Gannett called the book "saccharine," and Stolberg in the *Nation* attacked both the author and her subject with such vehemence as to produce a counterattack from the *Christian Leader*. As for the full-page review in the *Times*, Dr. Finley found so little to fault and so much to praise that Young wrote him to say he was almost persuaded to read the book himself.[10]

Whatever the pros and cons, both author and publisher were entitled to feel unlucky in their timing. A good fight among the reviewers was all very well, but the interest it excited now was nothing to what might have been. As for the economy, things had looked pretty grim only last September, with England going off gold, but that was nothing to the way things looked today. The magnitude of the intervening credit crunch had already been noted; during the same nine months, while unemployment soared, the business index fell off by another 25 percent, and any common stocks one had not been forced to sell at the outset would now have brought about one-third as much as then. And who now was buying books, at any price?

So—good luck to Owen Young as, like some uncrowned Canute, he now set out to reverse the apparently irreversible. His *ad hoc* group of big bankers and industrialists looked impressive enough on paper, but could they marshal the wisdom and the strength necessary to check, much less reverse, the downward spiral? Could they do all this on a nonpartisan basis, and in a presidential year?

iii

Well, they tried. Setting up offices in the Federal Reserve Building at 33 Liberty Street with a small staff of expert advisers, the Young committee promptly mounted exploratory attacks on several salients: home mortgage relief and possible mass construction of small homes; the creation through new investment agencies of a market for the bonds and basic commodities which were still being dumped for such cash as they might bring; projects for slum clearance, aid to the railroads, and such self-liquidating public works as new under-river tunnels or completion of the Triborough Bridge. For these latter, the committee's staff made estimates of the reemployment likely to ensue—directly in the building trades and indirectly in production of materials, especially steel. They also quoted the Society of Civil Engineers as estimating "that $100 million of construction—involving some 50,000 jobs—had been held in abeyance for New York City owing to the [city's] credit situation." (It was this, incidentally, which accounted for the stoppage of work on the Triborough Bridge.)[11]

Even more impressive were the figures supporting new capital loans to aid the railroads. As reported from authoritative sources, "approximately 45% of their [the railroads'] gross is spent in employment and they are now employing 400,000 to 500,000 under normal." As for their impact on other industries, "railroads are estimated to purchase 23% of U.S. bituminous coal production, 19% of fuel oil, 16% of total timber cut and 17% of total iron and steel output." Finally, "of railroad securities, national banks are said to hold one billion, savings banks $500 million, insurance companies three billion."[12]

Now set up in all twelve Federal Reserve districts, the B&I Committees could address such opportunities chiefly as catalytic agents; except as otherwise noted, it was the RFC that had the funds. But they could and did bring pressure to bear, especially after passage in early July of the President's version of the Robinson-Wagner-Garner bills, which gave the RFC new clout. And something of this survived both Governor Meyer's resignation as chairman of the RFC (which shortly followed Dawes's) and Young's refusal to head the agency himself.[13]

Meanwhile, the press was reporting definite action by the Young committee in support not only of bonds but also of mortgage refunding—together with some encouragement, at Walter Teagle's prodding, for "spreading" the available work. Presumably it was to meet with Teagle's subcommittee that Young had promptly extended an invitation to AFL president William Green to come over; what came of Green's acceptance is, unfortunately, not recorded. It is clear, however, that Young and Harrison were keeping in close touch with the other regional committees, and the end of July found them both in Washington again, working with Meyer and Mills to set up a central coordinating agency.[14]

To that end, a general conference of the chairmen and others was called to meet in the capital on August 24. After addresses by Mills and Young had set the stage, the establishment of a full-fledged central committee, with Henry M. Robinson as chairman, was approved with some enthusiasm. This, as the President hoped, would serve as a clearinghouse for new ideas and for directing the attention of all to measures which any given committee had found helpful. With offices in the treasury, it should also serve to promote close cooperation with the RFC and other government agencies.[15]

And already there were heartening signs that these efforts were paying off. In contrast with the dismal figures for the nine preceding months, "from June to September [of 1932] stock averages rose . . . from 35.9 to 61.5"—some 70 percent—"the rise incidentally validating a great body of security loans which had been under water." (Young's loans had yet to surface.) The same respected economist, B. M. Anderson of the Chase Bank, adds that "the curve of industrial production moved up rapidly . . . from about 58 to about 67"—or about 15.5 percent; even farm prices, he adds, "moved up very sharply though not enough." According to J. S. Davis, July and August also saw a "strong upturn in . . . corporate . . . bond prices in New York and London, and in the Harvard index of sensitive commodity prices. . . ." Davis indeed goes so far as to conclude that "but for the whim of the political calendar in the United States, mid-1932 might well have marked the definitive turn from contraction to recovery here and abroad."[16]

Setting aside this *obiter dictum* for what it may be worth, it is only fair to ask whether the summer's upturn was essentially the work of these committees, or was simply a predictable swing of the pendulum—touched off, perhaps, by congressional rejection of Wright Patman's extravagant bonus bill and passage first of the revenue and finally of the relief and reconstruction acts. So far, the latter is clearly the prevailing view—incidentally one that fully justifies the efforts that the administration, not to say Young, had been directing toward these ends. Europe too had finally made a potentially major contribution—here Young had kept hands off—in the Allied decision at Lausanne to transmute Germany's scheduled reparation annuities into a single—and almost nominal—lump sum, payable some three years hence. This happened in July; had the apprehensive French been willing to accept the inevitable a few months earlier, they might conceivably (according to Anderson) had saved the Brüning government and so staved off Hitler's triumph. Be that as it may, this virtual cancellation of the Young Plan was stated to be conditional on similar treatment of the Allied debts—a condition which the U.S. government was notoriously unprepared to meet. Even had it been, we have discovered no suggestion that this might have "saved the Hoover government" though it might, in Young's view, have had other and more beneficial consequences.[17]

But if it would be folly to ignore such positive forces and ascribe full credit for the rise to the Banking and Industrial Committees, we find it only less unrealistic to dismiss their efforts as unworthy of serious attention. The respective impact of all these varied and relevant factors—especially their psychological impact—defies quantification, and so distributive justice becomes at best a rough approximation. But if, for the committees' contribution, documentation is admittedly spotty, our testimony is based on something more than hearsay: both of us were watching and one of us was there.[18]

iv

It was a pity that September should have brought fresh distractions and interruptions—of which the political campaign was only one—because momentum was now all-important, and sufficiently hard to sustain. Young had no difficulty, for example, in securing a consensus of his committee in New York on the importance of proceeding at once with completion of the Triborough Bridge, but with the city's playboy mayor, Jimmy Walker, under fire and resigning under pressure from Governor Roosevelt, its still unsolved credit problems were not calculated to encourage any immediate RFC investment. Young not only sought the help of the bankers in pressing for solutions; he also consulted his old Baltimore friend Howard Bruce and, in search of helpful clues, inspected plans for the pending Chesapeake Bay Bridge. It was all to no avail: a full year and a certain amount of housecleaning in Tammany Hall would intervene before the RFC was prepared to do the necessary funding.[19] And to fund new under-river tunnels would take even longer.

In the case of the railroads, the problem was different but still vexing. Under prodding from Young and Alfred Sloan, the RFC did invest heavily in their future and with beneficial results; unfortunately it took time for the investment to become genuinely productive. Far more promising of immediate benefits was the Young committee's project for slum clearance, but it was here that the B & I Committees' built-in limitations were to prove most damaging. For all the impressive aggregates of capital represented in the New York group, this voluntary agency could act only through the persuasive force of unanimous agreement; like the eighteenth-century Polish parliament, it could be hamstrung by a single—or "liberum"—veto. And whatever slum area the committee proposed to attack, one bank or another turned out to be trustee for the owners, without whose permission it could not agree to the necessary condemnation proceedings. That the bank in question, acting in its capacity as trustee, could not be faulted only added to the frustration both of the staff and also of the industrialists, including the chairman, who found themselves powerless to move.[20]

In the meantime, there was politics—and the Radio suit. With the creation of the Central B&I Committee, Young's assistant had been transferred from New York to Washington, where, as its executive secretary, he was to assist the committee's chairman, Henry M. Robinson. Although the latter made every effort to preserve the nonpartisan character of this agency, it was no secret that his dominant concern was now the reelection of his great friend Hoover. This was equally true of the secretary of the treasury, Ogden Mills, who could not abide his Democratic Dutchess County neighbor. And since part of the secretary's office suite served as the committee's headquarters, and an old friend, James Douglas of Chicago, was at once assistant secretary of the treasury and secretary of the Central Committee, Case found himself quite literally in a hotbed of Republicans.

For an independent-minded Democrat in his early thirties, this situation was anomalous but by no means unrewarding. Supplemented as it was by weekends in New York to catch up with Young and the latest committee developments there (not to mention reunions with his wife, now expecting their first child), it did give him the feeling of knowing a thing or two about what was going on. But this feeling could sometimes prove deceptive.

For example, Case's notes for Saturday, September 10, were involuntarily cryptic because he was now out of touch with late developments in the Radio suit. Nevertheless, they do suggest how difficult Young was finding it to answer a summons from Governor Roosevelt while still keeping open his lines of communication with Washington:

Mr. Young had an appointment at 11 o'clock this morning at Hyde Park. About half an hour before this time, H. H. Adams [GE's experienced representative in Washington, and Philip Young's father-in-law] called from Washington to say that Henry Robinson was in his office and was very anxious to talk with Mr. Young. It was explained where Mr. Young was and Adams asked that a message be left for him to call Metropolitan 3600 at Washington between 12 and 1 (E.D.T.). Soon after this Mr. Neave called up to say that he had been talking to Mr. Robinson and would like Mr. Young to call him at Ossining after he talked to Robinson.

Mr. Young received the message and immediately called his own office to say that he couldn't talk from there. He then asked me (I was spending the morning at the Bank on B&I Committee matters) to call Robinson, explain his situation, and ask if there was any message I could take and where Mr. Young could reach [him] later in the afternoon. Mr. Robinson said he was leaving for Chicago soon after lunch and it was for that reason that he was anxious to reach Mr. Young. I got Mr. Young on the telephone myself before he and the Governor went in to lunch, and Mr. Young said I could tell Mr. Robinson that he would do whatever Mr. Neave recommended.

On his way back to Riverside Mr. Young stopped to see Mr. Neave at Ossining.[21]

Here ends the entry. Soon afterward Case learned that the government's antitrust suit against the Radio group was still set to open on October 10. He also learned that Young, advised by counsel that his attendance would consequently be required for the balance of the year, had promptly told Henry Robinson that this would force him to resign from both the B & I Committees and as director and deputy chairman of the New York Federal Reserve. As a GE director, Robinson could only approve; on the other hand, he feared lest this action hurt the recovery effort, and so Hoover's chances for reelection. Thus he was prepared to take off his coat to work out a solution that would obviate the need.

For want of tangible evidence bearing on Robinson's view of the optimum solution, the authors are teased by an undated, unsigned memorandum filed among Hoover's presidential papers which suggests that, in the mind of the anonymous writer, a solution more constructive than any mere postponement of the suit was both urgent and available. Given the strong probability that Robinson's views would have been at least consonant if not identical, it seems relevant to produce the substance of the memo here, beginning with its premise: "The proposed radio patent pool appears to have reached an impasse. Such a pool would be distinctly of value to the radio industry and it would be to the credit of the administration if such a set-up could be brought about as a result of the negotiations which have been carried on by the Attorney-General." Proceeding then to the options still available to the administration, the memo lists them as follows:

(1) Push through the pool under the best terms possible, trusting to time and patience to bring about correction of the imperfections, which after all are more theoretical than real . . . the so-called "restraint of trade" violation can be corrected by practical methods later . . . the principal thing being to get the R. C. A. to put all the General Electric and Westinghouse patents in the pool (which they are now willing to do).

(2) Continue efforts to bring about the attempt of the extremists for divorcing the General Electric and Westinghouse companies from the Radio Corporation, with a view to having a perfect theoretical legal set-up. This these companies will not agree to. . . . So, this course would result in disaster to many and good to none.

(3) Proceed immediately with the Department of Justice suit. Nonconstructive and bound to affect all interests adversely.

(4) Delay action by appointing a committee of practical government radio experts to make a constructive study of the situation, with orders to report direct to the President. This would save the President embarrassment, but would delay bringing a patent pool into effect beyond the time this administration would get the credit for it before election. On the other hand, it would be a logical step if this is necessary to prevent the catastrophe which would result if (2) or (3) must be followed. . . .[22]

Whether or not the hand or the voice was Robinson's, the notation to file bears Lawrence Richey's initials and so must have been ordered by his chief. Assuming that Robinson was at least privy to this document and its disposition, he would then almost certainly have sought postponement—as indeed he did. Of the effort and its outcome, Case's longhand note of September 20 speaks with a kind of guarded authority—his numbers *1* and *2* designating respectively the President and his attorney general:

HMR confided that numbers *1* and *2* were agreed that a postponement was called for and that *2* should explain matters to the Judge [Olney]. After a stormy two-hour session, the latter, it seems, was not only unconvinced, but declared that in the event of postponement he would resign and attribute his resignation to Wall St. pressure. . . .

HMR's perplexity about the Judge, however, [is] certainly not feigned, and *his* sincerity is transparent. He could not understand his attitude, he had the reputation of being a reasonable man, yet here he was suddenly stubborn, whatever his motives. . . .[23]

So, it was to be options two and three, however extreme and "nonconstructive." Two days later Young moved comprehensively to carry out his threat. His files contain letters of resignation to Robinson, George Harrison and Eugene Meyer, with copies and a covering note for Secretary Mills. These letters, however, are all originals, unsigned and never sent. Robinson's efforts having failed, how was Young persuaded to withhold them?

To this question David Sarnoff undoubtedly held the key. With sets and tubes a drug on the market, the Radio Corporation was now showing its first deficit, with only wireless and broadcasting subsidiaries reporting a profit. RKO, which had salvaged for RCA's Photophone some shares of the promising, if currently depressed, market for talking-picture equipment, was in receivership. In the face of such facts, Sarnoff was convinced that RCA could no longer afford the multiple costs of the protracted government suit, much less the risk of an adverse judgment and the costly private litigation which this would certainly invite. Thus a consent decree might offer the best way out, even if it did involve separation from, and competition with, General Electric and Westinghouse. After all, Sarnoff had worked hard for the independence promised for RCA in the 1930 unification agreement; this might now be realized in full, if only the manufacturing companies would agree to settle their outstanding advances and dispose of their large stock holdings in ways that did not harm RCA's other shareholders.[24]

Having convinced himself, Sarnoff's next step was to convince Owen Young, who held the key to the assent and cooperation required of the manufacturing companies. Just how quickly Sarnoff succeeded is not clear, but there is no doubt that he captured Young's interest and attention from the outset. Perhaps too the fresh possibility of settling the case by consent decree made the government—even to Judge Olney—less unwilling to consider a postponement, although this was not at once forthcoming.

Sarnoff, however, was in Young's office on Thursday, September 22— the day his resignations were dictated and at least temporarily shelved; presumably Young encountered Robinson the next day, first at the General Electric directors' meeting, and again at the Federal Reserve where the Central B&I Committee was convening. True, the day after that—a Saturday—found Young still saying—notably to B. C. Forbes— that he must now give all his time to the Radio suit, and his calendar for the following weeks attests that he meant business. Nevertheless, after two all-day sessions with Charles Neave, and Wednesday's succession of meetings with Neave and Thurlow Gordon, with Neave, Gerard Swope and A. W. Robinson, and finally with Sarnoff alone, Young wired Robinson that the previous three days, and more of the same through the following week, should so far complete his preparation for the suit that he could and would attend a meeting in Chicago which Robinson and Mills thought important. For the first time, the long tunnel had begun to show a faintly glimmering light.[25]

v

In its October issue *Forbes* presented its own editorial portrait of the man on whom these diverse pressures were converging. Wrote B. C. Forbes:

I met Owen Young the other evening after not having seen him for a long time. His appearance rather shocked me. He has aged. The lines in his face have deepened. In repose, his expression has become grave, not to say sad. His smile has lost some of its spontaneity, much of its sparkle.

He used to radiate vigor, buoyancy, enthusiasm, the joy of living. He now looks tired, burdened, contemplative.

Instead of saying, "Let George do it," this country—and even Europe—has developed the habit of saying, "Have Owen Young do it." No business man in America's whole history has shouldered as many appalling, public-spirited responsibilities. He is so constituted that he could turn down no opportunity for rendering important national or international service. The world should realize that he is paying a price for serving it.

Where Young was concerned, Forbes's pen was apt to be no less adulatory than Ida Tarbell's, and while Jo secretly agreed with this outpouring, she thought it best to sniff and so did Owen. To be sure, Paul Anderson could well have repeated his earlier observation that "Young has not been getting the breaks lately"; the summer's upturn in the economy had now been all but canceled and the personal pinch was more acute than ever. And with the Radio suit now approaching its climax he had still to prepare himself to take the witness stand if necessary, even while working overtime with all the affected parties on the new relationships and settlements involved in a possible consent decree.

Far from feeling sorry for himself, however, Young was finding in these unremitting pressures the kind of adrenalin he had so often found in happier times. Gone were the premonitory fears which in the spring of '32 had prompted the scribbled note found in his office: "the time has come for my books to go . . ." (where would he find a buyer?), or the more sententious but still poignant: "I would rather die surrounded with the broken hopes of an ambitious idealism than to live amid the ruins of . . . the belief that men can and will govern themselves wisely and unselfishly." Now, as reflected in a conversation at midnight on Friday, October 7, which Case (staying at the apartment) noted down, he was finding plenty to interest and excite him even in the new problems and difficult decisions with which a breaking up of the Radio group would certainly confront him. And the candor invited by the moment and his mood on coming home late makes his comments more than usually revealing:

"Well," he said, lighting his pipe, "I have had some interesting basic human reactions today. You know I lunched with [Winthrop] Aldrich, and I think we settled the Rockefeller Center situation. The settlement, however, was conditional on my remaining with the Radio Corporation. With me out of the picture they said the transaction was off, as they would not deal with Sarnoff on that basis.

"You knew I had gone up to see [Walter] Gifford at Yama Farms the other day? That was interesting too. Aldrich, you know, is a director of the

Telephone Company and they are pretty far along with the program of wired radio, by which they would bring "Red Seal" radio programs to telephone subscribers and charge them for it. As a public utility, however, they cannot go into the business of providing the artists or entertainment, because $5,000, or whatever it is that Lily Pons gets for a single performance, could scarcely be a proper subject for utility commissions to deal with. In describing his plan to his directors, therefore, Mr. Gifford had indicated that they had in mind a contract with the Broadcasting Company by which the latter would furnish artists and programs. Well, Aldrich inquired whether Mr. Gifford had taken this up with the Radio Corporation and Gifford replied that he would talk to me about it and to no one else. That is why I went to see him, and of course that has tremendous possibilities."

Here Young paused, as usual, to relight his pipe, but there was more to come:

"Well, Deac [Aylesworth] was in a great stew today because Sarnoff had apparently thought I might get out and indicated that he had some ideas about broadcasting, and if I got out Deac would take his orders from him alone. Deac telephoned me today and I could see he was upset, so I suggested that he dine with me tonight. [We did and] he said flatly that if I got out he got out too, that he was trying to do a job both in the Broadcasting Company and in RKO . . . but he did not have to stay as Sarnoff's man and that he would be damned if he would.

"I have been thinking about it, and it's just one of those basic human reactions that you can't get away from. It has nothing to do with me personally except as I represent a factor in the situation. Moreover, Deac has as little racial prejudice as I have. He can get along perfectly well with Sarnoff . . . as long as ultimately Sarnoff must report to me. Take that factor away and the balance breaks down."

Young paused again while several matches were ritually applied to his half-lit pipe. His auditor having seized the moment to suggest that this seemed to reveal a real weakness in the Radio setup, Young nodded and resumed:

"Undoubtedly. I have always had it in mind that so far as General Electric is concerned, as Mr. Swope and I had come in together we would retire together, but I had never thought it through in the case of RCA. I imagine that my withdrawal alone from General Electric might make matters difficult within the organization. In the case of RCA, its effect would be felt largely in outside relationships."

"Well," I said, "What are you going to do?"

Mr. Young laughed. "I told Neave, up at Ossining the other day, that I had solved the problem. I would resign from both companies, open my law office and get myself elected General Counsel by both."

I grinned and asked what Mr. Neave had had to say to that. Young grinned too and knocked out his pipe.

"He said [Young answered] it was the God-damnedest idea that might work that he had ever listened to."

Mr. Young got up and turned out the lights. "Well [he said] I think I will go to bed." At the stairs he turned and said with a quizzical smile:

"You know life these days is no bed of roses, but at least I can't complain that it's dull. Good night."[26]

Less than three days after this conversation, early on the morning of October 10, a speeding taxi safely deposited a very expectant mother at the Polyclinic Hospital, where by ten o'clock she had been delivered of her firstborn—a comely daughter. Fortunately for the father it was a Monday, so he was with her, and was indeed the first (except the doctor and the nurse) to see the child. Named Josephine Edmonds for her grandmother Young, the baby also had a late afternoon visitor who had cut short that day's Radio meetings especially to see her and her mother. So content was Grandfather Young with what he saw that he thereupon took the proud new father to dine with him at the Century, where they somehow contrived to find the potion most appropriate for a toast to welcome the newcomer. Nor did the natural course of these proceedings fail to do full justice to the absent mother and grandmother. In short, a memorable evening, undocumented and hitherto unrecorded.

vi

In the event, the government's suit against the Radio group—or its surviving members—never came to trial. After a series of postponements—the latest on November 15—it was finally settled by consent decree on November 21. In terms of the options offered in the anonymous memo quoted above, it was the government's insistence on "divorcing the General Electric and Westinghouse companies from the Radio Corporation, with a view to having a perfect theoretical legal set-up" which had delayed "bringing a patent pool into effect beyond the time this administration would get the credit for it before election." Evidently the Hoover administration had come to feel that this divorce must be achieved at any price; at least it had prevented Judge Olney's threatened resignation with its ascription of Wall Street pressure. And if the defendants found its terms harsh, they had at least had time to satisfy themselves that nothing better offered—now or prospectively.

The decree was hailed—and with good reason—by the independents and all of RCA's numerous and voluble critics as a notable victory for public opinion versus entrenched monopoly. GE and Westinghouse were directed to dispose of their RCA holdings by an equitable distribution to their shareholders and enjoined against their repurchase. Licenses under their pooled patents were no longer to be exclusive but open to all—ultimately including GE and Westinghouse—on payment to RCA of the same or equivalent royalties. After a two-and-a-half-year period of grace in which to consolidate its independent resources, RCA was to be subject to the open competition of its former parents, who were henceforth denied representation on any of its boards. (A special provision permitted Young and A. W. Robertson of Westinghouse to stay on for five months, and NBC's Advisory Council was not forbidden territory.) Even in the foreign field, contracts were to be shorn of certain exclusive features, but Sarnoff felt that they were still feasible.[27]

Of all these stipulations, the market took a predictably dim view, and Radio Corporation stocks were heavily sold. Editorial opinion varied widely and sometimes unpredictably—as witness the Republican *Herald Tribune*'s singularly independent-minded commentary of November 23. As a judicious recapitulation of issues, still imperfectly resolved, on which Young's views had been first challenged and finally overruled, it is here reproduced verbatim; it is for the reader to determine whether Young or Hoover must have read it with the greater relish. Entitled "Social Control," it reads as follows:

The consent decree which brings to an end the United States government's suit against the radio combine is being set beside the packers' decree of 1920 and the dissolution of the Standard Oil in 1911 as one of the few great achievements of the Sherman anti-trust act. No doubt it is; yet the nature of the achievement and the moral of the history leading up to it are alike questions only of doubt and perplexity. The story would seem admirably to illustrate the contradictory ideas of economic theory and governmental function in which this country's attempts to deal with modern industrial organizations have involved it. If it proves anything else, it is not easy to say what it is.

It was the government itself which originally urged the electrical companies to found the Radio Corporation of America as a patent pool which would prevent America's world radio communications from passing to foreign hands. That was in October 1919. But RCA had scarcely been set up before radio blossomed into a whole new industry of undreamed of domestic possibilities, and almost immediately the government started investigating its own creation. For a decade it continued to wrestle with the legal and economic problems presented. The Federal Trade Commission investigated from January, 1924, until December, 1928, only to report that it had no authority to pass upon possible violation of the anti-trust laws. The Department of Justice undertook the matter in 1929, only to discover at the beginning that the case arose out of a clash between two opposite ideas of governmental function:

"The case (said the Assistant Attorney General in charge) presents a conflict between the anti-trust laws enacted to prevent monopoly and the type of monopoly created by the government through the issue of patents. It is not an exaggeration to say that the case is one of the most complicated ever examined by this department."

On the one hand, RCA and its parent companies held a monopolistic position in the new radio industry which independents were denouncing as an illegal restraint of trade; on the other hand, Mr. Owen D. Young, the respected figure at its head, was arguing that it had only saved the whole radio business from a chaos of conflicting patent rights, and that if its use of its patents were in any way illegal the corporation itself would be the first to want to know about it. Suit was ultimately instituted in May 1930; it has now ended in a compromise, with the companies making no admission of illegality but opening the patent pool to the services of less restricted competition.

What, however, has happened to the industry in the meanwhile? Here is the case of an industry which the government has followed jealously from the cradle not, perhaps, to the grave but at any rate to a state of prostration. It presided at its birth and investigated at every subsequent stage. It failed, however, either to maintain that absolute free competition which the Sherman act theory would demand, or to secure that complete centralization which is supposed to smooth the business cycle and prevent the ills of overexpansion, stock speculation and collapse. The patent pool seems to have greatly assisted in developing the technical side of the industry; its financial and economic history, however, appears to have been quite as vivid as that of the most unregulated of the boom year industries. Finally, after the dizzy rise and fall, the government steps in about ten years late and insists upon unrestricted competition. As an essay in the social control of modern corporate enterprise, what could be more fantastic![28]

As for the settlement by the group of its own internal affairs, the current vulnerability of RCA was perhaps its greatest asset, and Sarnoff exploited it to the full. Of its nearly $18,000,000 of unfunded debt to the manufacturing companies, virtually half was canceled outright; against the rest GE, as the major creditor, was to receive the RCA building at 570 Lexington Avenue, valued for the purpose at $4,745,000, plus $1,587,000 in debentures; Westinghouse would receive $2,668,000 in debentures. In relieving RCA of this property—to which it would shortly move its headquarters—GE had also satisfied the new Rockefeller Center that RCA would be a reliable tenant and that the preferred shares it offered as compensation for a reduction in the space it was to have occupied should prove acceptable. And since all intercompany arrangements were subject to approval by the Justice Department, it was obvious that Sarnoff's proposals had had quite a gauntlet to run.[29]

That they emerged so nearly intact was by common consent a tribute first of all to Sarnoff's indomitable energy and negotiating skill, and second, to the unshakable support Young accorded him. Certainly Young's pride and satisfaction in comparing RCA's new balance sheet with that of December 31, 1931, and its unfunded debt, was obvious to his daughter and her husband when, on Sunday, November 20— best of all, bringing his wife—he paid his first visit to the old house in the Watchung hills to which they had just moved with their new daughter.

For the moment, it seemed, the human problems within the organization on which Young had reported some weeks earlier did not present any clear and present danger.[30] Nevertheless, the consent decree confronted Young himself with the hardest kind of choice: GE or RCA? He could have either but not both, and he had five months to decide. Apart from the personal equations already cited, RCA was very much his own creation; its precocity and more recent trial by fire had left its future much in doubt. The daring—and therefore tempting—course would be to stand by and take a hand in shaping its future, in contrast to which his role at GE seemed more like that of caretaker. This was duly noted in the press—for example by the *Herald Tribune*—and a few days later, George Harrison confided to Herbert Case that it would not greatly surprise him if Young chose the daring course.[31]

Shortly thereafter, Young took a step which suggested that he had by no means forgotten his conversation with Charles Neave; he got himself admitted, at long last, to the New York State Bar. Press reports of this event gave rise to a fresh spate of rumors: was he indeed about to become general counsel to RCA, or did he plan to resign as chairman of both companies to become their general counsel? Taking particular cognizance of rumors that Young might even resign as chairman of GE, the *Times* thereupon reported that these "were denied categorically by persons close to him."[32]

In the event, those "close to him" proved right. To his assistant Young confided that, considering the times, he had decided to do what the public would see as the "natural" thing; anything else would look quixotic. Known only to his wife—and Gerard Swope—was the perhaps determining influence of his own remaining indebtedness: $1,300,-000 to his broker; approximately half as much to the Bankers Trust Company; and $200,000 (which would just about cover the cost of the

Van Hornesville School's expansion) to Gerard Swope. The last, being unsecured, was the first to be paid off; assets securing the other two, now quoted at a fraction of their cost, had recently been buttressed by the assignment of most of Young's insurance policies—to which, in the following spring, his precious books were destined to be added.[33]

If Young still recalled the questions he had put to the graduating class at St. Lawrence only sixteen months earlier, he might well claim to have "enlarged [his] knowledge of obligations" even while his "capacity to perform them" was being steadily eroded. For his efforts to recoup, GE doubtless offered the surest foundation, but even at GE "extra compensation" was now a thing of the past, while basic salaries had twice been cut, beginning at the top. With prospects there so limited and his RCA salary about to be eliminated, with his wife's health precarious and his credit already strained, how could he ever hope to discharge these towering obligations?

Fortunately for his creditors, his faith that, given time, he would somehow find a way never flagged; fortunately for him they shared that faith. The true dimensions of his problem remained a closely guarded secret; other than Swope, his associates, like his children, were aware only that he, like others, was feeling the pinch. Still a "millionaire" in the eyes of the public,[34] he was presumed merely to be showing his own awareness of their all too common plight when he indulged—as he did early on—in a rueful jest or two about the mountainous burden of debt.

One such story, as reported to the *Washington Star* for September 15, 1932, goes back to those pristine days when the B & I Committees were still taking themselves seriously. A *Star* reporter, attending an all-day meeting of the Central Banking and Industrial Committee, had been impressed first of all by the atmosphere of grim determination that prevailed. "The job before them," he wrote, "was too serious, too tremendous for any attempt at levity. That is, until that lanky and friendly New Yorker—Owen D. Young—arose to speak."

Young, he reported, had been telling the conference that the prime purpose of the coordinated drive of business and government was to make more jobs. He also had been deploring and warning against exaggerated pessimism and its paralyzing impact. In the midst of his talk "a twinkle appeared in his eyes":

I can no better illustrate what I mean, [he said,] than to tell you a story I heard recently.

A man hard hit by business reverses met a friend of his one day and began to bemoan his plight.

"I am so badly in debt," he said, "my debts worry me so."

"Come, come," said the friend, "cheer up. It does not pay to be so depressed. Just imagine what you could do if you had all the money in the world."

"Don't joke with me that way," he replied mournfully. "My debts, my debts, they worry me so."

"But just what would you do," the friend insisted, "if you had all the money in the world?"

He thought for a moment, then replied in an even more mournful fashion: "I'd apply it to my debts—as far as it would go."

Chapter 31

Democratic Sweep
and the Interregnum
ODY, HH and FDR

F OR all Young's preoccupation with economic problems—national, corporate and private—the summer of 1932 afforded certain personal reminders that a political campaign of some consequence was under way. While Young told himself and others that his public posture would depend on F DR's stand on certain key issues, he had promised the governor that any call for help on a purely private basis would find him responsive. Less than a month after the Chicago convention the first call came—an "invitation" to Hyde Park for Saturday, July 23—and for reasons which perhaps included a test of Walter Lippmann's prophecy, Young was treating it very seriously indeed. Just how seriously is revealed in his son-in-law's Saturday morning transcript of what we choose to call Friday evening's undress rehearsal with the family on the porch at Riverside.

With his wife and the authors of this book playing the supporting roles, the curtain rises on Young removing his jacket, filling his pipe, easing himself into an underslung chair, and putting his feet up on the porch railing; business of striking two or three kitchen matches to get his pipe going properly while opening the conversation between puffs:

O D Y: Well, the Governor wants to see me.

J E Y: I suppose you know what you are going to tell him?

O D Y (stretching and sliding lower in his chair): Well, I've got two or three things to tell him. (Turning to E N C) You know I went over to see Floyd Carlisle yesterday. You don't know what it was about?

E N C (Shakes his head)

O D Y: Well, it seems that the utility people had a meeting after the Governor's article in *Liberty* came out. Carlisle said they decided that if the Governor was going to continue attacks of that sort on the industry they would have to oppose him and that they couldn't oppose him if Owen Young supported him. They concluded, therefore, that if Owen Young were to support him they could not give any more business to General Electric. Floyd said that he had been designated to break the news to me.

Here a pause to let this sink in, followed by a broad, slow smile; the smile suddenly disappears and Young becomes serious and animated.

ODY: This is what I said to him. "Well, Floyd, before we discuss this matter let's be quite clear about the basis of our discussion. The first thing I have to say to you is that my vote for the President of these United States is not for sale. The second thing I have to say is that if because of my vote or any of my activities I become a liability and not an asset to the General Electric Company I will resign and state the reason why. Now, if we are quite clear as to the basis of our discussion I am ready to talk to you."

Auditors exchange glances; Young takes stock of their reactions and, apparently satisfied, continues:

ODY: Then I told him that the Governor had asked me to come up on Saturday, that presumably one of the things he would want to talk to me about would be utilities, and that I thought I knew enough about the industry to be able to set him straight on a number of things. Carlisle replied very quickly that of course that would be fine and would undoubtedly take care of the situation.

So I thought over on the way out what I would say to the Governor if he asked me my views. This is what I am going to say. I am going to tell him that so far as I am concerned there are two fields in which my position is pretty well known, and where the American public have a right to expect that I will not compromise on any important article of my faith. These two fields are, first, the electrical industry, and second, the international situation. In both these fields I have a tremendous stake and a tremendous responsibility to the American people. I cannot ask the Governor in either of these fields to accept my views and to adopt them as his own. All I am going to say to him is that so far as they are concerned the question of whether I will support him or not depends not on me but on him, because in the nature of things I cannot support any views in these fields which seriously compromise my own. I shall not have to agree with all his views in other fields, because there one can balance the sum and if one is in general agreement that is all that is necessary.

Another pause for relighting of pipe while auditors prepare for an extended monologue.

ODY: So far as public utilities are concerned I am going to say this. Some of my associates in the industry are very much concerned over the article in *Liberty*. I read it three times. As an indictment of the industry it is no good. It is pathetic. It is less an indictment of the industry than of the writer. If you want to indict the industry I can tell you how to indict it.

You criticize it on the ground that bills to the consumer are too high. You propose to bring them down. The facts are that the household bill, which averages $30 a year, could not be reduced much more than ten or fifteen per cent if you provided the power free of charge. The real item of operating costs is service—installing and reading meters, repairing breakdowns, providing 24-hour service and so forth. Such an issue may be popular in a political campaign but it will be a boomerang if you are elected because you will not be able to deliver. If you really want to indict the industry why not indict its abuses? Look at this complicated system of holding companies, pyramided to the skies, where the assets of the sound operating company can be lifted out and put over into a bad situation full of watered stock. Look at the exorbitant service charges which they impose on the operating companies. That's the thing that ought to be indicted, and that kind of indictment which would reflect the statesman and the demagogue I would be quite ready to support.

Here Young pauses and says to Case in an aside, "That's the statement I should have made if I had been running. I would have had to go that far, to establish my independence and good faith and I would have been quite ready to because I have no sympathy with that kind of setup." Then, no one interrupting, he resumes.

ODY: I was also thinking over the foreign situation on the train and I believe I got for the first time a really clear understanding of what I had felt intuitively, namely the inter-relationship of debts, tariffs, gold movements and the fall in commodity prices. I think the statement that I make to the Governor will be something like this:

From the purely economic point of view neither the reparations nor the war debts are *of themselves* a major burden on budgets or taxpayers. They constitute too small a percentage of the total charges to be more than a minor factor in a reasonably prosperous world. When you introduce exclusive tariffs into the picture, however, what happens? Goods and services no longer flow freely; they stop at the border and are washed back. They meet a sign which says "No admittance." At the same time we demand full payment of the debts. Well, if they cannot be paid in goods, how can they be paid? The answer is in gold. Gold encounters no tariff barriers and is the only commodity which is admitted.

Now what does that mean as far as these debts are concerned in the realm of finance? Why, it means that gold is drained from the debtor countries and concentrated in the creditor countries in large bulk. Of course it soon exceeds the requirements of the creditor countries and is speedily sterilized. What is the result in a world functioning on the gold system? So far as the influence of gold is concerned, these huge sums that are sterilized might as well have been dumped in the sea. As a result the available supply of gold is seriously reduced. Suppose for the sake of argument, it is cut in half. The effect on commodity prices is obvious. Gold becomes so dear that the price of everything else in terms of gold is cut in half. As a result of the fall in prices it becomes no longer possible to do business at a profit. Trade stagnates because goods cannot move and the debtor countries can no longer make payments either in goods or gold. Then the whole credit structure which supports business is threatened, because it has been built up in terms of cheaper gold.

I think that gives us our present picture. Then debts become no longer merely a question of public psychology or sentimental resistance or nationalistic politics. Then their payment becomes virtually impossible and payments break down.

The real indictment of Republican policies during these post-war years is, therefore, that they have tried to eat their cake and have it too. If I were the Governor I would draw the issue there—namely, that you cannot expect to raise exclusive tariffs and at the same time collect the debts. You have got to give up one or the other. If you want to see the result of the Republican Party's refusal to give up one or the other, look around you.

Here Young stops and looks around; Case picks up the ball.

ENC: To my mind that's the only really illuminating statement on the subject I have ever heard. It not only deals with war debts. It deals with causes of the whole depression and really provides an agenda for any international conference which may be called. As you can see, I am most enthusiastic about it, but I have one criticism to make.

ODY: Well, out with it, that's just what I want.

ENC: It's too good for the Governor. (General laughter) No, I am more than half serious about it. It's important that such a statement be made well, and I really think you could make it better and more forcefully than anybody else. Moreover, it is appropriate that it should come from you.

JEY: In the first place, if you give it to the Governor he will mess it up.

ENC: Yes, precisely. In the second place, if he didn't mess it up but made it in that form—

ODY (laughing): People would ask who wrote it for him. (Thoughtfully) Well, I suppose there is something in that because he would not be expected to know the economics of it.

ENC: What I really have in mind is that you should say to the Governor, as you can quite honestly, that you are under great pressure to make a statement on this subject, and feeling that perhaps you should make one you wanted to take him into your confidence and let him know the kind of statement you would make. Then if he wished to deal with the political aspects of it and take issue politically with the Republican party on the question of debts and tariffs you would support him with a statement dealing with the economics of it. As your Assistant I am interested in that because I think it would be better for you, but I also think it would be better for the Governor and would have greater influence on the whole situation.

O D Y (after some thought): Well, I am not sure that you are not right. I'll think about it.

J E Y (getting up to go to bed): Well, I wish you joy tomorrow. I'm afraid it's a hard job to prop up a rag doll.

O D Y: These Republican cynics!

(Curtain)[1]

On that same Saturday morning, as Young was leaving for Hyde Park, Case had to return to the office on Banking and Industrial Committee business. Not until the following Wednesday did he have a real opportunity to ask his chief how things had gone. Press reports had not been notably illuminating, and his one clue to the outcome was Young's telegram to Bernard Baruch of Tuesday, July 26—which Young now described as telling the whole story.

He said the governor had been most cordial, but that he raised no question whatever regarding public utilities, nor, except in the most general way, about the foreign situation. He said that while their conversation was most friendly, he could not avoid the feeling—though perhaps this was not just—that the governor was avoiding real issues with him, that he not only failed to ask his views but did not want to hear them. When he left and got into the car he had felt quite depressed about their conversation and asked himself why, if the governor did not really want a frank discussion of important questions, he had invited him to come up. The only answer he could find was what he had given in replying to Baruch, namely, that it was useful for advertising purposes.

Case mentioned the "profound discouragement and disillusionment of the intelligent people [*sic*] in my generation so far as Roosevelt was concerned," saying that he felt the unanimity of it was striking. Young's response came quickly. "Yes," he said,

but your people are in a minority when it comes to the millions who will respond to the idea of a "new deal." I still think that Roosevelt is likely to be elected. Of course it doesn't increase one's faith in the processes of democracy if the hard and sober work and devotion which Hoover has given to his job, and the courage which, especially recently, he has shown are to go unrewarded. Still I am not sure in my own mind that Frank Roosevelt might not make a far better president than Herbert Hoover. After all, he is conscientious, serious-minded, and has a most intelligent wife.[2]

There were other calls, moreover, which found the governor just sufficiently outgiving to keep this particular friend in line. To quote Case's notes for September 19:

Mr. Young left today to attend the convention of the Association of Edison Illuminating Companies at Quebec. Before leaving he told Miss Morrison that she could say to an inquirer (and for general consumption) that Mr. Young had not seen the speech which Governor Roosevelt was sche-duled to make on the power situation. . . . Miss Morrison asked him if that meant that the Governor had not consulted him about the utility situation. Mr. Young said "Ah, that's a different matter. That wasn't the question you asked me before." Then, after a pause, he added "Yes, we did talk some about the utilities." Miss Morrison then suggested that perhaps this only left him in the same position as the various railroad officials whom the Governor had seen prior to his speech on the railroads—they had been consulted during the preparation of the speech, but none of them knew what the Governor finally decided to say. Mr. Young agreed that that was exactly his situation.

Others, however, were less patient, as Case's notes for September 13—also based on the testimony of this alert secretary of Young's—make abundantly clear:

Yesterday evening Mr. Young attended the dinner held in celebration of the fiftieth anniversary of the opening of Edison's first central station here in New York. He told Miss Morrison today that he sat next to Governor Smith. During the dinner the Governor turned to him and said "I see you've been visiting our friend the Governor at Hyde Park."

"Yes," said Mr. Young, "I went up to see him."

"Well, what did you think of him?"

"Oh, we had a very interesting talk. One of the things we talked about was when are you coming out in support of him."

"Hell," replied Governor Smith, "I want to know what he's going to do. I want to know how he stands on the bonus; I want to know how he stands on the sales tax; I want to know how he stands on the tariff. God damn him, he won't give me a peg to hang my hat on!"

ii

The grim determination noted by the *Star* reporter at the Central Banking and Industrial Committee's mid-September meeting was all very well, but all was not well with the committee. With Young in-creasingly preoccupied with the Radio suit and Henry Robinson with Hoover's campaign for reelection, the leaderless B & I Committees were losing much of their zip, and it was becoming an open question how and whether this could be recovered. From one point of view, Young might better have proceeded to carry out his planned resignations; from another, this might have come to look like abdication under fire. His earlier as well as his latter-day involvement in Samuel Insull's tangled affairs was now subjecting him to damaging charges, including some echoed by such responsible sources as Josephus Daniels's *Raleigh News-Observer.*

Young's letters of resignation, it will be recalled, were dated September 22; next morning the press carried a Chicago report featuring a list of Insull's so-called preferred investors, Young prominent among them. Charging that these men had bought into Insull Utility Investments early in 1929, at a price far below any public quotation for that year, the report implied that they had reaped large and largely unfair profits. The smaller print did state that at the time they contracted to buy, the stock had yet to be issued and that they were pledged to hold their shares for two years and a half, or sell them back to the corporation. Next to nothing was said, however, about their role as underwriters of a new and untested issue, or the losses actually suffered by Young and others who had loyally held their allotments.[3]

But with press and public eager for scapegoats, such niceties were apt to be forgotten or ignored, and Young's reputation for fair dealing ("Has this man no weaknesses?") made him a peculiarly inviting target. Daniels, indeed, had deliberately turned the spotlight on Young in order to ask what could be expected of ordinary mortals when a man of his character had shown himself so willing to accept "something for nothing."

For the moment, Young declined public comment but did write Daniels, whose good opinion he valued, a personal letter reciting the facts: How, in December 1928, Insull had called on him to say that his control of the properties that he had devoted his life to building up was now being threatened by speculative raiders. How he (Insull) was responding by setting up a new investment company that would take over his large family holdings and, supplementing these by public subscription, should be able to turn back the raiders and secure his family's continued control. How, having been asked to join on a modest scale in underwriting this new venture, Young had agreed to a fifty-thousand-dollar allotment, arranging with his office, before leaving the next month for the Paris conference, to make payment as the shares were issued and received. How nothing had been said about the price of these shares to which—since any sale was not to be thought of—he had paid no further mind. How he knew nothing of any "preferred" list, nor, having gone in to help a friend and customer, was he now about to cry over his losses. He simply wanted to tell Daniels the whole story, of which he could then be the judge.[4]

That was all very well, but before the year's end there was more to come. And in the meantime, thousands of "judges" who knew only what they read in the papers—or their headlines—were rendering their own verdicts. Nor did Young's year-end testimony in court concerning his efforts to stave off the Insull bankruptcy do much to change or even temper these verdicts. To the contrary, even his motives were to be impugned.

If Young's involvement in Insull's affairs was thus to bring him nothing but trouble—in seemingly endless installments—the reopening in New York on October 3 of the so-called Federation Bank and Trust Company rightly afforded him the kind of inner satisfaction which was becoming all too rare. Though the reopening was no doubt the work of many hands, those who had helped the most were first to insist that but for Owen Young it would never have been achieved. And this verdict, at least, was never questioned.

Certainly the event was a happy break in the tragic chain of failures which had followed the closing in December 1930 of the Bank of U.S. And because for some months after Herbert Case's surgery of the following spring, it had seemed all too likely that he himself might be a belated casualty of that frustrating battle, Young had been called upon, as already noted, to do double duty at the Federal Reserve. Partly on this account, but chiefly on his own, he had devoted considerable time to a critical examination of the various plans put forward for reopening the Bank of U.S., none of which, alas, passed muster. For any closed bank, the reason was always the same: the need for new capital, and who was to provide it? The commercial banks would not; the Reserve banks could not. As for the individual investor, what returns could an ailing bank offer that began to match his multiple risks? Nor was the Reconstruction Finance Corporation any panacea; its loans were designed to keep going concerns going; a bank already closed was out of bounds.[5]

Nevertheless, as Young's labor friends persuaded him to scan the balance sheet of the closed Federation Bank and outlined the remedial steps they were prepared to take themselves, he began to see in their plight an opportunity that was also a challenge. This bank, though relatively small, was a depository of organized labor's funds; indeed, unions which were AFL members had helped to organize it. To facilitate its reorganization, depositors had already agreed to cancel or defer 30 percent of their claims, thus providing (among other things) $500,-000 of new capital. Toward the $1,500,000 of additional new capital stipulated by the banking authorities, labor interests and certain philanthropically minded individuals were now pledging $500,000 themselves. What, then, about Young's concern for industry's unemployed capital and putting it to work? What if he could tap that source, for the remaining $1,000,000, beginning with GE?

Even before the close of 1931, Young was putting this to the test. By February 23, 1932, when he wrote A. W. Robertson for a Westinghouse subscription, he already had in hand the pledges of eight companies for $650,000; Robertson's response raised the total to $700,000.[6] By early summer Young had reached his goal, only to find that the planned reopening had been compromised by the continuing decline in the value of the assets. By early fall, however—thanks largely to the summer's upturn—values had recovered sufficiently for the bank to reopen, which it did with a modest flourish. Not least important was the fact that the bank's new president, Jeremiah D. Maguire, Jr., had himself put up $250,000 of new capital and so had a personal stake in its success.[7]

For Young, the happy outcome of this effort was it own reward. Except for the November issue of the photoengravers' union journal, the press had little to say of the part he played but it was known to those who counted, in industry and labor, in banking and legal circles, and of course in the Treasury Department. And it was bound to give a lift not only to labor but also to General Electric and the Federal Reserve —even perhaps to the half-becalmed B & I Committees.

Nevertheless, on the increasingly dismal banking and industrial scene, it was the merest flicker of light, and so far as recovery was concerned neither of the presidential campaigners—now going at it hammer and tongs—was doing much to help. Young still held himself aloof but he was not only disgusted but angered by Republican warnings that Roosevelt's election could only mean "grass growing in the streets." And so, on the eve of election day, before a huge crowd in the Metropolitan Opera House (not counting the radio audience) Young finally pocketed his reservations and made a powerful speech for Roosevelt.[8]

Beginning with the international situation, he repeated what he had said for Smith in 1928—the importance of electing the liberal party, to replace suspicion with confidence abroad. He attacked the Republican administration for vacillation and indecision, which "induced a false prosperity in the twenties and a very real catastrophe in the thirties which came near pulling down the whole economic structure of the world." This was no time for threats, he said, "but the President of the United States and his supporters have not hesitated to predict what would happen to securities and business if he were not elected. . . . We are told by the Republican party that it is dangerous for the United States to make a change." But, said Young, when the manager of the plant comes to think he is indispensable, it is high time for a change. Praising Roosevelt's very different "spirit of approach," he stated once more his abiding faith in American democracy: "What I hope for in this election is a true reflex by votes, uninfluenced by fear or favor, of the intelligence and intuitions of the great masses of our people. . . . What we need is a full and free and honest indication of how the millions of this country feel inside themselves."[9]

iii

The millions lost no time in making that clear, Roosevelt's sweep exceeding even Hoover's of 1928. But whether or not mid-1932 might have marked a definite turn in the economic cycle, at home and abroad, "but for the whim of the political calendar in the United States," it was in the postelection period that the truly whimsical aspects of that calendar were about to be demonstrated.

In "ordinary" times, no doubt, there was something to be said for a mandatory four-month interregnum during which a defeated and outgoing government might wind up its affairs in orderly fashion, while the victors engaged in unhurried preparations for the takeover. In critical times, as Senator Norris had not only foreseen but taken steps to remedy, it constituted a kind of power vacuum that no people could afford. And although the Norris-sponsored constitutional amendment to reduce it by half and get rid of the "lame duck" session of Congress had been approved by the Congress on March 3, 1932, ratification by the states occurred too late to make it applicable to the present crisis.[10]

Of Hoover as a lame-duck President, it must be said that he recognized the existing hazards and did what he could to minimize them. But it has also to be said that certain of the hazards were of his making—notably the impending threat of a general default on the Allied war-debts payments due December 15, the first to become due since the inception of his one-year moratorium. How deeply he may have regretted that he had not declared it for at least two years, we shall presumably never know; as he once told his friend Julius Barnes, "no President must ever admit he has been wrong."[11]

But that could not alter the fact that this President was now in deep trouble. In their joint communiqué of October 1931 he and the French premier Pierre Laval had agreed that the expiration of the moratorium would doubtless require some further (if temporary) agreement respecting intergovernmental debts, with the Allied powers expected to take the initiative and "at an early date." Though Hoover had avoided any firm commitment, this communiqué had almost inevitably been construed as a promise to talk turkey once the Allies took constructive action on German reparations. Unfortunately, as noted earlier, proposals for a prompt Allied initiative had encountered French resistance, and by July, when the Lausanne Conference finally convened, Hoover was embroiled in his own campaign. Thus the Allies' tardy conclusion that nothing less than an end to reparations would suffice to meet Germany's crisis—now political as well as economic—found Hoover otherwise engaged. No doubt his attention was duly called to the face-saving stipulation specifying a token payment of 3 billion marks (about $715 million) payable over the next three years (and never paid). But he did not fail to note the "gentlemen's agreement" making these concessions contingent upon similar treatment of the Allied debts on the part of the United States.[12]

For Hoover this was too much. His earlier proposal following Laval's visit, that Congress reconstitute the War Debts Commission, had not only been rebuffed, as noted; Congress had thereupon refused even to ratify the Hoover moratorium without adding gratuitous declarations against any further concessions whatever. That this hardly helped to avert default now that the moratorium had expired was only too obvious; so was the fact that the virtual cancellation of reparations had drastically reduced the Allied debtors' capacity to pay. On the other hand, having denounced the Young Plan's "annex" by which the Allies promised Germany a generous share in any relief the United States might one day grant them, Hoover was not about to be coerced into forgiving our debtors because—contingent on our doing so—they first forgave their own. Debt reduction was, after all, a matter of bilateral negotiation, and certainly the negotiating power of the United States would be greatly enhanced if the outgoing and incoming administrations were now to join hands.

Hoover's consequent invitation to confer found F D R not so much unresponsive as cagey. He would go, but he would go with Raymond Moley as adviser and without commitments in advance. The lame-duck Congress, including its Democratic leaders, was still opposed to further concession on the debts; to cooperate now in pulling Hoover's chestnuts out of the fire might be to compromise both F D R's influence with the Congress and his future freedom of action. And this, he felt, Hoover would not scruple to compromise where other issues too were at stake. Besides, he had no wish to be a "pre-President": until March 4, responsibility for action was all Hoover's.[13]

Except for a courtesy call at Roosevelt headquarters on election night Young had yet to see the new President-elect. Nevertheless, he had a pretty fair notion of the kind of approach which would find him most responsive. When, two days before the White House meeting of November 22, his assistant complained that F D R had not consulted him

on this of all questions, Young expressed mild surprise that he had not
sent Moley to see him but added that a more direct approach was
ruled out by the certainty that this would be regarded as tantamount
to an offer of either Treasury or State.[14] He went on to say that Ogden
Mills, fresh from the White House, had called him on Friday the
eighteenth to get his views on Hoover's next steps, which he proceeded
to rehearse as follows:

> Well, I said, there's no need for me or anyone else to tell you or the
> President what you ought to do, because that must be obvious to all of us.
> Clearly there must be postponement and some means of future discussion
> in our own interest. The President has a God-given opportunity to make
> a ringing statement on the situation which, regardless of Congressional ac-
> tion, will have fine repercussions abroad and be a real educational force at
> home. If Cleveland could make a place in history by his statement about
> gold, faced with this opportunity the President is really playing for a
> prominent place in history with the dice loaded in his favor. It is seldom
> that one's selfish personal interest and the welfare of the country are so
> completely in accord. Don't let him muff it, Ogden, and for God's sake
> write the statement yourself.
> Furthermore, the President should ask Roosevelt just one question. He
> should say "You have pointed out to me that immediate action is my re-
> sponsibility. I agree. I intend to act and I have only one question to ask
> you. This matter must come up for final settlement in your administration.
> How long do you wish me to make the postponement?"
> Such a proposition could not be turned down by the Governor, and
> as a matter of fact Democrats might be glad to have this issue postponed
> so that they would not have to deal with it at the very outset of the new
> administration.[15]

But Hoover, it appeared, had no stomach for an approach at once
so simple and so direct, nor was he prepared to let his successor off the
hook with a single question. Instead, at their White House meeting of
November 22, he elaborated his views on the complex interrelationship
of debts, disarmament and world recovery—and urged Roosevelt to
join him in the selection of a commission for dealing with all three. If
the response evoked by this approach was, for Hoover, predictably
unsatisfactory, who then was to blame?[16] Too disheartened even to
point the finger, Young's only comment on the outcome of this much-
advertised meeting at the White House was that it had "brought forth
another mouse."[17]

Two days later, on November 25, when T. W. Lamont called to ask
what advice he should give regarding debt payments by Great Britain,
Young replied, as he put it, "by anticipating events in the order of

their undesirability." Heading this list was "adoption of the President's brilliant suggestion that payments be made in sterling [than which] nothing could have a more unsettling or disastrous effect on the stability of currencies." Next to that he named payment by shipment of gold—which would persuade the American people that Britain's cries of distress were so much bluff. Then came default—which would at least lead to future negotiations and convince people that anything salvaged was so much gain.

Least undesirable, Young told Lamont, would be "a British offer to issue serial notes for the amount of the December payment. This would indicate . . . the desire to meet the obligation and . . . the impossibility of discharging it now. Future negotiations could then be conducted without prejudice." Young was so clear about this that he repeated it all to George Harrison when the latter called, at the instance of Mills, to get his views.[18]

A week later, after reading the British reply, his assistant expressed surprise at its evident rejection of this suggestion. Not true, said Young: not only did they welcome it, but through Lamont had conveyed their appreciation; the "present hitch is that Mills is insisting on the right to sell the notes in our markets immediately"[19]—which to the British must have seemed a stab in the back.

But it took a visit to Van Hornesville to produce Young's most original suggestion about the debts, which his assistant set down on paper on the very day he heard it (December 3). Admitting that he had come up with a "pretty good idea," Young had thought, he said, of writing Will Rogers as follows:

Dear Will: I see by the papers that you are interested in collecting the foreign debts. Obviously that is not a very easy thing to do, and so I want to tell you how I think it could be done.

You know, of course, that when we made these loans during the war we didn't ship our gold abroad—in fact we sent no money out of the country at all. What we did was to establish a credit in our banks here for the purchase by the Allied governments of American goods which they needed and which we produced. As they took our products they drew on their credit to pay for them. Therefore it was not our money but our goods which we shipped abroad.

Now they say to us it is difficult to pay because it is hard to ship the gold in such large quantities from one country to another. If you really want to see the debt paid, therefore, why not suggest that payment be made in the same way in which the loan was made; why not suggest that they establish a credit to our account in their banks for the purchase of their goods? That would obviously be fair because the two transactions would be precisely equal. Then all you would have to do would be to indicate the kind of goods which the American people, of whom 10 million are unemployed, would like to see imported from abroad in quantities large enough to discharge the debts. Then you would have solved the problem.— Very truly yours—

Not surprisingly, this delighted Case, who suggested that where a serious statement might increase the tension, this should actually relieve it. He further suggested that Young proceed to draft such a letter at once, to be signed and dispatched at the first likely moment.

Young thought a bit, then shook his head. "No," he said, "it's no good until we can learn whether or not they are going to pay on December 15, because if they do pay there's Will Rogers' answer."[20]

As for the December 15 payment, harassed Britain saw it as a Hobson's choice at best. Facing the stiffest repayment schedule of all the debtors, and having so lately been forced off gold, Britain had felt entitled to special consideration and so had hoped to make a separate plea. To this France not only objected but also applied coercion in the form of a threat to disrupt the Lausanne agreement if Britain did so. And when a joint appeal got nowhere, it was France (and Belgium) which defaulted, while Britain (and even Italy) contrived to pay.[21]

It was not until after the trauma of this partial default and painful payment that either the President or the President-elect sought Young's advice, and then it was the latter. On December 17, Hoover made another major effort to get F D R's cooperation on the same trilogy of problems. Apparently the White House not only dispatched a long telegraphic plea to Albany, but also sought to enlist such presumably influential Democrats as Lewis W. Douglas as emissaries of persuasion. It was not, however, at Hoover's prompting but at F D R's own invitation that Monday, December 19, found Young in Albany lunching with the governor. This visit lasted for three hours, and since Roosevelt and his aides were deeply engaged in drafting a reply to Hoover's message, one can fairly assume that Young was invited to take a hand and did.

Certainly this assumption finds support in Moley's call on Young next day, for help in drafting a reply to an even later Hoover message—this one occasioned by Roosevelt's response of the nineteenth. And since this time Hoover was urging F D R to designate "Owen Young, Colonel House or some other member of your party who is possessed of your views and confidence" to sit down with his White House advisers and try to clear the way, Moley would hardly have summoned Young—to the quality of whose help he gave high marks— had he doubted where his helper's sympathies lay or found him eager for this dubious assignment. As for F D R, we have it on Moley's authority that on December 23 the two leading candidates for secretary of state in Roosevelt's book were Owen D. Young and Cordell Hull.[22]

i v

Early in December, Herbert Case (now virtually recovered) reported to his son an exchange he had had with friends who had expressed the hope that Young would have an important post in Roosevelt's cabinet. He had told them, he said, that much as he would relish Young's being in the cabinet, he rather felt he could be even more useful if he were not. Reporting this to his chief as an interesting echo of Lippmann's letter, Young's assistant confessed that he had come to the same conclusion, and had even advised inquiring friends that the reasons dictating Young's withdrawal from the presidential race must be equally applicable to a cabinet post. Nodding his assent, Young had gone on to say that he "only hoped the Governor would not invite him, so that he would not have the onus of declining."[23]

At the time, and for some weeks thereafter, an invitation from that source seemed altogether likely. In the summer of 1931 Roosevelt had written Samuel Bertron, a private banker of Young's acquaintance, that "one thing we need is a real Secretary of State such as Owen Young or Newton Baker, in place of Henry Stimson." Shortly after the election, and Young's eloquent plea for *his* election, F D R told Adolf A. Berle that of the elder statesmen, only Young had "an adventurous mind." To be sure, he worried lest Young's close association with the utilities antagonize Republican progressives like Norris, and he had given Moley the impression that "he didn't feel he could run around in his mental carpet-slippers in Young's presence." Nevertheless, as late as December 23—and of course unknown to Young—the balance, as already noted, seemed to be tilting in his favor.[24]

In the meantime, beginning on the Friday and Saturday preceding his Albany luncheon, Young was being subjected to a kind of trial by fire: first in court, then—and far more heatedly—in the press. Samuel Insull, the great utilities mogul, now dethroned and defrocked and under indictment for embezzlement, had fled the country, thus establishing his guilt beyond peradventure in the court of public opinion. And this was the man whom Young had first exchanged favors with and then vainly tried to "save."

On this theme Young's interrogators—chiefly the attorneys for the rank and file of Insull's creditors—rang all the changes. As an "insider" who had been on Insull's "preferred" list, Young was clearly in Insull's debt; how else explain his readiness, in December 1931, to lend two million dollars "of his stockholders' money" to a customer whom he must have known to be all but bankrupt? And hadn't he subsequently conspired with the bankers to stave off the Insull companies' bankruptcy until such time as the general creditors' lien on the new collateral which the banks kept demanding had expired? Why else had they waited until mid-April?[25]

All this came through to the reporters loud and clear; not so the rejoinders of the witness who suddenly found himself a kind of unwitting defendant. He could and did explain, as he had to Daniels, the nature of his own original investment and his ignorance of any "preferred lists." He could and did protest that GE had traditionally—and profitably—helped its good but hard-pressed customers with timely loans, amply secured as this one seemed to be. He could and did insist that not until the following February, when at Insull's request he had first met with the bankers, had he become aware of any threat of bankruptcy. And he could and did dismiss with scorn any suggestion of a conspiracy to thwart the rights of creditors whom, indeed, he had been seeking to protect.[26]

Those who heard him out were few. This time it was not *his* words but those of his accusers which made the story—with one notable exception. Following his testimony of December 17 at Insull's bankruptcy hearing, Young had done the unforgivable by speaking charitable words about that same archvillain. He too privately deplored Insull's flight to Europe but was very much aware that, far from selling out to save his own skin, Insull had invested—and lost—his entire fortune in these same securities. Nor did Young relish striking a man when he was down. Thus his gratuitous and widely published comment to the reporters on leaving the hearing: "After all, the most you can say of that old man is that he had too much confidence in this country and his own companies."[27] (So of course had Young, but the losing bets he had placed in 1930 were purely personal and private.)

For the press, in its role of public censor, Young's comment was too much. While even the *New York Herald Tribune* made caustic editorial comments on "the large way of Mr. Young," the editors of the *Nation* promptly expressed their horror and dismay over his moral callousness, with the promise of more to come. And in their first issue of the new year—January 4, 1933—this promise was more than redeemed.[28]

Ostensibly wringing their hands over "The Loss of Owen D. Young," the editors proceeded to administer to this latest "fallen idol" a verbal castigation which was more suggestive of relish than of sorrow. And this was even more true of Norman Thomas's featured (and well-advertised) attack in their next issue, the most temperate and telling point of which was his conclusion that in the light of Young's iniquitous behavior "the new capitalism seems to be much the same sort of glorified racket as the old."[29]

That Norman Thomas, the widely admired if thrice defeated Socialist candidate for President, should have seized the opportunity to buttress his case against capitalism was, no doubt, fair enough. If, in the process, he assumed the dual role of prosecuting attorney and judge, that was no more than the *Nation's* editors had done. This time, Young wrote no letters, private or public, to the editor, even though Oswald Garrison Villard's father, as an early director of GE, would certainly have known of Charles Coffin's practice of trying to save his distressed customers and would hardly have expected Coffin's successor to do less for a former officer and large customer who had been an acknowledged leader in the industry. Such letters as he did write—to complaining stockholders or anxious friends like the Reverend Frank Oliver Hall—were more expository than defensive, even reflecting some bewilderment that his efforts, when he was apprised of the danger, to avert so major a catastrophe should have been so widely misconstrued.[30]

To his assistant, Young's one comment on the whole affair was shrewd enough: certainly he had been hurt by his involvement but far less than he would have been had he shied away and refused all help. What rankled as much as anything, perhaps, was that the deference which it was natural for him to show a respected and dominant figure, some fifteen years his senior, should have been misread—notably by the *Nation*—as "terror" of the man. To those who knew him, any such suggestion was simply silly. But some of them were nonetheless puzzled by Young's readiness to "go along" with Insull's original, and defensive, holding-company scheme, which seemed to lend itself to the kind of pyramiding Young was known to deplore.

This puzzle was resolved in part by Young's own obvious puzzlement over the tangled web with which he found himself confronted when, in February 1932, his help was sought. Called to testify again in February 1933—this time before Senator Peter Norbeck's Investigating Committee—his testimony was at once more telling and more searching, and so considerably more revealing. From the questions of Ferdinand Pecora there developed at one point a discussion of the holding company, its virtues and its dangers, especially the latter in such a witches' broth as Insull had finally brewed:

Mr. Pecora: When you refer to the structure of the Insull companies as being a very complicated one, will you tell the Committee just what you mean by that?

Mr. Young: Well, I confess to a feeling of helplessness as I began to examine, in February 1932, the complicated structure of that organization.

Mr. Pecora: Did you find that it embraced a large number of companies of various kinds?

Mr. Young: Great numbers of operating utilities, with holding companies superimposed on the utilities, and holding companies superimposed on those holding companies, investment companies and affiliates, which made it, as I thought then and think now, impossible for any man however able really to grasp the real situation. . . . And if I may add: I should like to say here that I believe that Mr. Samuel Insull was very largely the victim of that complicated structure, which got even beyond his power, competent as he was, to understand . . . you could not possibly get an accounting system which would not mislead even the officers themselves of that complicated structure.

Questioned then as to how this kind of situation could best be averted, the witness was ready with his answer: "I should like to see us work toward the final objective of not having more than one holding company superimposed on operating units in the public utility field."[31]

This exchange thus had a constructive outcome, and in the meantime, the very violence of the *Nation's* earlier attack had made it something of a boomerang. Though that liberal and righteous journal could "not conceive that, after these recent episodes [Young] will be considered available for further public service," his name over the next month was topping the lists in press speculation concerning the next secretary of state. That this was no longer true of Roosevelt's private list, Young had no way of knowing.

Few did. It is a matter of record, however, that on January 3, 1933, one of the two names that had topped this private list just ten days earlier was struck off: Hull's remained. By that time the *Nation's* issue of January 4 would certainly have reached the newsstands; in any event an advance copy would probably have reached the President-elect. The latter's apprehensions lest Young's appointment might alienate the Norris progressives were well known; on the face of it, the *Nation's* blazing thrusts would seem to have administered the *coup de grâce.* Cartainly F D R kept his own counsel, and even though pro-Young reporters like Frank Kent had mentioned the Insull affair as lessening any likelihood of his appointment, few seemed to be taking this seriously. Thus as January drew to a close, with the graph of his popularity clearly on the rise, and Clinton Gilbert writing that the quality of the cabinet depended on his heading it, Young became increasingly concerned lest he receive an invitation which he was in no position to accept but could not refuse without seeming to rebuff his old and newly eminent friend.[32]

On January 25, Young took a final and decisive step. However ironic, in retrospect, its timing now appears, his letter could only have come as a relief to F D R, who was enjoying a brief respite and welcome therapy at Warm Springs, Georgia. This is what it said:

Dear Frank:

On May 16 last, I wrote a letter to my friend John Crowley, up in Little Falls, of which I enclose a copy. It is all history now and has no bearing on anything except to enable me to say that the reasons which were so controlling then "as not to be open to argument" still exist.

Justification for this letter can lie only in our personal friendship. The reason for it is my great desire to avoid adding to your problems not only by any affirmative act of mine but even by my silence.

Sincerely yours—

On February 6 came F D R's reply. Dated February 1 at Warm Springs, it read:

My dear Owen:

I can only tell you that I am deeply sorry that the reasons which were not open to argument last spring are still in existence. I know, I think, the deep personal anxiety through which you have gone, and I can only tell you that I admire your courage and your devotion. Don't ever forget, however, that I count, and shall count, on you in many ways not only for advice and information but also to help out the Government in specific and general matters which are bound to arise.

As ever yours—

Young's letter had been released to the press on January 30; even after that his name kept appearing on cabinet lists, with the idea that he would certainly be drafted by the President-elect. Young knew better; Roosevelt's attitude toward him was always somewhat ambivalent. Friends since the days of the formation of R C A in 1919, they had never been close. Aware too of the political dilemma posed for his friend in appointing or failing to appoint him, Young suspected that his letter had been read without tears. Nor would he have been surprised to hear, as perhaps he did, that with Young at State, Roosevelt felt he would not be able to run foreign affairs himself—as he doubtless intended to do. Nevertheless, to be sure, Young wrote the letter.

A few days later, after a meeting of the National Broadcasting Company's Advisory Council, Elihu Root came up to Owen Young and, putting a hand on his shoulder, said, "My boy, you can decline more public offices which have not been offered to you with greater success than any one I have ever seen."[33]

Part V

*New Deal
and
Government Ascendancy*

1933–1939

Chapter 32

Roosevelt at the Helm:
The Hundred Days
and the Bombshell

Pᴜʙʟɪᴄ response to Young's latest refusal of "a public office which had not been offered" him tended to be less kindly and more acerbic. Dismayed and perplexed, his devoted admirers felt let down and many of them said so. If Senator Norris and Justice Brandeis were content with private expressions of their undoubted relief, not so Paul Anderson of the *Nation*, whose scathing comments were resumed in its issue of March 1. Nevertheless, Young's own relief was still the more palpable, for having escaped what he felt could only be for him at this point the crushing embrace of politics.

He had reason for relief on other counts as well. For better, for worse, both reparations and the Radio suit had now been *finally* settled; soon, perhaps, this would also be true of these vexatious Allied debts. (His own would take longer.) In any event, another few days would bring this disastrous interregnum to an end, with ꜰᴅʀ officially and actually taking charge; and this, Young hoped with all his heart, would make all the difference.

Best of all, his Jo had been steadily gaining strength and confidence. When, two evenings after Christmas, Rockefeller Center's much-touted Music Hall had opened with great fanfare, she had actually accompanied him to view the Rockettes—her first appearance in public for almost two years. And she had proved to be all the better for it.

For both there was satisfaction too in the stark fact of the center's completion—one constructive effort, providing work for thousands, which had not been blighted by a veto in Owen's ʙ&ɪ Committee or even by the city's fiscal squeeze. True, the committee could claim no credit for it—that belonged first and last to John D. Rockefeller, Jr.— but the popular nickname of Radio City was at least a reminder of the ambitions which Young had first entertained for it. If key elements of that vision—the new opera house and Philharmonic Hall—were missing it was not for want of effort; as attested by his succession of appointments with Otto Kahn and Myron Taylor (for the opera) plus master contractor John R. Todd (to keep plans flexible), Young had not given up easily. Just how the Music Hall, with Roxy in charge, was now to bring cultural riches to the masses was unclear, but there it was and by this time Young was ready to relax and enjoy it.

Not surprisingly, then, he welcomed the proposal of his daughter and her husband (whose Washington stint now seemed about over) that he join them on the visit to friends in Havana which they were tentatively planning. To get away from it all, the inauguration included, was a wonderful idea; after all, it was nearly two years since he had had a real holiday. But it was Jo who really made the whole thing possible; not only *must* Owen go, she said, but to be sure the Cases could, she herself would take care of their four-month-old daughter, her namesake, who would be good company for her. "After all," she added, to end all argument, "the baby is weaned and we both have our nurses."

And so it was arranged. The Cases' prospective host, Burnham Carter, was private secretary to the American ambassador; his wife, Jane, home for a visit, would return to Havana on their ship. As for Owen, he would put up in style, he said, at the Hotel Nacional. And by way of speeding their departure, the New York papers for February 11 carried front-page reports of the Young committee's "comprehensive plan for restoring New York City real estate to a sound basis through the refinancing of mortgages." This would be carried out, said the *Times*, by the newly organized Realty Stabilization Corporation, with ten million dollars of capital and William Church Osborn as its civic-minded head, armed with promises of cooperation from the banks, insurance companies and the RFC. Not a bad swan song—should that prove to be in order—for Young's Banking and Industrial Committee.

But in booking passage for February 16, the party of four had failed to take account of the absent Insull's lengthened shadow. That same day, and the day preceding, found Owen Young before the Senate committee in Washington to offer the testimony (already cited) on the bewildering maze of the Insull holding companies and the urgent need for measures to prevent any such proliferation. No one, of course, could have anticipated the near tragedy that rocked the nation on the evening of the fifteenth when, just after landing in Miami from his fishing trip, FDR narrowly escaped an assassin's bullet and the mayor of Chicago, who was near him, did not. That the hearing was resumed next day gave evidence of a determination to carry on as the President-elect was doing and asking others to do. Shaken as he was, Young could do no less.[1]

The hearing over, Young was inclined to agree with the *Herald Tribune* that this time he had come much closer to doing justice to himself as well as to Insull. While the *Nation* remained caustic, there was widespread acclaim for his declaration that for even the largest utility system the goal at which to aim should be a single holding company. According to the *Times*, the utilities themselves were now asserting this as their ideal—a report which Young could only have read with raised eyebrows.[2] Indeed, his luncheon guest of ten days earlier—his old and respected acquaintance, Bernard Flexner—has left a record of the views they exchanged on Insull and his fellows in which both despaired of the present generation of utility magnates, and even doubted their capacity to compromise, as they must, with the inevitable.[3] This conclusion did not, however, stop Young from continuing to urge them to do just that.

By the evening of February 18 the Havana-bound party was enjoying the comforts and seclusion of the Panama-Pacific's S.S. *Virginia*. Young, already relaxed, was content to bask in the company of his junior fellow-travelers, who—not excluding Jane Carter—were finding him excellent company. To him, if not to his daughter and son-in-law, the Caribbean was wholly new. All three now found it enticing enough to warrant further exploration. Soon after their arrival, with an assist from the embassy, accommodations were booked on a small cargo boat, the *Presidente Machado*, due to sail early in March for other Cuban ports and Puerto Rico. They were to be the only passengers, and the prospect was exciting.

But Young had first to get clearance from G E, R C A, and the Fed, as well as Jo's doctors. Asked to take care of this, Gertrude Chandler radioed on Friday, March 3, that only George Harrison had held back. Shortly thereafter Harrison phoned to say that the banking situation had become so critical that, unless it improved overnight, the United States would be forced off gold. Young replied that if by morning the party was going to be over, he was disposed to proceed with the trip.[4] And so, in forgathering next morning (March 4) in Young's rooms at the Nacional to listen to Roosevelt's inaugural address, the younger members present were still hoping against hope that the trip was on.

Reception was less than perfect, but most of the President's message came through clearly—especially his ringing words of assurance that "we have nothing to fear but fear itself." But his courage was contagious and Young was deeply moved. "When I think," he said, "of that boy [F D R was fifty-one, O D Y fifty-eight] facing the job he has to tackle at such a time and in such a magnificent spirit, my hat is off. . . . As I heard him, it was all I could do to keep the tears back." And when the others suggested that if he felt that way, the President might like to know it, Young's response was to send him the following radiogram forthwith:

I listened with eager interest and high hopes to your inaugural today and both were satisfied. The thrilling note of leadership and the courageous determination to meet a crisis within the limits of the Constitution impressed me more than anything that has happened in my time. It is the constructive program of the future rather than an indictment of the past which will secure for you the unified support of the people and so of all parties which is so vitally needed now. I send you, Mr. President, my heartiest congratulations, my best wishes, and within my limitations my tender of the best aid and support which I can give.[5]

Just before lunch Young talked again with Governor Harrison and decided to go back on a ship sailing that night. So, reluctantly, did the others. Evidently, Young reported, New York had finally fallen into line in declaring a "bank holiday," which the President would now make nationwide. Clearinghouse certificates were ready to be issued as a temporary currency; the country would not actually go off gold but there would be an embargo on gold shipments. During the previous two days, the New York Fed had paid out to the interior banks nearly a billion dollars in currency and its reserves were down to 22 percent. (They had been at 60 percent when the adventurers had left New York a fortnight earlier.)[6]

On Tuesday morning, March 7, Theodore met the returning travelers at the dock, reporting that the two girls they had left behind them were "doing fine." One of New York's finest, recognizing Young, inquired with a broad grin whether he had brought any money back with him. "Not a cent," he was told. "Well, Mr. Young," said the cop, "I guess your credit is still good." Smiling back, Young shook his head and said, "Don't know what I'll do if it isn't."[7]

It soon became clear that the cop's cheerful attitude was typical of the spirit pervading the city. The new President had done well; almost overnight he had established himself as a leader whom the people felt they could trust. In William E. Leuchtenburg's perceptive words, it was this plus "the very totality of the bank holiday [which] helped snap the tension the country had been under all winter. 'Holiday' was a delightful euphemism, and the nation, responding in good spirit, devised ingenious ways to make life go on. . . ."[8]

Nevertheless, time pressed, and the dimensions of the problem confronting the treasury and the Federal Reserve were truly formidable. For both, the preceding week had been frantically busy. Harrison, from

Washington, now reported to Young that recommended procedures for action had narrowed down to two: (1) the classification of all banks (some seventeen thousand) with immediate reopening of those certified as sound, or (2) the reopening of all banks, with initial restrictions on withdrawals—say at 50 percent—and a federal guarantee of deposits up to that amount. Harrison inclined to favor the former but said he was "so tired that he hardly trusted his own judgment." Others, Harrison reported, were even worse off, with Melvin Traylor "completely broken and useless and [Governor] Meyer petulant and uncooperative," but former Treasury Secretary Mills, still there, was proving "a tower of strength." Apprised of this report at luncheon that same day, Herbert Case confided to his son that on the day before the banks had been closed, Traylor's First National of Chicago had lost $100 million in deposits. And certainly Meyer's long-running battle with Hoover had left him physically and emotionally exhausted.[9]

Meanwhile, refreshed by his own brief holiday, Young asked Harrison to report to Treasury Secretary William Woodin that he was back and ready to come down if he could be of help. Before taking over the treasury at FDR's behest, the charming but frail Woodin had been president of American Car and Foundry, and, as a director of the New York Fed, one of Young's good friends and admirers. At the New York Fed, where Young's return was warmly welcomed, he was speedily immersed in sorting out and assessing proposed solutions. Herbert Case, as chairman, had drafted an agenda in rough outline which Young pronounced "the most sensible plan that I have seen." Beginning with a proposed declaration by the President of his determination to balance the budget, and urging the maximum use of checks in lieu of currency—especially in paying taxes—Case's plan embraced the second of the two options but with notable additions. First, in consideration of the government guarantee, all banks of deposit, state as well as national, were to become members of the Federal Reserve. Second, and assuming substantial agreement on the foregoing, the treasury should move to issue on March 15 one billion dollars in long-term $4\frac{1}{4}$ percent bonds, which, to hoarders of gold and currency, should have an irresistible appeal. Beneficial in itself, the success of such an issue might encourage conversion of earlier series, bearing the same coupons but shortly due to mature, thus relieving the treasury of another pressing problem.[10]

At two the directors were called into special session and approved the chairman's plan. But next morning's message from Woodin made it clear that Washington had opted for the other course and was looking to each Federal Reserve bank to classify all banks in its own district and certify the soundness of those to be reopened. This message caused consternation, with Case even threatening to resign. In view of the erosion of the past six months, he said, no man could certify the current soundness of most banks, and any list he was prepared to sign would be not only dangerously small, but notable for certain conspicuous omissions. Following another special meeting of the directors, Case was persuaded to transmit the requested lists but with a series of caveats included. This, it was hoped, would convince Washington of the folly of its course; but when Harrison loyally sought to reopen the question with Woodin, the latter finally threw up his hands, saying, "This way madness lies." So, Young reported after hearing Harrison out, that was that. There was no time to retrace steps already taken; for better, for worse, they must follow the lead.

This meant that the lists of banks to be reopened must be greatly expanded if the all-important confidence of the public was to be sustained. Fully aware of this, Young nevertheless threatened to resign himself when it appeared that the treasury might be dictating to the Fed which banks it was to certify. At the same time, he asserted that the Fed would clearly be minimizing the risks if, *of its own motion*, it were now to give key banks, in generous numbers, the benefit of the doubt. And at length, doubts and apprehensions having been largely dispelled by the President's bold economy message, and the swift response of Congress, it was so ordered.[11]

On Monday, March 13, with few and relatively minor exceptions, the Reserve city banks reopened; on the fourteenth and the fifteenth others on the "certified" list followed suit. Here, especially among the smaller country banks, casualties were not inconsiderable; but the very fact that numerous banks were not initially certified as sound enough to open lent credibility to the certifying process itself. Meanwhile, losses to depositors were relatively small, largely localized and, in cases where new capital was secured, temporary only.[12]

What the astonishing success of this delicate operation owed to the twenty-hour days of feverish activity put in by officers and staff at the treasury and the entire Federal Reserve System, no one who was not, in some sense, a party—or at least privy—to it all could possibly comprehend. But, however indispensable, all of the anxious sifting and sorting and decision making which these labors entailed could not, of themselves, have assured its success. That the public actually celebrated the reopening of the "certified" banks by depositing far more than it withdrew—and incidentally returning much hoarded gold—was essentially a triumph of confidence; and for that the President, not least by means of his Sunday Fireside Chat, could rightly take full credit. With even the financial capital now unstinting in its praises, Franklin D. Roosevelt stood, for the moment, as the unchallenged and indomitable leader of a united and grateful people.[13]

ii

The story of the famous "Hundred Days" that followed, and of the unfolding, then and later, of the New Deal in all its alphabetical—and increasingly controversial—ramifications impinges on this biography chiefly as Young himself became involved, whether as participant, critic or apologist. Of his role as participant, it can be said that it bore little resemblance to Walter Lippmann's generous prophecy, nor indeed to his own involvement in the councils of previous administrations. Was Woodin's failure to respond to Young's offer to come down perhaps the signal of F D R's determination to get along without him? Not necessarily. Young had been absent when the party started and there was no time for briefing late arrivals on what had gone before.[14] Nevertheless, as Roosevelt made successive and sometimes fateful decisions with no pretense of seeking Young's counsel, the question was bound to recur.

Asking himself, then, whether his chief was finding this a source of relief or a bitter medicine, Young's assistant tentatively concluded that it was both. But outward signs, certainly through the Hundred Days, continued to suggest that relief, not bitterness, prevailed. For one thing, the demands of the last two years had left Young bone tired, and if Gerard Swope's Washington involvement—notably with the National Recovery Administration—indicated an exchange of their customary roles, he was content to stay behind and mind the store. And Jo.

Moreover, in the President's program and more especially in his dauntless leadership, Young was finding much to cheer about. Having dramatically demonstrated its ability to control its own expenditures, the federal government had moved promptly to draw upon its newly strengthened credit resources to relieve the unemployed—so far as possible through making public jobs available. Strongly reminiscent of Young's plea of a year ago, this program's focus on youth, through creation of the Civilian Conservation Corps (c c c), was to Young especially heartening. So was the declared purpose of the Agricultural Adjustment Administration (a a a) to correct at long last the disastrous imbalance between farm and industrial prices. As for this act's so-called Thomas amendment, delegating to the President various inflationary options, this looked a good deal safer than leaving them to Congress.

Far from opposing, then, the President's assumption of extraordinary powers, Young quoted approvingly William Hard's wry suggestion that "it is better to go somewhere with a man than nowhere with a mob." He was amused by the *Times*'s editorial of March 10, recalling his February statement at Notre Dame about the possible temporary need to vest such powers in the President—the one item in that speech which had been roundly criticized—especially as the *Times* now went on to say that whether or not Young was responsible, we had certainly found a way. Nor did he criticize the President's action of April 19 in "taking the country off gold" by refusing to license its export; indeed, on the very day preceding, he had answered an inquiry from Senator Arthur Vandenberg by suggesting that of all possible inflationary measures (*reflationary* was becoming the preferred word) this step was clearly the least dangerous, and letting the dollar seek its own level might afford many advantages. Young's letter did stipulate, however, that the refusal to license gold exports should not apply to the "earmarked" gold held by the Federal Reserve Bank for the account of foreign central banks. Like Roosevelt, Young was currently looking for the least dangerous means of making it possible for the mass of debtors to meet their obligations, if only to prevent wholesale repudiation or bankruptcy. Because of the burden of his debts, however, Young had also to satisfy himself that any "reflationary" measure he espoused was first in the public interest and only incidentally in his own. In this instance he found reassurance in Walter Lippmann's—and J. P. Morgan's—public endorsement of Roosevelt's move.[15]

True, Young differed with the President on certain priorities: with ten or twelve million still unemployed, he felt that reform should wait upon recovery. Yet he explained to a GE colleague, equably enough, that the President was proceeding "on the theory that confidence could not be restored until [certain] situations were exposed and cleaned up." And significantly he added that "the excursion of government into business is not because the government wants . . . it, but because business invites it—and business being paralyzed the public approves."[16]

Thus he refused to join the rising Wall Street clamor against the Truth-in-Securities Act; little more than a year later he was to welcome the decision of his son Philip to join the staff of the Securities and Exchange Commission. As for the proposed Tennessee Valley Authority (TVA), he saw it as a bold and imaginative move, marred only—and deplorably—by the President's insistence upon duplicating existing power lines rather than selling to the utilities "at the baseboard." And if Young, as Roosevelt had initially, kept his fingers crossed on the so-called National Recovery Act, with its elaborate bureaucratic codes for the governance of business, September nevertheless found him making a nationwide plea for business cooperation in testing it out. The National Recovery Administration's embattled chief, General Hugh Johnson, had been insistent that he do this and perhaps he felt he owed that much to Swope as well as to the President. But as he confided to Ida Tarbell, his heart was not really in it. Only Title II of the act, with its ambitious program of public works, made the whole thing palatable; strengthened and reconstituted, this program was happily destined to survive the N R A's demise.[17]

Meanwhile, the early demise of the Banking and Industrial Committees relieved Young of what had become a thankless burden. Early in February, Adolf Berle had explored with Young's assistant their possible continued usefulness as agents of recovery, especially if F D R were to ask Young to serve as chairman of the central agency in Washington. Case's response had been at best lukewarm. In his view—and, more important, in his chief's—the significance of this particular "co-ordination of instrumentalities" now rested primarily in its demonstration of the impotence of business leaders to take concerted action, even when it was required by their own agenda. Not only did Young agree; he had come so far as to assert that if the economy were ever to get off dead center, some way must be found to coerce these recalcitrant and fatally obstructive minorities. If this meant invoking the powers of government, wasn't this, perhaps, what the New Deal—and even the N R A—was all about?[18]

Thus it was agreed that if anything of value was to be salvaged from what was left of these now-dormant agencies it would probably be found in the *ad hoc* studies of the experts who constituted the Young committee's able and increasingly frustrated staff. This suggestion, with its possibilities for quick action—on slum clearance, cheap housing and public works—Berle was conscientiously exploring when the banking crisis exploded, incidentally sealing the death of all committees on which bankers figured. Not until May, when Randolph Burgess of the New York Fed was called in to advise the framers of the N R A bill's section on public works, and so asked Everett Case for a memorandum summarizing the B & I staff's most promising projects, did these proposals reenter the picture as unheralded but by no means unwelcome reinforcement. By September, work on New York's Triborough Bridge was being resumed, the R F C was stepping up its aid to the railroads, and the new Home Loan Bank was doing far more to refinance homeowners' mortgages than had the new corporation set up by the Young committee, for all its promises of wide cooperation. But slum clearance and cheap new housing, for whatever reasons, continued to languish.[19]

iii

Never keen on volunteering advice to those in authority, Young had volunteered this quotable comment to his assistant as early as March: "I would like to go through these four years without having made any requests whatever of the Administration." RCA, however, had no such inhibitions, and had promptly petitioned the new attorney general, Homer S. Cummings, for permission to have Young remain as director for the two and a half years in which, under the decree, GE was not to compete in the radio field. On its face an entirely reasonable request, which the former assistant to the attorney general, John Lord O'Brian, and Judge Olney were reported ready to endorse, and Oswald Schuette of the independents was actively supporting, it was publicly denied shortly before the end of the month.

M. H. Aylesworth was particularly incensed and Young was perturbed that his friend Cummings had apparently failed to consult even the implacable prosecutors of the case. But to all the urging of his friends that he appeal the decision, Young turned a deaf ear. It was, he felt, a straight political decision, and as such could hardly be reversed. Even if it could have been, he told his assistant, "I don't think I could afford to have it reversed." So that was that.[20] Some five weeks later, on May 4, having reviewed and confirmed his earlier decision to stay with GE, Young resigned as director of the company he had created at the behest of the last Democratic administration. What this cost him is at least suggested in his acknowledgment of the resolution adopted by the RCA board at its June meeting.

Dear David [he wrote Sarnoff]:

I have often wondered whether the retention of consciousness after death was a thing to be hoped for or deplored; think of all the things that would be said of you, kindly and not, and then worst of all, a quick but enduring silence when one is forgotten.

After reading the resolution of the board of the Radio Corporation of America and looking back with rather misty eyes at the signatures of them who formerly were my associates in that undertaking, I am persuaded that a conscious interval of about twenty-four hours after death would be most satisfying.

In any event, I thank you and the Board for your generous testimonial and send you and them my affectionate good wishes.[21]

Earlier, Young had written Newton Baker that the latter's election to succeed him had almost reconciled him to resigning.

Two days later, at 9:30 on the morning of Thursday, June 8, Young was at the White House, to keep his first appointment with *President* Roosevelt. Of this much his calendar informs us. To what, or to whom, this appointment was owing, and as to what if anything might have come of it, the authors have no clue; the question does not figure either in Young's papers or the press, nor yet in any of the Roosevelt biographies we have scanned. That it had anything to do with the signing on June 5 of the bill abrogating the so-called gold clause from all contracts, public and private, we dismiss as most unlikely. Nevertheless, its context, especially in the light of the critical international problems now confronting the President, makes it a peculiarly teasing puzzle, not least because, so far, the President's "spirit of approach" had more than vindicated Young's November predictions.

On the following Monday, June 12, the World Economic Conference was scheduled to open in London; Secretary of State Hull and his mixed bag of U.S. delegates were either there or on the way. Meanwhile, at Geneva, after months of frustrating effort, the disarmament conference was floundering badly. Hitler, invested with full dictatorial powers on the day after F D R's inauguration, had officially denounced Versailles and all its works; German rearmament (already under way) would become official unless Geneva could come up quickly with a parity program satisfactory to him. Ostensibly to confer with the President on the economic conference—as Ramsay MacDonald and Edouard Herriot had done earlier—Hjalmar Schacht had appeared in Washington as Hitler's envoy and not so covert apologist. Alleged mistreatment of the Jews by the Nazis, he told Roosevelt and Hull in early May, had been greatly exaggerated by the press; thus any protests from abroad inspired thereby could only be counterproductive. As for the economic conference, his contribution was to warn the President that Germany was about to stop payment in foreign currencies on its external obligations, thus in effect defaulting on the two billion dollars of federal, local and industrial securities held by American investors. Roosevelt's strong if tardy protest occasioned nothing more than a few days' delay in making this effective.[22]

But if the President's sudden action of April 19 in taking the country off gold had taken the wind out of MacDonald's sails (he was then on the high seas, Washington-bound), Roosevelt's subsequent conferences with him, as with Herriot, had abundantly confirmed all that he had said—and he had said a lot—about the imperatives of making both conferences succeed. To be sure, they had not got far toward settling what Stimson called "those damned debts"; Roosevelt told them that this country would need a lot of educating first. But he also said nothing to indicate that the educational process might be working the other way. Thus Young had reason to feel that his own Philadelphia speech of May 15, in which he belabored previous administrations for insisting that our allies meet the letter of their bond, and then making its performance "utterly impossible," might be helpful to the President where help would be most welcome.[23]

Indeed, even as Young spoke, Roosevelt was eagerly awaiting word of the effect, especially on Hitler, of his bold message "to the world" appealing to the heads of all states to take off their coats and work together for genuine disarmament. And (not forgetting the other conference) to work for currency stabilization, the freeing of world trade, and the raising of price levels and living conditions everywhere. Certainly Roosevelt was living up to his pledge of being a good neighbor, even to the point of authorizing Norman Davis to assure other members of the World Disarmament Conference—in effect the League of Nations—that whenever, acting in concert, they pronounced a state guilty of aggression, and took measures against it, this country would, if it concurred, "refrain from any action tending to defeat the collective effort . . . to restore peace."[24] This, Young felt, was going pretty far, but recognizing, in view of the stakes, the President's perhaps salutary courage in offering such a pledge, Young kept his own counsel about it.

On the twelfth he had dictated to Woodin a letter suggesting the kind of trade-off we might offer Britain at the London conference; probably because he felt it wise to keep hands off, this note was never sent. A week later, on May 19, the press reported that Roosevelt might ask Young—along with Hiram Johnson, California's insurgent senator—to join the American delegation. Johnson declined; Young, to his unfeigned relief, never had to. On the twenty-second, a Washington dispatch reported that "it seems that the President wanted Young to go but on the basis of available information it was indicated that he could not go." Amused by this, Young confided to his assistant that he welcomed anything that took him off the hook; at this stage, an invitation from the President would have been a major embarrassment either to turn down or to accept.[25]

On May 26 Young's reservations about the President's disarmament message finally surfaced, but only in the presence of his current assistant and John Elwood, now an N B C vice-president. William Hard, a foremost correspondent and friend to all three, was sailing that night to represent N B C at the World Economic Conference; what, he wanted to know, did Owen Young regard as the critical questions at issue? According to Case's notes, dictated the same day, Young's reply was "substantially as follows":

I think the first question that Hard ought to ask himself . . . is whether the Economic Conference is dependent upon the success of the Disarmament Conference. Assuming that he finds the answer to be yes, then perhaps that suggests why the President has gone so far as he has in committing this country to assume such responsibilities abroad. . . . In virtually giving up our neutrality rights and yet retaining independence of action, [we would be] going further than to join the League, because if the League condemns a certain nation as aggressor, members have the protection not only of joint action but of joint decision; whereas a non-member, deciding independently, must bear a fearful onus and its decision is second only to a declaration of war.

Now I point this out not to raise any bogies, but because it suggests an approach that is worth examining. If the Economic Conference cannot succeed unless the Disarmament Conference first succeeds then the President is not making these overtures or committing us so far merely to aid Europe in keeping the peace, but actually to restore employment at home and make domestic recovery possible. That is something the people can understand, and unless they do . . . I am really fearful that we shall have another fiasco here similar to . . . Wilson's. [But] if it be true that disarmament underlies the economic problems, and if other nations are actually altering their armament program and framing their economic program on the basis of our commitments, then it would be nothing short of criminal for us to repudiate them. So if I were an observer I would want to look very carefully into that.

As for the economic conference, he continued, currency stabilization was basic, and France might well insist on settling this first. Here, recommendations were the job of the central-bank people, and they should have them ready.

Next, I would assume that on the question of ratio of the pound to the dollar, England's stake in the export trade was, after all, so much greater than ours that she would probably feel that a relatively low ratio was a real necessity. On the other hand, with our great domestic market and the terrific pressure of our domestic debts, a rise in prices is important to us. I would suppose, therefore, . . . that this whole question would turn around some such settlement as this: We, recognizing England's paramount interest in the ratio, might resolve doubts in her favor there, provided that she was willing to leave to us the question of the degree of inflation— and of course that would involve the pound as well as the dollar—of the currency units needed to establish higher prices. [This was the substance of Young's unmailed letter to Woodin, which at the time FDR would presumably have endorsed, at least in principle.] I mention that only so that Hard may have some criterion by which to test developments, because it would not surprise me if that was the way it went.

Case had one question. Suppose, he said, Hard found that the shoe was on the other foot, and the success of the disarmament conference depended primarily on the success of the economic conference, as Walter Lippmann had apparently decided. What then? "Well," Young replied, "that is what I would rather expect one would decide on examination. In that case the Disarmament Conference should be suspended pending the success of the Economic Conference."[26]

So much for Young's views. Had the President been giving serious thought to the relationship of London to Geneva, Young's analysis would have been his for the asking at their meeting of June 8. We find nothing to suggest, however, that the President sought his views and much to indicate that he did not.

iv

In the meantime, the ongoing Senate investigation of banking practices and conduct, led by its redoubtable counsel, Ferdinand Pecora, was further discrediting the public image of the "economic royalists," beginning at the top. That the interrogation of J. P. Morgan and others disclosed no illegal acts was beside the point; for the press and public, what counted was first of all the news that none of the Morgan partners had paid any federal income tax since 1929. (Neither had Young, but he was not interrogated.) Next Pecora unearthed a series of Morgan's so-called favored lists, on several of which Young's name appeared, and now made the headlines. The first, a veritable who's who of business and the related professions, plus certain political figures, recorded those invited (in 1929) to buy at twenty dollars (the cost to Morgan and Company) common shares in the new Alleghany Corporation, then priced by the market on a when-issued basis at a figure some twelve to fifteen points higher. So that was the way things went behind the scenes! Of what use to point out, as their spokesmen did, that the Morgan firm never made public offerings of common stock, and in this instance were simply helping to make a market for new issues in which they had an interest by placing in "responsible" hands—at cost to them—some part of their own holdings? All that the ordinary citizen could see in these revelations was the picture of how it was that the rich kept getting richer, while he was losing his shirt.[27]

If Young was puzzled—as he was—it was not by this public reaction. Nor was it by the disclosure of his *invitation* to subscribe for five thousand shares; after all, this would have been only natural at the time when he and J. P. Morgan were sailing together to "settle" reparations. He simply had no recollection of taking up these Alleghany shares, then or later; nor when his financial secretary was asked about it, did she. And if Miss Chandler, who wrote his checks and took scrupulous care of his accounts, had neither paid for these shares, nor even seen them, what was all this fuss about?[28]

More important, what was he to do about it? Issue a public statement denying that he had actually subscribed? No, for that would be to assume a holier-than-thou posture, first toward Morgan's and second toward the select company of those who had subscribed. He doubted that the public had shed any tears for William McAdoo, Newton Baker and Norman Davis when they cited their actual losses on this stock. In addition, he would have to be certain that he had never responded to any such offerings, or his denial of any part in them could easily prove a boomerang. No public statements, then; it was better to sit it out.[29]

But Pecora was by no means finished. By May 31 he was exploring the Morgan firm's late entry—in '28 and '29—into the burgeoning utilities sector. The disposal of its Electric Bond and Share stock in 1925 had left GE with no important utility holdings except for Mohawk-Hudson, into which GE's Schenectady power plant was tied. In June of 1928 J. P. Morgan and Company had shown sufficient interest in this property to warrant GE's proposing a sale of its 359,000 shares at $40 a share. Based on net earnings and the current market, the price was admittedly high, and Morgan would not buy. By fall both earnings and the market price had risen and, rejecting a Morgan offer to buy for less, Young and Swope stood by their original price—with interest added. On December 5 the deal was finally consummated on that basis, with Morgan also agreeing to buy preferred shares and option warrants held by GE's Employees Securities Corporation—payment to be made on or before January 15, 1929. GE's profit, as added to surplus and duly reported to its stockholders, was $13,471,402; the Employees Securities company's profit was $1,100,000, aside from its 2 percent interest in GE's.[30]

Those were the facts and Pecora did not dispute them. He did ask, however, whether by December 5 the market price was not already some three million dollars higher than the figure stipulated in the deal, adding that by the date of actual payment (January 10) it had risen a further twelve million. Didn't this suggest, he wanted to know, that Morgan, after all, was given a bargain? There were other and obvious explanations for this 1929 market's behavior, but some reporters, quick to catch the drift of Pecora's queries, were more interested in this loaded question than in the underlying facts, and so were the less-responsible editors. Thus in the *New York Evening Journal* for June 1, an article signed by its star reporter not only treated the deal as phony but bore the heading WORKERS' 12 MILLION DOLLAR LOSS BARED IN POWER DEAL. True, the text itself did not fully live up to the head-line, which disappeared from the later editions; even so it was a notable exercise in willful journalistic distortion.[31]

If Young was perturbed, his assistant was outraged, and immediately set out to draft a long letter designed to set the *Journal*—and its read-ers—straight. He thought he had done well until Young told him, kindly but firmly, not to waste his time. "You might as well learn," Young added, "that there is no use getting into arguments with the newspapers . . . first because no correction can really catch up with misrepresentation—especially in the headlines—and second because newspapers always have the last word."[32] But Young himself had not been idle, having already prepared a statement of the facts—not as a press release but for possible use in correcting either the committee's records or the misapprehensions of his stockholders, and especially the workers in the plants. And it might have other uses too, for on June 2 the press—including the *Schenectady Union-Star*—featured a list of those to whom, in 1929, Morgan had allegedly sold at $25 per share Niagara-Hudson stock then quoted at $36. This time Young was down for 6,000 shares, which looked like ample confirmation of Pecora's sug-gested *quid pro quo*. But here again neither Young nor Miss Chandler had any recollection or record of any such subscription on his part.

Ten days later, however, Young again was named (with Woodin, Norman Davis, Gerard Swope and two-score others) as having bought from Morgan's, back in 1927, 1,000 shares of Johns-Manville at $57.50—some 8 to 10 points below the then current quotation. This time Chan's records confirmed it, and the same year's federal income-tax returns (which she had prepared) further recorded its sale at a profit which would have been handsome even if it had been bought at the market price. With Chan's recordkeeping thus apparently vindicated, and our own exhaustive search disclosing nothing to impugn it, we can only conclude (1) that in terms of his actual investments, Young's name belonged on the Johns-Manville list and not on any of the others; (2) that he had nevertheless been right to refuse any public statement.[33]

v

In any event, June had its compensations. Aside from creating the NRA, public works and all, Congress's last act before adjourning on June 16 had been to pass the Glass-Steagall bill of 1933. Designed first to require commercial banks to divorce their investment affiliates, this measure had gone on to provide comprehensive deposit insurance and consequently to require all insured banks to become members of the Federal Reserve by January 1936. At least for the moment, Young could feel that his 1931 plea for a unified banking system had not been in vain. And everyone, beginning with the President, could now feel that a breathing spell was very much in order.[34]

Well before Roosevelt was free to take off on what was to prove his fateful seafaring holiday, Young was embarked on a round of commencements. It was not his year for honorary degrees, but on the sixth he had been on hand to congratulate Josiah Stamp on his Columbia award, leaving next day for the White House meeting of the eighth. On Monday the twelfth came St. Lawrence, which that year commanded special notice for reasons only partly academic. Present were the New York Giants (of nostalgic memory to one of the authors), incidentally to play the college team an exhibition game but chiefly to see their number-two pitcher, Hal Schumacher, receive his well-earned bachelor's degree. Ogden Mills, the commencement speaker, received an honorary degree and so did the poet Edwin Markham. But best of all for Owen was the B.A. degree awarded *in absentia,* and *nunc pro tunc,* to Jo.[35]

Nine days later he himself was the commencement speaker at Radcliffe College, of which Jo was a bona fide graduate and trustee. Business, he told the seniors, had failed to discipline itself, and so there was no escape from some political control. But before turning the kitchen over to the "lovely lady who talks so easily and so gracefully," he wanted to be sure that she could bake the bread. Responding to Dr. Finley's characteristic note of praise, Young said that he "did wish to suggest a note of caution in this . . . adventure of ours into that great unknown . . . without saying anything that might be embarrassing either to the Administration or to our worried representatives overseas."[36]

Finally, on June thirtieth, both authors were at Riverside to join Owen and Jo in celebrating their thirty-fifth wedding anniversary. Young and his assistant came out together on the train, the latter having taken in charge the two bottles of champagne which the faithful Tom Gairy was waiting at Grand Central to deliver. It was so hot that Young asked Case what he was "going to do if the heat popped the corks." Also, at Young's suggestion, they sat in the smoker, "where," as he put it, "if that happened, we would . . . at least avoid spraying the new spring hat on the head of the Greenwich Temperance Society."

Scanning the evening papers between glances at their precious package, Case reflected that his chief had more reasons than one for celebration. Since the banking holidays, when Young's precious books had been stored in a warehouse as collateral for his loans, recovery had been phenomenal. The Federal Reserve index of production had climbed from 60 to 100 (old series, 1923-25 = 100), with the Dow Jones stocks moving up even faster. Factory employment had increased by some 23 percent, payrolls by 35 percent. Capital goods and heavy equipment were, of course, the last to be affected, and for the first half of 1933, GE's sales and net income had been well below the corresponding figures even for 1932. Nevertheless, for the second quarter as opposed to the first, orders received were up 40 percent, and the company's future was looking definitely brighter. And so, no doubt, was Young's.[37]

True, a cloud or two had recently appeared, no bigger than a certain man's hand. If recent reports on the London conference were sufficiently disquieting to those who wished it well, the President's cavalier responses to inquiring reporters from his schooner, *Amberjack II*, and his summer home at Campobello were becoming even more so. Now, the conversation having turned to guesses in the press about the "real" message which, as the President's special envoy, Raymond Moley was carrying to London, Young confided that on the preceding day he had himself sent a message to the President from the Federal Reserve Bank. Based on reports that instead of joint action by the central banks, each armed with a stabilization fund, Moley was now to propose that the Federal Reserve should itself protect the dollar temporarily from falling below $4.25 to the pound, Young's message had warned that such unilateral action would require "an irrevocable Treasury licence to export gold and that the moment gold was exported it would be assumed that the dollar had reached its low. . . . Whereupon, there would be a rush of shorts to cover . . . the dollar would have a tremendous rise and the Fed, in order to check it, would have to assume the risk of large purchases of foreign exchange. . . . It was this risk," Young concluded, modestly enough, "that I felt the Federal Reserve should not assume."[38]

In their walk home from the train, the conversation touched lightly on the diverse and even contradictory views imputed to the President by the several reporters present at Campobello. Young was moved to suggest that the next day's statement by the President would probably propose no currency stabilization or international action at all, but only a program of "unilateral cooperation." But when, three days later, this lighthearted if caustic prediction proved all too accurate, Young was not so much sobered as stunned. On July 1, his interpretation of Ernest Lindley's apparently "inspired" piece in the *New York Herald Tribune* was that the President was not opposing concerted action by the central banks but at the same time wanted to create the public impression that the dollar was not about to be stabilized. He assessed this as an "exercise in tight-rope walking, which so far has been highly successful and might continue to be if he doesn't fall off." In handing his assistant, however, the early edition of the *World-Telegram* for Monday, July 3, this mix of admiration and apprehension had given way to a curious "deadness" in Young's whole attitude. "Maybe," he said at last, "maybe you can understand what the President means in this message. I have read it three times and I confess I can't."[39]

Speedily christened "the bombshell," the message in question had been dispatched, appropriately enough, from the cruiser *Indianapolis*. "I would regard it as a catastrophe," the President began,

amounting to a world tragedy if the great Conference of Nations, called to bring about a more real and permanent financial stability and a greater prosperity to the masses of all nations should, in advance of any effort to consider these broader problems, allow itself to be diverted by the proposal of a purely artificial and temporary experiment affecting the monetary exchange of a few nations only. Such action, such diversion, shows a singular lack of proportion. . . .

I do not relish the thought that insistence on such action should be made an excuse for the continuance of the basic economic errors that underlie so much of the present world-wide depression. . . .

The sound internal economic system of a nation is a greater factor in its well-being than the price of its currency in changing terms of the currencies of other nations.

It is for this reason that reduced cost of government, adequate government income, and ability to service government debts are all so important to ultimate stability. So, too, old fetishes of so-called international bankers are being replaced by efforts to plan national currencies with the objective of giving to those currencies a continuing purchasing power which does not greatly vary. . . .

Let me be frank in saying that the U.S. seeks [that] kind of dollar. . . . That objective means more to other nations than a fixed ratio for a month or two in terms of the pound or franc. . . .[40]

Reading this far, Case pinched himself; surely he must be dreaming? If not, what kind of sea change had the President undergone? Wasn't it in his fireside chat of early May that he had promised the "full cooperation" of the United States in realizing the four great objectives of the two world conferences: reduction of armaments, cutting of trade barriers, reestablishment of "friendly relations" and "stabilization of currencies in order that trade may make contracts ahead"? Now, having repudiated Hull's initial efforts to cut trade barriers, he was blasting all hope of a stabilization agreement, however innocuous, apparently lest it hamper unilateral efforts of the United States to raise domestic prices through depreciation of the dollar. Worse still, from a good neighbor, was the tone in which he proceeded to lecture all parties to the conference—while taking a sideswipe at "old fetishes of so-called international bankers" and heralding his own new fetish: the so-called commodity dollar.[41] As for reduction of armaments, Young's question to Hard—whether Geneva depended on London, or vice versa—was no longer moot. With economic cooperation now a casualty of American intransigence, what could disarmament expect at Hitler's hands?

Young, too, was lost in thought. When his assistant finally ventured the remark that "the worst of it is not that you don't understand what the President means but that he doesn't seem to understand it any too well himself," Young nodded. "Certainly he has shown such capacity," he said, "for stating clearly what he means when he does understand it that your assumption is a fair one." And when asked who, in Moley's absence, would vet such a statement before it was released, Young replied that he was lunching with Bernard Baruch and might find out. But Baruch, who—at Moley's suggestion and Roosevelt's request—had been standing by to advise on developments at London, reported that he had known nothing about the message until he read it in the papers and that the same was true of Norman Davis, the President's representative on disarmament.[42]

Monetary Experiments and the Federal Reserve

IT WAS not until late on the evening of July 5, 1933, that Young really unburdened himself, and then it was only in his home. Returning to the Riverside house at about 10:30 after dining out with friends, his daughter and her husband found him still up and in a mood to talk. As recorded next morning by Case the talk proceeded from the domestic to the global, substantially as follows:

O D Y: Well, in between listening for the baby—and I did not hear a peep from her—and taking the dog out—because he really requires more direct attention—I listened to Mr. William Hard this evening. [N B C broadcasting from London].

E N C: I am glad the baby didn't interrupt. I would like to have heard Hard tonight. I bet he was interesting because at last he could let go and more or less speak his mind.

O D Y: He was *very* interesting. He really gave a great picture of the situation there, a first-class job. Apparently there was not any word from Baruch or Harrison? (Looking at me; I shook my head.) I was rather expecting I might hear something from them. You know yesterday we formulated a little message to the President which they were going to send to him. We urged as strongly as we could that he spare no pains and leave nothing undone to keep France from going off gold, because such action on her part would inevitably reverse the trend of the dollar and so check the rise in prices and imperil the whole domestic recovery program. The effect might be so strong that he would actually have to use the inflationary powers of the Thomas amendment to counteract it, but that in turn might create such apprehension as to invite disaster . . .

E N C: Well, I am glad that you sent that message, whether or not it has the desired results. I know your reluctance to volunteer advice . . . but certainly there are things which must be brought to the President's attention by somebody. Bad as I think his message was, it seems to me its worst feature is that he apparently sent it without bothering to get anyone's reaction. . . . [In view of all that was at stake], that seems to me a really bad omen.

ODY: (nodding): Awful. You know, that is the first real evidence I have seen that what everyone predicted would happen to Roosevelt, if he were elected, is actually happening. Ever since Monday I have had my fingers crossed on that boy. As for the message itself, I could call it inadequate in substance and inexcusable in form.

Here Young paused to relight his pipe and reorder his thoughts. Then he resumed:

Well, we are seeing a curious development. Not only are obligations being broken down, but the whole machinery of international relationships seems to have collapsed. The role of ambassador is no longer important because it has sunk to a position merely of social distinction and political preferment. Then we resorted to sending specially accredited delegates to meet with other delegates in international conferences. Now that method has received the coup de grace. We find nothing left, not even good manners. . . . It is not too much to say that the President first repudiated obligations—because when we refused to pay foreigners in gold, having plenty of it, we knocked the bottom out of any reasonable contention on our part that they should recognize their obligations and pay their debts to us—next he repudiated his own appointees to London and put them in an impossible position; finally in the message on Monday he repudiated good manners.

There seemed to be little left to say, but Young was far from through:

I cannot understand that message. Its tone of petty politics for home consumption could have been justified only if he had been faced with an election next fall. In this situation, at the height of his power and popularity, with no election facing him and Congress not in session, there is no conceivable justification. As for the position of the American delegates, I should think Hull could do nothing except resign on his return, and I should think Cox [FDR's chief in the 1920 presidential elections] would just want to go home and find some quiet corner in Ohio and have nothing more to do with the Administration. You cannot treat a man of consequence like Cox that way. Lord, when I think of how near I came to resigning from the Young Committee because I thought that President Hoover and Mr. Mellon were making my position needlessly difficult, I can realize the way these American delegates must feel now, because what they did to me was child's play compared with what Roosevelt has done to his own official delegates.

There was another pause, while Young relit a pipe that as usual needed constant relighting. Finally he looked up and continued:

You see, in the field of international relations you have only good manners, for irritation ultimately leads to force. With your domestic organization you can enforce respect for obligations with your police or army or navy. Unless you are prepared to go to war, however, you cannot very well enforce such respect in the international field and you have to rely there on good manners and the faith of one gentleman that another will live up to his agreement. I don't suppose I will live to see the machinery of peace and the code of good manners re-established. You may, because things move very swiftly nowadays. Once the tradition that lies at their base is shattered, however, I think it will take a generation before confidence can be laboriously built up again. When you start a competition in bad manners there is only one thing can stop it, and that is that it becomes so flagrant that the great masses of people everywhere finally sense what is happening and repudiate it themselves.[1]

So ended the lesson. To Young's auditors it was doubly sobering because he was not given to Cassandra-like observations and also because they were less than sanguine about the masses rising to repudiate "a competition in bad manners." The more probable alternative that came to mind was not to be thought of.

It was only on reflection that they began to understand—or thought they did—the full force of the emotions prompting this purely private but unwonted outpouring. It wasn't only, they decided, that the generous if sometimes fragile hopes—like those for disarmament—which were rooted in the London conference had been blasted by the President of the United States; it was that they had been blasted by *this* President. Given the wise and liberal leadership which Roosevelt had seemed to promise, Young had been confident that through the process of give and take this country could bring home from London what Young, like Roosevelt, saw as its primary need. That this entailed due recognition of the needs of others was the kind of axiom that he had counted on Roosevelt to respect, as too often Hoover had failed to do. Wasn't it also possible, they asked themselves, that with his own renunciation of all political ambition, Young had transferred his own presidential aspirations to this fellow Democrat and fellow Yorker—speaking out in his support where others were hostile or at best silent, and embracing every opportunity to hail his courage and notable achievements? Was it farfetched to see in his attitude something of the pride and almost jealous satisfaction with which an older man follows the progress of his bright and more than willing younger surrogate? Something of the sort would go far to explain why Young's confidence and pride had now suffered such a humiliating blow.

But one thing they were sure of; what they had been listening to was not for public consumption. As had been his habit, Young would continue to support the President of the United States—and especially *this* President—wherever and whenever he could do so in good conscience. No longer able, however, to give this President his full faith and confidence, he would welcome and seek to maintain the arm's-length relationship which Roosevelt himself so evidently preferred.

ii

It was on July 2 (not the Fourth) that FDR had triggered the shot heard round the world, which the Hearst papers—and others—hailed as a new Declaration of Independence.[2] Before the month was over, the fabulous recovery of the spring and early summer was faltering or worse—the rest of the year, with its up and downs, was to show a decline that canceled more than half the gains.

Post hoc, propter hoc? Probably not, if one consults the evidence as well as the oracles. Like their President, the great body of Americans was preoccupied with concerns closer to home: the farmer with prices and the AAA; the unemployed with finding jobs or somehow getting a living; businessmen with impending new codes and the NRA. That a successful outcome of the London conference might have benefited those whose eyes were focused on such pursuits seemed too remote a possibility to bother with.

And so, no doubt, in any immediate sense, it was. Sensitive markets—and men—had inevitably felt the shock; investors were suddenly cautious and, as Young was soon explaining to his directors, sales of heavy equipment languished because the embattled utilities were in no mood to expand. But some such market reaction was clearly overdue, and there were other factors to sustain it. As the complex realities of the AAA and the NRA increasingly failed to match their early promise, and as securities markets and especially the utilities faced novel restraints and the prospects of more, it was not surprising that the euphoria of the honeymoon months should have given way to disenchantment. And for this, such internationally minded economists as the Chase Bank's B. M. Anderson blamed not London but first and chiefly what he felt to be the misbegotten NRA.[3]

Although Owen Young was not enamored of the NRA, the scope of his own apprehensions remained vastly more far-reaching. In assessing the probable impact of high policy, especially of the explosive sort, it was not enough to scan the surface for the splash. One must also have an eye for the long swells and deeper currents that help to shape the future. Accustomed as he was to assessing the unfolding prospect, in global terms, Young was now finding this exercise utterly dispiriting and chiefly for the questions it raised. In the absence of *agreement* to disarm, economically as well as militarily, who would? With no course now open to the democracies but to go their separate ways, how were Hitler, or the Japanese militants, or even Mussolini to be curbed? And if they were not, what then?[4]

Finding to such questions no tolerable answers, Young turned his mind resolutely back to the current domestic scene. In urging as he had a year ago that the United States had the resources to do a real job first of all at home, he had been preaching priorities, not autarchy; nevertheless, it was autarchy that was now to be the order of the day. Realist enough to face the fact, Young recognized too the importance of making the most of it. Working together and for each other, the American people should be able to achieve a better measure of recovery than most; besides, it behooved us to lose no time in rebuilding our strength. Thus, Gerard Swope, for one, was deeply involved in making the NRA work; its codes bore just enough resemblance—potentially at least—to those of his own earlier plan to give him special incentives.

Nor had Young himself been idle, though he went about his work with something less than his accustomed zest. He had not forgotten Cordell Hull; his radiogram of July 7 congratulated him on his "patience, courage and tact in handling a most difficult situation." On the twenty-ninth a perplexed and shaken Raymond Moley called at his office; so (some two months later and for reasons not disclosed) did Louis Howe. And he saw Moley again, but Moley was now "out," having resigned to become editor of *Today*, a new journal that was to be the forerunner of *Newsweek*.[5]

Meanwhile, Young was still trying to help closed banks—notably in the Mohawk Valley and Fort Wayne, Indiana—to reopen with new capital; in Fort Wayne, where GE had a plant, the company itself put in twenty-five thousand dollars. In August, GE advanced two million dollars to its Employees Securities Corporation which, in view of the phenomenally low rate of return on investments, had exchanged its old 6 percent bonds for a new 5 percent issue—GE's 2 percent premium for continuous holding becoming now dependent on the company's earnings. On the other hand the Advisory Committee, meeting in Bridgeport, reported that in accord with the new NRA code, two thousand would be added to the payroll, the overall cost increase of which would amount to some eight million dollars. As Young himself had written a few weeks earlier to the publicist Henry Goddard Leach, the NRA represented "a valiant effort to get people back to work . . . industrial managers should put away their doubts and cooperate fully in trying to get results." And this was the burden of his radio plea in September—of which the *American's* radio columnist said: "There's one big shot who knows how to use the microphone; he talks as though he were sitting across the table from you—most big shots talk as if they were on a soapbox in Union Square."[6]

How then did GE fare under the NRA? In contrast to the first half of 1933, sales billed for the third and fourth quarters were moderately higher than in the year preceding. Profits, however—reflecting the increased labor costs, paperwork and price restraints mandated by the code—were still unsatisfactory and dividends at ten cents per quarter were the lowest since the turn of the century. Although its shareholders, now numbering almost 200,000, were advised that GE was maintaining its accustomed share of the industry's business, Swope himself had become increasingly unhappy with the NRA—so much so that, as early as October, he had completed and submitted to Young for comment an ambitious plan for a new national economic council; this Young would have none of. As he wrote Swope on the fourth, he saw

no reasonable chance this country would commit itself to such a definitive setup as the memorandum proposes. Indeed if there were a chance, I should think, from the standpoint of the nation, it would be of questionable desirability. Taken at its best, it would be practically a separately organized economic government with power to coerce the political government. Taken at its worst, it would probably, as a practical matter, only mean a regimentation of industry with most of the other economic units aligned against it. It is difficult, for example, to see how argiculture could function in the face of that kind of industrial regimentation.

What then, would Young propose?

Something much more loosely organized. A coordinating economic council might be set up by the administration, perhaps without *de jure* recognition, whose business it would be to get the trade—and labor—organizations into cooperative action. . . .

I realize that you will think that this is unsatisfactory and probably would not function very well. I think that too, but if the President should put the right kind of men in it and it received and retained the support of public opinion, as I think it could if wisely handled, then we would start in the direction of a slow revolution in the organization of our economic forces. This, I think, is the safe and the American way to do it.

Then came his apologia: "As Josephine is waiting for me to go into the country, I am asking Miss Morrison to sign this letter and send it along to you. It gives my old-fashioned reactions to a very modernistic program. Neither in art nor business am I up to snuff."[7]

If this response illuminates the occasional disposition of even the best-matched team to pull in different directions, it also marks the candor which remained a salutary feature of the Young-Swope relationship. As Swope once remarked, he and Young "did not always agree" but they "never had a disagreement." And in this instance certainly Swope was greatly influenced by his partner's holding back.[8]

Although Young's June meeting with the President was to be his only White House call for 1933, Swope was a frequent visitor; the President liked his boundless energy, his zest and his down-to-earth concern for labor and the farmer as well as business. Thus Swope found himself involved not only with the NRA—proud as he had been, despite his growing disenchantment, that the code for electrical manufacturers was the second to be adopted—but also, and as chairman, with the newly sanctioned Business Advisory Board and the Coal Arbitration Board. In the latter post he came to know John L. Lewis of the miners' union; each earned the other's respect and trust. And because Section 7-a of the National Recovery Act finally mandated what Young and Hoover had recognized way back in President Wilson's time—namely, labor's right to organize and bargain collectively through an agency of its own choosing—Swope soon found that his involvement in labor disputes did not stop at the mines. He was a member of both advisory boards set up by the NRA—one for industry, one for labor—and on August 4 a joint meeting of the two had unanimously approved his proposal for a national labor board.[9]

Of this board, shortly set up with Swope a member and Senator Robert Wagner as chairman, Swope's biographer has written that, together with its regional branches, it "handled in six months 1,818 disputes and settled more than two-thirds . . . on the spot." This experience only confirmed Swope's long-standing conviction that workers in general were entitled to the benefits of such old-age, disability and unemployment insurance as GE had sought to provide; indeed, he fully shared Young's view that only as these became general—and so noncompetitive—could they ever be truly adequate. Thus by March of '34 the President was also consulting Swope about the social security bill which he was contemplating; they quickly agreed that it should insure all citizens against specified hazards "from the cradle to the grave." And if Congress, when it finally addressed the·matter in early

1935, so altered the original bill that Swope disclaimed paternity, he could not escape sharing the "garbage and the garlands" which marked the passage of the first Social Security Act.[10]

Since GE's top-management team still contrived to keep in close touch, it was first of all through Swope that Young was now keeping abreast of developments in Washington. But Swope was by no means his only source. In July a columnist remarked that Washington was quietly "putting the skids under George Harrison of the New York Fed";[11] but by October this patient and dedicated man was quietly conducting an almost daily White House tutorial by phone, often at the instance of the President himself, on gold purchases and commodity prices. In this delicate educational venture, Harrison relied heavily on Young, whom he saw often at the bank and on occasion at his apartment.

Mildly disconcerted by the post–London conference collapse of the "Roosevelt market," but far more by the sharp fall in commodities and the rising price of the dollar, FDR had determined that this latter trend must be speedily reversed. By October, further exposure to the doctrines of one George Warren, professor of agronomy at Cornell, had persuaded him that the persistent selling of dollars to bid up the price of gold would not only depreciate the dollar but would automatically raise, *pari passu*, all commodity prices beginning with farm products. So persuaded, he had promptly issued standing orders for the RFC to buy for the Treasury's account—and at prices to be specified by him from time to time—such quantities of gold as might prove necessary for the purpose.

Sympathetic though they were, and always had been, with the President's price objectives, Harrison and Young were deeply skeptical of Warren's equation. Moreover, while the order gave priority to newly mined domestic gold, it also provided for purchases in the international market through the agency of the New York Fed. And this, Young and Harrison agreed, not only compromised the independence of the Fed and its credibility abroad but carried with it the ultimate threat of forcing France off gold—an eventuality which, as Young had pointed out long since and Harrison was now reporting to the President, could only undermine his prime objective. Meanwhile, Harrison added, the government's credit was being seriously impaired and the depreciation in government bonds was becoming a major threat to the solvency of the banks.

Impressed, but unconvinced, the President nevertheless listened and sometimes asked for more; when, on more than one occasion, commodity prices not only failed to move upward as the dollar fell, but even lost their earlier gains, Roosevelt finally called off his experiment. This happened—almost conclusively—by the end of November, and just in the nick of time. Harrison, vindicated in his singularly diplomatic handling of a crisis that others would have met by denunciation, resignation or both, was now able to reassure the Bank of France, as well as his associates, that the party was over. And so, to all intents and purposes, it was; by January 1934 the value of the dollar was formally declared to be 59.09 cents in terms of gold—the price of which was fixed at $35 an ounce.[12]

Young's files make no mention of his supporting role in this critical endeavor, except to record the unusual frequency of his meetings with Harrison. At the Fed, however, it was common knowledge that Harrison made no move, if he could help it, without consulting Owen Young, and indeed their relationship was a happy combination of mutual trust and admiration. What Young's papers do disclose is his letter of November 17 to one of his senior Boston directors; certainly this reflects the kind of intimate knowledge and not uncritical understanding of what the President was about that could have come only from Harrison—flavored perhaps by a dash of Young's own brand of political acumen. "Dear Mr. Abbott," he wrote:

What I started to say to you yesterday has not been reduced to writing, but I have no objection to doing so, at the moment for your eyes alone.

In respect to the monetary policy, it seems to me that the President is on a teeter board with the Scylla of low farm prices on the one side and the Charybdis of impaired credit on the other. Naturally, he does not want to fall off into either. In order to prevent an incoming Congress from taking the money question out of his hands, he must at least keep the agricultural interest acquiescent, because due to our governmental setup, there are enough states in which agriculture is politically dominant to give them maximum power in the United States Senate. Of course the President would like to keep the affirmative support of agriculture, but at all odds, he must avoid revolt. The one way, and perhaps the only way, of avoiding revolt is to raise farm prices, and the mechanism which the President has adopted to do that is the depreciated dollar. The theory is, I suppose, that in agricultural products, the foreign price sets the domestic one, and so a dollar cheapened in the foreign exchanges should quickly reflect an increased agricultural price level.

The quickest and most effective means of depreciating the dollar is to frighten capital sufficiently to flee. That is exactly what has happened.

The program of purchasing gold abroad is not of so much influence because of the transaction as its threat to the dollar which induces the flight of capital. We have, as I said, seen rapid depreciation of the dollar and some increase, but no corresponding increase as yet, in agricultural prices.

But that was not all:

While the process was going on of frightening capital into flight and thereby depreciating the dollar, there was naturally a break in the prices of government bonds, and through it, a threat to the government credit. A secondary effect of the depreciation of bonds has been the loss in a relatively few days of something over $600,000,000 to the banks of the country which is just about the sum that the Reconstruction Finance estimated that it would take to repair the capital of the banks. This impairment of government credit and threat to the banking structure, of course, compelled the President to take a look at that side of the teeter board, and there is some evidence, it seems to me recently, that he is proceeding more conservatively, although the leave of absence of Mr. Woodin, the resignation of Acheson, and the appointment of Morgenthau, all conspired to create the impression to the public that the President was going through with the farm price situation regardless of its effect on the other side of the teeter board.

I think that impression is entirely erroneous. The President has practically been his own Secretary of the Treasury in determining monetary policies, and personally, I think the change in personnel is likely to be helpful rather than harmful.

How, then, did Young assess the prospect?

Naturally, [with the President] being on a teeter board and trying to keep in balance, no one can forecast what will happen next week or next month. I feel sure that the President himself could not do so. So long as he tries to do these mutually antagonistic things, he has the delicate job of staying on the board, and when he swerves one way or the other, it is only, as I construe it, to keep aboard.

Under the circumstances, Young added, any abrupt move toward stabilizing the dollar would so sharply reverse the flight of capital as to depress farm prices anew. Therefore, he concluded,

just how much uncertainty can be retained for the benefit of farm prices and how much certainty will be essential for the protection of government credit can only be determined from day to day. That means not only is the President on a teeter board, but all the rest of us, and to some extent, the whole world is on it too. They will remain on it with all its uncertainties as long as he does.

This is the penalty which you suffer from what I now know you will think was your own ill-advised request.[13]

iii

Young had taken no proper vacation that summer; he seldom did. On occasion, he would take a day off to fish from Little Point; and he did take his youngest son, Richard, off to Chicago to visit the world's fair, and congratulate his friend Dawes on its astonishing success. He also talked with Melvin Traylor, and again with W. S. Goll of the Fort Wayne plant about getting the bank there reopened, which he effectively followed up on his return. But he did want to get to Van Hornesville, and not only because the ugly mood of the midwestern farmers had spread to the upstate dairymen. Their milk strike, called for August 1, was soon over, but as a protest, it had not been ineffective in curtailing shipments to New York City; in Fort Plain, Young's Van Horne Farms milk had been dumped along with the rest. This was all right with him; he was not about to be a "scab," he said, when his neighbors whose very living depended on the price of milk voted to strike. But he did want to find out more about the facts; evidently the AAA was not providing the remedy which the plight of the dairy farmer called for.[14]

Back from Chicago, however, Young had first to cope with a typically crowded week in New York, beginning with a Sunday evening session with M. H. Aylesworth and Will Hays, the movies' "czar," on the future of NBC, on which he reported by letter to General James Harbord. He had two afternoon meetings—of the Executive Committee and the board—at the Federal Reserve and a long luncheon with George Harrison. He also lunched with Gerard Swope, in town for a flying visit, and followed this up with a series of meetings with GE officials. He wrote Clark Minor, now president of IGE, about the importance of meeting with the Council of the International Chamber of Commerce: "about the only place left at which there can be a free exchange between men of consequence in the different countries." To John Stewart Bryan, the genial and astute Richmond publisher who was the new chairman of the Committee on Mobilization of Relief Resources, he wrote asking for relief from further service; Bryan reluctantly agreed that he had earned it. Having suggested in vain that he be excused from reelection to the General Motors board, he did make its August meeting. And on Thursday Nelson Perkins came in for one of their long and rewarding visits.[15]

But Friday, August 11, was special. Boarding the New York Central's "Upstate Special" that afternoon, Owen was not alone; Jo was with him. It was the first time in more than two years that she had felt equal to the trip; now, with Owen at her side, she made it easily. Once at Van Hornesville, she stayed until after Labor Day, with her children and grandchildren stopping by for visits and Peggy Egan giving her special care. Owen could not stay, but Schenectady was only fifty miles away, and if he had to be in New York part of each week for Federal Reserve and other meetings, he managed to return for extended weekends. And when, soon after Labor Day, he and Jo went back to 830 Park, and thence to Riverside, their son Philip remained at the Home Farm which, he reported after listening to his father's NRA speech on WGY, was especially attentive to its master's voice. A few days later, Young himself was there listening to the broadcast of John D. Rockefeller, Jr.'s speech for the NRA; his subsequent message said it "sounded excellent in Van Hornesville."[16]

There was a change of scene awaiting Young when he returned to the city after Labor Day. RCA had already made the move to Rockefeller Center, though it would be some weeks before NBC's new studios were ready. Now GE had moved into the building at 570 Lexington Avenue acquired from RCA as part of the separation settlement. Young's new offices were high up, on the forty-seventh floor; on a clear day his windows commanded a view of the Sound that seemed to reach almost to Little Point. But he missed the familiar panorama of the harbor, with its ferries shuttling across and back and the great ships steaming past the Narrows to the open sea. He missed too the familiar bustle of the Street, and certainly the Federal Reserve was not about to desert its massive Florentine fortress at 33 Liberty for anything uptown had to offer. Thus despite the ostensible convenience of his new headquarters—on fair days it was just a good morning's walk from Park and Seventy-sixth to Lexington at Fifty-first—he clung to his old and now half-derelict office at 120 Broadway for at least occasional use during the few months that it remained available.[17]

Also, for the first time since joining GE, Young now found himself without an assistant. Philip, Faith and their small daughter, "faithie," were already living in Cambridge, where Philip was enrolled at Harvard Business School; now Jo and Everett, with their small daughter, "jo," were moving to a house not far from theirs. Jo's graduate studies took her to the Radcliffe library, Everett's to Widener—separate and unequal, Jo complained. But her husband, planning his thesis, had other concerns as well: How in the world was his former chief going to get along without him? Replacements, in such times, would be a dime a dozen, but would any of them be up to the job?

He need not have worried. When Young made no move to replace him, Case finally gathered that it was not because he had made himself irreplaceable. What, indeed, could a new assistant now do for Young that his surviving office staff could not—with the incomparable Lillian Morrison handling appointments and his important correspondence and dictation, and Gertrude Chandler taking expert care of his finances (and his wife's) while serving up his daily dosage of clippings from the press. William Packer was not well, but Case's able secretary, George Riddle—who could boast a Harvard degree—was well qualified to help at home or on the road, even to the point of noting down from time to time what Young was thinking or planning to say or do about the state of this and that. And for such *ad hoc* assignments as called for special and expert help, Young already had his eye on the young lawyer who, as assistant counsel to the Lamp Department, was proving himself a man to watch: Philip D. Reed.[18]

So for Young, even more than for Case, the transition was proving quite painless; and the returned graduate student's *amour propre* was given a boost from time to time by calls from his father-in-law, as well as from his father, for a critical review of the testimony they were asked to give on new banking legislation. During that fall and the next, moreover, Thanksgiving brought both of the senior Youngs back to their old Cambridge haunts for memorable visits with their children and grandchildren. And when, in the spring of '34, Young was asked by the University of Nebraska to speak and accept a degree at their commencement, he invited his former assistant to go along.

But there were other priorities on Young's agenda, beginning with the utilities, whose orders for heavy equipment were still conspicuous by their absence. With GE's vice-president in charge, his friend Charles Appleton, Young was spending long hours with their leaders—including S. Z. Mitchell's Bond and Share successor, Ned Groesbeck, and an engaging chap named Wendell Willkie—in vetting their grievances and other problems. He quite agreed that Roosevelt's policies had hurt their investors and so the industry, but held that these need not be fatal wounds unless the industry made them so. To Albert Shaw, who, as editor of the *Review of Reviews*, had sent him a relevant piece by David Lawrence, he confided that FDR had some reason to doubt the effectiveness of the regulatory commissions, thanks chiefly to the paralyzing impact on the rate-making process of court decisions which held reproduction costs to be the proper base. Now, with these costs down, he had some hope that the industry—and the judiciary—might see the light and substitute the "true" base, which, of course, was actual investment, and he made bold to suggest that "if [such] a program was sponsored independently, it might be that the administration and the utility people could be brought together on a sound and sensible plan of effective . . . regulation. This would be so much better than wasting public funds in duplicating facilities and . . . destroying billions . . . of private capital already invested. . . ." Where actual investment as the rate base was at issue, Young did not give up easily; but once again nothing came of his suggestion.[19]

In one development of the fall, however, Young found genuine cause for satisfaction: on November 20, the United States formally recognized the USSR. Six weeks earlier, when Colonel Hugh Cooper had been about to confer with Roosevelt on the subject, Young had advised him that the President already knew about his interest. Now, in response to a message from Saul Bron in Moscow, he expressed his pleasure that "all political obstacles to the freest possible intercourse have been removed." And he made a point of attending the ensuing dinner for Maksim Litvinov, the Soviet commissar for foreign affairs, at the Waldorf.[20]

Meanwhile, at home, Owen and Jo were adjusting to a suddenly diminished apartment; he had given up the library and its librarian when, in the spring, his books were put in storage as collateral for his loans.[21] But they were comfortable enough and, despite Young's explanation to the Council on Foreign Relations that Swope's absence kept him too busy visiting GE's various plants to be a regular attendant at their meetings, he still found time for family and extracurricular concerns. To Henry Robinson he wrote about Mme Curie's intended visit to California (she proved to be too ill to make it), and to Dean Jay in Paris he wrote to inquire about the status of her bonds. To his cousin Emma Young he wrote about Uncle Cyrus's estate in Alberta; there would not be much, but in selling the farm for what it would bring, he had reserved the mineral rights as an "interesting gamble for the children." To their clerical friend Frank Oliver Hall he wrote warmly of the proposed merger of the Unitarians and Universalists; certainly the latter must not be open to the charge of blocking this "federation of liberals." And he went to Choate for a Fathers' Day visit with Dick.[22]

But if ever Young and Swope kept a sharp eye on the research laboratory and the prospects for new business, it was now. The number of GE's shareholders had more than trebled since 1929 and, since dividends had fallen off in roughly inverse ratio, Young made a point of answering himself all the questions and complaints that came to his desk. Far worse was scanning the payrolls where, for 1933, the numbers employed averaged less than half of 1929's record total of 88,000, and some 5,000 less than 1932's 46,943. Nevertheless, between March 1 and the end of the year, 8,363 had been added and the annual payroll *rate* had risen by some $17.5 million. Even so, average annual earnings per employee were 17 percent below those of a decade ago— the one saving factor being that a 25 percent fall in the cost of living left *real* earnings up by more than 10 percent.[23]

True, the year ahead was to prove more encouraging to all hands, with the numbers employed averaging close to 50,000 and average dollar earnings up some 14 percent. Earnings per share rose too, from 38 to 59 cents, with dividends keeping pace. But Young and Swope had not waited for this improvement to reexamine the old profit-sharing plan for employees. Finding it too exclusively a scheme for rewarding continuity of service, they discarded it in favor of an extra-compensation plan which, like that long authorized for executives, was based on a designated share of profits in excess of 8 percent of the capital investment. It was a good time to present it for the stockholders' approval, as they did at the annual meeting on April 17, 1934; after all, profits were still so low that—again like the executives' plan— it would cost little or nothing for the present.[24] Duly approved, it served to illustrate how, by taking thought in the worst of times, management may build wisely for the future.

As for RCA, Young had perhaps not spoken the whole truth in saying that he "had retained his interest and discharged his responsibility." No longer on the payroll, he was still seeing Sarnoff often and Aylesworth even more so. Sometimes this meant fun as well as problems. With General Harbord and John Reith, head of the BBC, he celebrated the Armistice Day (1933) opening of NBC's new studios in Radio City as a party to a broadcast conversation with Sarnoff in London. And the Advisory Council's meeting of 1934 was a particularly lively one, with newcomers like Chicago's Robert Maynard Hutchins doing much to make it so.[25]

Of the Federation Bank, whose problems had not ended with its much-heralded reopening, Young never lost sight. For example, as it now felt the pinch occasioned by FDR's teeterboard act, it was Young who persuaded such industrial leaders as Alfred Sloan and Thomas J. Watson to come to the rescue with substantial new deposits. This bank, he wrote Lamott duPont, had much to teach industrial as well as labor leaders.[26]

In the meantime the pinch Young himself was suffering from his burdensome debts was not so easily abated. For '33 as for '32, his interest payments alone consumed his entire earnings; living expenses could be met only by sales in a buyer's market from his own and his wife's depleted holdings plus such uncommitted dividends as these still yielded. Not unnaturally his broker, George Pick, was a faithful and frequent visitor; not unnaturally, Young did what he could to help his broker.[27] From the scores who were *his* debtors, Young could look for little help or none; perhaps the only one who even called at his office was his enterprising friend Louise Clark, and she came as often as she could. Having admired her gumption when, left a widow in the Philippines, she set up her own business for the manufacture and sale of silk lingerie, Young had lent a sympathetic ear to her recital of the problems she faced in steering a luxury trade through the depression. He had no capital to lend her, but he arranged to endorse a loan for her at the Bankers Trust which, some years later, was entirely paid off when she gave up the business.[28]

A welcome break in the office routine was recorded on Young's calendar for October 2, when he and Clarence Woolley left at noon for the Polo Grounds to see the New York Giants beat the Washington Senators in the 1933 World Series opener ("G-4, W-2," noted the office boy in the office calendar.)

iv

In late October, Queen's University of Kingston, Ontario—just across the river from St. Lawrence—provided Young with an opportunity he was beginning to think he needed. Invited to be its convocation speaker and accept an honorary degree on the twenty-eighth, Young welcomed it, not only as a gracious gesture toward his alma mater, but even more as a challenge to sort out and reassess his own well-worn, and by this time somewhat battered, views on the shape of this "shrunken world" and its prospects for the future. Across the border, he felt, was a good place to test them for perspective.

Very well, he would begin by asking himself, and then perhaps his audience, a few obvious questions. Whatever had happened, for example, to the era of international cooperation—*economic* as well as political—he had once so confidently foreseen? Why had cooperation been eclipsed by the forces of national self-sufficiency and what now did these portend? It wouldn't do simply to generalize, much less to point the finger at the depression or the New Deal or both: something bigger and more fundamental than these was clearly at work. And it was time he took a hard look and gave a candid report on what he found, if only to prove to himself that his mind and arteries still functioned.

The resulting speech was hailed, locally at least, as good for Canadian-American relations, although it did not deal with them as such. For once the *New York Times* gave a Young speech relatively brief notice—until, some six weeks later, front-page headlines of its Sunday *Magazine* heralded the illustrated reprint that took up the whole of the first two pages. NATIONALISM REMOLDS THE WORLD, read the streamer, and under it: "As the Nations Become More Self-sufficient, Owen D. Young Foresees Extraordinary Changes in the Course of International Trade, and Makes a Plea for a Greater Exchange of Cultural Values."[29] In the speech itself, he started with the questions he had been putting to himself. Reviewing what now seemed his euphoric expectations of the twenties, he found them rooted in the notion that the very compression which science was effecting, with its consequent close contact, would ensure "a world more closely integrated in peaceful effort, in business interchange, in financial stability, in economic development, in psychological neighborliness." But would that notion scan? Not on the current evidence. To the contrary, compression seemed to be producing a whole series of opposite effects.

Asking himself why, he found a suggestive answer in his own experience. Near the farm where he was born, houses were widely separated: "It was a real undertaking to visit your neighbor, but the people were intimate and friendly. Each was interested in the others' affairs," both great and small. "Now," he continued, "I live in an apartment in New York. It may well be that I do not know even my [closest] neighbor. . . . My children may not know his. Life, death, sickness, all, all may take place without either of us knowing. . . . Congestion . . . does not necessarily insure, or even promote, intimacy, interest or understanding. . . . Possibly . . . with closer contact, one sets up barriers for his individual protection."

Very well then; the compression of our world may raise more barriers than it breaks down: "Perhaps nations are protecting their individuality as persons do. Perhaps we have a new problem on our hands . . . different . . . from what we thought we had. Mind you, I do not say we have; I only say perhaps . . . [but] one cannot look upon great nations drawing back within themselves without at least [raising] such a question."

The deep concern, amounting almost to despair, that Young had felt when FDR torpedoed the London conference could only have been aggravated by such predictable consequences as the final collapse of the Geneva conference and Hitler's rearmament and secession from the League. Certainly Young did not underestimate the hazards of unbridled nationalism when a Hitler arose to exploit them.[30] To play Cassandra from the public platform, however, had never appealed to him, nor—especially in speaking to students—did it now. Explicitly rejecting, then, any confession of hopelessness, he would concede only "that the road to a better-spirited and a more cooperative world is not quite so straight, not quite so easy, as I once thought it was."

What, then, of international trade? Raw materials, he asserted, would move across the seas regardless of isolationism or even a disturbance of the peace; as they were unevenly distributed, "he who has them to excess must sell; he who needs them must buy." Luxuries too behaved in somewhat similar fashion, especially because of their tendency to become "necessities." But in the case of fabricated goods, he looked for "barriers to be set up against [their] importation as rapidly as each country can produce its own."

The textile output of Shanghai has demonstrated that the looms of China can challenge those of England. Russia, without industrial experience or background is undertaking to . . . fabricate for her own needs [most of what she once imported]. Now if—with science and its machines—there be no God-given place for fabrication, I think it is inevitable that international trade in manufactures will grow less.

This indeed, a knowledgeable auditor might have reflected, was the real justification of the Young-Swope program calling for GE's substantial minority investments in, and exchange of patents and marketing agreements with, the world's leading electrical manufacturers. Perhaps he had this in mind as he summed up:

If it be true that the world has become very small, if it be true that increased propinquity tends to generate a more intense spirit of nationalism, if it be true that fabricated necessities will move less and less in the world's trade . . . if it be true that raw materials . . . luxuries and semi-luxuries . . . are to occupy the major place in our international exchanges, then every nation will be faced with the problem of gradually readjusting its domestic and international economy toward that end. It will be a slow process, and in many cases a painful one, but its harshness may be alleviated by careful planning in advance.

And he added that, for North America, temporary alleviation might also be found in the demand from abroad for engineers, technicians and skilled operators to install and handle new machines.

But his final word was a plea for enlarging the noncommercial "areas of common interest between nations." For example:

Public health is a national asset. Anything which threatens it, wherever it be in the world, is a national enemy. All nations being interested, all will cooperate to stamp out disease, to control harmful drugs [!], and to relieve suffering. Scientific research and engineering application are an asset to every country and cooperation should be widened and encouraged, and can be because there will be less competition in the world's market in the fabricating field. The interchange of students, the freedom of travel, the exchange of professors and the educational facilities should be enlarged. The movement of books and works of art for the purpose of developing and widening culture should be encouraged.

If this little world of ours must be dotted with compartments, each country seeking so far as possible to be self-contained in material things, at least we may keep the heavens above free for the interchange of those things which, after all, are the aims of an advancing civilization.[31]

Alas, if Young expected the heavens above to remain free for such civilized purposes only, he was to prove a poor prophet.

v

In leaving Jo the following June for a trip which was to take him on to visit old friends like Ralph Whelan in Minneapolis, and thence to Ottawa, Canton, and another commencement at neighboring Clarkson College, Owen did so not only at her urging—"It's high time you went off on a toot"—but with the knowledge that she was steadily gaining strength. This was one consequence of the bold step he had taken late in March. Knowing that his wife had loved sea voyages and ships since her early holidays, as a girl, on Martha's Vineyard and Nantucket—she still read books on voyages, and collected ship models— he decided to take her, her nurse and young Richard on a ten-day Caribbean cruise. The youngest member of the party remembers it as a delightful time; the *Mauretania* was one of the best ships afloat, and for this cruise she practically belonged to the Youngs. The Cunard Company saw to it that nothing was lacking for their comfort; even the sea was smooth, and Owen and Dick had some fascinating trips ashore. Best of all, Jo enjoyed it and it did her good.[32]

Jo understood that being the commencement speaker at the University of Nebraska would hold special attractions for Owen. Its seat was in Lincoln, where William Jennings Bryan and young Charley Dawes had long had their law offices in the same building. It was there that Dawes had become a friend of both Bryan and a young army officer named John J. Pershing. There too the innovative and impressive state capitol had been designed by Jo's old friend Bertram Goodhue. Not least, the chancellor's wife was a St. Lawrence alumna. And in Omaha, the Federal Reserve and utility people were eager to welcome him, even if Senator Norris stayed aloof. He would have a good time and he deserved it.

He had a good time and he made a good speech—widely reported, and reprinted verbatim (which was hardly news) by the *New York Times*.[33] Watching as well as listening, his son-in-law concluded that one reason why Young was still in such demand as a speaker was that, however commanding his presence, he never talked down to his audience. A second was that, despite his early exposure to Victorian oratory, and later to the law, science and technology, he despised all jargon and seldom indulged in rhetorical flights. Now, talking directly to the graduating seniors, he assumed that they shared his interest and concern about some of the more baffling—and therefore challenging— problems of the day, which he thereupon set out to interpret in plain English. And certainly he gained credibility by his insistence that no public issue could be as one-sided as its proponents and opponents would have one think.

This had special significance, of course, as he dealt with the New Deal, which, having made big business and especially the power trust its whipping boy, was being generously repaid in kind. Young now put it in its proper historical perspective. Even in choosing for his subject "Obsolescence in the Social Sciences," he was harking back to Woodrow Wilson's "lag of the law," which he then updated by applying it to the two intervening decades.

Recalling first of all the depression of 1893, in his own college days, he told something about the forces that had come to the rescue: chiefly the developments in the physical sciences and engineering, with their exciting new materials and new applications—automotive, chemical, electric. Seizing on these, his generation had done great things—all fine, he said, but for the fact that "the social and economic machinery was not being advanced in anything like" the same degree. Indeed, he continued,

the law stood still while business with its new weapons was going over the ramparts into no-man's land. To be sure, Theodore Roosevelt, sensing danger, tried to rally the progressive forces for an advance under the slogan of the Square Deal. Later he undertook to stampede the unperturbed front of reaction with the "Bull Moose." Woodrow Wilson, more learned in the history and theory of government, won in that important struggle by enlisting many under the flag of the New Freedom. Then came the great war, when our attention was given to other things, and after the war that great decade in which the accumulated advances of the technicians for a generation burst into flower. No one would listen to the New Freedom longer. The old freedom was good enough, and so we went on our way rejoicing.

Then·came the New Deal. It had to come. On the day it came into power, it was called on to make at once, yes, on that very day, the delayed improvements of a generation in government, in banking, in law and in innumerable parts of our social organization.

At pains to point out that he meant by "obsolescence" not a worn-out mechanism but one that has become replaceable by something better, he contrasted the prevailing attitudes of the physical and social sciences toward it. To the latter, especially in the twenties, "laws were laws, banks were banks, society was society in its heights and depths, the untouchables of our time. New ideas . . . were said to come from visionaries; experiments were revolutionary . . . [whereas] in the physical sciences [it] was being demonstrated daily that visions . . . were the motive power of progress and that experiments were the ratchets which hold the advance."

If here, as Case half suspected, Young was recalling the fate of his own visionary proposal—at Harvard in 1927—that labor hire capital, he gave no sign. Rather, with praise for Roosevelt's courage, he went on to ask why it was not logical for a President faced with the need for "delayed research and experiment" to create a "brain trust" for research, as the physical sciences had long been doing to great advantage. Stating that "I for one am their [the Brain Trust's] defender and ready to meet their critics," he added that

if I had one suggestion for the Administration, appreciating as I do its difficulties and sympathizing as I do with its aims, it would be to separate sharply the field of research from application. [Application engineering] interferes with research, and the spirit of research interferes with practical application. . . . Let the brain trust develop the principles. Let the experienced engineers apply them in the creation of the new practical working machines we need.

And let them do all this—here a fervent "please God" was all but audible—with a minimum of those bureaucratic and coercive controls that threaten our hard-won political and economic freedom. Nevertheless, he had so far assumed the role of apologist for the New Deal as to startle his midwestern audience into attention. But he was not quite through.

It will be for your generation, he now told the seniors, to determine

how much organized government must be enlarged, how much the free action of the individual must be curtailed. . . . Today we do not know. Great demands are being made to reduce the spread between the leader and the laggard. You must find the way without impairing the verve of them who lead. A social order within a nation must strive not so much for unattainable equality as manageable equilibrium.

What followed could be heard as a challenge to the President, to the Middle West's traditional isolationism, or to both. Weighing his words, Young now made a brief excursion into the international scene.

A world order must seek the same things, too. Nothing can be more incongruous or more certain of ultimate failure than the effort to reach social equalization within a nation and at the same time by a policy of reckless nationalism to leave the world outside in consequent turmoil and anarchy, where suspicion and distrust reign supreme and where arms are the only reliance of our faith, even when they blast our fondest hopes for security and peace in a better world.

Rather more disarming—even a bit old-fashioned—Young's concluding challenge was addressed directly, even exclusively, to the graduating class: "To you, young ladies and gentlemen, I come with confidence and with hope. My generation has had its victories and its failures. Today you inherit them. Our victories are your tools, capital for you to invest in a better world. Our failures are your opportunities. Them you must make your successes."[34]

Chapter 34

In Memoriam:
Josephine Edmonds Young,
1870–1935

O N THE eve of the '34 congressional elections, an essay by Young's erstwhile assistant on the role of the opposition party in making democracy work appeared in the *Atlantic* under the title "What Are Republicans For?" On the morning after, a commuter friend of the author's father was ready with his answer: "Well, Herbert," he said, "seems they're for Roosevelt."

If Young was more delighted with the retort than with the magnitude of the Democratic sweep, he was not about to join the opposition. Democrats who were "taking a walk," like Al Smith and John W. Davis, had become prominent figures in the so-called Liberty League, whose membership, consisting largely of disgruntled corporate tycoons, presented F D R with a made-to-order target. Young would have no truck with it whatever—nor, to his credit, would Herbert Hoover. And in fact the Democratic sweep confronted the President with so many clamorous demands from the extreme left as to incline him, briefly at least, to hold out the olive branch to "responsible" business.[1]

Alert as he was to such an opportunity and all that it could mean, Young bent every effort to persuade his business associates, beginning with the utilities, to seize it.

On November 27, he and Gerard Swope met in the latter's office with Floyd Carlisle, and Morgan partners Harold Stanley, George Whitney and Frank Bartow, to discuss Newton Baker's opinion questioning the constitutionality of the T V A act and the actions of the Authority under the act. Asked what course they should pursue, armed as they were with this opinion, Young advised that instead of making it public now, they should call on the President with a copy to discuss. They could say that while they had no wish for a long-drawn-out fight which might hurt recovery and the industry as well, they had to be concerned about protecting their rights. Thus they had sought the advice of eminent counsel and in view of his opinion and its implications, and as evidence of good faith, they were now laying it before the President in the effort to find a mutually satisfactory solution.[2]

Shortly thereafter the utilities saw fit to publish the opinion. Refusing to give up, Young tried another tack. In addressing the Association of Edison Illuminating Companies at their Fiftieth Annual Meeting in mid-January 1935, he recalled his long association with the industry, dating from 1896, as giving him some license for concern and for plain speaking. Having expressed his boundless pride in their achievements in "advancing the art and economy of service," especially in the period "when the leader was technology [and] finance was its aid"—instead of vice versa—he addressed their current predicament not as an outsider but as one of them: "I do not know much about bridge, but I have had some little experience with simpler and more plebeian games. One does not lose his money on bad hands or even mediocre hands; he loses it on the good ones because he overbids his hand." Lest someone miss the point, he proceeded to spell it out:

> We must confess, I think, that to some extent we have overbid our hand. We did our job too rapidly. We were too prosperous. The rapid advances of the art, the energy and skill of the managers, the ease with which technical improvement outran regulating authority, all led some to think that that process would go on forever. We must realize that if technical development has slowed down, regulation has been speeded up. While I doubt if the business will be as profitable as it has been in the past, and perhaps ought not to be in its own or the public's interest, yet I am confident that it is and will remain, one of the best business undertakings which exists or will exist in this great land.[3]

Still not sure that anyone was listening, he followed this up a fortnight later with a "personal and confidential" letter to Ned Groesbeck of Electric Bond and Share. This time he made a specific proposal: "I am satisfied," he wrote, "that the statesmanlike thing to do in the holding company situation is for the industry itself to make very promptly a complete survey of the entire country for the purpose of seeing how operating properties could be regrouped so as to get the maximum efficiency, economy, and service in operation."

He went on to suggest "territorial units" with central organization of generation and transmission of power, which would take over from current holding companies, leaving them as "merely finance" companies open to orderly liquidation:

I believe that such a program would be acceptable to the Administration and that, with the revised and simplified rate structure by which you would get a fixed minimum charge and then a reasonable rate for kilowatt hours varying only primarily with quantity, it would probably be enthusiastically supported.

I know this looks like a very difficult job . . . but if the industry is to be saved from these destructive attacks, I think we shall have to make a new approach with very large vision to the whole problem.

Aware of the risk he took in putting a "brainstorm in writing," he suggested that such a survey be announced at once, to be done by a group "acceptable to the President"—and in a handwritten postscript he said, "It is not defenses but a new and fresh attack that is required." Alas, like many of his suggestions, this was too extreme for the utilities to handle, especially as it required immediate action; at least we find no record that Groesbeck or any other utility head thought it worth taking up.[4]

Young remained philosophical. The country was trying, with considerable difficulty, he felt, to understand and assimilate the demands of the New Deal. As he put it to Samuel Crowther, the well-known journalist and commentator, "I think a very large share of the controversies which now center round our present policies arise from want of understanding both on the part of the proponents and of the opponents." Although to the public, especially the great numbers of unemployed, the skies were still dark, Young's New Year's letter to Sir Harry McGowan, head of Imperial Chemical in London, was guardedly hopeful as well as judicial:

I think we are making progress over here. . . . I confess it was even a greater job than I anticipated, but I believe now that we are on our way, due primarily to the economic pressure resulting from exhaustion of supplies. This, I suspect, has been retarded some by our experimental governmental activities, which I do not criticize, because I think they were necessary to our social stability, or, to put it another way, had they not been done social instability would have retarded economic recovery to a greater degree than the government activities.

And when the President—as in his ringing veto of Patman's inflationary bonus bill—took action that Young could praise unreservedly, he was quick to do just that.[5]

Like the President's wife, Young was now moving into action on the depression-caused problem which concerned him most—the plight of the young people of the country. Millions, perhaps a third of the country's total unemployed, were without jobs and with no place to go. Educational institutions could not take them, and at home their parents too were struggling to survive. All that remained for them to do was loaf, roam or steal. In the spring of 1935 Eleanor Roosevelt asked Owen Young to help, and he attended her meetings and worked with her. But the problem was far too great for individual efforts, and finally, in June, the President, under growing public as well as domestic pressure, established the National Youth Administration (NYA) by executive order, with a budget allocation of fifty million dollars. Young was appointed to the Advisory Council and made chairman of the Survey Committee.[6]

In spite of bureaucratic snarls and public criticism, the NYA effectively improved the situation of young people in the years before the war, not only in jobs and vocational training but in morale. It was so effective that Young, realizing that the problem was not going to disappear, even in wartime, fought hard with both the President and the Congress for a permanent program, but without success.

Young was also deeply involved at this time in the work of the American Youth Commission. At first chairman of the Executive Committee, and then, after Newton Baker's death, of the commission itself, Young put its work high on his schedule for the six years of its existence. Set up by the American Council on Education and funded by the General Education Board, the commission was a highly intelligent, diverse and strong-minded group.[7] With a competent staff, they set out to identify the problems and the needs of young people, to assess what was being done by other youth agencies, including the NYA and the Civilian Conservation Corps, and to cooperate with them. They concentrated on employment, education, health and citizenship. And it was primarily at Young's insistence that the problems of black youth were given special attention in a series of ground-breaking studies.

Young's constant attention, suggestions and criticism united the team and kept them moving forward. He demanded from the first "sharp, precise and definite inquiries in limited areas," never forgetting the basic importance of "fundamental economic remedies." The resulting publication, *Youth and the Future* (American Council on Education, Washington, 1942), was a report which won the President's praise and—more difficult—that of educators generally; it is still relevant, and readable, today. The introduction to the general report stated that it was not "the easy product of a group of like-minded persons . . . the possibility of unanimous agreement . . . at times seemed remote." That, of course, was the way Owen Young liked it, and the reason that, in spite of the hard and time-consuming work, he enjoyed the job.

In another field of concern, Young also made progress. He was deeply disturbed by the dangerous decline in construction, especially in the housing industry. To a Senate committee he said that spring that "if we would build one or two million $5000 homes, small homes, it would, in my opinion, do more than anything . . . in the way of restoration and the taking up of the slack in employment."[8] And he did not just talk—although the press was taking notice. With young Foster Gunnison (of the St. Lawrence family) he worked to set up a company called Houses, Inc. (actually a subsidiary of GE). which would do research and assist others—notably its subsidiary, American Houses, Inc.—in the manufacture of small prefabricated houses, of sound construction and excellent design. These were to be made in parts, which would be transported to the building site by trucks and set up in a few weeks. A sample house was exhibited in Grand Central Station for several months, and Young took almost everyone who called on him to see it. A model, called a "Motohome" (*not* a "mobile home") was exhibited at Wanamaker's store, where ceremonies were held and it was "dedicated" by Young and Mrs. James Roosevelt, the President's mother, with considerable fanfare.[9] Young even moved Jim Hagar, his manager in Van Hornesville, into Houses, Inc., to help Gunnison.

The support of General Electric in this project developed naturally from the prospective sale and installation of electrical appliances. Secretary of the Interior Harold L. Ickes, through his Public Works Administration (PWA), was tackling the problem of slum clearance and, despite the use of public funds, was finding it almost as baffling as had Young's B&I Committee. Young's small, inexpensive homes would meet needs of a different but not unrelated sort, while demonstrating too that private enterprise had not wholly lost its power to act. Government too seemed to be welcoming this private venture; the Federal Housing Authority now instigated a series of radio talks, which GE sponsored, on NBC stations. To participate in these, Young broke his rule, speaking on March 3 on "What Home Means to Me"—a brief and routine little talk which nevertheless brought him a pile of letters and clippings. At Purdue University on June 1 he spoke more formally to a conference on homes at the Purdue Research Foundation. Science had alleviated the isolation and drudgery of the modest home, he said, but its actual construction now required a wholly new art—new materials, new quality, new lower cost, along with new techniques, such as air conditioning, for health and comfort.[10]

In April something of Young's inherent optimism, which had been rather clouded over during the past few years, began to shine again. In Boston, at the centennial dinner of the New England Mutual Life Insurance Company, he made a call for action and progress, for imagination to meet the needs of our vast obligations by exploring new avenues to success: "The most valuable item on the balance sheet of America has been, and if nurtured will continue to be indefinitely, I predict, the things we do not know."[11] Though this was only saying in public what he had said to GE's research men, it was, perhaps, the most widely quoted sentence he ever spoke.

The first part of May saw Young moving rapidly from one place to another for a variety of meetings. Sir Josiah Stamp arrived from England and spoke at an Academy of Political and Social Sciences dinner in Philadelphia. He was introduced by Young, who, the night before, had attended a rather less formal dinner at the Penn Athletic Club "in honor of himself"—and of David Sarnoff, Merlin Aylesworth and Ed Wynn as well.[12] From Philadelphia he went to Canton for Charter Day, where his good friend Dr. John Finley gave the address; for a trustees' meeting where Laurens Seelye was elected the new president of the university; and for the presentation ceremony of his portrait by Leopold Seyffert, which was to hang in the new men's residence.

Young also took part with his old professor, Charley Gaines, in an impromptu dialogue in the lobby of the Hotel Harrington, attended, apparently, by curious passersby—and certainly by "Dr. John," for a full account (and an editorial as well) appeared in the *Times*, under the headline OWEN YOUNG TAKES ROLE OF SOCRATES. The subject was a comparison of democracy in ancient Athens and in the United States, and Young took great delight in needling his former teacher with questions such as "What do you think Demosthenes could have done for Greece if he had had radio?"—none of which fazed his eighty-year-old respondent.[13] One can imagine Jo's amusement when he told her about this. As Dr. Gaines's star pupil, who had read Plato and Demosthenes in the original, she probably said, "Owen Young, what do *you* know about Greek history and philosophy?"

ii

At the end of May 1935, Young was called to Washington to testify before the Senate Banking and Currency Committee on the so-called

Eccles banking bill. Increasingly regarded as a Federal Reserve spokesman, he took this in stride as a kind of return engagement. Through
1933, the series of New Deal measures which made gold no longer
lawful money had left the gold turned in for Federal Reserve notes
safely on deposit with the Reserve banks, as its traditional custodians.
But when the President, finally losing faith in the magic of his gold-
purchase program, advised Congress early in 1934 of his readiness
to stabilize the dollar at a figure between 50 and 60 percent of its old
gold parity, he also demanded that custody of, and title to, the nation's
gold reserves—not only the profits accruing from his "coin-clipping"—
be transferred from the Reserve banks to the Treasury.

To Senator Carter Glass this was sheer piracy; for the twelve Reserve bank chairmen, who, as Federal Reserve agents (of the board)
had legal custody of these reserves, it posed special problems—notably
those stemming from Secretary of the Treasury Henry Morgenthau's
conviction that he was already empowered to order this transfer forthwith. Mindful of their oath to defend these reserves against all hazards,
several chairmen were prepared to defy any such executive order,
Herbert Case of New York having armed himself with the opinion of
eminent counsel (Davis, Polk) that only an act of Congress could
override his sworn obligation to defend them. Thereupon Governor
Eugene Black of the Federal Reserve Board had persuaded the President that, after all, the wise and sensible course was to seek congressional authorization.[14]

So when Young, as deputy chairman, was called upon to testify on
the bill which became the Gold Reserve Act of (January) 1934, he
found himself engaged in a kind of balancing act of his own. Certainly, he told the senators, he welcomed the President's move toward fixing
the gold content of the dollar; this would now breed confidence and
so give recovery a boost. Certainly the profits that would ensue must
go to the government—indeed, where else?

Then Young shifted his balance. What, he now asked, was to be
gained by transferring the gold—or, for that matter, title to it—from
the Reserve banks to the treasury? Why not leave both where they
had been since the system (with a bow to Senator Glass) was first
established, with the profit credited to the treasury on the Reserve
banks' books? Of even greater moment, however, was the character of
the gold certificates which these banks were to receive in exchange for
any gold taken by the treasury. Restraint on the use of gold by regulation during the emergency was one thing; it was an altogether different

thing even to suggest a permanent currency redeemable in gold only at the option of the government. Ultimately a currency must be redeemable, not necessarily in coin or by the individual, but certainly in gold bullion and by the Reserve banks as its guarantors. This represented the one best hope of restoring stable exchanges and currencies worldwide; "and on that stability rests confidence at home and markets abroad."

It followed, then, that if any option not to redeem were to be vested in the treasury, it should be temporary only. Freely conceding the current need for a stabilization fund (to be created from the profit) if only to match those already operative elsewhere, Young urged that this too be declared an emergency measure, with the President himself empowered to determine when the emergency was over. This would give him the necessary leverage to rid the world of all such funds at the earliest possible moment—which of itself would do much to clear the air. In the meantime, and finally, lest this vast fund in the hands of the treasury be so used as to negate or cancel the responsibility of the Federal Reserve to restrain or expand credit in the public interest, it would be wise to make provision for some agency to coordinate policy.

Though he made a noble effort, the niceties of Young's little balancing act in the end availed little. As amended, the act of 1934 did indeed limit the life of the fund to an initial two years—renewable, however (and fairly sure to be renewed), at the discretion of the Congress. Also, the gold reserves were impounded in exchange for "gold certificates." Nevertheless, as his testimony ended, Senator Phillips Lee Goldsborough of Maryland paid him the compliment, rare on such occasions, of thanking him for his "very enlightening statement" and predicting that "even the man on the street will be able to comprehend it." And when Senator Robert Wagner strongly concurred, Young was pleased enough to say that "I have to make it that way because I cannot understand any other."[15]

Well, if with the new Banking and Currency Committee he was still *persona grata* in 1935, it would do no harm, for this time Young proposed to pull no punches. Appointed by the President late in 1934—in part, no doubt, to dramatize his total break with Wall Street—the new governor of the Federal Reserve Board was a western businessman hailing from Utah. His name was Marriner Eccles, and the bill which bore his name was clearly designed to centralize in the hands of a reconstituted Federal Reserve Board—to be known as the Board of Governors and headed by a chairman—virtually all of the powers hitherto exercised by the Federal Reserve System's Open Market Committee, or by the regional banks themselves. Even the chief executive officers of these banks—henceforth to be called president and first vice-president—were to be appointed only with the Washington board's approval—and this on an annual basis. Also explicit in the original bill but deleted by the House was the declared intent to make the chairmen of the regional banks, while still appointed by the board, purely honorary officers.[16]

This, for the system and especially for New York, was a New Deal with a vengeance, and the financial community liked it almost as little as Senator Glass did. Or Owen Young. As a witness, however, Young's strategy and tactics were peculiarly his own. First establishing his disinterest by pointing out that under newly instituted rules, he was not eligible for reelection as a director, he quietly and methodically took the bill apart. Certainly the nation's banking system cried *for reform from the bottom up*, but that was not the work of a day and this was working from the top down. Conceivably a central bank might be more effective than the regional system we owed to Wilson and Glass, but if the American people now thought so, they had yet to make it clear. Nor were they to be given that chance because, instead of posing the issue squarely, this bill would create a "central bank by indirection," leaving the facade—and only the facade—of the original structure intact. In such a maneuver, Young made it clear that he wanted no part.

Nevertheless, while recommending that the bill be shelved, *sine die*, Young still had to face the probability that in some form it was going to be enacted. What then? For one thing, no effort should be spared to insulate the Board of Governors against political pressure, especially from the executive branch; after all, the board must often do unpopular things. For another, governors (or presidents) of the regional banks must be given a responsible role, along with members of the central board, in the all-important Open Market Committee.

If we intend to retain fully the regional character of the System, [these regional members] should be in the majority . . . if we wish to overweight [its] centralized character but retain some of its regional characteristics and benefits, we might have a majority of one from the . . . Board. . . . If we create a larger majority than one and particularly if we make the election of the [regional presidents] subject annually to the approval of the Board, then we have almost as complete centralization as if the [regional banks] were not represented at all.

Young was enjoying himself—because this time he was not deferring to the President or anyone else but speaking out and speaking with authority. Aware of having the attention of his audience, and determined to make the most of it, Young went on to present in no uncertain terms his prescription for recovery in these uncertain times.

What we are concerned with today, Mr. Chairman, is to take up our unemployment. . . . The key to our whole situation . . . is business activity and particularly in . . . durable goods where most of our unemployment now lies. As durable goods have to be financed on long time, that market is particularly sensitive to drastic changes . . . in our financial structure. Business in durable goods . . . is still apprehensive about the political domination of our central banking system. . . . Whether business should be apprehensive over the pending bill . . . or whether it should not, views will differ, but the fact is that [it] is. Passage of the bill, therefore, either because it is not understood or because it is, will to some extent retard business recovery. . . . Seeing no reason for action now, I feel that . . . the way to get recovery today is to do nothing more and threaten nothing more to shake the confidence of business men. [With all needed emergency measures already taken and] the upward surge of a basic economic demand . . . ready . . . now to break through our doubts and fears . . . it is careful conservatism, not radical new departures, which will get now the activity which we so sorely need.

As for this bill, if nevertheless it was to be passed, some of the checks and balances of the regional system must be preserved, he said in conclusion, "so that the sensitive controls of money and credit may be vested in a body which is free from the fact and from the suspicion of subservience to any selfish interests, whether of profits or of votes."[17]

Judging by the ensuing exchanges, Young was not alone in enjoying the occasion. Asked by Senator James Couzens if he agreed with General Dawes's prediction of a marked upturn by July, Young said that he had "told the General it was all right to be a prophet but not to fix the date." And when Couzens, picking up Young's suggestion of a legislative holiday, asked, "Then you think we should adjourn and go home?" Young answered promptly, "It might be a good idea." This of course made excellent copy—hitting all the headlines and earning a few boos but mostly cheers.[18]

This time Young's efforts were not without effect. From his point of view and that of his associates, the bill as duly passed and signed on August 23, 1935, contained certain salutary amendments. The chief executives of the regional banks, once approved by the board, were appointed not for one year but for five. Also, five regional presidents were to serve on the Open Market Committee, along with the seven members of the Board of Governors. It was not quite Young's majority of one but could hardly have been closer; on the Open Market Executive Committee, moreover, the representation was two to three, and since the New York bank was still to execute the committee's policy decisions, its governor—or president—was virtually sure of a place on both committees.

In short, while the President and Chairman Eccles got the substance of what they wanted, the regional banks had by no means been reduced to ciphers. Certainly New York with its strategic location and central banking experience remained—at it should—a factor to be reckoned with.[19]

iii

Two days later Young was on his way to Purdue and the speech before the Housing Conference, then to plant a hickory tree in Beman Dawes's arboretum at Newman, Ohio, which Beman had been trying to get him to do ever since the days of the Dawes Plan. Invited by Charley Dawes to the centennial celebration of his own college, Marietta, Young spoke and received an honorary degree. It was a pleasant interlude. Marietta appeared to him much like St. Lawrence, and he spoke informally as he would have done at Canton; the general, delighted to have Owen there, was at his best. Then, back in New York, Young gave a farewell dinner to another dear friend, Josiah Stamp, gathering other friends together to hear and discuss Sir Jo's reactions to his American visit.[20]

At St. Lawrence, the 1935 commencement was one of those landmarks which punctuate the history of a college like old-fashioned milestones. Dr. Richard Eddy Sykes gave his last baccalaureate and last message to a senior class; President Seelye gave his first address; Owen Young, except for a few words at the commencement luncheon, said nothing—but carried the banner for '94 in the alumni parade. The only flaw in the occasion was that Robert Frost did not appear to receive his honorary degree.[21]

After these ceremonies, which marked not the end of Young's concern for St. Lawrence but the beginning of less involvement in its affairs, he spent two days in Van Hornesville, two days in the office, and several evenings and the following weekend with Jo in Riverside.

Then he was back in Canton to speak at the opening of the Canadian-American Conference. Sponsored by the Carnegie Endowment for International Peace with the cooperation of St. Lawrence and Queen's University in Ontario, and organized by that indefatigable worker for international comity, James T. Shotwell, this wholly unofficial meeting had had Young's special interest from the start. In his introductory remarks this veteran of international conferences distinguished sharply between political and "educational" conferences. They cannot be both, he said, for if they are political "they are likely not only to be non-educational but even mis-educational. . . . The only successful political conferences are those whose conclusions have been agreed to in advance. . . ."[22]

Young could devote only two days to the conference at the time, for he had both Federal Reserve and regents meetings in New York; and there was always the mail to catch up with. He had been mulling over the problem of housing, and wrote a long in-house letter to Theodore K. Quinn, a GE vice-president, on the subject, indicating not only careful attention to detail but excitement over this new project. Another letter—warm and affectionate—went to Bernard Baruch, saying how much he had missed seeing him lately—"I rather got the notion that possibly you thought that I was becoming too reactionary to make it worthwhile to talk to me in these progressive days. I have to leave again for a few days but shall be back the middle of next week, after which I am going to make it my business to see if I can get hold of you for a review of the world sufficiently to bring our minds up to date . . . there is no one whose friendship I value more."[23]

And with regret he wrote William F. Carey that he could not accept his invitation to the Louis-Carnera fight because he had to attend the commencement of the Van Hornesville School: "People will never know the sacrifices which I make for education."[24]

On June 22, he returned to Canton for the closing of the Canadian-American Conference, stressing in his final remarks "the moral and philosophical compatibility of the citizens of the two nations." From there he went home to Van Hornesville, to play for the fifth time his usual role in the school commencement, introducing the speaker—this time the new president of St. Lawrence—and handing out the diplomas. June is perhaps the most beautiful month of the year in this village, and to Owen Young the graduation of another class at his school was always the most satisfying and happy of occasions.

Then, with Richard, who had had his sixteenth birthday the day before, he returned to New York, ready for the week's work. But an early morning phone call changed both his schedule and his life.

iv

After her partial recovery—unexpected by her doctors—from the early and extreme stage of her illness, Josephine Young led a quiet and secluded life, at the apartment in New York, or at her beloved Little Point, or in Van Hornesville. As she grew a little stronger, her husband encouraged her to be up and about, to see friends as well as family. She went out very seldom in the city, but in the country she loved to be outside, to watch the gardens bloom at Riverside, the boats in the harbor, or in Van Hornesville the changing colors of the fall.

Owen refused all evening invitations, all distant trips; for almost two years he went no farther than Washington, Boston, Chicago or Canton—all only a night away on the sleeper. Not until February of 1933, when he had so briefly visited Cuba with his daughter and her husband, did he feel that Jo was strong enough for him to go farther. That summer, and the next, saw her back with him in Van Hornesville, and they were together in making their Thanksgiving jaunts to Cambridge, not to mention their own Caribbean adventure.

Late in June of 1934 Owen and Dick attended the Radcliffe commencement where Josephine received her master's degree; even though Jo could not be there, it was a great satisfaction to her—and to her daughter—that now they were fellow alumnae. In Van Hornesville that August the family was all present at one time; photographs were taken, at the Home Farm on the hill, of the grandparents, the four children, and the three grandsons and three granddaughters. And in the spring of 1935 Owen and Jo made a trip to Washington to visit Philip—now working for the SEC—and Faith and little Faith.

Throughout these four years, when the few trips were spaced by long quiet months at home, Owen and Jo had more time alone together than in all the previous years of their marriage. He had always kept her in touch with his life, and in these years more than ever she shared it wholly. Her sharp, clear mind, her definite opinions, her warm sympathies were directed to his concerns, public and private. She read a great deal, newspapers and periodicals and books, and kept him in touch with material he had no time to study. They talked of these things, and of older books and older times; they relived their lives with laughter and some tears. In a long and appreciative letter, written later to Owen, Frances Perkins spoke of an opportunity that she had had to talk "intimately for a good half-day" with Jo: "She spoke so simply about her affection for you, her faith, her sense of creative relationship to you and your work."[25]

Both Owen and Jo felt, that spring of 1935, that time was growing short. If the trips she enjoyed so much were weakening, they were the result of conscious choice. In May young Jo and baby Josephine came to stay with her at Riverside, sitting on the lawn among the flowers, talking of the past—and of the future, for another baby would be coming soon. If concern for this event, too, was a tax upon her strength, it gave her deep pleasure. "It will be a boy," she said, "we always have more boys. It is the girls that are special." And so it was.

She rarely talked of her illness, and almost never to her children. But to her intimate friends—Julie Hull, Charlotte Kruesi, who had been close since St. Lawrence days—she said she hoped she would not live on, incapacitated and feeble, but that she might go quickly at the end. And so it was.

Several swift heart attacks, beyond the power of the nitroglycerin pills to control; the doctor summoned, morphine given. She never recovered consciousness, and died at 5:35 A.M. on June 25. By the time Owen reached Little Point it was over.

The boys were soon with their father; the daughter was hurried off to the hospital, in New York, by the doctor, for he expected the baby would come immediately. (He was wrong.)

Then all the family, except for Everett and Josephine, gathered at Van Hornesville. The funeral was in the little white church where Owen had been Sunday school superintendent, where young Jo was married. Frank Oliver Hall, their friend from Southbridge days, and Dr. Sykes from St. Lawrence conducted the simple service, and the bearers were neighbors in the village. Far more people came than could enter the church; they stood quietly outside in the rain—relatives, neighbors, GE people, St. Lawrence people, regents. Owen was deeply touched that Nelson and Lulu Perkins came over from Boston, and persuaded them to stay the night with him.

Together, in the summer storm, family and friends walked up the hill to the cemetery, to the green slope where John and Eleanor lay, near Owen's parents, grandparents and great-grandparents.

The letters poured in: hundreds and hundreds of messages, from the President of the United States, from the porter on the private car they took to Arizona, from schoolmates of Southbridge days, from the stationmaster in Lexington, from governors and ambassadors, from colleagues abroad, from young people whom Jo had helped, from Morgan partners, from a New York State trooper who had known her in Van Hornesville. An especially loving letter came from Charley Gaines, who said in his gnomic way, "Bereavement . . . is the price of happiness and the penalty of living."[26]

Every single letter Owen answered himself, by a note, or by longer letters, many with special personal references. When his arm gave out, for he was not used to writing, he dictated letters, with apologies to the recipients. It was the labor of months.

Of his hundreds of replies, we quote only one, to Dr. Arthur F. Chace, Jo's doctor:

> Thank you so much for your comforting letter. You know that I do not yield readily or even gracefully to the inevitable—or at least I am never willing to admit inevitability. That was always true of the threatened loss of Mrs. Young and my hopes and will were aided by you these last four years more than by anybody in the world, for which I can never be sufficiently grateful. It is a comfort to feel that with your service we literally stole an additional four years of life together—not sad or depressed years, as might well have happened with a less wonderful woman, but buoyant and happy years—in many ways the happiest years of our life. I say all this in tribute to your part in it for you held Mrs. Young's confidence and faith and trust, all of which was so necessary. It was not the faith of an ignorant woman in some mysterious power of a man skilled in the art of medicine. It was the trust of a highly intelligent one in a man whose character she admired and whose ability she trusted to do all that was humanly possible to do—and beyond that lay her philosophy of life.
>
> I may say that I am accepting her philosophy now. I am very well, perhaps due to the fact that I am sleeping better than at any time in four years past—for then one carried as his last conscious thought of what might happen before morning.
>
> Thank you again.

When Jo, before they were married, told Owen she thought that he should be a "man of affairs," she got, in the event, rather more than she bargained for. To be sure, she had, through him, a life of rich rewards, in every sense; but she was without his company and care for a large proportion of their earlier years. She not only looked after five children, but capably managed several sizable establishments—all geared to giving him as little trouble as possible. Her own life, developed for the lonely times, included a few committees and boards, but she was not a "committee woman" except where she felt she could be of real help. It included also, in New York, constant attention to and appreciation of the arts; she rarely missed an important exhibition, especially of prints of any kind. She was a connoisseur of antique silver and furniture and, of course, rare books. She loved the theater, and went often. And in the country she spent many hours in the gardens, which grew and blossomed for her.

She read constantly all her life: her favorites were Dickens and Thackeray, George Borrow, Harrison Ainsworth, Fanny Burney, Fielding, Trollope; her modern ones, Conrad above all, Kipling, Galsworthy, Arnold Bennett, Shaw; and both old and new poets. Her avocations shaped her children's tastes, although they hardly knew it at the time. Only as they grew older did they realize how much not only their pleasures but their principles were learned from her example. She never preached, but they knew what she expected of them.

Her circle consisted only of family and good friends; she was glad to see acquaintances but she did not seek them out, except for young women and men to whom she thought she could be of service. To old friends she was always there, ready to help if needed, supplying not only funds but courage to go on, and humor to lighten dark days.

And courage for herself as well, to cope with death and illness, to maintain always an equable disposition in the face of tragedy and—sometimes more difficult—of small and large disappointments. Owen was always loving and considerate—she told an old friend that "Owen has never failed me"; but the demands of his life were often overwhelming for wife and household. She took the brunt of it, and enabled him to do what he had to do.

v

Young was back in the office on July 2, though for the first ten days he saw, for the most part, only those close to him—Gerard Swope, John Elwood, Stuart Crocker, Charles Appleton, Edward Adler—and the only business he did was with Foster Gunnison and Jim Hagar on Houses, Inc., which was now to be linked more closely with General Electric. By the middle of the month he was in Schenectady for the meetings of Camp General, where he spoke, informally as always, to his colleagues. This was his only talk for the second half of 1935; he refused all other invitations to speak. In this one he began with a curiously poignant figure—punctuation:

The printed page is not unlike life itself. The pause of the comma . . . the longer stop of the semi-colon; the question mark to express our curiosity and to suggest sometimes fear and doubt; the exclamation point to represent a great surge upward and outward of the emotions. . . . Finally the end of it, and we have that finality, that conclusiveness of the period, which carries assurance with it. And then you begin a new sentence, and [sometimes] a new paragraph. And when you go into the new paragraph you go into a new area of thought and action, and one by one the paragraphs are ended and you turn the page and begin anew.[27]

It was to be many months before he could turn the page. What remained of 1935 was filled with the jobs of his regular routine. His older children saw him, in New York or Van Hornesville, as often as possible, and he made every effort to keep in touch with Dick, at home or at school. Young Jo presented him with a new grandson, James Herbert Case III, and in September the Case family moved to Van Horne House to live, to raise children and write books. There Owen enjoyed visiting, and spent what time he could in Van Hornesville. But the apartment in New York—now reduced to two floors and three servants—was dismally lonely. His friends invited him for luncheons and dinners and weekends, but he had little heart for even such understanding efforts. The office was more comforting, where he could lose himself in the affairs of GE—which were now looking up. He wrote E. W. Rice, Jr.—now in his last illness—in September: "So far as the General Electric Company is concerned I feel that the storm is over. . . . Now I think we are running into a new period in which there will be again an opportunity for great constructive effort. To realize on that fully, we shall need to stimulate the imagination and ingenuity of the younger men, and filter their proposals through the experience of the older ones. . . ." He was talking to an elder statesman of General Electric, and he was beginning to feel like one himself.[28]

Perhaps nothing took him out of himself and his sorrow as much as his efforts on behalf of young people, which he had enjoyed so much discussing with Jo. In addition to the National Youth Administration and the American Youth Commission, he had begun, after his election to the New York State Board of Regents in 1934, a special project on education in New York State. He had soon discovered that this ancient and august body, having in its charge the supervision of all education in the state, was knee-deep in administrative detail and very short on up-to-date and well-ordered information; this was a serious barrier to policymaking, which the newest—and youngest—regent considered its most important function. Young thereupon proposed an outside and thoroughgoing audit—"The Regents' Inquiry into the Character and Cost of Public Education in the State of New York." He himself obtained half a million dollars from Rockefeller's General Education Board to fund it.

Young kept in close touch with the Inquiry throughout its course—the final report was issued in 1938—and also made it his business to see that everyone in the state from the governor down knew what was going on and why. In October of 1935, for instance, he set up a luncheon at the Waldorf for the press, to describe the Inquiry and to answer questions about it. This unprecedented behavior on the part of a regent delighted the editors and reporters present, and resulted in front-page articles all over the state.

Young had not thought of his youth-centered activities as "cover" for other affairs but apparently there were those who did. Coming up to Van Hornesville to vote in the off-year election, he told his daughter and her husband that the President had asked him to stop at Hyde Park on Wednesday "to talk about the National Youth Administration." Also, and for the same reason, Eleanor Roosevelt had invited him to supper at the White House the Sunday following.

Josephine asked how the President, "after three years of doing without your advice, could possibly get along without you for the four days between visits. He seems to think about you," she added, "when election day comes round." Her father's response was to say that Marvin McIntyre (a presidential secretary), insisting that both appointments stood, had finally confessed to Miss Morrison that there were one or two other things which the President had in mind for the Hyde Park visit.[29]

A week later, on Armistice Day, Young reported on his visit. The President, extremely cordial, had begun, he said, "by suggesting that 'we tell the newspaper boys that you and I have discussed the school survey by the Board of Regents.' What he really wanted to talk to me about, however, was 'this utilities mess.' He said he wanted my help and that I must tell him what to do."[30]

By the "utilities mess" the President meant the intensive campaign of opposition, lobbying and threatened appeal to the courts which had followed the introduction—early in the year and at his urging—of the Wheeler-Rayburn bill with its "death sentence" for utility holding companies. This bill had encountered hard sledding in the House but when, on May 27, 1935, a unanimous Supreme Court found the NRA and its codes unconstitutional, Roosevelt had been stung into action. Kept in session for what has been called the "Second Hundred Days," a hot and weary Congress had finally sent him for approval the new Banking Act, the Social Security Act, the Wagner Act with its far-reaching charter for labor, and a slightly amended version of the Holding Company Act.

As finally enacted—and neatly summarized by William E. Leuchtenburg—this measure "wiped out all utility holding companies more than twice removed from the operating companies, empowered the SEC, with whom all combines were compelled to register, to eliminate companies beyond the first degree that were not in the public interest." And with the registration date fixed for December 1, the big units were threatening to file suits instead of registering.[31]

All this, of course, Young knew, and except for its punitive overtones and arbitrary deadlines, the action government now called for was basically in accord with the recommendation he had made at the Insull hearings of early 1933. But this punitive "spirit of approach" had made all the difference. Responding now to the President, Young said that if he had been asked a few months earlier he might have been able to help, "but quite frankly, a settlement now looks hopeless." Nevertheless, if the President still wanted his help, he would do what he could. The President did.

"All right then," Young replied, "the first thing is for you to tell Landis [chairman of the SEC] and Cummings [U.S. attorney general] that you have asked me to take hold of this and let them come and see me. Once we are clear about what can be worked out from the government's angle . . . I will see what I can do with the utilities." This time, however, he had let the President know that General Electric's own business was threatened because "Gerard and I did not publicly denounce the act in question." It was true; Young's efforts to find a sensible middle course had subjected him to the increasing hostility of such utility leaders as his old friend J. F. Owens of Oklahoma and to nasty innuendos in such sections of the press as looked to the *Chicago Tribune* for guidance. He did not enjoy finding himself on the defensive but there it was. And the President, not unsympathetic, was still, he felt, "terribly anxious for me to take a crack at it."[32]

This Hyde Park meeting had an unexpected interlude. The President's mother had come to luncheon, and when she had asked if Mr. Young could stay and see her afterward, her son had expressed the hope that he could and would. And so, of course, he did. What Mrs. Roosevelt wanted turned out to be his advice about certain changes in the family's land holdings and some rearrangements of their private financial affairs. When their talk ended, the lady told him how grateful she was and how glad she was that he "was helping Frank." Young found her gratitude so genuine and so moving that he "doubted whether I could ever bring myself to vote against her son."[33]

Two days later Young went down to Washington to see Commissioner James Landis and the attorney general. Back in New York next day, he reported on the government's position to perhaps the most liberal-minded of the utility leaders: Wendell Willkie of Commonwealth and Southern, Ned Groesbeck of Bond and Share, and W. Alton (Pete) Jones of Cities Service—plus John Foster Dulles, appearing as counsel for the North American group. At the least, he was among friends who fully credited his good faith in presenting the government's position.

First, he reported, the Commission hoped that December 1 would not be regarded as the day for flinging down the gauntlet and taking irrevocable decisions by either party. To this the utilities agreed.

Second, the Commission was so anxious that the companies register first and discuss their difficulties afterward that it was ready to announce publicly its willingness to regard registration as in no sense prejudicial to any legal rights involved.

Third, the Commission urged that if two or three of the larger utility groups were to follow this procedure it might persuade the intractable groups to come along and so soften the atmosphere of conflict.

Fourth, and finally, Landis had offered to come to New York and sit down with any utility officials for full and frank discussion if this offered any likelihood of constructive results. Young had promised to advise him whether or not such a visit seemed in order and likely to be productive.

On all these points, the nub of the difficulty was that counsel to the utilities were wholly convinced that any such assurance as the commission was prepared to offer would have no standing in a court of law; and hence, that registration could only prove prejudicial to their rights. By no means convinced himself, Young persevered and the discussion went on for several days. In the end, however, he was left with no option but to advise Landis that his proposed visit looked to be futile.[34]

So Landis did not come, and on November 29 and 30, all of these groups publicly announced their refusal to register. And that would have been that, but for the special situation presented by American and Foreign Power. As a company whose operations were exclusively foreign—jointly owned by GE and Bond and Share, with Young a member of its board—it was presumably entitled to exemption. Young had told Landis, as he reported to Groesbeck, that he had no intention of permitting a company of which he was a director to be in the position of fighting its own government because its business was exclusively foreign; thus this corporation would be definitely filing claim for exemption before December 1.

Suggesting to Groesbeck, who agreed, that this afforded a fair basis for both of them to sit down and iron out the matter with the commissioner, Young had gone to Washington with his partner on the twenty-fifth. They had had a lengthy conversation with Landis, of which Groesbeck made a memorandum; next morning as they descended from the sleeper in New York, they were greeted by the news that the government had filed suit against Bond and Share, to compel its registration.

Surprise, surprise. Evidently, as Young remarked to Miss Morrison, it was not only in dealing with other governments that the New Deal was ruling out the ordinary decencies. Nor were matters mended when, over the next few days, Washington-based columnists delighted in reporting how the commission had "put one over" on Owen Young and "how everybody down here was enjoying the little joke." It was even presented as evidence that this administration was not about to be taken over—or even taken in—by Wall Street. End of story.[35]

The calendar of appointments for November and early December had been very full; Owen had endeavored to conduct "business as usual." Now, as Christmas approached, he knew that Dick would be in Van Hornesville with his sister and her family, and he need have no responsibility for him, or anybody else. On December 14, two days after attending what he now expected to be his last meeting as a director of the New York Federal Reserve, he went home to the apartment with a miserable cold and bronchitis and stayed there until the last day of the year. It was indeed the period at the end of this paragraph.

Chapter 35

The Utilities Again;
Louise and Washington Oaks

A T NEW YEAR'S, 1936, Young did spend a few days in Van
Hornesville with his children, but he was not feeling strong,
and on the ninth he left for Florida. The annual meeting of
the Association of Edison Illuminating Companies at Boca Raton was
a good excuse for making the change of climate which he badly
needed. The association always asked him to speak, he usually did
and gave 'em hell, and they did not like it; then next year they asked
him again. This year he said of the utilities, "This industry has lost . . .
its verve and its spirit, and its confidence . . . it has lost something of
its good temper" under political attack; to such attack, he said, resistance is not enough. Heavy taxes, the threat of inflation, yes, but "your
serious problems today are political"—what remedies could mitigate
those attacks? "The unruly few" must be controlled; the utilities must
accept regulation of holding companies; and because "some people
have accumulated enormous riches in a short time through the control of utilities . . . in these days of bitterness and envy" the situation
was made worse. Then he told a Van Hornesville story, about a hired
man he had on the farm, Joe:

He isn't very intelligent, but he is a good cow man and he is a great
eater, and on Sunday morning the boys try to have their breakfast after
their chores are done, so they get in the barn about five o'clock in the
morning and they get their breakfast about nine.

One Sunday morning I was up there and they had gone to breakfast.
When they came back, Joe, this very placid and lovable creature, slammed
the doors, was ugly to his cows—amazing to me. I said "Joe, what's the
matter?"

"Well," he said, "that Mrs. Van Deusen, as I was getting breakfast,
stood there with her hands on her hips and said, 'Joe, do you know you

have eaten twenty-six pancakes?' And, Mr. Young, I was so damn mad that I never finished my breakfast."[1]

Young's condemnation of the holding-holding-holding company in his Insull testimony, his letter to Ned Groesbeck in 1935, his speech at Boca Raton in that year, and this one in 1936, all emphasizing the need for truth and confidence and cooperation, within and without the industry, had little effect. The utilities fought the Wheeler-Rayburn bill tooth and nail, and the bitterness and antagonism which resulted from that contest, and from the endless line of suits brought under it against the SEC, continued to be deplored by Young in every word he spoke on the subject.

A month later he was in Florida again, to speak at Rollins College in Winter Park; there he used the same theme in a different context. He was tired, he said, of "prejudice and passion" in "these times of confusion and bewilderment"—especially at the beginning of a great political campaign. He spoke of the power of the radio—"one of the great central power plants of public opinion"—which magnified the effect of national speechmakers, so that

the same extravagance of statement, the same carelessness, the same appeal to emotions, which stirred the audience in the "ballroom" of the country hotel one hundred years ago is freely resorted to now, before the great central sounding-board of a nation. The jibe, the exaggeration, the exuberance—even though rhetorical only—which may have relieved the lonely pioneer on his way home over a muddy road, and so have been excusable, may become, when uttered by a voice of great authority before a master sounding-board while millions listen, an agency of irremediable injury.

And he quoted ill-timed, ill-judged statements from Herbert Hoover, Senator Joe Robinson and Al Smith to prove it, then ended with an appeal to the top: "To these great men, and even to the President of the United States . . . may we not appeal for the choice word and the measured phrase, spoken with malice toward none and charity toward all?"[2]

This appeal—somewhat rhetorical itself—was apparently welcome to tired ears all over the country, for the press gave it great play. A cartoon of Young carrying up the mountain the banner "MODERATION," under dark clouds of "Political Appeal to Prejudice and Passion," was widely reprinted, and *Newsweek* reproduced a cartoon from the *New York Daily Graphic* of March 15, 1877, showing a frantic, wild-haired orator shouting into a telephone box, from which wires ran to listening audiences in London, Dublin, Boston, the West, San Francisco, Pekin and the Fiji Islands, entitled "Terrors of the Telephone."[3]

After the Rollins speech, Richard Young arrived in Florida from Choate to spend his spring vacation and see, under the tutelage of his father, something of the state. They toured both the west and east coasts, visiting Henry Doherty and going to the horse races in Miami, calling on Edison's widow, and driving north together, visiting Civil War sites, at the end of March. Not least memorable to the son was his father's unwonted recourse to verse in response to Burma-shave's ubiquitous billboards, spurred no doubt by the prize they promised for the best couplet advertising that product. Young's couplet—alas, never submitted—ran: "Men are equal nowhere save / Before the law and Burma-shave."[4]

Business was better that spring of 1936, but the unemployment figures were still appallingly high. A request from Secretary of Commerce Daniel C. Roper for a statement on this problem from an employer's point of view produced a long letter (which the author described as "trite and commonplace"). Young asked first for "an intelligent breakdown of the figures of unemployment"—where, how much, and what kind? "Unemployment is not one problem—it is a hundred or a thousand problems. There is no magic formula by which we can deal with it in the large. We have to reduce it to small manageable sections and then tackle each intelligently and determinedly. . . ." And, of course, he spoke especially of youth, who must be trained so they might seize the opportunities for employment as they arose—as, eventually, they must.[5]

In fact, a census on unemployment was not attempted until late in 1937, when the federal government undertook it by mail. It was generally agreed that industry could not possibly take more than a million out of the estimated total of eight million unemployed. And Young urged, in another letter—again in search of facts—that the labor unions should make reports publicly on all their funds, for they are "organizations which have memberships of millions, and by their own statement exercise such vast power in the economic and social activities of the time, to say nothing of the political ones" that they should submit "to the same kind of publicity which other organizations much less influential are required to do." The reason for such disclosure, he went on, was that "I think that public opinion is the only effective agency with which to deal with such a sprawling and ever changing problem as that of unemployment. In order that public opinion may function, it is necessary to have public exposure of the facts."[6]

To the president of the McGraw-Hill Publishing Company, Malcolm Muir, shortly to become editor of *Newsweek*, he wrote, tongue in cheek, in answer to a request for a statement on "What Industry Means to America":

Why get out a special number to answer the question of what Industry means to America? Of course it means this:

That industry shall employ all the unemployed, nothwithstanding that that would be more than double the number that industry ever employed.

It means that industry should contribute to unemployment insurance, old age pensions and other pensions, so that no one would have to worry or save, quite regardless of whether the beneficiaries were participants in industry.

It means that investors in industry should not make a profit but supply a service, including such capital as is necessary to develop and maintain adequately plant facilities and turn-over funds.

It means that taxes should be raised sufficiently on industry so that municipal, state and Federal budgets can be balanced.

It means that reciprocal or other trade agreements should be made having the effect of reducing tariffs, so that American industry would not get a monopoly of serving the American people.

It means that prices to the consumer should not be raised, but lowered, in order that large quantities of goods should be consumed.

I think you can make an excellent number out of what Industry means to America if you will really devote yourself to that, instead of doing what I expect you to do and try to prove what Industry does not mean to America.

This letter is personal and confidential, and it does not mean that I am in favor of high tariffs or opposed to social security legislation, balancing the budget, high wages or low prices. I am in favor of all these things, but the general methods proposed to get them and the timing of the different steps seem to me to be as unworthy of our intelligence as the objectives are worthy of our aspirations.[7]

ii

The story, in these years, like his own concerns, returns always to the utilities. At the World Power Conference in Washington in September 1936 Young pointed out the enormous growth of "the business of power and the business of government, the output of both being the largest in our history."[8] He did not go on to say what was well known, at least in the United States: that a clash was inevitable between the two. To reduce this struggle to manageable proportions was one of the tasks he set for himself in the later 1930s.

Ever since President Roosevelt signed the Tennessee Valley Authority Act in May of 1933, the government and the utilities had been skirmishing incessantly over public versus private power. Young was inevitably drawn into this; he was to many, though not all, utility people their elder statesman, who could make himself heard nationally on any question, and was listened to by government and private agencies alike. Also, he knew, liked and respected the principal combatants on the battlefield—Wendell Willkie of Commonwealth and Southern and David Lilienthal of the T V A.

In September 1933 Young had written his friend Frank T. Post of the Washington Water Power Company, in the state of the great Bonneville and Grand Coulee projects, still on the drawing boards but threatening the future of the utilities there. Young praised his statement on "the injustice done to private power companies by government development," saying that he would guess that "after this temporary intoxication wears off, there will be a very considerable reaction in this country toward the re-establishment of respect for legal rights, certainly those embodied in fundamental rules under which any economic society or political organization based on it, must function if it is to survive."[9]

He may have had a suspicion that his guess was wrong. In any case, he met with Lilienthal, Willkie and others both in government and the utilities over the next years in an endeavor to accommodate, if not avert, the increasing role of government in the generation and especially the transmission of power. He also went to the top.

Waterpower, it will be remembered, had been a subject for discussion between Young and Franklin Roosevelt in previous years. Young had tried to educate F D R when he first became governor of New York, but it did not take very well. Young had recommended, in his discussions with Governor Smith on the development of the St. Lawrence River, public ownership and capital (that is, tax-exempt bonds) for the generating plant, but transmission and distribution by the private companies; this plan was included in the packet of information on waterpower that he had given Roosevelt in November 1928. But in 1933 Senator Norris and Interior Secretary Harold Ickes had persuaded the President that the T V A act must contain the right of the Authority to build its own transmission lines up to the point of distribution, even though they paralleled those of private companies. It was also empowered to offer municipalities low-interest loans to build distribution systems within their own limits.

By 1936 the situation was well heated up. Young saw the President on February 21; Frank Kent surmised in his column that Roosevelt was now trying to make overtures to "influential men from whom he has been practically cut off for three years."[10] Actually, it was one of the rare occasions on which it was not the President but Young who had asked for the appointment. We cannot prove that they talked waterpower, but Young had been seeing Willkie, and on the morning of the day he lunched at the White House he saw Morris Cooke, an enthusiastic supporter of Roosevelt's public power policy and later head of the Rural Electrification Administration.

When Young dined at the White House on April 29 the subject was youth—it was Mrs. Roosevelt's party—but the President asked him to return soon. This he did on May 5; at this meeting there is record that they talked about the Edison Foundation and the possibility of issuing an Edison stamp; indeed, said F D R, why not a series of stamps to honor American inventors?[11] What was said about public power, if anything, is not recorded; Young had had plenty of experience in trying to pin him down to a desired topic. However, he obediently got from the Research Laboratories at Schenectady a list of inventors who might merit stamps, and sent it to the President.

But something must have registered. As election day drew near, Roosevelt called a conference for September 30 on power. A large and representative group went to the White House: Willkie of Commonwealth and Southern, P. S. Arkwright of Georgia Power, Samuel Ferguson of Hartford Electric, among others; Young and Thomas Lamont; and for T V A, Lilienthal and Arthur Morgan, as well as Frank R. McNinch, the chairman of the Federal Power Commission, and other government officials. The advance press notice reported that the subject would be "a power pool."

Young wrote Henry Doherty on October 5, thanking him for his statement on

the basic principles affecting the industry [which I received] before going to Washington [and took with me] on the chance that there might be an opportunity to discuss them with the President. He limited the conference, however, at the very beginning to the very narrow area of exploration as to whether or not the transmission systems of the Commonwealth & Southern and the T V A could be unified and thereby avoid useless duplication of transmission lines. He said at once that the distribution problem as distinguished from transmission presented too many difficulties for a first approach, and similarly that that was true as to the generating problems because the costs of the government generating plants were so inextricably bound up in the navigation and flowage dams. He hoped, however, that we could find a basis for an agreement covering transmission, when we might then undertake further exploration in the other two areas in the hope of achieving some results there.

This was all; the group was dismissed within the hour. Willkie and Lilienthal met immediately with McNinch to attack the problem which the President had outlined; Young dined with his son Philip and his family and went back to New York.

It was a lost opportunity. A willingness on the part of the President to discuss the "basic principles" might well have changed the history of the power conflict. Once again Young's hopes were disappointed, but he looked forward to the further conferences the President had suggested.

Nevertheless, on October 14 Young answered an inquiry from Senator George Radcliffe; he replied,

Your information is quite correct. I am in favor of President Roosevelt's re-election and I do object to some of his policies. It is for that reason I have felt that it was impossible for me to speak in this campaign with justice both to the President and myself.

A political man who is part of a party organization is forgiven if he states affirmatively his reasons for support and conceals his reservations. In a word, he is regarded as a kind of professional advocate. That does not apply to me. If I speak at all, I must state both equally frankly and clearly. To do so would leave me to some extent critical of the President, and that I do not wish to be. After all he has been my personal friend for many years as he has been yours.

It is for these reasons that I cannot accept your invitation to speak in Maryland nor do I see how I can speak anywhere. . . .

Young also refused membership on an advisory committee to the Democratic National Committee, which Jim Farley had asked him to join. He pleaded his membership on the board of regents as a disqualification: "Mr. Roosevelt," he wrote, "when he was Governor criticized certain members of the Board publicly for such service."[12]

When election day arrived, soon after his sixty-second birthday, Owen Young was sick in bed at 830 Park—with a bad cold and bronchitis. The word *psychosomatic* was not used so frequently then as now, but it is possible to imagine that if he could not bring himself to vote *against* FDR he had a deep, if only half-realized, desire not to vote *for* him.

The further conferences of the power group never took place; on the twenty-sixth of January, 1937, Roosevelt "abruptly ended today elaborate studies which he ordered September 30 on the pooling of public and private electric power transmission facilities in the Tennessee Valley," because, he said, an injunction brought by the private power companies precluded such an arrangement. Letters were sent to members of the September meeting, and the President made his announcement at his press conference, "merely shrugging and assuming an attitude of one who bowed to the inevitable."[13]

Willkie made answer, pointing out that the litigation had been begun before September 30, and that it by no means prevented the pooling of transmission, the studying of problems, or the working out of a permanent solution. But the fiat had been issued, and that was that.

iii

Young's journeys to Florida in 1936 were not wholly for the purpose of enjoying the climate, making speeches, or showing the state to his youngest son. He found a warm welcome in St. Augustine from his friend Louise Clark. Her mother, Julia Powis, had decided to move south permanently, and had chosen northern Florida because she had spent some years there, in the 1880s, with her husband, Walter Van Rensselaer Powis. Young helped arrange, in 1936, for Mrs. Powis, the purchase from the Home Owners' Loan of a pleasant little house overlooking the harbor in St. Augustine, and it was there that he visited her and her daughter.

Owen and Louise, it will be recalled, had first met in the Philippines in 1921, on his way home from China, when she was Mrs. Elwood Stanley Brown. She and Brown had met at college in Illinois, married, and gone to the Philippines, where he developed a program in physical education for the YMCA—a career he continued for the army in France during the First World War. There were two children of the marriage, Virginia and Stanley. Mr. Brown died in 1924, and some years later Louise married an industrial engineer, Herbert Clark, by whom she had a son, Ward Clark. This was a brief marriage, for Clark died in 1929.

An active and ambitious woman of multifold talents, Louise had developed in the Philippines a cottage industry which combined the skills in fine hand embroidery of the native women and her own ability as a designer, with charming results. She also traveled through the Orient and Europe, as well as the United States, to find new ideas and new markets for her delicate lingerie and table linen. The firm, called Powis-Brown, had outlets in New York, Chicago and Paris, and made a major contribution to the support of the little family.

One difficulty from the first was the lack of sufficient capital to cover the long interval between the time the silk materials arrived in

Manila and when the finished product appeared on the counter at Saks or Pirie and Scott, for there was no air express. Missy Meloney, editor of *This Week*, the *Herald Tribune* magazine, was a friend of Louise, and also of Owen Young. It was first at her request that Young, in New York, had guaranteed for some years at the Bankers Trust a revolving credit, supported by orders ahead, for use in the interval.

In the depression, however, such a luxury business could not survive, for all the delicate beauty of the product and the talents and energy of the owner, and eventually Louise had to give it up. Her older children were grown, but she and little Ward lived with her mother, in New York and then in Florida. She tried her talented hands at sculpture, and in 1936 made a bust of Owen Young. But she was, perhaps, less interested in the art than in her subject, and when he came to Florida she showed him the ancient city, and drove him south along the sea.

Under this pleasant tutelage, Young found, somewhat to his surprise, that he liked Florida, especially some of the wild land they saw between Summer Haven and Flagler. It was good citrus country—the northern edge of the Indian River district—and the never-sleeping farmer in Owen Young responded to the healthy trees he saw in the strip between the sea and the Matanzas River. As he and Louise began to shape a common future, he inquired into the availability of a large tract, covered with big trees, on the coastal highway about twenty miles south of St. Augustine and three miles south of the spot where Marineland was just beginning to be built.

Florida real estate, especially jungly pieces far from anywhere, was not very high-priced in the 1930s; Young bought a strip of more than three hundred acres between the road and the river for six thousand dollars, putting title in Louise's name. Later he added more acreage, especially across the highway to the east, including some oceanfront. There were no buildings on the place except for one or two ramshackle frame houses near the road. The big plantation house, built under the live oaks by the river by cousins of George Washington (whose descendants owned the place until 1924), had long since disappeared, and the prolific growth had swallowed the original plantation. Only the name, Washington Oaks, remained.

There was no fresh water, no electricity and no telephone, but the pines and the palms, the hardwood trees and the banyans were enormous; one of the live oaks was reputed to be eight hundred years old. And it was a difficult choice which was more beautiful, the river where the white egrets fished and flew, or the seabeach with its fantastically shaped coquina ledges and the long horizon straight to Africa.

Louise and Owen were married on February 20, 1937, in the little Episcopal church on the marketplace in St. Augustine, in the presence of their families and a few close friends—including Missy Meloney, who prided herself on making the match. Mrs. Powis gave a reception in her new house, and that night the famous old Flagler hotel, the Ponce de León, saw considerable merriment. The secret of the marriage had been well kept beforehand, but when it broke there were a good many headlines.

The next day Washington Oaks was on exhibition, and Louise gave a wonderful party. In one of the cleared spaces an outdoor fireplace had been built, where Francisco, Louise's devoted houseboy from Manila, roasted whole one of the local wild pigs. Chairs had been set up, and long tables loaded with every delicious southern or Oriental dish imaginable. It was the Young family's first experience of the beauty of the Florida wilderness, and the cornucopia of mouth-watering food, with both of which Louise was to supply them for years to come.

The marriage was to last twenty-five years, the rest of Owen's life. When they were married he was sixty-two, his bride fifty. Their total of seven children were all grown except for the nine-year-old Ward Clark, who lived with Mrs. Powis in St. Augustine. It was a singularly happy partnership; there was not only much love between them, but great admiration and respect for each other's different and complementary talents.

For the first two years, they lived during their months in Florida in one of the old buildings on the place, while they worked at setting out citrus trees and gardens, and planning their new house. They chose for the site a slight elevation on the river side, looking west across the Matanzas to the wild islands and swamps beyond. Louise designed the house herself, for this was another of her skills. It was a small, one-story Spanish L-shape, containing a large living room with a great stone fireplace, a dining room, kitchen and two bedrooms, and with a terrace toward the river from which to watch, glass in hand, the sunset and the homing birds.

In this house, where, eventually, all the modern necessities were installed, last of all the telephone, Louise and Owen spent increasing time as his duties in the North became fewer. The children and grandchildren regarded it as a kind of wonderland, coming to visit every year, staying in the house, or in the cabana by the swimming pool, or at nearby Marineland, which had soon provided not only dolphins and marine research and exhibitions but a charming motel and restaurant. During the first years Louise, never at a loss for a new project, attempted a flower and fruit business; the products were beautiful and delicious, but the distance from markets, and then the war, kept it from success. She raised turkeys and chickens and hogs as well, but these too were not a commercial success, for the same reasons. The citrus, however, thrived; the trees bore well, and what they and their families could not eat was sold, or given to the St. Augustine Hospital. All this cultivation was centered not far from the house; the north and south woods were not touched, but remained the original wild forest which gave their house and lawns and gardens the sense of seclusion and remoteness they prized.

iv

Not all the renovation and cultivation and building took place at Washington Oaks in 1937 and 1938. Owen introduced Louise to Van Hornesville in May of '37, and from then on things in the village began to move. In the six years since his mother's death and his first wife's illness, Owen had had little time, heart or money to develop new projects in Van Hornesville. The farms were kept up and the breeding program went on much as before, as did the basic improvements in the village—lawns and spick-and-span houses, streetlights, the community water system. All these, like the old gristmill, the new milk plant and the original central school had been put in running order and paid for before Young's world fell apart in 1931; and if meeting the bills for the school and its subsequent expansion had strained his resources and his ingenuity alike, there was nothing in the finished product to suggest it.

By the time of Louise's arrival so much that was new looked weathered and natural that she could hardly have imagined the Van Hornesville of twenty years before. She quickly made herself at home, getting to know her neighbors, who, curious and shy, began in their turn to know and admire this big, snowy-haired woman with the beautiful dark eyes and smile; and, as much as you can like a stranger, they came to like her. The principal of the school and his wife gave a party for her, and little by little the new Mrs. Young became a citizen of Van Hornesville.

If Owen wondered how his active and ingenious wife would spend

AND THEN WHERE?

A. Ding in the *New York Tribune*, November 11, 1932. © 1932 New York Tribune, Inc.

North Shore Daily Journal, February 8, 1933

Albert Einstein and Owen Young at the convocation of the University of the State of New York, Albany, October 16, 1936. International News Photos

Owen and Louise Young, about 1940   Young in Florida, late 1940s

With the kindergarten at the Van Hornesville School, fall 1949; Young is showing them the big gold pocket watch he kept always, wherever he was, on Van Hornesville time. Alfred Eisenstaedt, *Life* Magazine, © 1949, Time Inc.

Owen Young and his children at the dedication of his office in Van Hornesville, September 1951; left to right: Philip, Richard, Charles, Josephine

In the new office with Sam and John Case

End of the day. Alfred Eisenstaedt, *Life* Magazine, © 1949, Time Inc.

her time in the place which was so wholly his—as Florida was hers—
he did not have long to worry about it. When, in that first summer,
the produce from the large vegetable garden began to come in, Louise
set up an operation in the old Grange Hall to can and preserve it. She
employed girls who were graduates or students of the school, under a
professional supervisor, and they put up seventy-eight varieties of food.
Some was used by the family, the rest donated to the school for lunch-
es. Louise was in her element; a gourmet cook in her own kitchen, she
delighted in this mass production and in the shelves of shining cans
labeled VAN HORNE KITCHENS—and so did her husband.

The next project, begun the following summer of 1938, was the renovation of the old house, which, except for the introduction of plumbing, a furnace, and electricity, was much the same as when it was built
in the 1870s. Louise was a skillful planner, as she proved at Washington Oaks, and she knew exactly what she wanted: a big new kitchen
and dining room, more bedrooms and bathrooms, a wide, curving
stair. The most ambitious and effective change of all was the addition
at the back of the house of a great room to be a library for Owen, with
space for hundreds of books, a grand piano, and a portrait of young
Jo over the fireplace. Untouched by the changes was the old living
room—Ida's "settin-room"—with its coal stove, old family pictures,
and the bay window where Ida used to sit to keep an eye on what
was going on in Van Hornesville. The bedroom above it, which had
been his parents', Owen preempted, and kept it much as it had been.

Behind the library, under the shade of the clothes-pole elm, Louise
made a terrace, and above that three levels of flower gardens where
Ida had had her sweet-pea and raspberry bushes and Uncle John his
chicken house.

While the renovations were being accomplished in Van Hornesville,
Owen and Louise stayed at Little Point when he had to be in New
York, and Ward Clark came north to spend the summer with them.
An adventurous boy of eleven, he climbed too high in the old trees
and was killed in a fall in June of 1939. Louise never returned there
to stay, and some years later the place was sold. Now, to all the family,
Van Hornesville was more than ever the family home.

When at last the extensive rebuilding was done, Owen and Louise
and young Richard—now at St. Lawrence—and Mrs. Powis made it
their summer house, furnishing it with a wealth of handsome pieces
from both their pasts. And at Christmas, when the elder Youngs were
in Florida, the young people took over—children and grandchildren
and friends—and made the rafters ring.

Once all this was done, Louise looked around for new projects. One floor of the Grange Hall (which had become the Odd Fellows Hall, owned by that odd fellow Owen D. Young) was turned into a weaving room. Louise provided looms and beautiful yarns, designs, and a teacher; the local women wove rugs and blankets, tweeds and shawls and table mats and curtains—all the result of charming and practical patterns from the hands of the experienced entrepreneuse from the Philippines. Across the street the old blacksmith's shop was made into a studio, for both pottery and painting; there the artist Leonebel Jacobs worked in the summers. Nor was literature neglected, for Louise provided a renovated old house for their Florida friend Marjorie Kinnan Rawlings. Indeed, over the years, Louise bought half a dozen old houses which were more or less falling down, and made them new and attractive. Her coming provided a kind of second renovation for the area, which delighted her husband, even if it cost him money.

v

In two respects Young's remarriage and the six-week honeymoon that ensued were singularly well timed. The first half of 1937 was witnessing the most marked surge of recovery since the beginning of the New Deal—and his own financial situation was notably eased.[14] GE's earnings in the first quarter, Swope reported to the stockholders in April, were forty cents a share as compared to twenty-five cents for the same period of 1936; orders were up 78 percent and it looked to be the largest first quarter in the history of the company. Some ten thousand men had been taken on, at wage rates even higher than in 1929. Small wonder that Chairman Young, back from his holiday, came out of the meeting with a big smile on his face.[15]

Nor was he unhappy to have escaped the furor created during his absence by the President's so-called Court-packing plan. FDR might well have been impatient with certain of the verdicts rendered by the Supreme Court's "nine old men," but the idea of a President's getting what he wanted through appointments to an enlarged Court horrified his enemies and dismayed many of his friends. Being out of reach of the press, and thus not publicly involved in the ensuing fracas, was something which Young could bear—especially since it was an issue on which he could not in good conscience have supported FDR. That much he did confirm in his response to a subsequent inquiry; dated June 8, this letter said:

I am not in sympathy with Executive coercion of the Supreme Court no matter how it is done, because I am a firm believer that we should keep the three departments of the government each independent of the other. However much I might disagree at any one time with the views or attitude of the Court or how much I might at the same time be in sympathy with the views and aims of the Executive, still I should not feel that the latter ought to be accomplished at the expense of the independence of the former. My reason for this is that some other time I might be greatly in sympathy with the views of the court and quite out of sympathy with the attitude of the Executive. So I prefer to take my chances on independence than to gamble on coercion.[16]

Certainly this move of FDR's did nothing to sustain confidence in either the President or the burgeoning recovery. After a serious fall in the market in August, business began to slide back into the depths. As Young reported to the Federal Reserve directors in New York at the beginning of October, "That there has been a substantial drop in business is shown by the fact that our orders received have fallen more than $2,000,000 weekly in September from the average for the first half of the year."[17] As the end of the year approached there was conviction in all quarters that a new program for recovery was essential. The press called for it, and leaders in both industry and labor were convinced something must be done. And in Washington, brain trusters Adolf Berle, Charles Taussig and Rexford G. Tugwell were telling the President that a program emphasizing cooperation between government, labor and industry must get under way without delay.

And how do we go about it? asked Roosevelt.

Well, they said [as Young told the story], perhaps the first step would be for us to get John Lewis and some leading industrialists together and see if they can agree on any sort of program.—And who, asked the President, would you ask him to sit down with?—They replied that possibly the heads of Steel and Motors might be invited and perhaps Owen Young. The President laughed and said they would never get John Lewis and Owen Young to agree on any sort of program.—Well, they said, if we can get Lewis to sit down with some industrialists and agree upon a program of collaboration, would you be interested enough to invite the group to meet with you? The President replied that he would, and told them to go ahead. Apparently he had no expectation that anything much would develop.[18]

So Berle and Taussig put the proposition to Lewis, who replied that he would be interested only if they could get Owen Young. Young, of course, was anxious for such a meeting, and suggested that Lewis bring in some of his people too; he himself suggested Lamont, which Lewis agreed to "if Mr. Young said it was all right." Both Lewis and Young were sure that no recovery could be achieved without better relations between the "lady in the parlor" and the "kitchen maid." And *sustained* recovery required *total* cooperation between politics and economics—about which both were doubtful. Roosevelt had indeed given special recognition to labor, but he had not shed his punitive attitude toward business.

On December 23, 1937, Berle and Taussig and Tugwell met with Young, Lamont, Lewis and Philip Murray at Taussig's office. Young's story continues: "There was considerable reserve on all sides at first, while the participants were busy smoking each other out. Lewis had been plainly skeptical and had thrown out various ideas to test the reaction of the others. Among other things, he suggested that business and finance were apparently insistent upon repeal of the undistributed profits tax, and he wasn't so sure he wanted it repealed. He looked around inquiringly." It was Young who answered him:

I doubt if you and I can get into a very serious quarrel on that point. As head of the General Electric Company, I can have no serious objection to such a tax. We can meet it, and the ones who really suffer are our competitors, especially our smaller competitors. It all depends on what you want. If the welfare of the country demands the strengthening of small business, then I would say the tax is vicious, because it falls most heavily on your little fellow who has no adequate reserves to fall back on. Personally, I doubt whether this country can afford to subject small business to such a handicap, but if you decide that it can, big business certainly has no cause to complain.

Then Lewis, turning to the brain trusters, attacked the administration: "How the hell can you cooperate with a President who faces in every direction at once? What does he want? First, he seems to be penalizing big business and then it turns out he is really penalizing small business. Why penalize any? I am just as interested as Mr. Young—maybe more—in seeing his company make a profit, because if it doesn't I haven't anything to fight for. You can tell the President that." And at the end of the first meeting Lewis said, "What I want is to see profits so large in this country that we can fight over them with safety."

Impressed by this remark, Young, before the next meeting, asked the economists at the Federal Reserve "to make an estimate as to how much increase in the national income would be required if the government was to be supported on anything like the present scale without placing a destructive tax upon enterprise." The answer was that it would have to be increased "from the present level of 68 billions to at least 88 billions." He reported this to the others, pointing out that it was no good continuing "a three-cornered fight when there was not enough in the pot to meet the requirements of any group. How would it be . . . to take these figures of the minimum increase required and agree to bend all our energies for the present toward providing such an increase in everybody's interest?"

Lewis's response was "immediate and vehement"; labor would co-operate 100 percent, if the others would too. But he did not think the government would. So they decided to go to the White House to find out, and Lewis agreed to go with them.

Berle's account of these preliminary meetings is less colorful. In his "Minute of a Conference" he lists ten points which the conference believed might alleviate distress and bring about recovery.[19] After the second meeting, however, he wrote in his diary: "It is extremely interesting that John Lewis is the man who wants peace in the country. If he means that, it will help considerably." And he went on to say that the really tough spot for agreement would be the utilities: "Today the utilities might be reasonable. In the early days of the discussion they were too arrogant for words. It is interesting to find Owen Young with this view. . . ."[20]

The meeting of the group with the President took place on January 14, 1938; beforehand they conferred in Young's rooms at the Mayflower, and agreed to emphasize the formula that "Industry, Labor and Government should concentrate their energies on raising the national income by 20 billions and agree to bury the hatchet until that had been done." Young told Lewis that he should make this statement to the President: "I wanted him to do this, because coming from such a source the statement would obviously have far greater weight with the President than if Tom Lamont or I made it."

With this understanding we went to the White House. The President came in smiling . . . and greeted us all by our first names. He said that he was curious to hear how far we had progressed toward an agreement and wanted to know what he could do. Berle rehearsed the circumstances of the earlier meeting and called on Lewis. Lewis said he thought we had progressed pretty far, and that the President ought to know how we felt about it, and that the best way for him to find out was to listen to Mr. Young. He passed the ball right back to me.

Well, so there I was. In one respect I really enjoyed the situation, because for once the President had to listen to me instead of doing all the talking himself. He had to listen because Lewis had told him to, and he knew that while I had no political power Lewis had plenty, and so he was all attention.

So Young gave, in some detail, their views and their recommendations, and concluded by saying that "I was very anxious lest I should have given [the facts] some color which did not reflect the real views of Mr. Lewis and Mr. Murray. . . . The President looked at Lewis who arose very slowly and, emphasizing every word, said "Mr. President, I wholly approve Mr. Young's statement and I approve it so strongly that I would not add or subtract a single word. As a matter of fact, I see no other basis for cooperation and unless we can find such a basis there won't be anything left worth fighting for for any of us.' "

The President said he would study the figures, and asked how this formula might be translated into a concrete program. Further meetings would be required, the group agreed, and they were ready to undertake them, *if* they could be assured of government cooperation—at which point Lewis "proceeded to denounce the want of coordination in the Administration's policies and emphasized the need for profits and Labor's deep interest in seeing profits assured."

As the meeting broke up, the President called out, "Oh, John, and you, Owen, come back here a minute." When we responded, he said that he wanted either or both of us to talk to the newspaper boys, and thought it better if no one else made any statement. As we were going out, Lewis said that I had made such a good statement in the meeting that I would better handle the reporters too. I said, "Not on your life. You passed the buck to me once, and that's enough. This is your job."

Thus it was John L. Lewis, in the center of the group outside the White House, who spoke briefly and noncommittally about the meeting. The press could not conceal its astonishment; no one else in the group said anything except to express total agreement: "such acknowledgement of labor leadership by men of interests so mixed cannot be recalled here," said the *Baltimore Sun* next day.[21]

News of a noncooperative action of the government awaited them, however, as they left the conference with the President. Just before their meeting with him, he had announced at his press conference his intention to do away with all holding companies. Apropos of a memorandum put before him by Wendell Willkie, recommending among other things that the holding company "death-sentence" provision of the law be modified, Roosevelt said that he saw no need for *any* holding companies, in the utilities or elsewhere. This singularly unfortunate timing caused wide comment; Arthur Krock wrote in the *New York Times* (January 16, 1938):

If the motivating idea of the group he summoned—with full knowledge of its general objective—is concession and teamwork until the national income makes it possible to support the full measure of the New Deal's social economics, why did the President usher in a peace conference with the trumpets of continuing battle? If, as Mr. Roosevelt himself admits, the thing to do is to restore confidence and bring about a resumption of buying and production, why did he shoot off a gun as the doves of labor and capital were settling?

In his own account of that memorable day Young recalled that when the *New York Times* man asked him for a comment on the President's statement on holding companies, he was totally surprised. This he knew nothing about. But he said, in his account to the family,

The President did ask me when he called me back after the meeting whether I was going to be around, and I replied that I had to go to Florida to attend the utilities meeting. I asked him then if he had any suggestions as to what I should tell the utility people. His reply, made with the wave of the hand, was that I knew what to tell them and he added that he wished I would clear up that situation. I told him there was a time when perhaps I might have been able to be of some use, but that just now nobody but himself could deal with it. "Oh well," he replied, "you go down and tell them anything you have a mind to, and then come back and tell me how they feel."

Young did indeed take off for Florida that very afternoon, and attended the meeting of the Edison companies in Boca Raton, where, as usual, he was expected to speak. He had serious misgivings, he told his family, because, as the audience knew well, "he had come straight from a widely publicized meeting with an Administration and a Labor leader both of whom were anathema to the utilities in general." But before he spoke, J. E. Davison of the Omaha Light and Power rose and said: "Yes, I think it is a real opportunity to hear what Mr. Young has to say, and it is only fair to remember that when he has given us the benefit of his knowledge and advice in the past we have sometimes resented and rejected it. If we are in difficulties today, certainly we cannot blame him for it, and if he can make any helpful suggestions now, we will owe him a vote of thanks"—which was an epoch-making statement in that forum. "So," said Young at the dinner table in Van Hornesville, "I got up and told them that a few of us had been holding meetings with John Lewis to see if we could arrive at some consensus of opinion." And he rehearsed the talks, and at the end read them the lesson: "I did not know, I said, what the government's decision would be, but it was certain that aggressive opposition at this stage would force its hand, and that the only real hope of a moderate and reasonable policy lay in the exercise of restraint and moderation on the part of the industry."

In February he was back in Washington for a National Youth Administration meeting on the eighth. While he was away Berle and Taussig had worked on the suggestion which had been made for a small continuing committee for what came to be known as the Lewis-Lamont-Young group. But they ran into a lot of flak from their own Brain Trust—"There has been no end of a split in Washington over our maneuvers with Lewis and Lamont," wrote Berle in his diary for January 31. "On Friday to see Lamont. Both he and Young are unhappy at the turn of affairs in Washington. They planned a real attempt to reach an understanding with the Government and apparently it had been used to make third-rate politics. Young is pretty well off the boat; so is Lamont . . . we will have another attempt . . . to see what we can do." In other words, this courageous effort was fizzling out, and as the Washington situation grew more confused, it was finally abandoned.[22]

At the NYA meeting on February 8 Young got word that the President wanted to see him, so he went to the White House immediately the meeting was over. This too he described to his family in Van Hornesville:

What followed made a great impression on me, because the general situation in the country was graver than ever and the press, having sensed some excitement and drama in the earlier meeting which Lewis had attended, was naturally hot on my trail when I called on the President again. Mind you, this was the first time I had seen him since that meeting . . . and the newspaper fellows are hanging about for some clue to the weighty questions which they supposed we were discussing.

When I went in I was told that the President was in conference with the Mayors but that he would leave that and see me at once. I suppose he was glad to have an excuse—even a poor one—to escape from that conference. As soon as he saw me he asked what progress we had made toward a program. I replied that I was the last person to know about that because as he knew I had been in the south ever since that meeting. He apologized with a wave of his hand and invited me to see some pictures which were on his desk. They were pictures of the Black Forest and he proceeded to expatiate at length upon the virtues of German forestry.

So, went on Young, "while the reporters waited and business marked time, the President proceeded to tell me all about his experiments in raising Christmas trees at Hyde Park." "But didn't the President have any other suggestions? Couldn't he find anything else to talk to you about without bringing up the subject of holding companies?" asked one of the family. Owen Young admitted that they did talk about small business—the President had just held a small-business men's conference and found they were worried about credit. Young, much concerned about this himself, as was the Federal Reserve, answered politely,

Well, Mr. President, I am interested in that problem, and I think the first step is to find out how many of these people are really entitled to credit and how many need capital. . . . If we find that a considerable percentage of applicants have been turned down not because they are not considered good risks but because they need advances for a longer term than the banks are able to advance, perhaps Jesse Jones could work out a plan by which the R F C might meet their requirements. . . . If it were able to find several hundred small enterprises to which it could furnish capital with reasonable safety, it might make a single bundle of these assets and issue debentures against them to the small investor who does not have time to investigate the claims of each individual company and is the last person who should gamble with his small savings—

Here the narrator was interrupted by laughter as he paused to light his pipe; "What was that?" he asked. "Certainly not. Who said anything about a holding company?"

Apparently Roosevelt's response to this was enthusiastic, and he asked Young to see Marriner Eccles and Jesse Jones. But Young told him that

that would be no good and that any request to be effective would have to come from him . . . he must have acted pretty quickly because I had hardly got to the office next morning [in New York] before I had a phone call from Jesse Jones saying that he was in town and asking what the devil I had been telling the President . . . he said the President had called him over . . . and told him Owen Young said he ought to make some loans to small business . . . what the devil was I trying to get the R F C into, and didn't I know that not one in a hundred of these fellows was entitled to credit, etc. You go to hell I told him. I know all that and you know it and if you came to New York just to tell me what we already know you're just wasting the taxpayers' money. The point is that the President doesn't know it and there is only one way to show him. That's what I am going down to Morgan's to say to them, and I'm going to say it to the Federal Reserve people here. As for you, you'd better go back to Washington and get busy.

At Morgan's some of his junior partners made serious objections to the kind of loans the President was talking about, "but Jack Morgan was remarkable . . . his support was so unqualified that I began to have some qualms not only about the responsibility that I was assuming in telling Morgan's what they ought to do, but also about the junior partners; and so not only to protect myself but in fairness to them I added that it was all very well for me to make these representations because I had none of the responsibility."

Here we include a part of Young's account which, at the time, was described as confidential and not to be quoted until after the deaths of the two participants. Not immediately apropos, perhaps, it seems to us an important indicator of how the wind blew in those days.

The firm meeting over, Mr. Morgan asked me to join him in his office. No one else was there. "I just wanted you to know, Owen Young," he said, "that I don't care a damn what happens to you or anybody else. I don't care what happens to the country. All I care about"—and here he became vehement, almost passionate—"all I care about is this business! If I could help it by getting out of this country and establishing myself somewhere else I'd do it—I'd do anything. In all honesty I want you to know exactly how I feel. And if things go on this way much longer I won't put up with 'em. I'll take the business and get out!"

I noticed that his hand was trembling; he was evidently under great emotional strain. He rejected my first remonstrances. Then I went over to him and putting my arm around his shoulder I said, "Jack, you don't know what you're saying, and furthermore you don't mean a word of it. If you'll just look back for a moment—or ahead—you'll see how true that is.

"This business was built up by men who had faith in America. It became great as this country became great, and because your predecessors, and especially your father, were ready to bet on this country's future. But for this country's development, and their faith in it, the business would have been nothing. Your father brought to it, as you do, great talents, great energy and unlimited devotion, but the prestige and power of the firm became unrivalled because his faith and loyalty were unshakable. So are yours—

"Your children and grandchildren are coming along and you are as proud of them as I am of mine—You have a magnificent heritage to transmit to them, and it's bigger than this business, bigger than any business that ever was or will be. You'll stay right here and outface these passing discouragements, because if you ran away you wouldn't be Jack Morgan. You owe it to the future and you owe it to yourself."

When I had finished, he was silent, and I was startled to find that his eyes had filled. "Well, Owen," he said, "I guess I needed some one to talk to me like that. And I guess you're the only one who could have done it."

It is interesting to note that, a week later, a financial columnist in the *New York Post*, under the heading "The Hostile Morgan Empire Adjusts Its Political Vision and Negotiates for Peace with the New Dealers," pointed out Morgan's increasing efforts to accommodate the interests of its own "constituents" to the political climate of the day.[23]

But to return to the dining room in Van Horne House. A question was asked about John L. Lewis—was he dependable, would he make good on his pledge that labor would keep the peace during a period of recovery?

To this Young answered that Lewis could no more guarantee, for a policy of peace, complete and universal respect by every element in labor than he himself could guarantee the cooperation of every unregenerate employer; the point was to know in advance what the policy was going to be so far as the responsible leaders were concerned. "As for his dependability, I think you need have no doubts whatever. I have met few people in my whole experience whose word, once given, I would value more highly than John Lewis'. I think"—he spoke very slowly, weighing his words carefully—"that I know of only two others in comparable positions of power who would go to such lengths to make good on their word. I think I would put Philip Snowden, Jack Morgan and John Lewis in a class by themselves . . . once they have made a commitment they expect to deliver, come hell or high water."

Chapter 36

The Tireless Mediator and Retirement

O
N NEW YEAR'S DAY, 1936, for the first time in thirteen years, Young was no longer a director of the New York Federal Reserve. Six months later he was serving once again as deputy chairman and as of January 1, 1938, he was named chairman—the first to hold that office since Marriner Eccles and his new Board of Governors had made it purely honorary. How had this come about—and why?

Curiously enough, the very circumstances which at first seemed to bar it had contributed largely to the outcome. The Fed's records are too impersonal to illuminate the character and quality of any individual's service there, but Young's long tenure had made him almost as familiar a figure at 33 Liberty Street as any of the bank's top officers. Alone among the directors, moreover, he had known and admired all of these—Governors Benjamin Strong and George Harrison, Chairmen Pierre Jay, Gates McGarrah and J. H. Case—and to each he had become a warm friend and trusted adviser. Thus he had been deeply disturbed by the Reserve Board's announcement of December 5, 1935, that incumbent chairmen of the regional banks would be reappointed only until March 1—in order that the new seven-man board, scheduled to take office on February 1, "might be represented at the different Federal Reserve Banks by Chairmen and Federal Reserve Agents of its own selection, chosen in accordance with its views as to how the chairmanships may best be made to fit into the changed organization of the Federal Reserve System."[1] Translated, this presumably meant that the office of chairman would thenceforth be honorary only, and for most of the regional banks, no doubt, this simplified structure had much to commend it.

For the New York bank, however, with its special monetary and fiscal responsibilities, foreign and domestic, it could only come as another blow—and not just because it would mean the abrupt termination of its sixty-three-year-old chairman's nearly nineteen years of service. With its governor, now to be called president, so often absent in Washington or Europe, the New York Fed had always felt the need for an experienced and full-time top-management team—failure to recognize which could only mean its further and deliberate downgrading by Washington. And if Herbert Case—twice acting governor while serving as Strong's senior deputy, and chairman since 1930—could now be dismissed so cavalierly, how were men of his capacity and dedication to be recruited?

With the new board's letters to the regional banks of February 26, 1936, and its public announcement of March 5, these fears became substantial facts: as of May (instead of March) 1, all regional chairmen's appointments were to be abruptly terminated—with six months' salary, regardless of their length of service, tossed in as a separation allowance. Young was then in Florida and did not return until April 1, but under the leadership of Clarence Woolley and Thomas J. Watson the bank's directors girded for action. By the time it was decided that a strong letter of protest signed by all the directors should go to the Eccles board, feeling was running so high that Case himself felt called upon to urge that his directors stress not so much the personal injustice as the adverse public—and staff—repercussions which the board's summary action entailed. Certainly the bank's junior officers were already restive, and the *New York Sun* had greeted the board's announcement by pointing out that the section of the Eccles bill which would have authorized it had been "deleted and with good reason." Now the board "is doing by indirection" what Congress declined to authorize, "and the reason is partly one of personal pique and partly one of mediaeval discipline."[2]

At once dignified and forceful, the long letter of protest signed and dispatched by all the directors on April 9 was all that Herbert Case could have asked. While it did not play down the injustice done him, it cited this chiefly by way of accounting for staff and public reactions, both injurious to the Federal Reserve System, which a more considerate board policy might still cancel and would certainly allay. On the seventeenth, the board rejected this plea—by no means curtly but with great finality. But when the directors made one further effort—this time on behalf of a separation allowance more nearly consonant with their chairman's long and devoted service—the board gave Watson and his committee its full attention and later voted Case a full year's salary.[3]

Young's part in these April proceedings is hard to determine; his interest and concern are not. Officially it was none of his business, but his office was open to Case whenever the latter—as he did—sought his counsel. Of the two letters the directors sent to the Eccles board, the principal draftsman was apparently Allan Sproul, then secretary and deputy governor, and shortly to become the bank's first "First Vice-President." Glad to be relieved of this accustomed chore, Young nevertheless assisted in their editing and George Harrison did too. Indeed, the unity that marked the entire effort on his behalf was to Case especially heartwarming. His one regret was that, as an ex-director, Young was not eligible to sign the handsome resolution honoring their departing chairman which a unanimous board adopted at Case's last meeting on April 20.[4]

On that same day Young received an invitation which had awkward implications. In Washington for meetings of the Chamber of Commerce and the National Youth Administration—not to mention the NYA dinner at the White House—he was asked to call on Eccles and M. S. Szymczak, the only carry-overs from the old Federal Reserve Board.[5] On May 6 he wrote a long letter to Herbert Case describing the meeting, explaining his dilemma, and asking how he should resolve it. Addressed to "Dear Herbert," the letter said:

> When I was in Washington Governor Eccles asked to see me. I went to his office and he said that the Board of Governors . . . acting unanimously, were requesting me to accept an appointment as Class "C" director of the New York Bank with my old designation as Deputy Chairman. He said also that it was the purpose of the Board to leave the Chairmanship vacant as he had understood from George Harrison that I would be unwilling under any circumstances to accept an appointment as Chairman. I told Governor Eccles that I would give him my answer in the course of the next week. . . . Frankly, my principal reason for delaying my answer was for the purpose of consulting you. . . . My initial inclination would be to accept no appointment from the Federal Reserve Board and thereby leave them or the public to feel that I condoned or even acquiesced in the sort of treatment which they had given you.

And on personal grounds, he went on, he was not keen to undertake the additional responsibilities and burdens on his time and strength which the rigid schedule of board meetings entailed.

> On the other hand, I am compelled to ask myself what my duty is in the matter. I have tried to follow the rule of not shirking a duty that was obviously mine, even though it involved sacrifice of time and effort or otherwise put extra burdens on me. Conversely, I have felt no hesitation

in declining offers where I felt that there was someone else equally or better qualified to do the job or where the job itself was of no great importance.

Not least because they had now lost Case, he continued, people in the bank, from George Harrison on, were strongly urging his acceptance;

some of them certainly feel that the problems of the immediate future, both political and economic, are of a kind which point their finger so decisively at me that I ought not to decline them. . . . So I need your help and advice, for you know the situation as well as anyone and probably better. . . . If I decide to accept, we should be prepared to make public an exchange of letters showing that you approve . . . lest there be some misconception of my willingness to accept. . . .

And he ended by saying, "I shall never cease to admire the magnificent spirit with which you faced and accepted a most difficult situation."

Herbert Case, now a partner in the investment banking firm of R. W. Pressprich and Company, replied immediately by phone, and on May 12 wrote an expression of his views to Young for the record. On the matter of appearing to condone his treatment by the board, Case said, "I understand and admire the delicacy and consideration you have displayed. But you know me well enough, I feel sure, to accept my assurance that so far as I am concerned this point or obstacle can be considered eliminated."

With Young's second point, namely, his reluctance to take on added burdens now, he was sympathetic but felt that the third point was, after all, determining. While only Young himself could decide it,

I should like to say frankly . . . that your especial training and business experience, your financial, industrial and international banking background, your relationship with the Federal Reserve System and the added fact that the relationship of the New York bank to the Board of Governors of the system as a whole, will, to some extent, have to be reset—all of these reasons to my mind indicate clearly that you are the logical person to accept the appointment.[6]

That this was far more than a *pro forma* exchange between equally doting grandfathers of the same two grandchildren, none who knew them would have questioned; for Young it meant the one reassurance he must have in order to proceed. But there was still another barrier, as he wrote Eccles on May 18:

I found last week that at least one or two directors of the General Electric Company had some reservations about the time and effort required of me in the performance of these duties. They were inclined to the view that such obligation as rested on me as a citizen to serve the institution in a quasi-public capacity had been discharged by my previous long service and that I had, so to say, been honorably retired. Accordingly, they were inclined to take it up as a new question involving new responsibilities rather than the carrying on of old ones. . . . And I would not be able—or wish—to accept the appointment . . . if a single director of the General Electric Company questioned its propriety.

The objection did come from a single director—the one of longest service on the board, elected in 1894—Gordon Abbott, who had been instrumental in bringing Owen Young to General Electric. Devoted to Young, his concern was certainly as great for him as it was for the company. But the formidable old Boston banker must have been finally persuaded that neither would suffer, and on June 15 Young wrote Eccles that he would accept, on the understanding that "even though the chairmanship be not filled, my duties and responsibilities are no greater in the contemplation of the Governors than they were when I held a similar office before."[7]

Governor—or rather, President—Harrison gave a sigh of relief and wrote Young an ecstatic letter:

I stopped by your office this morning, on the chance that you might be back, just to tell you how happy I am that you are to be back on our Board and how pleased I am in particular to have you to work with and your great wisdom and advice to guide me. I have missed you so much during your absence. Much of the fun of my work in recent years has been in working with you—in mulling things over with you. I am very happy in the prospect of having you to turn to again so please know how delighted I am to welcome you back. Already I have a long list of things about which I want to gossip with you. Thank you so much for making it possible—and legal! For me it will be both a joy and a comfort. All of us are much relieved that it is finally settled.[8]

The office of chairman of the New York bank was not filled until January 1938, when Case's original appointment would have terminated; at that time, to no one's surprise, Young received the title. He wrote Herbert Case thanks for his note of congratulation

on my designation as Chairman of the Federal Reserve Bank of New York, succeeding you. John Finley has a little quip to the effect that nothing succeeds like successors. I am very confident of my success because, as nearly as I can make out, I have neither duties nor responsibilities, notwithstanding that I signed a very heavy bond. That's my kind of job exactly . . . as you know I would not have gone back on the Board or troubled to take the chairmanship except to be of such aid and support to George as I could.

The question of whether I can be helpful is not important. The fact that George thinks I can is.[9]

On December 13, 1939, Young wrote Eccles asking him to designate another chairman, for, as he knew, he was about to retire from General Electric and would not be in New York much in the years to come. But pressure was again put on him to continue and he agreed to stay on through 1940—hardly the year, as it turned out, for the long and leisurely absences which he had stipulated at the outset. Sixty-six before it ended, Young could feel that he had fully and finally worked his passage; after all, his Federal Reserve stint of eighteen years almost equaled even Case's. And on January 2, 1941, the board he had served so long unanimously adopted and presented him with a resolution of appreciation, which, unlike many such, contains some exact truths:

Mr. Young's service to the bank has been longer than that of any other director. But his contribution to the bank's development cannot be measured in years. Its measure is found in his devotion to the public interest, in his ability to discern broad economic and social trends and in his wisdom which caused him always to seek and to give weight to the human factor in monetary and credit problems. For him to become a director of a central bank was to become a central banker by the study and practice of that profession. Through the most trying periods in the life of the Federal Reserve System he has been a dominant figure in the councils of the Federal Reserve Bank of New York, and he has contributed largely to the development of domestic and international banking and credit policy.

Young himself wrote Allan Sproul, now president of the New York bank in succession to George Harrison (who retired at the same time as Young), of what this long exposure to the central bankers' problems had meant to him:

It was not only a liberal education to serve on that Board, during the dramatic period of the '20s and the tragic one of the '30s, but it was a satisfying one too. There I saw the fidelity and intelligence with which men of diverse experiences and backgrounds served the cause of a sound currency and credit program for the Nation. During the latter years the Bank existed largely as an administrative institution and not as a central control reservoir of credit—that reservoir due to the deficit financing of the Government inevitably passed to the Treasury, and with it the responsibilities which only the projection of a long future can adequately measure. In addition to a fruitful experience, my service on the Board yielded me an enlarged acquaintance and deep friendships which I shall ever cherish.

Of the resolution, he said, "The generous recital is not more than I would have wished to have done and not more than I should wish my descendants to think I have done. For myself, I accept it with humility and gratitude, and I shall pass it on to my children and grandchildren with pride."[10]

ii

Events of the summer of 1936 had graphically illustrated Young's definition of the New York Fed as having become largely an administrative agency of the treasury. In September, armed with his Stabilization Fund, Treasury Secretary Henry Morgenthau could point with pride—and with good reason—to his achievement in negotiating a tripartite currency stabilization pact with Britain and France, which he saw as timely in itself and something of a check to Hitler's hopes of keeping the democracies divided. Young agreed, though there is nothing to indicate that he was so much as consulted in these delicate proceedings—in which the Fed's only apparent role was to execute the treasury's orders to buy and sell foreign exchange. As Young had told the Senate committee a year earlier, he had confidence in *this* secretary of the treasury, but he remained apprehensive about vesting monetary controls in an agency so politically oriented as to make even the Eccles board look independent. Nevertheless, stabilization as such was a good omen, especially since it would hardly have been achieved without the President's blessing.[11]

But as a central and controlling reservoir of credit—or at least an important factor in credit control—the Fed was not through. Even in the fall of '35, the vast reservoirs of so-called excess reserves, rising ever higher with the inflow of gold, had occasioned concern, private and public; could these be controlled, and if not, how was their potential for inflation to be curbed? At that time, both Harrison and Case had favored testing out the Fed's new powers to raise its member banks' required reserves and so absorb part of the excess; Young, like Parker Gilbert—and Eccles—thought it more likely to discourage the budding recovery and hence premature. But by August 1936, it was the consensus of Washington and New York and most of the other regional banks that the time had come, and required reserves were raised by 25 percent. The press generally applauded; Case hailed the move from his new post; and certainly it could only have helped Morgenthau's stabilization negotiations. Most important, the consensus itself offered proof that, thanks largely to the final composition of the system's Open Market Committee, New York and Washington could still communicate, and put to use this new instrument of credit control.[12]

Nevertheless, the New York Fed's new role and setup had brought their changes, including losses to the private sector. One deputy governor, Jay Crane, had already resigned in 1935 to become treasurer of Standard Oil (New Jersey). In 1938, Randolph Burgess—a likely successor to Case as chairman, had that office not become honorary—left to become vice-chairman of the National City Bank. Allan Sproul, however, was proving to be a tower of strength as George Harrison's right-hand man and probable successor; Young, his senior by twenty-one years, admired the younger man's quick grasp, energy and initiative, and certainly his admiration was warmly reciprocated. This was all the more heartening because 1937 was to take a grim toll of the old, and not so old, whose lives in one way or another had touched Owen Young's.

In January Gordon Abbott, his senior director, died. In February it was Elihu Root, full of years and honors. In April, it was Young's law-school roommate, "Squire" DeGoosh. Then the summer months took Hugh Cooper, Guglielmo Marconi and Andrew Mellon; September, Edward Filene and Charles Neave; October and December, Ogden Mills, Frank Kellogg and Newton Baker. But for Young the truly personal and irreparable losses came with the October death in Boston of his great and good friend Nelson Perkins, and only weeks later that of Henry Robinson in Pasadena. And he felt a special pang when, in February 1938, Parker Gilbert died at forty-five—less than half the age of Senator Root at the time of his death. Of all the Americans, young and not so young, who had figured prominently in the halcyon days of the Dawes Plan, it seemed that only Young and the general still survived.

Young had never been content to let the dead bury their dead. He could not attend the services for Henry Robinson or several of the others, but for Gordon Abbott's and of course for that of Nelson Perkins he made separate trips to Boston. To Elihu Root, Jr., he wrote that his father had been one of his boyhood heroes, his unbounded admiration for whom—as, alas, too seldom happens with the heroes of one's youth—had only been strengthened by the close association and friendship that came later. And as he confessed to the authors, Root was much in his mind as he prepared to broadcast on January 2, 1938, his singularly thought-provoking tribute to Newton Baker:

It has been the good fortune of America that during our whole history each generation has produced at least one man whose voice was so clear, whose mind was so penetrating, whose judgment was so wise, whose personality was so attractive and whose spirit was so all embracing as to command the respect of everybody. The influence of such a man results in a kind of invisible leadership which is always at work. It is not limited by a term of office—it is not created by political power—it does not rely on financial strength but only on sanity and charm and character.

One may call the names of that small and select company which has graced the pages of our history and which has contributed so much both to our stability and to our progress.

The last of that distinguished company to go is Newton Baker. The void which he leaves cries anxiously to be filled. A nation, grateful to him, will pray that a successor worthy of the place may again be found.[13]

In that same fall of 1937, a year or so after the abortive White House meeting to discuss a "power pool," Roosevelt appointed a new power-policy committee under the chairmanship of Secretary of the Interior Harold Ickes. This group "was drafting a bill for presentation to Congress designed to establish a government policy for administering all big power projects" and also studying, at the President's direction, "the whole field of policy." A long article by Ickes appeared in the *New York Times Magazine* of November 7, 1937, in answer to an article by Wendell Willkie in the previous week's number, which challenged the government's program.

Ickes began with a long quotation from Owen Young's famous speech before the National Electric Light Association Convention of 1926, on the special "class of water powers . . . the vast rivers" where development must be multipurpose and the government inevitably becomes involved. But Ickes's discussion of the government's purpose, in the TVA and other developments, was not wholly candid or temperate. It played down the generation of power, stressing conservation, flood control, navigation and irrigation—projects almost too diverse for even the harnessing of a great river to effect. And in regard to the utilities he used fighting words—"exploiting the people by lining private pockets," "selfish clique," "Red bogies" and so forth. The *Times*, heading a letter sharply criticizing the Ickes article, commented coolly SOME DODGING OF ISSUES SEEN.[14]

Young also wrote a letter to the *Times* in answer to Ickes; requoting from the same speech, he underscored his original and pointed question as more than ever timely: "May I not call for a broader view in the public interest from the representatives of both the utilities and the public?" He went on to say that he agreed entirely with the secretary, "assuming that the main purpose of the enterprise is the control of water." But, he continued, "the real question which is left unanswered in the Secretary's article is what the government is to do with the power." It could not be wasted; the government could sell it to private companies, or could distribute it itself—if so, how? Duplication was also wasteful: "To duplicate transmission lines where adequate ones exist already can mean nothing less than that either the taxpayers' money is wasted or the investment in the lines already built is impaired, if not indeed destroyed." He went on to detail the latter point: four million utility stockholders in the country, more than twelve billion dollars invested, much of it by life-insurance companies, savings banks and educational and other institutions. He described the enormous growth of the utilities industry, effecting great reductions in cost to the consumer; the great number of people employed—to all of these the waste of duplication would cause harm. And he ended by saying that even though "a great electrical manufacturing company" like GE would benefit by duplication, "no great concern whose fortunes necessarily rise and fall with the welfare of the nation can look with equanimity on waste, even though it might temporarily benefit from it."[15]

Perhaps this concluding statement of Young's was the most significant item in a letter which failed to solve the waterpower problem or even silence Ickes.[16] Throughout Young's labors on behalf of international peace and comity, GE's fortunes had been viewed in an international context; now the "national" was substantially all that there was left.

Meanwhile, looking back on his long and fruitless efforts to harness the St. Lawrence for the benefit of the people of New York State—either by public or private means, or both—Young must have had a sense of déjà vu. From his almost forty years of dealing with the utilities he felt an unfeigned pride in the prodigious expansion of their service, which (as he pointed out to Ickes) had also lowered charges to the point where they now averaged only 4½ cents per kilowatt hour. True, his efforts to persuade the industry to correct its own abuses had fallen largely on deaf ears; but, as he wrote ex-Congressman Herbert Claiborne Pell early in 1938, turning over "this vast industry to government" was *not* the answer. On the contrary, vesting the controls in a "bureaucracy with such enormous power might make it much more difficult for the people [ever] to correct abuses."[17]

But even these frustrating efforts brought rewards of a more personal sort: a growing friendship with another lawyer experienced in utilities, Wendell Willkie. Eighteen years his junior, Willkie had the qualities Young liked to see in a younger man, whether in the utility business or in politics. At the moment, business seemed by far the more important, for if the fall of '37 was a disappointment, 1938 was quickly becoming a disaster—and one which, given the ominous developments abroad, this country could ill afford.

iii

There must have been some carry-over from the meeting with the Lewis-Lamont-Young group in the presidential mind, for in his Fireside Chat of April 14, 1938, Roosevelt spoke of wanting cooperation with business and emphasized "teamwork." Since, in view of past history, this was not immediately greeted with outstretched hands by business leaders, Jim Farley got to work. He talked to John Hanes at the SEC, as the administration's "Wall Street man"; Hanes talked to Winthrop Aldrich of the Chase Bank, and Aldrich talked to Young. Hanes had drafted a statement, which was edited by Young, Clarence Woolley of American Radiator and Frederick H. Ecker of Metropolitan Life, and these three agreed to sign it, "provided there was a large enough group of representative people ready to sign so as to take off the appearance of the individual volunteer."[18] This there apparently was; a dozen others from banks, insurance companies and industries signed and it was sent off to Hanes.

The statement was brief and mild. Quoting Roosevelt's expressed desire for cooperation between government and industry, it called for business "to encourage the President in his efforts to restore confidence," and to support Congress in its efforts for a legislative program to build national recovery "for employer and employee alike, rather than toward the enactment of legislation based upon untried social and economic theories." It recommended "continuous consultation" by government with business leaders and pledged cooperation.[19] The press gave this little nonvolunteer move big headlines and editorials, although the papers did not fail to point out that previous efforts had had no effect. The President was in the midst of his new pump-priming program, which was strongly opposed by Henry Ford (who visited FDR the day after the statement came out) and by most business groups.

The *New Republic* greeted the statement with an article by John T. Flynn beginning:

Snow White Owen D. Young and the Fifteen Giants have decided to cooperate with the President to bring back recovery. The letter in which they convey their willingness to lend a hand breathes the spirit of goodwill and even goes so far as to reveal a suspicion of tolerance for the President himself. There is the thinly veiled suggestion that if he will put aside his nonsense and make an end of social and economic experiments they will be pleased to work with him to increase their profits.

But Flynn went on to attack the President, far more sharply, for inaction as "the more positive men of affairs close in on him."[20] Turner Catledge, in the *New York Times* for May 8, had a long discussion of the possibilities and impossibilities of government and business really cooperating on a recovery program, and the immediate prospects therefor, which he thought (fingers crossed) might turn out to be good, with this and other efforts on the rise. But like many far less well informed persons he realized fully the "unpredictable quality" of the President.

Young was also involved at this time with an informal group working on a peacemaking project with the labor unions in an attempt to end the infighting between the A F L and the C I O, which had been endemic in labor affairs since John L. Lewis had appeared on the scene. They had the assistance of Edward F. McGrady, one of labor's best-known and respected negotiators and now a labor consultant to R C A. McGrady, once Labor Secretary Frances Perkins's "ace strike mediator," did succeed in working out likely-looking terms for a truce between Lewis and William Green. But for all his skill, and the weight of the group behind him—John D. Rockefeller, Myron Taylor, Walter Teagle, Bernard Baruch, David Sarnoff, Thomas Lamont and Young— it could not be made to stick.[21]

In mid-April of 1938 Philip Young, now approaching twenty-eight, sent his father an article by one Paul Gourrich, the title of which posed two questions: "What Is the Matter with America and What Is to Be Done?" Philip had been with the S E C since 1934, and was now working closely with John Hanes, who had been appointed to head the S E C in January. Proud too of his son's progress in fields so different from his elder brother's, Young was ready to say what *ought* to be done, but added that the real and disturbing question was how—and even whether—we could do it.

He reiterated his idea—and by this time that of many others—that recovery required an increase in the annual national income of "something like 25 or 30 billion dollars. How are we to do that and do it quickly?" By producing more and lowering consumer prices, was his answer, which would require sacrifices on every side, including the government's waiving of "taxes at critical points." He had suggested to

Eccles at the Federal Reserve, he said, that relief from taxes for capital used for housing construction would stimulate the building industry and hence others—which Eccles had dismissed, arguing first that tax relief should go to homeowners, not capitalists, and second that "it would not be practical politically." Young went on to say, more frankly in this family letter than he ever said publicly:

I am not sure that our political organization will authorize action which might be economically desirable though temporarily politically unpopular. . . . It will take a long time to persuade a Democracy to accept unwelcome political medicine and my fear is that it may take so long that people will become impatient with a democratic form of government. The totalitarian state can and does act promptly . . . it still remains to be demonstrated that Democracy is strong enough to administer self-discipline to the extent needed when the disease is serious and the fever runs high. I hope with all my soul that our Democracy will make this demonstration. I believe it will.

Meanwhile, he was fearful that the more shots in the arm we took, the more we would be weakened in will and resources "for the final struggle which I fear we cannot avoid." He had sympathized with Roosevelt's experimental injections during his first term, because "temporary aids in large doses" were needed. But "it seems to me now that the President is now endeavoring to do on a much larger scale the very things which Mr. Hoover tried to do. Having seen them fail so disastrously . . . I have little confidence in the success of that policy now."[22]

Whether Hoover or Roosevelt would have been the less pleased and more surprised by this equation—so unorthodox at the time—it was not one which Young espoused in public. More characteristic was his succinct and graphic response to a worried letter from the head of a logging company in the state of Washington: "We are at present engaged in a tug of war, trying to stretch a canvas over an area which it is too small to cover, each group seeking to get more coverage at the expense of the other. While this continues we shall have animosity and bitterness and disintegration, which threaten the ruin of democracy more than anything else."[23]

And when M. H. Aylesworth, who had left N B C to become publisher of the *New York World-Telegram*, turned to him for help in January '39, Young really took off the gloves. Aylesworth's boss, Roy Howard (of the Scripps-Howard chain), had asked for his suggestions on how to respond to a query from an unnamed source (the President?) on what in this crisis Americans must do. Not having to sign the reply himself, Young could answer freely, and did:

. . . first I would rip hell out of both government and business. Then I would quote from the President's message to Congress that very telling passage: "Even a nation well-armed and well-organized from a strictly military standpoint may, after a period of time, meet defeat if it is unnerved by self-distrust, endangered by class prejudice, by dissension and by other unsolved problems at home." I would say that it is not enough to issue pronunciamentos but it was the business of the President to see that every man in the executive branch was on the job to accomplish that end and that his effectiveness would be measured by his success.

I would equally say that it was not enough for the National Association of Manufacturers to issue its handsome resolutions, such as it did at its last convention, but that every head of every business must be judged by his success or failure in their prompt and adequate execution.

I would say to all the rioters and trouble-makers that their time was over and that the public opinion of America would no longer tolerate the fomenting of hatred and bitterness between individuals, classes or groups of any kind; that they might freely speak, but that violent and unjustified attack might become just as injurious to society as libel and slander to the individual; that when we are trying to save democracy we have the right to demand prompt and effective execution of all handsome promises and a right to protect men from all subversive action having the intent to paralyze such efforts.[24]

The ruin of democracy—despite or because of the Munich pact—was the specter which haunted Americans as Hitler increased in power and arrogance—as the possibility of war for America grew clearer, as the numbers of unemployed again grew greater, as their own government seemed unable to cope with the persistently dangerous economic and human problems of the country. It was only occasionally that Young allowed any expression of the chill of fear; but it explains his long-continued emphasis on the care and employment of youth and on the essential cooperation of all segments of American society to revive not only prosperity but the spirit of the nation. Speaking again, in January 1939, at Boca Raton, he called for unified action on the part of all—beginning with the electrical industry—to assure the economic independence which was now so dangerously threatened. If economic freedom could not be maintained in addition to political and religious liberty, then dictators would move in and democracy would not survive.[25] It was, for him, an old theme but in a new and frightening context.

iv

All aid to the Allies short of war was also an old theme, but as it became more urgent, Roosevelt too was finding that the Neutrality Act placed it in a new and frightening context. While Young still urged support for the President in matters of foreign policy—with "no partisan politics [reaching] across the frontier of the United States"[26]—he was becoming increasingly wary of domestic programs which he held to be divisive and ill timed. Repeatedly excluded from active participation in the shaping of government policy, finding no real support in the White House for his efforts with the utilities or for the kind of cooperative venture he and John Lewis had been prepared to launch, Young's role as an apologist or mediator was giving place to that of critic. True, such domestic programs as he now proposed were always stated affirmatively, but they bore less and less resemblance to FDR's. There simply wasn't time, he felt, to fool around; whether in the hope of warning Hitler off or of giving him what for in the more probable showdown, we must spare no effort to recruit our strength—and fast.

In the affairs of General Electric, few additions were now being made to the creative program of employee benefits which had been the hallmark of the Young-Swope regime. True, the general profit-sharing plan adopted in 1934 was liberalized in 1937—incidentally the first year that promised anything worth sharing. But thanks to the Wagner Act, the initiative had now passed to organized labor, which was moving nationwide to capitalize on its newly assured collective-bargaining rights.[27]

Thus the CIO's United Electrical Workers needed no such invitation as William Green had once declined to move in and organize General Electric's workers. To top management, CIO's success, under their youthful leader, James Carey, came as no surprise; Swope and Carey had met and, taking each other's measure, discovered grounds for mutual respect. As for Young, if the adversary relationship of management and labor now mandated by the Wagner Act was nothing less than the kiss of death to his concept of a community of interest, he was philosophical about it. After all, he and Swope had had little support in their efforts to make that concept a reality; why shouldn't labor now welcome the strongest bargaining agency it could find? Nor need the so-called adversary relationship be fatally disruptive; on the contrary, the aim of collective bargaining was to reach a mutually acceptable accord, and here, taking careful aim, GE and Carey's union were to prove themselves on target. Certainly GE proved happily immune to the rash of strikes—sit-down or other—that broke out elsewhere.²⁸ By 1939, moreover, employment was up and both dollar and real wages were achieving an all-time high. Thus GE at least was not unready for whatever demands the future might be confronting it with.

On May 17, 1939, Young testified in Washington before the Temporary National Economic Committee (known as the "Monopoly Committee") as one of several corporate heads, including Edward Stettinius of U.S. Steel and Alfred Sloan of General Motors. They were invited by the SEC, whose purpose, as reported by the *Washington Post*, was a demonstration, from the mouths of a number of very knowledgeable horses, that big corporations are self-sufficient in capital and so would play no part in tapping the "stagnant pools" of idle savings which the President wanted to put to work. (It was indicated in some press reports that the hearing was a put-up job to enable the President to introduce a new big-spending program.) Young's letter of invitation indicated that this was an effort to "present cases of corporate financing . . . in terms of the history of individual corporations."²⁹

He gave them their money's worth. He read them a thirty-two-page paper on the "Growth of the General Electric Company . . . to show the origin and development of its capital," especially in its earlier stages. He pointed out that the General Electric Company could hardly have survived the panics of 1893 and 1907 "if a capital gains tax of the kind we now have had been in operation," and went on to pay his respects to the President's proposed new program of pump priming:

I am in favor of temporary deficit financing provided that it is supplemented by an affirmatively stimulating and helpful attitude toward the railroads, toward the utilities and toward the construction industry, and provided further that there be such revision of tax laws and a suspension of such threats and restraints as will really enable all stimulants to work. I do not believe in the policy of giving a stimulant and then immediately neutralizing it.

He spoke of the great men who had made General Electric, citing Thomas Edison and Elihu Thomson and Charles Coffin: "It was their energy and capacity, functioning largely without governmental restraint, that enabled them to build in half a century one of the most spectacular industries of the world. I am not now protesting against certain government regulation and restraints in this age, but I am saying that it should be exercised with the greatest discrimination and in such a manner as to conserve to the utmost the advantages of free and competent leadership." But the question he asked which the press emphasized the most was "whether artificial alleviations of the impact of depressions through government aid in the financial field are, in the long run, helpful to a nation's economy." It might be better to eliminate ineffective economic organizations "than to prolong the depression by a fruitless effort in their conservation."[30]

All this, of course, was definitely not part of the plan in holding the hearing; "presentation of this program by the tall, sedate business captain came as a surprise," said the *Washington Post*. Sloan also made some sharp remarks, agreeing with Young on taxes and the need for confidence. And the *Herald Tribune*, in an editorial early in June, began with the paragraph:

During the recent hearings before the TNEC (monopoly committee) on savings and investments Mr. Owen D. Young and Mr. Alfred P. Sloan, despite every precaution on the part of examining counsel, got "off the reservation" to the extent of introducing some rather pointed observations of their own concerning the cause of the stagnation of the investment market. Rumor has it that when the President read the news accounts of this hearing he was furious, and that he lost no time in getting one of the bright young men in charge of the investigation on the telephone. "See here!" he is said to have remonstrated, "this sort of thing has got to stop. These sessions are degenerating into a public forum!"[31]

Early in 1940 Raymond Moley, now contributing editor to *Newsweek*, raised the question of putting idle money to work more directly; to wit: (1) Do you agree that American savings have no place to go in private enterprise? (2) What is the chief factor blocking the flow of private savings into investment in industry generally? Agreeing with the first proposition, at least for the time being, Young went on to explain why in his answer to the second:

The forerunner for investment is adventure. Adventurous men and adventurous dollars in combination must be encouraged to take great risks in order that some percentage of their undertakings may be shown to be sound, useful and profitable. Then and not until then can savings be properly invested in such enterprise. Broadly speaking, savings may develop and carry on for profit, but they cannot and should not adventure. Therefore, to the extent which adventurous men and adventurous dollars are discouraged or paralyzed, you will have idle dollars awaiting investment and idle men awaiting employment. Indeed, you will have more, you will have stagnation of spirit, you will have so-called realism, which for the most part as now used is another name for destructive cynicism, in place of productive imagination and daring action.

And he went on to say that if productive enterprise is scorned rather than honored, and penalized by taxation, opportunity for investment of savings will be restricted.

Exploration and research will falter and our best brains and most vital energies will be devoted to mere survival in a static economy. . . . No people could push out the frontiers of productive knowledge and successful enterprise as far as we have in the last three generations without increasing the possibilities for new research and new enterprise on the perimeter of the now known. It is for that reason that I am sure, given stimulation for adventure instead of repression, there need be no idle men and idle dollars in America.

It was this he had in mind, he told Moley, when he emphasized adventure in his TNEC testimony, and cited the history of the General Electric Company "as one conspicuous example of adventure which had opened the doors for the profitable investment of large sums of American savings."[32]

v

In the meantime, Europe's second civil war of the twentieth century had begun in September. Reassured by the pact with Stalin, Hitler had sent his panzers into Poland, which the declaration of war by England and France could not save. Whether the relative quiet that ensued on the western front was a prelude to another Munich or a Nazi attack, who could say? Young and Swope were fatalistic about it; come what may, it was time for them to bow out of their posts at General Electric in favor of younger men.

On the morning of November 17, 1939, a Friday after a busy week of regents, Federal Reserve, and Academy of Political Science meetings, Owen Young sat down at the big desk in his office in the General Electric Company and wrote, by hand, a letter addressed to his board of directors. With only the most minor changes,[33] it was presented to them that same afternoon, and this is what they read:

To the Board of Directors   New York
General Electric Company: November 17, 1939

On May 16, 1922, we undertook at your election, the offices of Chairman and President, respectively, of the General Electric Company, and as a result of your annual designation we have held those offices ever since.

When we took office, we indicated our view that it would contribute to the morale and effectiveness of the organization if as a general rule men in important administrative positions would consider retirement when they reached the age of 65. We realize that there have been, are and probably will be exceptions, where it is desirable in the company's interest for men to continue in their place beyond that age.

Having adopted that policy of retirement during our administration, we now apply it to ourselves. We do so with no reservation, because there are younger men whose experience and capacity have been demonstrated to you, who are now available for those offices.

Accordingly, we now ask for retirement from the offices of Chairman and President, respectively, at the expiration of the present calendar year. We took up these offices together and we wish to lay them down together. We will remain as Directors and make ourselves available for such service as you and our successors may deem helpful to the Company.

May we express to you and through you to the organization our appreciation of the privilege of working so happily with you and them these many years.

Respectfully,
OWEN D. YOUNG
GERARD SWOPE

It was not a surprise. Nor was General Electric leaderless for more than minutes. The choice and training of successors had been one of Young's and Swope's most important concerns—and for far more than the past two years. General Electric policy was to fill positions from within, and the success of the Young-Swope team management indicated its continuance. Hence not just two men, but two men who could work together and who were well and favorably known within the company—or could be—had to be found. In 1937 Charles E. Wilson, just over fifty and with long experience in GE, was made executive vice-president. At the same time, Philip D. Reed, not yet forty, and eleven years with the company, was made assistant to the president. Soon after, they were made directors of the company, and at the November 17 meeting, they were elected, Wilson as president and Reed as chairman, to take office January 1, 1940.[34]

One member of the board of directors, on whom Young had called before the fateful day, objected when he was told of the plan. He argued that the older men were in good health, owed much to GE, and were too-valuable assets to let go. Young agreed on their debt to GE, and said, "I would like to think you're right about our being valuable assets," but pointed out that they were wasting assets. "Why not treat us instead . . . as a kind of insurance fund . . . against managerial contingencies? We plan to remain as directors, and if our health is as good as it looks, that fund should remain intact at least as long as there is any possible need for it."[35]

Whatever thoughts Young may have had as he penned that resignation—in writing that was, for him, clear, firm and legible—they were, for certain, mostly good.

That very afternoon he dictated a long and loving letter to his daughter in Cambridge, where her husband was now an assistant dean at the Harvard Business School. Retiring from a job, he said, "is fully as difficult as getting one. Now that it is done I am certainly as happy as I ever was in getting one. I enclose a copy of the communication which Gerard and I read to the Directors this morning and on which they acted. Everett may be interested in seeing it. He might use it as a thesis for establishing a course in the Business School on How to Retire."[36]

He went on to detail his plans for the next few weeks: he was going to Washington to speak to a group of Harvard Business School alumni and spend Thanksgiving with the Philip Youngs. Then he and Louise wanted to come to Cambridge for the weekend with Richard to see the Case family, and most especially his new grandson, Samuel, born October 28, a day late for his own birthday. These happy reunions, which, signaling the first rewards of retirement, took place as planned, were reassuring to him after this major landmark in his life, and to his children also, who could not help wondering how he would take it when retirement actually came to pass.

Release from obedience to the calendar and the clock was very welcome. There would be jobs to do, but these (he thought) he could arrange for his own convenience. And there would be months under the live oaks in Florida, on the farms in Van Hornesville. Best of all, he knew that he and Swope left behind a job well done.

Letters poured in, from twenty-one states and from foreign countries: from dozens of GE people, from co-workers in his other fields of action, from people he had never met. Most wished him well, some wanted him to run for President, many GE stockholders regretted his leaving, but one postcard read: "This is the best thing that has happened to [GE] in a long time." The columnist H. I. Phillips wrote a verse:

> There's nothing so strange
> And against all the dope
> As Gen'ral Electric
> Without Young or Swope

> The Company news
> As new praises are sung
> Won't quite seem the same
> Minus Swope and O. Young.

And Paul Cravath wrote that he recalled the day when Charles Coffin told him of "his decision to retire from active business, and mentioned the names of the two young men who were to succeed."

Among all the letters, Young wrote his friend Millard Jencks—who was also retiring, from Ginn and Company—were "suggestions, pleas, mental and moral coercions." But he had no qualms about getting rid of it all, moving into a smaller office, keeping only Gertrude Chandler and Lillian Morrison (who between them were quite capable of running the whole of GE, let alone an honorary chairman's office) and planning to go off to Florida for four months. He could leave with the added satisfaction of knowing that, unlike 1938, their final GE year had been a good one.[37]

But first there were numberless pictures to be taken, luncheons and dinners in honor of the two newly unemployed, both in New York and in Schenectady, with laudatory speeches to listen to—and all those letters to answer. Owen and Louise did get to Van Hornesville for Christmas with the family, but on the twenty-sixth Henry Doherty died and Owen came back to attend the funeral and speak about his old friend on the radio. He attended his last GE board meeting as chairman, then went back home for New Year's, where he and Louise gave a humdinger of a square dance at the Odd Fellows Hall for the whole community.

With the Annual Report for 1939, sent out to stockholders, went a booklet titled (not quite correctly) "Two Decades of General Electric Leadership" and signed by Philip Reed and Charles Wilson. This factual record presented the progress of the company in figures, charts and photos, without fanfare, emphasizing its overall growth in the areas of new uses for electricity, new appliances, rural electrification, industry, radio and broadcasting, international development, greater power generation and distribution, transportation, and especially employee relations.

The period of [the Young and Swope] administration encompassed two distinct eras—one of seemingly limitless expansion, and one of prolonged depression. Each brought problems of great magnitude for which there were few precedents to serve as guides. Possibly no better tribute as to how they met the many and diverse problems brought about by ever-changing conditions can be given than that contained in the January 1940 issue of the magazine *Fortune*: "when one recalls the storms through which they had to navigate their super-company, the magnitude of their accomplishments can be appreciated." In retrospect, the methods by which they dealt with these problems seem natural and logical; but, when first projected, to many, these methods appeared to be radical.

Part VI

"Freedom's Mighty Farm"
1940–1962

Chapter 37

National Defense,
the Dairy Farmer, and Pearl Harbor

REED, at least for the time being, from the twenty-seven years of demands from the General Electric Company, Young boarded the train for Florida on January 5, 1940. To Jesse Jones he confided that he was "prepared to face unflinchingly the arduous task of doing nothing for a while." He was suffering, he wrote Ferris Greenslet of Houghton Mifflin Company, from "a severe attack of exaltation"; he did not intend to write a book for him, or anybody else. Macmillan, Scribner's, Simon and Schuster, and most persistently Missy Meloney, were all trying to put the pen in his hand; all he refused. He had no ambition, he told his son-in-law, to compete with his daughter, in whose first book—*At Midnight on the Thirty-first of March*—he found sufficient cause for pride as an author once removed.[1]

But the publishers were persistent, and as late as December 3, 1941, he was writing Lincoln Schuster what he hoped would prove a sufficiently definite reply:

There is an area in a man's life of about fifteen or twenty years in which he should be exposed to "the grandeurs and miseries of power." In all the years before that period, he should be striving to qualify himself for them and to get them. At the end of the period, he should voluntarily slough them off and not wait for somebody to strip him. That is the only way he can best serve himself, his own generation and do justice to the next succeeding one. Incidentally, it is the only way that one man can be reasonably happy all along the line. Nothing is more tragic than the old man who hangs on too long. His juniors and even his contemporaries hesitate to tell him. So he goes blithely on believing himself indispensable.

The striving of the earlier years, the exercise of power midway with all its trials and sufferings and the relief which comes when the period closes all carry their satisfaction in their own time. To the last, one may add the fun of watching the generations after you undertake under new conditions their great adventure too.

I know of no higher compliment at my age than to have someone like you think I could write an acceptable book. I know of no better way to retain such a high opinion than not to write one.

In the meantime, the march of events, at home and abroad, had shut the door on the one post-retirement ambition to which he had confessed. This confession was made in the summer of 1936, when the impending campaign had prompted his son-in-law to warn him that if by 1940 he and F D R were both out of a job, he'd better look out. No, he said, he would be too old; one doesn't retire at sixty-five "to let himself in for the crushing responsibilities of the presidency. The worst of that job is that one has to make such a tremendous expenditure of energy and effort to accomplish even a little. But there is one job I would like to do," he added; "after my retirement maybe I can do it."

It is obvious to me that we have reached a point where the courts simply have to recognize that these national businesses demand Federal regulation. The case has been stated so often that there is no need to repeat it now, and I suspect the real difficulty has been that the courts have approached it in the past from the wrong angle and now are confronted with embarrassing precedents.

I think it might be possible to deal with that, however, if one were to make a different approach. Whenever Congress, recognizing the national character of the great corporate enterprises, has tried to regulate business that had hitherto been subjected only to state regulation, the burden of proof that they were engaged in interstate commerce has always rested on the government. I would like to hang up my lawyer's shingle again just long enough to argue a case before the Supreme Court in which I presented quite a different point of view.

Since the Constitution gives the Federal Government a clearly granted power over interstate commerce, and it is so clear to the layman that modern industry is largely national in scope, I would like to suggest that when Congress assumes the power to regulate business on the ground of its interstate character, the burden of proof should rest on those who challenge it. I believe it should, and I believe the Court would listen to me because of my long experience in industry, if not because of my profound learning in the law!

"That," he concluded, "is one job that I would really like to do, and if you will let me do that you can have your presidency."[2]

This colloquy, antedating by several months the President's ill-fated Court-packing plan, showed that Young too had not been happy with some of the Court's mid-thirties decisions. But by early 1940 it was clear that the justices no longer needed any such prodding. Besides, Europe was at war, and if, on the western front, the "phony war" still left the door to hope ever so slightly ajar, the Stalin-Hitler pact of the preceding August had made the totalitarian threat more total than ever. In developing effective answers to that threat it was the Congress, not the Court, with which Roosevelt must now cope.[3]

The United States being officially neutral, Young might make his elaborate pretense of doing nothing, though even in less critical times doing nothing had a meaning of its own for Louise and Owen. It had included, and still did, extensive farming and domestic operations at both their homes, plus building and renovation, and ever-present hospitality to relatives and friends. But now, with GE and the New York Fed both feeling the added pressures of war abroad and rearmament at home, Young was finding his role as honorary chairman of the one and chairman of the other to be no sinecure. In and out of directors' meetings, his counsel and advice were in demand; at GE, he and Swope had several long sessions with their successors. Only for the first two months of 1940, spent with Louise at Washington Oaks, was his hard-earned leisure respected; for the rest of the year it was to prove little more than a cherished illusion.[4]

For one who had never doubted that the looming war would overrun the world, this could hardly have come as a surprise. As early as December 1938, in a talk to the Economic Club of New York about the European crisis, Young had said, "I know the threat of force must be met temporarily with its only antidote."[5] Impatient with isolationists and the disunion they caused at home, and sick over the disarray of Europe, which he had spent so much time and effort to prevent, he spoke from the heart in two commencement addresses in 1940.

At Syracuse University he described the "despair we all feel about a world gone mad," tracing the cataclysm in Europe back to Germany's original disregard of "the solemn obligation of a great nation"—the "scrap of paper" of 1914. At St. Lawrence, where his youngest son was graduating *summa cum laude*, he spoke without preparation, pinch-hitting for Professor James T. Shotwell of Columbia, who was ill. Citing the long, unguarded border only a few miles away, he gave the young men and women of his own college a clear call for aid in the impending crisis: "I commend to you first the defense of this nation so that power can meet power and force meet force. Not to conquer but to tame. Not to take from others, but to restore to others what has been wrongfully taken. Not to break obligations, but to compel others to perform their own. Not to retire from a world so small that there's no longer a place to go, but to live in it and do your part."[6]

ii

Not yet ready to retire from the world, Young soon discovered that his retirement from office exposed him to various defense assignments. For a starter, in March of 1940, Roosevelt appointed him chairman of the presidential commission for a long-range study of transportation. This was under the National Resources Planning Board, headed by the President's uncle, Frederic A. Delano, and was the latest of numerous legislative and extralegislative commissions to study transportation problems, especially those relating to the railroads. A previous report had become a subject of controversy, and Young's appointment to take charge of a new study was, most likely, the President's way out, leaving him holding the bag.

Writing Tom Lamont from Washington Oaks on April 30, Young said only:

I undertook the transportation study at the request of the President because, as I wrote him, I knew nothing about it and so had no preconceived notions regarding its solution . . . when I get to the point I know enough about the problem to listen intelligently, I should like to sit down and talk it all over with you. . . . Doubtful as it may be as to getting helpful results, I feel that the undertaking is worthwhile, and I would rather be engaged in this effort than in many others where the information is less definite, and the opinions even more sprawling.

But the situation was further complicated by the presence of railroad legislation in both houses of Congress in 1939 which, characteristically, was agreed upon and passed as the Omnibus Transportation Act in September of 1940—well before the Young group had finished its study. The new legislation did authorize a three-man board for the purpose of continued study, and Young told Delano that he would like to have his report completed for their use—which he did. He was widely expected to head this new board, but he indicated to the President through Delano that he did not wish to do it; an unpaid coordinator was one thing, but a full-time government employee was quite different.[7]

In that same dark spring of 1940, as the Nazi blitz swept over Europe, the President tapped Young for another job—after which Young described himself as "a sort of handy man" for the administration. FDR was now setting up the organizational machinery that our own defense—including aid to Britain—would certainly require, especially as the war moved ever closer. These agencies were, for the most part, outside the regular governmental structure and were answerable to the President himself; the boards which headed them were largely made up of the dollar-a-year men who flocked to Washington, eager to be of service. Among them was the National Defense Advisory Commission, whose job was to provide materials and men for defense. For the mobilization of youth for civilian service under this agency, Roosevelt turned to Owen Young, because of his experience with the National Youth Administration and the American Youth Commission.[8]

A White House memo in Young's files discloses his twin assignment: the development of a plan for preliminary training and work experience, taking into account the needs of defense and future needs of industry; and second, the coordination of all agencies now employing and training young people—government, schools, industry and organized labor. And on May 21, 1940, the President wrote to say that "you are a component part in the development of the plan for coordination of training of young people."

Back from Washington Oaks for a GE board meeting, Young went at once to Washington in response to the President's letter, and met for some hours with Harry Hopkins, at that time still secretary of commerce. The following day, Sunday the twenty-sixth of May, Young called together the top group in the field: Aubrey Williams of the National Youth Administration, Commissioner of Education John Studebaker, Isidor Lubin of the Labor Bureau, James J. McEntee of the Civilian Conservation Corps, Arthur J. Altmeyer of the Social Security Board and Floyd Reeves of the American Youth Commission. From each of these he asked a report on facilities available for training youth in his area; this information was organized and presented within three days.

In a long letter to the President, Young reported that in the meeting there were two approaches discussed, one short-term, designed to meet only immediate defense requirements for labor;

the other approach was a much larger one, namely that any defense program could not contemplate the existence of large numbers of young people in the nation who are unemployed and restless and consequently either unmoved by national needs or receptive to subversive and disintegrating influences. This approach necessarily looked forward to getting these young people busy with something. If not a training of specific skills, then a general preparation so that any special facility could be quickly acquired.

This, he said, he was sure was what the President had in mind; it was certainly in his. He ended the letter: "My task, as I understand it, is only to aid the Secretary in the formulation of the plan. I think that you have in Washington men who can administer it satisfactorily once it is established. To the extent to which I might be helpful with the industrial groups, I should, of course, be glad to aid."[9]

This whirlwind effort, he hoped, finished his task, but a month from the day he had written the President he was called back, and lunched at the White House on June 28. Roosevelt wanted Young's services again and in the same field, but the picture had changed. The members of the National Defense Advisory Commission had now been appointed: for industry, William S. Knudsen of General Motors and Edward Stettinius of U.S. Steel; for labor, Sidney Hillman, vice-president of the CIO, chairman of the Executive Council of the Textile Workers' Union, and an outstanding figure in the field. Whatever the title and position the President pressed Young to accept, he emerged from the White House as an "advisory aide" to Hillman. The two men had already known each other, most recently on the Advisory Council of the National Youth Administration. Their relationship was cordial and admiring, and if Young's subordinate role caused comment in the press, it gave him what he wanted—freedom from primary responsibility.[10]

Nevertheless, the new aide spent much of the overheated summer of 1940 in Washington—overheated not only by the temperatures but by the confusion, anxiety and excitement of a nation gearing up for probable war. He sent his "boss" weekly memoranda on general plans, organization, specific approaches, seasoned with philosophic reflections. At the end of his first day at work, he wrote a long letter describing his conception of Hillman's job: what should be done and how to go about it, not only for efficiency and results, but in ways to obviate "existing apprehensions and potential criticisms."[11]

Young was assigned to organize an advisory group of labor and management to advise Hillman on training within industry and to aid him in setting up an appropriate mechanism to deal with that segment of the labor defense program. Such a group was set up, six on a side, and met for the first time with Young on July 25. He had asked especially not for top officers of companies or unions, but for younger men who would have time and will to give to the job of organizing the training of young people, not in schools but within industries themselves—a program in which the General Electric Company had been notably successful. With the organization of this committee, and the appointment of a director to do the work, Young was able to go on to the next problem.[12]

This was his recurring concern for the young people who were not— nor about to be—in military service, who did not have jobs or the prospects of any, and who were not in any kind of training. For the most part not included in statistics, their numbers were unknown but were certainly legion, and a large percentage lived in rural areas. "Looking after them is an important item of defense," he noted in his July 31 memo to Hillman; he suggested that a special director be appointed to organize programs on their behalf, using public schools after hours and volunteer teachers. Guidance and testing for aptitudes and community work projects would be an important part of these programs: "The important thing would be to put these young people on a job that was worthwhile and make them feel that they were doing their part in the Defense Program by getting training in fruitful community work. . . ." Such a program "would cover the agricultural areas primarily. It would first be established in some of the Southern states where there are large numbers of unemployed young people and diminishing need for them on the farm because of the inevitable curtailment . . . of the cotton and tobacco markets abroad."

In his final memo to Hillman before he left the Defense Commission in the middle of August, Young stated his concern even more strongly:

> Before leaving Washington . . . I wish to point out another area of defense which I regard as important, if not more important even, than the supplying of materials. This is the area of general morale, and particularly that part of it which has to do with several million youth now out of school and either unemployed or inadequately and unsuitably employed. We shall not have adequate and sustaining morale for any defense materials which you produce until we deal daringly and comprehensively with this problem.

And he reiterated, as a point of departure, the plan he had already proposed.[13]

During that summer of 1940, Young had been asked to join the group of Democrats who were supporting Wendell Willkie for the presidency. On July 30 Young sent his friend and sometime Democrat, now the Republican nominee, a long and thoughtful letter; he wanted, he wrote, to state his position directly:

> We have been friends too long and I am too devoted to you personally to run the risk of any misunderstanding. I understand fully that any declaration on my part is quite unimportant to you as a candidate for the Presidency, but it is important to me as your friend. When the occasion

arises, I shall make the same statement to the President, because he, too, has been my personal friend for more than thirty years.

He could not justify a breach of the third-term tradition, he went on, unless the world situation was so serious that Roosevelt, with his eight years' experience and his position in the world as well as the nation, would appear to be indispensable. If either Robert Taft or Thomas Dewey had been nominated, Young felt the tradition should have been broken. "When you were nominated the indispensability of the President under existing circumstances seemed to disappear."

But, he continued, "what will happen between now and November in this uncertain world, no one knows." And he weighed the advantages, in a world at war, between Roosevelt and Willkie as leader and spokesman of America: the President was known throughout the world, Willkie was unknown; but the President had aroused antagonisms abroad, which Willkie had not. "Faced as I am with these conditions, I do not wish to take a position."

In November, having resolved his problem by a vote for the losing candidate, Young thereupon sent Willkie congratulations on his "magnificent campaign"—it had been the closest race since 1916—"and particularly for the spirit of high statesmanship which your address showed. . . . It is inspiriting and refreshing to have such a note struck in this country by a business man."[14] And at the beginning of the following year, January 30, 1941, as Willkie had begun his travels, Young wrote suggesting that he visit Japan and China:

For three years at least I have regarded that area as not only the most sensitive and dangerous but also as the most hopeful place for us to act. It must be wisely and understandingly done. In a way I think there is less knowledge and judgment used by us in that area than in Europe. Something like three years ago, I urged that the United States and Japan come to an understanding in regard to Eastern Asia and the Pacific. As the war in Europe became imminent I urged it even more strongly. I felt that if we could reach an understanding with Japan and both of us say to the world that the Pacific Ocean would be truly "pacific," then we could release the energies of the English and the Dutch to deal with their European affairs. . . . Some solution of the Japanese-Chinese problem will have to be made and no effort is too great or prospects too remote to [keep us from making it]. . . . It might well be that such an exhibition of interest as your trip would make would be the best protection against unwise action by Japan. Indeed, action which might well precipitate the whole war on us.

Willkie replied, "You are dead right. I ought to take a trip to Japan and China. I would like to do it. . . ." But after the expense of his campaign the demands of making a living were pressing and he could not go everywhere. He did indeed visit western China on his world trip in 1942, but by then it was too late.[15]

iii

In late October 1940 Owen and Louise got away to Washington Oaks; after a ten-day interlude there he returned without her for a hectic round of activity which began with an election-day visit to Van Hornesville. Having broken the record of a lifetime by voting against his party's nominee, he came back to his office, apparently unrepentant, to devote the rest of the year largely to G E and the Federal Reserve, the board of regents and the completion of his Washington chores. After taking in—as a new director—a meeting of the Holstein-Friesian Association, he managed to spend Thanksgiving and the following fortnight at home in Van Hornesville, where the perennial problems of the dairy farmer were heating up again. Then came a crowded fortnight of meetings in New York and also with Sidney Hillman and Jesse Jones in Washington. Christmas in New York was not much fun but it kept him on hand for his—and George Harrison's—valedictory with the Federal Reserve directors next day. And on the twenty-seventh, having met all morning with the G E directors, and lunched with Gerard Swope, Philip Reed and Charles Wilson, he could take the overnight train to St. Augustine and Louise with a sense of virtue, if not of great accomplishment.

In responding as he had to the President's several defense assignments, Young found some relief from the agony of watching the progress of Hitler's unbroken triumphs. He had also demonstrated his mastery of the fine art of defining the job to be done, setting up the organization and leadership to do it, and then bowing out—remaining on call thereafter only as "rocking chair consultant." More than willing to leave the grind to younger men, he was also convinced that labor leaders like Hillman had earned the right to responsible public posts— and would be the better for taking them on.

Thus he could now devote himself in good conscience to cultivating his garden—this time his citrus grove. And there at Washington Oaks he stayed for the first four months of 1941, his only interruptions being a flurry of late February meetings in New York. Toward the middle of May, the Youngs left Washington Oaks for the long drive north to Van Hornesville, exchanging citrus groves and Louise's orchids for dairy cows and apple orchards. Young, however, was delayed in getting home by an endless chain of board meetings and a special trip to Washington, taken on his own initiative to talk with the secretary of agriculture, Claude R. Wickard. When he finally reached Van Hornesville late in June, it was to confront a problem, by no means unrelated to defense, which was not susceptible of delegation as he had been practicing that art. Indeed, this particular problem got so deeply under his skin that he had no heart to dodge or delegate it.

Young liked to insist, as he did to Russell Owens of the *Times*, that the press should label him not so much the retired industrialist as "the returned farmer." Now he was about to prove his point. It was all very well to have more time to devote to his prime herd of purebred Holsteins, which he found "a good deal more interesting than a lot of folks I know, and almost as good to the touch as calf-bound books." But the milk they produced so generously, and at such cost in equipment, feed, and labor, couldn't seem to pay for itself. And if he and his skilled manager and help couldn't make ends meet, what about his neighbors, whose living was at stake? Or the thousands of small farmers and their families—"the backbone of the nation"—thanks to whose joint efforts the total milk production of the Empire State was second only to Wisconsin's? It was better too, because, in order to qualify for New York City's great fluid market, York State milk had to pass a rigid inspection.

The problem was far from new, either to the other upstate farmers or to him. The thirties had been the era of "dollar milk," which meant that this was the return for one hundred pounds—a trifle over two cents a quart. Of this the consuming public, paying eight to ten cents a quart, was for the most part blissfully ignorant—so much so that if the price to them went up a cent or two they assumed that this all went to line the pockets of the avaricious farmer. Nor, to Young's dismay, did the urban press enlighten them by calling attention to the costs of distribution, or the fact that the "dealers' spread" typically absorbed most of any price increase.

Letting the "free market" dictate the farm price of milk had indeed left the state's fifty-eight thousand unorganized dairy farmers largely at the mercy of the dealers; the so-called State and Federal Orders established to correct this did at least assure all producers of returns equitably apportioned. Thanks, moreover, to the Federal Order's so-called equalization pool, all producers were assured a fair share of milk supplied to the fluid market, which commanded the highest price. But the nine different market classifications—and prices—which determined the "blend," or average price to the producer, were something else again. After all (as your neighbors never tired of pointing out), your cows "had only four tits and they all gave the same milk." And since, to qualify for the fluid market all your milk had to pass the same inspection tests, how come a third or more must compete with uninspected or "cheap" milk from the West? And why—oh why?—must the Department of Agriculture's bureaucracy administering the Federal Order be so slow to take account of changing conditions, especially rising costs, and disasters like the drought?

Here, in short, was a classically complex economic problem, with important political ramifications and grave social implications. It was the kind of challenge Young found irresistible, and even before his retirement—in 1938, and especially in the summer of '39—he had found himself involved. He initially tried, and with little success, to break down the barriers of suspicion and distrust that separated the several producer organizations. "If you want to be heard in Albany or Washington," he told them, "you will have to learn to speak with one voice." And he said to his fellow members of the local cooperative, that summer of 1939, "One day all you producers will get together and say what a fair price for your milk has to be—and that will be the price of milk."[16]

However satisfying emotionally, this was still a simplistic solution, as Young soon realized. But, as he kept insisting, there was something radically wrong about a setup which complained of an overhanging surplus and yet left children undernourished for want of sufficient milk, not only in the city but even on the farm. As matters stood, the farmer had no option but to ship every last ounce of his milk to the dealer, surplus or not, in order to get maximum—if still inadequate—returns from the blend price. Why not, then, limit each farmer's shipment, under the Federal-State Order, to his share of the *fluid* market, plus enough extra to ensure supply for that market at all seasons? For this shipment he would then receive the fluid, or highest, price. For the rest, why shouldn't he have the option of selling his "cheap," or surplus, milk in the open market or, if the bids were unsatisfactory, keeping it at home for the use of the family and extra feeding for his hogs?

Toward the end of 1940, Young had developed this plan sufficiently to write Governor Herbert Lehman about it at length in an effort to get him involved. He also consented to be interviewed at length by the editor of the *Holstein-Friesian World*. Published in its issue of March 1, 1941, as the lead article, complete with the author's picture, the piece was entitled "How to Make the Dairyman Master of His Own Business." It received strong editorial support and considerable notice in the upstate press, but it smacked of a "quota system," and although Young made his trip to Washington late in May expressly to discuss it with the secretary of agriculture and his dairy experts, the idea never really took. Nevertheless, it revealed his deep concern and willingness to work, and from then on the producer organizations sought his counsel at every step of the way. By the early summer of 1941 they needed counsel they could trust, for the dairy farmers' problems were acute.

In his May visit with Secretary Wickard, Young had warned him that trouble impended if something were not done; by July 1 the New York milkshed was in a turmoil. For one thing it had suffered the worst drought in years. True, wartime demands for milk and milk products had been depleting the surplus somewhat, and average returns to the farmer had more than doubled since the days of dollar milk. But so (and substantially more) had the cost of his feed and equipment, while labor, thanks to high industrial wages—at Schenectady, for example— was hard to come by at any price. Thus as it became clear that the producers' urgent pleas for higher returns had been largely brushed aside, the strike called for July 1 by the Dairy Farmers Union was widely hailed and by July 4 threatened to become general.

Young was in Van Hornesville, where his farms were withholding their milk. With this earnest of good faith, he made ready for the fray—marshaling his forces, planning his strategy, and finally exercising his clout with the same zest and attention to detail that had marked his creation of RCA or his efforts at untangling reparations. At his invitation, all the producer organizations sent their leaders to Van Hornesville during that same week for all-day sessions at the school. And at length a plan was evolved which—promising an end to a strike the dairy farmers could ill afford and a special hearing with the secretary of agriculture—commanded their united support.

Naturally, Owen Young's meetings with these striking farmers' representatives were news, even in the city; and when he suggested—by phone and very privately—that the governor might like to invite them all down to his office, Lehman was quick to respond. Not only was his invitation promptly accepted—and so reported by the press—but Young saw to it that, so far as the press knew, the initiative had been the governor's. This was also true of the governor's plea and promise at the meeting on July 6: end the strike, "put your faith in the orderly processes of democracy," and he would pledge his best efforts to secure an immediate hearing with the secretary of agriculture himself. Naturally, the governor was pleased when, at his urging, the strike was duly called off, and not least by praise from the media for his effective intervention. But he may have wondered what in the world Owen Young was up to; certainly he himself appeared to feel no great urgency about making good his pledge.

Young himself understood well enough that the governor, like the secretary, had other problems too, but the farmers didn't, and he was now feeling personally responsible to them. He was also irked by what he felt to be the governor's "European" tendency to regard the farmers as mere peasants. Lehman's pledge had been given on Sunday, July 6; by Tuesday the strike had ended and the leaders of the producer groups were hard at work on a joint petition for relief. By Saturday, July 12, this had been completed, signed, and filed in Albany and Washington; still no word had come from the governor.

This was too much for Young. That same day he made an appointment to see the governor on Monday; he also dictated a scorching radio speech which he threatened to make over w G Y if he got no satisfaction from this meeting. On Monday the governor told him he had been unable to reach the secretary, but when "as a matter of courtesy" Young showed him a draft of his speech, the governor blanched and issued peremptory orders to get the secretary on the phone at once, no matter where or how. This worked, and a meeting was promptly set up for the following Thursday. Young agreed to accompany the governor, and rather ostentatiously tore up "his only copy" of the speech. (and so—regrettably—it was.)

At this Washington meeting with Secretary Wickard on July 17 Young discarded his prepared statement, and stressing the desperate nature of the farmers' plight, urged the necessity of quick action to relieve it and restore their faith in "the orderly processes of democracy." Their grievances, he said, were genuine and deep-seated; it was time that they were heeded. On the following Monday, July 21, the secretary announced that hearings would be held on the farmers' petition, beginning in Brooklyn on Friday, August 1, and extending through the following week in Watertown and Albany. Attending all of these, Young held his fire for the Albany sessions, where he called on the secretary to determine the fair cost of production and, as a matter of elementary justice, see to it that returns to the dairyman were sufficient to meet it. At the same session, Professor "Ed" Misner of Cornell estimated fair cost to be $2.99 per hundredweight; stressing the drought, Young and his fellow producers were asking a blend price to the farmer of $3.00, for a rise of some 50 cents a hundredweight, or a little more than a cent a quart.

As the milkshed waited anxiously for Washington's decision, the farmers became increasingly restive; it was more than seven weeks since they had called off the strike on the promise of quick action. At last, on August 29 the decision was announced; a rise of 20 cents per hundredweight or a little less than half a cent a quart was the best the department could offer. And on September 5, with the farmers bitterly divided on how they should respond, Young did take to the radio but with a very different speech.

This time he spoke as one dairy farmer to another; others could listen in if they wished. (He hoped Washington was listening.) Explaining his own deep interest and concern, he rehearsed—with a certain wry humor—the frustrations of the several producer organizations in their efforts to get a hearing, and his suggestion that they might be heard through the noise in the department if they all shouted together—with the governor joining the shout. He reviewed the testimony they had given, as well as their patience and its wholly inadequate reward. As for the dilemma posed by the paltry rise now offered, he reported that after intensive discussion in Van Hornesville, their leaders were substantially agreed that the best course was to take it—after all, it was better than nothing—but immediately to petition for new hearings.

If they then did not get cost for their milk, they would somehow take the business back in their own hands. . . . Let no one think my recital flippant. The truth is that I feel so deeply the injustice to the dairy farmer that I do not trust myself to speak too seriously lest my bitterness appear and bitterness has never done anybody any good. Only a firm and serious determination to correct this situation by unified action of all dairy farmers in this milkshed can get us a price for our milk adequate to cover our costs. . . .

Dismissing as unrealistic the secretary's proposed fluid price of $3.11, Young added that he could "not believe that we have yet received the last word of the Department of Agriculture on all the prices which affect the blend. After all, it is . . . that price in which we are primarily interested. The blend depends not only upon the price of fluid milk but of products manufactured from the surplus." And:

The Secretary of Agriculture is charged with the responsibility of purchasing such products for Government defense needs and our lease-lend shipments abroad. Shortages in the lease-lend countries are rapidly becoming acute. Only yesterday I read that the milk ration for the coming winter in England will be a pint a day for children over six, with little or none for adults. And my daughter has shown me a letter from a young mother in China who says that a pound of evaporated milk for her baby costs $100 in Chinese money. This is about $5 per pound in U.S. currency. *So long as these conditions obtain in countries to which we have pledged all aid short of war it is silly to talk about a surplus production in the United States.*

The Secretary of Agriculture has recognized this and has asked for increased production as our contribution to defense. I said in my testimony, and I repeat now, that *when large industrial units are asked by the Government to produce for defense, they are not asked to do so at a loss. Why should the dairy farmers be asked to do so?* [emphasis added]. The record shows that the farmers of this milkshed are not getting their costs based on anything like a fair labor return. I am sure that the Secretary of Agriculture will not ask the dairy farmers to increase their milk production for defense at less than cost. I have great confidence in him. . . .

Then came a change of tactic: if flattery wouldn't move the secretary, perhaps a little humor would. So Young went on to put it to the test:

Professor Misner of Cornell said at the recent hearings that when a man is 5 foot under water he can be raised 2 feet and still find it difficult to breathe. We have now been raised about 2 feet and we would like to serve notice on the authorities and the public that we can't function very well as a producer of milk, or a consumer, or a citizen of the community until our head is really above water.

I think we must accept the new price on the referendum. I would rather be within 3 feet of the surface than 5 feet down. But under such conditions no one can expect us not to make a struggle, and if need be, a desperate one, to get to the surface. . . .

Then came his final appeal to the farmers themselves:

The task is now up to your producing organizations to formulate plans. They are acting together. They are led by able men. They have only one aim now; that is to get you a fair price. The task is up to you as farmers to support their plans. Let your support be unanimous.

We cannot afford the luxury of dissension until we cover our costs. Such is my appeal. I must not make an appeal unless at the same time I volunteer in your service. That I now do. And I will continue so long as the returns of the dairy farmer are out of balance with the earnings of other groups in the nation and so long as the farmers act together.[17]

It would be pleasant to report that this intensive and highly charged effort on the dairy farmers' behalf—unprecedented on the part of a mere industrialist—ended with a speedy and triumphant flourish. Having had some experience of bureaucracy, Young had no illusions that it would, nor was he through. But now his efforts as volunteer were interrupted by another urgent—and unrelated—call from Washington: a kind of draft to which his age was no barrier.

This, in September of 1941, was a request by William H. Davis, chairman of what was then the National Defense Mediation Board, to be their special representative in the dispute between the U.S. Gypsum Company and District 50 of the United Mine Workers–CIO, to "conduct hearings, take testimony and make findings of fact for the information of the Board."[18] The workers had struck two months before in a dispute over wages, vacations, arbitration of grievances and union security. The situation was confused by the number of Gypsum Company plants in various sections of the country, and the presence of some independent unions as well as the AFL and CIO; and the chairman of the Gypsum board was Sewell Avery of Montgomery Ward, an industrialist not known for his spirit of cooperation with either the unions or the government. Now the Mediation Board requested the union to end the strike, pending an investigation by Young of the issues on which the company had refused to bargain collectively. The men returned to work, and Young was given thirty days for his investigation.

"It was the first time," reported *Business Week* for September 13, "that anyone of such stature as GE's former board chairman had been pressed into service" by the Mediation Board. The special representative went to work immediately; meetings were held in New York and Chicago throughout September. It was a time when the shadow of war was growing darker for the United States, and Young began the first meeting by saying, "The issues are too inconsequential and unimportant to engage the time and effort of the men representing the company and the union in times like this . . . this I feel very deeply."[19]

But the differences between the two sides were sharp, and the Gypsum Company was wholly uncooperative. Young went to the top, but to no avail. As Marquis Childs was to report much later in the *Washington Post*: "Young had lunch with [Sewell] Avery in Chicago. They talked all afternoon, they talked until nine o'clock in the evening. Young really thought he was getting somewhere. Finally Avery said: 'You know you've made the best presentation of an indefensible case I've heard yet.' "[20]

So that was that. Young reported to the Mediation Board that further hearings would be useless and asked to be discharged. He held one more meeting, however, at the request of the union representatives; no results are recorded, but a letter in the Owen D. Young Papers expresses the union's "profound appreciation" of his services.[21]

In the meantime Young had not forgotten his pledge to the dairy farmers. He arranged for further and authoritative studies of cost of production as a basis for their new petition, which their leaders were now hammering out under his guidance. He also intensified his appeals to the court of public opinion, beginning with the metropolitan press, and notably the *Times*. There too he went to the top, insisting that their reports were parochial and one-sided and that it was high time they sent a special reporter upstate with a mission to explore in depth the problems of the milkshed and the reasons for the farmers' restiveness. By mid-November, the *Times* was finally persuaded to do just that, and "Young Jim" Hagerty[22] embarked on a three-week tour of exploration, not without an initial seminar or two with his Van Hornesville mentor. It seemed to work. As preliminary reports of his findings reached Van Hornesville, Young could envision a series of realistic and authoritative reports featured by the *Times* which would really compel the attention of the consumers. And as the December day drew near when Hagerty was scheduled to discuss his findings with Young, the aura of expectancy attracted other concerned members of the family to come home for the weekend.

Thus that Sunday, December 7, found Young, his son Dick, his son-in-law Everett Case, Jim Hagerty and Jim Beiermeister, the manager of Van Horne Farms, deep in talk in the big library which Louise had added to Ida Young's old house for Owen's books. The phone rang in the front room and Dick went to answer it; his old nurse, Margaret Egan, who now lived up the street, had been listening to her radio, and her first thought on hearing the stunning news of Pearl Harbor was to call her boy. It was the end of the milk conference, the projected series in the *Times*, and, among much else, of Owen Young's "retirement."

The new petition had nevertheless been duly filed and hearings called for January. Young kept in touch but had to leave further testimony to the producer organizations and his son-in-law, whose further education in these mysteries was entrusted to Jim Beiermeister, a Cornell graduate well acquainted with the intricacies of dairying. With the United States now actively at war, even bureaucracy was stirred to some semblance of action, and the next few months—and years— saw a steady increase in the dairy farmers' returns. If these never quite caught up with the persistent rise in costs, the producers could sometimes feel close enough to the surface to take a deep breath. As for Young, he could feel that he had at least led them out of captivity even though the promised land remained elusive.

iv

By the middle of March 1942, Young was back in harness at General Electric. Philip Reed, his successor, was already serving with the War Production Board; Reed had requested more than once to be relieved to go back to GE, where the pressure for production was enormous, but neither William Knudsen nor his successor Donald Nelson would allow him to leave. And when Averell Harriman's economic mission went to London, Reed went with it as deputy chief.

But that was not all. Early in March, with Reed still in Washington and General Electric moving into the massive production of war matériel with a billion dollars of government contracts, the government's legal arm brought a civil suit against the company, charging its lamp division—of which Reed had formerly been counsel—with violations of the antitrust laws. Reminded by Gerard Swope that a unanimous Supreme Court had dismissed similar charges in 1926, the assistant attorney general, Thurman Arnold, is said to have expressed his confidence that "this court" would see matters differently.

When the date for hearings was set, there was no doubt in GE's offices about what had to be done: Reed, with counsel, went to St. Augustine for a conference with Young. Two weeks later the latter was sitting in his old office at GE hard at work with the lawyers on a problem he thought he had seen the last of. Swope, who had served as chairman of the New York Housing Authority, and then gone to Washington as assistant to the secretary of the treasury, resigned the latter post and returned to GE; he too was a vital witness in the suit.[23] So the experienced captain and navigator found themselves once more on board. No public announcement of this was made, however, until September, when Charles Wilson was snatched from GE for the duration by the War Production Board, where he was made vice-chairman in charge of the aircraft production division. Young had been anxious that their return should in no way reflect upon their successors, and it was only when Reed's and Wilson's resignations were in the hands of the directors of the company that the reelection of the old guard took place. Now, formally, General Electric was cashing in on the "insurance fund against managerial contingencies" which Young had suggested in 1939.

A headline in the press read SWOPE AND YOUNG REVEL IN OLD JOBS. It was perhaps an overstatement, although Young was quoted as saying, "I like this resurrection so well that I'm less apprehensive about the next one." Whatever regret they felt for the loss of leisure at their time of life was certainly balanced by the pressing desire of both to do all they could to help their country in its uphill struggle. Young wrote a GE officer on the West Coast, "While I do not like to work and never did, I am still glad that such service as I can render to this war may be filtered through the General Electric Company. That is where I can do the most with the least nervous wear and tear of politics." He made a somewhat franker statement to his friend B. C. Cobb, now retired from Commonwealth and Southern, in thanking him for his word of congratulation: "I never had to have work to make me happy nor, on the contrary, has work ever made me unhappy."[24]

The company which Young and Swope took over for the second time was now a giant, producing not only stepped-up amounts of its regular products, but undertaking war contracts involving "products with which it had little or no previous manufacturing experience or for which the engineering designs had not been completed."[25]

In 1943 the company reported shipments of $1.4 billion and an increase in the number of employees from a prewar average of 67,000 to 171,000. The variety of war-related manufactured items was legion, running the scale from turbines for battleships and other navy craft— three-quarters of the navy's total propulsion power in the war was supplied by GE, or by others to GE design—to the development of bazookas, radar, heated goggles for flying and finally, in early 1945, the jet engine for the "world's fastest fighting plane," the P-80 Shooting Star. Such production, delivered to the government generally on time or ahead of schedule, was made possible, not only by new plants and employees, but by the use of subcontracts to some two thousand other firms scattered over the nation and involving over $400 million in orders.[26]

"These fantastic orders," as Young called them in a letter to General Dawes, required intricate negotiations and renegotiations of contracts, the supervision of new plants, equipment and workers. Although the pending suits had been temporarily shelved at the request of the armed forces, suspension was not dismissal and they still required attention. In sum, the old-new heads of GE were constantly on the job; Swope visited all the plants, keeping in touch with managers and men, new products, engineering and construction. Young dealt with the lawyers and the government on the more complicated contracts, making frequent trips to Washington. For a couple of caretakers, as they dubbed themselves, it all added up to a sufficiently formidable assignment.[27]

Nor were Young's trips to Washington confined to GE business. In November of 1941 the President had asked him to serve on the Patent Planning Commission. Designed to make the patent system an active stimulant to wartime invention, this commission had been the brainchild of Jesse Jones when he became secretary of commerce, and had been set up by executive order. Young accepted, suggesting that Charles Kettering of General Motors be made chairman of the group of five members, which was done.

The commission was concerned with the definition of "patentability," first for now, but also for the postwar period when new developments would be needed for employment. Young was also anxious for recognition by the Congress of organized research, that is, the "persistent and integrated study by large numbers of experts"—with which he was well acquainted—in contrast to the "flash of genius" criterion, which the courts had preferred in patent suits.[28]

This commission's members worked until June of 1945; their recommendations attacked current abuses and proposed procedural improvements for the protection of the public and the patentee alike. They took a strong stand against the compulsory licensing of patents, which, in the opinion of one expert, was perhaps the most effective result of their work, for it laid to rest the New Deal proposals for such a system. In general, however, their "affirmative proposals for change in the patent system had little effect."[29]

It was a job, however, which Young enjoyed—in contrast to some others in Washington. His experience in the early years with Stone and Webster, with GE when he was counsel, and with RCA in the tangled controversies over radio patents had given him a wide background on the subject. And he never lost his excitement over new inventions and the limitless possibilities of the future.[30]

Meanwhile, for all its characteristic ramifications, the Young-Swope team was finding that its new incarnation differed from the old in at least two important aspects. First, cultivation of new markets for GE was out for the duration; government demands were almost more than the company could handle. Second, while sales, payrolls and total revenues rocketed skyward, net profits remained earthbound. Nineteen forty-two's shipments were more than treble 1939's; in 1943, at $1,357 million, they were more than quadruple. Yet for each of these war years, *net* income after taxes was $45 million—only $3.5 million more than in 1939—and at $1.40, the dividend rates were the same for all three years. The inclusion of federal tax figures—$23 million for 1939, $193 million for 1942, and $206 million (provisionally) for 1943—serves both to resolve the puzzle and to eliminate any possible charge of wartime profiteering. As for Swope and Young, declining their former salaries and any claims to "extra compensation," they elected to draw their regular (and mostly taxable) retirement stipends only: a $30,000 pension plus an annual director-cum-consultant's fee of $67,000.[31]

v

In the course of his long and very private battle to rid himself of debt, Young might have reflected more than once that for one whose "knowledge of obligations" needed no enlargement, the decade of hard work had been notably stingy about increasing his "capacity to perform them." Jo, however, had left him all that remained of her estate, and it was thanks first of all to this that by the time of Owen's remarriage, close to $1 million of the original $2.5 million had somehow been paid off.[32] (Now, he might have said, he was only three feet under water instead of five.) But alas for the promise of that same spring of 1937 that the continuing rise in the value of his pledged collateral would shortly liquidate the debt which weighed him down most heavily—namely, the million and a quarter owed to his broker. By fall, business and the market were again in the doldrums, and the senior George Pick's summer trip to Europe had ended in his death. To his sons who, inheriting the firm, faced problems of their own, the proposed settlement which Young and their father had informally worked out before he sailed seemed far less than adequate and, for a time, unpleasantness threatened.

But in their new agreement, dated January 13, 1938, both parties made important concessions. This settlement owed much to the mediating skills of A. B. Siegel, Pick's attorney, whose nice balancing of the interests and concerns of the two parties Young was quick to acknowledge and commend. Young consented to sign a new three-year promissory note for $500,000, bearing interest at 2 percent and secured by the 4,800 shares of GE and the several insurance policies previously pledged against the old loan; Pick and Company accepted the remaining collateral in full discharge of any balance due, and—best of all—restored to Young full title to the books. If it fell far short of Young's hopes, this settlement (leaving him less than two feet under water) enabled him to face with less apprehension the prospect of retirement by the end of the following year.[33]

At $97,000, however, Young's retirement income from GE was better calculated to meet living expenses (including taxes and interest) than to retire debts, and in January of 1941 the note had to be renewed. The flurry of appointments which brought Young to New York in March, however, included an all-important one with Mitchell Kennerley, the rare-book expert and dealer, who was also a good friend. Kennerley had recently sold an important collection to the philanthropist Dr. Albert Berg, who had then presented it to the New York Public Library, to which he had already given his own collection. The book dealer thought the same could be done with Young's.

This prospect—with certain modifications—appealed to Owen Young, not least because it resolved what had become for him a peculiarly teasing dilemma. To give away, as he had planned, a collection which was now his most valuable asset, was a thing he could ill afford. On the other hand, he shrank from putting his precious collection up for sale to the highest bidder—especially after testing the market as he had in 1937, when Gabriel Wells sold for him a few valued items at a fraction of their cost.[34] And so he now suggested to his friend Frank Polk, president of the library, that if Berg were willing to buy—for the library—a half interest in his collection at (say) $375,000, he would gladly donate the other half himself. Thus the collection would remain intact and in hands which would tend it with loving care, while making it accessible to scholars and the interested public. Happily, Berg was a willing partner and on April 25, 1941, the agreement was signed. Its announcement ten days later was front-page news. Quoting a library official to the effect that this was the largest and most important collection ever given to the New York Public Library, the *Times* celebrated the event in a front-page article decorated by unflattering photos of Berg, Young and Shakespeare.[35]

Of Berg's welcome payment, Young now applied the first $150,000 toward his debt at the Bankers Trust, leaving a balance there (now amply secured) of $119,000. Part of the rest, we deduce, went to liquidate an earlier pledge to St. Lawrence, financed during the interim by a loan he had guaranteed; at least his regular payments of interest to the college ceased abruptly at this point. And by the following

January he had paid $50,000 against his $500,000 note to Pick and Company, executing a new three-year note for the balance.[36]

During the years prior to Pearl Harbor, then, Young had contrived to discharge almost four-fifths of his outstanding obligations. But the process had consumed virtually all of his negotiable assets except for those now pledged against the balance. And these hypothecated assets—especially his paid-up life insurance—were sorely needed if he were now to make adequate provision for his second, and younger, wife's security. With income sharply reduced and taxes sharply higher, his one hope, it seemed, was a rise in the market sufficient to pay off the final fifth and still restore to him a fair share of the collateral pledged against it. Even the substantial tax relief ostensibly accruing from the Berg–New York Public Library sale and gift was all too likely, if precedents meant anything, to prove a will-o'-the-wisp.[37]

It was shortly thereafter—earlier efforts having come to nothing— that the distinguished president of Johns Hopkins, Isaiah Bowman, reminded Young that some $70,000 was still due against his three-year underwriting of 1929 "to get the Page School started." In reply Young asked for further information about the school, suggesting that it had apparently failed to achieve momentum and "if that is so, the purpose of the underwriting [having] failed, I should think that my contribution in excess of $30,000 should be considered a generous gesture toward the enterprise." Bowman assured him that the school, now directed by Owen Lattimore, had "never been more healthy" but added (with a delicacy rare among college presidents) that he had no wish "to pursue you," and wondered whether "you desire to continue the discussion or . . . would prefer to drop it and request us to cancel the guarantee." Quick to seize the opportunity, Young said he would indeed be "pleased to have the Trustees cancel the guarantee because under the present and prospective tax program the burden is unduly heavy." He did express his "sincere appreciation of your attitude" and invited further information as a basis "for any future action I might be able to take."[38] But Bowman evidently chose to consider the matter closed, and Young did not protest. After all, his underwriting aside, he had played a major part in raising some $300,000 (net after the 1929 crash and accumulative fund-raising expenses) toward establishing the School, which had been turned over to the university in 1930.

Nevertheless for Young, as for Johns Hopkins, and the Page School in particular, it was a lame and sorry ending. Dedicated to searching out and making the public realistically aware of the "conditions requisite to peace," this hopeful enterprise had mirrored the idealism of the twenties at its best. Back in 1925, in accepting its leadership at the call of his fellow trustees—including FDR—Young had given the project a fresh and incisive definition of purpose, and his speeches had spread the gospel far and wide. Over two-thirds of the $600,000 he had hoped to raise outside New York had been subscribed by 1927, but as other demands insistently clamored for his time and attention, the psychological moment for a final whirlwind effort had been missed. It was only after returning bone weary from the Young Committee's sessions of 1929 that the chairman had pledged his three-year underwriting to get things started, confident that this would prove the key to the capital needed for endowment. And so it might have been, but for Judge Edwin B. Parker's untimely death—and the market crash—and especially the deepening depression, which had finally convinced the school's first director (former Minister to China John V. A. MacMurray) that not even the most timely and promising projects could command the necessary funding.

By that time the handwriting on the wall was doubly clear to Young, who admired MacMurray and had somehow contrived to meet his pledge for 1931. Unable to do so in 1932, he had authorized his assistant to suggest that the university seek a loan, which his chief would guarantee and service; this suggestion had politely been declined. Launched as it was not long thereafter—and by a Page School trustee—the FDR bombshell that shattered the London economic conference signaled (among much else) the death of the very concept which gave point to the whole enterprise, and Young, not unwillingly perhaps, had thereafter lost touch.

Now, with its grand design a casualty of the very war it was to have helped prevent, Young could see no hope of reviving it—Lattimore or no—merely by contriving to meet the letter of his bond. Thus he welcomed relief from further payment on a pledge that, for him, had lost its meaning. Far less welcome, however, was the implicit reminder of what he felt had been his real failure: missing the boat which, in the halcyon years, had promised to yield such rich returns.[39] But however this thought rankled, it became increasingly possible to view it in the context of a far more general failure: a parable, if you please, of the times.[40]

As for Young's remaining obligations, his $450,000 note to Pick, renewed on January 13, 1942, called for payment of $200,000 against principal by January 1945. Through the sale of the pledged shares of GE, this payment was made; and in the late summer of 1946 Young went on to prepay $208,000 of the balance, leaving only a paltry $42,000 still due. But if Young had almost surfaced, his retirement income now seemed smaller than ever, and it was not until the spring of 1950—on Patriots' Day, to be precise—that this residual payment was finally made and the account marked closed.[41]

World War II and After:
the Last Young Plan

Y OUNG's experience of the aftermath of the First World War led
him to think seriously about plans for the aftermath of the second. "If we wait until the war is won," he wrote Ralph Paine
of *Fortune* in the spring of 1942,

and the great reaction comes, we shall inevitably find what we did before,
a demand for vengeance on our enemies, a suspicion of our friends, and
a retirement from responsibility because we are tired. When a democracy
is in that state of mind, no responsible leader can do other than register
the public temper though he knows the terms of peace to be unwise. Mr.
Wilson tried and failed. Lloyd George and M. Clemenceau, more subject
to quick political penalty, did not try. As the years went on, it became possible to alleviate them some, but not fast enough.[1]

In June of 1942 Young spoke informally to a group at Harvard; the
talk itself was off the record, but in the notes he made for it are ideas
for the postwar world. He recalled a trip with Guglielmo Marconi on
his yacht in the English Channel, fifteen years before; Marconi was
communicating with Montreal, but Young noticed the directional
antenna faced east. To his question Marconi replied, "Mr. Young, the
distance from here to Montreal west is too short to enable me to experiment with these waves. I have to go round the world the other way to
get the needed distance."

"At that moment, gentlemen," said Young, "this world became too
small for the reach of the mind of man. At that moment, it became
too small for independent competing sovereignties which might throw
this world in each generation into conflict and the tragedies of war.
If this world is too small on which to experiment with the mind of
man, it is too small on which to loose the passions of men; too small to
permit the exploitation of men either for war or in peace."

In such a world, economic cooperation was all-important: currencies on a standardized base of interchangeability, leveling of trade barriers, the integration of power and transport systems—especially of electrical power. Throw the great switches, he suggested half seriously, whenever the power was being used to prepare for war. (He did not say who was to throw them.)[2]

Speaking to the U.S. Chamber of Commerce in the spring of 1943, he noted the current war-born unity and harmony between industry and agriculture "which I had advocated and dreamed of for a quarter of a century in my earlier incarnation. . . . Mr. Chairman," he asked, "what is the future of the present unity? What will happen after 'the duration'? And the duration, some one wisely said, would probably last longer than the war. . . . If buying power is the key to economic well-being, or the want of it to economic disaster, no two groups have greater reason for sympathetic and understanding cooperation." It should be voluntary, he argued, not forced by government:

Today politics may be our friend—tomorrow we may be its victim. . . . Some twenty years ago I was instrumental in having the National Industrial Conference Board make a study of the interlocking problems of industry and agriculture in the hope that we might have the sensible cooperation of free men in developing a sound economy. In the 'twenties, however, we decided to manufacture our wealth in the stock market rather than to rely basically on the factory and the farm. They were too slow. We have found it was not a good plan.[3]

By the same token, Young welcomed the initiative of a businessmen's group, led by Studebaker's Paul Hoffman, to anticipate and study ways to meet the economic and social problems of the peace. The resultant Committee for Economic Development did not list Young among its founding members—again he felt the responsibilities of active membership belonged to the next generation—but Hoffman himself (so he told the authors) found Young's counsel invaluable, especially when the CED concept was first taking shape.[4]

Closer to home, Young was thinking about St. Lawrence University and its place in the postwar world. Although he had been forced to resign from the board of trustees when he was elected a regent, he had—as he had then told President Richard Eddy Sykes he would—continued to spend much time and thought on affairs in Canton. Especially after Millard Jencks became president, in 1940, he worked closely with this old and valued friend on the wartime problems of the college. But again, his deepest concern was for the future.

On the occasion of the fiftieth anniversary of his graduation he made the commencement address at St. Lawrence to the class of 1944. In the Pacific the U.S. Fifth Fleet was battling the Japanese off the Philippines, in Europe American troops were moving on Cherbourg. Young quoted a sentence from his commencement oration of 1894 (when he had stumbled, forgotten and improvised, to the consternation and amusement of Professor Charley Gaines): "The distrust and antagonism between governments and the peoples suggest the need for some central force to bind them together." And today, he told the small class, mostly girls, this need was "a burning reality" and no longer "a cool generalization," as it was then. His generation, he said to them, had "not only compressed the world for you, but we gave you the tools with which you master and understand it. . . . Why do I say we failed when we gave you so much? We failed because we did not develop adequate controls of the titanic things we made." The lesson of this war indicated that "representative government must be established everywhere before moral controls can be relied on to keep the peace." Moral control and responsibility in this small world must be the work of the new generation.[5]

A typical commencement address, perhaps; but in the summer of 1944, in the crucial days that turned the tide of the war, it was listened to and widely commented on. The welcome words "moral controls" seemed to forecast a better world.

And in that postwar world, Young was anxious that his college take hold of the new developments that peace must bring: the returning veterans, with their education paid for by Uncle Sam, and the maintenance and advancement of the academic program they would require. Leadership was vital, he wrote Dean Murray Atwood in November of 1944 when it was clear that Jencks, on leave of absence because of illness, would not be able to return. Outlining the qualities needed in a new president, and suggesting several names, he moved on in a lengthy postscript to an optimistic and indeed grandiose vision of the future. With the expansion of the State School of Agriculture (which was on the St. Lawrence campus) and of the Clarkson College of Technology nearby in Potsdam, there might develop in the next ten years a great "University of the North Country," all this to come to pass under the leadership of St. Lawrence.

ii

There were few long, sunny, relaxing days at Washington Oaks or at the farms in Van Hornesville in the war years; Owen Young was away from the job only seventy-five workdays in 1943. Indeed, it was difficult to travel to either place, and not very comfortable when there. The Van Hornesville house was closed as soon as cold weather came, while in Florida shortages of gasoline and help for the groves and the turkey farm made it difficult to carry on. Fortunately the modest apartment Louise owned at 447 East Fifty-seventh Street was not rented, so they had a place in New York to lay their heads. Most fortunate of all, Dick, who had entered the army in July of 1942 and was assigned to counterintelligence, was stationed on Governors Island and lived for some of the time at this apartment, which was a great pleasure and satisfaction to his father.

The other sons were involved in war service of different kinds: C.J. in high-level research for the government at the RCA Laboratories, Philip as executive director of Lend-Lease in Washington, and later in the navy. The son-in-law, inaugurated as president of Colgate University in September of 1942, had been successful in obtaining several naval and marine training programs for the college, the care and nurture of which, together with postwar planning, occupied the war years. And two grandsons, C.J.'s eldest sons John Peter and David, were in the army after only months at Harvard. Owen Young's sixty-eighth birthday, October 27, 1942, was celebrated at the apartment in New York with all his children present; the difficulties of wartime jobs and travel were conquered by the deep-felt need for a family reunion in perilous times.

As though twelve-hour days and constant traveling on crowded wartime trains to Washington for war jobs in that uncomfortable city, in addition to the General Electric Company and the regents, were not enough, the press, in the spring of 1942, saw Young once again as a possible political candidate. Such reports could only have seemed to him like flies buzzing about his ears, distracting him from his proper work.

Jim Hagerty, Jr., in a front-page article in the *New York Times* of April 12, reported that Governor Herbert Lehman was about to be called to Washington by the President for an important wartime job. This would leave the field wide open in the gubernatorial campaign of the coming fall. Young was described as the leading candidate, and was considered to be Roosevelt's choice; on April 30 Adolf Berle wrote in his diary an account of a conversation with the President:

I raised the question of New York politics. He said that he had gone over the situation. Lehman did not want to run again; quite bluntly, he was sick of Albany. He had himself "invented" Jack Bennett, to whom Farley was pledged, but Jack could not win. . . . He had to consider that there might be one man who could work things out. This was Owen Young, who would have considerable strength among the business people and the voters. "He is not," says the President, "your type of liberal and mine. But he is a man who is more liberal at sixty-eight than he was at fifty-eight." . . .[6]

Whether Roosevelt's appraisal was correct or not, it was true enough that Young's continuing efforts on behalf of the dairy farmers had brought him favorable prominence in New York State. The press believed that even farmers who were Republicans—by far the majority— would vote for him. But to the *Watertown Times* Young wrote that he was not about to take on such a burdensome job. "I have only one real interest in the governorship and that is that next time we shall have a governor who really understands and sympathizes with the problems of milk producers as well as with the problems of milk distributors and consumers." And finally he told the Herkimer County delegation to the Democratic convention, who had been campaigning for him, that he would not permit his name to be presented. A week later he wrote his friend Tom Lamont, who was vacationing in Maine:

I think I have successfully said to the Convention that I would not permit consideration of my name for the Governorship. It was probably unnecessary anyway, but it was a matter of insurance against the risk of mortgaging an all too short expectancy for an uncomfortable job in Albany. Without in any sense depreciating the importance of the office or its high honor, I do not think that under present conditions it offers an opportunity for maximum service in these trying times. It seemed to me much better to help through the General Electric Company in any way I could. After all, I do know something about that, and whatever contribution one makes will be direct and effective in the prosecution of the war.[7]

Young actively supported Roosevelt's candidacy in 1944; as a Herkimer County member of a New York State group, Farmers for Roosevelt, he wrote friends and made statements in that autumn when the problems of peace were rising on the horizon:

I think that the crises in the next four years can be handled best by Mr. Roosevelt who has the accumulated experience of these last trying years and who, in a high degree, holds the confidence not alone of the leaders of the Governments abroad, but, what is more important, the confidence of great masses of leaders of opinion here. . . . There was [he pointed out] a great lack of confidence in the Republican party as a cooperator with other nations in a joint undertaking to maintain the peace.[8]

When the President's final term proved less than four months, rather than four years, Young shared deeply the shock and sorrow of the nation. Many of his high hopes for "that boy" had been more than fulfilled; there had been many serious disappointments too. If the warmth he felt for this friend, with whom he had much in common, was not wholly returned, and if their relationship in the White House years was never close, it was always cordial. The various jobs which Roosevelt asked him to do he did with skill and goodwill, and if he felt that he was not asked to help in fields of his special competence, such as foreign affairs and finance, he never said so. He supported the President wholeheartedly wherever he could, and where he could not, he said nothing in public. At the end, his admiration and grief canceled all else.

iii

At the General Electric directors' meeting of September 8, 1944, Owen Young and Gerard Swope presented their resignations for the second time. This time they resigned also as directors, effective at the end of the year—but signified their willingness to be of use in a consulting capacity. Charles E. Wilson had resigned from the War Production Board at the end of August, and was now reelected president. Philip Reed, still in London as chief of the U.S. Mission on Economic Affairs, resigned that post in December and was reelected chairman of GE on February 2, 1945. Thus December 31 saw Young's last formal connection with the General Electric Company severed after thirty-two years of service.

In anticipation of this second retirement and Young's seventieth birthday, Gerard Swope sent his old friend and associate the lately published biography of Justice Oliver Wendell Holmes, *Yankee from Olympus*, by Catherine Drinker Bowen. Like Swope's biographer, we find Young's response eminently quotable:

Dear Gerard [he wrote]:
I quote the final words from *Yankee from Olympus*: "Whether a man accepts from Fortune her spade and will look downward and dig, or from Aspiration her ax and cord and will scale the ice, the one and only success which it is his to command is to bring to his work a mighty heart."
This applies to you. . . .
Do you remember on our way back from the Orient [in 1921] you said "I will do all the work—I like it"? No promise has ever been more completely fulfilled—[9]

Young was not, however, wholly out of the business world, for he remained a director of American and Foreign Power until 1949, and spent considerable time on the problems of that troubled company. And in 1942 he had joined the board of the New York Life Insurance Company at the request of his old friend George Harrison, who, after his years of service at the New York Fed, had become first president and then chairman of this company. Young reported to his family that, on receiving the invitation, he had said to George, "You don't want an old fellow like me," to which Harrison replied, "On the contrary, I need you to reduce the average age of my board." (Nicholas Murray Butler, at the age of eighty, was still a member.)

With his GE service finished, and the outcome of the war daily more clearly defined, Owen and Louise spent four well-deserved vacation months at Washington Oaks before returning to Van Hornesville. But the days after the Battle of the Bulge in December 1944 were not happy ones for the Young family. John Peter Young, the eldest son of Owen Young's eldest son, was reported missing on that front. Months went by, and no one gave up hope. But after V-E Day, when daily reports of liberated prisoners were coming in, was the worst time of all, for John Peter's name was not among them. Now the grandfather learned what his mother had felt when his own son John was killed. But on June 4, 1945, C.J. received a message from Brussels: John Peter was there. He had been freed from an eastern prison camp by the Russians, and it had taken him, starving and weak, a long time to get to Belgium.

Young told the story of how he heard the news in a letter to his cousin John Elwood in California:

Charlie at once called me in Van Hornesville. I had just left for Utica to take the Empire to Cleveland for the Holstein-Friesian directors' meeting. Charlie talked with Jo in Hamilton and she had the bright idea of calling the Travellers' Aid girl in the station. When I walked into the station, which was quite crowded, the first thing I knew was this lady rushing up to me and putting her arms around my shoulders or around my neck and with tears in her eyes told me that my grandson had been found.[10]

The spring of 1946 saw the end of Young's term as a member of the New York State Board of Regents, and that summer his appointment by Governor Dewey as head of the Temporary Commission on the Need for a State University. Nor was he yet free from Washington jobs, for in June of 1947 President Truman appointed him to the President's Advisory Commission on Foreign Aid. This was set up (after General George Marshall's speech at Harvard had initiated the Marshall Plan for Europe) under the chairmanship of Averell Harriman, then secretary of commerce. The members, chosen by Harriman and

Dean Acheson at State, made up what the latter described as "an eminent, knowledgeable and representative Committee," and on June 22 met with Truman at the White House to hear him outline their task.[11] They were, Young wrote Philip Reed, "charged with the responsibility of advising the President as to how much and what kind of aid we may give to Europe and other foreign countries without impairing our own economy. The qualifying words of the President's authorization are 'safely and wisely.' "[12] Subcommittees were then appointed, of one of which, on economy and finance, Young was made chairman.

He worked closely with Harriman and with Senator "Young Bob" La Follette, the chairman of the Drafting Committee, and also set up meetings for his own committee with the National Association of Manufacturers, the U.S. Chamber of Commerce and the U.S. Associates of the International Chamber; of the last, Philip Reed was currently chairman. Drawing on his own experience in Germany, Young wrote Harriman a long letter voicing "some of my apprehensions and hesitations regarding the overall restoration of industry in western Germany." He agreed with the State Department's concern that, if we did not help Germany, Russia would take over, but not with the department's reported belief that the encouragement of socialism would prevent this:

The first items to be taken over in any socialized program are transport and power. I should have great hesitation about any setup that would enable a German government to take over railroads and the power supply at any time within the foreseeable future. In that I would see a serious threat to the future peace of the world. I do not regard Governmental treaties, however comprehensive and definite in language, as an adequate permanent safeguard against the misuse by a German government of its restored facilities to prove to the world the superiority and dominance of the German people.

Rather, transport and power should remain initially in the control of the United States or of an international organization, which would guarantee France's safety and assist all Western Europe.

The question may well be asked why I am so fearful of socialistic controls in Germany when I am complacent at least about similar ones in England. My answer to that is the capacity of the English people developed through centuries of training to so handle democratic machinery that Government will not become the master of the individual and destroy his freedom. That is not true of the Germans.[13]

When, in November, the Harriman Report was presented to the President, the Congress and the public, it was very well received. The press called it clear and hard-hitting, realistic, and praised its recommendations for an independent government agency to administer it, and for financing out of taxes. The cost was estimated at up to seventeen billion dollars for four years; the aim was the prevention of World War III. With this report and those of the other committees, and the setting up of the nationwide Committee for the Marshall Plan—of which Young was a member of the National Council—aid for Europe was under way. In April 1948 Truman signed the act setting up the Economic Cooperation Administration and the Marshall Plan was in business, with Paul Hoffman as director—an appointment Young warmly approved. Indeed, the work of this committee was stimulating and hopeful to Young. When the work was over, he wrote Harriman:

> The thing which impressed me most was the favorable contrast between the work of this Committee and of somewhat similar committees dealing with problems in the foreign field of twenty-five years ago. There was a much better understanding of the complicated problems, both of economics and politics, as they function in the international field than existed at the close of the First World War. Problems now are more difficult. They require more sensitive and intelligent handling and I sincerely feel greatly encouraged by the work of this Committee acting so industriously and competently under your direction.[14]

iv

Early in 1948 Young was invited by Herbert Hoover to serve on the Commission on the Organization of the Executive Branch of the Government; this bipartisan commission had been created by Congress in 1947 to study how to cut the costs and inefficiency of government services. To this Young replied: "I had personally resolved and firmly committed myself to Mrs. Young that when the work of the Harriman Commission and the New York State University Commission was completed I would not again undertake any new and additional assignment. You are the only person in the world, I think, by force of your own example, who could compel me to break such a firm resolution."[15] Hoover made him chairman of a small committee to survey the regulatory commissions: those of Interstate Commerce, Federal Power, Federal Trade, U.S. Maritime, Securities and Exchange, and Federal Communications; the Civil Aeronautics Board, the Federal Reserve Board, and the National Labor Relations Board. The other members were Professor Robert Bowie of the Harvard Law School, and Robert M. La Follette, Jr., now out of the Senate. To the latter Young wrote:

When Mr. Hoover asked me whom I would most like to have serve with me in the appraisal of the independent regulatory commissions, I said unhesitatingly—Bob LaFollette. I said that not only because I have such great respect and admiration for your character and ability but also because I felt that you with your legislative background and with your liberal views might advantageously be associated with me, a presumptive reactionary with no political background.

It seemed to me that we represented reasonably well the divergent forces which, fortunately, have a hold on the rope in the dramatic tug-of-war which has made America what it is.[16]

But to Young's disappointment La Follette was not well, and was not able to take part in the deliberations of the committee.

During the spring and summer of 1948 Bowie's small *ad hoc* staff prepared separate studies of the workings of each of the nine agencies. These staff reports were submitted for comment to a group representing a "reasonable cross-section of experience and point of view" in the field; their letters were sent to Young with the reports—he had four or five pounds of paper to read on each agency. But before he did so, he wrote Bowie a letter at the beginning of October, "to give you a brief indication of the spirit and background of my approach. I do this before reading the material or the observations of persons to whom it has been submitted because I have discovered that unless one sets his mind on some theory of approach, he is likely to get in such confusion that he never can emerge."

Likening the development of the regulatory commissions to the development in law to cope with "the expansion of human activities," he cited the creation of the Federal Trade Commission as an implementing mechanism for the Sherman act, of the Federal Reserve System as a necessary instrument for an expanding economy, of the Interstate Commerce Commission and the Federal Power Commission as overall agencies when state railroad and power legislation could not cope with interstate needs. "When each of these commissions was appointed, the pressing need for them was great. They were widely advertised, and it was possible to draft the most distinguished and able men to serve on them. They had to be, initially, very independent. They had to be closely in touch with Congress as well as the Executive. Their very nature required that they be free from departmentalization in their early stages." Later, he wrote, both personnel and procedure became rigid and routine; the result was "a mass of activities beyond the power of the Executive to coordinate and so interacting as to make it impossible for any legislative body to deal intelligently with the over-all picture."

Young concluded by asking Bowie to suggest which of the commissions under study could be included in one or another of the executive departments and hence more responsibly controlled by the executive and the cabinet, and which should remain independent and insulated from any political control. "When I come to talk with you about them, I should like to get a sort of over-all chart, not dealing with detail but with the kind of general grouping and relationships which you see in the picture. If that much insurance against confusion can be provided for me before I sink into the morass of detail, I may possibly survive."[17]

Talk they did, in nonstop sessions in October and November. "We have exhausted ourselves," Young wrote La Follette, "with consultations with the special investigators of each of these independent commissions . . . Mr. Bowie has drafted a report of our own."[18] In this they started out with three assumptions: (1) that independent commissions were necessary and desirable for certain jobs; (2) that they were not effective administrative agencies; (3) that the job of the committee was to guard their independence in the discretionary field, to relieve them so far as possible of administrative duties and to relate them to the executive for coordination with overall policy.

In their final report, they sorted out the nine agencies which they had studied to be either "departmentalized" or "insulated," and noted that "the chief criticism that can be made of the regulatory commissions is that they become too engrossed in case-by-case activities and thus fail to plan their roles and to promote the enterprises entrusted to their care."[19]

In spite of the long intensive sessions and the piles of paper, Young was much interested in the work; he had, after all, come in contact with most of these agencies during his career, and knew what he was talking about in that "chief criticism."

The reports of the Hoover commission—eighteen, plus a concluding one—were presented to the Congress, and the public, at intervals from February through March 1949; Young's and Bowie's appeared on March 12. There was considerable enthusiasm in the nation for the work of the Hoover commission, and the high caliber of the reports increased it. That on the regulatory agencies was no exception: under the heading "Regulating and Regulators," the *New York Herald Tribune* called it "one of the most compelling made thus far. It abundantly justifies the axiom that the development of administrative machinery by democratic, and essentially unplanned, methods needs to be resurveyed from time to time if basic objectives are not to be lost and wasteful practices not suffered to persist."[20]

This job Young took on, as he wrote in his acceptance letter, only as a result of his respect for the former President; for in spite of the rough treatment accorded him from the White House at the time of the Young Plan, and further instances of Hoover's want of confidence and consideration, Owen Young maintained throughout their later years a cordial, admiring and even affectionate relationship with Herbert Hoover. It was far less close than in the early 1920s, but it stemmed from those days of friendship when the then secretary of commerce needed all the help he could get on radio and broadcasting. Young's daughter remembers a visit she and her mother paid to Herbert and Lou Henry Hoover in Washington in 1924; as they parted Jo asked, "What message shall I give Owen from you?" "Tell him I love him," replied Hoover.[21]

Twenty-five years later Young wrote Hoover on his seventy-fifth birthday: "It is a great privilege for me to congratulate you, not so much on the attainment of 75 years of life as on the use which you have made of those years. . . . In making a review, as this letter encourages me to do, of the accomplishment of men who may be reasonably classed as contemporaries of mine, I know of no one who has done so much to help our country and the world as you in so many diversified fields. . . ."[22]

v

Radio and Holstein cattle and education—on all of these Young continued to work in his seventies. In 1948 he succumbed to the persuasion of his old friend Edward J. Noble to join the board of the American Broadcasting Company. Noble, the King of Life Savers, "the candy with the hole," was also the moving spirit of ABC, chairman of the board and holder of the controlling interest. Originally from the North Country, Ed Noble was a generous benefactor of the region and of St. Lawrence, and was chairman of the university board from 1941 to 1954. Joining the ABC board was for Young, whose work with broadcasting had been totally with RCA and NBC, a step outside the pattern, causing some public surprise, some satisfaction in the North Country, and some teasing in the family. He had talked it over with David Sarnoff, who naturally was not enthusiastic. But it is clear that he enjoyed the idea of a new and different relationship with radio. After he had accepted Noble's invitation he wrote Robert Saudek, vice-president of ABC, this brief letter:

When one has a child for whom he has hopes and even unreasonable ambitions and then the kid does so much better than the old man ever dreamed of, it is a great satisfaction to establish intimate associations with him again. So I feel about radio. My wildest dreams now look like child's play and demonstrate conclusively that I had only a most limited vision. I shall be happy indeed to learn from a renewed and intimate contact what a poor prophet I was.[23]

After his first directors' meeting, he wrote Noble a long letter full of questions. He needed to know, he said, "more clearly and definitely than you have ever told me, and probably more clearly and definitely than you have ever formulated your own ideas, what your ultimate conceptions are for ABC." What were they aiming at, he asked, what market, where, how were they going to get it? How were they going to compete with CBS and NBC? Did they want the cities, or a much wider audience from more outlets, programs with wider appeal? And what about television? For the city, or for "those vast populations . . . which make up the backbone of this country? . . . Sound puts us to sleep on the farms after the sun goes down but pictures (horrible thought) will probably keep us awake so that we will be late milking the cows in the morning." And now that, he concluded, "I have emitted such reactions as I have from the first meeting of the board, you will begin to realize what you are in for for the future."[24]

A year later Young was writing Robert E. Kintner, executive vice-president of ABC, in answer to a letter on the short-term prospects for the company—ABC had just opened its first television station in New York City:

I have felt from the beginning that television was being oversold, especially in the forecast which indicated that it would one day supersede sound radio. That has seldom been the history of new developments. I can recall the confident predictions that the telephone would completely supplant the telegraph; that electricity would make the gas plants worthless, etc. The new art seldom displaced the old; it merely forced a place for itself in an ever increasingly crowded arena.

After the novelty of television wore off, it would only be successful "if the programs are very superior and that probably means very expensive in production." He recalled the early days of radio, when its novelty produced enormous demands for sets. When the programs proved uninteresting and the newness wore off, the market collapsed, and the same could happen in television—"indeed, I think it is starting now." New kinds and types of programs would be needed "and possibly new types of . . . audiences." The letter ended: "I would like to persuade you *not* to be over-bullish on television or over-bearish on sound broadcasting."[25]

When, in need of capital, A B C merged with Paramount Theaters in the early fifties, Young found the new big corporation far less interesting than the independent project of his friend Noble, and resigned from the board in 1955. He had, perhaps, found less excitement and pleasure in his return to radio than he had anticipated. But in one important respect the directorship had done well by him. Noble was one of the very few people who knew how financially embarrassed Young had been and how limited his income was; the connection with A B C, including stock allocations, relieved him to some extent of these worries. He wrote Ed Noble in November of 1954, thanking him for his birthday message and saying, "There is no one to whom I am more thankful than to you for alleviating the major burden of these later years."[26]

Certainly the dairy business was far from lucrative, but as a result of his work with his fellow milk producers Young emerged not only as the best-known farmer in the state, but as a prominent figure in the national organization with which he had always been connected, the Holstein-Friesian Association of America. Beginning in the first year of his first retirement, he attended its meetings regularly; even during his second stint at G E he was able to go to three or four. The headquarters of the association were—and are—in Brattleboro, Vermont, but the meetings were held in different sections of the country, wherever men interested in black-and-white cows could get together—Chicago, Kansas City, San Francisco. These involved trips which gave him and Louise opportunity to visit friends—the Daweses in Chicago, St. Lawrence friends in California—and now they were free to travel at their own pace.

In June of 1948, at Kansas City, Young was elected president of the association; he had been a director and member of the Executive Committee for eight years, and now served as president for one. His picture, his cows' pictures, reports of his breeding program, articles and statements by him appeared in the *Holstein-Friesian World*. At San Francisco in 1949, in his presidential address, he drew, as in a series of fables, parallels between the farm and the troubled world of the present day—with a glance backward at his speech across the bay in 1930, which starred the mistress and the maid in the play called "Politics and Economics." He spoke of the four freedoms because he believed, he said,

that one great insurance of freedom lies in the hands of those who have

an anchorage to land, who have animals on the land and who have learned
to love them both. There is no such thing as regimenting breeders and
milkers of dairy cattle. Indeed, it is difficult to unite them even in their
own self-interests. . . . Freedom of speech . . . one can say anything in
a dairy barn so long as it is not so blatant and so loud as to irritate the
cows. Freedom of worship—yes, unadulterated wonder and gratitude for
the Great Creator and Conservator of animal life. . . . Freedom from fear.
Some one said courage is the product of fear after prayer. Many a prayer
is offered in a dairy barn. . . .

And of course freedom from want, which is in our hands, we "who
produce and control at its source . . . a basic necessity of life."

In this speech too he testified to the pleasure his herd had given him
over the years:

It is fun to have lived almost five decades with the Holstein cow; to have
known intimately, appreciatively, admiringly and always hopefully mothers
and grandmothers and great-grandmothers for more than a dozen generations. It is thrilling to have adhered for some years to a line of breeding
so that I have individuals now with a greater percentage of the basic
family blood than the first sire. I speak of this not with pride, nor in any
sense boastfully, but emotionally as I pay tribute to a long line of family
friends who played a major part in the basic satisfactions of my life. I
commend this kind of attainment to young men and women who must
inevitably live in a stormy and uncertain world.[27]

iv

The end of the war sent home thousands of veterans who wanted college education and wanted it now. The private colleges of New York
State took in as many of these mature and eager students as they
could handle—and often more. But many were still left outside the
door, and from Jews, blacks and even Catholics came charges of discriminatory admissions policies aimed at them. New "colleges" were
improvised, as at Plattsburg, but the pressures continued to intensify,
and in January 1946 Governor Thomas E. Dewey said in his message
to the legislature, "We should examine the need for a State University." In February he proposed a temporary commission to do just
this; the legislature agreed and appropriated $100,000 for the job.

Young had lunched with Dewey on October 31, 1945, before leaving for the winter and spring at Washington Oaks; they undoubtedly
discussed the governor's intended message, and possibly the chairmanship of the commission. On his return, Young met with Dewey on

June 13, 1946, at the home of State Senator Walter Stokes in Coopers-town, after they had all attended the famous annual exhibition base-ball game on Doubleday Field, played that year between the New York Giants and the Detroit Tigers. Dewey formally invited Young to take the chairmanship of the commission, and Young accepted. On July 14 the governor announced his sixteen appointees, which was fol-lowed by the announcement of two named by the Senate and three by the Assembly.[28] With the *ex officio* members, largely from the legisla-ture, plus Commissioner of Education Francis Spaulding and Chan-cellor William J. Wallin of the board of regents, the commission num-bered thirty-one, an unwieldy group with widely diverse backgrounds and convictions.

It would be untrue to suggest that Young was unaware of what he was letting himself in for; on the other hand, few could have foreseen the full force of the emotions excited by the complex and emergent issues now demanding resolution—and, as the demonstrators were insisting, "resolution now." There were marches and countermarches around the state capitol; fiery speeches and partisan bills in the halls of the legislature; and even among the existing colleges and universi-ties, mostly privately supported, diverse opinions and emotional as well as intellectual conflicts. A few saw in a state university the one answer that would take them off the hook; others, resenting wholesale allegations of their discriminatory practices, were concerned primarily to meet this issue once for all—as many of their own war-conditioned students were demanding. Finally, as against the few who resisted any change in the status quo, there was a saving majority who recognized that current needs required *both* a state university and more open admissions policies generally. For them the problem was to prevent a legislative "overkill," while quietly working for just and feasible solutions.

But if these crosscurrents and countercurrents—political, economic and moral—were all too reminiscent of the original Young Committee's Paris problems, the chairman, responding in his seventies to this new call from close to home, had no intention of becoming involved in the incessant daily turmoil. He could and did demand a younger but experienced deputy whom he could trust to carry the day-by-day bur-dens as vice-chairman; in Oliver C. Carmichael, sometime chancellor of Vanderbilt University and currently president of the Carnegie Foun-dation, he found his man. Young thereupon described his own role in words borrowed from General Dawes: "So far as the Chairman is concerned, he will do whatever is not assigned to Dr. Carmichael, in-

cluding receipt of the garlands and garbage which inevitably comes
to that kind of office. The Chairman has had sufficient experience with
commissions all over the world to realize that the garbage is likely to
be greater than the garlands."[29]

As on other commissions too, there were some in the group with
whom Young worked most closely, although he was careful always
to consult others, especially the politicians. Father Robert L. Gannon
of Fordham University was constantly helpful, as was Sarah Blanding,
president of Vassar. And he depended very much not only upon Carmichael but on Francis Spaulding and Cornell's Edmund Day. As for
the quickly recruited staff, he already knew and had worked with
Floyd Reeves on the American Youth Commission; and with Counselor Arthur Schwartz, rapport was immediate and lasting.[30]

The first meeting of the Temporary Commission—known generally
as the "Young Commission"—was held August 23, 1946, the last on
January 12, 1948. The complicated story of its career and the legislative battle which followed its report has been fully recounted by Carmichael's son; our interest is with the part played by its chairman.
In spite of his many other concerns, Young kept in close touch with all
that went on in the commission, and attended its full meetings and
public hearings. By September 1947 a draft report was ready for the
commission and staff to discuss in detail. Young suggested that the
group spend three days at a pleasant site on the shore of one of the
most beautiful lakes in the state—Lake George. He knew well that
the members of his varied and often antagonistic group could come
nearer to understanding each other, and could speak more frankly,
sitting on the wide piazzas of the hotel, glass in hand, than in the overheated atmosphere of Albany. "Throughout the three day meeting,"
wrote Oliver Carmichael, Jr., in his account, "Young urged that each
member must lay all the cards on the table and negotiations must be
conducted face to face without instructions from constituency or special interest. He conducted all discussion on an 'off the record' basis
and requested that they be considered as confidential."[31] Young also
demanded ultimate unanimity on the recommendations of the report,
knowing well that, on publication, any dissent would attract more
attention than the much greater areas of agreement.

Inevitably dissension arose, not so much as to whether New York
should have a state university or not, for everyone on the commission
agreed that it should; the questions were rather what kind, where
and—above all—how much would it cost? To this last was linked the

major issue: one big central university versus a distributive system. Young pushed for—and got—the second.

On another question agreement was reached with comparatively little difficulty; the commission came to realize, as its chairman had from the first, that the issue of discrimination was central to its work and must be settled before the final report was made public. To deal with this, Young appointed an *ad hoc* committee of three, drawn from the commission's minority members, with Father Gannon as chairman, and told them that the need for effective recourse in cases of discrimination, actual or alleged, was the important thing. Charges should be promptly investigated and their outcome reported to the board of regents: "a fair exposure of the facts and a disposition of the case by the Regents and the institution [involved] represents the best solution." And after a good deal of what Father Gannon described as "horse-trading," the committee brought in a report along those lines, which was adopted by the commission and became one of its most effective recommendations.[32]

The plan for a state university developed by the Young commission staff was by no means the only plan suggested; there was a plan from the administration, and one from the Democratic legislators. The commission had infinite difficulty in agreeing even on its own, with the result that the unanimous report its chairman demanded could be achieved only by compromise and the weakening of certain recommendations. On the evening of January 11, 1948, just before the final meeting of the commission next day, Young—who had come from Florida the day before—held an informal discussion with some of the more important members. "His strategy for the meeting on the 12th," wrote a historian ten years later, "was to attempt to get unanimous agreement on a brief statement of principle which would include the major features of the University plan both as to facilities and as to control. Details could be filled in later. . . ."[33]

In this he succeeded. On January 12 he pulled out of his diverse, overarticulate and combative commission, whose loyalties and interests were as varied as New York State could provide, a report. Because it was necessarily general in character, a committee of seven was appointed by the chairman to draft a final version (in which the administration had a hand). On February 11 Young telegraphed Dewey from Florida that the report was unanimous; it was presented to the governor on February 16, 1948.

This was, however, only the beginning. The effort to put into law the recommendations of the commission's report became a many-sided contest between the governor, the board of regents, the State Department of Education and the Association of Colleges and Universities of the State of New York—not to mention the Democrats and Republicans in the legislature. In this fracas Young took little part; deeply engaged in the cultivation of his citrus grove, he occasionally shot off a letter or a telegram to Albany. In March, just before the bills came up in the final legislative session, Dewey sent off a telegram which was a cry for help; the board of regents, jealous of its supremacy in education in the state, was preparing to fight the legislation embodying the recommendations of the report, because it set up an independent board of trustees for the new university—even though the recommendation stated that this board should report to the regents.

There was no telephone at Washington Oaks. Telegrams came by RFD mail next day. But the sheriff of Flagler County, impressed by the name at the end of the telegram from the governor, brought it down to Young from St. Augustine. Young replied in a soothing letter, saying the fault was in the drafting of the bill, which irritated the delicate sensitivities of the regents: the chancellor of the board of regents and the commissioner of education had, after all, approved the report.[34]

The legislation was passed, in spite of the opposition, on March 12, 1948, establishing the State University of New York as a public corporation with its own board of trustees, and enacting the Fair Educational Practices bill into law. Holding office until 1954, this "temporary" board was directed to plan for the development of the State University in all its components, including liberal arts colleges and professional and graduate schools. In the meantime it became responsible for the operation and development of existing state-aided institutions, including technical institutes and community colleges.

SUNY came into being on July 1, 1948, and the governor announced the board of trustees in August, with Carmichael as chairman. In December, after rejecting the title advocated by the regents, the trustees named the acting president of Stanford University, Dr. Alvin C. Eurich, as president of the State University. The regents continued their effort to circumscribe the authority of the new board, and Young, as head of the commission and a former regent, was appealed to by both sides. He wrote Carmichael at the end of 1948 from Washington Oaks; he had read all the material sent him, he said, and wondered what the shooting was all about: "Why is it necessary to go to the Legislature . . . for the purpose of clarifying the distribution of power . . . or . . . responsibility between the two Boards? Why not settle by a working agreement between the two. . . . To precipitate all these questions in the Legislature . . . is merely injecting politics into a great constructive program. With politics come heat and prejudice. . . ." He went on to suggest that the administrative problems should be dealt with by small committees made up from the two boards, "and thereby bring the experience of the Board of Regents, on the one side, and the fresh views of the planning Board on the other, into a unified and constructive program."[35]

Such a plan was too good to come true. In February 1949 a plan proposed by the regents was introduced in the legislature as the Condon-Barrett bill. In the controversy over it Young was also involved. On February 22, the *New York Times* published a letter from him expressing full agreement with its editorial of February 17, which ended, "let us bury present differences and suspend argument, while aiming for the real unity of educational development that is certainly possible under present law if a little tact, diplomacy and deference are employed on all sides." In March, just before the Condon-Barrett bill came up, Young allowed to be made public an answer he had written to Harvey Hinman of Binghamton, who had described the act creating the State University as "splitting the state educational system into two separate and distinct parts."[36]

The board of regents, Young replied, should be not an operating but a supervising body; his own experience was that the regents had too many administrative problems already. "I deplore the emphasis which the Board of Regents put on the loss of operation [of the new University] as evidence of their diminishing powers and prestige." He recommended that all proposed bills be withdrawn and that the two boards should work together in their respective fields until they were prepared to make "a joint request to the Legislature. . . . I shall decline to endorse any of the bills which have been shown me contemplating legislative action this year."[37]

The Association of Colleges and Universities of the State of New York, through its president, Everett Case of Colgate, expressed—not perhaps surprisingly—its agreement with Young's point, and suggested the immediate setting up of a conference committee by regents, trustees of the State University, and the association, which could clarify obscurities in the existing law and agree on future legislation. Informed public opinion also agreed (although sections of the press plunged rashly into the fray); a letter to the *New York Times* from Bethuel Webster, a prominent lawyer in New York City, discussed the controversy in judicial phrases, concluding: "It is the business of the

Board of Regents and the Board of Trustees to get along together, to make the thing work, to minimize the quest for power."[38]

It was too late. Sides had been taken and the possibility of cooperation and of peaceful and private resolution of differences which Young had hoped and worked for had disappeared. The Condon-Barrett bill was soundly defeated on March 23, 94 to 49. Then finally the regents recognized that cooperation had been forced upon them, and agreements were made between the two boards for working arrangements and an amicable—at least on the surface—development of the State University. The sound and fury which had echoed as far as Washington Oaks died away and the sheriff brought no more telegrams from Albany.

Chapter 39

Rocking Chair Consultant

R AYMOND FOSDICK, a close friend of Young's from the days when
he was head of the Rockefeller Foundation, was driving one
day in Florida along route A1A through a beautiful forested
area, when his wife, Betty, suddenly exclaimed, "Ray, Ray, there's
Owen Young!" Raymond looked briefly at a wayside stand selling
oranges and grapefruit, minded by a slovenly-looking character in old
clothes, a big hat, and boots. "Don't be silly, dear," said Ray and drove
on. But Betty was sure, and after a mile or so of argument they turned
back, to find that Betty was right. They received a warm welcome
indeed, and a tour of all the treasures of Washington Oaks, and an
hour or so on the terrace with Owen and Louise. "Do you know," said
Owen talking about the hat, "none of the hands on the place ever paid
any attention to me until I got this hat—Mrs. Young is the real boss,
you know. But I got the biggest hat I could find, and now they say,
'Yes sir, it's a fine morning, Colonel.' "[1]

Another visitor was less knowledgeable than Betty Fosdick; he asked
the fruit-stand keeper if this was Mrs. Young's place, and if she was at
home. "Yes to both," he answered, "I'll show you the way." On the
path from the road to the house the visitor admired the beauties of the
place and asked, "Do you work for Mrs. Young, my man?" "I'll say I
do!" was the emphatic reply.

David Lilienthal, stopping by on his way to visit his father in a hospital in Daytona, knew better. He did, however, report that he found
Owen Young "wearing a coat that looked as if it had been dragged
through brambles and then hauled through the city dump. Tickled
me," wrote Lilienthal, "to see that I am not the only one who loves
to wear old beat-up clothes. For luncheon Young put on a new jacket,
grinning: 'Just to show you that I actually have one that isn't so
torn up.' "

Philip Young, then dean of the Columbia Business School, was also there, and the three had lunch and talked for more than three hours. "Mr. Young," Lilienthal reported, "is a fine example of an old man who has given up the idea of elder statesman consciously and voluntarily, and for reasons of principle."[2] To this Young himself might have agreed, but he would have added that the "reasons of principle" included the lifelong one of never working any more than he had to. He always said that the fruit-stand job suited him fine.

He probably put on his better jacket, however, when one of his favorite visitors came to call: Charles Evans Hughes, who for a time spent his winters at Ormond, not far away. Meeting at his hotel, or, more often, at Washington Oaks, they would talk over the last half century. Although Hughes was twelve years older, they came to know each other when Young was practicing law in Boston. Later, when Hughes was practicing law in New York, Young, as counsel for GE, retained him on especially important matters for the company. Later still, when Young and Dawes were setting off for Paris in 1924, it was Secretary of State Hughes who gave them "an illuminating statement" before their departure. But it was at Washington Oaks, Young wrote Charles Evans Hughes, Jr., that "important as the early contacts were, later ones established a kind of personal relationship which will enable you to understand the personal sorrow which I felt on receiving the sad news of his death."[3]

There was no winter, after they were married, that Owen and Louise did not spend some time at Washington Oaks. Even in the 1940s, when Owen was unable to be there for the long, relaxing times he had so much looked forward to, he did manage a week here and a week there each year—days of rest (or at least change of occupation among the oranges) that made it possible for him to continue in New York and Washington.

During the war it was difficult to live there, because of gas rationing, the closing of the coastal highway—their only access—every night from dusk to dawn, and the scarcity of any help for groves and gardens. But after Young's "final" retirement and the end of the war, the Florida stays grew longer and longer. Somehow Louise had kept the place in shape, and although as the years went by her projects grew less ambitious, those for their own pleasure—and their friends'—were never neglected: oranges and grapefruit, flowers, the fishing pier, the pool, the winding paths.

To this paradise their children were always heartily welcomed; it was remarkable how often, in the cold North, in snowy February or March, or even April, the children felt compelled to go and see how the old folks were getting along. No other vacations were ever so good:

swimming, walking through the wildwoods or on the beach, picking and packing the fruit, then foregathering at the sacred hour of six, on the terrace overlooking the river or, if the evening were chilly, before the great fireplace in the high-beamed living room. There was a magic about the place which no one who stayed there has ever forgotten.

And how much they themselves enjoyed it; Young said to an interviewer who had come to ask for his thoughts about the later years, "This place means more to Mrs. Young and myself than you might think." He was giving him the big tour, through the gardens, by the little lake and the banyan tree, past the cabana and the pool to the grove where the fruit shone among the dark leaves; then back along the river under the enormous live oaks, past the old well which dated from the Washington plantation days, to the orchid house and the big tree where Peter the macaw flashed his colors and William the parrot croaked a welcome. "We acquired these acres," Young went on, "as a virtual wilderness eighteen years ago. We have planted and developed everything you see here. It is a part of ourselves. If we had bought something like this already set up, ready to turn on faucets and switches it wouldn't have meant much to us. This is a part of our lives during the years when we have more time to do and enjoy the things we like. Now here is a bed of very special hybrid roses we just set out this week. They're Mrs. Young's birthday present."[4]

They had many friends, in St. Augustine or other nearby places, some permanent residents, some just for the winter like themselves. These delighted in dropping in, for a walk to view the camellias or the amaryllis, for a bridge game (this was for Louise's pleasure; Owen never played anything but poker or pinochle, and those not in the later years), for a drink, or just to talk. Among those who came most often were Marjorie Kinnan Rawlings and her husband, Norton Baskin, and State Senator Verle Pope and his wife. Marjorie and Edith Pope, Florida's most distinguished novelists, were devoted to Owen and Louise, and there were always stories and jokes and laughter. Louise, artist herself in clay and textiles, enjoyed the company of artists, and brought them to paint or spin the potter's wheel at Washington Oaks. Her own daughter, Virginia, was a painter and married a painter, George Greene, in 1953, and they built a studio on the place not far from the main house.

Louise's elder son, Stanley Brown, lived in Daytona Beach, not far away, and his children, Kathan and Brad, spent many days at Washington Oaks with their grandmother. Kathan, who grew up to be an artist in several different fields, inherited her aptitudes from her mother, an artist herself, and her grandmother; in later years she published a book of etchings, both in color and black-and-white (the latter taken from photographs), with notes on her memories of Washington Oaks. It was done after the death of these grandparents, but they would have had to agree that no one ever caught better the spirit of their home— and of themselves:

My grandmother owned all the land from the river to the ocean. She had gardeners, and part of the land was exotic, with papayas, azaleas, orchids, beds of color interlaced with grass and little streams of sulfa water that bubbled up from springs. . . . There were paths and nooks with benches and oriental statues, places you could be and no one would know.

At my grandmother's the sunsets were behind the river, very calm, with long-necked egrets flying and the colors reflecting from rows of palm and huge scrub oaks dripping spanish moss. . . .

My grandmother's house was made of coquina, elegantly plain, rough, a large room joined by a large kitchen . . . the big room had one wall of fireplace, one of little tiny windows that opened with little turn handles, and the other two walls of books. Because of the books and all the wood beams and trim it always felt dark in there, but cool. And quiet. There was never any noise except voices. "You must," my grandmother would say to me, "learn to speak in a more lady-like manner. . . ."

Her grandmother was beautiful, Kathan wrote, and she told Kathan once that Mr. Young—as she referred to him to the children—was "the only man she ever loved."

He was, in fact, her third husband, but he was the only one who had been strong enough for her. A strong woman needs a strong man, she counseled me, and a strong man a strong woman. "Take your time, search for him, and when you find him, adore him." She did, obviously, adore him. In photo after photo her adoring profile is turned toward him. And he stands sure, confident, affable, perhaps a little pensive, but never mystified.

Under the etching of him standing on the seabeach, pipe in mouth, looking out to sea, Kathan wrote: "He knew he understood the world. He did not doubt himself, his human rightness, his (and others') ability to manipulate the world into rightness. Even tragedies—personal, like the death of a son, or public, like the depression—seemed not to weaken his confidence."[5]

ii

The annual schedule which the Youngs planned for their later years was to stay at Washington Oaks from mid-November to mid-May,

and sometimes they did just that. But more often there was interference. Definite engagements were few—Young resigned from the
New York Life board in 1951, and from the ABC board in 1955—and
he consistently refused invitations to join committees, make speeches,
appear at public functions or make public statements. But the health
of Louise's mother, Mrs. Powis, was not good in her last years, and
often kept them in the South after their usual date; and sometimes
their own health problems prevented traveling.

But Owen Young was just as glad to get to Van Hornesville in the
summer as he was to get away to Florida after the elections, and he
made every effort to keep to their schedule. Although by the 1950s he
had divided up his extensive holdings in and around Van Hornesville,
deeded their houses and lands to his children, and sold all the farms—
except of course the Home Farm, which went to Philip, and the original Young farm, dating from the 1750s, which went to C.J. (although
Richard managed it)—he still kept an eye on the cattle, and welcomed
the new calves of the umpteenth generation since he first started his
breeding program.

Friends stopped by at Van Hornesville too, to visit at the old house
or in the new office, to talk cows or politics or education. To all who
were new to the village he gave a conducted tour of the school, showing off not only the handsome buildings and excellent equipment but
what to him was the best and most important part—the children. They
all knew him, naturally, and greeted him eagerly, delighted to pose
with him if photos were being taken. And to each visitor he would
show the bronze tablet at the entrance, where his name was listed,
after all the names of those who built the school, as "Rocking Chair
Consultant."

In Van Hornesville summers his children were at hand, for as many
weeks as they could come. The next younger generation was there too;
by the time Owen Young was seventy the set of grandchildren was
complete—six boys and four girls, ranging in age, at the end of 1944,
from John Peter Young at twenty to John Philip Case, just born. By
the time he was eighty he had as well six great-grandchildren, three
boys, three girls. It was quite a crew to keep track of on the hills
around Van Hornesville or down the creek at the Stone Cave—or by
the sea or the river at Washington Oaks—and he was deeply interested
and concerned with the character and prospects of each one.[6]

A member of the family whose name does not appear in any records,
except the pages of the *Dumpling*, the family magazine, was Van
Horne Case. The invention of Owen Young and his granddaughter

Josephine Edmonds Case when she was very young, VHC—who is still around—exemplifies, in character and life-style, wickedness, waywardness, dishonesty and flamboyance; a world traveler, always in pursuit of cash—or a new wife—VHC, one must say for him, never gives up. Once the phone rang at midnight in Owen's bedroom in Van Hornesville; it was the telegraph operator in nearby Richfield Springs: "Mr. Young, I hate to call you so late, but this telegram—sent collect—appears to be very important—it's from a member of the family. It's from Pike's Peak, Colorado, and reads MAROONED ON PIKES PEAK NEED TEN THOUSAND DOLLARS AT ONCE and it's signed Van Horne Case." "Well," said Young dryly, "I guess it will wait till morning."[7]

The eightieth birthday was spent at home in Van Hornesville, with all his children and some of the grandchildren. After a long and dreary summer in Florida caring for Mrs. Powis, who died at the end of July, the Youngs came north in the first bright days of fall—fall comes at the end of August on these hills. On October 27, 1954, telegrams, letters, calls—and callers—appeared in profusion, from everyone who had ever known him, it seemed, and some who hadn't—with VHC in the vanguard. President Eisenhower wrote a letter from the White House, all the children from the Van Hornesville School serenaded him on the front lawn, the *New York Times* had an editorial as well as a news item, and dozens of upstate papers had articles and photos. *This Week* magazine's frontispiece was a picture of Young in his Van Hornesville office, with a brief statement from him on the theme of "the hills from which cometh my help." And to an interviewer, who had asked what advice he had for younger generations, he said with a grin, "An old man only sees the mistakes he has made and thinks he can tell some one else in a changed world how to make the same ones."[8]

The General Electric Company had already announced a tribute to its former chairman: the Owen D. Young Fund of a half a million dollars, for educational and scientific purposes. And St. Lawrence was planning a new library, to be named for him.

iii

Young was not able to visit St. Lawrence in the 1950s as often as in the past. President Eugene Bewkes was eager to have him there on all or any occasions, but he excused himself on various grounds. The truth of the matter was that he enjoyed traveling far less than he used to, and unless Louise or one of his St. Lawrence sons was available to drive him to Canton he would beg off. On one occasion—the observance in June 1956 of the centennial of the college—the university offered to provide a plane to bring him; but Young wrote, "I took a train in September of 1890 and I have not had time enough yet to face another thrill like that."[9]

In the eightieth birthday year—his sixtieth anniversary at St. Lawrence—he went to the fall homecoming; Louise drove him up from Van Hornesville, and Cliff Spurr came from Rochester with his daughter Laura, an alumna of the college. Young had refused the special birthday dinner planned for him, but he attended the laying of the cornerstone of the new building for the Theological School. The old one had burned in 1951, and Young had accepted the chairmanship of the campaign for $300,000 to build a new one, because he felt so strongly that the Universalist church and its Theological School had been the "father" of the college.[10] It was indeed its mainstay for decades, in the days when the Universalist sect counted thousands of members and many of the students in the college came there—as had Owen Young and Josephine Edmonds—because they belonged to Universalist churches. The money was raised, and it was a satisfaction to the quondam Sunday school superintendent of the church in Van Hornesville to see the cornerstone well and truly laid.

But the real fun of the visit was the reunion with Spurr; they talked till late into the nights, while Louise and Laura yawned and went to bed. Louise heard enough, however, to report that their recollections "seemed to center around the girls of that period."

Owen Young came back to Canton in October of 1956, at the time of the announcement that one million dollars had been raised for the Owen D. Young Library. When the campaign was started, in 1954, he had been—to use one of his favorite words—a little ornery about fund raising in his name. In November of that year he wrote Ed Noble:

> While I am greatly honored by the suggestion that a library on the St. Lawrence campus should bear my name, I am also very hesitant about a promotion statement that inevitably exaggerates my service to the College. I am hopeful that the brochure may be revised so as merely to show the growth of the Institution during these last sixty odd years. . . . A factual statement of the growth . . . will inevitably bring my name into the story, possibly enough to justify the naming of the building for me and for Josephine Edmonds, who I think was the most outstanding student at St. Lawrence in her time. I would like to eliminate all the florescent adjectives . . . I detest all that kind of bunkum promotion.[11]

Philip Young, a trustee of St. Lawrence at that time, was on the

Library Committee, and eventually he and the other children helped the college to concoct a statement for the brochures which contained a nice balance of straightforward history and "bunkum." The building was finished in 1959—a year in which the Youngs did not come north at all—and all four of his children took part in the ceremonies. Philip—at that time ambassador to the Netherlands—read his father's message from Florida, sounding and looking very much like him. The bust which Jo had had Jo Davidson make in Paris in 1924 now stood in the entrance hall of the library, the gift of the subject, who was pleased with the press photo of his four children grouped around it. But perhaps what pleased him most was the Josephine Edmonds Young Reading Room; this was close at hand, a light, bright room filled with comfortable places to sit and shelves of books not assigned for study, with a charming picture on the wall of the St. Lawrence student from Massachusetts who entered the college in 1891.

Young's visit to Canton in the fall of '56 was his last, but he kept in touch with St. Lawrence people, contributed to annual giving, and warmly welcomed any St. Lawrence graduates who appeared at Washington Oaks or Van Hornesville. From Philip he heard the news from the campus, and he was greatly pleased that both his daughter and her husband were given honorary degrees by the university.

In these later years, Owen Young felt more strongly than ever the lasting effect of the Universalist tenets in which he was brought up, at home and in the local church, then at college. The atmosphere of intellectual and spiritual freedom, and the belief in a loving rather than a vengeful God, in which his teachers lived left a permanent openness in Young's thoughts and attitudes.

It was not strange, then, that at the very end of the ten volumes of Young's collected speeches is his brief talk before the Universalist General Assembly in Andover, Massachusetts, in August of 1953. It was indeed a peculiarly appropriate occasion for his last speech. His first ones, after all, were Universalist-inspired, as early as 1880, delivered in the parlor to Grandpa Peter or in the barn to the cows, and in the style of the sermons he had heard in church.

The talk at Andover was not a sermon—at least not entirely. In fact, when he received the invitation to attend the banquet which ended the assembly's meetings, he stipulated that he would not speak "except to acknowledge very briefly the honor which you pay me as a special guest with my friend of many years Senator Leverett Saltonstall."[12] But he knew well that this was an especially important meeting; the Unitarians would be there too, and the subject was the Federal Union Plan for a merger of the two churches—a proposition upon which there was very little agreement on either side.

Owen and Louise drove over to Andover from Van Hornesville, and knowing that his "acknowledgment" would have to be something more, Owen scribbled notes on the writing paper of the Andover Inn. His writing, more illegible than ever, indicated that he felt strongly about what he wanted to say.[13] And he did; for he saw, and showed his audience in his talk, a procession of Universalist laymen and ministers emerging from his own past, beginning with his parents and grandparents and going on to the memorable elders of the church whom he knew and who taught him, especially Dr. Hervey. Boston too, in his days in the law, provided both distinguished Universalists and Unitarians whom he heard preach, for it was the headquarters of both churches. To all of these, he noted, he owed much of his education. "I speak of these personal relations and obligations which enable me to endorse not only unreservedly but enthusiastically the closer union between these two great liberal churches."

He had promised, he went on, not to say more than thank you on this occasion: "However, don't trust anybody on any platform after he is seventy-five." But these two churches, he pointed out, were now setting an example for all; and beyond that, "Isn't it time for the leaders of all religions to seek a way for united action to save the world? Perhaps our religious leaders will have to do what the scientists have done, and that is to throw overboard the bias and prejudice of the past." These leaders, he suggested, could convert what the scientists had produced into benefits, rather than destruction, for the human race. Politicians could not do it, for "nations have power only when the abiding religious faiths of their people are behind them."[14]

iv

Young's emphasis on the importance of religion in saving the world did not prevent him from keeping a sharp eye on what the politicians were currently doing. When the Youngs first lived at Washington Oaks after retirement, they had only the radio to keep them in touch. Young listened to it, far more than he had ever had time to before, and found he did not like it very much. A letter to Ed Murrow, praising his "Challenge of the '50s" program, indicates regret at the "prostitution of radio."[15] It was not long, however, before they acquired a television set; they were not sure they wanted one, and Louise disliked the tall

pole just outside the house. But she succumbed quickly to the fascination of TV; Owen watched mostly politics and sports. In 1954, after
some adjustment of the set and aerial, he got an excellent picture. He
wrote Philip that he had watched the McCarthy hearings: "I never
got so much irritation for so little money." But here again, as TV developed, he became very impatient with the poor quality, poor taste
and low level of the programs and commercials. Here is the finest and
most powerful instrument, he would say, that man has ever created for
the dissemination of education and culture—and look what we do with
it. Nevertheless, he continued, hopefully, to look at it; and in both
Florida and Van Hornesville he never missed a political speech or a
convention. His house in the north was tucked too closely under the
hill to get good reception, but Louise had acquired, and fixed up as a
guesthouse and inn, an old mansion a couple of miles away which
stood so high on the hills that the Mohawk Valley and the Adirondacks
beyond were spread out before it; and there the family repaired to
view such events as Owen deemed they must see.

There Young watched both of the conventions of 1952, sitting up
until 2:30 A.M. or later. Full of admiration for Adlai Stevenson's speech
of acceptance, he was nevertheless thinking—but not yet talking—of
voting Republican in the presidential election. A letter to an upstate
friend in that same year attests that he was a Democrat before he was
old enough to vote; "I remember well, that as a boy of 14, I felt that
the victory of Benjamin Harrison over Grover Cleveland meant the
ruin of the country. Fortunately the country recovered in 1892, when
I made my first political speeches for Cleveland"[16]—although he was
still not old enough to vote. But he had occasionally jumped the fence
in later years, voting for Dewey for governor in 1942, Willkie for
President in 1940, and John Foster Dulles for senator in 1949. Dulles
made the commencement speech at St. Lawrence in 1952—appropriately enough, for he came from the North Country; Young was not
able to attend, but wrote him a warm and appreciative letter. Dulles
replied with thanks: "As I told one of your boys, to me the high spot
of my 1949 Senatorial campaign was your coming out in my support."
And he said also, "I always cherish my association with you and my
very great regard for the tremendous contribution which you made in
the post-World-War-I era. If your views had been more faithfully followed, we might not have had Hitler and World War II."[17] When
Dulles was made secretary of state there was a renewed exchange of
letters.

To vote for Willkie had involved considerable soul-searching on

Young's part. It was the same in 1952; the family was divided over that election, for Adlai was a friend of the Everett Cases (and a classmate of Everett's at Princeton). Philip and his wife, on the other hand, were Republicans; he had worked closely with Eisenhower at Columbia, when they were, respectively, dean of the Business School and president of the university. There was a good deal of argument around the dinner table in the old house in Van Hornesville—Owen and Louise were there all summer long. But the head of the family did not tip his hand until close to the election; on October 30 he telephoned the Cases at Colgate that he would support Eisenhower. Mrs. Ogden Reid of the *New York Herald Tribune* had telephoned him at Van Hornesville to ask for a statement. The result was page-one news in all the leading papers: "Although I am a Democrat and an admirer of Governor Stevenson, I shall vote for General Eisenhower because I believe he can render greater service in the foreign field and will have less limitation in making desirable corrections in the domestic field."[18] An immediate telegram of appreciation came from the candidate on November 3.

The press, indeed, never ceased paying attention to Young and his opinions. Although his public appearances were few in the last decade, the reporters were always there to greet him. When, in the fall of 1955, New York Governor Averell Harriman set up a conference on the problems of the aging and to start it off invited a group of senior citizens to lunch at the Executive Mansion, Young's name was one of the two mentioned by the press. But he did have to share the limelight with an elder—Grandma Moses, who was ninety-five, while he was a mere eighty going on eighty-one. A press photo shows them with the governor, all smiles; and when luncheon was announced, she turned to Owen: "Young man, will you take me in to lunch?"[19]

Louise too took part in a number of conferences in New York State, in connection with her crafts projects at Van Hornesville. Owen went along, especially to Rochester, where he could visit with Cliff Spurr. There too the reporters appeared, asking for his opinion on this and that. Tall, still erect and handsome—and easily recognizable—he treated them with his habitual courtesy and friendliness and replied patiently to their questions.[20] Nor were his birthdays ever forgotten; a picture on his seventy-ninth, with the title "Rocking Chair Consultant," appeared in newspapers in most of the states of the Union—coverage surpassed only by that of the one taken on his eightieth.

Evidence that one—especially one who has been something of a celebrity in his active years—is not forgotten is surely welcome, however much Young pooh-poohed it in his own case. And every news item brought him letters—from friends happy to see his face in their local papers, from strangers, just admiring, or asking for advice, or money, or both; and when the "returned farmer" title was included, letters came offering to sell farms, cattle, horses and machinery.

His mail, indeed, throughout his retirement, was not light; he needed a secretary in both Washington Oaks and Van Hornesville. Whether in the cool wooden building under the live oaks—known as "Grandpa Peter's Oasis"—or in the stone office looking out over the milldam, he would smoke his pipe and dictate his answers. They reflect the value he attached to old friendships and the sympathy which moved him to help, if help was needed, both friends and others whose misfortunes distressed him. Unwarranted requests were briefly refused—although sometimes with a suggestion as to where else to go. For his "own" people, he was ready to guarantee a loan at the Herkimer bank, or to suggest an answer to a problem. Advice he never offered unless it was asked for, and then almost always to young people; to a student at Boston University who was writing a thesis on "Success," and had asked Young for a definition of success and the basic factors involved, he answered in four lines: "Success is something striven for and never obtained. A list of its basic factors, viewed in retrospect, would probably be the things which you fail to do."[21]

Many of the letters, inevitably, were of condolence, as the years sorted out which friends did not remain. Many of the oldest and the best were less long-lived than he: from the early days, his teacher Mark Hollister, his fellow law clerk Fred Weed, Frank Hall from Southbridge, Charley Appleton from St. Lawrence, all predeceased Young by many years. Others whom he came to know later, like Sam Fordyce, Thomas Nelson Perkins, Harry Robinson, Josiah Stamp— killed by a bomb dropped on his house in the war—he missed greatly.

In answer to a writer doing an article on the preservation of friendships, Young cited General Dawes's tireless efforts to keep in touch with friends and to be of service to them, no matter whether they were humble or great. He described an incident in New York, when he went with Dawes to the morgue, to identify an old fellow whom the general had helped for years, and to arrange for the funeral. Young and Dawes never grew away from the comradeship and affection begun in Paris in 1924; as the general said, it is not necessarily long years that make devoted friends, but what the two have been through together.

This last was true indeed, and for a longer period, of Young's friendship with Gerard Swope. Their unclouded partnership from 1922 to 1939, with the postlude during the war, is perhaps unique in business and personal annals. On Swope's eightieth birthday, December 1, 1952, Owen wrote him from Florida, recalling those years. He had just been reading Frederick Lewis Allen's *Big Change: America Transforms Itself, 1900–1950.* The book, he wrote Swope,

cannot tell either of us anything new about the period which it covers. We lived that period in the glow of the rising sun and not in the drab blacks and whites of evening. Our associates needed to have, and did have, great patience with us both. Perhaps Mary and you were discolored a little by your rather intimate contact with Jane Addams of Hull House and Lillian D. Wald of Henry Street. Perhaps I had gained a little understanding of color from Ida Tarbell and Lincoln Steffens. I mention them not as excuses for our behavior, but in gratitude for their help to us both.

As for their partnership over the years, "I cannot recall a single instance of irritation, of jealousy, of resentment. Our differences were always subjected to frank discussion, without reservation, and ended always in agreements as to what we should do and how we should do it."

Perhaps the friend that both Owen and Louise missed most was their Florida companion Marjorie Kinnan Rawlings—who became, as their friendship grew, also a Van Hornesville neighbor. One of the old houses which Louise bought and did over was a charming small one lost in the woods in the valley of the Otsquago, providing perfect seclusion for a writer. And eventually Marjorie bought a house of her own, where she lived summers, wrote *The Sojourner*, and gave fabulous parties for the Youngs and their families and friends. In 1953 she received an honorary degree at St. Lawrence, with the Youngs there to praise her. But six months later, in Florida, she died suddenly, leaving sadness both there and in Van Hornesville.

Whether with friends or family, Owen Young was usually more interested in talking about current affairs than in recalling the past. But his daughter remembers an evening in 1955, at Washington Oaks—a cold evening in February, when there was some concern lest the oranges freeze—when they sat before the big fireplace and Pops began to wonder about the pattern of his life, how it all came about "when I did not know what I was seeking, and never asked for a job; yet all came to me by a strange series of disappointments." He recounted his desire to go to law school, his efforts to persuade his parents that he *must* go, his guilty feeling of betrayal when they had counted on him to return to the farm; the total lack of funds, which caused his rejection at Harvard Law School, then the acceptance at Boston University, with a job attached; the invitation by Judge Burley to come into his office, and Burley's death soon after, then the offer from Charles Tyler, who had consulted the dean of the B.U. Law School about a likely candidate. Then the work for Tyler, and Stone and Webster, which eventually brought the invitation from Charles Coffin to join GE. Not new to his listener, the story, as he put together the links of the chain, did indeed coalesce into a pattern—a pattern which, even if he did not know what he was seeking, bound his long years together in a recurrent and coherent sequence, made up of readiness and right timing, luck—which he never discounted—and hard work.[22]

Another kind of reminiscence had been instigated, earlier in his retirement, by a letter from Allan Nevins at Columbia University, describing the Oral History project there and asking him to take part. Young replied that he thought it an excellent plan, and that he would be glad to "embark upon the adventure" at a later date.[23] But as it turned out, the recording which was made, in 1951, and deposited at Columbia, was not recorded by them. The head of the News Bureau at General Electric, C. D. Wagoner, an old colleague of Young's, had been delegated to write a "History of Radio in General Electric," and wrote his old boss asking if he could record what Young had to say about the early days, and offered to come to Florida to do it.

This was just the kind of setup Owen Young liked; how many times his children had wished that they had had a recorder under the dinner table. Now he could sit around with someone he knew well, who would ask the right questions, reliving the founding of RCA—his favorite topic—and at the same time fulfilling his promise to Allan Nevins. Wagoner spent several days at Washington Oaks, then went to Miami to listen to Commander (now Admiral) S. C. Hooper, then back to Young for the final section. The result of Young's talking added up to twenty-five closely typed pages when it was transcribed, and detailed many aspects of radio and broadcasting from the earliest days of RCA. Young spoke entirely from memory, without files or figures, and the result had an immediacy and liveliness which, as Nevins knew well, would have been lacking in a written account.[24]

v

During his active years, as he moved from engagement to engagement, meeting to meeting without pause, Young was asked constantly by the press, by friends and strangers for his opinion on every problem of the day. He had little time to discover what he *did* think. If he could get to Van Hornesville he could make some time, walking the mile to the cow barn or sitting in a field looking at the crops. But after his mother died, he did not get there so regularly.

There were, however, two other ways he used to explore his own mind. The first was a journey on a train. From his early days in law he had traveled constantly, and traveling meant trains—to Washington, to any one of the forty-eight states, for he went to all of them. Except during the wars, he was able to make himself extremely comfortable: a drawing room, a meal brought in—probably by a waiter or a porter whom he had known for years and who knew just how he liked it— a bottle of Scotch in the gladstone bag, and, if he wanted to work, a secretary—William Packer, or later George Riddle—to dictate to. Such journeys gave him time to stretch, not only his long legs but the long lines of his mind. Letters written thus, to friends and associates, occasionally to strangers who had asked him a question that set the wheels moving, often developed into five or six pages of speculation, suggestion and, sometimes, statements of his beliefs. He was like the child writing a composition, who said, "How do I know what I think till I see what I say?"

The second way was time with the family. We have indicated again and again how Owen discussed the problems, not only of his own life, but of the nation and the world, with Jo, and how much he depended on her brief and trenchant comments. The children too, as they grew old enough to listen without wiggling, became part of these discussions—which sometimes had the character of a monologue, but not always, for they too were asked for comments. Knowing from the earliest years that nothing said at home was to be repeated outside, they were talked to as frankly as adults, and responded with attention. Thus, within the circle, Owen worked out in talk what he thought should be done and how it could be managed. The talk dealt almost always with the future; constructive rather than destructive, it taught the young people by example how to attack their own problems—and to shed no tears over the past.

Perhaps these conversations at home had something to do with the fact that, as his children developed careers of their own, each moved into a different aspect of their father's concerns. This made for continuing rapport with each one, and genuine interest and understanding between child and father. In his eldest son, Owen Young saw the archetypical character of the inventor and research engineer upon whose work both GE and RCA had been founded. Although he was ignorant himself of such science in any technical sense, he was a dreamer and a prophet, expecting C.J. and others like him to bring the future into today—as indeed, in large degree, they did. He was proud of all his children, but perhaps most of his eldest, whose work he could not wholly understand.

As Philip moved from the Harvard Business School to the Securities and Exchange Commission and the treasury, spending war years with Lend-Lease and the navy, becoming dean of the School of Business at Columbia, following Eisenhower to Washington to head the Civil Service Commission and serve in his cabinet, then to the Netherlands as ambassador, his father was always in close touch, recognizing in these jobs aspects and problems with which he was well acquainted. Indeed, the burden of Owen Young's frequent and hardworking stays in Washington was greatly mitigated by evenings at home with Philip and Faith, talking of the problems and personalities of government.

The daughter, spending most of her life on college campuses, reflected her father's never-failing interest in education, and, as well, in the reading and writing of books. But no one ever succeeded in persuading Owen Young to write a book himself.

John, had he lived, might well have gone into law. So it was a special satisfaction when the late-born Richard went from St. Lawrence to the Harvard Law School—which his father had not been able to do—and thence, after his years in the army, into the field of international law. A permanent resident of Van Hornesville, where he built himself a charming house, Dick gave his father the feeling that the farm, the orchard, and the village were in good hands—at least when he was not in Saudi Arabia or elsewhere. Owen wrote him from Florida in 1949, after a message saying he was leaving for Dhahran:

It seems only day before yesterday that I used to send a message to Grammy in Van Hornesville saying I was sailing for Europe the next [day]. I used to wonder how she felt and how I would feel in her place. Now I know. Later, when I asked her, she would say "I was very proud that they needed you but I was never wholly happy until you came back. I am much happier than if nobody wanted you or if you did not have the ability or the courage to undertake the task."

Such words echo through succeeding generations of any family which is fortunate to have the conditions repeated—conditions mean deep affection, pride in accomplishment and abiding faith in each other.[25]

It was Richard who wrote the letter which expressed what all the children felt, but only he had the courage to put down. After his mother died, he had spent, in his late teens, far more time with his father than the others at that age. And when he got his law degree from Harvard, in 1947, he told his father what he thought of him:

I acquired a Harvard degree yesterday, and it started a train of thoughts which have been running around in my mind ever since. I thought you might like to know them.

I was thinking that, from my point of view at least, you're a successful father. So many fathers seem to bungle things. They mean well, but they fuss and fidget and try to coerce their sons into some pattern which they think is right. That you've never done: as I look back, my habits of mind were guided, yes, but never forced. . . . You might think me wrong—and say so—but opinions made no difference in our relationship. It would have made no difference, I think, had I turned Communist or Yogi, so long as I was an honest one; I suspect that's one reason I didn't turn. It's one of the best examples of the disarming influence of toleration I know.

They could disagree, he went on, because they were of different generations:

And while I may be more "advanced" than you are on some subjects, I have a notion that I still haven't caught up with you on others. But when it gets down to things that really count, things that don't change from generation to generation, I think we are not very far apart. It's funny, how ideas on these things have created themselves in my mind almost unconsciously, without preaching or sanctimoniousness. That's your doing.[26]

vi

Owen and Louise were fortunate in their love and their harmonious life in two beloved places; but in 1957 tragedy came to them once more. Louise had lost two husbands and her youngest child, Ward Clark; and in the spring of 1957 her talented daughter, Virginia, died very suddenly and unexpectedly. Married only four years, she and her husband were living happily at Washington Oaks in their studio-house, painting and looking forward to many years of productive work there and in Van Hornesville, where Louise had renovated an old house for them. It was a cruel blow to Louise, at seventy, and to Owen, who was very fond of Virginia, at eighty-two. He could only think of what his mother—at almost the same age—had said to him when John was killed—"If only it could have been me."

In the same year, in the fall, Owen himself fell seriously ill. His health, considering the burdens he had carried, had always been exceptionally good. When, in harassing times, he became too exhausted, he would quit for a few days and soon be back in shape. In fact, he paid little attention to his health; when he was seventy-six he said to B. C. Forbes, "The less one thinks about one's health the better. There is no surer way to become sick than to worry about your health."[27]

But in the fall of 1957 he was forced to worry, and went off to the hospital at Cooperstown—the first time he had been in a hospital for more than a checkup since his appendectomy in the fall of 1912. This visit disclosed an abdominal cancer and he was there for four months. Eventually he came back to moderate health, but he was never again as strong as before. The only gain, he said when he came home, was that the stay gave him an opportunity he had always wanted—to grow a beard. And a beautiful beard it was, snow-white and patriarchal, but he kept it only a few months.

When he and Louise returned to Florida they lived almost entirely in the little "townhouse" that Mrs. Powis had left them; daytimes they drove to Washington Oaks to see their gardens and groves. In 1959 they did not come north at all.

But in 1960 they came to Van Hornesville for a long and satisfying stay. Philip and Dick were home much of the time, and spent many hours driving their father over the hills to places long known and loved. It was a beautiful fall; the sun-warmed days kept the leaves on the trees in all their colors through October. Owen Young breathed the bright air, looked up at the hills, heard the water in the stream. It was his last stay in his native place, and a happy one.

Through 1961 and the first months of 1962, Owen and Louise lived quietly in the St. Augustine house, occasionally driving to Washington Oaks or to the St. Augustine seashore to watch the waves and feed the gulls. Louise herself was not very well, but their houseboy, the faithful Francisco, was with them, and nurses and other help were available when needed. The children came in turns, as often as they could, and the Youngs' own circle of devoted friends was always on call.

Owen Young died on July 11, 1962, quietly at home in St. Augustine. A service was held on the fourteenth, in the Universalist church in Van Hornesville, and he was buried in the cemetery on the hill above, next to his wife Josephine, near his son John, and only a few yards away from his parents and grandparents.

The radio—his radio—carried the news around the world, and the newspapers in every state in the nation, and in many foreign countries, carried a full obituary. In the *Times* of London for July 18 appeared a letter from Sir Andrew McFadyean:

I suspect that I am the last surviving mortal who was familiar with the work and personalities of the Dawes Committee, of which I was secretary . . . . May I therefore [he wrote *The Times*] because the Committee made a report of considerable historic importance and because Owen Young made a great contribution to it, add a few words to the obituary published in your issue of July 12?

With characteristic generosity, Owen Young averred that whoever made the report, General Dawes sold it. However much truth there was in that tribute to his colleague, I can truthfully say that Sir Josiah Stamp, as he then was, and Owen Young himself were its principal architects: there were other talented and even brilliant members of the committee, but their role was in comparison insignificant.

Owen Young's personality and appearance were as striking as his brain, which was a fine trained instrument eminently adapted to dealing with a problem which was economic, political and commonsensical. He had great and spontaneous charm, and I cannot imagine anyone working with or for him who would not quickly come to feel both respect and real affection for a great American.[28]

Letters came to the family from all parts of the world; no one had wholly realized, perhaps, how great his influence had been. He would have been particularly pleased with those, like McFadyean's, written by men who were young when he was in his heyday, and who said in letter after letter how much his life had affected theirs and how much they owed him. He wanted no other memorial.

Notes

All quotations and citations not otherwise attributed have their sources in the Owen D. Young Papers, now deposited and filed in the vault of the Van Hornesville Community Corporation, Van Hornesville, New York 13475. For the early years, these papers consist chiefly of Owen's correspondence with his parents—plus a few screeds from friends or others of the family that Owen or his mother thought worth saving. That the letters of Josephine Edmonds to Owen and her friend Blanche Winter were somehow preserved was no fault of hers; happily for us, both disregarded her injunctions to burn them, and they are here intact.

Because of the fire that destroyed the records of the Tyler firm, little written evidence remains for Owen's years at the Boston bar save his—and Jo's—letters to his mother, copies of certain notes and interviews taken from the Ida Tarbell papers by the authors, and a few drafts for important letters as dictated by Owen and written out by his wife. Most of these drafts and many of these early letters are undated, but the general chronology is usually clear.

To this sparseness the years with General Electric afford a marked contrast—the virtual disappearance of all that was consigned to Schenectady notwithstanding. Young's voluminous outgoing correspondence is preserved in the old-fashioned copybooks that only occasionally blot or blur their legibility. Originally there were two sets: business (BCB) and personal (PCB); a third (RCB) dates from the formation of the Radio Corporation. In the later years the distinction was largely lost and the use of the so-called Business Copy Book became all but general. Thus in the absence of notice to the contrary, Young's letters as cited are traceable to this source and inasmuch as each volume begins with an index and the order is chronological, further documentation is typically superfluous.

Nevertheless, full documentation becomes imperative as Young's career involves him in new and major responsibilities—industrial, financial and diplomatic, public as well as private. If this is sometimes less precise than we could wish, one reason is that certain categories of his papers—notably Radio and Reparations—are sorely in need of professional attention, having been inadequately sorted and indexed and even, on occasion, reshuffled. Thus at times we have had to make do with a categorical reference—e.g., to Reparations—without identifying the specific box or boxes in which the document in question is to be found. Such instances are, however, minimal and at worst may impose a slight added tax on the assiduous scholar's research.

Such incoming letters, messages and reports as were preserved and assigned to Van Hornesville are filed sometimes by subject, sometimes in boxes bearing the writer's name as indexed, and, in the case of those deemed most noteworthy, in boxes labeled "Special Papers." These we have sought to document according to their disposition, disregarding occasional overlaps. Where a speech or press clipping is cited, however, we have generally treated this citation as sufficient, both the voluminous clippings and the ten volumes of Young's speeches being chronologically ordered and each volume fully indexed.

To save both space and time, the following abbreviations are commonly used in these notes:

CJY:	Charles J. Young
ENC:	Everett Needham Case
HBR:	Helen B. Russell (cataloguer and writer who dealt chiefly with the Reparations files, anecdotes, etc.)
IBY:	Ida Brandow Young
JEY:	Josephine Edmonds Young
JHC:	James Herbert Case, Sr.
JYC:	Josephine Young Case
ODY:	Owen D. Young
PY:	Philip Young
RY:	Richard Young
BCB:	Business Copy Books
PCB:	Personal Copy Books
RCB:	Radio Copy Books
FRBNY:	Federal Reserve Bank of New York
HBS:	Harvard Business School
NYT:	*New York Times*
NYHT:	*New York Herald Tribune*
WSJ:	*Wall Street Journal*

CHAPTER *1. A Country Boyhood and a Country College*

1. The sleigh was much like a covered wagon, with runners instead of wheels. The Smith family lived in it all winter; Gersham (or Gresham) made cowbells for his neighbors, in exchange for food for his family.

2. The reason that Peter Young "took a scunner" against Seneca Herkimer, an upright and enterprising young man of the General Herkimer family, is not known.

3. This stone mill, built in 1835, has been in continuous use since that date. Electricity has replaced the big waterwheel, but the mill is still the center for the local farmers' cooperative.

4. ODY to Edward Adler 12/31/37.

5. John Worden Brandow, Jr., to ODY 9/17/1890, verbatim.

6. The quotations here and below from the letters of Ida Brandow Young to ODY, and his to her, are taken from the file of letters written from 1890 to 1898. Found in an old trunk, they are now filed and identified in the ODY Papers.

7. The quotations re school days are from a series of articles written by ODY for the Van Hornesville School *Highlights*, and appeared in January through March 1943.

8. From an interview with IBY in the *Knickerbocker Press* (Albany), undated. Ida was very unwilling to give interviews and this is one of the few to which she consented.

9. Many of these books were included in the Fundamental Library of English Literature which ODY suggested, funded and helped choose at St. Lawrence University forty years later.

10. The postcard is quoted in a letter from ODY to Mark Hollister 7/9/45.

11. Ibid.

12. A. B. Hervey to ODY 6/13/1890.

13. Ibid. 8/12/1890.

14. Ibid. 8/23/1890.

15. A letter of the time from a male student gives the picture:
    I nearly forgot to inform you that a number of ladies room in the building and most of the best-looking ones too. . . . It is some consolation to gaze upon their seraphic (?) countenances and to realize that you are living upon the same floor and breathing the same atmosphere that they are. . . . Yesterday some of the ladies . . . received a "lingual" castigation from the profs for being seen in the gentlemen's rooms in co. with certain of said masculine genders. I have not learned that anything serious was done, yet the profs affected to be greatly shocked thereat. . . . Just think of it . . . *4 young ladies and 4 young men all alone in a room and before dark too.* . . . Oh! horror of horrors, when will virtue be restored to the youth of the world?
This letter is quoted in *Candle in the Wilderness: A Centennial History of*

St. Lawrence University, 1856–1956, edited by Louis H. Pink and Rutherford E. Delmage (New York: Appleton-Century-Crofts, 1957), p. 18. Neither the author nor the date of the letter is given.

16. ODY to Hervey 2/14/23.

17. Clifford Spurr, "Anecdotes of Owen D. Young," ms in the ODY Papers.

18. "Struggle" by ODY in the *Laurentian* 1/1938.

19. Much of our information about the college and the town we owe to Atwood Manley '16, son and successor to Williston Manley '88, editor and publisher of the *St. Lawrence Plaindealer.*

20. From a talk by Charles Kelsey Gaines at the Hervey Anniversaries celebration; an account of this was published in a booklet, "The Hervey Anniversaries," October 12–14, 1928 (printed for St. Lawrence University). The anniversaries were the seventieth of Dr. Hervey's arrival at St. Lawrence as a student, and the fortieth of his return as president. Dr. Hervey himself, at the age of eighty-nine, attended this occasion, which was arranged by Owen and Josephine Young.

21. Spurr, "Anecdotes."

22. May Green to ODY n.d. (1931).

23. It was the rule at St. Lawrence in early days that when the roll was called at Monday morning chapel each student was expected to answer "present" if he or she had attended church the day before, and "absent" if not.

CHAPTER *2. A Bachelor's Degree—and Jo*

1. See Chapter 1, note 6.

2. A high point during their stay in the jail was the time that eighteen Chinese were brought in; they had been captured while attempting illegal entry at the border close by. While they were there the boys learned something about Chinese customs, language and music—all totally new to them. Another amusement, throughout their association with the sheriff, were games of euchre, with Young and Spurr against the sheriff and Chilton; some very fancy signals were worked out among both sets of partners. It was all perfectly fair, of course, since both sides were cheating.

3. This piece of juvenilia is quoted *in toto* in *Candle in the Wilderness: A Centennial History of St. Lawrence University, 1856–1956,* edited by Louis H. Pink and Rutherford E. Delmage (New York: Appleton-Century-Crofts, 1957), pp. 104–105.

4. "Anecdotes" furnished by James F. McKinney (1926; ms in ODY Papers).

5. Clifford Spurr, "Anecdotes of Owen D. Young," ms in ODY Papers.

6. Ibid.

7. Atwood Manley reports that "Canton was blessed with a remarkably able coterie of lawyers . . . a galaxy of legal talent" in those days.

8. Josephine Edmonds to Blanche Winter 9/1891. Subsequent quotations from Jo's letters are from this same correspondence, now in the ODY Papers.

9. Spurr, "Anecdotes."

10. Gaines also wrote two other novels of less value, and a collection of poems, which ODY arranged to have published in 1926 in a small, attractive volume, *Echoes of Many Moods*, printed by William Edwin Rudge with typography by Bruce Rogers.

11. ODY's college diary, kept only from January to September 1892, is in the ODY Papers.

12. Collection of JEY's letters in ODY Papers; all following quotations from her letters are also from this collection.

13. There are several accounts of this political meeting in the ODY Papers: one in Spurr's "Anecdotes" and another, "ODY and Political Debating," from the *Commercial Advertiser* of Canton, N.Y., 7/2/1929.

14. This anecdote was told the authors by ODY. Neither Owen nor Jo, for different reasons, could vote in that election; Jo was not celebrating, even though some of her best friends were Democrats. The Edmondses were a rock-ribbed Republican family, and she never switched her allegiance. In later years, when women had the vote, she and Owen went regularly to the polls together, traveling two hundred miles to Van Hornesville to cancel each other's votes.

15. This effort was remembered chiefly because ODY never took part in any activity of an athletic nature. The only exception was when he was persuaded to umpire a baseball game, and got a black eye for his pains.

16. This was ODY's first visit to Schenectady, where he was to spend so much time in later life. He had passed through it on the train when he was a child, when his father took him to Albany to see the Capitol and the State Museum.

17. ODY interview with Lawrence Thompson, the biographer of Robert Frost.

18. Josephine Augusta had been named for the empress by her father, Major George Clark, who was furious at Napoleon for putting away his Josephine.

19. It was a source of great pleasure to ODY later that his three St. Lawrence sons also became Betas.

CHAPTER *3. A Law Degree—and Tyler*

1. The spirit of the abolitionists was by no means dead, and the reformers stepped out of the ranks of old Boston: Wendell Phillips, on whom ODY had delivered an oration at college, Julia Ward Howe, Edward Everett Hale, Thomas W. Higginson. Newspapers, periodicals and books contributed to the public consciousness of the growing and apparently insoluble problems of the city; preachers and professors did not allow their listeners to relax into smugness. A leader among the last was Frank Parsons, whom Young certainly heard when he lectured at the Boston University Law School in the 1890s.

2. ODY to Ida M. Tarbell 2/3/34.

3. One of the plays he saw was *Rip Van Winkle* with Joseph Jefferson. He had seen it before in an amateur production in the Grange Hall at home.

He wrote his parents, "It has always been in my mind since then and now that I have seen it played so well it will doubtless hang in my mind forever."

4. Owen and Jo during this period always read the same books, and, indeed, had made a pact to read at the same time each night the same chapter in the current book.

5. ODY to Vere Goldthwaite n.d.

6. *Haverhill Bulletin* 9/24/1895.

7. His first case after he was admitted to the Massachusetts bar was the defense of a man accused of stealing a jug of cider; the man got six months.

8. Owen D. Young, "Professional Honor," Boston University Law School Archives.

9. Goldthwaite to ODY 7/30/1896.

10. Jo told her daughter, many years later, that she and Owen had agreed to burn their love letters; she destroyed his, but he cheated and kept hers.

11. William H. Young to Josephine Edmonds 3/6, 3/7/1898.

CHAPTER *4. Marriage and the Boston Bar*

1. The fields of Pumpkin Hook are one of the few even moderately level places around Van Hornesville where it might be possible to hit a golf ball. Thirty years later C.J. used them as a landing field for his airplane.

2. Charles H. Tyler to ODY 3/21/19; ODY to Tyler 5/5/16.

3. Much of Charles Tyler's collections can be seen today in the Boston Museum of Fine Arts, to which he left them.

4. Arthur M. Johnson and Harry E. Supple, *Boston Capitalism and Western Railroads* (Cambridge: Harvard University Press, 1967), p. 241.

5. Quoted in Wesley S. Griswold, *A Work of Giants* (New York: McGraw-Hill, 1962), preface, p. xi.

6. George Pierce Baker, *The Formation of New England Railroad Systems* (Cambridge: Harvard University Press, 1937).

7. As ODY reported to his parents, he had many conferences with Dr. William Seward Webb, vice-president of the New York Central, which was concerned about the future of the Ogdensburg and Lake Champlain as well as the Central Vermont itself; it also had a lien on the bonds of the Lamoille Extension.

8. *Burlington* (Vt.) *Free Press* 10/20, 10/26/1898.

9. Ibid. 3/22/1899.

CHAPTER *5. Ubiquitous Utilities: Tyler Takes a Partner*

1. Stone and Webster *Public Service Journal* 11/1908.

2. Russell Robb in ibid. 7/1907.

3. ODY's information in these letters (6/8, 7/10/01) was not nearly so

colorful or replete as that in the letters written to Smith Young from the West by his brother Cyrus Young at about the same time. For example, Cyrus wrote from Boise City, Idaho, on 6/29/1900: "We came here to Boise City the Capetell of Idaho A City of About 8 thousand Population we find heare is verey nice Valley with froot of all kinds Except Lemons and Oranges but Cheries peches plumbs proons Aprecuts Paires Apples quinces & all small froot all of these grow in perfusen . . . they raise 2 crops of teimethey & Clover & 3 of Alfalfa Hay . . . it is all dun by Eargation . . ."

4. Original notice of reorganization. ODY and Wadsworth were lifelong friends, and always remembered with pleasure their youthful expeditions afield for Stone and Webster. In the 1920s Wadsworth was assistant secretary of the treasury.

5. Dallas City Reports, 1900–1901.

6. Quoted in Ida M. Tarbell, *Owen D. Young: A New Type of Industrial Leader* (New York: Macmillan, 1932), pp. 79–80. We have no record that ODY and Louis Brandeis knew each other more than superficially in Boston in those early days. Nevertheless, this franchise is strongly suggestive of the Brandeis influence. ODY had certainly read of his efforts to protect the consumer against the politicians and the public utilities, notably in the case of the Boston Gas Company. The specifications of neither Brandeis nor Young were very widely observed in the decades when electric and gas utilities were first being set up; and it was some time before the laws—which owed something to both of them—caught up.

7. *El Paso Daily Herald* 4/24/01.

8. Tarbell, pp. 82–83. There the story is told in more detail, as ODY told it to her.

9. ODY's friendship with Charley Stone and Ed Webster survived the years and some difficult and unsatisfactory relationships with General Electric. Indeed, after ODY joined GE in 1913 he completed some unfinished business in Dallas for S&W.

10. Undated interview of Tarbell with ODY; Tarbell Papers, Reis Library, Allegheny College, Meadville, Pa.

11. Stone and Webster *Public Service Journal* 10/1907.

12. ODY to authors. For an account of this pioneer's colorful career see S. A. Mitchell, *S. Z. Mitchell and the Electrical Industry* (New York: Farrar, Straus, 1960).

13. Tarbell, p. 93.

14. E.g., ODY to R. E. Breed of American Gas and Electric 1/23/13, suggesting changes in the Indiana public service bill; ODY to C. N. Mason of the Electrical Securities Corporation, re proposed South Dakota bill, 1/24/13.

15. Undated interview, Tarbell with Burton Eames, Tarbell Papers.

16. *Exercises in Practice and Pleading*, collected by Homer Albers of the Boston bar and professor in the Boston University Law School, and Owen D. Young of the Boston bar and instructor in the Boston University Law School. Boston: Alfred Mudge and Son, Printers, No. 24 Franklin St., 1897. *Problems in Practice and Pleading at the Common Law* selected by Owen D. Young of the Boston bar and instructor in Boston University Law School,

and James T. Keen of the Boston bar. Boston: Alfred Mudge and Son, Printers, 1902.

17. Notes by George W. N. Riddle of a conversation with ODY on the train to Washington 11/20/29 (in ODY papers). Neither ODY nor the Law School gave up easily, as was evident in his reaction to their renewed offer of 1905, to teach corporation law, a subject he knew well and would have liked to teach. Writing Tyler, who was still opposed—the undated draft of the letter is in Jo's hand—he said (to convince Tyler, or himself?):

> I want very much to accept the position. It tickles my vanity, or to put it more seriously it enables me in a very small way to make my personality felt by the profession in Boston, in a manner in which you in a very marked way have done. That feature is important to you and this although it be very modest is likewise important to me.
>
> Don't you see that by its acceptance I am able to continue in the office longer than I can possibly do by refusing it—I've been there nearly ten years, I am more than thirty years old and the question of whether I shall ever amount to anything in the profession must be decided in the next fifteen years at the most. And every year that I remain represents quite a percentage of that total period. However pleasant,—or however lucrative, and I repeat what I have often told you that you have from the beginning, made it more lucrative than my services warranted—I shall from the nature of things be unable to stay very long. Money although a necessary concomitant to my plans, is not solely a determining force, in making them.

There is no evidence that this draft was ever copied and sent. But in June he wrote his parents that he would not be giving the course at the Law School in the fall—perhaps later.

18. Clement F. Robinson to ODY 2/27/46 (with parts of original letter); ODY to Robinson 3/15/46.

19. J. W. Elwood to Ida Tarbell n.d., Tarbell Papers.

CHAPTER 6. *And Loses Him to Industry*

1. ODY to E. H. Dollar, Heuvelton, N.Y., 8/10/09; to his uncle John Brandow the following year.

2. ODY was not satisfied to be separated from his pets for so much of the year, and brought a few of them to Lexington. There was no place for them on Warren Street, so he put them to board with a farmer in East Lexington, where not only he but the whole family visited them frequently, and of course drank their milk daily. When the family left Lexington in 1913 he had three cows, one heifer, one calf and one bull, all of which he shipped to Van Hornesville.

3. ODY to Abram Tilyou n.d.

4. GE's Annual Report for 1912 described this dividend as "out of surplus," for the stated purpose of "recouping the stockholders" in part for the dividends passed or reduced during the years 1893 to 1902; quoted by ODY in his statement to the Temporary National Economic Commission on GE's capital formation, Washington, 5/9/39. See John Winthrop Hammond, *Men*

and Volts: The Story of General Electric (Philadelphia: Lippincott, 1941), for full text.

5. *Electrical World*, vol. LX, no. 5 (8/3/12).

6. Quoted in Hammond, p. 90.

7. There were eleven directors: F. L. Ames, Charles A. Coffin, T. Jefferson Coolidge, C. H. Coster, Thomas A. Edison, Eugene Griffin, Frank S. Hastings, Henry L. Higginson, D. O. Mills, J. P. Morgan, Hamilton McKay Twombley. Edison remained on the board through 1901. ODY described GE's first directorate as a reflection of "distinguished and substantial backing" (R. B. Adams, *The Boston Money Tree* [New York: T. Y. Crowell, 1977], p. 212).

8. This account of the company's history is drawn mainly from Hammond.

9. J. R. McKee's name was so listed for 1913 only; it was his last year with GE. Until his death, Parsons had also been so listed.

10. Ida M. Tarbell, *Owen D. Young: A New Type of Industrial Leader* (New York: Macmillan, 1932), pp. 107–108: quoted from the unpublished ms of Hammond, which was nearly three times the size of the volume edited and published after his death. Hammond states that he may not be quoting verbatim, but the substance he most certainly recalls and vouches for.

11. For the history of these and other GE stalwarts, see Hammond's index. For the first fifty years of the research laboratory, see L. A. Hawkins, *Adventure into the Unknown* (New York: Morrow, 1950).

12. Tarbell, pp. 98–99, quotes ODY as saying that he accepted without qualifications at once, in the first interview. Surviving evidence, which follows, indicates that the definite yes came later.

13. There is no reason to believe that, like some letters dictated at home in the heat of the moment, this one was not sent. Coffin's answer confirms that it was. The draft is on the pink slips of paper which the Tyler firm still uses for memos.

14. Charles A. Coffin to ODY 10/21/12; again, draft of ODY's reply is in his wife's hand.

15. Tarbell, p. 99.

16. ODY to Charles H. Tyler 10/17/12.

CHAPTER *7. Lag of the Law: The Wilsonian Version—and Young's*

1. ODY to E. R. Stettinius 9/4/20.

2. ODY to IBY 10/14/13.

3. Herbert Croly, *The Promise of American Life* (New York: Macmillan, 1909). For its influence on the Progressives and especially TR, see Eric F. Goldman, *Rendezvous with Destiny* (New York: Vintage, 1956), especially pp. 159–60; also Henry F. Pringle's *Theodore Roosevelt* (New York: Blue Ribbon Books, 1931), pp. 540–41.

4. Woodrow Wilson, *The New Freedom* (New York: Doubleday, Page, 1914)—especially chapter 7, "Monopoly or Opportunity"; Arthur S. Link, *Woodrow Wilson*, vol. I: *The Road to the White House* (Princeton: Princeton University Press, 1947), pp. 489–93.

5. Western Electric was still at this time an active competitor in many lines; Westinghouse and many specialty companies remained so. In his Temporary National Economic Commission testimony of 1939, ODY maintained that in his time, GE's share of the market for electrical goods fluctuated between 20 and 25 percent.

6. Precisely when or where ODY heard or read this characteristic Wilsonian remark we cannot say, but there is no doubt that it delighted him. More than once we heard him quote it, always with relish, and sometimes with minor embellishments. Much later, in rehearsing it for Gerard Swope's biographer, David Loth, Young (then seventy-eight) even "recalled" that he had it direct from Wilson, "whom he had met early in 1913" (*Swope of GE* [New York: Simon & Schuster, 1958], p. 135). Unlike Loth, we have reason to doubt this latter-day recollection: first, because ODY's early records fail to support it, and second, because Wilson's biographer, Arthur Link, reports (in response to our inquiry) finding no trace of such a meeting in Wilson's papers of the time (Link to ENC 6/12/79). Perhaps the best— and notably disarming—clue to this small puzzle is to be found in ODY's letter of 7/6/53 to Bascom Timmons, whose biography of General Dawes, *Portrait of an American* (New York: Henry Holt, 1953), had just been published. Praising Timmons for relying as he did on the general's *contemporary* journals, ODY described himself as "old enough to know that one of the least reliable sources of information about a man's life is to get it from the man himself after he has reached or approximates the age of eighty."

7. For a succinct account of the rise and impact of "finance capitalism" and the trusts, see (e.g.) F. R. Dulles, *The United States since 1865* (Ann Arbor: University of Michigan Press, 1959), pp. 60–62. Most of the ideas here discussed were widely current among ODY's fellow students of the law, the economy and business, but few had identified the role of such active ingredients as the limited-liability concept. That ODY had done so *at the time* cannot be fully documented; but it is primarily to conversations with him and one or two friends like Wallace Donham and especially Chester Barnard—successively president of the New Jersey Bell Telephone and the Rockefeller Foundation—that the authors owe their initial understanding of its dynamic role.

8. Wilson, pp. 33–34. Students of intellectual history may find it interesting to speculate on Wilson's debt to Albert V. Dicey, whose *Law and Public Opinion in England* was first published in 1905, when Wilson was professor of jurisprudence at Princeton. See especially pp. 111 ff. (2d ed., London: Macmillan, 1914), where Dicey cites the "intolerable incongruity between rapidly changing social conditions and the practical unchangeableness of the law" as a prelude to the Reform Act of 1832. ODY's debt to Dicey, however, is not in doubt; attending in 1898 the beautifully structured Harvard lecture which was one of those on which the book was based, ODY took

handwritten notes—likewise beautifully structured—that reflect the young law lecturer's absorbed attention to the great man's argument. Happily these notes have been preserved together with ODY's copy of Dicey's book.

9. ODY to Josiah Newcomb 1/6/13. Newcomb was Stone and Webster's Washington representative.

10. ODY to A. G. Davis 1/29/13.

11. ODY to Allan Jackson 2/7/13.

12. But he wired Tyler on Tuesday, 2/11, that he could not leave Washington until Friday night. See also ODY to Charles A. Coffin 2/1/13 and ODY to Messrs. Baker, Botts, Parker and Garwood of Houston 2/3/13.

13. Included under "Other Income" in GE's financial reports. For ODY's much later version of the rise and role of these securities companies, including Bond and Share, see his statement of 11/17/39 to the Temporary National Economic Commission; text quoted in appendix to John Winthrop Hammond, *Men and Volts: The Story of General Electric* (Philadelphia: Lippincott, 1941), pp. 397–424.

14. Mitchell's stipulations and their rationale are fully presented in S. A. Mitchell, *S. Z. Mitchell and the Electrical Industry* (New York: Farrar, Straus, 1960), p. 66.

15. Copies of these documents are in the archives of the Department of Justice. Both are summarized in Hammond, pp. 340–44. The text of the consent decree is reprinted most recently in Robert Jones and Oliver Marriott, *Anatomy of a Merger* (London: Jonathan Cape, 1970).

16. ODY to Coffin 2/6/13. This letter of ODY's antedated by several months Brandeis's strictures on the money trust, the power trust, and interlocking directorates, which, first published in *Harper's Weekly* during November and December (1913), are discussed in our next chapter. Brandeis, after defending United Shoe Machinery as counsel, had denounced it as a monopoly, but his subsequent citation of the Court's decision in dismissing the antitrust suit brought against it in 1911 fully confirmed ODY's reading of the case. See Alpheus T. Mason, *Brandeis: A Free Man's Life* (New York: Viking, 1946), chapter 14, especially p. 546. For ODY's role as counsel to one of the plaintiffs in the 1911 suit, see ODY to E. S. Giles, letters of 5/1932, Box 333.

17. *History of Greater Dallas and Vicinity* (Chicago: V. H. Lewis Publishing Co., 1909), articles on Edward T. Moore, manager of Dallas Electric Light and Power. To consult this piece is to discover that it should be taken with *several* grains of salt.

18. The *Tangent* (Stone and Webster publication), Galveston, 4/1912; HBR notes in ODY Papers.

19. Submitted 2/28/13; text in ODY Papers, BCB. ODY evidently regarded this as unfinished rather than new business, despite the interest of GE's securities companies in the Texas situation.

20. ODY to Caleb Fisher 3/10/13.

21. ODY to Coffin 3/5/13.

22. Ibid. 3/7/13.

23. Ibid. 3/6/13.

24. Rice's original letter, with ODY's comment, was preserved by Mrs. Young (ODY Papers). The changes in GE's top management were approved by the board on 6/13/13, and made public the following day.

CHAPTER 8. *General Electric and "Fair Competition"*

1. From Wilson's first statement as President-elect, made on the day following the election; quoted in Ray Stannard Baker, *Woodrow Wilson: Life and Letters* (Garden City, N.J.: Doubleday, Doran, 1931), III, 412. See also Woodrow Wilson, *The New Freedom* (New York: Doubleday, Page, 1914), p. 180, for his campaign declaration: "I am for big business and I am against the trusts."

2. ODY to William McAdoo 3/18/13. McAdoo was then a widower; his marriage to Ellen Wilson occurred a year later.

3. For Coffin's attitude as contrasted with Young's see John Winthrop Hammond, *Men and Volts: The Story of General Electric* (Philadelphia: Lippincott, 1941), p. 387. As for Charles Steinmetz, ODY could not have made a better choice. A socialist refugee from Germany, this intrepid hunchback, with a wizard's head and hands, had single-handedly made alternating electric current, with its high potential for long-distance transmission, both practicable and vastly more efficient, and his subsequent research and experimentation on how best to protect the new high-voltage transmission networks against the hazards of lightning had produced in his laboratory the phenomenon of man-made lightning. Indefatigable in his role as GE's chief consulting engineer, this genial citizen and friend of socialist Mayor George Lunn also served on Schenectady's Common Council and for two terms as president of the school board (see *Dictionary of American Biography*, XVII, 565; *Who Was Who*, vol. 1).

4. Ida M. Tarbell, *Owen D. Young: A New Type of Industrial Leader* (New York: Macmillan, 1932), p. 112. See also below.

5. ODY to Allan Jackson 1/25/13.

6. ODY to Charles A. Coffin 1/29/13. In converting the old National Electric Lamp Association, with headquarters in Cleveland, into a fully acknowledged lamp division, GE had not yet consolidated it with its Edison lamp division; but all pretense that the two were competitive had now been dropped. For follow-up see ODY to F. S. Terry and B. G. Tremaine 3/14/13.

7. Hammond, p. 339.

8. In light of their future relationship, it is worth noting that subsequent efforts to settle this matter to the satisfaction of Western Electric, still an important "agent" in the distribution of its lamps, led to ODY's first meeting with the principal author of that company's lamp contract with GE, Gerard Swope. The meeting was arranged by an exchange of letters, ODY's response of 11/19/13 to Swope's note of 11/18/13 addressing him formally as "Dear Sir." ODY too had been unhappy about existing contractual relations with

WE. See ODY to F. P. Fish 5/29/13 suggesting that he call a conference with Leverett of AT&T and William Sidley of WE, with Jackson and ODY representing GE. Eventually Swope proved to be the key to a settlement.

9. ODY to Jackson 2/1/13; ODY to Darius Peck, acknowledging his helpful report, 3/8/13. "Based on its conclusions, I am preparing a communication to the directors," he wrote Peck.

10. ODY to Jackson 3/8 and 3/22/13.

11. Ibid. 2/28/13; ODY to Frank Y. Gladney 3/1/13.

12. See BCB, as indexed, for Gladney correspondence. An encapsulated version of this first encounter was given ENC by ODY, c. 1928, in support of his contention that in any sharp controversy one should be suspicious not so much of people as of what they assume to be the facts.

13. ODY to Anson Burchard 3/3/13.

14. ODY to M. M. Crane 5/6/13; see also ODY's earlier letter to Gerald Dahl of 3/21/13.

15. ODY to William J. Hughes 5/27/13. See also ODY to Charles E. Rowe for similar service 10/28/13.

16. ODY to Charles Neave 5/27/13.

17. ODY to Jackson 6/12/13; ODY to R. Moot (Law Dept.) 5/29/13.

18. ODY to Jackson 7/2/13; ODY to Neave 7/2/13; ODY to A. G. Davis 6/21/13; ODY to D. R. Bullen 7/1/13.

19. ODY to Bullen 7/19/13.

20. ODY to Coffin 8/1/13.

21. Published 3/1914 as *Other People's Money* (New York: Frederick A. Stokes Co.) with a preface by Norman Hapgood, these strictures of Brandeis took up where the Pujo investigation had broken off; his especially telling attack on interlocking directorates was presumably a factor in the New Year's announcement by the younger J. P. Morgan and the elder George F. Baker that, bowing to a "change in public sentiment," they were resigning from some thirty of their sixty-nine directorships.

22. Brandeis, pp. 155–61; ODY to W. J. Jenks 12/8/13; also—same date—ODY to Henry G. Bradlee of Stone and Webster. These articles in *Harper's Weekly* coincided with the efforts of President Wilson and Secretary Lane—supported by the House but blocked by the Senate—to secure a progressive federal waterpower bill (not enacted until 1920); Arthur S. Link, *Woodrow Wilson*, vol. II: *The New Freedom* (Princeton: Princeton University Press, 1956), pp. 128–32.

23. ODY to Arthur Page 12/26/13; ODY to S. Z. Mitchell 12/6/13.

24. ODY did advise GE director Gordon Abbott, 8/13/13, who passed the word to his fellow Boston banker Philip Stockton, that the Senate might recess until November before taking up the Glass bill. Cf. Carter Glass, *Adventure in Constructive Finance* (New York: Doubleday, Page, 1927), pp. 163, 164, ridiculing Stockton's August report to the NYT that "he had it on good authority that the Senate will not take up the currency bill at this session." Wilson, ignoring threats and importunities alike, kept the Senate in continuous session until the bill was passed in December.

25. Henry F. Hollis to ODY 11/10/13.

26. See Wilson, *New Freedom*, chapter 7.

27. ODY to Walter Kruesi of Schenectady 6/19/14.

28. ODY to J. M. Woodward 1/29/13; see also earlier letters of 1/4 and 1/13, BCB.

29. ODY to Coffin 4/21, 9/17, 10/7/13, BCB. Woodward enjoyed a regular retainer.

30. ODY to JEY 4/18/13; ODY to Coffin 4/21/13.

31. HBR notes in ODY Papers. For the development and expression of ODY's views on waterpower as both a state and a federal issue, see below, Chapter 19.

32. HBR notes.

33. BCB 1913–15, beginning with ODY to O. B. Willcox 6/24/13; ODY to George Hardie 1/28/15, PCB. Excellent statements regarding the purpose and rationale of these *Reports* also appear in ODY's letters to Daniel G. Tyler of E. and F. King and Company, Boston, 10/23/14; to L. P. Hale of the New York State Public Service Commission 1/13/15; to S. E. Barker, chairman of Massachusetts Gas and Electric Light Commission, 11/16/14; and to M. S. Decker of the ICC 11/16/14.

34. ODY to A. G. Davis 6/10, 10/23/14; ODY to Neave 11/25/14; ODY to Woodward 11/27/14.

35. ODY to Jackson 11/27/14; ODY to E. W. Rice, Jr., 10/29/14. Comprising all of the company's principal officers, the Advisory Committee was second in importance only to the board—of which very few save the chairman and president were members.

36. ODY to Jackson 7/10/13; ODY to Jesse Lovejoy 7/9/14; ODY to Jackson 7/9/14; ODY to Francis Pratt 12/9/14; ODY to Davis 6/11/14; ODY to John C. McClement of Allis-Chalmers 8/14/14.

37. ODY Office Schedule. The Manufacturing Committee met 6/23; the Executive Committee and the board 6/24; the Advisory Committee 6/25 and 6/26/14.

38. ODY to William H. Dunbar 7/31/13. A worn copy of *Other People's Money*, initialed ODY, is still on Young's shelves. ODY subsequently acknowledged to Susan Brandeis (12/12/56) an early professional debt to her father. See also ODY to Samuel Carr (of the Tyler firm) 3/4/13 re final settlement with Filene and Brandeis for services rendered (chiefly ODY's) in clearing the block required for Filene's new store. For Higginson's view of Brandeis, see Alpheus T. Mason, *Brandeis: A Free Man's Life* (New York: Viking, 1946), p. 393. Haldane, too, was unavailable.

39. ODY to M. F. Westover 12/24/13.

40. GE's Annual Report for 1913 (copy in ODY Papers).

41. ODY to his son Richard (and others).

42. See letters, as indexed, in PCB for 1913. Wadsworth's letter of introduction, beginning "Dear Judge," is dated 6/21/13; by October Fordyce had adopted this form of salutation. For his role re Gladney, see ODY to Coffin 10/22/13.

43. ODY to Caleb Fisher 11/24/13, PCB; ODY to Wallace Donham 2/7/13, PCB.

44. ODY to Coffin 2/7/13. Donham had assured him, wrote Young, that the setup had "the favor and support of the Labor Unions."

45. ODY to Nelson Perkins 10/28/13; Perkins to ODY 10/30/13; also HBR interview with Perkins c. 1926, HBR notes.

46. PCB, as indexed. ODY had already (5/2/13) resigned from the Middlesex County Bar Association.

47. ODY to the authors at various times. A slightly different version, as told to Ida Tarbell by Steffens's friend John Phillips, is in her papers at Allegheny College; her book omits all reference to the deal. See also Justin Kaplan, *Lincoln Steffens: A Biography* (New York: Simon & Schuster, 1974), p. 262.

48. These volumes are still a part of ODY's surviving library. Also, his papers include a Steffens folder, which segregates their varied but occasionally fascinating correspondence.

CHAPTER *9. War in Europe, Reform and Neutrality at Home*

1. Ray Stannard Baker, *Woodrow Wilson: Life and Letters* (Garden City, N.Y.: Doubleday, Doran, 1931), IV, 89–92. His summary of the President's peace proposal is quoted from John Bassett Moore's address to the Conference on International Arbitration at Lake Mohonk, 5/27/14. As Arthur Link points out in *Woodrow Wilson and the Progressive Era* (New York: Harper & Row, 1954), p. 147, American opinion regarding the aggressors was greatly influenced by the refusal of Austria-Hungary and Germany to submit the Serbian dispute to arbitration.

2. Baker, IV, chapter 8. For Root's position, see p. 398. A more complete account is in Philip C. Jessup, *Elihu Root* (New York: Dodd, Mead, 1938), II, 262–66.

3. Baker, IV, 334–52.

4. NYT 1/3/14. (See Chapter 8, note 21.) The elder Morgan had died on 3/31/13; neither Baker nor the younger Morgan was a GE director, although Baker's son, George F., Jr., was to be elected to the board in 1919.

5. Baker, IV, 367–75. Wilson also urged that "penalties and punishment fall not upon business itself, to its confusion and interruption, but upon the individuals [responsible]." Even Brandeis found this impracticable, and so, with few exceptions, did the courts.

6. NYT 5/14, 5/30/14; Link, *Progressive Era*, p. 68.

7. ODY to A. G. Davis 6/10/14.

8. See Link, *Progressive Era*, pp. 66–76, for a compelling exposition of this change in Wilson's emphasis if not indeed his philosophy—a change to which Baker signally fails to draw attention.

9. ODY to M. S. Seelman (of Brooklyn Edison) 11/4/14.

10. ODY to A. H. Jackson 7/9/14; ODY to F. P. Fish 8/17/14; see also ODY to F. C. Pratt 1/22/15.

11. ODY to Gilbert Montague 10/30/14.

12. ODY to Fish 11/19/14.

13. No complete texts exist of these speeches as delivered, but the ODY Papers contain enough typed and ms material to indicate their substance. See also ODY to S. O. Richardson 8/24/14, asking that the record of the Manufacturers Club meeting be corrected to make it clear that, far from indicting the courts, he had pointed out that they were merely interpretive of the law, business complaints about which should go to the legislative branch.

14. For text of Adler's article, see *Harvard Law Review*, vol. XXVIII, no. 2 (12/1914), pp. 252–62.

15. ODY to Joseph E. Davies 11/19/14.

16. ODY to Arthur Page 1/29/15. See also *World's Work*, vol. XXIX, no. 4. See also ODY to Barry Mohun 10/6/14: "This commission will certainly create a new jurisdiction and consequently a lot of new business."

17. ODY to H. C. Clark 2/27/15.

18. ODY to E. B. Parker 6/16/15.

19. ODY to O. B. Willcox 9/12/16, emphasis added.

20. ODY to Anson K. Burchard 3/21/17. In this view, ODY was following Hughes; cf. M. J. Pusey, *Charles Evans Hughes* (New York: Macmillan, 1951), I, 203.

21. John Winthrop Hammond, *Men and Volts: The Story of General Electric* (Philadelphia: Lippincott, 1941), pp. 367–71.

22. ODY to J. M. Woodward 10/4/15.

23. ODY to M. F. Westover 3/8/15.

24. Ibid. 3/10/15.

25. Hammond, pp. 364–67.

26. ODY to Charles A. Coffin 11/1/16.

27. ODY to JEY 2/4, 3/31/16. The *Times Herald* gave "Major General Young" quite a boost in salary, which, at this time, was $36,000; his total (gross) income was $47,315.

28. ODY to Coffin 11/1/16.

29. ODY to H. H. Adams 4/17/16.

30. ODY to Gordon Abbott 11/23/16.

31. ODY to J. F. Strickland 3/12/17.

32. ODY to Tom Finty (of the *Dallas News*) 3/15/17.

33. ODY to Tom Camp 3/15/17. The "Dallas Public Utility at Cost Franchise" became something of a model, and not for the moment only. Two years later, for example, a request for a copy came from E. N. Hurley, who had succeeded Davies as head of the Federal Trade Commission and was now chairman of the U.S. Shipping Board (ODY to Hurley 3/24/19).

34. ODY to Jeanette Belo Peabody 4/9/17.

35. ODY to JEY 10/18/17.

36. ODY to Coffin 12/19/17.

37. GE Annual Report 1897.

38. GE Annual Report 1901.

39. ODY to Maurice Oudin 8/7/14.
40. ODY to J. R. Geary 7/7/14.
41. ODY to Thomas Thacher 3/10/15.
42. ODY to H. A. Toulmin, Jr., 3/24/17.
43. ODY to Thomas Nelson Perkins 12/1/16.
44. ODY to E. W. Rice, Jr., 1/2/17.
45. Perkins to ODY 10/1/17.
46. ODY to Perkins 2/27/18. This letter was sent to Perkins at the War Department, but was returned undelivered, and ODY perhaps thought the time for it was past; but the tone and sentiments remain valid, and indicative of their relationship.

CHAPTER *10. The Yanks Are Coming:
Crusade and Its Aftermath*

1. ODY to K. M. Spende 9/14/16.
2. ODY to Thomas Chadbourne 10/25/16.
3. To Newton D. Baker and Josephus Daniels 2/5/17.
4. ODY to Goodwyn Rhett 5/28/17.
5. ODY to J. W. Kirkland 7/3/17.
6. ODY to Hugh S. Johnson 5/24/18.
7. ODY to Mrs. V. P. Starin 4/20/17; ODY to E. W. Rice, Jr., 4/26/17.
8. ODY to E. A. Filene 5/26/17.
9. ODY to E. N. Hurley 7/24/17. In this letter ODY also regretted the "want of personal accommodation between Mr. Denman and General Goethals." Goethals, the builder of the Panama Canal, had been put in charge of a program of shipbuilding. The idea at first was to build wooden ships; this was soon abandoned, but he and Denman were able to agree on nothing.
10. W. G. McAdoo, *Crowded Years* (Boston: Houghton Mifflin, 1931).
11. Thomas Nelson Perkins in interview with HBR c. 1926, HBR notes.
12. ODY to A. J. Stevens, vice-president of Barney and Smith Car Company, Dayton, Ohio, 8/11/16.
13. ODY to Paul Cravath 7/20/17.
14. ODY to JEY 10/18/17.
15. CJY to ODY n.d. (Probably late April 1918.)
16. ODY to CJY 5/3/18.
17. *The Autobiography of Lincoln Steffens* (New York: Harcourt, Brace, 1931), p. 584.
18. Ida M. Tarbell memo of interview with ODY, n.d. Tarbell Papers, Reis Library, Allegheny College, Meadville, Pa.
19. ODY to Henry Bradlee 3/24/14.

CHAPTER *11. Wireless versus Cables:*
Creation of RCA

1. ODY to Frank B. Kellogg 1/4/21.

2. Printed copies of ODY's testimony at the 1921 and 1929 Senate committee hearings are in the ODY Papers, Radio files, Boxes 117 and 120 respectively.

3. Erik Barnouw, *A History of Broadcasting in the United States,* vol. I: *A Tower in Babel* (New York: Oxford University Press, 1966), chapter 1.

4. Charles Neave to ODY 5/14/15; A. G. Davis to Neave 5/4/15; ODY to Davis 5/5/15; ODY to E. W. Rice, Jr., 5/28/15: ODY Papers, BCB and Radio, Box 71. ODY's first reference to Marconi occurs in a letter to A. G. Davis 2/10/13: "I have yours of the 5th regarding the Marconi–J. G. White & Co. agreement. Perhaps we can discuss the matter when you are down next time." The Marconi Wireless Telegraph Company Ltd. was founded and financed by the British in 1897; some five years later it established American Marconi, a subsidiary which apparently enjoyed considerable autonomy. Nevertheless, though its officers and directors were largely American, it was widely regarded—not least by the navy—as ultimately subject to British control.

5. 1921 Hearings on Cable Landing Licenses, subcommittee of Senate Interstate Commerce Committee; ODY's statement, pp. 331–33. See also for these and related developments John Winthrop Hammond, *Men and Volts: The Story of General Electric* (Philadelphia: Lippincott, 1941), pp. 372–74; Barnouw, pp. 47–52. Barnouw's account draws heavily on the *History of Communications: Electronics in the U.S. Navy* (Washington: Government Printing Office, 1963).

6. For this directive, signed by Franklin D. Roosevelt as assistant navy secretary, see Barnouw, p. 47, and G. L. Archer, *History of Radio to 1926* (New York: American Historical Society, 1938), p. 138.

7. Barnouw, pp. 53–55. For Secretary Daniels and his hopes for a government monopoly of wireless, see 1921 Hearings, ODY statement, pp. 334–35.

8. Hammond, pp. 375–77. Like Marconi, the navy had always wanted an exclusive contract; see E. P. Edwards to Anson Burchard 6/26/18, copy in ODY Papers, Radio, Box 75.

9. Davis to ODY 6/30/19, Radio, Box 75. Cf. 1921 Hearings, ODY's statement, pp. 332–33.

10. Davis to ODY 6/30/19, Radio, Box 75.

11. ODY to Davis 3/26/19. Pratt's draft was dated 3/27; for its signing and mailing see J. W. Elwood to Francis Pratt 3/29, copy in BCB.

12. ODY to Franklin D. Roosevelt 3/29/19, BCB and Box 75.

13. Roosevelt to ODY 4/4/19. The original is filed in ODY's Special Papers #1.

14. BCB.

15. ODY to Roosevelt 4/9/19, BCB.

16. Radio, Box 75.

17. Kenneth Davis, in his *FDR: The Beckoning of Destiny* (New York: Putnam, 1972), p. 575, has a simpler answer: "Young was easily persuaded: such a company—presumably exempt from the anti-trust laws, since the government itself had proposed it—would have a huge profit potential." This is a gross oversimplification, if not distortion, of Tarbell's account, the one source which Davis cites. That consideration of profit affects, when it does not dictate, business decisions is axiomatic; had it been the *dominant* factor in this decision, one wonders whether GE—or ODY—would so readily have exchanged the immediate and substantial profits assured by the Marconi deal for the labors and risks attendant upon creating, financing and developing a new communications company. As ODY himself observed, it was not the practice of General Electric to enter into competition with its customers.

18. This circumstantial account, as set down in Archer, p. 163n, was based on a 1938 interview with ODY. Archer is reliable enough in reporting the facts; it is his editorializing which is off-putting. See Ray Stannard Baker, *World War and World Settlement: Original Documents of the Peace Conference* (Gloucester, Mass.: Peter Smith, 1960), III, 425–28 ff., for messages directing the President's attention to wireless and its importance to the United States and to the League of Nations.

19. See ODY's testimony before the Senate Committee on Interstate Commerce, 12/9, 12/10/29. See also Admiral Cary Grayson's supporting testimony of 12/10, quoted in Archer, pp. 153–54. This whole episode is treated in context below, Chapter 25.

20. Davis to ODY 6/30/19, Radio, Box 75; 1921 Hearings, ODY statement, pp. 334–35.

21. Davis to ODY 6/30/19, Radio, Box 75; 1921 Hearings, ODY statement, pp. 334–35. Navy officials, including Roosevelt and Bullard, had made it clear that their cooperation was dependent on assurance of clear-cut American control of the new radio company (Kenneth Davis, p. 575; Frank Freidel, *Franklin D. Roosevelt*, vol. II: *The Ordeal* [Boston: Little, Brown, 1954], p. 28). Thus purchase by GE of British Marconi's large stock interest in American Marconi was imperative; according to A. G. Davis, this would reduce foreign holdings to 20 percent (undated Tarbell interview with Davis, c. 1930, Tarbell Papers, Reis Library, Allegheny College, Meadville, Pa.).

22. Davis to ODY 6/30/19, Radio, Box 75; 1921 Hearings, ODY statement, pp. 334–35. See also, re the attorney general, Sam Fordyce to ODY 5/20/20 (and below, Chapter 13), Radio, Box 95.

23. Barnouw, pp. 91–96. The ODY Papers have considerable data bearing on this chaos.

24. Barnouw, pp. 58, 59.

25. A. G. Davis headed this supporting cast; attorneys like Neave and Joseph P. Cotton were important to the later contracts, especially with

AT&T. Yeoman service was also rendered by ODY's assistants, A. W. Morton and (especially) John W. Elwood.

26. Burchard to ODY 5/17/19, Radio, Box 72. These files also contain ODY's penciled notes.

27. A lengthy memo of the Nally conversation, dated 5/14/19 and prepared by Elwood, is in Radio, Box 72, which also contains copy of Davis's penetrating analysis of American Marconi's patents and net worth.

28. Elwood memo of 5/14/19, Radio, Box 72.

29. ODY memo of 5/14/19, Radio, Box 72.

30. Elwood memo of 6/2/19, Radio, Box 72; draft of proposed contract with the navy dated 5/3/19 is in Box 75.

31. Elwood memo of 6/2/19, Radio, Box 72.

32. Davis to ODY 6/17/19, Radio, Box 72. Copies of Edwards's and C. E. Patterson's reports are in the same file.

33. ODY memo of 6/30/19, Radio, Box 72.

34. For this draft agreement, see Radio, Box 72.

35. The opinion was Cotton's; for copy see Radio, Box 72.

36. The amended $5 par for the Radio preferred equaled par for American Marconi, thus facilitating the proposed share-for-share exchange. As for the no-par common, such issues were prohibited in New Jersey—one reason for the new company's incorporation in Delaware.

37. Copy in Radio, Box 72.

38. Ibid., which contains copies of all cables exchanged.

39. Ibid., for records of preparations for the vote and its outcome.

40. Ibid.

41. Ibid. For attitude of U.S. government toward foreign control, see John W. Elwood to L.F.H. Betts 8/19/19, ODY to Davis 8/22/19; for British Marconi's South America proposal, see Davis to ODY 8/21/19.

42. Radio, Box 72, for copies of contracts. Purchase of British Marconi's 364,826 shares of American Marconi raised GE's stake in RCA to 600,000 preferred and 2,364,826 common.

43. ODY to Burchard 9/2/19, Radio, Box 72.

44. ODY to Davis 9/3, 9/16/19, Radio, Box 72.

45. Radio, Box 72. For minutes of the board meeting of that date, see Box 93.

46. The correspondence relating thereto—on motion of counsel to the committee—was made part of the record of the Senate Interstate Commerce Committee's 1929 Hearings; see p. 95 of the printed extract covering testimony of ODY and other RCA officials. If, as one might expect, ODY's Radio files contain the original letter nominating Bullard, submitted by Thomas Washington as acting secretary of the navy for the President's approval and countersigned by him, we have been unable to find it.

47. Federal Trade Commission, *Report on the Radio Industry*, 12/1/23 (Washington: Government Printing Office), p. 36.

CHAPTER *12. Public Business: A Bill of Rights for Labor*

1. Henry F. Pringle, *Life and Times of William Howard Taft* (New York: Farrar and Rinehart, 1939), II, 915–19. Pringle's account, based largely on Taft's letters, cites also the Bureau of Labor Statistics, Bulletin 287: "The National War Labor Board," especially p. 52.

2. Pringle, II, 919–24.

3. Ibid., pp. 917–18. As the supposedly conservative co-chairman—the other being the liberal attorney Frank P. Walsh—ex-President Taft had to "read the riot act" to the employers, who were "shocked and scandalized" at his stance. That the code was hailed by labor—with whom Taft found himself enjoying "curiously agreeable relations"—owed much to the scandalized shock he had experienced on being exposed to conditions in the southern textile and munition plants; his consequent conversion made him, as Walsh delightedly observed, "the most radical member of the . . . Board." According to Wilfred Sheed, "Whatever Happened to the Labor Movement?" (*Atlantic*, 7/1973), "Wilson's War Labor Board set the style for the New Deal."

4. Pringle, II, 919, 924–25; Irving Bernstein, *The Lean Years: A History of the American Worker, 1920–1933* (Boston: Houghton Mifflin, 1960), pp. 157–89.

5. ODY to Judge J. M. Woodward 1/6/19, breaking dinner engagement for the following evening. The War Labor Board, not yet liquidated, had called a hearing for Wednesday, 1/8/19, and ODY intended to be fully prepared. Pringle, II, 921–22, provides an illuminating glimpse of the immediate backdrop. When, during the previous summer, the board was completing protracted hearings on complaints from the Schenectady workers, Taft, it seems, had been responsible for an award of higher wages to the uncomplaining scrubwomen as well as to the others. He had noticed their low earnings but when he called their plight to Walsh's attention, the latter replied that the board lacked jurisdiction because these women had filed no complaint. Nevertheless, at Taft's insistence, they were given a break, and "the General Electric Company made no protest. A tendency toward illegality," Pringle concludes, "was growing in Taft."

6. Ida M. Tarbell, *Owen D. Young: A New Type of Industrial Leader* (New York: Macmillan, 1932), pp. 125–26. Elwood's report was among the files ODY consigned to Schenectady when he retired; it was subsequently (like so many other records) lost or destroyed. Happily, Miss Tarbell saw the original; so, at about the same time, did ENC, who also reviewed with Elwood the nature and scope of his mission. It did not, in ENC's judgment, reflect any conscious effort by organized labor to take the initiative, but rather ODY's conviction that managerial initiatives should take full account of the concerns and aspirations of the workers.

7. "GE & Labor Relations" in ODY Papers has unsigned copies of both versions of this report; the file of which they are a part identifies the

author, Atherton Brownell, for whose *vita* and credentials see *Who Was Who*, vol. I.

8. *Report of (Second) Industrial Conference* (51 pp.) 3/6/20; copy in ODY Papers, Conference files. See also below, Chapter 20, for ODY's 1923 interview with Brownell and its bearing on his 1927 speech at the Harvard Business School.

9. Tarbell, pp. 126–28. ENC assisted at this Tarbell interview with ODY but cannot date it.

10. See Bernstein, pp. 157–89.

11. Ibid., pp. 159–68, which cite Mackenzie King's special study and recommendations for GE (primarily at Lynn).

12. Ibid., pp. 162–68; Haggai Hurvitz, "The Meaning of Industrial Conflict in Some Ideologies of the Early 1920s: The AFL, Organized Employers and Herbert Hoover" (Ph.D. dissertation, Columbia University, 1971), pp. 245–48.

13. Margaret L. Coit, *Mr. Baruch* (Boston: Houghton Mifflin, 1957), p. 304.

14. Hurvitz, p. 7; see also Coit, p. 304.

15. Hurvitz, pp. 8–9; Samuel Eliot Morison, *Oxford History of the American People* (New York: Oxford University Press, 1965), p. 882. Wilson set out on 9/4; his thrombosis occurred at Pueblo on the night of 9/25. Governor Calvin Coolidge's statement is quoted in Morison, p. 885, which also cites his nomination for vice-president on the 1920 Republican ticket.

16. Hurvitz, pp. 27, 31–34; Coit, pp. 304–309. The First National Industrial Conference papers, chief source of these accounts, are in the Department of Labor Records (Record Group 174), National Archives, Washington. For an amusing account of Ida Tarbell's first meeting with Rockefeller, see William Allen White's *Autobiography* (New York: Macmillan, 1946), pp. 578–79.

17. John W. Elwood to E. J. Nally, ODY Papers, (First) Industrial Conference files (a fragmentary record); Hurvitz, pp. 31–33. For the dinner with Lane, see ODY Papers, loc. cit., H. H. Adams to Elwood 9/13/19.

18. Coit, pp. 307–308. ODY's hopes of moving the employers to a more defensible position are embodied in a typed memorandum, undated and unsigned, which was deposited among his other papers relating to the first conference. It may have been prompted by a front-page box in the *Washington Star* for 10/17/19 contrasting the respective stand of labor and the public groups with that of management. Aware that for most employers, the sticking point was dealing with a union as a force outside the plant, ODY was still striving to enlarge the room for compromise. "In the existing situation," his memo began,

would it not be wise—

First, to separate the questions in the pending resolution before the house into several parts and see if the Conference cannot agree to some of them and refer back the remainder to the Committee of Fifteen. [Five chosen by each group.]

For example, accepting Mr. James's suggestion, could not the Conference agree

1. That the right of employers and employees to bargain collectively is recognized.
2. That the right of employees to representation is recognized. Then refer the remainder back to the Committee.

I submit that this program has the advantage of recording the Conference, and particularly the employers group, in favor of collective bargaining, which is very important and, second, it records them in favor of representation which is also important.

If the Conference splits on the question of whether representatives shall be chosen inside or outside of the plant and employers vote against that proposition, it will not be a serious matter.

19. (First) Industrial Conference files. See NYT and the press generally of 10/21/19 for the story as published.

20. (First) Industrial Conference files.

21. Ibid. On 11/5/19, in response to an expression of confidence from his friend S. R. Bertron, ODY wrote: "The Industrial Conference broke up before I had an opportunity to demonstrate my unfitness. If I always could be so fortunate as this I would gain a reputation great enough to please such an ardent and charitable friend as you." The President's letter and copy of ODY's reply are in a special scrapbook, ODY Papers.

22. Not in ODY's letter-press copybooks, a copy of this letter to Coffin was sent to him in 1953 by his former assistant, John Elwood; his letter and the copy are filed with "GE & Labor," 1919, and also in Special Papers #1.

23. See note 21.

24. *Report of (Second) Industrial Conference*, 3/6/20; copy in files.

25. Ibid. A summary of the plan for prevention of disputes is on pp. 9–12; for their adjustment, pp. 13–14. For proposed treatment of public employees, see pp. 27–28, 41–44.

26. Former Attorney General Gregory, quoted by Tarbell, p. 141. Miss Tarbell, herself a member of the first conference, knew him well.

27. For the extent to which individual views were modified to achieve a unanimous report and the importance of such a consensus, see ODY to F. S. Hunting 3/20/20, also ODY to E. K. Hall and Julius Henry Cohen 3/29/20. The exception cited is noted on pp. 26–27 of the report.

28. ODY to Philip H. Gadsden 1/2/20.

29. Industrial Conference files.

30. Ibid. In extending in the drafting committee's behalf a unanimous invitation to Professor Henry R. Seager to attend the final session and lend his aid, ODY drew special attention to the committee's responsibility for "suggesting certain paragraphs . . . which are highly controversial . . . like the one on Collective Bargaining . . . and we need your assistance in presenting them to the Conference" (ODY to Seager 2/26/20). Of the outcome, Hurvitz writes (p. 175), "In its endorsement of collective bargaining as the *only* kind fair to employees, the Second Conference went even further than the Public Group had in the First. . . ."

31. Hurvitz, p. 222; see also, as cited by Hurvitz, AFL *Proceedings* 1920.

32. Copy of the report of the Bituminous Coal Commission is in Box 9. Hurvitz notes (p. 109) that the commission accepted the principle of a "living wage."

33. Hurvitz, p. 106. See also, for the content and consonance of Hoover's aims and those of AFL leaders, pp. 160–61, 190–92, 312–17.

34. Franklin D. Roosevelt to Hugh Gibson 1/20/20, cited in Frank Freidel, *Franklin D. Roosevelt*, vol. II: *The Ordeal* (Boston: Little, Brown, 1954), p. 57; ODY to Ralph Arnold of L.A. 2/25/20; ODY to Henry M. Robinson 6/21/20. For other Democrats supporting Hoover, see R. S. Baker, *American Chronicle* (New York: Scribner's, 1945), pp. 476–78; K. S. Davis, *FDR: The Beckoning of Destiny* (New York: Putnam, 1972), p. 609; Alpheus T. Mason, *Brandeis: A Free Man's Life* (New York: Viking, 1946), p. 530; Louis B. Wehle, *Hidden Threads of History: Wilson through Roosevelt* (New York: Macmillan, 1953), pp. 81–85. Wehle's proposed Democratic slate was Hoover and FDR.

35. Lane's resignation (see his *Letters* [Boston: Houghton Mifflin, 1922], pp. 337–38) was cleared 1/5/20 with Admiral Cary T. Grayson and tendered 2/5/20, to take effect 3/1. ODY's coded telegrams to Miller (copies in ODY Papers, Robinson folders) were dated 2/6/20.

36. Tarbell, pp. 142–45. ODY in turn paid high tribute to Secretary Wilson's services as chairman: ODY to R. W. Babson 2/25/20.

37. See note 18.

38. Hurvitz, pp. 175, 247, 248.

39. Tarbell, p. 147.

40. ODY at Boston University Law School commencement 6/1896, Speeches; *Report of (Second) Industrial Conference*, p. 30 (in the drafting of which ODY played a major part).

41. See Hurvitz's comments (pp. 32–33) on ODY as adviser to the employers' group, first conference: "a most progressive employer who sought ways for rapprochement between management and the AFL, provided the unions positively assumed the responsibility for higher productivity and maintenance of contracts." David Burner, in *Herbert Hoover: A Public Life* (New York: Knopf, 1979), p. 143, quotes an unidentified observer to the effect that "Hoover was perhaps the 'foremost' figure in the meetings." He also quotes an unidentified participant as remarking that Hoover and Young were "for pretty sweeping reforms" and, in chapter 8, note 10, rightly cites Hurvitz as "an important source for the conference."

CHAPTER *13. RCA: A Peacetime Patent Pool*

1. Hearings on S–6: U.S. Senate Committee on Interstate Commerce, 71st Cong., 2nd Session, 12/29 et seq., testimony of Captain S. C. Hooper. Copy of his letter, as signed by Admiral Hepburn, is in Radio, Box 95.

2. Federal Trade Commission, *Report on the Radio Industry*, 12/1/23, (Washington: Government Printing Office), p. 25.

3. See A. G. Davis to S. C. Hooper 12/29/19, citing Secretary Daniels's statement on the lapse of his wartime power to execute contracts (e.g., with new radio company). Davis "respectfully requests" withdrawal of recent naval *order* in favor of a less peremptory approach: Radio, Box 72.

4. Radio, Box 95. The Swope (Folk) memorandum—of which Swope admitted authorship in sending a copy to ODY 2/28/20—suggested that AT&T and GE collaborate in forming a new wireless company on substantially equal terms. For GE's several bids to recruit Swope see David Loth, *Swope of GE* (New York: Simon & Schuster, 1958), pp. 63–64, 78–79, 93–94.

5. The ODY Papers contain no written account of these initial conferences with Thayer. What was achieved can only be inferred from the first draft agreements prepared by the lawyers—e.g., by Charles Neave and A. G. Davis as forwarded to ODY in Washington by John W. Elwood and A. W. Morton 2/11/20. See copies of draft and letter in Radio, Box 95.

6. BCB: John W. Elwood to H. M. Francis (Ebasco) 1/10/20, to Bankers Trust 1/17/20, to RCA 1/17 and 1/21/20.

7. Charles Neave to A. G. Davis 1/24/20, Radio, Box 95.

8. Radio, Box 95.

9. Davis to ODY 4/15/20; George E. Folk to ODY and Neave to ODY 4/16/20: Radio, Box 95.

10. On 2/26 ODY had written to congratulate Admiral Benson and the country on his willingness to take on this job (PCB). Benson had been at the Paris conference with Secretary Daniels and President Wilson; Henry Robinson had previously served as commissioner of the Shipping Board.

11. See David Sarnoff to E. J. Nally, acknowledged by Nally, 11/9/16; also Sarnoff to ODY 1/30/20 and to E. W. Rice, Jr., 3/3/20, as cited at length in G. L. Archer, *History of Radio to 1926* (New York: American Historical Society, 1938), pp. 112–13, 189, and more concisely in Erik Barnouw, *A History of Broadcasting in the United States*, vol. I: *A Tower in Babel* (New York: Oxford University Press, 1966), pp. 78–80.

12. Ernst Alexanderson to Davis 4/12/20; Davis to Neave 5/4/20; Davis to Rice 5/13/20; Nally to ODY 5/7/20: Radio, Box 95.

13. Harry B. Thayer to ODY 5/5/20, Radio, Box 95.

14. Thayer to Neave 5/21/20, Radio, Box 95. See also note 15.

15. Davis to Rice 5/13/20, Radio, Box 95.

16. Elwood to W. W. Trench 6/4/20, indicating 5/28 as date of the GE meeting; the RCA board approved on 5/19/20: Radio, Boxes 95 and 93.

17. Davis to ODY 5/29/20, Radio, Box 95.

18. ODY to Herbert Hoover 6/19/20; ODY to H. M. Robinson 6/21/20, BCB.

19. ODY to Franklin D. Roosevelt 7/13/20, PCB. His note of congratulation to Coolidge, written "as a member of the Democratic Party," was sent just after the election.

20. PCB and General Motors files.

21. For GM's problems as here recounted, see Alfred P. Sloan, Jr., *My Years with General Motors* (Garden City, N.Y.: Doubleday and Company,

1964), especially pp. 25–45; cited fluctuations in GM stock and the Dow-Jones industrial average are charted on p. 41. A notably illuminating account of GM's organizational and administrative problems at this juncture appears in Alfred D. Chandler, *Strategy and Structure* (Cambridge: MIT Press, 1962), chapter 3.

22. Davis to ODY 6/9/20, Radio, Box 95; ODY to Newcomb Carlton, 9/13/20 (RCB); ODY to Carlton 10/21 and 10/30/20 (BCB). Although a traffic agreement of sorts was negotiated with AT&T and actually executed on 9/9/20, RCA did not pretend to find it satisfactory and copy of Carlton's letter of 9/9/20 to ODY was forwarded to Thayer at his direction on 9/18/20. Six weeks later, on 11/4/20, ODY told the RCA board of his ongoing negotiations with Western Union, which proved in the end futile. Radio, Boxes 113 and 93.

23. ODY to Jesse Lovejoy 9/22/19, BCB; GE Annual Report for 1921; see also Barnouw, p. 29n and pp. 72–73. A record of ODY's negotiations with United Fruit, chiefly through their George S. Davis, is in Radio, Box 85.

24. Sam Fordyce to ODY 5/20/20. The memo of the meeting with the attorney general is dated 5/12. Radio, Box 95.

25. E.g., Thayer to ODY 7/19/20; ODY to Thayer 7/21/20 (#1): Radio, Box 95.

26. ODY to Thayer 7/21/20 (#2). The RCA board formally approved stock issue as per this agreement on 8/18/20. Radio, Boxes 95 and 93.

27. ODY to Davis 7/9 and 8/4/20, Radio, Box 95.

28. Radio, Box 95; also Box 93 for minutes of RCA board meetings of 11/4/20 and 2/18/21. On 2/19/21, GE agreed to buy a half interest in Wireless Specialty for $248,000. Execution of the United Fruit agreements took place on 3/7/21 when their George S. Davis became an RCA director.

29. Minutes of RCA Technical Committee meeting 8/25/20, in Radio box so marked.

30. Barnouw, p. 65; Archer, pp. 193–96. Those who remember their Aesop will recall that the lion took *all* as his share.

31. ODY to Guy Tripp 9/2/20 (unsent), Radio, Box 114.

32. Barnouw, pp. 65–66; minutes of RCA board 10/20/20, Radio, Box 93.

33. For GE see William White, "Reminiscences," p. 19, 1951 (unpublished); W.R.G. Baker, "Reminiscences," p. 12, 1950 (unpublished). Cited by Barnouw, pp. 73–74, who also cites the effect on Sarnoff.

34. Godfrey Isaacs to ODY 11/27/20; James R. Sheffield to ODY 11/27/20: Radio, Box 72. See also minutes of RCA board 9/9, 9/15 and 12/1/20 (Box 93). Reasons for the delay included unsolved engineering as well as legal and financial problems.

35. ODY to Walter S. Rogers 11/17/20, RCB.

36. As the transcript of this testimony became available, Elwood and Neave saw to its strategic distribution, one of the first copies going to the new secretary of commerce, Herbert Hoover, to whom Neave also wrote at length. Somewhat later Gerard Swope sent copies to all key officials of IGE. Radio, Box 117.

37. ODY to Isaacs 1/24/21; Isaacs to Nally 12/27/20 (copy to ODY with

Nally's letter of 12/29) had indicated that the French and Germans were favorably disposed. On 1/19/21 the RCA board had empowered Nally et al. to negotiate, *provided* present RCA–British Marconi contract was fully respected. Radio, Box 93.

38. See, e.g., State Department report of 1/7/16, re Washington conference on radio, at which the "American Republics" agreed that "ownership and control of this vitally important means of communication between the American continents should . . . not . . . fall under non-American jurisdiction." (For reference to same, see Box 99.) Certain RCA directors, notably John W. Griggs and A. G. Davis, were even questioning whether Pan-American was not long since legally defunct, in accordance with a clause which voided its charter at any time that more than three-eighths of its stock was to be owned by foreign interests. See RCA board minutes 2/18/20 et seq., Box 93.

39. ODY did sit in on their meeting of 12/14/20, and wrote E. M. Herr occasional letters. In the meantime, at RCA's board meeting of 11/4/20, Young appointed Griggs and Walter S. Gifford (vice-president of AT&T) to investigate and report on the best new manufacturing arrangements, with Westinghouse included. Radio, Box 93.

40. ODY to Tripp, 9/2/20 (unsent), Radio, Box 114.

41. For Secretary Daniels's position, see his *Annual Report* published in the autumn of 1919. Regarding wireless, Daniels wrote: "The Government must be in exclusive control or it must make it a monopoly in private hands. No other plan, no divided authority, is thinkable in war. No other plan guarantees the greatest success in peace." Cf. ODY's letter of 11/17/20 to W. S. Rogers; also his testimony of 1/11/21 to the Kellogg committee in which he pointed out that if foreign companies or governments could play off competing American stations against each other, the controlling voice inevitably passed from American to foreign interests.

42. Davis to Rice 12/8/20; in his letters of 1/7/21 and 2/28/21 to ODY, however, Davis readily conceded the value of the Armstrong patents. Radio, Box 114.

43. Sarnoff agreed, however, to "interim" arrangements making GE and Westinghouse selling agents for RCA in dealing with their own customers; Alexanderson to Davis 5/21/21; Davis to Alexanderson 5/31/21; Rice to Davis 12/7/20: Radio, Box 114. After three to five years, in Rice's view, RCA might well assume all radio manufacturing, engineering and research functions.

44. Radio, Box 114.

45. The clearest account of the respective investments of Given and Westinghouse in the International Company as reconstituted is in Archer, pp. 193 ff. When the agreements were finally delivered, Tripp wrote ODY 8/10/21, enclosing the International Company's request that half of the RCA stock be issued direct to them or their nominees. Westinghouse must presumably have been their nominee (for what consideration?), because all subsequent listings indicate that one million shares of both common and preferred were *owned* by Westinghouse. For the allocation of RCA stock among its corporate owners, see Barnouw, p. 73.

46. This was handled largely by Davis, Neave and Cotton, in consultation with Rice and (when he was not abroad) with Nally. For pertinent data, see Radio, Box 114.

47. To the RCA board, meeting on 3/18/21, Nally reported on his European trip and new agreements re South America (Radio, Box 93). See also Nally to ODY 2/8/21 (from London); and copies of agreements of 2/10/21 with British Marconi, of 2/21/21 with Telefunken, and of 2/26/21 with the French companies (Radio, Boxes 99 and 118).

48. For Pacific Cables' and All American Cables' plans to lay new lines, see G. I. Kinney to Gerard Swope 5/17/20. (Kinney was chairman of the Cable and Radio Committee of the San Francisco Foreign Trade Club.) Letter refers also to Pacific Commercial Cables' plans and hails "return of the Marconi radio stations to private control," but asserts "there still remains the necessity for a very substantial increase in communication facilities to trans-Pacific territory." In his 9/29/20 letter to Nally, Sarnoff quotes from Trade Commissioner Paul P. Witham's report on transpacific communications, urging American initiative re China wireless service. Copies of both letters but not of the report are in Radio, Box 124.

49. See Radio, Box 124, for copies of correspondence with Fleischhacker, Schwerin, GE's Geary and Nippon Radio Telephone and Telegraph officials.

50. ODY to the authors, on several (undated) occasions. His first "Dear Gerard" letter was dated 3/7/21.

51. BCB for 3/1921 (as indexed). The Hoover correspondence is in a file so identified; engagements canceled included those with Stettinius and Thomas Cochran of Morgan's, A. C. Bedford of Jersey Standard, and meetings of the International Chamber of Commerce.

52. Joseph Cotton to General Electric Company 8/1/21; Davis to F. P. Fish 3/28/20: Radio, Box 114. The GE board approved "the arrangement" at its May meeting.

CHAPTER *14. International Dimensions: The Orient and Paris*

1. ODY to Josephine Young 3/31/21.

2. ODY to IBY 4/28/19.

3. ODY to Hale Mixer 4/28/19.

4. ODY to Frank Oliver Hall 12/16/18. ODY wrote George F. Baker, Jr., whose grandfather had laid the cornerstone of the first building at St. Lawrence, a long letter about the college and its needs: "I want this letter to be impersonal . . . because the last thing that I should want to do would be to presume upon my personal acquaintance with you." Some years later the university received a generous gift from George F. Baker, Sr.

5. Griffiths showed them his college, which—Owen wrote Jo—was most attractive; "Did you know that Bertram Goodhue was making a permanent plan for the School?"

6. The letters from ODY to JEY, from which the quotations in this chapter are taken, are dated as follows (all 1921): S.S. *Ecuador* 4/21; Fujiya Hotel, Miyanoshima, 4/30; Imperial Hotel, Tokyo, 5/3; same, 5/11; Miyako Hotel, Kyoto, 5/16; San Yo Hotel, Shimonoseki, 5/19; Grand Hotel de Pékin, 5/30; Shanghai Club, Shanghai, 6/5.

7. The *Brooklyn Eagle*, one of the best papers in the New York area, was the property of the Gunnison family of St. Lawrence. The interview with ODY appeared 8/7/21, and was reprinted in the upstate *Watertown Times* 8/9.

8. Japan's "rights" were confirmed at Versailles, which aroused a good deal of anti-Japanese feeling in the United States. It was not until some months after ODY's visit that, at the Washington Conference on world disarmament, an agreement was made for a return of most of the area to its proper owner.

9. *Brooklyn Eagle* 8/7/21.

10. In Peking Young and Swope had bought jointly a collection of blue-and-white antique porcelain, which, when it arrived in New York, Jo Young and Mary Swope divided, by alternate choices, on an evening of reminiscence and storytelling. That accounted for Owen's "spending all [his] money." Jo was never to see the Orient, and Owen never returned there. But a decade later their daughter and her husband, just married, were told in no uncertain terms by ODY that their invitation to join the Shanghai Conference of the Institute of Pacific Relations was on no account to be turned down. Hence the authors of this biography were able in 1931 to retrace many of the steps here recorded and to experience together the beauty of Peking.

11. *Brooklyn Eagle* 8/7/21.

12. ODY to Samuel Stow 7/18/21; ODY to Philo Parker 7/18/21.

13. ODY to Louise Powis Brown 7/18/21.

14. *Brooklyn Eagle* 8/7/21.

15. Godfrey Isaacs to E. J. Nally 7/12/21, reported to ODY on his return. See, for its background, RCA board's minutes, 4/15 to 6/30/21, Radio, Box 93.

16. Radio, Box 72.

17. For example, G. L. Archer (*History of Radio to 1926* [New York: American Historical Society, 1938]) seems to see ODY, if not quite as a Protestant David felling a Jewish Goliath, then as a kind of Young Lochinvar come out of the West to foil the machinations of the wily scions of the Empire. Except as otherwise noted, however, our account of the conference does draw heavily on his *facts*, as recorded in his chapter 14. For a concise and admirably documented version of this and subsequent efforts to achieve international cooperation in wireless development, see Michael Hogan, *Informal Entente: The Private Structure of Cooperation in Anglo-American Diplomacy, 1918–1928* (Columbia: University of Missouri Press, 1977), chapter 7.

18. ODY to Dr. Takuma Dan 12/12/21; ODY to Edwin Denby 12/22/21.

19. ODY to Elihu Root 1/9, 1/25/22.

20. ODY to Admiral William Bullard 3/6/22.

21. ODY's speech at Rocky Point appeared in the *Wireless Age* 12/1921; copy in ODY Papers, Speeches.

22. ODY to Herbert Hoover from Paris 9/13 and 9/15/21.

23. For this study and its outcome, see below, Chapter 15.

24. ODY on business arbitration (10/7/21); printed 10/15 by the International Chamber of Commerce as *Digest No. 3.* In his letter of 12/12/21 written in reply to a criticism that some definition of *moral* sanction should be made, he stated "that each country would have to define, impose and enforce its own moral sanction, which would be effective in that country— and there need not be necessarily any similarity in the character of the sanction imposed." ODY sent his daughter—then struggling with French in the ninth grade—a copy of the French translation of his talk: "This is just a sample of the facility with which I write French."

25. This too is treated further in Chapter 15.

26. For the role of Perkins's law partner, Roland Boyden, in enlisting ODY's efforts to settle the German reparations problem, see below, Chapter 16.

27. JEY to Josephine Young 3/22, 4/1 and 4/6/22, from Paris, Cannes and Avignon.

28. In his letter of 8/5/22 to W. G. McAdoo, ODY asserted that Coffin, by resigning while his faculties and influence were intact, was able to choose the entire new slate of officers and still, as a director, watch and judge their performance. Burchard, however, as the man who had brought Swope over from Western Electric, was not happy to be asked to step aside in his protégé's favor. Despite ODY's urging, he had remained abroad at the time of the meeting. On 3/9 and 3/11/22 ODY had wired Burchard in Paris of his own impending visit and arranged to see and brief him on the program. On 5/13 he wired that the program had the board's unanimous support and would be adopted at the meeting of 5/16, concluding his message with the words "regret exceedingly you are not here." On 5/16 ODY wired Burchard the full text of the board's press announcement of the new slate and on 5/28 sent a radiogram to his ship expressing the wish to see him "as early as possible after landing. Have not shown your messages to anyone because important first to discuss matter fully with you. So glad you are coming home." In the NYT for 5/17/22, Coffin, Young and Rice shared the headlines—in that order.

CHAPTER *15. GE: Young and Swope Find Room at the Top*

1. David Loth, *Swope of GE* (New York: Simon & Schuster, 1958), pp. 32–33, 37. Loth concludes that "Swope saw the business world essentially in the same light as most of his contemporaries who never entered Hull House." Perhaps, but only if one excludes his policies toward labor and assumes that "most" of his peers shared his sense of industry's obligations to the public.

2. ODY to GE Foremen's Association 2/14/23, Speeches.

3. International General Electric Company dinner for Anson W. Burchard, Schenectady, 7/26/22, Speeches.

4. Louis Brandeis, "Business a Profession," address at Brown University, 1910; R. H. Tawney's *Acquisitive Society* was a kind of bible for younger critics. For Swope's views see Loth, pp. 128–30.

5. See, e.g., ODY's remarks at GE Advertising Conference, Schenectady, 7/25/22 (Speeches), which hail this dependence on public confidence as something enlightened industry should welcome. See Chapter 20, below, for ODY's evolving concept of corporate management's new role as trustee for all parties at interest in industrial enterprise.

6. To these salaries there were added (for all save Rice) $25,000 in extra compensation, of which there had been none whatever in 1921—when, indeed, all basic salaries, beginning with Coffin's, had suffered a 15 to 20 percent cut. For both Young and Swope, therefore, the new totals added up to more than double their compensation for the year preceding, but the totals were not equal. Precisely how soon thereafter they became so, as they did, is no part of any record available to the authors, but it was within a very few years at most (Special [GE] Papers). Loth's only error here is his assertion that they "always" received the same amount.

7. Loth, pp. 139, 166. Cf. Alfred D. Chandler, *Strategy and Structure* (Cambridge: MIT Press, 1962), p. 9, for a suggestive rationale of this division of responsibility.

8. See note 5 above; also Loth, pp. 118–19, 144.

9. Loth, pp. 130–31. In its issue of 10/27/23 the NYT took editorial notice of Steinmetz's life and career, while his death was front-page news and his obituary filled several columns.

10. In the meantime, he had to put up with some flighty and highly romanticized versions of his life, about which his wife and mother taunted him unmercifully. He was the "Van Hornesville plowboy"—"plenty of them around these parts," sniffed his mother, while his wife pretended relief that at least he was not yet dubbed the "Van Hornesville playboy."

11. ODY to Pierre Jay 10/23/22.

12. Loth, pp. 116, 120.

13. Ibid., 121, 133.

14. ODY interview, B. S. Forbes, "Can You See Through Other Men's Eyes?" *American Magazine* 1/1923. The passages there "quoted" from ODY's remarks are the nearest thing to a text that the authors have discovered.

15. See note 2. GE's Annual Report for 1922—the first of the new regime— revealed that the *average* holding of its 28,155 stockholders was 62 shares.

16. ODY to W. G. McAdoo 11/9/23.

17. Loth, p. 118.

18. John Winthrop Hammond, *Men and Volts: The Story of General Electric* (Philadelphia: Lippincott, 1941), pp. 346–48.

19. Loth, p. 134. For an interesting discussion of the unions and "Taylorism"—which took its name from Frederick Taylor's "scientific" efforts to promote efficiency and eliminate waste—see Irving Bernstein, *The Lean*

Years: A History of the American Worker, 1920–1933 (Boston: Houghton Mifflin, 1960), pp. 102, 174.

20. ODY to ENC n.d. See also HBS case study of General Electric and Management Succession, 1942 (BP 411), p. 8; copy in the ODY Papers.

21. HBS case study, p. 8; Loth, pp. 154–56. See also GE Annual Reports for 1923–25.

22. ODY to ENC 1927. For the figures on employee subscriptions see GE Annual Reports for indicated years. Cf. Kim McQuaid, "Young, Swope and General Electric's New Capitalism, 1920–1933," in *American Journal of Economics and Sociology*, vol. XXXVI, no. 3 (7/1977); also his "Corporate Liberalism in the American Business Community, 1920–1940," in *Business History Review*, vol. LII, no. 3 (Autumn 1978).

23. Loth, p. 134.

24. Federal Trade Commission, *Report on the Radio Industry*, 12/1/23 (Washington: Government Printing Office), p. 37.

25. Ibid.; RCA Annual Report 1921, 1922, 1923. As reported by G. L. Archer, *History of Radio to 1926* (New York: American Historical Society, 1938), p. 189, and Erik Barnouw, *A History of Broadcasting in the United States*, vol. I: *A Tower in Babel* (New York: Oxford University Press, 1966), p. 79, 1923's sales equaled Sarnoff's early estimates; in 1922 and again in 1924 they exceeded his estimates.

26. Federal Trade Commission report, pp. 37–38. In its report the chapter following (pp. 39–50) contains an interesting discussion of patent rights and litigation.

27. This factor of technological obsolescence had much to do with ODY's earlier—and later—advice to the utilities that for rate-making purposes, the only sound base was *actual* investment rather than the frequently alluring cost of reproduction or even so-called prudent investment.

28. Barnouw, pp. 123–26; ODY to E. J. Nally 10/25/22.

29. Barnouw, pp. 123, 161; Archer, pp. 341 ff.

30. Federal Trade Commission report, pp. 1, 7, 10.

31. Ibid., p. 52.

32. Ibid., p. 69.

33. RCA Annual Report 1923.

34. Bernstein, especially chapter 2. For a brief account of the political and business scandals of the Harding administration, from which Coolidge emerged unscathed, see J. D. Hicks, *Republican Ascendancy* (New York: Harper & Row, 1960), pp. 74–77.

35. See ODY to Elihu Root 9/17/23. This letter of appreciation was sent at Hoover's prompting, Hoover having sought ODY's help in securing the grant. Carnegie was their obvious target, having recently financed the establishment of the National Bureau of Economic Research.

36. The committee's secretary, Edward Eyre Hunt, proved invaluable in a liaison capacity, as well as in taking care of the nitty-gritty. And ODY's assistant, Stuart Crocker, was helpful to him as well as to the chairman.

37. Aside from the economists he already knew—Edwin Seligman and

Henry R. Seager of Columbia, Frank W. Taussig and Charles J. Bullock, Edwin F. Gay and Wallace Donham of Harvard—ODY was meeting a host of others: Irving Fisher of Yale and Frank Fetter of Princeton, Alvin Hansen of Minnesota and Richard T. Ely of Wisconsin, Harold Moulton and Walter Stewart of Washington—the latter the director of the Federal Reserve Bank's division of analysis and research. With several of these, notably Stewart, Ely and Fisher, he was to develop warm and continuing relations; the group as a whole was sufficiently impressed with his stature to see to his subsequent election as a vice-president of the American Economic Association—an honor which he professed to prize as one always does "those that are least deserved."

38. "Business Cycles and Unemployment: Report and Recommendations of a Committee of the President's Conference on Unemployment." This appeared as a thirty-page Department of Commerce pamphlet (Washington: Government Printing Office, 3/1/23). The recommendations are summarized on p. 9. For its wide circulation and some of the comment it evoked, see the three cartons of data preserved in the ODY Papers. The hardcover edition, complete with the studies sponsored by the bureau, was published concurrently by McGraw-Hill.

39. "Arthur Bullard Interviews Owen D. Young: 'Will Prosperity Last?' " *Collier's Weekly* 5/19/23.

40. ODY to F. P. Cox 10/25/23. He had said much the same thing in his earlier letter to Root. On another occasion he questioned whether his own published warning had not been premature—the kind of question that inevitably haunts economic soothsayers.

41. The basic problem—how to increase circulation dramatically without compromising the standards which gave the *Post* its character—was of course not new; neither the associates (who included FDR) nor the editorial staff were able to solve it. For a full account see Herbert Heaton's admirable biography of Gay, *A Scholar in Action* (Cambridge: Harvard University Press, 1952).

42. Letters and press clippings are preserved in the ODY Papers. An especially moving account of John's fatal accident and its cause appeared in the *Hood River Glacier* 8/24/22.

43. Eleanor's great-grandfather, John Stebbins Lee, had been the first president of St. Lawrence; her grandfather, John Clarence Lee, was president from 1896 to 1899.

CHAPTER *16. The Dawes Plan: Adventure in Business Diplomacy*

1. For Dawes's nomination and election, see B. N. Timmons, *Portrait of an American* (New York: Henry Holt, 1953), pp. 228–30. William Jennings Bryan, an old friend of Dawes from their Nebraska days, covered the convention as a reporter; Timmons quotes him as saying that Dawes's nomination would give the Republicans "a Vice-presidential candidate who is abler than its Presidential candidate." Bryan's brother Charles, however, was later

named by the Democrats in a vain effort to balance the ticket headed by
John W. Davis. As for ODY, the several offices urged upon him editorially
ranged from that of police commissioner or mayor of New York City to the
presidency.

2. While this figure represented a considerable scaling down of earlier
Allied demands, it was still in large measure a sop to public sentiment in
the Allied countries. The A and B bonds, on which the Germans were expected to meet interest and amortization charges for thirty-six years, totaled
some 50 milliard marks; the C bonds, accounting for the rest, were held
in abeyance and in fact were never issued. Nevertheless, Germany's theoretical liability remained at 132 milliard marks—a convenient excuse for
paying nothing save under duress. Cf. Carl Bergmann, *History of Reparations* (Boston: Houghton Mifflin, 1927), especially pp. 76–77. This was the
author's translation of his *Weg der Reparation*, 1926. (N.B.: In European
usage, milliard=an American billion—i.e., 1,000 million.)

3. In Stephen Schuker's percipient phrase, "reparations . . . became the
vehicle for prolonging the Franco-German conflict," and so "took on a sym-
bolic significance that magnified . . . the economic and financial issues at
stake" (Stephen A. Schuker, *End of French Predominance in Europe*
[Chapel Hill: University of North Carolina Press, 1976], p. 6). See also
ibid., pp. 14, 15. Cf. James M. Hester, "America and the Weimar Republic
(Ph.D. dissertation, Oxford University, 1955), and Frank C. Costigliola,
"Politics of Financial Stabilization: American Reconstruction Policy in
Europe, 1924–1930" (Ph.D. dissertation, Cornell University, 1973); also
see Stuart M. Crocker, unpublished ms on the Dawes Committee and Plan
(Library of Congress, Manuscript Division; copy in ODY Papers). See also
Foreign Affairs, vol. I, as indexed for 1923.

4. For a succinct and notably fair-minded account of the causes and effect
of Germany's irreversible inflation, see Hajo Holborn, *A History of Modern
Germany, 1840–1945* (New York: Knopf, 1969), pp. 595–601. Joseph C.
Grew, *Turbulent Era: A Diplomatic Record of Forty Years* (Boston: Hough-
ton Mifflin, 1952), I, 467–74, gives a fascinating picture of Swiss fears of
Germany's total collapse and its devastating effect on Europe.

5. For editorials to this effect see, e.g., the New York *World* 12/16/23
and the *Chicago Journal of Commerce* 12/22/23, ODY Papers, Clippings—
chronologically arranged. The Crocker ms. quotes the *World's* editorial in
full. The announcement of American participation in an expert study of reparations was greeted with "a chorus of approval from a large section of our
press," said the *Literary Digest* 12/29/23, in joining the chorus. Hester,
citing this (p. 40), also quotes Foster Rhea Dulles on the paradox of
America's guilt complex about the League of Nations and its compulsion to
do something about world peace—short of any commitment for collective
security. See F. R. Dulles, *America's Rise to World Power* (New York:
Harper Bros., 1955), p. 159.

6. The Report of the Dawes Committee, in summary form at least, was
widely circulated by the press, including that of the United States. If
many journals, like the people, hailed the *fact* rather than the terms of the
settlement, thoughtful and generally favorable appraisals were by no
means confined to the East (Clippings). Certain pundits and economists

had their doubts, but banking approval was so general that a recent author chides the bankers for failing to push for a similar treatment of Allied debts: J. H. Wilson, "The Role of the Business Community in American Relations with Russia and Europe" (Ph.D. dissertation, University of California, Berkeley, 1966), p. 294. In his *Dwight Morrow* (New York: Harcourt, Brace, 1935), Harold Nicholson states, however, that Morrow thought the Dawes annuities unrealistically high (p. 273). Why, then, as Nicholson reports, should Morrow have coveted appointment as agent-general for reparations?

7. In view of Secretary of State Hughes's (and especially Hoover's) later insistence that war debts and reparations be kept separate, special interest attaches to Hughes's statement of 12/1922 at New Haven that "debtors to the U.S. . . . have unsettled credit balances and their . . . capacity to pay cannot be properly determined until the amount that can be realized on these credits for reparations has been determined" (quoted in H. G. Moulton and Lee Pasvolsky. *World War Debt Settlements* [Washington: Brookings Institution, 1926], p. 297). For an illuminating comparison of Hoover's original and later view of the Allied debts, see David Burner, *Herbert Hoover: A Public Life* (New York: Knopf, 1979), pp. 187–88.

8. M. J. Pusey, *Charles Evans Hughes* (New York: Macmillan, 1951), I, 579–87. The relevant developments are admirably set forth in Hester, chapters 4, 5 and 6. See also B. A. Hughes, "Owen D. Young and American Foreign Policy" (Ph.D. dissertation, University of Wisconsin, 1969), chapter 6, and Costigliola, chapters 1 and 2. For Allied debts, see Moulton and Pasvolsky, as indexed.

9. Pusey, I, 579–87; C. S. Hyde, "Charles Evans Hughes," in vol. X of *American Secretaries of State and Their Diplomacy*, edited by S. F. Bemis (New York: Knopf, 1928; reprinted, Pantheon, 1958).

10. Hester, pp. 387 ff., especially 390–92. According to the American ambassador, Myron T. Herrick, Poincaré said he felt exactly the same about reducing Germany's obligations as America did about canceling the Allied debts. Nevertheless, he was moving toward cooperation; according to B. A. Hughes, p. 184, J. P. Morgan's coolness toward any loan to France in the absence of a reparations settlement had a particularly beneficial effect. (In 1922 Morgan had been a member of the so-called Bankers Committee whose constructive proposals had met the same fate as others at the hands of the French.) See Schuker, however, especially pp. 108–15 and notes, for a convincing rebuttal of this (the prevailing) view of Morgan's conditions for making the loan that "saved" the franc.

11. See Hester, 383 ff., for Lloyd George's role and Coolidge's response; pp. 395–400 for Barthou's formulas. See also Pusey, I, 586–87, for a more condensed account. In his *Journey Through My Years* (New York: Simon & Schuster, 1946), Governor James M. Cox of Ohio recounts his own efforts to effect a settlement while visiting Europe in 1923.

12. For Poincaré's attitude, see Schuker, pp. 18–27; Hester, p. 401. Costigliola's and Crocker's opening chapters are also worth consulting.

13. Timmons, chapters 13–15, especially pp. 195 ff. and p. 222; Hester, pp. 375–76. Dawes's measured defense of the French occupation of the Ruhr.

as quoted in the *Literary Digest* 1/27/23, included a declaration that "the U.S. must face with courage instead of cowardice its unavoidable responsibilities [toward Europe, on grounds of] moral principle [and] the dictates of humanity as well as economic self-interest." The American occupation forces in the Rhineland having been withdrawn as the Ruhr invasion began, Dawes subsequently joined their commanding officer, General Allen, in raising $10 million to relieve starving German children (*Washington Herald* 12/27/23, Clippings).

14. See also above, Chapter 12, for Robinson's work with ODY and Hoover at Wilson's Second Industrial Conference, 1919–20.

15. The Crocker ms reports the call on Hughes. For the attribution of the suggested appointment to Morrow, see Nicholson, p. 273. Coolidge's reported consultation with General Harbord and Newton D. Baker gains added significance from ODY's and Baker's collaborative efforts in 1922 to establish the International Chamber of Commerce's new Court of International Arbitration (see *New York Evening Post* 11/6/22, Clippings). Robinson's name was suggested by Ambassador Herrick and, at almost the same time, acting through his chief, by Crocker (Crocker ms, p. 36). Crocker adds (p. 31) that Colonel Logan, acting on the advice of his predecessor, Roland Boyden, suggested ODY to Hughes, only to be told that ODY was already strongly recommended. ODY did spend an evening with Houghton on May 30 at the home of his colleague Anson Burchard, whose long letters also kept him abreast of developments in Europe: ODY to Burchard 5/26/23; Burchard to Charles Coffin 9/5/23 (copy to ODY).

16. Clippings (cited by Hester, pp. 402–04).

17. Ibid.

18. Charles G. Dawes, *A Journal of Reparations* (London: Macmillan, 1939), pp. 3 and 9. For his initial and characteristically generous assessment of ODY, see p. 5.

19. Ibid., p. 13.

20. Moulton and Pasvolsky are authoritative on all matters relating to the Allied debts. The pattern of the British agreement ignored Congress's stipulation that all these debts were to be paid in twenty-five years, and were to carry at least 4¼ percent interest, but it was nevertheless ratified; see their *War Debts and World Prosperity* (Washington: Brookings Institution, 1932), p. 78. Hughes's statement made in his New Haven speech is quoted in Hester, p. 353. For the impact of the Washington Conference of 1921 on British debt and diplomatic policies, see Roberta A. Dayer's illuminating essay, "The British War Debts to the United States and the Anglo-Japanese Alliance, 1920–1923," in *Pacific Historical Review*, vol. XLV, no. 4 (11/1976). Britain's case for more liberal terms had not been helped by the Balfour note of 1922, which committed Britain to pass on to its Allied debtors any reduction of its debt granted by the United States. Washington saw in this an attempt to shift to the U.S. the full onus attaching to the debt collector.

21. Dawes, pp. 21–24.

22. ODY's speech at testimonial dinner, New York City, 12/11/24, Speeches.

23. Ibid.

24. Ibid. See also text of the report as published (copies in ODY Papers, Reparations).

25. In his interview with Stuart Crocker, 5/16/25, Henry Robinson declared that ODY had given him essentially this outline of the Plan when he first arrived in Paris, six days after the Committee's initial meeting. Robinson believed that ODY had left the ship with these essentials already in mind; Crocker was sure of it (Crocker ms, pp. 50–55, also his interviews with members and staff of the Dawes Committee, Box R-14). But the most comprehensive tribute to ODY's role came from one who was neither a close friend nor an associate—Alan Goldsmith, the expert adviser from the Department of Commerce. Writing to Christian Herter on 1/28/24 (Leonard Ayres Papers, Library of Congress), Goldsmith said:

> Owen Young is a wonder. He has been the leader of the Committee, and I doubt whether they themselves know it. His quiet method of waiting out an argument and placing his ideas in another man's mouth has accomplished wonders. Not a plan, not an idea has been brought up in the Committee, which he has not discussed. As a matter of fact, the entire picture was in his mind when on the "America" coming over. Yet in almost every case the suggestion is advanced by a non-American member of the Committee.
>
> Thus far, Young has been able to put over his ideas, keeping the Committee clear of the amount of reparations, the Ruhr, and other topics which would have broken it up long since. He is getting unanimous agreements "en principe," but is going a step further. When details are then considered, none of them are to be hammered out in the Committee individually, until the entire picture puzzle is complete. He will, by that time, have every member of the Committee so committed, not only to the plan in general, but to many details, that nobody can back out.
>
> Under Young's method, dangerous questions will come up, if they do, in connection with some clearly defined economic part of the plan, and purely on an economic basis. The method per se reduces the possibility for acrimonious political and legal discussions [quoted in Costigliola, p. 105].

From the journal of Leonard Ayres himself, a very different picture emerges. Robinson told Crocker (interview of 5/16/25, Box R–14) that ODY's *modus operandi* was so strange to Stamp that it took the latter some time to appreciate his true caliber; apparently Ayres—also a statistician—never did. His is a record of frustration and disenchantment, principally on the part of the too often neglected economic advisers, but occasionally involving Stamp and even Robinson—whom he cites as sharing his own conviction that the Plan's maximum life would be three years. Ayres, vice-president of the Cleveland Trust and formerly chief statistician of the AEF and of the American Commission to Negotiate the Peace, was assigned to the McKenna Commission; but the disaffection of the advisers which he recounts seems to have been sufficiently widespread to suggest a serious flaw in the Committee's relations with them, clearly reflecting a failure in communication. If this is an indictment primarily of Rufus Dawes, as his brother's "chief of staff," neither the general nor Owen Young can be held wholly guiltless. See, however, Crocker's interview of 5/4/25 with Walter Tower, who reports that ODY had initially been at pains to consult the advisers but as pressures mounted his meetings with them had been less and less frequent. There are indications, moreover, that Young and Dawes became increasingly disenchanted with what they felt to be the doctrinaire approach of the economists.

26. Dawes, pp. 51–54. Prompt action was needed to support Germany's new and unorthodox—hence temporary—currency unit, the Rentenmark. But, as ODY was evidently aware, Schacht had been cooking up a scheme with Governor Norman of the Bank of England to establish a so-called gold-discount bank which might in effect tie Germany to sterling and the gold-exchange standard—currently London's fondest hope. See Hjalmar Schacht, *Confessions of the Old Wizard*, translated by Diana Pyke (Boston: Houghton Mifflin, 1956), pp. 179–91; Frank C. Costigliola, "Anglo-American Financial Rivalry in the 1920s," in *Journal of Economic History*, vol. XXXVII, no. 4 (12/1977).

27. Dawes, pp. 51–54.

28. Crocker ms, pp. 53–54; Dawes, pp. 56–57. Before they left Paris for Berlin, Houghton came to discuss "a tentative program there and what important men should be interviewed." Thus ODY's interviews were scheduled by Houghton in advance, and for those with Stresemann and Hugo Stinnes the ambassador made his own living quarters available (Crocker ms, p. 172). Certainly ODY felt Houghton's help to be invaluable. So, no doubt, was his own secret and timely message of reassurance to Stresemann, sent through Meinhardt of the Osram Company, on 1/13—the eve of Dawes's opening address designed to reassure the French. Not in ODY's papers, this significant message is fully reported and amply documented in Werner Link, *Die Amerikanische Stabilisierungspolitik in Deutschland, 1921–1932* (Düsseldorf: Droste Verlag, 1970), p. 220.

29. Dawes, p. 68. See also ODY's Memorandum on Berlin Visit, dictated immediately after leaving Berlin, in Reparations.

30. Dawes, pp. 76–77. ENC well recalls ODY's own verbal account of this session with Stresemann, and the latter's prompt response to the idea of sharing the burden—a welcome change from the war-guilt charge. See also—and especially—ODY Memo cited in note 29.

31. Dawes, pp. 76 ff.; ODY Memo. Allgemeine Elektrizitäts Gesellschaft (Germany's General Electric Company) had been founded by Rathenau's father, who had acquired Edison's European patent rights. The younger Rathenau, who had advanced ideas about labor's role in industry, was foreign minister when he was assassinated by nationalist fanatics on 6/24/22. For an illuminating study of Weimar's splinter groups, and the proximate causes and effect of Rathenau's assassination, see David W. Morgan, *The Socialist Left and the German Revolution* (Ithaca: Cornell University Press, 1975).

32. Dawes, pp. 76–77; ODY Memo. The quotation also appears in Ida M. Tarbell, *Owen D. Young: A New Type of Industrial Leader* (New York: Macmillan, 1932), p. 171. So, at some length, does Grasseman's moving plea on labor's behalf (pp. 171–74).

33. Tarbell, pp. 171–72; Dawes, p. 95. The question about agriculture, however, loses much of its point in the light of Ambassador Houghton's

cautionary suggestion—which ODY accepted—that if ODY sought to undermine the German reactionaries, it would be wise to placate the large landowners of the Right by eliminating the tax on agriculture (Houghton diary for 3/29/24), Houghton Mss. (cited by Costigliola, "Politics of Financial Stabilization," p. 174).

34. Crocker ms, pp. 250–52. For ODY's version of the story see his speech at the Stone and Webster dinner at the Harvard Club of Boston 6/25/25, Speeches (cited below, Chapter 18).

35. ODY to authors on various occasions. A not very different version was recorded by Stuart Crocker, who, as ODY's busy assistant, strove valiantly to keep his notes up to date; Crocker ms, pp. 83, 84. For Dawes's biographer's version, see Timmons, p. 225.

36. These letters from JEY are all in JYC's possession.

37. Robinson's interview with Crocker 5/16/25, Box R-14. One economic adviser, J. S. Davis, had so little understanding of ODY's negotiating tactics as to conclude that he was hopelessly wedded to the French figure of three milliard marks. See his otherwise useful *World between the Wars* (published posthumously in 1975 by Johns Hopkins University Press), p. 75. Bergmann knew better, as shown in his report of his 3/20/24 meeting with ODY, pp. 235–36.

38. See Dawes Committee report, Section X.

39. Dawes, p. 173. Robinson, whose help in drafting the chapter on the new German bank of issue, and in pinch-hitting when ODY was indisposed, had earned him a place on both commissions, told Crocker (interview of 5/16/25, Box R-14) that ODY had tried to escape the drafting chore but since no one else could have put things together in a way that would assure its unanimous acceptance, Robinson had virtually forced him to take it on. Of Stamp's role in preparing Part II, Crocker wrote (ms, p. 285) that but for him, "the Report would never have been written. . . . Mr. Young crouched by the fire and made suggestions but Sir Josiah . . . actually wrote each paragraph in its final form." In the meantime, it was ODY who suggested to Parmentier that he draft the clause re unity of the Reich. Thus the paragraph on the Ruhr was both constructive and sure to command French approval. It was actually included as drafted (Crocker ms, pp. 229–30).

40. ODY's personal copybook, Paris, 1924. For the discovery of this letter, the authors are indebted to a visiting research scholar, Kenneth Paul Jones of the University of Tennessee. M.I.C.U.M.=Mission Interaliée de Contrôle des Usines (factories) et des Mines. Dated 11/23/23, this agreement concerned deliveries in kind made during the Occupation and the means by which they were to be credited on reparations account.

41. Clippings for 4/29/24, Reparations.

42. ODY's Office Calendar; a copy of Dawes's message is in his Special Papers #1. Bergmann felt that the Committee's success could be traced to the fact that it "had the insight to build on the experience of the past. . . . It is to the everlasting credit of the experts, headed by Dawes," he wrote in his preface to the English edition of his opus, "that they assembled the best stones from the ruins [of previous efforts] and skillfully joined them into their ingenious structure."

Notes to Pages 294–300

Notes to Pages 294–300

CHAPTER 17. Germany in Receivership: "Owen the First"

1. ODY to Charles G. Dawes 5/29/24. Dawes's nomination, occurring on 6/12/24 after his friend Governor Frank Lowden of Illinois had declined it, was widely heralded in the Paris and Berlin press, samples of whose comments appeared in the NYT and the *New York Evening Post* for 6/14 (Clippings). Eckhard Wandel, *Die Bedeutung der V.S.A. für das deutsche Reparationsproblem* (Tübingen: Mohr, 1971), p. 11, declaring that Dawes and Young were received at home as "popular national heroes," characterizes the Plan (even as viewed in retrospect) as "a kind of economic bible which, in its logic and inner consistency, has virtually no peer" ("ein Bibel der Wirtschaft . . . die in ihrer Geschlossenheit und Logik kaum ein Beispiel hat"). Election day was to find ODY back in Europe, but he kept his "democracy" intact by publicly supporting his party's candidate, John W. Davis —who finished a poor second.

2. David Loth, *Swope of GE* (New York: Simon & Schuster, 1958), pp. 164–65; J. D. Hicks, *Republican Ascendancy* (New York: Harper & Row, 1960), p. 83.

3. Loth, pp. 164–65.

4. Ibid.; Erik Barnouw, *A History of Broadcasting in the United States*, vol. I: *A Tower in Babel* (New York: Oxford University Press, 1966), p. 201.

5. ODY to A. Lawrence Lowell 5/19/24.

6. Pip was Philip, her fourteen-year-old brother; Stuie was her father's current assistant, Stuart M. Crocker, Harvard '21.

7. This was the phrase borrowed by the NYT as title for its editorial hymn of praise 6/21/24.

8. Speeches. These remarks, together with Dawes's nomination by the Republicans, prompted a flurry of editorial suggestions to the Democrats, who were about to convene. Papers as far apart geographically as the *Montreal Star* (6/20) and the *New Orleans Times-Picayune* (6/21) thrust Owen Young's name into the arena. Judicious praise for the speech also marked the editorial pages of the *Boston Herald* (6/21) as well as the *Brooklyn Eagle* (6/20). Clippings.

9. ODY to C. L. Waddell 6/13/24. RCA had never made a public offering of its stock but over-the-counter sales by AT&T, Marconi stockholders and others had spread its shares fairly widely.

10. ODY to Alfred Lucking 6/25/24.

11. Hajo Holborn, *A History of Modern Germany, 1840–1945* (New York: Knopf, 1969), pp. 617–19, 636–37. See also Werner Link, *Die Amerikanische Stabilisierungspolitik in Deutschland, 1921–1932* (Düsseldorf: Droste Verlag, 1970), pp. 14–20; also pp. 201 ff. and particularly pp. 322–23.

12. Charles G. Dawes, *A Journal of Reparations* (London: Macmillan,

1939), pp. 231–32. This was a currently kept record, though published many years later.

13. ODY to Dawes 6/25/24.

14. Dawes, pp. 230–34. See also Harold Nicholson, *Dwight Morrow* (New York: Harcourt, Brace, 1935), pp. 273–75; Frank C. Costigliola, "Politics of Financial Stabilization: American Reconstruction Policy in Europe, 1924–1930" (Ph.D. dissertation, Cornell University, 1973), pp. 136–38; Stuart M. Crocker's interview with James Logan 5/15/25 (copy in Box R-14). Stephen Schuker's research convinces him that Coolidge's political henchmen were urging him to ditch Morrow lest the appointment of a Morgan partner alienate the German-American voters whose support was of first importance in key states of the Midwest. See Schuker, *End of French Predominance in Europe* (Chapel Hill: University of North Carolina Press, 1976), pp. 287–88, for his well-documented conclusions—which also were Werner Link's (p. 315n). Kenneth P. Jones, in "Discord and Collaboration," *Diplomatic History*, vol. I, no. 2 (Spring 1977), agrees about the influence of domestic politics but feels that Houghton's view of Germany's reaction was not unwarranted.

15. Dawes, p. 234; ODY to Montagu Norman 7/3/24.

16. See ODY to Dawes 6/23/24, urging him to come to the wedding. For ODY's plans "to settle down in Riverside," see JEY to IBY 7/1/24, written from Washington.

17. Reparations, London Conference files. In his authoritative and all but contemporaneous *History of Reparations* (Boston: Houghton Mifflin, 1927), Carl Bergmann (pp. 263–65) credits ODY with having exercised a salutary influence on the German delegation at London as well as in resolving the dispute between the bankers and the French. Cf. Frank C. Costigliola, "The United States and the Reconstruction of Germany in the 1920s," *Business History Review*, Vol. L, no. 4 (1976), p. 493, note 65.

18. Like her earlier letters, these from JEY are in JYC's possession.

19. D. R. McCoy, *Calvin Coolidge: The Quiet President* (New York: Macmillan, 1967), p. 192; Joseph Grew, *Turbulent Era: A Diplomatic Record of Forty Years* (Boston: Houghton Mifflin, 1952), I, 626–30. Wandel, p. 15, cites the first but not the second. All that the President would say to Kellogg was, "We didn't have to use it, did we?"

20. M. J. Pusey, *Charles Evans Hughes* (New York: Macmillan, 1951), I, 587–92. For one reporter's assessment of the determining role Hughes played, beginning with the Herriot luncheon, see New York *World* 8/2/24. According to Pusey, it was Chief Justice Taft who urged the American Bar Association to elect Hughes as its head prior to its London meeting.

21. Young Jo was to leave for college, and Philip for boarding school that fall—the first time either had been away from home to school—and Jo had their preparations very much on her mind. In the meantime, she wrote her daughter: "I have a beautiful autographed photo of H.R.H. the Prince of Wales for you—at least the Prince sent it to me, but I'll let you look at it!"

22. ODY to J. P. Morgan 8/4/24, Dwight Morrow Papers, Amherst College

Library, Amherst, Mass., which has kindly furnished us a copy. By way of background Logan reported to Crocker that back in June, on receiving Norman's inquiry, Morgan had invited ODY to list six men "who could do the job" (as agent-general) and on receiving the list had remarked, "That's funny. The only man I have recommended is not on your list: Dwight Morrow." Crocker reports this without comment. K.P. Jones, pp. 134–35, cites a Logan to Hoover letter of 9/5/24 in which Logan accuses a "humiliated" Morgan of "making every endeavor to break Owen Young." Certainly Schuker's "timetable" (*End of French Predominance*, pp. 285–89) makes it clear that Morgan had quickly changed his mind about the new slate (Young and Perkins) which he had tentatively approved; apparently the occasion was word from a trusted source in Germany which branded as baseless Houghton's warning about Morrow's appointment. Lamont even suggested to Morrow (on 7/8) that ODY, coveting the post for himself, had planted the idea in Houghton's mind. Schuker adds (*End of French Predominance*, p. 288) that not until 8/8 did Morgan learn who and what was really responsible for Coolidge's veto of Morrow (see above, note 14). For Morrow's lengthy and slightly petulant rehearsal of what transpired as he saw it, see his twelve-page letter to his partner Thomas Cochran, written 8/10/24 from his summer home in Maine (Morrow Papers, Amherst College Library). The letters re Norman Davis—a proposal which Russell Leffingwell evidently vetoed—are reproduced in Dawes, pp. 261–64. See also the helpful studies cited in notes 23 and 24 below.

23. Copies of the report of the London Conference including Annex IV, Interallied Agreement of 8/30/24, and report of Committee I as approved (see I, 93–94) are in the ODY Papers, Reparations. Minutes of the committee's eight meetings are included in the conference report, pp. 252–300. See also Schuker, *End of French Predominance*, pp. 302–04, 314. For ODY's much later account of one of his hassles with Norman and Lamont, see introductory pages of Crocker's Young Plan Diary (unpublished, copy in ODY Papers).

24. Jones, pp. 118 ff., especially pp. 133–39; M. P. Leffler, *The Elusive Quest: America's Pursuit of European Stability and French Security, 1919–1933* (Chapel Hill: University of North Carolina Press, 1979), pp. 100–109.

25. Gerard Swope to ODY 8/19/24, London Conference files.

26. Stephen V. O. Clarke, *Central Bank Cooperation, 1924–1931* (New York: Federal Reserve Bank, 1967), p. 57, says that Norman and Lamont "put forward" Gilbert's name. Costigliola, "Politics of Financial Stabilization," p. 137, states that "Mellon on August 22 imposed [the] settlement" involving ODY and Gilbert. Perhaps—but the authorities cited by Costigliola do not use this verb. See Schuker, *End of French Predominance*, p. 287, for Leffingwell's influence for—and on—Gilbert.

27. A long handwritten postscript which ODY labeled "Annex I" contrasts MacDonald and Philip Snowden, his chancellor of the exchequer, and adds: "Snowden does not like MacDonald and is not wild over the success of the Conference which greatly strengthens MacDonald's power . . ." The comment is interesting, especially in view of the equivocal role Snowden was to play in the ratification of the Young Plan.

28. Speech at testimonial dinner, New York City, 12/11/24, Speeches.

29. London Conference files. As early as March, ODY had sounded out the New York bankers, through Swope's good offices, on the terms and conditions they considered essential to the loan. See also Conference file of coded radiograms to ODY in London from Benjamin Strong and J. H. Case of the New York Federal Reserve. See Costigliola, "Politics of Financial Stabilization," p. 127, for changing status of the Morgan firm in the New York market, and Schuker, *End of French Predominance*, p. 350, for ODY's use of Clarence Dillon as a "stalking-horse" in London.

30. Reparations, Agent-General files.

31. Ibid.

32. Ibid.

33. Crocker interviews re Dawes Plan, in Box R-14.

34. ODY to Thomas Nelson Perkins, especially 10/3/24 (transmitted through Crocker), London Conference file; Perkins to ODY 10/7/24.

35. Justin Kaplan, *Lincoln Steffens: A Biography* (New York: Simon & Schuster, 1974), p. 277. The marriage, it appears, took place in August in a Paris registry office, with the William C. Bullitts and Jo Davidsons as witnesses.

36. The Jo Davidson bust is now in the Owen D. Young Library at St. Lawrence University, with a smaller version in the offices of the Van Hornesville Community Corporation.

37. A draft of ODY's "extempore" response is in his papers (Reparations). Both *The Times* and the NYT for 11/4/24 report the affair, and especially Balfour's tribute, at some length.

38. This letter too was addressed to Governor Crissinger of the Federal Reserve Board, with a copy to JHC of the New York bank. Thanks to JHC's files, and the bank's, a copy is now in the authors' hands, on deposit with the ODY Papers. As for the so-called Dawes loan, its terms as finally settled on 10/10/24 were as follows: Issue price: 92; interest, 7 percent. Sinking fund to provide redemption in 25 years—at 105 in the United States, at par elsewhere. Service of loan to be an unconditional first charge on German revenues and assets. Bergmann, p. 280, reports its issue a great success with the price quickly rising to par and above. ODY was especially pleased by oversubscription of the American *tranche*. See also, especially for the market's extraordinary response, the British Institute's *Survey of International Affairs*, 1924, part II, pp. 386–87. This entire section—"Western Europe: The Allies and Germany," pp. 266–403—is a notable contemporaneous account of the Dawes Plan in its full context, as observed and reported by Arnold Toynbee.

CHAPTER *18. American Ascendancy and Business Horizons*

1. ODY Papers, Radio. For this decision and its curious sequel, see Chapter 19.

2. J. D. Hicks, *Republican Ascendancy, 1921–1933* (New York: Harper & Row, 1960), chapters 2 and 3; also for agriculture, chapter 9; F. R.

Dulles, *Labor in America* (New York: T. Y. Crowell, 1949), chapter 14; Irving Bernstein, *The Lean Years: A History of the American Worker, 1920–1933* (Boston: Houghton Mifflin, 1960), especially chapter 2. Bernstein's prologue, "Revolt in the Piedmont," gives an illuminating account of the trek from farm to city and the plight of the farm worker looking for a job in industry—notably in the southern textile mills.

3. F. R. Dulles, *The United States since 1865* (Ann Arbor: University of Michigan, 1959), chapter 20, offers perhaps the best concise account. See also such general or special works as R. E. Spiller, et al., *Literary History of the United States* (New York: Macmillan, 1948), vol. III; Merle Curti, *Growth of American Thought* (New York: Harper, 1943); Henry S. Commager, *The American Mind* (New Haven: Yale University Press, 1950); William E. Leuchtenburg, *Perils of Prosperity, 1914–1932* (Chicago: University of Chicago Press, 1958).

4. Werner Link, *Die Amerikanische Stabilisierungspolitik in Deutschland, 1921–1932* (Düsseldorf: Droste Verlag, 1970). Concerned with the intertwining of political and economic as well as domestic and international factors in determining policy, Link sharply distinguishes economic cooperation from domination but adds, shrewdly enough (p. 16), that, like cooperation and competition, the two are not to be regarded as necessarily opposing concepts. Always there is some overlap—especially when cooperation involves a strong and a weaker partner (ENC's rough translation). An ODY memo to Charles Coffin and E. W. Rice, dated 8/11/23, proves that his postwar interest in AEG clearly antedated the Dawes Plan: prepared on the S.S. *Olympic*, on which he was returning from Europe, it recommends GE's participation in a proposed new issue of AEG shares on a scale sufficient to assure a voice in AEG affairs but only that.

5. Willis Whitney, in conversation with ENC, c. 1928. See also Ida M. Tarbell, *Owen D. Young: A New Type of Industrial Leader* (New York: Macmillan, 1932), pp. 258–62.

6. ODY to Gerard Swope 3/1924, Reparations files.

7. Swope to ODY 8/19/24, Reparations, London Conference files.

8. ODY to authors.

9. GE's announcement, made at 2:30 on Tuesday, 12/30/24, appeared in late afternoon editions of that day's evening papers and in morning papers next day. The headline and story cited here are taken from the *Financial World* 1/3/25, Clippings.

10. John Winthrop Hammond, *Men and Volts: The Story of General Electric* (Philadelphia: Lippincott, 1941), p. 388. See statement quoted by David Loth, *Swope of GE* (New York: Simon & Schuster, 1958), p. 134. Loth also reports (p. 164) the Senate resolution of 2/1925 directing the FTC to investigate monopolistic control of the utilities and the FTC's finding of "no monopoly of either power companies or supply of electrical equipment, nor control thereof in restraint of trade."

11. So great was the pressure that ODY's assistant, Stuart Crocker, reluctantly turned his own dinner ticket over to one of ODY's importunate admirers.

12. Only J. P. Morgan was missing; but five of his partners were present, including Russell Leffingwell, Dwight Morrow and Thomas W. Lamont.

13. Thanks to the indefatigable Crocker, ODY's files include a handsomely bound chronicle of all the evening's messages and speeches, plus press clippings. The full text of Hughes's message is there.

14. News and editorial columns gave the whole occasion top billing: in the *Sun* as well as in the NYT, the speech appeared verbatim. The *World*, the WSJ, the *New York Commercial*, the *Brooklyn Daily Eagle* and the *New York Journal of Commerce* reprinted major portions, and the NYHT joined the chorus of admiring editorials. All noted the tributes from high places and the notables attending; indeed, the NYT went so far as to publish an alphabetical listing of the 1,042 guests.

15. Speech at testimonial dinner, New York City, 12/11/24, Speeches. The concluding sentence was given particular attention by editorial writers and commentators.

16. ODY to Charles Evans Hughes 1/26/25; Hughes to ODY 1/31/25: Special Papers #1–4.

17. Special Papers #1–4.

18. Perkins file.

19. Henry Clay, *Lord Norman* (London: Macmillan, 1957), pp. 174–79. As governor of the Bank of England, Norman joined the chancellor of the exchequer, Stanley Baldwin, in negotiating the agreement. See also H. G. Moulton and Lee Pasvolsky, *War Debts and World Prosperity* (Washington: Brookings Institution, 1932), pp. 78, 84. As noted, the British settlement (which Congress ratified) spread payments over sixty-two years, with interest at 3 percent for the first ten and 3½ percent thereafter; for the other Allies, interest charges were to be much lower.

20. Josiah Stamp to ODY 3/31/25, Special Papers #1–4. Months before the New York rate was finally raised to 3½ percent at the end of 2/1925, Strong had asked Norman whether he preferred taking the lead. On 12/8/24, Norman cabled Strong that he much *preferred* to follow, and "so appear to have our hands forced by you" (quoted in Stephen V. O. Clarke, *Central Bank Cooperation, 1924–1931* [New York: Federal Reserve Bank, 1967], p. 88).

21. Alan Bullock, *Life and Times of Ernest Bevin* (London: Heinemann, 1960).

22. Clarke, pp. 103–06. Cf., e.g., J. S. Davis, *World between the Wars, 1919–1939: An Economist's View* (Baltimore: Johns Hopkins University Press, 1975), pp. 73–75. Hindsight critics, of course, have little difficulty in denouncing this whole effort—in which the Federal Reserve undoubtedly played the very role that ODY had urged and actively supported—as an exercise in futility or worse. Restored to its prewar level, they say (as John Maynard Keynes insisted at the time), the pound sterling was grossly overvalued; at best the action taken was hopelessly premature. As for restoration of the gold standard, not a few tend to dismiss it as mere fetish worship. What they seldom bother to answer are the questions which the men who were called upon to act in the context of the times could not possibly escape: what feasible alternatives were there to the course they elected and what, viewed *prospectively*, were the pros and cons of the options open.

23. Clarke, pp. 103–06. For Churchill's report, see *Parliamentary Debates* (Great Britain), House of Commons, vol. 183, 4/25/25, col. 57. Clarke (p. 81) quotes this passage following a well-documented review of the several factors and forces at work. Cf. Frank C. Costigliola, "Anglo-American Financial Rivalry in the 1920s," *Journal of Economic History*, vol. XXXVII, no. 4 (12/1977).

24. ODY to Stamp 3/3/25, Special Papers #1–4, including Stamp's reply of 3/31/25. For forces making for cooperation, see M. J. Hogan, *Informal Entente* (Columbia: University of Missouri Press, 1977), pp. 71–77.

25. Although it guaranteed the sanctity of west European boundaries only, and so disappointed earlier hopes of including eastern boundaries as well, Locarno was the first postwar political treaty to be freely negotiated between Germany and the Allies. Thanks to Ambassador Houghton, even the United States had a voice in urging initially hesitant parties to proceed; ODY's radiogram of 5/6/25 said that his Pilgrims' Society speech of a day or two earlier had won more nearly "universal approval" than any he could recall since the war. When, in October, the treaty was finally signed, ODY's message congratulating Stresemann brought (on 10/28) a warm rejoinder— flawed only by the fact that it came by cable, not by radio! Costigliola, "Anglo-American Rivalry," pp. 154–64, has an excellent account of Locarno in relationship to the Dawes Plan and the Geneva protocol; for its sequelae, see Jon Jacobson, *Locarno Diplomacy: Germany and the West, 1925–1929* (Princeton: Princeton University Press, 1972).

26. See, e.g., phrased rather more elegantly, ODY's speech of 1/26/26 to the American Bankers Association, Speeches.

27. ODY to ENC, c. 1928. JEY's caustic observations, frequently in the hearing of both authors, always delighted her husband.

28. ODY at Johns Hopkins 2/22/25, Speeches.

29. ODY at St. Lawrence University Club 3/6/25, Speeches.

30. Ibid.

31. Yale speech 6/17/25, Stone and Webster dinner 6/25/25, Speeches. Yale, like Johns Hopkins, awarded ODY an honorary degree.

32. ODY gives his own account of the press's version in his letter to Joseph Tumulty, the late President Wilson's private secretary, 10/6/25.

33. According to Moulton and Pasvolsky, pp. 100–102, the percentage "forgiven" ranged from some 20 percent in Britain's case to 70 percent for Italy. They compute the average at 43 percent.

34. Thomas Nelson Perkins to ODY 9/3/25 and 9/5/25; ODY to Herbert Hoover 9/17/25, enclosing the Perkins letters, Reparations, Box 35.

35. Hoover to ODY 9/18/25, which ODY sent Perkins 9/23/25, Reparations, Box 35.

36. ODY to A. G. Davis 10/30/25, BCB. Fortunately he quotes his answer to Caillaux, since we find no copy of the draft he sent on 8/26/25 to Clarence Dillon, through whom James Logan had evidently transmitted Caillaux's inquiry. In his letter to Dillon, ODY confided that Swope, his sole consultant, had reservations about his proposed answer but that it

faithfully reflected "my own feelings as nearly as I can put them into language."

37. ODY to Hoover 1/5/26; Hogan, chapter 9, treats this letter and the pricing of rubber in their larger context of conflicting U.S. and British goals.

CHAPTER *19. Private Enterprise or Public:*
Waterpower and Broadcasting

1. Although the Otsquago is not in the commercial class for generating electricity, in 1907 a local boy, Verne Miller, produced enough current to light the general store by means of a homemade waterwheel and generator. The village was not supplied with electricity until 1923.

2. Statement of ODY speaking for Manufacturers of Hydroelectric Machinery, hearing before the Federal Water Power Commission, 11/21/21, Water Power, Box 66; extempore remarks by ODY at meeting of Empire State Gas and Electric Association, 4/6/25, Speeches.

3. Radiogram from George T. Bishop to ODY in Paris 1/23/24, Water Power, Box 66. Bishop was president, later chairman, of the Frontier Corporation; he was a Cleveland financier and well known in public-utility circles.

4. ODY's address to NELA annual convention, Atlantic City, 5/18/26, Speeches.

5. Message to legislature from Governor Alfred E. Smith 3/5/23 (NYT 3/6/23). Smith was first elected governor of New York in 1918, served one term (two years at that time) and was defeated by Nathan L. Miller in 1920, but was reelected in 1922, 1924 and 1926. Independent and enterprising, liberal to the point of being called socialist by conservatives, he believed that the state of New York belonged to its people and that the state government existed to serve them.

6. ODY to Alfred E. Smith 2/16/23.

7. ODY to Ernest H. Abbott 8/15/28.

8. ODY to Smith 2/4/26. This letter was not sent, but served as an aide-mémoire for the meeting; there is no other record.

9. *Brooklyn Daily Eagle* 2/9/26.

10. ODY to Smith 2/9/26.

11. Statement by Smith on waterpower for release 3/1/26.

12. New York *World* 3/2/26; *New York Commercial* 3/4/26.

13. ODY to Herbert Hoover 3/2/26; ODY to M. H. Aylesworth 3/2/26.

14. Henry M. Robinson to ODY 7/27/26, two letters. ODY also heard from his friend George Bishop of Frontier, through a letter from him to Stuart M. Crocker, 8/6/26: "Each faction in politics has yearned for complete confirmation of his own ideas by Mr. Young, and failing to find it has circulated interpretations of his own. This is also true of a few public utility

men, whose vision extends backward to Franklin's kite, and forward not at all."

15. Charles J. Bullock to ODY 3/1/26; ODY to Bullock 3/5/26.

16. ODY to Crocker from London 4/4/26.

17. Radiogram from Crocker to ODY aboard S.S. *Duilio*, copied out by the ship's operator for ODY in a fine Italian hand, 3/16/26; New York *World* 3/16/26; NYHT 3/16/26.

18. NYHT 5/1/26.

19. Ibid. 5/6/26.

20. NYT 5/8/26; ODY to John Finley 5/12/26 (this is the entire letter). To Professor David Todd, the astronomer, whom ODY knew slightly from GE's participation in the study of eclipses, ODY wrote (6/15/26) in response to an enthusiastic letter: "It is a very great delight to hear from you again, and I am really much more interested in your comments on the eclipses than I am in politics. While I am as ignorant of one as the other, the heavens do extend my imagination and politics contract it, so let us talk about eclipses, and when you are in New York, come and see me in order that I may be stimulated to keep myself up to date in things worthwhile."

21. NYT 8/4/26.

22. New York *World* 8/5/26.

23. ODY to Eleanor Roosevelt 8/4/26.

24. ODY to the National Electric Light Association 5/18/26, Speeches.

25. Robinson to ODY 7/27/26.

26. ODY's statement appeared in all the New York City papers and others elsewhere 6/29 to 7/1/26.

27. NYHT 12/9/26.

28. ODY's statement was released 12/8, and printed in all New York City papers; this quotation is from the WSJ 12/10/26. But ODY had not told all; the companies, as he wrote Franklin Roosevelt two years later (11/26/28), "refused to accept the grant [of the lease] because the margins in it, already very narrow, would have been completely exhausted in the technicalities of litigation, to say nothing of the impairment of the public goodwill of the companies taking the grant."

29. Bishop to Crocker 12/10/26.

30. A copy of ODY's speech, typed in the fashion usual for his speeches (half page, triple spaced) exists in the files, marked: "In case Mr. Y. had to speak after Gov. Smith has spoken. Not given." Smith's speech exists in the files in a copy of a "verbatim" stenographer's report, which is full of misspellings and mistakes. Bishop's comment on the speech was, "How clever he is and how absolutely he obtains the sympathy of his audience" (Bishop to Crocker 12/17/26).

31. ODY's remarks got at least as much attention in the press as Smith's speech; see, e.g., *New York Evening Post* 12/14/26; the *Brooklyn Eagle* (12/15/26) added new interest by quoting the governor as saying he would

ask ODY to head the new power authority if the legislature created it. Neither of these things came to pass, however, and for the remainder of Smith's time as governor, no progress on waterpower was made.

32. Quoted in Matthew and Hannah Josephson, *Al Smith* (Boston: Houghton Mifflin, 1969), p. 351.

33. ODY to Bishop 1/13/26.

34. The letter is hastily typed, and "fact" at the end of the second paragraph quoted may be "face."

35. ODY to Franklin D. Roosevelt 11/26/28. Young was on his way to Arizona with his wife, stopping in Texas on the way to visit the King Ranch; the letter and material were mailed from San Antonio. See Frank Freidel, *Franklin D. Roosevelt*; vol. III: *The Triumph* (Boston: Little, Brown, 1956), pp. 101–12, for FDR and power. In mentioning the material which ODY sent FDR in 11/1928 Freidel describes it as written "from the General Electric point of view"; he does not refer to the public-private plan for development of the St. Lawrence upon which ODY worked with Governor Smith as described in the papers sent to FDR.

36. Freidel, III, 101–12; ODY to J. H. Cohen 7/31/29.

37. The most important books are: G. L. Archer, *Big Business and Radio* (New York: American Historical Company, 1939), and Erik Barnouw, *A History of Broadcasting in the United States*, vol. I: *A Tower in Babel* (New York: Oxford University Press, 1966). Archer's, written not long after the events described, is a most useful compendium; Barnouw's is not only accurate but objective and perceptive, and a pleasure to read. See also below, notes 39 and 40.

38. Undated memo, filed with 1922 letters; Radio, Box 127.

39. Otto S. Schairer, *Patent Policies of RCA*, quoted in Elmer E. Bucher's unpublished history of RCA, p. 644. The Bucher history is in the library of the David Sarnoff Research Center, Princeton, New Jersey; it is in manuscript form and special permission is necessary to see it.

40. ODY to Hoover 3/6/22. About this problem Bucher wrote: "Indeed, the situation was much the same as for the war materiel manufacturers at the beginning of the war, who were confronted with carrying on their experimental work, devising new types and at the same time producing the best they can in such quantity as they can, and they must do all this while building up their organizations, working out their policies and keeping an eye on the Government so that they can keep in accord with its regulations."

41. ODY to Francis C. Pratt 1/11/26; ODY to Isaac Marcosson 1/19/26.

42. Barnouw, pp. 184–85, has a succinct account of the concession and of AT&T's not exercising it. For an illuminating study of the stragetic uses of patents and—as illustrated by the AT&T hassle—of the impact on corporate policies of unanticipated developments, see L. S. Reich, "Research Patents and the Struggle to Control Radio," *Business History Review*, vol. LI, no. 2 (Summer 1977).

43. ODY to James G. Harbord 8/25/26.

44. While NELA had been charged with propagandizing unfairly for the

utilities, ODY had seen enough of Aylesworth in his previous capacities to be sure this was the man he wanted for NBC. Others were not so sure.

45. Announcement of formation of the National Broadcasting Company, 9/6/26, ODY Papers, Broadcasting.

46. Ibid.

47. Ibid.

48. Ibid.

49. ODY to John O'Hara Cosgrave 4/23/25.

50. ODY, in interview with C. D. Wagoner of GE, 2/1951; on tape in Columbia University Oral History collection, copy in typescript in ODY Papers, Florida file, 1951.

51. William Hard, "Europe's Air and Ours," _Atlantic Monthly_ 10/1932.

52. New York _Evening World_ 11/16/26; _Washington Post_ 11/17/26.

53. "Specifications of an American Citizen for a Broadcasting Company," memo to himself, n.d.

54. Barnouw, p. 204. The original members of the Advisory Council were:
Edward A. Alderman, president, University of Virginia
Walter Damrosch, conductor, New York Symphony Orchestra
John W. Davis, lawyer
Francis D. Farrell, president, Kansas State Agricultural College
William Green, president, American Federation of Labor
James G. Harbord, president, RCA
Charles E. Hughes, lawyer
The Reverend Charles F. MacFarland, general secretary, Federal
  Council of Churches of Christ in America
Dwight W. Morrow, J. P. Morgan and Company
Morgan J. O'Brien, lawyer and judge
Henry S. Pritchett, president, Carnegie Foundation
Henry M. Robinson, banker
Elihu Root, lawyer
Julius Rosenwald, president, Sears, Roebuck and Company
Mrs. Mary Sherman, president, General Federation of Women's
  Clubs in America
Guy E. Tripp, chairman of the board, Westinghouse Company
Owen D. Young, chairman of the board, GE, RCA
In addition ODY invited Mary Van Kleeck of the Russell Sage Foundation, and Melville Stone, advisory director, Associated Press, who were not able to accept. There were no medical or health names on the list, a fact which was noticed and complained about several years later. This lack may have resulted because broadcasting in its earlier years was extremely discreet: "a talk by a toothpaste company was delayed while executives argued whether anything so personal as tooth-brushing should be mentioned on the air" (Barnouw, p. 157).

55. ODY to list in note 54, identical letters, 11/6/26.

56. Elihu Root to ODY 12/12/26.

57. Quotations are from the memorandum of minutes of the first meeting

of the Advisory Council of the National Broadcasting Company, 2/18/27, taken by Stuart M. Crocker, secretary *pro tem* (in ODY Papers).

58. Ibid.

59. Barnouw, p. 191.

60. Message to the Advisory Council, third meeting, 1/30/29, Box 159.

61. ODY to M. P. Rice 2/18/25.

62. ODY to Hoover 12/1/25.

63. Barnouw, pp. 123, 218; ODY to NBC Advisory Council 3/7/28.

64. ODY to E. W. Rice, Jr., 3/15/23; ODY to David Sarnoff 1/25/28.

65. Quoted in Orrin E. Dunlap, *Radio's 100 Men of Science* (New York: Harper, 1944), p. 274.

66. Memorandum to the authors from CJY; he continues: "My development was proceeding at the GE Radio Department in Building 77. A facsimile scanner model was built which would handle 8½ x 11 inch sheets, and also a facsimile recorder to print out copies at the receiving end on a moving web of paper 8½ inches wide. The speed, as I remember, was about 6 lines of single space typing per minute." With this equipment C.J. and Ernst Alexanderson (of the Alexanderson alternator) put on a demonstration over a long distance: "The terminal apparatus was ready, and Alexanderson's group had established a short wave circuit from San Francisco to Schenectady. Alec and I watched the first sheets come out, an 8½ inch wide copy of part of the front page of the San Francisco Examiner."

CHAPTER *20. The Modern Corporation:*
Shall Labor Hire Capital?

1. JYC diary; ODY Papers, Dawes file. See also Thomas Logan to ODY 4/22/25, quoting Louis Coolidge of Boston as follows: "Charles Dawes is the only man in history who ever put an ancestor [*sic*] on the map." In her *Paul Revere* (Boston: Houghton Mifflin, 1942), chapter 8, Esther Forbes treats skillfully and judiciously the roles and respective claims of these two couriers; Revere emerges as undoubtedly the more important. Neither got beyond Lexington, however; a Dr. Prescott carried the news from there to Concord.

2. Stuart M. Crocker to CJY 6/3/25, New York and Richmond Gas file.

3. GE Annual Report for 1924; ODY to H. Campbell Graaf 1/7/25.

4. Untermyer's letter—dated 4/30/25 and missing from ODY's files—was featured in the NYT on Monday, 5/4.

5. ODY to ENC 1927. ODY's letter of 5/4/25 appears in his letter-press copybook and is cited in the NYT of the following day.

6. ODY to Raymond Fosdick 2/21/27. As a dedicated Wilsonian and president of the Rockefeller Foundation, Fosdick would be interested, ODY was sure, in his hopes that at Johns Hopkins, the Page School would serve as a clearinghouse for similar institutions and studies at home and abroad.

Naturally ODY hoped too for Mr. Rockefeller's interest and support. For ODY's travel schedule and addresses, see his Office Diary and Speeches.

7. GE and RCA Annual Reports, 1925 and 1926.

8. ODY to American Bar Association 1/26/26, Speeches, where the Page School speeches are also filed.

9. Ibid.

10. Ibid.

11. ODY to Mrs. William Brown Meloney 9/28/26.

12. Alfred P. Sloan, Jr., *My Years with General Motors* (Garden City, N.Y.: Doubleday, 1964), p. 64. For his emphasis on maximizing investors' profits, see p. 213.

13. Both authors had a thorough exposure to journalistic portraits of all types, examples of which—too numerous to cite—abound in the Clippings, as filed chronologically.

14. C. F. Weed file.

15. ODY to Felix Frankfurter 3/9/25.

16. ODY to Walter Lippmann 7/10/25.

17. ODY to J. O'Hara Cosgrave 8/26/25.

18. Nelson Perkins to ODY 11/11/26; Franklin D. Roosevelt to ODY 10/5/25. See also ODY to Winston Churchill 1/23/25, Churchill to ODY 2/10/25. It was three years later when ODY and Churchill finally met. FDR and Churchill had already met once—at a London dinner in 7/1918—but neither made much of an impression on the other (Frank Freidel, *Franklin D. Roosevelt*, vol. II: *The Ordeal* [Boston: Little, Brown, 1954], p. 354).

19. See above, Chapter 15. Among Rathenau's works, the more illuminating and to the purpose are: *Von Kommenden Dingen*, 1917; *Die Neue Wirtschaft*, 1918; *Der Neue Staat*, 1919. For his role in the German economy and polity of the time, see Hajo Holborn, *A History of Modern Germany, 1840–1945* (New York: Knopf, 1969), as indexed.

20. GE Annual Report 1926. Cost-of-living figures were the National Industrial Conference Board's, wholesale price index from the Bureau of Labor Statistics.

21. To National Electric Light Association 5/18/26, Speeches; emphasis added.

22. ODY to I. K. Russell 9/27/26; emphasis added.

23. Ibid. In a series of *Atlantic Monthly* articles, Professor Ripley of Harvard had also been pointing to the divorce of ownership from control; in his view, the danger of abuse on the part of management could be obviated only by devising some new scheme of stockholder control. When H. B. Swope of the *World* invited ODY's comment, the latter replied—not for publication—that stockholders were not interested in control and that no artificial device such as Ripley proposed could make them so; that the only way to curb or obviate abuse by management was to give wide and recurrent publicity to corporate policies and finances—so that the market could judge and rebuke the tricky or the irresponsible (ODY to H. B. Swope 11/22/26). Here certainly—and not only as a matter of hindsight—ODY would

seem to have been far too sanguine in his appraisal of his peers, or human nature, or both.

24. Wallace Donham to ODY 1/31/27; ODY to Donham 4/18/27: HBS file.

25. A. Lawrence Lowell to ODY 11/11/26; ODY to Lowell 11/22/26.

26. HBS and Adler files.

27. HBS dedication address 6/4/27, Speeches.

28. In answer to ENC's query of 6/11/75 as to whether the HBS record warranted such a verdict, Dean Lawrence Fouraker agreed that it did—and with good reason (Fouraker to ENC, handwritten on his note of inquiry; copy in ODY Papers, HBS file). If Dean Fouraker was suggesting that "Utopian" proposals such as Young's are less amenable to productive research and analysis than actual and identifiable developments in the changing business scene, his view would find powerful reinforcement in the publication two years later of Alfred D. Chandler, Jr.'s crowning study, *The Visible Hand: The Managerial Revolution in American Business* (Cambridge: Harvard University Press, 1977). Nevertheless, it is to us a matter of regret that the scope of Chandler's penetrating study, 1840–1920, precluded assessment of the Young-Swope role in this continuing revolution, including the revolutionary objective ODY found worthy of further study and research. It should be noted in any case that in its issue of 5–6/1977 (vol. LIII, no. 2) celebrating the golden anniversary of the dedication exercises, the *Harvard Business School Bulletin* devoted a full page to excerpts from ODY's address, including the key passage and its challenge to the faculty.

29. The passage quoted is from the *Manufacturers and Industrial News* 6/1927.

30. HBS file and Clippings. Conspicuously absent is any word, whether of praise or blame, from ODY's "fellow economists," including those—like Edwin Gay, Frank Taussig and Wesley Mitchell—with whom he had worked most closely.

31. Glass's comment was widely quoted; see, e.g., NYT 6/5/27. The excerpt from a Pacific coast editorial was reprinted in the *Fort Plain Standard* (7/14/27), which was strongly of Glass's persuasion. Since Fort Plain is in the Mohawk Valley twelve miles north of Van Hornesville, it is evident that ODY was not without "honor in his own country."

32. HBS file. Several copies of the reprint are still extant and from time to time a copy is still requested and supplied.

33. HBS file. Except for a copy of Lovett's letter, however, the whole lot was returned to Parker.

34. ODY to ENC in an unrecorded but well-remembered conversation, 9/1927.

35. HBS dedication address 6/4/27, Speeches.

36. Interviews, ODY Papers. Published in an obscure periodical, this had attracted curiously little notice.

37. Address at GE Camp General 7/1/26, Speeches.

38. According to David Loth, *Swope of GE* (New York: Simon & Schuster, 1958), pp. 168–72, the initiative was Swope's; he "asked Young to accom-

pany him . . . since the discussion might revolutionize the company's labor policy." ODY, for his part, had greeted Green's election by urging industry to support him—Green's problem, he said, would be to retain labor's support for his cooperative policies. But regardless of the original source of the suggestion that he be invited in to organize GE, no one who had seen the Young-Swope team in action could conceive of either making such a move without the other.

39. H. B. Dennison to ODY 12/13/27; ODY to Dennison 12/14/27: HBS file.

40. See HBS file for copies of letters cited or quoted here. Except for Aylesworth's, the originals were addressed to McDonald, who had sent copies of the speech to them and to others, and now sent the author copies of their responses.

41. Redlich's praise leaves one wondering why Adolf A. Berle and Gardner C. Means make no allusion whatever to this speech or to ODY's concepts in their study of *The Modern Corporation and Private Property,* first published in 1932.

CHAPTER *21. The Uses of Unexpected Wealth: ODY and Education*

1. For earnings and other income, securities sold (when and for how much, with date and cost of the purchase), taxes, interest and deductible contributions, the basic source is ODY's private file of U.S. income-tax reports. For ODY's salary and extra compensation as chairman, see Special Papers GE. Books and manuscripts purchased for the Young Collection are listed at cost in the box so entitled. For trust funds as set up in 1928, see New York and Richmond Gas files and personal copybooks as indexed. ODY's will of 8/26/30 (in Confidential file) bears eloquent testimony to the thought-out plans he and his wife had developed for the final disposition of his books and their remaining property, real and personal (see below, Chapter 26).

2. ODY to Josiah H. Penniman, president, University of Pennsylvania, 4/16/25.

3. Richard Eddy Sykes was born on a farm near Canton; when he was nine, in 1870, his father was appointed steward of the university. This meant that his parents "boarded" the forty students at $3.50 a week, and ran the college farm. The family lived in Richardson Hall; when Sykes became president, his office was one of the rooms in which the family had lived.

4. There was a through sleeping car from New York to Canton and return in those days.

5. When ODY's youngest son, Richard, went to St. Lawrence as a freshman in 1936, ODY persuaded Gaines, then eighty-five, to give him special lessons in Greek. This Charley consented to do, because the boy was Josephine Edmonds's son.

6. ODY to Clarence M. Woolley 8/20/25.

7. ODY to Stanley Gunnison 6/25/25.

8. ODY to Richard Eddy Sykes 8/6/25.

9. Ibid. 7/9/25.

10. Ibid. 5/12/26.

11. Ibid. 8/7/26.

12. ODY to Dean Edwin Lee Hulett 8/25/26; ODY to Irving Bacheller 9/21/27.

13. ODY to Sykes 11/2/25.

14. Among the Curie papers in the ODY files is a scrap of paper with a scribbled list—in English—of needs for her laboratory, in Mme Curie's handwriting.

15. ODY took advantage of these resignations to address a letter to "The Graduates and Friends of St. Lawrence University," suggesting that the annual Alumni Fund should be the largest in history "to celebrate this event." It was.

16. It is on this site, when ODY finally retired from GE, that his children built for him a small stone and wood office, with a vault for his papers and a big sunny room for him to work in. From the windows the view of the creek is the same that he saw in his school days.

17. Silas C. Kimm to ODY 12/17/26.

18. ODY to J. G. Wilson Corporation 3/14/27.

19. Ernest Sibley to ODY 4/12/27.

20. Remarks by ODY at the Van Hornesville School 7/4/28, Speeches.

21. ODY to Elmer Ellsworth Brown 12/27/27.

22. ODY to Sibley 3/6/27; ODY to C. E. Patterson of GE 12/14/27.

23. ODY to Mrs. George Hoague, president of the Massachusetts PTA, 8/9/31.

24. ODY to authors—and indeed to many others.

25. ODY to Maurice S. Hammond 11/27/33; ODY to Dean Thomas Ordway 10/15/31.

26. Ordway to ODY 2/27/32. When the Rockefeller grant was no longer forthcoming, the Albany Medical College had to give up the Van Hornesville project. A liaison was then formed with the Mary Imogene Bassett Hospital in Cooperstown, which sent, successively, two able doctors, Dorothy Shiedel and Anne Bahlke, to Van Hornesville.

CHAPTER *22. The Young Collection: "Next to My Family Come My Books"*

1. Charles Goodspeed, *Yankee Bookseller* (Boston: Houghton Mifflin, 1937). Goodspeed also reports a typical reaction of Charles Tyler: "When I unrolled for him a half dozen portraits—Sumner, Webster, Cass and

others—'Don't bother me with a few of these. Bring me a big lot—I want slathers of them' " (p. 127).

2. Gabriel Wells, "The Love of Collecting," *Saturday Review of Literature* 1/17/25.

3. When the family was again in England in 1927, the place chosen for a rendezvous for the parents and children, who were taking different sight-seeing routes, was Nether Stowey, in honor of Coleridge and Wordsworth.

4. ODY to James F. Drake 2/13/30.

5. ODY to Samuel W. Reyburn 11/29/27.

6. ODY to Drake 4/8/27.

7. James Fenimore Cooper to ODY 1/2/26.

8. Edwin Wolf II with John Fleming, *Rosenbach: A Biography* (New York: World, 1960), pp. 215–16.

9. Ibid., pp. 307–13.

10. JEY to Josephine Young 1/4/24, from London.

11. ODY to Howard C. Levis 8/3, 8/6/27, from London.

12. Walter T. Spencer to ODY 11/18/24; ODY to Spencer 2/17/25.

13. Spencer to ODY 2/9/25; ODY to Spencer 3/3/27; Spencer to ODY 3/31/27. A note on ODY's method of dealing with Spencer is brought out in a letter he wrote (12/21/28) in answer to a customs broker's question about the "special discount" which reduced the value of a shipment of books from Spencer from £25,142 to £17,560:

> The discount was wholly a matter of trade. My custom in dealing with Mr. Spencer is and has been for many years, to select from his stock items which I wish and to ask him to list them at the prices at which he marks them. When the total bill is made up we endeavor to make a trade on the total purchase. I usually expect to get from 25 to 33⅓ per cent off. If for any reason we are unable to make a trade on the total, then I begin to eliminate the items which are most uninteresting to me. This goes on until we finally reach a trade, and that accounts for the item of special discount which is carried on this bill. Insofar as the form of discount goes, it is a credit against all items. Of course, in fact, it means that I am willing to pay more for certain items than for others, and undoubtedly Mr. Spencer is willing to sell me certain items at a substantial discount and other items with very little discount. Our views on that matter frequently do not match, and therefore it is impossible to attach the discount to any particular item or group of items—

which must have given the customs broker a new view of the rare-book trade.

14. Spencer to ODY 1/6/34.

15. In a letter to Spencer, 2/3/28, ODY introduced Edgar Wells, and advised Spencer that Wells did not like "trading," and that Spencer should name his lowest price at once. "I would not want you to do that with me, because that destroys a lot of fun, and I have no fear really that you ever will."

16. That Christmas of 1928 was spent in Chandler, Arizona, where JEY was spending the winter because of her health. The family came for a

Christmas of sunshine, and the children never forgot the excitement of the gift of that manuscript. When, in 1895, Ida Young had sent Owen, at the Law School, a gift of two dollars on the thirty-ninth anniversary of her marriage, he bought a copy of Burns's poems with the money.

17. To look after his treasures, ODY had as librarian, at first, Mrs. Nelson Robinson, a St. Lawrence friend, who catalogued the expanding collection with painstaking care. When she had to leave because of illness, Young engaged a well-trained young woman, Sarah Dickson, who worked with the books for about three years with devotion and expertise. Even after the collection was put away in storage she was consulted on special problems, such as the *Tom Jones* case. "Certainly," she wrote in answer to one of these requests, "I take more interest in your library than anyone else in the world except yourself."

18. "An Explanatory Address" by Charles Kelsey Gaines, 11/3/29, printed by the university, copy in ODY Papers, Books.

19. NYT interview with Jerome Kern, 10/18/28. In 1927 Kern sent ODY as a gift a "Sterne memorandum"—a receipt for cash received—which they both believed was for money to go on the trip which became *The Sentimental Journey*, about which ODY had already some Sterne letters.

20. ODY to Jerome Kern 10/18/29.

21. John Livingston Lowes to ODY 9/22/28.

22. ODY to E. V. Lucas 12/4/34.

23. Edmund Blunden to ODY, Christmas, 1934.

24. Quoted in Goodspeed, p. 200.

25. See ibid., pp. 201–11, for Goodspeed's telling of this story.

26. ODY to Edward L. Dean 12/21/31.

27. ODY to the Reverend Cornelius Greenway 1/25/30.

CHAPTER *23. Unfinished Business, Private and Public*

1. *Annual Report* of agent-general, 12/1927, and supplemental report of 6/1928. Copies plus representative collection of press clippings are in ODY Papers, Reparations.

2. ODY address at Bryn Mawr commencement 6/7/28, Speeches; 1928 record of office appointments (chronological).

3. Charles G. Dawes, *Notes as Vice President, 1928–1929* (Boston: Little, Brown, 1935), pp. 155–57, makes it clear that he—and former Secretary Hughes—fully shared ODY's misgivings.

4. British industry—and labor—feared that with transfer protection removed, Germany's necessarily intensified efforts to increase its exports and diminish its imports would have devastating impact on Britain's still shaky recovery—notably on coal mining and foreign trade; see Clippings (arranged chronologically). Efforts to "rationalize" Britain's old-fashioned industrial setup, notably in textiles, had met with resistance, and if London's financial supremacy had been largely superseded by New York's, the pre-

carious stability of sterling now seemed threatened by the newfound strength of the franc and the Bank of France. See Stephen V. O. Clarke, *Central Bank Cooperation, 1924–1931* (New York: Federal Reserve Bank, 1967), pp. 139–42. Benjamin Strong's letter to George Harrison of 7/27/28, quoted in Clarke, p. 140, cites English resistance to "rationalization," and Sir Josiah Stamp's letter to ODY of 12/14/28 indicates his doubts —only lately resolved—about the course that he himself should follow if asked to tackle the reparations problem again.

5. RCA Annual Report for 1928. On 10/26/28 ODY wrote Thomas Cochran of Morgan's, briefing him on negotiations for a communications merger.

6. BCB as indexed. ODY's interest in Weir's taking the lead is partially disclosed in later communications to him: 10/17 and 11/21/28.

7. Appointments and Clippings. ODY's role in the proceedings is reported in the nearest local paper, the *Fort Plain Standard*, 10/25/28.

8. Arrangements for the private car were made 10/9/28. See also ODY to Richard Ellsworth 10/9/28.

9. Appointments, Speeches, Clippings, and BCB as indexed.

10. The Schenectady statement was reported but not featured—e.g., by the *Fort Plain Standard* for 10/25/28; others gave it short shrift (Clippings).

11. The *New York Sun* editorial appeared on 10/23/28. See also Speeches and Clippings.

12. *New York Telegram* 10/17/28. To Robert Treat Paine, a GE director, ODY gave an early account of the Russian negotiations; BCB 2/10/28.

13. ODY to Basil Miles (of the ICC) 1/9/28; also Clippings. For the James dispatches cited, see NYT 10/17 and 10/30/28.

14. Mildred Adams Kenyon, unpublished interview with ODY of 7/28 and 7/29/55, pp. 8, 9. At this writing the material she prepared for a history of the Federal Reserve is still in the custody of Brookings Institution, Washington, through whose courtesy—and hers—copies of the several ODY (and JHC) interviews are in the ODY Papers.

15. For an outside but not unknowledgeable report on the difficulties attending the selection of Strong's successor, see *American Banker* for 11/5/28. ODY's messages to Gilbert of 11/12/28 and later can be found in BCB as indexed; for his explanation of this demarche, see Kenyon interviews, second series, 9/15 and 9/17/55, p. 11. For John Brooks on Harrison, see his *Once in Golconda* (New York: Harper & Row, 1969), p. 153. ODY, also mentioned in the press as Strong's successor, wrote an enigmatic letter to Dwight Morrow, then ambassador to Mexico, on 10/17/28, the day after Strong's death, asking for word of any commitments he had pending for the next three weeks. Does this suggest he had Morrow in mind for the Federal Reserve, the Reparations Committee, or something else? Relevant to these questions is ODY's subsequent letter to Morrow of 11/14/28, also enigmatic until one equates the "Chicago friends" who may be waiting on him with ODY's earlier and confidential suggestion of Morrow for the presidency of the University of Chicago (ODY to Harold H. Swift 6/20/28, BCB). In his November letter, ODY also expressed the hope that Morrow might be named secretary of state, which would of course take precedence

over anything else. For ODY's later suggestion to Andrew Mellon that Morrow be named chairman of the new experts committees, see p. 428.

16. ODY to Lord Weir 11/21/28.

17. ODY to Franklin D. Roosevelt 11/26/28, FDR and Water Power files.

18. ENC to ODY 11/28/28.

19. Unless otherwise noted, ODY's appointments, activities and correspondence as recorded here and throughout the rest of this chapter are taken from the daily office schedules prepared and preserved by his secretary, Lillian Morrison; from press clippings—including the *Nation*'s "Open Letter"—prepared and filed by his financial secretary, Gertrude Chandler, and from correspondence files which, thanks to his old-fashioned copybooks, are far more nearly complete for outgoing than for incoming communications. Such of these as bear on reparations are also—for the most part—separately filed under that heading. The chronological file of ODY's speeches is an ever-present source. N.B.: ENC's occasional notes of conversations with his chief—uneven at best—are almost nonexistent for this period. Far more useful are JYC's chronological summaries prepared from the above sources and checked by her own recollections, especially where family affairs and relations are concerned. These are now a part of the ODY Papers.

20. For Weir's health problem and consequent acceptance of only a limited role, see ODY to Samuel Insull 12/13/28 (BCB). ODY had already consulted Insull (2/15/28, BCB) about GE's hopes and plans for Britain, and Insull had offered to help with Weir. ODY's view of GE's role in relation to the development of the industry worldwide is informally but suggestively set forth in his impromptu speech at GE's Camp General, 7/30/30 (Speeches). Perhaps his clearest and most comprehensive statement so far as Britain is concerned is to be found in his letter to Sir Felix Pole, dated 11/9/29 and marked "not sent." But the earlier letters cited here, and the still earlier ones to Sir Robert Kindersley (7/27/26) and Montagu Norman (4/4/27) are also illuminating; certainly they make no secret of the steps—including the purchase of a controlling interest in Metrovick—which, goaded by British inaction, GE had recently taken in order to effect a partial unification. Incidentally, the candor with which ODY outlined his plans in these letters hardly squares with the conspiratorial thesis advanced—not without certain evidential support—by two British journalists, Robert Jones and Oliver Marriott, in their *Anatomy of a Merger* (London: Jonathan Cape, 1970). See also below, Chapter 24.

21. Dawes, *Notes as Vice President*, pp. 224–26, 228.

22. Not surprisingly, this effort was for ODY not strikingly original, and read today, it has its points of unanticipated irony. For him the theme was familiar: the direction of large enterprise necessarily develops a certain largeness of thought, including a sense of broad trusteeship—for investors, workers and the public—which contrasts sharply with the days when management was the paid attorney for the owners. And to illustrate the point, he observed: "We have had much difficulty with questions of technical competence and moral responsibility in the offices of alderman, but we have had practically none in the great office of President of the United States."

23. After GE's distribution of its Bond and Share stock, ODY's directorship in the power company which served Schenectady stood as his sole official connection with any domestic public utility. From the days of the old Adirondack Power and Light he had actively sought, through mergers and enlightened management, to create a company sufficiently strong to meet and indeed anticipate GE's expanding needs and to do this out of its own resources. Thus he now welcomed the Morgan interest in Mohawk-Hudson and a further integration of the industry as assurance for the future and incidentally as affording him the opportunity to withdraw gracefully. Certainly he should not be a member of any board which moved—as he hoped this one might—to take over and develop the properties, and largely dormant assets, of the Frontier Corporation (ODY to T. W. Lamont 12/15/28).

24. When ODY first spoke in these terms, Perkins cited objections from abroad that advance discussion of the work of the committee could be prejudicial and resented. ODY's reply was that the President (Coolidge) had been doubtful about Americans participating in any new settlement until he had defined the job merely as completion of the familiar Dawes Plan. Thus ODY felt in honor bound to state the position publicly—reassured by the knowledge that only the committee could determine what might constitute such completion (ODY to Thomas Nelson Perkins 1/23/29, BCB; copy in Reparations, Box 30).

CHAPTER *24. The Young Plan and the International Bank*

1. See, e.g., ODY's private—and extempore—testimony to his GE colleagues at Camp General, 7/1929 (Speeches). Howard's commentary is taken from his *Theatre of Life* (London: Hodder and Stoughton, 1936), p. 570. For Morgan's biblical reference see Exodus 17:8–16; for the authors' commentary, Judges 3:12–14 and 6:2–5.

2. JEY saved these messages in a trunk which JYC first explored as these pages were written; they are now deposited (and properly labeled) with the ODY Papers, where they obviously belong.

3. The originals of the Coolidge and Hoover letters are filed among ODY's Special Papers; the inscribed and framed photographs of the two, especially of "Mrs. Young's president," had a place of honor in her living room as long as she—and her house in the village—survived. They are now in the vault where the ODY Papers are deposited. That ODY, in supporting Al Smith, still reciprocated Hoover's warm respect and admiration is conspicuously apparent in his letter of 10/11/28 to Missy Meloney of the NYHT. Asserting his faith in Hoover's "liberalism" but asserting also that "no one can be in a more uncomfortable place than . . . a liberal in a reactionary party," ODY wrote in conclusion: "It is not the diamond I am complaining about—it is the setting."

4. John W. Brandow to ODY 2/11/29, ODY Papers re farms.

5. Even before sailing, Crocker had complained to Mrs. Young: ". . . strange how these Vermonters make all men feel that they are kept"

(Stuart M. Crocker to JEY 1/19/29). Vercingetorix, so christened by Jo junior because of his blue eyes, blond hair and bushy mustache, had been the Youngs' chauffeur on her first trip to Europe in 1923, and ODY was delighted to find him again available.

6. Crocker's Young Plan Diary for 2/22–25/29, pp. 42–44, in ODY Papers.

7. Ibid.

8. Hjalmar Schacht, *My First Seventy-six Years* (London: Allen Wingate, 1955), chapter 32. An American edition (Boston: Houghton Mifflin, 1956) soon followed, entitled *Confessions of the Old Wizard*.

9. Crocker Diary, pp. 42–44.

10. FRBNY files; cited by Frank C. Costigliola, "Politics of Financial Stabilization" (Ph.D. dissertation, Cornell University, 1973), p. 607n. It should be noted that their response to ODY's summons automatically made Burgess, Stewart and Shepard Morgan members of "The Bellhops"—that exclusive club to which only the chairman's expert advisers and assistants could belong. The importance of the club arose from the fact that its self-imposed rule—"no member shall do any work"—was flagrantly and indeed systematically disregarded. Other violators, beginning with its wise and experienced chairman, Jeremiah Smith, Jr., included Leon Fraser, former counsel to the agent-general, Franz Schneider, Jr., dean of New York's financial editors, de Sanchez of the Morgan firm, Ferdinand Eberstadt and (later) David Sarnoff. Pierre Jay appeared often enough to qualify, and of course Stuart Crocker and Fred Bate, the committee's indefatigable secretary, were always present and active.

11. Walter Stewart, Shepard Morgan and Randolph Burgess to ODY 3/2 and 3/7/29; Stewart and Burgess to ODY 3/11/29: Box R–36.

12. ODY to Frank B. Kellogg 3/19/29, General Records, Department of State, File #462.00 R. 296/2771; copy in ODY Papers, Reparations.

13. ODY to Kellogg 3/2/29, copy in ODY Papers, Reparations, where there is also a copy of Kellogg's acknowledgment.

14. ENC to Crocker 3/11/29. Case was charged with making periodic reports by radiogram of U.S. press reactions to the news from Paris.

15. Allied and German press clippings, Reparations.

16. Original is filed in ODY's Special Papers: Reparations.

17. As Crocker's Diary notes (e.g., pp. 64–67, 94, and 126–29), both debtor and creditors shied away from opening the bids; their suspicions of each other must have reminded ODY of his earlier poker games in Texas.

18. Undated copy in translation in Reparations. The reference to "four weeks" suggests an issue of 3/11/29 or thereabouts. Incidentally, the chairman was accorded an honorable epitaph: "But even if the conference is interrupted without any seeming result, the merit of Owen Young and his honest endeavors will remain."

19. ODY to Herbert Hoover, enclosing T. N. Perkins's letters (1925) as previously cited, Chapter 18. The Hoover Presidential Library at West Branch, Iowa, has been good enough to send the authors copies of Hoover's memos re the French debt negotiations of 10/1925. ODY subsequently confided to his assistant how, much to his surprise, he had been forced to

conclude that the Allies preferred to count their war debts as part of Germany's "bill" for reparations, rather than to see them canceled and Germany's burden correspondingly reduced (ENC ms notes for 10/10/29, in ODY Papers).

20. Crocker Diary: for use vis-à-vis Schacht 4/23, p. 172; vis-à-vis creditors 5/18, p. 254; see also ODY to Henry L. Stimson 4/20/29, Reparations (Washington Correspondence).

21. ODY to Henry L. Stimson 4/20/29. Copy of the chairman's memo of 3/28/29, filed as Annex 7, is in ODY Papers, R–35.

22. *Commercial and Financial Chronicle* 3/16/29.

23. ENC to Crocker, radiogram of 2/7/29 (in ODY Papers); Lester V. Chandler, *Benjamin Strong, Central Banker* (Washington: Brookings Institution, 1958), p. 466. Chandler (pp. 465–70) has a judicious account of the dilemma confronting the Federal Reserve System in attempting to curb credit for speculative but not for other purposes. See also (p. 426) his chart showing loans to brokers by banks and by "others," 1925–29. See also J. S. Davis, *World between the Wars, 1919–1939: An Economist's View* (Baltimore: Johns Hopkins University Press, 1975), p. 181.

24. ODY to George L. Harrison 3/11/29; Harrison to ODY various dates but especially 4/11/29 (Reparations; also Box 265). See also Mildred Adams Kenyon, interview with ODY of 9/15 to 9/17/55, in ODY Papers. Mellon's attitude toward the board's direct-action policy was cited on the authority of a "High Treasury Official" in the evening papers of 2/26/29. For Mellon's report to the President on the board's rejection of his plea for a higher discount rate, see Harrison's memo of his telephone conversation of 4/26/29 with Mellon (Binder 45, G. L. Harrison Papers, Columbia University Library). Other sources—e.g., the Charles Hamlin Diaries in the Library of Congress—indicate, however, that Mellon's effort was halfhearted if not *pro forma*.

25. Harrison to ODY 4/11/29.

26. Crocker Diary, p. 69. Especially for family affairs an additional source for the next few weeks is the somewhat sketchy—and private—diary of JYC. In February Dawes had been asked by the President-elect to succeed Alanson B. Houghton at the London embassy. He had agreed to serve if Stimson approved; a few weeks later the designation became official and he sailed early in June (B. N. Timmons, *Portrait of an American* [New York: Henry Holt, 1953], pp. 274–78).

27. Crocker Diary, pp. 73–74.

28. Crocker Diary for 4/4/29; ODY to Gerard Swope 2/22/29; Packer's record of ODY's London appointments (filed with ODY's schedule of travels and office appointments). See also the highly colored account of Robert Jones and Oliver Marriott in *The Anatomy of a Merger* (London: Jonathan Cape, 1970), chapter 6, which presents the entire negotiation in a conspiratorial frame, with Gerard Swope as archconspirator. Although this chapter, characteristically enough, is entitled "The Easter Plot," ODY's role—even as there reported—seems more consistent with Packer's factual diary than with the title. Pp. 117–21, however, do give a useful and

objective account of Sarnoff's imaginative and almost successful efforts to carry on after ODY's return to Paris.

29. Crocker Diary, pp. 77, 89 ff. For the Germans' "conditional offer" and its reception, see Crocker, p. 128; Schacht, *Confessions*, p. 240. Schacht also reports (p. 238) on the creditors' proposals and his own role in checkmating "French raids" on the Reichsbank's reserves.

30. Reparations. For Crocker's account see his Diary for 4/9/29, pp. 94 ff. The message contained almost a thousand words—none of them to ODY's liking.

31. Crocker Diary, pp. 94 ff.

32. This digest of Root's advice is condensed from Lamont's extensive memorandum of their conversation of 4/9 (Lamont Papers, Baker Library, Harvard Business School, File 179-27). The same file includes Lamont's subsequent and coded message to Root—who had reached New York on 4/17. Rehearsing Washington's outright rejection of Root's two cardinal points, and the danger of a final breakdown occasioned by our government's intransigence, he urged Root to review the exchange of messages—leaving wholly to his discretion what if anything he might feel called upon to do about them. In his biography of Root (*Elihu Root* [New York: Dodd, Mead, 1938], II, 442) Philip Jessup gives a succinct account of the Paris session of 4/9 and Lamont's follow-up of 4/20. He also places all of this in the context of Root's patient efforts in Geneva to secure such amendments to the statute of the World Court as might disarm senatorial opposition to U.S. participation. In Root's negotiations, it was Secretary Kellogg who had been a major stumbling block; thus he now looked forward to the sympathetic support he could expect from his friend and admirer Stimson. And whether or not, in calling on Stimson, Root took occasion to enlighten him on the reparations problem as well, the secretary's messages to ODY, beginning with that of 5/2, reflected a very different spirit of approach.

33. Crocker Diary, 4/9/29; ODY to Stimson 4/11/29, Box R–35. Kellogg's letter is cited in B. A. Hughes, *Owen D. Young and American Foreign Policy, 1919–1929* (Ann Arbor: University Microfilms, 1969), pp. 303–04.

34. Crocker Diary 4/12/29. The account that follows—of Mellon's reception of the message and his reply thereto—is from ENC's "unwritten diary," for which the files supply supporting data.

35. ODY to A. W. Mellon 4/12/29. Full text (decoded by ENC) is filed in Reparations, Washington Correspondence (R–35).

36. Mellon to ODY, original in Special Papers #3, copy in R–35.

37. Copies of both Stimson cables are in R–35. For Stimson's ignorance of reparations, see Elting Morrison, *Turmoil and Tradition* (Boston: Houghton Mifflin, 1960), p. 374. His own avowal (Henry L. Stimson with McGeorge Bundy, *On Active Service* [New York: Harper & Bros., 1948] is quoted by Frank C. Costigliola, "The Politics of Financial Stabilization: American Reconstruction Policy in Europe, 1924–1930" (Ph.D. dissertation, Cornell University, 1973), p. 474. For Mills's warning of 4/6 that the BIS would mix up debts and reparations, see Treasury Department, Record Group 39, Box 78.

38. Crocker Diary, pp. 258–60.

39. The plenary sessions at which these figures emerged took place on 4/13, 4/15, 4/16, 4/17. Crocker's unusually full report on the objective and "subjective" gaps they reflected occupies pp. 104–40 of his Diary. For the near break, see pp. 142–47; for Revelstoke's death and the chairman's play for time, see pp. 148–50.

40. R–35. In his insistence that ever since the war, the United States government had consistently kept reparations and the Allied debts in separate compartments, Stimson had failed to note Secretary Hughes's statement at New Haven in 1922—as cited above, Chapter 16, note 7: "Debtors to the United States . . . have credit balances and their . . . capacity to pay cannot be properly determined until the amount that can be realized on these credits for reparations has been determined." So, alas, had ODY, for whom it would have served as a peculiarly telling point. The real, if apparently unconscious, *reductio ad absurdum* of the Hoover doctrine that the debts and reparations were never to be linked appears, however, in Henry Robinson's letter to the President-elect of 1/13/29—for which we have to thank Stephen Schuker, who brought it to our attention, and Robert Wood, for sending us a copy from the Hoover Presidential Library. Reporting to his chief on his own efforts to brief Mellon as well as ODY and Gilbert on the "understandings" that should govern American participation in the forthcoming Paris sessions, Robinson cites these two, which, with his concluding observations, we quote without further comment:

a) That no discussion of Allied indebtedness to us should be had, and if attempted, that the United States members of the committee should withdraw from further participation.

b) That in some manner an understanding should be reached that would give the United States assurance that the Mellon-Bérenger settlement of France's indebtedness to the United States would be finally ratified before, or as a part of [*sic*], the agreement fixing German reparations.

Mr. Gilbert expressed himself as in accord with (a) and believed that (b) could be accomplished. I understood that Mr. Mellon and Mr. Young were in accord with both (a) and (b), though I admit that neither was explicit in his reply.

I can only add that, should we participate and the German reparations payments be finally fixed and that then France failed to ratify the Bérenger settlement, everyone connected with the discussion, to put it mildly, would be embarrassed.

N.B.: Thanks largely to Poincaré, France did not fail; by a narrow margin in the Assembly, the agreement was ratified in late 7/1929. On this and all matters relating to war debts and reparations as viewed by the French, see Jacques Seydoux, *De Versailles au Young Plan* (Paris: Plon, 1932).

41. Crocker Diary, pp. 182–83; B. A. Hughes, p. 320.

42. R–35; Crocker Diary, p. 245 ff. Cf. also note 32 above.

43. Reparations, Confidential File, contains a copy of Gilbert's long memo of his conversation with Stresemann of 11/13/28, transmitted to ODY by Parker Gilbert on 3/9/29.

44. Crocker Diary, pp. 246–51. Moreau threatened to resign and blame it on the U.S. government's attitude toward the Bank for International Settlements. Kastl was only less exercised, saying that this played into the hands of the (German) Nationalists. Thus Morgan and Young had to swallow their own anger and disgust in the effort to placate the Germans and French.

45. Crocker Diary, pp. 103–04.

46. The "problem of the Belgian marks" was troublesome and special—special because it arose from the invading German army's willful depreciation of the Belgian currency; troublesome because it was not an integral part of the experts' agenda but Francqui refused to approve any report unless and until a settlement was assured. ODY told Crocker on 5/30 (Diary, p. 309) that if at all possible he would sail on the *Aquitania* and make the wedding even if he had to come back afterward. Happily the return voyage was to prove unnecessary thanks to the prompt settlement of this last divisive issue.

47. Interviewed by ENC (11/1977), Franz Schneider, Jr., reported that as Eberstadt's earlier magic in dealing with Schacht showed (perhaps inevitably) signs of fading, ODY had summoned to the task his friend David Sarnoff, who had more than vindicated his confidence. (ENC's memorandum of 11/1977 as corrected and approved by Schneider.) For Sarnoff's tireless efforts and unique contribution, as well as the handsome tribute ODY (and others) paid him, see Eugene Lyons, *David Sarnoff* (New York: Harper & Row, 1966), pp. 153–55.

48. Bearing a Washington dateline of 6/4, and featured in the NYT and especially the NYHT for 6/5/29, the message as transmitted through the Paris embassy was delivered by First Secretary Edwin C. Wilson on 6/6. That ODY found it so lacking in warmth as to be almost perfunctory came of course as no surprise. True, his primary concern was its probable effect upon the future of the plan, and here it was at least better than no message at all. Nevertheless, he could not fail to contrast it with Washington's enthusiastic reception of the Dawes Plan—and the contrast was hardly a heartening omen for the future.

CHAPTER 25. *Wall Street and Washington: The Crash of 1929*

1. For the "hero's welcome," see the *New York Telegram's* editorial proposal and news report of 6/11/29; for ODY's refusal, NYT (and others) 6/14. The *Evening Post* for 6/15 reports his "rescue," his statement praising the contributions of Morgan, Perkins and Lamont, and his timely appearance at the wedding.

2. In his tribute to two distinguished alumni who were present—Mark Hollister, his old teacher at East Springfield Academy, and Elihu Root—ODY omitted all mention of Root's aid in drafting his reply to Stimson's first cable, lest it embarrass Root's relations with the Hoover administration. He chose rather to stress the importance of sentiment in ending international

deadlocks: agreement at Paris seemed hopeless, he said, until word got around that they must get Owen Young home for his son's wedding and his honorary degree at Elihu Root's College.

3. The accord on acceptable procedure was reached in Washington after ODY and Harrison had conferred at length with the undersecretaries of state and treasury, Joseph Cotton and Ogden Mills. Much of the correspondence relating to the selection process is in the ODY Papers. For a succinct account and full bibliographical notes, see Frank C. Costigliola, "The Other Side of Isolationism," *Journal of American History*, vol. LIX, no. 3 (12/1972), especially pp. 614–18.

4. Against the "standard year" Dawes annuity of 2,500,000,000 deutsche marks, the Young Plan annuities averaged 1,988,800,000 for the first thirty-seven years (excluding 50,000,000 marks for service of Dawes loan), and 1,568,000,000 for the last twenty-two; their average for the first ten years was 1,735,000,000, or 30 percent less than the Dawes Plan's. For tables, see the Report of Second Committee of Experts, 1929. A convenient summary of schedules and plan is set forth in Leon Fraser, *The Reparation Settlement Signed June 7, 1929—International Conciliation for October 1929* (a publication of the Carnegie Endowment). The tables cited appear on pp. 88–91.

5. For an excellent recap of ODY's extempore Paris speech see Leland Stowe in the NYHT 6/10/29; also Arnot Dosch-Fleurot in the *World*, same date. See also John Maynard Keynes's praise of the plan in general and the bank in particular, in an interview with Irving Fisher, New York *Evening World* 6/24/29. Keynes, like Stamp's biographer, credits Stamp with having originated the concept of the bank. For ODY's earlier view of the bank's importance in relation to the outlook for economic advance, see above, Chapter 24, pp. 695–699; also, as cited there, his 7/1929 speech at GE's Camp General, Speeches.

6. Herbert Hoover to ODY 3/13/23; ODY to Hoover 3/16/23: Hoover file.

7. *Collier's* for 7/27/29, p. 62.

8. ODY to William Green 7/31/29; ODY to Ludwig Kastl and Carl Melchior 8/26/29; ODY to P. W. Litchfield 8/19/29.

9. Reparations (correspondence); Ochs's cable arrived 6/5/29, ODY's reply is dated 6/7. Young's press was at its peak in June and July, but the *New York Times Index* indicates that as late as October, November, and December (1929) he was featured in seventeen news items and four editorials (i.e., in the NYT). For the fact that Hoover's staff brought a marked copy of this index to his attention, the authors are indebted to the Hoover Presidential Library at West Branch, Iowa.

10. A voluminous sample of Respess's outpouring is preserved in the ODY Papers. While all alienists to whom these were shown by ODY's staff agreed that the writer's paranoia bordered on a dangerous psychosis, they were far from agreed on the question of whether his increasingly offensive letters constituted valid grounds for a forced commitment.

11. For details of Mme Curie's visit, see Chapter 21.

12. ODY to Josiah Stamp 8/26/29 (not sent). Ambassador Dawes's warm

letter to ODY of 9/9 did prove that at least one high government official had been active in curbing Snowden's intransigence.

13. ODY to Stamp 8/26/29 (not sent).

14. For press reports re GE and AEG, see (e.g.) NYT 8/3 to 8/5/29. For the broader context of their relationship, see Werner Link, *Die Amerikanische Stabilisierungspolitik in Deutschland, 1921–1932* (Düsseldorf: Droste Verlag, 1970), pp. 372, 380. Dwight Morrow once confided to a partner that Owen was so enamored of Germany's electrical industry as to view that country's industrial potential through rose-tinted glasses.

15. RCA Annual Report 1929; Eugene Lyons, *David Sarnoff* (New York: Harper & Row, 1966), p. 155–58; G. L. Archer, *Big Business and Radio* (New York: American Historical Company, 1939), as indexed.

16. Thomas W. Lamont to Russell Leffingwell 2/6/29 (Lamont Papers, Baker Library, Harvard Business School, file 103–13); ODY's testimony at Senate Interstate Commerce Committee Hearings 12/9/29 (Radio file, Box 120). RCA's 1929 Annual Report makes no mention of the ITT agreement.

17. See Chapter 21, note 1, for sources used in recounting ODY's private financial dealings.

18. ODY remarks at GE's Camp General 7/14/29, Speeches.

19. The "leading Chicago bank," quoted in the *New York Journal of Commerce* 8/26/29, was the Continental Illinois.

20. Curiously missing from the ODY Papers, the *Report on Recent Economic Changes* and its supporting studies are available in all good college libraries. J. S. Davis, *World between the Wars, 1919–1939: An Economist's View* (Baltimore: Johns Hopkins University Press, 1975), chapters 6 and 7, gives an excellent review of the prevailing euphoria and of "significant warnings" (including Wesley Mitchell's) which went unheeded. F. R. Dulles, *Labor in America* (New York: Crowell, 1949), chapter 14, has a judicious assessment of the workers' gains and problems during the twenties. (See also Irving Bernstein, *The Lean Years: A History of the American Worker, 1920–1933* [Boston: Houghton Mifflin, 1960].)

21. See Chapter 21, note 1, re ODY's private financial dealings.

22. *New Republic* 7/17/29. For evidence that Felix Frankfurter instigated this open letter, see Frankfurter to Bruce Bliven 6/22, 6/28, 7/3/29 (Box 25, Frankfurter Papers, Library of Congress). We thank Dr. Stephen Schuker for bringing this to our attention.

23. Office and Travel Schedules, letter copybooks (ODY to Charles G. Dawes 9/30/29). See also Dawes, *Journal as Ambassador to Great Britain* (New York: Macmillan, 1939).

24. ODY to Herbert Croly 7/25/29.

25. ODY to Association of Edison Illuminating Companies, Quebec, 9/9 to 9/11/29, Speeches.

26. ODY to A. W. Mellon 8/21/29 and—with thanks for prospective aid—to A. W. and Richard Mellon 11/22/29; also ODY to George F. Baker, Sr., 12/12/29. These letters include his promise to match: "I will strain my resources to the limit and do the same."

27. ODY to John Finley 8/30/29; ODY to Edward W. Bok and Edwin B. Parker 9/5/29. ODY's letter copybooks also contain his sympathetic if negative response of 8/13/29 to the request of the president of Agnes Scott College in Atlanta for an endowment for a "lectureship in international relations." Explaining that his prior obligation to the Page School precluded such aid to others, however worthy, ODY added that his own recent venture in international affairs had already cost him more than endowing the lectureship would require. Judge Parker's bequest—and its terms—was to be the subject of much hopeful but ultimately fruitless discussion between his trustees and those who were working on the Page School's behalf, including ODY's staff and ODY himself.

28. "Stocks up 2 to 12 on Young Accord," reported the *New York Evening Post* for 8/30/29. The Reparations files include congratulatory messages from Morgan, Emile Francqui and Alberto Pirelli but not from Schacht or —on this occasion—from Stamp. For ODY's reluctance to accept the Roosevelt Medal pending favorable action at The Hague, see his letter of 9/17/29 to Herman Hagedorn, BCB. Briand's government fell on 10/22; Jon Jacobson in his *Locarno Diplomacy: Germany and the West, 1925–1929* (Princeton: Princeton University Press, 1972), pp. 353 ff., speaks of this—and Stresemann's death—as marking the end of an era.

29. ODY to German ambassador Baron Friederich von Prittwitz und Gaffron 10/10/29, BCB. For an excellent German appraisal of the impact of Stresemann's death, see Hajo Holborn, *A History of Modern Germany, 1840–1945* (New York: Knopf, 1969), chapters 10 and 11, especially pp. 615–16 and 642–43. Walter Lippmann's sympathetic article on "Snowden at the Hague" (*Vanity Fair* 11/1929), explaining that Snowden had been no party to the political decisions demanding reparations and war-debts payments, said this was equally true of the experts: "The Young Plan, therefore," he concluded, "is a brilliant, ingenious and highly imaginative scheme for executing decisions that the Committee was not permitted to examine." See also, re Snowden, Dawes's *Journal as Ambassador*, pp. 42–44, 50–54.

30. See Chapter 21. The Edison celebration was given a great play by press and radio. Henry Ford was host; ODY made the opening remarks and the speakers included President Hoover, Einstein, John D. Rockefeller, Jr., and Edison himself. Mme Curie sat at the President's right. According to Will Rogers, "It was just like a big country picnic . . . a lot of my favorites were there" (NYT 10/22/29). ODY wrote Nelson Perkins 10/13/29 (BCB) that Churchill had expressed a special wish to see him before leaving for England; Perkins, however, was in the South and unable to make the necessary arrangements.

31. See, e.g., *Washington Post* and NYT 10/25/29. The full resolution as adopted by the Universalist General Convention is published in the *Commercial Advertiser* (Canton, N.Y.) for 11/12/29; a copy is in ODY's Clippings.

32. Speeches. For press reports see, e.g., NYT 10/28/29.

33. Office Diary and personal financial records. For behavior of the market, see any metropolitan paper for evening of 10/30 or morning of 10/31. Re bankers pool, see Goronwy Rees, *The Great Slump* (New York: Harper & Row, 1970), p. 49.

34. For Warburg's statement and its context, see J. S. Davis, chapter 7, especially p. 182. ODY of course was still in Paris at the time but working privately toward similar ends.

35. John Brooks, *Once in Golconda* (New York: Harper & Row, 1969), pp. 118–19. Sections of the press called the market "convalescent" as early as 11/16—see, e.g., the New York *World* for that date.

36. ODY to Samuel Insull 10/30/29; ODY financial records as cited. See Forrest MacDonald, *Samuel Insull* (Chicago: University of Chicago Press, 1962), pp. 279–82, for Cyrus Eaton's efforts to challenge Insull's control.

37. The locus of this meeting and the presence of Julius Barnes make one wonder whether the President had suggested it, perhaps to advise him on the timeliness of the White House conference announced on 11/16. If so, there is nothing in the ODY Papers—or apparently in the Hoover Papers—to confirm it.

38. ODY to Lena H. Salomon 12/3/29, BCB. GE stock was split 4 for 1 in early 1/1930. In terms of the old shares, 1930's earnings actually came to $7.80 and dividend payments to $6.30 per share (Annual Report 1930). For Insull companies' capital expenditures see MacDonald, p. 285.

39. Press clippings re JEY's activities are among ODY's, in chronological order.

40. ODY's Office Diary.

41. The exchange is filed under Radio, 11-14-1.

42. ODY's testimony is a matter of public record (see Senate Committee on Interstate Commerce Hearings 12/1929). While ENC has consulted the record to refresh his memory, his recollection of the confrontation and his part in the proceedings is still vivid.

43. The authors are indebted to Frank Costigliola for a copy of a letter Bernard Baruch wrote ODY on 1/5/29, in which Baruch said: "Grayson has told me often . . . the following story about President Wilson" and his wish "to send word to Owen D. Young . . . to look after the interests of America on the wireless" (Baruch Mss, Princeton University Library, Letter Book 1929, Vol XXIII). We can't believe this is not preserved among ODY's Papers but so far we have not found it.

44. Senate Committee on Interstate Commerce Hearings 12/9/29.

CHAPTER *26. The Pivotal Year: Convalescence and the Radio Suit*

1. *Time*, vol. XV, no. 1 (1/6/30). Almost daily reports on the problems of this conference appeared in the New York papers. See New York *World* 1/22/30 for one of the most illuminating.

2. Formal announcement of McGarrah's resignation and Case's designation was featured, e.g., in the NYT 2/28/30, but the *New York Telegram* of 1/31 had carried much the same story. Its antecedents, moreover, suggest

nothing so much as a game of musical chairs, involving Pierre Jay as well as J H C and McGarrah. In 1926 Parker Gilbert had urged J H C to head the Dawes Transfer Committee; his long letter of 4/17 was handwritten and also hand-delivered—by McGarrah. When J H C felt impelled to decline and Jay resigned as chairman to take the job himself, J H C was evidently offered and declined Jay's post at the bank, which McGarrah then took over. (See Jay's letter of 3/9/30, congratulating J H C on accepting the chairmanship "this time.") Copies of both letters, taken from J H C's files, are in the O D Y Papers, F R B N Y folder. A long letter from Benjamin Strong, dated 3/6/27, in O D Y's Confidential (F R B), Special Papers #5–6, indicates, however, that Randolph Burgess had been *his* first choice to succeed Jay.

3. O D Y to J. P. Morgan 2/28/30; E N C to J H C 3/1/30; O D Y to Governor Roy Young of the Federal Reserve Board 10/10/29.

4. N Y T 9/4, 11/16/29, 1/1/30; *Schenectady Gazette* 4/16/30. For the Hornblower and Weeks citation, see the W S J 2/28/30. For the early collapse of the market for cars and textiles and consequent unemployment, however, see Irving Bernstein, *The Lean Years: A History of the American Worker, 1920–1933* (Boston: Houghton Mifflin, 1960), pp. 254–55.

5. N Y T 1/4/30.

6. Ibid., 11/16/29, 1/1, 4/3/30. R C A's Annual Report for 1930 (p. 23) shows R K O's net earnings at $3,385,000, up from $1,669,000 in 1929.

7. Copies of Schacht's cable and the Security–First National *News Bulletin* for 1/15 are in the Young Plan folders. See also Eleanor Dulles, *The Bank for International Settlements at Work* (New York: Macmillan, 1932), pp. 20–34; Hajo Holborn, *A History of Modern Germany, 1840–1945* (New York: Knopf, 1969), pp. 640–48.

8. For the Respess letters, see above, Chapter 25, p. 458 and note 10. Three weeks prior to castigating O D Y the *Nation* had accorded him a prominent place in its Honor Roll for 1929.

9. O D Y to J. F. Cranston 1/15/30; O D Y to J E Y 1/17, 2/20, 2/24/30.

10. O D Y to J E Y 1/25/30; O D Y to Gerard Swope 1/24/30 and 1/28/30. O D Y's long radiogram to Swope of 1/24 spelled out the deal:

> Clarence Dillon has made arrangements to take debentures of Siemens which are to bear interest rate equal to the dividends paid on the stock but never less than 6%. The security takes this form so as to avoid the criticism [of] selling stock abroad. The total debentures will represent participation in earnings to the extent of 36% of the total. Dillon says stock is selling at 285% of par yielding around 4½% on present dividends, whereas debentures can be bought at price equivalent to 230% of par and will yield over 6% on present dividends. For $23 million we could purchase enough debentures to hold as security [for] 25% participation in earnings as Dillon figures it. He is ready to make public offering, but is holding it up until he hears from me. . . .

11. O D Y to Swope 2/7/30; for his Camp General remarks, 7/30/30, see his Speeches as indexed. G E's Annual Report for 1929 had already cited I G E's investment in Germany's A E G as well as Osram, "the largest manufacturer of incandescent lamps in Europe"; additional investments in Phillips (of Holland) and in the French Thomson-Houston Company were also noted.

Rounding out the picture of the industry's "international integration," GE's Report for 1930 added to the list the investment in Siemens and in Ganz of Hungary while noting IGE's "substantial interest" in England's Associated Electrical Industries. Patent exchanges accompanied these investments.

That Swope's active role in effecting this integration should have been ignored by his biographer is a matter for regret, not least because it was Swope's vigorous efforts to unite the English companies that cast him—posthumously, alas—as Robert Jones's and Oliver Marriott's archvillain. But David Loth—whose book (*Swope of GE* [New York: Simon & Schuster, 1958]) long preceded theirs (*The Anatomy of a Merger* [London: Jonathan Cape, 1970])—may himself have suffered from that dearth of company—or even personal—records which makes the true facts of Swope's progress abroad hard to come by. Our own correspondence with a subsequent IGE president, William Rogers Herod (now deceased), discloses little more than his own faith in Swope, and his consequent concern that Swope was no longer here to speak for himself. E. J. Kahn's account (*The World of Swope* [New York: Simon & Schuster, 1965], pp. 321–23) of the activities of Herbert Bayard Swope and his friend Thomas Chadbourne vis-à-vis General Electric Ltd. in 1929 does, however, lend some color to a part of these authors' freely expressed suspicions.

More important were steps taken by IGE at the close of 1930 to "incorporate" ODY's global concept. After an abortive effort in November, to which counsel objected, IGE tried again; on 12/13 there was executed at its Paris Office a so-called Notification and Compensation Agreement, signed by AEG and Siemens, one Swiss and four British companies, as well as Westinghouse International and IGE. Counsel still being dubious, IGE and Westinghouse International set up on 2/4/31 a Webb-Pomerene export association through which they might indirectly—and so legally (?)—participate in the Notification and Compensation Agreements. Although this cartel—as it was later held to be—proved no match for the depression and its operations were suspended with the outbreak of World War II, a postwar U.S. Government antitrust suit ended in the consent decree of 3/12/47 which enjoined further participation of the American companies, direct or indirect, in its activities (FTC report entitled "International Electrical Equipment Cartels," 6/30/48). Politics, it seemed, refused to follow here.

12. ODY to Henry L. Stimson 1/9/30; ODY to Dwight Morrow 1/10/30; ODY to Charles G. Dawes 1/21/30.

13. ENC ms Notes for 2/28/30 (in ODY Papers).

14. BCB and Office Calendar; ENC ms Notes 2/24/30; Bernstein, p. 355. To an emissary of Walter Teagle's who called to get his views, ODY had indicated his sympathy with the AFL's dilemma, but also reported William Green's rejection of GE's earlier invitation to come in and organize its plants. His caller at once identified Green's problem: how to justify to his associates and locals any dealings with company unions, and ODY agreed that industry could help him only as he solved it. Perhaps the consensus was that Green was still powerless to do so.

15. ODY to L. G. Myers 1/9/30. That Swope did not feel any such restraint in his personal dealings is evident in his biographer's allusion to his actions when, in the spring of '29, call money briefly commanded 20 per-

cent. According to Loth (p. 192), "Swope, who had been in the market with a million of borrowed money, now prudently sold all his stock holdings except GE . . . and invested the proceeds in the call money market." On at least one occasion the fact that GE invested its treasury funds in governments, rather than the call market, paid off affirmatively. On 10/29/29, JHC called his son from the Federal Reserve to say "that it was touch and go . . . whether they could keep the Exchange from closing its doors, and to do that they were putting as much money into the market as possible. He had just bought $50 million governments and . . . wanted to buy $20 million more at once. He thought GE might sell that amount." ODY, also at the bank, had agreed, but would not authorize it without Swope's approval. In a frantic half-hour's search ENC finally found Swope at the National City directors' meeting, located Jesse W. Lewis, the treasurer of GE, and the sale was authorized and made. "I was half an hour late for luncheon," wrote ENC in his memorandum of this affair, sometime later, "and I don't know whether Father ever did get any—but at least the Exchange did not close its doors!"

16. In calling it an "economic success" ODY was thinking primarily of the men in GE's plants and their larger take-home envelopes now that the saloon was no longer competing with their families for their wages.

17. ENC ms Notes 1/13/30.

18. New York *Evening World* 1/15/30; ODY to JEY n.d. (c. 1/16/30). For a fascinating account of the games FDR was playing with the Republican legislature to get his power commission, see Frank Freidel, *Franklin D. Roosevelt*, vol. III: *The Triumph* (Boston: Little, Brown, 1956), chapter 8.

19. Office Calendar; ODY's Tavern Club remarks were apparently not recorded.

20. BCB.

21. Office Calendar and Speeches; these remarks were recorded but not released to the press.

22. Minutes of NBC Advisory Council for 1/29/30 (in ODY Papers); ODY to Richard Ellsworth at St. Lawrence 1/30/30, PCB. The original reluctance of a few members—e.g., Elihu Root and Charles Evans Hughes—to accept any honorarium for membership on the Advisory Council had been overcome by ODY's explaining that it was hardly fair to some to ask their services gratis, and it might embarrass them to accept what others declined.

23. Office Calendar; ODY to JEY 2/5/30.

24. RCA Annual Report 1930; Federal Trade Commission Report of 1928, in re complaints against RCA; *Fortune*, vol. I, no. 2 (4/1930). For an able defense of RCA's licensing and royalty policies, see Eugene Lyons, *David Sarnoff* (New York: Harper & Row, 1966), pp. 112, 114–15.

25. ENC ms Notes 2/4/30.

26. ODY to Emile Francqui 2/6/30.

27. ODY to Josiah Stamp 2/6/30. Derso was a noted French cartoonist, a set of whose merciless caricatures of Young Committee members was presented to each one by the chairman.

28. ODY to Justice Harlan Stone 2/11/30; ODY to Page trustees 2/5/30; NYT 2/15/30.

29. Freidel, III, 122–23; Office Calendar, copybooks and Clippings for 2/1930, especially NYT 2/12 and 2/13/30. As for the meeting of the Finance Committee of the General Education Board, the authors have not seen the minutes, but would nevertheless wager that ODY's letter to the treasurer was not contested—and not only because the call market was now notably less attractive than it had been a year earlier.

30. JEY to ODY 2/26/30. The Yankee Republic was a nation invented by Richard Young, in the history of which various members of the family held important positions—some holding more than one; his sister, for instance, was both Archbishop and Major-General of Marines.

31. University of California Charter Day address 3/24/30, Speeches. The NYT, the NYHT and even (at Jesse Jones's suggestion?) the *Houston Chronicle* printed it in full. ODY's Clippings contain a good cross section of press coverage and comment. See also below, Chapter 29.

32. See, e.g., NYT 5/14/30.

33. ENC's recollections of the diverse reactions to the suit have been checked by reference to ODY's voluminous files on RCA and his press clippings. Evidently Swope's statement at the GE stockholders' meeting got wider press attention than his comment on the proposed further investigation of the Radio group. See, e.g., NYT 4/17 and 4/18/30; also 4/18 for Dill.

34. ENC ms Notes 5/3/30.

35. Ibid. 5/10/30.

36. Ibid. 5/12/30.

37. *New York Telegram* 5/15/30; ENC's *post hoc* analysis is the basis of much of this paragraph.

38. ODY to Glenn Frank 5/20 and 5/21/30.

39. RCB #4. That John W. Davis would be defending counsel for AT&T indicates that the original agreements had been adjusted to meet his interpretation rather than Roland Boyden's.

40. For Senator Reed's conduct of the case, and Grigsby-Grunow's meteoric rise, see R. Berry in the New York *Evening World* 6/28/30. For Grigsby's earlier complaints against RCA in testimony to the Couzens committee, see Erik Barnouw, *A History of Broadcasting in the United States*, vol. I: *A Tower in Babel* (New York: Oxford University Press, 1966), pp. 255–56.

41. Calvin Coolidge to ODY 5/9/30.

42. ODY to Coolidge 5/19/30. The Committee on Recent Economic Changes, in a later release, reported a 30 percent gain in public construction; see, e.g., *New York Evening Post* 6/27/30.

43. Data regarding ODY's finances are taken from his U.S. income-tax reports, the file of transactions with his broker, George Pick and Company, and his financial secretary's letters to commercial and investment bankers.

44. A copy of this will, marked "Cancelled December 16, 1930," is in a file labeled "Confidential."

CHAPTER *27. The Pivot Unhinged: End of an Era*

1. Herbert Hoover to ODY 6/10/30; ODY to George Akerson 6/10/30; ENC to Akerson 7/1/30: BCB and Hoover file.

2. A memo to the President, dated 8/25, from his loyal friend and supporter Edgar Rickard (of the Belgian Relief and Food Administration teams), does, however, suggest the contrary. Filed in the Hoover Presidential Papers at West Branch, Iowa, under the subject heading "RCA 1929–32," this Rickard memo begins: "George Baldwin tells me that Young feels hurt that his request for a conference with you and the Attorney-General was denied. I told Baldwin I could hardly credit a deliberate refusal to see Young; that I had never heard you express other than a friendly feeling for Young; that I knew nothing concerning the Administration's attitude toward the Radio Corporation other than what I read in the papers." While there is nothing in ODY's papers, or habits, to suggest that he had sought such a meeting, this testimony warrants something more than a summary dismissal. Now president of Hazeltine (Electronics) Corporation, Rickard would certainly have been following the Radio suit. George Baldwin, a GE vice-president, was an able executive whom ODY had once "lent" to Hoover when, as secretary of commerce, he had sought help in reorganizing the department. Knowing both men, Baldwin could well have placed his own construction on some remark of ODY's and decided that it called for immediate action on his part. Nor is it inconceivable that Young, knowing his man, might have dropped a deliberate hint in the expectation that Baldwin would indeed do something about it. Certainly ODY's Office Calendar records a visit from Baldwin on 8/25 and again on 8/26.

Admittedly, the circumstantial evidence suggests that the Rickard memo may well have *precipitated* the September meeting. In the absence of corroborative evidence from the Hoover Papers, however, we cannot accept at face value its purported revelation of an initiative which, for ODY, would have been out of character. As for the meeting itself, it is our considered conclusion, based on all the evidence at hand, that the President (1) would not have invited ODY down to discuss the Radio suit and (2) would have been most unlikely to introduce the topic once his guest was there. (Cf., e.g., *The Memoirs of Herbert Hoover* [New York: Macmillan, 1952], II, 246: "I told them to give them [the Radio group] both barrels.") And since, as we are in a position to attest, it was ODY's unvarying rule when visiting the White House to leave the initiative to his host, "one may safely assume," we now repeat, that the suit was not among the topics discussed.

We take the occasion, however, to acknowledge our debt to the Hoover Presidential Library at West Branch, Iowa, and more particularly to Robert Wood of the National Archives and Records Service, for calling our attention to the provocative memorandum which has occasioned this exercise. We are further indebted to the same sources for a copy of a letter to the President from Henry M. Robinson, dated 8/1/30 (White House: Robinson file), which suggests another possible subject for discussion at that same meeting. Because the subject was one on which the President and Young had not always seen eye to eye, it is doubtful that the President would have introduced it now unless he were seriously considering action; hence, we reproduce it here without further comment and for whatever it is worth:

Dear Mr. President [it read]:

Doubtless you are noticing that the discussion is beginning about the need for a reduction in the standard reparation annuities of 2,000 million marks and the argument, which is apparently sound, that the fall in gold prices since the adoption of 'the Dawes Plan has been about 28% and nearly 20% since the Young Plan was formulated. The discussion in all probability will grow stronger and stronger, with the creditor countries saying "yes" when America makes a like reduction.

In all probability, from an economic standpoint, a reduction should be made in the reparations and possibly at some other points. *To the American voter this will not have a strong appeal.*

I am merely suggesting for your consideration watchfulness as the *propaganda* takes more definite form.

N.B.: The emphasis was apparently not Robinson's but was added for the President by a member of his staff.

3. For the President's later message on commodity prices, see p. 520. That Meyer had seen both the President and George Harrison in early July and lunched with ODY on 8/12 is indicated by ODY's engagement schedule and letter from Robert Wood to ENC of 9/28/76. Also before leaving for Washington on 9/2, ODY conferred with the New York Fed's chairman, J. H. Case. In announcing Meyer's appointment on 9/5, the President said it was to be effective as of 9/15/30.

4. ODY NELA address 6/19/30, Speeches; ODY to ENC 7/1/30; ENC ms Notes (in ODY Papers).

5. NYT 6/20, 6/21/30.

6. NYT 6/20/30. The plan is recounted at some length in GE's Annual Report for 1930.

7. See, e.g., *New York American* for 10/12/30. Other Hearst papers, notably the *Boston Sunday Advertiser,* gave the coming interview advance notice, complete with photo of ODY, and then praised it editorially. See also *Philadelphia Record* and *Denver Post,* same date.

8. ENC ms Notes 4/18/30.

9. ODY to Henry L. Stimson 8/7/30—the very day of Cooper's call. On 9/16/30, a "hitherto unpublished letter" from ODY and Clark Minor of IGE to Amtorg, dated 10/9/28 and giving details of their own credit agreement with the Russians, appeared in the press and, notably, in the *Schenectady Gazette*; it was reprinted from *The Soviets in World Affairs* (New York; Cape & Smith, 1930), Louis Fischer's new book. In substance, GE had agreed to waive all claims for damages suffered through nationalization of the old Russian General Electric *provided* that, prior to 10/1935, the Soviets purchased at least $25 million worth of new equipment and met all credit payments when due. See Fischer, II, 766–67; also J. H. Wilson, *The Role*

of the Business Community in U.S. Relations with Russia and Europe (Ph.D. dissertation, University of California, 1966; University Microfilms, 1973), pp. 353–54.

10. ODY to P. S. Arkwright 7/15/30.

11. ODY to Frank B. Kellogg 8/7/30.

12. *Yale Review,* Fall 1930. See also *Knickerbocker Press* (Albany) 9/29/30 quoting undated NYT editorial, Clippings.

13. M. H. Aylesworth to ENC to ODY; ENC ms Notes of 4/16/30.

14. NYT 6/16/30; New York *World* 6/17/30.

15. NYT 6/16/30.

16. The two radio-in-education groups had confusingly similar names but very different orientation. The National Committee on Education by Radio, which saw no hope in the current broadcast setup, was based, significantly enough, in Washington; the other, based (also significantly?) in New York, was the National Advisory Committee on Radio in Education. The latter, financed chiefly by the Carnegie Corporation, was headed by Levering Tyson of Columbia University and the Adult Education Association.

17. For CJY and facsimile transmission, see *Schenectady Gazette* 4/4/30; ODY to Ernst Alexanderson 4/9/30; and ODY to B. C. Forbes 4/10/30, thanking him for notice of C.J.'s achievement.

18. ODY to J. R. Coleman 8/11/30.

19. The Camden and Philadelphia papers for 9/19 and/or 9/20/30 have the fullest account of this affair. For ODY's several letters, mostly dated 9/22, see his Radio copybook. Rukeyser's piece appeared in *Forbes* 9/15/30.

20. ODY to Charles G. Dawes 9/29/30.

21. ODY to Hjalmar Schacht 8/13/30; M. J. Pusey, *Eugene Meyer* (New York: Knopf, 1974), pp. 207–08. For the general tenor of Schacht's commentary, see Stuart Crocker's report of 10/9 to ODY on their visitor's speech of 10/6 to the Council on Foreign Relations (T. W. Lamont presiding). ODY had been "unable" to attend, but a copy of Crocker's report promptly reached the President (Henry M. Robinson to Akerson 10/10/30).

22. Pusey, *Meyer,* pp. 207–08.

23. ENC ms Notes 9/11, 9/29, 9/30/30. Tarbell repeated this observation in the preface to her book, *Owen D. Young: A New Type of Industrial Leader* (New York: Macmillan, 1932).

24. For sources of these financial data, see Chapter 21, note 1.

25. The *New York Daily Investment News* for 10/21/30 printed the comment on ODY and GE. An excellent summary of the continuing speculation by the press, both here and abroad, is in *London's Financial Chronicle* 11/22/30. See also Clippings.

26. ODY to Josephine Young 11/4/30.

27. JEY to Josephine Young 11/2/30 (original in JYC's possession).

28. Lillian V. Morrison to ODY 10/24/30. The Packer diary is in the ODY Papers.

29. ENC to ODY 11/24/30. Contemporaneous records of the FRBNY in-

clude an invaluable running commentary on the series of negotiations revolving about the troubled Bank of U.S. Prepared by several hands from day to day, these internal memoranda focus chiefly on the intensive negotiations extending from Saturday, 11/15, through Monday, 11/24; and again from 11/29 through the morning of 12/10. They will henceforth be cited by date and name (when name is appended) as FRBNY Internal Memo. The authors are deeply indebted to the archivist and to the bank's current officers and staff for permission to quote from these hitherto unpublished documents. The memo cited here, dated 11/20/30, was prepared by Deputy Governor L. R. Rounds as a summary of developments from late October through 11/19.

30. See, e.g., J. S. Davis, *World between the Wars, 1919–1939: An Economist's View* (Baltimore: Johns Hopkins University Press, 1975), pp. 203–4. He cites, however, the criticisms advanced by sources as diverse as Parker Willis and Milton Friedman.

31. JHC's personal memo of 10/28/30 records the offer; this and his refusal are confirmed in his letter of 11/25 to Governor Meyer of the Federal Reserve Board. (JHC's personal files are now in ENC's possession, pending their transfer to the Hoover Library at West Branch, Iowa.) A bank memo, prepared by Harold Bilby, then a junior officer, reports on the press stories of 10/28 and 10/29.

32. FRBNY Internal Memo by Rounds of 11/20/30. Burgess's role is implicit in his own memoranda as subsequently cited; a matter of common knowledge at the bank, it was attested by his chairman in no uncertain terms and witnessed at the time by ENC.

33. Dating from 1853, this voluntary association comprised mainly the well-established downtown banks and was notably chary of welcoming others. Thus admission of a new institution, representing a merger of several nonmembers, would be generally regarded as a guarantee of its viability and acceptability—especially important when at least one component had been under suspicion. And membership, if not a guarantee, was almost a *sine qua non* of aid from other members.

34. FRBNY Internal Memo by Rounds, as cited and continued through 11/24. Burgess's memo of 11/22 gives an excellent account of that evening's meeting.

35. FRBNY Internal Memo by Rounds 11/20 to 11/24/30. See Burgess's memo of 11/23 for Sunday's all-day and all-night sessions, consequent upon the Public National's second thoughts about the merger and its last-minute agreement to go along.

36. Forbes in *New York American* 11/26/30, Clippings. The numerous messages of congratulation preserved in JHC's papers include not only ODY's radiogram but also a handsome letter from President Hoover, who was well aware of the dangerous weakness of our multiple banking system (to which —in sheer perversity?—we the people still cling). See Hoover's *Memoirs*, III, 21–28. Cf. also ODY's remedial proposal in his Senate Banking Committee testimony of early 1931, as cited in the following chapter. Copies of Burgess's candid and illuminating letter of 11/25/30 acquainting the

governors of the other regional banks with the critical nature of the problem which the merger—and Case's crucial role therein—had finally solved are in JHC's papers and the FRBNY archives.

37. Office Schedule of appointments.

38. ODY's speech, with the others, was printed by the Lotos Club in a pamphlet entitled "In Honor of Owen D. Young" (copy of ODY's address in Speeches). See also Clippings for 12/4/30. ENC's ms Notes for 12/3 contain some references to it, including ODY's statement—no part of the speech —about the President; but the impressions of the occasion here recorded are based on ENC's recollections—far sharper for 1930 than for 1980.

39. The paper in ODY's files which records this statement is dated 12/31/30, but bears a penciled notation by ENC's then secretary, George Riddle, identifying it as delivered at the committee's luncheon 12/9/30.

40. FRBNY Internal Memos (anonymous) of 11/29/30; also and especially of 12/6 to 12/9/30, inclusive. Copy of the Public National's fateful "Ultimatum" of 12/7, in Burgess's handwriting, is in JHC's papers.

41. The FRBNY records cited thus far end abruptly with their notice of an officers' meeting at 10:00 A.M. on 12/10/30. For the fateful sessions which ensued, ending in the early hours of 12/11, our account is based largely on Broderick's testimony at his subsequent trial, as reported in the *New York Evening Sun* and the *New York Evening Post* for 5/11/32. Indicted for neglect of duty in failing to close the Bank of U.S. sooner, Broderick was (happily) acquitted. For Broderick's—and Governor Roosevelt's— earlier but futile efforts to save the bank, see Frank Freidel's admirable account in *Franklin D. Roosevelt*, vol. III: *The Triumph* (Boston: Little, Brown, 1956), pp. 186–90.

42. To the best of our knowledge this testimony of Broderick's was never challenged.

43. Copies in the authors' possession of Harrison's cables and replies thereto from Europe's central bankers—notably the Swiss—leave no doubt that this failure deepened Europe's fears of its own vulnerability to more of the same here. (These will go to ODY Papers, FRBNY file.)

44. Broderick's testimony as cited in note 41. Dated 12/11/30, an anonymous FRBNY Internal Memo records the runs suffered by these and other metropolitan banks. As for business and the market, the press bears witness to their sharp downturn; see especially the NYT's "Weekly Review of Business" and its Sunday market résumé for the last three weeks of 12/1930.

45. For historians of the period, we venture to suggest, this is a circumstance worth rather more attention than it has had to date. Certainly the consequent loss of confidence in this great quasi-public institution could only compound (as it did) the shattering impact, at once national and international as well as local, of this closing of a metropolitan "member bank." Why, then, once the merger had been publicly announced and JHC's name publicly involved, had its linchpin, the Public National, been permitted peaceably to withdraw? And why, in the ensuing showdown, with one or two of the clearinghouse banks "refusing to go along," had Harrison declared himself "in no position to press them"? While for our

part we may well pronounce further speculation fruitless, certain teasing questions do remain.

46. ODY to William P. O'Ryan 12/30/30.

47. Confidential files.

CHAPTER *28. 1931: Year of Adversity*

1. Printed copy of speeches at Lotos Club dinner for ODY; in Lotos Club file box.

2. Office Calendar; NYT 2/5/31; *Time*, vol. XVII, no. 7 (2/16/31).

3. The *Time* report explained in a footnote: "Of the 24,000 banks of deposit in the U.S., 7000 are national, 17,000 state. Five out of six failures occur among State banks not members of the Federal Reserve System."

4. For the early promise of recovery and its collapse see J. S. Davis, *World between the Wars, 1919–1939: An Economist's View* (Baltimore: Johns Hopkins University Press, 1975), pp. 258–59. On 2/16 the House passed the bonus bill 363 to 39; vetoed on 2/28, it was quickly passed over the veto. Hoover's concession in his veto message re help for needy veterans only had come too late, especially since Treasury Secretary Andrew W. Mellon had immediately rejected ODY's compromise proposal. For a particularly enthusiastic commentary on ODY's testimony, see Frank Kent in the *Baltimore Sun* for 2/6/31. Even the *New Republic*, which opposed the bonus, gave it grudging praise.

5. ODY speech at St. Lawrence dinner, 2/15/31, Speeches.

6. Office Calendar. In Van Hornesville 3/1–3/3, he attended services for Abe Tilyou; on 3/4 he was at Dr. Hervey's bedside on Long Island; five days later Hervey too was dead. In Van Hornesville on 3/10 for his mother's ninety-second birthday, ODY returned to New York and attended services for Dr. Hervey on 3/12 at the Church of the Divine Paternity. He arrived in Arizona (via Van Hornesville and Chicago) on 3/25.

7. Josephine and Philip Young went to Van Hornesville at once and learned of their mother's heart attack only on 4/10 when the Arizona contingent arrived. As for ODY's visit with the attorney general, he told his assistant he intended to ask whether the government was prosecuting RCA for technical breach of the law or as a vicious conspiracy in monopolistic exploitation of the public. If it was the first, and only so, quick settlement should be possible. (ENC ms Notes, 4/22/31; in ODY Papers). For the ensuing conferences and exchange of views by letter, see ODY's Office Calendar and Boxes 77–81 (RCA papers). Box 77 contains ODY's initial response to the proposal for an open patent pool (ODY to Charles Neave 5/15/31).

8. Clippings.

9. Office Calendar, Clippings; ODY speech at St. Lawrence 8/14/31, Speeches. The St. Lawrence speech was in great demand among the more thoughtful educators, including that "Master Quaker," Rufus M. Jones, of Haverford and Bryn Mawr.

10. ODY remarks at Van Hornesville School 6/22/31, Speeches.

11. The sources of information on ODY's personal finances are cited in Chapter 21, note 1.

12. Werner Link, *Die Amerikanische Stabilisierungspolitik in Deutschland, 1921–1932* (Düsseldorf: Droste Verlag, 1970), pp. 489–504; Eckhard Wandel, "Entstehung und Ratifizierung des Young Plans" (dissertation, Eberhard-Karls University, Tübingen, 1967), pp. 97–103; J. S. Davis, chapter 10, especially pp. 260–67; Stephen V. O. Clarke, *Central Bank Cooperation, 1924–1931* (New York: Federal Reserve Bank, 1967), pp. 182–85. See also Hajo Holborn, *A History of Modern Germany 1840–1945* (New York: Knopf, 1969), pp. 668–96, for an illuminating account—in English —of the economic and political tribulations of the Brüning regime (1930–32). To a great degree these stemmed from the orgy of borrowing which had followed the success of the Dawes loan; as early as 3/1928 the European correspondent of the *Chicago News* quoted ODY as expressing in an interview "his own alarm at German borrowing to finance extravagant home consumption." See Edgar Ansel Mowrer's *Triumph and Turmoil* (New York: Weybright and Talley, 1968), p. 167.

13. See note 12; also Elting Morison, *Turmoil and Tradition: A Study of the Life and Times of Henry L. Stimson* (Boston: Houghton Mifflin, 1960), p. 350, for Dwight Morrow's urging that France be consulted. At the last moment, Stimson did advise Ambassador Paul Claudel of the President's impending message but Paris did not regard this as "due consultation."

14. Office Diary. ODY's Confidential file contains his own recollection—dictated the same day—of the statement to be made by the President which he recommended on 6/13 to Ogden Mills. The short-term debts of the German banks remained an acute problem until the so-called standstill agreement of July-August provided temporary (six months) relief. See also M. J. Pusey, *Eugene Meyer* (New York: Knopf, 1974), p. 209. Stimson attributed Hoover's rejection of the two-year moratorium to fear of Congress (Morison, *Turmoil and Tradition*, p. 348).

15. Press coverage of ODY's statement on 6/22/31 was exceptional; even the *New York American* featured its full text. ODY's Clippings also include an editorial from the *Baltimore Sun* (sent with a covering note from the editor, John Owens, on 6/23) which asserted that "one reason why democracy . . . does seem to work . . . is that it releases and fosters intelligence, and in an emergency has a way of turning the chairman of a great electric enterprise, along with many other . . . first class men, into public servants whose words are heeded in political quarters." It was this kind of statement which prompted ODY's "apologia" to the President (ODY to Herbert Hoover 7/9/31, BCB).

16. See note 12. An admirably clear and concise account of developments in Europe both before and immediately following the Hoover moratorium is in R. H. Ferrell's chapter 7 of his *American Diplomacy in the Great Depression* (New Haven: Yale University Press, 1957). Clarke's account (his entire chapter 8) is also clear and knowledgeable, and the bibliographical scope of J. S. Davis's chapter 10 is impressive and exceedingly useful. For the role of the BIS—necessarily limited—see Eleanor Dulles, *Bank for In-*

ternational Settlements at Work (New York: Macmillan, 1932); her report
on the European scene of 1931 (chapters 11–15) is at once comprehensive
and lucid. See also Pusey, *Meyer*, pp. 209–11, for Meyer's intervention to
prevent a presidential statement in support of the German banks, which
he felt would merely leave the United States holding the bag.

17. The quotation is from Clarke, p. 219, who adds that "the value of
world exports in 1932 was about a third lower than . . . the year before
and only two-fifths that of 1929."

18. Wallace Donham to ODY 6/4/31; ODY to Donham 6/10/31 and 6/26/
31: BCB and Donham folder as indexed; *Outlook and Independent* 7/5/31
(Box 733).

19. David Loth, in his *Swope of GE* (New York: Simon & Schuster, 1958),
pp. 201–15, has an admirable summary and a not uncritical analysis of the
Swope plan and its reception at the hands of industry and publicists, government and the press. Consult also, for its background and antecedents,
Loth's pages just preceding (196–200). For briefer résumés, still in context,
see A. M. Schlesinger, Jr., *The Age of Roosevelt*, vol. I: *The Crisis of the
Old Order, 1919–1933* (Boston: Houghton Mifflin, 1957), pp. 182–83; and
J. H. Wilson, *Herbert Hoover: Forgotten Progressive* (Boston: Little, Brown,
1975), pp. 151–54. Wilson's apparent implication (p. 152) that the Swope
plan called for publicly rather than privately supported unemployment
insurance is misleading, but her treatment of the President's reaction is
most illuminating.

20. Loth, pp. 201, 205–06; WSJ 9/17/31, which also contains a long and
incisive summary of the plan itself.

21. WSJ 9/17/31.

22. For Swope's relations with President Roosevelt, see Loth, pp. 220 ff.
For the Swope plan's contribution to New Deal planning, see R. F. Him-
melberg, *Origins of the NRA* (New York: Fordham University Press, 1976),
pp. 127–31, 135, 157; also Ellis W. Hawley, *The New Deal and the Problem
of Monopoly* (Princeton: Princeton University Press, 1966), pp. 41, 44. In
his *Memoirs* (New York: Macmillan, 1951–52) Hoover pronounced the
plan sheer fascism and revealed that in first sending the plan to his attorney
general he had called it "the most gigantic proposal of monopoly ever made
in this country" (cited by Loth, pp. 208–09).

23. Some of these are in the authors' possession; not all make pleasant reading. During the fall of 1931, as we have reason to remember, Japanese
liberals who had opposed or questioned the Manchurian adventure were
largely silenced if not liquidated by the superpatriots of the military junta.
Recalling their own cordial reception in October by Dr. Takuma Dan of
Mitsui and Kengo Mori of the Young Committee, the authors were shocked
on their return stopover from China in December to find them both under
virtual house arrest. They were glad indeed to board their homeward-bound
ship. In March came the news that Dan had been assassinated.

24. ODY to Robert M. La Follette 10/15/31.

25. John Wheeler-Bennett, *The Wreck of Reparations* (New York: Morrow, 1933), chapter 6. In Hoover's message of 12/10/31, he expressly
opposed any cancellation of debts to the United States. See Morison, *Tur-*

moil and Tradition, pp. 424–26. Morison quotes Stimson's diary for 7/11/ 32 as evidence that Hoover himself still "thought that the debts to us could be paid, and that the European nations were all in an iniquitous combine against us." Stimson's entry goes on to say, quoting Drew Pearson, that "talking to Herbert Hoover about war debts was as futile as negotiating with last year's leaves." Stimson had reason to agree. This July entry was made just two days after the signing of the historic Lausanne agreement, virtually abrogating further reparations payments.

26. J. S. Davis, p. 285; Pusey, *Meyer,* p. 216, cites Meyer's role not only in pressing the President to act but also in drafting the bill: Senator Robinson pledged his support (Pusey adds) only if Meyer would also run the agency. According to Dawes's biographer (B. N. Timmons, *Portrait of an American* [New York: Henry Holt, 1953], p. 313), Speaker John Garner's opposition became support only with the assurance that the RFC would be administered by "Republicans like Charley Dawes and Democrats like Jesse Jones." ODY found it easy to support all three.

27. RCA Annual Report for 1931; ODY to the attorney general (8 pp.) 10/1/31. GE's action in reducing its dividend was reported by the press on 4/20/32. For ODY's effort to prevent AT&T's separate peace, see his letter of 1/20/32 to Walter Gifford (BCB). This letter, with its account of the helpful attitude of Oswald Schuette (of the Radio Protective Association, which had pressed hard for the government suit), admirably illustrates the rising interest of the independents in achieving a fair and speedy settlement for the benefit of the suffering industry.

28. ODY's Office Calendar records the series of calls, and meetings with the bankers, that his effort involved. For announcement of the Insull failure and its initial impact, see any paper for 4/8/32.

29. ODY's Office Calendar places him in Washington (with his son Richard) on 3/26–27; with Baruch on 4/24, where they saw Senator Robinson, Speaker Garner and Senator Pat Harrison. His purpose in returning on 4/30 is undisclosed but on 5/5/32 William Packer wired him at Van Hornesville that the House Ways and Means Committee had rejected the Patman bonus bill for full payment to all veterans, which he had opposed. On 4/27 he called on Al Smith; a fortnight later (NYT 5/12 and 5/13/32) the press was heralding the support of both for the Robinson-Wagner bill. For Hoover's original objections, veto and the outcome, see Schlesinger, I, 150–151. See also below, Chapter 30, for full development of ODY's program.

30. Schlesinger, I, 150–51.

31. NYT 4/29/32; *New York Journal of Commerce* 4/30/32.

CHAPTER *29. 1932: Climax of an Apolitical Career*

1. *Collier's* 7/6/23. Stuart Crocker sent off a radiogram to ODY in London, quoting the article, of 275 words. ODY replied in 20 words, saying he had no comment and hoped that others would say nothing.

2. ODY to John M. Stewart 9/14/23.

3. ODY to Governor Albert C. Ritchie 12/29/24. Ritchie was one of the leaders of the Democratic party and a prospective candidate himself.

4. Lincoln Steffens to ODY 5/24/26, from Casa Montague, Alassio, Italy.

5. ODY to Steffens 7/12/26.

6. ODY to John B. Miller 7/12/26.

7. ODY to Robert Wagner 10/11/26. Wagner's speech at Ilion, New York —an area ODY knew well—on 2/16/27 was pure ODY. This is the only instance of which the authors know when ODY acted as a ghost-writer.

8. ODY to Wheeler J. Welday 3/1/26.

9. ODY to W. McH. Howe 3/4/26.

10. ODY to Cordell Hull and statement sent to Hull 3/3/27. Hull himself drafted a statement, as did Norman Davis, and others.

11. Statement by ODY to reporters on 8/23/27 from the *Olympic* on his way home from the International Chamber of Commerce meetings in Stockholm.

12. NYT editorial 11/28/27; ODY to V. H. Hanson 11/28/27. In a long and interesting letter to Ida Tarbell, 5/12/31 (Ida M. Tarbell Collection, Reis Library, Allegheny College, Meadville, Pa.), Hanson tells the story of his initial nomination of ODY—for which he was still very active at the time this letter was written. During 1927 his campaign against the Klan was proceeding successfully, and the end of its power was in sight. The greatest danger to victory over the Klan was the nomination of Al Smith, which would give "a rallying cry that might save the Klan," as it appealed to the fundamental prejudices of the people against a wet Catholic. "Every move we made had been ascribed to our purchase by a slush fund raised by the backers of Al Smith, and thousands literally believed this to be true." If Hanson's newspapers supported Smith, "the effectiveness of the fight we had made and the sacrifices we had gone through would be lost." Then ODY appeared at the Jordan Dam, and Hanson lost his political heart to him: "The more I thought of the man, the bigger he loomed in my mind . . . this man had more of the qualities of high leadership than any man I had ever met. . . ."

13. ODY to Alfred E. Smith 11/28/27; Smith to ODY 11/30/27.

14. ODY to James W. Bullock 2/6/28.

15. Newton Baker to E. A. Filene 6/21/28; Filene sent ODY a copy.

16. Franklin D. Roosevelt to ODY 8/10/28.

17. Statement issued by the Democratic National Committee 9/29/28.

18. ODY wrote a long letter to Clifton B. Carberry of the *Boston Post* 9/10/28: he judiciously assayed the candidates and stated his reasons for thinking Smith would be able to do the better job; the *Post* came out for Smith. ODY also attempted to bring McAdoo into Smith's camp (ODY telegram to William G. McAdoo 10/17/28) but without success.

19. Little details like voter registration did not matter much in Van Hornesville in those days.

20. B. F. Sunny to ODY 7/18/28.

21. ODY to Sunny 7/25/28.

22. NYHT 12/11/29. Both the NYT and the NYHT printed the entire testimony.

23. Hard wrote two articles on the hearings, 12/11 and 12/12/29. They were syndicated by David Lawrence. The clippings in the ODY files are from the *Gary* (Indiana) *Post Tribune*.

24. *Washington Post* 12/15/29.

25. NYT editorial 3/25/30.

26. NYT 3/26 to 3/27/30. Rogers and ODY were old friends. Once on a train, as ODY was leaving the dining car after breakfast, Rogers came in: "Would you like my copy of the *New York Times* to read with breakfast?" asked ODY. "Hell no," replied Rogers, "I'm paid to write for the damn thing, not to read it."

27. *Schenectady Gazette* 5/1/30; *Collier's* 5/3/30.

28. Grayson's statement on returning to the United States, in the New York *World* 7/8/30.

29. New York *World* 11/29/30. The press photos taken on this occasion are excellent; they make it clear that the trip had done him good.

30. *Collier's* 12/6, 12/13/30; ODY to Hanson 12/9/30.

31. *New York Evening Post* 11/8/30.

32. *Review of Reviews* 2/1931.

33. *New York Daily News* 2/6/31; *Baltimore Sun* 2/6/31.

34. Clinton Gilbert in the *New York Evening Post* 2/19/31; "Gentleman at the Keyhole," *Collier's* 4/4/31, called it a "whiff of personality."

35. *Nation* 2/25/31.

36. Alpheus T. Mason, *Brandeis: A Free Man's Life* (New York: Viking, 1946), p. 601.

37. *Collier's* 3/7/31.

38. *New York Evening Post* 4/16/31.

39. *Annals of Internal Medicine*, vol. LXV, no. 4 (10/4/66). Dr. Wright entitled his article "The Man Who Declined the Presidency: Owen D. Young." ODY told Wright the story of the nonfunctioning turbine which none of the specialists could fix; ODY suggested that a nonturbine engineer look at it and he found the cause. "Experiences like this have convinced me that for many problems we need the men with the broadest view. You select them." The panel consisted of Dr. Richard Cabot of Harvard, Dr. W. S. Thayer and Dr. Walter Baetjer of Johns Hopkins, Dr. Walter Alvarez of the Mayo Clinic, and Dr. Chace. Dr. Wright, now Professor Emeritus of Clinical Medicine, Cornell University Medical College, and a good friend of the authors, designed this article "as an example of the significance of medical problems in influencing the course of history" (Irving S. Wright to ENC 1/9/79). It was published with the full consent and approval of the family —in spite of which a curious error in the printed version cuts JEY's years of survival in half. After the consultation she lived for nearly four years, vindicating the panel's prophecy.

40. *Collier's* 4/14/31. The Gentleman added, "Mr. Young is the least ob-

scure dark horse that ever was whispered about at the trackside of a Presidential race." And the column is headed by one of Haenigsen's most charming cartoons: two politicians with a lariat looking at a pasture full of light-colored, broken-down nags, among whom stands, alert and handsome, a beautiful black horse.

41. The series appeared in the *New York Daily News* 5/29 to 6/13/31. In regard to the quotation from part 9, see the first chapter of this book. A French reporter interviewing ODY at the time of the Dawes Plan had also suggested his resemblance to the "noble red man."

42. *Harper's* 8/1931. Frank Kent, who had given ODY a good chance for the nomination in an article in *Scribner's Magazine* 6/1931, noted in his column of 8/16 that Mayor Hague of Jersey City—who ran a machine as corrupt as any in the country—was an ardent advocate of ODY for President; "the biggest man in the Democratic Party and its best bet," said Hague.

43. NYT 9/3/31; *Baltimore Sun* editorial 9/3/31.

44. In his home county of Herkimer, however, ODY was defeated for membership on the local relief committee. The Board of Supervisors (fifteen Republicans, five Democrats) voted 15 to 5 against him. This bit of news made most of the newspapers in the nation.

45. Rogers spoke from Los Angeles; his speech was printed entire by most newspapers. The clipping in the ODY Papers is from the *Watertown* (N.Y.) *Daily Times* 10/20/31.

46. Joe Williams in the *New York World-Telegram* 11/18/31. This account was accompanied by a charming drawing of ODY in football uniform, carrying the ball, which is marked RELIEF—one of the best of the many cartoons depicting ODY. Actually ODY did not "invent" the idea; games had been played for charity before, but this was the first nationwide effort.

47. NYT 12/13/31.

48. ODY to Herbert Bayard Swope 12/21/31.

49. ODY to Louis Seibold of the *New York American* 2/2/32; Seibold in the *American* 5/15/32.

50. *Nation* 3/30/32.

51. ODY speech before the Northern Schoolmasters Club meeting at St. Lawrence 5/7/32, Speeches; Frank Kent in the *Baltimore Sun* 5/13/32.

52. *Newark Evening News* 5/11/32. This had its hazards. On 5/16 Franklin P. Adams (FPA)—who should have known better—wrote in the "Conning Tower" of the NYHT: "Owen D. Young, possible nominee of possible political party, traces depression to high wages in industry [*sic*]. Mr. Young, who traces well on Mondays, Wednesdays and Fridays would not reveal his favorite brand of tracing paper."

53. Esther Young wrote her mother, Mrs. N. A. Christensen, about this not long after the event; the quotations are from that letter (copy in ODY Pappers).

54. ODY to Roosevelt 7/5/32. His statement on party unity was released to the "Democratic Victory Campaign" on May 22.

55. ODY at Metropolitan Opera House 11/3/32, Speeches. The next day's

rise in the stock market "on a broad front" was widely attributed to ODY's reassuring words.

56. *Birmingham News* 5/17/32; *New York Evening Post* 5/17/32; ODY to Verne Barnes, Raritan, Ill., 6/16/32. One admirer of Young, however, had paid no attention to his refusal to run; this was Herbert Bayard Swope of the *World*. Politicking at the Democratic convention in support of Al Smith, Swope soon discovered that his favorite could not be nominated. He turned at once to ODY in his effort to prevent the nomination of FDR. E. J. Kahn, Jr., tells the story in *The World of Swope* (New York: Simon & Schuster, 1976), pp. 365–66:

> Swope kept his brother [Gerard] posted through a series of telegraphic communiques from Chicago. NEVER IN MY EXPERIENCE WAS A CONVENTION SO RIPE FOR THE PICKING AS THIS WOULD BE WERE MY HERO [ODY] FREELY AVAILABLE STOP. So Herbert wired Gerard at 4:43 one morning, after a night of furious politicking on Young's behalf: R. [Roosevelt] HAS MOST OF THE DELEGATES BUT NO FRIENDS THE OTHERS HAVE MOST OF THE FRIENDS BUT NO DELEGATES STOP AS I WIRED YOU WILL TAKE A MIRACLE TO BEAT HIM IF THAT MIRACLE OCCURS TWILL BE THROUGH A VOTE BLOC AND THEN THE NOMINATION OF MY CHOICE NONE OTHER CAN TURN THE TRICK HIS NAME ELECTRIFIES THOSE WHO HEAR IT THERE MUST BE A CHANCE FOR DRAFTING LOVE

57. *Providence Bulletin* 5/18/32.

CHAPTER *30. Banking and Industrial Committees: A Twice-flawed Effort*

1. NYT 5/20/32; *Commercial and Financial Chronicle* 5/21/32; NYHT 5/26/32.

2. Mortimer Buckner, Jackson Reynolds and Albert Wiggin will perhaps be remembered for their parts in the Bank of U.S. tragedy. The others were C. E. Mitchell of National City Bank, William C. Potter of Central Hanover and A. A. Tilney of Bankers Trust.

3. *Baltimore Sun* 5/18/32; see also Clinton W. Gilbert on the "Young Mystique," *Collier's* 6/25/32.

4. NYT 5/21/32; ODY Office Calendar; *New York Journal of Commerce* 4/30/32.

5. ODY to Herbert Hoover 5/11/32.

6. W. D. Mitchell to Lawrence Richey 6/14/32, Herbert Hoover Presidential Papers, Radio, West Branch, Iowa. Copy in ODY Papers, Radio.

7. See, e.g., "TRB" (its Washington correspondent) in *New Republic* for 6/22/32; also ODY to Charles G. Dawes 5/31/32, and ODY to Newton Baker 6/8/32. See also Governor Harrison's memo on 5/30 meeting (Harrison Papers, FRBNY) and B. M. Anderson, *Economics and the Public Welfare* (New York: Van Nostrand, 1949), p. 273. Hoover was puzzled and worried, long after the event, by Mills's "failure" to deliver to ODY by hand

(as instructed) his personal letter of 6/3/32, which he evidently thought would have been salutary. We are indebted to Robert Wood, assistant director of the National Archives, for calling this to our attention. A comparison of calendars for this almost frantic week suggests that Mills had been unable to make connections with ODY until matters were resolved, and the letter no longer relevant. Through Wood's courtesy and that of the Hoover Library at West Branch, Iowa, a copy of the letter is now filed in the ODY Papers, Hoover folder.

8. President Sykes of St. Lawrence, the "baccalaureate" speaker, observed to the authors that Van Hornesville seemed to be the real capital of the country.

9. See B. N. Timmons, *Portrait of an American* (New York: Henry Holt, 1953), pp. 316–22, especially for Jesse Jones's defense of the loan; also Anderson, pp. 274–75. Dawes's critics typically paid no attention to its context. For Meyer's defense, see M. J. Pusey, *Eugene Meyer* (New York: Knopf, 1974), p. 224.

10. ODY to John H. Finley 6/16/32. Copies of these and other reviews are in Clippings, 6–7/1930. After reading the ms, ENC and Stuart Crocker devoted several hours to a vain attempt to persuade the author that not even Owen Young could be *that* good; it only made her spring to his defense!

11. ENC to ODY, memo of 6/14/32, B&I files. Unless otherwise noted, this account of the B&I Committees' efforts is based primarily on fragmentary notes and memorabilia kept by ENC, plus occasional ODY or Federal Reserve letters and speeches, news clippings, and so on. If any systematic records were kept, they have evidently vanished; the files of the Federal Reserve Board and the New York bank reveal scarcely a trace. (For such scanty material as has so far surfaced in Washington, the authors are indebted to Merritt Sherman, sometime secretary of the board.) A happy exception to the foregoing, however, is the singularly illuminating entry for 6/8/32 in Agnes E. (Mrs. Eugene) Meyer's unpublished diary, which we owe to the generous thought of Meyer's biographer, Merlo Pusey, and—with permission—here reproduce verbatim (this is cited, with brief quoted excerpts, in the Pusey biography, p. 222):

I am excited this morning because I intended to see H [Hoover] and warn him of the danger he runs in trying to grab the com.s which E [Eugene Meyer] is organizing all over the country under the Federal Reserve Board. With the campaign coming on the danger to him is grave because some of the Dem. on the Com's might get off in a grouch and say that Meyer had formed these groups under false pretenses. The boomerang for H is too obvious to any one but a Pres. candidate which he now is. It is the kind of mistake he has made over and over again and I am not going to let him make it again if I can help it. My theme will be "The soundest political strength is a bi-product [*sic*] of right action."

Have just returned and got nowhere. He tried to tell me how this idea of the com's was his, how all the N.Y. men went on the com. because of him, that the Chicago man would not take the chairmanship until he asked him to, and that they were all telegraphing him "For God's sake let's have a meeting."—"Eugene thinks I am nothing but a politician but there has got to be leadership in this situation. I am the Pres. for better or for worse, and I have got to do the leading." He talked in loud angry tones. I respect him for being determined on one thing anyway— his leadership. When that, in his opinion, is threatened, he is certainly ready to fight. But alas his thinking is confused to say the least. One moment he tried to convey the idea that he was not thinking politically and the next he betrayed that—Owen Young was still a candidate for the Presidency and trying to use this Com. to further his cause! That is childish, of course, because Young could not possibly get anything out of the situation in the next three weeks before the Dem. Convention. His fears of possible rivals is something terrible to see. In this connection he mentioned that most of the R.F.C. staff are Dem. and that "we can't give the Democrats everything." Above all things *he* formed these local com's and he told me frankly I was under a delusion if I thought E. had organized them. From now on I shall know better than to reason with a Presidential candidate. When I saw that his talk of Owen Young had behind it the idea that E and Young were in cohuts [*sic*] I said to him "Don't ever think that I am more loyal to you than Eugene." That seemed to make him pause and think. I told him that since he was fixed in his purpose, I would take his point of view and work on it. Before I left he told me he was in trouble over the Dawes resignation because of the difficulty of getting somebody for the job whom Congress could trust. He actually doesn't seem to know that in reality it matters very little whom he puts in. For the first time I fully realize E.'s Difficulties with H. and his with Eugene. Poor Eugene is trying to save the country, and the Pres. is trying to save Hoover.

12. ENC to ODY, memo of 6/14/32.

13. Pusey, *Meyer*, pp. 224–25; Clinton Gilbert in the *New York Evening Post* 7/12/32.

14. ODY to William Green 5/31/32; Green to ODY 6/1/32; Office Calendar.

15. Speeches. ENC's fragmentary file includes a copy of Secretary Mills's speech, plus a few penciled notes taken at the meeting. Although we have not examined the co-called Secret History said to be included in Secretary Mills's papers, now in the Library of Congress, we have reason to doubt that it contains anything of importance on this subject which is not here reported.

16. Anderson, p. 276; J. S. Davis, *World between the Wars, 1919–1939: An Economist's View* (Baltimore: Johns Hopkins University Press, 1975), pp. 283–84. Secretary Mills in his *Annual Report* for fiscal 1932 limited the rise in industrial production from 58 to 66.

17. Anderson, p. 242, delivers the categorical opinion that "if the [Allied] governments had acted that winter [when Brüning would have reaped the benefits] Hitler would never have come to power and we should have saved the democratic regime in Germany." Cf. Hajo Holborn, *A History of Modern Germany, 1840–1945* (New York: Knopf, 1969), pp. 683 ff. As for

ODY, he shed no tears over what John Wheeler-Bennett dubbed the "wreck of reparations," saving them rather for our refusal to treat the Allied debts as realistically, and for Germany's virtual default on the Dawes and Young Plan loans.

18. Whether because documentation is so scanty or because, in the hectic fall of 1932, this final effort of big business to generate recovery was all but lost in the shuffle, the B&I Committees have so far been virtually ignored by historians of the period. For two reasons we find this a pity. The first is to be found in what proved to be the committees' fatal limitations; in demonstrating their impotence to act save by the often impossible road of unanimous consent, they were writing their own obituary—and with it the old order's—leaving a vacuum that could be filled only by some kind of New Deal. The second and less obvious is that the supporting data gathered by devoted members of their *ad hoc* staffs were found pertinent to certain unrealized objectives which the New Deal also found basic and was able to pursue. See the next two paragraphs of this chapter and notes 19 and 20; also Chapter 32.

19. ODY Office Calendar for 9/1932. For information re the Triborough Bridge—and much else—our thanks are due to Carl Backlund, archivist of the FRBNY.

20. For later outcome of recommended RFC aid to the railroads see Martin Dodge to ODY 8/31/42, enclosing a copy of Alfred Sloan's characteristic reply to Dodge's report to him (Banking and Industrial Committees folder). Dodge was consultant on the railroads to the New York B&I Committee. ENC retains vivid recollections of the impasse confronting the committee's projects for slum clearance and housing.

21. ENC ms Notes 9/10/32 (in ODY Papers).

22. For the discovery of this memo in the Hoover Presidential Papers, Radio, and for sending us a copy, the authors are deeply grateful once again to Robert Wood.

23. ENC ms Notes 9/20/32.

24. Erik Barnouw, *A History of Broadcasting in the United States*, vol. I: *A Tower in Babel* (New York: Oxford University Press, 1966), pp. 251 ff., especially pp. 266–68; G. L. Archer, *Big Business and Radio* (New York: American Historical Company, 1939), chapter 18; Eugene Lyons, *David Sarnoff* (New York: Harper & Row, 1966), pp. 162–67. A typographical error (p. 162) which dates the filing of the suit as of 5/31 instead of 5/13 appears in Carl Dreher's *Sarnoff* (New York: Quadrangle, 1977), p. 136; his account begins on p. 134 by stating that "two months after Sarnoff became President of RCA, Franklin D. Roosevelt was inaugurated as President of the United States." *Three years* and two months was the actual interval.

25. Office Calendar; ODY to B. C. Forbes 9/24/32; ODY to Henry M. Robinson 9/28/32.

26. ENC ms Notes 10/7/32, which include ODY's scribbled notes.

27. See note 24 above. Of all press notices for 11/22/32 the NYT has an unsurpassed report on the decree and its implications; it also contains the text in full, and Oswald Schuette's statement as executive secretary of the Radio Protective Association. The consequent selling wave in all RCA stocks was widely noted; since the filing of the suit, Radio common had slumped from almost 60 to 6.

28. Cf. Hoover's comments on the suit in his *Memoirs* (New York: Macmillan, 1952), II, 246:

Another task which I carried over from my post of Secretary of Commerce was radio. . . . The maintenance of freedom in this age of radio waves, kilowatts, and chemical synthesis keeps the lovers of liberty fighting off those who would have government ownership and monopoly on the one hand, and preventing private enterprise from creating monopoly on the other. The price of liberty thus becomes not only a matter of eternal vigilance, but of a good Attorney General.

On May 13, 1930, following a thorough investigation, and after an unsuccessful attempt at solving the problem by normal suasion, the administration started legal action to dissolve the "radio manufacturing trust." Attorney General Mitchell had laid before me the methods employed by the manufacturers of radio apparatus, and even broadcasting. I suggested to Mr. Mitchell that we place former Judge Olney of California in charge of the case. I directed the Attorney General to let them have both barrels. It took Mr. Mitchell and Judge Olney a year [*sic*], but within that time they made the concerns willing to accept a "consent" decree which, translated from legal terminology into plain English, was a complete admission of violation of law [*sic*]. Naturally I found some of these men, *possibly for other reasons*, publicly opposing my reelection in 1932 [emphasis added].

29. These too were accurately reported in the NYT story of 11/22.

30. See ibid. for RCA's new balance sheet. For ODY's satisfaction prior to its release, see ENC ms Notes 11/20/32.

31. As reported by JHC to ENC. ODY's dilemma was knowledgeably cited in the NYHT's story of 11/27/32, which surmised that he might choose RCA —unless he left both companies to join Roosevelt's cabinet.

32. NYT 11/30/32.

33. Financial files (see Chapter 21, note 1).

34. This was true despite an occasional knowledgeable comment in the press. On 11/28/32 the financial editor of the *New York Evening Journal*, Leslie Gould, noting that "the last three years had brought Owen D. Young probably his three biggest disappointments, right at the zenith of his career," also noted that "the pressure of his own business, due to the exigencies of the depression," had not only foreclosed "any dreams he might have had of . . . the White House" but might also "keep him from a Cabinet post *for Mr. Young no longer is a rich man*" (emphasis added). Aside from such dreams and the reality of the Radio decree, the third disappointment cited was the collapse of the Young Plan—surely, for its author, the least of the three.

CHAPTER *31. Democratic Sweep and the Interregnum: ODY, and FDR*

1. ENC ms Notes 7/23/32 (in ODY Papers).

2. Ibid. 7/28/32.

3. These press reports were nationwide. See, e.g., NYT 9/23/32; also Daniels's *Raleigh* (N.C.) *News-Observer* 9/24/32.

4. ODY to Josephus Daniels 10/6/32.

5. Papers relating to efforts to reopen the Bank of U.S. are largely segregated in ENC's files on that subject, now on deposit with the ODY Papers. The progressive impairment of bank capital as the depression deepened is widely attested, not least by the succession of bank failures. See also Russell Leffingwell's telling comment on the restrictions which limited the RFC's aid to secured loans when the need of the banks was for new capital: "For a fatal year and a half," he wrote to Alexander Sachs early in 1935, "the Reconstruction Finance Corporation continued to lend money to the banks on adequate collateral security and gradually bankrupted them in the effort to save them" (quoted in A. M. Schlesinger, Jr., *The Age of Roosevelt*, vol. I: *The Crisis of the Old Order, 1919–1933* [Boston: Houghton Mifflin, 1957], p. 237 and note, from copy in the Roosevelt Papers).

6. GE had led off with a $75,000 subscription; the final list (copy in ODY Papers, Federation Bank files) was a kind of blue-chip register.

7. According to the NYT 10/4/32, Maguire reported that the opening day's deposits exceeded withdrawals in the ratio of 10 to 1.

8. A few days earlier he had submitted a brief statement of support to James A. Farley to use if and where it might be helpful. At that time he said it was too late for supporting speeches; people were interested only in hearing from the candidates themselves (ODY to Farley 11/1/32, BCB). Evidently Farley—or someone—had strongly disagreed. For ODY's earlier aloofness, see his letter to FDR of 9/1/32.

9. ODY speech of 11/3/32, Speeches.

10. J. D. Hicks, *Republican Ascendancy* (New York: Harper & Row, 1966), p. 278; Frank Freidel, *Franklin D. Roosevelt*, vol. IV: *Launching the New Deal* (Boston: Little, Brown, 1973), p. 161.

11. J. H. Wilson, *Herbert Hoover: Forgotten Progressive* (Boston: Little, Brown, 1975), p. 154.

12. The text of the statement is quoted by B. M. Anderson, *Economics and the Public Welfare* (New York: Van Nostrand, 1949), p. 242; Elting Morison, *Turmoil and Tradition: A Study of the Life and Times of Henry L. Stimson* (Boston: Houghton Mifflin, 1960), p. 425–26, is illuminating respecting its context, and credits the original suggestion to Ogden Mills. See also re the double nature of Germany's internal crisis, Hajo Holborn, *A History of Modern Germany, 1840–1945* (New York: Knopf, 1969), chapter 11, especially pp. 682–96. Remarkably accurate as an almost con-

temporaneous account of Lausanne and its antecedents is John Wheeler-Bennett's *Wreck of Reparations* (New York: Morrow, 1933).

13. Freidel, IV, 25–36. As FDR's biographer, Freidel does an admirable job in presenting all sides of the Hoover-FDR contretemps, and may be forgiven the venial sin of confusing the Allied debt funding with reparations (p. 28) and the U.S. War Debts Commission with the Allied Reparations Commission (p. 33). See also, for the Stimson view, Morison, *Turmoil and Tradition*, pp. 424–36, and Henry L. Stimson and McGeorge Bundy, *On Active Service in Peace and War* (New York: Harper, 1948), pp. 211–19.

14. Cf. Raymond Moley, *The First New Deal* (New York: Harcourt, Brace, 1966), p. 27.

15. ENC ms Notes 11/20/32.

16. Freidel, IV, 25–36; Morison, 424–36.

17. ENC ms Notes 11/23/32. When this scribe allowed himself to wonder out loud whether one of the causes of the "decline of the West" (if Spengler had it right) would be found to be that "at a critical moment following a most disastrous war . . . the tremendous power and responsibility of financial leadership passed from the experienced and sensitive hands of Great Britain to the amateur and apparently insensitive hands of the United States," ODY suggested this brief addendum: "at a time when leadership in the United States was in part paralyzed and for the rest had largely abdicated."

18. ENC ms Notes 11/25/32.

19. Ibid. 12/2/32.

20. Ibid. 12/3/32. To be sure that *all* of Will's faithful readers got the point, ODY had also prepared this postscript: "Of course, you might add, if necessary, as much as is called for to make the point clear. You might say, for example, that this would not be very good for the American farmers or for American labor and industry. I agree. What happens to our trade, however, seems to be secondary in the minds of a good many people to collecting every penny of the debts. I am merely suggesting, therefore, a way in which they could be repaid, if this is our first object."

21. Morison, *Turmoil and Tradition*, pp. 435–36.

22. Freidel, IV, 144, citing as his authority Raymond Moley's *After Seven Years* (New York: Harper, 1939), pp. 111–13, and—especially for ODY—Moley's diary for 1/22/33 (Moley ms, Hoover Institute, Stanford University). In *The First New Deal*, Moley was less specific but the quotation from his diary recording FDR's views as of 12/12 (pp. 87–88) is much to the same effect; also on p. 31, Moley records his call of 12/20 for ODY's help in drafting FDR's reply to Hoover, adding that "Young was most helpful and we agreed upon the sort of reply Roosevelt should make." This, we submit, hardly supports Freidel's too-ready assumption (p. 39) that, at their 12/10 meeting, "Young must have tried to persuade Roosevelt to accept Hoover's view."

23. ENC ms Notes 12/3/32.

24. Freidel, IV, 112–14; Adolf Berle ms memo of 11/7/32, cited by Freidel, p. 141. See also note 22 above. ENC's notes of a telephone conversation (much later) with James A. Farley record his statement that for all

the President-elect's "great admiration for Mr. Young," he (Farley) "was not sure that Mr. Roosevelt didn't want somebody as Secretary of State whom he could handle," adding that "Owen Young was a strong character and . . . wouldn't be a yes man for anyone."

25. For the charges, see NYT 12/3/32. A transcript of the proceedings before the federal referee in bankruptcy, including ODY's testimony of 12/16 to 12/17/32, is on file with his papers (Box 15). This is also true of his later testimony in Washington on 2/16/33, before a Senate committee, of which the redoubtable Ferdinand Pecora was counsel. In 11/1934 Insull's belated trial ended in his acquittal.

26. NYT 12/17, 12/18/32; WSJ same dates. These papers did of course seek to do justice to ODY's answers, but some of these seemed only to make matters worse—as in his frank acknowledgment of having gone well beyond his original investment by taking up rights through 1931 to subscribe to several of Insull's new companies. (He estimated his total investment—actually $195,000—at "not less than $175,000 or more than $200,000.") And while the press had no way of knowing that in private sessions of the Edison group (which included Insull) and in private correspondence with its leaders ODY had been urging a critical examination of their financing methods, with special reference to the pyramiding of holding companies, awareness of this could only have added to editorial bewilderment over a personal involvement which was, on its face, so clearly at variance with such expressions of concern. As the hearings went on, moreover, dates were inadvertently but disastrously confused, as when *Time* in its issue of 2/27/33 quoted ODY as confessing to Pecora his feeling of helplessness "when I began in February 1931 [*sic*] to examine the [Insull] structure." Whether misled by this or similar errors of fact—the correct date being 2/1932— Hearst's *New York American* proceeded to castigate ODY editorially for GE's loan to Insull of 12/1931, "when he had known ever since February that bankruptcy impended." ENC, who knew the editor, did what he could but the damage had been done (ENC to E. B. Coblentz 3/20/33, BCB).

27. NYT 12/17/32; NYHT editorial 12/18/32.

28. *Nation* 12/28/32 and 1/4/33.

29. Norman Thomas in the *Nation* 1/11/33. Both Thomas and ODY had been listed on the *Nation*'s "Honor Roll for 1929."

30. ODY to Frank Oliver Hall 12/31/32; ODY to T. B. Macauley (president of Sun Life Assurance, Montreal) 1/12/33; ODY to Campbell Bosson (a Boston stockholder) 4/4/33 (BCB). Bosson's reply suggests a mind at once intelligent and fair; his original letter reflected the indelible impression headlines can make even on such minds. Both are in the ODY Papers, Insull folders.

31. WSJ 2/17/33; NYT 2/19/33; *Time* 2/27/33.

32. Freidel, IV, 144, cites the date on which ODY's name was struck "to the distress of Howe," but makes no mention of the *Nation*'s attack; the linking up of the two, so far undocumented, is a purely speculative adventure on our part but one for which, considering the striking coincidence in the dates involved, we offer no apology. For our other references, see

Frank Kent in the *Baltimore Sun* 11/2/32 and Clinton W. Gilbert in the *New York Evening Post* 1/30/33.

33. As reported to Ida Tarbell 2/2/33 by ENC, who was present and heard Senator Root's remark. Not surprisingly, ODY delighted in repeating it to his family and close friends.

CHAPTER *32. Roosevelt at the Helm: The Hundred Days and the Bombshell*

1. Frank Freidel, *Franklin D. Roosevelt*, vol. IV: *Launching the New Deal* (Boston: Little, Brown, 1973), pp. 169–74; A. M. Schlesinger, Jr., *The Age of Roosevelt*, vol. I: *The Crisis of the Old Order* (Boston: Houghton Mifflin, 1957), p. 466. Copy of ODY's testimony is filed with his papers, Box 15.

2. NYHT 2/18/33; *Nation* 3/1/33; NYT 2/19/33. From Greece came a handwritten note of appreciation from Insull, who went so far as to ask if there was anything he could do in those parts for GE (ODY Papers, Insull files).

3. For their copy of Flexner's lengthy memorandum of this meeting of 2/8/33—now in ODY's Special Papers #1–4—the authors are indebted to Professor Freidel, who in turn has acknowledged his earlier debt to Raymond Moley.

4. ENC ms Notes 3/3/33 (in ODY Papers); Gertrude Chandler to ODY, same date.

5. ODY to Franklin D. Roosevelt: ENC ms Notes 3/4/33. See, for impact on the people of FDR's inaugural, William E. Leuchtenburg, *Franklin D. Roosevelt and the New Deal* (New York: Harper & Row, 1963), p. 42; Freidel, vol. IV, chapter 12, especially p. 212.

6. ENC ms Notes 3/4/33. Some days later JHC confided to his son that the Chicago Federal Reserve had refused the New York Fed's request for a loan to cover this deficit and only after a lapse of several days had the Washington board ordered it to comply (ENC ms Notes 3/10/33).

7. ENC ms Notes 3/7/33.

8. Leuchtenburg, *Roosevelt*, p. 42.

9. ENC ms Notes 3/7/33; M. J. Pusey, *Eugene Meyer* (New York: Knopf, 1974), pp. 237–38.

10. ENC ms Notes 3/7/33; to these notes a copy of JHC's draft proposal is appended. Oddly enough it was Case, the conservative banker, who advocated a deposit guaranty which FDR opposed at the time and for some weeks thereafter.

11. ENC ms Notes 3/8 to 3/11/33; Freidel, IV, 219–29. (ENC's ms for 3/19 records his father's report that Harrison, sensing Washington's irrevocable commitment to option one, had intercepted the New York bank di-

rectors' missive of 3/10 signed by JHC as chairman, and returned it to its author.)

12. In New York City only eight small banks failed to reopen, but one—the Harriman National—was a clearinghouse member. Declaring that this wrote finis to all clearinghouse pretensions, ODY turned his attention to the task of finding new capital for key upstate banks—beginning with those closest to Van Hornesville and Canton.

13. As indicated in his ms Notes for the dates cited above (note 11), ENC was privy to most of the New York Fed's planning and subsequent cooperative efforts: his notes for 3/14/33 show him in a small way a party to the latter. Raymond Moley, *The First New Deal* (New York: Harcourt, Brace, 1966), chapters 10–15, gives a fascinating and largely firsthand account of the Washington scene, giving credit where credit was due and picturing FDR's poise and calm as the storm raged around him. Almost any daily paper gives for the week of 3/13 a progressive account of public confidence restored. We have relied principally on the NYT.

14. Two treasury "hangovers," Ogden Mills and Arthur Ballantine, did much to shape the program as adopted. See Moley, *First New Deal*, pp. 166–68, 171; Leuchtenburg, *Roosevelt*, pp. 42 ff.; Freidel, IV, 214–15, 220.

15. ODY to Arthur Vandenberg 4/18/33. Copy of this letter, written from Schenectady after a GE stockholders' meeting, and therefore not in the office copybook, will be found in ENC ms Notes for 1933. In his NYHT column for the two days preceding, Lippmann had strongly urged that the dollar be left to "seek its own level"; according to Woodlief Thomas of the New York Fed, the gossip was that Lippmann had been briefed not by Washington but at "the Corner," especially by T. W. Lamont and Parker Gilbert (ENC ms Notes 4/19/33). For J. P. Morgan's statement of support, see the NYT 4/20/33. Also, Russell Leffingwell sent the President a letter of warm approval: Freidel, IV, 336 and note. See also Freidel, IV, 331–39, for FDR's acceptance of the Thomas amendment.

16. ODY to F. S. Blackburn 3/30/33.

17. ODY radio talk of 9/13/33, Speeches; ODY to Ida M. Tarbell 9/15/33. Freidel, IV, 408–09, gives a succinct account of FDR's "conversion" to the NRA, reason for which he explains more fully in pp. 422–33.

18. ENC ms Notes 3/7/33. The need for dealing with these "recalcitrant minorities" is a recurrent theme of ODY's letters and speeches of the period.

19. ENC ms Notes 3/7, 4/21/33. Case's memorandum for Burgess, appended to the latter, suggests a close affinity in the recovery and reemployment measures of the B&I Committee and the *early* New Deal.

20. ENC ms Notes 3/28/33.

21. ODY to David Sarnoff 6/6/33.

22. Freidel, IV, chapters 22 and 23; especially, for Schacht, pp. 395–99. ODY's calendar for 5/12/33 records his presence at Sarnoff's private dinner at which Schacht repeated this performance; Sarnoff's other guests were Adolph Ochs, Bernard Baruch, Rabbi Wise, Judge Proskauer, Al Smith and John W. Davis. Schacht's credibility was low, but his warning that protests could only excite anti-Jewish reprisals could not safely be ignored.

23. Freidel, IV, chapter 22, especially (re the debts) pp. 384–85; Speeches; NYT 5/16/33. This speech to the National Conventon of the Junior League was made at the urging of ODY's daughter-in-law Esther Christensen (Mrs. C. J.) Young.

24. Freidel, IV, 400 ff. The text of the Geneva statement is on p. 404.

25. ENC ms Notes 5/22/33; the Washington dispatch was to the *New York Evening Post*. With Baruch as chairman—he had been FDR's first choice—ODY felt there would have been no problem. In the case of the lesser-known Hull, it was only too likely that his (ODY's) old friends in the European delegations would want to come first to him—which could create jealousies and misunderstanding for which he had no stomach. But if ODY had withheld his letter to Woodin for fear of becoming involved, he need not have worried; according to Moley (*First New Deal*, p. 408), who had sought to strengthen the U.S. London delegation by adding ODY's name, it "was crossed out . . . apparently by Roosevelt."

26. ENC ms Notes 5/26/33.

27. NYT (and others) 5/25/33; Freidel, IV, 348; Schlesinger, I, 434–39; John Brooks, *Once in Golconda* (New York: Harper & Row, 1969), pp. 186–91.

28. ENC ms Notes 5/25/33.

29. Ibid. The *Sun* had asked ODY for a similar statement. Secretary Woodin, whose name was on the list, had tendered his resignation to FDR, who declined to accept it. For the President's attitude toward Woodin—and Norman Davis (who apparently did not offer to resign)—see Schlesinger, I, 437. ODY did confide to ENC that he had stopped by at 23 Wall Street that afternoon to inquire how the list had been made up and that Parker Gilbert would be giving him the facts. Then, when the hearing was over, he might perhaps drop a note to the chairman which would clarify the record. We find no evidence that he ever did so.

30. NYT 6/2/33. See also, with ENC ms Notes, ODY's memo of the same date.

31. In all three of its editions for 6/1/33 the *Journal* carried E. C. Hill's signed story of this "iniquitous" deal; in each edition it carried a different headline.

32. ENC ms Notes 6/8/33.

33. Although Miss Chandler had undoubtedly been quick to confirm ODY's Johns-Manville subscription of 1927, it was not until the authors lately discovered it for themselves, in reviewing ODY's federal income-tax report for that same year, that they understood why he had apparently taken no steps to "clarify the record." This discovery, of course, gave fresh impetus to their detective efforts, and their search for the "missing" shares was extended to cover an alleged "favored" subscription to Morgan's United Corporation. Thus they diligently searched ODY's income-tax returns for the ensuing decade—also his wife's and, following her death in 1935, the securities held in her estate—only to draw a blank. No sign whatever of Alleghany or Niagara-Hudson; and while ODY's 1936 return did report sale of 1,000 shares of United Corporation at 6¾, its purchase at 35 on 1/29/30 was at the quoted market price. So was his second purchase of Johns-Manville in

10/1928, sale of which later in the year resulted in no gain, no loss. Nevertheless, the authors then extended their search for the "missing" shares to the list of securities held as collateral for ODY's two formidable loans. For Pick and Company the records are complete—and barren. For the Bankers Trust the list is hard to come by, until in 1937 securities sold to pay off some 70 percent of the principal appear on ODY's income-tax returns. Still nothing; and the same for 1941, when the balance was finally liquidated.

34. NYT 6/17/33. Freidel, IV, 441–44, makes it clear that Roosevelt had originally entertained serious misgivings about the Banking Act as well as the National Industrial Recovery Act, though he finally hailed both. Conservative journals like the *Commercial and Financial Chronicle* retained and paraded their misgivings about Glass-Steagall, especially the insurance of deposits (see its issue of 6/17/33). Opinion remained divided for some time, with few publicists recognizing the remedial provision for a unification of the banking system. In the event, this provision was first deferred and then eliminated. It has yet to be restored.

35. Office Calendar; *Watertown Times* 6/12/33; NYT 6/13/33.

36. ODY speech at Radcliffe 6/21/33, Speeches; NYT 6/22/33; ODY to John Finley 6/28/33. Young stayed for the Harvard commencement, at which Al Smith and Harry Emerson Fosdick were honored.

37. ENC ms Notes 6/30/33. ENC's recollections have since been quickened as well as verified by a review of press clippings and such reports on the marked recovery achieved that spring as appear in B. M. Anderson, *Economics and the Public Welfare* (New York: Van Nostrand, 1949), chapter 50, especially pp. 333–35. (The rest of his chapter inveighs against the depressing effects of the NRA.)

38. ENC ms Notes 6/30/33. Presumably ODY's message of 6/29 had been sent to Washington; cf. Acting Secretary of the Treasury Dean Acheson's message of that date to FDR (Freidel, IV, 476–77).

39. ENC ms Notes 7/1 to 7/3/33.

40. *New York World-Telegram* 7/3/33; ENC ms Notes 7/3/33. The full text of FDR's historic message, so widely published at the time, is reproduced in Moley, *The First New Deal*, pp. 464–65. To understand its destructive impact on the World Economic Conference, beginning with the U.S. delegation (James Warburg is quoted by Moley as simply not understanding what the President was saying) one would have to compare it, as Moley does, with Roosevelt's earlier instructions to these same delegates on the eve of their departure, and with the communiqués released by the White House after the May sessions with MacDonald, Herriot and Guido Jung (Italy's finance minister). As FDR's biographer, Freidel offers no apology for a turnabout so sharp and so sudden as to baffle many of the President's well-wishers; at the same time his exposition of the duality of FDR's concerns and his felt need to conciliate the congressional isolationists in the interest of his domestic reform and recovery program is singularly fair and illuminating. So is his assessment (IV, 487) of all the generous hopes and expectations that FDR had first encouraged and then blasted by his overkill.

41. Quoted from FDR's message of 7/3/33. For this in its full context, see Freidel, IV, chapters 27, 28.

42. ENC ms Notes 7/3/33.

CHAPTER *33. Monetary Experiments and the Federal Reserve*

1. ENC ms Notes 7/6/33 (in ODY Papers). A preliminary observation reads: "Jo sat down to knit, and gave a perfect imitation of a lady of the old school who says nothing while her men-folks talk but wears . . . [an] expression which indicates that she could say plenty if she wanted to."

2. Over the Fourth, the press had given the bombshell top billing, with the *Chicago Tribune* outdoing even Hearst in praise of the President. Roosevelt, indeed, professed himself delighted with the domestic reaction but could hardly have taken equal delight—unless it was sadistic—in the obvious distress of his own delegation—not to mention Prime Minister MacDonald's. As for the eastern press, he affected to despise it—with its talk of High and Mighty Language (Walter Lippmann), the Great Improvisator (editorial in the NYHT) and the NYT's editorial on the difficulty—well known to this Naval Person—of salvaging a torpedoed vessel. Actually the editorial tone was remarkably restrained—far more so than Clarence Streit's candid press report from London on the shambles which was all that was left of the conference.

3. Frank Freidel, *Franklin D. Roosevelt*, vol. IV: *Launching the New Deal* (Boston: Little, Brown, 1973), chapters 27 and 28; B. M. Anderson, *Economics and the Public Welfare* (New York: Van Nostrand, 1949), pp. 335–40.

4. In vol. II, chapters 12 and 13, of his *Age of Roosevelt* (*The Coming of the New Deal*; Boston: Houghton Mifflin, 1958), Arthur Schlesinger, Jr., successfully counters the widely held view that FDR's bombshell message was simply the product of a sudden inspiration—or "seizure"—by citing the manifold forces and influences which, in their cumulative effect, were convincing him that for the United States, freedom to manipulate the dollar and so raise prices was now an imperative. Conceding that Roosevelt's reaction "to the immediate issue" was "certainly out of proportion" and that his choice of delegates and "day to day management of American policy at the Conference was deplorable," Schlesinger doubts that the conference could have succeeded in any case and is not disposed to quarrel with John Maynard Keynes's dictum (which Winston Churchill promptly echoed) that "President Roosevelt is magnificently right."

Other historians—like Freidel, no less keenly aware of Roosevelt's domestic preoccupations, problems and pressures—hold rather different views (see above, note 3). Cf., e.g., Robert Dallek, *Franklin D. Roosevelt and American Foreign Policy, 1932–1945* (New York: Oxford University Press, 1979), pp. 49–58; on p. 78 Dallek unequivocally declares that "during the first two years of his presidency, Roosevelt met not intense isolationism in the country, but a general indifference to outside events which left him relatively free to seek expanded American ties abroad." Cf. also Melvin K. Leffler, *The Elusive Quest: America's Pursuit of European Stability and French Security, 1919–1933* (Chapel Hill: University of North Carolina Press, 1979), whose chapters 9 and 10 address with insight and balance the dual problems of economic and military disarmament in their full three-dimensional context, and trace to FDR's sins of omission as well as commission the failure of American leadership to salvage this last chance. Jeannette P. Nichols (*American Historical Review*, vol. LVI, no. 2, pp. 295–318), while doubting that the conference could have achieved much in any case, concludes that FDR's message spurred nationalistic competition and that failure of the democracies to cooperate played into the hands of Schacht, who "perfected monetary diplomacy as a means to a militaristic state."

But perhaps William E. Leuchtenburg in his *Franklin D. Roosevelt and the New Deal* (New York: Harper & Row, 1963), pp. 202–03, best voices the disheartening verdict which was also closest to ODY's. Conceding that much of the criticism of FDR's "bomb" was extreme, Leuchtenburg nevertheless concludes:

> Yet the failure of the London Economic Conference was deplorable. The United States may have been no more blameworthy than other countries, but, as the most powerful nation in the world, and as the principal creditor, it had a special obligation to lead. The meeting marked the last opportunity of democratic statesmen to work out a co-operative solution to common economic problems, and it ended in total failure. Henceforth, international trade would be directed by national governments as a form of bloodless warfare. In the very year that Hitler assumed power, the collapse of the conference sapped the morale of the democratic opponents of fascism. Roosevelt's policies strengthened those forces in Britain and France which argued the futility of international parleys and celebrated the virtues of economic self-interest. The Nazis hailed the President's message as a "bomb" which ended a futile meeting that was only a "remnant of an antiquated parliamentary order." Roosevelt, declared Hjalmar Schacht, had the same idea as Hitler and Mussolini: "Take your economic fate in your own hands."

5. David Loth, *Swope of GE* (New York: Simon & Schuster, 1958), pp. 222–23; ODY to Cordell Hull 7/7/33; see his Office Calendar for Moley and Howe visits. Raymond Moley, *The First New Deal* (New York: Harcourt, Brace, 1966), p. 501, gives an interesting report on the first of his calls.

6. ODY (Office Calendar) met with W. S. Goll, manager of the Fort Wayne plant, on 7/28/33; the $25,000 of new capital was authorized 8/8/33 as he wrote Goll; GE's Annual Report for 1933 updates the Employees Securities Corporation bonds; ODY to Henry Goddard Leach 7/19/33; Louis Reid in *New York American* 9/8/33; for GE's Advisory Committee report, see NYT 8/15/33.

7. GE Annual Report 1933; ODY to Gerard Swope 10/4/33.

8. Loth, who does not mention this exchange, reports only (p. 233) that Swope "kept urging self-governing bodies for industry even beyond those set up in the [NRA] codes," notably in a speech to the Business Advisory Council. Of this meeting Swope himself is quoted as saying "there was much discussion but little action." See also, for FDR's view and others', Ellis Hawley, *New Deal and the Problem of Monopoly* (Princeton: Princeton University Press, 1966), pp. 78–79.

9. Loth, pp. 223–33.

10. Ibid., especially pp. 233–39.

11. Drew Pearson and Robert S. Allen, "Washington Merry-Go-Round," *New York Mirror* 7/26/33. ODY sent a clipping with penciled inquiry to George Davison, president of the Central Hanover Bank, asking what he knew about it from his contacts with the Brain Trust.

12. The most vivid account of Harrison's reluctant involvement and beneficial role is in John Brooks, *Once in Golconda* (New York: Harper & Row, 1969), chapter 7, especially pp. 170–78. See also John Morton Blum, *Roosevelt and Morgenthau* (Boston: Houghton Mifflin, 1970), pp. 43 ff., especially pp. 47–48; on p. 49 FDR is quoted re dangers of a farm revolt. A shorter account of Harrison's role is in Matthew Josephson's *Money Lords* (New York: Weybright & Talley, 1972), pp. 160–63. For ODY's testimony re the 1934 act which fixed the dollar's gold value, see below, Chapter 34.

13. ODY to Gordon Abbott 11/17/33.

14. ODY Office Calendar; re milk strike and policy of his farms, ODY to authors.

15. ODY Office Calendar; ODY to Clark Minor and to John Stewart Bryan 8/8/33.

16. Replying to Philip's message on 9/16/33 ODY wrote at length on what it meant to know that his voice had reached the once isolated Home Farm; ODY to John D. Rockefeller, Jr., 9/19/33.

17. ODY Office Calendar.

18. Reed had already been called in more than once for help, notably re the Federation Bank. Certain of Riddle's notes are quoted in the next chapter.

19. Office Calendar; ODY to Albert Shaw 1/8/34.

20. ODY to H. H. Dewey of IGE 10/6/33; ODY to Saul Bron 11/21/33; Office Calendar.

21. The books had been stored by 3/20/33; Miss Dickson had stayed to tidy up the records for another six weeks.

22. ODY to Walter Mallory 10/4/33; ODY to Henry Robinson and Dean Jay 9/20/33; ODY to Frank Oliver Hall 10/17/33; also Office Calendar. As for "Uncle Cyrus's estate," if the "gamble" has not as yet paid off, it has not been written off either.

23. ODY letter copybooks; GE Annual Report for 1933.

24. GE Annual Report for 1934. Originally, however, eligibility was still limited to employees with five years or more of service; in 1937 participation was opened on a graduated basis, beginning after one year.

25. ODY Office Calendar; see also Report of NBC Advisory Council 1934, and ENC's scribbled notes on the meeting, in ODY Papers.

26. Office Calendar; ODY to Alfred P. Sloan and Thomas J. Watson 12/18/33; ODY to Lamott DuPont 12/23/33.

27. Office Calendar; see also (copies in tax files) ODY's U.S. income-tax reports for 1932 and 1933.

28. Office Calendar; also ODY files re Bankers Trust Company (incomplete).

29. *New York Times Magazine* 12/17/33 (copy in Clippings).

30. Hitler took Germany out of the League on 10/14/33 (Hajo Holborn,

A History of Modern Germany, 1840–1945 [New York: Knopf, 1969], p. 764). See also Freidel, IV, 406–07, for an excellent assessment of Hitler's skill in exploiting nationalistic policies of other leaders, including FDR.

31. ODY at Queen's University 10/28/33, Speeches.

32. When ODY and Richard planned to take a trip to Caracas for the day, ODY asked their very devoted steward (an Irishman from Liverpool) if he had ever been there. When he said he had not, ODY said, "Well, then, come along with us," and the three of them had a day's sight-seeing and a lunch together (from RY).

33. NYT (and others) 6/5/34 (Clippings).

34. ODY at University of Nebraska 6/4/34, Speeches.

CHAPTER *34. In Memoriam: Josephine Edmonds Young, 1870–1935*

1. William E. Leuchtenburg, *Franklin D. Roosevelt and the New Deal* (New York: Harper & Row, 1963), chapter 5, "Waiting for Lefty"; also pp. 146–47 for FDR's conciliatory turn toward business.

2. ENC ms Notes 1/4/35 (in ODY Papers).

3. ODY to the Association of Edison Illuminating Companies 1/16/35, Speeches. This was "printed but not published" by order of the association.

4. ODY to Ned Groesbeck 1/28/35.

5. ODY to Samuel Crowther 2/27/35; ODY to Harry McGowan 1/7/35. The President's message came later (5/22), and ODY's congratulatory telegram, not being in his files, must have been dispatched from the bank. He praised the veto, however, in his Senate testimony of May 29; see also John Morton Blum, *Roosevelt and Morgenthau* (Boston: Houghton Mifflin, 1970), pp. 127–28.

6. Leuchtenburg, *Roosevelt*, p. 129, without mentioning ODY, gives an admirable summary of the NYA's aims and important, if limited, achievements.

7. Among its members, for example, were Dorothy Canfield Fisher, the writer, Matthew Woll, the labor leader, and Robert Hutchins, president of the University of Chicago, with all of whom ODY became good friends.

8. U.S. Senate: Subcommittee of Banking and Currency Committee, Hearings on S. #1715 (Eccles bill) 5/29/35. For ODY's testimony in answer to questions see (e.g.) NYT and NYHT 5/30/35. Copy of his prepared statement is on file among his speeches.

9. Albany's *Knickerbocker Press* 3/27/35 gives an illustrated report on GE's prize awards for design of model homes. For the Wanamaker exhibit, complete with photos of the President's mother and ODY, see (e.g.) NYHT 4/2/35.

10. NYT 6/2/35; see ODY Speeches for his radio talk of 3/3/35.

11. Speeches. The dinner was held at the Copley-Plaza on 4/1; ODY had

to be on hand to speak because Gordon Abbott asked him to. The NYT 4/6/35 took cordial editorial notice of his statement on the "things we do not know."

12. See the Academy of Political and Social Sciences published reports; also "One Night in a Million" in magazine of Penn Athletic Club (ODY Papers, Box 153).

13. Newspaper accounts of this impromptu colloquy were printed, first by the *Watertown Times*, in connection with the St. Lawrence commencement of 6/9/35. The NYT of that date also featured it; "Dr. John's" editorial appeared the next day.

14. Raymond Moley, *The First New Deal* (New York: Harcourt, Brace, 1966), pp. 174–77—especially p. 176—gives an illuminating and authoritative report on the hectic processes of drafting the Emergency Act of 3/9/33, with special reference to the section (3) which Morgenthau evidently read as empowering him to act. This at least was the stated conclusion of the man who had drafted the original bill *without* this section, Wilson Wyatt, the highly respected counsel to the Federal Reserve Board. Wyatt is further quoted in Moley's note as declaring that Meyer's successor, Governor Eugene Black, was the man who persuaded Roosevelt to go through Congress. It was well that Governor Black—presumably armed with the Davis opinion—did induce Roosevelt to take that course, for Section 3, hastily drawn as an amendment to the Federal Reserve Act, raised questions that otherwise promised a formidable hassle.

15. Gold Reserve Act of 1934: Hearings before the Committee on Banking and Currency, U.S. Senate, 63rd Congress, 2nd Session, on S #2366, Part 3, 1/22/34. ODY's testimony begins on p. 261.

16. For Eccles, see Sidney Hyman, "Marriner Eccles" (Ph.D. dissertation, Stanford University Graduate School of Business Administration, 1976). According to R. L. Weissman, *The New Federal Reserve System* (New York: Harper's, 1936), it was Eccles's intention that the offices of governor and chairman of the regional banks be combined in that of the new president. The changes proposed in the Eccles bill he lists on pp. 120–21; for changes between the bill as introduced and as enacted, see pp. 122–23. See too, especially for Glass's role, Leuchtenburg's assessment—also quoting Walter Lippmann's—in Leuchtenburg, *Roosevelt*, pp. 160–61.

17. See note 8 above.

18. Ibid.

19. See note 16 above. Subsequent amendments made the president of the New York Fed a permanent member of the Open Market Committee, *ex officio*.

20. Beman Dawes was General Charles Dawes's younger brother, an oil company executive and former congressman. The guests at the dinner for Stamp included J. P. Morgan, George Harrison, Thomas W. Lamont, Parker Gilbert, David Sarnoff and Nelson Perkins. The date was 6/6 and the place the University Club. Stamp said that at this time he found the United States as Washington-oriented as it had once been Wall Street–centered.

21. A letter dated 6/11 to "Jo Edmunds" from Elinor Frost (St. Lawrence '95) says, "We were sorry not to go. I have not been at all well the last year . . . thought I might undertake the trip to Canton but . . . became worse last week. . . . Robert decided he would start Sunday morning without me, but when morning came he didn't like to leave me" (ODY Papers, JEY folder).

22. ODY in Canton 6/17/35, Speeches.

23. ODY to Theodore K. Quinn of GE and to Bernard Baruch 6/19/35.

24. ODY to William F. Carey 6/20/35.

25. Frances Perkins's letter, written after JEY's death, is filed with the other letters of condolence in the ODY Papers.

26. All these letters, and copies of ODY's replies, are filed in a special JEY folder in the ODY Papers.

27. ODY at Camp General (in Schenectady) 7/14/35, Speeches. During the depression the "Association Island" camp was closed.

28. ODY to E. W. Rice, Jr., 9/9/35.

29. ENC ms Notes 11/4/35.

30. ODY to authors.

31. Leuchtenburg, *Roosevelt*, pp 154–57. His summary of the act is on p. 156.

32. ENC ms Notes 11/11/35. See also ODY to J. F. Owens of Oklahoma Gas and Electric 5/9/35, and to Colonel McCormick of the *Chicago Tribune* 3/9/35. The latter takes exception to factual misrepresentation in the *Tribune*'s editorial of 2/5.

33. ENC ms Notes 11/11/35.

34. This account of ODY's Washington trip and its outcome is based on the notes of George W. N. Riddle (who often traveled with his chief) as typed and delivered to ENC on 2/5/36 and make a part of his ms Notes.

35. Ibid. The authors are also indebted to George Riddle for sending them a copy—here reproduced without comment—of the Pearson and Allen report on "this little joke," which appeared in their syndicated column for 12/5/35. Riddle adds that when this came to the notice of Henry L. Doherty of Cities Service, he wrote ODY a warm and sympathetic note from Washington, received 12/9, in which he said that this was all being hailed by New Deal supporters as evidence of what the power interests deserved and might expect, but that he nevertheless felt some good had been accomplished by virtue of ODY's efforts and was correspondingly grateful. As it appeared in the *New York Daily Mirror* 12/5/35, Drew Pearson's and Robert S. Allen's "Daily Washington Merry-Go-Round" read as follows:

UTILITY JOKE

Members of the Securities & Exchange Commission have a private joke on Owen D. Young and C. E. Groesbeck, heads of General Electric and the Electric Bond and Share Company.

One morning, during the barrage of suits against the SEC, on the Holding Company Act, Young and Groesbeck suddenly appeared at the SEC.

The report was flashed immediately over the news wires that the two men were negotiating with the Commission for a compromise in the holding company regulation battle.

Actually they had come to consult the Commission on securing exemptions, permitted under the law, for foreign subsidiaries owned by their companies.

Members of the SEC received them cordially and discussed their problem fully. At no time was the holding company fight mentioned. Young and Groesbeck, their business completed, returned that night to New York by sleeper.

Now for the SEC's joke.

While Young and Groesbeck were conferring with the Commission, its staff of lawyers was working furiously preparing the surprise suit against the Electric Bond and Share to compel it to register under the Holding Company Act. At four o'clock next morning, while the two utility men were rolling serenely homeward, the necessary legal papers were completed, rushed to a plane and shot to New York.

Young and Groesbeck, after leisurely breakfasts, arrived at their offices to be greeted with first news of the SEC's suit.

CHAPTER *35. The Utilities Again: Louise and Washington Oaks*

1. Speech before the convention of the Association of Edison Illuminating Companies, Boca Raton, Florida, 1/22/36, Speeches.

2. Founder's Day exercises, Rollins College, Winter Park, Florida, 2/24/36, Speeches.

3. *Newsweek* 3/7/36.

4. RY to authors. A friend since the early days of ODY's travels for Stone and Webster, Doherty had organized, and headed since 1910, that vast utility holding company, Cities Service. As an older man, he was one of the few who understood and actively encouraged ODY's efforts to effect a working compromise between the utilities and the New Deal.

5. ODY to Daniel C. Roper 4/13/36.

6. ODY to Webster Ballinger 8/25/36.

7. ODY to Malcolm Muir 4/22/36.

8. ODY speech 9/10/36 at World Power Conference 9/8 to 9/14/36, Speeches.

9. ODY to Frank T. Post, of the Washington (State) Water Power Company, 9/25/33.

10. WSJ 2/25/36.

11. ODY to Dr. W. R. Whitney 5/6/36.

12. ODY to James Farley 10/20/36.

13. NYT 1/27/37.

14. Thanks in large part to JEY's legacy, ODY's personal loan from Swope of $200,000 was by now fully repaid, and the loan from the Bankers

Trust had been reduced from $500,000 to about $270,000. His outstanding accounts with rarebook dealers—Rosenbach excepted—had been finally settled. This left the $1.3 million or so still owing to Pick and Company as the chief remaining problem, and here the value of his collateral was, at last, nearly equal to the loan.
News 4/23/37.

16. ODY to Charles S. Hammond 6/8/37.

17. ODY to George L. Harrison 10/4/37 (Box 270).

18. ODY told the story of this whole episode one evening—2/12/38—over the dinner table in Van Hornesville to a family group; this and the following quotations, unless otherwise specified, are from the record made by ENC shortly thereafter (filed in ODY Papers with ENC ms Notes). Unknown to ENC or ODY, Adolf Berle kept a "diary file" for the period in question, selected passages from which appeared some thirty-five years later in *Navigating the Rapids*, edited by his widow and Travis Beal Jacobs (New York: Harcourt Brace Jovanovich, 1973). With minor variations in emphasis and focus, the two accounts can fairly be said to substantiate, and sometimes complement, each other.

19. Lamont, in a letter to Berle, 12/14/37, pointed out that "the whole business community is one so far as it has the same general outlook and so far as it looks to Washington for intelligent understanding and general cooperation"—i.e., big and small business are one. He went on to describe the *methods* used by Washington to restore confidence as "fundamentally erroneous" (Lamont Papers, Baker Library, Harvard Business School).

20. Berle, pp. 152–59.

21. *Baltimore Sun* 1/15/38.

22. Berle, pp. 161–62. Berle also said in a letter to Lamont, 3/1/38, "I still think that the visit which John L. Lewis, yourself and Mr. Young paid to the President was productive. For one thing, it demonstrated that opposing interests can get together and discuss matters with a view to a practical solution—an attitude which I wish were more general in the United States just now" (Lamont Papers, Baker Library, Harvard Business School).

23. ENC ms Notes 2/12/38; Jay Franklin in the *New York Post* 2/16/38.

CHAPTER *36. The Tireless Mediator and Retirement*

1. NYHT 12/5/35; quoted in *FRB of NY Newspaper Review* for 12/7/35. The news ticker for 12/9/35 indicated Eccles's wish to keep ODY very much in the picture—even suggesting that the six-year rule could be waived for (honorary) chairmen. To such suggestions ODY had turned a deaf ear (Federal Reserve box).

2. JHC to Walter Teagle 3/4/36; *New York Sun* 3/7/36. The *Sun's* allusion to "personal pique" reflected the gossip current at the time that Washington had not forgiven Case for resisting the treasury's efforts to commandeer the bank's gold reserves by executive order.

3. Copies of these letters and accounts of procedure are among the JHC papers in ENC's possession.

4. Ibid.; ODY Office Calendar.

5. Office Calendar.

6. JHC to ODY 5/12/36, copy in ODY Papers, JHC box.

7. ODY to Marriner Eccles 5/18, 6/15/36. Philip Stockton, another Boston banker and GE director, wrote ODY early in June that he should accept, and that he himself would handle Gordon Abbott. He did.

8. George L. Harrison to ODY 6/19/36, Harrison box.

9. ODY to JHC 3/4/38.

10. ODY to Allan Sproul 1/21/40. Anticipating, as it were, the impact of his own devoted and dynamic efforts, Sproul's reply suggested possible ways to restore to the Federal Reserve System its powers as a central bank. The Eccles correspondence and the New York Fed's resolution—signed by B. Ruml as ODY's successor—are in the ODY Papers, FRB, Box 272.

11. John Morton Blum, in *Roosevelt and Morgenthau* (Boston: Houghton Mifflin, 1970), pp. 76–84, gives a lively account of the proceedings, admirably handled by the secretary, which eventuated in the tripartite pact. For the role of the New York Fed in executing the treasury's orders see pp. 84–85. Blum adds (p. 77) that FDR's insistence that management of the pact should rest in the three national treasuries and not in their central banks was "more than a matter of vocabulary." It emphasized his conviction that "monetary policy was the obligation of government, not of private [*sic*] finance."

That Blum's description of the President's conviction was strictly accurate, Roosevelt had already made clear. Nor was there anything novel about a political vocabulary which equated the Federal Reserve with "private finance," except for its use by the first Democrat to succeed Woodrow Wilson in the White House. It had long been the stock-in-trade of the Fed's inveterate critics, who could discover in the carefully structured system established by Wilson and Glass (with William Jennings Bryan's final blessing) nothing but the fact that its so-called member banks—compelled by law to put up all the capital for a limited return of 6 percent—were accorded the right to elect a majority of the nine regional bank directors: three bankers and three businessmen. This was control, wasn't it, and control by private finance? Never mind the fact that the central board, appointed by the President, had significant and recently augmented powers of appointment, supervision and control. Never mind that, as R. L. Weissman points out in *The New Federal Reserve System* (New York: Harper & Bros., 1936), pp. 125–27, "Federal Reserve Banks are not operated for profit" and that their net earnings after the 6 percent dividend must be used only for such specified public purposes as the law from time to time directs. Never mind that in its every function the system was so "charged with the public interest" that to serve it, public-spirited men and women turned their backs on the tempting salaries and other emoluments offered by *private* finance. It was this—or rather all these things—that made the familiar charge so misleading as to be exasperating to the Reserve banks' staff and friends, including ODY.

Mildred Adams (Kenyon), whose extensive interviews of 1955 with ODY on the Federal Reserve System are deposited, as of this writing, with the Brookings Institution (the ODY Papers have copies), has observed that "one of Mr. Young's most valuable abilities so far as the New York Board was concerned was his sense of proportion and his skill in analysis which reached to the heart of any situation." Faced with this vexatious but also peculiarly slippery problem, ODY's proposed solution was perhaps too obvious to qualify but it stood alone and, to some who heard it, it seemed to reach the heart. Politics was politics, the Federal Reserve was complex enough to seem mysterious, and the best defense was to make it less so. Then why not meet the charge head-on by giving the presidentially appointed Board of Governors the power to appoint five or even six of the regional banks' directors? That, he suggested, the public would certainly understand and the critics could not gainsay. Nor would he expect serious objection on the part of the commercial banks, which would still be free to choose their own minority representatives. Sound or not, nothing came of this suggestion. Like the proposal for a unified banking system under federal control, it was either lost or mislaid. Perhaps their time will come?

12. ENC ms Notes (in ODY Papers) and clippings for 11/1935 and 12/1935 and 8/1936; also ODY's Clippings. Parker Gilbert's earlier views appear in a letter to the NYT for 12/18/35.

13. ODY Office Calendar, letter copybooks and Clippings. A copy of his tribute to Baker is filed with his speeches.

14. NYT 11/14/37.

15. Ibid.

16. See NYT 11/21/37 for Ickes's reply.

17. ODY to Herbert Claiborne Pell 1/6/38.

18. ODY to Gerard Swope 4/25/38.

19. NYT 4/27/38, and all other metropolitan papers.

20. *New Republic* 5/11/38.

21. *Yonkers Herald Statesman* 4/20/38.

22. ODY to PY 4/20/38.

23. ODY to Warren T. Smith 5/27/38.

24. ODY to M. H. Aylesworth 1/10/39.

25. ODY speech to the Association of Edison Illuminating Companies, 1/1939, Speeches.

26. Ibid.

27. William E. Leuchtenburg, *Franklin D. Roosevelt and the New Deal* (New York: Harper & Row, 1963), pp. 150–52.

28. David Loth, *Swope of GE* (New York: Simon & Schuster, 1958), pp. 255–60.

29. Peter R. Nehemkis to ODY 4/22/39.

30. ODY's testimony before the Temporary National Economic Committee 5/17/39, Speeches.

31. *Washington Post* 5/18/39; WSJ 5/20/39; NYHT 6/8/39.

32. ODY to Raymond Moley 2/9/40.

33. The sentences were slightly reordered, and the paragraphs regrouped. Textual changes were negligible.

34. See below, notes 36 and 37.

35. Ibid. We cannot identify the director.

36. ODY to JYC 11/17/39. "Everett" established no such course but the suggestion bore fruit a year or two later, when he was asked to prepare a case, for the course in business policy, on continuity and succession in top management, using GE as his model. The result, "copyrighted 1942 by the President and Fellows of Harvard College," is on file in Baker Library; such case studies always remaining anonymous, its only identifying mark other than the title, "General Electric Company," is the notation "BP–411." It is cited here for the benefit of the few who may be curious to explore the processes by which GE's top management once sought and identified its own successors.

37. GE Annual Report 1939.

CHAPTER *37. National Defense, the Dairy Farmer and Pearl Harbor*

1. ODY to Jesse Jones 1/6/40; ODY to Ferris Greenslet 1/4/40. Published by Houghton Mifflin in 1938, JYC's book was dedicated to Ida Brandow Young, "who would have known what to do."

2. ENC ms Notes 4/15/37, recalling conversation of 8/1936 (in ODY Papers).

3. John Morton Blum, *Roosevelt and Morgenthau* (Boston: Houghton Mifflin, 1970), chapter 11; F. R. Dulles, *The United States since 1865* (Ann Arbor: University of Michigan Press, 1959), pp. 422–25.

4. ODY Office Calendar.

5. ODY to Economic Club of New York 12/12/38, Speeches.

6. ODY speeches at Syracuse University commencement, 6/3/40, and St. Lawrence University commencement, 6/10/40, Speeches.

7. At the end of his service, ODY wrote Delano (2/23/40) to say how much he regretted that the war had prevented "the complete realization of the program originally contemplated by the President and by you." It was an honor, he said, to serve on this committee as chairman: "I have discovered after long experience that when one is thrown with a group of able men, each of whom knows more about the subject in hand than you, the only safe and productive place under such circumstances is to be Chairman."

8. It was also suggested at the time that FDR, having about made up his mind to run for a third term, wanted to keep ODY busy and out of political mischief. (One author is inclined to believe this, the other is skeptical.)

9. The President's letter, ODY's letter and the White House memo are all in Box 495 of the ODY Papers. ODY's letter to the President of 5/27/40 reported on his visit with Hopkins: "It was a most satisfactory one because his

mind works with that clarity and definition which aids greatly in dealing with such a sprawling situation as this necessarily is."

10. R. E. Sherwood, *Roosevelt and Hopkins* (New York: Harper, 1948), pp. 157–58, lists the full membership, including Hillman, but not his "advisory aide"; he adds that no chairman was appointed until after Pearl Harbor. As for the press, see Frank Kent, in the WSJ 7/8/40, who wrote: "The idea of making Mr. Young the aide to Mr. Hillman seems so complete a reversal of their proper positions [*sic*] that it can be explained only by some queer notion of political expediency. . . ." ODY was amused but felt that Kent had missed the point, which was that with their recent rise to power, labor leaders should be encouraged to take on posts of public responsibility. To *Fortune*'s 11/1940 article on Hillman he contributed a striking if oversimplified description of his boss's *modus operandi;* he also defended Hillman and his work in a letter to Senator Robert A. Taft which, for ODY, was pretty sharp.

11. ODY to Sidney Hillman 7/10/40.

12. Richard Young, who was with his father in Washington at the time, reports that they met with the group of younger labor men, and that afterward his father asked him whom he thought to be the best of them. Richard had been impressed by Clinton Golden of the steelworkers' union, but ODY said the one he picked as the coming man was Walter Reuther, then aged thirty-two.

13. ODY to Hillman 8/15/40 (Box 495).

14. ODY to Wendell Willkie 11/15/40 (Box 34, Folder 1-307).

15. ODY to Willkie 1/30/14; Willkie to ODY 2/15/41 (Box 34, Folder 1-307).

16. Milk producers' meeting at Van Hornesville 6/29/39. For the text, see the (Little Falls) *Evening Times* 6/30/39 (copy in Milk folder).

17. ODY Papers, Milk; ODY radio talk on WGY, Schenectady, 9/5/41, Speeches. Both authors were active participants in the developments of that memorable summer, as documented in part by the Labor Day issue of the family magazine the *Dumpling*. See also Everett Case, "The Dairyman's Plight," in *Harvard Business Review*, vol. XX, no. 2 (Winter 1942), for a rather more serious-minded discussion.

18. Letter of appointment from the National Defense Mediation Board to ODY, signed by William H. Davis 9/3/41 (Box 489).

19. Stenographic record of Gypsum hearings, Chicago, 9/22 to 9/23/41 (copy in Box 489).

20. Marquis Childs in *Washington Post* 5/4/44, discussing the then-current battle between the government and Sewell Avery. When, in 1/1942, the National Defense Mediation Board was, by executive order, supplanted by the War Labor Board, ODY was appointed examiner and asked to continue with the Gypsum case. It is not clear that he did much examining; the workers, as indicated in the text, wanted his help, but—unlike the wartime controversy between John L. Lewis's United Mine Workers and the U.S. government—settlement of the Gypsum case was still blocked, not by the recalcitrance of the unions but by that of the employer. Throughout

1943 and 1944 Sewell Avery continued his defiance of the War Labor
Board, filing suits and resisting government takeovers. Thus the Gypsum
case was a kind of warm-up for the more spectacular Montgomery Ward
case, in which the stubborn Avery was removed from his office by the U.S.
Army—but that story does not belong in this book.

21. ODY's final report (Box 489). The note of appreciation came from E.
Gasaway, president, and Kathryn Lewis, secretary-treasurer, of District 50,
UMW, 11/22/41 (Box 489).

22. "Young Jim" was so called to distinguish him from his well-known
father, a senior NYT reporter; it was "Young Jim" who later became press
secretary to President Eisenhower.

23. David Loth, *Swope of GE* (New York: Simon & Schuster, 1958), pp.
279–83. Before this suit, which Assistant Attorney General Thurman Arnold
had launched in blithe disregard of Pearl Harbor, was brought to trial, it
was put off for the duration at the instance of the War and Navy departments.

24. Loth, p. 283; ODY to Franklin T. Griffith of Portland, Oregon, 3/30/43;
ODY to B. C. Cobb 10/1/42.

25. GE Annual Report 1942.

26. GE Annual Report 1943; John A. Miller *Men and Volts at War* (New
York: Whittlesey House, McGraw-Hill, 1947), pp. 220–21 ff.

27. ODY to Charles G. Dawes 7/30/42; GE Annual Report 1943.

28. ODY to Conway P. Coe, executive secretary of Patent Planning Commission, 4/24/42.

29. W. Houston Kenyon, Jr., to JYC 5/25/77. Kenyon, a Harvard classmate
of C.J.'s, was helpful to ODY on this assignment, and later served as research director for the Truman Committee on the Patent System. The records of the Patent Planning Commission, including ODY's contribution, are
in Boxes 463–4–5.

30. War manpower commissions, state as well as national, also called on
ODY for help. As a member of the national commission's Appeals Committee and chairman of its committee to select the colleges and universities best
equipped to provide special training programs for the armed forces, he met
often with Paul McNutt, the national chairman, or with his deputy. To
Anna Rosenberg's New York State Commission he could give less time,
but he so much admired her that he took great satisfaction in untangling
such snarls as he could for her. See his letter of 8/23/45, in which—as one
chairman to another—he praises her mastery of that sometimes tricky role.

31. GE Annual Reports for the years mentioned; ODY's U.S. income-tax reports; Loth, pp. 283–85.

32. See Chapter 35, note 14.

33. Pick and Company files and U.S. income-tax reports.

34. The $50,000 loss this deal involved was disallowed by the Internal
Revenue Service on the ground that, not being a professional dealer, ODY
had not bought these books for profit. Worse was to come, however. Wells
had sold to Lord Rothschild ODY's prize copy of *Tom Jones*, which he had
bought from Rosenbach following the sale in 1929 of the Kern Collection.

(Kern had bought it from Charles Sessler, who had it from none other than Walter Spencer.) Some years later, after war had broken out, Rothschild's bibliographer discovered that this much-touted copy contained certain "fraudulently inserted leaves" and Rothschild thereupon brought suit against both Wells and Young. Settled out of court in 1944, it cost ODY far more than the $2,500 paid as his share, with Wells paying $1,500 and the other two dealers $4,500 each. Later described as an "arrow to the heart of the rare book trade," it was the one known instance in which, as a collector, ODY had been duped. Nevertheless, he publicly absolved all the dealers involved of any fraudulent intent—like him they had been victims—and Rothschild publicly pronounced the settlement "entirely satisfactory." (See *The History of Tom Jones . . . Caveat Emptor*, Cambridge, England, privately printed for Lord Rothschild. The quotation is from Edwin Wolf II with John Fleming, *Rosenbach: A Biography* [New York: World, 1960], pp. 509–11.)

35. NYT 5/5/41. Although the transaction stipulated that ODY's books and manuscripts become an integral part of the Berg Collection, they have been fortunate in the respect and loving care they have enjoyed from the collection's two curators, John Gordan and Lola Szladits. When, on the centennial of ODY's birth, October 27, 1974, the library opened a representative exhibition to honor his generosity and "bibliophilic acumen," Mrs. Szladits personally supervised both the process of selection and the preparation of its handsome and specially printed catalogue. Her acumen was also evident in her foreword, in which she observed: "Several years ago, the scholar Richard D. Altick wrote that 'the Library's jewel, as far as literary research is concerned, is the Berg Collection.' One may surely add that the diamond in the jewel is the Young Collection; it shines in many colors, it increases in value, and it will never lose its lustre." And it was at her urging that JYC contributed to this publication the essay on her father as book collector which became the basis of this biography's Chapter 22. That this centennial proceeding would have been warmly applauded by John Gordan, as it was by his widow, Phyllis Goodhart Gordan, none who knew him would question.

36. See note 33 above; ODY to Bankers Trust Company 4/23/41.

37. And so in the end it did. ODY's 1941 tax folder tells the story.

38. Isaiah Bowman to ODY 2/9, 3/3/42; ODY to Bowman 2/23, 3/18/42: Page School files.

39. In our prepublication revision of this manuscript, considerations of space dictated a substantial abridgment of (among much else) our originally more comprehensive account of ODY's long and, on its face, ambivalent relationship to this once promising adventure. This is noted here because our original version had been "cleared," informally at least, with two long-suffering but invariably responsive Johns Hopkins archivists: Susan Tripp and Julia Morgan. It is preserved intact, however, in chapter 40 of our original manuscript—all of which is deposited with the ODY Papers in a specially marked file—and so remains open to inspection. Also open to scholarly research are, of course, the several cartons of Page School material in the ODY Papers which have been our principal reliance, first and last. We have *not* explored the voluminous but not yet sorted or collated

records on deposit at Johns Hopkins. We are indebted, however, to Ross Jones, the university's vice-president for institutional relations; to our friend Professor Stephen Schuker of Brandeis, who first made inquiries on our behalf; and again to Ms. Morgan for the following information: "By the close of World War II, the Page School had become little more than a funding operation for Owen Lattimore and a few graduate students; when Lattimore left, circa 1953, it was officially liquidated and its remaining funds were restricted for the use of the Political Science Department. The present School of Advanced International Studies, set up at the Hopkins circa 1950, was and is a wholly new, separate and more traditionally oriented establishment."

40. Once, during his later years, ODY wryly complained to his visiting son-in-law that he had not slept very well, having spent the hours from four to six in a wholly involuntary review of his sins. Asked whether it was the sins of commission or omission that troubled him the most, the answer was quick and almost scornful: "That's too easy; it's the sins of omission every time."

41. See note 33 above. No wonder his income seemed smaller; indeed it was. In 1945, when Young and Swope were no longer directors, their stand-by fees for special services were cut from $67,000 to $19,000. They remained at that figure until 1950's terminal payment of $35,000, after which they ceased and only the $30,000 pension remained.

CHAPTER 38. *World War II and After; the Last Young Plan*

1. ODY to Ralph Paine 4/11/42.

2. Talk to the Harvard-Cabot Conference group 6/20/42. The notes for this talk (in Speeches) are marked "materially changed when delivered."

3. Address to U.S. Chamber of Commerce 4/29/43, Speeches.

4. Paul Hoffman was not only a colleague of ODY's in this venture, but was also a fellow member of the Harriman Committee on Foreign Aid, and of the New York Life Insurance board; they were good friends and admired each other.

5. St. Lawrence commencement address 6/22/44, Speeches.

6. Adolf Berle, *Navigating the Rapids* (New York: Harcourt, Brace, 1973), pp. 412, 415.

7. ODY to Harry Landon 4/20/42; ODY to Thomas W. Lamont 8/20/42. There was never, as far as ODY's own files reveal, any direct word from the White House on the subject, either before or after his refusal. But in 1943 ODY was proposed for the office of lieutenant governor when this fell vacant; he was supported for it, of course, by the Young Democrats, but ODY announced that he had taken the chairmanship of the Independent Citizens Committee supporting Lieutenant General William N. Haskell for this post. The NYT intimated that Roosevelt had asked ODY to do this, in the hope that the election of a Democratic lieutenant governor might slow Governor Dewey's prospects in national politics. But ODY's campaign for Haskell

failed, which he probably expected with the Republicans now dominant in the state.

8. ODY to Jared Van Waggenen 9/29/44.

9. ODY to Gerard Swope 10/28/44.

10. ODY to John Worden Elwood 7/23/45.

11. Among Harriman Committee members were Randolph Burgess, James Carey of the CIO, George Meany of the AFL, Paul Hoffman, Robert M. La Follette, Edward Mason of the Harvard School of Public Administration, Dean William Myers of the Cornell School of Agriculture, and Robert Sproul of the University of California. See also Dean Acheson, *Present at the Creation* (New York: Norton, 1969), p. 235; Robert J. Donovan, *Conflict and Crisis* (New York: Norton, 1977), p. 341.

12. ODY to Philip Reed 8/21/47.

13. ODY to Averell Harriman 6/23/47.

14. ODY to Harriman 12/14/47. The files on this committee are in Boxes 483–86.

15. ODY to Herbert Hoover 1/14/48.

16. ODY to Robert M. La Follette 11/23/48.

17. ODY to Robert Bowie 10/5/48.

18. ODY to La Follette 11/23/48.

19. Report of the Subcommittee on Regulatory Agencies, 3/12/49. For the work of this commission see Boxes 451–56.

20. NYHT 3/27/49.

21. JEY and Lou Henry Hoover had remained excellent friends and served on some committees together; but Jo's feelings toward Hoover were never the same after 1929.

22. ODY to Hoover 8/26/49.

23. ODY to Robert Saudek 7/29/48. Such war and early postwar broadcasts as Edward R. Murrow's had cast radio in the responsible role ODY had envisioned for it.

24. ODY to Edward J. Noble 8/27/48.

25. ODY to Robert K. Kintner 8/3/49.

26. ODY to Noble 11/2/54.

27. ODY speech to Holstein-Friesian Association 5/30/49, Speeches.

28. Dewey's appointments, says Oliver C. Carmichael, Jr., in *New York Establishes a State University* (Nashville: Vanderbilt University Press, 1955), were generally representative "but weighted toward the professional educator; the non-Dewey appointees were overwhelmingly weighted toward the professional politician" (p. 55).

29. Minutes of the meeting of the Temporary Commission 8/23/46, ODY Papers. For the crosscurrents and countercurrents, see Carmichael, Jr., chapters 3, 6.

30. One of the two co-counsel to the commission, whom ODY had recommended for the appointment, Arthur H. Schwartz, was a young lawyer who had been associated with Dewey in the New York City District Attorney's

Office, and had remained close to him. (Schwartz had gained fame as the prosecutor of the famous racketeer "Legs" Diamond, in the 1930s.) Schwartz admired ODY very much, and kept him in constant touch with both the gubernatorial and legislative pulses in long and often amusing letters to Washington Oaks or Van Hornesville.

31. Carmichael, Jr., p. 119; we owe to this work the following details not otherwise attributed.

32. See, re ODY's *ad hoc* committees, Carmichael, Jr., p. 320. That the resulting bill as finally drawn won the support of the State Association of Colleges and Universities was owing in no small measure to the fair-mindedness and skillful mediation of its executive officer, David Berkowitz—a key figure in the subsequent development of Brandeis University, where, since 1949, he has been professor of history.

33. Frank Abbott, *Government Policy and Higher Education* (Ithaca: Cornell University Press, 1958), p. 262.

34. Thomas E. Dewey to ODY (telegram) 3/8/48.

35. ODY to Oliver Carmichael, Sr., 12/29/48. For the dispute over Eurich's title, see Carmichael, Jr., pp. 241–50.

36. Harvey Hinman to ODY 2/23/49.

37. ODY to Hinman 3/10/49. This letter was released from Governor Dewey's office, with ODY's permission, and perhaps was influential in defeating the Condon-Barrett bill. See Abbott, p. 301.

38. NYT 3/24/49. Bethuel Webster's junior partner, Charles Garside, had been named by the governor to the State University Board. As for the State Association of Colleges and Universities, its leaders' zeal to effect a compromise satisfactory to the regents had perhaps impaired its impartial standing—certainly in the eyes of the State University trustees (Carmichael, Jr., pp. 267–70).

CHAPTER *39. Rocking Chair Consultant*

1. The fruit stand was outside ODY's Washington Oaks Office, and when he was too cool inside he would come out to sit in the sun and admire his produce.

2. David Lilienthal, *Journals*, vol. III, 1950–55 (New York: Harper & Row, 1966), pp. 137 ff. The date of the visit to Washington Oaks was 4/7/51.

3. ODY to Charles Evans Hughes, Jr., 8/31/48.

4. Interview with John Prout 3/14/55, at Washington Oaks, in ODY Papers. Prout was planning a book to be called *Begin Living at Sixty-five*, the interview with ODY to form a chapter called "The Art of Relaxation."

5. Kathan Brown, *Album: A Memory* (Oakland, Calif.: Crown Point Press, 1972; unpaged). It is perhaps here, if anywhere, that one finds a clue to what many of ODY's admirers—including his Cooperstown barber and friend of many summers, Charles Navarro—have insisted on calling the "Young mystique."

6. At the time of the completion of this book, the total of ODY's great-grandchildren is thirty-three (no great-great-grandchildren as yet). Writing to Jo's niece Altha Stalford in 7/1957, ODY described Van Hornesville as "momentarily filled with more Youngs than my mother ever dreamed of in her most optimistic moments."

7. As for Van Horne Case, the only job that he has ever held on to (according to the *Dumpling*) is the presidency of the Alumni/ae Association of Flotsam and Jetsam College, whose seal, translated from the Sanskrit, reads, "Love to Learn and Learn to Love." VHC's latest scheme for making a quick fortune [*sic*], he confided in an article in the *Dumpling*, is to write the life of his great "backer and benefactor," the Van Hornesville plowboy-capitalist.

8. NYT 10/27/54; *This Week* 11/28/54; ODY to an interviewer on his eightieth birthday (clipping has no name or title).

9. ODY to Frances Cotter, secretary of the university, 3/17/56.

10. ODY to Atwood Manley 5/30/52 (in SLU box, 1949–).

11. ODY to Edward Noble 11/9/54.

12. ODY to Dr. Robert Commins 8/3/52.

13. Andover speech notes, Box 649, Universalist General Assembly folder.

14. The speech itself, given 8/24/53, Speeches.

15. ODY to Edward R. Murrow 1/6/51. The entire letter reads:

Down in the woods where I live we listen to you every night with gratitude and pride in your accomplishment. Your "Challenge of the '50s," I think, is one of the most impressive and distinctive programs I have ever listened to on the air. On the one side I feel keen disappointment in the prostitution of radio and on the other I get great satisfaction from many of its services, of which I regard yours among the most helpful.

I recall so frequently my original talks with Godfrey Isaacs in 1921 when he was saying that broadcasting could only be handled through a Government agency and supported by the Government tax. I was saying that we would not in this country submit to Government control of such a powerful agency unless there was no other way out and that we would try to see whether advertising could support it. The contrast between the two systems now is, of course, very marked. I still feel that we were right, but I have some reservations both about the taste and the ingenuity of these highly competitive and very profitable advertising agencies.

Murrow replied, "I feel that your early position was correct and that the abuses that have developed in this medium are an accurate reflection of this materialistic, mechanized civilization in which we live" (to ODY 1/24/51).

16. ODY to Edna F. Aney 11/18/52.

17. John Foster Dulles to ODY 6/11/52.

18. NYHT and NYT 11/3/52. ODY wrote to Gertrude Chandler on 8/5/52, asking her to come to Van Hornesville in September so they could work on tax returns: "I suppose we shall have to make them and pay even though we get a Republican president. This does not necessarily mean that I am voting the Republican ticket. Certainly I never would have gotten social security with a Republican administration." (Chan was a Republican.)

19. NYT 10/15/55.

20. Spurr sent ODY a clipping from the *Rochester Democrat Chronicle* 9/10/53 of an article by Henry W. Clune in which he reminisced about famous people he had met in the past: "Owen D. Young, poised, reserved, beautifully tailored in a double-breasted blue suit—as courteous to a reporter as he might have been to a king." Spurr noted that "you favored that type of suit even in college" (9/11/53; authors' note: seldom in later years). ODY replied (9/14/53): "All I can remember about my suit in college was that the coat sleeves were about 3 inches too short and my pants scarcely reached the top of my shoes." Nevertheless, he was asked for sartorial advice, when he was in college, by a classmate at East Springfield Academy: "Owen in as much as you [are] a traveling and around a good deal and in high society please write immediately at the best of your knowledge the color and latest stile of a suit of clothes and overcoat for fall and winter. Please grant an ever true friend a favor by answering my letter at your very earliest convenience And oblige Windsor Maxfield" (10/6/1892).

21. ODY was so pleased with this he repeated it to his daughter.

22. JYC diary 2/10/55, Washington Oaks.

23. Allan Nevins to ODY 11/15/49; ODY to Nevins 11/21/49.

24. There is a copy of the transcript in the RCA folder in one of the boxes marked "1949–," and it is so labeled on the outside.

25. ODY to RY (handwritten) 2/19/49.

26. RY to ODY 6/6/47.

27. Quoted in *Forbes* 3/15/51.

28. At age thirty-seven Andrew McFadyean brought to the work of the Dawes Committee long experience in organizing and recording such international undertakings, having served most recently as secretary to the Reparations Commission. Dawes (in his *Journal of Reparations* [London: Macmillan, 1939], pp. 188, 205) and Crocker (ms on Dawes Committee and Plan [Library of Congress, Manuscript Division; copy in ODY Papers], pp. 273–75, 285–86) cite his helpfulness in drafting the final Dawes report; he was knighted the following year. After thirty-seven years one might have expected Sir Andrew's impression of the man to have faded or become blurred; on the contrary, his portrait impressed itself on many who had known ODY well, early or late, as curiously undated.

Bibliography

For a full-length biography of Owen Young, the indispensable source is the thousand or so cartons of his papers—letters and copybooks, documents and records, speeches and memoranda, and not least the voluminous press clippings—which, pending other disposition, are deposited in the vault of the Van Hornesville Community Corporation, at Van Hornesville, New York 13475. Not included are the several hundred cartons of General Electric material which, consigned to Schenectady shortly after Young's final retirement in 1944, have virtually disappeared. Young urged at the time that the company consider setting up a full-fledged archives department, on the ground that "the history of this country is, to a substantial degree, the history of these great concerns like the General Electric," and that so long as this history must be written chiefly "from the records of Congress and especially from Committee Hearings . . . the historian . . . can only get a distorted picture" (ODY to W. W. Trench, secretary of the company, 7/24/45). But he must have had grave doubts about the fate of this suggestion; in the event, the compendious files relating to the formation and development of the Radio Corporation of America did not go to Schenectady as Owen D. Young had intended; rather, as a part of his personal papers, to Van Hornesville. Thus one phase of GE—and American corporate—history, in which (coincidentally) Young played the leading part, still lives in these personally established archives.

So too does much else, as visiting historians continue to discover and attest. Thanks in no small measure to Stuart M. Crocker, Young's devoted assistant at the time, the files relating to German reparations and the efforts of the Dawes and Young committees to negotiate an acceptable settlement are particularly full. Crocker's unpublished manuscript on the Dawes Plan is in the Library of Congress but the Owen D. Young Papers have a copy, together with Crocker's manuscript diary

of the Young Plan in the making. Less comprehensive but still rewarding are the records of Young's response to the numerous other
calls for service in the public and quasi-public sectors which—notably
in the case of the Federal Reserve—sometimes turned out to involve
a demanding and prolonged commitment.

Our exploration of related sources has been selective rather than exhaustive, being directed primarily toward filling inevitable gaps. One
such gap, a product of World War II, resulted from the decision of
Young's successors at the Tyler firm in Boston to store their records,
for safety's sake, in a barn near Andover, Massachusetts, where—
ironically enough—fire destroyed them. Ida M. Tarbell had seen them,
however, and her papers at Allegheny College proved helpful; so did a
Florida visit with Tyler's long-retired clerk, Karl Singer. Most rewarding, however, was one author's special trip to Dallas to explore from
contemporary material some of the problems Young encountered when,
as Stone and Webster's young attorney, he was called upon to cope,
there and elsewhere, with the legal and financial difficulties of the
burgeoning utilities. And such records as Young's papers now afford
concerning his role in President Wilson's Industrial (or Labor) Conferences of 1919, we owe to the library staff at GE's Schenectady plant,
who helped us discover and rescue from their dank abode in the basement these remnants—virtually the last—of Young's original consign-
ment.

While our Notes duly record our indebtedness to other sources, certain libraries, librarians and archivists deserve special mention here.
In fleshing out the family letters of Young's college days, the librarian
and staff of the Owen D. Young Library of St. Lawrence University
have been immensely helpful. To the Amherst College Library staff
we are grateful for their helpful response to several queries and not
least for sending us a copy of a Young to J. P. Morgan letter of August
4, 1924, which was missing from Young's files but not from the Dwight
Morrow Papers in their custody. We could ask no better guide to the
Thomas W. Lamont Papers in Harvard's Baker Library than its now-
retired Curator of Special Collections, Robert Lovett; nor in spotting
the occasional nuggets to be found in the reticent records of the Federal Reserve Bank of New York than its archivist, Carl Backlund. We
thank the librarian of the David Sarnoff Research Center in Princeton,
New Jersey, for making available the comprehensive but unpublished
manuscript on the history of RCA by Elmer E. Bucher. If this served
as a check on our draft manuscript, our own research was a check
on Bucher's, which, though an in-house account, is nevertheless com-

mendably objective. And if our visits to the Library of Congress were few, they were always rewarding.

With Robert Wood, of the National Archives and the Hoover Presidential Library at West Branch, Iowa, we have had a singularly lively and productive exchange of missing or elusive items, to the benefit of both collections as well as the enrichment of our book. This has been especially welcome in light of the comparative dearth of scholarly biographies of Hoover in contrast, say, to the plenitude that deal with Franklin D. Roosevelt. If, not to mention William Appleman Williams, such younger historians as Joan Hoff Wilson and (most recently) David Burner are taking significant steps to redress the balance, none has yet attempted (at this writing) to do for Hoover what Frank Freidel, Arthur Schlesinger, Jr., James MacGregor Burns, William E. Leuchtenburg and Joseph Lash have done for his successor. If, in preparing this study, we have paid scant attention to the riches of the Roosevelt Library at Hyde Park, it is because it seemed a mere pretension to rehearse the exhaustive and abundantly documented research that informs their published volumes—as well as certain more specialized studies.

Something of the sort applies as well to a significant fraction of the scores of books and articles—including a select few of the biographies of Young's contemporaries—that we have consulted and duly cited in our Notes. The temptation to present a critical listing of these secondary sources is one we are able to resist, in the hope that the ways in which we have used and cited them will speak for themselves. To our search for books that were missing from our own library, or for books that were scarce or out of print, the Colgate University Library and its librarian, Bruce Brown, provided without exception the answers. The Colgate Library made available as well newly published works and needed files of newspapers and periodicals, thus reducing to a minimum our demands on (for example) the New York Public Library.

Finally, we wish to cite our lasting debt to the score or more of visiting scholars, most of whom have consulted some aspect of the Young Papers while we were at work, and typically with such guidance as we could render. Several of these have given one or more of our chapters a critical reading, and we have also profited from the wide-ranging research that informs their dissertations, published books and other professional contributions. Thus it seems fitting to conclude this bibliographical note with a summary bibliography of *their* publications—insofar, at least, as the Young Papers were consulted as a primary source. To the scholar who seeks to go beyond our Notes and specific citations, we recommend due attention to theirs, and especially to their typically far-reaching bibliographical essays. Our listing follows, in chronological order dating from their initial visitations:

1. Hester, James McNaughton. "America and the Weimar Republic, 1918–1925." Doctoral dissertation, Oxford University, 1955.
2. Clarke, Stephen V. O. *Central Bank Cooperation, 1924–1931*. New York: Federal Reserve Bank of New York, 1967.
3. Hughes, B. A. "Owen D. Young and American Foreign Policy, 1919–1929." Doctoral dissertation, University of Wisconsin, 1969.
4. Link, Werner. "Die Ruhrbesetzung und die wirtschaftpolitischen Interessen der USA." *Vierteljahrshefte für Zeitgeschichte*, XVII (10/1969), 372–82.
    ———. *Die amerikanische Stabilisierungspolitik in Deutschland, 1921–1932*. Düsseldorf: Droste Verlag, 1970.
    ———. "Der amerikanische Einfluss auf die Weimarer Republik in der Dawesplanphase." In H. Mommsen, D. Petzina and B. Weisbrod, eds., *Industrielles System und politische Entwicklung in der Weimarer Republik*. Düsseldorf: Droste Verlag, 1974.
    ———. "Zum Problem der Kontinuität der amerikanischen Deutschlandpolitik im zwanzigsten Jahrhundert." *Amerikastudien*, XX (1975), 122–54.
5. Jacobson, Jon. *Locarno Diplomacy: Germany and the West, 1925–1929*. Princeton: Princeton University Press, 1972.
6. Hurvitz, Haggai. "The Meaning of Industrial Conflict in Some Ideologies of the Early 1920s." Doctoral dissertation, Columbia University, 1971.
7. Wandel, Eckhard. "Entstehung und Ratifizierung des Young Plans." Doctoral dissertation, Eberhard-Karls Universität, Tübingen, 1967.
    ———. *Die Bedeutung der USA für das deutsche Reparationsproblem, 1924–1929*. Tübingen: JCB Mohr (Paul Siebeck), 1971.
8. Schuker, Stephen A. *The End of French Predominance in Europe: The Financial Crisis of 1924 and Adoption of the Dawes Plan*. Chapel Hill: University of North Carolina Press, 1976.
    ———. "Frankreich und die Weimarer Republik." In Michael Stürmer, ed., *Die Weimarer Republik: Belagerte Civitas*. Königstein/Ts: Athenäum-Hain-Scripter-Hanstein, 1980.
9. Artaud, Denise. "A propos de l'occupation de la Ruhr." *Revue d'histoire moderne et contemporaine*, XVII (1970), 2–21.
    ———. "Le Gouvernement américain et la question des dettes de guerre." *Revue d'histoire moderne et contemporaine*, XX (1973), 202–29.
    ———. "Le Gouvernement des Etats-Unis et le Contrôle des empruntes européens, 1921–1929." *Bulletin de la Société d'histoire moderne et contemporaine*, XV (1973), 17–26.
10. Costigliola, Frank C. "The Other Side of Isolationism: The Establish-

ment of the First World Bank, 1929–1930." *Journal of American History*, LIX, no. 3 (12/1972), 602–20.

———. "The Politics of Financial Stabilization: American Reconstruction Policy in Europe, 1924–1930." Doctoral dissertation, Cornell University, 1973.

———. "The United States and Reconstruction of Germany in the 1920s." *Business History Review*, L, no. 4 (Winter 1976), 477–502.

———. "Anglo-American Financial Rivalry in the 1920s." *Journal of Economic History*, XXXVII, no. 4 (12/1977), 911–34.

———. *"Our Century": United States Political and Cultural Relations with Europe, 1919–1933*. Forthcoming.

11. Hogan, Michael J. "Informal Entente: Public Policy and Private Management in Anglo-American Petroleum Affairs, 1918–1924." *Business History Review*, XLVIII (Summer 1974), 187–205.

———. *Informal Entente: The Private Structure of Cooperation in Anglo-American Diplomacy, 1918–1928*. Columbia: University of Missouri Press, 1977. (Based on "The United States and the Problem of International Control: The Private Sector," doctoral dissertation, University of Iowa, 1974.)

———. "The United States and the Problem of International Economic Control: American Attitudes toward European Reconstruction, 1918–1920." *Pacific Historical Review*, XLIV (2/1975), 84–103.

12. McQuaid, Kim. "A Response to Industrialism: Liberal Businessmen and the Evolving Spectrum of Capitalist Reforms, 1866–1960." Doctoral dissertation, Northwestern University, 1975.

———. "Henry S. Dennison and the 'Science' of Industrial Reform, 1900–1950." *American Journal of Economics and Sociology*, XXXVI, no. 1 (1/1977), 79–98.

———. "Young, Swope and GE's 'New Capitalism': A Study in Corporate Liberalism, 1920–1933." *American Journal of Economics and Sociology*, XXXVI, no. 3 (7/1977), 323–34.

———. "Competition, Cartellization and the Corporate Ethic: GE during the New Deal Era, 1933–1940." *American Journal of Economics and Sociology*, XXXVI, no. 4 (10/1977), 417–28.

———. "Corporate Liberalism in the American Business Community, 1920–1940." *Business History Review*, LII, no. 3 (Autumn 1978), pp. 342–68.

13. Jones, Kenneth Paul. "Discord and Collaboration: Choosing an Agent-General for Reparations." *Diplomatic History*, I, no. 2 (Spring 1977), 118–39.

———. "Alanson B. Houghton and the Ruhr Crisis: The Diplomacy of Power and Morality." In Kenneth Paul Jones, ed., *U.S. Diplomats: America's Search for Peace in Europe, 1919–1941*. Santa Barbara: ABC-Clio Press, 1980.

14. Carroll, John M. "A Pennsylvanian in Paris: James A. Logan, Jr., Un-

official Diplomat, 1919–1925." *Pennsylvania History*, XLV (1/1978), 3–18.

————. "Owen D. Young and German Reparations: The Diplomacy of an Enlightened Businessman." In Kenneth Paul Jones, ed., *U.S. Diplomats: America's Search for Peace in Europe, 1919–1941*. Santa Barbara: ABC-Clio Press, 1980.

15. Leffler, Melvin P. "The Origins of American War Debt Policy, 1921–1923." *Journal of American History*, LIX (12/1972), 585–601.

————. "The Struggle for Stability: American Policy toward France." Doctoral dissertation, Ohio State University, 1972. (For a condensed but printed version, see *Perspectives in American History*, VIII [1974].)

————. *The Elusive Quest: America's Pursuit of European Stability and French Security, 1919–1933*. Chapel Hill: University of North Carolina Press, 1979.

16. Vlaun, Sister Joan, O. P. "Herbert Hoover's Economic Foreign Policy for Dealing with the Great Depression, 1929–1932." Doctoral dissertation, New York University, 1977.

17. Aitken, Hugh G. J. *Syntony and Spark: The Origins of Radio*. New York: Wiley, 1976. (Aitken is now working on the early history of RCA.)

18. Sudnick, Patricia. "Patterns of Multinational Enterprise, 1929–1941: An Alternative to the Open Door Paradigm" (tentative). Doctoral dissertation, University of Chicago, work in progress.

19. Schatz, Ronald. "Labor and Management in the Twentieth Century United States: GE and Westinghouse, 1911–1960." Paper read at the Fifteenth International Congress of Historical Sciences, Bucharest, Romania, 1980 (Rapports, II, 743–50).

20. Burner, David. *Herbert Hoover: A Public Life*. New York: Knopf, 1979. (Burner is one of several younger historians, including those listed below, who had made notable contributions to an understanding of various aspects of the 1920s and 1930s before discovering—or finding time to consult—the Young Papers.)

21. Hawley, Ellis. *The New Deal and the Problem of Monopoly*. Princeton: Princeton University Press, 1966.

————. *The Great War and the Search for a Modern Order, 1917–1933*. New York: St. Martin's, 1979.

22. Van Meter, Robert H. Jr., who is extending his earlier study, "American Policy and the Economic Reconstruction of Europe, 1918–1921" (*Journal of the Liberal Arts*, no. 16 [Fall 1968]) to take in the Dawes Plan and loan.

23. Woodard, Nelson E. "Postwar Reconstruction and International Order: A Study of the Diplomacy of Charles Evans Hughes, 1921–1925." Doctoral dissertation, University of Wisconsin, 1970.

24. Dayer, Roberta A. *Bankers and Diplomats in China, 1917–1925: The*

Anglo-American Relationship. London: Frank Cass, 1981.

———. "The British War Debts to the United States and the Anglo-Japanese Alliance, 1920–1923." *Pacific Historical Review*, XLV, no. 4 (11/1976), 569–95.

Hester's research was done largely in New York City, while relevant parts of the Young Papers were still there. Jacobson's research, and the earlier parts of Link's, Hughes's, and Schuker's, was undertaken in Van Hornesville with Richard Young's assistance; all the rest with the assistance of the authors.

Acknowledgments

A book so long in the making owes much to many, as our bibliographical and chapter notes attest; with rare exceptions these constitute our professional acknowledgments. For the rest, if a biography is in some sort a case history of a human life, the context of that life becomes at once integral to the case and to whatever judgments it invites. Thus in seeking to let the story of Owen Young's life tell itself as it actually unfolded in his time—a time which ranged from the fabulously promising to the ambiguous and tragic and, at long last (with cautionary footnotes) back to the fabulously promising—we have naturally solicited the help of those of Young's survivors, now alas too few, who had some firsthand knowledge of his life and of its ambience.

Our acknowledgments, then, go first to our families: to our other father, James Herbert Case, who not only treated us to reminiscences of meetings and visits with Owen Young, but kept urging us to get on with the book up to his death in 1972, only days before his hundredth birthday; and to Charles J., Philip and Richard Young, who have constantly encouraged us, read chapters, and given us corrections and additions. Our four children, too, have read chapters and, with their cousin John Peter Young, have been on the alert for relevant material we might otherwise have missed.

That Young's longtime secretary, Lillian Morrison (Mrs. Eugene Ehrhart), reviewed the chapters on his early years as chairman of GE and RCA—and the years immediately preceding—was for us doubly reassuring. Of those who saw him in action then, few survive and none could have been more knowledgeable. It is to her also that we owe the discovery of the early letter of resignation sent by Young to his chief, Charles A. Coffin, which is included in Chapter 12.

To others, now deceased, we are grateful for helpful responses to our questions in the early days of our project: among them, James A.

Farley, David Sarnoff, Lewis W. Douglas and Fred Bate—friends of ours as well as Owen Young's. To another who was both, Randolph Burgess, our debt cannot be measured. For the four years prior to his death in 1978 we were in close touch; no one else could have brought to our chapters on the Dawes and Young plans—and the subsequent failure of the grossly misnamed Bank of U.S.—not only his critical first-hand knowledge but his understanding heart and mind.

Another old friend and veteran of the New York Fed, Allan Sproul, wrote us from California: "If you should want me to look at a portion of your book on O D Y, I would be glad to do so. He is one of my heroes." Delighted, we dispatched three or four of the later chapters, asking him "to vet and criticize unsparingly." It was too late; death intervened, and for this our book must suffer with us. Likewise, from our closest friends, Burnham Carter and Louis Hyde, writers themselves, we can no longer receive their warm understanding and support.

Happily, we can acknowledge the help and encouragement of many others who still figure in the current census. George Harrar of the Rockefeller Foundation set us on our way in 1969 with a month at the Villa Serbelloni, where, in one of the most beautiful settings in the world, we first put pen to paper. Franz Schneider, now sole survivor of the "Bellhops"—as the Young Committee's Paris aides and advisers dubbed themselves—gave us a memorable account of Bellhop Sarnoff's key assist in persuading the last recalcitrant, Hjalmar Schacht, to sign the final report and so assure its requisite unanimity. Friends such as Dr. Irving S. Wright, whose special contribution is recorded in Chapter 29, have given certain chapters critical readings, as have Harold Loizeaux and Lorna M. Livingston. Experienced and generous biographers such as Frank Freidel and Merlo Pusey have brought important papers to our notice. Robert Calkins, sometime president of the Brookings Institution, Lola Szladits, curator of the Berg Collection, and Mildred Adams Kenyon and her husband have heartened us by their timely and pertinent suggestions. Our text and especially the notes owe much to the meticulous eye and purposeful red pencil of that copyeditor *par excellence*, Melissa Clemence. Nor do we forget the services rendered in deciphering and typing our first and revised drafts, respectively, by Phyllis Palmeter and Betsy Meggett, and re-typing our notes by Maria Zamelis of the neighboring New York State Historical Association.

To the four intrepid souls (other than our editor) who read our manuscript entire, we owe our special thanks. Two of these were volunteers: our youngest son, John—himself both editor and author—

and his wife, Quaker; at the risk of spoiling the parents they contrived to spare the rod. For the fact that no such example had been set by that most experienced editor and author and our tested friend, Edward Weeks, our readers—like us—have reason to be grateful. Reading our drafts, chapter by chapter, Ted kept insisting that we prune and cut —salutary advice that we did our valiant best, if not enough, to follow. Nevertheless, as was true of Philip Reed—another tested friend and Young's successor as chairman of GE, whose critical reading of our manuscript saved us from avoidable errors of fact—his enthusiasm for the final product was contagious enough to assist in securing for our publisher the two grants-in-aid that helped defray the soaring costs of publication. Thus to these two stalwart and knowledgeable friends we owe a double debt, as we join our publisher in thanks to the grantors: the Alfred P. Sloan Foundation and the General Electric Company. And to J. Richard Culliton of Buffalo, a longtime admirer of our subject, we are grateful for a timely and unsolicited gift to the Van Hornesville Community Corporation, earmarked to facilitate—as it did—completion of this study.

Our final word is reserved for our esteemed editor, William B. Goodman. Patient but firm, painstaking and perceptive, Bill has kept us alert to the rigorous requirements of what was for us a new and exciting venture, and has spared no efforts to make the published version worthy of its subject. Much of any praise and none of any blame that may accrue is rightly his.

Josephine and Everett Case
October 27, 1980

Index